Wars of Latin America,
1899–1941

as possible to Terán, while he led his mounted force of thirty men in a wild gallop against the Conservative positions. Upon approaching, he realized that the Conservative soldiers were too many to defeat even after his infantry had caught up with him. However, on noticing that the Conservative soldiers were not on alert and instead were relaxing, he quickly changed his plan. He ordered his men to remove their red insignia and to shout slogans such as "Long live the Conservative Party" and "Long live General Casabianca." Soon he reached with his men the headquarters of General Domínguez and took him prisoner. Uribe Uribe had the captured Domínguez order all his men to surrender, and although some units hesitated, the approach of Liberal infantry persuaded most to surrender. Only a few detachments secretly escaped and fled back to Ocaña. In spite of attempts by officers to control the men, the rebels celebrated the victory by pillaging stores and getting drunk with looted liquor in Gramalote. The plundering of properties suspected of belonging to Conservatives was standard practice for the rebels.[32]

By his bloodless victory at Terán, Uribe Uribe gained over 2,000 rifles and a considerable supply of cartridges. Popular enthusiasm for the Liberal revolt grew tremendously, and the fame of Uribe Uribe, already solidified by his heroic charge at Peralonso, reached new heights. Throughout the country Liberals were waiting for the arrival of Uribe Uribe to join the victorious rebels. Just as after Peralonso, the Liberals were poised again to drive the Conservative government from power. Exciting as were the prospects of a Liberal victory, the determining factor for General Vargas Santos was the fear that Uribe Uribe would turn into a tropical Caesar. Rather than more campaigns that could only enhance the fame of Uribe Uribe, General Vargas Santos returned the Liberal forces back to quarters after the victory at Terán, just as he had done after the victory at Peralonso and thus let pass the last opportunity to strike a decisive blow against the Conservative government.

Ecuador and the Liberal Revival in the Department of Cauca (March–July 1900)

The Liberal victory at Terán was responsible for reviving the revolt in the Department of Cauca. The situation in that department had seemed hopeless up to that moment, and even President Eloy Alaro of Ecuador had withdrawn his support from the Colombian exiles. The Department of Cauca should have remained free of invasions from Ecuador, but a fanatical religious fervor complicated matters. The Catholic clergy in southern Cauca, led by Bishop Ezequiel Moreno, decided that the time was propitious to overthrow the Liberal Alfaro because of the latter's hostility to the Catholic Church. Bishop Moreno in fiery sermons and pastoral letters began to agitate for an invasion of Ecuador. Local Colombian authorities shared the same religious fervor and were joined by Ecuadorian Conservative exiles on the border. President Alfaro, seeing the invading forces gathering on the frontier, had no choice but to renew his support for the Colombian Liberals as a measure of self-protection. A showdown between Ecuador and Colombia seemed inevitable.[33]

For the Liberals in Cauca, the news of the victory at Terán seemed the right signal to try again to revive the revolt, although the strategic equation in the Cauca had not changed. The key to success lay in getting weapons and ammunitions from Ecuador through the border garrisons and into central Cauca. Once the Liberals could arm the peasants and the Indian communities in the interior of that department, they believed that victory was certain. Instead, if the government could deal with these threats separately, then its highly motivated and well-armed troops could destroy the Liberals.

The first battle took place at Ipiales on 27 March. Liberal exiles supported by Ecuadorian battalions tried to capture this border town during three days of very heavy fighting. Ecuadorian Conservative exiles and Colombian troops fought off the attacks but by 30 March could no longer hold their positions. When defeat or surrender seemed inevitable for the defenders, a relief column appeared in the distance, and the exhausted Liberals decided to call off the attack and to withdraw back into Ecuador. In reality the relief column was nothing but a ruse, because women, children, and old men had dressed in soldiers' uniforms. They detonated firecrackers, shouted "long live Bishop Ezequiel" and carried on their shoulders sticks and brooms that from a distance seemed like rifles. The next day real reinforcements arrived, and the Liberals had lost their best chance to introduce weapons into central Cauca.[34]

Without outside help, the Liberals in central Cauca were no match for the army, as the second battle of Flautas on 16 April 1900 again showed. During the preceding days army troops had been maneuvering to surround over a thousand Liberals and their Indian allies at this ridge. On 16 April the army attacked at Flautas, but most of the Liberals managed to escape. However, the Liberals in central Cauca were very demoralized and did not want to take on the army again until they first received outside support.[35]

Bishop Ezequiel was still waging his holy war, and he renewed his plea for an invasion of Ecuador to overthrow President Alfaro. On 22 May Ecuadorian Conservative exiles and Colombian troops invaded Ecuador and tried to capture the border town of Tulcán. The Liberal exiles and Ecuadorian troops were able to repel the invasion, but when the Liberals tried to invade Colombia, the Ecuadorian troops refused to cross the border. President Alfaro was making his point that while he was willing to help the Liberals, he was not ready to commit his troops into a full-scale war with Colombia. The disillusioned Liberals tried one last time to cross the border at Ipiales on 20 July, but the unexpected arrival of army troops shattered this last attempt to reach central Cauca.[36]

As an uneasy truce settled over the border between Ecuador and Colombia, all hope of outside support seemed to have vanished for the Liberals in central Cauca. To their surprise, help came, but not from Ecuador but from the neighboring Department of Tolima. Under pressure from army troops in that department and short of ammunition, Liberal bands crossed the Andes Mountains and entered Cauca. The

Soldiers from Pasto, Colombia, in 1900. The religious fervor of inhabitants of southern Cauca Department made them excellent soldiers to fight for the Roman Catholic religion against the Liberals. The key person in the photograph is the Catholic chaplain (*Boletín cultural y bibliográfico*, 1985).

rebels from Tolima wanted to strike fast before their presence became known, so they decided to gamble everything on one wild attempt. The presence of these Liberals from Tolima rallied local sympathizers to make one last supreme effort. In previous campaigns the Liberals and their Indian allies had roamed widely trying to evade the army, but in October 1900 the combined Liberal forces, numbering over two thousand men, decided to head directly for Popayán, the capital of the department. Such a reckless move caught the government by surprise, and it desperately rushed units from other parts of the department to save the threatened capital. The advancing Liberals proceeded relentlessly towards Popayán, and only a few kilometers outside the city did army troops arrive in time to stop the rebels. The Liberals quickly used up their ammunition and then tried to withdraw to safety, but soon army troops were in hot pursuit. The rebel approach to the capital had scared and angered the local authorities, who were determined to prevent a repetition. The rebel bands from Tolima evaded reprisals by fleeing back home. As for the locals, the government's Indian auxiliaries proved tireless and merciless in tracking down Indian rebels; the army troops sometimes took prisoners among the whites but executed all Indian rebels.[37]

In central Cauca a wave of reprisals made sure neither Indians nor peasants ever rebelled again. The government was particularly ferocious, going so far as to take the wives and relatives of suspected Liberals as hostages. Officials also arrested many Liberals and carried out widespread confiscations. Suspects or prisoners were tortured and violent punishments inflicted on their families. In reality, these repressive measures were not necessary, because without outside support, any revolt in central Cauca had no chance against the army troops. The Liberals knew that the attack on Popayán in October 1900 had been the last gasp of the revolt in Cauca. However, a substantial group of Liberal exiles remained plotting in Ecuador and hoped that the Liberal offensive in Santander might still turn the tide.

The Final Campaign in Santander (April–August 1900)

From a military perspective, each month that passed diminished the rebels' chance for victory. The rebels confined themselves to one corner of the Department of Santander and left the rest of Colombia in Conservative hands. The rebels in Santander were all volunteers, but by February 1900 the supply of recruits from that department had run dry, because all who wanted to join the Liberal forces had already done so. The government was never able to attract adequate numbers of volunteers, but it enjoyed considerable powers to coerce peasants into the ranks of the army throughout Colombia. The enthusiasm and passion of the volunteer Liberals often offset the larger numbers of the less motivated army troops, but only if the rebels had ample quantities of cartridges. The decision of General Gabriel Vargas Santos to bottle up his army in Cúcuta gave the government plenty of time to marshal troops and resources against the rebels. The authority of the government remained firm throughout most of the country, and most Liberals were hesitant to challenge the local authorities. A curious mind frame set into the Liberal camp. While General Vargas Santos felt he did not need to launch an offensive because revolts throughout the country would soon topple the Conservative government, most Liberals outside Santander were waiting for the appearance of Vargas Santos's force before rising up in revolt. Months passed as Liberals looked to each other to take the first step.[38]

When Vargas Santos finally took his army south in late April, he did not have in mind any strategic maneuver. Because Liberals lacked funds to purchase supplies, the rebel force relied on confiscating cattle and foodstuffs from Conservatives to feed itself. As the weeks dragged on, many rebels became bored and devoted themselves to rowdy parties and drunken orgies. Cúcuta was at that time an unhealthy city, and many rebels soon had contracted yellow fever, malaria, and venereal diseases. By late April the supply of Conservative foodstuffs had run out, and General Vargas Santos decided to move his force to the south. To carry out this deployment required a wide flanking march around army positions. More importantly, Vargas Santos assumed the army would remain at Pamplona and take no action to counter the Liberal move. The army was under the command of General Próspero Pinzón, who had replaced General Casabianca when the latter became Minister of War. General Pinzón was a very patient and methodical person and was also a very devout Catholic who instilled religious fervor in his troops and persuaded them that they were fighting a holy war. As the Liberal forces were marching south towards the fateful rendezvous in the battlefield of Palonegro, for the first time in the war the combatants on both sides were equally motivated to fight to the finish.[39]

Army patrols detected the Liberal deployment, and in response General Pinzón began shifting the bulk of his army to Bucaramanga. The Liberals marched south past Rionegro and their forward elements reached Palonegro on 10 May (Map 5). When the rest of the Liberal force pushed into Palonegro, the army decided to stop them. On 11 May army battalions maneuvered to try to take control of key elevations and soon intense shooting erupted. On that day Uribe Uribe arrived to distribute the rebels along a line that stretched from Palonegro almost to the town of Lebrija. General Pinzón was dispatching units from Bucaramanga to face the Liberals, and in his most crucial deployment before the battle, he had a battalion drive out a Liberal picket from the heights of San Pablo. This position commanded the battlefield and was the heart of the army line stretching from Palonegro through San Pablo and to the Casa de Teja.[40]

The very rugged terrain full of hills and canyons put the Liberals at a disadvantage for an attack. General Vargas Santos stayed far in the rear in Rionegro and never inspected the field to reconsider the decision of giving battle in such an unfavorable site. The Liberals tried to improve their chances by a surprise attack on Casa de Teja after midnight in the early hours of May 12. The Liberals sneaked up and with machetes quietly slaughtered the first sentries, but pickets sounded the alarm and the army troops were able to beat back the rebel attack. When daylight came on 12 May, the army launched a series of attacks along the entire front and seemed to be winning, although the rebels were putting up a determined resistance. At this stage of the battle, the army troops were still eager to strike a determined blow to defeat the Liberals.[41]

On 13 May the army troops hoped to continue the previous day's success, but they did not realize that for the only time during the battle, they were outnumbered. The 7,000

rebels were preparing to launch an encircling maneuver to clear the army troops from the road to Bucaramanga when an army battalion arrived and began an assault on Palonegro. The troops had come close to the hamlet on the previous days, and with the support of artillery, they hoped this time to capture the objective, but did not know they were walking into a trap. Enthusiasm and the prospects of a quick victory drove the attackers forward without waiting for the rest of their battalions to reach the field, and they came close to the houses of Palonegro. Unfortunately, the gunners' insistence on firing at close range minimized the impact of army shelling. When Uribe Uribe arrived to lead another of his legendary charges, he broke the army front line and sent soldiers fleeing in retreat to the rear. For a while the artillery held back the Liberal avalanche, but because the cannons were firing at rifle range, they soon were put out of action. The soldiers dragged the cannons away to prevent their capture, and the gunners at last put one cannon to fire at 4,000 meters. This long-range shelling of Palonegro raised enough havoc among the Liberals to delay their attack until nightfall came to shield the Conservative retreat.[42]

For a while it seemed that the soldiers would fall prey to a panic like that after Peralonso in 1899, and even General Pinzón felt that his army was almost completely defeated. As he prayed his rosary, the belief that God was on his side reaffirmed his determination to stand firm and to fight on. The arrival of fresh battalions from Bucaramanga restored numerical superiority for the army, and General Pinzón came to command 21,000 officers and men in this battle. On the Liberal side, Uribe Uribe desperately asked for cartridges and reinforcements, but General Vargas Santos refused to shift units from other sectors in the front line. When the Liberals resumed their attack early on 14 May, the reinforced army troops easily fought off the weak assaults. The fresh army battalions counterattacked and recaptured all the positions lost in the previous day's combat. But something fundamental had changed, because henceforth the army troops, even though they again outnumbered the Liberals by at least two to one, became reluctant to launch any new attacks. The real effect of the Liberal charge of 13 May was to ratify a purely

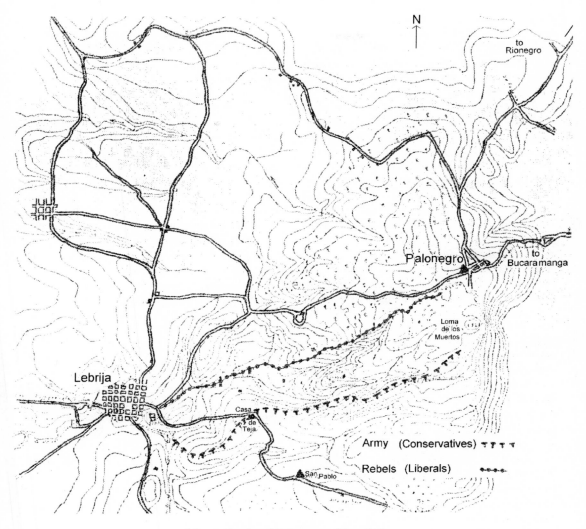

Map 5. Battle of Palonegro, May 1900.

defensive posture on the part of the army. Since the Liberals lacked the men and the cannons to shatter the army positions, the battle turned into one of attrition. A deadlock ensued, and in many ways Palonegro resembled and foreshadowed the battle of León during the Mexican Revolution.

The constant shooting and raiding over the next days necessarily wore down the Liberals, who could not replace their losses in men and ammunition. Particularly costly were the attacks and the counterattacks to capture Loma de los Muertos, an elevation between the two front lines. The casualties continued to pile up on both sides, and the stench of rotting cadavers became nauseating. After 14 May General

Vargas Santos should have broken off the battle, but characteristically he could not take any hasty action. Only on 25 May did General Pinzón consider the moment ripe for a limited offensive on his left flank. Troops converged from different directions on Lebrija and overwhelmed the poorly armed Liberal defenders. The army troops pushed forward and reached the road to the north of Palonegro and threatened to trap the rebels. General Vargas Santos at last decided to call off the battle. By daybreak on 26 May the Liberals had abandoned Palonegro and headed to Rionegro. General Pinzón sent a battalion to shadow the rebels, and he returned to Bucaramanga to celebrate a *Te Deum* giving thanks to God for the great victory. Although he has been criticized for letting the rebels escape the battlefield, he had correctly reasoned that the Liberals were finished in Santander and that there was no need to hurl his tired army at the retreating rebels.[43]

The Liberals down to 3,400 men dallied in Rionegro on 26 and 27 May as the leaders discussed their next move. When General Pinzón learned that the Liberal force was heading into the thick jungle to the northwest, he broke off all pursuit because he was confident that the jungle would ravage the rebel ranks. Instead, he sent his battalions on the cool and well-supplied highland roads to rebel-held Cúcuta, in an attempt to cut off the rebels' supply line to Venezuela. General Vargas Santos did not realize the danger threatening Cúcuta, and he believed his tattered force had plenty of time to make the trip to Ocaña. Almost from the start, the journey became a nightmare. Torrential rains made impassable the jungle trails for the Liberal column, and men sinking into the mud abandoned the ox carts carrying their food provisions. Soon the men, already suffering from diseases, began starving. As many as a thousand died, disappeared or deserted in this hazardous trip of over two weeks, and those who survived needed time to recover their strength.[44]

After the survivors straggled into Ocaña, General Vargas Santos learned that General Pinzón had laid siege to the Liberal garrison at Cúcuta. Because the rebel general knew he stood no chance in another battle with Pinzón's large army, General Vargas Santos decided to make a surprise move south to capture the undefended Bucaramanga. This odd decision forced the rapidly shrinking Liberal force to retrace its steps back to Rionegro along the same inhospitable route. This second time, however, the skeletons of dead rebels provided abundant guideposts through the dense jungle. The Liberals, down to no more than 1500 men and several hundred women camp followers, arrived in the first days of August near Bucaramanga, but they were already too late.[45]

Once General Pinzón had captured Cúcuta on 16 July, he returned with his army to find the Liberals, and on 27 July he reached Bucaramanga way ahead of the Liberals. General Pinzón sent patrols to track down the Liberal column, and in a first clash on 3 August, his troops sent the rebels fleeing in retreat to the west. General Vargas Santos decided to head south in a hopeless attempt to reach Bogotá, but with army troops closely following him, the survival of his by then less than 1000 men should have been his first priority. Meanwhile, General Pinzón correctly anticipated the spot where the Liberals would try to cross the Sogamoso River. The Liberals had only one canoe to ferry the men across the swollen river, and on 7 August army troops approached the site to try to destroy the rebels. For the first time in the war the army artillery shelled effectively from a long distance and halted the crossing. Only half of the Liberal force made it across the river, and that group under Uribe Uribe tried to struggle on. Army troops closely pursued the other half under Vargas Santos and Benjamin Uribe, and soon that other rebel band had disintegrated but its commanders miraculously escaped to Venezuela. The column of Uribe Uribe likewise disintegrated, and he with three companions only escaped capture by rowing secretly at night down the Magdalena River.[46]

The Liberal uprising in Santander was over, and never again did rebel bands rise in sufficient numbers to become more than a nuisance in that department. However, the three key Liberal leaders, Uribe Uribe, Vargas Santos, and Benjamin Herrera, had all escaped. The government had pacified the Department of Santander, but until the Conservatives could persuade these key Liberal leaders to lay down their weapons, the War of the Thousand Days would continue.

Venezuela and the Liberal Revolt, 1900–1901

The Conservative victory at Santander meant more than the pacification of that department. Any chance that the Liberals could overthrow the Conservative government had ended by July 1900. The Liberals had failed to rise up in numbers large enough to overwhelm the army. Instead in Mexico during the uprising of 1910–1911, rebels in overwhelming numbers were able to defeat the Federal Army and overthrow the regime. In both countries the ratio of soldiers per population was similar, but the Mexican army of 1910 had superior weapons and a much better trained officer corps than the Colombian army of 1899. The Federal Army should have been able to crush the Mexican revolt in 1910–1911, yet it was the badly equipped and poorly trained Colombian army that in July 1900 had saved the Conservative government. Clearly a threshold exists when superior weapons and training can no longer compensate for popular revulsion at a regime. In Mexico in 1911 a majority of the population had turned against the regime, but in Colombia at least a modest majority of the population accepted Conservative rule. In Colombia by August 1900 those Liberals who wanted to revolt had already done so, and most of them were in exile, wounded, or had died in battle. Simply put, the Liberals had failed to rally enough followers willing to take up arms against the Conservatives. The insurrection had spent itself and for all practical purposes was over in August 1900.

If the Liberal minority had been resoundingly defeated in battle by that date, how could the war last two more years? One major explanation has to do with the change of administrations on 31 July 1900. The sickly president no longer stayed in cold Bogotá, because he sought to improve his health by living in the warm climate of a nearby small town (Anapoima). From that town he ran the government, but soon accusations spread that favorites and not Sanclemente himself were taking the decisions. Rumors gained force that he was a senile and decrepit old man who could not even write his signature, and that the favorites used a signature rubber stamp to ratify whatever order they cared to issue. The consensus emerged among many Conservatives that Colombia needed a strong and dynamic government capable of bringing the war to a speedy conclusion. A civilian palace coup deposed Sanclemente and handed power over to vice president José Manuel Marroquín on 31 July 1900. Nobody can deny that the conduct of the war under Sanclemente had been far from ideal, but by that date the major victories in Santander and Panama meant that the deposed administration essentially had pacified the country. Instead the new Marroquín administration bungled the mopping-up operations, was slow to recognize dangers, and made tardy responses to threats. The unexpected and premature deaths from tropical diseases of Próspero Pinzón and Manuel Casabianca early

Piles of skulls remained as a grisly reminder of the Battle of Palonegro (May 1900) for thirteen years after the bloody battle (*Boletín cultural y bibliográfico*, 2000).

in 1901 did deprive the new administration of the two best Conservative generals. But repeatedly whether from inaction, tardiness, or simply blunders, the Marroquín administration prolonged the war and gave the Liberals many chances to revive the uprising.[47]

The Liberals could not know that the palace coup had made the Marroquín administration into their best ally. Instead they realized that the revolt had failed by August 1900. As had happened so often in the past in many other countries, the losing party turned to foreign help as the only way to attain victory.[48] In 1900 and 1901 the key foreign help came from Venezuela, and the support from that country made possible the three episodes this section describes. Venezuela was a sanctuary, and Lib-

Left: General Próspero Pinzón, the most competent army general of the Conservative government during the War of the Thousand Days (1899–1902) in Colombia (Henrique Arboleda, *Palonegro*; Bucaramanga: Imprenta del Departamento, 1953). *Below:* General Pinzón (seated on left) always considered himself a Roman Catholic gentleman and refused to wear army uniform except when military dress was indispensable. His general staff dressed according to this preference. Standing from left are General Rubén Restrepo, General Lázaro Riascos C., General Bernardo Caicedo, and General Gustavo García Herreros; seated at right is General Alcides Arzayús (Henrique Arboleda, *Palonegro*; Bucaramanga: Imprenta del Departamento, 1953).

erals could flee into that country and return at will back into Colombia. Venezuela was also a transit route for the weapons, supplies, and ammunition coming into Colombia. The rebels freely could use Venezuelan territory because President Cipriano Castro sympathized with the Colombians. President Castro, more than any other individual, was responsible for keeping the war going in Colombia through the end of 1901, although his motivations were complex and his support wavered. A man given to delusions of grandeur, he fancied himself another Napoleon Bonaparte or a Simón Bolivar, the South American hero who had won independence from Spain in the 1820s. Although he was not adverse to keeping Colombia weak through civil wars, he professed Liberal beliefs and detested both Colombian and Venezuelan Conservatives, the latter being his main domestic opponents. He also wanted a Liberal victory in Colombia as a way to form a loose confederation over the three countries of Venezuela, Colombia, and Ecuador. According to this fantastic plan, Castro would become president of this new confederation, while Eloy Alfaro of Ecuador and a Colombian Liberal would become vice presidents of their respective countries.[49] Whatever chance for success this scheme had, Castro realized that the strife in Colombia offered many opportunities to exercise influence. Initially he had expected the Liberal revolt in Colombia to succeed as easily and speedily as his revolt in Venezuela in October 1899. But once the Liberal revolt lost its momentum, he realized that he had to do more than provide a sanctuary and a supply base for the Colombian rebels. For the first time he gave direct support to the Liberals, who were preparing to launch an offensive in the Department of Magdalena.

The Liberal Campaign in the Caribbean Coast (June–December 1900)

The Conservative recapture of Riohacha in November 1899 had been a short-lived victory. The Conservative authorities never managed to extend their control into the interior, and meanwhile Venezuela was providing extensive support for the invasion of the Department of Magdalena (Map 2). Besides the capture of Riohacha and Santa Marta, the real goal of the Liberal expedition was to reach the Magdalena River and cut off that lifeline of the Conservative government. News of the approach of the large Liberal expedition under General Justo Durán persuaded army troops to abandon Riohacha. General Durán duly occupied that strategic port in February 1900, and his expedition was off to a very propitious start. Volunteers flocked to join the Liberal force, and soon he commanded nearly two thousand men, all well-armed with the weapons and supplies from Venezuela. The Liberals obtained and armed two steamships in Venezuela, and in May these two gunboats were in Riohacha. Thanks to support from Venezuela, the Liberals had regained the initiative and were poised to strike possibly deadly blows against the Conservative government.

Unfortunately for the Liberals, General Durán was a very passive individual who did not like to take any chances, and his inactivity had already consumed too much time. In June he finally agreed to assault Santa Marta by land

with the support of the two gunboats by sea, but before any shooting had started, he changed his mind and ordered the expedition to return to Riohacha. After this botched attempt, a Mexican traitor hijacked the gunboats and took them back to Venezuela. By then President Castro had become disillusioned with the Liberal expedition, and he did not allow the Liberal gunboats to return. Durán still had a powerful land force, but by then the outcome of the battle of Palonegro had totally changed the significance of this Caribbean offensive. Until May 1900 Duran's campaign had been a supporting operation, but after that date it became the Liberals' last chance to strike a serious blow before army reinforcements from the interior reached the Caribbean coast.[50]

The key to any Liberal success was control of the Magdalena River. Ever since the naval battle at Gamarra, the Conservative government had continually used that river to move troops and supplies. Sensing the urgency of gaining control of the Magdalena River, General Rafael Uribe Uribe decided to make one last effort in the Caribbean coast before trying to seek refuge in Venezuela. He had just barely managed to escape capture in Santander and with three aides rowed at night down the Magdalena River until he reached the Department of Bolívar. His plan had two parts. First he would take charge of the scattered guerrilla bands in that department and lead them to capture a town bordering on the Magdalena River. As the Conservatives would do everything possible to keep him from blockading the river, this was the hardest part of the plan and had a very high probability of failure. The easy part of the plan called for General Durán to march his large force south from Riohacha until he had linked up with Uribe Uribe in the Magdalena River. The latter urgently needed some of the many cases of cartridges Venezuela had abundantly provided to Durán. Once his men were well supplied, Uribe Uribe was certain that he could repel any Conservative attempt to regain control of the Magdalena River.[51]

Against all odds, Uribe Uribe was able to rally the guerrillas in the Department of Bolívar, even though General Gabriel Vargas Santos had already sent messages urging the local liberal leaders not to accept Uribe Uribe as their commander. The local leaders ignored the message from the exiled leader and enthusiastically recognized the already legendary Uribe Uribe as their leader. Soon Uribe Uribe seized major towns in the interior of Bolívar, not because of their intrinsic value but because this was his only way to obtain cartridges for his men. He knew that attacks against the two key cities of Cartagena and Barranquilla were impossible until he obtained ample ammunition. He completed his original plan when he captured Magangué, a strategically situated port town on the Magdalena River. Since the start of his campaign, Uribe Uribe had been sending urgent messages to Durán to hasten the march to Magangué from Riohacha, but the latter deliberately stayed away from the river to prevent any link up. The rivals of Uribe Uribe were afraid that if he received ample ammunition, he might still be able to capture the Caribbean cities and by himself win the war. Once again, blocking Uribe Uribe became more important for many Liberals than defeating the Conservatives.

The slow march of Durán south of Riohacha ended in disaster because of one of those comical episodes that have so unjustly stereotyped wars in Latin America. Upon entering into view of the opponent, both the Liberal and the army commanders panicked and ordered an immediate retreat without having fired a shot. The haste of Durán to flee was so great that he ordered his men to abandon all the cases containing the cartridges Uribe Uribe so desperately needed. Because Uribe Uribe never received the cartridges, he could no longer repel the army attacks on Magangué and had to abandon the town. Once again the government had full control of the Magdalena River. Uribe Uribe withdrew to the southwest and resumed his practice of capturing isolated garrisons to replenish his supply of cartridges. Soon many army units were hot on his trail, and the wretched condition of his men persuaded him to abandon the hopeless struggle. He believed that he could be more useful trying to secure supplies and ammunition for the revolt in New York and Venezuela. He deputized leaders to try to keep the guerrillas active in the Department of Bolívar until his return, and he reached Riohacha in December 1900 on his way to Venezuela. He knew that Venezuela had to be his base of operations, but like many other Liberals, he had already learned that President Castro could be a fickle patron. Uribe Uribe personally went to Caracas to request support from the Venezuelan ruler, but President Castro refused to cooperate.[52]

Uribe Uribe then took a steamship to New York, because like many Latin American exiles before and after, he cherished the myth of finding support in that city for the revolt back home. He had the recent example of the Cuban war of independence against Spain (1895–1898) when exiles had obtained resources in New York City to fit out expeditions against Cuba. But as Uribe Uribe knocked fruitlessly on door after door, he sadly reached the conclusion, as most Latin American exiles eventually did, that he could not repeat the fund-raising success of the Cuban exiles in their war of independence.[53] Militarily the Liberal uprising had failed by the middle of 1900, and only ample sums of money could revive the revolt. Realistically, he reached the conclusion that the Liberals had to end the war. He knew that he risked his position within the Liberal Party by being the first to publicly state the need to end the war. Consequently, he directed a famous manifesto urging peace not to the Colombian government but to the Liberals on 12 April 1901. Privately he discussed possible terms for a truce with Carlos Martínez Silva, a leading Conservative politician then Colombian minister to the United States, and conditions never seemed more favorable to end all hostilities.

Uribe Uribe wanted face-saving concessions from the Conservative government mainly to persuade all Liberals to abandon the war. His most important request was minority participation for Liberals in the legislative bodies in Colombia. Indignantly President Manuel Marroquín rejected the peace offers as a sign of weakness, and in public even the Conservatives openly ridiculed Uribe Uribe and called him a traitor to his cause. As expected, the faction within the Liberal party that had always opposed Uribe Uribe joined in the criticism. What was surprising was the arrogance of the Conservative government that insisted on unconditional submission without any concessions. The Marroquín administration believed that it was just a matter of months before the Colombian army finished destroying the last pockets of rebellion in the country. Even more rashly, the Marroquín government concluded that no real peace was possible until Colombia eliminated the Venezuelan sanctuary for the Liberals.[54]

Colombia was full of Conservative Venezuelan exiles who were seeking support to overthrown the Liberal Castro. The most prestigious Venezuelan Conservative was Carlos Rangel Garbiras, who with Colombian support was organizing fellow exiles for an invasion of Venezuela. When news of these preparations reached President Castro, he suddenly remembered Uribe Uribe and called him back from New York City. The president wanted the Liberal leader to organize Colombian exiles to stop the invasion of Rangel Garbiras. Uribe Uribe was at a crossroads in his career and in the history of his country. He could either submit unconditionally to the Colombian government, or he could accept President Castro's last-minute offer. If he submitted to the Colombian government, he might lose his prestige and probably sacrificed his leadership position within the Liberal party, but he would have spared his country of the suffering and disasters that the war still had in store for Colombia. His decision was perhaps inevitable, and he accepted Castro's offer to return to Venezuela. By the first days of July 1901 he was in San Cristóbal preparing the defense of that city against the expected invasion. In reality, Uribe Uribe's decision was a natural response to an earlier decision by the Colombian government. The Marroquín administration had not even entertained his peace proposals and had arrogantly rejected them. By refusing to negotiate with Uribe Uribe while he was in New York, the Marroquín administration set in motion the chain of events that revived the Liberal revolt and prolonged the war until 1902. A more disastrous decision on the part of the Colombian government cannot be imagined.[55]

The Colombian Invasion of Venezuela

By 15 July 1901 the support of President Cipriano Castro had allowed Rafael Uribe Uribe to organize 1500 Colombian exiles in Venezuela at San Cristóbal in Táchira province. The Liberal leader knew that this force was still too small to attempt any invasion of the Department of Santander, because just the Colombian troops stationed on the border numbered over 4,000 soldiers. Nevertheless, telegraph reports persuaded the Colombian government that Uribe Uribe's mobilization posed a major threat. Up to this moment Colombian authorities had been quietly supporting the plan of Venezuelan exile Carlos Rangel Garbiras to topple President Castro, but Bogotá concluded that Uribe Uribe's large force called for a more drastic response. The Marroquín administration authorized a preemptive strike by Colombian troops to go to the root of the problem and to end the Venezuelan sanctuary for Liberals once and for all. The invasion had the two-fold purpose of destroying Uribe Uribe's force in San Cristóbal and also of starting a Conservative uprising in Venezuela. Even if Rangel Garbiras failed to overthrow President Castro, Bogotá assumed that the task of pacifying Venezuela would keep Castro too occupied to be able to lend any support for the Colombian Liberals. Of course, Colombia was starting an international war by launching an invasion across the border, but Bogotá trusted that in the two most likely scenarios of either a civil war in Venezuela or the fall of President Castro, Colombia would escape any adverse consequences.

The Colombian units comprised the majority of the invasion force, and they were going to Venezuela supposedly as private citizens who had volunteered to help overthrow President Castro. An obsession with legalistic concerns persuaded Bogotá to take the extra precaution of placing Colombian troops under the command of the Venezuelan exile Rangel Garbiras. Although it was joked in Venezuela that he "did not even know how to fire a rifle,"[56] the Colombian authorities did not seem worried by his lack of military credentials. Meanwhile Uribe Uribe learned that regular Colombian troops were going to form the bulk of the invasion, but when he reported the news to President Castro and to his brother who was the governor of Táchira province, both dismissed the reports as Liberal fabrications to drag Venezuela into a war with Colombia. President Castro's refusal to reinforce his border province left the frontier wide open for the Colombian invasion.[57]

Rangel Garbiras considered military victory to be inevitable, and he devoted his efforts to the real task of preparing a new government in Caracas. He lavished appointments on his followers and soon had a shadow government in existence ready to occupy the important government posts in Caracas and the governorships. He spent a lot of time writing the mandatory manifesto, which he duly issued on 18 July 1901; in it he labored to reconcile the overwhelming desire of all Venezuelans to overthrow Castro with the need for Colombian intervention. The weighty task of preparing the manifesto did not keep Rangel Garbiras from neglecting the very important details of proper credentials. He had appropriate stationery printed up, and in letterheads he styled himself "President in campaign."[58]

With seemingly nothing left unprepared, the first Colombian troops crossed the border (where the railroad ended) at 0600 on 26 July 1901 for what promised to be a victory parade to San Cristóbal, the capital of Táchira province in Venezuela. Marching at a normal pace over familiar roads, the fresh and well-armed troops should have reached the town that same afternoon. Even with a long siesta after lunch, the troops should have reached their destination at the latest in early evening. Just the news of the rapid approach of an invasion force numbering over 5,000 soldiers was sure to send into a panicky retreat the 300-man garrison of San Cristóbal, and that town doubtlessly would have fallen without a fight. However, Rangel Garbiras saw no need for such unseemly haste, and in any case he had already divided his force into five columns and had given them orders to fan out across Táchira province prior to converging on San Cristóbal. Although the first Colombian troops reached San Cristóbal on the afternoon of July 27, units were still straggling on the last day of the eventual battle. Even worse was the absence of unified command, because the units took up whatever positions their commanders thought most suitable. Thus, the garrison of San Cristóbal faced not one large army but many units acting independently. [59]

Meanwhile, Uribe Uribe had been feverishly preparing the defenses of San Cristóbal, and he was the de facto commander. His spies reported the invasion even before the Colombian troops had entered Venezuela, and this early warning allowed the small border detachments to withdraw safely into San Cristóbal. He also ordered other Venezuelan units in the province to come to the defense of the town. Ultimately he commanded a respectable force of 2,500 men, comprised of 1500 Colombians and 1,000 Venezuelans. The numbers were still

2 to 1 in favor of the invading force, yet Uribe Uribe hoped to even the odds by rapidly shattering any illusion of an easy victory. The long perimeter he had to defend left particularly vulnerable the north and south sides of the town, but he counted on holding those weak points long enough to mount a flanking attack.

Shooting began at noon on 28 July, but the real fighting did not take place until the next day when most of the invading army dribbled in. On 29 July the invading forces attacked San Cristóbal from the north in the cemetery and were startled to receive deadly volleys from defenders in trenches. When a Colombian column that was supposed to attack the town from the south did not appear, Uribe Uribe concluded that the moment had arrived to mount a flanking attack. He marched around a hill to fall on the flank of the attacking troops and sent them reeling in retreat. By this time the Colombian troops were grumbling and did not understand why they should be fighting in a foreign country. The invaders made one last attack, but a second flanking attack by the defenders destroyed whatever will to fight remained in the Colombian soldiers who had already suffered the loss of 800 killed or wounded. By 1400 the Colombian troops were racing with the Venezuelan exiles to be the first to reach the border, and many threw away their equipment and weapons. The Liberals went on the pursuit but were able to take less than a hundred prisoners because the defeated army was fleeing so fast. Fearing that the Liberals would carry out their rumored invasion of Colombia, the government troops temporarily abandoned Cúcuta and rushed to seek safety by fleeing south to Bucaramanga.[60]

The Marroquín administration for a few days was in panic thinking it had carelessly started a war with its neighbor. President Castro wanted to reap a propaganda victory and was carefully gathering materials for an official publication or White Book denouncing the Colombian government. But because the Bogotá government had always prided itself on respect for international treaties, it desperately strove to find face-saving formulas to extricate itself from its embarrassing dilemma. Claiming that the invasion was carried out solely by volunteers, the Marroquín administration tried to wash its hands of the whole matter. By disowning the invasion, Bogotá had given President

Castro a good excuse to defuse an explosive situation. Once Castro calmed down long enough to realize that a war was not in his best interest, his enthusiasm for denouncing Colombia waned, and both countries let the invasion pass quietly into history.[61]

The Liberal victory at San Cristóbal briefly offered another good opportunity to end the war in Colombia. While many Liberals still hoped to overthrow the government, others such as Rafael Uribe Uribe realistically expected only to extract concessions at the negotiating table. Uribe Uribe should have used the panic in Bogotá over a war with Venezuela to negotiate his submission to the Conservative government. Since he was the most prestigious leader in the revolt, his defection necessarily would have condemned the rest of the Liberals to irrelevance or to submit to terms. It was a tragedy for Colombia that neither the Conservative government nor Uribe Uribe seized this fleeting opportunity to end the war. The victory at San Cristóbal also demonstrated that the Liberal uprising was far from over. As rebel bands revived and became more aggressive, the Conservative government could no longer believe that the country was pacified.

The Venezuelan Invasion of the Department of Magdalena (1901 August–September)

In spite of the Colombian attack on San Cristóbal in July 1901, President Cipriano Castro hesitated to plunge Venezuela into a full-scale war with Colombia and preferred a limited reprisal. Actually, the attack on San Cristóbal was not the only reason he wanted to strike back at the Colombian Conservatives. Many Liberal Venezuelans had died at the battle of Palonegro, and he had always wanted to avenge their deaths. Because the Colombian government was massing troops at the Táchira border and had reoccupied Cúcuta, any thrust in that direction meant major hostilities. Instead to the north an undefended border separated Venezuela from the Department of Magdalena, a Liberal stronghold. The many Liberal bands in that region had been trying to recapture Riohacha, but shortage of cartridges had always foiled their intentions. Providing weapons and ammunition to the Liberal guerrillas was the most obvious way to get back at the Colombian Conservatives, but President Castro felt that this response did not satisfy his honor or that of his country. He insisted on sending Venezuelan troops into battle inside Colombia as the minimal reprisal. In early August 1901 the first 200 Venezuelan soldiers crossed the border into the Guajira district of the Department of Magdalena, and they blended easily with the rebels. But when an additional 1200 Venezuelan soldiers crossed the border early in September, their number came to equal that of the rapidly coalescing rebel bands.[62]

This large Venezuelan force, besides being well armed with cannons and one machine gun, also brought additional rifles and many cases of ammunition to distribute among the Liberal bands. Because the army garrison at Riohacha numbered at most 400 soldiers, everything indicated an easy capture of that large town. As an additional precaution, Venezuelan gunboats came to block the harbor of Riohacha, so that the Conservative government could not send reinforcements to the beleaguered garrison. Unfortunately, fundamental

Rafael Uribe Uribe, the outstanding military figure of the War of the Thousand Days in Colombia. His extraordinary abilities saved the Liberal revolt on several occasions (*Boletín cultural y bibliográfico*, 2000).

flaws dogged the expedition from the start. President Castro appointed the incompetent General José Antonio Dávila, one of his loyal followers, to head the Venezuelan contingent. Secondly, he did not put the Venezuelan contingent under the command of local Liberal leaders and merely urged Dávila to work closely with the Colombian leaders. Of course, unity of command by itself cannot guarantee victory, but in Guajira a divided command created potentially fatal complications.[63]

Rather than a bloody assault on the entrenched garrison at Riohacha, the Liberal leaders argued for luring out the army troops to the east to Carazúa (Map 2) and then the main rebel force would make a flanking march in the rear to enter Riohacha by surprise. The army troops, seeing themselves cut off from their base and under attack in the front from another rebel force at Carazúa, were sure either to scatter or surrender. With very little fighting Riohacha would fall to the rebels, who wanted to save their men and ammunition for the big push to Santa Marta and then on to Barranquilla to cut off the vital waterway of the Magdalena River. The Venezuelan Dávila correctly emphasized that his troops would not follow the rebels that deeply into Colombian territory, but he was vehemently opposed to the plan to capture Riohacha without combat. He had come to fight to redeem the honor of Venezuela and not to occupy real estate, and only grudgingly did he appear to accept the rebel plan.[64]

On 12 September the combined force was duly in place to spring the trap. Early in the morning scouts reported that army troops were fast approaching Carazúa. Their haste was surprising, because the Liberal leaders had expected the force to advance slowly out of fear of being cut off from Riohacha. But before the army troops reached Carazúa, the Liberals to their consternation saw their main force returning from its hiding place near Riohacha to rejoin the rest of the Liberals at Carazúa. Why had this sudden change of deployment occurred? The Venezuelan General Dávila had ordered the entire detachment back to Carazúa, because he needed to have blood shed in real combat to vindicate the honor of Venezuela. Unfortunately for Dávila, he was in for a big shock. Unknown to the rebels, just a few nights before reinforcements had reached the Rio-

hacha garrison by sea. For unexplained reasons, the Venezuelan gunboats blockading the port had anchored to the northwest, leaving the entrance open for coastwise ships. The number of army soldiers had increased from 400 to nearly 1500, and more significantly, they came equipped not just with field cannons but also with several machine guns. The Venezuelan troops did have comparable field cannons but did not know how to use them effectively. Rather than using the cannon for long-range shelling, they remained tied to the Napoleonic tactic of putting the cannons in the front ranks to stiffen the morale of the infantry. And as for their single machine gun, a malfunction forced the Venezuelans to hide it in some bushes until a replacement part came.

When on 13 September at 1130 the opponents came within firing range, the mutual surprise caused tremendous consternation; neither side had expected to fight the biggest battle in the Caribbean coast. With perhaps as many as 3,000 men in the combined Liberal and Venezuelan force, the rebels still enjoyed a two-to-one superiority but not the eight-to-one they had originally expected. Normally the guerrilla bands would have fled, but enjoying for the first time ample ammunition and the support of the Venezuelan cannons, they were determined to stand and fight. For the army general, the situation was very straightforward; he realized that he had walked into a trap, and having been misled as to the size of the force facing him, he did not know what other rebel bands were still lurking in his rear. Saving his army by returning to Riohacha before another rebel force cut off his retreat became his only goal. However, he knew that any sudden withdrawal could easily turn into a bloody rout unless he first weakened the rebels. He thus was willing to engage in battle but just long enough to assure the escape of his army.

At 1130 both forces furiously began shooting and shelling each other out in the open field. The Venezuelan decision to place their field pieces in the front rank proved to be a costly mistake, as the army troops with their new Mauser rifles picked off the gunners until the cannons were left abandoned. Instead, the army cannons out of rifle range kept up a steady if not very accurate long-range shelling. The absence of any breastworks or trenches proved deadly to the Liberals and the Venezuelans, and the latter, as their casualties mounted, began to desert to the rear. Soon most of the Venezuelan units were in a panicky flight to the distant frontier; some were so terrorized that they took the northern direction into the desert regions where many perished leaving abandoned their weapons and ammunition along many kilometers. Although some Venezuelan units and the Liberals were still putting up with the murderous fire, the Liberal leaders wisely ordered a retreat but insisted that the men try to retrieve as much of their equipment and ammunition as possible. As soon as the first Venezuelan units began to flee, army troops marched forward into the collapsing line. The troops took hundreds of prisoners and also found the concealed inoperative machine gun with its cases of ammunition. The army commander received the news of this unexpected turnaround as a blessing from heaven, because he could claim a victory instead of a hasty retreat back to Riohacha. Had he ordered a forward charge, he could have destroyed the Liberal force completely and more importantly captured all their weapons and ammunition. Instead, he let pass the opportunity to pacify the Department of Magdalena.

He still believed that another Liberal force was ready to pounce on his rear and cut off his escape. Once he was certain about the Liberal flight, he ordered his soldiers to retreat quickly to Riohacha while the escape route was open. The fleeing rebels and the Venezuelans left abandoned almost all their ammunition and weapons over a vast area. The army commander was in such a rush to bottle himself back in Riohacha, that he did not have time to worry about any return of the Liberals to retrieve the scattered material.

The Liberals' Last Efforts, 1901–1902

The Liberal Resurgence in Panama (September–November 1901)

After the disastrous attack on Panama City in July 1900, the Liberal revolt in that region seemed to be over. The new administration of José Manuel Marroquín confidently transferred troops to other theaters and did not even bother to acquire naval vessels for the protection of that strategic department. Once again Bogotá was neglecting Panama and, not surprisingly, mopping up efforts faltered after July 1900. The rebels realized they could plunder, loot, and rape with immunity, and small bands proliferated in the interior of Panama over the next year. The rebels committed numerous atrocities in their search for plunder. The most notorious rebel leaders were the Indian Victoriano Lorenzo and Manuel Antonio Noriega, whose infamous actions were later overshadowed by those of his descendant and namesake in the 1980s. The impunity with which these rebel bands acted encouraged Liberal exiles to invade Panama again, but they needed foreign support to outfit expeditions. The president of Nicaragua, José Santos Zelaya was willing to support an expedition, but because he unjustly blamed Belisario Porras for the failure of the 1900 invasion, the Nicaraguan president insisted on supporting the weak and colorless Domingo Díaz.[65]

On 16 September Domingo Díaz landed on the coast of Panama not too far from La Chorrera, the town he selected for his base of operations. Many rebel bands joined his expedition, but other rebel groups continued to recognize Porras as their leader. Quarrels among rebel leaders soon weakened the Díaz expedition. Minor successes raiding government outposts helped keep the expedition alive, but the failure of Díaz to control the rebels confirmed his lack of leadership abilities. Díaz gradually faded from the scene, and a collective leadership assumed the task of taking decisions for the Liberal invasion. Although their undisturbed stay for months at La Chorrera made evident the government's weakness, the Liberals wanted more than a stalemate and remained on the lookout for a favorable opportunity to strike against the government.[66]

The Díaz invasion had not seemed threatening enough to the Marroquín administration, (that as usual dragged its feet sending reinforcements), and only very slowly did troops begin to arrive in Barranquilla for the trip to Panama. General Carlos Albán, the governor of Panama, had two choices before him. He could wait for the promised reinforcements to arrive and then after having garrisoned the Colón-Panama City corridor, he could launch an offensive to destroy the rebels. This was the soundest course of action, but waiting for

weeks or possibly months did not fit well with
his impulsive nature and grandiose concep-
tions. He decided instead to take the troops
garrisoning the railroad corridor on an offensive into the interior to surprise the rebels. He
left a token force in Colón and a modest garrison in Panama City, and then on 17 November he personally led the bulk of his troops
aboard ships to try to surprise the rebels at La
Chorrera. The measure was very risky and
could easily turn into a disaster, and in any
case no surprise was possible, because Governor Albán, a very trusting person, never realized that Liberal spies were promptly reporting
his every movement back to the rebels at La
Chorrera.[67]

The rebels immediately put into motion
their plan. The bulk of the rebel forces went to
the coast to try to delay Governor Albán's
troops as long as possible, and a detachment of
two hundred rebels marched north to try to
reach Colón while the city was weakly garrisoned. The rebels blocked the first attempt of
army troops to disembark, and when the
troops finally landed, the rebels kept them
under steady harassment. Governor Albán
should have realized he had lost all element of
surprise and that without enough troops for a
long and bloody campaign through the thick
forests, he needed to return promptly to
Panama City. Meanwhile the small rebel
detachment, with minute knowledge of the
operations of the Panama Railroad, had
marched north to catch a train. The rebels
boarded the wagons of one of the trains that
routinely waited in the station, and the rebel
officers took the precaution of purchasing
tickets for their men. The train duly entered
Colón, and the rebels overwhelmed the surprised garrison and took control of the city on
19 November 1901.[68]

The almost bloodless capture of Colón
was the high-water mark of Liberal success in
Panama. For the first time during the entire
war, the rebels prevented the government from
using the Panama Railroad. As soon as the
main Liberal forces heard of the capture
of Colón, they withdrew from their camps near
La Chorrera and marched north to set up road
blocks on the Panama Railroad. The rebels
allowed commercial and passenger service
to pass, but they did search trains to prevent
the passage of troops or war material. When

Governor Albán heard of the Liberal capture
of Colón, he was furious at having been outmaneuvered and fooled by the rebels. He
wanted to correct his blunder by rushing units
from La Chorrera back to Panama City and
then north by train to drive the rebels out of
Colón. Governor Albán failed to realize that
the rebel capture of Colón immediately opened
the door to foreign intervention. On 24 November the U.S. consul in Panama City concluded that conditions on the trains were not
safe for passengers, and he asked U.S. ships to
land forces for the protection of the railroad
service. U.S. marines began escorting the
trains, and the next day the railroad refused to
transport army troops north to the front near
Colón.[69]

The inability to ride trains forced the
army troops to travel on foot and gave the
rebels plenty of time to construct defenses
south of Colón. A rebel defeat was never in
doubt, because news of the loss of Colón had
finally galvanized the Marroquín administration into dispatching the troops in Barranquilla
to Colón aboard the gunboat *Próspero Pinzón*.
But upon its arrival, U.S. warships imposed a
delay of four days before the gunboat could
land troops to recover Colón. Governor Albán
meanwhile was leading the assaults on the rebel
defenses in the railroad route. Inexplicably, the
rebels abandoned their best positions and instead set up their defense on a line vulnerable
to a flanking movement. The U.S. navy had
also extracted an agreement from Liberal leaders requiring the latter to abandon Colón if
Governor Albán's troops cleared a path to the
city. When army troops sent the rebels fleeing
in retreat back into Colón, the Liberals signed
a capitulation on 28 November. In exchange
for no reprisals, the rebels agreed to surrender
their weapons and to abandon Colón. To avoid
incidents between the departing rebels and the
army troops, U.S. sailors temporarily held the
city before handing it over to Governor Albán's
troops.[70]

As the rebel bands disintegrated, and once
all danger to the Panama Railroad vanished,
the last U.S. troops withdrew on 4 December
1901. The unilateral intervention and the high-
handed actions of U.S. officials had generated
considerable anger in Colombia. An angry
Governor Albán went so far as to say he was
going to attack and disarm U.S. troops as soon

as he received reinforcements. Perhaps he was only venting his anger, but his outrage was shared by many in Bogotá who refused to recognize how far the balance of power had shifted to the U.S. government in recent decades. At no time did the Marroquín administration admit that its failure to garrison Panama adequately had caused the loss of Colón.[71] And once order returned to the Isthmus, the Marroquín administration, always lurching belatedly and clumsily from one crisis to the next, again neglected Panama and shifted its attention to other parts of Colombia.

The Liberal Invasion of the Llanos (1901 December–1902 April)

Rebel bands had gained control of the Llanos to the east of the Andes Mountains, while other rebel groups roamed at will through the Departments of Cundinamarca and Tolima (Map 1). Liberal exiles in Ecuador and Central America were busily preparing expeditions against the Departments of Panama and Cauca. Once again, the Colombian government was forced to spread its troops thinly to try to face both present and possible threats. Without the existence of a railroad network in Colombia, the deployment of troops was slow and kept the initiative in the hands of the Liberals.

At Táchira Rafael Uribe Uribe continued to build up his forces, and the Bogotá government, with no better clue as to his intentions, mechanically increased the number of Colombian troops facing him. His original plan had been to cross the border into Colombia at the same time that Liberal uprisings broke out in the Department of Santander. But as the weeks passed, the news from that region was uniformly negative. The last of the rebel bands in Santander had surrendered or been destroyed, and attempts to rally recruits had yielded few volunteers. Although some Liberals crossed the border to join the growing army of Uribe Uribe at Táchira, it was hard to avoid the conclusion that Santander, the original hotbed of the Liberal revolt, was exhausted and could not make any meaningful contribution to the war. The presence of large numbers of Colombian troops massed at the border served as a powerful deterrent and as a reminder that the Conservative government could still wield considerable military might. At the same time, President Cipriano Castro was finally realizing that the Liberals had no chance of winning the war, and he was gradually disengaging himself from Colombian affairs. He concluded that good relations with the Conservative government in Colombia were more important for him than continuing to support a dying Liberal revolt. Time was running out for the Liberal exiles in Venezuela, and when in November 1902 President Castro withdrew all support from the Colombians, Uribe Uribe knew he had to act fast before his exile force disbanded. He was down to the two options: he could march north and enter the Department of Magdalena or he could try the very risky move of going south to link up with the rebel bands operating in the Llanos and near Bogotá. The crushing Liberal defeat at Carazúa on 13 September made the first option unattractive.[72]

In any case, the lure of replicating the heroic ordeal of the Liberator Simón Bolívar was irresistible. In 1819 Bolívar had crossed the Llanos from Venezuela and climbed the icy Andes Mountains to win a smashing victory over unsuspecting Spanish troops in Boyacá. And the same reasons that had driven Bolívar to tempt the Andes Mountains were at work to push Uribe Uribe into a similar maneuver. Up to this moment the war had never posed a serious threat to the heartland of the country, but if he could bring the war to the national capital, he might just be able to strike a possibly fatal blow against the government. Even if the risky move was not completely successful, by prolonging the war he hoped to extract at least some concessions from a thoroughly scared Conservative government. The maneuver had to be carried out in complete secrecy, because otherwise the Conservative government would have ample time to transfer units away from the Venezuelan border to Cundinamarca. In theory, the movement of units seemed easier for the government, because it enjoyed shorter lines of communication than Uribe Uribe, who had to make a long flanking march around the Andes Mountains. In fact, the rugged mountains actually took longer to cross than the flat terrain of the Llanos. The railroad line from Bogotá extended only as far as Zipaquirá, where the large highland plateau ended.[73]

On 24 December 1901 Uribe Uribe set out from Táchira with his force and plunged into the dense forest to the southeast, and on 24 January 1902 reached Tame far into the Llanos. Everywhere his troops were well received, and many rebel bands joined his force. As usual, his magnetic personality made him very appealing to the local population. He drove his men at a steady pace marching south around the Andes Mountains until his column reached Medina which he turned into his base of operations for the difficult crossing of the high mountain peaks in front of him. Surprised army troops at Gachalá reported the approach of a rebel force and asked for reinforcements, but the Marroquín administration refused to believe that a large rebel column was so near. The Liberals attacked and defeated army troops in the battle of Gachalá on 12 March, but enough survivors escaped to report that none other than Uribe Uribe was leading the rebels. At last Bogotá woke up to the danger and promptly dispatched units to face the legendary Liberal hero.[74]

Unknown to Uribe Uribe, his expedition was already doomed. His first inkling of trouble came when recently incorporated rebel leaders proved lax about obeying his orders to cover the column's flanks. As he struggled with the indiscipline of the new rebels, he did not know that the decisive events near Bogotá had already ruined his invasion strategy. Even before the battle at Gachalá had revealed his exact location, news of the impeding arrival of Uribe Uribe to Bogotá had preceded him. Great as was the fear among the Conservatives, it was even greater among certain Liberals who had always resented Uribe Uribe. Intense envy made some Liberals fear that Uribe Uribe would turn into a modern-day Caesar and proclaim himself dictator of Colombia. The rebel chieftains near Bogotá who had enjoyed a free hand to loot and pillage to their hearts' content knew that the arrival of Uribe Uribe would not only stop the plundering but also would reduce them to insignificance. Bogotá Liberals urged the rebel bands to win a major battle before Uribe Uribe arrived, so that they would be in a position to control their tropical Caesar.[75]

The Liberal guerrillas had kept Bogotá practically surrounded but the machine guns of the government had prevented the rebels from capturing any important towns in the highland plateau. The Liberal chieftain Juan MacAllister

had been very successful as long as he stuck to raiding isolated villages and defenseless farms. Rather than waiting for Uribe Uribe to come with his cannons, MacAllister attacked Soacha on 23 February. Had he massed all his men for a simultaneous attack he probably would have won, but his bands dribbled in. The War Minister saw a chance to strike a decisive blow, and he promptly rushed reinforcements from Bogotá by railroad. A repulse turned into a panicky rout, and the guerrilla bands near Bogotá never recovered their morale after this disastrous defeat at Soacha. These disheartened guerrillas escaped to safety in the Llanos via the road from Quetame to Villavicencio. This very rugged road running southeast from Bogotá abounds in very defensible positions where small detachments can hold off large units for days if not weeks, yet the terror-stricken rebels fled at the sight of army troops even without having fired a shot. On 19 March the army troops entered Villavicencio as the remnants of the guerillas fled north to try to join Uribe Uribe; had the troops pushed north and captured the undefended base of Medina, they would have trapped Uribe Uribe's column. Fortunately for the rebel leader, news of his victory at Gachalá on 12 March persuaded the government to halt the pursuit at Villavicencio and to recall most of those troops for the defense of Bogotá. Because the force at Villavicencio numbered 4,000 soldiers and that facing Uribe Uribe's column numbered 6,000 soldiers, the government let slip away the opportunity to trap and destroy the rebel force before it could escape into the Llanos.[76]

Unaware that the defeat and flight of the Liberal guerrillas near Bogotá had deprived his expedition of any chance of success, the always optimistic Uribe Uribe continued to push ahead into the highland plateau. His victory near Gachalá on 12 March had boosted the enthusiasm of his troops and had also yielded large quantities of weapons and cartridges. He could put in the field over 2000 men, but unfortunately the new rebel leaders who had joined his column believed his orders to be merely suggestions, and Uribe Uribe felt that as far as discipline, he was back to the situation of 1899. He believed that both a distant covering force and a nearby unit were standing ready to support his advance guard, only to have his advance guard almost destroyed at Guasca on 21 March, and he himself barely escaped capture. He promptly pulled back, but the sight of large numbers of approaching army troops had already demoralized his men more than he realized. Uribe Uribe saw the opportunity to stop the troops by fortifying the defensible elevations at the farm of El Amoladero. As he had expected, on 22 March the army troops established a line in front of his defenses, but as a bad omen, not all the rebel forces showed up to take their assigned positions. After some skirmishing, the army troops mounted a vigorous assault, but meeting intense resistance, they retreated to regroup for a second assault. By then many rebels had decided to abandon the field as soon as the army troops began the second assault, and the rebel line rapidly crumbled. The advancing soldiers occupied one abandoned strategic position after another and were trying to surround the rebel force, but Uribe Uribe rallied enough men to stop the flanking movement until the remnants of his force could escape. He himself once again barely escaped capture or death as he fearlessly fought in the front lines as was his custom.[77]

He managed to calm his men down sufficiently to carry out a first strategic withdrawal to a new defensive line on 25 March. In hindsight he should have abandoned any thought of combat, but the apparently impregnable nature of the mountain peaks lulled him into thinking his men could still inflict a bloody defeat on army troops. The defensive line made the army soldiers pause and ask for reinforcements. The new army units brought cannons and machine guns, and soon those weapons were raking the rebel line. The strafing and shelling finished depressing the already demoralized rebels. When on 31 March Uribe Uribe ordered the inevitable withdrawal to the Llanos, the rebels ignored his detailed instructions for a safe and methodical withdrawal and instead rushed to escape. All discipline disappeared as rebel bands disintegrated and men threw away their weapons. Had the army troops attacked during the withdrawal, probably the entire rebel force would have been killed or captured. Apparently the army troops were not eager for combat either, for although they followed the collapsing Liberal column, they never came close enough to engage in combat or even random shooting.[78]

On 2 April 1902 at Medina the remnants of Uribe Uribe's column joined the guerrillas who had fled from the Conservatives at Villavicencio. The much-anticipated juncture of all the Liberal forces had finally taken place, but by this time it was a meaningless gesture because desertions and demoralization had shattered these forces beyond hope of any revival. To any disinterested observer it was amply clear that the Liberals had lost the war; the calculated risk of marching around the Llanos to catch Bogotá by surprise had turned out to be a dismal failure. The rebel leaders gathered in Medina held a formal council to decide their future course of action, but knowing well that army troops were slowly approaching, the meeting necessarily was brief. The lack of time perhaps precluded Uribe Uribe from using this occasion to persuade the local leaders that the war had to end. This conclusion was already evident in December 1901 before Uribe Uribe had set out from Táchira, but at the head of an apparently impressive column, he could not resist rolling the dice one last time to try his luck. Why risk everything again on an even riskier gamble? Both Liberals and Uribe Uribe should have insisted on ending their war when at Medina they commanded only a shadow of a shattered column. The continuation of the war could only bring irreparable damage to Colombia, yet the political passions were so high that the Liberals could not sacrifice their party for the good of the whole country. At Medina the rebel leaders agreed to unrealistic plans to return to Cundinamarca and other regions of the interior to raise recruits for new guerrilla forces; Uribe Uribe took the task of going to Curaçao to bring weapons and supplies to the Liberal forces in the Caribbean coast.[79]

His decision to make one last attempt in the Caribbean coast rather than to seek peace might seem inexplicable when in December 1901 he had rejected that option and instead had taken the southern road for the flanking move to the Llanos. But by April 1902 major new developments had taken place not only in the Caribbean coast but also in the distant Department of Panama. Given his perpetually optimistic nature, the changed situation in those areas made understandable — but not justifiable — his decision to make one last effort to save the Liberal revolt.

The Liberal Revival in the Department of Magdalena (1901 October–1902 April)

Very surprising changes had taken place in the Caribbean coast since the Conservative victory at the battle of Carazúa on 13 September 1901 (Map 2). Although Liberal guerrillas tried to survive after that disastrous battle, the apparently definitive eclipse of the Liberal cause influenced Uribe Uribe's decision to head to the Llanos and not to the Caribbean coast. In reality, the Conservative victory at Carazúa had been less definitive than at first appeared to be the case. Rather than pursue the defeated rebels, the Conservatives had promptly returned to Riohacha and left the battlefield littered with rifles, ammunition cases, and several cannons. Over the next weeks the rebels quietly returned to rescue the abandoned material and then slowly began reconstituting their bands. A few months later rebel bands were roaming again throughout the Department of Magdalena. Operating out of the Liberal stronghold of Valledupar, the guerrillas spread their control over most of the southern part of the Department of Magdalena. The rebel guerrillas, accustomed to a brutally hot climate in the region, continued to outmaneuver the sluggish army columns, whose demoralized soldiers lacked the will to fight in this inhospitable region. The Liberal leaders felt so sure of their growing power that they attacked and captured Riohacha on 16 April 1902. Because the fighting for the city had been heavy, the ability of the Liberals to carry a city by storm seemed to augur a resurgence of Liberal strength.[80]

Riohacha in rebel hands offered Uribe Uribe the easy entry point and the perfect excuse to make one last effort to save the Liberal revolt in Colombia. He honestly felt that he could not abandon war without taking advantage of this last opportunity. His specific mission in the Caribbean coast was to block the Magdalena River, because ample experience had shown that no Liberal victory was permanent as long as the government controlled this waterway. Blocking the Magdalena River acquired additional urgency, not just to prevent the victorious Conservative troops near Bogotá from coming to defeat the Liberals in the Caribbean Coast but also to prevent the depar-ture of expeditions to put down the Liberal surge in Panama.

The Last Liberal Invasion of Panama (1901 December–1902 August)

The capitulation of the rebels at Colón on 28 November 1901 turned out to be just a brief pause in hostilities, because exiles were busily preparing to send new expeditions to revive the Liberal revolt. The Liberals enjoyed the support of foreign benefactors, such as President Eloy Alfaro of Ecuador and President José Santos Zelaya of Nicaragua. The Panamanian Belisario Porras, the loser in July 1900, wanted revenge and was busily obtaining and smuggling weapons and ammunition into Panama. However, the army garrisons were too strong for any purely local revolt to succeed, and the apparent calm convinced the Marroquín administration to stop sending reinforcements to Panama. Even more damaging, the Colombian government dropped its plans to acquire a flotilla of gunboats on the Pacific side, even though Panama was more dependent on sea transportation than any other region in Colombia. The sole railroad in the department joined Panama City on the Pacific Ocean to Colón on the Caribbean Sea, and for the rest of Panama the nearly impassable trails forced the Conservative authorities to rely on coastwise shipping for troop deployments.[81]

The Liberal uprising of early 1900 in Panama had made military sense as part of a wave of revolts sweeping Colombia. But by late 1901 none but the most fanatical could doubt the Liberal defeat, and even Uribe Uribe publicly argued only for prolonging the war as the way to secure some concessions from the Conservative government. Uribe Uribe had assumed such a commanding position within the Liberal Party, that the eclipsed old chiefs (the "grandfathers") knew they had to act soon to regain their leadership. Rather than seeking to end a war that had become pointless and immensely harmful, this faction wanted victories to gain glory and prestige to maintain control over the Liberal party.

Because the government had a flotilla of gunboats on the Caribbean side and easy access to reinforcements from the interior via the Magdalena River, General Herrera necessarily based his plans on the Pacific coastline. His campaign strategy called for reviving the war in the departments of Cauca and Panama. However, time was running out, because on 31 August 1901 Eloy Alfaro was stepping down as president of Ecuador. Alfaro's successor was openly hostile to Colombian exiles and no longer would allow them to use Ecuador as a base. The Liberals planned two final expeditions: one by sea to try to capture Tumaco, and another by land to try to reach central Cauca. The Liberals hoped in these invasions to capture plenty of weapons and ammunition from the army garrisons. Herrera would then come with a flotilla to transport most of the rebels to Panama.[82]

General Herrera devoted his efforts to obtaining a gunboat more powerful than the modest craft the government had on the Pacific side. With his keen military intuition, he had realized that control of the ocean was the key to a Liberal victory in Panama. After much effort and only after having to pledge almost his entire personal fortune as collateral, he was able to purchase a small steamship. He had the ship fitted with cannons, and this rudimentary gunboat, which he christened *Almirante Padilla*, soon became the terror of the Conservatives on the Pacific Coast. In response, the Marroquín administration began scouring Europe and the United States for a superior warship, but none were on the market.[83]

Until the Colombian government found a gunboat, the Liberal *Almirante Padilla* was free to steam unopposed along the Pacific Coast of Colombia. The ship's first destination was not Panama but Tumaco on the extreme southwest of Cauca Department. When he arrived with his ships, General Herrera did not have to attack Tumaco, because the seaborne expedition of Colombian exiles from Ecuador had captured that port on 16 October 1901. Unfortunately, army troops defeated and completely dispersed the land expedition from Ecuador. The Liberals lost their last chance to reignite the revolt in central Cauca, and it was only a matter of time before army troops recovered Tumaco. General Herrera had never expected to stay for long in Tumaco, and he devoted himself to organizing men for his Panama expedition. At that time, the only comparable Liberal force in Colombia was the one that General Rafael Uribe Uribe had gathered in San Cristóbal with the support of Venezuelan President Castro. Yet like Uribe Uribe, Herrera had a force too small to face an army directly, and his only chance for success was to strike through a remote region.[84]

For reasons which can be fairly but not completely understood, General Herrera had from the start intended to invade Panama at a time when the Liberal revolt was irreversibly heading for complete defeat in mainland Colombia. Even the capture of all of Panama could not reverse the military tide, because it was just a matter of time before boatloads of reinforcements came from mainland Colombia to restore Conservative rule. General Herrera's real goal was to use Panama as a lever to bring pressure on the Colombian government either directly or through the U.S. government. Negotiations over a canal treaty between Colombia and the United States had been ongoing in Washington D.C. for years, and the Colombian government did not want to have its bargaining position weakened by losing control over Panama. General Herrera wanted to show the U.S. government that the Liberals controlled or at least threatened the canal route the United States wanted. Whether the Liberals intended to negotiate a treaty giving the U.S. government the canal route remains unclear but this option cannot be ruled out. Whether such an action would have made Panama independent in 1902 is one of several crucial points some Liberals have subsequently labored hard to bury in oblivion.[85]

On 24 December 1901, coincidentally the same day that Uribe Uribe set out from San Cristóbal on his expedition, General Benjamin Herrera arrived in Panama and landed his 1,500 men on an ill-fated mission that would cost Colombia that entire department. A network of spies informed him that Governor Albán had commandeered the *Lautaro*, a merchant ship of the Chilean Line. This large ship had the capacity to transport many soldiers and large amounts of supplies, and once fitted out with cannons, was more powerful than the *Almirante Padilla*. Herrera quickly realized that he had to take care of this threat before beginning any major campaigns on land.[86]

Governor Albán retained the original Chilean crew members, not realizing that they were very violent even by seamen's standards. The ship was not properly guarded and with Liberal sympathizers roaming around, the

outfitting of the ship took much longer than
normal. The *Lautaro* prepared to set out on the
night of 19 January 1902 with Governor Albán
and a battalion of troops aboard, but a minor
mechanical malfunction persuaded him to wait
until the next morning to depart, even though
the ship was capable of propulsion. That night,
someone mysteriously drained the boilers, and
this act of sabotage left the ship without any
steam. Keeping steam up was a normal wartime
practice, but meanwhile the crew fell into a
drunken frenzy, and officers had to call on the
troops to restore order. At dawn on 20 January,
an unknown ship steamed rapidly into the harbor of Panama but the *Lautaro* was without
lookouts and nobody sounded the alarm. The
deception continued longer, because General
Herrera had put his men to repaint the *Almirante Padilla* so that it resembled the many
merchant ships docked nearby. When barely a
kilometer away, the *Almirante Padilla* opened
fire, yet Governor Albán and his companions
believed those shots were only celebratory
salvoes. The next two rounds shattered the
bridge of the *Lautaro* and killed Governor
Albán, while the next round landed at the precise spot below the water line where the ship
was most vulnerable to sinking. The vessel
began to list heavily to one side and a mad rush
to abandon ship ensued. The *Almirante Padilla*,
its mission successfully completed, was by then
rapidly steaming away out of range of the
dreaded coastal artillery, whose first rounds fell
short as the ship disappeared in the horizon.[87]

The sinking of the *Lautaro* retained for the
Liberals control over the Pacific Coast, but on
land Herrera still faced the formidable army of
General Francisco de Paula Castro. The army
troops were better equipped and had ample
ammunition, yet Herrera felt he had to act fast,
because his spies reported that a Chilean warship Colombia was trying to purchase would
reach Panama by the end of February. With options fast running out, Herrera led his men to
attack the army troops at Aguadulce. The strategy might seem risky, but he sensed that General Castro was a mediocre officer who could
be easily intimidated. Herrera sent his men
charging through forests and thick bush against
the army troops on 23 February. But even before the attack had begun, General Castro was
already psychologically defeated. After brief
combat, he ordered his men to withdraw, but

he gave the order in such haste that a detachment of nearly 200 soldiers failed to receive the
order and continued resisting the Liberal assault for hours until it was completely surrounded and forced to surrender. No less surprising was the withdrawal route of General
Castro. Presumably he would have followed the
very rough but not impassable trails leading
back to Panama City by land, but he preferred
to take the even harsher route over the central
mountains to Bocas del Toro on the Caribbean
side.[88]

He returned by sea with his troops to
Colón and then by railroad to Panama City. Although he was reprimanded for having abandoned the battlefield so soon at Aguadulce, at
least he had saved most of his troops. The arduous army trek to Bocas del Toro had another unexpected consequence. After the victory at
Aguadulce, General Herrera had brought the region as far as the Costa Rican border under Liberal control but only on the Pacific side. He had
dismissed any crossing of the central mountain
range as impracticable for a large force, but General Castro's overland journey made him reconsider. Herrera dispatched a force of 500 men
from David to establish a base for launching expeditions at Bocas del Toro. General Herrera
imagined ships magically appearing to neutralize the Colombian gunboats on the Caribbean
side, and then the Liberals could use the sea to
attack not just Colón but also Cartagena and
Barranquilla. The tropics sometimes make persons lose touch with reality, and the Liberal
scheme was completely fantastic as the new governor of Panama, General Victor Salazar, realized when for once spies provided the Conservatives with good reports on the Liberals.[89]

General Salazar enjoyed tremendous prestige as the victor of Panama City in July 1900,
and immediately upon taking office on 27 February 1902, he tried to remedy the disastrous
situation he had inherited. A man of superior
ability and many talents, he was the best
Colombia could send; unfortunately, the critical situation in Panama required not just superior but extraordinary abilities. Without the
support of able subordinates, he simply was
overwhelmed with more problems than he
could solve. But the Liberal invasion of Bocas
del Toro rather than a problem seemed an opportunity. Deliberately General Salazar left
only police pickets defending the island capi-

tal of Bocas del Toro so as not to scare away the Liberals. The attackers did capture Bocas del Toro in early April only to discover that it was a trap. Government gunboats bringing reinforcements from Barranquilla soon blockaded the island, and the rebel force of 500 men had no choice but to surrender. Unfortunately, the Colombian general unwisely allowed himself to be persuaded by the commander of a U.S. naval warship to let the rebels leave unmolested with all their weapons. While this incident was not enough to prove a case of U.S. partiality towards the Liberals, it certainly prolonged the war. The excessive generosity of this Colombian general turned what should have been a morale-boosting victory for the Conservatives into another claim of Liberal success.[90]

Once the column from Bocas del Toro had rejoined his main force, General Herrera plotted his next move. He wanted to capture Panama City, but before he could make an attempt on the capital, he knew he had to weaken its garrison. At the same time in Bogotá the impatience with getting rid of the Liberals in Panama was growing, and General Salazar, who should have resisted the pressures, was on the lookout for any opportunity to strike a blow against the rebels. Because the *Almirante Padilla* kept the army troops bottled up in Panama City, General Herrera decided to open the door by sending the gunboat for routine repairs and outfitting to Nicaragua; he knew Conservative spies would promptly report the absence of the *Almirante Padilla*. He also pulled back his patrols to Aguadulce, in an effort to convey the impression that the Liberals were too weak to defend their territory.

General Salazar had received some reinforcements from mainland Colombia, but not as many as he wanted, and in one battalion most of the men had fallen ill with tropical diseases that confirmed the ill repute of Panama as a graveyard. Even under the best of circumstances the transfer from Bogotá of the troops who had recently defeated Rafael Uribe Uribe's expedition was necessarily slow. The government also was most reluctant to dispatch battalions until it first confirmed the location of the fugitive Uribe Uribe. Having only limited means, General Salazar should have waited until the arrival of a gunboat or of additional battalions. Instead, once spies reported that the *Almirante Padilla* was in Nicaragua, he devised a plan to trap the

Liberal garrison at Aguadulce. Coastwise ships and his remaining gunboat would transport a first contingent under General Luis Morales Berti to Antón and then a second contingent under General Castro to the Santa María River. Without realizing it, General Salazar had taken the bait of Herrera. The choice of these two commanders was most unfortunate. General Castro had bungled the previous campaign in Aguadulce, and no less worrisome, Morales Berti as a colonel had shamefully abandoned Cúcuta in that distant October 1899. Nevertheless, he had been promoted to general and in June 1902 was entrusted with this major expedition.

On 10 June the first army contingent landed at Antón. When the second detachment arrived under General Castro, it landed not in Santa María River but also in Antón. The route to the rear of Aguadulce remained open, and its Liberal garrison carried out an orderly withdrawal. General Herrera pulled back the rest of his men to Santiago de Veraguas, because he hoped to lure the army column deeper into his territory. When the army troops halted their advance, General Herrera realized that his only chance to gain a victory was to attack them. By the middle of July he began to close in on them, but the army troops merely hastened their retreat to Aguadulce. General Morales Berti did not even make token resistance along the way, and he abandoned easily defended positions such as the Santa María River. General Morales Berti seemed to be fleeing from Herrera just as had happened before in 1899. Actually, retreat was the only alternative left, because the rebel forces were well armed and by this time vastly outnumbered the army troops. General Morales Berti should have hastened the withdrawal, yet on 22 July he surprisingly requested more reinforcements to finish destroying the rebel forces. Governor Salazar, who already had ample evidence of a bungled expedition and knew the shameful combat record of both generals, should have recalled the expedition rather than send reinforcements. But the bait of ending the Liberal revolt in Panama was too great for Governor Salazar, and in a very risky move he dispatched troops aboard the gunboat *Boyacá*. When the *Boyacá* with other coastwise ships arrived near the coast of Aguadulce on 30 July, the *Almirante Padilla* was waiting and with its superior guns captured one merchant ship and, after a vain attempt by the *Boyacá* to flee, forced the surrender of the gunboat and of its troops on board who became prisoners.[91]

The naval victory thoroughly demoralized the troops of General Morales Berti, but there was still time to escape from Aguadulce, either by hacking their way through the dense jungle to Panama City or through the very harsh route to Bocas del Toro that General Castro had taken earlier that year. But Generals Morales Berti and Castro were both determined not to be criticized for failing to stand and fight, and they had their battalions take up positions inside a series of fortified redoubts in Aguadulce. General Herrera brought up his cannons to begin a daily shelling of Aguadulce, but because he did not want to lose his men in bloody charges, he relied on a tight siege to force the surrender of the troops. Once food supplies ran out, the famished army troops surrendered on 27 August. However, the siege had tied down the rebels long enough for reinforcements to reach Panama City from mainland Colombia, so that once again the elusive prize of Panama City was beyond the grasp of General Herrera.

The military campaign turned into a stalemate, and a large neutral zone stretching between Aguadulce and Panama City separated the opponents. Governor Salazar had learned a costly lesson in patience, and he postponed any offensive until a government warship able to destroy the *Almirante Padilla* first arrived.[92]

The Last Liberal Campaign in the Department of Magdalena (1902 August–October)

The Liberal success in Panama gave greater urgency to Rafael Uribe Uribe's mission of blocking the Magdalena River. Unfortunately, he still faced hostility from exiled Liberal leaders who were determined to prevent his military career from converting him into a Colombian Caesar. Gabriel Vargas Santos and other exiled Liberal leaders sent instructions not to recognize Uribe Uribe as the commander of rebels in the Caribbean coast. The local Liberals ignored these instructions and promptly put themselves under the command of Uribe Uribe as soon as he reached Riohacha on 14 Au-

The sunken *Lautaro* in the harbor of Panama City in January 1902. The men in the boats tried in vain to recover the body of Governor Carlos Albán (*Boletín cultural y bibliográfico,* 2000).

gust 1902. Yet even if the highest Liberal leaders had given their full support to the campaign of Uribe Uribe, he should have realized that even if the rebels gained control over all of Panama and the Caribbean Coast, the Liberals were still doomed to defeat. It was only a matter of time before the Conservative government brought large numbers of troops down the Magdalena River to crush the Liberals; blocking the Magdalena River could only delay but not prevent the inevitable outcome. The resources and population of Colombia were concentrated in the interior of the country; even the customs houses, the large source of revenue in the Caribbean coast, depended primarily on the trade between the interior and foreign countries. And as for Panama, it could not be expected to provide significant resources when it had generally been a drain on the government's resources. Uribe Uribe admitted that the uprising had failed, but he persuaded himself that prolonging the war was sure to extract favorable terms from the Conservative government. That argument had lost all validity after the failure of the Llanos invasion, and thus Uribe Uribe's decision to make one last campaign in the Caribbean coast was totally unjustified.[93]

He himself was not convinced of the need for this final campaign, but he needed a compelling persuasive reason to lay down his arms. Shortly after his arrival in Riohacha on 14 August, his determination to end the war became a solid conviction when he saw the ruin and misery gripping the Caribbean region. Abandoned villages, sickness, starvation, wild animals and poisonous insects were all that he could see in the formerly prosperous Department of Magdalena. Vegetation was overrunning formerly prosperous towns, unemployment was rampant, and basic necessities commanded exorbitant prices if available at all. Uribe Uribe realized that unless the war ended soon, Colombia risked falling into the most abject ruin.[94]

He should have promptly accepted one of the peace offers that government officials routinely forwarded to him during his military campaigns. However, he still believed that his reputation and that of the Liberal cause depended on demonstrating that he had really tried to block the Magdalena River. After toying with the impossible goal of capturing Bar-

ranquilla as the best way to block the Magdalena River, he settled on the more realistic target of taking and holding Tenerife further upstream (Map 2). He sent part of his forces north to keep the army garrisons tied down at Ciénaga and Santa Marta, while with about 1,000 rebels he prepared to capture Tenerife. He was not in a rush to reach that strategic place, because he wanted to give the rebels in neighboring Department of Bolívar plenty of time to arrive and to cover his western flank. He knew that the rebels from Magdalena Department were adequate to capture Tenerife, but to hold the town he needed reinforcements from Bolivar Department. His second reason for delay was to wait for the proper moment when the majority of the steamboats on the Magdalena River were north of Tenerife, and thus deprive the Conservative government of most of the vessels needed to rush troops from Bogotá to clear the blockade Uribe Uribe had established in Tenerife.

On 18 September Uribe Uribe easily overpowered the small garrison at Tenerife that had been caught by surprise. He placed his two cannons in an elevation overlooking the river so that they could fire from above into ships trying to run the blockade. The government gunboats were left in the disadvantageous position of having to fire blindly at a higher target. As attempts to force the blockade by the river route failed, the government brought troops from its garrisons on the Caribbean coast to capture Tenerife by land attack. Uribe Uribe counted on the arrival of the rebels from Bolívar to secure his exposed land flank, but in spite of repeated entreaties, these rebel forces moved at such a snail's pace that they never arrived in time. With the danger of being overrun becoming greater each day, early in the night of 2 October he evacuated his exposed forces. The Liberals blocked the Magdalena River for fifteen days, and because the previously stranded ships had to steam upstream to bring the troops destined for Panama, General Herrera had gained a respite of nearly two months.

Uribe Uribe, before his whereabouts became known, rushed north to join the rest of the rebels who with very little success had been trying to capture Ciénaga, the key town protecting the important city of Santa Marta. With his usual methodical care, Uribe Uribe carefully plotted a detailed plan to capture Ciénaga with the least number of casualties. In the attack on 13 October, the rebels entered the town and drove the garrison into the buildings of the central plaza. Uribe Uribe halted the attack to give time to distribute dynamite charges among the rebels and to position his cannons for the final assault the next day. Suddenly, the steamboat *Nely Gazan* appeared and with its small cannons began shelling the rear of the rebels. Uribe Uribe promptly put his gunners to point one of their cannons at the ship. The steamboat's wild shooting was not causing any harm but the loud explosions terrorized the rebels who panicked and fled. Only by making supreme efforts could he halt the rout and regroup his men to stop the counteroffensive by the army garrison. In the ensuing combat Uribe Uribe had his last brush with death during the war, as a bullet passed between his jacket and arm leaving him unscathed.[95]

The pitiful performance of the rebels in the Caribbean coast was the revelation that finally opened his eyes to the futility of trying to continue the war. At last Uribe Uribe recognized the inevitable, and he entered into negotiations with government officials to end his participation in the war. A truce was quickly signed ending hostilities in the Caribbean region, and on 24 October the Agreement of Nerlandia (the name of a farm owned by a Dutch immigrant) was signed. Essentially, in this capitulation the rebels agreed to surrender their weapons in exchange for safe passage back home.[96]

The End in Panama

The Nerlandia Agreement for all practical purposes ended the War of the Thousand Days in Colombia, because the ragged forces of General Benjamin Herrera in Panama could not even dream of standing up to the many victorious battalions the Marroquín administration was starting to send to that region. In an attempt to avoid needless bloodshed, one of the clauses of the Nerlandia Agreement required Uribe Uribe to plead with General Herrera to end hostilities in Panama. Uribe Uribe duly wrote a letter urging his Liberal colleague in Panama to lay down his arms, but months before his message reached Panama, both Liberals and Conservatives had been making con-

tacts to try to bring the war to an end in that region. Because the Liberals had always intended to use their campaign in Panama as a way to extract concessions that the Marroquín administration would not have granted to any other department, quite naturally General Benjamin Herrera made the first move to start negotiations in a brief message of 19 July to Governor Victor Salazar. This priceless opportunity called for a very generous counteroffer because of Panama's special condition as the isthmian canal route, but Governor Salazar on 28 July merely repeated the usual government terms. Because army troops had already landed at Aguadulce and were heading to Santiago de Veraguas, Governor Salazar believed that he was in such a strong position that he did not need to make any special offers. But his faith was misplaced, because as previous pages showed, by that date the military expedition of General Luis Morales Berti was already doomed and was heading inevitably toward surrender at Aguadulce on 27 August. Not surprisingly, General Herrera had not bothered to answer the 28 July letter and had concentrated on winning his important victory.[97]

The Liberal victory could still serve to start peace talks. With the canal negotiations in Washington D.C. entering into a critical phase, it was extremely urgent for the Colombian government to end the war even if it meant exceptional concessions to Panama. Yet neither side budged, and Governor Salazar preferred to wait until the arrival of the gunboat *Bogotá* restored control of the sea to the Colombian government. Little did he realize that each day that passed without peace shortened the time left for Colombian rule in Panama.[98]

Nobody doubted that the Thousand Days' War was coming to an end, but the question remaining was how to bring it to a close. Even General Gabriel Vargas Santos, the nominal leader of the Liberal revolt, realized the inevitable, and in an attempt to redeem his tarnished reputation, he came to Central America to try to negotiate peace in Panama. These complex negotiations ultimately failed but not without scaring General Herrera who felt that unless he acted soon, others would take the credit for achieving peace. He was glad that the negotiations with his close friend Vargas Santos floundered, because he could not openly defy the nominal leader. The panorama facing

General Herrera was bleak at best. His men had stripped western Panama of all cattle and resources, and he was fast running out of money to support his force. The constant confiscations had also made many local inhabitants angry and eager to achieve peace even if it meant a Conservative victory. He himself was being pressured hard to pay back the loan he had taken out to purchase the *Almirante Padilla*. He kept asking General Salazar to begin negotiations promptly, but the governor, an astute businessman too clever for Colombia's good, delayed any meeting until the arrival of the *Bogotá* returned control of the sea to the government. Even before the gunboat reached Panama City on 26 October, General Herrera had learned of its impending arrival and had asked to begin negotiations on terms the government had traditionally offered. Herrera hurried to hide *the Almirante Padilla* in a heavily wooded creek before the *Bogotá* could find and sink the rebel ship. Just as his world was collapsing, a messenger came confirming the meeting date and forwarding a message from Uribe Uribe urging him to sign an agreement to end the war on terms at least as favorable as those of the Nerlandia agreement.[99]

General Herrera was a cornered desperate man, but fortunately Governor Salazar proved very accommodating with Herrera's personal needs in everything except meaningful concessions. For example, Herrera asked Salazar to provide a government ship to take him to their meeting, but because the Liberal leader was supposed to command a flotilla of lesser craft besides the *Almirante Padilla*, Governor Salazar found the request odd but duly complied. More significantly, Herrera insisted on negotiating only aboard the U.S.S. *Wisconsin*, partly as a way to shift some of the responsibility for the agreement on the United States, and most reluctantly Salazar agreed. Although all participants and observers confirmed that U.S. naval officers were not involved in the negotiations, nobody could miss the powerful and portentous symbolism that this U.S. battleship conveyed for the future of Colombia and of Panama. As to the terms of the draft, both sides adapted the text of the Nerlandia agreement to local conditions in Panama. The governor as a businessman was also very sensitive to commercial deals gone sour, and in a secret clause

he agreed to make the Colombian government pay the loan for the *Almirante Padilla*. On 21 November 1902 both sides signed the *Wisconsin* Agreement bringing to an end the War of the Thousand Days.[100]

At the moment of signing the agreement, nobody could imagine that Colombian rule had less than a year to last in Panama. The Conservative government was so thrilled with its victory, that it overconfidently believed Colombia could return to the status quo ante bellum. But the War of the Thousand Days had profoundly affected the country and exposed the need for fundamental changes, including new institutions such as a navy and an army comprised of professionals and not of part-time amateurs. The question over the subsequent decades was not whether to make changes but how fast and how completely to transform the country.

Ironically, the most powerful stimulus for reforming Colombia came when Panama became independent on 3 November 1903 as a direct result of the weakening of Colombian authority during the War of the Thousand Days. The Liberal campaigns during the War of the Thousand Days more than anything else had undermined Colombian rule in Panama. The damage was not irreversible, but the Conservative response was woefully inadequate because the Marroquín administration never admitted that the survival of Colombian rule was at risk. After the *Wisconsin* agreement Colombia returned to its traditional policy of benign neglect for Panama and thus confirmed in the minds of many Panamanians that neither the Conservative nor the Liberal parties were the answer to that region's needs. From there it was only a small step to the false assumption that Panamanians could govern themselves better without Bogotá, and that if the opportunity for a bloodless coup presented itself on a silver platter, Panama should become independent.[101]

The Passing of 19th-Century Warfare

As the last war of the nineteenth century and the first one of the twentieth century, the War of the Thousand Days provides an ideal window to observe the appearance of a new type of warfare in Latin America. The War of the Thousand Days awkwardly shared characteristics of both nineteenth and twentieth-century warfare. After this war was over a new style of warfare based on the Mauser rifle and the machine gun spread rapidly across Latin America. This style would last until 1941 when new technological innovations once again forced the armies of the region to change the way they fought wars.

Technology defined the period from 1899 to 1941, but personnel remained the most important component of an army. Within personnel, officers played the crucial role, because good officers can make soldiers out of even very poor civilians, but bad officers can ruin even the best soldiers. During the nineteenth century, governments appointed civilians to be officers and promoted them on the basis of no clear or standard criteria. For many officers, the army was just a brief stage in their careers, and they had probably joined to participate in putting down a revolt or less likely to repel a foreign invasion. Although some officers had taken university courses and a few had been lawyers, the great majority did not have even a high school education. Once in the army, the officers received no formal education and little training. Maneuvers were rare, because combat was perceived to be the best school for officers and soldiers. Courage, boldness, and honor were believed to be the crucial values for victory in the battlefield, and most officers rejected the notion that studying books was the best preparation for warfare. The War of the Thousand Days found Colombia with typical nineteenth-century officers who were responsible for so many of the blunders in the war. And because Colombia lacked enough officers, the government repeated the traditional pattern of giving commissions to civilians who seemed to have military potential.

After 1899, the countries of Latin America moved forcefully to acquire an officer corps comprised of persons with the equivalent of a university education. Usually the officers graduated from military academies most countries either restored or created. The curriculum expanded over the years to become the equivalent of a university degree, with a concentration on military and engineering topics. Some countries, in particular Chile, had pioneered the creation of a professional officer corps since the 1880s, and in the early twentieth century the countries of Latin America strove to follow the Chilean model. A university degree, preferably from a military academy, became the indispensable requirement to hold officer rank. Curiously enough, Colombia lagged in adopting this system, so that when its war with Peru erupted in 1932, Colombia became the last country to appoint a civilian to head a major military expedition. As chapter 14 reveals, having an amateur in charge created needless complications in that war.

The rise of a professional officer corps was clear in government armies after 1899, but in rebel forces the continuity with the previous century remained the rule. Rebel leaders were generally very generous in distributing officer commissions to their followers. In many instances, rebel leaders simply proclaimed themselves to be of high rank, and self-promotion was far from uncommon. Outstanding combat duty received as reward an appointment as officer or a promotion to higher rank. For an individual who managed to stay alive, joining a rebel force offered many opportunities for a social mobility otherwise lacking in the civilian sector. The period of greatest opportunity for entry into officer rank and promotion lasted from the wars of independence (1810–1830) until the 1930s. Looking beyond the period covered in this book reveals an interesting development. Although lack of formal military education remained the rule among rebel officers in the late 1950s and 1960s, most of these men did have a university education. So while talented and capable rebels still had a chance to rise to officer rank in the rebellions of the second half of the twentieth century, the increasing complexity of warfare in an industrializing society gave those rebels with university degrees the inside track to become officers.

Continuity between the nineteenth century and the first half of the twentieth century was also present in the soldiers. In general, rebel forces relied on volunteers while coercion drove men into government armies. Some form of compulsion was usually present, even if in a subtle way. A landowner who had received an officer's commission from authorities usually would command a unit made up of his peasants. Criminals were often given the choice of either joining the army or going to prison, and those fleeing justice found a ready refuge in distant garrisons. Economic hardship or lack of any better opportunity often left the rations and meager pay of the army as the only chance to survive for many rural inhabitants. And many Latin American countries had adopted by the early twentieth century systems of conscription that forced at least a percentage of eligible young males to serve in the army, although the wealthy and the well-connected could escape this obligation.

However, coercion was not the only way the army obtained recruits. Perhaps the only case of genuine volunteers during domestic insurrections took place in Colombia because of religious zeal. During the War of the Thousand Days peasants volunteered to fight for the holy cause in the army. Other Conservatives joined armed bands that terrorized rebels and their sympathizers, but these irregular groups were outside traditional army discipline.[102] More frequent was the flood of volunteers who rushed to join the army during times of foreign invasion. War fever or *rage militaire* swept Costa Rica and Panama as crowds pleaded to be accepted into the army in 1921 as chapter 3 shows. The same occurred in Colombia in 1932 as countless young men desperately begged for a chance to repel the Peruvian invasion of Leticia (chapter 14). But except in these unusual cases, the rule remained that governments normally needed to apply at least some coercion to obtain sufficient numbers of recruits.

The rank and file of the rebels was almost the exact opposite of that in the army. While coercion sustained the army, volunteerism was the indispensable foundation of rebel forces. And even more than coercion for the army, volunteerism has remained the essential characteristics of rebel forces in Latin America from independence to the present. To organize rebel forces, the volunteerism not only has to be genuine, but it also has to be spontaneous and enthusiastic. Although rebel officers routinely traveled through sympathetic regions to find recruits, the eagerness of the peasants to join was the decisive factor. Without a formal government apparatus and the societal norms to bolster recruitment, the rebel officers needed spontaneous enlistments. Ultimately the motivation was political in the broadest sense. If a government had taken political decisions that adversely affected the daily life of the rural population, such as depriving villages of land or imposed harsh burdens, then young peasants

saw no reason to stay quiet and preferred to try their chances with any roving band that came looking for recruits.

Not all rebel forces were composed exclusively of volunteers, and coercion in different degrees sometimes crept in. The example of Pancho Villa in the latter years of his career (chapter 10) stands out because of his threats to villages if they did not supply recruits. Villa was the only rebel leader to have taken such extreme measures, but other rebel leaders used milder forms of coercion. In the War of the Thousand Days, prisoners sometimes had the option of joining the other side. Thus many Conservative prisoners from distant regions joined the rebel forces after the battle of Peralonso in 1899. Perhaps the prisoners were far from home, or perhaps they had enjoyed life as soldiers and did not want to return back home to the boredom of hard work on the fields. After Palonegro in 1900, General Próspero Pinzón sent the many Liberal prisoners back home on their word of honor not to take up arms against the government again. After 1912 as the Mexican Revolution entered its most savage phase, prisoners jumped at the chance to change sides, because by that date the normal practice was to execute all prisoners.

These exceptions did not modify the essentially volunteer nature of the rebel forces. Not unexpectedly, creating and maintaining discipline was tremendously difficult in these volunteer forces. Because the peasants had willingly joined, they felt they could leave at any time, so just keeping the rebel force from disintegrating was usually a constant ordeal for officers. During the campaign in the Department of Santander, the Liberal cause was so popular that officers could generally afford to ignore desertions because new volunteers were coming in. By the time of the campaigns in 1902 when volunteers were becoming scarce, the Liberals punished deserters in a vain attempt to keep the revolt going. Ultimately victory attracted many volunteers, while defeat drove away recruits.

Battlefield discipline was no less difficult but followed a generally predictable path in the rebel forces. Recent recruits, whether officers or men, were most reluctant to obey orders from superiors. The eagerness of the rebels to see combat was so great, that they sometimes rushed into battle and provoked major disas-

Signing of the peace agreement aboard the U.S.S. *Wisconsin*, 21 November 1902. This agreement ended the War of the Thousand Days in Colombia. Seated from left to right are General Victor M. Salazar, General Alfredo Vásquez Cobo, Dr. Eusebio A. Morales, General Benjamín Herrera, and General Lucas Caballero (Victor M. Salazar, *Memorias de la guerra, 1899–1902*; Bogotá: Editorial ABC, 1943).

ters, such as in the first failed attack on Bucaramanga in 1899. In the case of new rebel officers, once they learned that discipline was in their own best interest, they grudgingly accepted the need to obey orders. But insubordination among rebel officers remained a problem throughout the war, and as late as 1902 contributed decisively to such failures as Rafael Uribe Uribe's invasion of the Llanos.

Rebel officers quickly learned that to secure battlefield obedience, they had to allow their men to steal and plunder. The peasants who joined the rebels expected to receive a free meal starting the first day, whether it was given to them or they had to take the food by force. This practice of stealing from the rural population was endemic during revolts. What was different in Colombia was the care both sides took to steal or confiscate only from those of

the other political party. For the aggrieved party the difference was meaningless, because what the Liberals did not plunder the Conservatives confiscated. By the time of the Mexican Revolution, such distinctions had become meaningless, and the rebels were on the lookout for opportunities to loot all properties and to steal any animals still alive.

On the government side, as long as army troops received their pay and food, discipline was rarely a problem. Plundering by army troops was rare, and the officers generally kept tight control over their soldiers. Discipline inside the officer corps was another matter, and the army officers' refusal to obey orders had been a recurrent problem in the nineteenth century. In the War of the Thousand Days some army officers still did not obey orders, but the problem was never as serious as among the rebel officers. After 1899, as formal military education became universal among the officers, instances of disobedience of orders almost disappeared. Indeed, abject obedience sometimes killed any initiative and cost battles, as happened to the Federal Army in Ciudad Juárez in May 1911 (chapter 5). Examples of officer disobedience became very rare, and the only notable exception occurred in 1933 during the Chaco War (chapter 12).

After 1899, technological innovations made strict discipline and a formally educated officer corps indispensable. The technological changes affected not just weapons but also transportation and communications in the period 1899–1941. The amateur armies of the nineteenth century could not assimilate the new technology, and governments needed a skilled group of professionals to lead armies in war. The appearance of the Mauser rifle in the late nineteenth century promptly transformed the battlefield and made all other rifles obsolete. The very sturdy Mauser had a long range and the ability to sustain a steady fire over many hours even under harsh tropical conditions. At one swoop the existing tactics became obsolete, and the traditional combat at very close range and in open fields became suicidal, as the Liberal rebels in Colombia failed to learn. Officers steeped in traditional combat values were no less slow in trying to figure out the impact of this new weapon on the battlefield.

Because cash-strapped governments in Latin America were slow to acquire this relatively expensive new weapon, the fearsome power of the Mauser rifles was not always immediately felt. In the best example, the War of the Thousand Days found Colombia in the middle of a replacement program, and early in the war the government exhausted its small supply of Mausers and was never able to equip all its soldiers with this new rifle. Consequently, failure to have enough Mausers for the Colombian army was one major reason why the War of the Thousand Days lasted so long. In contrast, the Mexican army of 1910 was fully equipped with Mausers, but as mentioned before, the rebels multiplied faster than the rifles to shoot them.

Volleys from Mauser rifles were extremely deadly and sliced through wood effortlessly. At short ranges Mauser rifles could even penetrate metal sheets, but a rate of fire of five rounds per minute on the average was too slow to stop massed attacks by rebels. The ability of the machine gun to fire over a hundred rounds per minute made it the ideal weapon to stop charging lines of rebels, as the bloody experience at Calidonia Bridge in Panama City amply demonstrated in July 1900. Yet if the Mauser rifle had been a costly expense for most Latin American countries, the machine gun was even more expensive. The scarcity of machine guns in the Colombian army also contributed to the long duration of the War of the Thousand Days. Obviously machine guns would have turned glorious Liberal charges into bloody massacres. Yet inexplicably, the Mexican government failed to heed the lessons of the War of the Thousand Days. The Mexican army of 1910 had very few machine guns and lacked the capacity to stop large numbers of rebels. And by 1912 when the Cuban army in the Race War finally learned that machine guns defending towns released troops for the pursuit of rebels in the countryside, the Cuban government was able to put down the revolt quickly (chapter 4).

The Mauser rifle and the machine gun by themselves ended the style of war of the nineteenth century. Instead, innovations in artillery took much longer to have an impact on combat and no clear break occurred after 1899. If machine guns had been extremely expensive, purchasing new cannons with their valuable shells was almost prohibitive. Yet it was not just a question of money. The battle of Palonegro in May 1900 can be seen as one slow learning experience for the Colombian army. Had the army known how to use its artillery properly, its batteries could have blasted huge gaps in the Liberal lines and brought the battle to a quick close. Ironically, only in the pursuit of the defeated rebels did long-range shelling finally shatter the retreating Liberals. Artillery did come into its own during the Mexican Revolution and played decisive roles in many of the latter battles, but the lesson came only after scarcity of cannons in the northern battlefields made possible the fall of the Mexican government in May 1911.

The difficulty of hauling cannons over mountainous terrain and dense vegetation tremendously restricted the use of artillery. Not surprisingly, many governments were reluctant to spend large sums on weapons that seemed suitable only for defense of cities. The extreme case came in Peru, whose army concluded in the 1920s that artillery was unsuitable for jungle warfare. As long as earth-moving equipment remained scarce, little could be done to shape the terrain, but the vegetation proved more malleable. Urbanization and commercial agriculture gradually eliminated dense vegetation and thick forests in many battlegrounds of the nineteenth century. The most dramatic transformation was in Cuba: While Cuban rebels had successfully hidden in dense forests when fighting against Spanish troops in the 1890s, Cuban rebels of the 1910s found most hiding places converted to open cultivated fields. Obviously huge jungles and thick forests still covered many areas of Latin America, but safe forested sanctuaries near zones of high population density practically disappeared because of an incipient industrialization. Vanishing vegetation was one of the reasons considerably hindering the start of uprisings, and not until the late 1950s did rebel leaders figure out new ways to compensate for the huge advantages existing governments enjoyed.

Vanishing vegetation allowed governments to prevent or at least to put down uprisings faster than in the nineteenth century. But other equally important factors were present after 1899. Telegraph lines reported disturbances rapidly to the capital, and rebels only gradually learned the importance of cutting or otherwise intercepting telegraph lines. The telegraph became truly significant when combined with the railroad: The more extensive the railway network of a country, the less likely was a revolt and the easier it was for an army to crush rebels. A railroad network through the mountains would have made the War of the Thousand Days impossible in Colombia, and a railway line linking Panama City to Santiago de Veraguas would have made impossible a Liberal revolt in the Department of Panama. Mexico had a significant railway network in place by 1910, but quite significantly, those regions with limited or no railway service usually started the uprisings. More railroads, more machine guns, and more cannons would have made the Mexican Revolu-

tion highly unlikely if not impossible altogether.

Navies were another essential characteristic of the new warfare after 1899. After the wars of independence, the new republics had abandoned their navies as unnecessary. But the introduction of steam and steel on the seas made these countries very vulnerable to attacks from foreign countries, as Peru found out to its great regret in the War of the Pacific (1880–1883). The superior navy of Chile made possible a great victory over Peru in that war. Countries with seacoasts began to pay attention to their navies, but not Colombia. The failure of Colombia to have a modest navy prolonged the War of the Thousand Days and undermined Colombian rule in Panama. Mexico did acquire a modest navy after 1899, and although it could not stop the Mexican Revolution, the navy was a constant thorn on the side of the rebels and delayed their advance. After 1899 each country needed not a navy of capital ships like battleships but gunboats and light cruisers suitable to patrol coastlines and rivers. Any country that refused to consider a navy as an indispensable branch of government suffered serious consequences, as happened to Colombia. Perplexingly, that country was a very slow learner and still refused to acquire a navy after the disasters of the War of the Thousand Days. Consequently, the outbreak of the war with Peru in 1932 found Colombia again without a navy.

Innovations in warships, weapons, and transportation revolutionized warfare in Latin America after 1899. As the countries of the region found out, just buying the new technology was an inadequate solution, because skilled professionals in an efficient organization became indispensable to manage the new weapons and equipment. The ragged armed bands of the nineteenth century with civilians acting as generals were rapidly giving way to professionally trained armies. During the twentieth century, not all Latin American countries were equally successful in making the transition, and the struggle to master the new technology under the pressure of combat provides the underlying theme for the military campaigns appearing in this book.

PART I. BORDER CONFLICTS

1. War in the Amazon Jungle: The Acre Territory

We Brazilians cannot stop loving the Acre, where we have left a cadaver below each rubber tree. — Gentil Tristán Norberto[1]

During the last half of the nineteenth century, the most traumatic events in Latin America had been the French Intervention against Mexico (1862–1867), the War of the Triple Alliance of Argentina, Brazil, and Uruguay against Paraguay (1864–1870), and the War of the Pacific (1879–1883) of Bolivia and Peru against Chile.

Fresh on everyone's mind was the Cuban insurrection against Spain (1895–1898). Both the Cuban insurrection and the earlier Mexican struggle against France seemed to have eliminated the possibility of reducing Hispanic countries to colonial status. Thus in the heyday of imperialism, when colonial powers were scrambling to partition Africa and Asia, the Hispanic countries preserved their independence. However, an expansionist United States, which already occupied the former Spanish colonies of Cuba and Puerto Rico since 1898, loomed as an unknown factor. Would the United States replace departing European powers in their colonial role? The only certainty was that any deep U.S. involvement in the Caribbean and in Mexico was sure to provoke resistance.

In South America, the biggest dangers to peace came from the failure of the victors in the War of the Pacific and in the War of the Triple Alliance to settle the outstanding territorial questions completely. The most obvious

festering problems came from the War of the Pacific. Peru was determined to recover Tacna and Arica, the provinces it had lost to Chile. War scares between Peru and Chile maintained the area at a high level of tension. Bolivia, for its part, wanted to recover the maritime provinces it had lost to Chile in the War of the Pacific. Many persons incorrectly dismiss the War of the Pacific and the War of the Triple Alliance as border disputes, when in reality the future of Paraguay and Bolivia had been at stake. Argentina and Brazil accepted the existence of Paraguay but did not impose final boundaries. This oversight eventually gave Bolivia the opportunity to question the need for Paraguay to exist at all.

Bolivia was the link between these two major wars of South America, and again not just Bolivian boundaries were at stake. Throughout the nineteenth century Bolivia had been an anomaly, and its survival as a separate country was frequently in doubt. The War of the Pacific was really a first effort towards the partition of Bolivia among its neighbors. After the war a final partition could not take place because of Peru's obsession with regaining its two small provinces of Tacna and Arica. Knowing that knives were out to carve up the country did not prevent Bolivia from holding an exaggerated opinion of its own capabilities. By fits and starts Bolivia tried to

51

show its neighbors that it was worthy of belonging to the ranks of independent countries. The real reasons for its defeat in the War of the Pacific had been neglect of distant provinces and a denial of its weakness. In preparation for any new confrontation with Chile over the maritime provinces, Bolivia focused its efforts on establishing control over its remaining distant territories. Torn between the Chaco in the southeast and the Acre far to the north, Bolivia dribbled out its resources and ultimately jeopardized its chance of maintaining control over either region. Before Bolivia could even occupy these distant territories, the start of the rubber boom in the 1880s largely preempted Bolivian efforts in the Amazon region to the north.

The Acre Territory and the First Bolivian Campaign

After the fall of the Spanish and Portuguese empires in the early 1820s, the balance of power in the Amazon swung decisively to Brazil, the heir of the Portuguese empire in South America. Imperial Spain had been able to bring limited pressure on Portugal to restrain Portuguese penetration into the Amazon, but the independent Republics of Spanish South America lacked any leverage against a strong and unified Brazil. Bolivia, as one of the weakest of the new republics, did not seem capable of upholding its paper claims to the distant Amazon region in the north. In a frank admission of weakness, Bolivia realistically surrendered many Amazon territories to Brazil in a treaty of 1867. Although Bolivian nationalists denounced the 1867 treaty as a betrayal, in retrospect Bolivia should have forsaken its claims north of the Abuná River, a tributary of the Madeira River, and thus be rid of a costly and troublesome problem (Map 6).[2]

The Abuná River was significant because it offered the last easy water route to the Bolivian towns in the south. In the Amazon all transportation revolves around rivers, and quite naturally Bolivian colonists settled along the banks of those navigable rivers that had links with the interior. Bolivian colonists could not go north of the Abuná River, because falls and rapids in the Madeira River blocked downstream navigation for 424 kilometers. This natural barrier in reality benefited Bolivia, because the Madeira

rapids likewise prevented waves of Brazilians from going south into Bolivia. Not any special efforts by Bolivia, but rather the characteristics of the river system accounted for the strong Bolivian presence over jungle regions as far north as Villa Bella. Likewise, under the shadow of this natural barrier, Bolivia was able to retain the Mamoré-Guaporé River as the border with Brazil. This last river was one of only two stretches where the new South American republics succeeded in preserving the old boundary line between the Spanish and Portuguese empires; everywhere else Brazilian advance left behind the colonial paper boundaries, and usually by vast distances.[3]

The Madeira River diverted but could not stop the westward migration of tens of thousands of Brazilian colonists after 1877. In their overwhelming majority they came fleeing from the drought in the impoverished state of Ceará. This vast migratory current, as if hitting a peninsula, simply flowed around the Madeira rapids and sought openings to the west in the Purús and other tributaries of the Amazon. Bark from the quinine trees had been the lure originally attracting the immigrants, but soon tapping the rubber trees became the exclusive activity of the Brazilians pouring into the Amazon. The Acre River, explored by a Brazilian in 1860, soon had thousands of Brazilian immigrants settled along its banks. Steamboat service began in the river in 1879 and provided an outlet for the rubber and brought food for the colonists. However, the water was deep enough for navigation only from January to May.[4] At first rubber exports just covered the subsistence needs of the settlers, but as the price of natural rubber increased, many new colonists came to tap the rubber wealth. Each colonist hoped to beat the odds: "Swamps, miasmas, numberless mosquitoes and venomous insects, none but foul water to drink, insufficient nourishment, torrential rains—all contribute to a mortality which is conservatively reckoned at two lives to each ton of rubber exported."[5]

Not just hardworking colonists but also adventurers and criminals were among the nearly 80,000 Brazilians who had come into the Acre basin by 1898. Brazilian authorities exercised a weak control on their side of the border, and the absence of any Bolivian officials left Acre as a wild open place. Without any authorities, lawlessness and the survival of the

strongest became the norm in the Bolivian
Acre. The only rule in the region was nicknamed Article 44, a reference to the .44 caliber
of the Winchester repeating rifle, the almost
universal weapon in use among the colonists.
A shortage of women, who in the early decades
did not exceed 20 percent of the population,
deprived the region of the stability that only
family life can provide. Instead quarrels and
murders over women added more tension to
an already highly charged atmosphere. The
preponderance of young males was conducive
to frequent violent clashes and fits of rage. Although turmoil and greed were rampant, many
real colonists longed for some authority to restore order as the best way to develop this otherwise wild frontier.[6]

Had Bolivia really been interested in upholding its claim to the region, the government
should never have permitted this unrestricted
immigration to breed so much lawlessness and
disorder. The geographic isolation of the Acre
basin did not have to preclude Bolivian rule,
and sustained vigorous human action could
still overcome the natural barriers. But rather
than an intense official effort to colonize the
region, at the capital of La Paz the Bolivian
leaders wasted the decades in meaningless civil
wars and political intrigues. No Bolivian authority existed along the entire Acre River, and
Bolivian explorers rarely visited the region.
Only in the late 1890s, when the rubber boom
was in full swing, did the lure of customs revenue finally catch the attention of La Paz. Rubber from the Acre River was not paying any export duties, and the possibility of easily reaping
this huge windfall of revenue was too tempting to pass up any longer. Soon, however, La
Paz saw that establishing authority over a distant region was more easily said than done. Repeated attempts to send Bolivian expeditions
foundered, whether because of illness, death, or
scarcity of funds. After many attempts, a Bolivian commission steaming through Brazilian
rivers finally reached the region and formally
established Puerto Acre as the capital on 2 January 1899. At an elevation overlooking the river
and just five kilometers south of the Brazilian
frontier, Puerto Acre was well placed to collect
export taxes on the rubber leaving the region.
Prior to its arrival, the commission had pledged
future customs revenues to finance the costs of
the expedition. The customs house lived up to

the expectations of large revenues, and in
barely two months the tax on rubber exports
paid for all expenses and yielded a nice sur-
plus.[7]

Collecting the customs duties obviously
antagonized the Brazilian rubber exporters
who began looking for ways to escape Bolivian
control. The governor of the state of Amazonas,
Ramalho Júnior, was incensed, and he schemed
to preserve the revenue for his state. He secretly hired the Spaniard adventurer Luis
Gálvez and gave him resources to remove the
Bolivian authorities. Luis Gálvez, as an under-
cover operator, fooled naïve Bolivian officials
and went to Puerto Acre as a member of a Bolivian commission. Sensing the discontent
among the rubber merchants and seeing that
the defense of Puerto Acre was in the hands of
a handful of policemen and customs guards,
Gálvez carefully planned his coup. On 14 July
1899, the date he chose in a pantomime of the
French Revolution, Gálvez drove out the Bolivian officials and proclaimed himself the first
president of the Independent State of Acre.
Brazil was the northern limit of this new republic, and he claimed the Madre de Dios River
as the southern boundary. Gálvez appointed a
mock cabinet and issued fantastic decrees from
a crude shack he labeled the Palace of Government. Besides giving the title of colonel to
many of the locals, he sent appointments as
diplomatic representatives of the new republic
to surprised friends in Europe. The results had
exceeded the expectations of Governor Júnior,
who was extremely pleased with his hench-
man.[8]

His antics were grist more for a comic
opera writer than a historian. He labeled the
muddy paths in Puerto Acre with pompous titles such as *Hotel do Universo*, and *Praza da
Libertade*, and he really seemed to be living his
delusions of power. Unfortunately for Gálvez,
his followers soon tired of the sham theater and
deposed him, but in a counter-coup he returned to reoccupy his rightful post as president of this largely fictional republic. As the
new country was imploding, Bolivia asked for
help from Brazil in putting down the rebellion.
In the first week of March 1900 a Brazilian gunboat arrived to take Gálvez back to Manaus,
the capital of the state of Amazonas. Whether
the naval commander acted on his own, or
with encouragement from Rio de Janeiro, or

whether Governor Júnior recalled Gálvez, remains clouded in mystery. The effect of the removal of Gálvez was very clear: his jungle government collapsed, leaving once again a political vacuum. The Acre reverted to its previous state of lawlessness, and Brazilian colonists felt threatened by the many criminals and adventurers on the loose.[9] The disorder was an opportunity for Bolivia to satisfy this long standing need for protection and thus legitimize its rule among the many Brazilian rubber tappers. Just how would Bolivia respond to the succession of events?

The decision was in the hands of General José Manuel Pando, who become the president of Bolivia after its most recent civil war. The well-educated General Pando seemed ideally prepared to cope with the Acre crisis. Besides his extensive military experience, he was one of the few Bolivians who had explored the region. Pando hoped to make up the lost ground by sending substantial army units into the Acre, but if Bolivia for years had struggled just to send civilian officials, how could it expect to sustain a large army in that distant region? The La Paz government simply was incapable of mobilizing that large national effort needed to overcome the geographic isolation of the Acre region. The realistic alternative was to complete the strategic withdrawal Bolivia had partially begun in 1867. But President Pando could not resist the political benefits a victorious military campaign would bring, and in any case he did not want to challenge the strong nationalistic passions in La Paz. The President also harbored great illusions about transforming his agrarian country and imagined that a military campaign was a prelude to a much larger mobilization to transform the whole country radically.[10]

Service in the Bolivian army had always been odious because men did not want to die in meaningless civil wars. But because the country had never before sent men to fight in the jungle, the novelty of a campaign in distant frontiers captured the public imagination and evoked the curiosity of many who wanted to participate in this quixotic adventure. As this was a national war, the government counted on receiving contingents from each province. The government sent a small force north to open a direct route to the Acre down the Beni River, but the original plan called for

using Brazilian waters to send the main force by a steamship purchased in Europe for this purpose. Unfortunately, on 19 June 1900 Brazil closed the Amazon to Bolivian military expeditions. The Brazilian decision was the final warning to Bolivia to abandon any hope of reconquest, but President Pando did not for a moment desist in his goal of saving the Acre for Bolivia.[11]

Without access to Brazilian rivers, the task of getting troops and supplies to the Acre assumed formidable proportions. A single large expedition would strain the resources along any one route, so instead Pando decided to send three small columns by separate routes to converge eventually in the Acre. Patrols had already been surveying the Abuná region and in May 1900 picked the long trail of 120 kilometers between Mercedes on the Orton River (a tributary of the Beni River) and the Acre River as the best site to clear an overland route (Map 6). The commanders rejected the shorter trail of 80 kilometers linking Gironda on the Tahuamanu River (a tributary of the Orton) with the Acre River. Why had the Bolivians chosen Mercedes as the base of operations for their entire campaign? A main reason was that water levels were high throughout most of the year at that site, while further west at Gironda the lower water levels limited the navigation of steamboats. Another reason was that the trail from Mercedes linked into the network of trails hacked by the Brazilian rubber cutters near the Acre River; instead the terminus point of the Gironda route was simply an isolated shack distant from any other trails. These considerations might seem convincing, had not the Bolivian rubber tappers under Nicolás Suárez already opened a path to the Acre River at Cobija (then called Bahía) from Porvenir on the Tahuamanu River. The waters were even shallower in both rivers, but the land distance of 25 kilometers was the smallest of all the sites. Control of the shortest overland route to the Acre River at Porvenir explains why in this sector the Bolivians were successful in their military operations. Upon deeper reflection, the decision to use the longest and not the shortest of the three land routes to the Acre River practically doomed the Bolivian military campaigns. Bolivia burdened itself with the unnecessary effort of trying to drag soldiers and supplies through 120 kilometers of jungle rather than just 25 kilometers.[12]

Map 6. Acre Territory.

Quite heroically and striving mightily against their fate, hardy soldiers and Bolivian rubber tappers labored in the extremely hot and very humid weather to transform the long trail into a wide footpath. Clearing the jungle was already very arduous work, and in addition, the men had to build many bridges, two of them over wide rivers. Mercifully, the jungle was initially kind to the men, who so far suffered few deaths because of tropical illnesses. Good nutrition is the first requirement to preserve health in the jungle, but already the Bolivian government showed itself incapable of supplying the growing number of troops gathering at Mercedes. Repeatedly the troops had to go on half rations when foodstuffs failed to arrive on time. And to make things worse, throughout the war the Bolivian government relied on unscrupulous merchants who diverted, pilfered, and delayed the shipments of money and food for the troops. If near well-navigated and easily reached rivers La Paz could not adequately feed and supply its troops,

how could the government sustain an overland expedition into the distant Acre? The incompetence at La Paz, and not the harsh jungle itself would soon become the single most important factor contributing to the disasters in the expeditions.[13]

The men completed the footpath by early June, but shortly after the column unexpectedly received orders to halt and to await further instructions. The commanders used the extra time for training exercises, but the men began to fall ill and even to die because of tropical diseases. The reason for the halt was that with commendable caution, La Paz did not want the first column to proceed alone without having the other two columns nearby to provide support if bitter fighting erupted. These other two columns were following circuitous routes to reach the Orton River. The government failed to inform the first column of these deployments and left the troops in Mercedes feeling marooned. Officials at Riberalta, the nearest settlement, had stated that no more supplies were coming, and the troops knew that Mercedes had food stocks for only a few more months. After a council of war, the officers of the first column took the initiative and boldly decided to advance immediately.

Leaving all their heavy equipment and the many sick behind in Mercedes, the first column set out on 8 August 1900. The column had food for 25 days, but because pack animals were scarce, everyone, including the civilians, had to carry 25 kilograms of food and equipment on their backs. Walking with this crushing load in the exhaustingly hot tropical climate made the men suffer terribly. They repeatedly fell in the mud of the slippery jungle path. The night's sleep was not enough to restore the men, who had to take frequent rest pauses and a long break during the midday hours just to continue straggling forward. On 13 August the haggard column reached the Abuná River, the endpoint of the path. Not knowing that the rebellion of Gálvez had collapsed, the construction crews had not gone beyond Santa Rosa to avoid alerting the rebels to the approaching Bolivian forces.

The column took several days of rest to prepare itself for what the men expected to be the harshest part of the entire journey and the inevitable clash with the rebels. On August 18, after having crossed the Abuná River, the column resumed its march and for the first time the advance guard had to hack a way through the virgin jungle. At times the men got lost, but they persevered until they stumbled upon a trail of the Brazilian rubber tappers the next day. The network of trails and paths gradually widened and made easy their walk until at last on 22 August the expedition could gaze for the first time on the Acre River. Because of the season, the river was too shallow to navigate except by small canoes. The Brazilians were friendly and looked with curiosity at these ragged soldiers who seemed to have come from another planet. The column heard the news about the collapse of the Republic of Acre and sensed that the Brazilians welcomed the establishment of order. The column, oblivious to any danger, continued to march north at a leisurely pace along the well-traveled path that ran roughly parallel to the east bank of the Acre River. The local inhabitants sold some of their provisions to the column that by this time no longer had to carry heavy loads. After having

walked without any novelty, on 22 September the Bolivian expedition peacefully entered Puerto Acre. Without having seen any rebels or fired a single shot, the military campaign for the Acre appeared to be over. The peaceful tendencies of the Brazilians suggested that unless Bolivia provoked them, the region could remain Bolivian.[14]

Puerto Acre was little more than a collection of shacks and huts with a couple of warehouses. The new garrison devoted itself to fixing and cleaning the place and trying to establish some semblance of order in this region. The initial belief that the Brazilians were too timid to fight seemed to be confirmed. The garrison at Puerto Acre still lacked any communication with the outside world and continued to wait patiently for news about the other Bolivian units. The second column arrived at Mercedes on the Orton River on 26 September 1900, almost two months after the first column had set out down the cleared path. The second column was under the command of Lucio Pérez Velasco, the vice president of Bolivia, whom President Pando had designated as the highest ranking civilian official for the Acre. After a well-deserved rest, the Pérez Velasco column prepared to set out early the next month. On 7 October the third column arrived ahead of schedule in Mercedes. Under the command of Colonel Ismael Montes, the Secretary of War, the third column consisted of the Independencia Battalion, the only well-integrated unit of the campaign; a mélange of units from different regions of Bolivia had composed the troops of the first two columns. President Pando had appointed Colonel Montes as the supreme commander of the troops, while leaving civilian matters in the hands of Vice President Pérez Velasco; the situation potentially could be conflictive, but fortunately the two officials maintained a harmonious and supportive relationship throughout the campaign. Colonel Montes was impatient for action and decided to leave the next day with Pérez Velasco and the troops of the second column. The Colonel left the Independencia Battalion behind as a reserve at Mercedes.[15]

After a one-week march through the footpath, the second column reached the Acre River on 14 October. The Brazilian rubber tappers told Colonel Montes that the first column was already at Puerto Acre. Everything seemed so quiet and peaceful that Montes and Pérez Velasco saw no need to tire out their troops by marching through the jungle. The two officials left the troops behind and boarded a small craft that could navigate the Acre River during the dry season. Their plan was to inspect the region and to reach Puerto Acre to learn from the garrison whether any rebel activity remained. As the two officials were coasting downstream, on 22 October, Gentil Tristan Norberto persuaded fellow rubber tappers to proclaim him the president of a new independent state of Acre. Coincidentally, that same day Montes and Pérez Velasco had come to visit the new president, who promptly had them imprisoned. The president believed that he had in the bag quite a catch and departed to rally more supporters for his new republic. Montes and Pérez Velasco used the time to persuade their captors of the foolishness of their rebellion and promised them amnesty. Some of Norberto's followers were angry about his distribution of cabinet posts in the new republic, and they took advantage of the president's absence to depose him. The Brazilians released their prisoners and pledged loyalty to Bolivia in highly convincing expressions. This second republic of Acre ended on 22 October and lasted a mere four days.[16]

The episode of the second republic had provided comic relief before the Bolivian authorities had to face their first serious challenge. Colonel Montes, after his release, resumed his trip and reached Puerto Acre on 24 October. By then he realized that the rubber merchants were angry at having to pay export duties and were trying to incite the rubber tappers to take up arms against Bolivian rule. The rubber merchants spread rumors claiming that the Bolivians were coming to confiscate the rubber lands and to nullify the common-law marriages of many rubber tappers. To add more intrigue to the mix, the governor of the state of Amazonas was actively supporting a new rebel movement. The state of Amazonas was recruiting personnel, sending arms and supplies, and was even trying to delay the ships bringing supplies to the Bolivian garrison at Puerto Acre. The appearance of small rebel bands convinced Colonel Montes of the need to move the Independencia Battalion close to the Acre River. At Puerto Acre, so many men had contracted tropical diseases or died, particu-

larly from Beriberi, that he decided not to bring the second column into this unhealthy place. Instead, he ordered the second column to stay on the Acre River at Empresa. At this intermediate point he felt this second column was well positioned to move either downstream or upstream as needed. Colonel Montes himself began the long return trip to Mercedes to lead the Independencia personally to the Acre River. He traveled with a small escort and tried to stop as little as possible along the river to prevent a repetition of his earlier embarrassing capture.[17]

Meanwhile the rebel forces had been increasing and already numbered at least 1500 men. New adventurers and more criminals had been gathering on the Brazilian border to pounce on Puerto Acre, and Bolivian officers began to fear for the safety of their troops. The fears of an early attack proved unfounded, because the rebels had opted for starving out the garrison. The rebels established a blockade to keep any steamboat from crossing the Brazilian border into the Bolivian Acre. The strategy was well founded, because in the complex mercantile system then existing, rubber tappers received all their food from the steamboats in exchange for rubber. As the stocks of provisions in Puerto Acre and in nearby sheds declined, the garrison had to go on half-rations. Patrols in forays upstream found very modest amounts of food, and the garrison itself continued to dwindle because of disease. With so few soldiers left to bear arms, Puerto Acre could fall into rebel hands almost effortlessly unless reinforcements arrived soon.[18]

The early appearance of high waters allowed a steamboat to bring the second column at Empresa to Puerto Acre on 18 November. However, the arrival of the troops aggravated the scarcity of food, and already on 3 December at a council of war many officers recommended abandoning Puerto Acre. The worsening food shortage increased the pressure to evacuate, but the resolve of the men to suffer more hardship hardened when about a week later they received vague news that the Independencia Battalion had reached the Acre River. Fortunately for the garrison, Puerto Acre did not learn that the Independencia was actually fighting for its survival.[19]

By early December 1900 the number of rebels had reached nearly two thousand distributed in three main areas. The largest group stayed near the Brazilian border to enforce the blockade on Puerto Acre. A second group was at Empresa, which had become an important center for rebel operations. The third group was to the south near Riosinho and had the task of tying down and destroying the recently arrived Independencia Battalion on which all the hopes of Bolivia rested. Colonel Montes, who had safely completed his long trek to Mercedes, had set out with the Independencia on 24 November. After reaching the Acre, the battalion marched along the river and arrived at Riosinho on 6 December. All the inhabitants had fled the place, which was just a group of shacks. Scouts could not detect any rebels, but timely warning by a Brazilian sympathizer convinced Montes of the likelihood of an attack. He had the troops dig trenches all around the landward side and also provided an adequate defense facing the river. To the north, east, and west, a dense jungle began just 10 meters from the shacks, and the danger existed that the more numerous rebels could easily overrun the battalion before it had a chance to fire. To provide early warning, Colonel Montes established six pickets forming an arch deep in the jungle and linked them with a camouflaged trail that allowed soldiers to patrol the entire perimeter without being detected.[20]

On 12 December at 0600 the just awakened battalion was going through the procedure of morning roll call when shots rang out in the east. A sentinel had detected the approaching rebels, and although he was killed, his firing had so surprised the startled attackers that they momentarily halted and threw away any chance of easily overrunning the Bolivian force. The soldiers had ample time to grab their Mauser rifles and to take up their prearranged positions; even the military band played music to keep the troops in high spirits. The rebels launched a strong attack from the north, but their supporting attack from the other side of the river was one hour late. When their attack from the north died down, the rebels then tried to advance from the east but with no better results. The inability to launch a simultaneous assault on all the fronts deprived the rebels of the opportunity to win by simply overpowering the Bolivian defenders. The battle turned into a big firefight, as the rebels tried to bury the Independencia with bullets from their Winchesters. These rifles carried at least 15 rounds in their magazine, and soon the rebels had fired over 20,000 cartridges. At first glance the bolt-action Mausers carrying only five cartridges in their chambers were no match for the faster Winchesters. However, the constant firing of the Winchesters produced a blue smoke cloud that gave away the rebel positions. Officers told the Bolivian soldiers to calculate the height of a man and to fire below the smoke clouds appearing in the jungle; by firing only 3,000 well-placed rounds, the soldiers blunted the attack. After two hours of this unequal marksmanship, the demoralized rebels retreated into the safety of the jungle.[21]

Unable to destroy the battalion, the rebels did succeed in keeping the Independencia tied down. Montes tried sending out several sorties, but he was unable to drive away the rebels. Although the battle of Riosinho had been a morale-building victory for the Bolivians, for all practical purposes the battalion was immobilized. If all hopes had rested on this battalion, what chances did the beleaguered garrison at Puerto Acre still have? With its food supplies dwindling fast and more soldiers falling ill, its prospects were grim at best. The situation was so desperate that two Bolivian junior officers deserted and reported to the rebels the deplorable conditions of the garrison. The rebel leaders were convinced that their strategy of starving out the garrison offered the best chance for success. After having heard of the setback at Riosinho, they were not eager to test the Mausers of the Bolivian soldiers. Unfortunately for the rebel strategy, the return of high water was increasing the number of steamboats impatiently waiting at the border. The ships' captains saw their profits falling with each day's delay, and they demanded either free passage for their steamboats or an end to the military campaign. The pressure became unbearable for the rebel leaders, who seeing their time fast running out, reluctantly prepared for an assault on Puerto Acre on 24 December 1900.[22]

The rest of the rebels were not at all eager to engage in battle for the profits of others, and most of the rank and file had to be coerced into participating. As for the assault itself, the surest and simplest way to capture Puerto Acre was for the 600 rebels to attack the small and sickly garrison simultaneously from all sides. However, because many rebels were afraid of a Bolivian counterattack, they agreed only to attack from across the Acre River, the water thus serving as a natural defense. Under such an arrangement, the combat necessarily reduced itself to intensive firing. But the rebels had two aces to play: They had obtained a Hotchkiss machine gun and one small cannon. With these seemingly formidable weapons the rebels hoped to neutralize the Mausers.

The attack was scheduled to begin at daybreak on 24 December, but a dense fog delayed the operation. The dense fog did conceal the rebels who were able to take the best positions for combat without being spotted. The Bolivian garrison, after a meager lunch, sat down for a quiet afternoon siesta when a loud trumpet sound from across the river disrupted their rest. The trumpet had been the signal for the rebels to open fire; the Bolivian troops, including many of the sick, quickly took up their positions. Death, illness, and disease had reduced the garrison to 79 healthy soldiers and 73 sickly ones. The ammunition the soldiers had carried on their backs from Mercedes was scarce. The officers immediately halted the return fire and had the men stay low in the trenches as an incessant barrage flew over their heads. The noise and smoke were impressive, but gradually the Bolivians saw that the rebel fire was largely ineffective and at best was only damaging the shacks on higher ground above the trenches. The machine gun and the cannon kept rattling on, and in response a Bolivian officer lined up soldiers and ordered them to hold their fire until he called for a volley. At his signal the soldiers fired volleys that sounded like a gigantic cannon screaming. At such short range the high-velocity bullets of the Mausers cut through tree trunks and even metal plating. A few volleys from the Mausers sufficed to silence the probably defective machine gun, the cannon, and even the rebel trumpet.[23]

The rebels continued blazing away with their Winchesters, and soon the tell-tale smoke clouds appeared. The Bolivian officers told their men to fire an occasional volley below the blue smoke. In addition, as soldiers had done for thousands of years, the Bolivians shouted and roared to try to terrorize their opponents.

The ineffectiveness of the rebel fire emboldened the Bolivians to display false targets, at one point even sticking out rifle butts so that the rebels would have something to shoot at, but with no effect. Overconfident, the Bolivian soldiers made the mistake of taunting the rebels with insults. Steeped in the racist beliefs of the period, the Bolivians called the rebels monkeys and repeatedly mocked their abilities and courage.[24] Belittling the opponent is always dangerous, and in particular when the taunts can give the other side a reason to fight. The rebels, whose honor and courage had been insulted, for the first time were angry and at last were ready to charge the Bolivian trenches. For months afterwards the rebels remembered these taunts bitterly, so deadly in a region where the code of honor demands that blood flow over simple misunderstood words. Just as the infuriated rebels were preparing to make the final push across the river, the whistle of a steamboat sounded at 1400. The leaders of the rebels concluded on the basis of no evidence that the Bolivians were planning to cross the river to cut off the rebels. Panic seized the leaders who shouted every man for himself; their followers, left abandoned and with their heavy weapons destroyed, gradually retreated north to Brazil. The sudden departure of the rebels convinced the Bolivians that this was a ruse to lure them out of their trenches. Only at nightfall did the Bolivians send some scouts to explore, but by then the rebel force had long since vanished.

The Bolivians knew they had repulsed an attack, but the acute food shortage prevented them from realizing immediately that they had won a decisive victory. Stretching their remaining supplies gave food for only five more days; at another meeting the officers decided to wait until 30 December before beginning surrender parleys with the rebels. The garrison did not know that in their panicky flight, the rebels imagined seeing a Bolivian behind each tree. The rebel leaders blamed each other for the debacle as a ferocious power struggle erupted among them. Meanwhile the number of steamboats piled up at the border continued to increase, and their impatient ships' captains demanded passage into Acre. The rebels began to quarrel among themselves, and finally the leaders promised another attack on 28 December to capture Puerto Acre and to open the way for the steamboats. The promised attack never materialized, and the next day, the captain of the just arrived *Rio Affuá* persuaded the other steamboats to run the blockade. The constant sound of the ships' horns alerted the garrison, and the men took up positions to repel what they considered the inevitable rebel attack. Led by the *Rio Affuá* and hoisting large white flags, the twelve merchant ships arrived in front of Puerto Acre, whose confused garrison did not know what to make of the strange situation. Soon the confusion vanished, and the garrison went from suffering near starvation to feasting on delicacies as the ships unloaded their abundant cargoes.[25]

With the return of high waters, the steamboats continued their journey upstream to bring provisions to the rubber tappers and to collect the rubber shipments. In the wake of the ships the rubber tappers returned to their homes along the river, and gradually the rebel forces melted away. News of these developments failed to reach Colonel Montes, who remained pinned down at Riosinho. In spite of several attempts, he had been unable to strike a decisive blow at the rebel force at Empresa; meanwhile his men were wasting away from disease and their food supplies were running low. Colonel Montes decided to return with the Independencia back to Mercedes on the Orton River; there he hoped to find food, medicines, and replacements for his depleted battalion. The Independencia planned to leave on 4 January 1901, but constant noise from what the troops believe to be hunting horns suggested an imminent attack. In reality the sounds, heard for a long time because of the many bends of the river, came from ships' horns. The *Río Affuá* once again was leading the pack, and soon the ship was unloading supplies for the hungry battalion. The timely arrival of the steamer had prevented the departure of the battalion and hastened the collapse of the rebellion. Colonel Montes authorized the *Río Affuá* to return downstream to obtain the submission of the rebels at Empresa. On the promise of no reprisals, the rebels quickly signed a document pledging their unswerving loyalty to Bolivia.[26] The rest of the rebels vanished and rejoined the workers in the task of tapping the rubber trees. The revolt in the Acre was over, and Bolivia accomplished the seemingly impossible task of bringing the Acre territory under its control for the first time.

This campaign ranks among the finest in the otherwise bleak military history of Bolivia. A number of reasons accounted for this success. The officers had shown an unusual degree of initiative and had not hesitated to carry out dangerous actions; in many ways the whole campaign hinged on the decision of the first column to march into the unknown in August 1900. The well-trained Bolivian troops had a considerable advantage over the disorganized rebels who did not know how to coordinate movements. In the hands of competent soldiers, the Mauser rifle proved a decisive weapon; without this new rifle the Bolivians could not have won. The power struggles and divisions among the rebel leaders contrasted with the unified command in the Bolivian army, which worked harmoniously with the civilian authorities. The Bolivians consistently pursued their clear goal of bringing the region under control, in contrast to the rebel leaders whose motives did not remain constant. The urge for profits of the merchants and of the ships' captains proved instrumental in securing acceptance for Bolivian rule as the best alternative. Although the state of Amazonas had brazenly supported the Acre revolt, the Brazilian government had remained neutral and had tacitly approved the Bolivian campaign. Lastly, a considerable amount of good luck had favored the Bolivian troops, who at key moments seemed to be on the verge of losing. Many coincidences and unique events had made possible the miracle of a victory.

However, the victory had not been complete. The rebels had been dispersed but never destroyed; given the right conditions they could be rallied to make another attempt. The two foundations of the Brazilian presence in the Acre River remained intact: The Brazilian colonists and the many persons they had already buried in the region. Bolivia still had not made a commitment comparable to Brazil's in colonists and cadavers. Converting the path between the Orton and the Acre rivers into a wagon road was just a minimal step needed to facilitate the constant arrival of colonists, families, soldiers, and officials into the region. Only when Bolivians in substantial numbers were present in the Acre could Bolivia consider secure its control over that distant region.

Plácido de Castro and the Collapse of Bolivian Rule

A military occupation was the surest and most direct way to guarantee control over the Acre but was simply beyond the capabilities of Bolivia. Besides logistical difficulties and the high cost of supplying this distant region, the first Bolivian campaign had bled the Bolivian army dry. Sixty percent of the participants in the first campaign had perished, and many of those who survived were too weak to return to active duty. Bolivia needed to maintain a minimum of 1,000 soldiers in the garrisons on the Acre River and at least 500 more in nearby supporting bases. Because tropical disease relentlessly took its toll among the new arrivals, the Bolivian government had to keep a steady stream of replacements flowing into the Acre to maintain the garrisons at the minimum strength. Stationing a third or more of the Bolivian army in the Acre was not necessarily bad and could bring many benefits. Keeping the officers away from the poisonous political intrigues at La Paz was the best way to keep the army focused on its duties. If the parallel experience of Peru at Iquitos during the same decades was an indication, many soldiers had the tendency to stay in the region once their terms of enlistment were over, and in this way they would have increased the Bolivian element among the population. Most importantly, of course, large garrisons guaranteed Bolivian rule whose foundations otherwise remained dangerously shaky in the Acre basin.[27]

The customs revenue from rubber exports was more than adequate to cover the expenses of the large garrisons but left little profit for the national government at La Paz. President José Manuel Pando, who had aroused so many nationalist feelings among the population, quickly showed that all along he had intended to gain more than just the prestige of having the Bolivian flag wave over the Acre. He demanded that the Amazon adventure yield substantial revenue for the national government. The greed for revenue had been the driving force behind the initial Bolivian occupation and remained no less predominant. Rather than have large garrisons consume all the customs revenue of Puerto Acre, Pando sought a way to shift some of the costs of occupation into private hands. An earlier proposal to create a "Brazilian Syndicate" or trust to handle the rubber exports of Acre seemed the most promising way to reconcile Bolivian rule with Brazilian interests at a low cost. The members of this Syndicate or trust were the leading Brazilian rubber exporters who were very eager to obtain a share of the lucrative rubber trade. The Brazilian Syndicate proposal promised to turn any remaining opponents of Bolivian rule in the Acre into its most enthusiastic supporters. Regrettably, the Pando government let the proposal for the Brazilian Syndicate founder for the sake of a treacherous mirage.[28]

Instead of embracing the Brazilian Syndicate eagerly, President Pando decided on 11 July 1901 to sign a contract with U.S. investors who had incorporated a "Bolivian Syndicate." The agreement gave the U.S. investors considerable authority over the Acre region in exchange for a near monopoly on rubber exports, with Bolivia to receive a share of the profits. Although Bolivia publicly claimed that this was a purely financial arrangement, the real intention had been to use the United States as a barrier to block Brazil. The maneuver at first glance seemed to have come out of the pages of Niccolò Machiavelli's *Prince* but a close examination revealed that the Bolivian Syndicate was a formula for disaster. Pando failed to understand that a contract with U.S. investors did not automatically secure U.S. government support.[29] Reputable investors had refused to participate in the scheme, and only with great difficulty had Bolivian diplomats located some people willing to join but not to finance the scheme. These confidence men, for that was all they were, lured a naïve cousin of President Theodore Roosevelt into their board to highlight its supposed connection to powerful U.S. personalities.[30]

In reality, the Bolivian Syndicate was nothing but a sham, yet it seemed powerful enough to threaten the merchants of the state of Pará. These Brazilian merchants located downstream at the mouth of the Amazon River had controlled the rubber trade of the Acre until then. As long as their profits had not been threatened, the merchants of Pará had backed Bolivian rule in the Acre and pressured the Brazilian government not to support the rebels. In contrast, the merchants of the state of Amazonas, who were trying to dislodge the Pará merchants, had supported the Acre rebels since

1899. The balancing act between the interests of the states of Pará and Amazonas had shaped the policy of the Brazilian government until 1901. Once Pará also clamored for action against the Bolivian Syndicate, Brazil became more sympathetic to the rebels and less supportive of Bolivian rule in the Acre. However, the change in policy was not swift or complete, and Rio de Janeiro still hoped that the public outcry would force Bolivia to abrogate the ill-fated contract with the Bolivian Syndicate. To admit a mistake in time to take corrective action is unfortunately a quality all too rare among humans. A stubborn President Pando ignored all the warnings and relentlessly pushed ahead to obtain congressional approval for the Bolivian Syndicate on 21 December 1901. Little did he realize that he had signed the death sentence on Bolivian rule in the Acre.[31]

Not only had the Bolivian Syndicate pushed the Brazilian government down the path of intervention, but the threat of U.S. investors taking over the region galvanized the rubber tappers of the Acre in an electrifying way. During the first revolt against the Bolivians, the rebels had lacked a really convincing and universal grievance to sustain their movement. Instead in 1901 the news that U.S. investors were coming to squeeze the profits out of the rubber tappers sent the local population into panic. Pando had turned the whole Acre population against Bolivia, and he compounded the blunder by appointing the inept and rapacious Lino Romero to be the supreme authority in the Acre territory.

After the defeat of the rebel offensive in December 1900, Puerto Acre had enjoyed relative calm. Disease had driven the ranking civilian officials away to healthier climates, and authority over the region had devolved on the garrison commander. The two colonels who ruled Puerto Acre consecutively gained the sympathy of the Brazilian population, indeed one developed such close ties that months later he almost joined the revolt. Seeing that illness wasted away their troops and that La Paz failed to send timely replacements, these army colonels realized that trusting the Brazilians was the only way to sustain Bolivian rule. The colonels' attention and care gained the Brazilians' sympathy, and many settlers came to feel they were better treated in the Bolivian Acre than in their native Brazil. The rubber tappers

eagerly returned to their work in the belief that the Bolivian authorities were maintaining order and encouraging their efforts. These positive policies made many Brazilian rubber merchants come to live in Puerto Acre, and any ideas of avenging the humiliating insults of December 1900 seemed forgotten in the drive for personal wealth. Nevertheless, not all the former rebels had abandoned the movement. Discontented rebels continued to plot openly across the border in Brazil, and they enjoyed the staunch support of the new governor of Amazonas, Salvador Neri. Fortunately for Bolivia, their suggestions to revolt fell on deaf ears, and it became clear to the plotters that unless they could find a big issue to mobilize the population, no revolt could ever get started. That Bolivia needed to keep well-liked officials in charge of Puerto Acre was obvious to all but to President Pando who hand-picked the civilian Lino Romero to establish a formal governmental apparatus in the remote province.[32]

On 3 April 1902 Lino Romero arrived with a large civilian retinue of lawyers, clerks, and other followers. The apparent calmness at Puerto Acre was deceptive, and already the situation was becoming tense as news filtered into the region about the U.S. investors of the Bolivian Syndicate. Instead of practicing patient and skillful diplomacy to prevent any new outbreak, Romero jumped into the role of tropical dictator. His first order of business was to divide the Bolivians into two factions, as he strove to eliminate the previous employees in order to make room for his supporters. In the classic Latin American practice, he was the patron who had to find jobs and benefits for his clients or supporters. The creation of new jobs and the distribution of existing positions for his followers was just the starting point. When all Bolivian civilians and soldiers should have been united against the common danger, he managed to pit them against each other. His pernicious influence reached even into the garrison, and soon he had reduced its army commander to a figurehead. Even the deployment of the lowest ranking soldier required authorization from Romero, and his micromanagement of the troops sapped any initiative from its officers, who turned into passive observers of the unfolding drama.[33]

After dividing and demoralizing the Bolivians, Romero turned his attention to the

Brazilians. He issued decrees imposing new taxes to pay for the bureaucratic jobs of his followers, and soon he had his tax collectors harassing Brazilians up and down the Acre River. Bolivian rule, so comfortable under the prior colonels, had turned bothersome if not harmful. Initially, the petty abuses of Romero did not differ that much from those committed by the powerful bosses (*coronéis*) against the weak throughout rural Brazil, so that the patient Acre inhabitants still remained resigned to their fate. But when Romero issued decrees ordering all the inhabitants to pay a fee to register their rubber lands within six months, he changed from being a hindrance to a danger. In one blow Romero was striking at the root of all the prosperity of the Brazilians; the rumor spread that in six months the Brazilians would have to surrender their rubber trees to his followers. Obviously Romero himself stood to benefit enormously from this forced registration of the rubber lands, but it was not clear whether he was carrying out such a dangerous measure just for his own benefit or as part of the preparations for the Bolivian Syndicate that had yet to make its presence felt in the region. The Brazilians saw his decrees as a mortal threat and gradually began distancing themselves from the Bolivian authorities. The Brazilians avoided contact with most Bolivians, and in a very telling indication, those Brazilians who had earlier come to live in Puerto Acre quietly departed one by one until none were left. Romero, who afterwards tried to deny any role in starting the revolt, dismissed any concerns as groundless criticism from disgruntled Bolivians. Right down to the subsequent denials, Romero was a perfect example of the inept, corrupt, and petty politician who so often decides the destiny of Latin America.[34]

Romero had also shown himself in many instances to be a poor judge of character. The most famous case occurred when he ignored warnings about the loyalty of future rebel leader José Plácido de Castro. Rather than promptly arresting him, Romero allowed him to proceed south with a boatload of equipment to carry out land surveys. In reality, Plácido de Castro was carrying aboard weapons, ammunition, and supplies for a military campaign that he had agreed to lead. Because he could have avoided entering Puerto Acre, he was just trying to size up his opponent before proclaim-

ing a revolt. The chivalrous leader was ready to risk arrest, because he preferred to suffer personally than lead his men to disaster against a capable opponent. He appreciated but turned down Romero's offer to stay overnight and promptly returned to his boat to head south to complete the preparations for the rebellion.

The rebels of the earlier insurrection had correctly attributed many of their mistakes to poor discipline and deficient leadership; this time the plotters wanted to remedy the deficiencies by recruiting Plácido de Castro, a former army officer and a graduate of a Brazilian military academy. As he headed south on the Acre River, he did not have to recruit many followers because the rubber merchants had already persuaded their men to join the revolt. Generally mentioning the U.S. investors of the Bolivian Syndicate sufficed to overcome the doubts of skeptical Brazilians. Only in the upper reaches of the Acre River, where the Bolivian rubber tappers working for the merchant Nicolás Suárez were numerous, were the Brazilians hesitant to revolt; indeed many of these Brazilians fled south with the Bolivians after the revolt began.[35]

After Plácido de Castro completed his tour of the river, he returned to Brazil for one final meeting with the plotters on 1 July 1902. As he had done other times before, he bypassed Puerto Acre and took the land path for the last kilometers to avoid arousing the suspicions of the Bolivians who believed him to be busily surveying lands to the south. The meeting of 1 July 1902 was necessary because the plotters had to decide where to strike the first blow of the revolt. Based on his observations, Plácido de Castro believed that a surprise attack from the jungle side on Puerto Acre sufficed to overwhelm the defenders and end Bolivian rule in one swift action. Other than a handful of policemen stationed at Xapurí (Map 6), the weak and sickly garrison of 230 soldiers at Puerto Acre comprised the entire Bolivian military presence in the Acre region. The plotters remembered the disastrous attack of 24 December 1900 and were not so easily persuaded. A standoff occurred, and finally Plácido de Castro backed down and grudgingly accepted their strategy of leaving the attack on Puerto Acre for last. He then left for the south to organize the start of the revolt.[36]

Plácido de Castro decided upon a surprise

attack with 33 men to capture the Bolivian officials at Xapurí. He set 6 August 1902 as the date for the attack, and early in the morning, before the Bolivian officials had woken up, he captured them all without firing a shot. The Bolivians had been caught totally unprepared partly because of their failure to heed warnings during previous days and also because in a belated measure, Romero had ordered the detachment not to do anything that might antagonize the locals. The prisoners were deported to Brazil, and the next day Plácido de Castro formally proclaimed the independence of the Acre. He made sure that copies of the inevitable manifesto reached all the inhabitants, including the Bolivian authorities at Puerto Acre. In accordance with the strategy at the 1 July meeting, he went downstream rallying forces to join those already gathering in the north for what was assumed to be the final attack on Puerto Acre. Because supplies, weapons, and recruits were pouring in from Brazil, the strategy seemed to be working well.[37]

Less than a week after the proclamation of the independence of Acre, Plácido de Castro received a report that a large Bolivian force had reached the Acre River. The report turned out to be false, but the anxiety remained, and another report in early September confirmed that a Bolivian column was marching from the Orton River. The news aborted the planned attack on Puerto Acre and forced Plácido de Castro to deal with this threat to his rear. The news also rattled many of his men, who remembered the deadly volleys of the Mauser rifles and had no desire to face Bolivian army units. Many men deserted, and his original force of over 200 men shrank to 63. The adverse turn of events did not affect a determined Plácido de Castro, who planned to ambush the Bolivian column when it reached Volta da Empresa on the Acre River. He knew the Bolivians would be exhausted from carrying heavy equipment on their harsh march through the jungle path. Assuming that the Bolivians were unfamiliar with the terrain, he hoped to defeat them decisively on 18 September 1902. Success seemed assured, because the Bolivian Colonel Rosendo R. Rojas was taking only 100 replacements for the depleted garrison at Puerto Acre. In reality, as soon as Colonel Rojas learned of the new Acre revolt, he left his heavy equipment and most of

his ammunition behind in order to ease the burden on his soldiers. With his men traveling light, he could push them to complete an all-night march to catch Plácido de Castro by surprise on 18 September. A Brazilian guide familiar with the route led the soldiers through the jungle during the night, and they arrived in time to surprise the rebels still in their morning camp at 0800. Volleys of Mauser rifles from the jungle ripped through the rebels who lost fifty percent of their men and fled after three hours of unequal combat.[38]

In his first clash in the Acre, Plácido de Castro's gamble on an ambush had backfired, and he had suffered a disastrous defeat. With so many desertions and so few men left, the possibility loomed that he would have to abandon the rebellion that after all was starting to look foolish. All that Colonel Rojas needed to do was to let the news of the defeat sink into the minds of would-be rebels. Instead, he gave full vent to that arrogance that was emerging as a dominant trait of the Bolivian officer corps, as the Chaco War later showed. In a bombastic proclamation, Colonel Rojas accused the rebels of attacking him in a treacherous and ridiculous manner; even worse, he accused them and their leaders of being cowards. This direct insult ended any chance that Plácido de Castro would abandon the rebellion; his chivalrous code of conduct demanded that he either redeem his reputation or die in combat, if necessary alone. But he would not be alone, and the insolent manifesto of Colonel Rojas transformed the defeat into the start of the rebels' good fortune.[39] The rebels, already insulted at Puerto Acre in December 1900, could not stand being branded cowards again. Rubber tappers flocked to join Plácido de Castro, who soon was commanding at least five hundred men.

Success favors those who are in motion, but Colonel Rojas had already exhausted his supply of initiative. His soldiers were too exhausted after the clash and too few in numbers to pursue the fleeing rebels through unknown trails. His force was too small to try to repeat the sudden march of 1900. River transportation was impossible, because the only craft the rebels had left behind was the severely damaged steamboat *Río Affuá*. The combat of 18 September, although a resounding Bolivian victory, had not been without cost. Besides seven soldiers killed, Colonel Rojas had lost a disproportionate number of officers, with 2 killed and 2 wounded. His men had used up most of their cartridges, although the captured Winchesters with their ammunition provided an inferior substitute. Almost all the Brazilian residents had vanished as soon as they heard of the appearance of the Bolivian expedition and had cleaned out their shacks leaving no food behind. Faced with this hostile environment, at the minimum Colonel Rojas needed to retreat back to the Abuná River so that his force could recover the rest of its ammunition, equipment, and supplies. He also could drop off his wounded and collect whatever other recruits had arrived from the interior by then. Instead, in a totally perplexing decision that foreshadowed similar Bolivian blunders in the Chaco War of 1932–1935, he had his less than 90 men set up camp at Volta da Empresa (today Rio Branco). He sent messengers with requests for ammunition and weapons to Puerto Acre and to Riberalta, but even if the messengers made it safely, any help was bound to arrive too late. Being in such a precarious situation, how could he have issued the insulting proclamation? Had Colonel Rojas forgotten that in 1900 the rebels had pinned down an entire battalion well supplied with food and ammunition? Did Rojas not realize that his ragged unit was the only Bolivian force between Puerto Acre and La Paz?[40]

Because the soldiers had left their equipment behind and in reality had never come prepared for immediate combat, the men did not have any tools to build trench works. With too few men, he could not establish a continuous defense line from the river to the camp like what Colonel Ismael Montes had done at Riosinho. Colonel Rojas instead had to leave an isolated detachment guarding the damaged *Río Affuá*. After all the trouble Plácido de Castro had gone to set an ambush for the Bolivians, Rojas created and jumped into his own trap. Plácido de Castro could not believe his good fortune when he learned that Rojas was waiting patiently at Volta da Empresa. In the previous clash Plácido de Castro had correctly estimated that the Bolivian force did not exceed 100 soldiers. With his over 500 rebels he could not resist the temptation to try to overrun the Bolivians in one swift and simultaneous attack. Since he had become commander, he had been instilling the need for obedience on the always

restless and grumbling rubber tappers, and he believed that his force had become sufficiently organized to carry out his attack plans.

Plácido de Castro secretly surrounded the Bolivian unit at Volta da Empresa; with no local sympathizers left to forewarn the Bolivians as in 1900, the attack had a good chance of surprise. From jungle lookouts Plácido de Castro and his officers carefully observed the Bolivians, who had settled into a peacetime routine rather than aggressively patrolling the surrounding region. Plácido de Castro concluded that the garrison was most vulnerable at 1000 when the soldiers had finished their morning exercises and were waiting for their meal. Plácido de Castro insisted over and over that all his men attack from all sides simultaneously at 1000 on 5 October 1902, but unfortunately one unit panicked into firing at a Bolivian picket at 0930. As the shots rang out, any element of surprise vanished, and the entire garrison had time to jump into their crude trenches. At 1000 the simultaneous attack on all sides did begin and pressed the Bolivians so hard that they had to abandon two key trenches. The assault in no way had been barren of results, because the rebels surrounded the detachment at the *Río Affuá* and also deprived the main Bolivian camp of access to the river. Torrential rainfalls occasionally provided water for the soldiers but never in adequate amounts. Thirst came to add to the woes of the soldiers already suffering hunger and running out of ammunition.[41]

In spite of their losses, the Bolivians managed to hold their remaining positions, and Plácido de Castro started a formal siege. He taught his soldiers to build trenches in zigzag form, so that without taking casualties the rebels could move closer to the Bolivian lines. Not wishing to waste shots in sniping, the Bolivians saved their cartridges for another general attack and watched as the rebel trenches crept forward from the jungle into the clearing of the Bolivians. On 7 October the isolated detachment at *Río Affuá* ran out of cartridges and surrendered to the rebels. After a few more days of shooting, Plácido de Castro felt confident enough to invite the Bolivians to parley over surrender terms on 9 October; in his message, Plácido de Castro copied extracts from the messages Rojas had sent to Puerto Acre. Upon learning that his messengers had been intercepted, Colonel Rojas knew that he could expect no help and that his position was hopeless. His men had already exhausted the original sixty cartridges for each Mauser, and the soldiers were fighting off the rebel attacks with the Winchesters and ammunition captured from the rebels on 18 September. Any further resistance seemed pointless, but Colonel Rojas insisted on continuing the struggle because he feared punishment from La Paz if he did not prove he had done everything possible to save the unit. Also the Bolivian commander still underestimated the rebels and only when the rebels extended their trenches to barely six meters away from the defense lines did the Colonel finally accept the inevitable. A general assault was sure to overrun the Bolivian unit, but in a final attempt to avoid such a bloody outcome, on 13 October Plácido de Castro sent a captured Bolivian officer to take a final message for Rojas. On 14 October all the Bolivian officers urged Rojas to negotiate with Plácido de Castro. Rojas wisely insisted on going to negotiate to see for himself whether the rebels were also on the verge of exhaustion. When he saw how numerous and well supplied were the rebels, he agreed to sign the surrender terms on 15 October. The next day the unit turned over its weapons and began the long water route back to Bolivia by the Amazon River and the Atlantic Ocean.[42]

For all practical purposes the surrender at Volta da Empresa had ended any meaningful role for the Bolivian army in the Acre River. The small garrison at Puerto Acre was too weak and isolated to affect the course of events. Plácido de Castro was shifting his forces north to join the rebels gathering for the final attack on this last Bolivian bastion when news from the south again made him change his plans. According to fragmentary reports, a substantial Bolivian force had set up base at Santa Rosa on the Abuná River, the midway point in the path linking the Bolivian base in the Orton River to the Acre River. Secondly, he received very accurate reports about Bolivian victories in the Upper Acre. Under the leadership of Nicolás Suárez, the Bolivian rubber tappers had organized a column called "Porvenir" on 8 October; this column had returned to the Acre River and destroyed a rebel force at Cobija (then called Bahía) on 11 October. The combat had been particularly furious, and only after Suárez had his men fire incendiary arrows into the well-

fortified buildings did the explosions of stored kerosene and ammunition finally destroy the rebels. Plácido de Castro feared that this large force of Bolivian rubber tappers intended to join the Bolivian column at Santa Rosa de Abuná. With his best units he decided to return to the south to dispose of this potential threat before embarking on the siege of Puerto Acre.[43]

Suárez wanted to take the Bolivian rubber tappers downstream to capture the undefended Xapurí, the birthplace of the independent state of Acre. This offensive would gain extra time for Bolivia to send new troops against the rebellion. By the time Plácido de Castro returned south, to his surprise he learned that the expected attack on Xapurí had not taken place. The Bolivian rubber tappers were ready to die for their rubber trees but did not want to engage in distant operations. After some mutual raids, an uneasy neutral zone appeared in the Upper Acre with the Bolivians concentrated at Porvenir and the rebels at Xapurí. Out of the skirmishing a future international frontier line was taking shape in the Upper Acre; more to the point of Plácido de Castro's concern, the Bolivian rubber gatherers did not jeopardize his planned attack on Puerto Acre.[44]

As for the Bolivian column at Santa Rosa on the Abuná River, by early November Plácido de Castro had confirmed that it was nothing but a ragged picket and not a powerful force. The majority of its fifty men were untrained volunteers whose original mission had been to bring the ammunition to the trapped unit of Colonel Rosendo Rojas. When the small column learned on 20 October that Colonel Rojas had surrendered, it halted at Santa Rosa de Abuná. The commander of the column repeated the mistake of Rojas of staying at a vulnerable point rather than retreating back to the secure base of operations on the Orton River. Even worse, the commander left his men leaderless when he departed for a long trip to Riberalta to seek additional reinforcements. Nearly a month passed, and then the first one to arrive on 17 November was Plácido de Castro with nearly 500 rebels. The appearance of a force at least ten times larger on the north shore of the Abuná River should have persuaded the Bolivians to depart quickly that night, but without leadership they meekly awaited their fate. The next day under a covering fire the rebels easily crossed the river and soon the ill-prepared defenders were fleeing south on the footpath to the Orton River.[45]

Nothing stood in the way of the successful rebel drive south, and Plácido de Castro wanted to destroy the Bolivian base on the Orton River. However, his men, who only very grudgingly followed him as far as the Abuná River, refused to go further into what they considered Bolivia. His men, no less than those of Suárez, were primarily rubber tappers who did not want to fight far from home. Whether Brazilian or Bolivian, the rubber tappers set limits on how far the war could spread. As a consolation prize, Plácido de Castro destroyed all the bridges in the path, including the two long ones the Bolivians had so laboriously built. He then decided to return to the Acre River by swinging west through the jungle to the Tahuamanu River to try to destroy the Bolivian post of Costa Rica. A small detachment of Bolivian rubber tappers guarded this post, but the men had succumbed to heavy drinking to pass the long boring days. Only the timely warning of a mule driver gave the officer time to shout every man for himself, whereupon the drunken men fled in stupor before the rebels could reach them. Plácido de Castro entered the abandoned post, and after finally convincing himself that no danger lurked in this south, he returned to the Acre River.[46]

In reality his whole operation in the south had been unnecessary and actually endangered the completion of the military conquest of the Acre. The small haggard unit at Santa Rosa de Abuná posed to threat, while the Bolivian rubber tappers did not want to stray far from their lands in the Upper Acre. Instead an invasion to the south was sure to raise Bolivian fears that the rebels planned on seizing much more territory than just the Acre. News of the repeated Bolivian defeats had already reached La Paz, and President Pando was preparing to send the largest expedition ever to reconquer the Acre. The destroyed bridges on the path to the Orton River could not delay the Bolivian advance for long, and Plácido de Castro realized that he had to hurry his units north to crush resistance at Puerto Acre before the new expedition arrived.

Plácido de Castro was afraid that the Abuná campaign had given the garrison at Puerto Acre extra time to improve its defenses. Fortunately for the rebels, a negligent Romero had failed to take basic precautions. As a civil-ian who was the real commander of the garrison, his dictatorial antics had demoralized both the troops and the Bolivian civilians who had lost any desire to rally behind him in the face of the common danger. His minute control of the troops ruined a sortie against the rebels. Romero had not tried to bring more ammunition and weapons into the town while communications with Brazil were still open. Even more shockingly, he had failed to stockpile enough food to feed the garrison for at least a month. An industrious officer had managed to repair the small cannon captured in December 1900, but otherwise the garrison was in poor shape to face a determined attack. The ineffective actions of a garrison that sank into passivity emboldened many rebels to congregate around the town as skirmishing became more frequent. The rebels were still smarting from the taunts and insults of December 1900 and eagerly looked forward to the opportunity to redeem their reputation.

The soldiers, most of whom were sick with tropical illness, had maintained the old trenches facing the river. Well-drained bulwarks were really needed, but Romero considered them too expensive and unnecessary. Bolivian arrogance lingered in the belief that the rebels could only repeat the attack on the river front as they had done in December 1900. Instead, the rebels quietly surrounded Puerto Acre on 8 January 1903, and by then it was too late to remedy the situation. The weak soldiers hastily dug improvised trenches facing the jungle on the west, but these makeshift arrangements were inadequate to face a long siege. A garrison short of men and ammunition could not even harass the rebels as they tightened their ring around Puerto Acre. Because the elevation of the town precluded any surprise attack, Plácido de Castro took this additional opportunity to display his sense of honor by announcing on 14 January that the attack would begin the next day. He also proposed a joint ambulance service to collect all the wounded in both sides, but Romero, who believed he was immune to bullets, disdainfully rejected the humanitarian gesture of Plácido de Castro. As duly announced, at 0830 on 15 January the attack began, but because the attackers did not charge very boldly against the fire from the Mausers, the combat largely reduced itself to constant shooting. The next day the rebels resumed their incessant firing and eventually consumed over 600,000 cartridges during the siege. The goal of the massive shooting was primarily to draw return fire until the garrison depleted its limited ammunition.

Under cover of this heavy fire, Plácido de Castro put his men to dig zigzag trenches toward the Bolivian lines. Counter fire from the defenders could only delay the digging of these trenches. With over two thousand rebels to draw on, Plácido de Castro divided his men into shifts and rotated them in the front lines after a certain number of hours. The garrison easily detected the change in shifts, because both the replacement and the original unit fired simultaneously until the transfer was complete. Having to fight fresh troops all the time tired the garrison immensely, and soon soldiers were falling asleep in their trenches; eventually the narcotic sleep became so overpowering that the men fell asleep while firing their weapons. The mud-soaked Bolivian soldiers strained to stay awake day and night in their rain-filled trenches and continued to husband their dwindling cartridges until the end. The wind blew the stench from the decomposing bodies of dead rebels into the trenches and nauseated the defenders.

On 19 January rebel lines came close enough to fire incendiary arrows into the town, and soon several buildings were ablaze adding smoke to the other horrible smells. As their food supply diminished, the Bolivian soldiers were starting to suffer hunger. By 23 January with the rebel trenches less than 80 meters away and the Bolivians almost out of ammunition, the defenders could no longer hope to hold the town. Seeing the inevitable, on 24 January 1903 Romero agreed to surrender. Shortly later that same day, the garrison departed as prisoners to Brazil. A few days later a bitter Romero abandoned the Bolivians as he boarded a ship to go back home. Fortunately for the prisoners, the always chivalrous Plácido de Castro filled the leadership vacuum and made sure the Bolivians were well taken care of. Later the Brazilian government assumed the responsibility for returning the prisoners back to Bolivia by the sea route.[47]

The help Brazil provided the Bolivian prisoners reflected not just humanitarian concerns but also a new policy to Bolivia. Unknown to the combatants on both sides, the change in Brazilian policy meant that the siege of Puerto Acre turned out to be the last significant encounter in the Acre War. Although some combat later resumed around the Tahuamanu River, that perfunctory shooting was meaningless because diplomacy had already decided the fate of the Acre territory. The new Brazilian policy emerged out of the slow Bolivian response to the Acre rebellion. Even after the proclamation of independent Acre on 7 August 1902, President Pando let months pass by. Perhaps Pando still counted on the Bolivian Syndicate to leverage U.S. support for Bolivia; if so, his hopes were dashed, because Brazil was quietly negotiating to buy out the American investors and thus to eliminate the last possible chance of any U.S. intervention.[48] Only on 8 November, when news of the surrender of the column of Rojas reached La Paz, did the Bolivian government finally decide to respond. By then it was too late, because any large expedition needed at least four months to reach Acre. Bolivia had run out of time, because on 15 November 1902 a new administration took office in Brazil. The new foreign minister, the dynamic Baron of Rio Branco, had returned from Europe to take up his post on 1 December, and he wanted to settle the Acre dispute permanently.[49]

On 26th December the Baron of Rio Branco "had assumed a totally different attitude and tone: That now Brazil demanded the absolute rescission of the Concession [Bolivian Syndicate] and that the Brazilian Minister also suggested the purchase of the territory covered by the Concession by Brazil."[50] Subsequent telegrams from Rio de Janeiro confirmed that Brazil insisted on acquiring the Acre territory and wanted to offer ample compensation including some parcels of land. The Baron of Rio Branco in his offer reflected the frustration of Brazilians who had finally lost any hope that Bolivia could restore order to the Acre.[51] What Brazil wanted was not so much the Acre as stable borders with its neighbors. Bolivia had over the decades shown itself incapable of exerting authority over the region; thus Brazil insisted on a rectification of the frontier so that Bolivia would be in a strong position to control its remaining Amazon territory. Meanwhile, President Pando announced that he would personally lead the expedition, but domestic politics kept him from departing. His presence in Acre was unnecessary, because Secretary of War Is-mael Montes could lead the expedition compe-tently. Bolivia had intended to send a large force of 1750 men originally, but the bad fame of the Acre as a graveyard for soldiers made re-cruitment much more difficult than in 1900, and only on 19 January did Colonel Ismael Montes set out with 350 soldiers of the 1st Bat-talion. In blind disregard of all the warning messages from Brazil, the President set out with the 5th Battalion on 26 January 1903 in a des-perate attempt to rescue the beleaguered gar-rison at Puerto Acre that unknown to Bolivia had surrendered two days before.[52]

The total expedition was less than half of the expected strength, and even worse, Pando had not revealed to the Bolivian public that the Brazilian demands made the expedition mean-ingless. One day before Pando's departure, Baron Rio Branco increased the pressure when on 25 January 1902 he had the press publish a circular announcing that in response to the Bo-livian refusal to discuss the sale of the territory, the Brazilian president was sending troops to the two bordering states of Amazonas and Mato Grosso. Pando had already traveled nearly two weeks when on 5 February couriers brought him the news that Puerto Acre had surrendered and that Brazil was mobilizing troops at the Bolivian border. He returned to the capital and sent Montes ahead with only one battalion to defend the northern frontier at the Orton River. After a few days Pando changed his mind and sent Montes back to La Paz while the president himself with most of the troops set out for a last round of fruitless campaigning on the Orton and Tahuamanu rivers. Why Pando did not want to accept the fact that the Acre was lost remains inexplicable. By going into the jungle, he deprived himself of the opportunity to understand the unfold-ing Brazilian demands. The Brazilian determi-nation to go to war over the Acre was ab-solutely clear, but neither Pando nor the interim administration at La Paz could bring themselves to accept this reality.[53]

Because President Pando had set out on the expedition in spite of the repeated warnings from Brazil, Baron Rio Branco concluded that the time had come to unlimber the heaviest ar-tillery in the arsenal of diplomacy: an ultima-tum. In its ultimatum of 6 February, Brazil de-manded that Bolivia halt military expeditions

into the Acre. Brazil was not bluffing and even-tually mobilized several thousand soldiers in the region. The fear of a war with its powerful neighbor finally brought the interim govern-ment in La Paz to its senses. In the Protocol of 21 March 1903 the interim government capit-ulated and promised to recognize in a formal treaty that the Acre territory belonged to Brazil. Uncertainty existed over whether Pando out in the field might refuse the Brazilian ultimatum, but after his return to the capital, he duly ratified the Protocol. The president had seen the futility of opposing Brazil and finally ad-mitted defeat.[54]

President Pando was the person most re-sponsible for this Bolivian disaster. Unwilling to commit the resources and the prompt atten-tion the region needed to maintain Bolivian rule, he stubbornly refused to abandon claims to the Acre. His biggest blunder was to bring in the Bolivian Syndicate, a group of shady for-eign speculators. With this single action he shattered beyond repair the weak Bolivian hold over the Acre. Looking more deeply into the character of this president, at first glance a striking picture emerges of a person who had considerable education, much experience, and was one of the few high officials actually famil-iar with the Amazon region. But somehow he was unable to take the correct and timely deci-sions, and his career serves as a disconcerting warning to those who believe that sufficient ed-ucation and long experience always produce the right decisions. A stubborn refusal to alter course and bad judgment in selecting people reveal him to be a shallow person. Twists of fate accidentally promoted him to positions of power he could safely hold only in peacetime but never in a crisis. Outwardly competent, he was that rare person who could cause greater damage than a purely inept individual. A sec-ond culprit in the Bolivian disasters, of course, was Lino Romero. As a typical Latin American politician who merely wanted to milk the Acre position for his benefit, his actions are not hard to understand. The position in Acre, the most difficult in all of Bolivia at that time, required a person of extraordinary ability and utmost tact. For Bolivia to have sent Romero accentu-ated even more the bad judgment of the pres-ident who operated under politics as usual con-ditions.

The performance of the Bolivian officer

corps revealed serious flaws, but at this moment that Bolivia was at the mercy of Brazil it was too late to try to remedy command defects. To Bolivia's evident relief, it soon learned that Brazil was not looking to impose a victor's treaty but was actually seeking a carefully reasoned formula for lasting peace on the border. The negotiations to conclude the Treaty of Petrópolis on 17 November 1903 made clear the Brazilian priorities. Stable and secure boundaries and not additional territory became the primary Brazilian goal. Brazil had consistently supported the 1867 boundary line until it collapsed and became unworkable. But if Brazil demanded the boundary that the Acre rebels were insisting upon far to the south, then extreme territorial claims to the Madre de Dios River inadvertently opened the door to a partition of Bolivia. Did Brazil want in this sector a powerful country or a weak Bolivia? The Acre rebels felt betrayed when Rio de Janeiro gave up so much territory they considered theirs and could not understand that at stake was the survival of Bolivia. By limiting its territorial acquisitions to a minimum, Brazil prevented calls for a partition of Bolivia.

A weak Bolivia, however, revived the possibility of additional Acre style revolts in its remaining Amazon territories. Bolivia needed a minimal capacity to retain its frontier regions, and Brazil believed the solution consisted in finding the most stable border possible. Brazil was determined to stack the cards in favor of Bolivia, so that if any other rebellion broke out

in the remaining Bolivian Amazon, La Paz would enjoy every advantage to maintain its control. Not surprisingly, the Abuná River emerged as the main natural boundary between the two countries, and only in the area of Porvenir (in a tacit recognition of the efforts of Nicolás Suárez) did the Bolivian territory reach the Acre River. What was most surprising was that Rio de Janeiro agreed to give up 3,200 square kilometers of indisputably Brazilian land for the sake of giving the best navigation routes to Bolivia. Because Brazil still walked away with 191,000 square kilometers of land, Baron Rio Branco offered Bolivia additional compensation. Most importantly, Brazil promised to build a railroad around the rapids of the Madeira River as far as the Bolivian town of Villa Bella.[55]

The Brazilian diplomats crafted a solid treaty, and in the clearest sign of success, peace has reigned along this border ever since. A perhaps greater consequence of the Treaty of Petrópolis was less obvious. By this treaty Brazil formally stated its assumption that Bolivia would remain its neighbor and thus tacitly opposed any attempts to partition that troubled country. It remained to be seen whether other neighbors accepted the existence of Bolivia. The issue might not seem pressing, but as the next chapter shows, the future of Bolivia loomed as one large dark cloud hanging over South America as Peru struggled to gain control of Amazon territories.

2. The Struggle for the Peruvian Amazon

[...] my judgment is not to avoid the use of arms and force, but that they be saved as a last resort where and when the other ways are insufficient. — Niccolò Machiavelli[1]

The Acre episode in the previous chapter exposed how vulnerable South America's borders were. If clearly recognized boundaries like that of 1867 could collapse like a house of cards, then what hope existed for countries with ill-defined frontiers? Peru's situation was the worst, because it was the only Latin American country without a single definitive boundary treaty with any of its neighbors at the start of the twentieth century. Peru's Amazon borders were the most vulnerable, and its attempts to extend control over those distant regions form the topic of this chapter. The Peruvian effort advanced on two fronts. In the north, the existing town of Iquitos gave Peru an excellent base to push back Colombian and Ecuadorian colonists. In the south, in contrast, Peru's tardy and weak Amazon presence just barely sufficed to stop the westward drive by Bolivian and Brazilian rubber tappers.

The existence of so many visible boundary quarrels has created the false impression that only distant territories were at stake. Independent of the specific value of each frontier region, the struggle was not just over boundaries but also over the very existence of individual countries, because the countries themselves were no less fluid than the boundaries. As this chapter shows, the very hazardous initial decades of the twentieth century deter-

mined not just today's boundaries but also which countries would survive until the present.

Border Clashes and War Scares, 1900–1910

Peru's attempts to secure Amazon territory collided at every turn with Chile's determination to keep Tacna and Arica, two of the provinces Peru had lost in the War of the Pacific (1879–1883). Peru desperately wanted to recover those maritime provinces and saw the best opportunity in a war many expected to start between Chile and Argentina over their boundary line in the Andes Mountains. A Peruvian alliance with powerful Argentina could put at risk the very survival of Chile as a country. Maneuvering desperately to avoid this fatal threat, Chile attempted to protect itself from Peru by a most unorthodox maneuver. In 1895 Chile signed a treaty offering to transfer most of Arica and all of Tacna to Bolivia as a way to create a barrier against Peru. This treaty also satisfied Bolivia's insistent demand for an outlet to the Pacific Ocean. However, by the time the treaty came up for approval, the danger momentarily receded and the Chilean congress refused to ratify the treaty. Shortly after, the armaments and naval race with Argentina again heated up, and this time Chile tried a different tact to plunge any hostile coalition into disarray. In September 1900 Chile proposed the partition of Bolivia to Peru. In exchange for the recognition of Tacna and Arica as Chilean, Peru would receive in compensation most of Bolivia, including its Amazon territories.[2]

The Peruvian government faced a momentous decision. Chile was offering on a silver platter the opportunity to recreate the ancient Inca Empire stretching from Ecuador to Paraguay. Peru had still not signed a formal alliance with Argentina, so legally Peru was free to accept this tempting offer. Should Peru take most of Bolivia or should it wait for the outbreak of war between Chile and Argentina? In such a war Peru counted on recovering not only Tacna and Arica but also the southernmost province of Tarapacá also lost in the War of the Pacific. At Lima, the capital, wishful thinking prevailed over a unique opportunity, and Peru indignantly revealed the proposal to the public. For the sake of scoring a few fleeting propaganda points, Peru squandered away any chance of securing most of Bolivia and gaining a free hand over the Amazon. Any hope that Peru's loyalty had gained sympathy with Argentina proved illusory. Instead, the magnitude of the Peruvian blunder became clear in May 1902 when Argentina and Chile signed agreements that effectively eliminated the danger of war.[3]

Peru could no longer play the Argentina card against Chile, and the latter country was free to play the Amazon card against a very vulnerable Peru. Not a single one of the borders of Peru with neighboring countries enjoyed the protection of signed treaties. The competing frontier claims were so vast that they threatened to leave Peru without enough land to function as a country. Schemes like the partition of Bolivia in 1900 were far from improbable, and nobody could guarantee that much smaller Ecuador or even Peru itself were immune from grandiose partition proposals. The disputes over the Amazon were not just about borders but often turned into struggles over the survival of individual countries. Not surprisingly, the bordering countries had ready-made opportunities to promote their interests by taking advantage of clashes in the Peruvian Amazon.

First Clashes with Ecuador

Peru had been trying to define its Amazon boundary with Ecuador since 1887. In that year both countries signed a treaty agreeing to negotiate a boundary line and in case of failure to submit the whole issue to arbitration by the King of Spain. Negotiations had waxed and waned as both Peruvian and Ecuadorian colonists entered the disputed territories fitfully. The start of the rubber boom fueled hopes of wealth, even when many of the disputed zones lacked rubber trees. For Ecuadorian politicians, the goal of reaching the Amazon River was an integral part of their nation-building project, while for Peruvian officials the desire to dispose of another boundary dispute was the paramount consideration. The Napo River (Map 7) with its wide navigable waters was the least difficult route for Ecuador's drive to the Amazon River. Ecuadorian officials and colonists gradually pushed downstream as far as the juncture of the Napo with the Aguarico. They encountered Peruvian settlers who either ignored the Ecuadorian officials or left the region. Because a Peruvian ten-man post at the mouth of the Aguarico River blocked any further advance down the Napo River, Ecuador sent a force of 100 soldiers to drive out the Peruvians in early 1902. In reality, the troop movement formed part of a large diplomatic offensive against Peru, and Ecuador succeeded in persuading a panicky Lima to order the withdrawal of the Peruvian detachment. Thus without firing a shot, Ecuador took control of the mouth of the Aguarico and established the town of Rocafuerte, which became the base for the Ecuadorian penetration of the Amazon during the next forty years.[4]

Not for the last time Lima gradually realized it had been duped by Ecuador. It was too late to recover Rocafuerte but not to stop further Ecuadorian encroachments. The prefect of Iquitos established a new base at the mouth of the Curaray River, and when patrol boats reported that the Ecuadorians were establishing another base further south at Angoteros, he decided the time to act had come.

The prefect ordered the river gunboat *Cahuapanas* to carry a platoon of soldiers from Curaray to remove the Ecuadorian soldiers in Angoteros, peacefully if possible but by force if

Map 7. Ecuador-Peru Amazon Area

necessary. The *Cahuapanas* steamed up the Napo River and upon arrival on 26 June 1903, the Ecuadorian troops at Angoteros promptly began digging trenches facing the river and prepared to repulse a Peruvian attack. Rather than risk a direct attack, the naval commander Oscar Mavila decided to exploit the undefended left flank of the Ecuadorian defenders. He turned his ship around and steamed downstream 800 meters, where he found a secluded spot to land the soldiers who proceeded to march north. The *Cahuapanas* steamed back to Angoteros and approached land close enough for Mavila to shout to the Ecuadorian commander that they needed to talk to avoid combat, but the Ecuadorians replied no and promptly began shooting. The *Cahuapanas* fired its armament to draw the attention of the defenders, who failed to notice the Peruvian platoon advancing on the left flank. Caught in the cross fire that lasted barely 20 minutes, the defenders fled north, leaving two dead and five prisoners. After the battle, the *Cahuapanas* pursued the fleeing Ecuadorian soldiers and afterwards made sure that no Ecuadorians remained in Napo River south of the mouth of the Aguarico River.[5]

The battle demonstrated to both countries that direct negotiation had failed to preserve peace, and they agreed on 21 January 1904 to recur to the already agreed upon arbitration by Spain. Unfortunately, public opinion in Quito clamored for a reprisal against Peru, and Ecuador saw in arbitration a means to lure Peru into neglecting its defenses in the Amazon. To avenge the defeat at Angoteros, the Ecuadorian government sent over a company of soldiers and several small Krupp cannon down the Aguarico River. The hastily recruited troops were untrained and lacked any jungle experience, and during the trip the combination of heat, disease, and humidity soon decimated the ranks. Once they arrived at the last Ecuadorian outpost of Rocafuerte, their commander, Carlos A. Rivadeneira, concluded that the only chance his exhausted men had of defeating seasoned Peruvian veterans was to launch a surprise assault against Torres Causano, the northernmost Peruvian outpost on the Napo River.[6] A successful attack promised to open a path for Ecuador down the Napo River to the elusive Amazon River.

Spies reported the approaching Ecuadorian expedition to the prefect at Iquitos who had only slim material resources available to meet any invasion. He could spare only 15 soldiers to reinforce the 28-man garrison at Torres Causano, and he sent the men aboard the gunboat *Iquitos* under the command of Oscar Mavila, a hero of the previous clash at Angoteros. The *Iquitos* reached Torres Causano on 7 April 1904 and had orders to remain at that place until the Ecuadorian threat had dis-

sipated. The arrival of the Peruvian reinforcements complicated the original plan of Rivadeneira, who postponed the attack until 28 July, a Peruvian holiday, when he hoped that the Peruvian garrison would celebrate and thus let its guard down. The night before, he sent canoes downstream carrying nearly a hundred men and one Krupp cannon. The navigation at night and the fear of detection proved harrowing to the men, and only thanks to the help of a local guide did they manage to take positions along the jungle paths that led to the Peruvian camp; the Ecuadorians set up and disguised the Krupp cannon across the river but left no infantry to protect the gun crew.

At 0800 an Ecuadorian officer came aboard a canoe to deliver a note from Rivadeneira demanding that the Peruvians evacuate the position. The commander of the garrison, Captain Juan Francisco Chávez Valdivia, replied that he could evacuate only after he received orders from the prefect at Iquitos, who coincidentally was expected to visit any day soon. In the hostile Amazon men of all nationalities traditionally help each other, and Captain Chávez Valdivia offered to have the *Iquitos* take the Ecuadorian officer back to Rocafuerte saving himself from exhausting paddling upstream. The Ecuadorian officer declined the courteous offer and disappeared north on his canoe; this behavior seemed suspicious to Mavila who ordered the moored *Iquitos* to raise steam in its boilers and be ready to depart at a moment's notice. Captain Chávez Valdivia also put on high alert the pickets at the entrance of each of the paths leading to the Peruvian camp.

At 1340, apparently expecting the garrison to be in a deep siesta, nearly a hundred Ecuadorian soldiers rushed out of the jungle paths into the cleared area around Torres Causano. The pickets fired but could only delay the overwhelming attack long enough for the Peruvian soldiers to grab their weapons and return fire. The Ecuadorians charged into the open space of 100 meters between the river bank and the Peruvian camp, but before they could isolate the garrison, fierce fire from the *Iquitos* stopped their advance. The *Iquitos* distracted the Ecuadorian force long enough to allow Captain Chávez Valdivia to carry out a fighting withdrawal from the camp and thus to escape capture by Ecuadorian soldiers infiltrating his flank through a jungle trail. The small Krupp cannon across the river had been firing constantly at the *Iquitos*, and with almost all his crew wounded from small arms fire, Mavila steamed south and left the triumphant Ecuadorians the pleasure of hoisting their flag over the former Peruvian camp.

Ecuador had avenged the defeat of Angoteros, and at last the path downstream to the mighty Amazon lay open. However, Mavila refused to accept defeat, and in an unexpected move he steamed his bullet-riddled *Iquitos* to the other side of the river against the Krupp cannon. The Ecuadorian gun crew had very poor aim and only shattered the smokestack of the *Iquitos*, while the fire from the approaching gunboat scared the Ecuadorians who abandoned their cannon. The mad dash of the *Iquitos* had regained for Peru control of the Napo River, and on land events were taking a no less surprising turn. The victorious Ecuadorian soldiers had not slept or eaten the night before while waiting in the jungle and were very tired and hungry. Untrained soldiers who have been under immense strain will become careless once the pressure of combat has passed, unless vigilant officers enforce a rigid discipline. The Ecuadorians turned to looting the captured camp, some to obtain food, while others collapsed to sleep. The Ecuadorian officers failed to control their men and were unable to organize any pursuit of the fleeing Peruvians. Meanwhile, Captain Chávez Valdivia had regrouped his soldiers about 200 meters south of the camp. He had no trouble rallying his soldiers for a counterattack, because they knew that without the foodstuffs and tools in the camp none could survive alive in the hostile jungle lacking edible foods; they all preferred a swift death from a bullet than a slow and agonizing death in the jungle. At 1500 the Peruvians were able to take up positions nearby without alerting the pillaging Ecuadorians who in another mistake had neatly stacked their weapons outside in the open space. When the sound of gun fire sent the Ecuadorians madly dashing outside to retrieve their weapons, the accurate Peruvian fire cut them to pieces. The sight of their slaughtered comrades drove some Ecuadorians to flee unarmed down the jungle paths that had initially brought them to the Peruvian camp. The sight of some men fleeing triggered a hasty and panic-stricken withdrawal by the rest. Ri-

vadeneira and a few associates tried to halt the rout but to no avail. Actually, he was extremely lucky: taken prisoner and released one year later, he was among the fortunate few survivors who left the region alive. The rest of his panic-stricken men fled into the jungle, but without tools, food, or even weapons, the jungle quietly devoured the ill-prepared prey.[7]

Peru had restored its control over the Napo River as far north as the mouth of the Aguarico River and, with the invaluable aid of the jungle, had annihilated the entire Ecuadorian expedition. Ecuador considered the defeat at Torres Causano as nothing less than a national disgrace and desperately strove to repair its reputation, even though the government had agreed to accept the arbitration of Spain. In October 1904 a force with six cannon and 200 men carefully picked from the best units of the Ecuadorian army left for the Aguarico River. Peruvian spies in Quito detected the movement and gave plenty of time for the prefect in Iquitos to prepare a defense. Without any chance of surprise and not willing to risk another humiliating defeat like Angoteros or Torres Causano, Ecuador desisted from any attack and wisely decided to reinforce its small garrison at Rocafuerte.[8] Ecuador also concluded that before it could launch any offensive into the Peruvian Amazon, it needed the support of another country and confidently expected to find at least one ally among Bolivia, Brazil, Colombia, and Chile, the countries that had ongoing boundary disputes with Peru.

The Boundary with Brazil

The rebellion in the Acre territory (chapter 1) at last woke up Peru to the real danger of losing vast stretches of Amazon territory. In September 1902 the Peruvian government ordered the prefect of Iquitos to send reinforcements into the upper reaches of the Purús and Yuruá rivers (Map 6). After nearly a century of basing its territorial claims solely on colonial treaties, Peru belatedly realized that only effective occupation guaranteed possession of land. Peruvian rubber tappers were already active in many rivers, but the government was extremely slow in establishing any strong presence in the region. A Peruvian official established himself at the mouth of the Amonea River, a tributary of the Yuruá, but without troops he could not exercise any real authority and eventually this first Peruvian outpost vanished. On the Purús, Peruvian rubber tappers had already solidly occupied one of its tributaries, the Curanja River. Peruvian officials went downstream on the Purús to open a customs house at the mouth of the Chandless River on 23 June 1903 and about the same time opened a post at the mouth of the Santa Rosa River. Although Peruvian rubber tappers predominated in the Santa Rosa River, at the Chandless River the Brazilians were the majority. Even after receiving reinforcements in response to the Acre rebellion, these small and distant Peruvian outposts were extremely vulnerable to attack. The army counted on new Mauser rifles to give the small garrisons a chance against the more numerous but poorly armed Brazilian rubber tappers.[9]

Peru sent a second detachment to reestablish the post at Amonea River in October 1902, but the twelve soldiers encountered strong hostility from the Brazilian rubber tappers who already controlled the region. A clash just a few days after the arrival of the unit confirmed the value of the modern rifles. On 21 October 1902 over 200 Brazilian rubber tappers delivered a demand for the surrender of the small unit. The Peruvian sergeant in command replied that he would withdraw only after lowering the flag with all honors. Thinking that their task was accomplished, the Brazilian rubber tappers approached carelessly. The small Peruvian unit opened fire at the unsuspecting Brazilians who were even more surprised by the large volume of fire coming from the Mausers. The startled and outgunned Brazilians fled and gave the Peruvian unit time to withdraw with all its weapons. As soon as the prefect of Iquitos heard of the clash, he sent an additional 20 soldiers to join the original unit and gave them the duty of taking back Amonea. Upon their return, the soldiers this time encountered no hostility, but this isolated garrison in the midst of Brazilian rubber tappers seemed unlikely to survive for long.[10]

Peru needed to send many more soldiers if it expected to extend its control over regions already colonized by Brazilian rubber tappers. The success with the Mauser rifles also suggested sending machine guns to defend distant outposts. Because the Brazilian rubber tappers frequently impeded the arrival of boats bringing food for the Peruvian posts, the logistics of haul-ing supplies overland from Peru sharply limited any increases in the number of soldiers. The only two choices for Peru were either to send machine guns or to make a strategic withdrawal to positions more easily supplied. The failure to act brought the loss of the outpost at the mouth of the Chandless River. José Ferreira arrived with 150 Brazilian rubber tappers at this outpost and obtained the surrender of its small Peruvian detachment of 12 men on 7 September 1903. A small army unit with a large force of Peruvian rubber tappers returned early in March of 1904 to the mouth of the Chandless, but the embargo on food shipments soon made them suffer starvation and forced them to withdraw upstream on the Purús to the mouth of the Santa Rosa River. To finish driving them out, José Ferraira pursued and attacked them at Santa Rosa on 31 March 1904. The small Peruvian detachment was stationed across the river and the soldiers could only watch as the Brazilian rubber tappers pillaged the place and later executed many of the Peruvian civilians. The detachment did repulse the Brazilian attacks and remained in place. By this late date when rubber trees were becoming scarce, the ferocity of the rubber tappers became intensified as they desperately scrambled to acquire the last sources of rubber. Clearly the governments of Peru and Brazil were going to have to stop the mutual raids and atrocities of their rubber tappers.[11]

News of the savage behavior at Santa Rosa inflamed the Peruvian public against the Brazilian rubber tappers, and a war between Peru and Brazil began to seem imminent. Actually, the Foreign Minister of Brazil, the Baron of Rio Branco, had been making preparations for a clash with Peru since he had concluded the Treaty of Petrópolis with Bolivia in November 1903. Once he had settled the dispute with Bolivia, he felt Brazil could devote its efforts to obtaining a favorable boundary with Peru. Already in January 1904 Brazil was readying troops at Manaus and at other garrisons in the Amazon for a military campaign. In a revealing contrast, while against Bolivia Rio Branco had been most hesitant to threaten the use of force, against Peru he based his whole policy on military preparations to awe the opponent into submission. On 9 March he obtained from the War Ministry the assignment of an army captain to be the Brazilian consul at Iquitos, because Rio Branco wanted a military professional rather than a civilian diplomat reporting on Peruvian troop movements. Upon hearing in early April that Peru bought Krupp cannons, he badgered the War Ministry to hasten its purchases of the new rapid-firing cannons; he also wanted the Navy Ministry to buy gunboats for the Amazon. The War and Navy ministries did not share the sense of urgency of Rio Branco, who revealed that he needed to have a force of 4000 Brazilian soldiers ready to occupy Iquitos and the Ucayali River. He saw this offensive as necessary to deprive the Peruvians on the Upper Yuruá and the Upper Purús of their supply routes from the Ucayali River.[12]

The ragged Peruvian outpost at Amonea in the middle of the jungle appeared to be a formidable fortress to Rio Branco. By late May on the basis of no credible information, he concluded that the Peruvians were heavily fortifying their post with machine guns and cannons, and that more artillery was on the way. He felt that only a large Brazilian force could overcome the 150 Peruvians he said were well entrenched at Amonea and the additional 200 Peruvians he imagined stationed in the overland trail to Ucayali. To complement the lack of activity from the sluggish Brazilian military authorities, Rio Branco since early 1904 had been seeking allies for the war against Peru. He hoped to tempt Chile into joining Brazil in a combined war that was sure to crush Peru. But Chile was fresh out of settling its disputes with Argentina and hesitated to enter an alliance that might trigger a continental South American war. Ecuador instead had no hesitation, and this tiny country concluded negotiations for a secret treaty of alliance with Brazil on 5 May 1904. The treaty was in reality an executive agreement calling on each country to help the other defend itself from attack by Peru. In case of war, both executive branches would submit the treaty simultaneously to their congresses for ratification. This secret treaty once again showed how vulnerable Peru was to a hostile alliance by its neighbors. Peru still had not settled even one of its disputed boundaries, and the longer this uncertainty prevailed, the greater the risk that its neighbors would unite to destroy Peru.[13]

The preparations for the preemptive war Rio Branco wanted to launch against Peru gradually began to unravel. He was trying to repeat in South America the power politics he had learned in Europe but without adequate

means. The idea of making a demonstration in the Amazon with the warships of the Brazilian navy proved impossible, because not a single warship was fit for service at sea. The army was not in much better shape either.[14] With little leverage left against Peru, in May Rio Branco closed the Amazon River to arms shipments for Peru. Brazilian officials impounded a shipment in Manaus, but with such bad luck that the ammunition belonged to an U.S. company and the Baron soon received a barrage of diplomatic protests. Rather than bringing pressure against Peru, Rio Branco had created an embarrassing diplomatic incident.[15] To complicate Rio Branco's strategy even more, the unexpected death of the Peruvian president on 7 May led to a cabinet reshuffle in Lima. Alberto Elmore, the new Peruvian foreign minister, was extremely pro–Brazilian and wanted to end the border dispute as soon as possible under any terms he could sell to an angry public in the Peruvian capital. Rio Branco could not impose a harsh policy on Peru when its foreign minister was looking to Brazil to provide leadership for South America. To make things worse for Rio Branco, although public opinion in Lima remained at a fever pitch against Brazil, in Rio de Janeiro the press did not want a war and seemed if anything pro–Peruvian.[16]

As the strategy of Rio Branco to launch a military offensive crumbled, he still hoped that U.S. support would persuade Peru to accept his conditions. To the Baron's surprise, the United States supported the Peruvian demand that both sides withdraw from the disputed territories and leave the administration of this neutralized zone in the hands of a mixed commission composed of officials of the two countries.[17] "Baron Rio Branco thinks, as he has said to me, that Peru is attempting to bluff Brazil into giving something for peace, and all the Baron is doing, I am confident, is intended as a bigger bluff."[18] On 6 June Rio Branco stated to Peru that he could not grant any more territory, but he soon had to change his mind. He was hard pressed to refuse the request of Foreign Minister Elmore for the Santa Rosa River as the indispensable condition to secure acceptance from the Peruvian public.[19] The U.S. government continued to press Brazil to avoid any war and encouraged Brazil to include the extra strip in the neutralized zone: "Baron Rio-Branco told me yesterday he would concede enough of a change [of territory] to Peru to practically cover their desires, so at this time it seems as if an agreement should very soon be reached."[20] On 12 July 1904 Brazil and Peru signed a Modus Vivendi agreement that withdrew all officials from the neutralized territory. By this agreement, both countries entered into negotiations to define their boundary. The agreement included one last-minute request from Foreign Minister Elmore that bound both countries to submit the matter to mandatory arbitration if they did not reach an agreement through negotiations. Up to this moment, Rio Branco had been firmly opposed to arbitration, nevertheless "he expects to find some way to reach an agreement that will entail less of chance."[21]

As diplomats began long and tedious negotiations, an incident at the Peruvian outpost at the Amonea River almost wrecked the prospects for peaceful settlement. This outpost had not been included in the neutralized zone so Peru should have withdrawn the detachment. Peru evacuated all units and authorities from the neutralized zone but left the Amonea detachment forgotten and isolated in the north. The Peruvian captain of the 40 soldiers did not receive the order to evacuate or any news for that matter. Similarly, officials at Manaus were slow to implement the Modus Vivendi. Two Brazilian river steamers arrived on 2 November 1904 carrying a large force. The Brazilians marched around the Peruvian outpost and attacked with overwhelming force on 4 November. The Peruvian captain, who did not have any cannons or machine guns as Rio Branco had believed, defended his position until his scant supply of rifle ammunition ran out. The next day he agreed to abandon the post and return with his men to Peru. Both countries dismissed the incident as an unfortunate accident and remained firm in their determination to negotiate a final boundary treaty.[22]

The negotiation for a boundary treaty took years. The lack of precise geographical knowledge had constantly plagued all attempts to draw boundaries in the Amazon, and until surveying expeditions returned with sufficient information and maps, both sides realized that any attempt to draw lines was pointless. Rio Branco (who had served as a diplomat in the Kaiser's Germany) could not resist hurling one last disguised threat to the Peruvian diplomat to try to extract concessions: "never would

Brazil arbitrate the differences between his country and Peru."[23] In 1905 ill-will over a romantic affair gone awry threatened to derail the negotiations, but the arrival of a new Peruvian diplomat eased the tension.[24] More serious was the Brazilian insistence on keeping half of the neutralized zone, and because no agreement was possible, the dispute seemed headed to mandatory arbitration. The Brazilian position changed drastically when on 9 July 1909 Argentina issued its award recognizing most of the Peruvian claims to the territories in dispute with Bolivia. Rio Branco's deep-seated fear of adverse arbitration in this case became real, and he promptly decided to cut his losses. In a remarkable reversal, he offered the entire neutralized zone to Peru.

Would Peru accept the very generous but not perfect Brazilian offer? Arbitration might give Peru the Amonea River and other strips of land but might also take away areas Brazil was willing to grant. Arbitration took years and meant postponing settlement of the longest boundary line of Peru. The long delay also opened the more dangerous possibility that some or all of its neighbors might form a coalition to crush Peru. Arbitration might not even be final, and already Peru was in the middle of negotiations with Bolivia to make adjustments in the Argentine award. Although from July to September 1909 Peruvian diplomats simultaneously labored to settle their boundary disputes with Brazil and Bolivia, Peru was in the greatest rush to reach agreement first with Brazil, as happened in the treaty both countries signed on 8 September 1909.[25]

By the treaty with Brazil, Peru decided to accept the neutralized zone and to abandon any other claims. Both countries duly ratified the treaty, but its significance was different for each country. While for Brazil the treaty of September 1909 settled one of its last boundary disputes, for Peru the treaty was its first boundary agreement. Peru hoped that the settlement with its biggest and most powerful neighbor would be a positive precedent to help secure other boundary treaties, starting first with Bolivia.

The Boundary with Bolivia

The prospects of a boundary treaty with Bolivia had seemed the most promising to Peru because the two countries were the most similar in cultural and ethnic characteristics. The debacle of the Acre region (see chapter 1) had made Bolivia reluctant to risk another test of arms, and instead it agreed to submit the boundary dispute to arbitration by Argentina in December 1902. Decades of diplomacy had revealed the futility of trying to use vague imperial charters to draw boundary lines, yet the treaty of arbitration still directed Argentina to examine the relevant colonial documents to complete the task.[26] "It is quite astonishing to find these ancient limits still seriously being revived by the two litigants at the beginning of the twentieth century."[27] After nearly seven years of trying, the Argentine arbitrators gave up on the colonial documents and instead fell back mainly on geography to draw a fair and solid line. An obvious boundary line for a long stretch was the Heath River (Map 6), but once it flowed into the Madre de Dios River, the Argentine arbitrators lost any easy landmark between its mouth and the Brazilian border in the Acre River.

Bolivia had not adequately documented the activities of its rubber tappers under the merchant Nicolás Suárez, and in the absence of that information, the Argentine arbitrators traced a sensible line between the Acre and the Madre de Dios rivers. The arbitrators submitted their findings to the President of Argentina who incorporated them into the arbitration award he issued on 9 July 1909. Peru promptly accepted the award as satisfactory, but in Bolivia the announcement triggered angry outbursts in the capital of La Paz. After the loss of the Acre territory in 1903, the Bolivian politicians had promised the public that they would obtain territorial compensation by pushing the Bolivian frontier westward to the Andes Mountains. In 1903 this false promise had helped secure congressional approval for the Treaty of Petrópolis but in July 1909 fueled the outrage of an enraged population that justifiably felt betrayed. A mob attacked the Argentine and Peruvian legations in La Paz on 10 July, and the Argentine diplomats had to flee for safety. Rioting resumed the next day, as the mob turned its anger at the shops and business of Peruvian residents. The Bolivian government called out troops to protect the foreign diplomats and to patrol the city, and the disturbances died down after a few days. Argentina and Bolivia broke diplomatic relations, but the conflict was not between them; the real decision was whether to accept or reject the Argentine award.[28]

To reject the award almost certainly meant a war with Peru that could only end up much more disastrous than the failed Acre campaign. To try to even the odds, on 11 July 1909 Bolivia sounded out an unlikely ally to learn whether "we could count upon the sympathy of the Chilean Government in case the award were rejected."[29] Chile restrained itself and cautiously replied the next day that it wanted to proceed in accord with Brazil to ease the tension. All caution vanished on 13 July after Chile heard a rumor that Peru was massing troops on the Bolivian border:

> Ministers and leading men have expressed intense sympathy for Bolivia. They advise me that enthusiasm is restrained for fear that Bolivia may place them in an awkward position. They offer to launch Ecuador against Peru and to furnish many well-known officers who have studied Peru; that to bungle matters or show signs of fear would today be the loss of Bolivia and perhaps her ruin, and that a foreign war is better than a civil war. They believe that if Bolivia shows determination for war Peru will draw back.[30]

Chile even offered its own diplomat in Quito to negotiate an alliance between Ecuador and Bolivia until the latter country could open its own legation in Quito.[31] Because fear of antagonizing Argentina prevented Chile from openly joining the anti–Peruvian coalition, the possibility of having Ecuador and Bolivia unite to defeat Peru was particularly attractive to Chile. To hurl Bolivia into the war, Chile astutely played upon Bolivian desires to recover an outlet to the Pacific Ocean:

> This is the opportunity to achieve our dream of an outlet to the sea. Chile guarantees our victory and furnishes money, armament, officers, and men. Secures the assistance of Ecuador and of Brazil and the neutrality of Argentina; and although it might be only to prepare for any circumstance, I beg you to accept the offer. This moment brings us the most important opportunity in our history. Chile asks for nothing in return; she only wishes to put an end to the Tacna-Arica matter and thus to eliminate a common border with Peru.[32]

Bolivia requested 15,000 Mauser rifles, 24 machine guns, and 20 cannons, all with abundant stocks of ammunition. In addition, Bolivia needed a large loan to finance the war with Peru. The weapons were ready to ship to Bolivia and the negotiations with private bankers for the loan were far advanced when the Chilean game plan suddenly collapsed. On 23 July 1909 the newspaper *El Comercio* of Lima revealed that Chile was goading Bolivia into a war with Peru. A startled public refused to believe such preposterous reports, although the newspaper promised to prove the accusation. On 24 July Brazil tried to head off the crisis by consulting the United States and Great Britain about all three countries making an appeal to Peru to modify the Argentine award slightly in Bolivia's favor. The two countries refused to support the Brazilian proposal, which, however, had introduced a promising solution. Meanwhile *El Comercio* began the publication in installments of telegrams inciting Bolivia into war against Peru; the Peruvian government had broken the code of the Bolivians and had been distributing copies of the incriminating telegrams to foreign diplomats. The revelation that Brazil supported the Argentine award left Chile alone and with no other option than to drop its Machiavellian maneuver. A totally discredited Chile tried vainly to retrieve its reputation by trying to make a scapegoat out of the Bolivian Chargé d'Affaires in Santiago.[33]

The exposure of the Chilean machinations had provoked a continental outrage at such a blatant practice of power politics and forced Bolivia on 26 July to accept negotiations as the only way to settle the boundary dispute. To bolster its shaky bargaining position, on 27 July Bolivia still insisted on receiving the weapons and money Chile had supposedly promised to provide. Wrongly believing that Bolivia still enjoyed Chilean support, La Paz reiterated its extreme demand for the Andes Mountains as the western boundary. Would Peru bargain away the Argentine Award? Although Bolivia was diplomatically isolated, just a few days before Peru had faced alone the threat of a two-front war against Bolivia, Ecuador, and possibly even Chile. Peru seized upon the Bolivian demand as a tacit admission of a willingness to negotiate a final boundary.[34]

The risk of war remained lurking, and the diplomatic pressure upon both countries was intense. Bolivia and Peru entered into direct negotiations to adjust the Argentine Award to the reality in the Amazon. Instead of making fantastic claims or citing ancient documents, the two governments narrowed down their differences to one strip of land to the west of the Argentine award (Map 6). Rather than arguing, the negotiators located the two main rubber outposts in that strip. They then drew a slanted line between the Bolivian and Peruvian outposts and extended it northwest to the Acre River and southeast to the mouth of the Heath River. The diplomats signed the agreement in La Paz on 17 September 1909 and hoped for a speedy ratification.[35]

Bolivia could cite this favorable modification of the Argentine Award to the public as evidence of a diplomatic triumph, and almost unanimously the Bolivian congress ratified the treaty on 25 October 1909. Bolivia was eager to end its last Amazon dispute, and the government instead wanted to concentrate its resources on what seemed a much more promising drive into the Chaco to the southeast. The lure of securing a second border in the Amazon proved no less irresistible for Peru, and it ratified the modification of the Argentine Award. A few minor incidents still occurred in the vast jungle region, and Bolivia always found it hard to resist the temptation to meddle in Peru's conflicts with other neighbors. In spite of these shortcomings, Peru had succeeded in solving a border dispute on favorable terms, and Lima hoped to make similar progress with its smallest and weakest neighbor.

The Showdown with Ecuador

Two down (Brazil and Bolivia) and three to go (Chile, Colombia, and Ecuador) was the score card for Peru as it strove to define boundaries with its neighbors. In the same manner as the Argentine award of 1909 had ultimately led to a boundary agreement with Bolivia, so in early 1910 Peru expected the imminent award of the King of Spain to settle the boundary dispute with Ecuador. The similarity and the optimism were unfounded, because for Ecuador the arbitration by Spain was simply one more maneuver to try to gain territory extending to the Amazon River.

Drawing a boundary line across the disputed territory should not have been a cumbersome or forbidding task, because already some key geographical markers already stood out. The two terminal points for any demarcation were Rocafuerte on the Aguarico River and the mouth of the Yaupi River on the Santiago River. Rather than engaging in negotiations with Peru to fill in the line between these two points, Ecuador instead eagerly welcomed Chilean offers of support as a way to extract additional territory from Peru. However, Chile stopped short of making a formal alliance, and Ecuador continued to search for additional support. In February 1907 the government of Eloy Alfaro signed a contract with Count Charnacé to build a railroad in the Pacific coast of Ecuador and a strategic railroad from Ambato to the Curaray River in the Amazon. As an incentive to build the unprofitable railroad to the Amazon, Ecuador offered large land grants and very generous benefits to the French investors. The Charnacé Contract, as it came to be called, generated immense hostility and contributed to sparking major riots in Quito on 25 April 1907. President Alfaro cancelled the contract that day, and while it was not certain that the French investors would have built the railroad, no doubt existed about the determination of Ecuador to obtain as large a part of the Amazon as possible.[36]

The inauguration of the railroad from Guayaquil to Quito on 25 June 1908 gave Ecuador a major logistical advantage. A project to build a railroad into the Amazon was the next step to link the highlands with the Amazon territories, which the Quito government confidently expected the King of Spain to recognize as Ecuadorian. Unfortunately, early in 1910 the Ecuadorian legation in Madrid learned that the King of Spain in his award accepted most of the Peruvian claims and deprived Ecuador of any land bordering the Amazon River. The legation leaked the news to the press in Spain, and newspapers in Ecuador were reprinting and wildly exaggerating the reports in early February 1910. The public outcry turned violent as riots broke out in Ecuador's cities in March. The mobs attacked the consulates of Peru and then turned against the businesses of private Peruvian citizens. Counterdemonstrations occurred in Peru, and in early April Ecuador called for volunteers to enlarge its army. Peru sent troops to its northern border and delivered an ultimatum demanding that Ecuador accept the award of the King of Spain in its entirety.[37]

War seemed imminent as troops from both countries faced each other at the Zarumilla River, the common border on the side of the Pacific Ocean (Map 29). The paper strength of the army of Ecuador was 5,140 soldiers, but because the officers padded the rolls to receive the pay of non-existent soldiers (a practice then present in Mexico also), the actual strength was 25 percent less or about 3800 soldiers. Hastily recruited levies soon increased the army to 20,000, but the fighting quality of the new units was questionable at best. Five thousand new Mauser rifles from Germany armed the regular army, but the new levies received old ruined rifles Chile had sold to Ecuador in 1907. Chile tried to make amends by rushing 15,000 rifles and numerous sea mines to Guayaquil; shortly after this shipment's arrival on 12 March, Ecuador placed mines in its coastal waters to try to check the overwhelming superiority of the Peruvian Navy.[38]

New rifles and raw recruits do not suddenly make an army. Peru mobilized nearly 30,000 soldiers and was confident of victory. But Peru still hesitated to attack first, because the breaking of diplomatic relations between Peru and Chile on 22 March counseled patience. A two-front war against Chile and Ecuador was too high a risk for Peru; instead Ecuador had nothing to lose by bluffing a war.[39]

Alfaro raised the stakes by moving most of his army to Zarumilla River, a region itself in dispute over which river bed constituted the real boundary between both countries. The deployment was particularly risky, because the Zarumilla region at that time depended on coastwise shipping for its links with the rest of the country, and the Peruvian navy could easily blockade the sea coast. Instead in the Amazon, the logistics at first glance seemed more favorable to Ecuador. The possibility existed that a rapid deployment into the Amazon just might allow Ecuador to overwhelm the outermost Peruvian outposts before Lima could send reinforcements. After the Peruvian legation in Quito reported that Ecuador had dispatched armed contingents to the Napo River in early April, the prefect of Iquitos, Francisco Alaiza Paz Soldán, reinforced the frontier outposts and put the Peruvian river flotilla on patrol.[40]

President Alfaro went personally to Zarumilla and on the border talked about capturing

Tumbes, a city Ecuador also claimed, but this bravado was simply smoke to hide the true Ecuadorian intentions. Deeply disappointed over the failure of Chile to join in a war against Peru, on 10 May Ecuador signed a military alliance with Colombia. The legislative branches of Ecuador and Colombia approved the treaty, but upon realization that a war with Peru was inevitable if the treaty went into force, at the last minute the executive branch of Colombia delayed ratification of this treaty. Ecuador had failed to drag either Chile or Colombia into a war with Peru and was fast running out of options. Already the threat of bankruptcy had forced Ecuador to demobilize some troops. Ecuador could not afford to support its remaining troops on the Zarumilla border and needed to find a way to demobilize gracefully and still salvage something from the war scare.[41]

At this moment the United States appeared with an irresistible offer. Secretary of State Philander Knox had been following the evolving crisis since February 1910 and gradually came to the conclusion that he needed to mediate to prevent the outbreak of war. The United States had major economic investments in Peru but almost none in Ecuador, so the reason for the U.S. involvement was not clear. Most likely Secretary Knox wanted to improve his prestige as a peacemaker, but he knew that to play a meaningful role he needed the participation of other countries. Without too much difficulty he persuaded Argentina and Brazil to join the United States in offering their mediation to Peru and Ecuador on 22 May. Ecuador enthusiastically accepted the next day and appealed to Knox's vanity by "sincerely congratulating your Excellency on the brilliant diplomatic triumph you have achieved."[42] The Peruvian foreign minister hesitated to accept the mediation, because he feared it threatened the imminent territorial award by the King of Spain. The foreign minister overcame his initial doubts and accepted the tripartite mediation. Less than eight days later he regretted his decision, and eventually he had to resign because of his blunder.

The Peruvian foreign minister's slip had given Ecuador the opening to play the card of the small country bullied by the larger one. The game plan called for pressuring Peru to give up its positions as the only way to keep the larger country from appearing hostile or threatening to the mediators. The mediators imposed as their first condition that both countries withdraw their massed troops from the Zarumilla River by 4 June. The Peruvian troops duly withdrew and in most cases embarked for the long trip back home to the interior. Quite revealingly, Ecuador proved unable to comply with the 4 June deadline because the units were so incompetent that they could not complete a peaceful withdrawal in good order before the deadline. The delay in withdrawal conveniently served as a pretext for Ecuador to bluff the demand that Peru withdraw its garrison from Tumbes, nearly 50 kilometers from the Zarumilla border. The mediators, fearing that Ecuador might attack and unaware of the long-held Ecuadorian claim for the return of all of Tumbes province, naively accepted the Ecuadorian demand to separate the forces of both countries an equal distance away from the border. Under this formula, Peru had to withdraw its garrison from a city it had peacefully occupied for nearly a century.[43]

The tripartite mediation was providing very fruitful for Ecuador, which demanded as a condition for its demobilization that Peru hasten the disbandment of its troops. Peru too was groaning from the high cost of maintaining a large army and did not need much convincing to return to a peacetime footing. However, the many demands from Ecuador were not propitious for fruitful negotiation and provoked "some mortification" because "the deep-rooted pride of the Peruvian leads him to express the most profound contempt for his northern neighbors. He calls the Ecuadorians 'the monkeys' and seems to consider them to be in a less advanced stage of civilization."[44]

On 7 July Ecuador denounced a Peruvian invasion up the Aguarico River in the Amazon and demanded that Peru withdraw because of its wanton defiance of the mediation efforts. Ecuador had overreached and at last had revealed its intention to manipulate the tripartite mediation into forcing Peru to abandon its Amazon outposts. Peru was not about to abandon the positions its troops had won on the Napo River and calmly explained the nature of its defensive movements in place since April. What had so incensed the Ecuadorian government was the blockade the Peruvian river flotilla imposed south of the mouth of the Aguarico River, but because the Peruvian boats stayed in their waters, the mediators could not see in these patrol activities any type of invasion. The United States had always been the heart of the mediation effort, and in spite of repeated fulsome and bombastic praise by the Ecuadorian diplomats, even Secretary of State Knox realized he had been duped and refused to be manipulated any more.[45]

Ecuador realized it had overplayed its hand and made profuse apologies to try to keep the tripartite mediation going as long as possible. Meanwhile the appearance in the press of many diplomatic notes about the tripartite mediation persuaded the King of Spain that in the highly charged atmosphere any award granting most of the land to Peru was sure to lead to war. Consequently, the King of Spain refused to issue the much anticipated award and thus formally ended the arbitration procedure. Ecuador had definitely outmaneuvered its rival and revealed an extraordinary ability to extricate itself from the mandatory arbitration award. This diplomatic coup was of the first magnitude but ultimately turned bitter, because in the definitive territorial settlement in 1942, Ecuador lost extensive territories it would have received under the award of the Spanish King. But that harsh reality lay in the future. It was now up to the tripartite mediation to find a solution to the border dispute. Nor surprisingly, once the mediators made clear their refusal to force Peru to abandon territories in the Amazon, Ecuador lost interest in the tripartite mediation that gradually faded in 1911.[46]

Peru's frontier with Ecuador remained as undefined as it had been in previous decades. The prospects for direct negotiations had always been slim. Peru reluctantly concluded that settlement of the border with Ecuador depended on first solving the disputes with Chile and with Colombia. While the threat of a war to recover the lost provinces of Tacna and Arica was always present in dealings with Chile, Peru did not expect major complications with Colombia. Thus, quite unexpectedly one of the memorable battles in the Amazon suddenly erupted.

Colombia and the Battle of La Pedrera

Unlike Ecuador, Colombia had made no effort to extend its authority over the Amazon region. Some Colombian rubber tappers entered the Caquetá and Putumayo rivers but made little headway against the near-monopoly of the Peruvian Julio César Arana. His firm, the Casa Arana, worked closely with the authorities in Iquitos to extend Peruvian control into the Putumayo and Caquetá rivers. The Bogotá government did nothing besides cite ancient documents in its feeble diplomatic protests.[47]

The key to rubber extraction in this section of the Amazon was the exploitation of Indian labor. The scarce population meant that the Casa Arana could earn profits only if it forced the Indians to collect the latex from the rubber trees. Torture, imprisonment, and even death became standard fare. Brutality against the local Indians became so widespread that reports of the atrocities reached the outside world. The Putumayo River and the Belgian Congo became the two regions of the world that most shocked the Victorian public prior to World War I. Sensationalist journalism spurred the U.S. and British governments to investigate the accusations, and the inquiries fueled public demands for action. International pressure mounted on Colombia to stop the atrocities the Peruvian rubber tappers were committing inside its Amazon territory. The international outrage found strong echo among Colombian nationalists who had long clamored for action in the neglected Amazon region. With extreme reluctance the Bogotá government temporarily exchanged its beloved diplomatic notes for military deployments.[48]

In November 1910 the Bogotá government dispatched an armed expedition to the Caquetá River. The dual mission of the expedition was to protect the Indians and to establish Colombian control in the region. General Gabriel Valencia had the duty of protecting the Indians and of compiling testimonies on the Peruvian atrocities. The task of establishing Colombian control fell to General J. Isaías Gamboa who planned on establishing posts along the Caquetá River. General Gamboa had under his command about 100 military police (*gendarmes*) rather than regular army troops, but as the Peruvians later quipped, it seemed "too many generals for 100 cops."[49] Originally he had requested 500 soldiers, because he knew that many men would become sick or die during the journey. A government still reluctant to abandon ancient documents as the only defense of a frontier refused his request for more men. Gamboa also wanted cannons and machine guns, but the Bogotá government, in 1911 as later again in 1932, felt that heavy weapons would only provoke a Peruvian retaliation. Brand-new Mauser rifles comprised the only armament of the police.[50]

The expedition was inadequate for either military or police functions and if anything was best suited to make Colombia look ridiculous. The only way the country could avoid embarrassment was to send General Gamboa secretly with his men to the Caquetá River via the overland route. Instead the government sent the expedition by sea around the Atlantic and up the Amazon River. Secrecy was impossible, and already on 5 January 1911 the Peruvian minister in Bogotá informed his government of the impeding expedition. He knew Lima was certain to react to the news that Chilean military advisors had helped plan the expedition. As expected, the arrival of the minister's report on 11 February in Lima sent the War Ministry scrambling to make the best possible response.[51]

Small as the number of 100 policemen might seem, Iquitos could not spare a comparable force to oppose the Colombians. A Peruvian expedition by sea would normally have been the preferred choice, but the voyage through the Straits of Magellan (the Panama Canal was under construction) took much longer than from Colombia. As a faster response, the War Ministry in a memorable decision dispatched the 9th Battalion from Lambayeque in the Andes Mountains to Iquitos in the Amazon jungle. This was the first time that Peru had tried to move a large army unit overland into the Amazon region. The War Ministry was confident that the brilliant and resourceful Mayor Oscar R. Benavides could carry out the difficult deployment successfully.[52]

The 9th Battalion marched through jungle trails and often had to hack its way with machetes. Over 50 Indian porters helped carry its equipment, but even with their help the battalion could only bring two of its four machine guns. Upon reaching navigable waters, the battalion boarded river boats and reached Iquitos on 13 May after having completed a trip of 1200 kilometers. Mayor Benavides assumed command of the Iquitos garrison and promptly dedicated himself to meeting the Colombian threat. The mission seemed more urgent than ever, because an unconfirmed report stated that Colombia was trying to buy 100,000 Mausers in Germany, and he had to strike fast before Colombia could field such a large army. A severe shortage of steamboats forced him to leave one company behind in Iquitos as a reserve force. He was confident that his remaining companies were more than adequate to overcome any Colombian resistance.[53]

As Mayor Benavides completed the careful preparations for his expedition, the Colombians under General Gamboa were facing many difficult complications in the Caquetá River. The General had reached La Pedrera on 11 April barely a month ahead of the arrival of Mayor Benavides at Iquitos. A second Colombian force of about 80 men was soon to follow the original expedition up the Amazon River. A small overland detachment was also supposed to travel down the Caquetá River. Once these three forces united, General Gamboa was confident that his at least 200 men could withstand a Peruvian attack. He promptly put his men to construct buildings, barracks, and paths along the river (Map 8). He also established two outposts away from La Pedrera, one to the west (Puerto Córdoba) and another near the Brazilian border to collect customs duties on rubber exports. General Valencia, who was in charge of the customs house, also began to collect testimony on the atrocities of the Casa Arana. The Indians enthusiastically welcomed the Colombians as liberators from the exploitation of the Casa Arana. The friendly Indians reciprocated by reporting on Peruvian activities, and soon the Colombians learned of the impending Peruvian attack. General Gamboa had always expected an attack, and already from the first day of his arrival he had selected the site and the installations with defense as his main concern. In response to the warning, he put his men to dig trenches running parallel to the river and to cut tree trunks for breastworks, all well camouflaged under the jungle canopy.[54]

Tropical diseases soon started ravaging his policemen, who were not accustomed to work in the intense humidity and stifling temperatures of over 40 degrees centigrade (104° F). Extreme torrential rains produced a massive flood and damaged many of the installations the men had laboriously constructed. The flooding, the worst in twenty years, did not recede immediately and brought instead a greater prevalence of malaria, yellow fever, and dysentery. General Gamboa had expected to lose many men from climate and disease, but after the flood the rampant sickness surpassed anything previously experienced in these tributaries of the Amazon. Almost all his men fell sick, and they could not work to improve the defenses. The dwindling survivors became so weakened that they dreaded the exhausting toil of having to dig a grave for the new cadaver each day inevitably brought. The infirmary was full of the very sick and the dying, while General Gamboa himself fell sick and struggled just to remain conscious. Had not a party of 10 men returned in July from an exploration trip, the battle of La Pedrera could not have taken place because General Gamboa simply could not man the trenches without the returning patrol. The men in the exploring party had been away for nearly two months and not yet contracted the deadly sicknesses of the garrison.[55]

On 28 June Mayor Benavides left Iquitos with the 9th Battalion of 250 soldiers. Besides the armament aboard the steamers, the troops carried two rapid-firing cannons and four machine guns. Because the outnumbered Colombian garrison lacked artillery or machine guns, the prefect of Iquitos predicted that "the outcome of our expedition will have to be obviously a complete success."[56] The expedition traveled aboard the gunboat *América*, the large river steamer *Loreto*, and the smaller steamers *Tarapoto* and *Estefita*; these ships also towed three barges loaded with coal and other supplies. The long detour through Brazilian waters delayed the arrival of the flotilla at La Pedrera until 10 July at 1230. Mayor Benavides sent an ultimatum demanding the withdrawal of the Colombian garrison to the north bank of the river (Peru claimed the Caquetá River as its northern border) within two hours. General Gamboa negotiated an extension until 1600 that gave his sickly and weak men barely enough time to crawl and drag themselves to the trenches. He struggled out of a hammock and staggered around the defense lines trying to rally his dying men. Shooting started at 1600, but the cannon and machine guns fire failed to scare the well-dug defenders. Instead, the Peruvians standing on the decks of their boats

made easy targets for the highly accurate Mausers of the Colombians. Although the Peruvians hastily erected barricades aboard the ships, it was clear that the naval bombardment was not going to shatter defenses. Mayor Benavides devoted the remaining hours of daylight to look for a possible landing site for his soldiers. In front of La Pedrera the river turned into raging rapids and further downstream the record flood had not left any solid ground. As night approached, the flotilla withdrew out of rifle range.[57]

On 11 July under the protective fire of the *América*, Mayor Benavides sent the *Loreto*, the river steamer with the most horsepower, to try to reach the best landing spot suitable for its company of soldiers. The *Loreto* came within a few meters of the spot, but the current proved too strong. Meanwhile, the Peruvians continued to take heavy casualties from the Mauser fire of the sickly Colombian soldiers. With just a couple of cannons the defenders could have disabled the Peruvian flotilla. As the third day began, Mayor Benavides was increasingly desperate. His soldiers and sailors had taken serious casualties, and one of his favored officers had been killed. After two days of combat his previous ultimatum was starting to sound like idle bombast, and he was starting to look foolish. Then Mayor Benavides learned that upstream on the Caquetá the 9th Battalion could land on solid ground west of a creek behind La Pedrera. Unfortunately to steam upstream required forcing the rapids, something that no steamer had ever done before. He ordered the *Loreto* to force the rapids and to disembark its army company on land, while the rest of the flotilla kept a strong covering fire to tie down the defenders. Unfortunately steaming upstream required passing right in front of the Colombian defenses; a volley of Mauser bullets ripped through the main steam tube of the *Loreto*, which limped helplessly downstream and to the north bank of the river.[58]

Any other commander would have abandoned the attack, but a determined Mayor Benavides decided to gamble everything on one last try. He ordered the *América* to increase the steam pressure until its boilers were at the bursting point and then to force the rapids. Under incessant Mauser fire from the Colombians the bulky *América* labored mightily against the rapids of the Caquetá, and after half

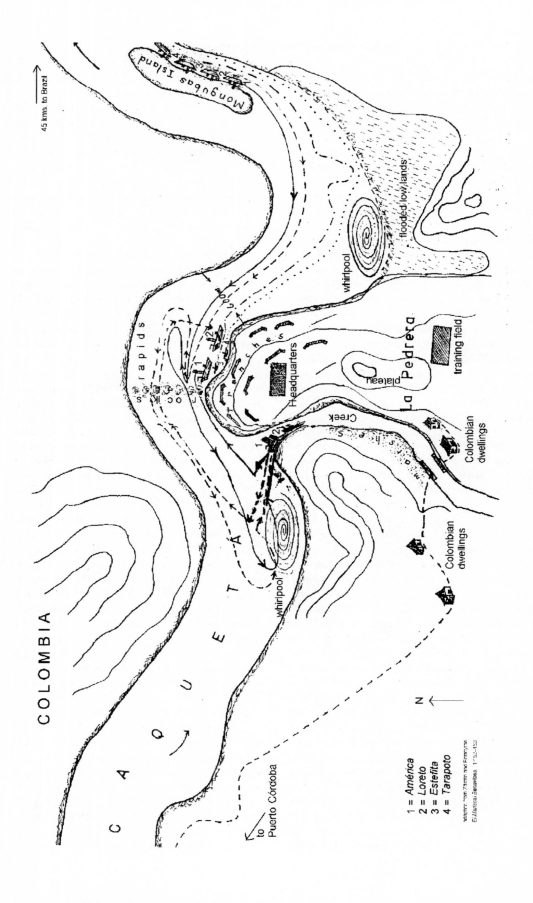

an hour of standing nearly still as the steam engine and the river current matched their strength, the gunboat at last broke free and crossed into the calm waters west of La Pedrera. After the *América* disembarked its troops, it returned downstream to shell the Colombian garrison caught in a cross fire between the gunboat and the Peruvian company coming from the west. Meanwhile the *Loreto* had fixed its steam pipes, and its commander, eager to equal the achievement of the gunboat, likewise forced the rapids and disembarked another company.

The Colombians knew they were outflanked and began an orderly withdrawal along a jungle trail they had partly cleared to the Brazilian border (Map 27). Only some men in the rear guard fell prisoner when they stayed behind too long covering the retreat of their companions. Because all the Colombians were very sick, they could carry very few items, and the abandonment of their equipment led the Peruvians to conclude that a precipitate rout had ensued. When the Peruvians troops attempted to pursue the retreating Colombians, unfamiliarity with the terrain and obstacles the retreated Colombians had placed soon forced the pursuers to desist. The Peruvians believed they had won a resounding victory, but the real winner was yet to emerge.[59]

Mayor Benavides sent the *Loreto* to take possession of the remaining Colombian outposts on the south bank of the Caquetá River. He had already ordered the gunboat *América* back to Iquitos for urgent repairs, because the bullets from the Mauser rifles had perforated the thin steel skin and riddled all the gunboat's compartments. He correctly concluded that two well-situated cannons made La Pedrera impregnable to an attack from the east. The news of the Peruvian victory reached Iquitos just after the prefect had received orders from Lima to recall the expedition. Between the departure of Benavides and the battle of La Pedrera, Lima had changed its mind and no longer wanted a war with Colombia. However, for the prefect, the news of the victory changed the situation entirely: "After bloody victory and delirious enthusiasm of the local population, I must regard the abandonment of La Pedrera to be extremely inconvenient. According to Be-

navides, the defense of that position is simple and completely guaranteed."[60] The rejoicing at Iquitos was contagious and soon spread throughout the country. Because the order halting the expedition had come too late, Lima had to decide whether to take the highly unpopular decision of withdrawing the 9th Battalion from La Pedrera. Any attempt to make the Caquetá River the northern boundary of Peru meant war with Colombia, and already the prefect of Iquitos was urging Lima to send a second battalion from the highlands to reinforce the depleted 9th Battalion.[61]

The population of Iquitos hoped to sway Lima to retain La Pedrera, but already on 1 August 1911 the plans for a permanent Peruvian occupation were collapsing in a totally unforeseen way. The Caquetá River had turned out to be the unhealthiest place in the entire region. "I am profoundly disturbed to learn how critical has become the situation of your brave troops" commented the shocked prefect of Iquitos.[62] An unknown plague had attacked the Peruvian soldiers already weakened by the traditional tropical diseases. Mayor Benavides could not understand what was happening to his men who fell sick and died at alarming rates. In desperation he burned the infirmary built by the Colombians and moved his men to a new infirmary, but to no avail. He himself traveled constantly on the river from one outpost to another to see what orders he could give to save the soldiers who continued to die. He was among the last to come down with malaria, so apparently travel inside the river provided some protection from the illnesses. However, a new disease seemed to be at work, because even locals already with considerable immunity to the tropical diseases also fell ill, although less seriously than the newcomers from the highlands of Peru. Because most of the soldiers of the 9th Battalion came from the Andes Mountains and had little immunity, only a quick departure from the deadly region could save the troops. On 19 August, barely a month after the Peruvians had celebrated their victory, Mayor Benavides and most of his sick soldiers departed aboard the steamers. He left a skeleton garrison behind with one cannon and three machine guns, but the disease-infested force continued to dwindle.[63] A telegram of Septem-

Opposite: **Map 8. Battle of La Pedrera, 10–12 July 1911.**

Top: The Peruvian gunboat *América.* During the battle of La Pedrera in July 1911, the bullets from the Mauser rifles of the Colombian soldiers made the holes visible in the gunboat (Archivo Histórico Militar del Perú, Lima, Peru). *Left:* General Oscar Benavides, the heroic commander of the victorious expedition to La Pedrera in July 1911. In 1933 as president, he extricated Peru from a hopeless war with Colombia (Archivo Histórico Militar del Perú, Lima, Peru).

ber to the newspaper *El Comercio* broke the news to an incredulous and stunned public in Lima: "The camp at La Pedrera has become a large hospital and cemetery."[64] The jungle, and not any country, had been the real winner at La Pedrera.

The Foreign Ministry in Lima had long since abandoned any claim to the Caquetá River, but just as happened again in 1932, the frenzied popular enthusiasm made any withdrawal have very high political costs. Mayor Benavides, himself on a convalescent trip to Europe, realized that La Pedrera was not as defensible as the site had first seemed. The natural defenses and the artillery emplacements all faced east but were nonexistent for the west. Any Colombian expedition sailing down the Caquetá River could easily repeat the flanking maneuver Benavides had performed. Supplying the Peruvian garrison was slow, costly, and ultimately depended on Brazilian willingness to keep the rivers open to navigation; instead the Colombian forces could easily obtain supplies from the fertile regions in the headwaters of the Caquetá River.

A final reason for withdrawal came from the captured archive of General Gamboa. Incriminating documents revealed that Colombian officials had been trying to plan a joint attack with Ecuador, and indeed a treaty of alliance existed but had not been ratified.[65] Because Chile had helped send the Colombian expedition in the first place, a coalition of two and possibly three countries against Peru was threatening to become a dangerous reality. Peru had to extricate itself gracefully but quickly from this adventure before the Caquetá River threatened to engulf the whole country in a disastrous war.

The Lingering Disputes Over the Northern Boundary of Peru

As late as October 1911 Iquitos was making extraordinary efforts to sustain the dwindling Peruvian outposts in the Caquetá River. The Peruvians on the lower Putumayo River were themselves struggling to survive and could not send much help through the jungle trails leading north. All supplies had to come from Iquitos, but the collapsing rubber market sharply reduced the customs revenue available to the prefect to outfit supply ships. Poorly fed soldiers fell ill and died in large numbers in the lower Caquetá, a region unusually fatal even by the standards of the Amazon. In contrast to the dire situation of the Peruvian garrison, Colombia enjoyed the benefit of having navigable rivers to carry foodstuffs and troops downstream from the Andes.[66]

Victory in the battlefield could not change the logistical realities, a lesson that Peru had to relearn painfully in a later war with Colombia in 1933. In 1911 Oscar Benavides, who received the promotion to Colonel because of his victory at La Pedrera, concluded that a timely withdrawal rather than a shameful expulsion was the only option for Peru. A stable and easily defended boundary with Colombia was more important than a futile attempt to retain distant territories. Peru accepted the inevitable

and on 23 October 1911 signed an agreement with Colombia abandoning all Peruvian claims to the Caquetá River. As a goodwill gesture to try to erase bad feelings, Peru returned all the items its troops had captured at La Pedrera. The officers were at best resigned to the outcome, but no officer wanted to appear on his curriculum vitae the task of having commanded the last detachment at La Pedrera. The few soldiers gradually melted away, until finally a minor police official formally abandoned La Pedrera on 10 December 1911. Eventually Colombian officials established a weak presence in the unhealthy region.[67]

Cordiality returned to the diplomatic relations between Colombia and Peru as both countries strove to erase even the memory of the battle of La Pedrera. The collapse of the rubber boom deprived the region of its main economic value. Without the lure of either revenue or profits from rubber, the environment became much more favorable for peaceful relations. Both countries seemed poised to settle their territorial dispute, but serious negotiations did not begin until Fabio Lozano Torrijos came to Lima as the new Colombian minister in May 1920. Lozano was determined to conclude a boundary treaty with Peru, and the new president of Peru, Augusto Leguía, shared the same determination.[68] The prospects for a peaceful outcome seemed favorable as negotiators labored to draft a treaty in the 1920s.

Colombia and Peru had turned away from war and adopted diplomacy as the best way to settle their outstanding differences. In contrast, Ecuador continued to use a dangerous mixture of diplomacy and war to try to reach the Amazon River. During the tripartite mediation Ecuador falsely accused Peru of sending reinforcements in defiance of the wishes of the mediators. The accusation was really a covering smoke screen to disguise the ambitious plans for Ecuador's expansion into the Amazon. Blocked in the Napo River, Ecuador decided to direct its advance into zones not yet defended by Peru. This new policy of silent penetration eventually reached dangerous extremes in the 1930s (see chapter 15) but at this moment seemed like a safe gamble. As an additional precaution, Ecuador decided to press forward only in the company of European investors. The Quito government granted the newly constituted Franco-Dutch Colonization Company

These Peruvian officers went to the Amazon in 1911 to fight against Colombia. Oscar Benavides is the fourth person standing from left; the remaining officers could not be identified (Archivo Histórico Militar del Perú, Lima, Peru).

the right to bring immigrants from the Pyrenees Mountains in Europe into the valleys of the Santiago and Morona rivers (Map 7).

This ingenious attempt to use a foreign company to block Peruvian advances was reminiscent of the similar effort by Bolivia to use U.S. investors to defend the Acre territory in 1903 (see chapter 1). But the Bolivian disaster of 1903 had in no way deterred Ecuador from carrying out a similar scheme. The president of the colonization company, Julian Fabré, raised enough capital to take a steamer with immigrant families from Europe up the mouth of the Amazon River; at the Santiago and Morona rivers, the steamer was supposed to meet an overland column descending from Riobamba in the Andes Mountains.

An advance party composed of peasants, Indian carriers, and soldiers did establish several temporary camps near the Morona River in 1910. The main overland column had not arrived by the time Peru learned of the Ecuadorian scheme and took countermeasures. Peruvian officials detained the steamer and arrested

Fabré and the immigrant families at Iquitos. Without the supplies aboard the steamer, the advance party could not survive for long at its temporary camps in the inhospitable jungle. The large follow-up column from Riobamba never came and left the first expedition abandoned to its fate. An immediate evacuation was the only way to save the men who were already falling ill from tropical diseases, but the leaders obstinately insisted on staying. Once the last of their food supplies ran out, these victims of hunger learned at first hand how deadly the Amazon could be. To make things worse, the Indians in the region were among the most hostile in the upper Amazon. The disintegration of the expedition came too late to save the men. Although a few dragged themselves miraculously back to the Andes Mountains; most men simply disappeared in the jungle.[69] Peruvians soldiers found no trace of the Ecuadorian expedition when they arrived to establish their first permanent garrisons in the Morona River in May 1911. The Peruvian Army had long since learned how hostile the Amazon was and had adopted the standard practice of providing at least four months' rations of food staples for the soldiers. River boats supplied the army posts throughout the Amazon, but to remain healthy, the army expected the soldiers to gather or grow in gardens (*chacras*) the fruits and vegetables needed to complement the dry foodstuffs.[70]

The Franco-Dutch Company did not bolster Ecuador's claims and ultimately harmed them by forcing Peru to change its policy. Until then Peru had believed that its control of the vital waterways sufficed to safeguard the upper Amazon. The establishment of a base in the Morona River marked the start of a deliberate policy to erect an extensive defensive line on land, and soon a string of new Peruvian posts guarded the Curaray River. Peru had concluded that any serious invasion from Ecuador would most likely come through the Curaray River, and consequently Peru wanted to create a chain of posts and trails not just along the river but also linking it with Peruvian positions in the Napo River. To minimize the possibility of clashes with the nearby Ecuadorian outposts, the prefect of Iquitos ordered the soldiers in the farthest Peruvian outposts in the Curaray and the Napo rivers to dress in civilian clothes and to pretend to be colonists after July 1910.[71]

The Peruvian precautions helped keep the Amazon peaceful. No less important was the collapse of the rubber boom. Both countries lost interest in the region during the 1910s and the 1920s. The Amazon region languished and entered a decades-long period of decline. With the end of opportunities to earn revenue or profits in the Amazon, the incentive to clash over a largely worthless region virtually vanished. Once the world economy did not need the products of the Amazon, the region drifted back into its traditional poverty and subsistence living. This economic collapse had already contributed to ease the tensions with Colombia. The whole Amazon seemed to be falling into a deep sleep.

The tensions with the Indians remained a lingering problem, however. In the prevailing atmosphere of savage exploitation, the rubber tappers had treated the Indians brutally. In contrast, relations of the Indians with the Peruvian army had generally been satisfactory, and many officers and soldiers had become friends of local tribes. The platoon stationed in the Morona River was under the command of a captain who was extremely friendly with the Indians. He became such a good friend of the chief (*curaca*) of the Guambisos Indians that he refused to believe the reports about their ferocious and independent nature. He invited the Indian chief to test a new Mauser rifle the captain had recently received. The Indian chief came with a small party and secretly surrounded the camp with a large number of Indians. When the captain showed him how to fire the Mauser, the Indian chief fired the first shot at the captain and promptly killed him. At the sound of the shot the rest of the Indians rushed into the camp and massacred everyone they could find; fortunately about half of the platoon had been at work in their gardens or hunting in the jungle, and most of these managed to escape. As soon as word of the massacre reached Iquitos, the prefect sent a 100-man company to rebuild the post and to capture the Indians.[72] The only consolation was that the troops found nothing to report that would link the Morona massacre with Ecuador. However, because later Ecuador claimed the Indians were its allies, even some Peruvians believed that the Ecuadorians instigated the Indian uprising. In reality the Morona massacre was just one more episode in the tragic history of the destruction of the Amazon Indians.[73]

After the embarrassing defeat of Torres Causano in 1904, Ecuador no longer dared attack existing Peruvian positions. But rather than abandon its ambitious goal of reaching the Amazon River, Ecuador searched for more promising avenues of attack and believed to have found them in the weak logistical situation of Peru. Although a Peruvian flotilla at Iquitos seemed capable of controlling all the navigable rivers in the region, in reality the Peruvian situation was very fragile. Until the late 1930s, Peru had no direct, reliable and fast way to send large quantities of supplies and armaments by land to Iquitos. The water route from the Atlantic Ocean via the Amazon took months and was subject to Brazilian approval. The downhill roads from the Peruvian Andes were in very poor condition and could not supply adequately the river traffic in the tributaries of the Amazon. Thus, paradoxically, although Peruvian gunboats and troops provided a formidable initial defense, the logistical shortcomings threatened to weaken and finally exhaust any sustained military action in the Amazon, as Peru learned to its regret during the war with Colombia over Leticia in 1933.

Unlike in Colombia whose navigable rivers flowing into the Amazon passed fertile regions, in Ecuador the navigable rivers began further to the east. A gap existed between the Andes Mountains and the navigable headwaters of the rivers flowing into the Amazon. Only after Ecuador bridged this gap could supplies and equipment easily reach its troops, who at last could overwhelm the poorly supplied Peruvian forces. Even before the completion of the railroad linking the capital city of Quito with Guayaquil in the Pacific Coast on 25 June 1908, Ecuador had been preparing to build a railroad into the Amazon. The government employed American engineers to trace a route to the Curaray River in 1906, but lack of funds delayed the start of construction. The limited commercial value of the railroad did not justify a large capital investment, and the project required lavish subsidies. The most economical route was from Ambato to Baños and then to the start of the navigable stretch of the Curaray River. This route avoided having to climb mountains and at 450 kilometers in length was the shortest of all the alternatives to the navigable tributaries of the Amazon River. American civil engineers directed the construction work and by late 1917 had managed to lay 46 kilometers of track beyond Ambato. The normal gauge track communicated Ambato with existing railroads leading to Guayaquil and to Quito. The government had hoped to reach Baños in January 1918, but World War I caused a shortage of rails and halted operations. If Ecuador could not complete even the easiest and smallest segment of the railroad, how could it build the remaining 400 kilometers of track passing through extremely dense jungle? Meanwhile Peru hoped that the jungle and the shortage of funds would keep the proposed railroad far away from the Curaray River. Each meter the railroad advanced into the jungle was one less meter of safety for Peru.[74]

The lack of progress on the Curaray Railroad did not keep Ecuador from endorsing an even more ambitions project on 7 November 1919. A law of that date authorized the government to grant a Chilean Syndicate immense privileges, including land on each side of the track, to build a railroad of nearly a thousand kilometers from Puerto Bolívar on the south coast of Ecuador through Cuenca and Loja as far as the Amazon River. No commercial reasons justified such a fantastic scheme, which the Chilean Syndicate continued to promote vigorously in public as late as 1921. The motivations for the railroad lay in another realm:

> Perhaps Chile thought that Peru would so strenuously object to even such an agreement between Chile and Ecuador that the situation would develop into a war in which Ecuador would be her ally and an easy defeat of Peru would bring about the settlement of her old question with Peru on terms favorable to Chile. [...] in analyzing the benefits to be derived by both Ecuador and Chile against the common enemy, it is not difficult to understand that both countries would be eager to see the proposition an accomplished fact. [...] However, [...] one still retains considerable doubt as to a South American government putting through a proposition of such proportions as this one. These governments are fully capable of conceiving such ideas, but the matter of making them accomplished facts is a different matter.[75]

Chile's chance for a preventive war with Peru vanished as the latter country calmly watched the fantastic railroad proposal languish and fade away in the early 1920s. With railroad construction in the Amazon virtually paralyzed, Peru's control over the rivers meant that Ecuador needed at least several decades to prepare for any war. Hopefully the long delay would calm down Ecuador to the point that it would be willing to trace and recognize a border following natural landmarks and existing outposts. However, Peru knew that as long as Ecuador relied on support from Chile, no meaningful negotiations were possible. To try to bring Ecuador to the negotiating table, Peru had to bury the hatchet with Chile. Peruvian President Augusto Leguía concentrated on settling the Tacna-Arica dispute with Chile as the first indispensable step to securing Ecuador's approval for a treaty defining the Amazon border. The future of the Amazon hinged on the parallel negotiations President Leguía was conducting with Chile and with Colombia during the 1920s. The ongoing negotiations made the threat of war recede continuously into an ever more distant future.

3. War Between Panama and Costa Rica

One of the principal qualities of a commander in all times has been the power of forming a right estimate of his adversary's character, and of basing his own plans upon the defects of the enemy, upon those of the enemy's general, and upon the conditions of his army. — Albrecht von Boguslawski[1]

By the late 1910s the threat of war was receding from the Amazon jungle. As the likelihood of clashes among Latin American countries diminished, a spreading pacifist movement hoped to eliminate war as an instrument of national policy. To everyone's consternation, war made a surprising comeback in a forgotten corner of Latin America. Most disturbingly, the armed clash between Panama and Costa Rica in February 1921 revealed that even the smallest and poorest countries were still willing to use force to solve their disputes. An analysis of how troop deployments escalated into military operations offers insights into how wars start and provides a comparative framework to analyze the renewed outbreak of wars in Part III of this book.[2]

The War Over the Coto Region

Costa Rica and Panama went to war over the small village of Coto. The territory in dispute was tiny compared to the vast extensions at stake in the Amazon wars of the first two chapters, and no war seemed justified over such a minuscule parcel of land. But precisely because both countries were so small, the piece of land loomed much larger than its actual size.

Large countries used such small parcels as sweeteners to conclude boundary negotiations, but for Panama and Costa Rica this small plot of nearly worthless real estate was the only thing to fight over.

Behind the dispute lurked a fundamental shift in regional power: until November 1903, Panama had belonged to the large and rich country of Colombia. Under Colombian protection, Panamanian colonists had gradually pushed the border westward until Coto represented the westernmost penetration. Costa Rica did not want to risk any war with Colombia and relied on diplomacy to conserve Coto. Costa Rica persuaded Colombia to accept arbitration, and on 11 September 1900 the Loubet award by the President of France established the approximate boundary and specified Punta Burica on the Pacific Ocean as the southernmost divide (Map 9). Incomplete geographical information had prevented the Loubet award from specifying all the coordinates for the boundary, but Colombia and Costa Rica were confident that they could trace a mutually acceptable line on the ground.

Regional power shifted dramatically when U.S. intervention made Panama independent in November 1903. The new republic inherited the undefined border with its western neighbor.

Panama negotiated a satisfactory line with Costa Rica on the Atlantic or northern boundary but failed to reach an agreement on the southern sector. Both countries submitted the disputed portion to arbitration by the Chief Justice of the U.S. Supreme Court. The White award of 12 September 1914 accepted the Costa Rican interpretation of the earlier Loubet award and assigned Coto to Costa Rica.[3]

The award seemed fair because, among other reasons, the geography and the mountainous terrain weakened the Panamanian claim. Both land and water routes to Coto were easier and faster from Costa Rica than from Panama. Only a mud trail requiring a day to cross under the best of circumstances linked Panama to the 27 families and two officials who lived in the village.[4]

President Belisario Porras of Panama should have seen the inevitable. His obligation was to order the evacuation of Coto and to offer compensation to the local families, but such a move amounted to political suicide. He knew that his partisan enemies would use any abandonment of Panamanian territory to accuse him of treachery, and he could not bring himself to take the risk of ruining his future reelection to the presidency. Political enemies had already attacked him furiously for having been too generous when he settled the northern stretch of the boundary with Costa Rica in 1910. Further complicating the picture, his wife was from Costa Rica, "and was surrounded up to the acute period of the crisis in February 1921 by a small court of Costa Ricans holding office under the Republic of Panama."[5]

For Porras the easiest alternative was to let matters drift; the hardest and truly statesmanlike course required that he prepare his people for the loss of Coto, even if the withdrawal meant the end of his political career. After the White award of 1914, Costa Rica was more than willing to grant Panama ample time for a leisurely withdrawal, but as the months turned into years, the bordering country became more impatient. A civil war in Costa Rica gained more time for Panama, but Porras took no steps either to abandon or to defend Coto. Although a 1916 commission had recommended stationing a police force of ten men in the village, the sole defense remained one policeman.[6]

Any defense of Coto was doubtful at best and not just because of the isolation of the village or because of the absence of any garrison. U.S. pressure and fear of the political pretensions of military officers persuaded Panama's rulers to abolish the army in November 1904, barely one year after the independence of the country. The former soldiers joined the Panamanian national police created the previous year. Around 1000 policemen armed with revolvers and some carbines maintained internal order. Of the modest arsenal inherited from the Colombian bases in 1903, Panama had sold most of it abroad. Of the rifles left, the United States under threat of military occupation had forced Panama to surrender them in 1916 after a stray rifle bullet killed an American policeman during street disturbances. President Porras had surreptitiously hidden fifty rifles and 60,000 cartridges in the basement of the Presidential Palace, but because the United States did not let Panama purchase any additional weapons, for all practical purposes the country was unarmed and lacked troops to defend its borders.[7]

The trump card of President Porras was the territorial guarantee that the United States had given Panama under the Canal Zone Treaty. The U.S. obligation to preserve Panama had kept Colombia from reoccupying Panama, and Porras believed that the same treaty protected Panama from Costa Rica. Porras and the Panamanian public naively believed that the United States would defend with zeal the Panamanian borders, much as Colombia had done until 1903. The war over Coto was sure to be another learning experience for Panama about exactly what constituted the obligations of a client state that existed only for the benefit of a powerful patron.

After the civil war ended in Costa Rica, Julio Acosta García was elected president on 7 December 1919. His rule did not begin smoothly, and by the end of 1920 his many followers were restless and fast running out of patience. With support for his presidency crumbling, he needed to find some issue to restore his popularity. As his officials reviewed the file on Coto, they could not understand why Costa Rica had failed to occupy the village. The president asked for an inspection of the region and for additional reports before making up his mind. He also insisted on consulting with the United States before taking any action. In November 1920 President Acosta personally told

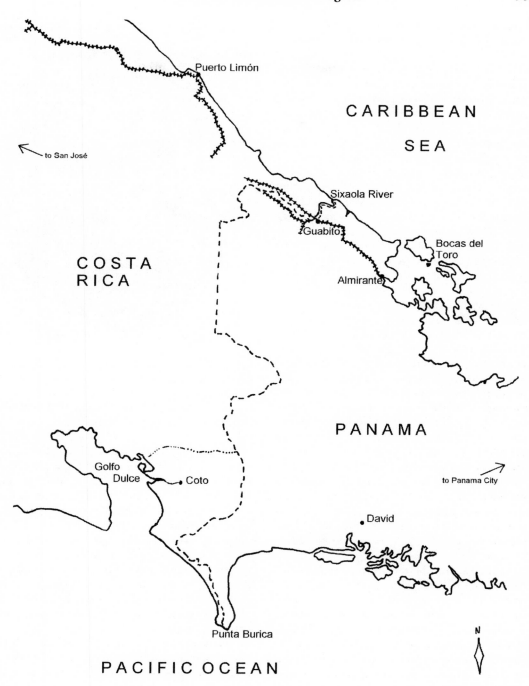

Map 9. Panama and Costa Rica Border

the U.S. ambassador that Costa Rica intended to send a military unit to occupy Coto under the terms of the White award; the Costa Rican ambassador in Washington D.C. reiterated the message to the U.S. State Department. The dilemma for the State Department was clear: either the U.S. government tried to explain why Costa Rica could not enforce the award of the U.S. Chief Justice or the U. S. government persuaded Panama to withdraw peacefully. Washington had to adopt one of the formulas, yet inexplicably the State Department failed to reply.[8]

Costa Rica bore no blame for the glaring failure of the State Department to respond. Perhaps the confusion associated with the coming change of administrations in Washington was responsible for letting the matter slip through the cracks. After waiting several months and hearing nothing adverse from the U.S. government, President Acosta decided on 20 February to send a unit of 28 soldiers to occupy Coto. He sincerely believed that he was not starting a war, and all he wanted was to bring pressure on Panama to negotiate a formal withdrawal. Just like Daniel Salamanca later in the Chaco War, President Acosta believed that after releasing a small dose of force, he could then put the genie of war back into the bottle.[9]

Militarily, President Acosta was in a position of clear superiority over Panama. Although the army of Costa Rica numbered only 400 soldiers, it had well-stocked arsenals. Most of the weapons were in good condition and were the physical remains of a previous policy to create a large conscript army patterned on the French model. Like so many foreign formulas imported into Latin America, the experiment was a dismal failure, and Costa Rica was gradually shifting its budget away from the army and towards education. But the arsenals still had thousands of Mauser rifles, dozens of machine guns, and even some artillery pieces. In a striking paradox, Acosta had an army but wished to use it like a police force, while Porras had a police force but wished to use it like an army.[10]

At dawn on the morning of 21 February 1921, 28 soldiers and officers of the Costa Rican army traveled upstream on the Coto River from the Golfo Dulce aboard the motorboat *La Estrella* until they reached the village of Coto. Had Panama increased the police force to 10 men, President Acosta would have needed a much larger force or perhaps he would not have attempted the maneuver at all. Instead, Acosta confidently could issue orders to avoid combat. By sheer numbers the Costa Rican soldiers effortlessly took control of the village from a Panamanian official and a lone policeman. The Costa Ricans had no intention of keeping the seizure quiet; on the contrary, they hoped to use the news to restart the negotiations. At

Belisario Porras, the Liberal leader in Panama during the War of the Thousand Days (1899–1902). He was president of Panama during that country's war with Costa Rica in 1921 (*Boletín cultural y bibliográfico*, 2000).

0700 they sent the Panamanian policeman to report the occupation to his superiors. Extremely familiar with the rugged path, favored with good weather, and highly motivated, the policeman reached the next Panamanian town in record speed by 1700 that afternoon. The governor of David, the provincial capital of western Panama, soon knew of the invasion, and by 2000 that night drums were convoking the city dwellers to mass rallies. A spontaneous outburst of nationalistic frenzy seized David, as citizens volunteered by the hundreds to fight to defend Coto.[11]

The decision for war, of course, was ultimately the responsibility of President Porras, who soon received telegrams reporting the news. He plunged into the preparations to make a quick response to the Costa Rican "invasion." To make sure the executive branch was behind him, he convoked a cabinet meeting in Panama City largely for morale purposes at 1800 on 22 February. He proposed to keep the matter secret as long as possible, so that troops could depart undetected and thus catch the Costa Ricans at Coto by surprise. As expected, the cabinet endorsed his plan passionately. No less predictable was the Latin bravado, and in a dramatic gesture, Porras offered to lead the troops in person to the front. Arguing that his presence was indispensable at the capital and that his departure would alert the Costa Ricans, the cabinet members persuaded a reluctant Porras to stay behind. General Manuel Quintero, a famous veteran of the War of the Thousand Days, received command of the expedition.[12]

Once the theatrics were over, the realization sank in that no troops existed to take to the front! Porras hastily improvised and ordered the police force to transform itself into an army. To patrol the city, he deputized the firemen as policemen. Soon news of the Coto invasion reached the public, and spontaneous demonstrations much larger than those of David erupted throughout the capital. Volunteers offered themselves by the hundreds to go serve in the front. The National Assembly, normally a check on the authoritarian tendencies of Porras, swiftly approved all requests to mobilize Panama for war.

Keeping secret the departure of the troops had panicked many Panamanians into believing that the government had sold them out. A huge crowd marched to the presidential palace in Panama City on 24 February to demand action against Costa Rica. With great difficulty Porras calmed the angry demonstrators who finally went home satisfied with his explanations.[13] The utter impossibility of obtaining any weapons abroad and the diplomatic isolation of Panama made Porras reconsider, and he began to search for a way out of the conflict. On 28 February he floated as a trial balloon the statement that "war between Panama and Costa Rica over valueless land was an absurdity"[14] and hoped to return the country to the path of reason. With only the inexperienced firemen patrolling the city, a rampaging mob soon formed outside the presidential palace. A furious crowd crashed through the back entrance of the palace. Coincidentally, the U.S. ambassador to Panama and the governor of the Canal Zone were paying a courtesy visit to Porras; on seeing the rampage, the two officials ordered U.S. troops to enter Panama, and "American troops arrived at the home of President Porras just in time to save the President's life."[15] U.S.

troops stayed on duty in the presidential palace until 12 March when the threat of additional violence in the capital had subsided. The mob attack of 28 February had made stark clear the choices before President Porras. He had to pick either his political survival or the defeat and humiliation of Panama. Realizing that he could do nothing to control the violent nationalistic outbursts of the population, he hoped by remaining in power to find some opportunity to halt the conflict.[16]

For the moment, he resigned himself to supervising the expeditions going by sea and then upstream by river to Coto. With considerable delay Costa Rica was learning of the Panamanian intention to counterattack and tardily sent small reinforcements. The superior espionage network of Panama alerted President Porras to the departure of Costa Rican units to the front, and on 27 February he ordered General Quintero to capture Coto promptly even though only 100 policemen were ready to take part in the attack. At 0800 on 27 February the Panamanians arrived to surround the village. Because the Mausers of the Costa Ricans were vastly superior to the old rifles of the policemen, combat was sure to last until the Costa Ricans ran out of ammunition. However, according to earlier orders of the Costa Rican President not to engage in combat, the garrison had remained in a peace time routine, and the two ranking officers were out hunting. The capture of these two officers eased the task of regaining control of Coto, and after some confused events, the garrison surrendered and gave up its arms.[17]

No fighting had yet taken place, and President Porras hoped to keep the conflict bloodless by ordering the blockade of the mouth of the Coto River or of Golfo Dulce, so that Costa Rican reinforcements could not return to the disputed territory. Costa Rica had only motorboats made of wood, and they could be rammed or driven aground by Panama's steel-hulled coastwise ships. General Quintero considered the plan feasible, but relying on a little leeway in his orders, he opted for a different strategy. His real problem upon his departure from Panama City had been lack of weapons, and the shortage became worse as thousands of volunteers clamored to join the expedition. General Quintero concluded that he could obtain weapons only by capturing them from the

Costa Ricans, and he proceeded to set a trap accordingly. He did not send his coastwise vessels to establish a blockade and deliberately left the routes open for the Costa Rican wooden launches to navigate up the river to Coto. Meanwhile, General Quintero ordered his men to entrench themselves and to build breastworks on the banks of the river.[18]

The Costa Rican launch *Sultana*, bringing 29 Costa Rican soldiers and one machine gun, duly motored upstream into the trap late in the afternoon at 1730. The Panamanians first allowed the *Sultana* to proceed unmolested to a narrow segment of the river. Then when the launch was at very close range, the Panamanians from their protected positions began raking with fire the uncovered deck of the launch. Although the surprised *Sultana* turned around and tried to escape, the Panamanians kept up their fire on the launch until the Costa Ricans still alive surrendered. Unaware of this event, *La Estrella*, carrying another 100 Costa Rican soldiers, was returning upstream on 1 March. With the captured weapons and reinforcements General Quintero had sent, the Panamanians stood a chance against La *Estrella*. The combat raged for an hour and a half, and the defenders were running out of cartridges; only the Mausers the Panamanians had previously captured from the *Sultana* gave them the edge to force the surrender of La *Estrella*. The debacle for Costa Rica could not have been more complete, and President Acosta, who had wanted only a police action, had suffered a terrible humiliation and had to act fast to remain in office.[19]

President Acosta had seriously underestimated the Panamanian response and faced the angry reaction of his own people. When news of the defeats reached Costa Rica, the outrage was immense in San José, the capital, and in other towns. The passionate public demonstrations and the outbreak of war fever surprised the government. The defeats were particularly insulting to Costa Rica, which until then had regarded Panama not as a real country, but as a puppet of the United States, as little more than a paper republic. To avenge the humiliation, Costa Ricans flocked to the colors in the thousands as war fever spread from Panama to Costa Rica. Volunteers soon had enlarged the ranks until Costa Rica had a large and well-equipped army.

In contrast, Panama simply lacked weapons to arm the many volunteers and was critically short of cartridges. The government had depleted all its meager arsenals and had already scavenged the country for arms to outfit the expeditions to Coto. Panama could find no weapons to purchase in the international market, and the United States pressured countries not to sell to either belligerent. Only by smuggling could Panama hope to acquire weapons, but arms merchants were still rare in this period, and much time, effort, and money was wasted into acquiring very few weapons. Costa Rica with its existing arsenals clearly retained the overwhelming military superiority.[20]

An offensive to recapture Coto seemed most in accord with the original goal of the war, but lack of shipping delayed the deployment of any large force, and a small force risked another humiliating defeat. As Costa Rica struggled to mount an effective response, unfounded rumors scared the government into believing that Panama was planning to attack the Caribbean coast.[21] Initially neither side had expected the Panamanian province of Bocas del Toro to experience any hostilities, but fearful of a surprise attack from Panama, Costa Rica as a precaution sent 25 policemen to reinforce the border post facing the Panamanian town of Guabito on the Sixaola River. Radio intercepts reported this very small deployment to the Panamanians, who had only 33 policemen to defend the entire province of Bocas del Toro. Their commander, Captain Herminio J. Pinzón, gradually transferred his 33 policemen and some volunteers to the border to try to forestall any Costa Rican advance. As an additional deterrent, the Panamanians planted false radio messages reporting the arrival of hundreds of reinforcements from Panama City. These false messages backfired, because they gave Costa Rica the evidence to confirm the imminent Panamanian attack. In a panicky response, Costa Rica rushed hundreds of soldiers to the border to ward off the expected Panamanian invasion. As the mobilization took a life of its own, eventually Costa Rica mustered over 2,000 soldiers as well as cannons and machine guns near the border on the Atlantic side.[22]

Costa Ricans soldiers with machine guns already defended the boundary line with Panama at the Sixaola River. The Costa Rican commanders concluded that to guarantee a successful defense against the expected Panamanian invasion, they had to launch a preemptive strike across the border to seize Guabito. In contrast to the Panamanians who had excellent intelligence, the Costa Ricans generally were in the dark about their opponents. The only suitable crossing point over the Sixaola River was a steel railroad bridge, the property of the United Fruit Company. Because the U.S. company was also the owner of the banana plantations on both sides of the border, Panama did not dare blow up the bridge. Captain Pinzón, with only 33 policemen, wisely decided to withdraw the night before as soon as he heard an attack was imminent. The Costa Ricans had planned to capture Guabito after 2200 on 3 March, but quarreling among some officers who feared the operation was too risky delayed the attack until 0630 on 4 March. The Costa Rican attackers rode aboard a banana train they had commandeered from United Fruit. As the banana train entered the bridge, the Costa Rican troops in the trenches opened an intense covering fire with their machine guns. They raked the other side of the river, but because they were firing at such close range, some bullets ricocheted off the steel beams of the bridge and ended up killing a few Costa Rican civilians and soldiers. The banana train eventually reached the other side, and the Costa Rican soldiers easily secured the town.[23]

As the Costa Ricans were setting up a defensive line at Guabito, they received orders to continue by train forty kilometers south to capture Almirante, the main port in the region. The order to shift from the defensive to the offensive had come from President Acosta, who had become convinced that an invasion could secure Coto for Costa Rica. He had wanted to know the U.S. attitude towards the ongoing war, and the United States had replied it would remain passive as long as the hostilities remained localized at Coto. President Acosta then took the bold decision to order the invasion force to advance deeply into Bocas del Toro province in the hope of provoking U.S. intervention.

As the Costa Rican force rolled down the tracks towards Almirante, all Panamanian opposition vanished. Originally Captain Pinzón had wanted to make a stand at Almirante, where he expected to meet the reinforcements

coming from the Panamanian capital. President Porras himself gave a strict order to hold Almirante at all costs, but the failure of any reinforcements to arrive made pointless any defense. Captain Pinzón took away all the craft in the port except for two large lighters and left with his small detachment to Bocas del Toro, the island capital of the province. At the town of Bocas del Toro, the governor had been busily organizing volunteer units, but the shortage of rifles and ammunition severely handicapped his efforts. Meanwhile the Costa Ricans leisurely rode the train until they entered Almirante around 1600 that same day. Almost simultaneously, the long-promised Panamanian reinforcements arrived by sea under Colonel Alejandro Mosquera, who now became the ranking military officer at the town of Bocas del Toro. Although he had brought only 110 hungry, poorly clothed, and badly armed policemen, the news of their arrival seemed to confirm to the Costa Ricans that this was the long-expected large expedition. The Costa Rican soldiers at Almirante began to panic and clambered aboard the trains to rush back to their defensive positions at Guabito; conflicting orders assured a long period of confusion until the Costa Rican commanders restored discipline and returned their men to Almirante.[24]

A second small Panamanian contingent had arrived to reinforce Bocas del Toro, but even counting the volunteers, the garrison was still vastly insufficient to defend the island. The Costa Ricans brought more troops aboard the United Fruit Company train until by the morning of 6 March they had 1,200 well-armed soldiers at Almirante. Although each of the two barges could carry 400 men, the Costa Ricans preferred to distribute their force among a larger number of craft they were bringing from Puerto Limón. The attack plan called for keeping 400 soldiers at Almirante while the main force of 800 men boarded the flotilla for a landing later that night. Three cannons and 17 machine guns aboard the flotilla provided ample cover for the troops. A U.S. military observer concluded that

> The Costa Ricans would have captured Bocas del Toro without difficulty, as it was occupied by only 300 unorganized Panamanian troops, and their plans were then made to proceed in a steamer to attack Colón. There would

have been nothing to prevent their reaching Colón, but there the United States would be caught in a most humiliating position, and would be forced to use military measures to prevent their landing.[25]

The Costa Rican troops had duly boarded their craft at 1800 on 6 March and were preparing to steam out for the attack when half an hour later the order arrived to halt operations and to return to Costa Rica. Timely U.S. diplomatic intervention had saved Panama from the humiliating loss of Bocas del Toro. In reality, the clever use of false messages had backfired on the Panamanians who had only themselves to blame for the near disaster. The inhabitants of Bocas del Toro did not realize how lucky they had been, and instead in one last burst of bravado, they threatened to fire at the United Fruit Company steamship returning the Costa Ricans home. President Porras at last had his opportunity to cool the war fever, and he gave the firm order to allow the steamer to depart unmolested. Without any mishap, the ceasefire remained in place.[26]

The invasion of Bocas del Toro had given Costa Rica a great negotiating card to persuade the United States to force Panama to abandon Coto. Essentially, the United States imposed the award of Chief Justice White as the valid boundary line, in exchange for a Costa Rican withdrawal from the province of Bocas del Toro. President Acosta had not expected to start a war, and the hostilities turned out to be very different from anything he had imagined. Nevertheless, by recourse to force, he had finally obtained his limited goal. No less important, his popularity soared and his government received a much needed boost.[27]

Panama clung desperately to Coto, and President Porras took the final step of seeking U.S. permission to fight a war with Costa Rica to defend Coto. He did not have to worry about a renewal of the hostilities because the prompt and predictable U.S. response shot down this bluff. The United States instead issued an ultimatum for the evacuation of the village, but Panama continued to delay. With U.S. marines on their way to occupy the country, Porras could rightfully claim that a military ultimatum from the United States had forced him to abandon Coto. On 5 September 1921, Costa Rican authorities took control of the region permanently. The transfer of authority did not appear traumatic at all to the local residents; only six families abandoned the region to receive compensation in Panama, while 21 families were quite happy to remain under the rule of Costa Rica. Curiously enough, President Porras had managed to rally nationalist feelings for his own benefit. By informing the Panamanian public minutely of all his efforts to save a lost cause, nobody condemned him for launching Panama into a hopeless war. Instead, Porras had extracted the maximum political capital out of the territorial dispute with Costa Rica. Although Panama had lost, in a very rare occurrence the presidents of both countries won politically from the war.[28]

Some Reflections

If rulers always benefited politically from war, they would rarely hesitate to start a war. But because military defeat has almost always ruined political careers, rulers have generally been most reluctant to launch their countries into war. The political genius of President Belisario Porras lay in extracting political victory out of a military defeat. Very few politicians ever have had the talent or enjoyed the exceptional conditions to repeat such an extraordinary feat. The general principle has been that the loss of a war means the weakening and usually the eventual fall of a defeated government.

Some of the almost theatrical aspects of the war between Costa Rica and Panama may inadvertently hide the deadly seriousness of the determination to wage war on both sides. The outburst of passionate feelings easily could have led to carnage similar to the Chaco War. Perhaps most disturbingly, the willingness of popularly elected leaders to risk war for personal political reasons casts doubts on the widely held belief that democracies are inherently less prone to war than military or dictatorial regimes. The commanding presence of the United States obviously determined the flow of events in this war, and as explained earlier, the war only occurred because in November 1920 the State Department did not respond to the advance warning from Costa Rica. The United States ultimately imposed the solution, and President Julio Acosta García accurately sensed that the U.S. decision had to favor Costa

Rica. President Porras instead miscalculated when he felt that Panama's status as a client state gave it special privileges with the U. S. government. Nonetheless, his whole doomed attempt to retain Coto did serve to create a sense of shared experience among the population. Panama has always been an artificial construct as a country and as a nation. The modest victories in the south and the long agonizing struggle to delay the inevitable loss of the territory helped shape a distinct national conscience. Not a single country supported Panama in its territorial claims, and this sense of being totally alone as the helpless victim fostered strong emotional bonds among the population.

How successful was Porras in creating a fully developed Panamanian nationalism? Although the complete answer falls beyond the scope of this book, the question of whether war remains the best way to create a national conscience is worthy of more reflection. For example, President José Manuel Pando had seen in the Acre campaigns a way to rally his country of Indians around a national purpose, but the results were disastrous as Chapter 1 has shown. Panama instead was extremely lucky in its brief fling with war and miraculously escaped with almost no suffering or loss.

In many ways the war between Panama and Costa Rica besides being unnecessary was also tardy. The wave of international armed conflicts in Latin America had crested by the early 1910s, yet the war between Panama and Costa Rica came ten years later. Because Central America is often regarded as being behind the rest of Latin America, perhaps the delay could have been the result of the usual lag. The preponderant U. S. influence in Central America also helps to explain why this war stands in isolation between the first wave of conflicts in the early twentieth century and the second wave in the 1930s. Its very awkward existence serves as a warning to those who insist on categorizing human phenomena too rigidly.

Whatever the exact reasons why the conflict did not take place earlier, the war definitely marked the start of a period of seemingly permanent peace. In the eyes of pacifists, the war between Panama and Costa Rica lurked as an insignificant aberration that could not detract from humanity's relentless march towards world peace. Many believed that the swift end to the conflict meant that war among Latin American nations had disappeared. The countries of the region rushed to sign the anti-war treaties so fashionable in the 1920s, most notably the Brian-Kellogg treaty outlawing war as an instrument of national policy. Although threats and rumors of war continued to reappear with disturbing frequency throughout the 1920s, Latin America had never seemed closer to reaching the goal of universal peace.

About the end of domestic disturbances, not even the most committed pacifists held any illusions. At first glance, endemic disturbances seemed to grip Latin America almost constantly during the first four decades of the twentieth century. In reality, after the War of the Thousand Days in Colombia of 1899–1902, sustained and determined military campaigns occurred only in a very small number of cases. Only in Cuba, Mexico, and Nicaragua, the countries that comprise Part II of this book, did insurrections turn into generalized warfare.

PART II. DOMESTIC INSURRECTIONS

4. Cuba: Demobilization and War

An observant and perceptive government is one that looks at subtle phenomena and listens to small voices. — Zhuge Liang[1]

Domestic turmoil had been a traditional characteristic of Latin America since its independence in the 1820s. Although the number of revolts, mutinies, and coup d'états declined after 1880, many disturbances still shook the region from 1899 to 1941. Real military campaigns were rare, however, because almost all the disturbances were political movements with little or usually no combat. From 1899 to 1941, only in Colombia, Cuba, Mexico and Nicaragua did the upheavals become wars. The War of the Thousand Days (1899–1902) in Colombia was the forerunner of the violent insurrections in Cuba, Mexico, and Nicaragua. The Mexican Revolution, a savage war raging for nearly two decades, was the most brutal and destructive of all.

The best introduction to the Mexican Revolution is this chapter on uprisings in Cuba. Striking parallels between Cuba and Mexico suggest ways the events might have proceeded differently in either country. Had the Mexican government drawn the correct lessons from the August 1906 revolt in Cuba, it might have been able to prevent the outbreak of the devastating and inhumane Mexican Revolution. The fruitful comparisons between the two countries apply also to the period after the Mexican Revolution and help to explain why the Cuban government remained vulnerable to a revolutionary upheaval after 1941. In the 1920s Mexico created an army capable of savagely crushing any renewed outbreaks of violence in the

rural hinterland, but Cuba failed to create a similar force to keep the rural interior under submission. Because Cuba did not learn the lessons from the Mexican Revolution, an armed revolt capable of overthrowing the government remained a possibility in the island. Yet surprisingly, it was the insurrection in Nicaragua (chapter 11) that provided a bridge between the Mexican Revolution of 1910–1929 and the Cuban Revolution of the late 1950s.

The First U.S. Occupation of Cuba (1898–1902)

Unlike the rest of the Latin American countries, 1899 found Cuba under U.S. occupation. After the defeat of Spain in 1898, the United States acquired Puerto Rico and Cuba in the Caribbean, and Guam and the Philippines in the Pacific Ocean. The acquisition of these island territories was an unexpected outcome of the Spanish-American War of 1898. The United States was not sure what to do about its new possessions, indeed the strong opposition to this new empire could easily become a powerful political force in U.S. domestic politics. Few doubts existed about the future of Cuba, because the primary reason for the war of 1898 had been to obtain the independence of Cuba from Spain. For its other island possessions considerable freedom and leisure existed to organize a colonial government, but for Cuba the United States felt obligated to re-place the military authorities with a new republic in a few years.

Part of the haste to withdraw was fear of rebellion similar to the Filipino Insurrection. The outbreak of a savage and bloody guerrilla war in the Philippines in February 1899 made U.S. officials determined to prevent a similar insurrection in the island. Cuban rebels had fought a quarter of a million Spanish soldiers to a standstill from 1895 to 1898, and the United States had to diffuse a potentially explosive situation. As a first inducement to disband, the military government offered free rations to the starving rebels but only if they abandoned their units. The military authorities also gave each of the 50,000 rebels $75 as muster-out pay. The sum was considerable for the time, but for destitute veterans lacking everything for their families, it could only go so far. U.S. officials placed veterans in the bureaucracy and also provided many temporary opportunities for employment in the public works program the military government undertook. In general, U.S. officials hoped that the reconstruction of the economy would provide many employment opportunities. For those unable to find jobs, President William McKinley and most U.S. officials assumed that the creation of a Cuban army was necessary to employ 10,000 Cuban veterans. To everyone's surprise, the demobilization of the Cuban rebels proceeded very smoothly, because they were essentially exhausted civilians who were most eager to return to their families. Consequently, U.S. officials postponed any plans to establish an army until the exact nature of Cuban independence became clear. In reality, economic reconstruction was what Cuba desperately needed the most.[2]

Unlike in the Philippines, in Cuba the population received U.S. rule well, always, however, on the understanding that full independence was coming in a timely manner. In spite of the highly successful disbandment of the rebels, the United States did not reverse the previous decision to cut short its military occupation of Cuba. The insistence on a precipitate withdrawal was unfortunate for both countries. Of all the island possessions, Cuba was the closest and the most valuable for the United States. The U.S. Navy had long envied the strategic position of Havana as a site for a

large base, while the fertile fields of Cuba already attracted the largest amount of U.S. investment in Latin America. The United States purchased most of the sugar exports of the island and also supplied most of Cuba's imports.

The island suffered massive destruction during its war for independence from Spain in 1895–1898. At least 200,000 died during the revolt and the population declined by nearly 20 percent. Livestock suffered a catastrophic decline, dropping from 3 million animals to 200,000. In 1898 almost all the roads, bridges, and buildings in the countryside were no longer standing. The U.S. Army received a ruined and devastated country in 1898 and by 1902 transformed the island into a prosperous and safe place. A large part of the credit for what was the most successful U.S. military occupation in Latin America goes to the governor, the extremely capable General Leonard Wood, a future chief of staff of the U.S. Army. Impressive as was the economic reconstruction of Cuba, the political transformation of a society steeped in authoritarian traditions required more than a couple of years. All the U.S. Army officers clamored for more time to complete their work, but Washington was insistent on ending the occupation. President Theodore Roosevelt, already preparing for his reelection in November 1902, wanted to turn the island over to the Cubans before the military occupation became an issue in the presidential campaign. However, the rapidly growing private U.S. investment meant that the United States no longer could ignore any collapse of the soon to be inaugurated Cuban Republic.[3]

To preserve order in the island once the military occupation ended, Washington imposed two obligations on the island. The most famous was the Platt Amendment, a law passed by the U.S. Congress in 1901. The crucial clause of the Platt Amendment gave the United States the right to intervene in Cuba to maintain order and to protect property. Several other clauses guaranteed U.S. strategic interests: The United States could buy or lease naval bases anywhere in the island and also retained a claim on the large Isle of Pines south of Cuba. To forestall any intervention over defaulted foreign loans, another clause gave the United States the power to supervise finances and specifically to approve any foreign borrowing. The underlying assumption in the Platt

Amendment was that if the Cuban government maintained internal order and managed its finances wisely, the United States would not have to intervene militarily again. Thus the virtual protectorate was more an insurance policy than a program for intervention: Only if something went terribly wrong would the United States recur to its right to land troops. Implicit in the clauses was a U.S. guarantee to protect Cuba from foreign invasion. In effect, the Platt Amendment also doubled as a defense treaty between the United States and Cuba. The United States largely assumed the burden of defending Cuba and thus liberated its government from having to maintain large military forces.

Without the heavy cost of an army, the Cuban government was free to channel its customs duties (its main source of revenue) into the improvement of the economy and the betterment of the society. But how was Cuba to preserve internal order? Very early in the military occupation the U.S. governor wisely decided not to have U.S. soldiers in daily contact with the civilian population. Cuban city policemen preserved law and order in the urban centers. The city police likewise patrolled the rural areas because in accordance with the Spanish laws, the 132 municipalities then existing (corresponding to counties in the United States) had jurisdiction over the surrounding countryside. Over two-thirds of the population in this agrarian society lived in the countryside, so the responsibility upon the urban police was immense. Not surprisingly, around 100 municipalities could not police their rural areas effectively. Some lacked the funds and others the population, while in the eastern provinces the municipalities covered vast areas. Already under Spanish colonial rule lawlessness in the rural areas was excessive, and to try to fill the void the Spanish government established the *Cuerpo de Guardias Rurales* in 1889 to police the countryside. After the end of Spanish rule, the full burden of policing the countryside fell to the municipalities.[4]

All but one of the U.S. military governors of the provinces adopted the policy of increasing and strengthening the municipal police as the best way to maintain law and order in both rural and urban areas. The one exception was General Leonard Wood, who as governor of Oriente Province created the first rural guard

General Leonard Wood. As military governor of Cuba (1899–1902), this dynamic individual conducted one of the most successful U.S. occupations (Library of Congress, Prints and Photographs Division).

force independent of the municipalities and reporting directly to him in late 1898. Because Oriente was the most isolated and turbulent of the provinces, this extraordinary measure seemed justified by the extreme regional conditions. In addition, he felt the need for an agency reporting directly to him to speed up the social and political transformation of Cuba. But when he became governor of the entire island in 1899, in a fateful decision for Cuban history, he pushed for the creation of a national rural guard for the entire island. He found the existing channels inadequate to Americanize Cuban political life and institutions. As an efficient and non-partisan body, he saw this new rural guard as performing the invaluable function of bringing the Cuban countryside into the twentieth century. Significantly enough, the rural guard Wood envisoned was not an import or a direct copy from the United States, because nothing similar existed back home. Instead, he inspired himself in the tradition of the earlier Spanish body and in particular he drew extensively from the *rurales* in Mexico; the reality that those two organizations were integral parts of highly authoritarian regimes did not bother Wood.[5]

Other U.S. Army officers and civilians in Washington were not convinced of the wisdom of the proposal and pointed out the dangers a national police force could pose to the political stability of the country and the freedoms of its citizens. By keeping the proposed rural guard limited to only 1,250 men, Wood expected to eliminate any danger of militarism and coup d'états. The completion of the first railroad network linking all the main urban centers in any Latin American country influenced Wood's belief that the small number of men was more than adequate: Havana could swiftly rush reinforcements to crush a revolt at its outbreak. Wood also counted on having U.S. troops stay behind in Cuba for many years as a final defense. Because his proposal was a substitute for the creation of a local army, momentum for his idea grew. With the impending proclamation of the Cuban Republic fast approaching, the need to leave some national military force became urgent, and Washington duly authorized Wood to issue a decree creating the Rural Guard on 10 April 1901. U.S. officers carefully selected the best men from the roughly 50,000 Cuban veterans and trained them intensively. Observers were impressed at how well the small force of only 1,250 officers and men was fulfilling its duty of maintaining law and order throughout the countryside. In reality, Wood knew that the simultaneous presence of U.S. Army units barracked in the cities served as the ultimate shield for the military government. He expected the republican government to enjoy the same benefit, and he planned on leaving three army regiments behind. Unfortunately, Washington did not find attractive his plan to station U.S. regiments in Cuba for an indefinite number of years. The full burden of preserving internal order fell on the diminutive Rural Guard, and all that Wood could do was appoint General Alejandro Rodríguez as its first commander in April 1902.[6]

In a lesson from the Spanish-American War of 1898, U.S. military officers insisted on stationing U.S. artillerymen in Cuba after independence. In perhaps the only Spanish success of the entire war of 1898, fire from coastal artillery had prevented the U.S. Navy from im-

posing a tight blockade on Havana. The terms of the Treaty of Paris ending the war of 1898 required Spain to leave behind all its shore batteries. Although the United States retained the responsibility to defend Cuba, U.S. officials feared that a foreign power could shell Havana with impunity. To gain enough time for a U.S. fleet to arrive, Cuba had to maintain respectable coastal batteries. Consequently, when Cuba formally became independent on 20 May 1902, the withdrawal of U.S. troops did not include the coastal artillery unit. The U.S. artillerymen were supposed to stay until Cubans completed a technical training lasting for years.[7]

The United States committed three major mistakes during its occupation of the island. The greatest blunder was ending the occupation prematurely. U.S. officials had too little time to prepare the Cubans for self-rule. The election of municipal officials in 1901, the election of legislative bodies in 1902, and the election of a president in 1903 seemed the fastest possible schedule to make a smooth transition from military government to a democratic republic. Inauguration of the republic in 1904 or better in 1905, were the earliest reasonable dates. A longer occupation would have increased the flow of capital into Cuba and thus generated more employment. As prosperity and wealth increased, the likelihood of discontent and armed uprising would decline.[8] Secondly, the United States rushed the withdrawal of all its troops. U.S. units had been unobtrusive, their spending helped the local economy, and the Americans enjoyed considerable popularity among the local population.[9] A long and gradual withdrawal of the units throughout the decade certainly would have bolstered the position of any Cuban government. Lastly, the United States needed to leave behind a force adequate to preserve order, but as mentioned earlier, the 1,250-man Rural Guard was woefully insufficient to fill the void left by the departing U.S. troops. In a self-fulfilling prophesy, U.S. Army officers confidently predicted the return of U.S. troops to the island. Some Cubans shared the same view. General Rodríguez told Governor Wood when embarking on his voyage home "that if anything happened to bring us (the Americans) back, he and the Rural Guard would always be loyal to the Government which had done so much for Cuba."[10]

The August 1906 Revolt and the Second U.S. Occupation (1906–1909)

The U.S. government gave the highest priority to negotiating a trade agreement with Cuba even before the inauguration of the Cuban Republic on 20 May 1902. Cuba likewise wanted an agreement but ultimately realized that the proposed terms were too favorable to the United States. In exchange for a 20 percent tariff reduction on imported sugar, Cuba basically sacrificed the rest of its economy to U.S. exports. The first president of Cuba, Tomás Estrada Palma (henceforth Don Tomás) felt that this was the best deal Cuba could get, and in December 1902 he signed the Reciprocity Treaty. In reality, Don Tomás wanted to do everything possible to strengthen Cuban links with the United States. He had been a teacher in New York and was a naturalized U.S. citizen; he had never hidden his sympathies for annexation to the United States as the best long-term solution for Cuba. Although the Reciprocity Treaty was essential to guarantee the profits of U.S. investors in Cuba, surprisingly strong opposition erupted in the U.S. Senate. Not until one year later, after President Theodore Roosevelt invested major political capital, did the U.S. Congress in a special session finally ratify the Reciprocity Treaty in December 1903. This arduous struggle assured that no U.S. administration would want to reopen the thorny issue of relations with Cuba in a long time.[11] The Reciprocity Treaty, the Platt Amendment, and the Rural Guard emerged as the three pillars of U.S. relations with Cuba.

Many Cubans still resented the imposition of the Platt Amendment and decided to take out their frustration on the easily visible U.S. artillery unit in Havana. Already in the summer of 1902 the Cuban Congress asked Don Tomás to hasten the training of Cuban soldiers so that the last U.S. troops could leave the island. For a few months politicians gained popularity by playing this issue to the maximum, and in a vain attempt to placate the political opposition, Don Tomás unwisely caved in. The U.S. Army had already imposed the rule that only whites could serve as officers, but the organization of this unit, the most intellectually demanding branch of the army, had barely

started when the U.S. artillerymen departed in early February 1904. Sensing the historical significance of the withdrawal for Cuba but not for his regime, Don Tomás and his cabinet attended a military review for the departing troops. In a very emotional speech he expressed his deepest appreciation for all the United States had done for the independence of Cuba.[12] Once the last U.S. troops withdrew, the defense of his regime depended exclusively on the Cuban artillery unit and the diminutive Rural Guard.

Don Tomás believed that an honest administration and economic prosperity were all that his presidency needed to keep the support of the Cuban people. He plunged tirelessly into administrative details and strove to continue the work so well begun by General Leonard Wood. He believed that the financial solvency of the Cuban Republic was the best guarantee for prosperity. He was parsimonious with the budget and routinely reduced the sums allocated to specific expenditures. In one very dangerous decision, he reduced the bonus the veterans wanted as compensation for their services during the war of independence, because he felt the treasury could not afford to borrow so much to pay the veterans. His pessimistic calculations proved wrong, and as the foreign trade of Cuba grew by leaps, its customs revenue, the main source of income for governments before the introduction of income taxes in the 1930s, grew dramatically. Soon the Cuban treasury was awash with funds, and the government generated surpluses year after year. But Don Tomás did not waver on his practice of relentlessly reducing costs, and he refused to consider another bonus payment to the veterans (as eventually happened in the next decade). Under immense pressure to provide government jobs, only grudgingly did he allow the payroll to expand slightly. His presidency gained the well-deserved title of being the least corrupt of the first Cuban Republic (1902–1958), and he himself was the only president to have died in poverty.[13]

Afraid of doing anything to strengthen the militaristic tendencies he saw rampant in Cuba, he always opposed the creation of an army. The Rural Guard was manifestly inadequate to perform routine police duties in the countryside, and in response to intense pressure from the sugar planters who demanded protection for their properties, he most reluctantly consented to increase the Rural Guard to the still vastly inadequate number of 3,000 men in 1905. General Rodríguez, its commander, pleaded constantly for additional increases for the Rural Guard but to no avail.[14] Instead, the only area Don Tomás singled out for large annual increases in expenditures was education. As a former teacher, he had huge faith in the transformative powers of education, and with tremendous pleasure he enthusiastically expanded the public education system General Wood had established. In one of the most eloquent restatements of the saying "the pen is mightier than the sword" Don Tomás explained that he wanted "more teachers than soldiers."[15]

The very success of his presidency convinced Don Tomás to run for reelection in 1905 against the Liberal party. His supporters were desperate to save their jobs and committed considerable fraud to guarantee his victory at the presidential elections on 1 December 1905. The outraged opposition party demanded a second election, but the Liberals exhausted their legal appeals and could not stop the second inauguration of Don Tomás on 20 May 1906. Seeing themselves shut out of the public payroll, the angry Liberals started to organize a revolt under their leader José Miguel Gómez. The Liberals were so sure of winning any fair election held under U.S. supervision, that fear of a second U.S. occupation did not deter them. A revolt was not a far-fetched idea, because the Liberals, unlike Don Tomás, realized that the country was seething with discontent. Not all Cuban veterans shared in the prosperity of the island, indeed many were losing their lands to encroaching U.S. corporations. Foreign managers and Spanish immigrants took the best jobs and left many veterans unemployed and often poverty-stricken on the island. As word of the bulging surpluses in the treasury spread, the images of booty to distribute reappeared in the manner of the nineteenth-century revolts in the Spanish-American republics. Early in 1906 some isolated incidents occurred, but the seasonal employment of the sugar cane harvest kept the rural population too busy to participate in a revolt. As the cane harvest ended by July and released large numbers of persons into the ranks of the unemployed, the allure of rebellion was fast becoming irresistible. Belatedly

Don Tomás announced a public works program, but in his obsession to preserve the budget surpluses, he made sure the funds were too little and came too late to make any major impact on the island's unemployment.[16]

Liberal leaders concluded that this was the moment to act, and they hatched a conspiracy to seize the police stations in Havana and to take prisoner Don Tomás. The supposedly secret plot was the talk of cafés in Havana by 1 August, but curiously enough Don Tomás refused to take any precautions. At least six months earlier he had learned that the Liberals intended to revolt if they did not win the elections, but he did not take their threats seriously. Don Tomás still had time to increase the Rural Guard, and certainly an immediate doubling or better a tripling of the 3,000–man force would have deterred any rebels. The recruitment of additional rural guards also necessarily depleted the ranks of the disgruntled. Between accepting immediate employment from a legally constituted government and believing in promises of future jobs after a revolt, most would take the concrete offer.[17]

One Liberal congressman and veteran, Faustino "Pino" Guerra, could not wait any longer, and with several hundred followers he raised the banner of rebellion on 16 August 1906 in Pinar del Rio, the province to the west of Havana (Map 10). Veterans flocked to his banner, and soon "Pino" Guerra was leading two thousand rebels. In Havana Province at least 8,000 rebels were roaming the fields, and in Las Villas Province a comparable number was threatening the cities. The veterans had kept spare weapons after turning in arms to the U.S. military government in 1899, so most of the over 15,000 rebels were armed, although some had only machetes. The spontaneous turnout surprised even the Liberal leaders.[18] Once the people perceived that the government was weak, volunteers rushed forward to join the winners, as Pino Guerra revealed:

> The secret of revolutions is the fact that there has not been an effective army. A small band would go out to say in Santiago, for instance, strike a few effective blows, and as the government had no efficient force to turn against it, the people began to believe that the victory was on the side of the insurgents, whose number gradually increased until there was a large revolutionary army, when if in the begin-

ning a sufficient force could have been turned against it the revolution would not have lasted 48 hours. I say that if the government has well organized troops and if a revolution is immediately opposed by them, it will not receive converts, but if it is permitted to grow, it will soon have thousands of adherents.[19]

Cuba failed to learn this lesson, but perhaps neighboring Mexico would learn from the August revolt and take precautions in time to prevent a similar upheaval against the regime of Porfirio Díaz. In Cuba, Don Tomás with only 600 artillerymen in Havana and 3000 rural guards scattered in 244 posts each of usually only 12 men could do little against the massive uprising. Because the city police in Havana openly sympathized with the Liberals, the capital would have immediately fallen to the rebels if the artillerymen had not taken defensive positions in the suburbs. The defection of the Havana police thus destroyed any chance that the artillerymen, the only trained and disciplined military force in the island, could sally forth to strike blows against the spreading rebellion. Don Tomás still did not realize how serious the threat was, and instead of doubling or tripling the strength of the Rural Guard, he authorized the hiring of only an additional 2,000 men. Finding these men would have been easy a few months earlier when many applicants struggled to land any position in the Rural Guard, but by this moment a remarkable reversal had taken place. The political stock of the government had declined so drastically that not enough persons were willing to enlist for the full 4-year enlistment period. As a desperate alternative, the government created on 25 August a militia for 90-day volunteers. Because public opinion sensed that victory was on the side of the rebels, volunteers were slow to join the militia but fast to disappear and to desert. Because the Cubans lacked expertise in handling the few Colt machine guns in the arsenals, the government created a foreign legion comprised of Americans, Germans, and Englishmen to handle these new weapons.[20]

In spite of the overwhelming numerical preponderance of the rebels, the Rural Guard did not collapse or surrender. The detachments fought off attacks, and when later regrouped into larger units, the Rural Guard pursued the rebels vigorously. In late August Rural Guards tracked down and killed Quintín Banderas, the most prestigious black veteran leader. His death left a leadership vacuum that had fatal consequences for the black community as the next section will show. In spite of occasional government successes in skirmishes, rebel forces roamed at will through the western half of Cuba and could at any time destroy valuable private property including U.S. investments. Initially the rebels had limited their actions to demanding food for themselves and forage for their horses but they made no secret of their intention to burn cane fields and ravage private property if Don Tomás did not step down.[21]

Only a smashing victory by the Rural Guard could stop the downward spiral of the government. On 8 September 1906 Pino

Map 10. Cuba

Guerra ambushed the armored train carrying the foreign legion near Consolación del Sur but obviously could not overcome the intense fire from its machine guns. The armored train had come from Havana to reinforce Rural Guard Colonel Avalao Acosta, who hearing of the ambush, came to attack the rebels from the rear. The opportunity to trap and to destroy the rebels could have saved the government from falling, and the clash at Consolación del Sur foreshadowed the later battle of Casas Grandes in Mexico in March 1911. The government forces failed to take advantage of this last opportunity to shatter the aura of invincibility surrounding the rebels, just as would later happen in Mexico. The Rural Guard did not press the attack vigorously at Consolación del Sur and merely relieved the surrounded train. Guerra withdrew in good order and soon was in nearby towns bragging about how his men had resisted the firepower of the machine guns.[22]

The return to Havana of the armored train riddled with bullet holes only served to demoralize Don Tomás who concluded that his government could not put down the revolt. That same 8 September at the request of Don Tomás the U.S. Consul-General Frank M. Steinhart (the U.S. minister had the misfortune to be on vacation in Europe) telegraphed President Theodore Roosevelt requesting the dispatch of two warships as a show of force. Don Tomás said that after the ships arrived, he would ask the Cuban congress to invite U.S. forces to restore order in Cuba.[23] Up to this moment the United States had remained aloof as the political crisis evolved into a revolt, but this urgent request ended all passivity. President Roosevelt, then vacationing at Oyster Bay was outraged: "I am so angry with that infernal little Cuban republic that I would like to wipe its people off the face of the earth."[24] Not the revolt itself but what he considered the arrogant attempt of the Cubans to manipulate the United States made Roosevelt furiously angry. In effect, he refused to accept that Cuba had cornered a powerful country like the United States into having either to support Don Tomás or to start a second military occupation. Because Roosevelt refused to occupy Cuba, for the moment the only option was to support Don Tomás. The United States already sent 10,000 rifles and five million rifle cartridges to

Cuba on August 25, and by this support Roosevelt hoped to gain enough time to find a third option, when in reality no other choices existed. Don Tomás knew that only the landing of U.S. forces could save his government because the Liberals, who were most eager to have the Americans run new elections, had no intention of fighting against the Americans. This was what happened in Cienfuegos, where as soon as the U.S. Navy commander on his own initiative landed armed sailors, the Liberals promptly consorted with U.S. troops and the revolt was over in that city.[25]

The same outcome as in Cienfuegos was starting to appear in Havana. When on September 12 the U.S. Navy commander posted armed sailors to defend the presidential palace, the political stock of Don Tomás soared, only to collapse hopelessly the next day when a direct order from President Roosevelt ordered the embarkation of the sailors. A similar order would have gone out to Cienfuegos if Roosevelt had known about the landing of sailors in that port. The swift withdrawal plunged Don Tomás into a melancholy gloom, and he felt betrayed; why had Roosevelt abandoned this close American friend?[26] Essentially because Roosevelt did not want to pick one of the only two choices Cuba had imposed on him, and instead he insisted on a third choice. In the face of all contrary evidence, the United States wanted to mediate an agreement between the warring factions as a way of avoiding the unpalatable decision of having to support one side over the other. A stubborn Roosevelt sent Secretary of War William H. Taft and Assistant Secretary of State Bacon to Havana to negotiate a peaceful solution to the Liberal revolt. Both sides wanted to make the best possible impression on the Americans, and cheering Cubans greeted the negotiators when they disembarked with cries of "Viva Taft y Bah-con … Viva Mis'tah Roo-velt" on 19 September.[27] The enthusiasm was genuine, and both sides announced the suspension of all military operations as another sign of good faith. The Peace Mission seemed to have begun on a hopeful note, but as many accounts have narrated in great detail, the envoys were trying to do the impossible.

The amiable and talkative Taft immersed himself with gusto into his tropical task, and he too shared the American belief in the possibility of finding a compromise or a common middle ground. After many rounds of talks and intense negotiations with both sides, the same two options resurfaced. The only revelation was that Don Tomás had agreed to the mediation believing that the Americans needed to make an appearance of impartiality before formally backing him. At an angry meeting on 24 September, Cuban officials put aside their usual politeness and bluntly said that if they had known the Americans intended only to mediate, they would not have invited them at all. Don Tomás sensed that the Americans did not want to make the inevitable decision, so in a final favor to the United States, he made the decision for Roosevelt. Don Tomás explained to the Americans there was nothing left for him to do but to resign and to leave all the responsibility for maintaining order and protecting property in the hands of the United States. Not even this last threat to resign could budge the U.S. officials, so Don Tomás formally sent his resignation to the Cuban congress on 28 September. The Cuban congress could have picked a replacement, but it too decided to dissolve. The Cuban government had disappeared, and Secretary Taft, in consultation with President Roosevelt, had no choice but to proclaim the establishment of a U.S. occupation on 29 September 1906.[28] The prophets of doom during the first military occupation had been right, and U.S. troops returned to Cuba just four years after they had left. Would the second U.S. military occupation be the last one in Cuba's history?

The Creation of the Cuban Army and the Race War of 1912

The need to return to Cuba so soon after the United States had departed revealed that the Platt Amendment, the Reciprocity Treaty, and the Rural Guard, the three pillars of U.S. relations with Cuba, were not working adequately. Unfortunately, U.S. domestic political pressures prevented creating a whole new structure for relations with Cuba. U.S. policy makers were free to reshape only the vastly undermanned Rural Guard. In December 1906 a specially convened U.S. Army board searched for a solution and recommended an increase of the Rural Guard to 10,000 men. Nobody

Cuban president Tomás Estrada Palma, who despite hard work and selfless dedication proved unable to prevent the outbreak of the August 1906 revolt in Cuba (Library of Congress, Prints and Photographs Division).

doubted the need for more manpower, but the Liberal Party and notable Cuban personalities totally disagreed with the recommendation to enlarge the Rural Guard. Instead, they proposed that the entire increase go into the many municipal police forces then numbering just 2,332 men. With a prophetic glimpse into the future of the island, these persons wanted to avoid the creation "of a large armed body available for enforcement of the desires of a single individual."[29] Instead, with the police power distributed over many municipalities, no chance of a military coup existed, because the city mayors and the police chiefs could not coordinate themselves to overthrow the government. By keeping the police close to the people, the diffusion of power would give democratic practices a chance to spread in the island. Even though increasing the municipal police forces resembled the structure existing in the United States, between support for democracy and the protection of U.S. property, U.S. officials did not even consider the proposal to strengthen the municipal police worthy of attention. Perhaps the thought of having to negotiate with many mayors seemed forbidding to U.S.

officials, but whatever the exact reasons, Washington was determined to impose a centralized government in Cuba as the best way to obtain compliance with U.S. requests to protect private investment.

Critics often blame the United States for trying to impose mechanically on occupied countries formulas from back home; in the case of Cuba, the U.S. officials studiously avoided copying domestic law-enforcement practices. So when in February 1907 President Theodore Roosevelt ordered the increase of the Rural Guard to 10,000 men, it was perfectly clear that the United States was shaping a particular institution suitable for its informal empire in the Caribbean. However, the Cubans were not completely helpless victims, and the August 1906 rebellion if anything kept alive the fears of another Filipino insurrection in Cuba. Havana newspapers raised an angry howl when the order to increase the Rural Guard reached Cuba. The Liberals who had led the revolt of August 1906 profoundly distrusted the Rural Guard because it had stayed loyal to Don Tomás until the end. U.S. authorities retained General Alejandro Rodríguez as the commander of the Rural Guard, but because he had been so close to Don Tomás, the Liberals feared that any enlargement of the Rural Guard threatened their political prospects. Because Washington rejected the proposal to increase the municipal police forces, the astute Liberals knew that besides making lots of protest, they needed to come up quickly with an alternative hopefully acceptable to the United States. In a remarkable turnaround, Liberal leaders like José Miguel Gómez came up with the proposal to create a Cuban army.[30]

This new proposal unleashed an outcry in Havana. U.S. officers strongly opposed a Cuban army: "An army dominated by politics is ruined. In proportion to its freedom from interference by politicians is its proficiency proclaimed. History repeats itself from Rome to South America and the use of politics has ruined every army, every military force, with which it has been connected."[31] The new party line for the Liberals was the demand for an army, and the issue became so red-hot that Secretary of War William H. Taft himself returned to Havana in April 1907 to try to find a solution. Once back in the United States, Taft hammered out a compromise formula with President Roosevelt. For both men the immediate concern of preventing another U.S. occupation outweighed the long-term fears about army involvement in domestic politics. The United States authorized the increase of the Rural Guard by 700 men but more significantly also created a separate Cuban army on 4 April 1908. As recruitment and training progressed, the plan called for the two forces to rise eventually to a combined strength of 12,500 men, a number U.S. Army officers considered adequate to halt any partisan revolt. The main function of the slightly enlarged Rural Guard was to patrol the countryside on horseback much more thoroughly than it had been able to do in August 1906. A process of reducing the outposts from the excessive number of 244 made possible concentrating large numbers of rural guards to face any threat of rebellion. If the Rural Guard failed to deter an insurrection, the army stood ready as a reserve force to defend the cities and to sally out to crush any revolt. U.S. officials were confident that this strategic deployment at last guaranteed that no partisan revolt could ever again overthrow a Cuban government. What Washington did not want to realize was that the dangerous creature Leonard Wood had created in 1899 was beginning its transformation into a monster.[32]

The hope remained that by having two armed bodies in the island, each would serve as a check on the political ambitions of the other. To try to minimize the political role of these bodies at least in the beginning, Cuban leaders agreed to have the U.S. provisional governor, Charles Magoon, appoint the first chiefs of the two bodies. General Alejandro Rodríguez had continued to serve as head of the Rural Guard during the U.S. occupation, but his past links with Don Tomás made him unacceptable to the Liberals. Magoon retired Rodríguez with every possible honor and replaced him with General José de Jesús Monteagudo, one of the Liberal leaders of the August 1906 revolt. Magoon ratified "Pino" Guerra, the most famous Liberal rebel of the August 1906 revolt, as the head of the new Cuban army.[33] The presence of this Liberal General was expected to inspire fear: "This puts an end to insurrections; nobody will want 'Pino' to go after them; he would not bring in prisoners."[34]

President José Miguel Gómez and Vicepresident Alfredo Zayas took office on 28 January 1909. Although Governor Magoon stepped down that same day, by mutual agreement the last U.S. troops did not leave Havana until 31 March.[35] The U.S. government felt confident that this had been the last military occupation, but some high officials were more pessimistic: "The United States will have to go back. It is only a question of time."[36] The fears were not groundless, and almost immediately any hope of keeping the new army out of politics evaporated. Less than a week after Governor Magoon handed power over, the Liberals began purging the Rural Guard of any persons suspected of ties to Don Tomás. The Liberals began to fight among themselves over patronage and split into pro–Gomez and pro–Zayas factions. General Monteagudo, the chief of the Rural Guard, was pro–Gomez, while General Guerra, the head of the army, was pro–Zayas. The split widened and became so nasty that by 1910, General Guerra "has on several occasions, more or less openly, ridiculed President Gómez."[37] As both sides jockeyed for power, rumors began to circulate that General Guerra was plotting a coup to force Gómez resign and thus give the office to Zayas, the vice-president.

In a power play, the Zayas faction on 27 June 1910 obtained unanimous passage from the Cuban Senate of a bill to place the Rural Guard under the army. The Cuban lower House was expected to approve the bill that would essentially put all the armed forces of Cuba under the pro–Zayas General Guerra. Politically too weak to stop the bill by himself, President Gómez appealed to the United States for support. The State Department heeded the call and concluded "that for President Gómez to allow army bill to become law would be dangerous, under present circumstances, to the continued peace and order of Cuba."[38] The U.S. Minister in Havana promptly visited the speaker of the Cuban House of Representatives and persuaded him to oppose the bill.[39]

Prompt U.S. pressure kept the Rural Guard and the Cuban army separate, but the success was more apparent than real, because Cuban politicians had actually manipulated the United States in this complex power play. By blocking the bill, the United States gave President Gómez time to consolidate his political position among Liberals. Equally important, he had most army units report directly to him, thus bypassing General Guerra who became

little more than a figurehead. Then Gómez brought intense pressure upon General Guerra to resign, which may have included an assassination attempt on 22 October 1910. Finally in December 1910 General Guerra resigned as head of the army.[40]

President Gómez gained full control over the army and the Rural Guard, but rather than keeping the two under separate commanders, on 11 February 1911 he placed both under the command of his trusted supporter General Monteagudo. Henceforth the army and the Rural Guard were separate branches of what was called the Armed Forces of Cuba, which later in the year also included a small navy. Such a momentous change seemed to clamor for congressional debate, but Gómez claimed that in accordance with the precedent of Governor Magoon, executive decrees sufficed to carry out the consolidation.[41] The legal interpretation was questionable, but by presenting a fait accompli, he faced only symbolic protests rather than a bruising congressional fight. Much more troubling was any possible reaction from the U.S. government which so far came off appearing as easily manipulated if not foolish. Would the United States insist on keeping the two forces separate or would it accept this reversal of policy? Any chance of controlling the political involvement of the officers depended on keeping the Rural Guard and the army as independent bodies, but once they were under the same commander, the new Armed Forces of Cuba became the real source of power. Neither the U.S. minister in Havana nor the State Department officials relished a fight, and tacitly they acquiesced in the unilateral Cuban modification of the structure of the armed forces. The transformation of Wood's innocuous Rural Guard into a harmful Praetorian Guard was nearing completion.

President Gómez spent lavishly on the army, which soon was at full strength and boasted the latest weapons. "Gómez was resolved that nobody should do to him what he himself had done to Estrada Palma."[42] Wisely he requested the presence of his friend Captain Frank Parker as the advisor to the Rural Guard. Captain Parker repaired the damage from the purge of 1909 by training and shaping the cavalry units of the Rural Guard into a battle-ready force. Once the men completed their practice, they were assigned to the many outposts throughout the island. The Army initially stayed entirely in Havana to defend the capital from any likely rebel attack. Although later the government posted garrisons in the five other provincial capitals, the bulk of the army remained in Havana closely enmeshed in the intense political life of the island.[43] As his presidential term was nearing its end, the possibility of his reelection in 1912 became the dominant concern. Just like in 1906 with Don Tomás, the efforts of President Gómez to position himself for reelection triggered a revolt but of an altogether different stripe. With the Liberal party split into two hostile factions, President Gómez could not defeat the Conservatives unless he first found allies who could deliver or steal votes for him.

Examining the political landscape, President Gomez could find as possible allies only the black leaders Evaristo Estenoz and Pedro Ivonnet of the Partido Independiente de Color. Turning to these two was a very dangerous and possibly ineffective move, because in the past they seemed to have lacked any large following among black Cubans. By attempting to form a political alliance with these black leaders, President Gómez, who had already shown considerable incompetence, started rolling the chain of events that eventually culminated in the Race War of 1912. As so often happens with revolts, the Race War of 1912 was the result of miscalculations by mediocre politicians. Full responsibility for the start of the war rested equally with President Gómez, Estenoz and Ivonnet. All were inept politicians ambitious for power. In exchange for supporting Gómez in his reelection bid, Estenoz and Ivonnet wanted more patronage jobs for blacks and the repeal of the Morúa Law passed two years earlier. In February 1910 the Cuban Congress had adopted the Morúa Law prohibiting any political parties or movements based on race or color. Estenoz and Ivonnet seized upon the repeal of the Morúa Law as the issue most likely to mobilize black support behind them. The author of the Morúa Law had been Martín Morúa Delgado, then the most prominent black personality in the island. His sudden death in April 1910 left a leadership vacuum the new black leaders aspired to fill.[44]

In a meeting in February 1912, President Gómez told Estenoz that if the Partido Independiente de Color dropped the "*de color*" or "of color" from its title, he could welcome them as political allies but if not, "he would put every possible obstacle in their way."[45] A defiant Estenoz boasted to the press "that the Colored Party was all-powerful and that no political party could hope to win at the polls without its help."[46] The open challenge by Estenoz later led to his arrest and to prohibitions on the activities of the Partido Independiente de Color. The matter did not end there, because the temptation of black votes was irresistible. President Gómez released Estenoz from jail in March 1912 and agreed to obtain the repeal of the Morúa Law on the condition that the party support him in the elections. Gómez had called the bluff of the black leaders who had to deliver their part of the bargain with the president. Unfortunately for them, the majority of blacks did not support the Partido Independiente de Color, which had done very poorly in the polls and at times had not even received enough signatures to be placed on the ballot. Estenoz was playing the dangerous game of offering the votes he lacked to President Gómez and in turn using promises from the president to rally black supporters. Estenoz desperately needed some dramatic event to show Cuba that he had a large following among black voters.[47]

Besides organizing large demonstrations in the cities, the two black leaders decided to stage an armed protest in the countryside. The mobilization of thousands of blacks, even if poorly armed, was bound to make the white Cubans pay close attention. The black leaders did not intend to start a real revolt and did not want to shed blood or to damage property. What they wanted was a show of strength adequate to boost the efforts of President Gómez to repeal the Morúa Law. In sincere gratefulness, blacks would enthusiastically vote for Gómez whose reelection was thus assured. No doubt exists that the black followers of Estenoz and Ivonnet believed that this was the game plan, although after the Race War President Gómez strove to destroy all evidence of his participation in this devious arrangement. In any case, to carry out such intricate maneuvering would tax the skills of even the most talented politicians, and the incompetent Gómez, Estenoz, and Ivonnet were sure to bungle the maneuver.[48]

Whatever might have been the original plot, events immediately slipped out of the control of politicians. Two unexpected responses transformed the armed protest into the Race War of 1912. The first came from the black peasants who comprised around 40 percent of the rural population in Oriente Province and who turned the armed protest into a social insurrection. Although the new economic expansion had favored urban blacks, rural blacks saw their situation steadily deteriorate as they increasingly lost their lands to U.S. corporations. When Estenoz and Ivonnet toured the island to whip up support for their armed protest, rural blacks rallied to the movement enthusiastically. Estenoz put his speaking talents to good use to galvanize the crowds he invariably attracted. The message the black leaders preached was straightforward: They wanted demonstrations in the cities and an armed protest in the countryside to occur simultaneously throughout the island on 20 May 1912. Because that date was also the holiday of Cuba's independence, the black leaders naively assumed that their protests would easily blend into the festive atmosphere of that day. The nearly public nature of the preparations meant that government officials throughout the island immediately gained a detailed knowledge of the armed protest far in advance of the 20 May target date. In the most damning evidence against President Gómez, he took no action even after receiving overwhelming and irrefutable proof of the coming armed revolt.[49] Both he and the black leaders were so blinded by political ambition that they refused to recognize a fundamental characteristic of revolts: "In Cuba, once a revolt is successfully launched, it is very hard to keep it from extending, for there are always thousands of idlers and dissatisfied 'heelers' ready to flock to the standard upon the first sign of success."[50]

The extremely enthusiastic and very numerous black participation in Oriente Province triggered a white backlash as the second unexpected response. Newspapers learned of the impending black protest and promptly labeled it a Race War before it had even started. The press began publishing highly sensational accounts designed to instill the greatest fear in whites; "Rapes" became the daily headline titles as the press affirmed the worst stereotypes of the sexually predatory black rapists. In the most extreme case, the press reported first that a young white schoolteacher had been raped,

then that she had been gang-raped and killed. The press was still not satisfied and later reported that her body had been cannibalized, a clear reference to scares in previous years about black *brujos* (warlocks) and *santería* (criminal witchcraft practices). Teachers in Cuba declared fifteen days' mourning for their desecrated colleague, only to have the supposedly cannibalized teacher write a letter denying all the reports. However, the hysteria did not die down. The steady stream of lurid accounts of rapes and destruction kept the white population terrified and fit into the larger scheme the press constructed of a struggle between civilization and barbarism[51]:

> [The black rebels] follow the natural bent of all armed people without aim and driven by atavistic, brutal instincts and passions; they devote themselves to robbery, pillage, murder, and rape. [...] And everywhere, the voice of the guns, which is the voice of civilization, answers and has to answer them. [...] Civilization is arming itself against barbarism and is getting ready to defend itself against barbarism.[52]

In such a supercharged atmosphere with passions at a fever pitch, the newspapers could not report the scheduled black protest accurately. While black leaders busied themselves organizing for the demonstrations in the city and for the armed protest in the countryside, the press reported a sinister conspiracy to seize all the Rural Guard posts on 20 May. Although President Gómez reiterated his orders to stay quiet, the effervescence over frightful rumors of massacres prompted many local officials to take action on their own. The Rural Guard and the municipal police arrested all the know leaders of the Partido Independiente de Color in the three western provinces of Pinar del Río, Havana, and Matanzas. Local officials later claimed that their timely action saved the Rural Guard posts from capture, but in reality the black leaders had never intended to take such a drastic step. In Oriente Province, where the blacks participating in the armed protest soon numbered into the thousands and where local officials had not arrested any blacks, the rebels did not attack Rural Guard posts on 20 May or in the subsequent week.[53]

Public opinion clamored for the prompt crushing of the black rebellion, and President Gómez, unlike Don Tomás in 1906, had at his disposal the new Cuban army and the crack cavalry units of the Rural Guard. Already in the night of 20 May he dispatched the first units to Oriente by train; others followed by ship and by train in the next few days. By the end of May every available soldier of the regular army and the cavalry units of the Rural Guard in Havana had left for Oriente. The transfer of troops still fit within the President's original political play, because he too needed to make a show of force in his negotiations with the black leaders. In the stereotypical Latin American pattern, the opposing forces were expected to strut in front of each other, perhaps exchange a few shots, avoid any real battle, and then resume negotiations. If no agreement was reached, then the process was repeated, and if any engagement occurred, it was suddenly broken off on the verge of victory to allow negotiations to resume. Except for some crucial exceptions, this desultory style of civil war had been the rule in the Latin American republics, but the collective frenzy among the whites was making it increasingly unlikely that President Gómez and the black leaders could choreograph this delicate minuet. Until the end of May the army and the Rural Guard merely tried to locate but did not attack the black rebels; whenever a decisive engagement appeared imminent, orders immediately came halting the attack on the rebels. For their part, the black rebels in the field in Oriente under Estenoz and Ivonnet carefully avoided contact with the government forces and refrained from attacking any towns or Rural Guard posts.[54]

Gómez and Estenoz had some final days to extricate themselves from a violent confrontation, but they had to act fast because Gómez could not detain the mounting white onslaught for much longer. Even before 20 May the outpouring of public emotion had been so great that thousands of whites were volunteering to campaign against the blacks. Gómez refused to accept the volunteers, and he claimed that with the existing forces he could settle the matter in ten days. Undaunted by the official refusal to arm the volunteers, many groups of armed whites spontaneously began to appear throughout the island and were already starting to attack the blacks in Oriente. The unanimous condemnation of the black revolt and the collective hysteria among the whites should have suggested to Estenoz and Ivonnet that

a massive and ruthless repression was fast coming.[55]

Unfortunately, the ferocious white response came too late to deter many blacks who had trusted the promises of their leaders. Had the armed protest fizzled, Estenoz and Ivonnet would have had no choice but to flee for their lives abroad. But for the first time in their political careers, thousands of blacks had heeded their call. Although the press multiplied their numbers into the tens of thousands, at the start the rebels did number at least ten thousand in Oriente. However, it was clear that the rest of the island had not rallied to the revolt and that the government was free to concentrate all its forces against the rebels in Oriente. The indications of a savage clash between the black social revolt and the white backlash movement were overwhelming, but Estenoz and Ivonnet, who at last controlled thousands of blacks, could not bring themselves to abandon their one moment of glory. When victory is impossible, the final responsibility of a commander is to save his men. With all the signs pointing to a suicidal struggle, the black leaders had the obligation to disband their followers and send them back home. Probably at least a thousand rebels realized the futility of any revolt and quietly returned home on their own, but the many who remained were more than adequate to confirm the worst white fears.[56]

What chances did the black rebels of 1912 have of repeating the earlier success of the Cuban guerrillas against Spanish troops in 1895–1898? During the war for independence from Spain small rebel bands had inflicted heavy losses on Spanish soldiers who could never trap and destroy the Cuban bands. The black rebels at first glance appeared to enjoy some of the same advantages. They were skilled veterans who knew every corner of the land; accustomed to the harsh life in the countryside they had not grown soft in the cities and could endure the hardships of a military campaign. However, almost everything else had changed. Most of the thick forest had given way to sugar cane fields. The earlier trails had become roads, and railroads also reached many previously remote places. As the population increased, new towns appeared in previously isolated areas, while new sugar mills dotted the countryside. The thick tropical forest in the flat lands, the preferred hiding place for the Cuban rebels during the war for independence, was largely gone; only in the mountainous regions of Oriente did thick woodlands still exist, but even there coffee and cacao cultivation had begun to open up previously inaccessible areas. Invisible to the rebels was the presence of the technological innovation of wireless telegraph. The wireless stations appearing throughout Oriente kept the government forces fully informed of rebel movements even if the latter destroyed telegraph wires.[57]

Not only had terrain and transportation changed to the detriment of the black revolt, but the tropical diseases that had so decimated and demoralized the Spanish troops of 1895–1898 no longer posed a major threat. Like the Cuban rebels of 1895–1898, all the government forces in 1912 were well armed with new rifles, plenty of ammunition, and machetes. Instead most black rebels lacked any weapons other than the machete, and those armed usually had worn-out rifles and were short of cartridges. The Cuban forces, unlike the Spanish army, also had machine guns, which released more soldiers to pursue the blacks because a small detachment with a machine gun sufficed to defend most towns. Also most Cuban soldiers in 1912 were either mounted or had access to horses, unlike the soldiers of the Spanish army who normally trod on foot and could not pursue the rebels vigorously. The Cuban soldiers were themselves veterans of the war of independence and knew just as well as the black rebels all the hiding places and the secret trails through what was left of their former forest haunts. The high spirits and self-motivation of the government forces in 1912 contrasted sharply with the demoralization of the Spanish conscripts often forced into battle at pistol point. Lastly, the Cuban government, unlike the Spanish government in 1895–1898, was able to eliminate the rural bases of support for the rebels. The Spanish troops had tremendous difficulty rooting out rebel sympathizers and in desperation turned to forced relocations of the entire rural population at immense human and political costs. Instead in the Race War of 1912, identification of rebel sympathizers was easy: The government forces did not waste time with interrogations and simply concluded that any black person living in the countryside was either a rebel or a rebel sympathizer.[58]

On both the white and black sides the

pressure for more extreme solutions was rapidly mounting. President Gómez wanted only the Cuban army and the Rural Guard carrying out military operations, and he refused early offers of volunteers. But the collective madness was too great to ignore, and he relented on 23 May. Many white veterans flocked to join the volunteer units departing Havana for service in Oriente. Other veterans spontaneously formed groups of volunteers in their municipalities and received over 9,000 rifles from the government. Even more ominously, many former Spanish soldiers, who had stayed in the island after independence, joined the Cuban forces out of a desire to settle old scores with at least the black rebels who had so bedeviled the Spanish Army. Whether Cuban or Spaniard, all the soldiers were skilled and battle-tested veterans of the forest war who were eager for combat and confident of victory. Any hope for negotiating a truce with the rebels was rapidly vanishing, and President Gómez could only see in the departing troops the end of his bid for re-election.[59]

The acceptance of 90-day volunteers on 23 May meant that the Cuban government was rapidly moving to a policy of repression as the only way to crush the black revolt. For their part, Estenoz and Ivonnet were fast losing any freedom to negotiate a peaceful solution, because the almost minuet-like maneuver they had envisaged was transforming itself into a peasant uprising. The hardening of positions on both sides crystallized in the last days of May. Estenoz and Ivonnet could no longer offer any hope of a negotiated solution and in desperation began to attack towns and foreign properties. The worst depredations occurred in the large valley of Guantánamo Bay. Black bands tried to destroy sugar mills, buildings, stores, and railroads, but their lack of weapons and of dynamite limited their ability to inflict major damage. The rebels began torching cane fields, the tactic most dreaded by foreign corporations. Whenever the rebels captured towns, they took out their anger at having lost their lands by burning the property registers and all records of land transactions. The black rebellion had all the characteristics of a peasant uprising, but their actions did not suggest or even imply any racial hatred. The black rebels concentrated on pillage and the destruction of property but generally left the white peasant families unmolested. A class war solely over land and property did not fit well with the journalistic prejudices, and the newspapers insisted on printing lurid accounts of a destructive black horde bent on slaughtering the whites and raping the white women. This rampage of killing and rapes was purely imaginary, but the sensationalized press accounts were enough to provoke a first wave of migration, as the frightened white population in isolated or remote areas fled to the safety of the towns and the cities.[60]

The attacks on foreign property doomed the black rebellion and hastened its end. Ever since 20 May foreign property owners had been asking for protection from the expected black disturbances, and once the attacks materialized, the foreigners demanded troop detachments from the Cuban government. Because in the first week of the revolt the little damage blacks inflicted on property mainly occurred in the valley of Guantánamo, the urgent requests of foreign companies might seem exaggerated but actually reflected the Mexican experience (see chapter 5). In Mexico, foreign investment had been somewhat complaisant if not passive about the initial outbreak of the Francisco Madero insurrection in 1910. When Mexican rebels finally appeared outside U.S. or British installations, by then it was too late to obtain any help from the collapsing government. An earlier foreign demand for protection just might have shaken the Porfirio Díaz regime out of its somnolence in time to crush the revolt, and in any case U.S. investors were not going to repeat in Cuba the mistake in Mexico. These two countries hosted the largest U.S. investment in Latin America at that time, and the U.S. investors did not want to suffer in Cuba the heavy loss they had already taken in their Mexican investments in 1910–1911. When the profits of sugar mills and the very survival of large capital investments were at stake, the leisurely pace of the random clashes of a preindustrial society became totally unacceptable. Foreign investment generated the prosperity and the revenues for the host country, but in exchange the Cuban government assumed the obligation to use its resources to crush any threats to the profits of corporations.

Cuban officials were most reluctant to garrison the foreign properties, because dribbling out units for guard duty meant repeating the mistake of the Spanish Army in 1895–1898. Only a vigorous pursuit of the black rebels could end the revolt swiftly, even if that meant leaving some properties temporarily unprotected. The Cuban government could not afford this luxury, because the Platt Amendment gave the United States the right to intervene to maintain order. Already talk of a third U.S. intervention was frequent, and some even called for the return of General Leonard Wood this time to stay for ten years until the island was at last cleaned up. The Cuban government tried to avoid an intervention by presenting excessively favorable accounts of the campaign against the black rebels. In reality the U.S. pressure was superfluous, because the collective white hysteria clamored for an immediate end to the black revolt. On 3 June President Gómez suspended constitutional guarantees and put Oriente under military rule. Feelings were running so high that the volunteer units took matters into their own hands. Many of the white volunteers had obviously come to kill blacks and turned against peaceful blacks after not finding any rebels. Sometimes the patrols fired at any approaching blacks, and in other occasions the volunteers started the practice of hanging any suspicious blacks. Lynching became so widespread that newspaper articles asked with undisguised pleasure whether "Mister Lynch" had found a home in Cuba. The worst show of brutality came from the Cuban army, when General Carlos Mendieta invited newsmen to observe a demonstration of his machine guns as they slaughtered black families in a small village. The massacre confirmed the popular perception that the whites were butchering all the blacks in the countryside. The news triggered a second wave of migration, as black families fled in panic into the cities for protection. The cities in Oriente swelled in numbers to the point that foreign consuls feared the outbreak of epidemics, but no major diseases broke out. Only those blacks living in foreign installations or among white families who vouched for them dared to stay behind in the countryside.[61]

Outrageous as was the frequent slaughter of innocent civilians, the terrorist massacres achieved the military goal of almost instantly depriving the black rebels of any rural base of support. The whites in the countryside were generally well protected by the volunteers, and no black peasants remained to help the rebels. General José de Jesús Monteagudo, the head of the Cuban Armed Forces, arrived to take personal command of the campaign on 29 May. When he learned of the presence of a large force of 2000 rebels under Estenoz and Ivonnet halfway between Guantánamo and Santiago de Cuba, he launched an operation to surround and capture this large black force. Monteagudo moved detachments from the coast and from two cities, while other units moved south from the railroad on 2 June. The plan resembled the encirclements the Spanish army had carefully crafted to catch the Cuban rebels in 1895–1898, and just like those plans, it too failed to catch the black rebels as they doubled back behind the advancing forces and marched north after burning a town in their escape. The setback did not deter General Monteagudo, because he felt that the operation gave him a true measure of the rebels and that the next time they would not be able to escape. An impatient U.S. consul did not share the optimism and exclaimed in frustration, "These people cannot be caught."[62] The failure of this operation and the memory of Spain's inability to crush the Cuban rebellion moved the United States to land 1,050 marines in the valley of Guantánamo Bay on 5 June. The marines remained on Cuban soil throughout the Race War to protect U.S. sugar mills and to serve as a reminder that if Cuba did not act swiftly and effectively, the United States was ready to land more troops to finish crushing the black revolt. [63]

Compared to the over 8000 Cuban troops gathering in Oriente for the campaign against the black rebels, the number of marines was small, yet they sufficed to release Cuban soldiers from any guard duty. Already on 6 June General Monteagudo was so sure of success that he offered an amnesty to those blacks who surrendered before 8 June. He had his troops patrol the countryside extensively, and he was careful to isolate the rebels from any access to the towns and cities. Monteagudo extended the amnesty offer until 22 June, and daily many rebels were surrendering. On 12 June his units did find the main force under the command of Estenoz and Ivonnet. After a brief engagement, the rebels split into smaller bands and fled to evade capture. No large concentration of rebels remained in Oriente, and to track down the small, demoralized, and largely unarmed bands, Monteagudo

divided his forces into small units to find the remaining black rebels. By 17 June Monteagudo believed that the revolt was over, and that only its leaders (excluded from the amnesty offer) were still at large.[64]

In an engagement on 27 June Evaristo Estenoz was killed, but Ivonnet remained on the loose. Although some officials still feared Ivonnet, the white peasants crowded in the cities concluded that the revolt was over and in early July began to return to the countryside. The black peasants were more cautious and waited another month before daring to return to their abandoned homes in the countryside. General Monteagudo, who had directed the successful campaign, returned back to Havana on 17 July and left the task of finding Ivonnet to subordinates. The next day government forces captured Ivonnet, but while in route to Santiago de Cuba to face trial, a mulatto army lieutenant applied that Mexican invention, the *Ley Fuga* ("killed while trying to escape") to the black leader. The cold-blooded execution was unnecessary, because long before the death of the two major rebel leaders the black revolt had fizzled out completely. In the victory celebrations in Havana to welcome the triumphant returning troops, the government claimed to have killed at least 2,000 rebels and to have lost only 16 dead soldiers, including those killed by friendly fire. Unofficial estimates put the toll of black deaths at least as high as 5,000 just in Oriente. Even without knowing how many unreported black deaths occurred in the other provinces at the hands of the volunteers, a massacre of major proportions had taken place.[65]

The crushing of the black rebellion ended any chance of repealing the Morúa Law still in force today. Most surprisingly, the savage repression did not bring any hardening of the policy towards blacks. During the frenzy of the revolt, proposals surfaced to reproduce the segregationist system of the southern United States, but no formal action ever emerged. Instead, the belief in "Cubanness" and in the fundamental equality of all persons who considered themselves Cubans finally triumphed. The outburst of collective white frenzy during the revolt marked the last gasp of a dying white racism in Cuba. Never again did the island experience such an outpouring of racist hatred, and successive Cuban governments relentlessly and ceaselessly strove to erase any traces of racist differences in the island. For all practical purposes, the Race War of 1912 eliminated race as a factor in later Cuban history. Paradoxically, the Cuban army and police forces that had so persecuted rebels in 1912 became a favorite source of employment for blacks.[66]

Militarily, the Race War of 1912 seemed to demonstrate that a rebellion no longer had any chance to overthrow the government in power. The victory of the Cuban government had been so overwhelming that the question arises of whether the application of similar methods by Spain could have crushed the Cuban rebels in 1895–1898. Obviously the late nineteenth century did not know how to prevent tropical diseases and lacked the wireless telegraph, but otherwise Spain disposed of the same technology. Whatever might be the conclusion as to Spain's chances, no doubt exists that had the Cubans delayed their revolt until the 1910s, the economic expansion and the technological advance would have made an insurrection impossible. Instead of Spain, it was the Cuban government of 1912 that enjoyed such a commanding advantage over any insurrection. The success of Cuba contrasted starkly with Mexico, where as the next chapter shows, the regime did not use technological advantages to immunize itself from the threat of a domestic insurrection.

An additional consequence of the tragic Race War of 1912 for the later history of Cuba deserves mention. The migrations from the countryside contributed to the urbanization of Cuba. Large numbers of peasants came for the first time into the cities, and while many gladly returned to the countryside, others eventually became urban dwellers. Ultimately economic forces made possible the rapid urbanization of the island, as Cuba joined Argentina in the ranks of the most heavily urbanized countries in Latin America. The armed forces created in the first decade of the twentieth century for an overwhelmingly agrarian society did not seem to fit well the needs of an increasingly urbanized society. The question of whether Cuba needed an army at all reappeared as the next section shows.

The Revolt of February 1917

The Race War of 1912 showed that the armed forces of Cuba were capable of crushing domestic insurrections. This new strength promised to guarantee the survival of any Cuban government and also allowed the United States to meet its goal of distancing itself from direct involvement in Cuban politics. Above all, the United States wanted to avoid any situation that might require another occupation under the terms of the Platt Amendment. The United States was trying to elude its self-imposed obligations, when the most obvious solution was simply to abolish that agreement. But no U.S. administration wished to expend the political capital needed to repeal the Platt Amendment. The reluctance of the United States to intervene gave the Cuban government considerable leverage but could also encourage rebels to adopt destructive tactics to make a third U.S. occupation unavoidable. In retrospect, a third U.S. occupation would most likely have benefited both countries; the relations between the two nations contained too many unresolved points, and at the very least the drastic social and economic transformation ongoing in Cuba required an updating of the arrangements of 1901.

What the U.S. government did not want to realize was that a strong Cuban army capable of putting down internal revolts could also serve as an excellent partisan tool. In a replay of the circumstances leading up to the August 1906 revolt, the Conservative Mario G. Menocal, the President of Cuba, sought reelection in 1916 even in the face of an overwhelming Liberal majority among the voters. Menocal turned to the new army and the Rural Guard to try to win reelection, even though in the four years of his first term he had not succeeded in purging all the Liberal officers from the army. The Liberals were determined to elect their candidate, Alfredo Zayas, who had been one of the leaders of the 1906 revolt. Zayas seemed to have a good chance at winning because all factions of the Liberal Party united behind his candidacy. Most importantly, ex-president Miguel Gómez had agreed to back Zayas although with such onerous conditions that Gómez would become in effect the power behind the throne. Victory for the Liberals was far from assured, because World War I brought a sugar boom and ushered in the period of greatest prosperity in the history of the island. High world prices for sugar fueled a remarkable business expansion, and the increased customs revenues financed government expenditures and widespread patronage. Even many persons not directly benefiting from official money saw no compelling reasons to change the president.[67]

Not surprisingly, the elections on 1 November 1916 were hotly contested. Each side committed massive fraud. Over one million persons voted, although three years later the census of 1919 (carried out under U.S. auspices) reported that less than half that number qualified to vote. In spite of the massive fraud, by all indications Zayas had won. Initially President Menocal was willing to admit defeat, but the female members of his family became hysterical, and they emboldened him to fight to retain the presidency. Once Menocal claimed victory, a clash seemed inevitable with the Liberals. Because the inauguration date did not come until 20 May 1917, both sides agreed to repeat the election in the most contested districts in February, the winner to be declared the next president of Cuba.[68]

The Liberals soon lost any hope of winning these partial elections. Menocal was spending furiously to secure votes and was also using the army and the Rural Guard to intimidate Liberal voters. With a Conservative victory at the partial elections a foregone conclusion, the Liberals saw in a revolt the only way to stop the reelection of Menocal. Their decision to start an uprising came as no surprise, because even before the elections of 1 November the Liberals had threatened armed protest. The Liberals believed that they had a great chance of overthrowing Menocal by force, but that even if the revolt sputtered, the threat to property was sure to provoke a third U.S. occupation. The Liberals were sure they could win at the polls, just as they had done during the U.S. occupation of 1906–1909.[69]

The Liberals were closely following the script from the August 1906 rebellion, and similarities existed besides the obvious one of an incumbent president seeking a second term. Don Tomás Estrada Palma and Mario Menocal were both staunchly pro–American, both having lived in the United States for years. Menocal had faithfully served U.S. officials during the first occupation and then worked as a manager for the Cuban-American Sugar Corporation. The prevailing opinion was that "The President of Cuba is much more American than Cuban."[70] Yet in spite of similar signs of devo-

tion to U.S. interests, Washington had failed to support Don Tomás in 1906, and the Liberals expected the same fate to befall Menocal in 1917. Over less serious matters the United States occupied neighboring Haiti and the Dominican Republic, and the Liberals believed that a revolt in Cuba was bound to trigger an intervention to protect U.S. investments. But the continuing U.S. occupation in Haiti and the Dominican Republic was making Washington reluctant to assume another commitment. The Woodrow Wilson administration had just ordered the Punitive Expedition out of Mexico early in 1917 and was in the middle of an intense debate over entry into World War I. Even assuming that a new deployment would not require more than the 6,000 soldiers of the 1906–1909 occupation, on the eve of declaring war on Germany Washington did not want to divert any U.S. Army troops away from the European war. President Menocal read the U.S. position correctly and concluded that if he acted resolutely and swiftly, he could win his second term in office.[71]

The Liberal leaders were no less sure of their chances of success, and in the first days of February 1917 Gómez and Zayas gathered to plan the revolt. The leaders believed that the veterans were just waiting for the word to start another march on Havana like in 1906. The Liberals did not set a fixed date for the uprising, but at the urging of Zayas agreed to postpone a decision until after the partial elections. Other Liberal leaders had the task of raising the banner of revolt in the provinces near Havana. The Liberals expected thousands to flock to the insurrection as the rebels made their final triumphal march towards the capital to depose Menocal.[72]

The Liberals were organizing an armed protest rather than a real revolt. They knew that in contrast to 1906, they faced a Cuban army and a Rural Guard that had proven to be brutally efficient in the Race War of 1912. The many machine guns of the army were sure to tear the rebel volunteers to shreds unless the Liberals first neutralized most of the army units. Consequently, the Liberals devoted most of their efforts not to organize the mobilization in the countryside but rather to recruit army officers. José Miguel Gómez, who had promoted many officers during his presidency, actively recruited many plotters. Eventually the

Liberals counted on three-fourths of the army joining the revolt. By the simultaneous revolt of army units and of the countryside, the Liberals hoped to give the impression of enjoying overwhelming support.[73] As one plotter commented, the revolt was "truly a bluff" designed to fool Menocal officials into capitulating.[74]

The plot called for the two main Liberal leaders, Gómez and Zayas, to announce the revolt from Las Villas province at the appropriate moment. Under the cover of going on a fishing trip in the Caribbean, Gómez left Havana by train on 7 February to go board his yacht on the south coast of Cuba, and that day Zayas also left by train to attend a provincial Liberal convention at Las Villas. After the inevitable betrayal of the conspiracy took place, on the night of 9 February the alerted government ordered the police of Havana to round up suspected civilians and officers. Upon hearing of the arrests, several Liberal leaders, including Pino Guerra, fled the city and raised the banner of revolt to the west on 10 February, the date regarded as the start of the uprising.

With Pino once again in the field and rumored to be leading thousands of rebels, the August 1906 revolt seemed to be repeating itself. However, in reality his band never numbered more than ninety followers. Unlike in the revolt against Don Tomás, the response to the Liberal appeals was very weak. With the sugar cane harvest or *zafra* just having begun, the Liberals could not have picked a worst month to launch a revolt. The August 1906 revolt benefited from its timing at the start of the dead season when employment dropped off dramatically after the sugar cane harvest was in. Instead in February 1917 few were willing to abandon the high wages of working in the sugar cane harvest for the potentially greater but immensely riskier gamble of a revolt. The veterans of the war of independence, the backbone of the August 1906 revolt, rarely took to the field, while a substantial number of veterans solidly backed Menocal. As the wave of arrests in Havana came closer to the army officers, some plotters tried to seize Camp Columbia near Havana in the early hours of 11 February. The troops at the largest army base in Cuba refused to join the revolt, and the plotters with only forty soldiers had to beat a hasty retreat into the countryside to escape capture.[75]

The premature discovery of the conspir-

acy strongly suggested to many Liberals that they should desist from their original goal of overthrowing the government. Angry that the revolt had begun without his approval, Alfredo Zayas was among the many who decided to await developments. The Liberal presidential candidate returned quietly to Havana. He stayed as a guest of a wealthy female benefactor in a sumptuous castle-like palace and kept out of public view for the duration of the revolt. Leadership devolved exclusively on Gómez, who arrived on the south coast of Camagüey on 10 February and then issued orders for all plotters to join the revolt. Many army conspirators failed to detect any mounting groundswell against Menocal and decided to remain quiet after receiving the orders from Gómez to revolt. However, some middle-ranking officers decided to gamble the rest of their military careers on one wild adventure.[76]

The officers at Camagüey were the first to strike, and on 11 February they gained control of that provincial capital. Although the fighting was brief, loyal and rebel forces suffered in total 22 casualties among killed and wounded. Instead the capture of Santiago de Cuba, the capital of Oriente and the second largest city in the island, took place bloodlessly and with precision at 1500 on 12 February: "The movement was carried out so stealthily, suddenly, and effectively that no resistance was manifested sufficient to cause serious trouble."[77] The small army detachments in the two provinces were far from being formidable, and the rebels, to bolster their chances, distributed two thousand rifles to their followers in Camagüey and 1,500 rifles in Oriente. The rebel officers released the prisoners from the military and the civilian jails and incorporated them into their units. The next day the garrison at Guantánamo joined the revolt, and soon additional bases in Oriente joined the uprising.[78]

The relatively easy rebel seizure of most of the two easternmost provinces gained tremendous momentum for the revolt popularly known as "La Chambelona." Liberals in Las Villas, the traditional bastion of Gómez, felt the time had come to rise up, and they took control of many towns but not of the provincial capital. At Santa Clara Menocal loyalist Colonel Wilfredo Ibrahim Consuegra had purged his regiment of Liberal sympathizers and remained in control of the city and its railroad links. As the furthermost loyalist outpost in the middle of hostile Liberal territory, his position was precarious at best. Unless he received ample reinforcements, the rebels approaching from the east could easily overwhelm him. Santa Clara became the key to the advance to Havana, and as long as Colonel Consuegra held firm, the Menocal regime was safe.[79]

Some rebel leaders, in particular Major Luis Solano Álvarez, understood that every minute counted and were in a rush to reach Havana before Menocal could rally his badly shaken supporters. The plots in Havana and the rebel capture of two major provinces thoroughly rattled the Menocal regime, and many of its worried officials were seeking a negotiated solution. As late as 15 February high officials still feared the defection of additional units, and not until ten days later did the government regain confidence in its strength. Menocal himself never wavered, and he correctly realized that the only chance to secure his second term in office was by means of a victory in the battlefield. He gathered troops to rush to threatened Santa Clara, but time was against them because they could not reach that city ahead of the rebels who were right next door in Camagüey Province.[80]

Fortunately for the government, its best ally in the struggle was ironically the rebel Gómez himself. He was regarded as the most Cuban of the presidents and belonged to the Latin American tradition of preferring desultory engagements over real combat. Gómez wanted an armed protest and not a war, but he needed to have men in the field to have something to bargain with in negotiations with the government. A display of force was all that he wanted, and he never prepared for anything other than scattered skirmishes. Had he been up against a like-minded opponent, his strategy probably would have resulted in some negotiated solution to the presidential succession, an obviously political problem. Gómez was trying to show the government that it needed to heed the Liberal majority in the country. Instead Menocal knew that battlefield victory was the only way for the Conservatives to remain in office. The President, perhaps because of his close assimilation of American values, wholeheartedly endorsed the doctrine of victory in decisive battlefield combat. The clash of personalities reflected a diametrically opposed conception of the type of warfare that should be waged in Latin America.

The crucial day for the revolt was 13 February 1917. To remain a credible threat and to maintain their momentum, the rebels needed to complete a trio of successes: Camagüey on 11 February, Santiago de Cuba on 12 February, and the next day had to be Santa Clara. A rebel train, steaming from Camagüey to Santa Clara, was intercepted not by government troops but by Gómez himself at 0200 on 13 February. Speed was of the utmost urgency, because in addition to the strategic reasons to strike fast, a rebel officer had been fooled to reveal the rebel objectives by telegraph. Up to this moment a panic-stricken Havana government had been in the dark and could only guess where the rebels would strike next. Menocal saw an opportunity to gain time, and he enthusiastically approved Colonel Consuegra's plan to rush a train to destroy the bridge at Jatibonico, the most vulnerable point in the Santa Clara-Camagüey railroad. However, the chance of reaching Jatibonico was slim because the rebels had such a head start. Fortunately for the government, Gómez detrained the cavalry and sent it to inspect the path ahead. Normally the cavalry could cover the distance in three hours, but the commander did not want to tire his horses so the cavalry took twelve hours to cover the distance that the train could steam in 45 minutes. The rebels were still in time, because the government troops lacked explosives to blow up the Jatibonico bridge. Instead, the loyal troops set fire to the bridge, but the wood burned so slowly that only after many hours would the beams suffer damage, and at any moment the rebels could arrive to put out the fires. At 1700 when the rebel train moving at a snail's pace encountered the cavalry, Gómez did not load the horses on board and instead disembarked the men for a long and sumptuous dinner. Needless to say, when the rebel train finally reached the burned bridge, the damage required repair work of no less than two weeks.[81]

Time was what Gómez did not have. The burning of the Jatibonico bridge slowed the rebel advance to a crawl and gave the government a breathing space to rally forces and to rush ample reinforcements to Santa Clara from Havana by train. Equally significant, the

United States publicly announced its support for Menocal on 14 February. The Liberal calculation that Washington preferred to intervene rather than to support the Havana government had backfired; Menocal received the backing the United States had denied to Don Tomás in 1906. Those Liberals who were still waiting for the right moment to revolt stayed quiet after the cue from the State Department. At Havana Province Pino Guerra and his followers, who had never numbered more than ninety, disbanded. The United States also rushed weapons and ammunition to the government, which was enlarging its forces. To augment its firepower, the Menocal government purchased 28 additional machine guns for its units. The Menocal government also enlisted 90-day volunteers and stepped-up recruitment for the army and for the Rural Guard. The government waved entrance requirements such as literacy and Cuban citizenship, indeed the government accepted any volunteer who just looked healthy. And if the rebels were opening up prisons to secure recruits, the government could not be far behind when it received into the army persons with criminal records.[82]

The rebels faced an increasing number of discouraging signs. Many officers had refused to join the movement at Santiago de Cuba and at Camagüey. The officers and soldiers that did join the revolt generally showed little enthusiasm. As a matter of fact, the revolt had barely begun when officers and soldiers started to desert. Why had the coup part of the Liberal insurrection achieved very modest success among army units? Police actions, such as the arrest of suspected plotters, naturally played a role, but something more fundamental was at work. The officers who had participated in the revolt were disgruntled because Menocal after 1912 had appointed mostly Conservatives to key positions. Promotions and key assignments went largely to the loyal supporters of Menocal, while others within the army saw their careers languish. All the plush assignments were in Havana and these naturally went to close supporters of Menocal. Officers in disgrace remained holding minor positions at Havana or the less desirable commands of provincial garrisons. With their careers stuck or sinking, the disgruntled officers knew that another four years of Menocal meant the end of any hope of advancement as Conservatives continued to fill the officer ranks. Armed revolt was the only way to revive their flagging careers, but their command of small and distant units in the provinces meant that their defections reduced but in no way destroyed the ability of the Cuban army to put down domestic insurrections.

Enjoying complete U.S. support, Menocal had to decide on the best way to employ his growing forces to put down the rebellion. The three western provinces were completely quiet and did not require any attention. The simplest and most obvious way to take the offensive was to send troops east by railroad to Santa Clara. At Las Villas, the home base of Gómez, the government needed a large army presence to subdue the many rebel sympathizers in that province. But the destruction of the rail bridge at Jatibonico meant that if all army reinforcements went to Santa Clara, then the campaign against the two easternmost provinces could not start for at least two weeks and possibly as long as a month. Great as was the mobility the railroad offered for troops, an exclusive reliance on trains could turn into a dangerous dependence if not a trap as the Federal Army in Mexico found out to its great misfortune. In Cuba, Menocal bypassed the trap and did not wait for the repair of the damaged bridge. Instead, he sent troops aboard his gunboats to Camagüey Province. The expedition to Camagüey aimed to test the strength of the rebels in that province and possibly also to demoralize them. On 17 February loyal troops disembarked at Júcaro on the south coast and two days later reached Jatibonico. The sudden appearance of this force caught the rebels in Camagüey by surprise, and they became too demoralized to put up any effective resistance. The rebel officers put the men to destroy the culverts and small bridges of the railroad track, but even defensive precautions could not keep the rebel forces from melting away. Without any opponent to fight, the advancing loyal troops acted more like a repair crew than an army. Long before the entry of his troops into the provincial capital of Camagüey on 26 February, Menocal realized that the rebels no longer posed any threat to this province.[83]

This first test of the rebel strength persuaded Menocal that the whole revolt was tottering and just needed one good push to collapse completely. Although he was unaware of

Cuban army officers aboard the warship *Cuba*. The Cuban navy transported troops and kept control of the sea for the government during the revolts of 1912 and 1917 (Library of Congress, Prints and Photographs Division, George Grantham Bain Collection).

the exact location of Gómez, he felt that Las Villas had enough government forces to control the situation. Menocal sent troops east to begin an offensive, but instead of landing more units in Camagüey, he had his gunboats take the soldiers to Oriente. The first intention of Menocal had been to land the troops directly in Santiago de Cuba to strike the uprising at its root. Because the naval cannon aboard his ships outclassed the weak coastal batteries in that port, a sudden landing in Santiago de Cuba was the fastest way to bring the revolt in Oriente to a swift close. The rebels knew their vulnerability to a sea-borne attack and in response were preparing to sink block ships at the bay's entrance and to mine the surrounding waters. U.S. corporations bitterly protested this measure, and at one point the U.S. Navy was about to take over the bay to keep the navigational channel open to merchant ships. An arrangement was reached whereby the rebels in exchange for not blocking the navigational channel received the guarantee that the U.S. Navy

would not allow Cuban gunboats to enter the bay. With their sea front well protected, the rebels took the offensive to try to expel the last government troops from Oriente. The rebels easily captured a number of towns to the north and west of Santiago de Cuba, but their drive ran into unexpectedly strong resistance at Bayamo on 22 February. Menocal knew the importance of maintaining a strong government presence in Oriente Province, and he hastened to save the beleaguered garrison. The troops he had originally intended to disembark at Santiago de Cuba he shifted to Manzanillo, the port nearest to Bayamo. The loyalist troops landed at Manzanillo on 24 February, and the next day they marched to lift the siege of Bayamo. Heavy combat between the relief column and the rebels lasted for three hours until the superior firepower of the loyal troops forced the rebels to retreat. In the north, government troops disembarked at Nuevitas and began pushing south into Oriente Province. A simultaneous drive from Bayamo in the west and Nuevitas in the north was converging on Santiago de Cuba where a major battle was looming, and in preparation the rebels busily fortified the approaches to the city.[84]

The rebels seemed determined to make a last stand at Santiago de Cuba at least during the start of March, but soon events in Las Villas Province drastically changed the prospects for the revolt. After the destruction of the bridge at Jatibonico, the column of Gómez proceeded on foot and on horseback into Las Villas Province on 15 February. Gómez with most of the rebels proceeded westward from Jatibonico, while a smaller detachment went south to capture weapons at Sancti Spiritus for distribution to volunteers. Government reinforcements had not yet reached Sancti Spiritus, so after some shooting the more numerous rebel force easily overwhelmed the 135 defenders who surrendered on 15 February. The haul of 200 captured rifles and 20,000 cartridges had not been worth the effort, and many of the rebels began to desert. The attack at last revealed to the government the exact location of at least some rebels; and lacking any other target, Menocal sent troops to recover Sancti Spíritus. Three columns converged on the town, and one of them passed close to the main force of Gómez but incorrectly concluded it was just a mounted rebel patrol. One squad and a machine gun took up positions to keep the rebel cavalry at a safe distance away from the rear of the main marching column. Gómez ordered his cavalry armed primarily with machetes to drive this squad away prior to preparing a larger attack on the rapidly departing government column. The tactic of Gómez was highly questionable if not suicidal. Machete-waving cavalry charges against Spanish troops armed only with Mauser rifles had been rare in the independence war of 1895–1898 and only used as a desperate last resort. To try to repeat this tactic against government troops who unlike the Spaniards had a machine gun was an invitation to disaster. Upon hearing the lone machine gun firing, the horsemen instinctively dismounted to take cover on the ground, when in reality they should have turned around and fled out of range. The machine gun sprayed the crouched rebels liberally with bullets and inflicted terrible losses on the men and their horses. Once the machine gun crew was convinced it had neutralized the rebel cavalry, the

squad, still unaware of the presence of the main force under Gómez, packed up, resumed its march formation, and hastened to rejoin the main column heading for Sancti Spíritus. The anticipated battle to recapture that town did not take place, and the three columns entered Sancti Spíritus unopposed on 19 February. Desertions had so decimated the rebels that on 17 February they evacuated the town and headed north to rejoin the main force under Gómez.[85]

In spite of these setbacks, Gómez still hoped to reconstitute a powerful force. "The most potent factor in this insurrection is undoubtedly José Miguel Gómez and, should he be eliminated from the situation from any cause whatever, it is probable that the insurrection would lose a considerable number of its present adherents and might even collapse entirely in a short time."[86] The rebels and even Gómez himself did not realize that the political revolt survived only thanks to his presence. Rather than keep the entire rebel force united around Gómez as a huge personal guard, the rebels split up into two columns heading west for Santa Clara. The larger force of about 800 men marched close to the north coast of Cuba, while the smaller force of about 600 men under Gómez proceeded in a parallel line about 20 kilometers south. Both columns were supposed to link up near Santa Clara with the supposedly large force of fellow veteran and future president of Cuba Gerardo Machado. Once reunited, the combined rebel forces then planned to make their final assault on that key city. The main reason for splitting into two columns was to recruit over a wider zone; the new recruits were desperately needed as replacements for the many youths who had tired of the revolt and deserted. By this time the revolt generated little excitement, and the recruitment efforts failed to yield enough men to offset the tactical blunder of dividing the rebel force. Army units of about 1000 soldiers each were searching the region and could single-handedly destroy any of the two rebel columns.

In a skirmish on 6 March near Placetas, loyalist troops confirmed that Gómez was present in the southern rebel column. At a strategy meeting that night in Santa Clara, government officials decided to leave that city defenseless and to send all their available troops in an all-out effort to trap Gómez the next day. Officers drove the men and the horses hard until the government forces were near the marching column of Gómez in the morning of 7 March. To overtake a marching column is never easy, but Gómez conveniently halted for a very early lunch near the hacienda of Caicaje and thus gave the 3,000 government soldiers the time to set up their machine guns. When the rebel pickets reported the presence of government forces in his rear, Gómez merely dispatched a patrol of 100 men to scatter what he concluded was just a harassing band. The patrol immediately detected a very large government force and observed how it continued to increase in numbers. Gomez dismissed the first reports about this threatening force and threw away the chance to escape before the encirclement was complete. Loyalist cavalry surrounded the two flanks of the rebel force while the infantry had time to place its machine guns on a hill overlooking Caicaje, the site of the battle. Behind the rebel camp was a river, which unknown to the rebels was already closely held by another government column. None of the very accurate reports his scouts sent could budge Gómez, who indifferently awaited his fate as the trap shut tight around him. Thus, when the government machine guns opened fire, panic struck the surprised rebel camp. Only the 100-man patrol was replying, but its rifles could not match the fire from the machine guns and the massed loyalist infantry.[87] The fire from the machine guns was so intense that bullets riddled the bodies of the defenders and in one case "the bullets decapitated the head of a soldier as cleanly as a slicing knife."[88] Obviously the improvised defense line quickly collapsed, and the rebels desperately tried to flee their camp. Only a handful managed to escape through small gaps in the army lines, and all the rest were either killed or captured.

Among the prisoners was Gómez, and his capture meant the end of the political revolt. Upon hearing the news of the disaster at Caicaje, the northern column halted its advance and eventually disintegrated from desertions. The youths who had joined the revolt in search of excitement and a coming-of-age experience fled to their dull but safe homes in the countryside. Isolated

rebel bands continued to be active for another month in that province, but any danger to Santa Clara or to Menocal had passed.

All that remained of the revolt was Oriente Province, but even there the Menocal offensive was well advanced. As stated earlier, loyalist forces were converging on the capital of that province, and it was clear that even before Menocal had time to redeploy his forces from Las Villas, the Cuban army vastly surpassed Oriente's rebel garrisons in numbers and in firepower. By March 7 loyal troops had entered the suburbs of Santiago de Cuba and fierce fighting over the city seemed certain. To avoid unnecessary destruction and deaths, Admiral Reginald R. Belknap obtained the withdrawal of the rebel forces on March 8 and landed sailors and marines to maintain order. On 16 March government troops entered the city, but the last U.S. Navy forces did not leave Santiago de Cuba until 25 March.[89]

Cuban president Mario Menocal and family. His wife and the other female members of his family gave Menocal the determination to crush the revolt of 1917 in Cuba (Library of Congress, Prints and Photographs Division).

The rebel evacuation of Santiago de Cuba on 8 March and the capture of Gómez at Caicaje the day before ended any last hopes of military victory for the uprising. However, the Liberals still had their backup plan of inflicting enough destruction on property to trigger a third U.S. occupation. The Liberals still wanted to use the U.S. occupation to regain power just as they had done before in August 1906. In any free and honest elections the Liberals knew they had the votes to win, and to return to power they were more than willing to pay the small price of several years of U.S. military rule. The peasants in Oriente extremely enthusiastically heeded the calls of the Liberals and attacked not only U.S. property but also the land of wealthy Cubans. In effect, just like during the Race War of 1912, the Liberal revolt sparked a social uprising in the countryside. Peasants who had lost their lands to U.S. sugar corporations and who had to work for starvation wages wanted to regain the independent lifestyle of their former subsistence agriculture. In an attempt to reverse the commercialization of Oriente, the peasants were more than glad to destroy property. Dockworkers even managed to burn the sugar cargoes aboard steamships.[90]

By the middle of March the peasants had joined the last remaining rebel officers to create a formidable position 23 kilometers north of Santiago de Cuba:

> The main revolutionary command under General Rigoberto Fernández was located at [Alto] Songo. These forces are well armed and equipped and composed mostly of Negroes. They carry modern Springfields and have ample ammunition; every man had approximately 150 to 200 rounds and the way they are fighting this supply will last them a long time. Their methods being strictly guerrilla warfare they are separated into bands of from 10 to 50 men. They are fully supplied with horses, which makes them a cavalry force, permitting them to spread over considerable territory. Regarding food supplies they have commandeered staples from the different stores where they have been operating and as they are used to living on the produce of the country this will keep them going for some time.[91]

The Cuban army could not respond immediately because a hostile peasant population provided little information on the whereabouts of the rebels. When the government at last learned the location and size of the main rebel force, the army brought up a substantial force and heavy weapons. Forewarned of the impending attack, the rebels dug three lines of trenches and strung up barbed wire. The Cuban army attacked with rapid-fire cannon and machine guns on 29 March. After heavy shelling, 600 infantrymen charged, and the rebels gradually withdrew after seven hours of heavy combat. The cavalry tried to pursue the retreating rebels who escaped to find refuge deep in the mountainous forest. In April peasants bands were still descending from the mountains to burn the sugar cane fields, and the most determined bands raided sugar mills and ripped up railroad tracks. Whenever the peasants raided villages and towns, just like the black peasants in the Race War of 1912, they also destroyed the property registers and municipal archives in an effort to halt the land grabs by U.S. corporations and wealthy Cubans.[92]

The Liberal revolt in Oriente was becoming a social revolution, and unceasingly the U.S. government pressured Menocal to crush the peasant revolt. For their part, many Liberal leaders were likewise horrified, because they had become wealthy landowners and did not want their properties damaged. In spite of the mounting pressure to crush the resistance, the Cuban army and the Rural Guard were most reluctant to track down the often unarmed peasants. Not surprisingly the pacification of Oriente dragged out during the summer of 1917. To prod the Cuban army to assume a more vigorous persecution, U.S. consuls suggested attaching small detachments of U.S. officers and soldiers to the Cuban units. Despairing of Cuban promises to protect private property, in August 1917 the United States stationed marines to guard the most important U.S. investments in Oriente and in Camagüey. The presence of the marines safeguarded most U.S. properties, yet the last U.S. forces did not withdraw until 1922.[93]

The End of a Mission

The long stay of U.S. troops reminded the Cuban government of its obligation to protect private property under the Platt Amendment but was also a confession of the failure of U.S.

policy. The Cuban army was supposed to prevent a third U.S. occupation, yet U.S. troops still had to serve in Cuba from 1917 to 1922. What had gone wrong? Was the Cuban army too small or did it need major changes? The Cuban armed forces had ruthlessly crushed a revolt during the Race War of 1912 but could not stamp out a peasant revolt in 1917. It was not just a question of conventional warfare versus counterinsurgency, because even against rebel columns the army's performance depended on massive firepower and had been far from flawless. U.S. training and the forceful personality of General José de Jesús Monteagudo had kept the army and the Rural Guard fit for combat in 1912, but by 1917 the armed forces had deteriorated considerably. Captain Frank Parker departed in 1912, and after Monteagudo the latter heads of the Cuban armed forces neglected military preparedness for exclusive concentration on partisan politics. As U.S. Army officers had feared in 1908, the Cuban army became a major threat to the stability of the island. Proposals to abolish the army surfaced, and even the U.S. military attaché in prophetic language strongly argued for ending the existence of the harmful Cuban army.[94]

Was the proposal to abolish the Cuban army sound? Because the United States protected Cuba, the island did not need an army to repel foreign invasions. Of other reasons to have an army, only two were applicable to Cuba. One was that the army was needed to provide employment. Because of the extreme concentration of income, jobs have traditionally been scarce in Latin America, and unemployed people are most likely to participate in disturbances. Each person working for the government is one less disaffected person interested in revolting; of course, placing civilians in the official payroll generates similar employment opportunities, but without the benefit of providing the government with a means to apply force. Unfortunately, the governments could not resist turning the army and the Rural Guard into partisan instruments to impose a particular candidate or political party. Cuba was still in time to reverse Leonard Wood's fateful 1899 decision and to replace these national armed bodies with greatly enlarged municipal police forces. Not only did strong municipal police units bring government close to

the people in each locality, but the many mayors and police chiefs were most unlikely to agree among themselves to overthrow a national government. Not national armed bodies but local forces were most likely to keep politics democratic and to prevent dictatorships.

The second reason for having an army was the need to use force to repress disturbances, be they large scale or just from criminal bands. In Cuba the two overlapping groups of veterans and peasants were responsible for the domestic disturbances during the first two decades of the twentieth century. The veterans of the war of independence had the military skills to lead a full-scale insurrection against the government as happened in August 1906. The failure to appreciate the military potential of the veterans was the mistake U.S. planners made during the first occupation of Cuba (1898–1902). The small Rural Guard General Wood left behind was adequate to deal with isolated disturbances in the countryside but not to crush a coordinated revolt by vigorous veterans. Don Tomás had worsened the problem by keeping the Rural Guard small and hence made inevitable the success of the August 1906 revolt. To prevent another collapse of the government during the first two decades of the twentieth century, either a substantial force had to exist or the United States needed to station troops in the island. Cuba could combine these two basic solutions in varying proportions or could rely on only one. Obviously the ideal solution was an enlarged municipal police. Not only would powerful municipal forces serve a deterrent function against any insurrection but they provided employment to those veterans who otherwise would have been the persons most likely to support a revolt.

By the February 1917 revolt, the situation had changed in the island. The majority of veterans had entered the political system and had profited either on the government payroll or had received generous bonuses and other benefits. Although not exactly pampered, the veterans had become a privileged group in Cuba. Only those veterans deep in the countryside who had not learned to profit from the new Republican system or who genuinely wished to live in the countryside as peasants showed any willingness to rise up in arms. Many veterans stood ready to participate in the February 1917 revolt but only as part of the bandwagon effect to make sure they were on the winning side. Some veterans did campaign in that revolt, but they were among the first to desert when they saw the rebellion falter. Dispossessed peasants in Oriente and naïve youths in search of adventure provided the bulk of the followers for the 1917 revolt. The untrained civilians who joined the February 1917 were not as threatening as the battle-hardened veterans had been in August 1906. By the late 1910s, the veterans were generally in their forties and no longer posed a military challenge. In the twenty years after 1898, many veterans (including the major leaders) had died, and whether because of illness or of having put on too much weight, most were no longer fit to campaign in the field. The disappearance of the veteran threat removed a major reason for the existence of the Cuban army.

The only other military justification for the army or for the Rural Guard was to put down peasant revolts, but because the officers refused to consider the needs of the countryside, the armed forces of Cuba lost their initial capability to conduct counterinsurgency operations. The inability of Cuba to retain a capacity to repress rural populations contrasted sharply with the success the Mexican army would have in the 1920s against the Cristeros. After years of upheavals, the Mexican government learned the costly lesson that any revolt, no matter how small, could not be left to fester even in remote and isolated regions. By the 1920s the Mexican army would learn how to repress rural rebels by savage and brutal means. Instead after 1917, the Cuban army faced the future without any real ability to destroy rural insurgencies. The difference in the armed forces of both countries helps to explain why Mexico closed its cycle of revolts in the late 1920s, while Cuba left open the possibility of a rural insurrection in later decades.

Since the end of the second U.S. occupation in 1909, the Cuban army turned into the battleground for competing political factions. The February 1917 revolt ultimately hinged on the loyalty of individual army units. The way to power by force lay no longer in the dangerous practice of rallying peasant rebels but by gaining the support of army garrisons. The February 1917 revolt precisely had captured the moment of transition from the old civilian insurrections to the new military coups. The only

remaining justification for the Cuban army was to provide jobs to reduce the high unemployment rate. Indeed many of the veterans had remained loyal to the government precisely because they belonged to the Cuban army. The idle troops in the barracks were too much of a temptation for the government that increasingly used them for police duties. In a major example, army patrols frequently protected sugar cane fields from incendiary fires particularly during harvest time. More disturbingly, the government also placed soldiers in voting places supposedly to safeguard the electoral process. Needless to say, the army presence intimidated voters and frequently contributed to fraud at the polls.[95]

The army performed police duties at best and partisan acts at worst. By 1920, the end of the threat from the veterans and the inability to repress peasant revolts left the army without any military justification for its existence. Only the employment function remained valid, but the government could provide jobs in less harmful ways. The transfer of all the soldiers and officers preferably into the municipal police or at least into an enlarged Rural Guard adequately protected jobs. The authorized strength for the Cuban armed forces of 12,500 men was the minimal number the Rural Guard needed to police the countryside. The Rural Guard garrisoned hundreds of posts, and duty in these remote and scattered detachments was vastly different from service in the large army barracks in the cities. The Rural Guard was in constant touch with the rural population, unlike the army units generally unaware of urban problems when living inside their barracks. The idleness of the officers left them with lots of time to participate in factional strife and sundry intrigues. The repeated army involvement in partisan politics was a major reason for the failure of first Cuban Republic (1902–1958). The glamour of living in the large cities could not compare with the boredom of duty in remote villages, and not surprisingly service in the Rural Guard outposts had the worst reputation and was seen as punishment or a demotion. Sometimes the rural guards extorted and robbed the peasants. The most ignorant and brutish members ended up in these remote outposts, and the personnel rather than uplifting the peasants often adopted their worst habits. Close to the daily life of the peasants, the Rural Guard was the opportunity for the government to learn about the real conditions in the countryside, but unfortunately Havana preferred not to look.[96] For the civilian politicians and the army officers involved in a world of money and politics in the cities, it was easy to overlook the many dispossessed peasants living in wretched conditions throughout the island.

Indeed, the Cuban peasants in Oriente continued to resist after the collapse of the Liberal revolt of February 1917. Left with few targets to attack and pursued by government forces, the die-hard peasant rebels gradually withdrew into remote fastnesses in the dense forests in the high ranges of the Sierra Maestra Mountains. The army's heart was not in this campaign, and the government did not want to spend more money on this costly pacification effort. Rather than pursue the bandit rebels into the mountains, the government wanted to end the operation. The peasant rebels for their part lacked the weapons and ammunition to hold back the troops and had settled on the very modest goal of just being left alone. A modus vivendi gradually emerged: Because the rugged mountainous lands lacked almost all commercial value, the peasants could remain as squatters eking out a miserable existence on the slopes. In exchange, the peasants halted their bandit raids on the valuable properties in the fertile lowlands. These runaway peasants remained fiercely Cuban, intensively committed to the ideals of equality, and violently hostile to the U.S. corporations that had expelled them from their lands in the fertile lowlands.[97] Once the last bandit raids ended, Havana and the Cuban army lost all interest in these isolated peasants, who remained forgotten for over 35 years. When in 1956 a fleeing Fidel Castro stumbled upon these isolated peasant communities in the Sierra Maestra, he found the initial supporters for the most remarkable revolution in the history of Latin America.

5. Mexico: The Fall of the Ancien Régime

The chief foundations of all states, new, old, or composite, are good laws and good arms; and as there cannot be good laws where the state is not well armed, it follows that where they are well armed they have good laws. — Niccolò Machiavelli[1]

The August 1906 revolt in Cuba had toppled a defenseless president and made obvious the need for a substantial army in that island. Subsequent Cuban governments learned the lesson of 1906, but an unperturbed Mexico continued to reduce its army. From 40,000 soldiers in the 1880s and substantial reserves, the Mexican army declined to a nominal strength of 29,000 and no reserves in 1910. With an army barely twice that of Cuba's, Mexico pretended to control a population seven times larger and to maintain order over an area almost twenty times larger than Cuba.[2]

Just to provide coverage comparable to Cuba's 12,500 soldiers, Mexico needed 100,000 soldiers. Unfortunately, the administration of Porfirio Díaz had been reducing the size of the army since the last decade of the nineteenth century. Lower expenditures on the military gave the government more funds to finance the transformation of the agrarian society into a semi-industrialized country. The economic growth did take place, but at the cost of concentrating the wealth in the top five percent of the population. The risks of upheaval became greater, but the wealthy minority refused to sacrifice any of its profits for the sake of enlarging the army. As an economical alternative, Bernardo Reyes, the Secretary of War, established a "Second Reserve" on 1 December

1900. Under his ingenious plan, civilians met periodically for drills and target practice.[3] The volunteer program caught the mood of the moment, and soon 30,000 men had enlisted enthusiastically in the Second Reserve. Although the costs were minimal, the additional expenses to build barracks and acquire weapons irked José Limantour, the Secretary of the Treasury. Limantour also feared Reyes as a rival to succeed the aging Díaz, and a power struggle raged between the two cabinet officers over the Second Reserve. On 22 December 1902 the loser Reyes had to resign as Secretary of War.[4]

Besides mobilizing enthusiastic supporters for the regime, the Second Reserve had temporarily reduced the pool of candidates willing to join a revolt. Unfortunately, Díaz distrusted the enthusiasm of the reservists, and the next year he abolished the Second Reserve. The final barrier holding back a possible revolution had vanished. If politicians failed to prevent the outbreak of an armed uprising, then the entire burden of restoring order fell on the 29,000-man army which Limantour refused to enlarge even as the population of Mexico grew. He shared the belief of most civilians that the Federal Army, because of its prestige and reputation for invincibility, was more than capable of putting down any revolt.[5]

The Start of the Insurrection

The political system ultimately rested on Porfirio Díaz, who exercised his power with remarkable tact and consummate skill. In political talents he was superior to his contemporaries. However, he, like the rest of the Mexican upper class, had no experience in selecting a successor. Because of his advancing age (he was born in 1830), Díaz could no longer postpone taking some steps to find a suitable replacement.

> The president has taken good care to permit, in fact to cause, a general expression of public opinion on all political matters, whether of national or of state importance, his idea being [...] to educate the people to the point of self-control as fast as it is possible for this to be done [...] As the president has on various occasions said to me, personally and confidentially, his very great hope is to leave the Mexican people in such a state of mind and of self-government, either at the end of his term of office or his natural life, that national and state affairs will go ahead without him as they have been going in the past few years under his guidance.[6]

One consequence of the Reyes-Limantour power struggle was the decision in 1904 to create the office of vice-president under the assumption that whoever held that position was the heir-designate. The term of office for president also increased to six years, so it was almost certain that the vice-president elected in 1910 would replace the aging Díaz. The upper class was happy to see Díaz run for reelection in the 1910 election, but unexpectedly a dispute arose over the candidate for vice-president. Some members of the upper class and significant numbers of the middle class wanted General Bernardo Reyes, the former Secretary of War, to run for vice-president. For the second time Díaz had the opportunity to anoint Reyes as the successor, and for the second time the president let pass the opportunity. Instead, Díaz was quite content to retain the incumbent vice-president, Ramón Corral, who had amply demonstrated his incompetence and who suffered chronic illness. Blind loyalty and fawning obedience made Corral the choice for Díaz, who still resented years later the independent actions Reyes had taken as Secretary of War.[7] The preference for obedience over ability or initiative revealed the fundamental weak-

ness of the regime. In the high spheres of government the Reyes candidacy never had any chance of success. The loss for Mexico was immense, not only because he was the most competent person for successor, but also because his age (only 10 years younger than Díaz), promised an eventual rotation of high political office and even the hope of a transition toward an open and democratic system.[8]

The vice-presidential candidacy of Reyes was a missed opportunity for Mexico. The old president was losing his deft touch, and politics rather than providing stability was opening the doors to eventual rebellion. However,

Mexican president Porfirio Díaz created present-day Mexico, and his long rule brought peace and prosperity to the country. His failure to carry out an orderly succession in 1910 was responsible for the start of the Mexican Revolution (Library of Congress, Prints and Photographs Division).

Díaz had not been completely wrong about the defects of Reyes, whose campaign self-destructed in an embarrassing way. The former Secretary of War never proclaimed his candidacy, and a caring Díaz provided a graceful exit to Reyes, who went to Europe on a military mission in October 1909.[9] Upon the sudden departure of Reyes, his many spontaneous followers (Reyistas) were left looking like fools. A political void had appeared, and a new figure, Francisco I. Madero, seized the opening to launch his political career. A wealthy landowner from Coahuila, Madero had studied abroad in France and in the United States. The publication of a small book calling for open and honest elections had gained him limited prominence. After the fiasco of the Reyes campaign, members of the upper and the middle class asked Madero to run not for vice-president but for president in 1910. Former Reyistas such as José María Maytorena from Sonora and Venustiano Carranza from Coahuila now became followers of Madero (Maderistas). The new candidate went on the campaign trail across Mexico and his tours culminated in his nomination to the presidency in Mexico City in April 1910.[10]

The large crowds Madero had drawn in his rallies aroused the curiosity of President Díaz, who met Madero for the first and only time on 16 April 1910. Some of the loyalists of Díaz were already trying to arrest the opposition candidate, and the president had to take a decision. Díaz wanted to use the Madero campaign to neutralize the popularity of Reyes in the army, in the upper class, and in northern Mexico. However, Díaz was afraid that the Madero movement might get out of hand and wanted to reach some agreement or at least an understanding. In the conversation, Madero, the cocky young upstart, kept challenging the statements of the president and even went so far as to point out contradictions. Díaz was furious, but the patient old man maintained his control as he tried to explain that he had reserved a place for Madero in the president's plans for a future Mexico. Madero for his part refused to disclose any of his intentions, so the meeting was barren of any agreement. The interview gave Madero the opportunity to size up his opponent: "The impression that General Díaz left me was that of being really decrepit and of having little vitality [...] I felt I was

dealing with a child or with an ignorant and skeptical rancher [...] I can assure you that after the interview my hopes of victory have increased."[11]

Shortly after the interview, the supporters of Díaz, without a counter order from the president, felt authorized to arrest Madero. Because the government controlled the voting machinery, the outcome of the election was never in doubt; the press announced the "practically unanimous"[12] reelection of Díaz and Corral for a six-year term in June 1910. Madero obtained his release on bond on 22 July, but on the condition that he stay within the city of San Luis Potosí. Once he made up his mind to rebel, he jumped bail on 6 October and fled to Texas to organize the revolt. In a published manifesto of October 1910, he called on Mexicans to rise up against Díaz on the announced date of 20 November 1910. Smugglers brought copies of his manifesto, the Plan of San Luis Potosí (named after the city where he had spent time in jail) across the border. Soon the plan reached most provinces of the country, but the question remained: Would the Mexicans heed the call to revolt? The plan promised to replace Porfirio Díaz and his henchmen with new persons elected in open elections, but it was silent on other issues. The change of rulers was appealing to many in the upper and middle classes, but was meaningless to the illiterate Mexican peasants who comprised over 80 percent of the population.[13]

Madero never promised or intended any revolutionary changes in economic or social structures. He even hoped to avoid an armed insurrection by appealing to the Federal Army (the formal name of the national Mexican army) to switch sides. In a proclamation he addressed to the Mexican army in the early days of November, he warned the soldiers and the officers that they could only delay the triumph of the revolt and urged them to join his movement to avoid needless bloodshed.[14] The government had paid scant attention to the Plan of San Luis, but the proclamation to the army hit a raw nerve in the War Department. At a time when the army should have been feverishly preparing for a campaign in the north, the War Department engaged in a witch hunt among the officers to weed out those with Maderista sympathies. "Officers were transferred from one military unit to another, some suspect officers were removed from command, orders were sent to relocate some battalions, and discipline was taken to the extreme."[15] The obsession with political loyalty did prevent any major defections but inevitably disrupted army operations.[16]

Any chance to prepare the army for a campaign in the north evaporated when riots shook Mexico City on November 8 and 9. A mob in Rock Springs, Texas, had burned to death a Mexican accused of raping and murdering a white woman. In protest, university students in Mexico City staged demonstrations that degenerated into riots. Although the police (under the command of Félix Díaz, the nephew of the president) controlled the disturbances the next day, the fear of new outbreaks made the regime hesitant to deplete the army garrisons in the cities. Had adequate police forces existed in the cities, many troops otherwise tied down would have been free to fight in the countryside. In still another unfortunate consequence, the Mexico City riots had redirected attention towards central Mexico and away from the more vulnerable northern provinces.[17]

From his refuge in Texas, Madero was busy constructing a network of collaborators to start the revolt at many places. The police was the first line of defense against the announced Madero revolt, but in spite of many accusations to the contrary, "the Díaz Regime had never developed the kind of all-powerful secret police that emerged in many countries later in the twentieth century."[18] The closest Mexico had to a national police force were the less than two thousand mounted *rurales*, whose corruption and drunkenness made them woefully incompetent.[19] The *rurales* served at best as auxiliaries to the federal troops. In Mexico City the police had been making arrests and taking other precautions since October to prevent any organized uprising.[20] Intense policing should have prevented the outbreak of any urban revolt, but city police traditionally starved of resources were unable on their own to detain all the plotters. In the states of Sinaloa and Tlaxcala, and in the cities of Guadalajara, Guanajuato and Pachuca timely arrests did abort planned revolts. In Puebla on 18 November the local police learned that Aquiles Serdán had collected weapons in his house for the planned revolt. The attempt to arrest him failed, and the local police needed the help of

the *rurales* and garrison troops to overcome the resistance at his house. The attackers killed the 22 rebels, including Aquiles Serdán, and only spared the four women who had also participated in the combat. This blow to the conspirators did keep Puebla quiet for months but at the cost of creating the first martyr of the revolt. News of the heroic defense at Puebla by Serdán and his female relatives quickly spread by word of mouth across the country and predisposed many to sympathize with Madero's cause.[21]

The inadequacy of the police response paralleled the lack of military preparations. Because Treasury Secretary Limantour had killed the Second Reserve of Reyes, the army could not summon any reservists in this critical time of need. Therefore, once Madero chose war in early October, the only realistic option for the government was to increase the size of the Federal Army, even if only with short-term enlistments. Any increase in troop strength had the additional salutary effect of drawing from the same recruiting pool as the rebels. At this early stage, each additional soldier meant one less rebel: Good pay for the volunteers was the most potent weapon available to the regime of Porfirio Díaz. Again Limantour rigidly blocked any increase in army expenses, and keeping the budget balanced remained a higher priority than preventing the start of a revolution.

A vigorous redeployment of existing units promised to deter the rebels, but in trying to carry out this response, the War Department ran into difficulties. Although nobody expected Chihuahua to become the key battleground, Madero was sure to have sympathizers in his native Coahuila.[22] Sending additional army units to Coahuila and reinforcing the border posts along the Rio Grande River seemed the obvious minimum steps to contain the Madero uprising. The show of force was sure to scare off many men thinking of taking up arms. In addition, the deployment itself would also reveal that many units were seriously undermanned. The practice of "padding" the muster rolls so that corrupt officers received the pay and allotments of non-existent soldiers meant that the size of the army was a fraction of its authorized strength of 29,000. In October plenty of time remained to bring the undermanned units up to strength and to chip away at Limantour's ban on any more army expenditures, but unfortunately a fast redeployment proved too cumbersome for the War Department. The failure to mount an adequate show of force in the north confirmed that the greatest weakness of the Federal Army was the same as that of the regime it served: The insistence on blind obedience to the exclusion of competence or initiative.[23]

The army deficiencies emerged starkly during the campaign for Ciudad Guerrero, Chihuahua, the first major military operation of the insurrection (Map 11). The revolts in northern states either fizzled out or failed to appear except in Chihuahua, the largest state in Mexico. Resentment against the Terrazas-Creel clique ruling and owning that state for decades made rebel recruitment easy. At least eight rebel bands coalesced in the week before 20 November, and they threatened small towns like Ojinaga and even bigger urban centers like Hidalgo del Parral. However, the center of the revolt was in Ciudad Guerrero, on whose outskirts mounted peasants had been gathering during the previous week. Their leader was the later notorious Pascual Orozco, Jr., who resented the favoritism the Terrazas-Creel clique had shown to a competitor in the freight-hauling business. The army captain at Ciudad Guerrero had promptly reported the threatenening concentration of Orozquistas to Chihuhua City, which was just a couple of hours away by a comfortable train ride. Because he commanded only 62 cavalry men, at least since 18 November he repeatedly telegraphed for reinforcements from the thousand-man garrison at Chihuahua City. However, General Manuel M. Plata, the commander of this military zone, pondered the matter at leisure and then sent a telegram to the War Department asking for instructions. Mexico City authorized the transfer on 20 November, but in the relaxed peacetime atmosphere, the reinforcements did not depart until the next day.[24]

All the time Urbano Zea, the civilian district official or *jefe político*, had been directly telegraphing Mexico City with desperate pleas "to amass war formations because this place is worth more than any other location in the Republic."[25] The district official had realized that the key to halting the entire revolt was in Ciudad Guerrero, but even this prophetic insight could not convince Porfirio Díaz or anyone else in Mexico City of the urgent need to reinforce

Chihuahua. The active district official armed 43 volunteers who joined the small cavalry army unit to stop the first attack by rebel forces on 21 November. That same day 175 soldiers had finally set out from Chihuahua City, but the long delay ruled out an easy train ride. A rebel force under the later notorious Pancho Villa fired at the train and in the skirmish killed the unit commander. The second in command, after the fuel for the locomotive inexplicably ran out, decided to proceed on foot the next day. On 27 November the relief column fell into a trap of Pascual Orozco and his 300 rebels. The soldiers initially fought back, but because General Plata had allotted only 60 rounds per soldier, the defense collapsed when the ammunition ran low.[26] The second in command was killed and "Only the valor of some regulars, who collected bullets from the cartridge belts of their dead and wounded comrades, in order to continue the fight, prevented annihilation of the federals."[27] Nearly seventy fell prisoner and only thanks to the cover of night did the third in command manage to lead 28 wounded survivors back to Chihuahua City.[28]

The victory gave the rebels an important psychological boost, and hundreds flocked to join Orozco and Villa. Orozco returned with 800 men to intensify the siege of Ciudad Guerrero. After heavy fighting, civilians persuaded the army garrison to surrender on 4 December 1910 on promises of safe passage. Although the brutal carnage of later revolutionary years had not yet begun, the captain realized his soldiers were dead men if they did not leave immediately. To save their lives, he told them to flee quickly in small parties to their homes. He urged the civilian officials to do the same, but they did not share his fears. In a decision they later regretted, the civilian officials did not accompany the captain to Chihuahua City.[29]

The capture of Ciudad Guerrero provided the rebels with their first major victory: For the first time in memory, the Federal Army had failed to save one of its outposts from a slowly mounting attack. On 5 December, as soon as Porfirio Díaz heard of the loss of Ciudad Guerrero, he fired General Plata and replaced him with General Juan A. Hernández. The War Department tried to send reinforcements to Chihuahua, whose rebels had revealed how weak the regime was. Many previously fearful sym-

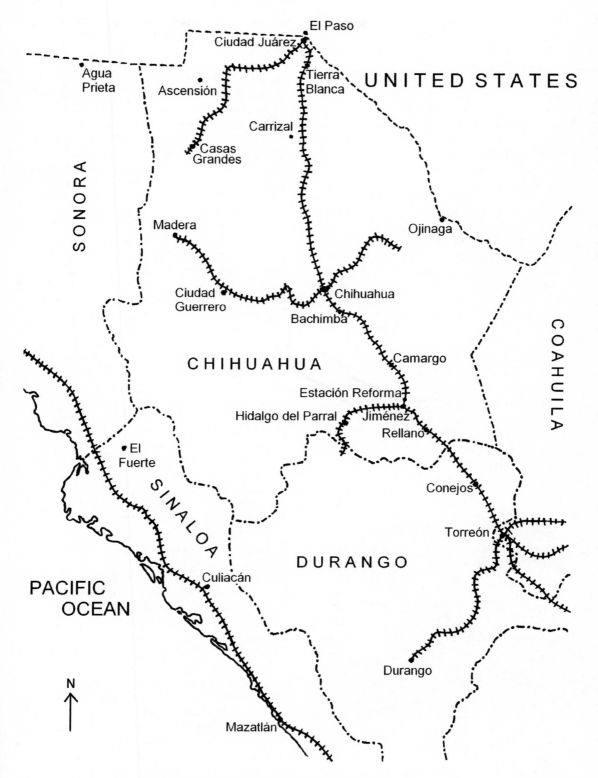

Map 11. Chihuahua and Surrounding Regions.

pathizers gained confidence to take up arms on behalf of Madero. A thousand armed rebels threatened Ojinaga in eastern Chihuahua, and about 5,000 appeared west of the state capital. The new rebels sensed a chance to win and also discovered the many attractions of campaigning. After years of disastrous crops, the granaries and farms of Chihuahua and most of Mexico were full of foodstuffs from an abundant harvest in 1910.[30] The temptation to plunder and thus to compensate for years of hardship was ever present, and as early as December 1910 Pascual Orozco was accusing some followers "of going around with the sole object of robbery"[31] rather than fighting the Federal Army. By simply proclaiming the name of Madero, rebel bands gained license to take cattle, horses, and foodstuffs from the haciendas.[32] The "Revolution" had become an easy way to earn a livelihood when little other employment was available. The collapse of property rights was essential to finance the revolt and to attract fol-

Pascual Orozco was the principal rebel leader in Chihuahua and led with Pancho Villa the attack on Ciudad Juárez in May 1911 (Library of Congress, Prints and Photographs Division).

lowers. Weapons and ample ammunition were no less vital if the rebel bands were to deter the Federal Army.

On the border, the Mexican consuls and spies enjoyed ample cooperation from the U.S. government and should have been able to halt the supply activities, but unfortunately Díaz had become "careless in the management of his consular spy and police systems."[33] Soon Madero found financial resources to obtain and deliver weapons and ammunition. In the process he created a network that "included the services of competent lawyers, a revolutionary secret police, hired detectives, paid informants."[34] He even managed to bribe several Mexican consuls. Madero's network became operative in December, by which time he knew that the revolt in Mexico had taken a very different turn than he expected. Although he had financial support from a handful of wealthy landlords, almost unanimously the upper class had remained loyal to Porfirio Díaz. His appeal to the Federal Army had failed to convince any units to switch sides. The biggest blow was the failure of his native Coahuila to join the insurrection. Madero himself came to lead the revolt in Coahuila, but when early in the morning of 20 November he did not find masses eager to acclaim him leader, he had to cross the border hurriedly to the United States to escape capture. All his plans for the revolt had failed, and instead his appeal had found an echo only in Chihuahua. None of the leaders of the rebel bands were from the upper class, and very few had some claim to middle-class status; many were cattle rustlers, bandits, and murderers, including Pancho Villa.[35] Madero faced a turning point: Did he abandon the revolt that had turned into an attack on property rights, or did he supply ammunition and money to the rebels? Without his support the rebels in Chihuahua were just looters and criminals; the Federal Army, no matter how slowly, eventually could pursue and exterminate them. Instead, with his support, the bandits of Chihuahua were miraculously transformed into revolutionaries, who now could rally the other Mexican states to join the sacred struggle for freedom. Already on 3 December 1910, a day before the rebel capture of Ciudad Guerrero, Madero had made his pact with the devil when he wrote his father: "The news published from Chihuahua is reassuring and makes us hope that the place will, rather than extinguish itself, become the base to set ablaze the rest of the Republic."[36] With his boundless optimism, Madero believed that after the revolt was over, with words he could convince the Chihuahua rebels to return to peaceful pursuits.

The Spread of the Insurrection

Because the insurrection by early December appeared confined to Chihuahua, the Díaz government ignored the flickering sparks in other regions and committed the blunder of not enlarging army strength. Again Secretary of the Treasury Limantour blocked any increase in the numbers or the pay of the army. The Federal Army had just begun to acquire machine guns and needed many more. Rush orders for machine guns and for artillery pieces could still tilt the balance of victory to the Federal Army, but Limantour, who was concerned exclusively with refinancing the foreign debt of Mexico, blocked any increase in military expenditures. Only a rapid redeployment of most of the army units could strangle the revolt in Chihuahua, but the government was reluctant to leave central and southern Mexico totally undefended and not just because of the fear of urban riots. In supposedly somnolent Tabasco the local garrison had to crush an outbreak on 31 December 1910; not until the initial wave of revolts had spent itself could the government have a sense of which units were not needed in their usual postings. When the transfer of troops north began in January, the government, which still had a railroad network at its disposal, showed no haste. Miscellaneous units and fragments of battalions drifted into Chihuahua during January and February in a haphazard fashion. Even the government realized these reinforcements were insufficient and shifted several units from neighboring Sonora to Chihuahua. As the northward redeployment continued, the shortage of men in many units could no longer remain hidden. As early as February rumors had circulated that the army rolls were padded with non-existent soldiers, and gradually the government moved to fill the ranks. No urgency accompanied the task, because the government deluded itself into believing that bringing the units up to full strength sufficed to meet the crisis. Without

any need for extraordinary or rush efforts, the army stayed within budget. Until April the Treasury Department blocked all attempts to increase the numerical strength or the pay of the army.[37] In contrast to the complacency of Mexico City, the rebels had already realized that victory in the north depended on who could bring more fighting men into the field. The tardy and inadequate response of the federal battalions gave the rebels the "opportunity to recruit our armies and train our eager recruits. Every day increases our strength."[38]

The redeployment of the Federal Army to the north was arduously slow and paradoxically also revealed signs of hastiness. For a winter campaign, the army had failed to provide many of the arriving soldiers with warm clothing and some lacked even blankets. Many soldiers who had come from a hot climate found themselves in an outdoors campaign in the coldest part of Mexico; soon men suffered frostbite and became sickly. More time was needed not just to bring adequate numbers of soldiers, but also to prepare them properly to fight in the very cold conditions. At times the freezing wind blew so hard that the men could not walk upright, and the officers believed the weather was worse than in Siberia.[39] In spite of the hardships, some units were ready for combat, and the government felt it could not afford to wait until the build-up in the north was complete. The government was determined to avenge at once the loss of Ciudad Guerrero, even when it lacked enough soldiers to guarantee the defense of the remaining cities in Chihuahua.

In any counterinsurgency strategy, strongly defended cities and aggressive patrolling were the indispensable conditions that had to precede the final mopping-up campaign. Ciudad Guerrero had become a symbol of defiance the government had to stamp out, but because the rebels also understood the symbolism, substantial resistance was inevitable. The premature attempt at recapturing Ciudad Guerrero was compounded by the blunder of General Juan A. Hernández, the new commander in Chihuahua City, who put General Juan Navarro in charge of the expedition.[40] On 8 December 1910 General Navarro, who will figure prominently in the rest of this chapter, marched with over 900 men from Chihuahua City. He did not take the railroad in the vain hope of trying to conceal his movements from the nearly ubiquitous rebel cavalry. As additional army units were marching from other directions, Navarro conceived his mission to be more than recapturing Ciudad Guerrero. On paper he prepared a strategic pincer movement to surround and destroy the rebels, the only possible justification for what was otherwise a counterproductive offensive.[41]

How he would carry out this encirclement was not clear, because he refused to send out his well-equipped cavalry on reconnaissance. Like most Mexican infantry officers, he did not believe that cavalry or artillery had any useful role to play in a campaign. Not surprisingly, his column marched unawares into an easily avoided ambush at Cerro Prieto on 11 December; only a quick flanking movement by one of his colonels saved the force from disaster.[42] General Navarro now had to decide whether to continue the march along a long open route where no ambush was possible, or to go to Ciudad Guerrero via the shorter route through the canyon of Malpaso. He chose the latter, and when he reached the canyon on 16 December, rebels numbering over 1200 stopped his advance guard. Six hours of fighting ensued until somewhat unexpectedly the rebels gave up their high ground. The entrance was open, and General Navarro plunged forward and established camp halfway into the canyon. After the heavy combat, his column was low on ammunition, so he decided to wait until a supply convoy of 450 men brought 150,000 Mauser cartridges. This convoy came by train and as additional protection carried two 80 millimeter cannon. The rebels, who meanwhile had reoccupied the heights at the entrance of the Malpaso canyon, greeted the train with intense rifle fire on 18 December. The colonel commanding the convoy shared with General Navarro the belief that only brave infantry won battles. Thus, rather than reverse the train out of rifle range to unlimber his artillery pieces, he insisted on detraining his soldiers and hurling them against the massed fire of the rebels in the heights. He himself was wounded, and a subordinate finally ordered the supply train to retreat to Chihuahua City, where the colonel later died of his wounds. The slaughter lacked any sense, because the fractured rocks on the hill easily splintered into dangerous fragments upon impact by artillery shells. Furthermore, the intense shooting had roused the lethargic General Navarro to send units to link up with the supply convoy. Greater speed by General Navarro or a longer resistance by the supply convoy sufficed to catch the rebels in a crossfire, but by the time Navarro's units reached the entrance, both the convoy and the rebels were gone. Gross incompetence had destroyed a precious opportunity to inflict a major defeat on the rebels.[43]

The one in a trap was General Navarro, whose troops were running out of food and medicine and lacked enough ammunition for a major engagement. The official history gave the most charitable interpretation of his predicament: "The column of General Navarro was entirely isolated because all its lines of communications were cut. It could not move because of the large quantity of impedimenta and because of the wounded soldiers."[44] General Navarro calmly awaited rescue from a quandary he himself had created. His total passivity revealed a general unable to take any independent action. His age of 68 probably slowed him down, and in any case his inability to respond forcefully to events clearly disqualified him from any further command. For the moment, to extricate the general from the trap, the War Department hurriedly rushed troops from Torreón and other places to avert a potential disaster. A force of 750 men with two mortars and two machine guns was finally on its way on 24 December. Expecting heavy fighting, the column carried 300,000 Mauser cartridges and many supplies. The commander decided this time to take the long route around Malpaso canyon and reached the camp of General Navarro on 28 December. Facing only scattered skirmishers along the way, General Navarro resumed his leisurely march and entered Ciudad Guerrero on 6 January 1911 without firing a shot. He immediately settled into winter quarters and only a couple of times allowed the cavalry to patrol the surrounding region. Instead of pursuing the rebels aggressively, General Navarro immobilized his forces more effectively than when the rebels had him trapped in Malpaso canyon.[45]

The recapture of Ciudad Guerrero had lulled many besides Navarro into a false sense of victory: "It is the general opinion among those best informed that the government has the situation well in hand and that the revolution, as such, will end very soon."[46] The rebels, short of ammunition, quietly slipped north to seek plunder in weakly defended towns and ranches. About the middle of January 1911, Madero called on the rebels to gather outside Ciudad Juárez for an attack on that city. From Ciudad Guerrero came Pascual Orozco, his forces riding north with impunity and leaving a trail of looted towns and sacked ranches in northern Chihuahua. In effect, the government began to pay the price of leaving so many places defenseless for the sake of the earlier campaign against Ciudad Guerrero. For the U.S. military attaché, the significance went much deeper: "The inability of the federal forces to quell the movement when confined to Chihuahua forebodes much pending trouble."[47] Both Casas Grandes and Ciudad Juárez were in danger of capture. By 1 February 1911 Orozco had gathered over a thousand men thirty kilometers south of Ciudad Juárez, which was defended by only 90 soldiers. Nothing could stop him from capturing the city, but his tendency to delay taking decisions manifested itself for the first time. Inexplicably, he limited himself to ripping the railroad track south of the city. The delay gave enough time for a relief column under Colonel Antonio Rábago to repair the damaged railroad track and, after a hard day of fighting, to enter the city at 2200 on 5 February.[48]

The Federal Army had won the race for Ciudad Juárez. A disappointed Orozco concluded that the best option for him and his men was to return to their villages to rest and to recover. Enough rebels stayed behind harassing Ciudad Juárez to show that the insurrection was far from over: "This revolt of Chihuahua has greater importance than what Mexico City believes. This is the nucleus that has to be crushed immediately, and once done, the rest of the country can be taken care of in days."[49] The solution was simple: "An effective cure is needed urgently. The Treasury must be opened, there is no other way to handle the matter."[50] But Díaz still refused to overrule Treasury Secretary Limantour, and thus left the army unable to garrison the key cities in Chihuahua. In a tacit admission of a past blunder, the War Department decided on 30 January to abandon the hard-won Ciudad Guerrero. The withdrawal was a great opportunity to replace the inept General Navarro with a more vigorous commander, but instead the War Department ordered Navarro to take his detachment to Ciudad Juárez. He abandoned Ciudad Guerrero on 2 February and reached Juárez on 15 February; one more crucial piece fell into place to make possible the disaster at that border city in May. Orozco, whose revolt was at a low ebb, received an unexpected boon. Without firing a shot he had recovered Ciudad Guerrero. He now appointed his followers to run this town and the surrounding villages.[51]

The offensive to crush or at least contain the rebel bands of Orozco had clearly failed by mid–February. In the chess game of moving units across Chihuahua, the isolated rebels had outmaneuvered the government in spite of its railroads and telegraphs. The success of the rebels had emboldened persons in other Mexican states to rise up. The contagious nature of the Madero insurrection precluded containment and required the immediate destruction of the Chihuahua revolt. In early February the U.S. ambassador regretfully reported "a decided recrudescence of the revolutionary movement throughout Mexico."[52] The capture of the otherwise insignificant town of Nieves in Zacatecas on 4 February generated sensationalized press accounts and spawned rebel bands in nearby Durango and Coahuila.[53] Far away Sonora experienced the first rebel activity, and even southern states like Veracruz, Chiapas and Oaxaca saw scattered rebel bands coalesce into larger units able to capture villages and to threaten cities. In most cases the Federal Army failed to respond aggressively to the attacks. The district official at Torreón, the key railroad link for Chihuahua, complained that:

> Many times I or others have reported to the local army commander that the enemy is burning this or that bridge, but only nine or more hours after the notice does a detachment set out to pursue the bandits. By the time the detachment arrives at the scene of the events, the crime has already been committed and the brigands are carrying out similar acts somewhere else. Is this long delay proper and convenient? The neglect and the laxness in these important matters have reached such a degree that last February 13th, when a patrol was setting out to pursue the rebels, I had to furnish 5000 cartridges out of the city stocks, because the soldiers lacked sufficient munitions. In such a manner, can we expect to defeat the enemy?[54]

With so many rebels rising in arms throughout the country in February and March, the government had to abandon the original strategy of hurling the entire Mexican army at Chihuahua. The last reinforcements reached Chihuahua in February, but as early as January 18 the army had to return a unit originally from Sonora back to face rebels in its home state. The new danger was that the War Department might uselessly disperse troops. The only possible strategy was to concentrate the troops in the places most likely to yield clear victories, even at the cost of abandoning marginal regions.

The decision hinged on the deployment of the 8th Battalion, the last one President Díaz felt he could spare from the garrison of Mexico City for service elsewhere. Amidst the myriad of desperate pleadings for more troops pouring into Mexico City from almost every corner of the country, militarily the most insignificant was Baja California. A group of Mexican anarchists and American adventurers had crossed the U.S. border and captured the virtually undefended Mexicali on 29 January. Under tremendous diplomatic pressure from the United States, the War Department ordered the incompetent colonel of the small garrison at Ensenada to march across the desert to drive out the invaders. Not surprisingly, the army attack on Mexicali failed on 15 February, and the defeated unit returned to Ensenada. More Mexican rebels and American adventurers crossed the border to reinforce the anarchists in Mexicali, who threatened to capture the rest of Baja California. The War Department hoped to draw forces from the battalions stationed in neighboring Sonora, but the zone commander explained that he too needed more troops to deal with the rebel bands proliferating in that state. Clearly the government was stretched thin and if anything had to concentrate its forces. Mexicali was temporarily lost and perhaps Baja California as well. To prevent an embarrassing surrender of the troops in Ensenada, the gunboats of Mexican Navy did stand ready to evacuate the small garrison to the south.

In response to incessant U.S. diplomatic pressure and to the groundless fear that the United States planned to annex Baja California, the government sent the last spare battalion to that remote territory. After a long trip by rail and ship, the 8th Battalion arrived in Ensenada on 9 March and soon engaged in extensive and inconclusive combat; the only clear result was to tie down troops better used elsewhere. The expedition to Baja California repeated the mistakes of the campaign of Ciudad Guerrero; the government insisted on dispersing scarce troops to capture secondary objectives. The 8th Battalion, if sent to Chihuahua, just might have provided that slight margin crucial for victory.[55]

By March the failure to stamp out the insurrection had tarnished the image of invincibility the Díaz regime had enjoyed for decades. The Mexican peasants who joined the "Revolution" gained a license to steal and take private property: "they can get as many recruits as they can arm, while the federals are constantly losing in numbers."[56] In spite of the wave of revolts spreading throughout the country, the government still did not enlarge the army. Insistent requests for soldiers poured into Mexico City from many threatened places, but no troops were available. Higher pay was indispensable to attract recruits, but the Treasury Department still refused to authorize any additional hiring, much less any pay increases. As a substitute for soldiers, requests also poured in for machine guns, but the Treasury Department refused to pay prices it considered outrageous.[57] Deprived of an increase in the number of soldiers and machine guns, the army could not stop the momentum of the insurrection. The last chance to halt the rebels was in early March when the army still could win a major victory in Chihuahua.

The urgency came because by this date the insurrection was spreading on its own, and time was on the side of the rebels. Madero himself was pessimistic, and he was right, because time was running out for him as a leader. Rebels clashed daily with federal soldiers, yet Madero remained safely in the United States. To maintain his leadership he knew he had to reinsert himself into the insurrection. On 14 February, with U.S. agents hot in pursuit, he crossed into Mexico about 15 kilometers south of Ciudad Juárez. This entry was not a repeat of the fiasco of his attempt on 20 November; this time rebels flocked to his standards, and after a week he had over 700 men under his command, including a contingent of Americans. When Madero learned on 21 February that a garrison of only 338 soldiers defended

Casas Grandes, he decided to capture that town. His force continued to attract recruits as he moved south at a leisurely pace. Should the federal garrison at Ciudad Juárez attempt any sortie, he left behind roving bands to protect his rear. With 800 men he set up camp three kilometers south of Casas Grandes on 5 March and prepared to attack the next day. He was confident of victory, not just because of his numerical superiority, but because the American volunteers trusted their dynamite to shatter the town's defenses.[58]

Colonel Agustín Valdés, in command in Casas Grandes, had meanwhile been preparing the defense lines and had already managed to increase his force by 138 auxiliaries and volunteers. Because rebels had cut his telegraph communications since 1 March, he had not been able to request reinforcements from Ciudad Juárez. He had managed to chart the movements of Madero's column and realized that he could count only on his men for the defense; he did have, however, a secret weapon: a well-positioned machine gun. Colonel Valdés was certain that he could defend the town as long as his ammunition lasted.[59]

One of the bands that Madero had left behind to cover his rear installed itself comfortably in the village of La Ascensión. For General Navarro, this was a great opportunity to get rid of Colonel Samuel García Cuéllar, who had made a pest of himself by insisting on rapid strikes against the rebels. On February 27 General Navarro ordered Colonel García Cuéllar to dislodge the rebels from La Ascensión; that day the colonel with 576 men set out first by train and then continued by rapid marches. His cavalry reconnoitered incessantly and accurately reported the rebel movements. By the time the main column reached La Ascensión on 2 March, the small rebel bands had already dispersed and returned home; the only large rebel band was fleeing over the mountain range into Sonora. The colonel confirmed the next day that a large force under Madero himself was south of Casas Grandes. On 4 March the colonel led his well-rested troops on forced marches to try to intercept the rebel leader. When he learned that Madero was planning to attack Casas Grandes, García Cuéllar swung his column east to avoid any contact with the rebels outside the town. At 2030 his column camped six kilometers to the east of Casas Grandes, at the hamlet of Nuevas Casas Grandes.[60] A telephone line the rebels had failed to cut brought the good news to the beleaguered garrison. By phone the two colonels coordinated their plans to smash the rebels the next day.[61]

For the only time during the insurrection, the rebels were in the dark about the federal troops. Unaware of the danger hovering over them, Madero's men prepared for the attack at dawn on 6 March. The rebels diverted the waters from the irrigation ditch that flowed in a straight north-south line to the east of the town. Then they began to occupy isolated houses outside the defense perimeter Colonel Valdés had established. The plan called for first advancing silently along the ditch. Then under covering fire from the houses, the rebels would jump from the ditch and rush to capture the town. The dynamite charges would take care of any army resistance.

At 0500 small groups of Madero's men began the battle by attacking from the north and the south in what were obviously diversionary attacks. After 0600 the main rebel force jumped out of the irrigation ditch to attack the town from the east, only to be stopped by the deadly fire of the lone machine gun. The Americans hurled their dynamite, but it exploded harmlessly because the distance to the federal defense lines was too great. After an hour the bulk of Madero's attacking force returned to the irrigation ditch. Between 0715 and 0730 the relief column suddenly appeared in the rear and caught many rebels in a crossfire in the irrigation ditch. Colonel García Cuéllar had not thrown his entire column into this assault, but he had wisely diverted his cavalry south to intercept the escape route and to seize the rebel camp. Heavy fighting ensued, and not until the two 80 mm mortars began raining explosive grenades on the ditch did the rebels begin to retreat. As the rebels fled to the south, the army force broke through the ditch and entered Casas Grandes. By twelve noon the rebels were in full flight to the south, and only those left trapped in the houses continued to resist. Colonel García Cuéllar had over six hours of daylight for the pursuit, and he expected to capture or kill all the rebels, who were fleeing on foot.[62]

Madero himself suffered a wound, and the future of the insurrection hung in the balance.

Francisco Madero after Casas Grandes. A wounded Madero was extremely lucky to have escaped alive from the March 1911 battle (Library of Congress, Prints and Photographs Division).

Colonel García Cuéllar, sensing the opportunity to shatter the insurrection, plunged forward on horseback to direct his men to the pursuit. At this fateful moment, a bullet struck him, and to save his life his men dragged by force a protesting colonel away from the battlefield; eventually his hand had to be amputated. Command fell by seniority to the artillery colonel who promptly and inexplicable abandoned the pursuit. Madero and the rebel force were able to walk away to the south unmolested and to gather some days later in the town of Galeana.[63]

The defeat and near death of Madero had an electrifying impact on the insurrection. When Madero entered Mexico in February, the rebel leaders had largely ignored him. His brush with death made the rebel leaders realize that without Madero, they were little more than brigands. Instead, under Madero, the rebel leaders belonged to the sacred cause of the "Revolution" and miraculously gained absolution from any past crimes. Fully conscious that the death of Madero meant their trial and execution as common criminals, Orozco and the rebel leaders rallied to his side and pledged loyalty and obedience. In one week Madero commanded a larger force than before the battle. His numbers had more than doubled by the end of March. On 2 April Pancho Villa came with over 500 men he had recruited.[64]

The momentum Madero gained showed that the battle of Casas Grandes, rather than a defeat, had been a catalyst for spreading the insurrection. Not just in Chihuahua, but throughout the country sympathizers flocked to the movement. What action could the government of Porfirio Díaz take to halt the rapidly spreading insurrection? The convalescent Colonel García Cuéllar as early as 10 March had urged that flying columns coordinate their movements to inflict decisive blows against the rebels, but General Navarro limited himself to forwarding the Colonel's recommendations to the War Department. The Federal Army resumed its usual pattern of tardily responding to rebel thrusts. Meanwhile, Madero slowly gathered over a thousand men for a second attempt on Casas Grandes, and he deployed hundreds more to distract the federal garrisons. He ordered the rebels to cut the railroad lines and in particular the track to the south in Torreón. His goal was to isolate Chihuahua City, so that its large garrison could not threaten his rear. Madero's precautions were unnecessary because on 7 April Colonel Agustín Valdés evacuated Casas Grandes and headed to Chihuahua City, in response to orders from the War Department. As with the abandonment of Ciudad Guerrero on 2 February, strategic movements had again gained the rebels another valuable town without any combat The rebels enjoyed undisputed control over nearly half of Chihuahua. The rebel territory included even a railroad, which proved very useful for the later campaign on Ciudad Juárez.[65]

From a military perspective, the evacuation of Casas Grandes on 7 April was another turning point in the campaign. The abandonment of Ciudad Guerrero on 2 February had exposed the acute shortage of troops. The evacuation of Casas Grandes revealed that the Federal Army barely could defend the largest cities in Chihuahua. From a political perspective, the evacuation of Casas Grandes also reflected the decision of Díaz to seek a political solution to the revolt. The president was among the first to realize that the destruction of the rebels was no longer possible. However, Díaz still wanted to preserve a strong Federal Army as a bargaining chip in the negotiations with Madero. Although on 11 April he had at last overruled Limantour and authorized an increase in the number of soldiers and in their pay, he harbored no illusions about destroying the rebels.[66] The president was trying to save as much as possible of the ancien régime, but ultimately battlefield events and not negotiations would dictate the terms of any agreement. Just recently the survival of the Madero insurrection had hung on the one bullet that fell Colonel García Cuéllar at Casas Grandes. In late April the fate of the Díaz regime rested in the hands of General Juan Navarro at Ciudad Juárez.

The Battle of Ciudad Juárez

Porfirio Díaz had received so many reports about the utter incompetence of General Juan Navarro that just the presence of the latter in Ciudad Juárez was reason enough to abandon the city. But the preference for loyalty over ability, the endemic flaw of the army and of the ancien régime, again determined the outcome. With so many reasons to remove General Navarro, the one recalled was the victorious Colonel Samuel García Cuéllar. Although the War Department promoted him to the rank of Brigadier General, it could not appoint him the commander at Juárez without jumping over senior generals. No matter how incompetent the other generals, President Díaz did not want to antagonize them, because he needed them to keep in check the junior officers who already had hatched a small conspiracy in late March.[67]

Patient attention had taken care of dissension within the army in the past, but time was what Díaz now lacked. Sending units north from their home bases had left the south open for rebellion. The deployment of troops from

An early photographs of Pancho Villa (Library of Congress, Prints and Photographs Division).

the south was too slow to achieve decisive victories in the north, but fast enough to encourage rebels to rise up and raid haciendas and villages in the states of Morelos, Guerrero, and Puebla. Again the small size of the army severely limited the responses of the government. Small-scale fighting had begun in Morelos in February, and the revolt in that state formally started on 10 March 1911. The rebels learned that by uniting into large bands, they could overwhelm the defenses of the isolated haciendas. Soon the peasants in quest of rich booty were ransacking haciendas and looting villages. Through his self-driven quest for power, Emiliano Zapata imposed himself as the leader of the bands in the state of Morelos. The frightened hacendados and the terrified city dwellers sent desperate pleas for protection to Porfirio Díaz. The relatively small number of rebels at Morelos south of Mexico City threatened the national capital and thus gave Zapata unusual political leverage.[68]

With the rebels pressing hard on so many fronts, the War Department played another round in the fateful chess game of troop movements across Chihuahua. Casas Grandes, along with Chihuahua City and Ciudad Juárez, had formed a triangle of supporting garrisons that disrupted rebel movements. When the War Department concluded that Casas Grandes was too exposed for effective defense, how could it overlook the greater vulnerability and isolation of Ciudad Juárez? The latter city needed for its defense the entire column that had left under García Cuéllar, but only 223 soldiers with a machine gun and two mortars, had set out for Ciudad Juárez a few days prior to the evacuation of Casas Grandes. When this small fraction returned to its base on 6 April, many soldiers were sick or wounded. The War Department had foolishly split up the Casas Grandes garrison, with most troops heading for Chihuahua City as replacements for the departing 29th Battalion, which was to head south to face the rebels in Puebla. The troops were needed in Chihuahua City not for its defense but to constitute a relief column for the beleaguered garrison at Ojinaga to the east. The recently promoted Brigadier General Rábago left with 1000 soldiers on 17 April for that distant outpost on the Rio Grande River. For the sake of saving marginal Ojinaga the government had sacrificed vital Casas Grandes; a more far-fetched military maneuver was hard to imagine. All that Ojinaga needed was money to procure food and ammunition from the U.S. side, but just because the Mexican treasury had been remiss in sending funds did not justify the large relief column. The only valid military options were either a simultaneous withdrawal from Ciudad Juárez and Casas Grandes, or a determined defense at both places.[69]

Poor reconnaissance had led the government to conclude erroneously that Madero was concentrating rebels to the northwest of Chihuahua City in preparation for an attack on that state capital. In fact, his original intention had been to capture Casas Grandes, and on the way to that city he heard about its evacuation of 7 April. He might have tried to intercept the retreating garrison, but instead he summoned the rebel bands to congregate near the very vulnerable Ciudad Juárez. Already on 11 April the *jefe político* or district official in that city, who had been pleading urgently for reinforcements and ammunition, reported that 3,500 rebels were threatening Ciudad Juárez. The district

official had sounded the alarm constantly about the danger of an attack, but the commander of the garrison, the immutable General Navarro, did not share the concern and limited himself to requesting additional ammunition. While Madero ably carried out strategic movements, General Navarro remained passive. Madero was gradually tightening the noose around the garrison of Ciudad Juárez, yet General Navarro calmly expected the government to rescue him from any predicament, just like when he had been trapped in the Malpaso Canyon in January.[70]

A repetition of the rescue was not possible because the government did not realize promptly the danger threatening Ciudad Juárez. The War Department received news from the front with considerable delay and was very slow in responding with orders. It was Díaz who first discovered the dangerous intentions of the rebels, and on 21 April he recalled General Rábago back to Chihuahua City. The President also ordered Rábago to pick up additional men at Chihuahua City and to march immediately to the relief of Ciudad Juárez. Wanting to emphasize the urgency of the movement, Díaz also sent a construction train to repair the damaged track so that the relief column could advance faster. General Rábago had acquired a reputation for arriving just in time to save endangered units, and even though the infantry normally required 20 days to march through the barren terrain, he hoped to reach Ciudad Juárez sooner by riding the railroad on the repaired stretches of track. His optimism was well founded, because on 26 April he was already at Terrazas, about a third of the way on the trip. His large and well-armed column surely would have reinforced Ciudad Juárez before the end of the month had he not received that same day an order from the War Department to halt immediately. The War Department cited the terms of the truce Madero had signed with General Navarro as the reason for halting the relief column. Only on 7 May, after the expiration of the truce, did General Rábago receive the order to resume the march.[71]

In what initially had seemed like a great idea, General Navarro had entered into negotiations for a truce with the rebels. Rather than limiting any truce to the forces near Ciudad Juárez, he disastrously included in its provisions a prohibition on any troop movements

Battle of Ciudad Juárez: rebels fire from positions near the city (Library of Congress, Prints and Photographs Division).

north of Chihuahua City. The prohibition benefited the rebels who could easily detect any relief column coming from Chihuahua City. Instead, who would keep stray bands from joining the large rebel forces outside Ciudad Juárez? How could a weak Madero make his followers comply with the provisions? Navarro's truce of 23 April was a fatal mistake, because the rebels gained time to collect more supporters and to familiarize themselves with the defenses.[72]

General Navarro had placed great faith in the fortifications of the city, because his second-in-command, Colonel Manuel Tamborrel, enjoyed the reputation as the army's leading authority on fortifications. The colonel had begun to ring the city with trenches, but his haughty arrogance blinded him to the need for more extensive fortifications. He dismissed the rebels as cowards who would never stand and fight but would flee as in the past. His arrogance influenced General Navarro who likewise ignored the warning signs; only at the very last moment did Tamborrel order erecting some crude breastworks. He had not con-

structed a defense in depth, because initially he had wasted time and resources building useless defenses at the city center. He shaped some bastions for the artillery and placed sandbags and rock to block the town entrances. Even if the fortifications on the outskirts had been more solid, the shortage of soldiers made for a precarious defense. Nominally General Navarro had over 850 men under his command (including 130 government employees and private citizens who as volunteers fought ferociously) a number just barely sufficient to man the trenches against the over 3,000 rebels under Madero. In reality, sickness and wounds reduced the fighting strength of the garrison to 631 soldiers.[73] To make coordination more difficult, the soldiers hailed from eight different battalions and other sundry miscellaneous units. This hodgepodge of units in Ciudad Juárez was not unusual and reflected the government's desperate attempts to strip detachments from any battalion for service in the north.[74]

At first sight General Navarro's defenses seemed solid. The key to Ciudad Juárez was the

Battle of Ciudad Juárez: rebels having dinner (Library of Congress, Prints and Photographs Division).

trench line in the west overlooking the open space south of the Rio Grande River (Map 12). The soldiers with their long-range Mausers controlled the entire approach, and the rebels with their short-range Winchester 30–30 rifles could only watch helplessly. A large frontal assault against the army trench line was suicidal, and as an alternative, the rebels had devised a more complex plan to capture the city. First, Pancho Villa and his spirited cavalry would make a diversionary attack from the south on Ciudad Juárez. Then the rebels would attack simultaneously from the east and the west until they broke into the city and could overwhelm the garrison. Whether the rebels could coordinate such synchronized attacks remained to be seen. No doubt existed, however, that a major battle was imminent. Almost all the civilians fled to the U.S. city of El Paso with as many belongings as they could transport. The Mexican Foreign Minister, sensed the momentous consequences of the battle, and asked for hourly telegrams no matter what their cost.[75]

Stray bullets had already crossed the border, and the indignant U.S. Army Colonel Edgar Steever threatened to intervene in Mexico if the American city suffered any damage. Both Madero and Navarro took very seriously the threats from Colonel Steever. International complications were issues beyond the grasp of General Navarro, who for the sake of satisfying the U. S. officer exposed his command to fatal consequences. It never occurred to General Navarro that a decision to intervene had to come from Washington, D.C., and that perhaps the American colonel had exceeded his authority and was bluffing. Anyway, Navarro should have welcomed and not feared U.S. intervention as a radical way out of his predicament.[76]

Watching events unfold faster than he could comprehend them, General Navarro left his fate to his subordinate colonels, as he had done before in the Ciudad Guerrero campaign. Unfortunately, at Ciudad Juárez he did not have resourceful colonels like García Cuéllar or Rábago and instead depended exclusively on

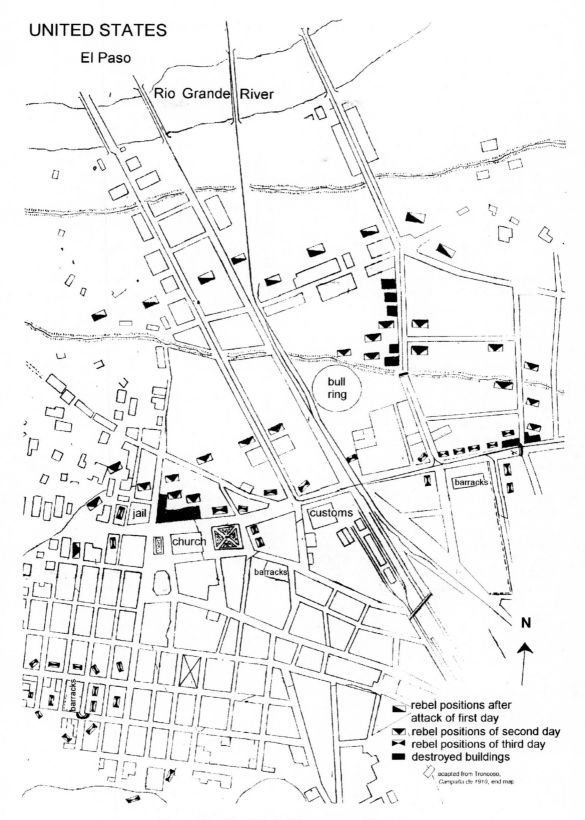

Map 12. Battle of Ciudad Juárez, 8–10 May 1911.

the impetuous Colonel Tamborrel. The arrogance of the latter continued to intensify. Perhaps because he saw the war ending without having any chance for real combat experience, or perhaps because he had not bothered to inform himself fully on the rebel tactics, he had become obsessed with engaging in combat. His arrogant contempt for the rebels may have bolstered the will of his soldiers but also inspired a false sense of confidence in General Navarro. Tamborrel went too far when he broadcast through the newspapers of El Paso that the rebels would not fight because they were cowards, who could only steal chickens from defenseless farms. Insulting an opponent has always been counterproductive; the machista code of honor required that the angry rebels redeem their sullied reputation.[77]

Madero, fearing complications with the Americans on the border, decided to take the rebel force south to attack Chihuahua City as soon as the last truce expired. He believed that so many would rally to his cause, that he could conduct a triumphant victory march all the way to Mexico City. His followers were not so eager to march through the barren desert and had their hearts set on looting wealthy Ciudad Juárez. Nevertheless, late in the afternoon on 7 May Madero coaxed the rebel contingents to start moving to the south, only to be surprised early the next day by the news that President Díaz had agreed to resign. The excited rebels hurriedly returned to their former positions in front of Ciudad Juárez. A little later Madero, Orozco, and Villa learned that the news was false and that President Díaz had promised to resign only when convenient.[78]

The war had not ended, and Madero wanted to resume the march south, but first he had to halt the shooting near the U.S. border. At 0800 intense rifle fire had erupted near one of the bridges in the U.S. border. As they had done many times before, rebels had walked along the river to the bridge to receive provisions from the United States. A Mexican army officer spoke coarse words to a female rebel sympathizer, tempers flared, and soon the verbal dispute turned into shooting. The decisive battle of the Madero insurrection, perhaps quite fittingly and in the best machista tradition, had started over a perceived insult to a young woman. The rebels were too few to pose a serious menace, but if their numbers increased, they could outflank the army trench line facing west. The soldiers from the trench opened a very effective fire that kept the rebels pinned down; as long as the army held that position, Ciudad Juárez was safe. Inevitably some shots (almost certainly from the rebels) fell on the U.S. side. Like clockwork, U.S. Army Colonel Steever promptly sent a message threatening intervention if the shooting did not stop. The U.S. side teemed with thousands of curious spectators who had gathered in El Paso to watch the long-anticipated battle from the best viewing spots.[79]

Madero and Navarro entered into crisis management to defuse the conflict, and soon both had ordered their troops to cease firing. Here the excessive discipline of the Federal Army backfired: While Navarro's troops obeyed the order, the rebels continued shooting and resumed their advance. The enraged rebels, who had long wanted the spoils of the city, could no longer resist the temptation to attack. Orozco and Villa sensed the mood and disobeyed Madero: Instead of conveying his order to halt, they told their men to press harder the initial attack.[80] At 1000 the rebels poured out of their positions and headed to the army trench line. After the initial incident at 0800, Tamborrel had rushed an artillery piece to bolster the defense, but before it could reach the position, it received the order to return because of a new cease-fire. The soldiers, trapped in iron discipline, could only watch helplessly the following scene unfolding in the open space south of the Rio Grande:

> Like a flock of sheep, no, better like a teeming ant pile, almost like spreading gunpowder, we could see from afar the rebels coming down from the heights. They proceeded along the creeks and low spots to take advantage of the natural curves in the terrain to come closer by giant footsteps towards the city.[81]

No matter how anxious, no junior officer dared to give the order to open fire on the many easy targets. By the time the cumbersome consultation process brought new orders from General Navarro to resist, the army soldiers had barely had time to escape capture in the trench line. The rebels rushed forward along the river and seized the two bridge crossings into the United States. Not only had the rebels gained the decisive position for the defense of

Battle of Ciudad Juárez: A rebel camp outside the city (Library of Congress, Prints and Photographs Division).

the city almost without shooting, but they had also cut off the electricity, telegraph, and supply lines coming from the United States. Without electricity for the pumping station, the city was also left without water. Inexplicably, General Navarro had not stockpiled food or collected water in the army barracks.[82]

The rebels pushed south from the international bridges, captured the bull ring, and were approaching the center of the city when they ran into the army's secondary defense line anchored on the city jail, the main church, and the barracks. The rebels stopped their advance for the night and surveyed the defense line in preparation for the next day's attack. Colonel Tamborrel angrily talked of a counterattack to crush the rebels completely. His arrogance blocked any consideration of a fighting withdrawal from the city, the only realistic alternative to save the garrison. With disdain General Navarro even rejected a rebel offer of safe passage for the troops as a means to spare the city from wholesale destruction. Two junior officers

with pro–Madero sympathies took the opportunity to defect to the rebel side. Afraid of more desertions, the army officers kept their men in large contingents, rather than spreading them out thinly as was advisable for the block-to-block fighting inside the city.[83]

When on 9 May the rebels resumed their attack on the north and on the outskirts to the south, they were joined by fifth columnists or sympathizers who opened fire on government troops from inside the supposedly abandoned houses. Although the estimate of General Navarro of over 500 was too high, at least a hundred were sniping at the defenders. The first rebel advances down the streets encountered murderous artillery and machine gun fire. Armed with dynamite and long iron bars, the rebels turned to burrowing through the walls of the abandoned townhouses as the best way to outflank the army positions. Colonel Tamborrel and the men he personally commanded were trapped behind, and they escaped only by jumping through a window to another building. The Colonel was certainly a very brave man, and even after he was wounded, captured, and rescued, he insisted on returning to the frontline where he finally met his death around 1900. Inside the city the rebels had gained ground, but in the open south artillery had shattered their attacks.[84] "Ah, if only we had the cannons of the Federal Army, already we would have won completely, exclaimed the rebels!"[85]

The macho tradition exaggerated the already excessive emphasis most armies of the world then placed on personal bravery. Rather than brave heroics in the frontline, what the garrison of Ciudad Juárez needed was calm thinking to devise a survival strategy. The crumbling of the army defenses in the urban north and the successes in the open south indicated the path to follow. By noon on 9 May, Navarro had ample evidence that he could not continue to hold his position much longer, and that instead the road for a retreat was wide open to the south. Had ample water and food been available, further resistance was still possible, but famished and thirsty troops could not endure much longer. The late afternoon of the 9th was a perfect time to prepare an orderly withdrawal either during the night or before daybreak. The rebel offensive had started to flag in the north, and the federals were able to recapture some positions. What most slowed down the rebel advance was looting. With their daily allowance weeks in arrears, the rebels avidly rummaged the captured homes and buildings in search of any valuables. Others took the excuse of leaving the front line to grab a bite to eat, but in reality the meal turned out to be a bout of drunkenness. The capture of alcoholic beverages was having a deadlier effect on the rebels than the bullets of the army troops. The rebels were desperately trying to smuggle ammunition from El Paso, but they were running out of cartridges. The federal garrison might have resisted long enough until General Rábago, who had resumed his march on 7 May, arrived with his relief column. If Ciudad Juárez held out, Díaz could extract less harsh terms from the rebel negotiators.[86]

Knowledge that Rábago was coming emboldened the rebels to press their attacks with greater fury. To capture the key position of the main church in the central plaza, the rebels set fire to the nearby post office. After resisting dynamite charges and flames from the fires, the soldiers in the church, who were nearly surrounded, withdrew by 0800 on 10 May. General Navarro could no longer postpone his final and irrevocable decision.[87] His artillery and his machine gun still had plenty of ammunition, and he could use them to blast a path through the thin lines of rebel cavalry to the south. Once outside the city, the Mausers would keep the rebels at a safe distance, allowing a withdrawal in good order. Water and food were available in ranches to the south, and a link-up with the relief force of General Rábago was a matter of a day or two at most. The discipline of the troops had held up remarkably well, but should Navarro feel that their morale had collapsed, then crossing the Rio Grande River to seek internment in the United States was the only other option. With no irreparable harm to the regime, on 13 April the small garrison at Agua Prieta in Sonora already had interned itself in the United States when faced with overwhelming force; other garrisons along the border had recourse to this practice in later years.

Incredibly and in a final display of his incomparable incompetence, General Navarro ordered all his troops to gather at headquarters and to leave their animals in nearby corrals. Without the animals the garrison could not move its heavy weapons and was effectively immobilized. Like a rancher leading animals to the slaughter pen, General Navarro had trapped the soldiers at headquarters more effectively than the rebels could ever have done. With almost no water left and little food, the surrender of the garrison was inevitable, but General Navarro believed that extraordinary acts of bravery could still retrieve the garrison from its desperate situation. The sighting of a large approaching force mercifully brought the meaningless resistance to an end: The hope that it was the relief column of Rábago made the spirits of the defenders soar, but upon confirming that it was a rebel force, the bitter disillusionment so demoralized the troops that they demanded a halt to the fighting. The anger of the troops was so great that according to one account "Navarro's surrender probably was due more to knowledge of his officers that their soldiers would turn on and kill them if fight continued another day than to other causes, such as shortage of water and provisions."[88] A cornered General Navarro asked to negotiate

Battle of Ciudad Juárez: On the streets of Juárez, in front of the Monte Carlo Hotel, rebels waiting for the surrender negotations to conclude (Library of Congress, Prints and Photographs Division).

for terms. The rebels, who remembered how haughtily he had rejected their previous generous offer of safe passage out of the city, insisted on an immediate surrender. With his troops on the verge of mutiny, General Navarro had to surrender at 1430 on 10 May. The rebels, angry that they had found so little booty in the evacuated city, threw themselves with fury at the army buildings to take everything removable, down to the most insignificant items. Whatever the rebels could not use they sold in El Paso; insignia, buttons, and identification pieces from the Federal Army glutted the display cases of stores in El Paso for years afterwards.[89]

The major in charge of the federal artillery had buried the firing pins of the cannons and the machine gun and then planned his escape. Even before the shooting had stopped, curious Americans had come to inspect the smoldering ruins. The light-skinned major duly dressed himself up as an gringo tourist; equipped with the mandatory camera and stammering a few Spanish words with a very heavy English ac-

cent, he took photographs of the rebels all the way to the safety of the U.S. border.[90] For General Navarro, a marked man, no such escape was possible. The General, who had done so much to undermine the Díaz regime, could not leave the public stage without weakening Madero. The rebels wanted the firing squad for General Navarro in reprisal for the executions he had supposedly ordered at Cerro Prieto; the rebels also threatened to kill all officers should General Rábago continue his march on Ciudad Juárez.

Madero totally opposed any reprisals. However, Pascual Orozco and Pancho Villa were so insistent on the execution of Navarro, that they prepared a coup against Madero. Besides disarming Madero's personal escort, they almost fired pistol shots at the rebel leader. By a miracle Madero escaped alive, but wishing to avoid further complications, he swiftly spirited General Navarro to the safety of El Paso. The inability of Madero to control the rebels was out in the open.[91]

Was the loss of Ciudad Juárez and its garrison the crucial battle that toppled the regime of Porfirio Díaz? Complete as had been the victory for the rebels, the battle by itself did not end the war, because the Federal Army continued to fight throughout Mexico. Why then was the battle so significant? Important as was the role of Ciudad Juárez as an entry point for munitions from the United States, the real impact lay not with the loss of the city but what its capture revealed about the strength of the rebels. The change in perceptions was swift. On 13 May public opinion still believed that General Rábago could save Ciudad Juárez, yet scarcely two days later, "it seems to be accepted as a foregone conclusion that the rebels can capture Chihuahua [City] when their forces gather from both the north and the south."[92] The conventional wisdom had been that the rebels fled as soon as army troops arrived. The battle of Ciudad Juárez demonstrated that not even the garrisons of large cities were safe. It was only a matter of time before the rebels overwhelmed the other federal garrisons one by one.[93]

The Collapse of the Ancien Régime

If Ciudad Juárez had been the only city lost, the rebel threat might seem to be nothing but a local affair confined to the state of Chihuahua. In reality most cities of Mexico were under the threat of attack and of capture, as Torreón to the south well illustrated. To blockade or to capture the vital railroad link for Chihuahua City, Emilio Madero, a brother of Francisco Madero, had gone to the region of Torreón to raise rebel bands. The experience of Emilio near Torreón paralleled those of his brother Francisco near Ciudad Juárez. In the most dangerous similarity, both brothers faced defiance and disobedience from their armed followers.

Rebels had isolated Torreón by the end of April, and Emilio with over 4000 men prepared to attack the besieged city. The federal garrison consisted of about 700 men but lacked artillery. Two machine guns, instead of just one at Ciudad Juárez, more than compensated for the lack of cannon. The commander, General Emiliano Lojero, had fortified the heights on the outskirts of the city and had accumulated ample

supplies of food and water. However, rebel control of the railroad to Mexico City meant that ammunition stocks were low. The rebel attack began at noon on 9 May and coincided with the second day of battle at Ciudad Juárez. As proof of the superior abilities of General Lojero, the garrison at Torreón outlasted that of Ciudad Juárez, and as late as 14 May the rebels had not captured any of the key redoubts. However, the federal troops had fired over 55,000 rounds and were running out of ammunition. Late in the afternoon under a heavy rainfall, the defenders prepared for evacuation during the night. In spite of being surrounded, the garrison escaped to the south in the early hours of 15 May. "The evacuation was very precipitate and showed great anxiety on the part of General Lojero to get away, while several days previous he stated that he would fight to the last drop of blood and only deliver the town in ruins"[94] The most basic military principle required a spirited pursuit, but the retreating troops easily slipped away because the rebels had come with a different agenda. At Ciudad Juárez the residents had moved all their valuables to the safety of the United States, but the lack of a nearby refuge had left a rich Torreón bulging with goods and luxury items. As the rebels entered the city:

> The pandemonium on the streets was beyond any description. Shouting, yelling and the most promiscuous shooting in the air with rifles, [and] revolvers by the crazy masses surging through the streets. My first idea was to go to assist the banks as the mob by this time was absolutely crazy. [...] I heard the reports of dynamite which spelled to me a general robbing of the stores. I met a lot of men and women carrying typewriters, sewing machines and all kinds of articles. [...] The mob on foot and horseback had gotten by this time beyond control. [...] To give an excuse to plunder a certain store containing desirable goods, somebody only had to cry that shots had been fired from the roof and immediately the mob would break in the door and plunder. [...] About 9 o'clock or thereabouts the killing of the poor misled Chinamen commenced, and the killing of these harmless people will always remain a blot in the history of Torreón.[95]

By the time Emilio Madero entered the city in the afternoon and began to restore order, the mob had butchered as many as 300

Chinese.[96] The tragic anarchy of 15 May had revealed again that plunder, and not any particular ideology or even hatred of the Díaz regime, was the basic motivation of the rank and file. As long as prospects for booty existed, the temptation to join the rebel forces was hard to resist. Large bands of rebels hovered outside most of the cities of Mexico, ready to pounce their prey at the first opportunity.[97] Almost simultaneously the rebels repeated their performance in another captured city: "Pachuca, capital of the state of Hidalgo, was taken by the revolutionists last night amid indescribable scenes of violence, looting, and debauchery. Many buildings were burned and four banks demolished."[98]

The government had no choice but to order a redeployment into the largest cities. Control of the countryside passed to the rebels who roamed at will. The large army units at Sonora had not suffered a defeat comparable to that of Ciudad Juárez, but their many victories had been Pyrrhic: "Our troops have won every time in combat, but in each clash they suffer irreplaceable losses, while the enemy easily replaces his, because people addicted to robbery and disorder flock to the rebels wherever they pass."[99] Seeing his forces dwindle and fearing that isolated garrisons were too vulnerable, the commander in Sonora ordered the abandonment of Agua Prieta on 10 May. The withdrawal from Agua Prieta was particularly painful, because after bitter fighting the army had earlier driven out a larger force of rebels from that border town. The abandonment of Agua Prieta confirmed again that while the army with its superior firepower and discipline could generally capture any objective, the federal troops lacked the numbers to defend all the positions. By 13 May the Federal Army held only the railroad line running between the capital of Hermosillo and the port city of Guaymas. The rest of Sonora was in the hands of the rebels, who were already linking up with Maderistas to the east in Chihuahua and to the south in Sinaloa.[100] In early May five thousand rebels roamed at will in Sinaloa. In that state the government held only the capital city of Culiacán and the port city of Mazatlán with its small garrison of 360 soldiers and policemen. Barrages from the gunboat *Tampico* shattered the rebel attacks on Mazatlán and saved that port city from pillage. For the inland city of Culiacán

beyond the range of naval cannon, no salvation was possible. On 30 May the rebels entered the capital city of Sinaloa to the by now usual tune of rampage, looting, destruction, and killing.[101]

The Madero insurrection was no longer just a northern phenomenon. In Puebla the rebels had overrun the state, and only the timely arrival of the 29th Battalion from Chihuahua City had saved that provincial capital. On 16 May the governor was confident that the 1,200 well-trained soldiers could hold off the nearly 10,000 rebels in the outskirts of Puebla. When the War Department insisted on recalling the 29th Battalion for the final last stand in Mexico City, his optimism vanished, and the governor confessed that he had to negotiate with the rebels to avoid a bloody rampage and the release of the criminals from the prisons.[102] No less worse was the situation in the state of Guerrero. A special commissioner concluded on 2 May that:

> The pacification would require a solid army of no less than six thousand soldiers, in addition to considerable time, constant expenditures, and the destruction of the villages. I thus propose instead a conciliatory approach as the most urgent and practical. No time can be lost and the negotiations cannot be left hanging, because the rebels impatiently await their outcome.[103]

In the supposedly loyal state of Michoacán, the rebels had overrun almost all the districts. The interim governor of Michoacán reported on 15 May that "only the prompt arrival of federal troops" could save the state capital, Morelia, from capture by the rebels.[104] In Morelos, the power-hungry Emiliano Zapata, who out of pure political expediency had proclaimed support for Madero, was overwhelming the few remaining army garrisons. With a 10-to-1 superiority in numbers, Zapata had hoped to capture Cuautla on 12 May, but the determined garrison blunted his attack. Zapata laid siege to Cuautla, unaware that the dynamic General Victoriano Huerta was leading a relief column and hoped to attack Zapata by surprise. Because the garrison was running out of ammunition for the machine guns, the fateful encounter between these two personalities did not take place yet. The Cuautla defenders, taking advantage of the carelessness of the rebels, managed to escape to Cuernavaca on 19 May.[105] The stubborn defense had angered Zapata, whose victorious followers vented their fury by going on a rampage of destruction, reprisals, and killings. Before the siege started, Zapata had promised to eliminate all trace of Cuautla, although subsequently he moderated his fury.[106]

Already the government had written off Morelos and Guerrero, and on 16 May the War Department ordered the surviving garrisons to return to Mexico City for the final last stand in the capital. The order to withdraw came too late to save the main army unit in Guerrero. Its commander with 500 men tried to escape to the north to Morelos to find safety with the likewise retreating garrison of Cuernavaca. The Guerrero unit, demoralized from weeks of inconclusive campaigning and marching over unfamiliar terrain, fell into a trap and surrendered to the rebels. For the first time a Federal Army unit had surrendered on the open field. This action foreshadowed the collapse of the rest of the army.[107]

No one doubted the overwhelming rebel victory, "even Mexican army officers admit that the government is beaten."[108] Madero's priority had shifted from overthrowing the regime to controlling his followers, who were on a rampage of destruction throughout Mexico. To restore order an agreement to halt the fighting was imperative. Both sides kept negotiators meeting in Ciudad Juárez after the rebel capture of that city. On 21 May 1911 they reached an agreement whereby President Díaz, his cabinet, and almost all high officials (including the governors of the states) resigned. To conduct new national elections in October, the agreement called for a provisional government under Francisco De La Barra to take office on 25 May. With his army defeated and the whole country overrun with rebels, President Díaz had lost all bargaining power and duly resigned on 25 May. The Madero insurrection had toppled the old man, who even in his defeat remained wiser than his opponents. As he boarded the steamship *Ypiranga* bound for an austere exile in France, he remarked "Madero has released a tiger; let us see if he can control it."[109] As the tired Díaz prepared to spend the last years of his life in Paris, nobody doubted that the youthful Madero would outlive the sickly octogenarian.

6. The Struggle to Restore Order

Nothing is more difficult to harness than a people that has thrown off its burden. —
Napoleon Bonaparte[1]

Francisco Madero genuinely believed that the resignation of Porfirio Díaz automatically meant the end of the insurrection. He concluded that the rebels were looking forward to returning home to enjoy their new civil liberties. He believed that political rights such as freedom of the press and honest elections to choose new officials had more than satisfied the rebels. He assumed that ideological or political convictions had motivated the illiterate peasants to join his revolt. He could not accept the reality that the prospects of booty and plunder or at least of a daily allowance had been the primary reason attracting most peasants into the insurrection. He did worry about the loyalty of leaders like Pancho Villa and Pascual Orozco. Nevertheless, Madero, with his boundless optimism, believed that presidential authority and his personal popularity sufficed to restore order and peace to Mexico. He simplistically concluded that the rebels were eager to return to their harsh work as peasants, even after they had tasted the excitement of campaigning and the pleasures of travel and plunder. He also failed to realize that the insurrection had aroused political ambitions in many rebel leaders who did not want to return to their previous insignificance.

The Revolt of Emiliano Zapata

After the resignation of Porfirio Díaz on 25 May 1911, not Madero but Francisco de la Barra became the provisional president of Mexico. Mexicans justifiably feared that any incumbent would rig the elections of 1 October 1911 to assure an electoral victory as had happened repeatedly in the nineteenth century. The prevailing view among both contemporaries and scholars has been that Madero committed a major blunder by not assuming office after the Ciudad Juárez Accords of 21 May. This account takes the diametrically opposite view that the De la Barra presidency bolstered the incoming Madero administration and delayed the latter's self-destruction.

De la Barra understood that the most urgent task facing Mexico was to restore order. The Madero revolt had unleashed primeval forces that threatened to ravage Mexico and to destroy its cities and all signs of civilization. Having stood on the precipice of anarchy, De la Barra urgently wanted to disarm the rebels and return them home. Local and state officials had to regain their authority to guarantee peace and stability indispensable for economic growth. The task was easiest in a state like Sonora, where local hacendados had used the rebel bands to drive Porfirista officials from power. If Madero could mobilize peasants to drive out President Díaz, why couldn't hacendados do the same to drive out governors and district officials (*jefes políticos*)? Once the Ancien Régime had fallen, hacendados in Sonora no longer needed a rebellion, and they dis-

157

persed their rebel bands. As the disarmed peasants returned to civilian life, new men who protected property rights came into office. The entry of new persons into office had been easy in Sonora and elsewhere because so many Porfirian officials had fled or abandoned their posts. Throughout Mexico the provisional government enjoyed many opportunities to make appointments or to encourage new persons to run for local or state offices. As for the rebel leaders, a financial gratification persuaded most to return to private business. Other rebel leaders were content with their appointment or election to important positions. Whatever the exact solution, the central goal was to demonstrate convincingly to all the rebels that the time for armed violence had passed.[2]

The policy adopted in regard to the disbandment of the Maderista troops seems to be a very good one, viz.: to buy their firearms; to retain the better element for a newly organized Rural Police [*rurales*]; and to pay off the others,

Francisco L. de la Barra. As provisional president in 1911 after the resignation of Porfirio Díaz on 25 May, De la Barra struggled to prevent the disintegration of Mexico (Library of Congress, Prints and Photographs Division).

discharging them with certificates of service and recommendations—where deserved—whereby they may obtain civil employment. In connection with this last feature, Dr. Vásquez Gómez has appealed to the factories and larger commercial establishments for their cooperation.[3]

Inevitably incidents, sometimes bloody, occurred during the process of discharging the rebels; but by August, De la Barra had managed to demobilize the rebels in most of the states in Mexico. In a simultaneous process, he had encouraged the Federal Army to rise to its budgeted strength of 29,000; additionally, he drew on former rebels to increase the number of *rurales*.[4] Quietly, the military force of the provisional government came to surpass that of Díaz, yet in the small state of Morelos the political ambition of Emiliano Zapata prevented a full demobilization. In contrast to rebels in many states, the Zapatistas had lacked the opportunity to plunder cities. Only when the insurrection was almost over did the Zapatistas finally capture and sack Cuautla on 19 May, but the wealth of this looted city, rather than satisfying their desires, merely inflamed their appetite for greater booty.[5] The Peace Accords of 21 May in principle revoked the rebels' license to steal at will, but by then it was too late: Zapata had already made the discovery that by allowing his men to engage in looting, he could create a power base for himself.

The long-standing traditions of Morelos made the state particularly suitable for Zapata's ambitions:

Morelos in the late 1860s and until the early part of the Díaz regime was a particular hotbed of outlawry. There was an organized band of robbers, about 600 strong, who levied regular tribute upon all who dwelt within the region of their maraudings, even being so bold as to have an agent in the capital, who would sell safe-conducts to stage travelers for a corresponding purse of gold. Those caught without one of those safe-conducts were not only robbed, but killed or tortured or both [...] Zapata's horde is undoubtedly composed largely of descendants of these older bandits [...] and their program throughout has been one of murder, arson, loot, and rape.[6]

De la Barra concluded that by restoring order in Morelos he would benefit the incoming Madero administration enormously. Zapata had already shown himself to be a cunning foe, and his men were intimately familiar with the terrain. Any military campaign against him was sure to be difficult, and only by calling upon the most talented general in the Federal Army could De la Barra hope to crush the rebellion. On 8 August 1911 at 1230, the president summoned General Victoriano Huerta and gave him the task of restoring order to Morelos. The general jumped with joy at the task, not just because he knew he could complete the mission, but more significantly because the presidential summons saved his career. The general had languished in obscurity ever since the fall of his patron the former Secretary of War Bernardo Reyes. The disgraced general distracted himself during his forced retirement by visualizing surprise attacks and outflanking moves to crush the rebels in Chihuahua. He watched in disbelief as the inept General Juan Navarro let slip the precious opportunities to strike decisive blows at the rebels. At last Huerta had a major command to prove himself and to redeem the tarnished image of the defeated Federal Army.[7]

The next morning on 9 August his units left Mexico City for Cuernavaca, the capital of Morelos; Huerta knew how to inspire his troops who left the train station confident of victory and in high spirits. Once at Cuernavaca, Huerta devoted himself to a careful study of his opponent, and soon he had a plan ready to present personally to President De la Barra. Huerta concluded that he had underestimated the task ahead, and he requested that the 29th Battalion under Colonel Aureliano Blanquet come join the campaign. Colonel Blanquet had fought before in Morelos, and his name inspired fear among the rebels who remembered his relentless persecutions. Huerta had 3,000 men under his command, but he did not want to strike in the void, so he carefully constructed a network of informants. More than any other general in the Federal Army, he valued intelligence and paid generously for timely information on the rebel movements. At the same time, he made sure his soldiers and their camp followers (*soldaderas*) had plenty of money to purchase their provisions; Huerta wanted to make a sharp contrast between the rebels who came to loot and the soldiers who came to buy from the locals. Huerta himself commented upon how some villages had greeted his troops icily but then upon reaping

good business, did not want the troops to leave ever.[8] Huerta later claimed in his inimitable style that his column went "sowing trust, if the word is fitting, in all parts, and preaching by words, by the Republic's rifles and by its cannons a message of harmony, peace, and brotherhood among all the native sons of Morelos,"[9] Whether to buy provisions, information or loyalty, money was the most powerful weapon in his arsenal.

The abrupt appearance of Madero shattered Mexico's best chance to destroy the Zapatistas. A Madero out of touch with reality did not limit himself to sending messages, but personally came to Morelos on 14 August to mediate a negotiated solution. Just recently his meddling in Oaxaca had nearly sparked a major revolt, and only careful doctoring by De la Barra diffused the crisis in that state.[10] The Oaxaca episode confirmed how inadequate Madero's political skills were. Why then did he intervene in Morelos when everything suggested the benefits of keeping his distance? The rebels had called themselves Maderistas during the revolt against Díaz, but their penchant for lawlessness made then unattractive followers. Other than make perfunctory public denunciations of Huerta and De la Barra, Madero just had to sit back and let the army conduct the operation. If the military campaign against the rebels failed, Madero stood to gain in popularity. If Huerta succeeded in crushing the rebels in Morelos, then Madero had one less problem to worry about once he was inaugurated as president on 6 November. Unfortunately, Madero could not admit that force was the only solution for Morelos. Naively he believed that his mere presence sufficed to bring the warring parties to the negotiating table.[11]

General Huerta soon tired of Madero's ramblings and refused to see him any more. Huerta ordered his column to march forward, but when the rebels on 19 August put up a fierce resistance, he managed by an encircling movement to destroy the rebel force and to clear the road to Cuautla.[12] Once again Madero obtained an order from De la Barra to halt Huerta, but by then the many messages of Madero had irked President De la Barra who confessed "that Madero's interference has been most embarrassing as he [De la Barra] had intended to act with all possible vigor."[13] Supposedly Madero had come to protect the rebels from the army

Francisco Madero. During his presidency of Mexico (1911–1913), he proved incapable of controlling the revolutionary forces he had unleashed (Library of Congress, Prints and Photographs Division).

peace was the ambition of Zapata. When De la Barra received information that only a few followers protected Zapata, the provisional president saw the chance to strike a deadly blow. On 29 August he authorized Huerta to launch a surprise attack. On 1 September federal troops marched through Cuautla and reached Zapata's home town of Ayala. Zapata barely escaped after running into the surrounding cane fields to elude his pursuers. The federal troops met some resistance, but henceforth the rebels avoided combat and tried to return to guerrilla tactics. Huerta had anticipated their response, and he had created three flying columns to hunt down the rebels. As he advanced, he also left garrisons in the six main cities in the state and along the main railroad lines. The garrisons sent out patrols ten or more kilometers away from the base, while the flying columns as necessary split up into smaller units to track down the rebels. For the first and only time in his life, Zapata felt afraid, and he ordered his men to lie low and to pretend to be passive peasants. Disguise alone could not work for Zapata, who had to flee into the neighboring state of Puebla with Huerta hot on his trail. The general was pumping his agents not just for information but for defections, and gradually he persuaded rebel leaders to abandon Zapata. By the end of August peace had returned to Morelos, and the rebel menace had receded.[15]

onslaught, but even they tired of him. Unlike the northern rebels who accepted money, Madero's bribe offer of a hacienda had angered Zapata, whose driving passion was for power and not for money. In contrast to Huerta, who merely avoided contact with Madero, the Zapatistas were already shouting "Death to Madero" and wanted to execute him. Zapata, not sure he could control his turbulent followers who were only acting out what he was wishing, insisted that Madero depart promptly for Mexico City on 23 August.[14]

Madero continued his dilatory tactics, but by then both De la Barra and Huerta had reached the conclusion that the real obstacle to

Once the towns were safe, the outside world learned of the Zapatista excesses as journalists filed stories about the rebel atrocities. The destruction had reached such an extreme that even the battle-hardened Huerta wrote "I have been shocked by the atrocities committed by the Zapatistas, because walking through the streets I have had the misfortune to see smashed safety boxes and pianos and sundry household objects and the whole town reduced to bits by the bandits; I have never seen anything like this before."[16] The savagery of the Zapatistas went beyond mere looting and extended to wanton destruction of any property they could not carry or convert into cash; in their urgent rage to destroy the cities, the Zapatistas seemed to be responding to something deeper than mere greed for booty.[17]

Huerta hoped to end this primitive rampage by offering a pardon to rebels who surrendered and by catching Zapata in the state of Puebla. In the first week of October Huerta was about to pounce on Zapata, when Madero extracted an order from De la Barra on 1 October recalling or in effect firing Huerta as the military commander. Madero had just won the presidential election and De la Barra knew that he was no longer indispensable. If the interim president did not comply, Madero could easily have the inauguration date moved forward. An anguished De la Barra had most reluctantly accepted the recall of the victorious General Huerta, who was formally relieved of his command on 3 October. To soften the blow, De la Barra received Huerta publicly and signed special dispensations for the general. A bitter exchange of letters in newspapers between Huerta and Madero followed, and the victorious general sank into disgrace, his military career apparently over.[18]

The firing of Huerta was already a psychological victory for Zapata. The dismissal also allowed Zapata to escape from the trap, because the replacement of Huerta, although competent, needed some time to familiarize himself with the strategy and to reconstruct the intelligence network Huerta had operated. Indeed, one of the reasons Huerta had been so successful in his all-too-brief command in Morelos was that besides relying on paid agents and scouts for information, he benefited effortlessly from the network of merchants, hacendados, and middle-class persons who had most suffered the rebel depredations.

Without the hawk's eyes of Huerta upon him, Zapata sneaked back to Morelos and rallied his followers for one more round of raids. Zapata targeted towns outside Morelos in the hope of catching their smaller garrisons by surprise. The lure of loot was enough to attract followers for the march, and in a series of bold moves his bands went into the Federal District

and raided towns like Milpa Alta near Mexico City on 24 October. Although the next day troops drove away the small bands, the raid triggered a final cabinet crisis in the De la Barra administration.

Clearly, Zapata had made the most of the breathing spell Madero had provided, but the rebel leader had no illusion about defying for long the entire Federal Army. The bribing away of some of his leaders had demoralized and undermined Zapata, whose raids were last-minute gasps to try to demonstrate enough strength to secure a pardon for himself and his close associates. To his credit Zapata had made one last effort to avoid the destruction that left Morelos in ruins for decades. Zapata put out feelers first to De la Huerta and then to Madero after the latter's inauguration on 6 November. Understandably the hacendados were outraged at any suggestion of an amnesty for the Zapatistas. Had the landlords realized this was their last chance to safeguard their properties in Morelos, they certainly would have accepted the proposals. But without a glimpse into the future, they insisted on bringing the rebels to justice. Madero himself did not want to appear weak in the face of the Zapatistas, and although he was willing to grant an amnesty to most followers, he could not pardon Zapata and his close associates.[19]

The refusal to grant an amnesty permanently marked the personality of Zapata. His life became a constant ordeal for personal survival; he concluded that as long as he remained a regional war lord his life was safe. His power and his life became inseparable and coalesced into two sides of one personality: Any attack on his power necessarily endangered his life. He well knew that in Morelos he kept power by providing opportunities to loot for his followers, but how could he keep his followers fighting once the plunder ran out? As a first solution, he pioneered the extortion of protection payments from the wealthy as a substitute for the inefficient and destructive looting. Rather than destroying the haciendas at one swoop, Zapata expected to milk them gradually to death. He even instituted a system of weekly collection payments from the hacendados, who at some moment were sure to abandon their ruined land holdings. When the protection payments dried up, Zapata's power base necessarily had to disintegrate.[20] He then needed something to attach the peasants permanently to his unceasing quest for power. On 25 November 1911 Zapata issued the Plan of Ayala that denounced Madero for betraying the Revolution and proclaimed a still loyal Pascual Orozco, Jr. as the head of the revolt. The plan promised to restore all illegally seized village lands and to confiscate one-third of the land of the haciendas. The plan did not outlaw looting or ravaging and did not offer any guarantees for private property or commerce.[21]

Plunder in the present and land in the future, this was the formula that gave Zapata the foundation for a long-term political career as a regional war lord. First he had to regain control over Morelos, because even without the crucial leadership of Huerta, the Federal Army still held a commanding presence in the state. Fortunately for Zapata, Madero had rejected Huerta's request to organize *rurales* both as a necessary part of the army's pacification campaign and as an effective ploy to deplete the pool of recruits for the rebel leader. Without a local police force, the transfer of army units for service in the north necessarily left defenseless the countryside of Morelos. The Zapatistas plunged into this power vacuum with a vengeance and hurriedly recovered all the ground they had lost under General Huerta. The atrocities of the rebels resumed at an even greater scale than in 1911, because this time Zapata was determined to root out all the merchants, hacendados, and any other person of means who might denounce the movements of his followers. The elimination or expulsion of hostile groups was more than vengeance and conveniently tied in with Zapata's own vision for Morelos. His ideal state consisted of himself surrounded by passive peasants; he did not want to deal with other social classes or economic groups whose existence he in any case did not accept. Obviously he wanted a return

Emiliano Zapata and unidentified followers. Zapata (seated, both hands on table) always appreciated the finer things of life for his own use (Library of Congress, Prints and Photographs Division, George Grantham Bain Collection).

to a very simple agrarian life style of the past based on idealized ancient village traditions. Of indusstrial society, he cared only for its weapons; otherwise he had no use or place for an urban society of merchants and industrialists. He instinctively assumed the role of the regional war lord determined at all costs to preserve the "rural anarchism" of Morelos.[22] The very existence of Zapata posed a permanent threat to a strong and unified Mexico

Seeing the rebellion still festering in Morelos, why did President Madero pull troops out and send them to the north? The explanation lies with General Bernardo Reyes, a prominent figure of the Ancien Régime. The previous chapter had left the former Secretary of War in Europe in an exile disguised as a military study mission. President Porfirio Díaz, seeking someone to diffuse the Madero insurrection, had recalled him early in 1911, but Reyes had made it only to Havana when the Ancien Régime fell. On 9 June a cheering crowd welcomed him back to Mexico City, and because he renounced all political ambitions, Madero offered him a cabinet post in his future administration. The position was none other than his old job of Secretary of War, the only arrangement likely to have spared Mexico the subsequent years of rampage and destruction. Madero's followers condemned the political deal, and seductive voices finally persuaded Reyes to run for the presidency. Four days before the election of 1 October, he withdrew his candidacy, thus guaranteeing the victory of Madero. A few days later Reyes was in San Antonio, Texas, plotting to overthrow Madero.[23]

To face threats like the Reyes invasion, Madero had agreed to increase the army to 40,000, but not willing to use the pressgang, recruitment went very slowly. Without additional new soldiers, President Madero could strengthen the garrisons in the north only by transferring units from the large army in Morelos. Reyes was bound to cross over into Mexico from Texas into the state of Nuevo León, his traditional base for support. In reality, the Madero administration had overestimated a Reyista menace that barely merited police measures. The U.S. government hounded Reyes in a way it had never done with the rebel Madero. For their part, agents of the Madero government reported all the movements of Reyes in the United States, and local officials

monitored closely any suspected Reyista activity in Mexico. The United States arrested Reyes for violating the neutrality acts, but free on bail he fled to Mexico on 4 December. No crowds of supporters welcomed him in his homeland, and finding himself totally alone, he surrendered on 25 December 1911; soon he was in a Mexico City prison awaiting trial on charges of treason.[24] Although the Reyista threat turned out to be harmless, "the disturbance nevertheless strained the financial equilibrium and dissipated the energies of the central government" as "the members of the cabinet devoted much of their time for a period of three months to discussing the problems of protection."[25] Among other consequences, the gambit of Reyes had saved Zapata from destruction and had blinded the Madero administration to the most dangerous threat lurking in Chihuahua.

The Revolt of Pascual Orozco

The Madero administration, obsessed with the Reyes plot, had failed to devote enough attention to the greater danger emerging in Chihuahua. Madero, forgetting that he owed his victory to the rebels in that state, rewarded them miserly. The rebels each received 50 pesos, an additional 25 pesos if they turned in a rifle, and a one-way train ticket to their home town. The assumption was that since one peso sufficed to provide sustenance for at least one day, the 50 pesos should last until some job eventually materialized. For the many rebels in arms, the most obvious employment was as federal mounted police or *rurales*, whose new head in Chihuahua was Pascual Orozco, Jr. However, the Madero administration put no more than 10 percent of the former rebels into 350-man units of *rurales*. Leaving over 90 percent of the former rebels to fend for themselves seemed like an open invitation to revolt. Because the government had withdrawn the Federal Army from Chihuahua, the need to have a larger than usual federal police force was obvious. But, just like Porfirio Díaz, Madero preferred balancing the budget to arming the regime. The Madero government did try to buy off the rebel leaders; Orozco received 50,000 pesos and Pancho Villa 10,000 pesos.[26] The payment worked well for Pancho Villa who, in another reflection of his complex personality, was content to be a wealthy businessman. With his brothers he opened four butcher shops in Chihuahua City and supplied them with cattle from his ranches. The Revolution had given him a chance to have a new start and to erase his past of cattle rustler and murderer. For Villa, running a successful business and enriching himself were more than satisfactory alternatives to a political career.[27]

Villa was an exception, and private business alone did not satisfy most rebel leaders who also coveted political positions. The Maderista governor of Chihuahua, Abraham González, was able to place 100 rebels into state jobs in the capital; no purge had been necessary because most Porfirista officials had fled. In district towns Governor González found more jobs for rebels in the state bureaucracy. Equally significant, the abolishment of the hated post of *jefes políticos* or district officials in Chihuahua and the introduction of popular election for mayors created numerous political opportunities. In their home towns many former leaders won municipal elections, and once in office, they rewarded their followers with employment and favors.[28]

Orozco as head of the *rurales* and owner of lucrative businesses had achieved success unimaginable in 1910, yet he was dissatisfied. He had tasted political power and longed to return to prominence. He set his sights on becoming governor of the state, but Madero instead wanted his close friend and supporter, Abraham González, to become the governor. Whenever possible, Madero tried to have his loyalists elected as governors. For example, he supported Venustiano Carranza for the governorship of the neighboring state of Coahuila. But Carranza in his home state did not have to deal with a rebel figure of the power and prestige of Orozco. On the pretext that Orozco was still a few months short of the constitutional age requirement of 30 years to be governor, he was disqualified as a candidate, and González almost effortlessly won the election for governor of Chihuahua. Orozco was in no way out of a job, because he remained in his former post as head of the *rurales* in Chihuahua.[29]

The arrangement of González as governor and Orozco as head of the *rurales* was fraught with friction but was not necessarily unworkable. Governor González was a skilled negotiator and had an affable personality; he was certain to build coalitions and to avoid clashes with Orozco. Unfortunately, barely a month after he took office as governor, President Madero persuaded González to come to Mexico City to become Secretary of Gobernación, the key political post in the cabinet. Behind every domestic insurrection or civil war lies at least one inept politician, and Mexico certainly had many in the Chihuahua imbroglio. A reluctant González accepted the cabinet position and thus left a dangerous power vacuum behind. Naming Orozco interim governor was the easiest alternative, but appointing a nonentity could only exacerbate the resentment.

With González away in Mexico City, Orozco was free to extend his base of support. In an unexpected twist, the flattery and attentions the wealthy showered on Orozco powerfully affected the former rebel leader. The conservatives and the Porfirians realized they could use a popular leader like Orozco to manipulate the masses for the benefit of the upper class. Soon Orozco was fanning the resentment of the former rebels. His task was easy because so far prosperity had not returned to Chihuahua. Employment was hard to find, and most peasants barely scraped together enough work to earn their meals. The rebels longingly recalled how easy it had been to take food at gun point from rich haciendas and from the wealthy towns. Only a small step separated daydreaming from action, and stray marauding bands appeared in January 1912, not unlike what had happened at the start of the Madero insurrection of November 1910. The situation became explosive in January 1912 when Secretary of Gobernación González ordered the units of *rurales* to reduce their numbers from 350 to 250 men. Although the discharge of the men would take place at the end of February, by this order Secretary González showed that he had failed to understand the true motivation of the rebels. More than any other single action, the order to discharge the *rurales* triggered the Orozco Revolt.[30]

To contain the Chihuahua disturbances within that state, President Madero called on citizens to join volunteer units. The governors of northern states like Coahuila, Durango, Nuevo León, and Sonora busily organized their own militia units. Volunteers for the militia units were plentiful, because many felt an obligation to defend the political freedoms the

Madero regime had brought to Mexico. However, the individual states lacked the resources to finance these forces, so the governors of the states, in particular Venustiano Carranza of Coahuila, took the lead in securing federal funds to support their state militias. Soon most of the northern states had militia units sometimes larger than the local army garrisons.[31]

In Chihuahua itself, banditry, disturbances, and mutinies among the *rurales* forced the interim governor to resign. Madero belatedly pleaded with Orozco to accept the governorship, but in a decision the rebel leader later regretted, Orozco declined the offer because he already had set his sights on bigger goals. In a last attempt to prevent a major revolt, González resigned as Secretary of Gobernación and resumed the governorship of Chihuahua in 12 February 1912. No longer trusting the *rurales* whose loyalty he had effectively undermined, Governor González made an appeal for volunteers to form a state militia. He specifically asked Pancho Villa to organize a militia unit, and in response to governor's call, Villa forsook his business ventures and resumed his long political career. The number of outlaw bands roaming the state had continued to grow, and plots were rife in the air. On 27 February the *rurales* in Ciudad Juárez mutinied and took control of the city. As their nominal commander, Orozco went to try to persuade the *rurales* to return to obedience, but upon his arrival at Ciudad Juárez, he faced a dilemma: Either he headed the revolt or the movement would find another leader. The turn of events had been faster than even Orozco expected, and after some hesitation he accepted the leadership by 1 March 1912. A military uprising had not been in Orozco's prior plans, for otherwise he would not have allowed the cartridge reserves of his *rurales* to run dangerously low in the previous months.[32]

In the first days of March the surprise had been complete even for Orozco, who lacked even the indispensable manifesto! His first proclamation announcing his resignation as head of the *rurales* on 1 March contained "a series of trite remarks that revealed the lack of

Here Pascual Orozco, standing third from right with a wide-brimmed hat, is issuing the inevitable manifesto in his revolt against the government of Mexican president Francisco Madero in March 1912 (Library of Congress, Prints and Photographs Division, George Grantham Bain Collection).

ideas and the inferiority of the syntax,"[33] and a second proclamation on 8 March was no better. To fill the gap, Orozco's advisers trolled for ideas to compile a worthy document. The result of their labors was a formal manifesto of 25 March, an unwieldy document whose vitriolic anti–Americanism later proved harmful to the revolt. In spite of being a confused catalogue of whatever ideas were floating in the air, some of the proposals in the manifesto, such as the large-scale distribution of land, resurfaced years later in the Mexican Constitution of 1917.[34]

Independent of the promises in the manifesto, the illiterate peasants saw more practical reasons to join the revolt. The news that the popular Orozco was leading a movement brought thousands to join his ranks; eventually he managed to attract over 10,000 men. Just as significantly, very few rallied against him. The lone holdout was the rival Pancho Villa, who rejected the offers to join and on the contrary recruited men to fight for Madero. Why did Orozco gain control of almost all of Chihuahua so easily? For the former rebels of 1910–1911 the new campaign promised a return to the good days of plunder and booty. At the very least, the rebellion guaranteed veterans and newcomers a good daily meal; many peasants joined because they were hungry and knew that as rebels they would eat well. Instinctively Orozco sensed the motivation, and in an action that in a few months backfired, he offered each volunteer a daily allowance of two pesos, twice the normal allowance of the federal soldiers.[35] In the absence of gainful employment, the opportunity to earn a livelihood by marching across the terrain was irresistible and certainly much more agreeable than the hard toil on a farm: "Pure lawlessness, reckless bravado, and desire to earn a livelihood by some easier means than working have been the controlling motives in the entire movement."[36]

The above reasons applied to most of Mexico as well, yet the Orozco revolt was able to draw few recruits from other states. Why? Essentially because Orozco, who had enjoyed a brief flurry of national popularity in 1911, remained a regional leader who had little appeal outside his native Chihuahua. But the reason had a deeper side and was not simply a public relations failure or a lack of communications. When other Mexicans saw Orozco as more

Chihuahuan than Mexican, they indirectly sensed that he was not above sacrificing the rest of Mexico for the sake of Chihuahua. For those less perceptive, one manifesto went so far as to state that Orozco was ready for national office, "provided that the sovereign will of the Chihuahuan people does not choose independence for the state, a desire that all Liberal Mexicans will have to respect."[37] Orozco harbored the idea of taking Chihuahua, and perhaps other northern states, out of Mexico, a possibility that may have helped him receive financial backing from the upper class of the state.

The possibility of a new republic helps to explain why Orozco, in spite of frequent talk of marching to Mexico City, never pressed hard for a southward military drive. Other reasons also blocked his southward advance, the most important being shortage of weapons and ammunition. So many volunteers flocked to his ranks that he exhausted his supply of weapons and had to turn away those who did not come with their own rifle. Modern cannons or machine guns were unavailable in Chihuahua. Orozco had counted on purchasing weapons and ammunition in the border, but on 14 March 1912 the U.S. Congress passed a very stringent neutrality law. Over the next months U.S. officials vigorously enforced the law against a movement proclaiming its anti–Americanism. Orozco's agents had to turn to smugglers to procure an irregular supply of cartridges.[38]

Before Orozco's forces could complete their rearmament, the Federal Army wanted to attack with its superior firepower. President Madero was most eager to crush this challenge to his administration. On 4 March he accepted the resignation of his Secretary of War, José González Salas, who instead took command of the newly constituted Division of the North. For the Mexican army, this was the first use of the division structure in the twentieth century; until then, battalions, regiments, and brigades had comprised the largest combat units.[39]

General González Salas made the railroad junction of Torreón in Coahuila his staging area for the operations against Chihuahua (Map 11). He did not wait for all his troops to arrive, and instead with only 2,150 soldiers he took the Central Railroad (which runs from Mexico City to Ciudad Juárez) north of Torreón on 18 March. His advance slowed down because the engineers had to repair the damage the rebels had done to the track and the bridges. The advance parties skirmished with the rebels, who retreated to prepared positions at Rellano 176 kilometers north of Torreón. Orozco had at least 3,000 men dug in at Rellano, and he had other large groups in the vicinity. González Salas, unaware of the large rebel forces in front of him, ordered the infantry and the artillery to proceed along the railroad under his command. He also divided the cavalry into two columns, one to march to his east and the other to the west. On paper this deployment seemed solid, because the cavalry covered the flanks of the main force. However, the column of General Fernando Trucy Aubert, containing most of the cavalry, soon roamed ahead. González Salas did not recall the large cavalry column and instead sent Trucy Aubert ahead to rendezvous with the main force at a point north of Jiménez. He also allowed the smaller cavalry column under General Joaquín Téllez to scout ahead out of range of the main force. Without knowledge of the terrain or of the rebels, he assumed all three columns would converge simultaneously at Jiménez.[40]

By splitting up his small force into three, he ran a real risk and tempted the larger rebel army to try its chances in battle. González Salas was nearing Rellano when the rebels sent a locomotive full of dynamite against the repair trains on 24 March. The troops had received word that the locomotive attack was coming, and in precaution, the American engineer, Mr. Colvin, had removed one rail; everyone trusted Mr. Colvin so much that none dared suggest any other precautions. When the dynamite train appeared, it came at such a tremendous speed that it jumped the missing rail and regained the track crashing into the lead repair train. Some men suffered wounds, but because most soldiers had enough time to scatter before the explosion, the units remained ready for combat.[41]

All the infantry detrained and marched north; about 1000 the rebels at Rellano opened a heavy fire from the surrounding hills. General Aureliano Blanquet led the 29th Infantry Battalion in a flanking attack against the rebels and was about to capture the heights when he received word to retreat quickly. Another rebel force of about 1500 men had appeared to attack the trains, and all the federal infantry had to form a protective circle to avoid being over-

run. Rather than the three federal detachments converging in Jiménez, two large rebel forces had trapped one of the federal detachments at Rellano. No disaster had occurred because General Téllez accidentally was nearby, and upon hearing the gunfire, he had rushed with his cavalry to the rescue. General González Salas ordered the infantry back into the trains and directed the cavalry under General Téllez to form a rearguard to cover the withdrawal; at 1430 the trains were heading back south to Torreón. Téllez conducted the fighting withdrawal in good order, and under his cover the troops retrieved almost all of their equipment and lost only 2 cannons. However, the troop trains, once loaded, steamed away so hurriedly, that the cavalry rearguard of General Téllez fell way behind. The next day González Salas still had not received any word about the whereabouts of either the cavalry under Trucy Aubert or of the rearguard under Téllez. Fearing the worst fate for the other columns and unable to face the humiliation of an inquiry, General González Salas, in a fit of depression, shot himself with a pistol on the morning of 25 March.[42]

The retreating troop trains returned to Torreón, leaving isolated in the north the cavalry of General Trucy Aubert, who had managed to reach Jiménez. Once the commander learned of the defeat at Rellano, he tried to turn back to Torreón, but by then several thousand rebels were trying to cut off his retreat. He lost all his equipment, nearly half of his men, and barely escaped. The heavy losses of this cavalry column and the suicide of González Salas created the image of a military disaster, when in reality the Division of the North arrived largely intact in Torreón.[43] Orozco boasted about marching to Mexico City, but plagued with ammunition shortages and aware of the real strength of the Federal Army, he did not push south. Probably with his bombast Orozco was trying to send out peace feelers for some sort of accommodation with the Madero government, be it as a regional war lord or perhaps even independence for Chihuahua.[44]

Indirect confirmation of the military weakness of Orozco came from his inability to eliminate Pancho Villa. Most of Villa's men had deserted after running into a large Orozquista force on 15 March, but Villa soon reconstituted his band. In a surprise move he captured Parral on 24 March as part of the first federal offensive, but the defeat of the federal forces that same day at Rellano left him very vulnerable. Rather than retreating, Villa fortified the city, and his men easily defeated the small force Orozco had sent to capture Parral. Outraged by this setback, Orozco sent 3,000 men to crush Villa. With only 500 men, Colonel Villa defended Parral during daylight on 5 April from a vigorous attack, but at nightfall he gave his force the order to break through the besieging line and to escape.[45] A determined pursuit might have destroyed the fleeing Villistas, had not the Orozquistas revealed the real reason why they had come to Parral:

> At about 7:30 P.M. the Orozquistas reached the center of the town and this was the beginning of the most dreadful night Parral has known. The looting began at once. The doors of the stores were blown in with dynamite bombs, and the same means used to burst open the safes. The soldiers took the pick, and then invited the populace to carry away what they did not want. The saloons were opened and there was free drink for all. The Banco Minero building was dynamited and then burned up. [...] Soon a spirit of destruction marked the looting, and what could not be taken away was broken into pieces—desks, counters, show cases, all were destroyed or badly damaged. [...] The looting went on all night with little or no attempt to stop it [...] the houses of many citizens were entered forcibly, as well as stores.[46]

The sacking of Parral spread terror among the neighboring states but proved counterproductive to the Orozco revolt. Fear of Orozquista outrages temporarily rallied citizens around the Madero administration. Federal reinforcements continued to pour into Torreón, and any chance that the rebels might capture that city passed by 10 April. The government also had to select a new commander to replace the deceased González Salas. Madero brought his entire cabinet into the decision, and in a momentous session the cabinet members discussed the respective merits of each possible candidate. If military victory was the goal, then General Victoriano Huerta was the only qualified candidate, explained the new Secretary of War. Madero opposed the appointment of Huerta, but seeing no other way to calm the terrified citizens, he finally relented; by 26 March the public knew that General Huerta, who had been in disgrace, was the new commander of the Division of the North.[47]

With a sense of vindication General Huerta accepted the appointment, but on the single condition that he have a free hand to conduct the offensive. Obviously Huerta did not want a repeat of the political meddling that had crippled his campaign against Zapata in Morelos in 1911. Huerta did not depart promptly for Torreón but instead devoted himself to picking the units and the commanders he knew to be most competent. Huerta originally expected to conduct a campaign against guerrilla bands, but as he carefully gathered information from spies, scouts, and civilians, he was struck by the willingness of Pascual Orozco to engage in pitched battles. To wage regular warfare, he transferred to Chihuahua most of the artillery batteries stationed in Mexico City; he was not going to repeat the mistake of Porfirio Díaz who had kept the cannons largely in the capital in 1911. Huerta also realized that Orozco's only chance to survive was to invade neighboring states, and to prepare for that eventuality, when the general left Mexico City on 10 April, he rode the train not to Torreón, but to Monterrey. Once Huerta confirmed that the army troops and the new state militias sufficed to block any rebel move to the east, he went to Torreón to take command of the Division of the North on 15 April.[48]

Unlike the previous commander of the Division of the North, Huerta was in no hurry to rush northward. To restore the shattered morale of the troops, he dedicated himself to improving the combat capabilities of the men under his command. Upon his arrival, he found soldiers from many different units, a fragmentation typical of the Federal Army. He obtained permission from the Secretary of War to consolidate the infantry into battalions and the cavalry into regiments all with full complements. He devoted fifteen days to training his men, who had never before had the opportunity to practice in the large formation of a division. He placed the artillery batteries under the command of Lieutenant Colonel Guillermo Rubio Navarrete, whom he considered the best artillery officer in Mexico. He wanted the batteries to practice laying down concentrated fire in a synchronized manner and in barrages, while having to make repeated displacements. Just in case Orozco tried to attack in the rear, Huerta strongly supported the efforts of the *jefe político* (the state of Coahuila had not yet abolished the position of district official) to have convicts build fortifications. He remembered that the Mexico City arsenal had some very large artillery pieces; although they were unsuited for a field campaign, he had the War Department ship these big cannons to bolster the defenses of Torreón.[49]

Huerta did not try to conceal his preparations from Orozco, who correctly sensed a major offensive was imminent. Orozco, who was constantly short of cartridges for his over 10,000 men, decided in the last week of April to make a preemptive strike on neighboring Coahuila. He sent 1500 mounted men to ride across mostly desert in the hope of taking Monclova by surprise; from that city the Orozquistas could threaten Saltillo and Monterrey. The surprise came to the Orozquistas, who 85 kilometers west of Monclova ran into a state militia unit of 180 men on 30 April. Its commander, the later famous Pablo González, conducted a fighting withdrawal and on subsequent days continued to delay the advance of the Orozquistas. Reinforcements raised the numbers of the defenders to over 300, and González already revealed his special talent to hold off and harass larger attacking forces. In spite of all his efforts, the rebels had pushed him back to a position 35 kilometers west of Monclova by 6 May.[50]

On the afternoon of 5 May General Huerta concluded that the situation called for reinforcements, and he dispatched 1000 soldiers (mostly the 23rd Battalion, and the rest state militia and *rurales*), two cannons, and four machine guns under General Trucy Aubert. Riding comfortably at night by railroad, the relief force reached Monclova at 0700 on 6 May. Upon learning that the state militia was under heavy attack, General Trucy Aubert promptly ordered the train to continue west to the site of the combat. The railroad tracks took Trucy Aubert's men virtually into the battlefield, and his fresh troops barely had to detrain to attack the surprised Orozquistas.[51] As the federal infantry advanced,

> the formidable attack began that showed the enemy how superior the government forces were in tactics, weapons, discipline, and courage. After the enemy took direct hits from the salvoes of the cannons and the volleys of the rifles, the Orozquista rabble lost all hope and fell prey to the most frightful panic. They scat-

tered themselves totally and ran away in full flight, leaving the field covered with dead bodies and the wounded [... the cavalry] forced them to hasten their flight across the burning desert, where they abandoned many horses dead from exhaustion and lack of water. The Orozquistas were in horrible conditions and lost hundreds of men who deserted because they had totally lost the will to fight.[52]

The collapse of the Coahuila invasion was a major setback for the Orozquistas. Already on 6 May General Huerta had begun advancing north of Torreón along the Central Railroad. To stop him Orozco on 8 May sent two flanking columns of 1500 men each into the federal rear. The first column marched east and was supposed to cut off the rail and telegraph links to Monterrey, while the second column marched west to cut off the Central Railroad to Mexico City; with his supply lines threatened, presumably Huerta would have to retreat back to Torreón.[53]

The plan was not far-fetched, and the western column proceeded undetected across barren mountains. Huerta quickly discovered the eastern column, and the night after it set out, he sent Pancho Villa with over 400 cavalrymen to stop the Orozquistas. At the rail head of Tlahualilo in Durango, Villa quietly placed his men that night in irrigation ditches. At daybreak of 9 May, the Orozquista column launched heavy attacks to clear Villa from its path. The rebels had neglected to cut the railroad track, and at 1100 General Antonio Rábago with 800 soldiers rode a train into the battle. Caught in the crossfire, the rebels hurriedly fled, abandoning 600 horses and many wagons with supplies; in an innovation, the rebels used automobiles to evacuate some of their wounded.[54]

Unaware of the existence of the second Orozquista column to the west, Huerta ordered the Division of the North to resume its northward advance along the railroad. Huerta wanted an engagement to show his soldiers the value of all their training; he himself was eager to test his tactics on the rebels. Still in the state of Durango, on 11 May 1912 the Division of the North encountered strong rebel defenses at Conejos, a train station 86 kilometers north of Torreón and in the middle of a canyon. Banderas Hill on the west dominated the position; the Orozquistas had dug trenches and established a defensive line over one kilometer long starting from Banderas hill and running across the railroad track into the lower hills to the east. Huerta did not have enough cavalry to try to outflank the whole canyon, and the rebels were confident they could stop any frontal attack in the mouth of the canyon. That same day the detachment of General Trucy Aubert arrived by train from its victory at Coahuila; the returning soldiers were in high spirits and boosted the morale of the other units of the Division of the North. Huerta devoted 11 May to reconnoitering the enemy positions and making the proper dispositions for an assault the next day.

Huerta was confident of victory, in contrast to the rebels, who in the morning of 12 May kept the steam up in their locomotives in their rear to assure an immediate withdrawal. The artillery under Lieutenant Colonel Rubio Navarrete opened fire at 0700 and soon had neutralized the few cannons of the Orozquistas. The infantry marched towards the train station and for the first time in the history of the Mexican army followed under the protection of a rolling barrage of artillery fire. The

shells zoomed so low over the advancing infantry, that even Villa was worried that his men might be killed; he did not calm down until he verified that the shells accurately fell on the Orozquista lines. When small arms fire from Banderas hill halted the frontal infantry advance, the batteries shifted their hail of exploding shells into the Orozquista positions on that hill; Huerta also sent the battalion of Trucy Aubert on a flanking attack against Banderas hill. At 1400 Trucy Aubert's battalion was part of the way up the hill; Huerta sent more reinforcements to rush the last heights and to complete the capture of Banderas hill shortly afterwards. The Orozquistas still did not give up and tried to recapture the key hill, but when the counterattack failed, panic seized the rebels. The Orozquistas abandoned their three cannons and fled in a rout to the waiting trains in the rear; they were so afraid of the federal artillery fire that they forced the conductors to leave without waiting for the last units to board, some of whom had to march back across the desert.[55]

Huerta and his fellow officers watched with great satisfaction through binoculars the

The cannons of Pascual Orozco proved no match for the efficient Federal artillery (Library of Congress, Prints and Photographs Division).

disintegration of the rebel force, but they could not savor their triumph for long. The next day Huerta received word that a large rebel force had appeared south of Torreón in the state of Durango. This was the Orozquista western column that after nearly a week had finally resurfaced and in a surprise attack on 14 May had overwhelmed a small federal outpost. When this western column cut the links to Mexico City, Huerta had to take a strategic decision about his campaign. If he continued marching north, his Division of the North risked isolation, while if he returned to Torreón then Orozco could claim an easy victory without having fought at all. Huerta reasoned that the fortifications he had built were more than adequate to defend Torreón. As Huerta analyzed the information about the western Orozquista column, he concluded that the long march over barren terrain must have weakened considerably its combat capability. Indeed, the rebels were so desperate that they had taken out their frustration by promptly executing sixty federal prisoners. The executions foreshadowed the routine practice of killing prisoners after February 1913, a custom that still had not become generalized.

Without the victory at Conejos on 12 May, Huerta probably would have retreated after hearing of the appearance of the western Orozquista column south of Torreón. With the victory, he sensed that he still had the chance to crush the revolt, provided he continued pushing north. Huerta telegraphed urgently to the Madero government asking for only one more battalion to clear the path between Mexico City and Torreón. The Madero government approved the request and diverted the 29th Battalion, which was preparing to leave for Morelos. The diversion of this battalion granted Emiliano Zapata still another reprieve. Huerta counted on the counterinsurgency experience of General Aureliano Blanquet, the commander of the 29th, to put down the rebels in Durango. Although the Orozquistas outnumbered the 29th Battalion, General Blanquet relentlessly pursued the rebels and wore them down. With their ammunition low and short of supplies, the Orozquistas abandoned the state of Durango after 28 May and returned north to try to rejoin the main force of Orozco in the state of Chihuahua.[56]

No longer facing a threat in his rear, it was now the turn of Huerta to push north along the Central Railroad. The advance went slowly because the Orozquistas had destroyed large stretches of track and blown up every bridge and culvert; the repair crews had to contend not just with the damage but also with the intense scorching heat. As Huerta's forces trudged laboriously to the north, Orozco had plenty of time to prepare his defenses at Rellano, 176 kilometers north of Torreón. Twin hills commanded the heights at either end of the canyon at Rellano. Orozco dug in his men along the crests and placed his remaining artillery pieces in the western hill, but the loss of the 3 cannons at Conejos had left him without artillery to defend the eastern hill. At 1500 on 22 May the artillery of Rubio Navarrete opened covering fire for the advancing cavalry brigade of Pancho Villa, whose task was to discover any weak points. The probing attacks of Pancho Villa failed, but not without first having revealed the defense's positions.[57]

Huerta realized that the eastern twin hill was lightly held by only infantry. Meanwhile the Orozquistas descended into the plain to try to surround Huerta's force, but the federal cavalry counterattacked and drove the rebels back up to their positions in the hills. Huerta took advantage of this confusion just as night was falling on 22 May to shift Villa's brigade to the right in an attempt to capture the eastern twin hill. To disguise the maneuver, he had one battery fire almost continuously upon the rebel positions during the night. Once Villa's cavalry and the federal infantry had seized the eastern twin hill, Huerta moved all his other batteries to the newly captured position. At daybreak he ordered his 36 cannons to pound the remaining defenses. From the heights the federal artillery poured a flanking fire directly into the Orozquista trenches. Orozco, seeing his men about to panic, gambled everything on a final valiant attack. He sent his men to try to recapture the eastern hill by means of a turning movement to the east; if successful, this counterattack could stop the entire federal advance. Huerta responded by trying to rush reinforcements to save the threatened eastern hill, but before they could arrive, the intense shelling from Rubio Navarrete's artillery had shattered the attackers. Then the federal artillery resumed shelling the remaining Orozquista positions, until at 0945 Huerta felt it was safe to have General Rábago lead a cavalry charge. At first the Orozquistas resisted the cavalry but not vigorously enough to deter Huerta from launching a general assault. By 1300 the federal troops had occupied all the defensive positions. The Orozquistas were running to board the waiting trains in the rear and abandoned their artillery and equipment. Orozco's force had left at least 600 dead in the field, while Huerta's troops had suffered only 140 casualties in both dead and wounded.[58]

A desperate Orozco concocted one final scheme to stop the advance of the Division of the North. After Rellano, shortage of supplies had delayed the march of the large federal force, and Orozco used the time to place powerful mines under the railroad tracks. The federal engineers repaired or replaced the damaged track and culverts, but they did not excavate under those portions of the track that seemed in good condition. Orozco hoped to use this omission to blow up the railroad cars carrying the artillery; he felt that his soldiers were man enough to defeat the federals with-

out cannons. In case that any cannon survived the mine explosions, the terrain was particularly rugged around Bachimba and heavily forested, so even Colonel Rubio Navarrete would be hard pressed to locate the targets. Orozco still had plenty of infantry, but because since May he had not been able to pay the daily allowance on a regular basis, he knew he needed to win soon to prevent his army from melting away. Orozco's plan depended on the success of the hidden mines, but when one of them exploded prematurely on 29 June without causing any serious damage or even casualties, he lost the element of surprise. Huerta ordered his engineers to revise every inch of track, and they soon uncovered nine more mines.[59]

Once his engineers had declared the route safe, Huerta resumed the march. On 2 July his cavalry tried unsuccessfully to cross the rebel defenses at Bachimba. The next day the main Federal Army arrived at Bachimba. The terrain was rugged with many hills, but was not impenetrable and even had flat areas. Although

Orozquista rebels preparing to depart by train for the front. Deployments of troops and rebels strained the capacity of Mexico's incomplete railroad network (Library of Congress, Prints and Photographs Division).

some trees occasionally coalesced into small forests, most of the vegetation consisted of scattered bushes. With the rebels short of ammunition and terrified of the federal artillery, Orozco should have conducted an orderly evacuation that night. Meanwhile, Huerta prepared with Rubio Navarrete an attack plan that called for the artillery to relocate forward by steps in order to provide a steady covering fire for the advancing infantry. On 4 July at 0800 the federal artillery began a bombardment at a range of 3000 to 4800 meters. The rebel cannon replied but its shots fell short and by 1100 had fallen silent. Shortly after the federal artillery advanced 500 meters and resumed fire; the artillery repeated the maneuver twice until it had moved forward 1500 meters in total during the battle. Huerta concluded that the shelling had demoralized the defenders to the point that they could not withstand an assault. But when he sent his infantrymen to climb the ridges to the west of Bachimba station, the federals ran into heavy rifle fire. Huerta quickly pulled back his men out of the range of rifle fire and ordered the artillery to resume its incessant artillery barrages. Late in the afternoon Huerta judged the moment had come to launch a general assault on the defenders. The shell-shocked rebels did not wait for the attack but earlier had fled to board the waiting trains in the rear. The battle came to an end when the victorious federal troops swept unopposed into Bachimba station at 1900.[60]

Huerta promptly sent mounted *rurales* in hot pursuit of the rebels. Aware of accusations that he was deliberately dragging out the campaign, Huerta entrusted the pursuit to Emilio Madero, a brother of the President. However, thirsty and tired horses could not overcome the head start of the rebel trains. The rebels were so terrified of the federal artillery, that in their haste to flee they accepted Orozco's proposal not to stop at Chihuahua City. The residents, who had feared a sacking worse than that at Parral, thankfully watched the rebel trains steam through the city. The last train blew up large stretches of the Central Railroad to try to delay the advance of the Federal Army. In spite of frequent halts to repair the track, the Division of the North made a triumphal entry into Chihuahua City on 7 July. The reinstated Governor Abraham González almost immediately clashed with Huerta, who so far had enjoyed absolute authority over the campaign. Huerta had issued an amnesty offer shortly after his arrival in Torreón, and he wanted to reissue the offer in Chihuahua City, but the governor insisted on heavy punishment for all suspected rebel sympathizers. Up to this moment, the governor had followed conciliatory policies as befitted his amiable personality, so this display of a vengeful side was quite surprising. Perhaps the governor did not like Huerta or was just looking for any issue to show the supremacy of civilian rule; whatever the exact reason, he appealed to Madero. For the moment the president sided with Huerta, but the governor's pleas had not fallen on deaf ears. The general, believing he still had a free hand to conduct the operation, resumed his campaign to finish the Orozco rebellion.[61]

The Orozquista Invasion of Sonora

The campaign against Pascual Orozco was coming to an end in the state of Chihuahua, but the revolt was not over, because the Orozquistas had a chance to regain strength in Sonora. Neither the Madero administration nor General Huerta realized until too late the menace facing the neighboring state. By the time the government began to respond, the Orozquistas were already invading Sonora.

After the recapture of Chihuahua City on 7 July, Huerta put into place a strategy to eliminate the last remnants of the rebellion. By garrisoning the main cities and patrolling the railroads, he deprived the rebels of plunder. Fortunately, no danger of guerrilla warfare existed, because the rebels were not fighting for political changes. The Orozquistas wanted to plunder the cities and to have an easy life without having to work. Huerta reasoned that raiding ranches and farms could not sustain the rebels for long, and inevitably the rebel bands either would disintegrate or surrender.

The immediate task for Huerta was to decide how to recapture Ciudad Juárez, the last major city still in the hands of Orozco. The shortest and most direct route was straight north, but the rebels had damaged extensively the Central Railroad. The repair crews worked furiously, but the very high summer temperature retarded their progress. Preliminary reconnaissance revealed that the railroad running west from Chihuahua City through Ciudad Guerrero had suffered only slight damage. However, this railroad still lacked 130 kilometers of track beyond the town of Madera. The rail line resumed near Casas Grandes and curved eastward into Ciudad Juárez. Huerta sent the bulk of the Division of the North by this longer and more circuitous route. By looping westward he also hoped to close the escape route to Sonora.

The rebels had too much of a head start for the federal maneuver to be successful. As early as 13 July (nine days after the battle of Bachimba) Orozquistas were already gathering in western Chihuahua in preparation for the invasion of Sonora. Orozco himself retreated north to Ciudad Juárez; presumably he planned to take the railroad line to rejoin the rest of his forces at Casas Grandes and there to take command of the invasion of Sonora. On 14 July most of the rebels abandoned Ciudad Juárez, and the U.S. consul worried that too much time might elapse between the departure of the last rebel units and the arrival of the Federal Army. The task of rebuilding the totally destroyed track turned out to be so staggering, that the federal advance north of Chihuahua City slowed down to a crawl. During these extra weeks Orozco succumbed to his character flaw of indecision and tarried at Ciudad Juárez too long. By the time he heard that federal troops had reached Casas Grandes on 12 August, it was too late for Orozco to escape to Sonora.[62]

The failure of Orozco to join the invasion force split the Orozquistas into two main groups. The majority of the rebels were heading for Sonora, but a second group remained behind under the command of Orozco. This second group at Ciudad Juárez was in danger of being trapped and destroyed by the two advancing federal columns. Desperately looking for a way out, Orozco sent a cavalry patrol to discover if federal forces were marching to reinforce Ojinaga on the Rio Grande River. The patrol returned to report that no federal troops had reached the large bridge under construction at the Conchos River, which was the eastern terminus of the railroad coming from Chihuahua City. Orozco jumped at this last opportunity to escape, and with about 1400 men he abandoned Ciudad Juárez on 15 August. Five days later the federal troops from

Casas Grandes (reinforced by the column from Sonora under General Agustín Sanginés about which more shortly) entered Ciudad Juárez. Orozco seemed to have disappeared, but when a federal outpost near Ojinaga reported an attack by an unusually large rebel force, General Huerta immediately realized one day ahead of the local commander that the rebel leader was headed to this destination.

On 30 August Huerta ordered two columns to converge on Ojinaga. Meanwhile, the small garrison of 250 soldiers and policemen tried to defend the town against the 1,400 attacking Orozquistas. The local commander, although short of ammunition, felt he could hold his position perhaps long enough for the promised reinforcements to arrive. Orozco began repeated attacks on 9 September, but only on the night of 12 September did the garrison withdraw to the U.S. side. The first relief column of 500 soldiers arrived on 14 September at 1100. Its commander, Colonel Manuel Landa, took a quick glance (the famous *coup d'oeil* of European warfare) and decided not to wait for the arrival of the second relief column under General Fernando Trucy Aubert. Colonel Landa deployed his troops for the attack, and by 1800 his soldiers had captured the outer line of rebel defenses. Some rebels began to flee in the dark at 2100, and Colonel Landa sent his cavalry to try to cut off their escape. The next day Colonel Landa effortlessly entered Ojinaga at 0600, because the rebels had all fled across the border. At 1000 General Trucy Aubert arrived with 500 more soldiers, and he immediately sent his cavalry to hunt down the fleeing rebels. Orozco and most of his officers had escaped by crossing the Rio Grande River into the United States.[63]

In spite of General Trucy Aubert's efforts, at least 400 Orozquistas galloped into Coahuila. The failed invasion of early May did not seem to deter the rebel force that collected stragglers and soon numbered 800 men. The Coahuila state militia under Pablo González was more than a match for the demoralized rebel force. However, the government mistakenly concluded that the rebel force numbered over 2,000 men and could threaten Monclova. The War Department rushed 1100 soldiers of General Aureliano Blanquet from Durango to Coahuila by railroad, but their presence quickly proved unnecessary. General Blanquet's troops returned to their original base, their trips having demonstrated again the immense potential of railroads for swift troop deployments. The state militia diligently hunted down the Orozquista bands, and few were the rebels who managed to return to Chihuahua in the first week of October.[64]

With the destruction of rebels in eastern Chihuahua and in Coahuila and with Orozco himself in exile, the only large Orozquista force left on the field was that poised to invade Sonora (Map 13). Since 13 July the Orozquistas had been readying a three-pronged invasion of the neighboring state: In the north close to the U.S. border one column aimed to capture Agua Prieta and then proceed west to loot the other rich border cities; in the center the main force was to march west from Casas Grandes and had as its target the state capital of Hermosillo; in the south the last column was to march west from Madera in the direction of the rich port city of Guaymas. The Orozquistas resembled the wandering tribes of barbarians who had poured into the Roman Empire seeking to plunder and to ravage. Because Orozco had not been able to pay the daily allowance since May, the booty became essential to keep the men from deserting.[65] As a preview of the plunder awaiting the rebels in Sonora, "At Madera, Pearson, and Casas Grandes the retreating army known to be without ammunition was given time to loot and rob everything moveable, and allowed ample time to visit the ranch properties."[66] The plundering delayed considerably the start of the Orozquista invasion. Only one of the three columns had set out, and it had not yet crossed the Chihuahua state line by late July.

The long delay to launch the invasion had given Sonora considerable time to make defense preparations and in particular to increase its own forces. Traditionally, Sonora had used the threat of raids from the Yaqui Indians to secure federal funds. Governor José María Maytorena persuaded Madero that Sonora needed two state militia battalions to stop the Indian raids. The funds the governor pried from the federal government allowed him to hire many veterans of the 1911 revolt in militia battalions Nos.1 and 2. Like the governors of other states, he also incorporated many 1911 veterans into the *rurales*, the federal mounted police. As soon as Orozco revolted on 1 March, Maytorena ob-

tained additional funds from the Madero government to pay the volunteers in the new militia battalions Nos. 3, 4, and 5. A similar recruitment drive in 1911 had failed because the stingy regime of Porfirio Díaz had wanted the volunteers to serve without pay and away from their local communities. Governor Maytorena corrected the earlier defects by dividing the volunteers into two groups. Those who received the daily allowance of 1.50 peso had to agree to serve the state government anywhere, while those without the allowance stayed in their local village as self-defense units and bore arms only when the Orozquistas threatened the immediate vicinity.

Under these revised conditions, recruitment proved easy, because in Sonora the Madero regime had opened the door to the political and economic advancement of many new men who wanted to preserve their gains. The opportunity to join the militia battalions or the *rurales* had the additional beneficial effect of exhausting the pool of disgruntled veterans and thus deprived the Orozquistas of any recruits. Almost no inhabitants of Sonora joined the Orozquistas, although the Yaquis later took advantage of the general confusion to resume their raids on villages and ranches.[67]

Rather than wait for the long-delayed invasion, Governor Maytorena decided to take the war to the Orozquistas to protect Sonora from the plunderers. He sent state militias and *rurales* to Chihuahua, but because state officers lacked experience handling such large forces, he assigned the command to General Agustín Sanginés of the Federal Army. The general fortunately worked very harmoniously with the state officers, and he successfully led the force of over 900 men into Chihuahua. Sixty kilometers to the northwest of Casas Grandes at a hacienda called Ojitos, the Orozquistas attacked him on 31 July. General Sanginés had taken proper defensive precautions, and the rifle volleys from his troops soon showed the startled Orozquistas that this was not a defenseless hacienda ready for plundering. General Sanginés sent his infantry to outflank the Orozquistas on the right, and on the left he sent the cavalry under Lieutenant Colonel Álvaro Obregón to pursue the fleeing rebels. The other state officers broke off the pursuit, but not Obregón, who for a day relentlessly tracked down the rebels until he captured their six artillery pieces.[68]

Map 13. Sonora.

    General Sanginés marched east to link up with the advancing Division of the North at Casas Grandes. These tardy maneuvers had failed to bag any substantial number of rebels, who were quietly slipping over the mountains into Sonora during August. On 8 September the northern Orozquista column was threatening the small garrison of Agua Prieta, and other rebel bands were starting to menace southern Sonora. Governor Maytorena demanded the prompt return of the Sanginés column, but an overland journey was bound to take considerable time. Fortunately for Sonora, Washington agreed to the request of the Madero government to transport Mexican troops aboard U.S. railroads; after a brief train ride, the Sanginés column arrived in Agua Prieta on 12 September. Any danger to Agua Prieta had thus passed, and General Sanginés immediately sent his men to pursue the rebels to the south.[69]

The Orozquistas found Sonora to be an extremely hostile state. No villages had welcomed them, and the self-defense units had resisted the rebels long enough for the militia units to arrive. The rebels were short of ammunition, had not received pay in months, and had not found the much promised opportunity to plunder and ravage. On 19 September Lieutenant Colonel Obregón learned that the largest Orozquista band with over 500 men was just starting to set up camp less than 4 kilometers from the railroad track at the hacienda of San Joaquín. The tired rebels were aware of Obregón's presence but did not feel threatened by his small force and planned to attack him the next day. Obregón did not wait patiently, and at 1500 he loaded his 4th Militia Battalion of only 200 men aboard a train and headed at full steam to the rebel camp. He counted on surprise and sudden movement by his well-rested soldiers to crush the rebels. Marshes and wire fences made San Joaquín unsuitable for the Orozquista cavalry and favored the militia infantry, which Obregón promptly detrained and hurled against the center of the camp. No pickets guarded the rebels, and the sudden attack came as a complete surprise. The 4th Militia Battalion poured a vigorous fire on the Orozquistas, who decided to withdraw to a ridge to the east. Obregón's men began to outflank the ridge, and after an hour the rebels fled; by 1900 all combat had ceased. The rebels had abandoned their camp and lost all their baggage and supplies, including 228 saddled horses.[70]

The defeat of the largest Orozquista column in Sonora earned Obregón his promotion to Colonel. Most of the rebels decided to return to Chihuahua after the loss of so many supplies and horses. A splinter group did insist on pushing south, but soon pursuing *rurales* were hot on its trail, and by 12 October the rebel group was heading for Chihuahua. The few stray bands of Orozquistas still remaining eventually negotiated their surrender to the authorities. The attempts to enlarge the base of the Orozco revolt by invasions to Sonora and to Coahuila had ended in complete failure.[71] The Madero administration, which in March

had trembled for its survival and feared a drive to Mexico City, had weathered the revolt. Just like the alarm had been excessive in March, so the rejoicing was extravagant in October. The government could not resist the political temptation to issue vastly exaggerated claims that the rebellion had ended completely.

Madero believed his own propaganda and mistakenly concluded that he no longer needed Huerta. The president had become impatient with the independence of Huerta and began to direct the campaign in Chihuahua from Mexico City in a manner reminiscent of Porfirio Díaz. The general, whose only precondition had been independence from political control, felt hurt and betrayed. Huerta knew that he needed to keep Chihuahua well garrisoned to remove the temptation for easy looting, but the president did not want large idle garrisons and insisted on hunting the rebels in the barren desert. The president believed that Huerta was not conducting a vigorous campaign and began to see in the delays something more sinister. When Madero learned that an eye was causing Huerta pain, he ordered the general back to Mexico City for the needed cataract surgery. During the long convalescence of Huerta, Madero abolished the Division of the North on 16 December, and in effect left Huerta without a command. As modest compensation, Madero promoted Huerta to the highest rank in the Mexican army and offered a study mission in Europe. Huerta asked for more time to recover before he could decide on the Europe offer. At grave risk do governments treat victorious generals shabbily.[72]

With Huerta out of the way, Madero was free to confirm his victory claims by recalling most army units from Chihuahua. Inevitably the precipitate withdrawal left many areas defenseless, and the Orozquistas came out of their hiding places to resume their brigandage. The bands attacked ranches and isolated towns, and in January 1913 the Orozquistas were boldly threatening to capture and loot Ciudad Juárez and Chihuahua City. Public opinion in Mexico City could not understand how after so many declarations of victory, the Orozquistas again posed a threat. And the problem was not just in Chihuahua, because the Zapatista revolt in Morelos had revived with intensity in September 1912. The Madero administration seemed unable to restore the order that Mexico had enjoyed under Porfirio Díaz.[73]

The Final Battle of Francisco Madero

With the exception of the farcical Reyes plot, until October 1912 the revolts against the government of Francisco Madero had come from his disgruntled followers. Madero had unwisely demobilized most of his followers after May 1911, and many of these, without any stable employment, were ideal recruits for ambitious leaders offering daily pay and plunder. The rebel demobilization also left Madero largely dependent on the Federal Army to maintain order throughout Mexico. When on 16 October 1912, Félix Díaz, the nephew of Porfirio Díaz, persuaded many federal units in the state of Veracruz to support a rebellion against the Madero government, no doubt should have remained about the existence of many disloyal elements inside the army. Madero needed to take swift action, but the almost bloodless collapse of the Felicista revolt on 23 October reassured the trusting president

Félix Díaz, nephew of Porfirio Díaz. None of Porfirio Díaz's children went into politics, but his nephew tried to become a national figure in Mexico (Library of Congress, Prints and Photographs Division).

that the army was completely loyal. Eventually Félix Díaz ended up in a prison in Mexico City, and the government treated him and his many sympathizers in the Federal Army very leniently. In spite of the Felicista revolt and many other warnings, a Madero sliding into self-delusion refused to purge the army.[74]

Madero still had in the state militias another alternative to the Federal Army. During the Orozquista revolt, he had most reluctantly allocated federal funds to finance additional state militia units, but once Huerta broke the back of the revolt, Madero sharply reduced these budget lines. All the governors pleaded for the restoration of the funds, and two were so insistent that they came personally to Mexico City to argue with President Madero. José María Maytorena, the governor of Sonora, explained to Madero that the state militia needed months to control the Yaquis, who had taken up arms during the Orozquista invasion. In spite of having this excellent argument, Maytorena secured federal funds only after he threatened to resign as governor. The task for the other governor, Venustiano Carranza of Coahuila, was even more daunting because he did not have any Indians to use as a pretext. Extensive pleading failed to budge a stubborn Madero, until the revival of the Orozquista revolt in late 1912 at last gave Carranza the convincing argument to save his state militia. Madero agreed to fund the state battalions, provided that most of them serve under federal command in Chihuahua to fight the Orozquistas. Up to this moment Carranza had adamantly blocked sending the militia battalions outside his state, but the precedent of Maytorena, who had sent his state militia to Chihuahua, undermined the position of Carranza. The governor of Coahuila, seeing no other way to prolong the life of his state militia, grudgingly accepted the departure of Colonel Pablo González with the best militiamen for the campaign in Chihuahua.[75]

Some other states out of their meager funds and with small budget lines from the federal government also maintained modest state militias, but in early 1913, only Sonora and Coahuila had sizable and experienced militia battalions.[76] Although the *rurales* were a federal force, many of its members were former Maderista veterans who were loyal to the government. Because Madero had kept the *rurales* and the state militia so small in numbers, he lacked any counterforce to balance the Federal Army. Thus, he remained dependent on the ten times larger Federal Army to maintain his authority in Mexico. By the end of 1912, most of the army officers had become disenchanted with Madero and blamed him for the continuing unrest in the country. The feelings of the army officers turned from contempt to bitter hatred, and they interpreted any conciliatory gesture, such as the leniency to the Felicista conspirators, as another sign of weakness. The angry officers blamed Madero for aborting the successful offensives against the rebels first in Morelos in 1911 and then in Chihuahua in 1912. The revolts in those two states rekindled with intensity in January 1913, and bandits appeared to loot and plunder in other states. Actually, the situation seemed much more serious than it really was: Mexico enjoyed economic recovery during Madero's first year in 1912. Foreign trade and revenue figures exceeded those of the last year of Porfirio Díaz, and prosperity was spreading.[77]

The Madero administration counted not just on an expanding economy to pacify Mexico, but also on support from the newly elected president of the United States. Although the supposedly unsympathetic William H. Taft administration had repeatedly helped the Mexican government put down the revolts, Madero had reason to expect more spontaneous and solid support from Woodrow Wilson whom he regarded as a kindred spirit. The change of administration in the United Sates worried the army officers and conservative elements, who in a monstrous miscalculation concluded that the economic recovery had to be saved from the inept Madero. Curiously enough, the most aggrieved party, General Victoriano Huerta, refused offers to participate in a coup d'état. During the early stages of the planning Huerta was still convalescing from his cataract surgery, but even when his health improved he stayed distant from the plotters. While some claim he did not participate in the coup because he knew others had already taken the key leadership positions, a more complete explanation has to take into account his status in the army. If the coup failed, Madero had already promoted him to the highest rank of the Mexican army and promised him a grand tour of Europe as the proper way to end a long army career prior to retirement. If the coup was successful, then the next president of Mexico would be his patron Bernardo Reyes, who was sure to call on Huerta for his services. Either way, Huerta had no incentive to run the risk of joining the coup.[78]

As Huerta waited quietly for the best career prospects to unfold, the coup d'état against the Madero government began in the dawn hours of 9 February 1913. The plotters first released Bernardo Reyes and Félix Díaz from prison in Mexico City. The freed leaders then headed downtown to join other rebel forces who were simultaneously taking control of government installations. The chain of events had been too swift for Reyes to assimilate, and he naively believed that a bloodless coup was possible once all the remaining army units joined the movement. When Reyes reached the National Palace, he learned that General Lauro Villar had retaken the building from the rebels, a sure sign of a determination to fight. Rather than attack or bypass the National Palace, Reyes made his final political mistake and approached the large central gate of the National Palace. He asked to talk to General Lauro Villar, a former acquaintance, to try to persuade him to join the revolt. General Villar, who had previously posted two machine guns to cover the entrance, in reply demanded the surrender of Reyes. The standoff ended in a firefight that left many dead, including Reyes, and many wounded, including Villar. The disconcerted rebels abandoned their plan to capture the National Palace and withdrew in disorder.

A presidency of Bernardo Reyes could have been immensely beneficial to Mexico. As a friend of Carranza and of Maytorena, he was the only one who could have persuaded those governors to accept the overthrow of Madero. His upper-class credentials promised at least a veneer of respectability, and it is hard to imagine Bernardo Reyes shabbily treating the deposed Madero. The death of the talented Reyes tragically ended a life that at many moments had offered so much promise to Mexico. The mantle of leadership fell to Félix Díaz, who led the rebels to the southwest of the city to capture the military arsenal at the Ciudadela. By this surprise move the rebels gained virtually unlimited ammunition, many machine guns, and most importantly, the bulk of the artillery. Díaz had the pieces unlimbered and was rap-

A Federal soldier in Mexico City. Soldiers like this one engaged in combat when troops mutinied in February 1913 (Library of Congress, Prints and Photographs Division).

idly constructing a defense perimeter around the Ciudadela.[79]

The coup attempt found a surprised Madero in his official residence at Chapultepec Castle on the outskirts of the city. That morning of 9 February he proceeded downtown with an escort into the National Palace; along the route in a very strange twist of fate, he ran into Huerta. The general spontaneously offered his support to Madero and advised the president to return to Chapultepec Castle to avoid exposing himself needlessly. Madero welcomed the support but did not heed the advice and soon was in the National Palace having to take a decision. The wound of the loyal General Lauro Villar was serious, and he could no longer remain in command of the troops in the capital. Remembering the offer of Huerta on the street, Madero proposed naming the general the new commander. The Secretary of War could have taken command of the troops himself, but in a

suspicious move that should have served as a warning, he actively supported Huerta. Madero believed that with Huerta as commander of the loyal forces in Mexico City, the revolt was as good as finished. The president increasingly retreated into a fantasy world of acute self-delusion and until the last minute refused to heed the repeated warnings from his political allies, his close friends, and his many relatives.[80]

The rebel artillery shelled the city indiscriminately, leveling many buildings and making any recapture of the Ciudadela impossible. At least one thousand civilians died in the incessant shelling, as Mexico City for the first time experienced the ravages of war. On 11 February and again the next day the Madero government sent mounted *rurales* in charges down a street against the Ciudadela whose machine guns reaped a frightful slaughter of at least one thousand killed. This suicide charge has been called "unique in the annals of world military history,"[81] but less accurately has been imputed to General Huerta on the ground that he was trying to kill the loyal supporters of Madero. The general had command only over army units and not over the *rurales* who were under the Secretary of Gobernación. What was becoming clear to Huerta was that the Federal Army did not have its heart set on capturing the Ciudadela, and in fact units had continued to defect to join the rebels, who gradually extended the area under their control in the neighborhood.[82] Less clear to Huerta was the political situation, because the death of Bernardo Reyes had left the general adrift without a compass. Huerta needed time to figure out a solution for his career. If he waited too long, the army might rally behind someone else, but if he struck too soon, the country might not be ready to accept him. As he waited for events to set the course to follow, he found refuge in increasingly frequent bouts of drinking alcoholic beverages.

The incessant cannonade turned into ten days of destruction (the *Decena Trágica*). The U.S. ambassador Henry Lane Wilson (no relation to President Woodrow Wilson) loathed Madero from the beginning and wanted to do everything possible to remove him from office. The new threat to American lives and property only made Ambassador Wilson even more eager to find a way to obtain the resignation of Madero. Huerta realized that he had to move

From heights overlooking Mexico City, a federal battery is firing at mutinous troops in February 1913. Because the troops were most reluctant to shoot at each other, most of the shells fell on the city and caused over a thousand civilian deaths (J. Figueroa Domenech, *Veinte meses de anarquía*; Mexico: n.p., 1913).

fast to prevent the rebel Díaz from winning the support of the ambassador. On 17 February the General made preparations for his coup, and the next day by noon his troops had arrested Madero and all the high government officials. Quite naturally the first person Huerta informed of this accomplishment was the U.S. ambassador, who still had a crucial role to play in bringing the rebels in the Ciudadela under the control of Huerta. Ambassador Wilson invited Díaz and Huerta to the U.S. embassy for negotiations. Later than evening the Pact of the Embassy emerged: in exchange for most of the cabinet positions and other benefits in the new government, Díaz agreed to support Huerta as the new interim president of Mexico.[83]

After obtaining the resignation of Madero and his vice-president, Huerta took the oath of office as president the next day. Mexico City, whose press had constantly published malicious attacks on Madero, greeted the overthrow of the government with relief. Many saw in

Huerta the only hope to restore order in the country. Conservative elements began to pledge their support to the new government, and very soon almost all the units of the Federal Army proclaimed their loyalty to Huerta. For the rebels in the field Huerta prepared initial offers of amnesty, with the understanding that much worse would follow if they did not lay down their arms. In spite of Huerta's ultimate fate, his policy of conciliation had a very good chance of gaining the support of most Mexicans. He prepared many reforms and began to spend heavily on education. He realized that the peasant masses needed land, and he eventually espoused a reform program much more radical than Madero's. Inevitably Huerta saw himself as another Porfirio Díaz, who would complete the task of bringing peace and prosperity to Mexico: not a revival of the old dictatorship, but a new and improved version.[84]

Huerta never had a chance to consolidate

his dictatorship because of a fatal blunder on 22 February. Overwhelmed by the many items of organizing a new government, Huerta had not paid close attention to the fate of the deposed president and vice-president. He knew the danger, because already Gustavo Madero, a brother of the deposed president, had been brutally killed after the coup. To prevent the same fate from falling on Francisco, Huerta promised foreign diplomats a safe-conduct for the deposed president. Huerta saw no danger in the diminutive Madero and had failed to realize the deposed leader's significance as a rallying symbol. Since many army officers and civilian conservatives loathed Madero, the danger to the ex-president's life was very real. In addition, many plotters wanted to avenge the death of Bernardo Reyes or other fallen comrades. Another motivation of the murderers was the natural desire of subordinates to impress the new superior. Huerta bore the responsibility of failing to take extra precautions to protect the lives of Madero and Pino Suárez. Under mysterious circumstances never cleared up, the defenseless Madero and his vice-president José María Pino Suárez were brutally murdered in accordance with the infamous *Ley Fuga* (killed while supposedly trying to escape) on the night of 22 February. This single action shattered whatever chances Huerta had to win the support of Mexicans peacefully.[85]

7. The Revolt Against Victoriano Huerta

But there is one thing that has not been dwelt upon, and one thing that anyone who has not stood face to face with the present distressing situation in Mexico may fail to understand; and that is the pure, deep, deadly HATE which possesses and controls completely the actions in this tragedy which is destroying a nation. — U.S. Consul John Silliman[1]

Between February 1913 and August 1914 Mexico faced the most intense war it had ever seen. Throughout the country rebel bands rose up to oppose the military dictatorship of General Victoriano Huerta. The war quickly degenerated into a savage contest marked by executions and reprisals. During this extremely bloody stage in the history of Mexico, men were willing to butcher each other because the stakes were so high. Would the military dictatorship succeed in its goal of restoring the rigid political controls of the deposed ruler Porfirio Díaz? Or would the rebels be able to introduce a more open and participatory political system? Dialogue and discussion were useless: only victory in the battlefield could decide the future of Mexico.

Venustiano Carranza and Sonora

Right after General Victoriano Huerta deposed Francisco Madero, the new ruler announced the change of government to Mexico and to the world. As expected, the army generals and the federal bureaucrats promptly telegraphed their congratulations to the new regime. Mexico City certainly welcomed with relief the fall of Madero. The governors of the states, who less than a week before had sent messages of undying loyalty to the beleaguered Madero, abruptly changed their tune and rushed to pledge support to the new ruler. Huerta believed that the general population, tired of the disorder under Madero, wanted a return to the quiet days under Porfirio Díaz. Once he demonstrated that he controlled Mexico completely, he expected foreign countries to extend diplomatic recognition.[2]

The growing momentum to accept Huerta hit its first snag on 19 February 1913, the day after the fall of Madero. The governor of Coahuila, Venustiano Carranza, obtained from the state legislature a resolution rejecting Huerta and repudiating all the measures of his regime. Such an immediate act of defiance stood out in stark isolation and in contrast to the other governors who enthusiastically recognized Huerta as the new president. Large federal forces were present at Torreón and Monterrey, only hours away by train from the capital of Coahuila, Saltillo, so the danger was very serious. What drove Carranza to take such an immediate and apparently suicidal step? His inflexibility, already evident in his quarreling with Madero over the funds for the Coahuila militia, was one character trait that helps to explain his decision. Another personality trait that came into play was his penchant for risk-taking. Lastly, he also knew that northern Mexico had welcomed the Madero regime as a relief from the Porfirian tendency to centralize power in Mexico City. With remarkable foresight, Carranza sensed that a revolt against Huerta could gain substantial support in the north.[3]

Through a series of delaying messages Carranza fooled the Huerta regime into thinking that some deal was still possible. Carranza needed to gain time to organize the resources at his disposal for the revolt. His main assets were the state funds and the Coahuila militia. The first order of business was to recall Colonel Pablo González who, under the terms of the agreement with the deposed Madero regime, was in Chihuahua fighting the Orozquistas. With his 200 militiamen, Colonel González secretly fled Chihuahua City and crossed the desert instead of riding the railroad under federal control. Carranza meanwhile gathered the other scattered detachments of the state militia. Once Colonel González returned, the governor counted on a grand total of 500 men. In contrast, just the federal garrison at Torreón numbered over 2000 soldiers. Carranza recruited additional followers for the long war ahead and also prepared to abandon the state capital. He knew he could not hold on to Saltillo, and before his retreat north to Monclova (Map 14), the governor withdrew all the state funds in specie from the local banks.[4]

Besides the obvious need to gain time to make the military preparations, in the days immediately after the coup Carranza also wanted to give his negotiators time to secure guarantees for the life of the imprisoned Madero. Carranza did not want to start hostilities until Madero was safely abroad. At that point, the governor planned to create a beachhead in Coahuila to drive out Huerta. The restoration of Madero to power was the original goal of Carranza, but when on 23 February the governor received the tragic news that Madero and his vice-president had been murdered, the uprising acquired a radically different nature. The death of Madero lifted Carranza to another level; it was almost as if the departed president's spirit had descended on the governor. Filled with righteousness, he assumed a dig-

nified demeanor in all his subsequent dealings. With the death of Madero, Carranza considered himself the only legitimate and duly constituted civilian authority left in Mexico. He acted not as one more general, because that would have lowered him to the level of Huerta, but as the guardian of the civilian tradition in Mexico. As a member of the upper class, his aristocratic bearing effortlessly provided an aura of respectability and legitimacy to the revolt. His commitment to the cause was total, and he knew the high cost of failure. The governor of bordering Chihuahua, Abraham González, also intended to defy the military regime, only to be arrested and brutally murdered by Huerta's henchmen. General Antonio Rábago became the new governor of Chihuahua, and in Sonora that state was reported to have recognized Huerta. Carranza stood alone against Huerta, the political elite, and the Federal Army.[5]

Huerta concluded that the moment to snuff out this flicker of rebellion had come. On 5 March over 800 soldiers and two artillery pieces under General Fernando Trucy Aubert left Torreón by train. Carranza knew all along that Saltillo was untenable, but the Coahuila militia under Colonel González wanted to try to stop the advancing federal column. A brief skirmish at El Anhelo near Saltillo on 7 March was the first formal clash between his followers and the Federal Army. The superior firepower of the federal troops soon forced the rebels to withdraw in a hurry, after only a handful of casualties on both sides. The road to Saltillo was open, but then General Trucy Aubert received orders to proceed east to help stamp out the bands of rebels that spontaneously were appearing north of Monterrey. Consequently he did not return to occupy abandoned Saltillo until 13 March when Carranza was already safely ensconced at Monclova.

The next logical step was to pursue Carranza in his hideout, but the Huerta regime believed its own propaganda and concluded that the "battle" of El Anhelo had decisively shattered the Carrancistas (or followers of Carranza). Believing that the threat from Coahuila was over, the government left only 350 soldiers and two artillery pieces at Saltillo.[6] When Carranza learned how weak the garrison was, he saw the opportunity to show the country his

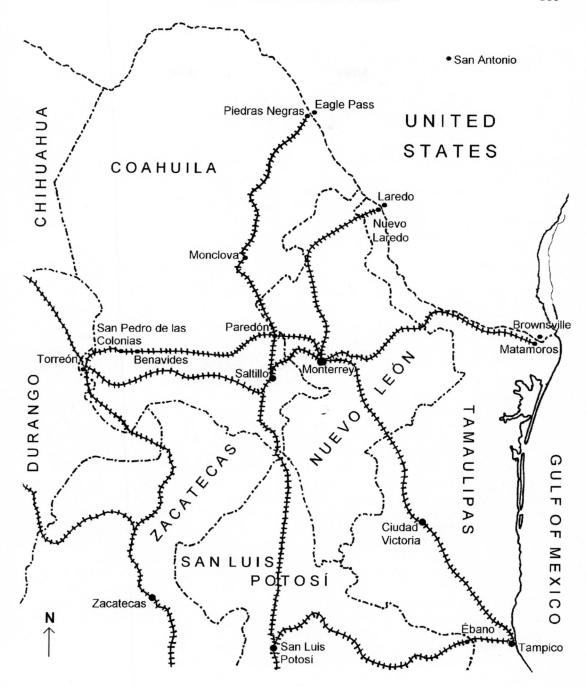

Map 14. Northeast Mexico.

revolt was alive. He authorized an attack on Saltillo for 22 March:

> The engagement was essentially a bold, badly planned, wild, cowboy attack by the followers of Carranza. It was a surprise to the federals, and had it not been for the arrival of 480 infantry from the south under General Casso López on the afternoon of the 21st, Saltillo might have been taken. The federals wasted an enormous amount of ammunition — their firing being principally from the Cathedral and

from roofs of the taller buildings in the central part of the city.[7] The rebels manifested very poor military training and judgment in their attacks. They confined their operations to desultory firing and unorganized attacks. The federals displayed good training, coolness, and generalship, thus sustaining slighter losses in all engagements.[8]

The higher than expected casualties forced Carranza to halt the attack the next day. The rebels withdrew to the north in good order the next day because the federals made no attempt at pursuit but contented themselves with executing most of the prisoners.[9] The setback at Saltillo turned out to be a blessing in disguise, because the Huerta regime mistakenly concluded that the Carranza revolt was finished. In reality, the attack on Saltillo emboldened many sympathizers to come and join the movement. By early April Carranza had so many volunteers at Monclova that he could not feed them. He had spent all the specie he had brought from Saltillo, and he received only a trickle of revenue from the customs house at Piedras Negras on the U.S. border. Food and fodder were very scarce in this barren region.

To try to escape his predicament, Carranza opted for extreme solutions. He sent most of followers to the states of Nuevo León, San Luis Potosí, Tamaulipas, and Zacatecas. Their mission was to spread the revolt in what turned out to be very fertile recruiting grounds. Sending the rebels to fend for themselves in other states constituted an implicit authorization to engage in plundering and looting. Left with no other alternative, Carranza reached the same conclusion as Madero had in 1911: Namely, that he had to authorize his followers to take what they needed at gunpoint. To give an air of legality, Carranza insisted that the rebels issue receipts for the value of the goods. He promised to repay those sums after the defeat of Huerta. Foreigners and wealthy property owners duly collected many receipts from rebel leaders, but the peasants normally could expect to receive nothing from the usually illiterate foraging parties. As long as the looting was not excessive, and as long as foreign-owned properties remained immune, Carranza had to allow his followers to raid ranches, farms, and towns just like in the revolt of 1910–1911. Not surprisingly, the easy life of plunder proved an attractive employment al-

ternative as many joined the rebel bands multiplying all over northern Mexico. Rebel bands proliferated, and after several months they began to have a decisive impact on the military operations in the northeast.[10]

The seeds Carranza was planting in other states could grow only if he remained a valid and real alternative to Huerta. In the crucial months of April and May, Carranza needed Monclova not so much as a base of operations as a rallying symbol for rebels in northern Mexico. Fortunately for Carranza, the Huerta regime failed to realize the urgency of stopping the uprising before it could spread. After the failed rebel attack on Saltillo of 22–23 March, the federal commanders needed to pursue the Carrancistas relentlessly. Instead, inaction seized the federal troops who let slip the fleeting opportunity to strike a mortal blow against the rebels when they were most vulnerable. Only after reinforcements finally arrived and after leaving a strong garrison behind in Saltillo, did 800 federal soldiers begin their northern advance on 19 April. The month-long delay gave Colonel González plenty of time to organize his 500 rebels for the defense. Because the advancing federal column insisted on repairing the slightly damaged railroad track, Colonel González had plenty of opportunities to excel in his specialty, the fighting withdrawal. He also launched surprise cavalry raids on the federal column and in its rear. The weary federal troops, despairing of ever reaching Monclova by train, finally abandoned the advance. By the end of May the federal column was back in Saltillo after having accomplished nothing except to confirm the inability of the Huerta regime to eradicate the principal Carrancista base.[11]

The rebel success at Monclova partially compensated for the unfavorable situation elsewhere in Mexico. Chihuahua State had been the foundation of the Madero insurrection in 1910, and Carranza expected a similar outpouring for his revolt. The arrest of Governor Abraham González on 22 February and his subsequent murder dashed those hopes. More bad news came on 27 February, when Pascual Orozco announced his full support for the government of Huerta. The combination of Orozquista bands and federal garrisons was sure to overwhelm any Carrancista rebels. The Huerta regime, always eager to exaggerate success, enthusiastically proclaimed that state's pacification.

The regime's grip on Chihuahua, however, was more apparent than real. Huerta distrusted Orozco and dispatched his armed bands to other states. Orozco himself came to Mexico City on 12 March to enter into negotiations with Emiliano Zapata, who had not ceased his revolt against Mexico City. Some Zapatistas wanted to submit, but predictably Zapata blocked any recognition of the new regime. The collapse of the negotiations forced Huerta to divert troops against Zapata. Moreover, Huerta's maneuver to use Orozco to obtain the submission of Zapata had backfired. The absence of Orozco from Chihuahua at this crucial moment left a power vacuum in that state. News of the Carrancista revolt in neighboring Coahuila was all the encouragement rebels needed to create bands. Already in late February Colonel Toribio Ortega had refused to recognize the military dictatorship and with his unit seized the frontier town of Ojinaga. The rebel leaders of 1910–1911 returned to campaign in 1913 and soon were making raids throughout Chihuahua and neighboring Durango. All was not lost for Huerta, however, because many of the rebel leaders were considering recognizing the new government in exchange for generous payoffs. Negotiations between the Huerta regime and the rebel leaders began in late March. Both sides had agreed to a truce, and as the negotiations dragged on into April, Carranza could only watch helplessly as the Chihuahua rebels tried to make up their minds whether to support him or Huerta.[12]

The news from the distant state of Sonora was not very encouraging at first. Carranza learned that Governor José María Maytorena of Sonora had recognized Huerta as president of Mexico, but in reality that report came from a devious schemer who had also told Sonora that Carranza had recognized Huerta. Because the Huerta regime controlled the railroads and telegraph lines, it had been able to keep the real news away from Maytorena and from Carranza. In reality, Sonora never recognized Huerta but took a long time to turn against him. The indecision was exclusively the fault of Governor Maytorena, who had sunk into a state of depression and inactivity when he first heard that Madero had fallen. Before taking any decision, his political instincts told him to can-

vass his supporters. Among others, he summoned Colonel Álvaro Obregón, who having heard that Madero had fallen, promptly came with armed followers to Hermosillo, the capital of the state, ready to do battle against Huerta. Maytorena was angry at that response and stated "I don't need warriors."[13]

When Huerta let pass through the telegraph the reports on the death of Madero, the news had an electrifying effect on Sonora. Town after town rose up and demanded to fight against Huerta. In a last effort to contain the anti–Huerta momentum, Maytorena revealed the telegram he had received stating that Carranza had recognized Huerta. Maytorena's plea that Sonora was alone in opposition to the central government did not dampen the enthusiasm. Many in Sonora felt that the governor was hesitant to proclaim the revolt because his ailments made him too frail to campaign in the harsh outdoors. Colonel Obregón tried to reassure the governor: "I do not need you to come in person in the campaign; the only thing we need is your last name because in these moments you represent the legally constituted authority."[14] Maytorena sensed the political effervescence but was unwilling to break with Huerta. Instead, the governor asked for a leave of absence from his post on 26 February and left that same day for the United States. Fleeing like a coward totally discredited Maytorena, and an angry state legislature punished him by appointing Ignacio Pesqueira, a bitter enemy and fellow landowner, as the interim governor.

The presence of large federal garrisons to the south in Guaymas and to the north in the frontier towns made Pesqueira hesitant to start hostilities. The absence of a federal garrison at Hermosillo prevented the immediate arrest of governor Pesqueira, as had befallen his counterpart Abraham González at Chihuahua City, but the danger of federal reprisals remained lurking. The interim governor also engaged in last-minute negotiations to avoid a rupture, but at the same time he had to ask the legislature to consider a bill rejecting Huerta as president of Mexico. On 4 March Pesqueira brokered an agreement to preserve peace with Huerta in exchange for continued federal payment of the state militia and the withdrawal of federal troops from Sonora. The U.S. consul strongly urged the military regime to accept the

As a forceful general, Victoriano Huerta was very successful in his earlier campaigns, but as president of Mexico (1913–1914) he proved incapable of dealing with Venustiano Carranza's revolt. Huerta is in the center here; on the left is José V. Delgado and on the right is Abraham F. Ratner (Library of Congress, Prints and Photographs Division).

ment was strapped for cash. Obviously Huerta halted the payments from the federal treasury for the state militia, and unless the men received their daily wage, they would return home to obtain other employment. The best way to guarantee the daily wage of the men was to seize the federal customs houses in the north. The rebels also needed the customs revenue to purchase adequate quantities of ammunition. Otherwise, the 60,000 cartridges in the Hermosillo arsenal were insufficient for a formal battle.[16] However, sending the 1800 militiamen to the north left the rebel government very vulnerable. The state government was neatly sandwiched between numerically superior federal troops. From the port city of Guaymas to the Yaqui River over 2,000 federal troops maintained their patient vigil over the restless Indians in the south. To the north near the U.S. border nearly 2,000 federal troops garrisoned Naco, Agua Prieta, and Cananea (Map 13). Should the federal troops in the north and the south simultaneously converge upon Hermosillo in the center, they could crush the rebel government. Much as Colonel Obregón wanted to attack the north, he knew that if he left Hermosillo unprotected, the federal troops in the south could easily march unopposed to capture the state capital.

Spies brought highly valuable news. The federal soldiers at Guaymas were very disgruntled, did not wish to fight, and were deserting from units as large as thirty men after having killed their officers. Both Governor Pesquiera and Colonel Obregón concluded that the federal garrisons in the south were in no condition to mount an offensive against Hermosillo. Meanwhile, new rebel bands eventually numbering over a thousand men had spontaneously appeared in the south, and they constituted a more than adequate barrier to protect Hermosillo. Colonel Obregón could safely take the state militiamen to begin the campaign in the north.[17]

Colonel Obregón, whom Pesquiera had appointed as the commander of all the state militia units, left Hermosillo on 6 March for

agreement in spite of its lack of a clear recognition of Huerta. Mexico City should have accepted the agreement, but blinded by arrogance, Huerta rejected the proposal. The next day the state legislature, at the insistence of the state militia commanders, formally defied the Huerta regime.[15]

The Sonora rebels had to decide where to begin their military campaign but could not take too long to think because the state govern-

the frontier with the United States. Damage to the railroad north of the capital meant that the trip to reach Nogales took six days instead of the normal half a day. The journey would have taken even longer had not Obregón made his men march the last day through a snow storm and freezing rain to bypass the damaged track. New rebel bands had formed in the north, and they reinforced his column. Reconnaissance confirmed that Nogales, the first objective, had 200 federal defenders, Cananea, the second, had 350, and Naco had the largest number with almost 800 men under General Pedro Ojeda. This General, as commander of the northern sector, had to take a decision on how to face the approaching rebels. Because Obregon's force would soon number over a thousand men, any decision of General Ojeda required concentrating his scattered forces, an easy task because only three hours of travel time by train separated his most distant garrison. He then had to decide whether to confront Obregón in one decisive battle, or, more in keeping with past federal passivity, to concentrate his forces for a determined defense of Naco. Instead, he chose to do nothing, and by default left the initiative to Obregón, whose cold and tired men took up positions outside Nogales on 12 March.

Because Nogales was right on the border, Obregón could attack only from the east to minimize the risk of bullets falling into the U.S. side. To reduce his casualties, he launched a night attack in the early hours of 13 March. His inexperienced men bungled the attack and achieved little by daybreak. Obregón planned to wait until the next night to resume the attack, but the first combat experience made some of the soldiers so enthusiastic that their forward momentum continued the advance. Obregón had no choice but to order a general assault, and his men gradually began to seize outposts. At 1600 the federal commander learned that his three key defensive positions lacked enough cartridges to repel the expected night attack. After an hour, he ordered a retreat to the U.S. side. The next day the rebels entered Nogales.[18]

The Sonora revolt had gained its first customs house and a path to the outside world. The victory became sweeter for Obregón when he read in U.S. newspapers for the first time that Carranza had defied Huerta and was leading a successful rebellion. Huerta's censorship

had kept the Sonorans ignorant of the Carrancista revolt. An excited Obregón could not hide his joy telling everyone that Sonora was not alone! The enthusiasm spread to his men who wanted to finish driving out Huerta's forces from the northern towns.

Colonel Obregón marched his men from Nogales to Naco and hoped that General Ojeda would accept battle outside the border town to avoid incidents with the United States. No doubt existed in the mind of many of the Yaquis in Naco over who would win eventually, and over 200 Indians deserted the federal garrison and crossed over to the U.S. side on 18 March.[19] General Ojeda was left with barely 550 soldiers, and not surprisingly he rejected an offer to come out in formation for a battle. Leaving a small covering force behind, Obregón returned to capture Cananea, which he wanted to secure before attempting the much more difficult siege of Naco.

Cananea made an attractive target in many ways. It was 50 kilometers south of the United States and thus no gunfire could reach the border. The hilly terrain provided many vantage points to control the town, while the army garrison of 350 men was too small to protect anything other than its barracks and one outpost. The town lacked defenses, because the officers felt so confident that no attack was possible. Not only did the soldiers fail to make rifle slits in the barracks and to dig a network of trenches, but they also neglected to stockpile food and water for a prolonged battle. The enthusiastic support of the inhabitants allowed the rebels to occupy the town without firing a shot on 23 March. The rebels promptly cut off the flow of water and foodstuffs to the barracks.[20]

Only the next day did the attack begin, and although the rebels kept the garrison under pressure, they were not able to overcome the resistance. A crisis in authority erupted when Colonel Salvador Alvarado, who still refused to recognize Obregón as his superior, made a brief truce with the federal commander. Governor Pesqueira promptly ratified the authority of Obregón, and a grudging Alvarado reluctantly complied. Once the truce expired, Obregón resumed the attack. Without water and food the morale of the federals collapsed, but because of the brutal discipline typical in the army, the fear of reprisals kept the men from expressing their views. The *soldaderas*, the female companions of the soldiers, were outside the chain of command and thus freer than the soldiers to speak the truth. A delegation of *soldaderas* told the commanding officer he must surrender because the soldiers could no longer fight. After consulting with his fellow officers, the commander agreed and surrendered to Obregón at 1800 on 26 March. A few officers did manage to escape and ran into the relief column that General Ojeda was belatedly bringing to Cananea, but when he heard that the rebels outnumbered him, he returned hastily to Naco.[21]

Obregón had hoped that the attack on Cananea would lure the federal garrison out to make a sortie, but Ojeda's prompt retreat left the rebels with no alternative but to prepare for a formal siege of Naco. The federal commander up to this moment had shown little initiative, but at last he took the basic precautions to defend the town. He blocked all the street entrances into Naco with sandbags and stone blocks to form a continuous perimeter around the city. He placed men and machine guns behind barricades on the rooftops and opened rifle slits in the walls of the houses facing the open fields. Lastly, he placed his two 80 mm mortars in a way that they could lob exploding grenades into the attackers. The terrain surrounding the city was flat and offered an excellent field of fire for his soldiers to shatter any daytime attack. In case of a night attack, he piled up firewood at strategic places so that when lighted, the huge bonfires would illuminate the attackers and provide easy targets for his gunners. His defenses were so impressive that had he previously summoned the lost garrisons of Cananea and Nogales to join him, he could have held out for months as long as he had plenty of ammunition.

Colonel Obregón had never before faced such a difficult objective. On 8 April the attack on Naco began, but the rebels failed to advance and suffered heavy casualties. Huerta was so impressed by the successful defense that he promoted Ojeda in rank. Meanwhile the real battle broke out in the rebel camps at Naco, as Obregón faced the last challenge to his authority. The forces under his command were very numerous, and not all the rebel leaders recognized his authority; at one point they were about to kill him, but he overcame this danger

and gained their reluctant obedience. The internal bickering took the pressure off the federal garrison, and as the days passed, the morale of the rebels was falling. Obregón knew he had to do something dramatic to revitalize the spirits of his men, who had erroneously expected another easy victory like Nogales or Cananea.

He proposed a night attack to surprise the defenders with a simultaneous attack from the east and the west (to prevent shots from falling into U.S. soil, he did not attack on the south side). His fellow officers accepted the plan, but because the attackers would have to cross an open space of 800 meters, only his loyal Yaqui soldiers volunteered for this dangerous mission. Obregón placed his men in the farthest trench and gave them hours to sleep before the night attack set to begin at 0300 on 13 April. After 0100 his Yaqui troops abandoned the trench and with painted faces silently slid across the vast space under cover of darkness. Around 0300 the federals at last sensed something and fired their first volley into the pitch darkness, and General Ojeda lighted his bonfires to illuminate the area in front of his trenches. His machine guns and mortars fired furiously but only managed to raise huge dust clouds in the desert sands. Gradually the light from the fire gave way to heavy black smoke that darkened the battlefield, but not before Obregón caught a glimpse of his Yaquis engaged in hand-to-hand combat with the startled soldiers in the federal trenches. Instinctively, Obregón ordered reinforcements to follow up the attack, but the smoke, din, and bullets scared the men who advanced only at daybreak. The war whoops from the painted Indians had terrified the federals, who were in no condition to oppose the second wave of rebels. The federal soldiers ran from their positions, and General Ojeda himself fled to the U.S. side after setting fire to an ammunition dump. Unaware that their commander had already abandoned them, a few officers continued to resist, but by noon of 13 April the rebels had full control of Naco.[22]

In a campaign of thirty-nine days, Obregón had cleared the north of all federal garrisons. No looting accompanied the capture of the towns, and civilian authorities continued to operate normally. Obregón was insistent on maintaining order and severely punished any criminals who tried to take advantage of the confusion to engage in looting. Throughout the war Obregón made sure that his forces (always paid their daily wage of $1.50) never engaged in the plunder and marauding actions that so characterized rebel bands in most other areas of Mexico.

The Sonorans were clearly able to control their own state, but they still needed to legitimize their war against Huerta. Sonora could not be a loose cannon singly defying Mexico City. Maytorena, the only legally constituted authority, had refused to provide the authorization the Sonorans craved. When delegates from Sonora went to visit Carranza to obtain his mantle of legitimacy, what they saw made them awe-struck. Carranza's courage and determination transformed him into an ideal leader, and his position as a legally elected governor legitimized his uprising. The aristocratic air and refined manners of Carranza naturally generated prestige, while his eloquence with the Spanish language made him an effective advocate for the revolution. The crude warriors of Sonora saw in the dignified and elegant Carranza the answer to their needs, and on 19 April they enthusiastically recognized him as the leader of the revolt. This recognition gained Carranza the best warriors of Mexico, including the best officers in the country. Although he had just acquired his most important army, Carranza himself did not take any military rank. He properly considered himself the direct inheritor of the civilian rule of Madero. He limited himself to taking the title of First Chief, with the provision that once Huerta was overthrown, Carranza would take the job of provisional president until elections could take place.[23] Much as the rugged warriors of Sonora needed the polished Carranza, years would elapse before they realized that he needed them even more.

The Offensives of Victoriano Huerta

Long before the rebels had captured Naco on 13 April 1913, Victoriano Huerta had decided to make Sonora the target of his first major offensive against the rebels. The president could have turned the Federal Army first against Coahuila, but he concluded that the

garrisons near Saltillo sufficed to keep Venustiano Carranza in check. Mexico City enjoyed good rail links with Coahuila but not with Sonora; paradoxically, the easy transportation to Saltillo became another reason to postpone a federal offensive in that region. Huerta reasoned that should any rebel surge occur in the northeast, the railroad could easily bring reinforcements from Mexico City. He failed to realize that First Chief Carranza had acquired a symbolic significance and that the government could not leave the rebels free to expand in Coahuila. Taking a narrowly military perspective, Huerta concluded that the rebel army in Sonora posed the most immediate threat to his regime. In hindsight, he should have limited his efforts in Sonora to holding the port city of Guaymas. After the Federal Army had crushed the Carrancista movement in the rest of Mexico, a huge expeditionary force could then at its leisure subdue the remote province.

Sonora

The victorious march of the rebels through northern Sonora so angered Huerta that he insisted on sending reinforcements to crush the rebels. A first large contingent departed by rail from Mexico City on 22 April and boarded troop transports two days later; under the escort of two gunboats, this contingent reached Guaymas on 1 May and immediately dashed Colonel Obregón's hopes of capturing the port city (Map 13). The rebels had only two small artillery pieces (captured in Naco) and feared the naval gunfire. As soon as Colonel Obregón heard of the gunboats' arrival, he ordered his troops to withdraw inland. The War Department ordered the federal commander to begin the march to Hermosillo promptly and not to wait for more reinforcements. General Manuel Gil, in spite of his misgivings, reluctantly loaded trains with almost 2,000 soldiers and began to move north on 2 May.[24]

As the federal troops occupied one railroad station after another on their northward trip, Colonel Obregón carefully set up a trap on 4 May. The perspicacious General Gil suspected something and halted the advance of the federal troops for three days. On 7 May he was recalled to Mexico City and replaced by the newly arrived General Luis Medina Barrón, a veteran of the Yaqui campaigns. Upon hearing of his return, the Indians in droves joined the rebels to seek revenge against their former tormentor. Obregón did not have enough rifles for the Yaquis, who fought initially with their extremely accurate bows and arrows.

General Medina Barrón was most impatient to reach Hermosillo, because he knew that General Pedro Ojeda was coming from the United States to take charge of the campaign. General Medina Barrón realized he had to move quickly to gain a smashing victory. Eager for glory, on 8 May he ordered the federal column to resume its northern advance. By then Colonel Obregón was sure that the federals had detected his trap, but he believed that the influx of the Yaqui volunteers still kept his plan feasible. His general goal was to isolate the federal column from food and water. Obregón first sent strong detachments to defend the main sources of water near the railroad track. On 9 May he launched a massive attack from three sides on the federal advance guard at the Santa Rosa train station; he aimed to lure the rest of the federal column forward into the trap. General Medina Barrón, in the dark about the rebel dispositions, led his main column forward to relieve the hard-pressed advance guard. Rather than waiting for his infantry to arrive and to advance under the covering fire of his artillery, the federal commander sent his cavalry ahead to charge into the waiting machine guns of the rebels. The cavalry took heavy losses of almost 150 casualties in less than 30 minutes, and although the suicidal attack finally was called off, the wounded cavalrymen and riderless horses spread panic as they retreated through the advancing infantrymen. As this sorry mayhem was taking place, rebel parties quietly slipped in the rear and established roadblocks to the south. The rest of 9 May passed in costly charges and countercharges by both sides; incredibly, the federal commander still did not realize that he was surrounded, and he insisted on attacking to the north to try to reach Hermosillo.

Fierce clashes resumed on 10 May, but the failure of a supply train to arrive with food and water at last made the federal troops worry about their survival. General Medina Barrón immediately needed to make a wide flanking movement around the southern rebel roadblocks. Instead, the federal commander continued to attack the rebel positions to the north

on 11 May, only to have a flanking rebel maneuver capture a position one hundred meters from his artillery. With the federal batteries under heavy rifle fire, and with his men short of water and food, General Medina Barrón at last accepted the necessity of fleeing by night.[25] Fortunately for the federals, the rebels were out of cartridges, and not until an ammunition train arrived from Hermosillo the next morning could Obregón send cavalry to try to cut off the retreat. Even without the prompt rebel pursuit, General Medina had to abandon six machine guns and considerable quantities of equipment and ammunition to make his hurried escape possible. He did manage to extricate the crucial artillery pieces, but he still lost over a third of his force. The officers suffered a disproportionate number of casualties; the rebels afterwards claimed they gave their sharpshooters orders to try to pick off the federal officers. The quest of General Medina Barrón for glory had turned into a near disaster. The Federal Army had suffered a serious defeat at Santa Rosa, and as late as 12 May ragged stragglers were still drifting into Guaymas. Although the rebels remained inferior in artillery, they had shown themselves to be superior in infantry and cavalry tactics; Obregón had emerged as an outstanding commander, who received the well-deserved promotion to the rank of General.[26]

Lack of water and intense heat had already plagued the federal column in May, and the climate worsened as the scorching summer began in June. The emergence of serious threats in other states of Mexico counseled adopting a defensive stance at Guaymas. Instead, the Huerta regime became obsessed with avenging the defeat of Santa Rosa and sent additional units to Sonora to replace the battlefield losses. The urgency to subdue the state overrode even military considerations, and rather than wait for all the reinforcements to arrive, the War Department pressed for a speedy advance on Hermosillo.[27] The risky operation required a dynamic commander, yet Huerta had already made up his mind to appoint General Pedro Ojeda to lead the new expedition. Apparently Huerta felt that General Ojeda bristled with a desire to avenge his earlier defeats, when in reality his lack of aggressiveness did not bode well for the new offensive.

By late May General Ojeda was training

and reorganizing his troops in Guaymas. The defeat at Santa Rosa had shattered their morale, and the soldiers did not want to attack the apparently invincible rebels. The federals had lost so many locomotives and railroad cars at Santa Rosa, that the infantry had to march north under the broiling summer heat. To instill confidence in his men, General Ojeda had two new 75 mm cannons installed on railroad cars. He also brought five additional pieces of field artillery and eight machine guns; the rebels had 14 machine guns but were virtually without cannons. The federal column numbered around 2,250 soldiers and was smaller than the rebel force of about 3,500 men. General Ojeda wanted to wait until the last of the reinforcements arrived, but under orders to begin the offensive at once, he left Guaymas on 28 May.

A force of 300 rebels deliberately stayed in view to the front of the federal column but out of firing range. The federal advance went slowly, because work crews had to repair the culverts and bridges the rebels had meticulously destroyed. By 8 June the column had traveled only the 38 kilometers to Ortiz station. Fearing a repeat of the ambush of the battle of Santa Rosa, General Ojeda advanced in a cumbersome way. He did not sent scouts or patrols over the countryside but kept his cavalry in two parallel columns close to the railroad track. He sent the armored railroad cars forward and then had the cannons on the flatcars shell any suspected rebel patrol or position within sight. The shelling could last for hours, and when it finally stopped, the federal cavalry sallied to inspect the targets. Meanwhile, a repair crew examined the railroad track carefully to see if the rebels had placed any mines under the crossties. Once the all clear was sounded, the main body marched forward, but the troops halted to set up camp for the night no later than by 1800. This ponderous routine stopped at Ortiz station, because there the reconstruction of a fallen bridge over 70 meters long required no less than two weeks of strenuous toil. General Obregón kept his men pouring a steady harassing fire on the repair crews to disrupt even more their work. The federal column was stuck in the middle of a dry plain, and General Ojeda did not realize how vulnerable he was to rebel encirclement.[28]

An American aviator flying a biplane reported to General Obregón that a large portion of the railroad track to the south was unguarded.[29] This was the first time in the Western Hemisphere that an airplane provided intelligence during a military campaign; the information was all that General Obregón needed to finalize his plans to surround and destroy the federal column. In the early hours of June 19 he sent troops to seize all the key watering spots near the federal forces and to destroy large stretches of the railroad track between Guaymas and the federal column. Without having to fire a shot, the rebels set up their machine guns in the crucial road blocks. Because it was important to destroy the railroad track quickly before daylight, the rebels detonated huge dynamite charges. The explosions heard as far away as Guaymas naturally woke up General Ojeda, who ignored this last warning of imminent disaster. The federal commander believed that a stray band had caused the damage; instead of moving south with his whole army, he contented himself with waiting until morning to send a repair crew. Another repair party also set out from Guaymas, but unexpectedly stiff rebel resistance blocked all attempts to reach the damaged track. In spite of all the evidence, General Ojeda still refused to conclude that a large rebel force was blocking his retreat south. Had he abandoned his advanced position at Ortiz and immediately marched south with his entire force, he still could have blasted his way to safety. Not realizing that the survival of his army was at stake, he let pass the last chance to escape the encirclement. He knew that a retreat, no matter how successful, meant disgrace in the eyes of Huerta.

Combat engagements had begun on 19 June and continued with growing intensity in the coming days. Lacking any good reconnaissance, General Ojeda had to learn the hard way through attacks the strength of the rebel positions. After giving up on his attacks to the south, he turned most of his forces to the west to try to capture several key water holes. His men took heavy casualties as they charged the rebel machine guns covering the water holes, and the federals managed to capture only one shallow well that was fast running dry. In a desperate move, on 22 May he launched an attack to the north around the fallen bridge, in the mistaken belief that he could still reach Hermosillo if his men just tried. The attack failed miserably and cost high casualties. He returned to making attacks to the east, but by then his men were getting exhausted; many were running out of water and had not eaten in days. On the night of 24 June, General Ojeda finally accepted a retreat as inevitable, and belatedly he gave the orders to carry out a simultaneous withdrawal beginning at 0300 on 25 May.

The first part of the withdrawal along the railroad track went smoothly because the men had a clear path to follow, but once the column reached the damaged track and abandoned the last locomotives and railroad cars, confusion took over. Sandy soil and the uneven terrain slowed down the horse wagons and the field pieces. The cavalry and the infantry continued to retreat at an adequate pace and could have escaped, but were slowed down to the snail's pace of the impedimenta. Dawn found the retreating column still in sight of the rebel lookouts, who promptly reported the movement to General Obregón. The retreating army was headed to the hacienda of Santa María, already defended by a rebel detachment, but Obregón knew the unit was too small to hold the position. He ordered reinforcements to ride and march at full speed to the hacienda of Santa María. Meanwhile, an ineffective artillery shelling had not dislodged the defenders at Santa María, who were well protected in the many covered irrigation ditches in the hacienda. The federal attacks against Santa María failed, and any chance of capturing the water holes in this hacienda ended when the reinforcements Obregón had sent arrived at 1230. The rebel machine guns took a fearful toll as the desperate federal soldiers charged forward craving a drink of water. Under the rebel guns lay a patch of watermelons, and delirious soldiers, in defiance of the orders from their officers, raced across the field in a desperate attempt to outrun the bullets. After the battle the rebels found watermelon in the mouths of many of the bullet-riddled bodies.

The desperate federals tried to outflank Santa Maria to the west, but their movement ran into entrenched rebels; the line of battle soon extended from Santa María to the damaged railroad track in the west. Obregón feared that if the federals jumped the track and went further west they would reach a water hole, and to preclude that possibility he posted his last reserves to the west of the track. When he realized that he lacked troops to protect one last ridge, he and his general staff personally manned the position rifles in hand. Only a few stray federal soldiers wandered in front of Obregón's position, and the federals insisted on attacking directly to the south. By nightfall General Ojeda knew that many soldiers were collapsing from insolation and were dying from lack of water. With no other option left, at 2230 of the night of 25 May he ordered his men to escape by making a wide sweeping movement east of Santa María. The hilly terrain meant that they had to abandon all their equipment and the valuable artillery. The retreat in pitch darkness turned into a rout as men and animals lost their way and took days to make their return to safety in Guaymas. Many soldiers fell into rebel hands, and the abandoned wounded found a miserable death in the barren hills.[30]

Unaware of the federal rout, General Obregón prepared for the renewal of fighting the next day. He ordered his units on the far west to march east to the railroad track at 0300, and on the way they ran into stragglers who reported the federal withdrawal. Obregón's natural instinct was to begin a relentless pursuit into Guaymas, but his commanders pleaded with him not to order the exhausted men to advance. Obregón later blamed himself for not leading whatever men could still march and ride on a hot pursuit, but he was really being too hard on himself. He did fail to bag additional fleeing prisoners, but as long as naval gunfire protected Guaymas, no land attack stood any chance of success.

Obregón formally placed Guaymas under siege on 28 June, and after thirty days of desultory attacks and shelling, he concluded that the effective naval gunfire made too costly the attack. Just to maintain the siege consumed a large number of cartridges, which had to be smuggled across the border from the United States. Instead, a small covering guard sufficed to keep the federal garrison trapped in Guaymas. Although the disaster of Santa María forced the Huerta government to postpone its plans to reconquer Sonora, Huerta wanted to keep Guaymas under federal control to keep alive the hope of a future reconquest. To safeguard the port, Huerta sent one additional battalion, a deployment that finished locking a large federal force in the city more effectively than any trap could have. Rather than reinforcing Guaymas, Huerta should have withdrawn the garrison and thus released those troops for duty in other battle fronts; the strategic equation remained the same in August as in March: Once the rest of the country had been pacified, Mexico City at its leisure could subdue this distant state.[31]

The large federal garrison locked up in Guaymas was powerless to stop General Obregón from advancing south into other states, and he was sure to win equally smashing victories against the Federal Army. This swift advance would have ended the suffering in Mexico much sooner, but unfortunately local politics and not the Federal Army halted any offensive by Obregón. The root of the problem lay in the decision of José María Maytorena to resume the governorship once the six-month's leave of absence he had taken on 26 February expired. A ferocious power struggle ensued, and to patch things up the presence even of First Chief Venustiano Carranza proved necessary.[32] The bickering among the men from Sonora gave a respite to the Federal Army to try to destroy the rebels in other places in Mexico.

Northeast Mexico

Had General Álvaro Obregón lost the battle of Santa María, the Federal Army would still have needed months to finish subduing the entire state of Sonora. Thus whether the federals won or lost in Sonora, their army remained unavailable for redeployment to face the new threats erupting in Mexico. Yet even before the federal disaster at Santa María on 26 June, the outbreak of other serious uprisings confirmed how erroneous had been Huerta's decision to subdue Sonora first. The followers Carranza had sent to other parts of Mexico in April found ample support for the revolt in the rural areas. The insurrection acquired ferocity more intense than in any of the previous revolts. To make matters worse, bloody reprisals proliferated, and Carranza tried to legitimize the rebel actions by reviving on 14 May the law of Benito Juárez of 25 May 1862. The Juárez law had sentenced to death all persons who collaborated with the French invader, and in 1914 Carranza extended the harsh penalty to all who supported the Huerta regime. Initially the bru-

tal practice applied only to captured officers, but soon all prisoners risked facing the firing squad. The Federal Army reciprocated in full and no longer limited itself to sporadic executions of prisoners.[33]

Rebel bands roamed across northeast Mexico and were coalescing into large units: For the first time towns and even cities were in danger of rebel capture. The first breakthrough was the work of General Lucio Blanco, who explained his plan to capture the border city of Matamoros:

> My military operations against Matamoros proceeded slowly, mainly because almost all the people who will participate in the attack were scattered around in guerrilla groups throughout the states of Nuevo León and Tamaulipas. By now I have gathered together most of these bands, and at this moment I have 700 men under arms. Another reason for my delay in attempting the attack has been the scarcity of ammunition for the veteran fighters and the lack of weapons for the new recruits. Now almost all my men have ample munitions and adequate weapons. My scouts are virtually next to Matamoros, and my advance guard is about 20 kilometers from the city; as soon as my rear guard returns from Reynosa this afternoon, I intend to issue the order for the attack.[34]

Carranza approved the attack but did not share the heady optimism. The First Chief cautioned that the most important thing was to avoid a failure and that if the attack appeared too risky, Blanco should instead bring his men to join a forthcoming rebel attack on Nuevo Laredo. Carranza's misgivings proved unfounded, because Blanco had chosen his target wisely. Rebel control of the countryside blocked the rail links of Matamoros with the rest of Mexico, but in spite of this imminent danger, the Huerta regime had not considered the situation threatening enough to send reinforcements. The federal garrison of roughly 400 men might have put up a more vigorous defense, but its commander, an ancient major who had held that same rank since 1878 was not very aggressive. The lack of machine guns crippled the defenders who, however, were not without creativity: They erected an electrified fence around a key part of the perimeter. But Blanco foresaw this barrier and supplied his men with plenty of dynamite. He launched the attack on 3 June, and he had his men hurl dynamite bombs to blast holes in the electrified fence and to terrify the soldiers in the trenches. Still, the defenders resisted, even after the wounded federal major fled to the U.S. side. Other officers took command of the scattered federal units, and at 2000 they began a night withdrawal. The next day, 4 June, the forces of Blanco formally took control of the entire city.[35]

The rebel capture of this border city opened another route to smuggle weapons and ammunition from the United States. For the Huerta government the loss of Matamoros was a serious political blow and was followed a few days later by an even bigger setback. Rebel leaders learned that only a small federal garrison protected the capital city of Zacatecas. The rebels infiltrated troops disguised as civilians into the city and then began an attack in the morning of 5 June. The main rebel force entered the city and hurled dynamite bombs into the defense lines. The next day the rebels continued their attacks, and fires started to break out in the city. The last federal troops withdrew, not wishing to see the city reduced to ashes, and the rebels gained control of the city on 7 June. The immediate benefit for the rebels was the capture of 1000 rifles, 3 cannons, and 80,000 cartridges, but the impact on Mexico City was much greater.[36]

Zacatecas was the first state capital to be captured by the rebels (Hermosillo had never been in the hands of Huerta), and its loss reverberated powerfully through the regime that was still reeling from the loss of Matamoros. The first casualty was Secretary of War Manuel Mondragón, whom Huerta blamed for the inept handling of the campaign against the rebels. The appointment of General Aureliano Blanquet as the new Secretary of War could not stop the search for more scapegoats, but the most urgent business was to counter the recent rebel advances. After extensive discussion at the cabinet meeting of 13 June, Huerta belatedly decided to make Coahuila the objective of the next federal offensive. Once the Federal Army had driven Venustiano Carranza from his home state, the rebel bands would lose their rallying symbol; the recapture of the lost territories was then inevitable. Compelling as the rationale had been in February or even March, by June the rebel movement had spread so far as to make meaningless the federal offensive

against Monclova. Carranza could easily slip away to other rebel regions to keep alive the banner of rebellion.

A complex plan of operations promised a federal victory. A first column setting out from Saltillo under Huerta's nephew Colonel Joaquín Maass had as its objectives the capture of Monclova and then the border town of Piedras Negras. The War Department rerouted a part of this column to Zacatecas; only after the recapture of that state capital would those units rejoin Maass at Saltillo. A second large column under General Guillermo Rubio Navarrete, the artillery expert, had the task of marching north from Monterrey to Nuevo Laredo; this parallel drive was supposed to support the advance of Maass. Because the column of Maass required more time to reach full strength than the column of Rubio Navarrete, the latter was to veer sharply to the east from Monterrey to retake Matamoros. After the capture of that city, Rubio Navarrete was supposed to return to Monterrey to launch his northern advance; by that time Maass almost certainly was sure to have captured Monclova. As the defeated rebels fled east, they were expected to fall right into the advancing forces of Rubio Navarrete. The offensive promised to catch the rebels in a gigantic pincer movement.[37]

Initially the offensive unfolded according to plan. The recapture of Zacatecas proved surprisingly easy, because the rebels had evacuated the city prior to the entry of the federal column on 16 June. The Huerta government had recovered its state capital, only to lose two days later another state capital, Durango. Tomás Urbina, a particularly vicious rebel leader from Chihuahua, had answered the call from local guerrilla groups to come help capture the city of Durango, the last place in that state still in federal hands.[38] The rebel attacks began on 15 June with dynamite blasts, but soon it became clear that the small and demoralized federal garrison wanted only to escape. On 18 June the incompetent commander withdrew, and by 1100 Urbina's men had taken control of the city and started to plunder the city meticulously:

> The scenes which followed the triumphal entry of the rebels into the city almost beggar description. They came pouring in from all sides by twos and threes, by fifties and by hundreds; they rode through the streets shouting and yelling and discharging their firearms at will.

Mexican Federal soldiers escorting rebel prisoners. The prisoners were likely well aware that at this stage of the war both sides routinely executed captives. However, it is possible that the presence of the photographer saved these men from the usual fate (Library of Congress, Prints and Photographs Collection).

[…] They were not long in beginning the work of pillage, destruction, and arson which had been promised them for many months past. Practically every commercial house in the city was forcibly broken into by a plentiful use of dynamite bombs and were stripped bare of all merchandise and other movables of value. The rebel hordes were ably seconded in the general looting by the lower element of this city, who followed in their wake with sacks, carts, and other conveniences to obtain their share of the plunder. The women vultures were particularly voracious and could be seen fighting and clawing their way through the entrance of every store, from which they issued a few minutes later literally bowed down by the weight of their booty. After the stores were completely sacked, the torch was applied to the remains, and tonight some six or eight blocks of Durango's principal business section are in ashes. These scenes were repeated through the night which followed, with sickening monotony, the rebels constantly becoming more intoxicated and punctuating their crimes with blood-curdling yells and the continuous discharge of firearms. […] When business houses offered no further inducements, attention was directed to private residences, and there scarcely remains a house in Durango tonight which has not been forcibly entered and such articles as suited the fancy of the invaders appropriated. Their particular penchant has been for horses, saddles, arms, ammunition, and money, although nothing has escaped which served to gratify a passing whim.[39]

The sacking at Durango seemed to confirm the propaganda charges in the Huerta press that the rebels were nothing but murderous looters bent on destruction. In response, Carranza reiterated his orders to prevent the pillaging of cities, but his generals did not always manage to restrain their troops[40] Of course, the requisitioning of food, clothes, and fodder continued unabated throughout the Revolution.

The propaganda points the Huerta regime scored over the looting could not hide the fact that the capture of Durango had disrupted the federal offensive. The troops that had recovered Zacatecas received the new mission of recapturing Durango. The federal troops ran into determined rebel resistance, and as they struggled vainly to reach Durango, any hope of joining the column of Maass in Saltillo faded. The need to modify the original campaign plan was obvious, yet an unperturbed Huerta still insisted on making a full-scale effort to recapture northern Coahuila. Colonel Maass needed more troops to launch the offensive, but the only available troops were under General Rubio Navarrete, who was poised to recover Matamoros. Curiously enough, Huerta's real reason for the offensive against Matamoros had been his desire to save all the glory for his nephew, but in the changed circumstances, Huerta relented. The War Department ordered General Rubio Navarrete to march north from Monterrey along the railroad to Nuevo Laredo and then to swing to the west to catch the retreating Carrancistas, who should have been fleeing from the parallel advance of the column of Maass.

Colonel Maass left Saltillo for Monclova in late June, and General Rubio Navarrete set out from Monterrey toward Nuevo Laredo in early July. The rebels under Pablo González had carried out their usual destruction of the tracks. In a very unusual practice for the normally slow Federal Army, both federal commanders detrained their men and marched them forward. General Rubio Navarrete deployed his force in separate columns, only to have one of them badly mauled on 8 July. The chance encounter had revealed the location of the main rebel force of Pablo González. A jubilant General Rubio Navarrete rushed west with all his units to close the trap and to capture Monclova ahead of the advancing column of Colonel Maass. Huerta, still not wanting to deprive his nephew of the glory, urgently ordered General Rubio Navarrete back east to the railroad track. The fleeting chance to destroy the army of Pablo González disappeared, and the rebels conducted a leisurely withdrawal to the north. On 10 July Colonel Maass entered the abandoned Monclova, by then just a piece of worthless real estate. An aggressive pursuit could still disrupt the retreating rebels, but the march to Monclova without trains had physically and psychologically exhausted Maass. Not even his promotion to the rank of general could goad him into action.[41]

General Maass loitered in Monclova waiting for reinforcements. Only a month later, on 12 August, did he march north with two columns to the border town of Piedras Negras. Pablo González tried to halt this federal advance, but "during each engagement [...] the federals used their artillery to the exclusion of other arms and the rebels could not stand under the fire."[42] Unable to use his numerical superiority effectively in a formal battle, Pablo González resorted to harassing the enemy columns by skirmishing, sniping, and raids. The tactics of González aimed to delay and to wear down the advancing federal column of General Maass, who was already predisposed to proceed very slowly. Pablo González concluded that he did not need his whole army to harass the slow-moving federal column. Instead, he quietly transferred the bulk of his army east to the state of Nuevo León to look for opportunities to strike decisive blows. Unaware of the changed rebel strategy, on 7 October General Maass finally entered the abandoned Piedras Negras:

> The scattered rebel forces appear to have simply opened out in front of the advancing enemy and allowed the federals to pass through. After this passage they closed in again and are said to be occupying several of the towns just vacated by them a few days earlier. [...] Meantime no steps have been taken by General Maass to hunt them out.[43]

The entry into Piedras Negras on 7 October marked the end of Victoriano Huerta's offensive against the rebels. The four months of campaigning seemed to have captured considerable territory, but the federal soldiers held only the ground they garrisoned. Although federal casualties had been light, the Huerta government had failed to inflict any serious damage on the rebel forces. The offensive had tied down large numbers of federal soldiers who remained in isolated garrisons throughout Coahuila.[44] The military genius of General Obregón had gained brilliant victories in Sonora at the early date of June, but even more tellingly, average rebel commanders had managed to outmaneuver the Federal Army in northeast Mexico. Huerta and his top generals continued to plan more offensives on paper, but the anticlimactic capture of Piedras Negras on 7 October meant that the initiative had passed to the rebels.

The Rebel Offensives

Northeast Mexico

The redeployment of rebel forces from Coahuila to Nuevo León marked the start of the offensive against Huerta. General Pablo González decided to capture the lightly defended Monterrey, the most important city in the north. By early October his units had begun to cut off the rail and telegraph links of that city and seemed to have isolated it. González gathered over 6000 rebels for the attack, and since the federal garrison in Monterrey numbered barely 1700 men and had little artillery, he stood an excellent chance of success. As rebel units slowly moved closer to the city, the federal commander realized he could not defend the entire urban perimeter and instead deployed his units at strategic points in downtown. Very ingeniously the federals mounted a machine gun aboard a Protos automobile for easy movement to any threatened position. Less wisely, the federal commander dispatched a unit nine kilometers to the north to block the large force of General González. On the afternoon of October 22, the rebels overran the federal unit and most significantly captured its two artillery pieces. Since the Monterrey garrison had only two other cannons, the federal artillery this time could not deprive the rebels of victory. The isolation of Monterrey had not been complete, however, and the federal commander had managed to dash off requests for reinforcements. Relief columns were on their way from Saltillo and from Nuevo Laredo, and unless General González struck quickly, he might lose the coveted prize.

The rebel attack on Monterrey began smoothly from the north at 0630 on 23 October. The federal pickets withdrew in good order and soon the rebels were inside the city. The capture of the army barracks in the outskirts proved surprisingly easy, because many of the conscripts switched sides and joined the attackers. By noon the rebels were near the inner defense perimeter but had failed to encircle the federal troops in downtown. Some flanking moves brought the rebels to the east and west of the city's center, but as nightfall approached, the rebel advance petered out on its own. Not Federal Army resistance but the temptations of the city had proven deadlier: "This night the worst element of the rebels and the mob of the city engaged in considerable looting and destruction of private property."[45] Drunkenness cut short the rampage as the rebels fell under the influence of massive doses of alcohol. The drunken rebels proved easy targets for the well-

entrenched federal soldiers, who effectively halted all attempts to resume the advance in the morning of 24 October. General González desperately tried to rally his men for one last effort to capture the relatively weak center of the city, but the arrival of the first federal reinforcements at 1500 persuaded him to desist, especially when he learned that the federal troops were the advance units of an approaching relief force.[46]

Fortunately for the drunken rebels, the federals did not attempt any pursuit. As the rebels slowly withdrew, they systematically destroyed any items that might be of use to the Federal Army. The rebels put to the torch the railroad repair facilities and all the captured rolling stock. To deprive the Federal Army of the ability to withstand a siege, the rebels burned all the granaries. In the barracks, the rebels seized over a thousand rifles and 400,000 cartridges, enough to support a large offensive. Paradoxically, the rebel army emerged stronger from the embarrassing defeat. The propagandists of Huerta transformed the repulse of the attack into a catastrophic disaster for the rebels; the propaganda was so persuasive that federal generals mistakenly concluded that the rebel threat in northeast Mexico was over.[47]

A well-chastened Pablo González gradually withdrew to the east and immediately began the difficult task of persuading his men to avoid drunkenness and looting. As he tried to discipline his men, during the first week of November the rebel general was quietly moving his forces toward a new objective: Ciudad Victoria, the capital of the state of Tamaulipas. The garrison of Ciudad Victoria consisted of 700 soldiers and 500 volunteers; the latter promptly deserted as soon as combat started. General González with over 5,000 rebels began the attack at 0500 on 16 November. His plan was not particularly original and called simply for a simultaneous attack on the outer defenses of the city. In spite of the desertion of the volunteers and the ineptness of the army commander, the small garrison with two cannons defended itself stoutly for 49 hours. The overwhelming rebel numbers finally forced the tattered garrison to fight its way south at 0200 on 18 November. General González immediately ordered a chase, but most of the retreating federals eluded their pursuers.[48]

The capture of Ciudad Victoria gave a

much-needed boost to the rebel cause and helped to compensate for the earlier setback at Monterrey. Ciudad Victoria became after Durango the second state capital to fall permanently into rebel hands, and its capture gave Carranza ample proof to bolster his claim that the revolt was far from sputtering. General González gained the opportunity to redeem his tarnished military reputation if he followed up the victory with other successes. What should be his next objective after the capture of Ciudad Victoria? He continued to maintain a strong force covering Monterrey, but another attack against its reinforced garrison seemed premature. His options boiled down to two. He could take the railroad south and try to attack Tampico before the federals could reinforce that valuable city. Or, he could backtrack and take the much longer route around Monterrey to surprise the garrison at the border town of Nuevo Laredo. Making a decision was difficult, because each site offered advantages and drawbacks; even with the perspective of time no right answer to these riddles that life sometimes presents is readily apparent. A perplexed González tried to evade the dilemma by assigning *both* cities as objectives for subordinate commanders. Consequently about 2000 men went south to try to capture Tampico, while the rest began the long trek to reach Nuevo Laredo. By this decision, he dispersed his units and violated the principle of concentration of forces. The distances also deprived him of direct control over these campaigns conducted by subordinates.

The rebels reached nearby Tampico first. That city, nearly surrounded by the Pánuco River and a lake, had only three narrow and easily defended land approaches, two of which brought the railroad lines into the city. The rebels arrived on the railroad line from Ciudad Victoria but inexplicably failed to block the other railroad leading west to San Luis Potosí. González believed that the 2000 rebels he had sent were more than adequate to overwhelm the small garrison of 350 soldiers, in spite of the presence of a coastal battery. Although the odds in numbers were not as favorable as the 10-to-1 superiority in Ciudad Victoria, the rebels decided to repeat the same tactic of a simultaneous attack on all fronts. The rebels began their assault on 10 December, but because the garrison needed to defend only three

land approaches, the weak attacks failed. With a smaller force than at Ciudad Victoria, the rebels needed to concentrate their men in one spot, but the local commanders, no less than González himself, failed to grasp the principle of concentration of forces. The coastal battery proved particularly effective in stopping the attacks, and the gunboat *Bravo* also came to shell the attackers. A few hours after the attack began, 580 soldiers arrived on a train from San Luis Potosí. The rebels should have desisted, but recalling that the failure to persevere at Monterrey had cost them a victory, they did not quit. Mounting losses did not deter the rebels who continued their attacks during the subsequent days. But the arrival of 640 additional soldiers aboard the gunboat *Veracruz* on the afternoon of 12 December ended any chance of capturing the city. On 13 December the persistent rebels tried to run a train loaded with dynamite into the defenses, but the train exploded harmlessly. A federal counterattack under the covering fire of the *Bravo* and the *Veracruz* finally forced the rebels to lift the siege.[49]

The attack on Tampico had failed, but as in the recent attempt on Monterrey, the rebel force withdrew in good order and largely intact. Just like in many other places in Mexico, bands of cavalry stayed behind to keep the garrison of Tampico trapped in the coastal port during subsequent months. Indeed, González had counted on federal troops being so tied down that they could not send reinforcements to his other target, the isolated garrison of Nuevo Laredo. He himself commanded a large force, eventually numbering almost 8,000 men, to threaten Monterrey and thus to prevent the federals from sending any reinforcements to their small garrison of 600 men at Nuevo Laredo. He dispatched around 2500 men to the north and gave them orders to attack Nuevo Laredo in the early morning hour of 1 January 1914; perhaps he hoped to catch the garrison asleep or drunk from a night of celebrations for the New Year. At the last moment the federals discerned the intentions of General González and rushed through a train with 600 soldiers to Nuevo Laredo; the train arrived in the afternoon of 31 December just a few hours ahead of the rebel band whose task had been to tear up the track. The rebel commander requested permission from General González to postpone the assault on the well-entrenched garrison, but General González ratified the order to attack as planned. At 0500 on the very cold morning of 1 January 1914 the rebels desperately tried to dash across the wide open spaces that separated them from the federal trenches. The waiting federal machine guns opened a deadly fire and stopped the assault cold. The rebels continued partial attacks that day and the next, but finally abandoned the operation on the night of 2 January after having taken a thousand casualties in dead, wounded, and missing.

The attack had been a disaster but had in no way altered the strategic situation in northeast Mexico: In the states of Nuevo León and Tamaulipas, the rebels controlled all the territory except for Monterrey, Tampico, and Nuevo Laredo. Trapped federal garrisons could only suffer demoralization inside those cities, and it was only a matter of months before the large army of General González began to pick off one by one the remaining federal bastions.[50] The ineptness of General González, who had not used to the best advantage the resources at his disposal, contributed to prolonging the suffering and increasing the casualties. General González stood in start contrast to General Obregón, who in a few Napoleonic moves had rid Sonora of federal troops and thus spared that state from the savage destruction the Mexican northeast suffered.

Militarily Huerta was finished in northeast Mexico. Only by bringing at least 10,000 more soldiers into the northeast could he hope to restore the military balance, but the outbreak of revolts across Mexico prevented him from reinforcing either Sonora or the northeast. Although Huerta had a much larger army than Porfirio Díaz, the situation resembled that of 1911: Too many revolts and not enough troops. Huerta kept his best troops in central and southern Mexico, and instead he sent hastily promoted officers and raw conscripts for the expeditionary forces to the north. The results in Sonora had been disastrous and in northeast Mexico the federal position was crumbling. But before Huerta could try to contain the rebels in the northeast and in the northwest of Mexico, he first had to face a belated and violent onslaught from Chihuahua.

Chihuahua

As mentioned in the first section, the rebel bands in Chihuahua had been considering recognizing the Huerta regime, but the negotiations collapsed in early April and the rebels resumed hostilities. On 13 April they captured Jiménez and on 23 April Camargo, the two key towns in the railroad line between Chihuahua City and Torreón. In effect, the rebels had isolated both the capital of Chihuahua and the city of Parral. The rebels had already tried previously during three days (5 to 7 March) to capture Parral. Although the troops under General Salvador Mercado repulsed the furious attacks, the intense combat had consumed most of their ammunition. The Parral garrison had not received any pay since March, and the inhabitants were openly hostile to the Huerta regime. The commander pleaded repeatedly for help and for instructions but to no avail. With food becoming scarce and with over 3000 rebels starting to gather for the final assault, General Mercado decided to evacuate Parral on 6 May. The departure of his 600 soldiers left the entire southern region of Chihuahua in rebel hands. When Mercado arrived at Chihuahua City on 17 May, he feared that he would be court-martialed because of his unauthorized withdrawal. He was pleasantly relieved to learn that on 31 May the War Department had appointed him commander of all federal troops in Chihuahua and governor of that state. He was replacing the demoted General Antonio Rábago, whom Huerta did not trust.[51]

Simply reshuffling commanders could not stop the rebellion. The rebels under the savage Tomás Urbina, not feeling strong enough to attack the capital city, went south and joined in the capture of Durango on 18 June. As mentioned previously, the capture of Durango was a military success but a political disaster because of the savage sacking of the city. Powerful as the Chihuahua rebels were, their image as bloodthirsty looters weakened their popular support. The Chihuahua rebels were also divided into many rival bands, whose leaders were more concerned with maintaining control over their own bailiwick than in defeating the Federal Army.

In spite of the tremendous potential Chihuahua offered to cripple the Huerta regime, nothing could happen until a decisive leader

A grim and determined Pancho Villa (right), accompanied by unidentified aides, is riding to the front (Library of Congress, Prints and Photographs Collection).

but the astute Maytorena, who immediately detected in Villa a rival more independent and dangerous than the Sonora officers, cleverly gave money to keep him in Chihuahua. For Villa, who never forgot anyone who helped him in dire times, that money symbolized a sacred obligation to repay. Probably also Villa saw in Maytorena, a wealthy landowner, the substitute for the figure he had idealized earlier in the deceased Francisco Madero.[52]

When Villa with a handful of followers crossed the Rio Grande, no one appeared to greet him as the leader. However, his bandit skills, always lurking in the background, sufficed to consolidate a group of desperadoes in northwest Chihuahua. Once he had a core group of followers, he reduced the bandit raids to just what his men needed for subsistence. He began to play the Robin Hood card by distributing some of the wealth of a village among the inhabitants. He knew he needed much more money

shaped the quarrelsome and divided rebel forces into a coherent whole. In Sonora the state government had organized the revolt, and Obregón commanded a unified army, yet at the start even he had faced occasional challenges to his authority. Much more difficult had been the task of General González in northeast Mexico, who struggled to impose some order and discipline over his very independent followers. In the fiercely individualistic Chihuahua, only a person of ruthless determination and extraordinary personal abilities could hope to impose his leadership of the rebel bands. That man was Pancho Villa, who crossed into Mexico from the United States on 6 March 1913, after José María Maytorena, the governor on leave from Sonora, had given him money to buy weapons and supplies. Villa had been so eager to return that he was willing to start all over in Sonora,

than what the dirt-poor villages of northwestern Chihuahua contained, and here again his bandit skills came in handy when he knew exactly when to intercept a train carrying 150 silver ingots on 10 April. By May he commanded 700 men, a number comparable to those of other rebel leaders in Chihuahua but not enough to challenge Mercado's federal garrison then withdrawing from Parral. Villa wisely decided to put as much distance as possible between himself and the column of General Mercado. In June the first rebel leader to join Villa brought 500 more men, and afterwards Villa's brigade was the largest in Chihuahua. But his force was still too small to threaten the federal garrison in Chihuahua City and lacked the indispensable artillery. Furthermore, with almost all the towns and villages already in rebel hands, Villa did not seem to have much of a chance to score the spectacular battlefield success that he needed to consolidate his authority over the rest of the local leaders.[53]

Villa soon found an opportunity to shine. He had been near Ciudad Juárez trying to smuggle ammunition across the border. He obtained some but not enough cartridges, and then he quickly returned to the vicinity of Chihuahua City. Upon hearing that only 900 federals were at the train station of San Andrés (90 kilometers west of Chihuahua City), he rode his over 1200 men hard at night and in an attack on the unsuspecting federal force at 0500 on 26 August 1913, he captured all the strategic positions around San Andrés. He halted the attacks during daylight and restricted the shooting to conserve ammunition. The sporadic firing by the federal soldiers confirmed that most were the usual press-gang recruits with little stomach for fighting. As Villa observed the federal positions, he realized that their two 75 mm cannons were the heart of the defense. He decided to gamble everything on one massive cavalry charge to capture the two field pieces after nightfall. Conveniently for Villa, the federal commander had failed to provide an adequate infantry cover for the artillery. Once the cavalry charge captured the two cannons, resistance collapsed and the federal unit disintegrated. In the inevitable execution of prisoners that followed, Villa wisely spared the artillerymen whom he incorporated into his brigade.[54]

The victory gained Villa artillery pieces and so enhanced his prestige that rebels in the south asked him to take charge of the attack against Torreón. VIlla was originally preparing an assault on Chihuahua City, but the arrival of Pascual Orozco with his brigade on 22 July had made that state capital virtually impregnable. Instead, the departure of Orozco's brigade from Torreón on 1 July had left this last city vulnerable. To take advantage of this momentary weakness, Villa accepted the offer to lead the attack on Torreón but left behind a detachment of 600 men to tear up the track south of Chihuahua City. Believing his rear was safe from a federal attack, he moved his brigade to the south, and after his arrival the rebel leaders elected him their supreme commander on 26 September. Henceforth this force became known as the División del Norte. He commanded over 8,000 rebels to hurl against the Torreón garrison of 2,700 soldiers.[55]

Villa continued to enjoy his customary good luck. The federal commander had let the Torreón defenses deteriorate and had failed to build any new fortifications. Because the War Department was incessantly ordering garrison commanders to take to the field to attack the rebels and not to stay holed up in the cities, the federal commander picked the worst possible moment to send a unit out on patrol. On 29 September a federal column of 550 soldiers ran into the main Villista force 25 kilometers to the west of Torreón. In a lighting charge, over 4000 Villistas overwhelmed the federal unit and captured its two artillery pieces. As the *soldaderas* of the fallen soldiers streamed into the city, they spread wild rumors about the huge size of Villa's army.

Desertions began and left the federal commander with barely 2000 men to try to hold off Villa's victorious army. Villa had four good cannons, but still not enough to silence the massed federal artillery. Because his plan called for a simultaneous assault against federal positions, he timed the attacks to begin just at nightfall. His men approached the federal trenches in the waning daylight of 30 September. Because the federal commander had placed most of his artillery in the heights overlooking Torreón, VIlla sent waves of his men to their death in attacks against those well-defended heights. The very modest gains Villa made persuaded him that his chances for victory were slipping away. He hurled all his men in a last desperate attempt to break the federal resistance on 1 October. The incessant waves of rebel attackers began to take their toll not so much physically as psychologically on the wearied defenders. More soldiers deserted, but if the officers could rally enough men, Villa could still suffer a bloody and probably fatal defeat. The garrison had begun a counterattack, but the psychological pressure had been too much for the federal commander who cracked under the stress and fled before nightfall. Just as the second in command was restoring the battle line, Spanish civilians suddenly bolted and fled for their lives to the east. This stream of refugees panicked the remaining troops, who now abandoned their positions and joined in the mad dash to flee. Although a flooded creek protected the fleeing federals from the Villista cavalry, the panic-stricken troops still did not feel safe. As an additional precaution, the retreating federals opened the irrigation canals and flooded the region causing immense damage to its cotton plantations.[56]

In spite of the escape of most of the demoralized federal garrison, Villa had won the victory he so desperately needed to impose his leadership on the recalcitrant local rebel leaders. After the battle of Torreón, no rebel leader from Chihuahua ever challenged or questioned his authority again. To the happy surprise of the inhabitants of Torreón, Villa permitted no looting and kept all his men in good behavior in the city. The wealthy did not escape without having to make forced contributions, but for political and international reasons, Villa saw the need to halt the destructive and uncontrollable plundering of previous years. Of course, the remembrance of the rampage and the veiled threat of a revival of looting remained highly effective tools to extort forced contributions from the wealthy.[57]

Villa was particularly pleased with the 11 artillery pieces his men had captured at Torreón. The largest was an 80 mm piece baptized as El Niño, which Huerta had first used in his 1912 campaign against Orozco. With ample artillery and even larger numbers of followers than ever before, Villa felt he at last could achieve his original goal of capturing Chihuahua City. However, he considered Torreón too far south to hold permanently against the expected federal counterattack. He ordered the local rebel leaders to harass any advancing federal column, but if necessary, they could abandon Torreón. Villa accurately estimated that Huerta could mount only one relief effort at a time, and thus any federal drive against Torreón left Villa free to concentrate his División del Norte against Chihuahua City.[58]

By the first days of November, Villa had collected over eight thousand highly motivated rebels to overwhelm the 6,300 demoralized men defending Chihuahua City.[59] Although the odds were not as favorable as in Torreón, he counted on his newly recruited artillerymen and the captured pieces to bring him victory. His plan of assault was the same as at Torreón. Toward nightfall on 5 November Villa launched his attack on Chihuahua City "which was strongly fortified with a complex network of trenches, formidable redoubts, concealed batteries and machine-gun nests."[60] The night attack was a failure, and the waves of attackers he sent in the following days could not even get within rifle distance. The rebel artillery failed to silence the federal cannons, whose shrapnel shattered the Villista cavalry charges. On 7 November Villa launched some final attacks, but seeing his men running short of ammunition, he quietly withdrew to the south that night. He left behind at least 800 dead and had suffered a setback but was far from destroyed. The next day General Mercado sent a cavalry unit in pursuit, but it soon had to beat a hasty retreat to escape destruction. On 9 November patrols reported that the rebel force seemed to have disappeared to the south.[61]

Only on 13 November did General Mercado learn that Villa's force was headed north toward Ciudad Juárez. In effect, on the night of 9 November Villa had backtracked and taken his forces around Chihuahua City to turn against the only other federal garrison in the state. He also hoped to obtain some ammunition once he was closer to the U.S border. He had no choice but to try to revive his flagging fortune by a bold move against Ciudad Juárez, although he well knew the risk of complications with the United States in that border city. Fortunately for Villa, the federal garrison was only of 500 men, and he hoped to reach the city with 2000 cavalrymen before any federal reinforcements arrived from Chihuahua City.[62]

General Mercado publicized extensively the repulse of the Villista attack on Chihuahua City. His intention was to bolster the sagging morale of the soldiers and of the Orozquista irregulars, but the propaganda created a false sense of victory throughout Mexico. Mercado himself harbored no illusions about his precarious position. About three-fourths of the garrison consisted of irregulars who fought well but only when paid on time. Since the arrival of Orozco's relief column on 22 May, the War Department had not sent reinforcements, supplies, or ammunition. Villa's capture of Torreón had accentuated the isolation of Chihuahua City, while Villa's assault had depleted the supply of artillery shells. With few artillery shells left, the troublesome irregulars became the heart of the city's defense. Orozco and the other leaders of the irregulars repeatedly quarreled with General Mercado. The federal general detected strong currents of sympathy for Villa everywhere in the city except among the wealthy. General Mercado felt that Mexico City

At headquarters the Mexican federal officers are plotting on a map their moves to stop the rebel advance (Library of Congress, Prints and Photographs Collection).

had abandoned him again, just like it had in Parral in May.[63]

He decided that his only chance to survive was to try to save Ciudad Juárez from Villa's expected attack. In a sense, both Villa and the federal commander were gambling their last cards on Ciudad Juárez. On 13 November General Mercado sent 2,400 men north on the railroad to Ciudad Juárez under the command of General José Inés Salazar. In retrospect, if he had taken personal command of the force, Villa's fate would have been different. But with the joint appointment of governor and military commander, he felt no other person could keep the city quiet if he went away on a campaign. Furthermore, the rigid military code deprived Mercado of the freedom to select the most competent officer to head the column and mechanically forced him to appoint the person with the highest rank and seniority.

While the federal column steamed slowly north along the railroad, an extraordinary good bit of luck fell on Villa that very same 13 November. At 1700 his men captured a coal train headed for Chihuahua City and either he or

some of his followers came up with the plan to use the train to seize Ciudad Juárez. Essentially, he rode with his 2000 men aboard the train after sending false telegraph messages saying that the train was returning to Ciudad Juárez because rebels blocked the road. This Trojan Horse contributed immensely to the legend of Pancho Villa, but the legend has made it difficult to understand the real reasons for the success of the bold plan: "The federals felt so secure from the reports that Villa was besieging Chihuahua that they failed to send out the customary scouting parties or to place sentries."[64] While the federal soldiers were asleep in the barracks that cold night, the officers were enjoying the bars, casinos, and brothels in Ciudad Juárez. The carelessness of the officers was inexplicable, because all knew that capture meant execution. Villa's train arrived on 18 November at 0130 and by 0200 under the helpful moonlight, his men had quietly taken positions around the barracks and other key points in the city. When the firing started, in less than two hours the Villistas had defeated the federal troops, who tried desperately to escape to the

U.S. side. Villa had beforehand sent a detachment to secure the bridges; without an easy escape route, many soldiers were captured and executed; only by wading across the sometimes treacherous waters of the river did some federals reach safety on the U.S. side.[65]

The sneaky capture of Ciudad Juárez powerfully fed the Villa legend but proved less decisive in military terms. The booty turned out to be meager, with the biggest disappointment being the 100,000 cartridges, not enough for a day's fighting for the nearly 8000 men he had under him. The federal garrison had spasmodically constructed fortifications, but because Villa did not want complications with the United States, he felt the risks of a rebel defense of Ciudad Juárez were too high. Furthermore, it was not his style to fight cornered in a border city, he always longed for the wide open spaces to maneuver his cavalry with speed. He decided to defend the city at the train station of Tierra Blanca, 31 kilometers south of Ciudad Juárez. The sand dunes in this region made for excellent defensive positions. His infantry and artillery could remain hidden and move furtively behind the sand dunes, while his cavalry could raise large dust clouds to confuse the federals. Villa needed a quick victory, because with his men's bandoleers three-quarters empty, he soon would run out of cartridges.[66]

On 17 November, when the federal relief column was 130 kilometers south of Ciudad Juárez, news came that Villa had captured the border city. The chance to trap Villa between the federal column and the garrison at Ciudad Juárez had vanished. However, to abort the advance when Villa might not even want to fight risked conveying an impression of weakness and fear. Rather than return to the safety of Chihuahua City, in another fateful decision both Generals Salazar and Mercado agreed to proceed north to recapture Ciudad Juárez. On 22 November the federal column ran into the Villista cavalry at the train station of Tierra Blanca 31 kilometers south of Ciudad Juárez. Upon receiving news of the arrival of the federal column, Villa left Ciudad Juárez with 6,200 men to reinforce his detachment near Tierra Blanca. He ordered his men to leave behind their *soldaderas* or female followers, but many women still jumped aboard the departing trains and fought alongside their men during the battle. "It was a richly picturesque sight, but the complete silence, the stoic and yet anxious faces of the women was depressing, as it gave the impression that all were going to a tremendous funeral, or their doom."[67]

Villa knew he was betting everything on one battle. He counted above all on his good luck to give him the chance to use his overwhelming numbers to crush the smaller federal force. He deployed his nearly 8,000 men in a line cutting across the railroad track for a distance of over 8 kilometers and then waited for the federal commander to make the next move. Had the federal commander known the true strength of the Villistas, he should have immediately wondered why it did not attack and overrun his trains. Like most federal commanders, General Salazar lacked intelligence on the rebels. Although he could see the sand dunes all around him, he did not even have an exact topographical knowledge of the terrain, unlike Villa and his commanders who had repeatedly ridden on horseback and on automobile across the sand dunes. General Salazar faced two options. He could return in his trains back to Chihuahua City; ample precedents and reasons for such a withdrawal existed. However, many of the irregulars, buoyed by the successful repulse of Villa at Chihuahua City, were extremely eager for battle and predicted an easy victory. The federal commander forgot the maxim that those soldiers who are most insistent on combat are usually the first to break and run. The second option was for General Salazar to give full rein to his artillery and try to win a decisive engagement by pounding the Villista positions. This approach was what Huerta had used in his 1912 campaign against Orozco, but Salazar did not have as many cannon and was short of artillery shells.

In violation of the principle of concentration of forces, on 20 November General Salazar detached a force of 400 soldiers. This column was supposed to protect a train station 100 kilometers to the south from marauding rebels. The column he detached was too small to stop a determined rebel attack but sizeable enough to weaken the main federal force. On 24 November he sent his cavalry to try to outflank the left Villista wing, and after that attempt failed, he had his artillery open fire on the rebel right flank. He had already prominently displayed his artillery near the track, but he did not order the general bombardment needed to shatter the will of the rebels critically short of cartridges. His artillery had the range to pulverize the Villista center, but instead he ordered some of his cannons to move forward to support an infantry attack on the rebel right. The Villista right began to give way, and to halt a disastrous rout, Villa, who lacked a reserve, took men first from his center and then from his left to save his right flank. The movements of these reinforcements made great targets for the federal cannons in the center, but General Salazar, still husbanding his scarce shells, did not order the artillery to open fire. The weakening of the rebels' center and left also opened the chance for a general assault along the entire front, but General Salazar let pass the opportunity as nightfall fell. "Their chance for a complete victory — yes, indeed, our annihilation — was forfeited. It was a grave tactical blunder by the federal general for we were completely at his mercy."[68]

The spirited resistance by the desperate Villistas was frustrating the federal soldiers and especially the irregulars, whose hopes for an easy victory were vanishing. Hunger, cold, and thirst were sapping the strength of the federals, unlike the Villistas, who were continuously replenished with food, water, and fodder from Ciudad Juárez. The federals suffered tremendously from the blowing sand, which reduced the visibility and jammed their machine guns. The field pieces almost sank into the sand, and dragging them across the dunes had exhausted the artillerymen. In comparison with the rebels, the federal infantry still had plenty of cartridges, but the federal soldiers, who had become psychological dependent on massive firing to sustain their morale, had become uneasy as the visible reserves of cartridges dwindled. General Salazar failed to send out scouts or reconnaissance patrols, and without accurate information on the Villista positions, his only valid option was to board the trains and return for replenishment at Chihuahua City. Instead, in a totally inexplicable maneuver, he pulled back his flanks to the railroad tracks that night, in effect exposing his force to encirclement. At some moment General Salazar must have realized he was somewhat vulnerable, but rather than a speedy retreat aboard the trains, he telegraphed the column 100 kilometers to the rear to come quickly to join him; apparently he counted on the arrival of these fresh troops to win the battle.[69]

Mexico's federal officers at Ojinaga observe the rebel advance (Edith O'Shaugnessy, *A Diplomat's Wife in Mexico*; New York: Harper & Brothers, 1916).

A desperate Villa counted on a massive cavalry assault at night to retrieve his sagging fortunes. When his Indian scouts reported at 0200 on 25 November that the federals had taken positions along the track, he saw the first glimmer of victory. He prepared to attack and encircle the federals by means of a night attack from both sides. Unfortunately his cavalry was not ready to attack before daybreak, and to his amazement in the morning the federals launched an infantry attack straight up his center; presumably the federals wanted to clear a path to Ciudad Juárez. Under heavy covering fire from their artillery, the federals advanced deeper into their self-constructed trap. As the Villistas ran out of ammunition, they gradually gave ground. The Villista cavalry was taking longer than expected to attack, and as his center collapsed, Villa despaired and could only order his cavalry to attack simultaneously along the entire front. The stress on Villa became unbearable, and suffering a horrible headache he left the battlefield.

Into this leadership vacuum stepped his subordinate General Maclovio Herrera, who personally led a cavalry charge against the federal infantry breaking through Villa's center. The sudden charge by cavalrymen riding two to a horse spread panic among the federal soldiers who broke and ran to the trains in the rear. Herrera's cavalry divided into two and pressed the retreating federal center to the left and to the right against the rest of the Villista cavalry at last appearing in the flanks of the federal trains. The retreat turned into a panicky rout as the federal soldiers threw away their weapons and some even vainly tried to hide in the sand. Only the artillery units held their ground and on the verge of being surrounded tried desperately to save their field pieces. In spite of the wheels sinking deep into the sand, the artillerymen managed to load some cannons aboard the trains, but to no avail as these trains fell into rebel hands. The Villista cavalry galloped after the fleeing federals, but the horses were too exhausted to capture all the departing trains. At nightfall the arrival of the federal column from the south saved the remnants of General Salazar' force from complete annihilation. Barely a thousand thoroughly demoralized men returned to Chihuahua City on 27 November.[70]

The day before General Mercado heard the news, and he accurately judged the changed strategic situation. Villa had captured so many cannons that even if General Mercado could compensate with the superior performance of his artillerymen, the supply of shells in the city was inadequate to fight off an attack. The panic of the defeated troops had spread among the garrison, and the unpaid irregulars were starting to return to their old habits of looting. With these demoralized troops he could not expect to repeat the previous defense of the capital, and evacuation was the only alternative left to General Mercado. He was among the first high-ranking officers to realize that Huerta could not win, and he was certainly the first to realize that not just Huerta, but the entire system of the dictatorship, including the Federal Army, was structurally flawed. Since he had been a commander of the garrison at Parral in April, Mercado all alone had to struggle against the indifference of Mexico City. When he became commander at Chihuahua, the situation did not improve, and increasingly he felt that the Huerta government had abandoned his command. He needed reinforcements, supplies, and funds, and since April he had rarely received any. Continuing the struggle could not alter the outcome, and all he could hope to do was to reduce the bloodshed and destruction.[71]

Only the wealthy persons pleaded with him to defend Chihuahua and offered him large sums of money, but General Mercado knew that the majority of the population strongly sympathized with the rebels. An evacuation was the only solution, but where could the federals go? Two reasons ruled out any withdrawal south to Torreón. First, this city remained in rebel hands until December 9. Secondly, after his victory at Tierra Blanca, Villa had ordered the rebel leaders of Torreón to join him for what he expected to be a second furious attack on Chihuahua City. The demoralized federal column was in no condition to face in battle the rebels coming from the south.[72] The U.S. border to the east beckoned as the only safe escape route. General Mercado began the evacuation on 27 November, and the last units left Chihuahua City on 30 November. The destination was Ojinaga, a border town on the U.S. border. The few rebel bands in the largely desert area could not pose any resistance. Once he reached Ojinaga, General Mercado hoped to receive funds and supplies from the Huerta regime via the United States.[73]

General Mercado planned to ride the first 120 kilometers aboard the trains to the end of the track at the Conchos River and then to march the rest of the way to Ojinaga. However, sabotage by railroad employees forced his troops to detrain almost immediately and to march in the cold desert almost the whole way. Mercado divided the retreating soldiers into three columns so that they could forage over a wider area for food and fodder. The retreating columns lost most of their equipment, while soldiers had been deserting continuously since Mercado announced the evacuation from Chihuahua City. Somehow the general straggled into Ojinaga with 4,500 men and 12 artillery pieces. Upon his arrival on 13 December, he found that the Huerta regime as usual had made no preparations to send money or supplies to his exhausted force. With great exertions he managed to repel sustained rebel attacks on Ojinaga from 31 December 1913 to 4 January 1914. The morale of his troops was by then very low, and unable to resist more, the defense collapsed when Villa came personally to lead a general assault at nightfall on 10 January 1914. After 45 minutes of furious rebel attack, Mercado, his soldiers, and their *soldaderas* crossed the Rio Grande into the United States.[74] With the capture of Ojinaga, Villa was in full control of all of Chihuahua. The rebel offensives had permanently wrested most of northern Mexico away from Huerta. Whether they could also march south into the rich central areas remained to be seen.

Huerta's Last Stand and the U.S. Occupation of Veracruz

At the start of 1914, the greatest danger to the Huerta regime came from Pancho Villa. He commanded the largest rebel force, and his fame magnetically attracted many followers. Of the three main rebel commanders, he was best positioned to begin the southward advance to Mexico City. First Chief Venustiano Carranza shared the same strategic assessment and supported Villa's plan to capture Torreón. He rejected the proposal of General González to have Villa march secretly to Coahuila to join the attack on Monterrey. Instead, Carranza in-

structed Pablo González to keep the pressure on Monterrey, so that Huerta could not draw troops from that garrison to reinforce Torreón.[75]

Unlike General Salvador Mercado, almost all the federal commanders and Huerta himself still believed that it was possible to defeat the rebels in the north. Indeed, a few entertained themselves with fanciful plans for counterstrokes, not realizing that by the third quarter of 1913 the regime had exhausted its abilities to mount any offensive. Strategic withdrawals offered the only opportunity for success, but a disintegrating regime could no longer respond rationally to the impending rebel advances. Instead of concentrating forces in central Mexico for the final clash, Huerta insisted on sending troops north to recover Torreón. On 10 December a federal column under General José Refugio Velasco recaptured that city over two months after Villa had first seized it on 1 October. The local rebels had delayed and harassed the entry of the federal column:

> The rebel plan is then to cut off all railroad communication and to place the city in such a close state of siege as to prevent the introduction of supplies or provisions, thus starving the federal garrison into submission. That the above plan is to be followed is borne out by the fact that several train loads of provisions, etc., have been brought into Durango yesterday and today from Torreón [...] so the Federal Army may find the city untenable unless they can maintain communication with their base of supplies at Saltillo.[76]

General Velasco initially did not realize that he had fallen into a trap, and he busied himself preparing the defenses of Torreón. He included the neighboring towns of Lerdo and Gómez Palacio within his defense perimeter as part of his plan for an in-depth defense of Torreón. These preparations, however, could not match the remarkable expansion of the Villista army. Not only did Villa have many more men, but the unbroken string of almost incredible victories had made them highly motivated. The Villista artillery, under the former federal General Felipe Ángeles, had improved tremendously in quality, and both sides had about the same number of cannons at Torreón. General Velasco obtained unusually good intelligence on the rebel preparations in Chihuahua City, and his analysis showed that the federal garrison of 7,000 soldiers could not hold Torreón without reinforcements. Already at the end of January he dispatched a lieutenant colonel to Mexico City to plead for prompt reinforcements, but the trip of the officer starkly confirmed the isolation of the garrison. The officer reached Saltillo without too much mishap, but because rebel bands had destroyed large stretches of the previously safe track to the south to San Luis Potosí, he took the circuitous but faster route of Piedras Negras, Galveston, Havana, and Veracruz to Mexico City. By the time the lieutenant colonel delivered personally his message, Torreón was under heavy attack.[77]

As General Velasco too patiently waited for reinforcements, he did everything within his power to prepare Torreón for the expected onslaught. He dug in his cannons, and he erected many adobe walls and blockhouses to bolster his already extensive network of trenches. He knew these fortifications could not stop Villa, but they could gain time for federal reinforcements to reach Torreón. Completely out of Velasco's hand was any increase in the number of men, machine guns, cannons, and cartridges. The isolated Torreón could not withstand a determined siege and increasingly resembled Chihuahua City in November 1913. Instead, when the United States lifted the arms embargo on Mexico on 3 February 1914, Villa, like other rebel generals, was able to import weapons and ammunition.[78] Under similar circumstances, General Mercado had wisely decided to evacuate Chihuahua City in November 30, but General Velasco was too far away from the U.S. border to save his army or to find safety from the wrath of his superiors. From a military perspective, Velasco should have withdrawn to Saltillo or to Zacatecas; otherwise, his only chance of saving Torreón depended on Villa's good luck running out. Had Velasco possessed ample ammunition, he certainly could have shattered the rebel attacks, because Villa "says he would rather lose a thousand men in three hours than in ten days."[79]

The rugged terrain of Torreón did not offer Villa much room for his by then legendary cavalry charges, but he still counted on waves of rebels to overwhelm by sheer numbers the federal positions. The attacks on the outer perimeter of Gómez Palacio and Lerdo began on 22 March, and the Villistas took very heavy casualties. The federals repulsed the attacks, but

The camp of federal soldiers right before the rebel attack at Ojinaga. The photographer in the foreground is crouching to have a good shot at the combat (Library of Congress, Prints and Photographs Division).

The federal soldiers try to repel the rebel attack at Ojinaga. The soldiers are furiously working their Mauser rifles and the standing officer is trying to instill confidence in his men, but the dead soldiers suggest an unhappy ending. This is one of the finest combat photographs from the Mexican Revolution.

suffered the grievous loss of three of their best generals. As the federal outer positions crumbled, Velasco rushed his reserves to try to restore the defense line; instead of trading land for time, he insisted on defending the outer perimeter. By the time he evacuated Gómez Palacio and Lerdo on 26 March, the intense fighting in the outer perimeter had seriously depleted key units necessary for the defense of Torreón. Unlike Velasco, Villa was receiving constantly reinforcements. While the rebels began the attack with over 8,000 men, their number rose to 10,000 and eventually exceeded 12,000, in spite of very heavy losses. All the federals could do to compensate for their smaller number was to fire even more cartridges and shells. The rebels with fresh forces launched repeated attacks and could afford the luxury of rotating units to the rear for rest and sleep. The constant attacks and shelling instead wearied the tired federal troops whose endurance was truly remarkable.

A stroke of good luck gave Villa the opportunity to end the slaughter and capture Torreón. On 27 March a rebel scout found the federal plan of defense, but Villa, rather than immediately taking action, made little if any use of this valuable document. News of an approaching federal relief column did worry him, and he sent 2000 men to slow down its advance. Afraid that time was running out, Villa launched his most ferocious attack of the entire siege as night fell on 1 April. This bloody assault cost him over 800 rebels in dead and wounded. The defenders had not cracked, and with the impending arrival of the relief column, Villa felt he had no choice but to lift the siege on the afternoon of 2 April. The wisdom of the decision seemed confirmed when the federals opened up the heaviest artillery bombardment of the siege. In reality, that same day Velasco had decided to abandon Torreón under the cover of a raging dust storm. His men were exhausted, and he had only 20,000 cartridges left in the arsenal for the infantry. The federals set fires in the city to help cover their retreat, but in a very strange decision, Villa decided not to pursue the withdrawing army.[80]

Velasco was leading the Torreón garrison eastward to San Pedro de las Colonias, but rather than attack him, Villa decided to travel a longer distance by another route to attack the relief column first. Villa could not transport his entire army with him, yet he insisted on attacking the substantial relief column on 10 April. Velasco hurried to join the relief column, and the junction of the two forces gave the federals for the first time a numerical superiority over Villa. Velasco had two options: Either the federals attacked and defeated Villa or they conducted an orderly withdrawal to Saltillo. The troops from the Torreón garrison were exhausted and demoralized, while the raw recruits in the relief column recently had been pressganged into the army and did not want to fight. Obviously the correct choice was to retreat, even at the risk of provoking the wrath of Huerta. For several days Villa could do nothing but wait quietly in the outskirts of San Pedro de las Colonias until the rest of his army arrived from Torreón.

On 13 April he regained numerical superiority and launched his whole army on a full-scale assault on San Pedro de las Colonias. The ferocity of the onslaught sent many federals fleeing from their trenches, and officers halted the rout by using their pistols against the men. Villistas almost reached headquarters and managed to wound General Velasco, who finally realized the hopelessness of the defense and ordered a hasty retreat to the trains under cover of his artillery. The trains later had to be abandoned, and the badly mauled force reached Saltillo only on 23 April, after having lost most of its equipment; many men had died of thirst in the walk across the barren desert. Repeatedly Villa had the federal force within his grasp, but he allowed Velasco to escape; these blunders were not fatal at this time, but they revealed fatal flaws in his generalship.[81] In an attempt to cover up Villa's blunders, General Felipe Ángeles tried to paint the outcome in a favorable light by claiming that if the troops of General Pablo González attacked the retreating army of General Velasco "they could annihilate it completely and this perhaps would bring to an end the campaign."[82]

The last thing General González wanted to hear was that another Federal Army was heading toward his theater of operations. During January 1914 the federal garrisons at Nuevo Laredo and Monterrey had attempted to reach Matamoros and Ciudad Victoria, and although González had managed to restrain the federals, they disrupted his plan to capture Monterrey. A weak and indecisive personality, he had difficulty keeping his men under discipline. One of his units roamed through the towns of northern Mexico and refused to obey "the repeated orders to rejoin the main force, and instead continued in their lax attitude and even degenerated in many cases into banditry."[83] General González received a much-needed boost when on 3 February 1914 President Woodrow Wilson lifted the arms embargo on Mexico. The abundant ammunition he obtained through Matamoros allowed him to tighten the noose around Monterrey. In a series of small engagements he strove to isolate the federal garrison at Monterrey, the key to northeast Mexico, while he amassed a force large enough to overwhelm the defenders.

The rebels were confident of capturing Monterrey this time. With over 8000 men, González launched on 20 April his attack on the garrison of 2500. The rebels with abundant ammunition began overrunning the defenses until the federal commander decided to evacuate at 0100 on 24 April. A vigorous pursuit would have made the victory complete, but by the time González decided to act, the federal column was safely away. The loss of Monterrey was significant enough and left dangerously isolated the remaining federal garrisons in the northeast. Even before the fall of Monterrey, the garrison at Piedras Negras had sensed the inevitable and began on 22 April its long trek back to Saltillo. After struggling to capture Piedras Negras for nearly a year, the federals evacuated the prize without a fight.[84] The federal garrison at Nuevo Laredo did not want to go so quietly and decided instead to bring the war to an unheard of level of ferocity during the withdrawal on 24 April:

> Three trainloads of Mexican Federal troops departed from Nuevo Laredo and simultaneously therewith a dynamite bomb was exploded in the American Consulate and the town was fired in various places. The work of the incendiaries continued until night fall. All of the prin-

This photograph of rebels burying dead federal soldiers serves as an epitaph for Mexico's Federal Army (Library of Congress, Prints and Photographs Division Collection).

cipal buildings in the city have been burned, at the time of the report it appeared that a greater portion of the residential section had also been destroyed.[85]

Troops under attack had routinely set fires to cover their escape, but with no rebels in sight and no reason to terrorize the population, this wanton torching ranks among the most senseless in the campaigns of the Mexican Revolution. Previously on 1 January Nuevo Laredo had been the site of the last federal victory, and on 24 April the town had the misfortune to witness the disintegration of the Federal Army.

The rebels were unable to play up in their propaganda the torching of Nuevo Laredo, because the U.S. occupation of Veracruz on 21 April and the fear of a U.S. invasion preempted public attention. In a well-intentioned attempt to keep weapons and ammunition from reaching Huerta, President Wilson had used a minor incident in Tampico as a pretext to occupy Veracruz. The surprised federal commander de-

ployed his garrison to defend the port city while he consulted Mexico City. To avoid the destruction of Veracruz by the naval cannon of the U.S. warships, the Secretary of War ordered the federal garrison to withdraw. By the time the troops received and promptly obeyed the order, some units had already begun firing on the American sailors and marines. The decision to abandon Veracruz was correct on military and humanitarian grounds, but made the federal soldiers appear as cowards who fled from a foreign enemy and fought only against fellow Mexicans. To make the humiliation of the Federal Army complete, Mexican civilians and released convicts had spontaneously taken up arms and joined the cadets of the Mexican Naval Academy in a hopeless attempt to stop the landing of the U.S. sailors. This heroic defense produced martyrs and became a rallying symbol for Mexican nationalists, who now expected a repeat of the full-scale U.S. invasion of 1847.[86]

Carranza condemned the U.S. occupation, as did the rest of rebel leaders except for Pancho Villa, who promptly rushed to the U.S. border to reassure American officials that "he is too good a friend of ours and considered us too good friends of theirs for us to engage in a war [...] as far as he was concerned we could keep Veracruz [...] and that he could not feel any resentment."[87] Villa was more guarded in his public statements, but as the only leader to support the U.S. occupation, he instantly became the favorite rebel of the Wilson administration. The nationalist outcry throughout Mexico had surprised Washington, and was so real that U.S. officials dropped any consideration of sending troops inland from Veracruz to hasten the fall of Huerta.[88]

The U.S. occupation of Veracruz affected the civil war decisively but not necessarily in the most obvious ways. Huerta tried to shift some units to stop the expected invasion of Mexico City, but by May the Federal Army was incapable of any coordinated deployments on a large scale. From a purely military perspective, the lifting of the arms embargo on 3 February and the subsequent policy to halt arms sales to Huerta were much more important for the rebel success than the U.S. occupation of Veracruz. From a financial perspective, the capture of the port city deprived Huerta of his richest customs house and plunged the regime deeper into insolvency. Most importantly, the U.S. occupation of Veracruz precipitated the final break between Villa and Carranza. Villa's independent actions in the past had angered the First Chief, who had limited himself to trying to restrain the warlord. Villa's support of the U.S. occupation was an entirely different matter; henceforth Carranza considered him a traitor unworthy to lead Mexico. As a first step Carranza maneuvered to keep the warlord from reaching Mexico City but without endangering the campaign to topple Huerta.[89]

The political break between the two men started to impact the rebel offensives almost immediately. Just 75 kilometers southwest of Monterrey, Saltillo appeared at first sight as the next natural target for González, but the city was heavily defended. The column of General Velasco from Torreón had joined the remnants of other federal garrisons in the northeast, so that a respectable force of at least 10,000 soldiers under the command of General Joaquín

Maass blocked the advance of González towards Saltillo. Carranza did not want to tie down the men of González in a costly attack on Saltillo and preferred to send them by rail to capture Tampico. This somewhat abrupt change in strategy reflected Carranza's preparations for the coming conflict with Villa. The First Chief had concluded that the petroleum royalties from Tampico and the customs revenue from the ports were more important than any inland city. The major drawback to this new strategy was that no rebel offensive against Tampico could succeed as long as a large federal garrison in Saltillo was threatening the rebels at Monterrey. In a very devious maneuver, Carranza used every last ounce of his remaining influence with Villa to persuade the warlord to attack Saltillo before proceeding against Zacatecas. Although Villa did not want to delay his advance to Mexico City through Zacatecas, he could see the advantage of eliminating this large federal force also capable of threatening his rear. Not wishing to break openly with Carranza yet, Villa agreed to attack Saltillo.[90]

On 11 May Villa left Torreón with his División del Norte, just two days after General González had begun his attack on Tampico. As mentioned previously, Tampico had only three entrances by land, and federal gunboats on the Pánuco River blocked the water route into the city. The sudden appearance of the large army of González had caught the garrison by surprise, but the natural positions were still too strong to be taken by assault. González piled up heavy casualties until lady luck finally smiled on him on 13 May. A ferocious tropical storm poured such a downpour that federal soldiers had to flee to high ground to avoid drowning in their flooded trenches. As the raging curtains of rain continued, General González realized this was his only chance to capture the city and ordered a general assault all along the front. After ferocious hand-to-hand fighting near the flooded trenches, the rebels broke through the federal lines and headed towards the city. Two gunboats put out to sea carrying some soldiers, but the bulk of the garrison boarded trains to retreat westward under the covering fire of the *Veracruz*; this last gunboat steamed upstream 10 kilometers west of Tampico, and there its commander removed the artillery on board and scuttled the vessel.

The U.S. occupation of Veracruz. U.S. marines have just disembarked from boats and are preparing to head for the firing line (Library of Congress, Prints and Photographs DIvision).

The garrison rode railroad cars for 55 kilometers but had to detrain at the later famous station of Ébano, where the rebels had damaged large stretches of track. The remnants of the Tampico garrison reached the Valley of Mexico after a month of trudging through harsh terrain.[91]

After González entered Tampico on 13 May, he was free to advance further into the interior of Mexico. He did not have to backtrack to protect his rear at Monterrey, because Villa, who had left for Saltillo on 11 May, was taking care of that problem. By 15 May Villista trains had moved 10,000 men and 38 cannons to a point 40 kilometers west of the jail juncture of Paredón but could go no further because the federals had thoroughly destroyed the track. Ahead the nearly 15,000 federal soldiers defending Saltillo loomed as a serious obstacle. However, Villa's good luck held up: General Joaquín Maass, the federal commander,

had violated the principle of concentration of forces and scattered his troops around the region. Maass had placed 5,000 soldiers at Paredón as part of his planned offensive on Monterrey, but they were too numerous to be a scouting force and too small to wage a formal battle. The morale of the federals, in their majority pressganged, was very low, and the officers were so sure of their safety that they did not even bother to post pickets or conduct regular patrols. The Villistas arrived near Paredón early in the morning of 17 May. General Felipe Ángeles was just starting to unlimber his artillery, when Villa realized that if he acted quickly, a sudden cavalry charge could destroy the unsuspecting federals. At 1000 he signaled his 8,000 cavalrymen to charge; the speed of the assault was such that the federal artillery barely had time to fire a few rounds. The sight of the galloping wave of horsemen panicked the infantry, and in half an hour the

U.S. sailors guard the Mexican Naval Academy after it was shelled by the U.S.S. *Chester* (Library of Congress, Prints and Photographs Division).

federal force had ceased to exist. The federal cavalrymen had tried in vain to turn Villa's flank, but seeing the debacle in the camp they turned and fled to Saltillo. The demoralized cavalry spread panic and fear among the garrison troops, and left General Maass no choice but to abandon Saltillo on 20 May. To try to save what he could of his dwindling force, he evacuated the region but unable to use the damaged rail track, he took his men on the long and difficult trek by foot to San Luis Potosí.[92]

As Villa returned to Torreón, Carranza was already preparing the next steps in the southern offensive. The First Chief had to revise his previous strategy of having Obregón advance in the Pacific coast, González on the east, and Villa in the center, because he did not want Villa to reach Mexico City ahead of the others. At the same time, simply halting Villa removed too much pressure from Huerta's center and risked prolonging the war. To shape a new strategy, Carranza traveled to Durango on 10 May for an inspection of the front. Based on his observations, on 25 May Carranza ordered his loyalist General Pánfilo Natera to capture Zacatecas. Carranza felt this attack met his new strategic needs, because the capture of Zacate-

cas would keep the pressure on Huerta and at the same time block Villa's advance into central Mexico. Unfortunately, when General Natera began his attack with 7,000 men on 9 June, the federals put up an unexpectedly vigorous resistance; already on 10 June Carranza had no choice but to telegraph Villa to be ready to send reinforcements to Natera on a moment's notice. On 11 June Carranza ordered Villa to send three thousand men, and the next day he increased the number to five thousand. Villa exploded in rage when he at last saw through the ploy of Carranza. On 12 June Villa refused to obey the order. Carranza then tried to remove Villa as the commander, but Villa's generals refused to serve under any other person. The long-expected break between Villa and Carranza had at last taken place, and the struggle for power between the two men was soon to drive Mexico into its bloodiest warfare.[93]

No reconciliation was possible between the two men, but they did not want the dispute to become public until Huerta was safely out of power. Villa himself left Torreón on 16 June and took his entire División del Norte to capture Zacatecas. The rebels now numbered over 23,000 men and had 39 cannons against 5,000 federals and 10 cannons. As in Torreón in late March, the federal commander, seeing the approaching avalanche, should have withdrawn his command to Aguascalientes or to Guadalajara. General Luis Medina Barrón deluded himself into a false sense of optimism and very naively trusted the promises of Huerta to send reinforcements. General Pascual Orozco (who had escaped from the Ojinaga debacle) was on the way with 3,000 men, a number too small to make any difference. Villa and his trusted artillery commander Felipe Ángeles had prepared a generalized assault on all fronts to capture the city. Under cover of ferocious artillery shelling, the massed cavalry and the waves of infantry stormed the outer federal defenses on 23 June. Short of ammunition, outgunned, and outnumbered, the federals never had a chance and were annihilated in mass. From the doomed garrison, only 300 managed to escape.[94] In a throwback to the early days of the Revolution, the Villistas could not resist throwing themselves into a rampage of looting, rapes, extortion, and brutal killings of civilians including ecclesiastics; the atrocities in the city were so bad that to try to save his reputation, Villa ordered 60 of his soldiers shot the next day.[95]

The battles of Zacatecas and Paredón confirmed Villa in his tactical conviction that whenever cavalry did not have open spaces to charge, then overwhelming numbers and artillery sufficed to secure victory. Meanwhile, Carranza was doing everything possible to stop Villa from marching south against Aguascalientes. Carranza sent repeated telegrams to Generals González and Obregón ordering them to hasten their southern offensives; he also halted the shipments of coal from the mines in Coahuila. Although Villa could have bought coal for his locomotives from the United States, he immediately used the coal shortage as an excuse to withdraw the División del Norte from Zacatecas to Torreón. To add to Villa's complications, after the occupation of Veracruz the United States had restored the embargo on the shipment of ammunition and weapons to Mexico. A few weeks later, Washington relaxed the restriction on selling arms and weapons to Carranza, but not to Villa. Why the U.S. government punished the only rebel leader who had supported the U.S. occupation of Veracruz remains a mystery.[96]

Had Villa remained in Zacatecas with most of his troops, his mere presence posed a constant threat to Huerta. Instead, his hurried withdrawal to the north took the pressure off Huerta's center and left Obregón exposed to a massive counterattack by the Federal Army. By his sudden retreat, Villa and not Carranza was the first one to put in jeopardy the rebel advance on Mexico City. He could have bought coal from the United States, and even without trains, did not Villa have the famous cavalry and abundant fodder to take him to Aguascalientes? Did Villa intend all along to take the pressure off Huerta? Militarily a mistake, politically the retreat was a blunder of the first magnitude. By his withdrawal, Villa thought he was sending the political message that his active participation was indispensable to settle the future of Mexico. In reality, he revealed that he was still incapable of thinking beyond the confines of a regional warlord. The supposedly weak and old Carranza had shown more courage than Villa and seized the opportunity to fill the military and political vacuum left by the rival's hasty retreat to the north. Carranza was in a very precarious position and was taking the huge gamble that the distant Obregón and the weak González could finish off Huerta.

The poor generalship of González left all hopes for a Carrancista victory riding on the distant General Obregón. Sonora politics and not the Federal Army had prevented Obregón from launching an offensive after the resounding victory at the battle of Santa María in June 1912. The return to the governorship of José María Maytorena had plunged Sonora into bitter political struggles. Months passed before Obregón marched again, and not until 14 November 1913 had his army moved south to take Culiacán, the capital of the neighboring state of Sinaloa. He then turned to Mazatlán, the port city of that state, but its capture was impossible as long as the Mexican navy could supply the garrison by sea. With Guaymas further north, Obregón had two thorns in his rear. To try to regain control of the sea, Obregón tried something that made world history. In the first recorded case, he ordered his observation plane to drop bombs on the Mexican gunboats on 15 April. Although the bombs missed their targets, the water splash of the explosions scared the crews who put their ships out to sea temporarily. Mechanical failure kept the pilot from trying again, and the gunboats resumed their normal duties. A frustrated Obregón decided to bypass Mazatlán, and he marched south to capture Tepic on 15 May.[97]

When Carranza's order to advance on central Mexico reached Obregón, the general realized that a march across the Sierra Madre offered the advantage of surprise and eliminated the need for a supporting push from Villa at Aguascalientes. The federal garrison in Guadalajara was not expecting any attack until the Carrancistas first secured a railroad line. After he collected 200 wagons and 2000 mules, he set out from Tepic on 10 June with 14,000 men. Because of the harsh and slippery terrain, he limited his heavy equipment to eight 75 mm cannon and four machine guns. His force arrived safely at the plateau of Guadalajara by 25 June. During the journey he had been out of contact for several weeks, but when he at last heard the first rumors of the break with Villa, Obregón spontaneously offered his full support and that of his soldiers to Carranza on 2 July.[98]

Between Obregón and final victory in Mexico City stood the federal garrison of 12,000 men in Guadalajara, which most surely would receive reinforcements from Mexico City. The garrison was under the command of José María Mier, one of the oldest generals in the Federal Army and a veteran of the war against the French in the 1860s. In recognition for his past services, both Carranza and Obregón gave the strictest orders to save the life of the old general. As Obregón received reports from his mounted patrols and carefully observed the federal positions scattered in three places, he increasingly became apprehensive. General Mier, besides keeping a strong garrison in Guadalajara, had placed most of his soldiers at the train station of Orendáin. He

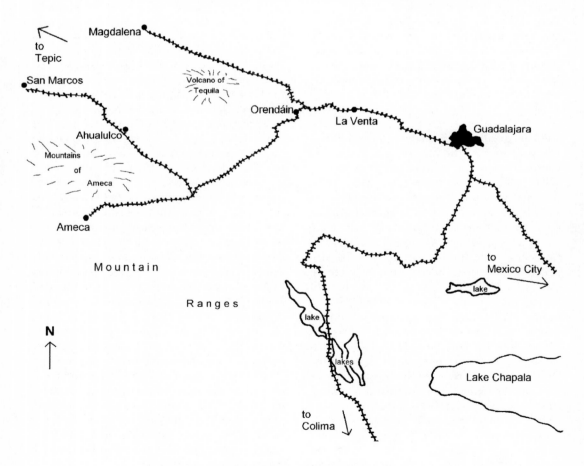

Map 15. Guadalajara Campaign of 1914.

kept only a small unit at the train station of La Venta to keep the force at Orendáin in communication with Guadalajara (Map 15). The federal deployment was better suited to hold off cavalry charges of a Villa, who could be expected to attack first the outermost contingent.

Obregón had a different approach, but in a mistake he later admitted, he erroneously estimated the federal force at Orendáin to number 12,000 men, when that was the total figure for all federal soldiers in the region. Obregon's initial plan called for luring forward the federal force toward his position and into a trap. He had noticed that the many ridges on the hills provided perfect cover for his men, who could hide until the federals entered the trap. He had provided bait to lure the federals forward, but at the last moment one of his officers blew up a culvert in the railroad track. The explosion spooked the advancing federals who retreated to repair the damaged culvert.

Not even a strong reprimand to the officer could rescue the original plan, and fortunately for military science, Obregón had to devise a more ingenious approach. He stripped his front line of troops and sent them in two detachments into the federal rear. Most of the cavalry took a long detour to points south of Guadalajara at night; its mission was to rip up large stretches of track to prevent the arrival of any reinforcements from Mexico City or from Colima. A larger contingent of infantry and cavalry took a detour to surprise the federal detachment at La Venta at dawn on 6 July. Obregón stayed with his few remaining troops in front of Orendáin and did his best to prepare his men to resist a counterattack on what was the Achilles' heel of his plan. His worry was unfounded, because his deployments caught the federals by surprise. When the federals at Orendáin heard shooting in the rear at the train station of La Venta, rather than attacking the weak line of Obregón, they promptly retreated to help the small unit at La Venta. The federal withdrawal to La Venta caught the attacking rebel column in crossfire. Fortunately for the rebel column, a heavy rainfall slowed down the federal movement. Under cover of the downpour, Obregón positioned his main force for an attack on the weak points in the federal rear. Close to midnight Obregón hurled his troops to the attack, and by daybreak they had taken

the main federal positions along the railroad track. Obregón moved forward two of his field pieces, and then the stranded federals, seeing their escape route to Guadalajara closed, fled in disarray over the hills at 1000 on 7 July. Rather than follow the federals into the rugged terrain, Obregón moved his men along the track until by nightfall they had taken positions blocking the entrances to Guadalajara.

Throughout the night federals desperately tried to break the rebel line in a futile attempt to reach Guadalajara; so many federals preferred to surrender that some units of Obregón had more prisoners than soldiers. Upon hearing of the disaster at Orendáin, General Mier ordered his remaining 1,500 men to evacuate Guadalajara on the night of 7–8 July, but with the track destroyed, they had not walked far when the rebel cavalry surprised them at noon on 8 July. The sudden cavalry charge shattered the remaining federal soldiers, few of whom managed to escape. Among the survivors was not General Mier: By the time the rebels found him, one of his own sergeants had killed him for refusing to give the order to withdraw immediately. The battle of Orendáin had been a total victory for Obregón. The rebels took over 5000 soldiers taken prisoners; in contrast to the bloody battles of Villa, Obregón's distaste for slaughter and his superior military talents had kept combat deaths slight on both sides.[99]

The victory at Orendáin opened the road to Mexico City. Upon hearing the news of the disaster, Huerta on 8 July made up his mind to resign. He kept his decision secret until 15 July, when he presented his formal resignation to his rump Congress. Actually, he had had left Mexico City hours earlier, because with Veracruz in U.S. hands, he knew he needed more time to leave the country. He and his entourage reached Coatzacoalcos safely and on 20 July departed for exile to Europe.[100] The rebels had accomplished the apparently impossible task of driving Huerta from power and thus had partly avenged the overthrow and death of Francisco Madero. The fall of Huerta evoked many moments of delirious joy among the rebels. However, the departure of the hated general in no way signified that peace had returned permanently to Mexico. As the next chapter shows, Mexico still had some of the fiercest and bloodiest battles ahead.

8. The Struggle Against Pancho Villa

Villa's record is unlovely, viewed from any angle whatever. Butcher by trade, it is really a matter of indifference to him whether the shambles be filled with his own kind or with bullocks and lambs. He has hunted throughout almost the length of his whole life his fellow men, and they have hunted him. [...] The stern necessities of his peculiar life bred in him daring, cunning, animal craftiness and alertness [....] He is today the same brutal, overbearing, and untamed savage that he was when first he took up the trade of highwayman. — U. S. Consul Marion Letcher[1]

The resignation of Victoriano Huerta on 15 July 1914 promised to bring peace to a war-ravaged Mexico. First Chief Venustiano Carranza had led the rebels to a surprising victory, and once his government solidly established itself in Mexico City, the new president could embark on the daunting task of economic reconstruction. However, these happy prospects for the country clashed with the personal ambitions of Pancho Villa who, as the last section of the previous chapter showed, wanted to remain the warlord of his home state of Chihuahua. The virtual independence of Pancho Villa in the largest state of Mexico bolstered the position of fellow warlords in other places and necessarily meant turning Mexico at best into a confederation of warlords and at worst into petty republics like Central America. In direct opposition, Carranza insisted on unifying Mexico under a strong national government. Between these two mutually exclusive alternatives, no compromise was possible. Only war could decide which of the two visions would shape the future of Mexico; when an impatient Villa launched an offensive in September, he plunged the country into the bloodiest phase of the Mexican Revolution. For two years savage warfare raged to determine whether Mexico was to be a confederation of regional warlords or one unified country.

The Path to War and the Start of the Villista Onslaught

Venustiano Carranza and Pancho Villa had kept their struggle for power so secret, that when the dispute finally emerged into the public view in late June 1914, the majority of generals on both sides could not believe the news. The naive assumption that all revolutionaries were good had led the generals to believe that a simple misunderstanding had caused the rift. Representatives from both sides met in Torreón on 4 July to find a way to diffuse the dispute. In the agreement of 8 July, the generals decided that all rebels had to work together to defeat Victoriano Huerta. Once the Huerta regime had fallen, the generals pledged to meet at a convention to determine the future ruler of Mexico. This artificial agreement disguised the power struggle and preserved a united rebel front against Huerta at least outwardly. After the decisive federal defeat at Orendáin in Jalisco, Huerta regretfully concluded that the split among the rebels had come too late to save his collapsing regime. He resigned the presidency and left Mexico City on 15 July 1914. The Chief Justice of the Mexican Supreme Court, Francisco Carbajal, became the interim president, and he appointed General José Refugio

Velasco as the new Secretary of War. These personnel changes forced the rebels to reconsider their campaign against the still considerable Federal Army near Mexico City.[2]

The interim government put out feelers to sound out Villa about the possibility of an alliance, a proposal that militarily was very attractive. The Federal Army was solidly entrenched around Mexico City and could gain enough time for Villa with his 30,000 men to launch a devastating attack on the Carrancista rear. An alliance with the Federal Army offered Villa a first great opportunity to gain national power. But because at this moment he still could not think beyond the confines of a regional warlord, he made no attempt to conclude this Machiavellian bargain. Hostility toward the federals had not influenced Villa, because in contrast to the rest of the Carrancistas, he reserved his hatred for the fallen Huerta. Perhaps because he had once served in the Federal Army, Villa harbored no ill-will toward its members, and this tolerant attitude attracted soldiers in droves and quite significantly many ex-federal officers into the Villista ranks.[3]

As the remote possibility of any deal with Villa vanished, interim president Carbajal resigned. The fate of the Federal Army was in the hands of its last commander, General Velasco, who had to decide whether to surrender unconditionally to the hostile Carrancistas or to continue the war. Combat had not ceased after the resignation of Huerta, so it was not a question of resuming hostilities. At first sight the advantage lay with the Federal Army. General Álvaro Obregón could muster at most 18,000 men, while the garrison of Mexico City numbered 30,000 soldiers. The arsenals had a thirty days' supply of ammunition and many artillery pieces. A final stand in the capital was certainly possible, but General Velasco knew well that ultimately the Federal Army was doomed. Many additional Carrancista units were on the way to Mexico City, and Villa had ratified his offer to return with his over 30,000 men as soon as Carranza supplied the necessary coal for the locomotives. The Federal Army had suffered so many defeats that the deep demoralization threatened a sudden collapse. Military history, in its haste to praise the victors of bloody battles, often fails to commend generals like Velasco who avoided a needless disaster. To save his men from annihilation, General Velasco

agreed to negotiate with Obregón on the sole condition that the lives of the federal troops be spared. Given the practice of executing all prisoners, saving the lives of the members of the Federal Army was no small concession. Obregón, always receptive to arguments based on reason, could see the logic in the request and readily agreed.[4]

By the Accords of Teoloyucan of 13 August 1914, the Federal Army ceased to exist. All units across the country were to disband after turning over their weapons to the nearest Carrancista forces. As for the large garrison at Mexico City, all the soldiers were to receive a final payment and free passage back to their homes. The *leva* or press gang of Huerta had forced many into the Federal Army, and those who were looking for an opportunity to desert saw the disbandment as freedom to return home. But for most men, home was at best a crumbling adobe room, exhausting toil, and the constant specter of hunger. A more attractive alternative was to join the Carrancisctas, who were always looking for volunteers to fill their ranks. A steady allowance, entertainment, and occasional booty had originally enticed many to join the ranks of the rebels and were equally attractive to the former federal soldiers. Once he had a rifle, the man had no difficulty finding a young female to cook for him and to take care of his emotional and sexual needs; his allowance was enough to feed both, and the women traditionally performed miracles as scavengers of food and other items. Harsh as today might seem a life of marching across the country and of fighting for causes the illiterate men never bothered to understand, the rebel armies offered enough attractions to lure many former federals into staying. While no national figures are available, at least one half of the federal rank and file near Mexico City joined the Carrancistas. Foolish was the Carrancista general who did not avail himself of the opportunity to replenish his unit with veteran soldiers.[5]

Not so simple were the choices for the former federal officers, who supposedly could stay in Mexico City to await reassignment from the new rulers. Junior officers supervised the disbandment of their units and often joined the soldiers returning to their homes. The highest ranking generals, including Velasco himself, prudently departed for the United States.[6] A handful of officers refused to accept the

Teoloyucan Accords and continued to fight against the Carrancistas. A small number of officers left military service altogether. The largest share of federal officers reported back to Mexico City to await reassignment, a sure sign that few expected any reprisals from the troops under Obregón. The most natural choice for Carranza would have been to incorporate as many as possible of the former federal officers into his army, but almost all of his officers were violently opposed to accepting the former federals. Sparing their lives had been such a huge concession that the Carrancista officers vehemently drew the line at their absorption. The Carrancistas had been successful in attracting enough men of middle-class background to fill their officer ranks, unlike the Villistas who suffered acute shortages of officers. Not just principle, but competition for plumb assignments also fueled the Carrancista hatred of the former federals. The intense struggle for promotions was understandable at the higher ranks, but not for junior officers who traditionally suffered heavy casualties in combat. Instead of using the ex-federals as replacements, the Carrancistas drove them into the Villista army. The influx of former Federal Army officers helps to account for the remarkable staying power of the Villista army over the coming year; only in 1916 did the Carrancistas begin to correct the earlier mistake of rejecting the Federal Army officers.[7]

In August 1914, only the officer corps of the Mexican Navy survived intact. Carranza trusted the Navy's pledges of obedience, and the admirals remained loyal to him because they knew that their ships could not survive without land bases. The Accords of Teoloyucan had cleared the path into the capital, so Obregón and his advance guard entered Mexico City at 1430 on 15 August to the shouts of a wildly joyous crowd. But his troops still had one unfinished matter to tend to. The Accords of Teoloyucan had also stipulated that the federal units facing Zapatista bands in the south were to remain at their posts defending the city until Carrancistas arrived to relieve them. As more units of his army arrived, Obregón secured the surroundings and prepared the city for the victorious entry of Carranza into Mexico City on 20 August. The struggle the First Chief had begun in February 1913 against impossible odds had finally culminated in his tak-

ing triumphal possession of the capital as the new ruler of Mexico. Yet Carranza knew that the long trip to national power was still not over, and while the crowds celebrated the victory enthusiastically, he began to prepare for what he considered the inevitable showdown with Pancho Villa.[8] Some of his followers, unaware of the storm clouds in the north and eager to end all conflict in Mexico, had been trying to secure the submission of Emiliano Zapata even before the Carrancistas had entered Mexico City.

Zapata had already been in revolt against every government in Mexico City; would he also rebel against Carranza? Zapata operated in the minuscule state of Morelos, which derived its strategic significance from its proximity to Mexico City. The defense of the capital against the Zapatistas pinned down many troops better employed in other regions of the country. Carranza was wrestling with ways to solve the strategic dilemma Morelos posed, but unlike some of his followers, he harbored no illusions about an arrangement with Zapata. Carranza considered the Zapatistas to be nothing less than bandits, looters, and criminals; perhaps better than anybody else, Carranza realized that Zapata had wrapped himself in the mantle of land reform to perpetuate his personal power. Carranza also felt that Zapata was too weak militarily to merit courting as an ally. The logical strategy called for eliminating the powerful Villa first, and afterwards there would be plenty of time and resources to dispose of Zapata in a leisurely manner. Not surprisingly the negotiations between Zapata and Carrancista delegates were barren of results. On 5 September Carranza released the inevitable announcement confirming the failure to reach an agreement with Zapata.[9] The tension between the forward Carrancista outposts in the south and the Zapatista sentries increased during September, but both sides wanted to avoid combat and concentrated on watching the events unfolding in the distant northern state of Sonora (Map 13).

The troubles at Sonora ultimately all sprang from the envious hatred of Governor José María Maytorena for Obregón. The previous chapter had revealed how bitterly Maytorena resented Obregón's rise to prominence. Maytorena, a large landholder, always saw himself as the rightful ruler of Sonora and passionately despised the upstart Obregón. Ever since Maytorena had cowardly fled the state in February 1913, he had been desperately striving to recover his power. In contrast, as Obregón increasingly moved into the national arena his interest in Sonora waned, and he was willing to end the feud with the governor. However, Maytorena could not bring himself to bury his hatred for his former subordinate, and each successive triumph of Obregón merely intensified the determination of the envious Maytorena to seek revenge. The governor did realize that by himself he could not destroy Obregón who had become too powerful. Maytorena canvassed for allies and detected in Carranza a willingness to keep Obregón in check. But Carranza had no intention of destroying his best general, and Maytorena concluded that the only other person left in Mexico able to stop Obregón was Villa. Maytorena had financed Villa's revolt against Huerta in March 1913, and Villa never forgot a favor. Villa himself was looking for allies after Carranza had blocked the coal shipments in June 1914. In early July Villa and Maytorena were closely coordinating their next moves.[10]

The pieces were falling into place to start the next war in the Mexican Revolution. Although Maytorena was responsible for launching Mexico into years of destruction for his own personal goal, the clash between Villa and Carranza over raw political power was inevitable. Mexico was not big enough to fill the political ambitions of these two men. What was not preordained was the exact incident that triggered the war, and here was where Maytorena took the most decisive action in his entire life. Although he was governor of the state, the Carrancista troops in Sonora were not under his control. Those in the northern border towns were under the command of Colonel Plutarco Elías Calles, and those in the southern part of the state were under the command of his superior, General Salvador Alvarado. Calles, after some initial disagreements with Obregón, had forged a friendship with the general that eventually matured into perhaps the most important relationship in Mexico's history. Once the alliance between the two men solidified, not surprisingly, Maytorena also directed his fury against Calles.

General Alvarado, who had always harbored resentment at fellow native Obregón,

seemed a natural ally for Maytorena who, however, turned him into a bitter enemy. At least by July 23 Obregón had learned of the intentions of Maytorena to join Villa, so in anticipation Obregón had ordered as many of the troops and artillery in southern Sonora to depart for the siege of Mazatlán. Wise as a precaution to deprive Villa of these units, their departure left Alvarado at the mercy of Yaqui soldiers in Hermosillo. Maytorena who "does nothing openly but all underhanded work"[11] took advantage of the opportunity. Alvarado explained that "The governor has been doing his best to gain over the Yaquis and officers in his command and has spent money freely in his efforts."[12] With the Yaqui garrison under his orders, Maytorena was free to carry out a coup in Hermosillo on 9 August. He had all Carrancista loyalists arrested, including General Alvarado.[13]

The Hermosillo coup of 9 August came just as Obregón was negotiating the surrender of the Federal Army in Mexico City and thus came to put a damper on the impending Carrancista triumph. Maytorena controlled all of Sonora except for the border garrisons in the north under Colonel Calles. Maytorena forced the two thousand imprisoned federal soldiers to join the army he was gathering for the campaign in the north. Upon learning of the rebellion of Maytorena, Obregón ordered the 4,000 soldiers in Mazatlán to return to Sonora, but Villa promptly checkmated him by stating that if Carrancista troops went to Sonora, he too would come with a larger force. A stalemate had ensued as the two rival groups faced each other in Sonora. Up to this moment no combat had taken place, but as the soldiers of Calles gazed intensively to the desert south from their border towns, nobody was sure how much longer peace could last.[14]

By bringing Villa into the dispute, Maytorena had gained time to consolidate his rule in Sonora, but the governor could not be satisfied as long as Colonel Calles remained in control of the northern desert towns. Carranza had long since expected a civil war with Villa and did not really care whether the initial spark took place in Sonora or anywhere else. Many generals still could not bring themselves to believe that the Mexican Revolution was not over. Trapped in the clichés of manifestoes, many generals could not really understand why fellow revolutionaries would want to fight each other. Propaganda had depicted Huerta as such a monster and the source of all evil, that once he was gone, what justification remained for Mexicans to continue killing each other? Obregón, who was making slow progress in his learning curve as a politician, naively believed that he could broker a deal to diffuse the tension in Sonora. He obtained the reluctant permission of a cynical Carranza, who saw the propaganda value of a peace mission. Carranza certainly did not want the burden of starting the war to fall on him, and he saw the political advantages of having the impulsive Villa attack first.

Obregón came to Chihuahua City on 24 August and persuaded Villa to accompany him on a peace mission to Sonora. Obregón's trip caught Villa by surprise, and he later commented that had not the visit taken place, his troops would have been firing already. At Nogales the two men met with Calles and Maytorena to complete an agreement on 30 August, not without first overcoming major difficulties. The accord (*acuerdo*) appointed Maytorena to be the commander of all troops in Sonora, but accepted that Obregón was his superior. Colonel Calles remained in Sonora, but under General Benjamín Hill, whom Obregón promised to send to take command.[15] Of all the high officers from Sonora, General Hill had the closest friendship with Maytorena, and Obregón, who strongly believed in friendship, hoped the two men could work together. When General Hill arrived to take command, Maytorena immediately demanded that Hill renounce the loyalty to Obregón. The friendship of years instantly evaporated as Maytorena gave vent to his passionate hatred for Obregón. At Maytorena's request, Villa on 8 September ordered Hill to depart with the northern garrisons for Casas Grandes in Chihuahua. Upon closer reflection, Villa had felt duped by the agreement of 30 August and became determined to support Maytorena in Sonora as his unconditional ally. General Hill, not surprisingly, refused to leave, because he did not want to be at the mercy of Villa's large army at Casas Grandes. As Villa repeated his orders to Hill to withdraw, war became imminent: "Hill says [he] will not fight unless attacked [...] unless Hill can be induced to withdraw immediately, it appears fighting must ensue."[16]

Patrols exchanged shots on 10 September and suffered casualties, but the skirmishes did not suffice to start the new civil war.[17] Maytorena, who controlled larger contingents than Hill, was eager to attack, but Villa was hesitant to unleash the governor. A second surprise visit from Obregón caught Villa still undecided. In one last effort to preserve the peace, Obregón had rashly decided to return to Chihuahua. He ignored the many warnings that he risked execution and, undaunted, he hoped to woo over to Carranza's side many of the Villista generals. Villa for his part hoped to overawe Obregón sufficiently to shake him from his allegiance to Carranza. The Mexican holiday of independence, 16 September, coincided with the arrival of Obregón in Chihuahua City, and Villa could not resist showing off his military might. For three hours the Villistas paraded before delirious crowds; Obregón and his chief of staff quietly counted the Villista units, whose very slow march disguised their modest numbers. After the parade, Villa then gave a tour of his armory to Obregón, who was well familiarized with the captured federal arsenals in Mexico City and calmly concluded that the Villistas did not excel the Carrancistas in either quantity or quality of armament. Obregón also calculated that if the large number of men Villa claimed for his army was true, then the supply of cartridges was too small to support any long campaign.[18]

Neither the military parade nor bulging arsenal overawed Obregón into submission; not surprisingly the rest of the visit turned out badly. In one of the most famous episodes in Mexican history too well known to narrate in any detail, the discussions over Sonora and Carranza became very heated, and a furious Villa took Obregón hostage; Villa considered executing his prisoner and his staff, and their fate remained in the balance for days. Villa finally released his prisoners, but their train to Mexico City failed to arrive on time. The start of hostilities seemed imminent, and Carranza wrote off Obregón as dead and made the final dispositions for war. Because up to this moment Villa enjoyed the freedom to strike from his excellent bases at Torreón and Zacatecas, military logic required that Carranza take some preventive steps. In an attempt to delay the Villista advance, Carranza on 22 September ordered the destruction of the railroad tracks west of Saltillo and north of Aguascalientes. Unfortunately for Carranza, the governor at Aguascalientes was a closet Villista who waffled on carrying out the order; even worse, telegraph operators had intercepted Carranza's order and immediately transmitted a copy to Villa, who exploded in one of his violent outbursts. For Villa this order meant war, and on 22 September he sent a telegram to Carranza openly rejecting his authority; the next day Villa issued the inevitable manifesto to the Mexican people to try to justify his rebellion. Villa also ordered the train taking Obregón back to Mexico City to return, but by a matter of minutes his order came too late, and Obregón escaped execution.[19]

The confused accounts over Obregón's fate left Carranza unsure about how to respond, but for the moment he relented on his orders to destroy the key railroad tracks. The repeal of the destruction order might seem like a mistake, but in reality the decision did not matter, because a forewarned Villa was already on the move and had preempted any chance the demolition crews had of destroying the tracks.[20] Deficient as Villa was in national strategy, his grasp of the regional situation was superb. He knew that saving the tracks south of Zacatecas and east of Torreón was just a first step to launch an offensive; he could not advance safely until he first had secured his flank at Durango. On 23 September he sent an ultimatum to the Arrieta brothers, the rulers of Durango, asking for their support against Carranza. The evasive answer of the brothers angered Villa, who replied by ordering nearby Villista troops to seize Durango.[21] The operation began at night on 26 September as Villista troops

> entered Durango last night from the east and north, while the forces of Generals Mariano and Domingo Arrieta departed at about the same time towards the south and west to take refuge in the nearby mountain fastnesses. Both the entry and departure were accomplished in perfect order, not a single shot being fired.[22]

With Durango subdued, Villa was free to deploy his forces to the south. Because no fighting had taken place in the Durango operation, the honor of hosting the first engagement in the war fell to Sonora. Previously Carrancista troops had evacuated Nogales, which

Maytorena promptly occupied. General Hill controlled Naco, Cananea, and Agua Prieta. Skirmishing had taken place on 10 September but then both sides had held back. Upon hearing of Villa's rebellion, Maytorena promptly issued his own supporting manifesto on 23 September. More significantly, he took the Villa revolt as the green light to send his troops to drive out the Carrancistas from Naco. General Hill, for his part, had sent a small detachment to patrol the approaches near Nogales at the point called Martínez. Shortly before 0900 on 25 September, the Yaqui Indians of Maytorena ran into the Carrancista covering force. The major in charge of the Carrancistas, rather than prudently withdrawing, insisted on giving battle. After two hours of fierce combat, the Yaquis overran the unit and killed the obstinate major; the survivors fled in panic.[23] The disaster tested the mettle of General Hill, who promptly abandoned Nogales and desperately strove to rally his demoralized troops for a final defense at Naco. Except for the garrison at Agua Prieta, he recalled all units in the field to Naco. He put his men to dig a network of trenches around the town, with the ends resting on the U.S. boundary line. Meanwhile Maytorena massed his forces for the attack, and on 30 September he had sealed off Naco. After some sorties to test the defenses on 4 October, the siege settled into a routine:

> The firing between the trenches and Maytorena's force is kept up day and night; generally very light but at times rather severe. [...] there is no possible way of telling at present when this conflict will end. It seems to be a case of each side trying to wear out the other by continual, annoying firing [...].
> There seems to be no limit to the amount of small-arm ammunition in each force, which they use most liberally. As far as can be determined by observation there is very little aimed firing from either side, Maytorena's men frequently firing from the hip and off-hand.[24]

Maytorena tried his luck with night attacks on 10–11 and 16–17 October, but illumination from two search lights gave the defenders an excellent field of fire. Having found Naco too hard to capture for the moment, he accepted the propositions of a delegate from the Convention of Aguascalientes (about which more later) for a truce. He withdrew his troops 35 kilometers away from Naco. He had agreed to the truce supposedly to give the Convention of Aguascalientes one last chance to patch up a peace, but in reality his real goal was to replenish and refurbish his troops. On 9 November Maytorena resumed the effort with the help of 75 mm. cannons. General Hill had not been idle either and had by then obtained heavier weapons from the United States.

Two night attacks did not go well, and worse, the former federal soldiers were taking advantage of the darkness to flee. Not willing to risk more desertions, Maytorena attacked in broad daylight on the morning of 18 November. The ex-federals marched in parade formation, and the charging lines made great targets for the defenders. The huge losses crippled any chance of capturing Naco, unless Villa sent large reinforcements. The defenders for their part were too weak to drive off the besiegers, and consequently the siege settled into desultory shooting. Casualties piled up on both sides of the border, leading the U.S. government to pressure Villa to lift the siege. Once Villa ordered Maytorena to abandon Naco, the governor had no choice but to enter into negotiations. By the agreement of 11 January 1915, both sides declared Naco a neutral town. Maytorena first withdrew his forces south, and then Calles (who had taken command from Hill) removed the garrison to Agua Prieta, which remained as the sole Carrancista outpost in Sonora.[25] Just like Carranza had postponed the final offensive against Zapata, in a similar strategic decision Villa delayed the Sonora invasion until after he had destroyed his rivals in central Mexico. Little could Villa foresee that one year later his destiny would bring him to Sonora.

As an ally Maytorena was nominally a Villista, but his troops were not under the direct command of Villa, who preferred to leave local matters in the hands of the regional warlords. Elsewhere in Mexico, the Villista and Carrancista troops had still not engaged in combat, and many generals hoped to contain the warfare inside Sonora. Obregón realized that war was inevitable, but many other generals strove to maintain the peace. The conference at Torreón of 8 July had promised to convoke a convention, and the generals pressed for the gathering to take place. On 1 October Carranza inaugurated a convention of generals at Mexico City; in attendance were only his followers, because the Villistas and Zapatistas refused to

participate. Carranza duly resigned on 3 October, left the chamber, and prepared to return to private life; in his absence, his followers enthusiastically and unanimously elected him their leader. Later that evening he resumed his duties as provisional president.[26]

At that moment the military campaign against Villa should have begun, but the majority of generals, including many Carrancistas, still believed war could be averted. According to the generals, the absence of Villista representatives at the Mexico City convention had not given negotiations a fair chance. Obregón strongly supported the proposal of convoking a second convention with Villista representatives present, not because he expected to avert war, but because he hoped that a careful exposition of arguments would persuade some of Villista generals to switch sides. Carranza opposed a second convention, but because he could not afford to antagonize the generals who had just supported him, he tolerated their participation while he prepared for the inevitable war. Villa also was busily readying his offensive, but he eagerly accepted the proposal to convoke a convention at the neutral ground of Aguascalientes. Villa had leaped at the chance to participate, because he felt the Convention of Aguascalientes provided an excellent forum to repair his image badly sullied by the attempted execution of Obregón.

When the Convention opened at Aguascalientes on 10 October it immediately captured the imagination of the Mexican masses who have remained fascinated at the spectacle of generals legislating for the country.[27] The Convention appeared to be a complete success for Villa as well: Rather than Obregón winning over Villista generals for Carranza, Villa attracted Carrancista generals over to his side. Obregón later admitted he had badly blundered when he had supported the Aguascalientes Convention. Again he had overestimated the power of reason to sway others and had underestimated the charisma of Villa who easily charmed many into believing he was the savior of Mexico.

As an added bonus, the Convention of Aguascalientes had brought Villistas together with Zapatistas. As will be recalled, Carranza had never expected to reach any agreement with Zapata. Difficult as it had been for Villa to think in national terms, for Zapata it was impossible; nevertheless, a common enemy, Carranza gradually drove the Zapatistas towards the Villistas.

As news of these proceedings reached Mexico City, Carranza with incredible insight grasped the true nature of his predicament. Having to maintain an army in Mexico City against Zapata deprived the Carrancistas of mobility to face Villa; to make matters worse, the general in charge of the cavalry in the capital had succumbed to the charms of Villa. The betrayal of this general deeply hurt Obregón, who could rely only on his infantry. The defection of the cavalry also left Carranza very vulnerable, and he planned his escape from Mexico City. Not wishing to appear to be fleeing, he announced his intention to take rest trips on Sundays after a hard week's work. On Sunday 25 October he left and returned the next day. The next Saturday afternoon, he said he was going with his private escort to spend a day visiting the pyramids at Teotihuacán; his trip aroused no suspicion when he left on 1 November, and this time he did not return but remained with his troops in the field. His intention was to set up a new government in Veracruz, but because that coastal city was still under U.S. occupation, Carranza had plunged into a highly risky maneuver. He had gambled on the United States fulfilling its promise to evacuate Veracruz; meanwhile Carranza had ordered General Salvador Alvarado to proceed with the evacuation from Mexico City.[28]

Alvarado had returned from Sonora after the Convention of Aguascalientes obtained his release from prison. Time was running out for goodwill gestures, and the Convention issued an ultimatum: If Carranza did not resign by 1800 on 10 November, war would begin. That very night Villista troops began boarding their trains and were on their way south of Aguascalientes on 11 November (Map 16). This Villista advance was the last straw for Obregón, who resolutely denounced Villa. Carranza appointed Obregón to command all the forces withdrawing from Mexico City, including those of Alvarado. The Carrancistas shipped their arsenals and equipment to Veracruz and tried to carry all they could from the capital.[29] Why had Carranza so willingly exchanged cool Mexico City for steamy Veracruz? As the largest port in Mexico, Veracruz generated customs revenue and was a natural entry point for war material. However, Veracruz by itself could not produce enough funds to defeat Villa. Carranza also had to hold two other regions at all costs: Yucatan with its large revenues from the export of henequén, and Tampico with royalties from its petroleum fields. With the Mexican Navy solidly behind him, Carranza could move troops easily along the Gulf of Mexico and thus maintain control over the three coastal areas most vital for the war with Villa.

Once Villa had sent his army of nearly 40,000 men south from Aguascalientes on 11 November, a major engagement with the 20,000 men of General Pablo González seemed inevitable. To the surprise of the Villistas, all resistance vanished, and any Carrancista troops who appeared in their path fled after exchanging some shots. Villa's advance was more like a triumphal march than an invasion, and he peacefully occupied León on 16 November and Querétaro on 18 November. The road to Mexico City was clearly wide open, but what had happened to the army of Pablo González? Many generals and units had defected in mass to Villa, and the disintegration of his forces made González desist from any battle. He gathered the remnants of his army at Pachuca on 20 November, but because he had only 6,000 men left, he knew he could not tarry long in that vulnerable position. With masses of Villistas to the south and west, it was too late for him to backtrack to Toluca, where General Francisco Murguía had rallied scattered Carrancista units; Murguía himself considered his position at Toluca too exposed and on 24 November left for Guadalajara to try to join the army of Diéguez. For General González, only two options remained. He could fight his way to the east to try to reach the troops evacuating from Mexico City under Obregón, or he could go north to Tampico. As was his custom, González took a long time to ponder the options, until attacking Villistas closed off all but one escape route and forced him to beat a hasty withdrawal from Pachuca on 29 November. After receiving reports that the paths leading north could comfortably carry his army, he plunged into the rugged mountains in the direction of Tampico. Obviously he had been badly informed, and the trip through barren and harsh terrain sorely tried his army and lasted nearly a month.[30]

The sudden collapse of Gonzalez's army

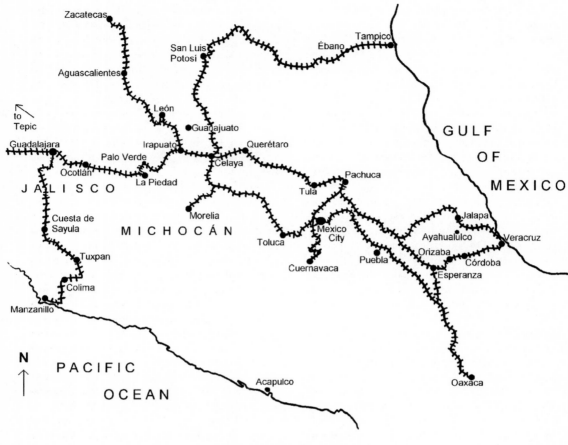

Map 16. Central Mexico.

forced Obregón to hurry the evacuation of Mexico City. The first military trains began departing on 18 November, and in the following days trains rumbled out of the capital at a continuous pace. At 0700 on 24 November Obregón left with the last train, and already the night before Zapatistas had occupied the outlying towns of Xochimilco and San Ángel. Around 2200 of 24 November the Zapatistas established a weak presence in Mexico City. The Villistas started arriving by train on 29 November and soon had established a tight grip on the entire city.[31] The revolutionary excesses that had so bothered the inhabitants during the Carrancista occupation paled in significance compared to "the reign of terror"[32] that Villa imposed on the capital. His men went on a rampage in Mexico City and committed countless cruelties and atrocities. General Tomás Urbina, the most dreaded of Villa's subordinates, used torture and executions in his greedy

quest for loot. Under Villa's supervision, Urbina routinely kidnapped wealthy persons to extort sums of money for their release. Mexican citizens and foreign residents lived in terror of the Villistas and longed for the mild rule of Carranza. The occupation of Mexico City, rather than the climax of the career of Pancho Villa, in reality marked the start of his decline.

Each day Villa wasted in Mexico City reduced his chances of striking a knockout blow against Carranza. The U.S. occupation of Veracruz left the Carrancista trains stranded between the capital and the port city. When the United States finally evacuated Veracruz on 23 November, the trains did start to roll into the port city, but to clear the backlog of sidetracked convoys required weeks. Heaps of merchandise lay strewn along the tracks, and wagons full of equipment and troops clogged the rails. The confusion reached extreme proportions because Carranza had evacuated a government and not just an army. Even if the cargo and the personnel could be sorted out, the task of restoring the morale of the Carrancista troops was daunting. The Villistas had earned a reputation of invincibility, and the Carrancista troops no longer wanted to challenge their formidable opponents. General Felipe Ángeles urged Villa to take advantage of the Carrancista demoralization to pursue aggressively. If in early December Villa had struck at the Carrancista forces strung out in the railroad to Veracruz, most likely he would have won the war just by sheer momentum. Obregón with his accustomed care had been scouting the possible Villista advance routes to prepare a spirited defense, but even he seemed resigned to execute a fighting withdrawal. As another indication that victory was within grasp, on the night of 15 December a panicky General Alvarado abandoned Puebla after lightly armed Zapatistas appeared. Obregón was already rushing to the front with reinforcements, but Alvarado had lost the will to fight; militarily the loss of Puebla marked the lowest point for Carranza.

The day before on 14 December Villista troops had driven Diéguez out of Guadalajara, while General González was presumed lost after his flight from Pachuca. With the capture of Puebla by the Zapatistas, the road was clear for Villa to make a final push into Veracruz precisely when the Carrancistas were at their most vulnerable moment. The situation seemed so bleak that even Obregón studied a final evacuation route via the Tehuantepec railroad to the Pacific Coast, should such a retreat prove necessary. Presumably the remnants of the Carrancistas expected to make a final stand somewhere in the Pacific Coast.[33]

Fortunately for Carranza, no Villista offensive against Veracruz ever materialized. Not lack of troops or ammunition, but the failure of Villa to forge a satisfactory alliance with Zapata had been the primary reason for the Villista inaction. Zapata was extremely sensitive to any outside interference in his region, and Villa did not want to antagonize his would-be ally by an independent offensive on Veracruz. As a substitute to joint operations with Zapata,

Artillery of Pancho Villa, who was always fascinated with cannons but did not always know how to use artillery properly in the battlefield (Library of Congress, Prints and Photographs Division).

Villa prepared a grand strategy that called for creating a large army to march to Guadalajara and from there to subdue the rest of the Pacific Coast. Another large Villista force was to march north to capture Saltillo and Monterrey with the ultimate objective of reaching Tampico. Villa with considerable doubts assigned the drive to Veracruz to Zapata, whose offensive had stalled at Puebla; supposedly Zapatistas in Veracruz and Villistas in Tampico would trap between them any remnants of the Carrancistas. The plan looked good on a map, but rested on the entirely unfounded assumption that the Zapatistas could campaign effectively far beyond their home grounds. Zapata for his part left the field and returned home to enjoy his absolute power in Morelos. No local leader from the state of Veracruz had offered support for Villa, who considered this remote state as beyond his area of knowledge; as he had stated to the Americans in April 1914, he really did not care about Veracruz. Villa's grand strategy was more a patchwork of partial offensives, as befitted a regional warlord. Standing within reach of national power, Villa shuddered and returned to his familiar territory: Chihuahua and its bordering states comprised his known universe. He had never gone as far as Pascual Orozco who had mentioned the independence of Chihuahua from Mexico, but his world view was just one step short of separation. When Villa had the chance to rule a unified Mexico, he preferred to fight for a confederation of regional warlords.[34]

When news reached him that the Carrancista garrison in Saltillo was threatening Torreón, Villa immediately bolted into action. Unable to understand the strategic significance of Veracruz, he was all too familiar with Torreón, the gateway to Chihuahua. His best general, Felipe Ángeles, protested this mistaken strategy, but Villa insisted on having him take troops to the north. The reports turned out to be exaggerated, because the Carrancistas in Saltillo were only strengthening their defenses. Rather than recall Ángeles from the north to attack Veracruz directly, Villa remained dallying in Mexico City during the last weeks of 1914.[35] Villa was so calm because he was very confident that his new offensives were sure to destroy Carranza in the new year of 1915. The Villista troops had the reputation of invincibility, all resistance collapsed upon their ap-

pearance, and Carranza seemed too weak to stop them. Likewise, many foreign observers believed that Villa had gained so much momentum that his victory was just a matter of time.

The Turn of Destiny, January–April 1915

Nothing at the start of the new year of 1915 suggested that the unbroken string of victories of Pancho Villa was about to end. His threefold northern strategy seemed very promising. He sent Felipe Ángeles, his best general, with 10,000 men to capture Saltillo and Monterrey. He planned to send General Manuel Chao with 10,000 men to pierce the defenses at Ébano and capture Tampico. To reinforce the sweep against Tampico, he also sent a smaller Villista force to Ciudad Victoria. Once he had taken the Tampico oil fields, in effect he had won the war.

General Ángeles, upon arriving in Torreón, reported that the nearest Carrancista troops were too weak to pose any danger to the city, but even this information failed to budge his boss, who insisted on driving out the Carrancistas from Saltillo and Monterrey. A skeptical Ángeles did his best to comply with what he considered a mistaken strategy. In a textbook maneuver, he lured most of the Carrancista garrison of Saltillo away from that city. Ángeles left a small detachment to distract them, while he sent the bulk of his troops rapidly by train down the main track to Saltillo. The surprise was complete, and the few Carrancista troops at Saltillo fled north. General Ángeles entered Saltillo on 7 January 1915, but he well knew that his clever maneuver had gained only real estate and had not really destroyed the Carrancista force, which was busily taking up positions between Saltillo and Monterrey at Ramos Arizpe.[36]

General Ángeles decided to attack the Carrancistas the next day at Ramos Arizpe before they received more reinforcements from Monterrey and before they had time to consolidate a defense line. A very heavy fog enveloped the bitterly cold battlefield on 8 January, and directing the troops became virtually impossible. The ferocious battle saw not only hand-to-hand combat, but often soldiers shooting at their own troops. General Ángeles at least had the chance to give his troops general instructions before he lost contact, but the Carrancista general, Antonio Villarreal, never understood what was going on. He could have aborted the battle until the weather improved, or he could have tried to take charge of the battle. Instead, the orders he issued compounded the problems of the Carrancista side; for example, he sent into battle tired units not ready for combat. Ramos Arizpe turned out to be the most confused battle of the Mexican Revolution, and many of its aspects remain unclear to this day. The Carrancistas were successfully pushing the Villistas back to Saltillo when suddenly one Carrancista unit in the center withdrew. The unexplained gap in the line plunged the Carrancistas into panic, and in the headlong flight they carelessly abandoned many trainloads of weapons, munitions, and supplies. The utterly demoralized Carrancistas were in no condition to defend Monterrey, and on 14 January 1915 they evacuated the city. The next day General Ángeles entered the city, and Villa himself came a few weeks later to celebrate the triumph.[37]

The Villista victory at Ramos Arizpe had been more apparent than real. Huge as had been the losses in material and weapons, Carranza still had the resources to purchase replacements abroad. Most of the Carrancista soldiers had escaped, and although General Villarreal never recovered from the defeat, General Maclovio Herrera worked hard to restore the morale of those units under his command. The very brave General Herrera was famous for his inspiring leadership and was fast rebuilding the army. As for Monterrey itself, the capture of the industrial capital of Mexico should have been a major coup for Villa. The enthusiastic support of Monterrey for Villa could have gone far to offset the superiority of Carranza in resources. However, even before his entry, most inhabitants had major reservations about Villa. By his precipitate and typically harsh actions, Villa lived up to the worst fears of the city residents. He duly antagonized all segments of the population, and not just by his forced contributions. A cowboy-bandit figure from the previous century could not evoke any sympathy in a city fast striving to catch up with the industrial United States. Villa's actions created many bitter opponents who avidly supported the return of Carrancista rule.[38]

Until January 1915, the Carrancistas had been on the run: Besides suffering defeats, desertions had weakened their army, and many units had defected. In spite of these apparently fatal setbacks, Villa failed to strike mortal blows against the Carrancistas. Even as Ángeles was winning victories for Villa in the north, an almost unperceived revival of the Carrancistas was underway. On 20 December 1914, General Pablo González, who appeared to have vanished in the mountains northeast of Pachuca, surfaced with his army near Tampico. In an almost epic march through some of the harshest terrain in Mexico, three thousand men had survived the ordeal and the desertions. The men and the horses were so haggard, that to hasten their recovery General González distributed them among neighboring haciendas for food and fodder. Unfamiliar with the terrain, one unit of 500 soldiers lost its way and went west 11 kilometers too far only to hear the sound of gunfire at dawn on 23 December. Upon learning that the Villistas (under the Cedillo brothers) were attacking Ébano, the unit commander rushed his troops to reinforce the defenders who were preparing to evacuate. Because Ébano was the last barrier before Tampico, the chance arrival of this unit saved this city. On 26 December the Villistas abandoned the attack on Ébano and withdrew back to San Luis Potosí. Given the modest size of the forces on both sides, the encounter passed largely unnoticed and at first glance seemed unimportant.[39] In reality, Ébano was indispensable for the Carrancistas. Veracruz, Yucatan, and Tampico formed the essential tripod of revenue sources; to have a chance at defeating Villa, Carranza could not lose any of the three legs.

Ébano blocked the invasion path to Tampico from San Luis Potosí, and in response Villa, as part of this three-fold offensive, had decided to try a different invasion route. He sent 5000 men to capture Ciudad Victoria and thus open the northwestern avenue into Tampico. Although he had assigned 5000 men to this expedition, only 2000 arrived to face 1500 Carrancista defenders. After trying to capture the city for two days, the Villistas withdrew on 7 January 1915. The strong Carrancista resistance not only had saved Ciudad Victoria, but also kept blocked this other invasion route to Tampico. Just like the defense of Ébano on

23 December, this small Carrancista success at Ciudad Victoria on 7 January passed largely unnoticed. Indeed, the Villista capture of Monterrey on 15 January appeared to have overshadowed the modest Carrancista successes. The large army of Ángeles was sure to resume the offensive against Ciudad Victoria soon and thus fall on the unprotected northern flank of Tampico.[40]

General González did not want to wait helplessly for the Villista attack to come. The Villista General Chao had still not arrived with his expedition to attack Ébano, thus giving González enough time to carry out a counterstroke. After González had verified that no large Villista advance from San Luis Potosí was imminent, he decided with the approval of Carranza to transfer most of his army north to launch a preemptive strike. By a swift and unexpected movement, González hoped to recapture Monterrey and then Saltillo, thereby safeguarding Ciudad Victoria. In a surprise attack on 6 February, his troops seized strategic positions within Monterrey and were on the point of driving out the Villista garrison. As soon as General Ángeles heard of the attack, he rushed troops by train from Saltillo. After the arrival of the reinforcements on 7 February, González, who had not taken the precaution of blockading the railroad track, withdrew his troops from the city.[41] Although the Villistas had saved the city, the attack had fooled General Ángeles into believing that the Carrancistas were preparing a major offensive against him, and he requested reinforcements from Villa.

The changed circumstances persuaded Villa to revise his original plan. He demanded that General Chao begin his advance from San Luis Potosí to Tampico, and by the last days of February the Villistas succeeded in slowly driving the Carrancistas back to their defenses at Ébano. The failure of General Chao to advance promptly against Tampico in January left González free to attack Monterrey in early February, but Villa realized that correcting just this flaw no longer sufficed to drive the Carrancistas from Tampico. The request of Ángeles for reinforcements found Villa short of coal for his locomotives, and Villa seized the opportunity to solve two problems at once. He conceived another three-pronged offensive. A first column was to turn north to secure the coal fields between Saltillo and the U.S. border. A second

column was to march southeast from Monterrey to capture Ciudad Victoria, while the last column had the task of capturing Matamoros on the U.S. border. The last two Villista columns would then converge on Tampico to link up with General Chao who was pounding away at Ébano. The imaginative plan violated the principle of concentration of forces: One large united force could overcome any Carrancista resistance, but three columns risked destruction in a piecemeal fashion. Furthermore, the plan aimed more at capturing real estate than destroying the Carrancista forces. What Ángeles wanted to do was destroy the demoralized forces of González before they could recover, but Villa's rigid plan precluded any aggressive pursuit.[42]

The only chance for success with the revised plan was to launch the three attacks simultaneously, but initially the Villistas were only able to mount the campaign to secure the coal fields. The Villistas turned north from Saltillo and soon ran into very strong Carrancista resistance; the campaign to take the mines and key towns in the coal district dragged on. The Villistas could consider the region partially secured only when the Carrancistas abandoned Piedras Negras on the U.S. border on 9 March.[43] Because the population was generally hostile to the Villistas, Ángeles had to place large garrisons in the towns and cities to prevent Carrancista uprisings. In a curious parallel, the Carrancista control in the countryside resembled the similar situation during the campaign against Huerta in 1913–1914. Ángeles was stretched thin, and the incessant Carrancista raids delayed Villa's plan to send columns against Matamoros and Ciudad Victoria. For Villa, northeast Mexico, rather than a source of revenue and supporters, had proved a drain on his resources.[44] To offset his high costs in Monterrey and Saltillo, he needed to make smashing gains elsewhere.

The setbacks in northeast Mexico were just the beginning of Villa's problems. In Guadalajara the Villistas experienced their first major defeats; to Villa's surprise, the Carrancista Francisco Murguía, who had been given up as lost like General González, also reappeared with his army in early January. As will be recalled, he had left Toluca on 24 November 1914 to begin a harrowing march plagued with many defections and fierce engagements. He eventually reached the state of Jalisco and joined with General Manuel Diéguez on 6 January 1915. Their combined forces were large enough to carry out offensive operations, and after defeating Villistas in several engagements, Diéguez and Murguía entered Guadalajara in time for supper on 18 January.[45] This victory could not have come at a better moment for the despondent Carrancistas, who realized they could defeat and rout the supposedly invincible Villistas. Equally remarkable was the successful partnership between Generals Diéguez and Murguía; of roughly equal rank and enjoying the personal loyalty of their own units, the initial tension promised bitter quarrels. Perhaps because the overwhelming odds they faced brought them together, the two men patched up their differences and worked effectively as partners. In harmony with each other, rather than as a divided command, the two minds functioned as one. In contrast to the more frequent personality quarrels in the revolutionary armies, the partnership between equals Diéguez and Murguía stood out as an extremely rare case of effective cooperation, almost as the exception that proves the rule.

The loss of Guadalajara deeply angered Villa, but in the long run the failure of the Zapatista alliance was an even more serious blow to his cause. Villa had wanted Zapata to make a determined push towards Veracruz or at the very least to keep the Carrancistas out of the Valley of Mexico. When on 5 January 1915 Obregón easily overcame the weak Zapatista resistance and recaptured Puebla, Villa began to realize that Zapata was not going to make any major effort outside his home state of Morelos. Villa continued to request the full-hearted cooperation of Zapata for years to come, but usually the Zapatistas hesitated to wander too far or to stay away very long from their home state.

Obregón's capture of Puebla brought his army within striking distance of the Valley of Mexico, and he diligently sent patrols and spies to report on the Villistas. Meanwhile the Convention of Aguascalientes had shifted locale several times and rather than a check on Villa had become his pliant tool. Villa no longer felt the need to hide his violent temper, and his savage outbursts antagonized many officers. Many generals were looking for an excuse to

General Pablo González. Although not so brilliant as other famous generals of the Mexican Revolution, he always displayed a tremendous ability to rally his men even in very adverse situations (Library of Congress, Prints and Photographs Division).

return to the Carrancista camp, and the advance of Obregón into Puebla provided the cue. In November 1914 the defections had hit hard the Carrancistas; now in January 1915 it was the turn for the Villistas to see their ranks thinned; around 10,000 soldiers bolted to join the Carrancistas. These January defections marked the end of the stage of massive shifts. Although lower-ranking officers still managed to switch sides in the coming months, the generals had already made their personal commitment for the rest of the civil war.[46]

Obregón, who had carefully fostered the defections, cautiously pressed forward into central Mexico. As he marched through one town after another seeking battle, he realized that the Villistas were disappearing upon the approach of his army. The Villista defections had left such a large gap that Villa feared his garrison at Mexico City might be cut off and ordered its withdrawal. By the last week of January, Obregón learned that only the Zapatistas maintained a weak hold on the capital; they too retreated south when on 28 January Obregón entered Mexico City. Obregón was pleased with the return to Mexico City, but Carranza saw the occupation more as a symbolic gesture to let the world know that the Carrancistas were still major players. The defections from Villa had made possible the occupation of Mexico City, but Carranza realized better than Obregón that the capital from a military perspective was more a burden than a benefit. Carranza made no move to return to Mexico City; indeed, he ordered Obregón to complete the evacuation left unfinished by the hurried departure in the previous November. Troops dismantled the machinery of the cartridge and powder factories for shipment to Veracruz, while others scavenged the city for anything else of military value. For example, the troops recovered the plates for printing paper money that they had inadvertently left behind in November. The allure of Mexico City soon wore out. The Zapatistas had willingly abandoned the city, but to the south in San Ángel and Xochimilco, they maintained a steady pressure. Almost incessant clashes against the Zapatistas consumed over 40,000 cartridges each day and required 5,000 soldiers to defend the city from the Zapatistas, who constantly disrupted the supply of food and necessities. The urban residents complained about the shortages, and the mounting difficulties confirmed Carranza in his initial belief that the occupation of Mexico City could be only a brief affair. Pachuca, the vital rail link with Veracruz, had a greater military significance than the capital. Carranza pressured a hesitant Obregón to capture Pachuca on 10 February, thus setting the foundation for the start of the first Carrancista offensive in central Mexico.[47] Up to this moment, the Carrancistas had fought the Villistas in more distant fronts, and combat in central Mexico had not risen above skirmishing.

Carranza in particular wanted Obregón to engage the Villista army in central Mexico, but outside events forced a change in plans. Villa himself proved uncooperative. Rather than rushing south with reinforcements to recapture Mexico City, he instead headed west to Guadalajara to repair the tarnished image of his army. Unless Obregón went out of his way to attack the Villista rear, Villa preferred to save

him for later, precisely because the lack of combat in central Mexico had eliminated the need to redeem any sullied reputation. Carranza had been prodding a reluctant Obregón to attack Villa, but the outbreak of a rebellion at Yucatan on 9 February forced an immediate change of plans. Because of its henequén exports, Yucatan was one of the three indispensable sources of revenue for Carranza. The loss of Yucatan meant inadequate funds to purchase ammunition abroad and virtually guaranteed a Villista victory. Yucatan had been in turmoil since early January, but as long as the revenue flowed smoothly to Veracruz, Carranza relied solely on political channels to restore order. When on 9 February Yucatan virtually proclaimed its independence, Carranza knew any delay in responding was fatal to his cause. Much to his regret, he halted the advance of Obregón and even recalled the troops under Salvador Alvarado for the Yucatan expedition. Removing Alvarado brought the added benefit of eliminating the latent tension between these two generals.[48]

The departure of the troops left Obregón desperately short of soldiers. Volunteers and captured prisoners had traditionally provided enough recruits for the Carrancistas, but the sudden departure of Alvarado's army called for extraordinary measures to fill the gap. Where could Carranza find additional volunteers? Nobody wanted to return to the press gang of Victoriano Huerta. Fortunately, an innovative agreement Carranza signed with the labor unions on 17 February eased the shortage. In a memorable coup, Carranza obtained volunteer recruits from the labor unions in exchange for support against business. Known as "Red Battalions," they partially offset the overwhelming numerical superiority Villa enjoyed.[49]

Against the backdrop of the Red Battalions feverishly organizing in many cities, General Alvarado set out on 19 February for Campeche aboard the ships of the Mexican Navy. His original destination had been Mérida, the capital of the state of Yucatan, but he had to change course and sail for Campeche, because the rebels had invaded that neighboring state in an attempt to carve out a greater Yucatan. After landing in Campeche, his army easily put to flight a small rebel force on 14 March. The main rebel force was further north in Yucatan, and General Alvarado marched into the state. On the morning of 16 March he learned that the rebels were digging in at Halachó, and he decided to attack immediately before they had a chance to complete their defenses. His veteran troops were up against a hastily organized rebel force. The local volunteers included students from wealthy families of Mérida who dreamed of acquiring glory and fame in their first battle. Alvarado divided his force into three columns, and at 1100 the columns on the left and the center began the attack; soon the battle degenerated into an intense exchange of fire, with the Carrancistas slowly capturing advance positions. At 1500 Alvarado saw that the column on the left had penetrated farther than the others, and he then ordered a simultaneous assault on all fronts. In twenty minutes the defenses collapsed, and the Yucatecans fled in panic.

Normally this would have been the end of the battle, but at least two hundred mostly student volunteers barricaded themselves in a row of houses and poured a few volleys into the advancing Carrancistas rather than using the houses as cover for a safe retreat. The Carrancistas in their haste to celebrate the victory had let their guard down and suffered needless casualties. The volunteers were totally unaware of the routine practice in the Mexican Revolution of fleeing rapidly after a battle was lost in order to escape execution after capture. The encircled students surrendered after their ammunition ran out only to face the soldiers' wrath. The Carrancistas promptly lined up and began executing the prisoners, but when the officers saw that most of the prisoners were white, the officers tried in vain to stop the executions, so determined were the soldiers to avenge the lives of their fallen friends. Only the timely arrival of General Alvarado in person as a savior finally spared the lives of the volunteers from the soldiers' vengeance: Alvarado magnanimously returned the sons, fathers, and husbands to their homes. The tremendous goodwill he gained served him well during his long and very successful governorship in Yucatan as the proconsul of Carranza.[50]

The smashing victory of Alvarado had ended any hopes for Yucatan's independence and guaranteed the steady flow of henequén revenue to Carranza. Meanwhile the cost of maintaining large armies had mushroomed to the point that Carranza could not import am-

munition fast enough to supply the frontline troops. Ammunition shipments arrived just in time to prevent a retreat by Obregón, but the amounts were insufficient to launch an offensive. The ammunition shortage was worst in Jalisco, where Generals Diéguez and Murguía faced the impending Villista avalanche. At all costs Villa was determined to recapture Guadalajara and to redeem the reputation of his forces. Carranza had ordered Diéguez and Murguía to abandon Guadalajara rather than lose their army in an unequal contest with Villa. With little ammunition, they had no intention of holding Guadalajara anyway, which they abandoned on 12 February.[51]

Villa was pleased with the swift recapture of Guadalajara, but in a primeval belief, he felt that not until blood was shed could he restore his army's honor. Murguía and Diéguez were fast retreating into the mountains, but the Villistas insisted on pursuing closely. A huge Villista force caught up with the Carrancistas the night of 17 February at Cuesta de Sayula and prepared to attack the next day. Diéguez and Murguía were loading their equipment and artillery aboard trains in the rear and needed to fight a delaying action long enough to complete their withdrawal on 18 February. The crest they had selected offered an impregnable position, and had the defenders enjoyed ample ammunition, Cuesta de Sayula would have turned out no differently than the latter battles of Celaya. To make their ammunition last, the defenders held their fire until the Villista cavalry was within close range. Their volleys stopped the initial cavalry charges, but once the defenders were down to five cartridges per soldier, the Carrancistas abandoned their positions. Bottlenecks in the canyons detained the withdrawing troops, giving Villa time to send his cavalry crashing into the immobilized and helpless infantry. For unexplained reasons Villa did not follow up his victory, and gradually the Carrancista infantry made its escape by clambering up the departing trains or scurrying up the mountains. Thus, although defeated, the army of Diéguez and Murguía escaped almost intact. Exhausted and without ammunition, the main task of the soldiers was to protect their weapons. Yet it remained a potential army, and if Mauser cartridges arrived, the generals could count on their hardened troops to resume the offensive. Villa savored his last major victory and the last time a cavalry charge won a battle. Even more dangerously, Villa exaggerated the magnitude of his victory and really believed that he had inflicted a devastating blow on the Carrancistas.[52]

Villa could still have pursued the Carrancistas to the Pacific Coast and forced them to scatter, but rather than trying to gain full control of the state of Jalisco, he opted for a different strategy. As March began, Villa faced the Carrancistas in Monterrey and Obregón in central Mexico. Villa held Obregón in great contempt and did not regard him as a serious threat. However, in case the Zapatistas failed to cut off the supply lines of Obregón to Veracruz, Villa felt that the capture of Tampico sufficed to cripple the Carrancistas. Without the petroleum wealth, Carranza could no longer afford to buy ammunition for his army. On 10 March Villa devised still another plan for three simultaneous advances on Tampico. He sent his main force to Ébano, but to prevent the Carrancistas from shifting units from the north to defend that key bastion, he dispatched two other expeditions against Ciudad Victoria and Matamoros. The capture of any of these last two cities also opened up additional routes for the final assault on Tampico.[53]

The key to Tampico was Ébano, a railroad station 56 kilometers to the west of Tampico on the rail line to San Luis Potosí. Two rustic soldiers had on their own discovered the immense strategic value of this elevation. Through the rugged terrain in this region, passage was possible only through a narrow area of five and a half kilometers; the flanks rested on a mixture of rivers, swamps, and dense forests. The Villistas, in their renewed drive to Tampico, had already pushed the Carrancistas away from their advance positions into Ébano. General Jacinto Treviño arrived to take command of the defense; although General González sometimes came to supervise the operations, General Treviño remained the local commander. The soldiers hurriedly rebuilt the crude trenches of December 23 and spread out barbed wire to detain the Villista cavalry. Carrancista engineers and artillerymen had carefully surveyed the entire area and plotted on their maps the coordinates for all the likely Villista emplacements. These coordinates turned out to be extremely useful for the Carrancistas, who had managed to bring to the front only one 80 mm.

cannon when the first Villista attack began on 21 March.

Treviño did have an adequate number of machine guns, so when General Chao launched his cavalry to the attack at 0600, a murderous slaughter ensued. Without any prior reconnaissance or observation, Chao had expected his cavalry to overwhelm the Carrancistas. At least 600 Villistas died in the initial charges. Stunned by the repulse, Chao at last had his artillery open fire on Carrancistas, but it was too late to save the day. The resourceful Treviño pushed two rail cars full of machine guns and soldiers down the tracks, a surprise maneuver that finished destroying the will of the Villistas to attack. By 1800 the shooting died down, and at 2000 the arrival of the first of many artillery batteries from Tampico ended the one advantage the Villistas had enjoyed.[54]

The following days witnessed considerable skirmishing, and Treviño put his men to deepen the trenches and to construct a network of bunkers and tunnels immune to artillery shelling. While the men fought at the trenches, the women prepared food, healed minor wounds, and mended the clothing of the men in the underground bunkers where they all slept. Malaria initially threatened to wipe out the defenders, had not the medical service performed wonders to keep the soldiers healthy for the battle. While the Carrancistas duplicated the trench warfare then raging in the Western Front of World War I, the Villistas failed to discover the reasons for their initial setback. Villa correctly realized that he had hit a raw nerve the Carrancistas were determined to fight for, but in keeping with the cowboy tradition, Villa attributed the defeat to poor leadership and insufficient courage among the troops.[55]

He put his most sanguinary general, Tomás Urbina, in charge of the offensive against Tampico and gave him additional units. Word of the slaughter at Ébano had already reached the Villista rear and made recruiting impossible. To refill the units, Urbina became the first Villista to use the hated press gang to obtain enough men, a practice more typical of the vanquished Victoriano Huerta. At 0400 on 2 April, an artillery barrage signaled the imminent start of the attack, but the strong response of the Carrancista artillery promised a tough fight. At daybreak the cavalry charged in waves towards the silent Carrancista trenches; Treviño had ordered his men to hold their fire until the horses reached the barbed wire. At the same moment the simultaneous fire of the rifles and the machine guns stopped the attack in its tracks. Urbina hurled four more cavalry charges, but with the same disastrous results. The defenders, restless in their trenches, jumped out and attacked the Villistas; in some cases even bitter hand-to-hand combat ensued. By 1900 when the shooting had stopped, the magnitude of the Villista disaster was clear.

In subsequent days and weeks Urbina tried everything possible to overcome the defenses at Ébano. Night attacks fared no better, because cleverly hidden search lights illuminated the field of fire for the Carrancista machine guns. Attempts to outflank the defenders by crossing the swamps and rivers ended in total failure. Carranza kept the defenders well supplied and sent one of the Red Battalions as reinforcements. The arrival of a Carrancista flotilla of planes to bomb and reconnoiter ended any chance of a surprise Villista move. The drive on Tampico had not only failed miserably, but Villa had sacrificed thousands of troops and considerable prestige on his failed attempt to capture Ébano.[56] In spite of the huge Villista losses, the siege of Ébano had worried Carranza immensely; since February he had realized that the loss of Tampico was worse than the loss of an entire army. Carranza rushed troops and weapons, but no matter how much he sent to Ébano, he never could feel secure as long as Villa continued to pound at the gates of Tampico.

The determined resistance at Ébano shifted the burden of capturing Tampico to the two other Villista columns advancing in the north. The column heading for Matamoros aimed to deprive Carranza of his last effective land link with the United States and to open the door for a southward thrust along the Gulf of Mexico to Tampico. Late in March a large Villista force set out from Monterrey to drive out the Carrancistas from Matamoros. The Villistas were sure of an easy victory, not just because the garrison numbered only 307 soldiers, but also because they expected the Carrancistas to defect. The Villistas did not know that the garrison commander, General Emiliano Nafarrate, was busily making preparations for the defense of the city. He constructed canals

linking the irrigation ditches with the Rio Grande and installed sluice gates to hold back the river waters. He camouflaged the deployment of 16 machine guns he had received from the United States. Although he had also received four million cartridges, he ordered his men not to begin the usual premature shooting at long range and instead to hold their fire until the Villistas were within a range of 200 meters. On 27 March the Villista cavalry confidently approached down the road from Monterrey only to fall into a well-prepared trap. The twelve machine guns pointing in that direction mowed down the cavalry so fast that it seemed that the horsemen were jumping down one at time to take cover in the ground when in reality they were already dead. The stunned attackers withdrew and settled down to a siege of Matamoros. The besieged were really the Villistas, because marauding bands constantly harassed their rear. On 12 April three hundred Carrancistas broke through the Villista lines and entered the city to reinforce the garrison. Seeing the Villistas flagging, Nafarrate concluded the moment had come to launch a counterattack. On the morning of 13 April the defenders jumped from their trenches to attack the besiegers who, startled, began to retreat. At that moment Nafarrate opened the sluice gates and flooded the escape routes of the Villistas. Those who escaped did so by wading out with water up to their necks, only to find the marauding bands waiting to finish them off. Even their commander perished, and few survivors straggled back to Monterrey.[57]

The Villista disaster at Matamoros left all hopes riding on the offensive against Ciudad Victoria, the last possible route to Tampico. On 10 March Villa sent a large force south to attack Ciudad Victoria, but the expedition began inauspiciously as the Villistas had to fight their way out of Monterrey, by then practically a besieged city. Under constant attack the expedition slowly fought its way south. The Carrancista garrison of 400 men felt too weak to hold Ciudad Victoria and instead took up positions to the north along the road to try to ambush the approaching Villistas on 15 April. The Villistas foiled the attempt and entered Ciudad Victoria on 16 April. Supposedly the road to Tampico was open, but in reality marauding bands kept the Villistas trapped in the city. The pattern of the Villistas garrisoning cities and the Carrancistas controlling the countryside repeated itself. Any talk of an advance against Tampico vanished, as the Villista garrison in Ciudad Victoria just struggled to survive.[58]

From Piedras Negras to Ciudad Victoria, the Villistas faced unrelenting opposition. The failure of Villa to attract this region to his cause was a major factor in his downfall. Only in the revolt against Victoriano Huerta did the inhabitants of that region demonstrate a similar passion and determination. But except for those two major cases, the region generally remained peaceful. Not even the revolt against Porfirio Díaz had aroused comparable hostility. States in nearly constant rebellion like Chihuahua and Morelos are only part of the answer to explain the Revolution; the behavior of this region bordering Texas makes for a more accurate predictor of the ultimate winners.

The triple setbacks at Ébano, Matamoros, and Ciudad Victoria had shattered Villa's original plan. Although Urbina continued hurling men to their deaths against the trenches of Ébano until late May, Villa sensed that he was losing the initiative. The northeast had proved so inhospitable that Villa could not imagine pouring more troops down that bottomless theater of operations. He knew he had to do something fast before the Carrancistas regained the initiative, but he was not sure what exactly to do. On 12 March Villa was gathering forces in Querétaro, apparently for an attack on Obregón's army, but again he succumbed to his nasty habit of letting matters drift. By the time he finally made up his mind, it was too late to do anything but respond to the Carrancista thrusts.[59]

Quite unexpectedly for Villa, the challenge came not from Obregón, but from Diéguez and Murguía. Villa had fooled himself into believing that Cuesta de Sayula had annihilated the Carrancistas, and he dismissed reports that they were regrouping. As soon as Carranza managed to send cartridges via the Tehuantepec Railroad and by the gunboat *Guerrero* to Diéguez and Murguía, they reconstituted their scattered forces into a fighting army. The generals resumed the offensive, and at the battle of Tuxpan on 26 March they decisively defeated the Villistas, who lost most of their equipment and ammunition. As the defeated Villistas fled south to Michoacán, the

Carrancistas reestablished control over southern Jalisco. On 1 April Diéguez and Murguía were back in Cuesta de Sayula for another clash, but this time they were the victors. Then the two generals began preparations for a final push on Guadalajara. Villa exploded with rage when he heard about the defeats in Jalisco. He promptly sent 6,000 men to contain the damage until he himself came with a much larger force. Villa's swift response arose out of his complex frontier code of honor: He considered Diéguez a nobody, a person unworthy to be an opponent. Underestimating an opponent is always dangerous, and Villa did not want to recognize that Diéguez and Murguía had successfully rallied their soldiers. Instead the troops Villa sent to Guadalajara were demoralized and short of ammunition. Diéguez and Murguía had initially wanted to attack, even though their troops had the bare minimum of 120 cartridges per soldier. Upon reflection the two generals decided not to risk everything on one battle and preferred to wait until Carranza dispatched more ammunition.[60]

Given the high spirits of their men, if Diéguez and Murguía had pressed on, they probably would have defeated the Villistas and gone on to capture Guadalajara. But the lost opportunity did not really matter, because they had already performed the much more valuable task of diverting Villista units away from Obregón, who since February was under heavy pressure from Carranza to march north against San Luis Potosí. By this maneuver a deeply worried Carranza hoped to halt the incessant attacks on Ébano, his vital lifeline. Even if Obregón did not march north, Carranza wanted to prevent the easy transfer of Villa's forces from one front to another. Carranza's fears were largely unfounded, because Villa in over three months of shifting his forces around had only worn them out and had not accomplished anything decisive. Instead, hurling Obregón's force at the considerable larger army of Villa was extremely dangerous and risked a disastrous defeat. Carranza, who up to this moment had displayed an uncanny strategic grasp, for the first time faltered. Instead, Obregón accurately realized his vulnerability and moved forward slowly; only on 4 April did his army enter Celaya after having driven out Villista patrols. Obregón then entrenched his army at the rail junction of Celaya and waited for Villa's next move. To keep Carranza off his back, Obregón justified his defensive posture on the valid explanation that he could not advance because Zapatista raids threatened his supply line to Veracruz.[61]

General Ángeles had urged Villa to ignore the advance of Obregón and instead to finish the campaign in the northeast. Villa disagreed, and by early April he had brought over 32,000 men south to his base at Irapuato. He now faced two choices: Either he sent all the men to Jalisco or he hurled them against Obregón at Celaya. In a violation of the principles of war, he split his force into two: a larger one of 20,000 men and a smaller one of 12,000 men. The smaller force was more than adequate to recapture Jalisco, but in an indication of his priorities, he sent the larger force to Jalisco. He even had intended to lead the Jalisco campaign himself, and only at the last minute did he change his mind and decide to command the attack on Celaya before returning to head the campaign in Jalisco.[62]

One strategic blunder after another augured badly for Villa as he drove to meet his destiny at Celaya. But his good luck held up one last time at the start of the first battle of Celaya. Obregón had placed 1500 soldiers under the command of General Fortunato Maycotte west of Celaya and had left strict orders to withdraw if any large Villista force appeared. Early in the morning of 6 April, when the Villista cavalry crashed into the Carrancista advance guard, Maycotte was away momentarily at Celaya, and his subordinates did not promptly withdraw. The Villista cavalry surrounded Maycotte's unit so fast that only the cavalry escaped. To retrieve the infantry, Obregón rushed with 1500 soldiers to the front; he had his train blow the horn repeatedly to attract the Villistas, who turned to attack Obregón and left a gap in the line wide enough for the trapped infantry to escape. By 1600 the troops and the train had completed the retreat; shortly after Villa launched his first cavalry attacks against Celaya, while during the night the Villista infantry surrounded the town and kept up a steady volume of fire. Many officers strongly urged Obregón to withdraw, because they felt their force was too small to withstand the dreaded cavalry charges. Obregón explained that precisely because the cavalry of Villa was so strong, the infantry stood no

chance out in the open field, and that their only chance of survival lay behind their trenches and their machine guns.

Villa confidently expected on 7 April to encircle Obregón's force in the same manner he had encircled the advance guard the previous day. Had Villa come with all his 32,000 men and not just 12,000, his maneuver would have succeeded, because the Carrancistas barely had enough ammunition to stop the smaller force. When he renewed his cavalry charges early in the morning of 7 April, the many cadavers and dead horses strewn in the field from the previous night slowed down the advance and turned his men into great targets for Obregón's gunners. The relentless fire from the trenches and the outrageous consumption of ammunition stopped all the cavalry charges, but at the cost of depleting the supply of cartridges of the defenders. After 0900 Obregón and his staff went to inspect the defense line where the fighting seemed most intense, only to discover that four battalions were withdrawing into the town in panic because they had run out of ammunition. Obregón promptly gave orders to bring ammunition from the last reserves of his army and for another battalion from a quiet part of the front to man the abandoned trenches temporarily. With the Villistas preparing to attack, Obregón lacked the time to rally the retreating battalions, and instead, he summoned a trumpeter (actually a 10-year old boy) to play a victory tune. The Villistas, already reluctant to make further suicidal charges, only needed the excuse of hearing the victory tune of the trumpeter to abandon their attack.

The arrival of ammunition restored the morale of the battalions who returned to their trenches and kept up a steady fire. But the reserves of cartridges were running out, and Obregón, sensing that the Villistas were staggering, decided to end the battle by a daring maneuver. At 1310 Obregón sent his cavalry in a movement around the left and the right flanks of the Villistas. The cavalry attack triggered a rapid withdrawal of the Villistas back to Irapuato, and at times the retreat turned into a rout. Most Villistas escaped aboard departing trains and rescued their artillery but not without leaving at least 2,000 dead and countless wounded behind. The Villista casualties were considerably larger than the 600 dead of Obregón's army. More significant was the loss of many officers who had recklessly led the assaults on the machine guns; Villa could never find equally spirited and loyal replacements. Nevertheless, the Carrancistas, in spite of having won a clear victory, were so low on ammunition that Obregón during the coming days was seriously considering a withdrawal, an action that would have diminished the impact of the victory. Only with the arrival on 12 April of ammunition in what was dubbed "The Victory Train" was Obregón in any condition to face Villa again in battle.[63]

Carranza believed that the ammunition made possible an immediate offensive by Obregón's army. Carranza was so certain about the capture of Aguascalientes, that he even suggested to Obregón the next possible objectives after the occupation of that city. By this moment Obregón's strategic grasp surpassed that of Carranza, and the general rightfully dismissed any attack as wishful thinking. Obregón was not going to underestimate the Villista strength, and he knew that until Diéguez and Murguía could link up with him, the Carrancistas simply lacked the manpower to attack Villa. More disturbing was the prospect of stalemate, a very likely outcome unless Villa committed a horrible blunder. Obregón concluded that the best strategy was to fortify himself in Celaya and to await what he considered the inevitable attack. Obregón knew his opponent very well and expected a furious Villa to insist on revenge.[64]

Villa stopped dispatching units to Jalisco, but he did not recall the troops he had already sent to defend Guadalajara from the coming Carrancista offensive. Still, the 30,000 men Villa gathered at Irapuato were more than what he had at the first battle of Celaya and should have assured his victory. Unfortunately for Villa, Obregón also had a larger army. The arrival of reinforcements, including the Red Battalions, had increased the Carrancista army to 15,000 men, much more than for the first battle of Celaya. From outward appearances, however, the Carrancista army did not seem much larger, because as part of his preparations for a master stroke, Obregón kept only 9,000 men inside the trenches of Celaya. The other 6,000 mounted soldiers he kept about 7 kilometers away hidden in a dense forest. Obregón had studied the first battle of Celaya carefully and

had concluded correctly that he had failed to strike a decisive blow because he had not cut off the retreating Villistas. He was determined to prevent a similar omission in any rematch.

Instead, Villa had concluded that all he needed to win was more cavalry; Obregón's assessment that he faced a brutish and crude opponent seemed borne out. At 0600 on 13 April huge clouds of dust revealed the approach of Villa's columns across the dry terrain; the infantry came aboard trains, while the dismounted cavalry and the artillery advanced forward in columns. Not until 1600 did the first Villista units reach the Carrancista trenches; obviously this very visible approach eliminated any chance of surprise. Indeed, the Villistas had wanted to display rather than hide their advance to overawe the defenders. At 1800 rifle and cannon fire broke out throughout the line, while the Villistas raced to surround Celaya. The front stretched for 12 kilometers, but curiously enough, the Villistas did not surround the defenders completely. In their attacks on cities, the Villistas often did not destroy either the railroad track or the telegraph line, a tactic they hoped would tempt the garrison to use the escape route to flee. During the night the Villistas established positions as close as 400 meters to the defense line and appeared to be digging trenches. This was the most dangerous time for Obregón, who knew he could not withstand a long siege of Celaya; his troops fought well as long as they had ample cartridges, but days of incessant shooting and cannonade would exhaust the supply of ammunition and melt the will of the garrison to resist.

A very impatient Villa was in no mood to wait, and he wanted his cavalry to crush Obregón quickly. Starting at daylight on the 14 April, wave after wave of cavalry crashed against the trenches of Obregón. The cannons and the machine guns wreaked havoc on the charging horsemen, and the immense slaughter indicated that the moment to counterattack was fast approaching. Late in the afternoon, Obregón sent orders to his cavalry column of 6,000 men to take up positions not far from the Villista rear starting at nightfall but to attack only at dawn the next day. On 15 April the cavalry Obregón had kept hidden struck the rear of the Villista left by surprise, and the flank collapsed at 0900. The Carrancista cavalry blocked the retreat to Irapuato and pressed the panic-stricken Villistas against the center, where Villa himself managed to reconstruct a new defense line by 1000. One hour later Obregón ordered his infantry to jump from their trenches and charge across the fields, while he sent his remaining cavalry to the rear of the by then very weak Villista right flank. The infantry running in the front and the cavalry charging in the rear caught the Villistas in crossfire. Panic seized the trapped Villistas as they realized that no escape route remained open. The desperation reach such extremes that whole units surrendered, and in this battle Villa lost all his 32 cannons. In contrast to barely 200 killed in Obregón's army, Villa had suffered casualties of over 4,000 dead and more than 6,000 prisoners, plus countless deserters and wounded. No less serious was the sacrifice of so many of his horses, which although unsuitable for charging against machine guns, were superb for irregular warfare in rough terrain.[65]

Celaya was not the only disaster to fall on Villa. The next day, on 16 April, Diéguez and Murguía defeated the Villista force in Jalisco, and on 18 April they entered Guadalajara. After leaving a garrison behind, Diéguez and Murguía set out with 11,000 soldiers to join Obregón. On 22 April the two forces linked up, and Obregón commanded an army of nearly 30,000 men.[66] By any strategic estimate, Villa had lost central Mexico, and a concentration of his remaining forces in his home grounds seemed the best option. Ángeles, the former federal who was Villa's best general, recommended a withdrawal at least to Zacatecas and preferably to Torreón. Each kilometer Villa retreated to the north shortened his supply lines and extended those of the Carrancistas. With his remaining cavalry he could raid the rear of the Carrancistas and disrupt their lines of supply. A stalemate likely would ensue, and at some moment proposals for a negotiated settlement were sure to arise on the condition that Villa remained the warlord of Chihuahua.

Strategically valid, the argument of Ángeles overlooked the political implications for Villa. A withdrawal to Torreón besides being a public confession of his weakness also left a vacuum for the Carrancistas to fill at their leisure. If his status dropped to that of a regional rebel, he knew he could no longer prevent the revival of the central government.

Villa astutely sensed that if he remained in central Mexico, he retained a much stronger bargaining position to obtain his recognition as warlord of Chihuahua. He refused to retreat to the north, and more than his usual obstinacy was at play. The strong centralizing tendencies under Porfirio Díaz were too recent for Villa to forget, and he more clearly than others understood that inevitably Mexico City would try to reestablish control over distant provinces. If he quietly retreated to Chihuahua, he merely postponed the inevitable reckoning. The longer he remained in central Mexico, the more he weakened the Carrancistas and the more he improved his chances to rally allies to try to stop the revival of the central government.[67] Thus, political-economic calculations rather than narrow military considerations shaped the next phase of his campaign.

The Campaign in Central Mexico

After the second battle of Celaya, General Álvaro Obregón seemed well poised to pursue the demoralized Villistas. With the arrival of Generals Francisco Murguía and Manuel Diéguez from Guadalajara, Obregón for the first time enjoyed a numerical superiority over Villa. A relentless Carrancista pursuit promised to deprive the Villistas of time to bring reinforcements from other fronts. But because the Villistas were tearing up the railroad tracks so thoroughly, only the cavalry could conduct an aggressive pursuit. Even after the staggering losses at Celaya, the Villista cavalry was vastly more numerous, so the Carrancista horsemen risked destruction if they strayed too far ahead of the infantry. The farther north the Carrancistas advanced, the longer became their supply lines from Veracruz and the closer Villa came to his home base in Chihuahua. Inevitably Villa would stand and fight at a ground of his choosing far in the north. Faced with these prospects, Obregón wisely decided to advance north at the pace that his work brigades repaired the damaged track. Because a long campaign in northern Mexico was beyond the resources of the Carrancistas, Obregón aimed to destroy Villa's army in one grand battle of annihilation.

At first the requirements for a classic battle of annihilation seemed to be falling into place. Villa converted Aguascalientes into his new home base and constructed a defense line south of the city of León.[68] The initiative did not immediately pass to Obregón because he did not know what Villa intended to do. Obregón's excellent network of spies this time failed him. As his army slowly advanced northward beyond Irapuato, the last Villista patrols vanished from view and left Obregón groping in the dark.[69] To try to locate the Villista units, Obregón sent General Maycotte north to León and another force northeast to Guanajuato. On 25 April, after having passed Silao (Map 17), Maycotte ran into a larger than usual Villista force, but he still managed to press his advance forward. As Villista resistance intensified in the following days, Obregón rode with infantry units aboard the trains to reinforce Maycotte and sent General Murguía with cavalry to make a flanking movement to the west via Romita. Obregón arrived with the trains on 29 April, just in time to extricate Maycotte who was under heavy Villista attack. Fire from cannons aboard train platforms and from rifles in the passenger wagons covered the retreat of Maycotte. Obregón's train was in danger of capture, but his troops on board repeatedly fought off Villa's cavalry until they reached safety at Silao. The flanking attack to the west had not fared better, and Murguía, after running into a larger Villista cavalry force, had to beat a disorderly retreat back to Romita on 1 May.

Intense as had been the fighting, the Villista forces were still not numerous enough to block the Carrancista advance, and Obregón concluded that the fighting had been nothing but a rear guard action. He brought up more battalions from the rear to overcome the intensifying resistance, and, after heavy fighting, his forces pushed their way to the train station of Trinidad on 7 May. Using the irrigation ditches and canals as trenches, his men formed a defensive line facing to the north. To the east and west Obregón placed other units, and he brought Diéguez forward to cover the rear with his troops. The Carrancista army thus formed a large square defended on all four sides. Lookouts detected a Villista airplane taking off, and promptly the officers selected the best Yaqui and Mayo sharpshooters to fire at the airplane. The bullets wounded the pilot and damaged

the plane extensively; for the rest of the battle Villa lacked aerial reconnaissance.

A furious Villista cavalry charge on 8 May persuaded Obregón that Villa had decided to defend León. Obregón deployed more soldiers to face León, and his line north of Trinidad came to stretch 16 kilometers. He had prepared an attack, but the failure of the ammunition train to arrive from Veracruz forced him to suspend the operation. Villa, who had been bringing supplies and troops from Aguascalientes, had regained numerical superiority and launched the first blow on 12 May. At noon Villista cavalry poured out from the dense forest and rushed to cross the two and a half kilometers separating the Villista and Carrancista lines. No surprise was possible because in the hot and dry climate the horses kicked up clouds of dust. The Carrancista cavalry pickets numbering only 125 men quickly retreated back to the main line of defense. The Dorados, the most prestigious Villista unit, led the cavalry charge. Villa had obtained a shipment of brand new Colt .45 caliber automatic pistols, and he had hoped that this new weapon in the hands of his best cavalry could crush the Carrancista center. The Dorados rode unopposed until they were within close range of the defense lines, and then the defenders opened up with their machine guns on the hapless cavalry. The concentrated fire stunned the horsemen who reeled from the losses but then resumed the charge hoping to find a weak point to make a breach in the defenses. In the few spots where the Dorados reached the trench line, they flashed their .45 pistols and shouted at the infantry to surrender, but steady fire from the Mausers soon killed the intruders. The last waves of cavalry found the machine gun fire no less withering, and the carnage was finally too much for the horsemen who broke and ran for the rear. The Villista officers fired their pistols at the retreating soldiers to force them to charge again, but nothing could stop the panicky flight of terrified men who feared their officers' pistols less than the machine guns.[70]

Obregón knew this was the moment to launch the counterattack and destroy the Villista army, but because his men had exhausted their ammunition, he could not replay the second battle of Celaya. Random fighting and lesser attacks continued during the following days, but Obregón could not undertake an

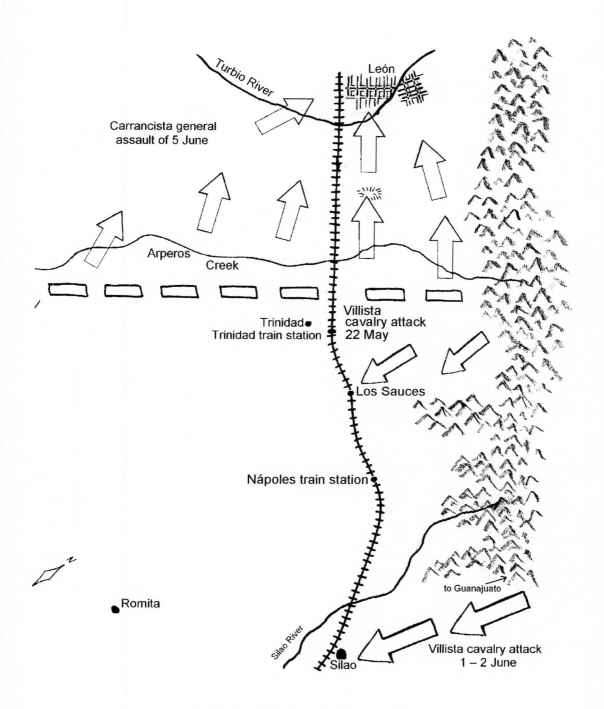

Map 17. Battle of León, 7 May–5 June 1915.

offensive until the trains carrying ammunition arrived on 20 May. By then the defense lines stretched for over 28 kilometers as the battle for León became the largest engagement of the entire Mexican Revolution. The shortage of cartridges had plagued earlier battles, but by this battle the scarcity reflected a much deeper problem that was not simply a matter of broken track or late trains. Years of warfare had so weakened the Mexican economy that it could no longer produce the resources to support large armies at an intensive level of combat. During World War I the industrialized economies generated huge volumes of supplies to keep the destructive warfare of the Western Front going for years. Mexico, in a very incipient stage of industrialization, had never been able to afford the large standing armies of Western Europe, and the widespread fighting had disrupted production throughout the country. The signs of economic exhaustion were first appearing in the battle of León; their message was that Mexico had to stop its fighting and shift its attention to the reconstruction of its shattered economy.

By his quest for a battle of annihilation Obregón was seeking to end the costly war in Mexico, but unfortunately León threatened to become a battle of attrition. Villa likewise wanted to break the stalemate, and once he received ample ammunition, he busily engaged in implementing a very complex attack plan. He first made available to Obregón's spies reports that the Villistas intended to attack Celaya and thus cut off the supply line for the Carrancista army attacking León. Obregón believed the false information and on 21 May ordered Murguía to take most of the cavalry out of the front line to begin a march back to Celaya that same day; however, Obregón did not order the cavalry to rush to its mission, and this determination not to hurry ultimately prevented a disaster. That same day early in the afternoon he began to receive reports of unusual activity in the Villista camps. After personally inspecting the front, he concluded that a large Villista attack was imminent, and he put all his troops on high alert. His anguish was real, because he did not know whether he should recall Murguía or whether the Villista activity was just a ruse to keep him from securing his supply line at Celaya. What he did not know was that a large contingent of Villista cavalry had set out secretly to make an outflanking movement around the Carrancista right flank.

The night passed quietly until at 0400 on 22 May the Villistas launched a large attack on the Carrancista left. In spite of the pitch darkness the attack did not keep Obregón from seeing clearly what was happening. He immediately transmitted orders to Murguía, who had reached only Silao, to march the cavalry back urgently to the Nápoles train station, a reverse movement that required the whole morning to complete. Obregón already suspected that the Villistas had made only a diversionary attack on his left flank, and he braced his troops for

the main attack. At 0800 the full fury of the Villista attack materialized against the Carrancista right flank. Three assault waves charged enthusiastically and were confident of victory because of several innovations. Villa had obtained hand grenades for his soldiers, who were supposed to race forward and hurl the grenades at the Carrancistas in the fox holes. In another innovation, Villa had two soldiers ride each horse, so that if one man was hit, the other could still continue the charge. Unfortunately, the infantry never had a chance to get close enough to thrown their hand grenades. Instead machine guns and Mausers feasted on slaughtering each of the assault waves whether the soldiers were mounted or on foot.

The frightful carnage had not been in vain, because the tempting targets had so captivated the Carrancista gunners that they saw only too late the Villista cavalry racing to the rear and seizing the Los Sauces train station. The cavalry Villa had sent around the night before around the Carrancista right flank had waited until the fighting in the trenches was at its most intense moment to make the fast sally to the rear. Belatedly the Carrancista artillery at Trinidad began laying barrages on the Villista cavalry, but the harsh reality was that part of the Carrancista army was surrounded and risked a destruction that could well drag down the rest of the army. All seemed lost until at 12 noon Murguía's cavalry arrived at Nápoles train station. A confident Obregón gave the order for Murguía's cavalry to charge north into the massed Villista force near Los Sauces. The heavy artillery barrages had already demoralized the Villista horsemen who still managed to resist the first charges of Murguía. But caught under intense shelling from one side and the Carrancista counterattack from the north, the Villista cavalry turned around and fled back. So terrified had the Villistas become of the Carrancista artillery that many riders stopped to surrender to the pursuing cavalry rather than continue the flight under the hail of the deadly artillery shells. The survivors returned to their usual positions, although after night fell stray Villistas were still trying to fight their way out of the Carrancista rear.[71]

The intricate offensive maneuvers had come very close to yielding a smashing victory but still could not disguise the harsh reality that the attacks of 12 and 22 May had cost Villa dearly in men and horses. Villa was losing this battle of attrition, and Obregón again had the opportunity to launch a crushing counterattack against the demoralized Villista army. The spontaneous surrender of Villista units on 23 and 24 May confirmed that the situation was ripe for a counterattack, but once again shortage of ammunition precluded any action. Not until 30 May when the Carrancistas received the most recent shipment of cartridges from Veracruz could Obregón prepare his final assault. At a meeting on 31 May he discussed with his generals the date of the operation. Murguía argued for an immediate attack, and Diéguez wanted to attack soon. Other generals were more skeptical, and Hill preferred to wait until the next train brought more ammunition. Obregón decided to wait a few more days before launching a general attack. He hoped that the impatient Villa would become weaker in another costly attack.

Merely waiting to respond to the opponent did not sit well with a restless Villa who always wanted to retain the initiative. Villa enthusiastically explained to a skeptical Felipe Ángeles a new plan to send all the cavalry in a wide flanking movement nearly as far east as Guanajuato to make a surprise attack in Obregón's rear at Silao. Meanwhile as a diversionary tactic, the Villista infantry would make modest attacks to the south against the Carrancista trenches. A month before the plan might have won victory, but after his many costly assaults had deprived him of numerical superiority, his front line was too weak to resist a counterattack from the larger Carrancista army. Initially the plan worked well, and on 1 June his cavalry completed the wide flanking movement, successfully captured Silao, and raised havoc on the Carrancista rear. Obregón calmly responded, and after some strategic withdrawals that night, he ended the threat to his rear on 2 June. The cavalry raid had caused more alarm than damage, and the weak Villista attack in his front line showed Obregón that the time had finally come to counterattack. On the morning of 3 June, as he came close to the front to make the final dispositions, an artillery shell wounded him; he survived but lost his right arm.[72]

Hill assumed command but could not master the battlefield situation, and soon a leadership vacuum emerged. The next day, Hill

proposed withdrawing to avoid being cut off by the Villista cavalry still at Silao, but Murguía violently objected. At the insistence of Murguía, the generals agreed belatedly to implement Obregón's plan for a counterattack. On 5 June the Carrancistas launched a general assault along the 28 kilometers of Villa's lightly defended line. As Obregón had predicted, the Villista line crumbled, and by noon Carrancista units were entering León. But without the master hand of Obregón to guide and adjust the movements, the results were disappointing. Villistas conducted an almost leisurely evacuation of León and withdrew with their artillery and supplies aboard the trains. The Carrancista cavalry column sent early in the morning to block the railroad line got lost, and all the Villista trains escaped safely. The next day Hill sent troops to clear the Villista cavalry from Silao and Guanajuato; the troops secured those rear areas but failed to strike any decisive blows against the cavalry, which retreated in good order. Had not Murguía partially filled the leadership vacuum, León would have been an embarrassing defeat for the Carrancistas. Such a setback would have vindicated Villa's strategy of remaining to fight in central Mexico. Villa had lost many men, but less than in Celaya, and the number of Villistas taken prisoner was also modest.[73] León, rather than the battle of annihilation Obregón had wanted, had turned out to be a Pyrrhic victory; Carranza could not afford another victory like León. The battle of León, the longest and largest of the Mexican Revolution, had merely postponed the inevitable reckoning. Once Obregón recovered from his wound, he had to find another way to destroy the Villista army before the Carrancista resources gave out.

General Ángeles counseled Villa to retreat at least to Zacatecas and preferably back to Torreón; Obregón himself had expected Villa to withdraw to Zacatecas. However, Villa did not want to retreat so far to the north and decided to make his stand at Aguascalientes, the next major city north of León. He believed that if he held that city and Zapata kept Mexico City, victory against Carranza was still possible. Another battle of attrition like León seemed to be beyond the capabilities of Villa, but undaunted, he scrambled desperately to obtain the resources. Villa engaged in massive requisitions, including the seizure of cattle for sale to the United States. He generalized the practice of kidnapping wealthy persons to extort sums of money. The funds he extracted replenished his arsenals; he hoped that new weapons and abundant ammunition would help revive his soldiers utterly demoralized by repeated defeats and retreats. He could not raise any more volunteers, and Villa had to revive the hated *leva* or press gang to fill his depleted ranks. At Aguascalientes he trained and drilled his new men, a sure sign that he had lost most of his veterans. He put his recovering army to construct a network of trenches, barbed wire, and mine fields three kilometers south of the city; he had his soldiers install the many machine guns and cannons he was bringing from the north. This strong defense line reached to the hills at both ends of the valley. Any direct attack was bound to turn into another long and inconclusive clash like the battle of León. Good luck favored Villa in his task of rebuilding his army, because the shortage of ammunition slowed down the Carrancista advance. The booty at León had been sparse, and scavenging the corpses in the battlefield had not yielded enough cartridges to refill the bandoleers of the Carrancista troops.[74] Furthermore, the long supply line to Veracruz was too exposed to attacks. To compound the Carrancista difficulties, the Zapatistas were making a tardy appearance.

After the second battle of Celaya, Emiliano Zapata finally realized he had to destroy the Carrancista supply route from Veracruz. Until then, Zapata had limited himself to skirmishing south of Mexico City, but at last in late April he sent detachments as far north as Tula and Pachuca to intercept the Carrancista trains. Had he taken this action earlier in the year, Villa would probably have emerged as the leader of Mexico. Why he did not is a fascinating question whose answer exposes the true nature of Zapata. Aware of the limited power of his small state of Morelos, Zapata knew that he could preserve his independence as a warlord only as long as Villa and Carranza were fighting each other. When Villa seemed on top in January, Zapata, by his relative inactivity, had given decisive help to Carranza by default. By late April when Villa was losing, Zapata tried to even the odds by taking the offensive against Carranza. Perpetual war and strife among warring factions were the only means Zapata conceived to preserve his personal power in Morelos. His Machiavellian policy makes him the most sinister and selfish of the revolutionary leaders.[75]

The Zapatista attacks on Obregon's supply line delayed any offensive against Villa. As long as the Zapatistas held Mexico City, they enjoyed an excellent base for their raids to the north. The Carrancistas realized that they could not advance faster to the north until they had first regained Mexico City. The elimination of the Zapatista threat and the recapture of Mexico City melded into one single problem in the mind of Carranza. After the Villistas had abandoned their hopeless siege of Ébano in mid–May, Carranza felt that General Treviño on his own could recover northeast Mexico and no longer needed the supervision of General González. Consequently, on 23 May Carranza appointed González to lead the recapture of the capital; by late May the general was scraping together a small a force at Puebla. Unknown to González, the long occupation of Mexico City had sapped the energy of the Zapatistas, who although supposedly fighting for land, had easily succumbed to the tempting pleasures of the capital. A desperate Zapata had to shake his commanders away from the "theaters, cantinas, and brothels"[76] of the capital. González advanced cautiously against sporadic Zapatista resistance but when he reached the outskirts of Mexico City on 22 June, his force of only 5,000 soldiers could go no further. The Zapatistas managed to stop him at a defense line they had established behind the Gran Canal, the large drainage canal near the capital. Rather than take heavy casualties in a frontal assault, González waited for additional troops to arrive, so that he could make a flanking movement around the Gran Canal further south. The Carrancista delay gave Zapata time to rally his demoralized men. At least for the moment, the Carrancistas had not reached Mexico City[77]

The Zapatista resistance boosted the spirits of Villa, who believed that his strategy of staying in central Mexico was serving to rally opposition against Carranza. To regain the initiative, Villa dispatched three major expeditions. He was confident that whatever their outcome, all at least kept the Carrancistas off balance and on the defensive. His first expedition headed to Saltillo with the intention of regaining the coal fields. Previously, Villa had evacuated Monterrey on 19 May to obtain additional troops. The Carrancistas, not satisfied with entering Monterrey on 23 May, boldly pushed on to capture Saltillo by the end of the month and cut off Villa from the coal fields. To reopen the supply route, Villa sent six thousand soldiers under Raúl Madero (a brother of the deceased former president), who on 14 June entered Saltillo after the small Carrancista force had fled north. The easy victory persuaded Raúl to press on to Monterrey, only to fall into a Carrancista trap just to the north of Saltillo at the canyon of Icamole. The Carrancistas had cleverly hidden themselves in the sides of the canyon, and their 40 machine guns cut down the unsuspecting and trapped Villistas in a frightful slaughter. In spite of this Villista disaster, the Carrancistas could not break the grip of the Villistas over the coal mines. Sporadic fighting continued in the front line between Saltillo and Monterrey for the rest of the summer, but at least Villa had assured the supply of fuel for his locomotives.[78]

The second expedition aimed to retake Guadalajara and to turn the state of Jalisco into a bastion of Villista support; Villa believed that the expedition would also divert Carrancista troops away from the Aguascalientes front. As soon as Obregón learned that a Villista column aimed to recapture Guadalajara, he sent General Diéguez to defend the city. By the time Diéguez reached the city on 16 June, the garrison had already repulsed the Villista column. With Guadalajara safely under Carrancista control, Diéguez returned to Obregón's army. Clearly this second expedition had been but a momentary distraction. The third expedition consisted of sending a column under the generals Rodolfo Fierro and Canuto Reyes in a wide flanking movement to fall on the unprotected sections of the Carrancista supply line to Veracruz. Scouts reported the movement of the hostile column to Obregón, who promptly dispatched Diéguez to protect the incoming munitions train from Veracruz. Diéguez successfully defended the munitions train on 30 June, but suffered a serious wound; the Villista attackers took heavy casualties and then disappeared. The third expedition seemed to have fared no better than the second, but later events showed that this verdict had been premature.

For the moment at least, none of the three Villista expeditions had halted the Carrancista advance against Aguascalientes. The last expedition, however, had made Obregón aware of how precarious his advance position was. He now realized he faced the classic dilemma of many armies in history: Either seek a decisive battle or retreat to safe supply bases. On 5 July he laid out the bleak situation to his senior officers and asked them to express freely their opinions as was his custom. The trains, which had fuel for only four hours, were useless, because Villista raiders had ripped up the tracks to the south. The food supply was running low. Although each soldier carried the normal quota of ammunition, the reserve was only of 100,000 or roughly 5 additional cartridges per man. Spies had described the Villista defense line in detail and revealed that the north was unprotected; therefore a long march of several days around Aguascalientes had every chance of outflanking Villa. All the senior officers were aware of the serious risks of the maneuver, but agreed to support the plan as the best chance to save the army.

Early in the morning on 6 July the army set out on its epic march through the arid terrain; each soldier received rations for 5 days. The convalescent Obregón felt strong enough to lead the column in person, while the likewise convalescing Diéguez remained behind with 1,500 men protecting the trains; should anything happen to Obregón's army, the small force of Diéguez, without any possible escape, necessarily had to be engulfed in the disaster. After having marched barely 8 kilometers, the army ran into Villista patrols. Over the next four days the Villistas desperately tried to block the march of Obregón, but his soldiers shattered the hastily thrown up defense lines one after another. Each clash proved costly in scarce ammunition, and by the night of 9 July, his men had cartridges for only one more attack. On 10 July at 1000 Obregón sent his infantry on a running charge on a front 25 kilometers long against the weak Villista positions, while he kept his cavalry to the north to cover his rear. The large number of soldiers racing down the hills soon broke the center of the defenses, and as the Villista flanks crumbled, the Carrancista soldiers quickly refilled their bandoleers with cartridges from fallen Villistas. The attacking soldiers pressed forward against collapsing resistance, and at 12 noon they entered Aguascalientes from the north as the Villista army disintegrated into small groups fleeing in all directions. Although the number of dead, wounded, and prisoners was not as large as in Celaya, Aguascalientes marked the last time Villa could place in the field a force capable of engaging in battle the combined Carrancista army.[79]

In the past Villa with his ruthlessness and his personal magnetism had been able to make amazing comebacks after military disasters. Much as Obregón wanted to deprive Villa of the opportunity to rally his forces, lack of ammunition threatened to halt the pursuit. A stroke of good luck suddenly changed the situation. To try to intercept the retreating Villistas, Obregón had sent General Murguía with the cavalry in a flanking move to the north of Aguascalientes. Murguía drove his cavalry very hard and set up road blocks to stop the trains that had been desperately trying to escape from the defeat at Aguascalientes. The cavalry of Murguía captured the Villista artillery intact and even more significantly found four million cartridges. By forced requisitions Villa had scraped the funds to import seven million cartridges from the United States, but why he had stored so many at the vulnerable front line has never been explained. The capture of these four million cartridges immediately and irreversibly altered the strategic balance and as a first consequence made possible a swift Carrancista advance to the north.[80]

Obregón's decisive victory at Aguascalientes on 10 July coincided with the Zapatista withdrawal from Mexico City. When General González completed the flanking movement around the Gran Canal, the Zapatista defense line crumbled. Rather than risk a pitched battle, the Zapatistas abandoned the city. On 11 July General González entered the capital and promptly pushed the Zapatistas back into Morelos.[81] Whatever chance had existed of stopping Carranza vanished. The struggle against Pancho Villa assumed a different nature. While before Carranza had been trying to eliminate a rival for national power, henceforth he was struggling against a rebel. Although still the most powerful of the regional warlords in July 1915, Villa was no longer able to overthrow the national government. Obregón was most eager to resume the advance into the north, but before he could bring the war into Chihuahua, he first had to take care of an unexpected danger in his rear.

The rejoicing at the defeat of Rodolfo Fierro and Canuto Reyes on 30 June had been premature. This third expedition of Villa had not fled north after its defeat but had quietly slipped back south in early July. Through tricks and clever maneuvering Fierro and Reyes went on a rampage of destruction in central Mexico. Instead of trying to capture the heavily escorted supply trains, Fierro and Reyes concentrated on completely destroying large stretches of track; not only did they dynamite the bridges and culverts, but they usually used the crossties as fuel for their retreating trains. During their campaign, they occasionally seized cities, first Tula and then Pachuca on 17 July. The two Villista generals united scattered groups until they led over 8,000 men. Their bold movements made General Pablo González fear for his own supply lines. Afraid that he would be trapped between the Villista raiders and the Zapatistas, a panicky González began a hurried evacuation of Mexico City and the last of his troops departed on 18 July. González with his whole army marched north while Obregón was coming south with troops against the Villistas who in the meantime had captured Querétaro. After rapid moves, González defeated the Villistas at Pachuca on 28 July, and that same day Obregón drove them out of Querétaro. Carranza had insisted that González reoccupy Mexico City as soon as possible, and on 2 August the general entered the city; never again did the capital change hands. Obregón continued to pursue Fierro and Reyes until the last remnants of their forces had abandoned central Mexico.[82]

With the elimination of this last major threat in the Carrancista rear, Obregón could now resume his advance to the north. After the battle of Aguascalientes, the Villistas had abandoned San Luis Potosí in 16 July and the Carrancistas entered the next day. In Zacatecas, after the Villista garrison fled, the cavalry of Murguía entered on 28 July. The Carrancistas in Zacatecas soon were in contact with the Arrieta brothers who throughout all the months of Villista supremacy had maintained a steady resistance in Durango. With Zacatecas in their grasp and Durango about to rejoin the Carrancista fold, the paths into Chihuahua were wide open.[83] A week after the Villista disaster at Aguascalientes a despondent Villa arrived at Torreón, but he was not sure how long he could defend that city. "It is his earnest desire to have peace and I believe he will accept any reasonable proposition."[84] The powerful Villa, who had shaken Mexico to its foundations, had been humbled, and meekly requested some decent terms. In a rare case for Latin America, no negotiations ensued, perhaps because the message was never delivered; at least no Carrancista rejection is known. Certainly some arrangement to spare Mexico further bloodshed and destruction was highly advisable. Villa had been completely defeated but not destroyed; he retained considerable resources and could drag out the war for months. Mexico needed to begin its reconstruction from the ravages of war as quickly as possible. But if the Carrancistas did not eliminate Villa soon, the Chihuahua leader, known for impulsive and wild actions, was still capable of springing surprises, as the next section reveals.

The Villista Invasion of Sonora

In the first days of August 1915 General Álvaro Obregón pondered over the best strategy to liquidate the Villista rebellion. Specifically, he had to select an invasion route for his army already seriously hampered by ammunition shortages. The four traditional paths to the north had been the Atlantic and Pacific coastlines and the railroads leading north from Zacatecas and from San Luis Potosí. His field army of over 30,000 men had been adequate to win victory in Central Mexico but was too small to cover the wide open spaces in the north. Ideally he required armies of at least 20,000 soldiers for each of the four invasion routes, but even if he could recruit the men, Carranza could not extract the resources to maintain them from a depleted Mexico. The traditional invasion route to the north had been Zacatecas, but with the Villistas furiously burning every bridge and crosstie, Obregón did not want to duplicate the slow march of Victoriano Huerta in 1912. In addition, Pancho Villa was not given to wait patiently until a column ponderously trudging across the desert arrived to destroy him. Yet abandoning the pursuit took all the pressure off the Villistas, so consequently Obregón decided to leave a few infantry battalions and most of his cavalry in the Zacatecas route. The aggressive General Francisco Murguía was sure to prosecute the pursuit vigor-

ously, at the risk, however, that should Villa suddenly halt and hurl his entire army against Murguía, the entire Carrancista center could collapse. Obregón understood the danger very well, but he concluded that he had no alternative other than to run this calculated risk.

Any renewed Villista drive required coal, and Obregón planned to paralyze the Villista trains dead on their tracks by a swift campaign to recapture the coal fields in Coahuila. He had decided to take the bulk of his army east to San Luis Potosí before Villa had a chance to strike a counterblow against Zacatecas. Because work crews had repaired the damaged track as far as Aguascalientes, Carrancista troops could return by train fast enough to stop Pancho Villa before he could push very far to the south. On 5 August Obregón rode ahead to Monterrey to finalize the details of the offensive against Saltillo. The plan called for General Jacinto Treviño make a diversionary attack to the north to distract the Villista garrison of Saltillo, while Obregón quietly advanced from San Luis Potosí to surprise the defenders from the south. A few days later reports from spies forced Obregón to modify his strategy radically. Scouts and deserters had earlier reported a general retreat of the Villistas to Chihuahua, but it was not clear how far north Villa would withdraw or whether he planned to defend Torreón. When the spies reported that Villa was concentrating many of his retreating troops at Casas Grandes, Obregón instantly realized that Villa intended to launch an invasion of Sonora. Obregón backtracked by train on 9 August to Guadalajara and promptly began dispatching reinforcements to Sonora. He appointed General Diéguez to command the Sonora expedition and sent all the nearby units to the Pacific Coast for the long trip by rail and sea to Sonora. Obregón knew that the Pacific Coast was a much faster way to send reinforcements than the land route via Zacatecas. The possibility loomed of catching Villa in an anvil between the Diéguez force in Sonora and the pursuing Carrancistas, but the wide deserts of Chihuahua had foiled many clever strategies before.[85]

Obregón then rode back to lead the campaign to deprive Villa of the coal from Coahuila. Of course, Villa with his dwindling funds could try to purchase coal from the United States, but unknown to Obregón, a secret ally was doing everything in his power to halt or at least delay coal exports to Mexico. Zach Lamar Cobb, the Collector of Customs at El Paso, was determined to stop Villa at any cost. Cobb passionately believed that Villa was extremely harmful to both Mexico and the United States. Filling the policy vacuum Washington left, Cobb was able to harass, delay, and eventually halt Villista imports of coal, supplies, and ammunition. Villa himself was fast running out of money, because his rapacious policies had bankrupted Chihuahua; already starvation was appearing in the Villista territory. The old bandit habits resurfaced as his demoralized men became looters stripping the haciendas and villages of anything of value. In such a wretched economic condition, the loss of the coal mines of Coahuila was bound to hasten the collapse of the Villista rebellion.[86]

In late August Obregón's army marched from San Luis Potosí into the long and barren desert to the north. The Villistas had taken up positions at the natural defensive line of Angostura, the site of the famous battle against the Americans in 1847. Inspired to do justice to this historical battlefield, Obregón prepared another of his brilliant maneuvers. He was disappointed to see that only five thousand Villistas with a single cannon were defending Angostura, but their determination to resist kept alive his hope for a memorable battle. On 4 September as he began to position his units, the Villistas opened fired prematurely and wounded a popular Carrancista officer. In anger and seeking vengeance for their fallen comrade, the 21st Battalion charged recklessly against the main Villista defense line. Not wishing to sacrifice the battalion needlessly, Obregón ordered his artillery just starting to unlimber to lay covering barrages on the Villista position. He also ordered all his other troops forward to support the exposed battalion. The precautions were unnecessary because in 30 minutes the 21st Battalion had breached the defense lines, while the artillery shells had sent the rest of the Villistas into a panicky flight. Alas for Obregón, the precipitate action of the 21st Battalion had spoiled his brilliant plan, and he had to content himself with having his five-to-one superiority win the easiest victory in his military career.[87]

That same day General Treviño defeated and sent into headlong flight the Villistas at Icamole. At noon on 4 September Obregón's cavalry entered Saltillo unopposed, and later that day came the infantry. Obregón sent General Treviño to take possession of the coal fields. By 7 September Treviño's troops had reached Piedras Negras, and soon the Carrancista trains were hauling coal shipments.[88] But the retreating Villistas had destroyed the track to the west of Saltillo so thoroughly, that no train travel was possible for at least a month. Obregón did not want to wait until the repair crews finished their work, and on 17 September he set out across the hot desert with his infantry and cavalry. Reports reaching him suggested that the Villistas could not make any determined resistance, so he left his artillery behind. The march over the barren and hot terrain was slow, and before Obregón could reach Torreón, General Murguía with his cavalry had entered that city on 28 September. The Villistas had left earlier, after having destroyed all the track both east and north of the city. Carranza, who was in a hurry to declare the war over, prematurely concluded that the need for military campaigns had passed. Only after long conversations with Obregón did the president accept the need to pursue Villa relentlessly until his final destruction.[89]

The Villistas were in retreat, because in a strategic redeployment, Villa had decided to withdraw his forces even before the arrival of the Carrancistas. Although he was sorry to lose the coal from Coahuila, by then he had thoroughly drained those regions of men, animals, and food. To replenish his demoralized army, he needed the plunder of a rich region. Of the wealthy states in Mexico, only Sonora had escaped the ravages of the revolution. Once he had refurbished his army in Sonora, Villa planned to push into Sinaloa. He believed that after a southern advance of three months he could join his many supporters still fighting at Tepic and Jalisco.[90] The plan was highly risky but not impossible; just a few Carrancista mistakes sufficed to tip the balance of victory over to Villa. A traditional gambler like Villa could not let pass his last best opportunity to cripple the central government. The Orozquista invasion of Sonora in 1912 had ended in disaster, but Villa believed that he had learned from the mistakes of Pascual Orozco. Villa planned to keep his men together in one large force, unlike Orozco who had sent many small units over three main invasion routes and had given Sonora time to rally and to defeat the invaders piecemeal.[91] Villa brought many cannons with him, unlike the Orozquistas who had lacked artillery. Lastly, Villa enjoyed the support of Governor José María Maytorena, in contrast to Orozco, who had to fight his way through every town. No less encouraging was the weak Carrancista presence in Sonora: To the south, an invasion from Sinaloa had stalled at Navojoa in January 1915, while the only other Carrancista garrison was in Agua Prieta under the command of General Plutarco Elías Calles (Map 13). The troops at Agua Prieta had earlier distinguished themselves in the defense of Naco from October 1914 to January 1915. By a curious twist of fate, the struggle against Villa returned to its starting point in Sonora.

The retreating Villistas had thoroughly destroyed the track east of Torreón, including every bridge and culvert. As they withdrew north into Chihuahua they became even more meticulously, going so far as to burn every crosstie. The destruction of the track seemed to have delayed any Carrancista pursuit until the end of the year, yet the Villistas had not gained much of a head start. Lack of coal hampered the movement of the troop trains from Chihuahua City to Ciudad Juárez until late September, and the train crews, who originally had been great supporters of Villa, refused to work if paid only in worthless Villista paper money. Thousands of soldiers took advantage of the delays and the confusion to desert, while many officers slipped across the U.S. border. With difficulty the remaining Villistas eluded the vigilance of Customs Collector Cobb to scrape enough U.S. coal and local firewood to make a final train journey from Ciudad Juárez to Casas Grandes, the terminus of the railroad. A distance of 250 kilometers still remained to Agua Prieta, and even more to Naco; from this last place Villa's troops could ride trains south to Hermosillo and to the port city of Guaymas before continuing their invasion down the Pacific Coast (Map 11).[92] At last by early October the first detachments of his large army were ready to march to the west, but meanwhile the original situation had vastly changed in Sonora.

Governor Maytorena had been trying to drive the Carrancistas out of northern Sonora, bit in spite of some initial successes, he fared badly. By late September Calles had gone on the offensive and was threatening Nogales on the U.S. border. Maytorena could have retreated back to the capital of Hermosillo and waited until Villa arrived to reverse the military situation, but the governor's power base had virtually disintegrated. His white supporters gradually deserted him, and he became dependent on the Yaqui Indians, who comprised almost all his troops. The leader of the Yaquis was their chief General Francisco Urbalejo, who had become the de facto ruler of Sonora. Maytorena had even complied with the Yaqui demand that all whites be disarmed: "This is the most outrageous action done by this government but as I have before reported the Yaqui is running this state and the authorities are afraid of them. Not a day passes but that someone is killed or [a] girl stolen or people robbed."[93] Not surprisingly in such chaotic conditions economic activity halted, and the state revenues evaporated. The perspicacious Villa was sure to realize that Maytorena was powerless and thus useless as an ally. Unwilling to be a pawn of Villa and without funds to pay the restless Yaqui Indians, Maytorena decided to escape while the Nogales border was still open. He appointed an interim governor, and at 2015 on the night of 30 September he crossed into the United States; quite ironically he was repeating his shameful flight of February 1913. Real power was in the hands of the Yaqui Indian Urbalejo, the commander of the troops in Sonora.[94] For the first and only time since the appearance of the Spaniards in the sixteenth century, the Yaquis were in control of Sonora. "Here in Hermosillo there is absolutely no law or order and everything [is] in the hands of the Yaquis."[95] Anguished as were the cries of the whites, it was more remarkable that the Yaquis did not carry out any large scale reprisals or massacres. The collapse of Maytorena had been so sudden and so unexpected that the Yaquis did not know what to do with their new power.[96] Perhaps confirmation of the imminent entry into Sonora of Villa's huge army counseled the Yaquis to wait for orders from this powerful leader; in any case Urbalejo and his Yaquis shifted their alliance from Maytorena to Villa without a moment's hesitation.

As Villa tried to complete his preparations for the Sonora invasion, no longer at his side would be the wise Ángeles, who had settled in the United States after their relationship had cooled. Not missed at all was the brutal Tomás Urbina, whom Villa had executed on 4 September. He publicized the execution as a way to reassure Sonora that the inhabitants had nothing to fear from his invasion.[97] The Villista army finally set out for Sonora early in October. Villa had tried to send part of his forces ahead, but clashes with long-distance patrols from Agua Prieta persuaded him to keep his army together for the departure ín mid–October. A wagon road provided a well-marked route to Agua Prieta, and with the passing of the burning summer heat, the cool temperatures of October promised ideal marching weather. In a decision that later had many adverse consequences, Villa for the first time in his career forced all the female camp followers or *soldaderas* to stay behind at Casas Grandes. Crossing over virtually uninhabited areas, the *soldaderas* had no chance to carry out their scavenging activities. Traditionally they had bought or extorted food, firewood, and fodder in the populated regions of Mexico, but in the Sierra Madre mountains, Villa concluded they were just more mouths to feed. Henceforth the soldiers would do their own scavenging and cooking, but once they had reached populated areas, the soldiers found it hard to take only food and also helped themselves to women. The *soldaderas*, often rape victims themselves, had performed the invaluable function of keeping rapes to a minimum during campaigns, but this time without the restraining influence of the *soldaderas*, Sonora was at the mercy of Vandalic hordes bent on pillage, plunder, and rape.[98]

Ten days after the invasion force set out, Villa left his herd of cattle behind, because it was slowing down his march and consuming too much water. The route of 250 kilometers was not arid, but water sources were too far apart. After thousands of men and animals drank, the wells usually ran dry, and thirst began to plague the Villista army of 12,000 men. For food, hunting of small game like rabbits was adequate to feed patrols but not a whole army, and soon the men were both hungry and thirsty. In spite of legends to the contrary, only at Pulpit Pass near the Sonora border did the path become perilously narrow; although seven cannon and their teams of animals fell down these precipices, the bulk of the artillery made it through safely. It was not the

hostility of the terrain but Villa's insistence on keeping the army together that made the journey harsher than usual.[99]

As the Villista army laboriously approached Agua Prieta, he began to receive disconcerting news. The sudden departure of governor Maytorena irked Villa. The Yaquis did not worry Villa, and he was sure that the Indians would rally to his side once they saw his large army and his many cannon. Instead, news that on 19 October the United States had recognized Carranza and placed an arms embargo on Villa fell like a bombshell. A deeply offended Villa felt betrayed: Of all the Mexican rebel leaders, he had been the only one to support the U.S. occupation of Veracruz. For as long as he did not need the resources, he had spared U.S. citizens and companies from forced contributions. Poor Villa did not understand that whatever earlier sympathy he had enjoyed with the U.S. government, he had squandered it away when he had begun to extort U.S. citizens after his defeat in Celaya.[100]

The U.S. recognition came in time to save the Agua Prieta garrison. Calles and his three thousand men had retreated to this town to face the approaching onslaught. His small garrison had few machine guns, and worse had only 4 cannons to face the 32 of Villa. Once artillery shelling shattered the trenches, Villa was sure to capture Agua Prieta. To save the otherwise doomed garrison, Carranza asked the U.S. government for permission to have Mexican troops ride U.S. trains from Piedras Negras to Agua Prieta. President Wilson instantly agreed, and soon the garrison increased to 7,000 soldiers and received 22 cannons and 65 machine guns. Obregón also sent steel beams to build underground trenches and bunkers covered with thick layers of sand. The soldiers had soon strung out the new rolls of barbed wire to have many lines protecting the trenches. Calles even managed to electrify one barbed wire fence running around the town.[101]

The open U.S. support for Carranza was the worst news for Villa, but he soon received more bad news. The troops Obregón had presciently sent to Sonora were fast approaching from the south. On 9 October General Diéguez with a substantial force steamed out from Mazatlán and headed for Guaymas, still in Villista hands. The inhabitants of that port city feared a bombardment from the gunboats of the Mexican Navy, but to their relief Diéguez landed in a lightly defended beach further south on 12 October. The landing force routed the Villistas, and by nightfall the defenders, in their majority Yaquis, were evacuating Guaymas. On 13 October at 1100 the Carrancistas entered Guaymas before the Villistas could sabotage the rolling stock; indeed, the Villistas had fled so fast that they had failed to load enough coal aboard their trains that soon ran out of fuel and stopped. Diéguez had no intention of rushing forward because he remembered the disastrous offensives of the old Federal Army against Obregón in 1913. Diéguez waited until the rest of his units arrived by sea and then with a force of 12,000 he slowly started a methodical march toward Hermosillo. He expected the offensive to require at least one month and possibly two. In another curious parallel with the 1913 campaign, recycled federals, including the military band, comprised a large part of his initial units.[102]

In spite of the similarities, the 1913 campaign did not repeat itself in 1915. The retreating Villista troops disintegrated, and all those who were not Yaquis fled to the east or melted into the civilian population. With General Urbalejo in the north about to join Villa, the Yaquis in the south were left leaderless, and they began to quarrel among themselves. A conventional defense of Hermosillo did not fit with their traditional style of warfare, and gradually the Yaquis split up into bands, some returning to their home grounds in the Yaqui River, others going north to join Urbalejo. The Carrancista force at Navojoa had meanwhile marched north and linked up with Diéguez. Even with these additional forces, Diéguez still hesitated to push north and with excessive caution continued to await reinforcements.[103]

The deteriorating prospects in Sonora did not augur well for Villa when he finally arrived near Agua Prieta on 31 October. He gave his thirsty and hungry men some time to rest, while he prepared his plan to attack the garrison the next day. As he surveyed Agua Prieta, he should have concluded that only a protracted siege could overcome its formidable defenses, yet instead he believed that a furious attack sufficed to capture the town. In reality, he had no pressing reason to attack Agua Prieta, and instead he should have marched his men to Naco to board the train and reach Hermosillo

before Diéguez arrived with his force. (Already General Urbalejo and the Yaquis were coming). Between attacking the heavily entrenched garrison at Agua Prieta and the army of Diéguez out in the open, the right answer should have been obvious, but not to Villa who insisted on first destroying Calles and then turning south to deal with Diéguez. His enthusiasm for an easy victory infected his staff officers who believed they could capture Agua Prieta in five hours. At 1335 on 1 November the Villista artillery opened fire on Agua Prieta and did not stop until nightfall. The only noticeable impact of the shelling was to detonate some land mines the Carrancistas had buried beyond the barbed wire perimeter.[104]

Villa saved the costly frontal assaults for the night, and he selected the eastern and southern sectors for the main efforts. At 2000 and 2200 he made some feints to keep Calles guessing as to the direction of the main Villista assault. Then after midnight Villa ordered his artillery to resume firing, but his gunners preferred to shell the deserted town buildings rather than the Carrancista trenches. At 0050 on 2 November his troops rushed forward to storm the trenches. Unfortunately for Villa, two searchlights illuminated the charging soldiers who made easy targets for the defenders' machine guns and rifles; buried land mines also set off large explosions. The few Villistas who came near to the town suffered ghastly deaths electrocuted in the barbed wire. Frightful slaughter had never deterred Villa who wanted to try again the next night, but his men refused to repeat the death charges and were about to mutiny. The Villistas were also desperately short of food and fodder because Calles had stripped clean the area near Agua Prieta. Reluctantly Villa took his army to Naco on 4 November in preparation for the advance on Hermosillo. South of Naco his men replenished themselves and found pastures for their animals; many, however, were just waiting for the first opportunity to desert, and at least 1500 crossed the border to safety in the United States in the following days.[105]

Villa wanted to give his men plenty of time to recover their strength and their spirits, and he was in no rush to have them make the train ride into Hermosillo. By the time he decided to ship his army south, bad news had again overtaken him. On 6 November the slow-moving Diéguez finally entered Hermosillo; that same day, Álvaro Obregón, the old nemesis of Villa, showed up at Agua Prieta to take command of the operations. Obregón had initially contented himself with sending reinforcements to Sonora, but the slowness of the movements of Diéguez and Calles persuaded him that he needed to be there personally to prod the campaign. In reality, the strategic situation had not changed, because Villa still had the largest army in Sonora; if he hurried south with his entire army, he could still smash Diéguez. However, having Obregón on his rear worried Villa, who committed the blunder of splitting his army into two forces. The larger one under General José Rodríguez had the duty of keeping Obregón bottled up in Agua Prieta. Villa himself led the smaller army to Hermosillo to destroy Diéguez and then to push south to Guaymas.[106]

The arrival of more reinforcements from Guaymas emboldened Diéguez to attack the Villista detachment at Alamito on 18 November. In this clash the Villistas suffered large losses and retreated, but subsequently Villa arrived with the bulk of his army to halt the rout.[107] The large force of Villa persuaded Obregón to authorize Diéguez to withdraw to Guaymas if a defense of Hermosillo seemed impossible. Diéguez, who had received 28 cannons and an "exceptionally large supply of machine guns,"[108] was unsure about his course of action. When scouts intercepted a message for Villa saying that 2,000 of his cavalry could not participate in the attack because the horses were too weak to travel, Diéguez made up his mind and hastily began to fortify the city. Villa, plagued with desertions, was finding it almost impossible to motivate his men to attack. The time for squeamishness had passed, and sensing himself cornered, he played his last card. He told his men that Hermosillo was famous for its beautiful females and was full of booty; in a throwback to the early days of the revolution in 1911, he promised his men that during 48 hours they could do whatever they wanted in the city. Villa launched his attack on 21 November, and had not his men turned to looting and raping almost from the first hours, Villa might have captured the city. Instead, the determined Carrancista resistance wore down the Villistas, who after thirty hours of failed attacks finally left in retreat on 22 November.[109]

Villa correctly concluded that the attack had come very close to success, and he attempted to correct his earlier mistake by ordering Rodríguez with the other half of the army to join him. The reunion of the two forces was imperative, because on 26 November Obregón had captured Nogales after he moved troops via U.S. railroads from Agua Prieta. Obregón hoped to trap Villa between Nogales and Hermosillo, but before he could have his units in place, Rodríguez surprised everyone and refused to go south. A furious Villa could only fume as his subordinate headed as fast as possible to the east; it was not just Rodríguez, his men also were angry at Sonora and wished to return home to Chihuahua. A surprised Obregón reacted promptly to the maverick Villista column, and to save the undefended Agua Prieta from the inevitable sacking, he rushed troops by U.S. railroad. Obregón saw the opportunity to destroy the Rodríguez column, and he deployed most of his soldiers south of the town to try to cut off the escape route of the retreating Villistas. The Rodríguez column had no heart for combat and split up into many small groups. These fugitives suffered many casualties and lost all of their equipment, but in the vast spaces of Sonora the Carrancistas were spread too thin to prevent most Villistas from slipping through and fleeing across the Sierra Madre back to Chihuahua.[110] The retreating Villistas took out their frustrations on the inhabitants of the scattered towns: "This force was ordered [to be] pursued but they got away meanwhile ravishing women and girls, murdering, looting, and carrying into the hills the young girls of Morelos, Bavispe, and Baserac."[111]

The flight of the Rodríguez column had rid Sonora of a horde of barbarians, but Pancho Villa himself was still on the loose. When the Carrancistas captured a train carrying most of the wives and children of the Yaqui soldiers, all but the two hundred under Urbalejo abandoned Villa, whose force was rapidly shrinking through desertions. Defeated armies like to retreat through their route of advance, but Villa knew this was not an option for his tattered force. His whereabouts remained unknown for some days as he marched north and then briefly turned east before beginning a long march south past Hermosillo, all the time losing men through desertions. He decided to plunge east into the upper reaches of the Yaqui River, at first under the guidance of his Yaqui scouts. In a rage of violence Villa engaged in a massacre in a small mining town. On December 1 Urbalejo and the last Yaquis abandoned Villa and returned to join the Carrancista army; all sides immediately incorporated into their forces the Yaquis who were too valuable as soldiers to waste before an execution squad. Villa pushed on into unknown territory eventually losing all his artillery and equipment. At San Pedro de la Cueva he committed perhaps the worst massacre of his career, when he ordered the cold-blooded slaughter of all the men in the village. Pancho Villa had reached a new low point in his life as he took out his frustrations on hapless civilians. On December 8 he straggled over the Chihuahua state line, and on 11 December he reached the rail head of Madera to take the train back to Chihuahua City. He had lost all his equipment and weapons and had returned with less than 2000 men, a small fraction of the army that had departed in October. The Sonora invasion had been a complete disaster for Villa, but he was far from finished.[112]

Obregón was preparing to take his army from Sonora to Chihuahua, when bad news from the south came to upset his plans for the close pursuit of Villa. In the middle of November a Yaqui insurrection was beginning in the tribal homelands, but Obregón hoped that either negotiations or local troops could contain the Indian revolt while he finished off Villa. Unfortunately, two additional complications shattered Obregon's holding strategy. First, the Yaqui raids threatened the property and lives of a handful of U.S. citizens and provoked immediate demands from the State Department for protection. Carranza and Obregón gave orders to send some units, but the raids from the rapidly spreading Yaqui insurrection multiplied. Into this volatile situation plunged the bellicose U.S. Navy Admiral C. McR. Winslow, who since the first Yaqui raid had been itching for any opportunity to land U.S. sailors and marines in Sonora. The Woodrow Wilson administration did not want any repeat of the Veracruz landing of April 1914 but was under intense political pressure not to appear "weak" in the defense of U.S. interests abroad. In a virtual ultimatum dated 23 November and delivered several days later, the State Department expected Carranza to reciprocate the permission to ride aboard U.S. railroads: The Mexican government could either promptly dispatch troops to the Yaqui region or else accept the landing of U.S. forces.[113]

Carranza indignantly rejected any landing of U.S. forces in Sonora, and Obregón immediately realized that the ultimatum closed the U. S. railroads to his troops and destroyed any chance of a quick pursuit of Villa. Obregón placed his army aboard trains bound not for Chihuahua but for the Yaqui territory in southern Sonora. A handful of American civilians and an aggressive admiral generated such political pressure as to sidetrack the original U.S. policy of rendering Villa harmless. Obregón came to Guaymas to calm down Admiral Winslow, and when 12,000 Carrancista soldiers arrived to pursue the Yaquis on 21 December 1915, the Admiral at last abandoned his insistence on landing U.S. forces. The threat of Indian raids ended, but final victory proved elusive. After some months the Yaquis resumed the peaceful appearance they traditionally adopted when confronted with overwhelming force. The Yaqui threat remained simmering.[114]

The Yaqui insurrection and U.S. pressure destroyed the western or Sonora half of the trap against Villa, and left the entire burden of destroying Villa to the Carrancistas advancing from Torreón. General Murguía in a lightning dash forward with his cavalry had captured that city on 28 September. If Murguía kept up the pace of his advance north into Chihuahua, he could catch Villa emerging from the Sierra Madre Mountains after the escape from Sonora. But more good luck came to save the rebel from Murguía just like good luck had saved Villa before from Obregón. In one of the strategic decisions of the war that revealed the true intentions of Carranza, the president refused to appoint the dynamic General Murguía and instead named General Jacinto Treviño to complete the pacification of Chihuahua. Treviño seemed outwardly competent because of his successful defense of Ébano. In reality, capable subordinates and close supervision by General Pablo González and Carranza himself had made possible the victory of Ébano.

Carranza, who in September 1915 had tried unsuccessfully to dissuade Obregón from pursuing Villa, again attempted to abort the campaign by appointing the incompetent Treviño. Why did Carranza give Villa a new lease on life, by appointing the thoroughly inept Treviño? Paradoxically, to maintain his power, Carranza needed Villa on the loose as a rebel. Carranza joined the long list of historical personalities who used or prolonged a war to bolster their political fortunes. The removal of the dynamic Murguía reeked of opportunism and also coincided with Carranza's beliefs. The president wanted the people to turn to civilian politicians for solutions to their needs and never to generals. A symbiotic relationship arose between Carranza and Villa: The president kept within bounds and squeezed the Villista rebellion for political gain but never hard enough to crush the prey. Carranza could not imagine that his cunning political maneuvers had inadvertently plunged Mexico into a collision course with the United States.

U.S. Military Intervention: The Punitive Expedition

Only in early November 1915 did General Jacinto Treviño timidly begin to repair the railroad track north of Torreón, but troops advanced no faster than the very leisurely pace of the repair crews. The sluggish pace was remarkable because in contrast to Victoriano Huerta who in 1912 had to engage in combat repeatedly to rebuild the track, Treviño encountered no resistance. Treviño's troops had barely crossed the Chihuahua state line on 2 December. Pancho Villa, upon his return from the Sonora disaster, was puzzled by the failure of the Carrancistas to have reached Chihuahua City. The rebel leader immediately decided to take advantage of this stroke of good luck. He entered the state capital to try to rally his troops and his generals, but it was too late; Chihuahua was desolate, war weariness had set in, and nobody wanted to stop Treviño. With remarkable foresight, Villa grasped the type of war Carranza was willing to let him fight. Villa had plenty of time to bury large caches of ammunition and weapons. Although Villa no longer had the men willing to fight, by burying arms and ammunition he planted seeds for a future when men would spring from the ground to brandish the weapons. On 22 December Treviño finally entered Chihuahua City; the day before the Villista garrison in Ciudad Juárez had surrendered to the Carrancista consul of El Paso. More

significant than the capture of real estate was the eagerness of the Villistas to take advantage of the amnesty. The men seemed genuinely tired of war and wanted to resume peaceful work. A total of 16,104 men returned to civilian life, but only half surrendered their weapons. The lawlessness in Mexico advised keeping some arms whether for self-defense in their ranches or as insurance against any Carrancista reprisals and did not necessarily mean a desire to fight for Villa again.[115]

The amnesty offer excluded Villa, his brother Hipólito, and only three other persons. The massacres of peasants and of Americans in the Sierra Madre were too fresh in the minds of Mexican leaders to bring themselves to pardon Villa, whose crimes appeared too savage to leave unpunished. Nevertheless, the failure to extend the amnesty to Villa was a major blunder. Just the need to crush the Yaqui revolt counseled obtaining quickly the submission of Villa. The true test of statesmanship was to pardon Villa, but understandably the Mexican generals wanted him either dead or in exile. Carranza could have overruled his generals, but he had his own reasons for keeping the Villista rebellion alive. Curiously enough, President Woodrow Wilson did pass the test of statesmanship when he authorized offering refuge for Villa in the United States as the easiest way to end the turmoil in Mexico. Mexican rebels usually jumped at the opportunity to obtain refuge in the United States, but not a Villa who regarded even Veracruz as too foreign. He could not imagine life without being either a regional warlord or a successful businessman. Unlike other Mexican leaders, he did not need daily doses of political power to be content, and he was more than willing to give up his role as regional warlord. To lay down his arms, all he insisted upon was the revival of the 1912 arrangement, which had granted him a ranch and related businesses to run with his family. He remained a rebel until at last in 1920 the government accepted his conditions. He was in a strong position to bargain, because he had mastered the secret formula of starting revolts and was willing to fight until the death.[116]

Chihuahua was ready to calm down, but only under the direction of able leaders. Ignacio Enríquez, the new Carrancista governor, pursued very conservative policies that failed to create a broad base of support for Carranza.

General Treviño, the zone commander, added corruption and abuses to his usual ineptness, until he had antagonized many persons. The only employment the Carranza regime offered the former Villistas was enlistment in the new national army, but the low pay and poor conditions persuaded only the most hungry to enlist. The situation seemed ripe for Villa to make another of his surprising recoveries. In one of his flashes of insight, he concluded that he needed something more spectacular than an attack inside Mexico to regain national status. Because his followers had dwindled to less than five hundred, in any case he lacked the men to attack any major town. Instead, he had more than enough men to overrun any of the small U.S. towns on the Mexican border. He felt Washington had betrayed him in October 1915, and ever since Villa developed a hatred of the United States. He originally picked Texas for an attack and headed to Ojinaga, but because most of his men deserted when they learned about the plan, he had to scrap the attack.[117]

Before selecting another target, his first order of business was to recruit more soldiers. Volunteers were very scarce, so he turned to the press gang or *leva*, which the Villistas had previously used. From here on, compulsion became the usual way for Villa to obtain recruits. Some of the men came to like the campaigning, but most eventually deserted, and to find replacements necessitated a renewed use of the press gang. Although Porfirio Díaz had occasionally used the *leva*, the supposedly brutal dictator seemed benign compared to Villa who threatened to burn the houses and kill the families of the men who refused to join and stay in his army. At least for Villa, the Revolution that had intended to liberate men had become more oppressive and brutal than the original dictatorship. Villa could always count on a core of hard-core fanatical followers, but for his final years, fear and compulsion were the dominant characteristics of his fighting force. In a sure sign of war weariness, the Revolution no longer attracted enthusiastic followers as in 1911 and instead terrorized men into fleeing at the first opportunity.[118]

The stakes were very high for Villa, for Mexico, and even for the world when he attacked Columbus, New Mexico, at 0445 on 9 March 1916. Because he did not want his men to desert as had happened in his aborted raid to Texas, he had kept his destination secret to all but a few of his closest confidants. He restricted his reconnaissance drastically to make sure the men did not suspect he was thinking of attacking the United States. Most of his men believed they were attacking merely another sleepy and dusty Mexican village. Unfortunately, the failure to scout properly proved disastrous to the attack, because Villa did not know that a large U.S. cavalry force was garrisoned at Columbus. His men caught the cavalry unit by surprise, but they did not press the attack and instead turned to looting the town. Soon U.S. officers returned to rally their men and to counterattack. The Villistas failed to obtain booty, money, or arms; over a hundred died and many were taken prisoner. Only 17 Americans died, most of them civilians. Tactically the attack had been a disaster, but Villa was confident that he had scored a major strategic success; at that moment his optimism did not seem justified, but unfolding events made come true even his wildest dreams of success.[119]

President Woodrow Wilson vainly tried to detain the irresistible pressure to launch a military response. Bluntly, his cabinet told him not to run for reelection in 1916 if he did not send an expedition to catch Villa. General John Pershing crossed the border on 16 March leading a large U.S. Army force usually referred to as the Punitive Expedition. After the United States had given repeated permission for Carrancista troops to ride U.S. railroads during the Sonora campaign, Mexico could not immediately condemn the U.S. reaction. Trying to put the best face forward, Carranza likened the U.S. response to the hot pursuit of hostile Indians, a privilege both countries had enjoyed since the 1880s. Carranza realized that his failure to prosecute the campaign against Villa had backfired and had exposed Mexico to the risk of war with the United Sates. Carranza could not bring himself to take the politically costly decision of removing Governor Enríquez and General Treviño. The president had to do something, and with great reluctance he appointed General Álvaro Obregón to be the Secretary of War on 13 March. Initially Obregón did not realize how rotten and ineffective was the Carrancista regime in Chihuahua, so he did not insist on the immediate removal of high officials in that state.[120]

As the large Punitive Expedition pushed

south, Villa fled ahead of it. He had too much of a lead for the Americans to catch up with him, but Pershing could certainly restrict Villa's movements. The American invasion immediately helped Villa, who portrayed himself as a champion in the struggle against the United States; he was not the first or last Latin American leader to discover that anti–Americanism could generate strong popular support. Initially Mexicans joined his ranks, but inevitably many of these patriotic volunteers deserted when they realized that Villa wanted to fight only fellow Mexicans and not Americans. But by then Villa was mouthing the same anti–American slogans in the next village. With his replenished force, on 27 March Villa drove the Carrancistas out of Ciudad Guerrero, the town that proved again to be as decisive as it had been at the start of the Madero insurrection in that far distant November 1911. The Carrancistas counterattacked, and although repulsed, in the fighting they wounded Villa in the knee. He was in great pain and could be carried only very slowly. He knew either the Carrancistas or the Americans would soon catch up with his slow column, so he disbanded his force and retreated into a camouflaged cave to convalesce. Only two cousins knew the location of this cave, and they kept him supplied with food and water. Two months passed in this forced boredom, although he was able to break the monotony one day by watching march the Punitive Expedition in the plain below.[121]

Villa seemed finished, and it was a miracle that without any medical attention his knee wound healed. During his forced convalescence, all Villista attacks had ceased, and both U.S. and Mexican officials urged President Wilson to withdraw the Punitive Expedition in April. Up to this moment the right of hot pursuit still vaguely covered the American troops, but any longer stay implied an occupation and possibly a war with Mexico. No better opportunity ever came to withdraw the Punitive Expedition, which had achieved its original goal of destroying the Villista bands. After April the pretext for the U.S. intervention changed to the goal of capturing Pancho Villa. A divided cabinet made the decision difficult for President Wilson, who with deep misgivings authorized Pershing to continue the search for Villa. The U.S. decision to stay provoked massive hostility in Mexico. While Villa emerged as the leader of nationalist sentiment against the invaders, Carranza appeared as a puppet of the Americans. The problem became public when on 12 April a mob at Parral attacked some soldiers. Elisa Griensen rallied the locals to throw stones at the Americans. The mob shouted the inevitable cries of "viva Mexico" but what worried Carranza most was that the crowd also shouted "viva Villa." Carranza duly began to protest the U.S. intervention, and he tried to regain public support by releasing the texts of the angry notes he sent to the U.S. government. Washington ignored him and also quietly imposed an embargo on shipments of arms and ammunition on 1 May, thus crippling the Mexican army for years.[122]

National feeling in Mexico clamored for the expulsion of the Americans, and Carranza could not fall too far behind public opinion. In early June Carranza took the decision for war when he told American troops that if they moved south, east, or west they risked Mexican attacks; the only direction open was north back to the United States. On 16 June General Treviño communicated the warning to Pershing, who replied that he had not yet received any restrictions on his movements from the U.S. government. The next day Pershing summoned Captain Boyd, and according to the general's recollection, told him to reconnoiter to the east and to avoid combat; however, the noncommissioned officers of Boyd recalled him saying that his orders were to test whether the Mexicans intended to attack if U.S. troops moved in a direction other than north.

At 0700 on 21 June, Boyd's cavalry troop approached the Carrancista troops posted at the village of Carrizal. The Mexican second in command asked why they were here, and Boyd replied they were looking for bandits; to which the Mexican replied that none were in the area. Boyd then said he was going to recover a deserter in a town further east of Carrizal, whereupon the Mexican told him he could not proceed. Boyd replied that the Americans were going to shoot their way through. A few minutes later the Mexican general personally came to plead one last time with the hot-headed Boyd not to attack and asked for three or four hours to send telegraph messages to his superior to try to clear up the situation. Boyd foolishly interpreted this last gesture for peace as a sign of weakness and concluded that the Mexican general was just playing for time. As soon as the Mexican general returned to his troops, Boyd hurled his cavalry troop at the massed Mexican infantry. By 0800 the cavalry charge was almost over, with all the men of Boyd's unit killed, captured, or fleeing. A war seemed inevitable, but presidents Carranza and Wilson maneuvered deftly around the clash. Carranza returned all the prisoners and the captured equipment, while Wilson halted any further American advance.[123]

Wilson, however, still did not feel politically strong enough to recall the Punitive Expedition. Lengthy negotiations with Mexico ensued, and by then Villa had emerged from his cave and rallied enough supporters to capture villages. Although only by force could he recruit men, his control over the countryside was increasing. To show his newly recovered strength, on 16 September he attacked Chihuahua City. He knew he could not overcome its large garrison, but expected enough of a surprise to liberate the prisoners from the penitentiary and to kill General Treviño. The Carrancista commander had ignored the many warnings of an imminent attack and had unwisely sent on leave most of his soldiers to celebrate the Mexican national holiday. The Villistas duly captured their objectives, including the officers' quarters, but because Treviño with his newfound wealth lived in a private residence, he escaped alive. As the Carrancista soldiers hurriedly reported to duty, they mounted a counterattack that drove back the Villistas, who withdrew in good order loaded with booty and recruits from the penitentiary. The failure to kill Treviño was a disguised blessing for the Villistas, who otherwise would have lost their most incompetent opponent.[124]

The near capture of Chihuahua City on 16 September provided U.S. diplomats with just the excuse they needed to justify the continued presence of the Punitive Expedition in Mexico. Pershing prepared his men for winter quarters and distributed them in grids occupying northwest Chihuahua. Meanwhile, Villa continued to revive his fortunes under the banner of anti–Americanism and as usual avoided U.S. forces and attacked only the weaker Carrancistas. On 23 November Villa made another attempt on Chihuahua City and again caught Treviño by surprise. The Carrancistas repulsed

the assault and even counterattacked successfully, but in the process they used up most of their scarce ammunition. Rather than realizing how precarious his situation was, a triumphant Treviño prepared to celebrate the victory and neglected to reinforce his artillery at Santa Rosa, the key hill that dominated Chihuahua City. The Villistas returned to the city at full strength on 26 November and in the pre-dawn hours of 27 November in a ferocious charge they captured Santa Rosa hill. Treviño panicked and fled in such haste that he failed to tell all his units to withdraw to the railroad station. Most Carrancista troops escaped by train, but some remained behind fighting in the penitentiary. With food, water, and cartridges running out, the defenders of the penitentiary agreed to surrender when Villa offered them the chance to fight against the Americans. Like so many of the Villistas, most subsequently deserted at the first opportunity.[125]

Villa had been in a hurry to capture the equipment and artillery in the city before the fast approaching relief column of General Francisco Murguía arrived. The Villistas had damaged the track to delay the forceful Murguía, who did not let the destruction stop him. Murguía pushed ahead of the repair crews and was closing in fast on the state capital. At Horcasitas right in front of Bachimba, Murguía defeated a small Villista force on 1 December. The next day the Villistas, loaded with plunder, supplies, and cannons, evacuated Chihuahua. As soon as the Carrancistas returned to the city, General Murguía relieved the incompetent and corrupt Treviño as the zone commander. Murguía, a brilliant general, had the fatal flaw of letting arrogance cloud his judgment; in many ways he resembled the old Díaz commanders, most notably General Antonio Rábago. After his arrival, Murguía did not grasp the magnitude of the Villista military threat. In a notable omission, he failed to reinforce the beleaguered Torreón garrison at once in spite of direct orders from Secretary of War Obregón to do so. Villa seized Torreón on 22 December, and his army regained the strength of those he had commanded in 1915.

This remarkable comeback persuaded Villa to shift from a guerrilla to a conventional war and to risk everything in one decisive battle. Murguía was more than glad to comply, and in another show of overconfidence, he split his army and sent 3,000 of his soldiers to destroy the Villista supply bases at Ciudad Guerrero. With his weakened army he himself marched south to meet Villa at Estación Reforma near Jiménez on 3 January 1917. The two sides were equally matched and a draw seemed the most likely outcome, had not Villa become even more arrogant than Murguía. Villa believed that the Carrancistas were so demoralized that headlong cavalry charges sufficed to win the battle. The result was a predictable replay of Celaya, with Murguía's machine guns and rifles mowing down Villa's horsemen. Murguía counterattacked, put the Villistas to flight, and entered Jiménez. Although he failed to pursue the Villistas as furiously as he could have, this battle largely finished Villa as a major threat in the north.[126]

The column Murguía had sent to Ciudad Guerrero did destroy the supplies of Villa, who never again was able to field a large force, but who maintained irregular warfare for years. From 1913 to 1915 Villa had been a popular figure who could rebuild armies after crushing defeats, but by January 1917 even the flagging anti–American wind could not revive his faltering movement. His forced impressment of men and his repeated brutality had angered many inhabitants of Chihuahua. Probably the worst massacre took place a few days after the battle of Horcasitas; in a fit of rage, he ordered the execution of ninety *soldaderas* of a captured garrison. Just like before at the massacre of civilians at San Pedro de la Cueva in 1915, so again at Horcasitas Villa proved he could push the limits of bestial savagery.[127]

Atrocities and massacres could only hasten the disintegration of the Villistas. With Villa in headlong retreat, the continued presence of the Punitive Expedition became pointless. For the United States, the crushing Villista defeat at Estación Reforma was the cue to evacuate. On 18 January 1917 President Wilson gave orders for an orderly withdrawal, and on 5 February the last of Pershing's troops left Mexico. The Punitive Expedition, by reviving Villa, prolonged the upheavals and the conflicts that had ripped Mexico apart since 1910. Rather than bringing peace and order, the Punitive Expedition worsened a desperate situation. Although usually consigned to a footnote as a non-event in U.S. history, the Punitive Expedition had a major impact on world history. The inability to catch Pancho Villa exposed the U.S. Army to ridicule. The failure of the Punitive Expedition made the German high command confidently conclude that the United States could not stop Berlin from winning World War I.[128]

9. The Revival of Mexico's Central Government

Boys, let us pray that the revolution may continue forever as then we will continue to enjoy life, women, wine, and music. Once it is over, then back to work for us. — General Juan Carrasco addressing his soldiers[1]

The defeat of Pancho Villa at Estación Reforma on 3 January 1917 did not mean the end of his career. His remarkable comebacks and exploits as a guerrilla cum bandit leader continued until 1920, and their narration can easily fill another chapter. But without any radical changes in technology, tactics, or strategy, only admirers of Pancho Villa would delight in reliving his later local adventures.[2] This chapter has the much more important task of revealing the crucial role the army played in the revival of the central government.

Since the disintegration of the Huerta regime in early 1914, Mexico had lacked a central government. Even before Pancho Villa dropped to the level of being a regional nuisance, President Venustiano Carranza began the long and difficult task of reconstructing the central government of Mexico. The authoritarian character of Carranza suggested that he planned to restore the oppressive system of Porfirio Díaz, but the changed circumstances counseled otherwise. After 1916 Carranza kept the army campaigning against minor rebels, but its usually languid efforts rarely produced smashing successes. He preferred conciliatory arrangements to battlefield victories, and he displayed an extraordinary patience in his dealings with the rulers of the individual Mexican states. His light touch seemed to be what a tur-

bulent Mexico needed to calm the revolutionary passions, but the danger of disintegration remained lurking. By 1919 the country finally was tired of waiting for his negotiated formulas to restore peace and order. A new regime very eager to bring the full weight of the army to crush rebels emerged in 1920. The army made sure that no more popular insurrections ever again overthrew the central government, but who could keep the generals from revolting?

The Exhaustion of Mexico and the System of Venustiano Carranza

Very powerful reasons made possible the rise of the system of Venustiano Carranza in 1916. The financing of the war and the recruitment of armies are the two areas that best demonstrated the disastrous conditions in Mexico. Traditional accounts emphasize that the national government financed the warfare of 1911–1916 by printing paper money and by allocating most of the budget to the army. Paper money and budgetary priorities were just the two outer layers for cost reduction and the shift of expenses to the private sector, the two real mechanisms that financed six years of bloody and destructive warfare. No other solu-

261

tions were possible, because the government lacked the ability to increase revenue in any significant way. Booms in henequén and petroleum prices did bring windfall revenue but not enough to compensate for the decline in customs revenue. At that time, the customs houses were the largest source of revenue for governments, and Mexico was no exception. Customs revenue declined after 1912 because of the disruptions of the war, and not surprisingly, governments readily printed paper money to offset the decline.[3]

Paper currency rapidly depreciated and was really a way to shift the war expenses to the private sector. Reducing costs was the second mechanism, and the large bureaucracy of the army was the first to suffer budget cuts. Under Porfirio Díaz, orders flowed from one of many sections in the War Department through the ten military zones and then to the individual units, a slow and cumbersome process at best. The battlefield required officers in the front and not behind desks; by 1914 the ten zone commands melted away, and the War Department itself was disintegrating. Small staffs in the field armies assumed the administrative duties, much as the rebels had done from the start. The collapse of the War Department in the second quarter of 1914 merely reflected the disintegration of the central government. Not until late 1916 did Carranza begin the laborious task of reconstructing the principal governmental organs in Mexico City. Under the initial direction of General Álvaro Obregón, the War Department slowly began to revive.[4]

One major reason why so many staff officers could join combat units was that the army no longer needed to provision the soldiers. Under Porfirio Díaz a quartermaster bureaucracy was slowly replacing the female camp followers or *soldaderas* as the main source of cooked food and clothing for the soldiers. The rebel forces of 1911 made no attempt to establish a quartermaster system but did not rely to any large degree on the *soldaderas* either. Because the rebels of 1911 generally fought near their villages and rode horses, they could return home easily and thus did not need many *soldaderas*. By 1912 as units routinely traveled long distances, all the contenders relied on women to find and prepare food, firewood, and clothing for the soldiers. The female scavengers became adept at finding any scrap of food that

could be found in a village. Supposedly they bought the provisions from merchants and peasants, but paying in usually depreciating currency, the purchases were more in the nature of forced requisitions. When American soldiers paid their purchases with specie in 1916, they gained grudging acceptance for the Punitive Expedition in Chihuahua.[5]

The Punitive Expedition was but a rare exception to the prevailing pattern of requisitioning from the countryside to support the marching armies. Although the Carranza regime strove to pay its soldiers, from 1911 to 1916 the outright confiscation of cattle, horses, fodder, clothing, and foodstuffs was the normal rule. The practice began as open looting in 1911, and although plundering continued throughout the period, Emiliano Zapata was the first to impose forced contributions as the usual way to finance his army. Forced contributions were more orderly and less destructive than looting. Then if the revolutionary band became sufficiently stable, the forced contributions and ransoms necessarily evolved into a system of taxation. Only the Carrancista regime managed to accomplish the transition from looting to taxation. The Carrancistas from the start had tried the hardest to keep their soldiers from looting, and if never completely successful, their behavior contrasted with the drive for plunder in the other revolutionary groups.

The Carrancista units were always composed of volunteers and usually received their daily wage or allowance to acquire food, even if with depreciated money. As the Carrancista currency became stronger, the combination of volunteer soldiers and adequate wages gave that side an advantage over its rivals. The *soldaderas*, however, never received a cent and had to make their partner's allowance stretch to feed them and their children. In effect, the revolutionaries had shifted a large part of the burden of financing the war upon the backs of these poor and ignorant women. Some could be as young as twelve years. Abductions were frequent, and the soldiers routinely forced women to follow the army. "One of the most barbarous crimes committed by the forces in the fields is the taking of Mexican women, whose husbands have joined the enemy, and also single Mexican girls, forcing them to join the ranks of the *soldaderas*."[6] Some women did follow their men out of love, but most joined because they lacked any other alternative. With their villages destroyed or all the men in their lives dead, joining the army was often the only way to escape starvation. "It was either follow the army, starve, or get raped."[7] And with so many women getting raped during the pillaging of villages and haciendas, the life of a camp follower was the only option for women shamed into fleeing their communities.[8]

Real bonds of attachment often arose between the men and the *soldaderas*, and many women fired rifles to help or to avenge their partner. Women actually fought as soldiers, sometimes disguised as men or in separate all-female units. The majority of the females were free to leave, but generally stayed on even after the death of their companions. The unattached *soldaderas* were in the worst condition, because they did not receive the regular allowance of their companion, yet many still stayed for lack of a better alternative or to wait for the right man to appear. Women, usually disguised as men, became officers and a few reached even the rank of colonel.[9] During the intense campaigning of the years 1912 to 1915, women on the average provided at least 1 percent and perhaps as much as 5 percent of the rifle fire, the figure naturally varying greatly by army and region. The most common combat role of the women was much less glamorous but not less significant. No soldier felt comfortable going into battle with less that 120 cartridges, but carrying more than a hundred already put a tremendous weight on the men, or if they happened to be mounted soldiers, on their horses. Except when riding trains, the *soldaderas* walked on foot and carried heavy bandoleers for the soldiers, who either marched alongside the women or rode horses. During combat the women reloaded rifles and scurried for cartridges and rifles from fallen soldiers.[10]

Prisoners were not a luxury Mexico could afford. The random executions of 1912 escalated in early 1913 until the execution of prisoners taken in battle became the standard practice on both sides. This brutal policy eliminated the expense for prisoner of war camps and also permanently reduced the numbers of the opponent. Not surprisingly, soldiers learned to flee as fast as possible from the battlefield as soon as defeat seemed imminent. After the fall of Victoriano Huerta in July 1914, a growing number of exceptions restrained the

practice of executing the prisoners. So many were the prisoners taken at battles like Celaya, that a wholesale slaughter was out of the question, and only the officers faced the firing squad. But in engagements by small units or even larger units in isolated areas, the execution of all prisoners remained the tragic norm. And what about the *soldaderas*? Whether combatant or not, as women they were exempt from execution. Although they were free to leave after being taken prisoner, most women joined the victorious army. When Pancho Villa in one of his frequent rages had *soldaderas* executed in 1916, his barbaric action seemed unusually bloody and cruel to men accustomed to the horrors and savagery of the Mexican Revolution.

Looting, forced contributions, executions, and the exploitation of women financed the war, but in a Mexico drained of resources by 1915, more resourceful ways had to be found to keep the war machine going. To reduce costs, officers put the *soldaderas* and sometimes the soldiers themselves to search battlefields for empty cartridge shells. Just the purchase of millions of cartridges abroad had become a crushing expense for Mexico. Villa, Carranza, and even Zapata tried to produce their own munitions, but only Carranza, who had inherited the installations from the Díaz regime, had some success in producing cartridges. By recycling empty shells to produce new if inferior cartridges, Carranza did not have to import as much ammunition and thus gained both a financial and a military edge over his rivals. Complete victory should have been his had not the United Sates prohibited ammunition exports to Mexico in May 1916. Because of the U.S. arms embargo, the temporary boost Carranza received from recycling served only to prolong the incessant irregular warfare of the years 1917 to 1920. The chronic shortage of ammunition crippled the Carrancista campaigns against the poorly armed rebel bands.[11]

With such a scarcity of resources and under the threat of execution if captured, how could the armies find men motivated enough to stay and fight? The dregs of society had traditionally ended up in the armies of Diaz and Huerta, who had relied on the *leva* (levy) or the press gang to bring their units up to strength. With the men ever willing to desert, the officers had to maintain constant vigilance to keep units from vanishing. These coerced soldiers fought surprisingly well, but the ultimate defeat of Diaz and Huerta discredited the press gang. Of the rebel leaders, only Pancho Villa gave the press gang another chance after 1915, but with the predictable results of constant desertions. Except for the Villista bands in their last years, volunteers comprised almost all of the armies in revolutionary Mexico.

The best inducement for men to join the army was regular pay, and the Carrancista regime with its control over the best revenue sources enjoyed a distinctive advantage over the other revolutionary rivals. Already in 1916, it was not low pay but the need to escape starvation that primarily drove many men into the Carrancista ranks. The proximity to the United States made the monetary consideration most acute in the troops from Sonora. There the men coldly calculated their options: Much as they liked the excitement of campaigning across the country, if the pay did not equal what they could earn in the civilian pursuits of mining, farming, and ranching, they refused to join the army. Because Sonora escaped any major destruction, the alternative of private employment really existed for these men. Sonora was an unusual case; for the rest of the soldiers from other ravaged regions of Mexico, joining the army was the only way to escape starvation.[12]

Boys provided a significant percentage of the recruits for the revolutionary armies. A large number of children accompanied the troops and reinforced the image of the army as a wandering tribe of nomads. The girls grew up to become *soldaderas*, and as soon as they could carry a rifle, the boys joined the troops and became indistinguishable from their much older companions. A stage of observation, when the boys carried weapons and cartridges as their only toys, generally preceded their formal entry into the ranks. Although conceivably a boy born to a *soldadera* in 1911 could have fought in the campaigns of 1919 and 1920, no such case can be recorded. With so many fathers killed and mothers abducted or dying, the huge number of orphans often had no other place to go but to the armed units, which also served as crude orphanages. The natural attraction of boys to guns and combat made the army life seem less cruel and more fascinating than it actually was. An analysis of the available ev-

idence suggests that boys 14 years or younger comprised at least one-fifth of the rebel forces. If 16 is considered the age limit for boys, then the figure can well rise to one-fourth. When in 1916 the War Department ordered the discharge of soldiers less than 18 years of age, a tremendous outcry arose among the field commanders. General Francisco Murguía claimed he could not comply, because he did not want to lose 40 percent of his soldiers.[13] It should be noted that in contrast to world military history, the standard association of drafting boys with the depletion of the supply of adult males did not hold in Mexico. The army took the boys because they were easier to incorporate than the surviving adult males who were learning fast to hide or flee when armed groups passed nearby. The armies were able to beguile the naive youths with the glamour of soldiering but not the adults who feared for their lives and usually had seen enough of the horrors of war.

The prospects of plunder were indispensable to encourage enlistment in the rebel armies, but as places to loot became scarce, the lure of booty waned. One of Villa's reasons for invading Sonora in 1915 was precisely to tap one of the last wealthy regions in Mexico. With plunder fast running out as an inducement after 1914, not surprisingly the supply of idealistic souls supposedly willing to die for a cause was also drying up. Even in the early years when great prospects for plunder had attracted many volunteers, the supply of really able soldiers had remained limited. The peasants from central and southern Mexico did not take well to campaigning in distant regions, even though they could fight superbly to defend their home grounds. Skilled soldiers willing to fight anywhere in Mexico and accustomed to army discipline were not abundant. Although most of the population of Mexico lived in the center and south of the country, the overwhelming majority of the best soldiers came from the sparse population in northern Mexico. Converting the crude, ignorant, and taciturn peasants of central and southern Mexico into disciplined fighting soldiers was a slow, difficult, and often impossible task, even if they had volunteered to join.[14]

For an immediate supply of skilled and enthusiastic soldiers, the generals relied on two main sources of volunteers. The first and best known were the Red Battalions mentioned in

Boy rebels in Chihuahua. No less than in the War of the Thousand Days (1899–1902) in Colombia, boys were an important source of recruits for the rebel forces in Mexico (Library of Congress, Prints and Photographs Division, George Grantham Bain Collection).

the previous chapter. The workers at factories and at other industrial establishments had acquired skills and usually an urban experience that set them apart from the more backwards country folk. Carranza pulled a coup when he signed an agreement with the labor organizations in February 1915. They agreed to provide workers as soldiers, and in exchange Carranza pledged to support labor unions against business. The agreement could not have come at a more critical moment for Carranza, who was desperately short of soldiers because of the Yucatán uprising. Not only did Carranza receive soldiers when he needed them most to save his movement, but in addition, the workers were eager to fight well in combat. The great victories of Obregón and the defense of Ébano could not have occurred without the Red Battalions. Although they were not a large percentage of the Carrancista army, their skills, dedication, and enthusiasm provided that additional edge required to make victory possible.[15]

Before the organization of the first Red Battalions, another source was already providing a larger number of good soldiers and continued to supply recruits long after the disbandment of the Red Battalions. Indian warriors, sometimes under promises of land or booty, at other times just for a chance to strike back at the Federal Army, joined the maelstrom of the Mexican Revolution as early as 1911. The Indians usually but not always came from the isolated regions of the north, and often they came armed only with bows and arrows. Whether they were the Zapotecs from Oaxaca, Ocuila from Durango or Pimas, Papagos, and Tarahumara from Coahuila did not really matter. Rebel armies successfully recruited large numbers of Indians, who found campaigning to be an attractive activity in its own right. Almost every large rebel force inevitably ended up incorporating significant numbers of ethnic Indians into its ranks.

Of all the Indians, the Yaquis and the

Mayos of Sonora and northern Sinaloa were the most prominent throughout the Mexican Revolution. These last two groups spoke the same language, and their fundamental difference (besides living in separate river valleys) was that the Mayos had long since made their peace with the white man, while the Yaquis remained locked in a struggle over whether to accept the Mexicans or drive them out. Superb warriors who could withstand the extremes of cold and heat, they were much more than scouts and came to comprise some of the best combat battalions. Always officered by their own leaders, the Yaquis and the Mayos were extremely loyal, and they abandoned their allegiance only when that side stood no chance of winning. If any soldiers read the endless manifestos of their generals, the Yaquis and the Mayos certainly did not, and thus they could fit comfortably in any revolutionary army whatever its cause or leader. The Yaquis and the Mayos seemed to be present in all the revolutionary armies, and at least in Sonora these Indians were sometimes found fighting each other on opposing sides. The Yaquis and the Mayos were much too valuable as soldiers to execute if taken prisoner, and instead the winning side promptly incorporated them into its ranks. The almost complete immunity from execution helps to explain why from 1911 to 1929 the Yaquis and the Mayos appear to have been more numerous than they actually were; in reality the same modest number was recycled through the revolutionary armies.

Indians, children, and women were a nearly constant presence in the armies of Mexico. Not indignation or ethical constraints halted the exploitation of the weakest and most vulnerable members of society. Only the exhaustion of material resources by 1916 finally brought the destructive warfare to a halt. The rapacious campaigning of 1911–1916 had stripped the country of the wealth laboriously accumulated under Porfirio Díaz. An agrarian society like Mexico, despite benefiting from the stimulus of an expanding U.S. economy, could not support indefinitely the warfare of the industrial age. Ammunition shortages had plagued the last battles of General Álvaro Obregón, and the economic collapse limited immensely the capacity of the Carranza regime to sustain a large and efficient army. Hunger was stalking Mexico, and diseases were decimating the population. The railroad network was in shambles and served only the army instead of the economy. The civilian population was weary of war and longed to see the end of the destructive military campaigns. Mexico needed a long period of peace to repair the ravages of the war, but without resources, how could it maintain a strong government?[16] To achieve the peace, the generals wanted to finish destroying all the rebels quickly; Carranza opposed the military solution and preferred to wear down the rebels until they accepted a political arrangement. A fundamental division emerged between Carranza and his generals over how to bring peace to Mexico.

Ever since the break with Villa in 1914, Carranza developed a strong distrust of his generals. In 1913 he had welcomed them into the revolt against Huerta, but the realization that political power gravitated to the generals and not to civilians like Carranza cooled his enthusiasm. Each additional battlefield victory increased the power and prestige of the generals. Yet he could not disband the army while so many rebellions were still swirling around the country. What Carranza needed was to pacify the country in a way that preserved his own position and the preeminence of civilian leadership. Hence, when Obregón was preparing to leave for Sonora to block Villa's invasion, Carranza considered it more important that the general accompany him on political tours of already pacified regions. The Punitive Expedition had forced Carranza to appoint Obregon to be Secretary of War, but the president did not give freedom of action to the general. Most notably, Carranza refused to remove Treviño as zone commander in Chihuahua and agreed to replace him only when the danger from Villa had become overwhelming. Not surprisingly, Obregón grew increasingly frustrated with Carranza's interference in the campaigns to destroy the rebels. Obregón took advantage of Carranza's inauguration as president on 1 May 1917 to leave the War Department and to return to private business in Sonora.[17] With Obregón no longer present to insist on military victory, the president was free to pursue a more leisurely policy toward the rebels. Carranza did not receive a blank check, however, and the resignation of Obregón left explicit a deadline. If Carranza did not restore order and peace to Mexico during his term, the generals were ready to step in to impose a solution by force.

Carranza took office as elected president for a term of four years under the just promulgated Constitution of 1917. Its clauses gave the president many powers, but the authority of the central government was often more nominal than real beyond Mexico City. The largest cities of Mexico, such as Monterrey and Guadalajara, and the main customs houses were under firm government control. Carranza kept a tight grip over Yucatán with its henequén exports. He was less successful in the petroleum fields of Tampico where the rebel Manuel Peláez (initially using the Villista label) had cut into the oil royalties since late 1915.[18] Villa maintained a lingering revolt in Chihuahua, while Zapata continued his protracted resistance in Morelos. Felicismo, the movement of Félix Díaz, the nephew of Porfirio Díaz, had taken root in parts of Veracruz State. Other lesser rebels, such as the Cedillo brothers in San Luis Potosí, harassed many regions. Most difficult to identity were the fluctuating groups of bandits who seemed to terrorize almost all of Mexico. This lawlessness and these late rebellions were particularly hard to put down because of their seasonal nature. Rebels and bandits fought when agrarian chores were lightest but then returned to the countryside for harvests and plantings. With the rebels and the bandits easily melting into the rural population, any campaign to destroy them necessarily had to be long and costly.[19]

The rebels and bandits were a serious but not the most dangerous challenge to the authority of Carranza. The Mexican constitution established a federalist system similar to that of the United States, and in accordance with that principle, the individual states enjoyed for the first time in their history considerable independence from the central government. To bring the states under his control, Carranza tried to elect as governors individuals personally loyal to him, and in over half of the states he was successful. However, in many of these states, his imposition of official candidates aroused considerable resentment, and the latent hostility was just waiting for a favorable moment to explode into a violent revolt. In over a third of the states the governors were either openly hostile to or indifferent to the president. In spite of Carranza's deliberate efforts to

favor civilians, many victorious generals converted states into their personal fiefdoms. The most notable was Calles, who ruled Sonora in virtual independence of Carranza. Although the Arrieta brothers had passionately fought for Carranza, once in power they ruled Durango practically on their own. The most blatant example of independence was the federal territory of northern Baja California. The president had the constitutional authority to appoint the governors and officials of territories, but in Baja California, a former federal officer, Esteban Cantú, reigned supreme. Not even his earlier alliance with Villa could persuade Carranza to authorize an invasion of Baja California to depose Cantú. The President contented himself with tardy protests of loyalty even when Cantú kept the proceeds from the customs houses. The brisk trade with the United States made dollars the legal currency in that practically independent territory.[20]

Cantú was an extreme case that revealed the real danger that Mexico might break up into smaller countries. Baja California would most likely be absorbed into the United States, while large states such as Chihuahua could proclaim independence. Once fragmentation began, a domino effect was sure to produce a coterie of petty republics resembling the Central American countries. Comfortably at least a dozen countries could have emerged out of Mexico to complete its Central Americanization. Because Carranza had blocked the final military campaigns, he left Mexico extremely vulnerable to political disintegration. His fear of the generals drove Carranza to preside over a confederation of nearly independent states. The result was quite ironic, because the struggle with Pancho Villa had been mainly about the allegiance of a regional warlord to the central government. Had Villa kept at least outward submission to Carranza, he probably could have remained as warlord of Chihuahua. Villa's open defiance and his pro–American stand over Veracruz made an accommodation impossible, but his goal of a weak central government came closer to realization than even Carranza wished to admit.

By 1919 Carranza had been able to weaken most of the remaining rebellions. His access to customs revenue gave his army a staying power over the rebel bands, which gradually retreated into remote areas or more likely disbanded. Zapata's insatiable need for personal power precluded any peaceful settlement, and this regional warlord blocked every attempt to find a negotiated solution. To dispose of the Zapatistas and the remaining rebels, Carranza needed more time. With his four-year term rapidly coming to a close, he knew that he could not run for president again, because reelection was the most hated concept in Mexico. As the next section explains, Carranza came to believe that he had found a path around the barrier of no reelection.

The Overthrow of the System of Venustiano Carranza

From 1917 to 1919 Carranza lived the heyday of his political career. As president he faced little political opposition in Mexico City and had a free hand to direct national affairs. To his credit he astutely kept Mexico out of World War I, but national issues of such a momentous magnitude were rare. With no other field of action left, Carranza, in the tradition of Porfirio Díaz, dabbled in the politics of the individual Mexican states. In what remained a characteristic of his governing style, he spent considerable time touring many parts of the country. He used these trips to bolster loyalists and to give his blessing to local candidates. In Mexico City he surrounded himself with sycophants, and the inevitable adulation of subordinates had a deleterious effect on Carranza whose stubbornness and inflexibility grew by bounds. Not wishing to hear bad news, the president increasingly grew out of touch with the country. The cronies around him soon were involved in many scandalous cases of fraud and corruption. Porfirio Díaz for decades had resisted the temptations of adulation, but for Carranza, a few years in power sufficed to foster the conviction that Mexico could not survive without him.[21]

The Constitution of 1917 had codified the principle of no reelection to the same post, and as Carranza saw his four-year term winding down, he searched for a way to perpetuate himself in power. The public seemed eager to participate in presidential politics, and to try to gain time for himself, on 15 January 1919 Carranza appealed to the country to delay the start of the presidential campaign. The public re-

ceived the appeal surprisingly well, but Carranza knew he had to do something more substantial. When General Pablo González sought authorization to ambush Emiliano Zapata, Carranza saw in the elimination of this bothersome rebel leader an opportunity to bolster the political fortunes of his increasingly unpopular regime. Zapata's personal quest for power had prevented any negotiated solution to the rebellion in Morelos, but the destructive campaigns of the army had made his followers much more amenable to an arrangement. When Zapata was ambushed and murdered on 10 April 1919, Carranza at last could bolster his claim that he was bringing Mexico closer to peace. But the Zapatistas, who for the first time were free of the dictatorial control of their warlord, were also watching the shifting presidential winds. The Zapatistas wisely decided to wait before reaching any agreement with Mexico City to lay down their arms.[22]

Carranza did not want to realize that the blatant corruption of his cronies had thoroughly discredited his regime. He could not believe either that the army, the real source of political power, no longer supported him. In 1917 the army accepted Carranza as the first constitutional president, but soon the generals felt ignored and even betrayed by his blatant preference for easily manipulated civilians. A serious clashed loomed had not General Álvaro Obregón graciously retired to private life in May 1917. The life-long goal of Obregón had always been to attain the status of a wealthy businessman in his native state of Sonora. He applied to his business dealings the same care and skills he had formerly devoted to this military campaigns and not surprisingly shrewd deals made him a millionaire. The widowed Obregón remarried and was enjoying a very happy family life with his children. He rejected repeated requests to return to political office and even declined to run for governor of his state. In spite of his modesty and his desire to enjoy his new family and to concentrate on his business affairs, he was already a legendary figure in Mexico, the true life hero who vanquished even Pancho Villa. Not surprisingly, political and military leaders constantly urged Obregón to run for president, and after repeated entreaties Obregón finally announced his candidacy on 1 June 1919. By the end of the month it was clear that another general, Pablo

González, was also interested in running for president. The latter made a good opposition candidate, but no one doubted that the popular Obregón was the overwhelming favorite to win any honest election.[23]

By the time Carranza's term ended, he would be over sixty and rightfully could claim to have saved Mexico on repeated occasions. An approach to Obregón, who had always been most deferential to Carranza, promised to provide the ex-president any suitable position such as the governorship of his native Coahuila. But like many other Mexicans, holding high office had become an incurable disease only partially calmed by daily doses of power. Rather than negotiate a dignified retirement, Carranza plunged Mexico into another decade of turmoil. To succeed him, Carranza picked the pliable Ignacio Bonillas, a helpless civilian then ambassador to the U.S. Bonillas was a figure who immediately inspired ridicule and soon was nicknamed "Tea Blossom"; his many years abroad fed the accusation that he would be the first Mexican president not fluent in Spanish. The power play of Carranza was obvious; in effect he wanted to rule through a puppet.[24] Extreme as were the pretensions of Carranza, they were not totally without foundation; indeed, he was the first to realize that the presidency included the authority to pick a successor, a power that lasted until the year 2000.

As early as October 1919, Plutarco E. Calles warned that "if the government [...] tries to impose the engineer Bonillas, I am sure, and I regret it with all my soul, that the country will fall again into a civil war."[25] Carranza counted on the old Porfirian practice of stealing elections to secure the victory for Bonillas. This part of the maneuver should have been successful had not the disintegration of the president's authority reached the point that he no longer controlled enough of the electoral machinery to guarantee the election for Bonillas. In a replay of the Porfirian precedent that had provoked the revolt of Francisco Madero in 1910, Carranza decided to lure Obregón back to the capital and then have him arrested on trumped-up charges, thus eliminating the rival candidacy. Obregón received a court summons to declare in a military trial, and if he refused to come, he faced arrest. The danger of arrest was no less if he came, but if he had dared before to risk execution at the hands of Pancho

Villa, Obregón was confident that this new crisis somehow would rebound in his benefit. As soon as he arrived in Mexico City, the police put him under round-the-clock surveillance, and he felt almost like a prisoner.[26]

News from Sonora soon showed the path for Obregón to follow. The state government of Sonora was engaged in a bitter quarrel with Mexico City over lands in the Yaqui River and tempers were already running high. At this volatile moment, the Carranza government announced the creation of a vast military zone, which included Sonora, on the Pacific Coast. As commander of the new military zone, Carranza appointed General Manuel Diéguez, whose real mission was to displace the Obregón sympathizers from the electoral machinery in those states. By turning to the army to impose the civilian candidacy of Bonillas, the Carranza regime had been the first to threaten force. The outrage in Sonora was enormous, and Governor Adolfo de la Huerta vainly tried to persuade Carranza not to send General Diéguez. On 6 April the state legislature unanimously declared to the president "that the deployment is an immediate and direct attack on the state's sovereignty, and that if the Executive insists on the deployment, you will be the only one responsible for all the consequences."[27] Carranza refused to reverse course, and in reply on 10 April the state legislature authorized the executive to take all actions to defend Sonora. De la Huerta appointed Plutarco E. Calles commander of the military operations, and the army units in Sonora joined the rebellion.[28]

Thrilling as was the repetition of Sonora's earlier revolt against Huerta in 1913, Calles knew that unless many army units in other states joined the movement, Sonora alone stood no chance against the reviving power of the central government. Calles hurriedly contacted his allies to try to convert the state rebellion into a national movement. The news of the revolt of Sonora was the signal Obregón in Mexico City had been waiting for. At 0100 on 13 April he escaped the police surveillance and in disguise boarded a train for the state of Guerrero to the south; by the time the police discovered his flight, he was safely away. The zone commander at Guerrero, General Fortunato Maycotte, offered his support to Obregón, who in turn asked him to pretend to be loyal to Carranza a few more days until Obregón

Disguised as a railway employee, in May 1920 Obregón fled Mexico City to escape the arrest order of Venustiano Carranza. Here the disguised Obregón is in the center, flanked by two of the followers who helped him escape (Clodoveo Valenzuela and Amado Chaverri Matamoros, *Sonora y Carranza*; Mexico: Editorial Renacimiento, 1921).

could quietly rally more supporters for his movement. The nearby Zapatistas, in an effort to secure the political agreement their leader had steadfastly opposed, were among the first to support Obregon eagerly. On 20 April Obregón publicly declared his support for the revolt of Sonora and put himself under the orders of Governor De la Huerta; with the troops in Guerrero and the Zapatistas in Morelos, Sonora was no longer alone. By then local sympathizers helped by troops from Sonora had gained control of Sinaloa. The Carranza regime still had a chance to put down these widely separated revolts, but General Diéguez, who should have been vigorously leading troops against Sonora, dallied in Guadalajara.[29]

Before Obregón's announcement of 20 April, army commanders throughout the country had been pondering whether to join the rebels or to remain Carrancistas. Zacatecas had joined the revolt on the 15th, followed the next day by Michoacán where individual units had

been abandoning the government: "The revolutionary movement in Michoacán, even though all of us were determined to support it, did not have any preparation, because there was no prior agreement among the different officers who carried it [...] each officer based first on his own initiative and his own beliefs, carried out separately their revolts, and then put themselves spontaneously at the orders of this commander."[30] At the oil district of Tampico, General Arnulfo R. Gómez joined the movement on 18 April and made an alliance with the rebel Peláez. On 21 April their combined forces invaded Veracruz State and attacked Tuxpam, defended by the loyal forces of Cándido Aguilar, the son-in-law of Venustiano Carranza. The combat lasted 18 hours, and although the rebels were not able to dislodge Aguilar, he decided to abandon the city and retreated to Veracruz, in effect granting the rebels their first major victory.[31] More than any other rebel General Gómez knew how crucial it was for the revolt to score a victory quickly at any cost. When he heard on 1 May that "soldiers of the 65th Battalion have deserted without any reason and only because of the fear that hesitant spirits feel and thus showing their cowardice," he consequently ordered that "any deserter will be executed." [32] Although this revolt did not revive the practice of executions of prisoners normal in the bloody years of 1913–1916, the readiness to use whatever means were necessary to win ratified the deadly seriousness of the revolt.

Calles was eager to push south from Sinaloa to link up with Obregón in Guerrero, but the danger of a Carrancista offensive from Chihuahua kept most of the rebel troops tied down in Sonora. The turning point came on 26 April, when all but one of the army units in Chihuahua City joined the revolt. Only the 62nd Regiment remained loyal to Carranza and entrenched itself in its barracks. The rebels, not willing to leave the 62nd Regiment as a rallying point, shelled the barracks intensively until the Carrancistas surrendered. Elsewhere in the state of Chihuahua the army units joined the revolt; only in Ciudad Juárez did General José Gonzalo Escobar delay taking his garrison into the rebellion until 3 May. Even without Escobar's adherence, General Calles concluded that the victory at Chihuahua City had eliminated any danger of a Carrancista thrust against Sonora. Calles was free to begin his southern advance against General Diéguez who was concentrating Carrancista troops in Guadalajara. The impending clash at Guadalajara was sure to make or break the revolt, because even after the defection of Chihuahua, the central government still had more than enough troops to crush the revolt.[33]

In reality most units were wavering in their loyalty. Carranza himself sensed something was not right, and in a half-hearted measure, on the night of 27 April he summoned General Pablo González. The President asked his protégé and until then loyal supporter to renounce his candidacy and to cast his support behind Bonillas. General González replied to this suggestion by pleading with the president to repudiate Bonillas as the only way to avoid further bloodshed. Before the visit of the General, many persons had begged the president to ditch Bonillas, but a tragic flaw in Carranza's character kept him from heeding arguments once he had determined to take a course of action. The generals under González had already told him they would no longer obey Carranza, and González struggled to reconcile the loyalty of his supporters with his loyalty to the president. After anguished soul-searching for three days, at last on 30 April he took the painful step of publicly breaking with the person who had made possible his entire career. Most of the army units near Mexico City rallied to General Gonzalez, although the substantial garrison in Mexico City outwardly remained loyal to Carranza. Because González could easily overwhelm the Mexico City garrison and take the president prisoner, the defection of González tipped the military balance to the side of the rebels for the first time. All that Carranza could do was to flee immediately to Veracruz to escape arrest. The last hope of his disintegrating presidency was the plodding army of Diéguez.[34] Diéguez was stalled at Guadalajara because army units kept defecting to the rebels: The end finally came on 12 May when the remaining troops mutinied and arrested Diéguez on 12 May.[35]

Carranza, who should have left Mexico City promptly in the first days of May, had lost that acute ability to sense danger that had saved him in November 1914. González could have surrounded or captured Mexico City at any moment, but he could not bring himself to take this final step in his betrayal of Carranza. González withdrew his troops to nearby Texcoco, and his reluctance unintentionally gave Carranza the opportunity to play out one final fantasy. The president had repeated many of the precedents of Porfirio Díaz but could not admit defeat, unlike Díaz who promptly had grasped his imminent collapse in May 1911. Carranza read history differently and believed he could repeat his legendary retreat to Veracruz of 1914. At Veracruz, where his son-in-law Aguilar was the governor, Carranza hoped to lead the struggle against the rebellious generals and gradually to restore civilian rule over turbulent Mexico. In a theatrical replay of 1914, Carranza ordered the entire federal government to board the waiting trains. Troops and bureaucrats were to pack and take with them munitions, weapons, airplanes, archives, money, and anything else of value. The evacuation orders even included all the machinery and equipment of the arsenals and of the military factories because Carranza expected a long struggle against the rebels: "The government could not take many things from these establishments owing to the sabotage, which is the true reason, done by directors, employees, and workmen, the latter especially who refused to continue work the last few days leaving no one to take down and load the machines as was ordered."[36] At the artillery foundry and the gunpowder factory, the directors "had received orders to take down the most indispensable machines and take away the important parts of the others, and upon abandoning their establishments, to blow up with dynamite the installations."[37] The directors refused to carry out the dynamiting and instead decided to wait and surrender to the rebels. Not all the troops wanted to follow Carranza; for example, almost all the officers of the 6th Regiment hid in private houses until the rebel troops had entered the city.

At 1000 on 7 May 1920 eight long trains, reputedly stretching for twelve kilometers, finally left Mexico City. But one officer was determined to deprive Carranza of the dismantled airplanes which were on crates aboard the trains. This officer rammed a wild locomotive into the fifth train, causing innumerable casualties aboard the wagons full of troops and *soldaderas*. The resulting confusion delayed the march of the last trains, which soon fell into the hands of rebels.[38] The 4,000 soldiers left in the remaining trains were soon under rebel attack. At Algives in the state of Puebla the trains mysteriously ran out of water and could not advance any more. Attacks on 13 and 14 May shattered the presidential column, and almost all the troops and civilians surrendered to the rebels. Both González and Obregón had given strict orders that Carranza was to be taken alive, but the fleeing president haughtily spurned their repeated written offers to turn himself in. He detrained from the stalled wagons and with a small party fled on horseback into the rough countryside. Many followers deserted him, until in a confused skirmish a group of rebels ambushed the presidential party. Five soldiers heroically died trying to save Carranza's life, but his high-ranking officers fled and shamefully abandoned the fallen president to his death. This tragic and ignoble end to a memorable career impacted the country. Because he angrily rejected the many opportunities to escape alive, the only plausible explanation for his death was that like Francisco Madero, Carranza was deliberately seeking a martyr's crown so that legions of followers would spring from the ground to avenge his death.[39]

In his self-delusion, Carranza was cruelly mistaken, because his regime had become so unpopular and corrupt, that not thoughts of revenge but concerns over a peaceful succession were uppermost in the public mind. Just hours after the departure of Carranza's trains, General González occupied the city, and he immediately appointed officials to replace the vanished Carrancistas. No one questioned the need to pick municipal officials to maintain order in the city, but in making appointments to cabinet positions in the federal government, González had dangerously overreached himself. The action was not politically fatal, had he obtained the approval of Obregón after the latter entered Mexico City on 9 May. Yet in obfuscations typical of González, at a meeting on 12 May he explained using very calm and measured words that he rose up against Carranza

but did not join the Obregón movement. González was slow to grasp that his career had died with the death of his patron Carranza. What González could not realize was that to salvage any political or military career he needed to transfer his allegiance to Obregón swiftly and enthusiastically. Of course, the defiance of González did not set off Obregón into a rage as would have been the case with a violent person like Pancho Villa. Instead, the always patient Obregón did not challenge the independent actions of González and approved all the appointments in Mexico City.[40]

Obregón afterwards explained that with only two thousand soldiers, he preferred to wait until more of his troops arrived rather than risk a confrontation with the much larger army of González. Obregón also worried needlessly about the loyalty of the troops of González: "Among the military element the great majority of sympathy is with General Obregón, there being many cases of officers under General González requesting transfers to troops under General Obregón or Hill."[41] González finally realized that he had blundered, and on 15 May he issued a manifesto explaining his reasons for withdrawing from the presidential race, thus leaving Obregón as the only candidate. Had González planned to retire to private life, his announcement of 15 May, as well as his promise to hand over the administration of Mexico City to the provisional president on 5 June, were more than appropriate final gestures. But to save his political career this resignation came several days too late, because in the meantime Obregón had come under intense pressure from the Zapatistas to hang González for the murder of Emiliano Zapata. González did not realize how lucky he was that Obregón spared his life, and in an extremely dangerous move he demanded the consolation prize of the provisional presidency before retiring from politics. When the Mexican Congress convoked on 24 May to elect the provisional president, González suffered the humiliation of receiving only 29 votes against 224 for De la Huerta. A prompt and enthusiastic support of Obregon in the first week of May certainly would have secured some important position for González, at the very least governor of his native state of Nuevo León, but his inept bungling had ruined him. This much-maligned man of considerable administrative

General Álvaro Obregón (bearded, center) addressing a crowd in Mexico City, 1920. A national hero and the most brilliant general in the history of Mexico, Obregón was president of Mexico from 1920 to 1924. An easygoing and very friendly person who detested war, he considered himself first a businessman and a civilian. His tragic death doomed any chance Mexico had for democracy during the twentieth century (Library of Congress, Prints and Photographs Division).

ability still could make valuable contributions in a subordinate post, but regrettably for Mexico the death of Carranza sunk González back into the obscurity from which he had come in 1911.[42]

On 1 June De la Huerta was formally inaugurated as provisional president. The next day almost 40,000 soldiers paraded with their artillery in front of the National Palace to celebrate the inauguration. Mexico had never seen such an imposing display of military power, and although the desire to celebrate was genuine, the new government wanted to send a strong message to anyone still in defiance or contemplating revolt.[43] Not even Porfirio Díaz at the height of his power had ever dared mount such a spectacle of military might; the men from Sonora, who in effect were the new rulers of Mexico, set out to complete the task Don Porfirio had begun of creating a strong and unified central government in Mexico. The new rulers resumed the drive to centralization and eventually went much further than Díaz in his wildest ambitions had ever thought possible.

Just like during the Porfirian era, Mexico had no place for rebel bands or regional warlords. Fortunately for the new rulers, Manuel Peláez of Tampico and the Zapatistas in Morelos had joined the bandwagon against Carranza, thus eliminating the two most irritating rebellions. Other lesser rebels also submitted to the authorities, but two major figures could still create major complications for the new regime: Pancho Villa in Chihuahua and Colonel Esteban Cantú in Baja California. Both had been given the chance to join the revolt against Carranza, indeed Pancho Villa received several offers, but studiously stayed neutral. Villa believed his good luck had returned, and he saw an opening to regain power while Carranza and Obregón fought themselves to a standstill. Villa looked wise compared to Colonel Cantú, who committed the greatest political blunder. In spite of his years of quietly defying Carranza, Cantú was the only leader who raised the banner of avenging the martyr president. The battle cry of avenging Francisco Madero had worked wonders in 1913, but in a war-weary country sick of the corrupt Carranza regime, the plea fell flat.[44]

Not surprisingly, the new regime set its highest goal in eliminating Colonel Cantu and Pancho Villa, not only for their intrinsic importance, but also to send a powerful message to political bosses throughout the country that the age of regional warlords was over. Military campaigns against Villa and Cantú were the most obvious solutions, but came at the high cost of sustaining an excessively large army. The men from Sonora knew that before any economic reconstruction of Mexico could begin, the army had to shrink in size, but that any new campaigns necessarily postponed the inevitable demobilization. The provisional president De la Huerta, who had been a rather passive figure as governor of Sonora during the revolt against Carranza, suddenly displayed a burst of energy to try to secure the submission of Villa and Cantú. Not being a general, he preferred negotiation, and unknown to his colleagues from Sonora, who should have noticed the warning signs, De la Huerta wanted successes to justify his claims to have a full term as president in 1924.

Pancho Villa meanwhile realized he had blundered in rejecting the offers to join the revolt in April and tried to make amends by sending out peace feelers. De la Huerta enthusiastically seized the opportunity in June, but as word of the talks leaked, generals, such as Joaquín Amaro, categorically stated that the army would rather revolt than accept Villa and his followers in its ranks. De la Huerta correctly read the protest as a limitation on but not a rejection of an agreement with Villa and proceeded with the negotiations. In exchange for submitting to the government, De la Huerta offered to give Villa a very large but remote and

isolated hacienda; the federal government also assumed the cost of maintaining 250 of his followers for one year and 50 men of his bodyguard indefinitely. Villa accepted the terms, but insisted on having any agreement cosigned not only by the De la Huerta administration, but also by Calles, Hill, and Obregón; the first two promptly agreed, but Obregón was adamant and wanted personally to lead an expedition to avenge the many crimes Villa had committed during his long bloody career. On more practical grounds, Obregón and others raised the objection that any deal with Villa was probably meaningless, because the U.S. government had every right to demand Villa's extradition for the attack on Columbus, New Mexico once he turned himself in.[45]

The opposition of Obregón seemed to have killed the agreement, but fortunately for Mexico both Villa and De la Huerta did not give up. Villa decided to flex his military muscles one last time, and he set out with his followers on a daring raid to neighboring Coahuila. After making a spectacular crossing of a desert nearly 1100 kilometers long, his men began to plunder the rich ranches in prosperous Coahuila. When Pascual Orozco had tried a similar maneuver in 1912, the railroad had brought federal troops to stop his advance, but in 1920 the Mexican army proved unable to carry out a similar deployment. At the very least the reputation of General Joaquín Amaro, who was supposed to be pursuing Villa in Chihuahua, was tarnished; more significantly, the Coahuila raid proved that any campaign of extermination against the wily Villa was bound to be long and costly. Villa remembered the Orozco raid of 1912 and knew he had little time before the government brought reinforcements by train. He wired his willingness to close a deal to De la Huerta, who shared a similar urgency. On 28 July the victorious Villa signed the agreement stipulating the terms of his submission to the government. De la Huerta had taken a risky move, because although Calles and Hill strongly supported him, Obregón was opposed, and the attitude of the U.S. government was unknown. Villa, a born charmer, sent fawning letters to Obregón asking that they become friends again; the stern Obregón waited to see how Villa lived up to the agreement and finally on 29 September communicated his approval. In a remarkable display of statesmanship, the U.S government expressed its great satisfaction at seeing peace return to Mexico and promised to hold any extradition proceedings in abeyance.[46]

The submission of Villa was the greatest success of the De la Huerta presidency. The agreement could be misunderstood, however, as an indication of a weak government that could only buy off opponents. Unless a dramatic display of military might took place, other rebels might be tempted to rise up in the hope of securing lucrative deals. On a personal level, Secretary of War Calles, who also was aiming for the presidency in 1924, had been the first to sense the political ambitions of the provisional president. De la Huerta was busy sending out feelers to Colonel Cantú, but the latter lacked the political talents of Villa and did not realize how crucial it was to avoid any incident that might provoke a harsh response. When Mexico City tried to appoint its own officials to the customs offices in Baja California, Colonel Cantú refused to give up these lucrative sources of revenue he controlled since 1914.[47] By trying to preserve the de facto independence he enjoyed under Carranza, Cantú gave Calles a great pretext to use military force. On 20 July Calles appointed General Abelardo L. Rodríguez to head an expedition to Baja California. The first troops left Mexico City on 26 July, and soon General Rodríguez was moving up the Pacific Coast collecting additional units along the way. He himself brought 3,000 soldiers to Sonora, other units were pouring into the state, and over a thousand Yaquis joined for the campaign, until the expedition came to number nearly 6,000 soldiers. Mexico had never before deployed a force of this size to remote regions, and it was larger than the expedition General Salvador Alvarado took to subdue Yucatán in 1915.[48]

Pancho Villa in retirement. He had always preferred the life of a rancher to a warrior, and he was very glad to retire to a hacienda in 1920 (Clodoveo Valenzuela and Amado Chaverri Matamoros, *Sonora y Carranza;* Mexico: Editorial Renacimiento, 1921).

Colonel Cantú, to defend himself, desperately tried to recruit more soldiers but to no avail. He placed orders for arms and ammunition, but the U.S. government refused to authorize their export.[49] Foiled in his efforts to increase his forces, Cantú counted only with the 25th Battalion:

> This 25th Infantry is the last of the Díaz regime to retain its original organization. Both officers and men are of the old Federal Army. Having been ordered to this isolated part of Mexico, its identity has been preserved through the vicissitudes of the revolutions. These soldiers have been in Ensenada six years and are of the old soldier type averaging thirty to forty-five years old. [...] Morale is absent. The troops are mainly criminals from interior sites of Mexico sentenced years ago to serve in the army, and are there now partly because of these sen-

tences and partly because they are paid $2 gold per day. They are loyal to Cantú only because of the $2 and would serve any other Mexican quite as willingly.[50]

At Ensenada Cantú could not muster 100 soldiers, and while he had detachments scattered in other parts of Baja California, the real strength of the 25th Battalion could not have been over 500, considerably below the usual estimates of 1,000. Corruption was rampant among the officers, and Baja's taverns, casinos, and brothels had weakened the combat spirit of the troops. The end did not come quickly, because the suspicious sinking of the gunboat *Guerrero* at Mazatlán on 5 August frustrated the government's plan to send the expedition of General Rodríguez to Ensenada by sea. Cantú used the extra time to lure an American aviator to fly his planes, but in the face of U.S. opposition, the Colonel was unable to obtain enough pilots and planes to be able to bomb the approaching expedition from the air. General Rodríguez, undeterred by the loss of the *Guerrero*, pressed north along the Bay of California and reached Guaymas, Sonora on 12 August. The American pilot turned out to have an unexpectedly beneficial effect, because his reconnaissance brought daily reports to Cantú on the mounting military might of General Rodríguez. Seeing the inevitable end, Colonel Cantú on 14 August reached an agreement with the agents of De la Huerta for the orderly transfer of power. Four days later, on 18 August, Colonel Cantú resigned and left for exile in the United States. Although De la Huerta managed to persuade many sympathizers that his negotiations had been responsible for the peaceful outcome, the expedition of General Rodríguez, the work of General Calles, had been the decisive action that ended the independence of the recalcitrant Colonel.[51]

Baja California was once again under the control of Mexico City, and the promise of guaranteeing peace and order throughout the country gave still another boost to the presidential campaign of Álvaro Obregón. As the only major presidential candidate in the elections of 5 September, he received 96 percent of the votes cast. Upon his inauguration on 1 December 1920, he became the ruler of a country that seemed fully pacified. Correctly President Obregón concluded that economic reconstruction and social improvements were the highest

priorities for Mexico. Tremendous euphoria greeted the inauguration of Obregón as president; the masses were celebrating not just a new president but the end of the violence and destruction that had so plagued the country.[52] On 1 December 1920, just days after the tenth anniversary of the Francisco Madero revolt on 20 November 1910, Mexico seemed at last to have regained the benefits of peace.

The Revolt of Adolfo de la Huerta, 1923–1924

The revolt against Carranza was notable for its lack of reprisals. No executions of any kind took place, and the only major figure to die was Venustiano Carranza himself, all because of his vain attempt to gain the martyr's halo. The unexpected death of the former president made the new government keen to prevent any further bloodshed. Any Carrancista loyalists were free to leave the country, and the harshest punishment for officers was discharge from the army. Even then, the government hesitated to expel all the Carrancista officers out of fear they would start minor rebellions or turn to banditry. The only Carrancistas in prison were those who had been with Carranza at the moment of his death; the charge against them was failure to protect the ex-president. The magnanimous policy to the thousands of Carranza loyalists reflected the sincere desire of General Álvaro Obregón to bury the violence of the Revolution. Unfortunately, the benevolence of the new regime communicated the impression of weakness. Without any bloody and exemplary reprisals, many generals felt that a rebellion was a safe way to promote their careers. They did not need to fear deadly penalties if the revolt failed, but the rewards were immense in case of success.

When Obregón assumed the presidency on 1 December 1920, he was determined to keep the army out of politics. The first and most urgent task for the new government was to reduce troop strength. The army of over 100,000 men was a crushing burden on the budget, and the sooner the men and their *soldaderas* returned to civilian life, the faster the economic reconstruction of Mexico could take place. By 1920 war had ceased to fascinate all the soldiers, and more than enough volunteers were eager to return to civilian life. In contrast to the early years of the Revolution, a train ticket and a lump payment sufficed to lure many soldiers back to their villages in 1920. An entirely different matter was the highly sensitive discharge of the officers. The government could only facilitate but not force their return to civilian life out of fear of fostering revolts or banditry. By 1 December 1923, the predictable result was a top-heavy army with officers comprising 20 percent of the 70,879 men. The percentage was excessive even when making ample allowance for the many officers who served in fact but not in rank as substitutes for scarce non-commissioned officers. Deducing officers from the army total, its 508 generals stood out strikingly as almost one general for every 100 soldiers.[53]

The generals did not appreciate their privileged position and insisted on grumbling and complaining. President Obregón and later President Plutarco Elías Calles tried to facilitate the return of the generals to civilian life and were successful in many cases. As a final safeguard and as a throwback to the traditional practices of Porfirio Díaz, both Obregón and Calles allowed the generals to acquire wealth and land; in many cases Obregón went so far as to authorize payments as thinly disguised bribes to keep the generals loyal. Why then did the generals still insist on revolting? Obviously a few had caught presidential fever and were on the lookout for any chance to gain power; however, these were too few to mount a really serious challenge to the government. Others had bitterly resented the enlargement of military zones from 20 to 35 on 21 February 1923. By this measure Obregón gained more positions to reward loyal followers and also diluted the power of individual zone commanders; not surprisingly, the generals affected opposed any reduction in the size of their territorial jurisdictions.[54]

Obregón wanted the zone commanders to observe but not to participate in local politics and to be a final safeguard for the preservation of order in the individual states. Obregón totally condemned any interference of his generals with the agrarian and labor movements sweeping the country. His insistence on supporting agrarian reform was the single most important factor angering the generals. On ideological grounds some generals opposed giving land to the peasants, while most had been seduced by the siren calls of the wealthy and the landholding class (among the earliest cases had been Pascual Orozco in 1912). In many instances, generals had taken control or ownership of confiscated lands that the peasants claimed as their own. Obregón tolerated the land acquisitions of the generals, but he insisted that the generals not support the land claims of hacendados. Clear as this distinction was in theory, in practice the difference became blurred. Many generals were involved so tightly in business deals with local hacendados that the interests of the landowners and individual generals became indistinguishable; often the deals were precisely over the lands in dispute with the peasants. At least one-fifth of the generals were so thoroughly co-opted into the upper class that they adopted its values and violently opposed the populist policies of Obregón.[55]

The irony was that the upper class had emerged basically intact from the ravages of the Mexican Revolution. Obregón as a millionaire businessman and owner of large stretches of land was not in a rush to distribute plots to the peasants. Nevertheless, he knew better than most of the landowners that the system of Porfirio Díaz, although basically sound, needed key changes to survive. Most notably, the president recognized that some popular participation and a limited distribution of land were inevitable. Obregón was building for the century, but the wealthy persons saw only their immediate gain.[56] The task of gaining acceptance for modest changes as being in the best long-term benefit of the upper class proved extremely arduous. A dangerous nostalgia for privileges made many large landlords long for the years of Porfirio Díaz. As hard as Obregón tried, he realized that the construction of a lasting structure for Mexico required more time than one presidential term. Who among the men of Sonora could complete the consolidation of the new regime? Although Obregón delayed the formal announcement, Calles in the number two place among the men of Sonora was the certain successor. Obregón was the first president to implement what Venustiano Carranza had botched in 1920. The power of the Mexican presidency was starting to include the right to appoint a successor after pro-forma elections.

The mysterious death of General Benjamín Hill by poisoning two weeks after taking office as Secretary of War had eliminated one of the most promising men of Sonora and the third in power after Obregón and Calles. Hill's replacement in third place was Adolfo de la Huerta, the most lackluster of the men from Sonora and the only one who had not been a general. Mistakenly, De la Huerta concluded that from being number three he could jump to being number 1; his tenure as provisional president in 1920 merely fueled his presidential ambitions. In Obregón's cabinet De la Huerta served as Secretary of the Treasury and vainly tried to undermine Calles, who held the position of Secretary of Gobernación. Calles parried the blows and then deftly maneuvered with the Secretary of Foreign Relations to orchestrate the departure of De la Huerta from the cabinet on 24 September 1923. Not just the political intrigues, but the ineptness of De la Huerta as Secretary of the Treasury contributed powerfully to his fall. De la Huerta had almost bankrupted the Mexican state when he bungled foreign debt negotiations; he also siphoned government revenue into his future presidential campaign and in the process created a huge deficit. The blunders of De la Huerta forced a visibly angry Obregón to adopt an austerity budget and to cut the salaries of all federal employees by 10 percent on October 16. The perquisites of the generals sheltered them from any hardships, but those below the rank of general had fewer opportunities for graft and corruption and thus resented the pay cut and became more likely to support their generals in a revolt. The 10 percent cut was largely insignificant for the soldiers, who were accustomed to living in miserable conditions, but when the financial crisis delayed their daily allowances for over a month, at that moment the rank-and-file grumbled and became willing to follow their officers in an uprising.[57]

As was long expected, on 19 October 1923 De la Huerta formally announced his candidacy to become president. Although Calles had also resigned as Secretary of Gobernación to campaign for president, the Obregón administration supported his candidacy and controlled the electoral machinery. Only the wealthy rallied to De la Huerta who lacked any chance of winning even if the elections had been free.[58] In the typical Latin American pattern, De la Huerta could be expected after the elections of

July 1924 to stage a revolt in protest of the rigged elections, but in reality the initiative was in the hands of the impatient generals. General Rómulo Figueroa jumped the gun on 30 November 1924 when he revolted in Guerrero. The government bribed his subordinates to stay loyal and forced an isolated Figueroa to flee into the hills with a small band of followers. The ease with which the government seemed to have quashed the Figueroa revolt without any bloodshed created a false sense of security.[59]

Obregón had loyalists in command of most of the 35 military zones, but in spite of many warnings, he kept Guadalupe Sánchez in Veracruz and Enrique Estrada in Guadalajara. In the case of Estrada, the reduction of the area of his military zone in February 1923 had increased his resentment against Obregón. Estrada actively recruited fellow generals for the expected revolt, but when copies of his incriminating correspondence reached the president, Obregón still refused to heed insistent requests, including a rare plea from his wife, to remove Estrada from command. Neither could Obregón bring himself to remove Fortunato Maycotte from the command of any troops because the president could not forget that this general had saved his life in the 1920 revolt. When political survival is at stake, gratitude is a dangerous luxury. Obregón did take the precaution of moving Maycotte from Puebla to Oaxaca; without this fateful transfer as zone commander, Mexico City would have been defenseless.[60]

Some scholars have speculated that Obregón followed a Machiavellian policy of passively waiting for his enemies to expose themselves.[61] If that were so, he needed to prepare himself by replenishing his depleted arsenals, but he did not make any significant purchases of arms or cartridges prior to the rebellion. The reality was that his trust in friends and his sense of justice had failed to protect him from bitter surprises. Had he taken action against generals whose disloyalty was well know in many circles in Mexico City, then De la Huerta would not have been tempted to depart the capital secretly at night to contact a disgruntled Guadalupe Sánchez. And had this general known that other garrison commanders were not ready to strike, De la Huerta would not have dared risk a repetition of the

Félix Díaz fiasco in October 1912. When the presidential candidate arrived in Veracruz on 5 December, he still hesitated; instead, General Guadalupe Sánchez, joined by the Navy admirals, quietly took control of Veracruz. To De la Huerta's surprise, he read in the morning in the local newspaper that the revolt had broken out and that he was its leader. The bizarre occurrence has led one historian to deduce that perhaps Obregón learned of the revolt before its supposed leader De la Huerta. In any case, the rebel leader started to make up for the lost ground by issuing the inevitable manifesto on 7 December. The rebels hastily cribbed the manifesto from the proclamations of previous revolts. The attention the plotters devoted to each of the words in the manifesto revealed the unreal nature of the movement, when all knew that not words, but bullets, would determine victory. A first glitch in the revolt came when at the state capital of Jalapa, the garrison commander remained loyal to the government in spite of having earlier sympathized with the rebels. The Jalapa garrison received minor reinforcements by train from Mexico City, and Guadalupe Sánchez had to engage in extensive combat for 17 hours until he overwhelmed the beleaguered garrison on 8 December. The Veracruz rebels had opened the path into the interior, but they hesitated to push beyond Esperanza, out of fear they might be encircled by government forces attacking from the rear (Map 16).[62]

At Guadalajara General Estrada had been waiting only for the spark in Veracruz to proclaim his support for the revolt, and on 8 December he telegraphed his defiance to Obregón. Commanders and troops in the large zone Estrada had previously commanded placed their forces under his direct control in Guadalajara. Miguel Diéguez and Salvador Alvarado, among the few generals with Carrancista sympathies dismissed from the army, made a final attempt to revive their flagging careers by joining Estrada. The large size of the forces under Estrada persuaded President Obregón to destroy the Guadalajara rebels first before turning his troops against Veracruz. He began concentrating units at the large army base he had previously constructed at Irapuato. Any campaign to defeat Estrada required considerable time, which Obregón hoped to gain by blocking the Veracruz rebels at Puebla.

Meanwhile Calles had taken full control of operations in northern Mexico and throughout the revolt he made sure that the railroads to the United States remained open to carry supplies and weapons. Calles was also responsible for transferring loyal troops from the north to the combat fronts in the south; much more subtly, Calles by his presence helped to reaffirm the loyalty of commanders in those distant regions and thus prevented a wholesale defection of the army towards De la Huerta as had happened in May 1920. In many ways, Calles retook his role of 1920 as that of a dynamic personality forcefully pushing for victory.[63]

Before Obregón had gathered enough troops at Irapuato to launch the offensive to the west, the defection of a third general forced the president to change his plans. On 14 December Fortunato Maycotte rose up against the government but did not recognize the authority of De la Huerta. General Maycotte acted vigorously by leading his forces north toward Puebla, and because General Sánchez was advancing from Veracruz, the loyal forces in Puebla risked being caught in a trap. On the night of 14 December the government evacuated Puebla and retreated for a final defense in Mexico City. The same day that Maycotte revolted, Estrada's forces reached La Piedad, one-third of the way between Mexico City and Guadalajara. The rebels were starting to encircle Mexico City, and the defection of Maycotte's troops considerably reduced the numerical superiority of the loyal army.[64]

The government faced a major challenge: Any battlefield setback could force it to withdraw the candidacy of Calles as part of a negotiated solution. Inconclusive campaigning might also sap the will of the government as had happened to Porfirio Díaz in 1911. Fortunately for the government, the rebel situation was far from ideal and suffered serious handicaps. Obregón exercised undisputed supreme command, while the rebel generals operated largely independently. The government controlled the central railway network and could shift troops from one front to another in a matter of hours, while geography left the rebels largely isolated from each other. The government also kept the railroad lines from the United States open, but control of the ports was largely meaningless for De la Huerta because of the U.S. embargo on the rebels. Last and certainly not least, Obregón was the most gifted of all Mexican generals; only if the rebels mustered comparable talent could they hope to neutralize the military genius of Obregón.

The capture of Puebla turned out to be the high point of the rebellion. Even though the rebels retained the initiative, their drive to the capital stalled. Maycotte was already insisting on his prerogatives in the new government and did not want to risk his troops in heavy campaigning. Generally Maycotte and the other rebel leaders believed that the loyal army would melt away through defections, as superficially seemed to have happened in 1920.[65] Whatever forward movement was left in the rebellion remained with the much larger units General Estrada was bringing from the west. Even if the defenses at Irapuato delayed Estrada, his offensive threatened to press Mexico City between his advance and that of the rebels from Puebla. Sensing a momentous decision, General Estrada convoked his fellow generals to a crucial meeting to select

> The route that the column should take, in effect the campaign plan that should be adopted. General Diéguez explained that immediately the column should march rapidly and with energy on the road to the capital; the column could count on numerous sympathizers at Irapuato, Celaya and other places through which it would pass. On the contrary, General Estrada argued that no enemy should be left either in the flanks or in the rear; it was necessary to carry out a "general sweep" beforehand. The majority of those present agreed with the opinion of General Estrada, and consequently the column decided to advance to the right to attack Morelia.[66]

Estrada's southward turn took the pressure off the government and gave it a breathing spell to prepare a counterblow. Obregón, who spent most of the time traveling aboard a yellow campaign train, quickly rerouted to the east the units previously headed towards Irapuato. Equipped with plenty of artillery, the reinforcements blasted through a roadblock outside of Puebla on 21 December. A major battle seemed to be shaping up for Puebla the next day, but General Maycotte, angry that he had not been recognized as supreme leader, left in a huff with his troops. Around 3,000 soldiers of the Veracruz garrison remained to face the onslaught of over 9,000 army troops under General Eugenio Martínez. Although the artillery

shelled the rebels intensively for hours, the decisive event came when airplanes dropped 74 bombs on the forts of Loreto and Guadalupe. The aerial bombardment panicked the defenders who attempted to flee but most fell prisoner. The recapture of Puebla was the turning point of the rebellion, because the government had won its first major victory and regained the initiative. However, the government did not press far beyond Puebla, even though the bombardment had shocked the rebels into pulling back to Esperanza. Instead, General Martínez had most of his units board trains for a return trip to Irapuato, where they took up their defensive positions.[67]

The government cautiously interpreted General Estrada's southward turn as a delay in the rebel march towards Mexico City. Once aerial reconnaissance confirmed that General Estrada was moving south, Obregón seized what he believed was a momentary opportunity to strike in the east beyond Puebla. But first he had to secure his western front. Although the nearest rebel positions were 160 kilometers west of the defenses at Irapuato, the government did not want to leave itself exposed for too long. Obregón first took the precaution of trying to delay General Estrada, and to keep him under harassment, the President sent General Lázaro Cárdenas with over two thousand cavalrymen against the rear of General Estrada. General Rafael Buelna, the best field commander in the rebellion, detected, surrounded, and destroyed the column of General Cárdenas on 27 December 1923. Having lost its scarce cavalry, the army infantry abandoned its advance positions and retreated back to Irapuato, in effect leaving the region to the rebels.[68]

The rebel victory opened the road to Morelia, which Estrada wanted to capture because supposedly Obregón had stockpiled a large arsenal in that city. Estrada advanced slowly in the hope that other army units would defect. Apparently Estrada had the illusion that the generals could mount a relatively peaceful coup and had not expected a tiring campaign mostly on foot in the cold winter. By his long delay in attacking anything, he in effect forfeited the initiative to Obregón. When aerial reconnaissance confirmed that Estrada's slow southward turn was definitely headed for Morelia, Obregón ordered its small garrison of

600 men to evacuate. Even though a plane dropped the order by air, the commander felt it was too late to withdraw and rallied the volunteers for a spirited defense.[69] The attack began at 1900 on 21 January 1924, but the unexpectedly stiff resistance from the garrison soon cost the life of General Buelna. General Estrada never recovered from the loss of his best general, and "demoralized and downcast, he wanted to withdraw immediately from Morelia."[70] After Estrada retired to his train on the night of the 23rd, General Diéguez ordered preparations for a dawn assault to capture the city, which fell into rebel hands on 24 January. Victory came only because the 65th Regiment joined the rebels, yet the attack was weak enough to allow the governor, many officials, and at least 100 soldiers of the garrison to escape. The rebels had captured the state capital of Michoacán, but the effort had thoroughly demoralized Estrada and had seriously depleted his supply of ammunition; the large arsenal turned out to be nothing but a false rumor that Obregón had spread to lure the rebels away from Mexico City.[71]

Serious as was the failure to capture weapons and ammunition, the real irreplaceable loss was the time Estrada had wasted in his Morelia diversion. The government did not watch the unfolding of Estrada's campaign passively but once again took advantage of the time to send troops by train from Irapuato back to Puebla. After the loss of that city the rebels withdrew to a new defense line at Esperanza. The rebels hoped that the rugged terrain would allow them enough cover to use their rifles effectively against the more numerous cannons and machine guns of the government. The rebels had meanwhile consolidated their control over Yucatán, Campeche, and Tabasco. In this last state, control of the seas had deprived the loyal garrison of reinforcements or supplies, so that once ammunition ran out, the loyal troops numbering 2,000 surrendered. The prisoners were offered the opportunity to join the rebellion, which they pretended to do when they were shipped from Tabasco to Veracruz. De la Huerta, against the unanimous advice of all his officers, insisted on sending these 2,000 former prisoners to man the defenses at Esperanza. De la Huerta even rejected a suggestion to distribute the Tabasco soldiers among his other units. Soon the Tabasco soldiers con-

tacted the government to say they remained loyal and would return to their normal allegiance at the most advantageous moment. The opportunity came on 28 January when General Martinez launched a ferocious attack on the train station of Esperanza. As the heavy artillery barrage began, the 2000 Tabasco soldiers turned and attacked the rebel rear, in effect trapping most of the rebel force. General Sánchez barely escaped capture, but only after having lost his trains and all his equipment. The next day General Martínez attacked and occupied Esperanza against crumbling rebel resistance. The easy recapture of Córdoba on 4 February was the last blow for the rebels. When on 5 February De la Huerta decided to abandon Veracruz, panic seized the shocked rebels who had expected their vacation stay in Veracruz to yield an easy victory. For those who wanted to continue their revolutionary adventure, the navy took the rebel government to its new seat in Tabasco. The troops of General Martínez entered Veracruz on 12 February, and the starting point of the rebellion was back under government control.[72]

President Obregón concluded that final victory was inevitable for the government but at the same time put the highest premium on subduing the rebels swiftly. As the army grew, the burden on the budget increased and afterwards demobilization became more difficult. He even opposed the recruitment of temporary volunteers, and most reluctantly he authorized the creation of auxiliary units serving only for the duration of the conflict. Instead, he very enthusiastically welcomed weapons and ammunition coming from the United States. The arrival of 5 million cartridges in early January 1924 confirmed the contrast between the government's abundance and the rebels' shortage of ammunition. Even more significant was the arrival of airplanes coming from the United States during that month. The impact of U.S. armaments seemed so great that observers and even scholars have attributed the government's victory primarily to timely support from Washington. Such a conclusion, besides depriving the Mexicans of any role in their history, overlooks the rebel mistakes and the adroit government responses. The limited quantity of cartridges had never stopped the offensives against the rebels whose supply of cartridges was considerably smaller. By late December the rebellion was doomed, even before the arrival of the first arms shipments from the United States. The real effect of the U.S weapons and ammunition was to make possible a swift end to the revolt. From a long-term perspective, the U.S. shipments dispensed with the need to mobilize many men for a large army.[73]

When Estrada finally decided to return north after eight days in Morelia, he was the first to experience the government's new arsenal. Airplanes not only reconnoitered carefully but more significantly strafed and bombed his column repeatedly. The demoralized soldiers hid during the day and marched at night to escape the danger from the air, but they could not avoid suffering from irregular meals and infrequent sleep. Gradually Estrada shifted to a defensive but not completely passive strategy. He sent a column under General Diéguez to destroy the lines of communication of the army troops near Irapuato, while he took up defensive positions with the rest of his forces along the Lerma River. General Estrada's dispositions to delay the government advance were sound and were the most likely to frustrate Obregón's desire for rapid victory. The longer Estrada could prolong the war, the greater the likelihood of a negotiated arrangement for the rebels.[74]

Obregón was itching to engage the rebels in a decisive battle like that of Celaya in 1915, but each time that he was ready for a set piece during the first week of February, General Diéguez sprung from the trap. In the most notable case, on 3 February the rebels, "as soon as they detected the advance parties of our columns [...] fled to escape, and the retreat was a real disaster because it lacked any order [...] our pilots having noticed that the rebels went in disorganized groups by different routes."[75] Obregón perceptively noted that the hasty retreat "will delay the military annihilation of the rebels, but will hasten their moral annihilation, because they have accepted a defeat without even fighting."[76]

Morale was a major concern for General Estrada, who realized that his men knew the rebellion no longer had any chance of overthrowing the central government. Inactivity bred despondency and thoughts of surrender, so he was afraid of leaving his men too long behind the defense line they were rapidly constructing along the Lerma River. He put his men to destroy sections of the four bridges over this river and on the west bank to dig a network of trenches stretching between each of the fallen bridges. In some sectors the rebels had constructed four lines of trenches; tunnels linked the blockhouses and the chambers hiding their eight machine guns and two cannons. The rebel soldiers were very eager to dig these extensive works, because they were well aware of the government's superiority in artillery and in shells.[77]

Everything indicated that General Estrada stood his best chance of success by staying behind his impressive fortifications. Estrada thought otherwise and felt his troops had to stay on the move to maintain their morale. He took 1,500 soldiers out of the Lerma River defense line and personally led them in a march to join the column of General Diéguez. The purpose of this maneuver was to rip up the railroad track between La Piedad and Irapuato and thus to destroy the supply line of the army troops. Unfortunately for the rebels, that stretch of railroad no longer supplied the loyalists, and sending out such a large detachment was not the way to accomplish a task better performed by small units. In any case, the maneuver of Estrada did not even manage to distract government troops, because General Joaquín Amaro had already received orders from Obregón to prepare the attack on the rebel defenses of the Lerma River. If anything, the discovery that the rebels had sent out two columns made Obregón and Amaro want to hurry their attack while the trenches were undermanned.[78]

The apprehension that the rebel columns might return to disrupt the river crossing explains the haste and determination of General Amaro to ford the river. Artillery was already in place to shell the 1,900 rebels who were entrenched on the west bank; the idea was that as the soldiers attempted to capture the bridges, a heavy covering fire from the artillery would keep the defenders pinned down and unable to reply from their supposedly uncovered trenches. Intermittently, airplanes would drop bombs to shatter the defenses or at least the morale of the rebels. Very ingeniously, the Mexican sappers had constructed pontoons out of wood and automobile tires; once the pontoons were linked in a row, they would provide a makeshift bridge for the infantry to walk over. Poncitlán, the site Amaro had selected for the main attack, had the added advantage of offering three ways to cross the river: over a bridge and a dam, or by fording some shallows. As an additional precaution, the attack was scheduled to begin at night in the early hours of 9 February.[79]

For reasons never explained, the attack took place not at the Poncitlán front, where the line of trenches was only 250 meters long, but at Ocotlán, where the trench lines were 800 meters long. A long delay in taking up positions may have explained the switch, and in any case the attack did not begin at dark but at dawn when the defenders had an excellent view of the soldiers trying to cross the river. Although the nine army cannons thundered away the whole day, the artillerymen performed poorly and did not have enough cannons to lay down a devastating barrage. Not sufficiently shelled, the defenders were able to repel all the attacks against the bridges near Ocotlán. With casualties mounting and the hours passing, Amaro was risking a bloody repulse that could only raise the fallen hopes of the rebels. Fortunately for Amaro, recently arrived Yaquis and Mayos under Roberto Cruz saved the day: Under intense rifle fire, they swam across the Lerma River carrying a cable in their mouths. The Indians tied the cable to a tree in the west bank and latched the pontoons to the cable to form a crude bridge. By 1600 over five hundred infantrymen had crossed the bridge and established a beachhead on the west bank. The rebel commander lacked any reserves to throw against the penetration, and with ammunition running low, he wisely gave the order for an orderly retreat before the government troops outflanked and surrounded his force. Well-protected in the subterranean trenches, the rebels had suffered at most thirty casualties and withdrew in good order. The many wounded soldiers weighed down Amaro who was in no condition to pursue the retreating rebels. In addition, he had to explain to Obregón why the well-prepared crossing had cost over 400 casualties, admittedly a small number compared to Pancho Villa's bloody attacks. Obregón, who detested the senseless loss of life, demanded explanations, and in a most unusual move, he ordered a formal inquiry into this battle to find out what went wrong. Obregón could not punish Amaro whose loyalty he needed, but at least the pres-

ident wanted to warn him and to teach lessons to other generals for any future battle.[80]

The bloody battle had spared the rebels from physical harm but had inflicted a tremendous psychological defeat. The relentless determination of the army soldiers to die rather than fail in the deadly river crossing had impressed the rebels, who almost without ammunition, did not want to engage their death-defying opponents again. The disintegrating rebel forces retreated into Guadalajara, and on 10 February grabbed all the trains to evacuate the city as fast as possible. The next day loyal troops entered Guadalajara, just as their fellow soldiers were approaching Veracruz in the east. The two main rebel bases had fallen to the government almost on the very same day.[81]

The rebellion was finished for all practical purposes, even though Generals Estrada and Diéguez were still on the loose. The defeat at Ocotlán and the capture of Guadalajara left the columns of Estrada and Diéguez hanging in air, and their earlier mission of destroying railroad track in the rear lost all meaning. Estrada had the obligation to extend peace feelers to the government for surrender, and in case it rejected his offers, he then had the obligation to disband his men to spare senseless bloodshed. Instead, General Estrada was increasingly gripped by a death wish or a martyr complex similar to what had befallen Venustiano Carranza in 1920. Fully cognizant that defeat was inevitable, he sank into a deep depression and total pessimism; only a glorious death seemed to offer him an escape from his adversity. On February 12 his force came near the train station of Palo Verde in the Irapuato–La Piedad railroad line and was very close to General Diéguez whose troops were busy destroying track. Rather than combining the two forces, Estrada sent his troops to continue tearing up track at one end, while several kilometers away Diéguez continued to destroy track in the opposite direction. Again, once the news of the Ocotlán defeat arrived, the ripping up of track lost all meaning.[82]

In the early morning hours of 13 February the troops of Estrada moved to the Palo Verde train station, in effect the rear of General Diéguez. Because loyal troops were stationed barely twenty kilometers away at La Piedad, most of the troops of Estrada occupied the nearby hills to provide cover for the demolition parties near the track. As the troops set up camp for a quick breakfast, at 0915 observers reported army cavalry barely visible with binoculars about 4 kilometers away. The troops in the hills immediately prepared for battle and took the best defensive positions. The unit commander José Ramirez Garrido reported to General Estrada that the army force was very large and that the rebels in the hills had little ammunition. Estrada had to decide upon either prompt reinforcement or more likely an immediate withdrawal, but he did neither. He could have ordered General Diéguez to rejoin him to escape together, but any full-scale battle was doomed to failure because the government troops were more numerous, were better armed, and had more ammunition than the combined rebel forces.[83]

By 1100 intense firing broke out along the front line, but both sides kept their distance. Around twelve noon the army cavalry decided to try new tactics to capture the rebel positions. The U.S. government, in a show of its strong support for Obregón, had rushed many types of weapons to Mexico; among them were many .45 caliber automatic pistols. Unlike the Mausers and the carbines that required working the bolt and pressing the trigger to fire each bullet, the cavalryman by just pressing the trigger of this pistol could fire until the clip ran out. The brilliant idea appeared that if all the cavalrymen fired their .45 caliber pistols simultaneously, no defender could withstand the hail of lead. In spite of the fact that the elevation of the hills was at least 7 degrees and thus not suited for an uphill charge, the cavalry, without any element of surprise or a prior artillery barrage, charged up the hills. In one hill the dash was so sudden that some cavalrymen reached the defense line and used their pistols to wound ten rebels, but otherwise the rebels' machine guns and Mausers mowed down the cavalry. The charge turned into a rout, and the rebels even managed to take prisoner some of the dazed cavalrymen. Another attempt to revitalize cavalry as a vital combat force had failed miserably.[84]

The remaining cavalrymen stayed safely out of Mauser range until the first infantry battalions began to arrive around 1300. As long as the rebels had adequate ammunition, they were confident of holding back the infantry until the column of General Diéguez arrived. But what appeared were more infantry battalions, and as the steady Mauser fire spraying the rebel positions increased, the rebels knew that the dreaded artillery was not far behind. Unknown to the rebels in the hills, no help was on the way because General Estrada had never summoned General Diéguez. As the rebel situation deteriorated, Estrada merely kept on repeating with fatalism the order for his men to stay in their positions.[85] Any chance of saving the force of General Estrada rested on the independent initiative of General Diéguez who could clearly hear the firing far to his rear. Diéguez had received a message from Estrada merely saying that combat had started. Any hope that Diéguez might rush to the rescue ended when a fleeing rebel colonel arrived shortly after. The rebel colonel had panicked at the sight of an impending cavalry charge, and in a terrified voice he told Diéguez "All is lost! The first shots killed General Estrada, others were taken prisoner [...] only I escaped by a miracle but I could see the execution of the prisoners. Our forces have been defeated and flee in utter disorder."[86] The story seemed believable because already other rebels were streaming to the rear. In the absence of orders or additional information, General Diéguez prepared to escape as soon as night fell.

In reality, no flight had taken place, and the rebel soldiers valiantly resisted the army infantry pressing upon the hills. The rebels were hungry, tired, and sleepy from days of wandering and were stretched to the breaking point. The collapse came when one officer ran out of ammunition for his machine gun and hurled his useless weapon to one side after shouting depressing words.[87] Panic ensued as the rebels rushed to the rear on foot and on their horses. A veritable stampede ensued, and only much later did the officers manage to slow down and eventually to stop the terrified men. As his force was melting away, a mesmerized General Estrada almost mechanically kept repeating the order to stay at their positions, and when his orderlies tried to take him away, he insisted on dying there. The General was truly dazed and was not just performing theatrical heroics; the pleas that his orderlies would also stay and die with him finally persuaded him to leave. Even then the orderlies had to place Estrada upon a horse and send him galloping among other riders to escape the grasp of the rapidly closing cavalry.[88]

The debacle of Palo Verde finished destroying any chance the rebellion had of surviving. Over the next month betrayals and defections hastened the inevitable disintegration of the rebels. Central Mexico returned to government control, and the north remained solidly loyal. The rebellion had lost all credibility, even though it still held Tabasco, Campeche, and Yucatán, thanks to rebel control of the sea.

The Mexican Navy was the only remaining rebel asset, and it had retreated to the ports of Yucatán. Even in the midst of the land campaigns, the government had not lost sight of the rebellious Navy and had been combing the world to purchase warships. Brazil sold the battleship *Deodoro*, which was commissioned as the *Anáhuac* in April 1924. But before a fascinating naval battle could take place between the large *Anáhuac* and the many small warships of the rebel navy, the United States imposed an embargo on coal exports to rebel ports. This crippling blow left fuel for only 15 days, and on 8 April the marooned rebel fleet accepted offers to surrender on the condition that the lives of the crews be spared. The government lived up to the agreement and actually paid a nice sum to the crews but obviously dismissed the rebel ringleaders from the navy. The remaining officers strove to prove their loyalty by transporting and escorting troops diligently to the east, starting with Tabasco. Then loyal troops disembarked in Yucatán on 16 and 17 April and with almost no fighting restored the authority of Mexico City. Gradually the Mexican army eliminated the pockets of rebel resistance throughout southern Mexico.[89]

Already as the government took the first large batches of rebel prisoners in January, the question of reprisals emerged. Clearly the leniency after the May 1920 revolt had backfired; rather than being grateful, those spared had become emboldened to hatch new plots. Nevertheless, a return to the wholesale execution of prisoners as in the period 1913–1916 did not seem advisable either. Not only would the world confirm its image of Mexico as a land of barbaric savages, but shedding so much blood conveyed the impression that the government was too weak to remain in power other than by recourse to brute force. By sparing many of the rebels, the government demonstrated it was powerful enough to remain in office without the need for widespread executions. The officers below the rank of general and the enlisted men benefited most from the leniency of the government. Prisoners gradually returned to civilian life, and discharge from the army was the harshest punishment for enlisted men and officers below the rank of general.

For the rebel generals, rarely was escape possible. After a drumhead court-martial, they faced the firing squad. The government spared the lives of only those generals who betrayed their former rebel associates. Mexico witnessed the dreary spectacle of army troops hunting down formerly prestigious generals through the jungle and forests. Just to name a few, Salvador Alvarado and Miguel Diéguez vainly tried to escape their pursuers and the inevitable appointment with the firing squad. Many generals desperately tried to flee to the United States, but not all reached safety, because the government did not facilitate or otherwise encourage their flight abroad. Only the very elusive Guadalupe Sánchez proved impossible to track down, and a government impatient to have all of Mexico pacified relented for once in its policy. In an agreement of January 1925 the government agreed to spare the life of his followers and allowed the former rebel general to depart openly for the United States.[90]

With this firm but not excessively harsh policy of punishments and reprisals, the government hoped to have rid Mexico of the threat of army rebellions. As the presidential term of Obregón came to a close in November 1924, he was handing to his successor Calles a central government much more powerful than what had existed in 1920. Obregón accomplished what Carranza failed to do because the latter's soft policies toward the rebels and bandits had kept Mexico weak during the years 1917 to 1920. The failure of Carranza to return peace and stability to Mexico, rather than any presidential ambition of Obregón, was the real reason for the overthrown of Carranza in 1920. The country gave Carranza four years to try his conciliatory policies on rebels and bandits, but found the results wanting. Ever since Carranza refused to pursue the campaign against Pancho Villa with vigor in 1916, Carranza consistently tried to avoid using military force. Instead, the men of Sonora had no hesitation about using the army to awe the rebels into submission.

As the threat of rebellion receded, Obregón looked to a future when armed bands and bandits no longer terrorized the country while army and police forces protected the rights of peaceful citizens. A modest-sized army of great versatility was all that Mexico needed, but the process of reducing the large and motley revolutionary forces into a smaller army was fraught with risk, as the De la Huerta rebellion revealed. Because the possibility of genuinely spontaneous popular insurrections like in 1910–1911 seemed to have vanished, the government believed optimistically that controlling the generals sufficed to prevent any renewed outbreak of disturbances. Obregón certainly knew what had to be done to maintain peace in Mexico, and as he returned to private life, he hoped that the incoming President Plutarco Elías Calles had learned the secrets of keeping stability and strengthening the central government.

10. The Pacification of Mexico

But a close inspection brings to light from under the ruins an immense central power, which has gathered together and grouped all the several particles of authority and influence formerly scattered among a host of secondary powers, orders, classes, professions, families, and individuals, and which were disseminated throughout the whole fabric of society. — Alexis de Tocqueville[1]

Starting a war is always easier than returning to peace. Time, effort, and wisdom are just the basic requirements to achieve peace. The task is even harder for revolutionary wars which generate the most intense passions and unleash countless ambitions. The Mexicans who had eagerly rushed into rebellion in 1910 could never have imaged that to bury the revolutionary fury required a very delicate balancing act.

This last chapter on Mexico could easily have been titled Plutarco Elías Calles, who came to play a pivotal role in the country's history. His presidency of 1924–1928 should have been peaceful had he followed the policies of the outgoing president Álvaro Obregón. Instead for unfortunate Mexico, Calles insisted on new departures, and his initiatives triggered one last popular insurrection. He never accepted that his own bungling had caused the bloody uprising, and mistakenly he concluded that Mexico was inherently prone to revolt. He felt that only an extreme solution could pacify Mexico. He overcompensated by imposing a rigid political system that stifled the country for the rest of the twentieth century.

The Cristero Rebellion and Other Armed Revolts

The relatively mild reprisals after the revolt of Adolfo de la Huerta suggested that the revolutionary fury had at last spent itself by 1924. Nobody could have imagined that the most sanguinary violence, even exceeding that of the bloody 1913–1916 period, was yet to come. During the years of 1927 and 1928, brutality, savagery, and destruction reached levels unknown until then. For the first time the Mexican army waged a war against its own people and not just against armed rebel groups. How could such extreme violence have erupted in a ruined country that had seemed weary of war?

The Mobilization of the Catholics in 1926

The Mexican Constitution of 1917 is famous for its many unfulfilled promises. This constitutional outcome is not at all surprising in Latin America, where the law is generally assumed to be an ideal to strive for rather than a rule to obey scrupulously. No harm generally comes from printing on paper lofty principles more suitable for heaven than earth, but in the rare instances when rigid doctrinaires insist on following the letter of the law, the consequences can well be disastrous. As a bargaining sop to rabid atheists, the 1917 Constitution had included clauses hostile to the Roman Catholic Church. Presidents Venustiano Carranza and Álvaro Obregón had wisely decided to ignore those restrictions, as had the vast majority of state governors.

The lack of enforcement of the anti–Catholic provisions seemed to parallel the erosion of revolutionary principles. By the time Plutarco Elías Calles became president in 1924, he felt the decay had gone too far and that something had to be done to revive the revolutionary spirit. Out of a personal obsession to try to justify that he was still an idealist, Calles devoted all his remaining revolutionary fervor to try to destroy the grip of the Catholic Church on the population. He received ample warnings from home and even from abroad not to tamper with religious matters, and for the first time in his life, he refused to heed the advice of his friend and ex-president Álvaro Obregón to leave alone the religious question. On 24 June 1926 an unperturbed Calles resolutely issued decrees imposing crippling restrictions on the Catholic Church and punishing any infractions with criminal penalties. His action could not have come at a worse moment, because as part of the healing process from the spiritual and material ravages of the revolutionary wars, large segments of the population were experiencing a religious revival.[2]

Catholics throughout Mexico protested the measures and took all the available nonviolent steps to try to get the Calles government to reverse its policy of religious persecution. A petition with over 2 million signatures went to the Mexican Congress but to no effect. The Catholic bishops most painfully concluded that the Church could no longer operate and in a final act of desperation ordered all Catholic services to halt on 31 July 1926. This extreme action was not enough to persuade Calles to relent or to seek a compromise; the president was convinced that the bishops were bluffing and that the peasants were too imbued with revolutionary ideas to listen to fanatical clergy. In the last week before the 31 July deadline, as Mexicans made long lines outside the churches to obtain baptism and matrimony, the charged tension was evident to all. Rather than try to diffuse the explosive situation, the Calles administration provoked a confrontation by issuing new and harsh orders to take over all the church buildings after 31 July. In Sinaloa and Coahuila officials saw the absurdity of these orders and established arrangements for the buildings satisfactory to local Catholics. Not surprisingly, those two states did not experience uprisings and served as the north-

ern limit to the rebellion that was about to break out.[3]

To the south of Sinaloa and Coahuila, the authorities bungled the takeover of the church buildings; often it seemed that the local authorities, in their zeal to impress President Calles, had gone out of their way to antagonize local Catholics. Protests gave way to riots and disturbances as many crossed the line from peaceful protest into violent actions. Arrests became frequent and soon protesters were dying in spontaneous clashes outside the churches. The Catholic hostility to the government was strongest in the states of Jalisco and Colima, and resistance was spreading to nearby states. Already in August 1926 Pedro Quintanar emerged as an important regional leader when he took control of a zone in Zacatecas. Quintanar was the first of many leaders who began to form bands and to take sporadic actions in states ranging from Michoacán and Oaxaca in the south to Guanajuato and Aguascalientes in the east. However, no serious fighting had occurred yet, and the localized outbursts did not amount to an insurrection. Time to abort the movement still remained if the government relented on its harsh policy. Although the fanatically anti–Catholic Calles could not abandon the religious persecution, the supposedly astute politician should have listened to another argument. In September 1926 the Yaqui Indians rebelled again in Sonora, but because Calles continued Obregón's policy of reducing the army, fewer troops were available. Specifically, Calles did not have enough battalions to fight a two-front war: He could eliminate the Yaquis or he could enforce his anti–Catholic measures, but he could not do both. When he ordered most garrisons in Jalisco to redeploy to the north for the final campaign against the Yaquis, he gave the Catholics time to organize and to launch an armed insurrection.[4]

The Yaqui Campaign of 1926–1927

The elimination of Catholic influence and the destruction of the Yaqui tribe were essential parts of Calles's drive to strengthen the central government. To transform Mexico, all obstacles to the power of the government had to disappear, and among these obstacles the most irritating was the open defiance of the Yaquis.

The Mayo Indians to the south, identical in language and culture to the Yaquis, had agreed to live under the rules of the Mexican government and were a valuable element within the local community. For reasons not quite clear, the assimilation of the Yaquis into Mexican life had not gone smoothly. Many Yaquis were trying to incorporate themselves into the local Mexican society, but a sizeable minority refused to abandon their semi-nomadic life for the hardship of planting and growing crops in their valley. At stake was not just the transition into Mexican rule and society but also into an agrarian life. Since the time of the Spanish colony military campaigns to subdue the independent Indians had repeatedly failed. The last one took place in the late 1910s and culminated in an arrangement to pay the Yaquis a stipend to remain peaceful. Governor Adolfo de la Huerta had gained considerable popularity among the Indians by his support for this generous agreement.[5]

Allotting the Indians a monthly stipend was cheaper than waging a military campaign, but the policy harked back to the bribes the Spanish monarchy paid Indians not to attack outposts in the eighteenth century. The Mexican government felt humiliated and was looking for a pretext to scrap the stipend policy and to solve the Yaqui problem once and for all. The opportunity came on 12 September 1926 when in a brazen act, for 16 hours Yaquis held hostage the passenger train carrying none other than ex-president Álvaro Obregón. Calm reactions and patient handling by General Obregón avoided a bloodbath, while a providential downpour soaked the Indians so thoroughly that any desire for combat faded by the time army reinforcements arrived on 13 September. The train incident was probably enough justification for Calles to launch a furious campaign against the Yaquis; when in addition he learned that one of the grievances of the Indians was that the religious persecution threatened their annual pilgrimage to a Catholic shrine, Calles concluded that whether in Jalisco or in Sonora, he was fighting the same Catholic influence everywhere. As if the reasons were not enough, the Indians claimed to have the support of the exiled De la Huerta; with his revolt still fresh in everyone's mind, no argument was needed to destroy any allies of the rebel.[6]

President Calles promptly authorized his close friend Obregón to supervise the campaign against the Yaquis. Obregón was only a retired general and did not want to be in the chain of command, but his immense personal prestige as Mexico's military hero assured immediate compliance with his always reasoned and modest suggestions. In what was to be the final military campaign of his life, General Obregón did not take to the field and left command of the troops to others. Instead, he concentrated on devising a successful strategy. From his study of the many previous offensives against the Yaquis, he correctly concluded that extensive patrolling had failed to subdue the Indians. The Yaquis were just too swift and too familiar with the terrain to catch, and they easily eluded combat. He welcomed the help of airplanes to discover the Yaqui camps but was not sure aerial reconnaissance could reveal the presence of small bands of Yaquis hiding in the thick underbrush.[7] Obregón focused all the army's efforts on completely isolating the rebel Indians. He created five lines of troops to blockade the Yaquis in the rough mountainous terrain of northeast Sonora. Although occasionally Indians slipped through individually, the lines did their job of trapping the Indians in the most barren part of the state during the last quarter of 1926. Obregón wisely left the decision on when to pursue to the local commanders, and he returned to devote his attention to his private business matters. Excessive control from headquarters helped spoil many previous offensives, and Obregón knew too well that only if the local officers had freedom of action could they destroy the hostile Indians when the conditions were right.[8]

After over a month without regular access to food supplies for themselves and their families, the Yaquis began to suffer tremendous hardship. The first surrenders of families came in late October, and the trickle increased over time.[9] In preparation for an offensive, the army increased its mobility by bringing trucks to the region; the Indians, in spite of their traditional attachment to horses, soon followed suit and obtained automobiles from the United States, although in smaller numbers. Perhaps fittingly, the last Indian war in North America utilized motorized vehicles for the transport of men and supplies.[10] With a more practical sense, the officers resumed the old practice of pocketing funds destined for the campaign. The spread of corruption and the lack of clear victories created impatience in Sonora by the start of 1927, when in reality the blockade just needed time to make its effects felt. At last a clear indication of imminent victory came when on 19 January 1927 a nearly starved Yaqui family brought a peace offer from the tribe. The Indians agreed to accept army troops in railroad stations and in Mexican towns, but wanted no soldiers in their camps. The Indians also did not want the school to take away their children, whom they needed at home to help with the work. The absence of any request for a stipend was the bait for the government, but President Calles, aware that attempts at living peacefully as neighbors had failed in the past, rejected the peace offer. The government insisted on the unconditional surrender of the Indians and the enlistment of all the male rebels into special Yaqui battalions of the army. The government felt that tours of duty in the army were the best way to begin

the process of assimilation into Mexican life. After their discharge, the Yaquis could reunite with their families and apply what they had learned to enter into the mainstream of Mexican society.[11]

Since the negotiations failed, Obregón and the local commanders felt that the time had arrived to increase the pressure on the Indians. In early February 1927 at least 15,000 soldiers began to chase the cornered Yaquis estimated to number no more than 2,000 armed men.[12] Since the blockade remained in place, the Indians could not escape and continued to suffer starvation. In desperation, the Indian chiefs summoned their followers to one of their remotest strongholds in the mountains at Zamahuaca in early March. The commander of the fifth line, the nearest to Zamahuaca, was General Agustín Olachea, who either through aerial observation or from deserters learned about the Indian gathering. In swift and quiet moves, his troops approached the Indian en-

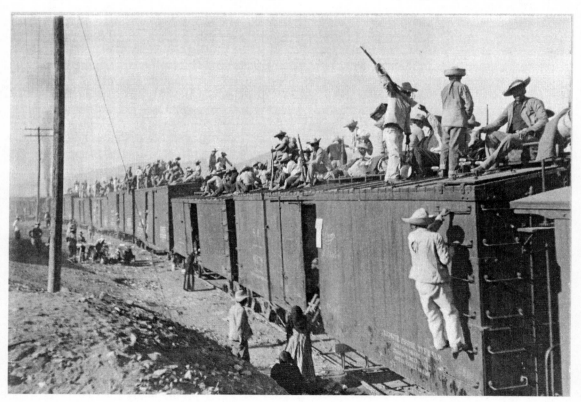

Yaqui troops, enlisted in the Mexican Army, are being transported in boxcars. All sides prized the Yaqui Indians as great warriors (Library of Congress, Prints and Photographs Division, Frank and Frances Carpenter Collection).

campment at night and then early in the morning of 19 March began an encircling attack.
While his field artillery kept the Indians distracted, his troops climbed rocky heights and
pushed back the Indians in savage combat until
the Yaquis were trapped in a large rocky escarpment. The troops set the main Indian
camp on fire, and ferocious combat ensued for
two days; the Indians were fighting for the survival of their way of life and neither side took
prisoners during the combat. The next day
hunger and thirst pushed the soldiers to the
point of collapse, and the chance existed that
the Indians might escape through the weakened army lines. But the arrival of airplanes to
bomb the Indian positions restored the morale
of the troops and drove the Yaquis into panic.
As the Indians jumped from the escarpment in
a desperate attempt to flee from the exploding
bombs, waiting cavalry below took most of
them prisoner, including 200 women. The battle of Zamahuaca broke the Indian resistance
and was the decisive engagement of the campaign. Quite revealingly, the airplane ended the
last Indian war of North America.[13]

Only small groups of rebel Yaquis remained on the loose, and they desperately
headed through the mountains to try to reach
the U.S. border before aerial reconnaissance exposed their location. Ground patrols confirmed
the victory, and in July an army colonel reported that "In my opinion this campaign is
nearing the end, because in the recent expeditions, we have not been able to find any tracks
that reveal the existence of any large Indian
groups."[14] With the forced enlistment of the
men into the army and the deportation of at
least 1500 Yaquis, mostly women, the Indian
menace disappeared permanently.[15] The military campaign gave way to police functions
more appropriately performed by local authorities who dealt with the occasional robbery and
cattle rustling. Although army garrisons remained a permanent fixture in Sonora, the government no longer needed to maintain so large
a force and could redeploy many battalions to
face the rapidly spreading Cristero Rebellion.

The Start of the Cristero Rebellion

The departure of most army troops for the
campaign in Sonora gave the Catholics the
indispensable freedom to launch an armed in-

surrection. Their most famous slogan was
"Viva Cristo Rey," which soon earned them the
name of "Cristeros." However, Catholics did
not rise up in arms in every state. The heart of
the revolt was always in the states of Jalisco,
Colima, and Nayarit. Second in intensity were
the states of Aguascalientes and Michoacán.
Sometimes quite determined bands existed in
other nearby states, and as mentioned previously, Sinaloa and Coahuila as peaceful states
were the northern limit of the rebellion. Much
as the Cristeros tried, they never generated
enough national momentum to topple the
regime as had happened in 1911 against Porfirio
Díaz. The geographical concentration in west-
central Mexico was far from accidental: West-
central Mexico was the last heavily populated
region not to have experienced a spontaneous
mobilization. Contending armies had fought
over the region for years, and the capture of
Guadalajara had always been a prize objective
of many a military campaign in the past. The
war had come to west-central Mexico and the
leva had carried off some of its inhabitants, but
the region had never before plunged wholeheartedly into any rebellion. Even against
Porfirio Díaz in 1911, the popular insurrection
had been weak, tardy, and largely ineffective. In
contrast, northeast Mexico, the region centered
in Monterrey, twice decisively shaped the
course of the country's history by rebelling
against Victoriano Huerta and by opposing
Pancho Villa. In the late 1920s the turn to revolt had come to west-central Mexico.[16]

In the absence of a strong army presence,
the Cristeros seized small towns and isolated
posts throughout west-central Mexico. Success
attracted more followers, and by November
1926 the movement gained considerable
strength in the west-central states of Mexico.
Since March 1925 the League for the Defense of
Religious Liberty, an organization of lay
Catholics, had been trying to stop the anti–
Church persecution, but the failure of its
peaceful measures forced it to shift tactics. The
League issued a manifesto urging all Catholics
to rise up in armed revolt against the Calles
government on 1 January 1927. This call to
arms strikingly resembled Francisco Madero's
appeal in that distant November 1910. The
Catholic bishops opposed any recourse to violence, but they managed only to delay the is-
suance of the manifesto. The League defied the

bishops on the solid argument that the insurrection in the field was already a reality and that the League had to provide leadership for an otherwise fragmented movement. The League's appeal brought new regions into the Cristero revolt in January 1927, most notably Los Altos, the most fertile and productive district of Jalisco. Los Altos emerged as the very core of the Cristero rebellion, and was the target of many army campaigns.[17]

As one town after another joined the Cristeros in Jalisco, the rebellion enveloped the entire state by 11 April. The rebel tactics of avoiding combat except in surprise attacks were effective: "The federals decidedly lack control of the situation, they being wholly now on the defensive, their efforts being exerted in putting down uprisings rather than to take the offensive to eliminate rebel activities."[18] Although fear spread that the Cristeros intended to cut off Guadalajara, the government did not adopt harsh measures until the Cristeros perpetrated a major atrocity on 19 April. On that day under the leadership of a fanatical priest, the Cristeros captured and torched a train headed to Mexico City from Guadalajara. Most of the passengers on board died either from gunfire or more gruesomely from the flames of the burning cars.[19]

The Cristeros never repeated an atrocity of this scale, but their action nicely confirmed the government's worst stereotypes about the fanatical rebels. Since aggressive patrolling had failed to keep the movement from spreading, the government switched to the forced evacuation of the inhabitants of Los Altos. This policy of reconcentration imitated similar policies of European powers in their colonies such as in Cuba between 1895 and 1898, but Mexico was the first country to apply this barbaric measure to its own people. As the Cristero movement spread into other states, so did the policy of reconcentration of rural civilians; soon the cities were swollen with floods of destitute refugees from the targeted areas. Although the Mexican government at times relented and was not always diligent about enforcing the reconcentration policy, enough evacuations took place to disrupt farming and thus to make food scarce in the countryside. Even in places where the government did not insist on evacuation, the troops always very diligently destroyed any food supplies in the countryside including the seed corn for the next planting season.[20]

Starvation was a key weapon the Mexican government used against its own people, but this brutal reprisal required several years to make its effects felt. Indeed, during the first semester of 1927 the Cristero movement continued to expand, in spite of the best efforts of Secretary of War Joaquín Amaro, who personally came to the rebellious regions to try to invigorate the army offensives.[21] A good part of the problem for the government came from incompetent officers such as the zone commander of Colima, General Rodrigo M. Talamantes. Rather than waging a vigorous campaign against the Cristeros, Talamantes "spent most all of his time in a certain saloon in Colima; orders and correspondence would be brought to him at the saloon and he would sign them there."[22] When finally pressed to take action against a Cristero stronghold at the base of a nearby volcano, "his expeditions were nothing more than picnic parties [...] on these expeditions he would purchase the best provisions the market afforded for himself and staff, and would take along plenty of wines, liquors and beer. He would be out from two to three days and would return and report a victory over the rebels [...] when, perhaps his troops had not fired a short or seen a rebel."[23] Mexico City recalled the incompetent Talamantes who had very ably practiced graft on a considerable scale. Although his replacement was more aggressive, the Cristeros easily eluded any decisive engagement. Even the presence of Secretary of War Amaro, who came with reinforcements and airplanes to prosecute the campaign against the Cristeros in Colima, failed to produce significant results.[24]

At least 8,000 Cristeros were in revolt in July 1927, but before they could make their numbers felt, the defeat of the Yaqui Indians released army battalions for duty against the Cristeros. Starting in June, General Amaro was returning troops from Sonora to Jalisco by train and in addition, the army counted on five new battalions of surrendered Yaqui fighters. With the many troops under his command, General Amaro was preparing a large offensive to smash the Cristeros. Seeing the imminent army onslaught, the League for the Defense of Religious Freedom concluded that the Cristeros desperately needed a single commander to save the rebellion.[25]

Where could the League find a suitable

military commander? Of the many leaders of the Cristeros, all, like their soldiers, were tied to a particular region; they had risen to command precisely because they inspired local respect. In need of a commander with a national perspective and solid military credentials, the League searched for persons not connected with the regimes of Calles, Obregón, or even Carranza. General Enrique Gorostieta, a graduate of Chapultepec Military Academy and a proud member of the old Federal Army of Porfirio Díaz, emerged as the best candidate. He came from a Monterrey family, and thus was not related to any of the regions in revolt. He had been close to Victoriano Huerta, and his father had even been a cabinet member of the deposed president. In exile after Huerta's fall, Gorostieta despised the new revolutionaries who ruled Mexico. Although an amnesty allowed him to return to Mexico, his contempt for the new regime remained very intense. In reality, he had been bit by the revolutionary bug; like many others struck by this usually fatal disease, he believed that only large doses of power for himself could save Mexico from its many problems.[26]

Gorostieta with his strong conservative background was quite comfortable with the Catholic Church, although he himself had not manifested any great religious devotion during his earlier life. His initial status was that of a mercenary. The League for the Defense of Religious Freedom in July 1927 signed a contract offering him a salary and a life insurance policy payable to his wife. Once he lived closely with the Cristeros, their passionate religious devotion so impressed him that he underwent his own spiritual conversion. The Cristeros' dedication led him to conclude that these were the best soldiers he had ever commanded, and soon a genuine bond based on military and religious principles sprung up between the men and Gorostieta. However, he never lost sight of the larger political goal and soon was filling the power vacuum in the Cristeros' leadership. By the time the League tried to halt his drive for power, it was too late, and Gorostieta was already the visible head of the Cristeros and not just its military leader.[27]

However, his power was not absolute, because Gorostieta, the League, and the regional leaders formed a system of co-government. As the field commander, Gorostieta cultivated the regional leaders and soon had gained tremendous popularity. He traveled widely to familiarize himself with the region and its people. He stepped up recruitment, formed new units, and appointed officers to key commands. Most importantly, he brought organization to the scattered Cristero units. He replicated the structure of the Mexican army among the Cristeros whom he grouped into squads, platoons, companies, and battalions. At the same time, he preserved the essential qualities of a guerrilla force; for example, although he insisted in discipline, he tolerated the frequent return of the Cristeros to their homes and towns. He eventually succeeded in shaping a guerrilla force well suited for the irregular warfare he considered to be the first stage of the campaign to overthrown the government.[28] However, his preparations were far from complete when starting in August the government began to return the battalions from the Yaqui campaign. Before the battalions returning from Sonora could launch their planned offensive against the unprepared Cristeros, good luck smiled on Gorostieta. The outbreak of the Gómez-Serrano revolt in October 1927 forced Secretary of War Amaro to recall many battalions from Jalisco to Veracruz, and this unexpected transfer gave Gorostieta the extra time to strengthen the Cristero military organization.

The Gómez–Serrano Revolt of October 1927

The Cristero Revolt was the greatest blunder of the Plutarco Elías Calles presidency. He had received a recovering country from Álvaro Obregón in 1924, but by 1927 Mexico seemed on the verge of collapse. This obvious failure deprived his inept administration of influence over the selection of the next president of Mexico. The crisis was so bad that many persons inside and outside the government implored Obregón to abandon his private life and return to save Mexico. The Mexican congress approved a constitutional amendment allowing the non-consecutive reelection of persons to the presidency, thus authorizing the former president to run again. On 26 June 1927 Obregón formally announced his candidacy for the presidency. As the only living hero of the Revolution, Obregón commanded widespread sympathy throughout the country, and Calles, seeing his power ebbing, had no choice but to put the wholehearted support of his administration behind the Obregón candidacy. Unfortunately for Mexico, the ineptness of Calles tempted other generals to dream of becoming president. Two of them, Arnulfo R. Gómez and Francisco R. Serrano, went so far as to declare their candidacy for the presidency in what the public dubbed the Generals' election. Calles initially tried to keep Serrano in the cabinet and even offered him the post of Secretary of Gobernación, which the general unwisely declined. Because proposals had already surfaced that the government should subsidize or otherwise encourage opposition parties for the purpose of creating some semblance of democracy, the Calles administration put its best face forward and welcomed the two candidates as clear proof of an open electoral process.[29]

Generals Gómez and Serrano resigned from the army to run for the presidency, but after the elections they could expect reincorporation or some other compensation for having performed the useful function of loyal opposition candidates. The two generals did not comprehend their only possible role in the emerging political system and foolishly believed that they had a chance to win the presidency. For his part, Serrano quickly depleted his campaign funds in scandalous expenses and riotous living. Both he and Gómez finally realized their sputtering candidacies had no chance to win, but their common hatred of Obregón brought them together in August 1927 to begin planning a military coup. The lynchpin of the coup was General Eugenio Martínez, the zone commander at Mexico City, who had been an early associate of Obregón but had become somewhat distant from his former superior. General Martínez, an inveterate drinker, soon was bragging in bars about the proposed coup. When word of the plot reached Obregón, he persuaded General Martínez to resign his command post and instead to accept a study mission in Europe as a grateful exit from an awkward situation. Without General Martínez in command of the troops in the Mexico City military zone, the coup lost any chance of success, or at least that was how the too logical Obregón reasoned.[30]

General Héctor Almada, the chief of staff

of General Martínez, temporarily assumed command of the troops in the Valley of Mexico and had no intention of dropping the coup. Almada met with Gomez and Serrano on 30 September, and although they could not agree on the final form of the coup, the Calles government soon learned about the preparations and issued orders for the arrest of Gómez and Serrano. The last two fled the city supposedly to rally provincial garrisons. A reckless Almada hatched the plan to seize both Calles and Obregón when they appeared to observe scheduled military maneuvers in Balbuena Field at 2000 on 2 October. Forewarned of the plot, neither came, and only Secretary of War Joaquín Amaro briefly appeared with an impressive escort. A desperate Almada ordered the four battalion commanders involved in the coup to leave the city with their soldiers for an extended campaign. Over a thousand soldiers left with the rebel Almada, but unless Gomez and Serrano could obtain large numbers of followers from other army units, the revolt was doomed. For Serrano, any chance of help came too late. Calles had already ordered the arrest of Serrano, who was captured in Cuernavaca early in the morning of 3 October and executed later than same day.[31]

An even harsher fate awaited the 16th Infantry Battalion just three days after its arrival at Torreón, Coahuila. Calles sent orders to make sure that all army garrisons remained loyal to the government, but overzealous subordinates stopped at nothing to impress their superiors. Previously the War Department scattered units of doubtful loyalty, such as the 16th Battalion, among more reliable garrisons. At 0300 on 3 October, the 43rd Artillery and the 18th Cavalry battalions launched a massive surprise attack on the 16th Infantry Battalion as most of its soldiers were sleeping on the floor, many next to their wives and children. Indiscriminate machine gun fire killed many of the women and children, while other soldiers came to finish off any survivors still alive; at least 200 died in this massacre. The authorities claimed that the 16th, originally of 300 men, had intended in the name of Gómez to overwhelm the garrison of 3,000 soldiers at the new army base. To make sure that this cover story held, all officers and any soldiers who escaped the initial massacre were executed so that they could not talk. The hideous brutality of this totally unjustified action appeared to fore-shadow the return of Mexico to the barbarity of the savage years of 1913–1916.[32]

Certainly for the leaders of the revolt no mercy was possible. General Aldama fled to the state of Veracruz, where he managed to join with General Gómez who was trying to rally supporters near Perote. Unable to interest the locals in the revolt, the rebels forced ethnic Indians to join their ranks. Afraid that the revolt might spread, the government began to pull units out of the Cristero front to send to the state of Veracruz. General Gonzalo Escobar with a column of 3,000 men pursued the rebels, while the government rushed troops to the region until over 8,000 soldiers and 9 airplanes were looking for the rebels. At Ayahualulco the army troops located the rebel column of over 1200 soldiers and Indians; after a brief combat of 15 minutes on 9 October, the demoralized rebels fled, and over 500 soldiers and officers surrendered to the government.[33] The failure of General Escobar to continue a vigorous pursuit gave the rebels a lease on life; "his lack of aggressiveness has caused much dissatisfaction in the War Department, which, however, maintains him in command."[34] The government feared the appearance of guerrilla warfare, but the rebels were simply trying to hide. The capture of General Gómez on 4 November and his execution the next day triggered the final collapse of the revolt. The remaining rebel generals tried to reach the safety of the United States, but only the bold General Almada made it safely across the border.[35]

The Gómez-Serrano Revolt was over, but it had revealed that Mexico still did not have an army completely loyal to the government. Too many generals still believed that the Mexican Revolution had not properly rewarded their merits. The discontent within the officer corps boded ill for the pacification of Mexico and already had given the Cristeros a breathing spell to reorganize under their new dynamic leader Enrique Gorostieta.

The Cristero Rebellion at Its Height

With the army momentarily distracted in Veracruz, Enrique Gorostieta seized the opportunity to expand the revolt. The number of armed Cristeros reached 20,000 by the end of December 1927 and peaked at almost 25,000 in February 1928. To solidify their control over the civilian population, the Cristeros tried to root out government sympathizers, thus provoking a flight of local officials into the cities and in many cases to the United States. Army troops returned in December to resume the offensive and they were reinforced by armed peasants (*agraristas*) brought in from quiet states in particular from San Luis Potosí. The government gave those peasants land and in return demanded military services from them. The large numbers of persons massing on both sides promised bloody clashes, but the Cristeros generally avoided combat because they were critically short of ammunition. Skirmishes took place every day but rarely any major encounters. Lack of artillery also foiled the attempts of the Cristeros to capture large towns or cities. Assaults on fortifications were out of the question, and even the bell towers of churches in small towns posed a generally insurmountable obstacle. Repeatedly after gaining control of a town, the Cristeros saw their victory spoiled by solid resistance from soldiers holed up in Church towers. Artillery would have quickly leveled the towers, instead dynamite charges failed to dislodge the troops from the towers and even from their barracks. The Cristeros were never able to capture arsenals and could only strip cartridges from either dead or captured soldiers. Whenever possible, the Cristeros substituted the use of the machete for the scarce cartridges.[36]

Except in the rocky volcanic region of Colima where horses were not suitable for travel, the Cristeros normally rode their own horses and easily avoided the soldiers usually walking on foot. General Amaro, a passionate lover of horses, tried to improve the mobility of the troops by buying animals in the United States, but the large imported horses lacked the stamina of the lean and hardy Mexican breeds. The slow-moving soldiers could not hope to pursue much less catch the mounted Cristeros. Not surprisingly, the army usually lacked good information on the Cristeros, who enjoyed the sympathy and support of almost the entire civilian population. The Cristeros seemed unbeatable, but in spite of the best efforts of Gorostieta, they still had some weaknesses. Turnover in the Cristero units remained high, as many men returned to their homes and villages permanently. Sometimes family members took turns serving in the Cristero units, but the high turnover meant that Gorostieta was never sure how many men might show up for a particular operation. Worse, the Cristeros did not like to campaign outside their home grounds, and this reluctance eliminated any chance of a concentrated attack on a major city like Guadalajara. Each of the units was locally recruited and enjoyed the enthusiastic support of the neighbors, but at the same time the exclusively local recruitment created other complications. The men generally chose the officers, and unless they were popular in the community, they could not be effective leaders. Gorostieta had to walk a fine line in making officer appointments; he wanted competent and loyal commanders, but they had to be popular as well. Except in a few unfortunate cases, Gorostieta managed to ratify as officers the most appropriate local leaders.[37]

The village support was indispensable, because the war was more against the rural population than against the armed Cristeros. The government extended the reconcentration policy beyond Los Altos, and soon many regions in neighboring states were suffering the ravages of the forced evacuation. The army was supposed to give ample prior warnings about the districts to be evacuated, but local commanders acted on their own as they saw fit. Army officers had seen in the reconcentration policy a great opportunity for personal enrichment, so that the troops, even when they located Cristeros, headed instead for the villages and rural dwellings. The troops seized whatever they needed for their immediate use without any payment; afterwards they began to interrogate and then to torture locals to identify sympathizers. Inevitably some executions resulted, and worse, many died as a result of sadistic extremes. The soldiers burned, scorched, hung, pulled, cut, strangled, and submerged suspected sympathizers to extract information or just for the pleasure of forcing them to renounce the Catholic faith. Frequently the troops skipped the fatal tortures to take away relatives of known sympathizers as hostages; the hostages rarely returned home alive. Then the soldiers began to steal anything of value they had seen in the village and in the farms; eventually whole railroad trains full of looted merchandise came to Mexico City from the Cristero regions. Machine guns finished

slaughtering any animals that the officers could not carry away. But the ravaging expedition was not yet over: The soldiers only departed after having conducted mass rapes against the women in the villages. Sometimes the soldiers raped the women inside their homes in front of their families, in other instances the soldiers locked the men in the church building and then proceeded to rape the women left in the town.[38] The *agraristas*, like the plundering tribes of the ancient world, remembered fondly that among the booty they brought home were "beautiful horses and handsome women."[39]

More than reconcentration, what the army and the *agraristas* were conducting was a policy of scorched earth. By destroying the agriculture and ranching in the region, the government was depriving the Cristeros of a food supply. The burning of planted fields and the destruction of seed corn became standard operating practice as the government strove to starve out the Cristeros. Emaciated refugees by the tens of thousands crowded into the cities fleeing the devastation in the countryside. The Cristeros themselves became very ragged looking and often went around almost naked because they lacked clothes or even blankets to keep them warm during the shivering nights. Surrender was out of the question, because the government ordered the execution of any persons suspected of Cristero sympathies. The policy of executing all prisoners returned Mexico to the bloody practices of 1913–1916 and reversed the more humane practice of selective executions during the De La Huerta Revolt in 1924. The Calles government bears the responsibility for reviving the brutal policy of summary executions. In spite of their supposed fanaticism, the Cristeros themselves were much more humane with their persecutors. Although Gorostieta himself was personally inclined to execute all prisoners, fortunately the local leaders showed more compassion. Exceptions occurred after incidents of particularly bloody government savagery, but normally the Cristeros executed only the officers and released the captured soldiers after some religious education. The lenient attitude towards the prisoners reaped immediate rewards, because many soldiers allowed their *soldaderas* to sell cartridges to the Cristeros.[40]

The pocket change the soldiers earned by selling cartridges to the Cristeros paled with the large sales corrupt officers in Mexico City made to the urban network of the Cristeros early in the conflict. When army units captured Mexican cartridges not yet issued to the army, the government at last put a stop to the scandalous sale in Mexico City. The Cristeros captured ample numbers of Mauser rifles and pistols, but remained critically short of ammunition. A brisk black market in cartridges sprung up in the cities as the urban networks tried to supply the ammunition. The role of female supporters was crucial for purchasing the cartridges and then for smuggling them out. Women sowed special dresses and garments suitable for hiding large numbers of cartridges. Traveling as quietly as possible, the women (organized in brigades) went from the cities to the countryside to deliver the cartridges. As the police increased the inspections at road blocks in the city exits, this approach became too risky even for the women, who turned to the no less pressing task of smuggling food and other vital necessities to the starving Cristeros in the countryside. To bypass the vigilance, some women contacted with a sympathizer to bring munitions from the United States via Monterrey aboard an automobile. The lack of roads made the trip a harrowing experience, but at least in this instance the shipment of cartridges did reach the Cristeros.[41]

A very ambitious group planned to have an airplane land in Durango carrying a large shipment of cartridges from the United States. The women had gone so far in their preparations as to obtain flight directions and land signals from a local leader, although it is not known whether the supply by airplane ever took place.[42] Conversely, army airplanes routinely bombed Cristero villages and suspected hideouts, doubtlessly inflicting many casualties on civilians and animals but never hitting any Cristero units. Although some of the terrain was suited for air bombardment, most of the region was so thickly covered with vegetation as to make the airplane mainly a nuisance for the Cristero units.[43]

The relative ineffectiveness of the air campaign was the only setback in the government offensive. The relentless army campaign was taking a heavy toll on the Cristeros, whose numbers had declined to under 12,000 men by May 1928.[44] As a professional officer Gorostieta could sense that victory was slipping away,

because the acute shortage of ammunition repeatedly crippled any Cristero countermoves. Gorostieta learned that gathering many Cristeros for a major combat with the army was pointless, because as soon as the ammunition ran short, the Cristeros withdrew. In frustration Gorostieta repeatedly stated "Give me three million cartridges, and I will control this region of the Bajío."[45]

To secure a large shipment of ammunition, Gorostieta assigned to Jesús Degollado, one of his best regional commanders, the task of capturing Manzanillo on the Pacific Coast. The plan was to hold the port town long enough for a cargo ship bringing munitions and weapons to unload. Only 60 soldiers defended Manzanillo, and so as not to alert the army, the Cristeros in Colima had remained quiet during the preceding weeks. The surprise was complete when 1000 Cristeros arrived on the outskirts of the town in the morning of 24 May 1928. Not all was good news, however, because the gunboat *Guerrero*, scheduled to depart the previous night, was still in port. Once the attack began at 0700 the defenders put up a tremendous resistance joined by police and customs officials, and soon the *Guerrero's* guns opened fire on the attackers.[46] Manzanillo, with the sea on three sides, was well suited for defense against Cristeros not accustomed to attacking fortified cities. Their lack of experience showed, as the Cristeros did not cut the city's telegraph line until 1330, a fatal oversight. At Colima, the dynamic General Heliodoro Charis promptly learned by telegraph of the Cristero attack and set out personally with two battalions to the relief of Manzanillo. In anticipation of that reaction, Gorostieta directed another large Cristero force to block the advance of the relief column; as a further precaution, he entrusted to a third Cristero leader the destruction of bridges and railroad track. But the response of General Charis was so swift that his troop train passed before the blockading force was in place. The third Cristero leader barely damaged the track and caused a delay of only fifteen minutes for the quick repairs. Thus when the Cristeros had finally breached the defenses and entered Manzanillo at 1545, the relief column was almost upon them. The troop train arrived at 1600, but by then the Cristeros were rapidly abandoning the city. At least eight did not escape in time, and the loss of these

Cristeros thoroughly demoralized the rest because they were not accustomed to suffering casualties of this number in a single engagement.

Unrivaled in small-unit actions, the Cristeros had not yet mastered the techniques of seizing cities or of coordinating large deployments on separate fronts. The failure to seize Manzanillo deprived them of a last chance to obtain cartridges and cannons on their own. Gorostieta desperately tried to find another solution, but he knew that time was running out for the Cristeros, whose numbers dwindled down to around 5000 men by the end of 1928. The battalions were fast closing in on the last Cristeros when the outbreak of a political crisis miraculously saved the rebels from destruction. Once again the government recalled its battalions and gave the Cristeros the opportunity to recover their strength. The rebels hurriedly took advantage of the pause to prepare for what they knew was the inevitable return of the army.

The Escobar Rebellion and the Last Battle of the Mexican Revolution

When a Cristero fanatic assassinated president-elect Álvaro Obregón on 17 July 1928, Mexico lost its most gifted and tolerant leader. The fatal consequences of this hideous act shaped the rest of the twentieth century. During the six years of his upcoming presidency, Obregón planned to restore prosperity to Mexico and to construct an open and participatory system. Perhaps the goals were unattainable, but it was Mexico's last hope. With his tragic death, the less capable Plutarco Elías Calles concluded that Mexico's only salvation lay in the imposition of a rigid and stifling structure of abject submission.

In the short run, the assassination plunged Mexico into a simmering political crisis. The immediate question was to find a replacement for Calles once his presidential term expired on 1 December 1928. Calles cobbled together diverse deals and was able to arrange a peaceful transfer of power to the provisional president Emilio Portes Gil on 1 December. Calles dedicated himself to creating an official political party to govern the country. As the real head of the rapidly spreading official party,

Calles quietly operated in the background and in effect became the real power broker in Mexico, independent of who occupied the presidency.[47]

Much as Calles considered the political crisis to be over by the start of 1929, not everyone shared that assessment. Many generals who had complete faith in Obregón distrusted Calles and feared for their future careers. Discontent increased among generals who had harbored probably exaggerated illusions of promotions under an Obregón presidency. These generals felt bypassed and began to plot against Calles and the provisional president Emilio Portes Gil. Leading the plotters was General Gonzalo Escobar, the zone commander of Coahuila who had fallen into relative disgrace after his inept campaign against the rebel Arnulfo Gómez in October 1927. Not satisfied with the meager pickings at Coahuila, Escobar saw no other way to rehabilitate his fortune than by starting a revolt.

Spies reported that at secret meetings at the Regis hotel in Mexico City, initially the conspirators had wanted to repeat the coup d'état of February 1913 by taking prisoner the government leaders including Calles in Mexico City. The coup planners then shifted to a simultaneous uprising of the majority of the zone commanders in the country. The conspirators were oblivious to denunciations and brazenly went so far as to contact generals throughout Mexico. On 25 January 1929 Governor Fausto Topete of Sonora wrote a letter to his colleague Abelardo Rodríguez of Baja California inviting him to join the conspiracy. With great carelessness, the letter listed many plotters, not just General Escobar but also General Jesús M. Aguirre, the zone commander of Veracruz. Even after obtaining a copy of this letter, the government refused to arrest the plotters. Hasty action in October 1927 had resulted in the massacre of the 16th Infantry Battalion at Torreón, and the government did not want a repetition of that shameful and messy incident. Secretary of War Joaquín Amaro instead was quietly removing the main plotters from command positions, but at this critical juncture an accident he suffered while playing polo incapacitated him. He went to the United States for medical treatment, and his absence provided a breathing spell for the plotters to conclude their plans. Calles could still have had the plotters removed from command, but he trusted Aguirre as much as Obregón had trusted Enrique Estrada in the De la Huerta revolt of 1924. Again like Obregón, Calles could not bring himself to believe that a trusted general was about to betray him. The failure of the government to take preventive action in early 1929 has led many to speculate that Calles wanted to purge the army of disloyal elements and thus deliberately allowed the generals to revolt. But such a Machiavellian maneuver was too risky for Calles, whose political skills were less than commonly believed. His sense of timing failed him, and he simply waited too long to arrest the coup suspects. Thus, the outbreak of the revolt on 3 March 1929 caught Calles by surprise. To face the crisis, he immediately accepted appointment as Secretary of War to replace the convalescent Amaro.[48]

The trigger for the revolt was a routine order from the War Department reassigning two units stationed in Veracruz to other posts. General Aguirre misinterpreted the order as an attempt to weaken his power base and reported his fears to the plotters in Sonora, who decided to start the revolt on 3 March. Proclaiming General Escobar as their leader, the rebels easily gained control of most of the northern states of Sonora, Chihuahua, Coahuila, and Durango. About 17,000 men out of a total army of over 50,000 soldiers rose up against the government.[49] General Escobar realized that for the revolt to succeed, he had to strike quickly before the government could bring its larger forces to bear. He ordered General Francisco Manzo in Sonora to push rapidly south into Sinaloa and to capture Mazatlán at least. General Manzo had been a firebrand who had most passionately prodded other generals to join the revolt, and consequently Escobar expected bold and decisive results from him. Escobar also sent the Yaqui General Francisco Urbalejo to push south from Durango into Zacatecas. Upon learning that the government had withdrawn most of the garrison from Monterrey, Escobar took advantage of the opportunity to attack that city. The high point of the revolt came on 4 March when Escobar surprised the small garrison at Monterrey and thus captured the most important city in the north.[50]

The rebels, riding an apparently unstoppable wave of successes, harbored the simplistic notion that rebel units from Veracruz and Oaxaca could converge easily on the capital to seize the leaders of the Mexican government. Unfortunately for the rebels, the revolt at Oaxaca had fizzled, and at Veracruz complications arose almost immediately. Although the Mexican Navy supported the revolt, many army units refused to obey General Aguirre, who could not begin his drive on the capital. Even before loyal troops reached the port city, other army units defied Aguirre and forced him to flee into the bush on 6 March. The Veracruz part of the rebellion lasted barely three days and its collapse ended any chance of easily overthrowing the government. The campaign against Veracruz that had consumed two months during the De la Huerta revolt required only three days in 1929. However, the Escobar rebellion was far from over, and the large numbers of rebel troops in the north presented the Mexican government with a situation strikingly similar to what Victoriano Huerta had faced in 1913. If the drive to centralize power in Mexico City was to succeed, the country had to learn that not even the north could defy the orders of the central government.[51]

The sudden self-destruction of the Veracruz revolt caught Calles by surprise, and the Secretary of War hastily recalled the troop trains on their way to that port city back to Monterrey. General Escobar, upon learning of the approaching large forces, abandoned the city on 5 March, but not without first looting funds from the official Banco de Mexico. Throughout the northern states the same pattern repeated itself, as rebel generals looted banks in an attempt to assure a comfortable exile in the United States. Clearly the desire to enrich themselves was the primary motivation among the generals who led this revolt. Although universally known as the Escobar revolt, this movement should have been more accurately titled "The Generals' Revolt" because they were the instigators and the real driving force.[52]

Defections of soldiers and junior officers from the ranks repeatedly plagued the rebel generals who often had to struggle to keep their forces from melting away. The *pronunciamiento* originated exclusively in the army, and as far as arousing enthusiasm among the civilians, "The Mexican people as a whole have manifested considerable apathy."[53] The spontaneous gathering of roving bands to form a revolutionary army as in 1910–1911 did not repeat itself. Why did the popular participation in warfare end? By 1929 the attractions of rebelling had wilted considerably among a population weary of revolt. An army larger and better equipped than that of Porfirio Díaz existed to deter a new generation of would-be rebels. As the campaign against the Cristeros revealed, the ruthlessness and brutality of the army vastly exceeded anything ever imagined under the unjustly maligned Díaz. The death of so many of the earlier revolutionaries also served as a reminder of the risks of rebelling. At the same time, hundreds of thousands of men had either died in combat or fled into the United States, and their absence left many vacancies for unskilled workers needed to reconstruct a ravaged Mexico. The greed and selfishness of many previous revolutionary leaders had certainly disillusioned many Mexicans, and when the generals of 1929 issued the mandatory manifesto, its trite phrases and vague promises could not persuade any to join the revolt. The generals' revolt was exclusively over power and wealth at the highest levels, and the Mexican people wisely stepped aside from that clash as too remote from their daily struggle to survive.[54]

After evacuating Monterrey on 5 March, the rebels took up positions to the west of that city and to the south of Saltillo. Their grip on railroad lines seemed to give them a solid defense, but General Juan Andreu Almazán realized they were vulnerable to encirclement. The strategic maneuver he devised was sure to succeed, had not General Saturnino Cedillo, who was advancing with troops from the south, bungled his approach. Early on 12 March the rebels at last realized they were in a trap and hurriedly boarded their trains for a mad dash to Torreón. Belatedly General Cedillo attacked the fleeing troops, but a screen of rebel cavalry gained time for the troops to board the departing trains. The clash ended that same day with the entry of loyal troops into Saltillo at 1530. The rebels tore up the track completely as they withdrew to Torreón and counted on the dreaded Mapimí desert to delay any government offensive from Saltillo for weeks.[55]

The news on the other fronts was no better for the rebels. In spite of repeated orders from Escobar, General Manzo hesitated to push south into Sinaloa. Manzo, who had demanded the revolt so strongly, became depressed and sank into inactivity. The advance south into Zacatecas proved disastrous for the rebels, who put their control of Durango at risk. Units defected, the rebels failed to form an alliance with the Cristeros, and rivalry erupted among the rebel generals in Durango. The approaching column of General Lázaro Cárdenas was sure to drive out the rebels unless General Escobar arrived in time to save Durango. Escobar realized that if he took his large combined force south, he could overwhelm the column of General Cárdenas and then have enough time left to face General Almazán when the troops finally crossed the Mapimí desert.[56]

A decade before the strategic maneuver of Escobar had every probability of success but a unique combination of horses and trucks made the desert less impenetrable. General Almazán promptly put work crews to repair the damaged track, but he knew that time was of the essence to destroy the rebellion. After a good day's rest, he sent all his cavalry (in reality mounted infantry) to cross the 154 kilometers of the Mapimí desert in two days. The cavalry could carry only enough supplies for one day, and the men with their horses collapsed exhausted after the long ride in the broiling sun. Later that night trucks arrived carrying food, water, and fodder. Suitably replenished and rested, the cavalry rode hard the next day and reached Benavides where the desert ended (Map 14). The mounted infantry arrived in no condition to wage a battle, but fortunately General Escobar had not garrisoned that village. Mistaking the cavalry for a patrol, the rebel general sent a meager force to try to recapture Benavides on 16 March, but solid resistance showed him that he faced a serious threat. As the cavalry pushed on to San Pedro de las Colonias, rebel pilots reported that infantry was also marching across the desert. Escobar risked facing a whole army to his rear, but he hesitated to move, because he wanted to use the great natural defenses of Torreón as the site for a decisive battle. When he finally realized he was trapped and gave the order to evacuate Torreón on 17 March, his last units fled to the north just one hour before Almazán's army blocked the railroad track.[57]

Calles arrived in Torreón on 19 March and took a fundamental strategic decision on the future campaign. Once the armies of Almazán and Cárdenas completed their concentration in a few days, this huge army could crush everything in its path as far as the U.S. border. The most obvious option was thus to advance north from Torreón against Chihuahua as Victoriano Huerta had done in 1912 and then turn west to subdue Sonora, possibly by riding on U.S. railroads as Obregón had done in 1916. However, some rebels in Sonora were pushing south into Sinaloa and threatened to capture Mazatlán. In an indication that the danger was not so serious, General Manzo, one of the rebel commanders in Sinaloa, was already putting out peace feelers to the government. But the risk that the rebels might gain an easy victory was real enough, and the government did not want to slow down the disintegration of the rebellion. The government decided to send troops to Mazatlán, but the only question remaining was how many to send. The government already enjoyed such superiority in numbers and equipment that it could detach some units in Torreón for duty in Mazatlán without in the least hindering the steam roller marching north to Chihuahua. The decision to send the majority of forces north and only a relief column to Mazatlán seemed the best course to follow, yet Secretary of War Calles decided otherwise and split the forces at Torreón. The army of Almazán remained to continue the advance to the north, while all the rest of the reinforcements went with Cárdenas to relieve Mazatlán. Calles had eliminated the numerical superiority on the northern front, because although Almazán's army had been larger than the rebel force at Saltillo, the scattered rebel forces regrouping under Escobar roughly equaled Almazán's army.[58]

The government tried to justify this division of the army as necessary to make a two-pronged attack on the rebel stronghold of Sonora; supposedly Almazán would come from the east and Cárdenas from the south. The maneuver required sending the army of Cárdenas first by railroad to Mazatlán and then by sea to Sonora, but such a long and convoluted trip merely deprived the government of these troops at a most critical moment. Why had Calles insisted on a strategy not justified on any military grounds? Calles from his many years of association with Alvaro Obregón had come to recognize the traits of military genius, and he saw too many of them in Almazán. Also,

Cárdenas was a competent general, but leaving him command of the entire northern force risked giving him too much political temptation. Better to split the forces, so that no one general could claim credit for putting down the rebels and thus launch his political career. The preference of loyalty over ability meant that after two decades of revolution, Mexico had come full circle to the basic principle of Porfirio Díaz.

The cold political calculation of Calles deprived Mexico of an immediate end to the rebellion and also made possible one last major battle to close the cycle of warfare begun in 1910. General Escobar breathed easier once he learned of the departure of most army troops to the south. He could not believe this unexpected good turn of fortune and realized he had a chance of defeating Almazan's army. Since both opponents were fairly evenly matched in material resources, victory depended on superior generalship. A very calm Escobar knew very well the impetuous nature of Almazán and wanted to use it to gain a victory. The rebel general prepared to lure Almazán further north and hoped to create the illusion that only one fierce push was needed to shatter the rebel army. Then at an unexpected point the rebels would make their stand and soundly defeat Almazán. The army troops for their part were tired of pursuit and were afraid that the rebellion might end without any chance to engage in battle.

On 24 March Almazán left Torreón and resumed the northward offensive along the railroad line to Chihuahua. He believed that the rebels planned to fight delaying actions at every defensible position, so he did not expect to advance very far. To Almazán's surprise, Escobar abandoned one defensive site after another and did nothing else but rip the track to shreds in a leisurely retreat north. Aerial reconnaissance revealed that General Escobar was concentrating his forces at the train station of Rellano, because the narrowness of the canyon at that point made it the best place to stop an advancing army. Rellano! Twice the fate of Mexico had hung on a battle in this place. Would Mexico's future be decided a third time at Rellano? General Almazán definitely believed so, and he prepared his army for a difficult assault against the rebel positions on 28 March. He planned an early morning attack on 30 March, only to learn that his cavalry patrols had peacefully overrun the abandoned defensive lines of the rebels. Immediately he ordered his infantry forward and sent his cavalry in hot pursuit of the retreating rebels. The army cavalry eventually caught up with the rebel cavalry screening the rear guard of Escobar, but random skirmishing only confirmed that the rebel army had safely escaped to Jiménez.[59]

Almazán concluded that the rebels for the first time were willing to stand and fight at Jiménez, but he was afraid that if he waited until the track was repaired, the rebels would have plenty of time to fortify themselves and wage a costly battle. As was his custom, Almazán decided to retain the initiative and sent his cavalry and infantry across the desert at 0300 on 31 March. The troops reached their assigned objectives seven kilometers south of Jiménez in the afternoon but were exhausted and without water. To quench their unbearable thirst, units marched around the city to a river, but then, rather than return to the positions Almazán had told them to take, the troops decided to halt a rebel train leaving the city. Soon the troops had spontaneously attacked a suburb (*caserío*) of Jiménez to the west, but when thousands of rebels counterattacked, the advance elements with tremendous difficulty extricated themselves from the trap. As the rest of his infantrymen arrived, Almazán deployed them to the south of Jiménez facing the rebel line of trenches and fox holes. At last a major battle seemed to be imminent between the roughly 8,000 rebels and the 8,613 soldiers.[60]

Cavalry comprised about half of the rebel force, and General Escobar kept this mounted infantry at Jiménez close to the front line to be ready to deliver the final blow against the army troops. According to Escobar's scenario, those troops would waste themselves in a suicidal attack against the rebel front line. Then, as they retreated in disorder, the rebel cavalry would launch a furious counterattack, much as Obregón's cavalry had done at the legendary battle of Celaya. A crushing defeat comparable to Pancho Villa's in 1915 was the inevitable fate for Almazán in 1929. As the army general sent on 1 April some units to attack the flanks of the rebel defenders, at first Almazán appeared ready to play the role of willing victim. Inconclusive fighting lasted the whole day, but the

soldiers gained the mistaken impression that the rebels were ready to crack after one good shove. The many weeks of pursuit had created tremendous frustration among the army officers who were afraid that the revolt might end without any major battle. For his part, Almazán was so sure of a victory, that he concerned himself mainly with the pursuit of the fleeing rebels after the battle. Already on the night of 31 March he sent most of his cavalry around Jiménez with orders to destroy a large stretch of track to the north at Estación Reforma. When the cavalry commander replied that he lacked the tools to do a proper job, Almazán bluntly said to use bare hands if necessary. Almazán imagined the rebel infantry desperately streaming north of Jiménez aboard the trains and then having to halt to repair the track. The delay would give enough time for his pursuing infantry to catch the rebel infantry at Estación Reforma.[61]

After the failure of the morning attacks on the rebel flanks on 1 April, that afternoon Almazán ordered his commanders to prepare for a general attack on the central rebel fox holes early the next morning of 2 April. In a fateful decision, at 1600 Almazán changed his mind and cancelled the assault orders; instead he warned his generals to prepare to resist a massive rebel attack early the next day. The two generals had changed roles: While initially Escobar was the calm Obregón waiting for the attack, at this moment Almazán was Obregón and Escobar would try to emulate Pancho Villa. Escobar had realized that time was not on his side, and that if he did not win a battle soon, shortages would force him to retreat to the U.S. border; conversely every day that passed brought more supplies to the loyal army. Out of desperation, Escobar gambled everything on massive attacks early on 2 April. After inadequate artillery shelling, he sent his cavalry to attack both flanks of the army line, while the infantry charged across no-man's land to try to break the center. Machine gun and artillery fire hacked to pieces the rebel cavalry, but the rebel infantry managed to come to within 80 meters of the trenches. At that exact moment Almazán rushed his reserves to the threatened spot and halted the rebels.[62]

That whole morning of ferocious combat virtually annihilated the rebel cavalry, yet as the afternoon began, the rebel infantry in its fox holes continued to resist vigorously. Around 1500 the first rebel trains departed to the north, and shortly before night fell the rebel infantry swiftly abandoned its fox holes and ran to waiting trains in the rear. As long as any daylight remained, the army artillery pounded the departing rebels, but once darkness set in, Almazán decided against a night pursuit. His men were exhausted, and night combat in a confused situation could result in unexpected complications and certainly needless casualties with units wandering lost in the dark. Besides, Almazán had received confirmation that his cavalry had tore up a large stretch of track near Estación Reforma to the north of Jiménez. Confident that this time the rebels could not escape, Almazán had his men rest for the night at the town to be ready for the hard march across the desert the next day.

Early on 3 April Almazán sent half of his cavalry along the west side of the track and the other half along the east side of the track; he himself marched with the infantry north and left his work crews in the rear laboring furiously to repair the damaged track. The mission of the cavalry was to take up positions to the north of the stalled rebel trains at Estación Reforma and to delay the rebel retreat long enough for the infantry to march from the south. When the cavalry on the west side arrived sooner than expected, it found the rebels detraining and decided to use this vulnerable moment to launch a charge. The startled infantry with difficulty fought off the attacks for two hours, but when the cavalry on the east arrived to attack the rebel column from the eastern undefended side, all discipline collapsed and "a veritable butchery" ensued.[63] Estación Reforma, the site of the decisive defeat of Pancho Villa in 1917, once again shaped the destiny of Mexico. At 1400 the combat was over, and so many rebels died that the cadavers were too many to be buried and had to be incinerated in mass piles. Missing among the prisoners was General Escobar who with the last two hundred horses rode away to safety. For all practical purposes the loss of Escobar's army meant that the rebellion was over. With extreme difficulty Escobar mustered in Chihuahua over 2,000 men, not enough to face the victorious army of Almazán.[64] In their steady retreat to the U.S. border all the rebel generals could do was loot the major banks to assure themselves enough booty for a comfortable exile abroad.

The one large unfinished business was the sizeable rebel army of Sonora. As mentioned earlier, the rebels from Sonora had invaded Sinaloa and were heading toward Mazatlán. By 8 March in their drive to Mazatlán the rebels had reached the state capital of Culiacán. Initially the government had planned to abandon Mazatlán, but by 7 March the reinforcements from Guadalajara were heading by rail to the beleaguered port city. However, because the Cristero revolt raged fiercest in Jalisco and Colima, the government could not remove all the garrisons from those states. If the rebels from Sonora rushed south, they could still capture Mazatlán before the reinforcements from Jalisco arrived. The hurriedly erected trenches seemed at first sight impressive: "Mazatlán is apparently well fortified against an attack of infantry and machine guns, but probably a death trap if artillery was brought into action as none of the fortifications are constructed so as to withstand artillery fire."[65] Fortunately for the government, the many rebel generals bickered among themselves and let valuable time pass. Although rebel scouts came within 18 miles of Mazatlán on 13 March, they quickly retreated and gave the defenders time to receive more reinforcements and to harden the fortifications against artillery. The defenders under General Jaime Carrillo also received artillery batteries and enjoyed naval support from the gunboat *Progreso*. In spite of these obvious preparations, the rebels remained "fully in the belief that the capture of the port of Mazatlán was only a question of a short but hard attack on the federal forces."[66]

Finally on 21 March after some skirmishing the rebels took up positions around Mazatlán and cut off the city's fresh water supply. The next day at 1630 the rebels opened an intense rifle and cannon fire on the defense trenches and then suddenly sent their cavalry to charge from the north side. The cavalry dismounted and was advancing briskly on foot when the gunboat *Progreso* appeared and shelled the walking rebels who retreated in disorder. At 0600 on 23 March the rebels launched an attack on the landward side out of range of the *Progreso's* cannons, but even then the rebels suffered heavy casualties and came only within 600 meters of the defense trenches. By then the impossibility of breaching the defenses was obvious, but to goad the men to a final effort, one of the rebel generals, the Yaqui Roberto Cruz, "had offered the Yaqui and Mayo Indians of the column four hours of free looting in Mazatlán as an incentive to enter the city as quickly as possible." The rebels tried a night attack at 2330, only to run into electrified wire and intense machine gun fire. At daybreak on 24 March a final attempt to rush across the 600 meters ended in a frightful slaughter. The rebel generals turned to accusing each other for the setback and during an angry meeting concluded "that the trenches were impregnable and so cleverly constructed that it was impossible to take them."[67] The failure at Mazatlán finished discrediting General Manzo, whom General Escobar relieved of his command and recalled to Sonora. Manzo, afraid for his life, prudently fled to safety across the U.S. border on 12 April.[68]

The rebels also learned that the advance elements of the large expedition under General Lázaro Cardenas had reached Tepic, less than a day's train ride away. Wisely the rebels decided to retreat to Sonora rather than risk a major battle so far from their home base, but in withdrawing, they surrendered all initiative to the government. When news of the disaster at the battle of Jiménez of 3 April reached the Sonora rebels, whatever justification had existed for the fighting withdrawal immediately vanished. Even if the Sonora army managed to block the northern advance of the huge force of Cárdenas, any serious defense required all the rebel troops and thus left unprotected the eastern border of Sonora. As the victorious army of General Almazán advanced rapidly through northern Chihuahua, it was sure to turn west into Sonora. Faced with a two-pronged invasion from the south and from the east (and not counting a nuisance advance from Baja California), the rebels stood no chance. Negotiations or exile were the only two realistic alternatives left for the rebels, who, however, recalling the time when Sonora under Obregón had defied Victoriano Huerta, believed they were in a position to repeat the extraordinary deeds of 1913.[69]

The rebels prepared to stop the advance at Masiaca near the Sonora border, and as they abandoned Sinaloa, they destroyed all the bridges, culverts, and tracks. The rebels constructed successive lines of trenches in Sonora where they hoped to wear down the advancing army in a long drawn out campaign. Only on 17 April did General Cárdenas cross the border into Sonora. The rebel withdrawal to the north did not proceed smoothly, however. The gunboats *Progreso* and *Bravo* repeatedly shelled the fleeing rebel trains and disrupted all rebel movements within range of naval gunfire.[70] As Cárdenas continued the inexorable northern advance into Sonora, the government concentrated most of the Mexican air force for this final offensive. Air planes had strafed and bombed the rebels in the past, but for the first time the rebels felt the full fury of air power:

On April 24th, they dropped 135 bombs on the rebel entrenchments at Masiaca completely demoralizing the morale of the troops, and officers as well. Orders were given to fall back on Navojoa that night. [...] Large numbers deserted at Masiaca and on the road here, they are yet coming in and giving themselves up to the Federals [...] the Yaqui valley where the American colony is situated is overrun with deserters and those who have surrendered. The retreat from Masiaca developed into a disorganized rout. [...]

General Roberto Cruz came overland with his cavalry and while resting at the station of Fundición the Federal airplanes dropped bombs on them and scattered them in every direction [...] several hundred of the horses broke away and were never captured and large numbers of the men deserted. [...] His command was completely disorganized and demoralized.[71]

The air bombardment had also shattered the ranking rebel commander: "General Topete was a crestfallen, broken-spirited man, entirely different from when he went south with his troops a few days ago. While talking with some of his officers in the hotel here, tears were running down his cheeks."[72] The rebel generals desperately looted money from local banks and then rushed to safety across the U.S. border. On 3 May the president of Mexico proclaimed that the revolt was over, exactly two months after it had begun. Air power was decisive in ending the revolt without the need for another bloody battle like that of Jiménez. But great as had been the impact of air power on this rebellion, air planes played an even greater role in preventing any future outbreaks. The northern states of Mexico, the veritable hotbeds of rebellion, were most vulnerable to attacks by air. As long as the government controlled the air, no revolt in the barren and easily patrolled regions of northern Mexico was possible. In addition, trucks made possible a swift army response to any rebellion and liberated the army from that abject dependence on railroad lines so characteristic of the old Porfirian army. Although Mexico still needed ground troops, the airplane more than anything else had ended rebellions in the north and brought the violent phase of the Mexican Revolution to a permanent close. Would the airplane be as effective against the Cristeros in the heavily forested and dense regions in central Mexico?

The End of the Cristero Rebellion and the Pacification of Mexico

Impressive as the performance of airplanes had been against the rebels in the north, the government counted on much more than air power to defeat the Cristeros. Taking advantage of the war footing of the country, the government had been redeploying its units to the Cristero zones "as rapidly as railway facilities would permit."[73] The haste to crush the Cristero rebellion was new, and contrasted sharply to 1927, when the government allowed the military campaign to slacken and to settle into a routine. The Escobar rebellion shook the complacency of the government that saw itself surrounded on all sides by hostile enemies. Although another rebellion of the generals seemed unlikely, the efforts of the Escobar rebels to establish an alliance with the Cristeros meant that the latter remained as tempting allies to any would-be revolutionary. Smashing the Escobar revolt in two months was an indispensable but incomplete response; only by crushing the Cristeros could the central government make sure that Mexico ceased to be the land of rebellions. However, the large cost of an all-out effort against the Cristeros did make the government receptive to a more economical way to end the revolt. Consequently, while the army proceeded with its full-scale campaign, in an independent but parallel track, the government agreed to negotiate a peaceful solution with the bishops. The government believed that the combination of massive force and serious negotiations was bound to weaken the determination of Catholics to sustain the rebellion.[74]

Peace talks with the Catholic bishops reflected the change of policy under provisional president Emilio Portes Gil. Actually, Plutarco Elías Calles had taken the first steps toward a negotiated solution late in 1928 but his extreme demands precluded any meaningful discussions. Portes Gil set a new tone in January 1929 when in a radical departure, he prohibited the execution of Cristero prisoners. Field commanders followed this new directive except in the case of Cristeros caught destroying railroad and telegraph lines. The president also prohibited violent reprisals by army troops and by the *agraristas* against civilian sympathizers. Full compliance with these new orders was impossible, but at least the atrocities and the reprisals diminished to the point that by January 1929 and for the first time ever, rebels began to surrender. Although at first only a trickle, these submissions would have been inconceivable in the previous years of summary executions.[75]

The Cristeros might have seen the new leniency as a sign of weakness, and to prevent such an erroneous misconception, the government simultaneously bolstered its military effort. The capture of the archive of the rebel leader Manuel Ramírez de Oliva in December 1928 allowed the government to dismantle his entire support network in Aguascalientes and the bordering region of Jalisco. The police in Guadalajara began a massive effort to identify and arrest all those who were supplying the countryside. The government began sending off to prison not just men but many of the female sympathizers who had formed the core of the urban networks. Through a system of checkpoints, the police established tight controls on the entrances to the cities. For the first time the government was targeting the urban supply network and not just the elusive rebels in the countryside. Police measures thus prepared the way for a larger army effort. In Jalisco the army imposed the policy of forcible removal of the inhabitants from remote areas, in order to free up troops for campaigns in other parts of the state. The government also sent reinforcements to the rebel areas.[76] In Jalisco the army mounted a large campaign on 1 February 1929,[77] while in Colima reinforcements of 900 soldiers gave General Heliodoro Charis adequate forces to strike real blows against the Cristeros.[78]

As the combined army and police offensives proceeded, the trickle of Cristeros surrendering began to grow in numbers. President Portes Gil seemed to be close to attaining the success that had eluded Calles during his many military offensives, only to have the outbreak of the Gonzalo Escobar revolt on 3 March shatter any hope of destroying the Cristero rebellion. Just to cite one of many examples, on 6 March Colonel Charis had to halt the offensive he was personally leading with great success in Colima. As mentioned in the previous section, the government stripped Jalisco of most of its garrisons, thus leaving 94 of its 110 municipalities without any protection. The troops the War Department left in Jalisco and Colima were barely adequate to defend the largest cities and the rail lines. As the Cristeros effortlessly occupied vast rural areas, they seemed poised to mount a major offensive.[79]

Some worried that Guadalajara was in danger of capture, and Gorostieta did seize the moment to plan a combined offensive with his men and the force of Jesús Degollado from southern Jalisco. Unfortunately, Degollado was unable to elude the army troops concentrating in the south for the campaign against the Escobarista rebels in Mazatlán. Undaunted, Gorostieta pushed ahead on his own, and carefully deployed his units to ambush the passenger train coming from Mexico City to Guadalajara on 23 March. He planned to send all his men into Guadalajara in the captured train, much as Pancho Villa had done at Ciudad Juárez in 1913. The plan had every chance of success, but Gorostieta lacked timely information on the troop movements. Rather than just a passenger train with its usual escort of 100 soldiers, what arrived right on schedule at 0700 was the first of several troop convoys. The trains were carrying troops under General Lázaro Cárdenas headed for the Sonora campaign, but by the time Gorostieta realized the mistake, it was too late to stop all his units from attacking the train. One whole day of combat ensued, and once their ammunition was exhausted, the Cristeros disappeared in good order that night.[80]

The Cristero failure to capture any city and their endemic shortage of cartridges meant that any chance for success depended on the support of the Escobar rebels. Gorostieta wanted to join with the army rebels, but the civilian leaders in Mexico City were more cautious. Had Gorostieta pushed harder for an alliance, and had the civilian leaders been more receptive, the creation of an effective axis between the two rebel groups would have posed a formidable threat to the government of Portes Gil.[81] Mexico could easily have sunk into another long cycle of warfare and chaos. But the government knew it was vulnerable and hence strove to bring the Escobar revolt to a quick end. The unexpectedly swift collapse of the Escobar rebels precluded any effective alliance with the Cristeros; cooperation remained sporadic, and at most some army rebels joined the Cristeros. The Escobar rebels made no effort to supply cartridges or artillery to the Cristeros; without this indispensable support, the Cristeros could only watch helplessly as the government redeployed its battalions.

After the collapse of the Escobar revolt President Portes Gil resumed his previous policy towards the Cristeros and resisted the temptation to switch to pure repression. As he continued to negotiate with the hierarchy of the Catholic Church, army troops poured in large numbers to reoccupy the abandoned areas. By 1 May Jalisco was fully garrisoned, and the army was preparing to resume the offensive campaigns. In the middle of May 4,000 soldiers arrived at Colima, much more than the small state required. In reality the large force at Colima formed part of a vast strategic maneuver: While General Andrés Figueroa pressed south from Jalisco and General Lázaro Cárdenas north from Michoacán, the only escape for the Cristeros was Colima where the large army force was waiting to trap them. The offensive began in Jalisco on 24 May and soon rebels were surrendering under the amnesty terms of the government.[82] General Charis began his offensive in Colima in early June and deployed flying columns to pursue the rebels in the six sectors of the state. Military officials claimed that "if the campaign in question should have carried on in full force for another month that much more blood would have been shed but that the government forces would have succeeded entirely in destroying the revolutionists in this state [Colima].[83]

The government had heard these claims of imminent victory before, and preferred to seek a negotiated solution. Portes Gil wanted to get away from a policy of repression and strove to dispel the foreign image of Mexico as a violent and barbaric place. In addition, just talk of negotiations demoralized the Cristeros, who increasingly defected rather than face the relentless army onslaughts. A final stand at Los Altos in Jalisco did not take place, because Gorostieta, in his greatest mistake, had supported a rival against the popular leader Victoriano Ramírez or "El Catorce." The murder of "El Catorce" by the rival on 16 March 1929 had so demoralized the inhabitants of this vital bastion of the Cristero revolt that they disbanded and proved receptive to peace offers.[84] Throughout the remaining fronts, the Cristeros suffered under dire conditions, and the tight police circle deprived them of ammunition, food, and clothing. In barren areas like Zacatecas, the shortage of food was acute, with the rebels eking substance out of cactus leaves.[85] By the first days of June the likelihood of an agreement with the government was so great that Gorostieta himself saw the handwriting on the wall and urged his followers to surrender or to disband. He summoned his main rebel chiefs for a final meeting to iron out the details of the disbandment.[86] Unfortunately for Gorostieta, the army had an old score to settle with him. Spies reported the upcoming meeting at Hacienda el Valle in the Los Altos region of Jalisco, and on 2 June a battalion took up positions:

> When Gorostieta discovered that they were surrounded, he directed his other chiefs to surrender themselves. He mounted his horse, tied the reins to his belt, took an automatic in each hand, and ordered the gates to be thrown open. When this was done, he rode out, firing right and left, until he was mortally wounded.[87]

The death of Gorosteita deprived the Cristeros of their most talented general and certainly hastened the inevitable military defeat. Henceforth not just rank and file but also chiefs were streaming to surrender to the authorities.[88] Meanwhile negotiations between the Catholic bishops and Portes Gil had been moving to an agreement. When the matter was referred to Rome for final approval, the Pope insisted on less harsh terms for Catholics. Even though military victory seemed within grasp, the appeal of a negotiated settlement was too great to resist, and Portes Gil accepted the conditions of the Pope. On 22 June 1929 the pres-

ident and the archbishop announced the settlement; in less than a week religious services resumed at most of the Catholic churches in Mexico. The announcement of the agreement had a cataclysmic effect on the remaining Cristeros, who surrendered in droves. The government gave them all safe-conducts and train tickets to return to their villages. The army mistakenly believed that the parallel strategy of combat and negotiations was continuing under the form of combat and amnesty, but the government immediately cleared up the confusion. The surrender would be completely peaceful, and the War Department halted any offensive; all troops on the field were to return to their bases and to move only when ordered. Over the coming months the garrisons in the Cristero regions returned to their normal peace-time complements.[89]

The abrupt ending of military operations may well have been premature because in the 1930s another bout of Cristero violence resurfaced. But the violence of the 1930s did not threaten to overthrow the government and never required a comparable mobilization of troops.[90] As the Cristeros finished surrendering in 1929 and returned to civilian life, they may not have realized they were closing the final chapter of the Mexican Revolution. The call of Francisco Madero to rise up against Porfirio Díaz on 20 November 1910 had unleashed nearly twenty years of savage warfare, chaotic disorder, and brutal destruction. By 1929 a new political system had emerged that was more solid and considerably more oppressive than the original Porfirian structure. The Revolution had come full circle to return to its authoritarian origins. Mexicans were willing to pay any price to restore peace and stability. Freedom and democracy, the rallying cries against Porfirio Díaz, had fallen by the wayside. To prevent any further outbreaks of war, Mexicans paid a very high price; not until the twenty-first century did democracy start to reappear in Mexico.

For the rest of the twentieth century, Mexicans no longer settled their political quarrels with machine guns and Mauser rifles. But instead of the bullet that could only kill once, lies and deceit came to destroy men's souls for their entire lives. Executions no longer threatened citizens who could become non-persons through political ostracism and relentless blacklisting. The use of force to recruit into the army disappeared but remained to compel citizens to vote for the official candidates. Looting and rampage gave way to fraud and corruption. No longer did strategic moves decide a campaign, instead rigged or stolen elections henceforth brought victories. The platforms of political parties replaced the manifestoes of the rebel leaders. Loyalty displaced ability as the key condition to hold public office. Intrigues in dark corridors rather than combat in the open battlefield determined the rulers of Mexico. As Venustiano Carranza had so insistently wanted, the population learned to look to politicians and not to generals to settle its political quarrels.

11. Nicaragua: The Insurrection Against the United States

The guerrilla chief always has the invaluable advantage of not having to engage in combat and of attacking only when the probability of winning is on his side. — Evaristo San Miguel[1]

As Mexico was striving to prevent revolts in the late 1920s, further south in Nicaragua an insurrection broke out in 1926. Under its leader Augusto C. Sandino, the insurrection in Nicaragua lasted until 1933 and became the most famous military conflict of Latin America in the first half of the twentieth century. Many in Latin America, in Europe, and even in the United States found very appealing the struggle of one leader in a small and poor country against the United States. In addition to the traditional sympathy that the underdog evokes, the Nicaragua revolt was a classic David and Goliath story, with the weak Sandino daring to defy the all-powerful United States. As a symbol for all those struggling against impossible odds, the Sandino revolt became a legend in its own time and inspired countless persons during later decades.

From a military perspective, the Sandino revolt had major resemblances with the Mexican Revolution to which it provides a weak sequel. The Sandino revolt came out of a Latin American tradition of irregular warfare, most recently in the Mexican Revolution. The most notable of many examples were Emiliano Zapata in the state of Morelos and Pancho Villa during his latter career in Chihuahua. Both bore striking resemblances to Sandino in Nicaragua. Like Zapata and Villa in his last

years, the Sandino revolt never aimed to overthrow a government. The many similarities with the spontaneous revolt against Porfirio Díaz in 1911 are also striking, particularly in the second stage of widespread Nicaraguan insurrection in 1930–1933. In Nicaragua the goal of driving out the U.S. marines substituted nicely for the aim in Mexico of overthrowing the aged dictator. Although withdrawing in the face of overwhelming force was standard practice in the Mexican Revolution, the warlords eventually tried to bring towns and territory under their permanent control. In an important difference with Mexico, even in the period 1927 to 1929 when his activities were largely confined to Nueva Segovia Department, Sandino did not strive to hold that territory permanently and was content to wander around hidden camps. Not only did he show little interest in controlling land, but most remarkably and in apparent violation of all the principles of war, he was not interested in defeating or much less destroying his enemy.

The style of guerrilla warfare that emerged helps to explain the unorthodox practices of the rebels, but a major part of the explanation for the Sandino revolt lies elsewhere. The Sandino revolt was the first media war of Latin America; as journalists reported and invented battlefield accounts, the Sandino revolt came to take on a life of its own in a parallel dimension often far distant from the actual events. While this chapter will stay close to the reality of campaign operations, occasional glimpses into the fantasy world are necessary to come to a closer understanding of this otherwise baffling revolt.

The First Phase of the Sandino Revolt, 1926–1929

Starting in 1909 recurrent civil wars ravaged Nicaragua. But the disturbances were no different from what the rest of the Central American countries routinely experienced. The Mexican Revolution and a turbulent Central America seemed to confirm the impression that all the countries south of the United States border were trapped in perpetual turmoil. Nicaragua soon stood out because the nearly constant U.S. intervention distorted and eventually made that country diverge from the Mexican or even the Central American pattern. Supposedly out of concern for a possible Nicaragua canal, U.S. marines routinely landed to restore order in that country. A similar pattern in Haiti and in the Dominican Republic finally culminated in U.S. military occupation of those countries, but in Nicaragua the United States never felt the circumstances were right to establish direct rule. The parallel presence of a civilian government and U.S. marines became the standard pattern in Nicaragua.[2]

The United States repeatedly withdrew the marines from the country only to have to return them again. All the marines again left in August 1925, but this time the United States believed that the organization of a combined police and army called the *Guardia Nacional* sufficed to preserve order. The United States was trying to repeat in Nicaragua the earlier success with the Cuban army (see chapter 4) as the best way to prevent another U.S. intervention. But even in Cuba where the U.S. occupation enjoyed widespread popularity, the task of creating a really effective army took some time. Although the United States flooded Nicaragua with weapons and ammunition, the new Guardia Nacional needed much more than armament to be able to cope with the revolt that broke out shortly after the marines departed in August 1925. General José María Moncada of

the Liberal Party rose up in arms against the ruling Conservative Party, and although at first the uprising spread slowly, the Guardia Nacional failed to respond adequately. By December 1926 the uprising against the Managua government gained such momentum that the United States reluctantly dispatched marines and navy bluejackets back to Nicaragua but only to protect U.S. lives and properties. Although ostensibly Juan Bautista Sacasa headed the revolt, the driving force behind the rebels was Moncada, the most important Liberal general.

Once U.S. forces were guarding exposed installations, the best policy seemed to let the revolt run its natural course, but a paranoid United States sensed a sinister Mexican influence lurking in the background. Mexico publicly declared its sympathy for the Liberal revolt, and the United States resented this verbal Mexican intrusion into an otherwise exclusive sphere of control. Furthermore, Washington feared the spread of radical and revolutionary influence from Mexico, a totally unfounded fear when Mexican rulers were trying to harness the revolution into a conservative channel. In a manner typical of U.S. policies to Latin America, Washington refused to support the Conservative leader who was ferociously anti–Mexican and anti-radical. With a mystique bordering on the incredulous, the U.S. government believed that free and honest elections were the panacea to Nicaragua's political problems.[3]

To end the civil war, President Calvin Coolidge sent Henry L. Stimson as a high-ranking emissary to Nicaragua in April 1927. His mission was to force all Nicaraguans to lay down their arms in preparation for new elections. At sixty years of age, at first glance the mild Stimson seemed the best person for this delicate assignment. However, he did not speak Spanish and could not even pronounce the word Nicaragua correctly.[4] Perhaps the tropical heat made him impatient, and in any case he wanted to dispose of his Nicaraguan assignment quickly so that he could return home. In no way was he a mediator, and instead he spoke bluntly if not brutally to the Nicaraguans in early May 1927. The key figure was General Moncada, who although he was old and did not relish any more campaigning in the harsh wilds, needed something to persuade his followers to lay down their arms. As a bare minimum, he insisted on U.S. supervision of the presidential elections. Stimson resented having any Nicaraguan impose conditions on the United States, but on 11 May he reluctantly signed an agreement to have the United States supervise the elections.

The revolt was not yet over, because Moncada first had to secure the adherence of his principal followers to what became known as the Tipitapa accords. Not all of Moncada's generals had been eager to sign, because they felt the accords cheated them of their victories. But faced with the threat of having to fight against the United States, on May 12 all but one agreed to disarm. Sensing the resistance, the United States as a powerful incentive offered to pay $10 for each rifle turned in. As the Liberals rushed to exchange their rifles for a sum of money very large at that time, the rebel units melted away rapidly. It seemed that once again, like many times before and after, the United States could impose its will with impunity on the Caribbean countries.[5]

The one general who did not accept the Tipitapa accords was Augusto C. Sandino. Why did he refuse? What made him think that he could defy the United States? No easy answer is possible, but some considerations help to understand his decision. Although he was the illegitimate son of a wealthy farmer and a maid, since early in his life he had harbored illusions of grandeur; for a middle name he adopted César instead of his maternal Calderón to achieve the unmistakable imperial flair of Augusto César. Like many Nicaraguans, he aspired to the presidency, although this goal gradually suffered modifications. He had spent time in Mexico, particularly in Tampico, were he became acquainted with radical and Communist ideas. However, his commitment to nationalism soon triumphed over other ideologies. His defenders have strongly emphasized his anti–Americanism, but in spite of countless later declarations, it was far from clear that the desire to drive out the Americans from Nicaragua was paramount in May 1927. More revealing was his stormy relationship with Moncada; the latter never liked him and saw Sandino as a loose cannon and a source of unnecessary complications. To win Sandino over, Moncada offered him the post of *jefe político* or district official at Jinotega, and as a further

persuasion, had Sandino's father try to convince him to lay down his arms. After all, Sandino was a minor figure in the Liberal revolt, and Moncada felt the offer was more than adequate. In many ways Moncada's lurking fears about Sandino were right, because the rebel harbored much larger ambitions. Alone among the Nicaraguan Liberals, Sandino perceived that anti–American feeling was widespread among the population because the U.S. marines had stayed too many years in Nicaragua and gradually wore out their welcome. He saw the opportunity to lead a movement, and he was sure that the people would sympathize with a liberator who promised to drive out the Americans.[6]

Anti-Americanism could certainly be the source of power for a politician like Sandino, but unfortunately his followers were more interested in accepting the $10 for their rifles than in fighting the marines. Sandino hoped to rally the morale of his followers by withdrawing to Jinotega, where he issued the inevitable manifesto announcing his defiance (Map 18) The high-sounding phrases were not enough, and to keep his force from totally evaporating, Sandino withdrew to the fastness of San Rafael del Norte. There he married his fiancée Blanca Arauz on 16 May, but because his men were more interested in celebrating the wedding than in fighting, he had to retreat further north to prevent the rest of his men from deserting. Blanca stayed behind as a telegraph operator and kept in touch with him through the wires.

Hot on the trail of Sandino were the marines who established a base at Jinoteca on 23 May. To try to find a way out of the closing trap, he wrote to Moncada and sounded out the marines at Jinoteca about his possible submission. His only condition was that the United States formally declared a military government, because otherwise he felt the Liberals did not stand a chance in the promised elections. For a supposedly bitter anti–American to demand the establishment of U.S. military government seems paradoxical. Perhaps it was just a ploy to justify his defiance, knowing as he certainly did that the United States could not accept such a condition. If he was an extreme nationalist, perhaps he saw in the U.S. military government a way to galvanize the country into a struggle for liberation from colonial rule. For this last possibility, the precedents were not encouraging, because U.S. military governments had crushed revolts in Haiti and in the Dominican Republic. Perhaps most likely he wanted to be able to claim that he made one last effort to negotiate a settlement before embarking on an armed revolt. The offer to negotiate did suggest to Moncada that Sandino was wavering and the rebel leader later confessed that this was the most trying period of the entire revolt. In a last attempt to abort the revolt, Moncada sent Gregorio, Sandino's father, to try to persuade Sandino to lay down his arms. By the time the father arrived and wasted four hours trying to persuade his errant son, Sandino had already made up his mind and regained his earlier confidence and defiant attitude.[7]

What made Sandino suddenly confident of attracting enough followers to lead a revolt? From his sojourn in Mexico he had learned how the revolutionary generals raised forces. To counter the one-time $10 offer of the United States, Sandino offered the chance to loot and plunder to peasants who saw an immediate economic benefit to joining the revolt. Sandino began confiscating coffee in the region and reselling it in Honduras; he also captured and looted the gold mine at San Albino. With the proceeds from these raids, more peasants willingly joined him lured by the prospects of greater booty.[8] The practices of the Mexican Revolution surfaced again in northern Nicaragua. In these the most trying days of the revolt, his leadership qualities proved essential. Many found his personality quite appealing, and since he naturally disguised his ambitions with an air of unpretentiousness and familiar language, peasants found him to be a sympathetic figure. In reality he was not a strong leader, so although he could attract followers to fight, he had tremendous difficulty controlling them. An inspiring but not a commanding figure, his inability to impose his will on his subordinates doomed many military operations.

Effective as the lure of plunder was for recruiting, Sandino knew that he had to take some action soon to dispel his image as a marauding bandit. In response to the raids of Sandino, the marines extended their occupation of Nicaragua to the far north. On 8 June, 39 marines established a post at Ocotal and later were reinforced by 48 men of the Guardia Nacional under marine officers. At this time the strategy called for the marines at Ocotal and other outposts to hold their positions but not to provoke the rebels by hostile action; the hope was that gradually the rebels would turn in their rifles. Ocotal had many stores full of goods, and since most of the residents had fled, Sandino had no trouble raising a large force of possibly as many as 800 peasants eager to strip the town clean of its belongings. The overwhelming numbers were misleading, because most of the peasants were unarmed, and many did not have even the basic machete. About 60 followers with rifles and 3 machine guns formed the real core of Sandino's force. He had been trying with little success to obtain additional weapons, but upon hearing that marine reinforcements had left Managua and were on their way to Ocotal, Sandino decided to risk an attack with his poorly armed and ill-trained force. The local Rufo Marín enthusiastically embraced Sandino's cause and was the real commander of the operation, while Sandino spent most of the battle observing from a nearby hill.[9]

Rufo Marín wisely decided to infiltrate most of the peasants into the town after nightfall on 15 July. At 0115 on 16 July 1927, a marine sentry detected something unusual, and minutes later shooting began. The premature discovery of the rebels deprived the attack of the element of surprise, but Sandino still hoped to win. The peasants enthusiastically threw themselves into looting the buildings in the town but not into attacking the barracks. Both sides settled into a random pattern of exchanging rifle and machine gun fire for the rest of the morning. In the afternoon marine airplanes arrived from the airfield at Managua, and shortly after 1430 they began dive bombing and strafing the rebel positions in the town. Lacking any prior experience with aerial bombardment, the peasants conveniently bunched themselves together, providing ideal targets for the marine pilots. After 45 minutes the planes exhausted their bombs and ammunition and returned to their base. The bombs and the strafing sent the peasants into panic and they began fleeing Ocotal. The retreat turned into a rout, although the dedicated small core of followers tried to provide covering fire. By 1730 the rebels had left, but with nightfall fast approaching, the marine commander wisely postponed any pursuit until the next day.[10]

The airplane had revealed its fearsome power at Ocotal, a battle that by any military measure was a resounding victory for the United States. The rebels had lost at least a hundred killed and possibly as many as three hundred wounded, while the total losses of the Marine Corps and the Guardia Nacional were one dead, four wounded, and four Nicaraguans taken prisoner. Yet for Sandino, the attack on Ocotal was an enormous political success, because he instantly became the hero who dared defy the United States. On July 20 when he issued a manifesto explaining why Ocotal was really a victory for the revolt, he began the invariable pattern of reporting battles and victories that existed only on paper. News of the attack spread throughout Latin America, and the heroic figure of the Nicaraguan David battling the Goliath of the United States inspired many to come and fight next to Sandino. Eventually volunteers came from almost every country in Latin America to fight alongside Sandino; among the famous was Agustín Farabundo Martí, the Communist leader from El Salvador. The battle of Ocotal was an instant publicity success for Sandino, who saw himself gradually transformed into a larger than life figure. To cultivate his image abroad, Sandino appointed the Honduran poet Froilán Turcios to be the representative of the revolt abroad. Turcios published a magazine and distributed florid accounts that stirred the emotions of Latin Americans throughout the region; the poet Turcios knew exactly what to say to cast Sandino in the most stirring poses; when Sandino did not himself create the victories, Turcios was there to magnify the military campaigns. Incessantly the United States labeled Sandino as a bandit, but to no avail, because Sandino was rapidly entering the pantheon of larger-than-life heroes in the Latin American imagination.[11]

Much as Sandino enjoyed the favorable propaganda, he knew that after the disaster of Ocotal he needed to restore his fallen military prestige, especially because in July 1927 the foreign volunteers still had not arrived to supplement his meager forces. Enjoying excellent intelligence on the movements of the Americans, he learned that U.S. marines with some Guardia Nacional personnel were heading toward the village of San Fernando, about 15 kilometers from Ocotal. On 25 July he deployed his men for an ambush that had every likelihood of inflicting heavy casualties on the marine force. His followers, however, still did not take the fighting very seriously, and in the hot afternoon most drifted off into deep siestas. Most fatally, the sentry who was supposed to give advance warning of the approaching marines left his post to amuse himself with a peasant girl in a nearby shack. The tired marine force of about 100 men thus entered San Fernando undetected, but was roused into a combat posture by the unusually quiet appearance of the town. As shooting started, it was clear that the ambush had failed, and the rebels who fled in disorder lost at least 11 dead; this was the only engagement in the war in which Sandino feared for his life. Two days later near the town of Santa Clara, another ambush attempt badly backfired on the rebels who were caught between air bombardment and an advancing marine column. The marines reoccupied the gold mine and even a town the rebel leader had immodestly renamed Ciudad Sandino.[12]

With the rebels fleeing in every direction, the marines split their large columns into smaller patrols to track down the last fugitive Sandinistas. The marine commander, however, still smarting from the many failed ambush attempts, did not want to see his men cut off in small isolated engagements and in any case felt that the campaign was over. Marine headquarters at Managua shared the same view and did not send the reinforcements needed to complete the mopping-up operations in Nueva Segovia Department. At the moment the Sandinistas were closest to complete destruction, good fortune had saved them. The United States needed more marines in China, and already in June Washington shipped one thousand marines from Nicaragua to China. Although headquarters at Managua argued strenuously for keeping the force level at least at 1200 marines until the elections, Washington pointed to the string of victories in July as ample proof that the campaign against Sandino was over.[13]

The start of the rainy season in June ruled out any major operations through the often impenetrable jungle trails; the last deployments for the engagements in July had proved exhausting for the men and ruined much of their equipment and supplies. The lull in the fighting proved a godsend to Sandino, who had time to reconstruct his forces and to revise his strategy. The inability of the rebels to engage successfully in combat against the marines was a reality; in spite of sporadic attempts to improve the combat abilities of the rebels, the marines remained throughout the war the superior fighters. The rebels were notoriously bad shots and thus could not count on hitting their targets. Scarcity of ammunition, obsolete weapons, and poor care of their rifles were mainly responsible for the inaccurate firing; however, none of the available accounts report Sandino himself ever devoting time to instruct his men in any way. Without any training or rudimentary organization skills, even the simplest of infantry maneuvers were beyond the abilities of the Sandinistas. Accustomed to fighting in very small units, the rebels had tremendous difficulty coordinating movements. The answer of Sandino to these tactical deficiencies was to avoid combat whenever possible and to limit engagements to at best harassment of the marines. Hit-and-run tactics became the norm, with the emphasis on the "run" part. One rule the rebels followed scrupulously after July 1927 was never to leave the bodies of their dead comrades behind; thus the marines were never sure about rebel casualties. Hiding bodies was just one way that Sandino strove to keep the numbers and activities of the rebels hidden from the marines, thereby maximizing the benefits from the accurate knowledge he had of the marine deployments.[14]

Aviation proved the most difficult challenge for the Sandinistas, who nevertheless learned how to deal with the marine planes. In the mountainous jungles of Nueva Segovia Department, where visibility on the ground rarely exceeded seven meters, the rebels escaped detection by air, but in lowlands, farms, and any clearings, the marines seemed to be ready to pounce. A veritable cat-and-mouse game evolved between the rebels and the marine aviators; by flying low, the marine planes could generally approach the rebel camps unheard, but if detected risked more damage from ground fire. In another tactic, planes dived straight down from high altitudes and then dropped their bombs from a height safe from ground fire, but the sound of the engines usually gave the rebels enough time to scurry for safety. Because the rebels preferred to stay in

shacks whenever any existed, the marine pilots developed techniques to bomb the shacks without alerting the occupants. Inevitably many civilians and their dwellings were inadvertently bombed, and this bombing campaign more than anything else discredited the United States in the eyes of the world. Needless to say, the rebels promptly executed any pilots shot down. In contrast, the rebels welcomed the many marine deserters from the infantry and sent them on their way to Honduras where the U.S. government tried to obtain their arrest.[15]

A special characteristic of the jungle and forests in northern Nicaragua made possible the recovery of Sandino's extenuated forces. Unlike the Amazon jungle, the soil was fertile enough to support edible plants, and over the decades banana groves and clumps of sugar cane had taken root in many parts. An abundant variety of fruit trees naturally grew, so the rebels who knew where to find food did not have to fear hunger. Looting village stores and bringing supplies from Honduras over trails provided a more diverse diet. At least in 1927 Sandino had his men plant beans and corn to assure a food supply.[16]

As the rebels expanded their network of trails, Sandino established his headquarters on a hilltop he called Mount Chipote. From this base he sent patrols to raid the surrounding region. His attacks, particularly a strong attempt to capture Telpaneca on 19 September 1929, demolished the claims that his rebellion was over. The booty from each raid brought much needed supplies and equipment to the struggling rebels. More importantly, the newspapers magnified each raid a hundredfold, thereby turning Sandino into a veritable mountain lion leading a determined army of rebels. Word gradually filtered to the marine detachments about this mysterious base, and at first the marines dismissed Mt. Chipote as a local superstition. Only when a marine plane located Mt. Chipote on 23 November did headquarters accept the existence of the rebel base by then somewhat mythical. That same day the marine planes began bombing the camp, but in spite of almost daily air bombardment, it became clear that only a ground operation could destroy this rebel stronghold completely. Both the local rumors and the foreign newspaper accounts emphasized that the destruction of this formidable mountain base was sure to crush the Sandino revolt.[17]

As the rainy season came to an end in December, marine headquarters at Managua prepared to launch an offensive. The operation was risky because of the reduced size of the marine force in Nicaragua. To gather enough men for the operation, the marines had to deplete the garrisons in other nearby towns. In Managua rumors circulated that the whole Mt. Chipote fortress was just a trick to lure the marines deep into the jungle and then attack the unprotected rear. In spite of the risks, the prospect of knocking out the Sandino revolt in one blow was too irresistible for the marines who set out in two columns. Their movements were reported to Sandino who decided to spring some ambushes again. On 30 December the larger marine force of 114 men walked into an ambush; about a third of the men were wounded, including the commanding officer; had a rebel machine gun been properly mounted, the entire detachment could have been wiped out. The presence of foreign volunteers, many of them skilled and better shots, was making a difference. As soon as the marines counterattacked, the rebels quietly vanished, but the marine detachment prudently decided to return to its base. A similar fate fell to a small marine column of sixty men, and it too had to withdraw. At least for 1927, Mt. Chipote remained firmly in rebel hands.[18]

In reality Sandino never intended to hold on to Mt. Chipote, and had the marine columns pushed on, they could have easily taken the prize. In January 1928 the marines decided to try again, this time with a single large column of 300 men. Marine planes bombed the rebel camps constantly in preparation for an impeding assault. Sandino had by then withdrawn most of his followers and left only a small covering force behind. Aerial reconnaissance reported on 19 January that the camp seemed deserted, and by the time the first marine patrols reached the summit on 26 January, they found only small amounts of food to destroy. Sandino and his rebels were far away and were engaging in a campaign of plunder in the coffee growing regions of Nicaragua. He entered San Rafael del Norte while other followers raided the district of Matagalpa. The hope of plunder lured hundreds to join his ranks, and once the looting was over, they effortlessly melted back into the local peasant population. These victorious raids through the towns the marines had left undefended in

their obsession to capture Mt. Chipote restored the morale of the rebels. Weak in tactics, the rebels proved superior to the marines in strategy. The raids of January and February generated enough prestige and plunder to tide Sandino over comfortably until the start of the rainy season in July largely impeded marine operations.[19]

Sandino needed all the boost his successful rampage could provide, because the failure of the first marine offensive against Mt. Chipote finally demonstrated to the Coolidge administration that the rebellion in Nicaragua was far from over. To reinforce the 1,414 marines in Nicaragua, an additional 1,148 men left the United States on 9 January 1928. Once the marines garrisoned most of the Nicaraguan towns, Sandino realized that any large raids became impossible. But he could not stay still and needed to maintain the momentum. Not willing to face the marines, he found in Carleton Beals, an American journalist, a safe and effective avenue to advance the rebel cause. The propaganda efforts of Turcios had turned Sandino into such a Latin American hero that even the American public became curious about this would-be David. Turcios saw a chance to strike an even bigger propaganda coup, and he arranged to provide safe passage for Beals to interview Sandino in the jungle. The visit of Beals foreshadowed the even more memorable trip in 1957 of the journalist Herbert Matthews to interview a rebel Fidel Castro in Cuba. Although Sandino was a beginner in the game of press manipulation, he did quite well in the interviews. Beals returned to present a glowing picture of the rebel in the magazine the *Nation* and later compiled his findings in a book. While Beals tried to report truthfully, and his accounts fell far short of the excessive embellishment and exaggerations of Turcios, the American public did learn for the first time that anti–Americanism was a reality in Nicaragua and that Sandino was not a bandit as the U.S. government insisted on portraying him.[20]

Sandino enjoyed being the center of world attention and was relishing every moment of his newly found prestige. The marines carelessly contributed to his fame:

> Sandino would have been finished long ago had the marines not lost their heads after the Quilalí fight and broadcast the statement that he

had appeared there with a real army and all sorts of modern weapons. That, naturally, made him a real object of admiration and encouraged him tremendously, but it was entirely untrue. The whole thing turns out to have been based on that fact that he fired on the planes with anti-aircraft machine-guns, which were nothing but his same three guns on some mounts which he made himself in Yuscaran.[21]

In reality, only three small detachments comprised his entire army after March 1928: a field force of eighty men under Manuel Girón, a general staff of 6 officers and ten guards, and the personal group of Sandino. Like the Mexican *soldaderas*, women came to support these three wandering columns that generally stayed separate; orders went from Sandino through the general staff and then to the field force. Among the women who had joined the column was the Salvadorian Teresa Villatoro, who soon caught the attention of Sandino and became his mistress. However, this new relationship did not keep Sandino from corresponding by wire with his wife who still was a telegraph operator. The three detachments changed locations every week or so to foil aerial reconnaissance, and while tracking around northern Nicaragua the rebels demanded contributions from the local population. Some skirmishing took place, and marine planes routinely bombed suspected rebel hideouts. When the rainy season began in June, the marines took to canoes and small boats in an attempt to catch the rebels by surprise.[22]

Always enjoying excellent intelligence on U.S. movements, Sandino decided to set a trap for the flotilla of marine convoys on 7 August 1928. The plan called for Girón's main force and Sandino's personal group to ambush the marine canoes at a bend in the Coco River. Marine planes spotted Sandino's group, but rather than abort the entire mission, he simply withdrew his group without informing the other force. Girón was having troubles of his own, because the rebels he sent to cover his left flank took the wrong trail in the jungle and only a part of the force under Girón reached the ambush position. His men were trigger happy and did not wait for the canoes to come within firing distance. Instead, the rebels opened fire on a marine patrol that was hacking its way through the river bank. Alerted by the shooting, the marines disembarked from the canoes

and after three hours of combat outflanked the vulnerable left side of Girón. The rebels fled after losing 10 dead; Girón correctly concluded that Sandino abandoned him, and although the rebel leader later promoted him to be the head of the general staff, a strong tension between the two men was evident.[23]

The defeat so demoralized the Sandinistas that by August 1928 they lost the ability to ambush marine patrols. Sandino directed bands of fugitives and not of fighters. Already in September "the men were mostly Hondurans, and thugs and bandits of the worst type."[24] Paradoxically, the defeat of 7 August 1928 in no way hurt the reputation of Sandino. As always, Turcios reported that the battle was a smashing Sandinista victory, that the rebels sank many canoes and that the blood of dead marines colored the shores of the river. But as more accurate reports of incontestable validity revealed to Turcios how desperate the Sandinista situation was, his commitment wavered and he began to seek a way to end his participation in this largely fictional revolt. The Nicaraguan elections scheduled for 4 November 1928 provided a good opportunity to bail out. Sandino wavered in his response to these presidential elections, but when the Liberal Moncada won, any possibility of a return to Conservative rule vanished. Sandino attempted to contact Moncada, who put out feelers in spite of his despotic personality. However, neither man made a determined effort to seek an accommodation and both seemed to be largely guarding appearances. Moncada was in no rush to compromise because he knew he could count on the United States to back him completely and that Sandino was virtually finished.[25]

While the animosity existing between the two men prevented any arrangement, within the Sandinista ranks the election and inauguration of the Liberal Moncada provoked deep splits. Many followers and supporters abandoned Sandino, including almost all the Mexican volunteers. The most visible defection was Turcios himself, who perhaps remorseful of having created a world figure, no longer could support Sandino. The poet tried everything to convince Sandino of the need to abandon the struggle but to no avail. A frustrated Turcios resigned on 28 December 1928 and later accepted a posting as Honduran diplomat to Europe. Never again did Sandino have such an efficient propaganda machine at his disposal.[26]

Some hoped that the defection of Turcios finally would convince Sandino to abandon his struggle, but the rebel leader remained obstinate. On the military front, the news continued to deteriorate. A disappointed and wounded Girón silently abandoned the Sandinistas, but he accidentally strayed into a marine patrol and was taken prisoner on 3 February. Eventually the marines turned him over to the Nicaraguans, and Girón had the misfortune of falling eventually into the hands of the Mexican Juan Escamilla, who under the authority of President Moncada was leading a volunteer force against the rebels. Escamilla, an exiled general, operated in the style of the Mexican Revolution, and promptly had prisoners like Girón executed. Shortly after the defection of Girón, the rebel general staff deserted in mass to cross the border into Honduras. The field force, the main combat unit of Sandino in 1928, had disintegrated after the election of Moncada, and only the personal group around the Generalissimo (a title Sandino liked to use) still managed to survive.[27] In a premature epitaph in April, U.S. Army intelligence reported that "The original Sandino situation, the one which might have kept the United States in trouble with Latin America for years, has ceased to exist. Sandino, as a Latin American hero fighting the whole power of the United States as represented by the marines, is finished."[28]

The mounting defections and setbacks were having an effect on Sandino. As early as 6 January 1929 when he wrote to the president of Mexico, he was already thinking of a trip to that country. One of the few remaining Mexicans among the Sandinistas was Captain José de Paredes who passionately admired Sandino. Captain Paredes went on a mission to learn what possibilities Mexico offered to support the Sandinistas. Captain Paredes based on no reliable evidence returned from the mission to report to Sandino that Mexico was willing to provide weapons and ammunition. In reality, President Portes Gil had offered only the traditional Mexican hospitality to Latin American exiles, namely that Sandino could stay peacefully in Mexico and if necessary receive political asylum. Knowing how irrational Americans were about any hint of Mexicana

involvement in the U.S. sphere of control, President Emilio Portes Gil went out of his way to explain the exact situation to U.S. ambassador Dwight Morrow. Mexico had traditionally supported the Liberal Party in Nicaragua, and with the election of the U.S.–backed Moncada, Mexican policy had achieved its goal and was in perfect harmony with U.S. policy. Support for Sandino had no place in the official Mexican agenda.

Unaware of the bleak prospects that awaited him in Mexico, Sandino was in high hopes when he left Nicaragua and crossed the border into Honduras. He left behind rebel activities in Nicaragua almost at a virtual standstill. The revolt of 1927–1929 never managed to spread and ultimately failed.[29] The exile of Sandino to Mexico was a fitting end for a misguided and ill-conceived adventure. Nobody could have imagined that Sandino's departure simply reflected a lull after the first phase of the revolt. Unknown even to the rebel leader, extraordinary circumstances were appearing to revive the flagging insurrection.

The Revival of the Sandino Revolt, 1930–1933

Good fortune did not smile on Augusto C. Sandino in Mexico. After his arrival in June 1929, the Mexican government allowed him to stay in a hacienda near Mérida, Yucatán, a sign of hospitality he initially misinterpreted as an early indication of support. In reality, the Mexican government wanted him to stay in Yucatán and not come even to Mexico City, because President Emilio Portes Gil realized how emotional an issue Nicaragua was for the United States. Unfortunately, the propaganda campaign of Turcios had made him into such a hero that the Mexican public was very enthusiastic about Sandino. After months of waiting, he received permission to visit the capital and talk with the Mexican president and other officials in January 1930. The United States by then decided to encourage Sandino to stay in Mexico, because Washington judged that it would be easier to keep an eye on him in Mexico than in one of the Central American republics. According to revolutionary legend, the United States (and possibly even Mexico) offered Sandino a large sum of money to purchase a hacienda in Yucatán, provided he agreed not to return to Nicaragua, a condition he indignantly rejected. Mexico was too busy buying off its many generals to spare money for a Nicaraguan rebel, so that part of the story cannot be true. The available reports reveal a Sandino trying to buy a property in Yucatán but unable to raise the money for the purchase price. Just like a bribe offer from the United States cannot be ruled out, the possibility that Sandino was willing to settle down permanently in Yucatán if he had received the money cannot be dismissed either.[30]

Facing financial difficulties in Mexico that eventually would have forced him to return to the jobs of day laborer he held during his youth in that country, Sandino heard with satisfaction the good news that the revolution in Nicaragua was not dead and was in fact reviving. As has often been the case in Latin America, "Revolution" as a business is a valid economic alternative for those who are unable or usually unwilling to obtain more traditional employment. He also received the bad news that in his long absence, other rebel leaders, in particular Miguel Ángel Ortez, were starting to usurp the position of visible head of the insurrection.[31] The two choices before Sandino were very clear: Either he returned to Nicaragua to reclaim his rightful leadership role or he stayed in Yucatán and by default abdicated control over the insurrection to new rebel leaders. For whatever the exact reasons, he no longer found Mexico appealing and left in late April. Prior to his entry into Nicaragua in May, he announced to his followers that he was bringing weapons, ammunition, and many men. Effortlessly he had slipped back into the world of fantasy, when in reality other than a few weapons smuggled in hidden suitcase compartments; he did not bring the promised arsenal. The rebels as before continued to rely on captured weapons and ammunition. About 15 men came with him, including two marine deserters skilled in handling machine guns. Obviously he was not bringing anything substantial to reinvigorate the insurrection, whose revival clearly had come from factors distinct from Sandino's efforts.[32]

When Sandino suddenly left for Mexico in May 1929, he had not been able to impose his temporary replacement; the person he chose declined the task, but fortunately for Sandino,

the very loyal Pedrón Altamirano forcefully took the leadership role. The episode confirmed again that Sandino was not a commanding personality and also revealed the degree of disintegration among the rebels who were more interested in scurrying to safety across the Honduran border than in fighting. Because the decline in rebel activities had manifested itself early in 1929, precipitously the U.S. government decided to reduce the number of marines in Nicaragua from over five thousand early in 1929 to 3,100 by May. Precisely when the remnants of the Sandinista rebellion were most vulnerable to destruction, the United States government abruptly abandoned the final campaign. By July the number of marines was further down to 2,555, and in a dramatic move, Washington ordered their reduction by August to 1,300. American officials in Nicaragua both diplomatic and military argued vigorously against the hasty withdrawal, and an unexpected raid to the south in Matagalpa Department on 1 June 1929 showed that their fears were well founded. Washington with its distant wisdom dismissed the raid and pointed to the subsequent lull in rebel activities as clear proof of the success of the withdrawal policy. In reality the start of the rainy season had imposed a halt on military operations.[33]

Washington believed that the marines could shift the burden of conducting the final mopping-up operations to the rapidly expanding Guardia Nacional. Marine units still garrisoned the cities and served as officers in the Guardia Nacional. After the rainy season ended in late 1929, the Guardia Nacional began patrolling in January 1930, and over the subsequent months clashes and skirmishes became more widespread in northern Nicaragua. In contrast to the situation in 1927, large numbers of peasants were starting to join the revolt in 1930. Sandino, shortly after his return, took to the field with four hundred men and marched to attack Jinotega by surprise on 19 June 1930. Marine planes spotted and bombed the rebels, while Guardia Nacional reinforcements rushed to attack the exposed rebels. At night the rebels escaped with their wounded, among whom was Sandino himself. To take care of the convalescent Sandino, his mistress Teresa Villatoro returned from El Salvador. This failed attack was the last time Sandino himself personally led men into battle. Henceforth he devoted himself to being the political and philosophical leader of the rebellion, and he granted virtual freedom of operation to his subordinates. Under this nominal supervision, even General Ortez could accept Sandino as leader. Sandino increasingly devoted himself to writing proclamations and reports. In addition to his earlier practice of describing imaginary victories, he formulated long philosophical musings. He had a facility to string together high-sounding words into pompous phrases that impressed his peasant followers.[34]

After the defeat of Sandino in June, the Guardia Nacional conducted sweeps in Nueva Segovia Department, but without adequate numbers to patrol the region effectively, the rebels easily escaped. President Moncada expected that outcome, and as early as May 1930 he ordered the forced resettlement of the inhabitants of Nueva Segovia Department. The idea was to depopulate the entire region, that way the marine planes could strafe and bomb at will whenever they saw any signs of human activity. The immediate result was a flood of refugees heading towards the cities of Nicaragua. Moncada then extended the program, and by mid June the government finished evacuating the departments of Nueva Segovia and Jinoteca. The resettlement resembled too much the brutal techniques of colonial powers, most notably the reconcentration of civilians in Spanish Cuba, to be palatable to the American public. The protests of U.S. ambassador Hanna obtained the cancellation of the resettlement program, and in July the inhabitants were free to return to their homes.[35]

The resettlement program at least spoke to the need to do something beyond relying on the still too small Guardia Nacional. In honesty to Ambassador Hanna, since May 1929 he had repeatedly urged a program of road building as the best way to weaken the rebels. Hanna realized that the growing numbers of unemployed were providing the largest number of new recruits for Sandino, and if the government could provide meaningful employment the need to take up arms to gain a livelihood vanished. Even before the United States experienced budgetary pressures, Henry Stimson, who at this moment was Secretary of State, blocked the proposal as too costly. Not even the enthusiastic backing of the marine commanders who realized the military benefits of

being able to crisscross the region on good roads could budge the U. S. government. The Nicaraguan government started some road building on its own, but sorely short of funds, the program could have a marginal impact at best. The Guardia Nacional itself began to suffer cutbacks, as the drop in customs revenues forced the government to scale back its expenditures to keep the budget balanced.[36]

The decline in customs revenue was just one of many indications of the massive impact of the Great Depression. Foreign companies in Nicaragua and Honduras were laying off workers and unemployment was increasing. The number of really desperate people looking for any way to earn sustenance was rising. Deprived of any economic alternatives, many saw in revolution the only way to survive. The deteriorating economic conditions provided Sandino with the many followers he had desperately tried to recruit during the first phase of his rebellion. In a manner reminiscent of Francisco Madero in Mexico in 1911, bands of rebels much larger than anything seen before appeared under new leaders and all proclaimed their nominal loyalty to Sandino. Just as in Mexico, the main attraction was plunder. Joining the rebel movement gave the participants a license to loot, steal, and destroy. The only way for civilians to escape pillage was to pay a contribution to the rebels. The forced collection of contributions soon degenerated into torture and death by horrible means. This outbreak of violent passions and barbaric actions threatened a breakdown in civilization as the number of rebels increased during the rainy season of 1930.

In response to the many savage and brutal assaults, the Guardia Nacional resumed its campaign in the field in November 1930. The goal this time was to cut off the supply route to Honduras; the rebels had developed a sophisticated distribution network to take booty such as coffee, cattle, and gold to Honduras and to bring back supplies and ammunition. The undermanned Guardia Nacional trudged through the jungle trials without being able to cut off the supply routes or to destroy the rebels. But the Guardia Nacional did manage to harass the Sandinistas so much that the rebels began to look for other opportunities to plunder without having to worry about hostile pursuit.[37]

The end of the rainy season in November

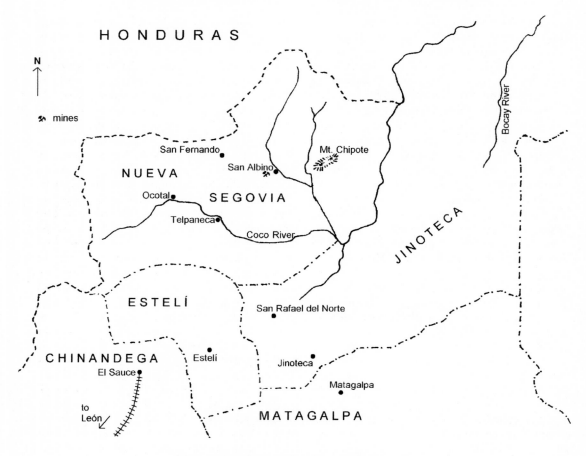

Map 18. Northern Departments of Nicaragua.

coincided with a deepening of the Great Depression. In desperation, the rebels "being able to move over the trails unhampered by weather were able to get together into bands for the purpose of getting something to eat."[38] As the large bands roamed over northern Nicaragua with apparent impunity, the marines could not remain passively garrisoning the cities and increasingly had to assume patrol duties in the countryside. The fateful engagement took place on 31 December 1930, when one of the very rare successful rebel ambushes took place near Ocotal. A ten-man marine squad was out on patrol repairing telephone lines, when a rebel attack killed all the marines except two who managed to escape wounded. The news was a front-page sensation and had a major impact on Washington. Senator William E. Borah, the Chairman of the Foreign Relations Committee, openly and for the first time called for the withdrawal of all U.S. forces from Nicaragua. Secretary of

State Stimson began a process of consultations inside the government to give himself time to reflect on the options. The Great Depression was also hurting the U.S. budget, and Stimson realized that to end the Sandino revolt required sending large number of marines at a high financial cost. On 13 February 1931 Stimson announced the withdrawal of one thousand marines from Nicaragua. He also stated that the rest of the marines, including the pilots and those serving as officers in the Guardia Nacional, were to leave after the presidential elections of 6 November 1932.[39]

Under the shadow of this impending U.S. withdrawal, the most dramatic rebel offensives took place in 1931. Sandino already had more rebels than what the loot and plunder in Nueva Segovia Department could support, and he continued to receive fresh contingents of Hondurans from across the border. His many recent recruits gave him the opportunity to shape a national strategy for the first time. He kept enough rebels active in northern Nicaragua to tie down Guardia Nacional garrisons, while he sent three large columns to the Atlantic coast of Nicaragua. In that region influential local leaders were eager to rally to his side. The local population, a mixture of English-speaking Blacks and Indians, had been hard hit by the onset of the Great Depression. Foreign businesses, in particular the gold mines and the Standard Fruit Company (a banana exporter) had laid off many workers, and discontent was rife and ready to explode in a violent way.[40]

The northernmost column of rebels under the local leader Abraham Rivera was the most successful of the three. Rivera gained the support of the Indians at the Bocay River, a tributary of the Coco River. Aboard their canoes the

Indians took the 40 rebels down the Coco River in early 1931. Rivera easily overran the isolated villages along the river; the high point of the expedition came when he captured Cabo Gracias a Dios early in the morning of 15 April (Map 19). The rebels and the locals thoroughly plundered the undefended village and stripped all its stores of anything of value. The rebels left after 1530 when marine planes arrived to drop bombs. After the Sandinistas and their many local sympathizers divided the booty, Rivera took his column up the Coco River for the return voyage back to Nueva Segovia.[41]

The Rivera column had been more a plundering raid than a military expedition. The second and largest rebel column heading towards the Atlantic Coast was that of Pedro Blandón. His expedition set out in early March and ini-

Map 19. Nicaragua.

tially consisted of at least one hundred guerrillas. By late March Blandón was looting the gold mines at Pis Pis River. However, the real objective of this second expedition was the Standard Fruit Company, whose banana plantations and logging operations promised ample plunder. The company had built a small-gauge railroad linking the export harbor of Puerto Cabezas to a rail head at Logtown 90 kilometers into the interior. Any possibility that the Guardia Nacional could send reinforcements to the threatened Atlantic Coast ended on 31 March 1931, when a destructive earthquake leveled Managua. Almost fifteen hundred died in the earthquake, and the resulting fires, destruction, and disorder absorbed all the energies of the Guardia Nacional. Sandino was soon citing the earthquake as divine punishment, and he pointed out that only Managua where his enemies were concentrated suffered from the tremors.[42]

By early April Blandón reached Logtown and began the systematic looting of all the properties of Standard Fruit and of local merchants. The locals flocked to join him, but weapons were scarce and Blandón had to act quickly to capture Puerto Cabezas, the main prize. He did not move fast enough and gave time for the small Guardia Nacional garrison in Puerto Cabezas to come by railroad to Logtown. In a bold attack on 13 April, the Guardia Nacional under marine officers attacked and routed the rebels, whose most important loss was the death of Blandón himself. Left leaderless, the rebel group melted away to the west. Meanwhile another part of the rebel force was fast approaching Puerto Cabezas. Joined by locals, the rebel force damaged track and burned a crucial bridge so that the victorious Guardia Nacional unit could not return in time to save the threatened town. For the first time in the entire insurrection, the rebels were on the verge of capturing an important town; the flight of the panic-stricken inhabitants to boats in the harbor confirmed that the loss of the town was imminent. To forestall an easy victory for the Sandinistas, the United States had previously sent the USS *Asheville* to Puerto Cabezas. On 15 April bluejackets and marines disembarked to protect Puerto Cabezas temporarily until the stranded Guardia Nacional returned by canoe to take up its posts. Once the prospects of plunder vanished, the rebels either melted into the local population or tried to rejoin their other companions likewise retreating to the west.[43]

Some scattered Sandinista activity continued in the Atlantic Coast, and in perhaps a high point, the rebels managed to shoot down a slow amphibian plane on 22 July, although the pilots escaped alive. For all practical purposes, the expeditions failed to establish any Sandinista presence in the Atlantic region. Just like in northern Nicaragua, the rebels could hide and flee but could never capture an important town and rarely could defeat even very small Guardia Nacional units. The seemingly spectacular Sandinista offensive to the Atlantic Coast merely served to confirm the military inferiority of the rebels. In northern Nicaragua the rebels went back to pillaging and looting the area as their only means of support. All persons of any wealth had to pay forced contributions, and kidnapping persons to extract ransoms became a standard practice. Special rebel units were in charge of collecting the ransoms and the forced contributions. Extremely sadistic tortures and painful executions terrorized the local inhabitants. What had been a campaign to drive out the Americans degenerated into the persecution of anybody with any possessions, be it simply a few head of cattle or some bushels of coffee. The extreme measures reflected the desperation of the rebels who could no longer support themselves in the ravaged northern departments.[44]

The Sandinistas knew they had to stockpile supplies for the long rainy season, and consequently they launched another series of raids into other departments during the months of May through July 1931. The most ambitious was that of Miguel Angel Ortez, who believed that enough rebels were trained and equipped adequately to take by storm an isolated Guardia Nacional barracks. But the attack of 15 May was virtually a replay of the attempt on Ocotal in 1927 and confirmed that the Sandinistas could not overwhelm even small outposts. Ortez himself died in the attempt, and Juan Pablo Umanzor became the new leader of this defeated band. The only options for the rebels were to capture undefended places or to ambush small patrols. Following that strategy, Altamirano successfully raided the gold mines to the west at the Pis Pis River in May and then turned south to raid gold mines in the hitherto untouched department of Chontales in July. The other rebel leaders likewise managed to gather enough supplies to maintain their forces during the rainy season. Meanwhile, an important change took place at Sandino's camp. He finally broke with his mistress Teresa because of her bad temper, and in March 1931 his wife Blanca came to live with him. She enthusiastically supported Sandino, yet quietly she began to make her influence felt as became evident a year later.[45]

When the rainy season came to an end in November 1931, the rebels resumed raiding, and having picked clean northern Nicaragua, for the first time they attacked more populated areas linked by railroad to Managua. Their attacks caused considerable consternation in the capital, when in reality they revealed how desperate the rebels had become. The raids had to yield enough booty to trade for arms, ammunition, and supplies in Honduras, but attacks on easily reached targets exposed the rebels to clashes with the Guardia Nacional. On 22 November a rebel column temporarily occupied an undefended station on the railroad between Chinandega and Managua, but soon Guardia Nacional units were fast closing in on the rebels. In a series of engagements from 25 to 29 November, the rebels managed to hold off the first wave of Guardia Nacional attacks, but as more government troops poured in, the rebels wisely returned to the north.[46]

The raids of November 1931 were not followed by expeditions comparable to those of the previous years. No new attempts to invade the Atlantic Coast or to seize towns materialized. January was an unusually quiet month, with virtually no contact with the rebels. Activity began to increase in February, and between April and September 1932 the Guardia Nacional clashed 104 times with the rebels. A pattern of small-unit engagements became the norm as the rebels tried to extract goods and services from the terrorized local population. Only those who were abjectly poor felt safe, otherwise the rebels searched shacks to steal even used clothing from poor women. The claims of fighting against the foreign invader transformed themselves into licenses to steal and loot, much as had happened during the Mexican Revolution. Plunder was the essential motivation of the rebels who had discovered in revolution an exciting way to earn an easy living.[47]

As the date of the presidential election scheduled for 6 November approached, the question of what would happen to Nicaragua after the departure of the marines loomed ever larger. Stimson accepted U.S. supervision for the presidential elections, but categorically stated that the last marines had to leave by 2 January 1933, the day after the new president was inaugurated. Moncada maneuvered to try to amend the constitution to permit his reelection, but the Great Depression caused so much discontent that the population clamored for a new ruler. Sandino proposed an exiled general as his own candidate for the election of November, but the Nicaraguan politicians ignored his suggestions and instead nominated Juan B. Sacasa to be the Liberal candidate. An angry Sandino wanted to make demonstrations of strength by encouraging his generals to take to the field and launch an attack. But the Guardia Nacional attacked first, and after tracking down the band of Altamarino, badly mauled the rebels on 25 September. The rebel General Umanzor accepted Sandino's suggestion and led an expedition to capture a village on Lake Managua on October 2 and then backtracked to attack a small isolated village near Chinandega on 28 October. With the Guardia Nacional hot on his trail, Umanzor retreated back into the mountain hideouts. The rebels could still harass the government, but as far as the necessary display of might to overawe the Nicaraguan politicians, the rebel military performance fell far short.[48]

With weak battlefield results, the only hope left to keep the revolt alive was a Conservative victory in the November 6 election. In that case, Sandino could continue to lead a Liberal revolt against Conservative rule as had happened in 1926–1927, although of course without the additional prestige of leading the struggle against the United States. But when the Liberal Juan B. Sacasa won the election to president, Sandino was fast running out of political options. Not only was Sacasa a Liberal, but Sandino originally rose up in arms to support Sacasa. If Sandino wanted to save his reputation as the hero of the insurrection against the United States, he simply could not revolt against Sacasa. Sandino had to use the last remaining months of the Moncada presidency to try to secure the most favorable terms for his submission.[49]

Adverse as the political situation was to any continuation of the Sandino revolt, other factors pushed him toward seeking a negotiated peace. The money he occasionally received from abroad was never enough to acquire a steady flow of weapons, ammunition, and supplies. If he could not provide his armed followers with either supplies or booty, they were sure to return gradually to their homes in Honduras and Nicaragua. Although not necessarily without able subordinates, the loss of several leaders had slowly deprived him of key loyal followers. The threat of insubordination remained latent, and as a reminder, on 7 November, the day after the elections, Juan Gregorio Colindres, one of the rebel leaders, proclaimed himself president of Nicaragua. Fortunately for Sandino, the second-in-command agreed to arrest Colindres who subsequently abandoned his claim. The next time Sandino might not be so lucky, and with his always lax discipline over his generals threatening to collapse, it made sense to seek a peace before his followers turned against him.[50]

Accusations that Sandino had all along wanted to create a separate country just for himself were frequent. He toyed with the idea of proclaiming the independence of northern Nicaragua, and only after he realized that no foreign government would recognize him did he drop his plan to create still another republic in the already highly fragmented Central America. Any alternatives to negotiations were running out for Sandino, and the new government of Nicaragua likewise was running out of choices. Without any U.S. support, President Sacasa knew that his only options were either to obtain an agreement with Sandino or to mobilize the country for a relentless pursuit of the rebels. To show its determination, the new government authorized the Mexican General Juan

Escamilla to recruit volunteers in early January 1933; it was understood that he would be free to apply the methods of the Mexican Revolution, in particular summary executions, to destroy the rebels.[51] Before the bloodshed could begin, Sandino's wife personally went to negotiate with the government and obtained a cease-fire on 23 January 1933. Blanca in pleading letters begged Sandino to accept the cease-fire, and the rebel leader finally agreed. In the discussions over peace terms, Sandino demanded an amnesty for his followers and the control of the Nueva Segovia Department. He flew in by plane to conclude the negotiations with the government on 2 February 1933, and by the agreement he signed on that date, his followers received an amnesty and land. He was allowed to keep a personal guard of 100 men, but all other rebels were to turn in their weapons and disband.[52]

Sandino claimed victory in the war over the United States and proclaimed himself the liberator who had expelled foreign troops from Nicaragua. But the rejoicing did not last for long, because Nicaragua most tragically learned that U.S. occupation was far from the worst fate. As the country sank under the grip of the dictatorship of the Anastasio Somoza family, Sandino's campaign against the United States began to appear if not foolish and counterproductive, at least quixotic. Only unusual factors and extraordinary good luck had allowed Sandino to sustain for so long his campaign against the United States. Indeed, the revolt assumed significant dimensions only after the Great Depression made its impact felt in Central America. As the next chapters of this book explain, the effects of the Great Depression were far reaching and touched even the most remote places in the South American interior.

12. The Chaco War: The First Phase, 1932–1933

Victory does not lay in the battle, but in the pursuit, because the art of war consists not in winning in the field, but in extracting benefits from the outcome of the battle. [...] In choosing the moment to retreat lies the life or death of an army. — Francisco Villamartín[1]

The Chaco seemed to be the region of Latin America least likely to provoke a ferocious war. The inhospitable region lacked valuable resources and was virtually worthless. In spite of repeated claims that the war started over oil, the petroleum deposits were outside the Chaco proper, in the region of the Andes Mountains between Santa Cruz and Villa Montes. The Chaco itself was a vast harsh wasteland stretching between the fluvial plains of the Paraguay and the Parapetí rivers (Maps 20 and 24). The scarce local population consisted of semi-nomadic Indians rarely numbering more than a thousand in total. The place names in the maps were never populated villages, but merely assorted collections of shacks for soldiers and civilian assistants of the army. Beyond the fluvial plains of the Paraguay and Parapetí rivers, not only settlers but wildlife virtually disappeared; the rarity of birds left most of the Chaco in eerie silence. The thick forests gave a false impression of abundance, but just like in the Amazon jungle further to the north, the soil lacked the nutrients to sustain food crops. Although the flood plains of the Paraguay and Parapetí rivers and to a lesser extent of the Pilcomayo had grasses for cattle, mules, and horses to graze on, everywhere else the scrub vegetation could not support the an-

imals that soon perished without imported fodder. "The Chaco must certainly be one of the most inhospitable places on earth. Not exactly desert and not exactly jungle, it manages to combine the worst characteristics of both."[2]

At first sight the Chaco seemed just a southward extension of the Amazon jungle, but the soldiers quickly found this comparison to be false. At times the jungle could be as dense as that of the Amazon, but the occasional clearings with only scrub vegetation were unique to the Chaco. Not surprisingly these clearings frequently witnessed flanking movements and became the sites of fierce fighting. In contrast to the eternal heat in the Amazon, the Chaco experienced intense cold during its brief winters, and cold snaps also appeared during the spring and fall, seasons otherwise characterized by hot days and frigid nights. At least during the few winter months the cold helped quench the thirst of the soldiers who otherwise consumed huge volumes of water during the long and scorching summer months. Any savings in water was crucial, because the scarcity of that precious liquid was the most important difference with the Amazon. The traveler is rarely far from abundant water in the Amazon jungle, but in the Chaco, in spite of seasonal torrential downpours, the rainfall rapidly evaporates and leaves the land parched dry. Once inside the Chaco and away from the tributaries of the three bordering rivers, wells tapping underground aquifers were the only reliable source of the precious liquid. Not surprisingly, the struggle for the control of these wells produced the most decisive battles of the war. While neither the Amazon nor the Chaco could feed armies, the consequences from scarcity of food were different in each region. In the Amazon, soldiers without food slowly starved as happened in the war between Peru and Colombia (see chapter 14). In the Chaco, soldiers without water went mad and soon died but not fast enough to escape excruciating agonies.[3]

Without rubber trees or any other valuable resources, the Chaco escaped those economic pressures that had triggered wars over the Amazon in the 1900s (see chapters 1 and 2). The Chaco was a drain on resources rather than a source of revenue, and so was ideally suited for a negotiated partition. With no pressing economic interests at stake, diplomats operating at a leisurely pace should have been able to draw boundary lines across the barren region. Unfortunately after 1870 the Chaco ceased to be a purely boundary dispute and became part of the struggle for strategic supremacy in South America. Most significantly, the failure of Argentina to pursue a forceful and aggressive foreign policy was responsible for the Chaco War. The Treaty of the Triple Alliance of 1865 granted Argentina the Paraguay and the Paraná rivers as its boundaries with Paraguay. After the defeat of Paraguay in 1870, Brazil no longer wanted to border Argentina on the Paraguay River and tried to restrain Argentina from taking control of the entire region to the west of the Paraguay River. Brazil did not want the territory and was looking for a way to provide a graceful escape for Argentina. Most ominously for the future, Brazil encouraged Bolivia to press its claim to the Chaco region. Argentina, never firm or sure about its policy towards Paraguay and caught between pressures from Brazil and Bolivia, decided not to exercize its rights under the Treaty of the Triple Alliance. Argentina first withdrew its frontier claim south to the mislabeled Verde River (really a seasonal creek) and then finally accepted the Pilcomayo River as the boundary.[4] Had Argentina vigorously defended its national interests and insisted on the Paraguay River as its

eastern boundary, then obviously an Argentine wedge of territory would have physically isolated Bolivia from Paraguay and prevented any border war. Had Argentina at least made the Verde River its northern boundary, the possibility of a clash would have been extremely unlikely.

Argentina's retreat to the Pilcomayo River made possible the Chaco War. The Argentine boundary itself exerted a powerful pull in military operations, and commanders of both sides constantly had to take into their plans the existence of this international border in the Bolivian rear. As Bolivia slowly pushed deeper into the Chaco over the decades, the Pilcomayo gained a new importance as a source of supplies. The Argentine towns on the Pilcomayo River were very convenient supply bases for the Bolivian outposts in the barren Chaco. Eventually, and in response to the Bolivian advance, the Paraguayan government gradually pushed its outposts farther west into the Chaco. At first, supplying the outposts near the Paraguay River was easy, but as the distance from the river increased, logistics became difficult. A private logging railroad line running 160 kilometers into the interior from Puerto Casado emerged as the lifeline for the Paraguayan penetration of the Chaco. The railroad was by far the best transportation, because its solid embankments resisted all but the worst floods. Instead the Chaco's unpaved roads turned to mud channels at the first downpour.

A reasonable alternative to war was to draw lines linking the existing military posts of both countries. The resulting boundary line would give Bolivia slightly more than half of the Chaco, and a poverty-stricken Paraguay was more than eager to settle on those terms the simmering dispute with its rich neighbor to the west. But the insistence of Bolivia on the Paraguay River as its boundary doomed all the efforts of the diplomats. The Bolivian demand for the Paraguay River had its origins in the War of the Pacific (1879–1883), when Bolivia had lost its Pacific coastline to Chile. Just as in the 1900s Bolivia had tried to compensate its losses to Brazil in the Acre with Peruvian territory (see chapter 2), in the 1920s Bolivia wanted to compensate for its losses to Chile in the Pacific with Chaco territory. Instead, for Paraguay keeping Bolivia away from the Paraguay River was a matter of life and death.

Once Bolivian troops reached the Paraguay River, what would keep them from crossing over to the other shore to capture Asunción, the nation's capital? The partition of Paraguay among its powerful neighbors was then just one step away: At stake for the country was its very existence. The perspective each country brought to the war was radically different. A colonial campaign was the image Bolivia had of the conflict, but Paraguay always saw the war as a struggle for national survival.[5]

The Decision for War

As each country pushed its outposts deeper into the Chaco, inevitably armed clashes occurred. Historically, diplomacy had diffused any incident before a crisis erupted into a war, but the armed clash on 5 December 1928 was different. North of Bahía Negra near the Paraguay River, Bolivian forces had established the outpost of Vanguardia. When a Paraguayan patrol discovered the outpost, a clash ensued and a Paraguayan officer died. The later famous Rafael Franco, the commander of the garrison at Bahía Negra, was outraged at the news. In a first indication of his preference for swift action, Captain Franco immediately sent a large force to drive the Bolivians out of Vanguardia. The Paraguayan unit demanded that the Bolivians abandon the outpost in ten minutes; once the time elapsed, the Paraguayans promptly attacked and captured or killed all the defenders. The news of this sudden attack shocked the Bolivian public and ignited war fever. Because Paraguay refused to back down, six days later Bolivia retaliated by occupying Boquerón in the south (Map 20). Frantic diplomatic efforts tried to stop the apparently inevitable war, but because both countries had already begun the full mobilization of their army reserves, the prospects for preserving peace were bleak.[6]

On 16 December 1928 Paraguay called up its reservists between the ages of 20 to 29, but after issuing the decree nothing seemed to go right. Without any prior experience or planning, the army was at a loss as to what to do. The reservists came to their home towns but found nobody to direct them. Spontaneously all the reserve units marched to the nation's capital. Soon the public buildings in Asunción were overflowing with reservists, all without uniforms, equipment, or even food. In an attempt to relieve the congestion in the capital, the army distributed the reservists among many towns, but the dispersion delayed any chance of putting together combat units. The men arrived hungry after having spent days without any meals, and in desperation starving soldiers looted stores for food. The mobilization had brought forth not an army but a hungry mob; "a complete chaos [...] an indescribable confusion existed."[7] Before its eyes Paraguay saw disintegrate any chance of waging war against Bolivia. After three months the angry reservists returned home in rags, tired and hungry. With no other option left, Paraguay handed over its fate to the diplomats, who surprisingly cobbled together a satisfactory arrangement. In exchange for the Paraguayan withdrawal from Vanguardia, Bolivia agreed to abandon Boquerón. As diplomats congratulated themselves on what they considered their triumph, the hope reappeared that negotiations could find a permanent solution to the Chaco dispute. In a favorite past-time of foreign offices in Spanish America (but not in Brazil) diplomats pored over moth-eaten colonial documents to find the formula for a boundary settlement. As the negotiations dragged on, the Bolivian diplomat Daniel Salamanca walked over to his Paraguayan counterpart and stated: "Don't even dream about finding a solution in these moth-eaten documents; the Chaco problem will be resolved by gunshots [*cañonazos*]."[8] Perhaps the statement was just a casual remark born out of frustration, or more likely it was a diplomat's ploy to intimidate the opponent.

Independent of its original intention, the statement turned out to be prophetic. Later in 1932 that same Salamanca, as president of Bolivia, based his decision to go to war on the conclusions he had drawn from the Vanguardia incident of 1928. Both he and the Bolivian public believed that a war with Paraguay would be an easy victory. The larger size, population, and wealth of Bolivia compared to Paraguay were additional indicators that promised victory. The disastrous Paraguayan mobilization of December 1928 convinced most Bolivian army officers that Paraguay was too chaotic to put up any organized resistance. Bolivian officers dismissed the ferocious and desperate resistance of the Paraguayans during the War of the Triple Alliance (1865–1870) as ancient and ir-

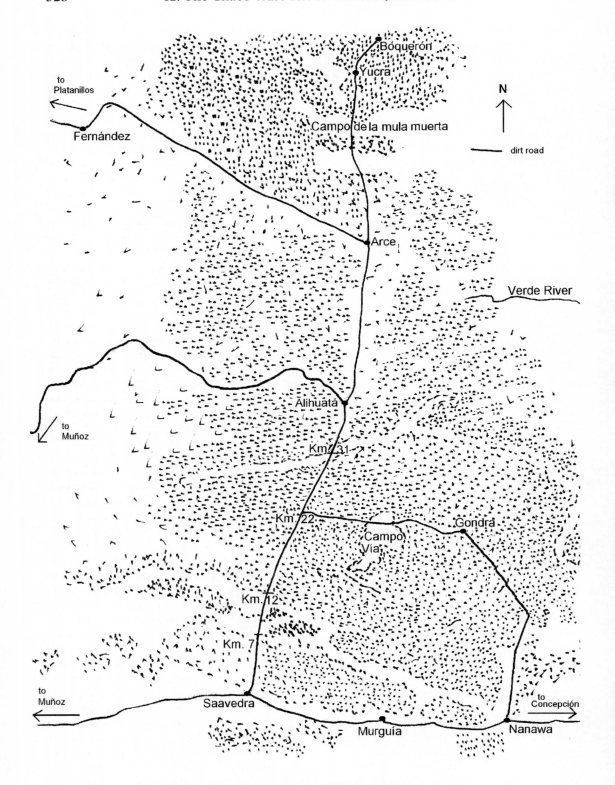

Map 20. Chaco Theater of Operations, 1932–1933.

relevant history at best. The harshness of the Chaco did counsel caution. The Bolivian officers planned on a swift offensive to the Paraguay River to avoid the barren region devoid of food and water. To intimidate the Paraguayans into submission, nothing was better than overwhelming firepower from the most modern weapons. Bolivia enthusiastically embraced aircraft and came to believe that air power alone sufficed to defeat the Paraguayans. In any future showdown, Bolivia believed itself ready to win a war, although the Bolivian General Staff recognized that the huge logistical obstacles demanded a campaign of at least six months.[9]

The Bolivian penetration into the Chaco was in the hands of the 4th Division in the south and the 3rd Division in the north. By 1931 these two units had pushed their outposts near those of their Paraguayan counterparts; for a time it seemed that the Bolivian government was ready to accept this string of posts as the boundary line. If the resulting boundary line was fairly straight, the Bolivian government was willing to face the nationalistic outcry in La Paz about the failure to reach the Paraguay River as the price to settle the territorial dispute. The government and the General Staff of the army continued to talk about the Paraguay River as the proper boundary, but they seemed willing to compromise along a line down the middle of the Chaco. Unfortunately, a gap of at least 300 kilometers lay between the 4th and 3rd divisions, both of whose wings ended in thick forests. The huge gap between the 4th and 3rd divisions had not been an oversight or accident, but instead reflected the absence of water in that sector. Exploring parties lost their way in the jungle of the gap and soldiers perished when their water supply ran out. The jungle dulls perceptions so much that Bolivian officers in the field had not even realized that such a large gap existed, but to the armchair strategists pouring over maps back in La Paz, the gap loomed dangerously large. Until the Bolivian army had first closed this supposedly vulnerable gap, no Bolivian politician stood a chance of surviving the political backlash that the abandonment of the claim to the Paraguay River already entailed.

Bolivia learned that in July 1931 the Paraguayans had established a post west of Toledo (Map 21) in the direction of the Pilco-mayo River. This flanking movement appeared to threaten the rear flank of the 4th Division and seemed to make untenable all the Bolivian forward positions. As 1932 began, Bolivia felt itself under increasing pressure to close the gap in the middle. A misunderstanding had already led to a break in diplomatic relations with Paraguay. To keep the two countries talking instead of shooting, diplomats had hurriedly convoked a conference of neutral countries in Washington, D.C. To bolster its case before the conference, Bolivia wanted to present as a fait accompli an unbroken line of posts along the entire disputed border. But the Bolivian troops could not occupy the gap until they first discovered water.

The jubilation in La Paz was immense when aerial reconnaissance discovered a lake in this gap on 24 April 1932. Verbal accounts said that the lake, which the Bolivians baptized as Lake Chuquisaca, was teeming with ducks and was a veritable oasis for wildlife in the desert of the jungle. From the airplane the observers spotted two buildings but could see no signs of humans near the lake and the site the Paraguayans called Pitiantuta (Map 21). This body of water became the key for the entire Bolivian effort in the center, because the nearest water holes in Bolivian hands were 200 kilometers away at Camacho. In discussions with President Salamanca, the General Staff of the army reached the conclusion that the buildings were most likely abandoned or belonged to "savages."[10]

The lure of water proved irresistible, and the General Staff ordered a land expedition to reach the site. The coordinates from the aerial observation proved useless, and in the dense jungle the initial expedition missed the lake and had to return to base in a wretched condition. With the information that the first patrol had gathered, a second expedition under Mayor Óscar Moscoso finally arrived at Pitiantuta (Map 22) on 15 June only to discover six Paraguayan soldiers occupying the buildings. Moscoso promptly ordered an attack, and his platoon killed the Paraguayan corporal and sent five privates fleeing into a jungle trail. The survivors took days to cross the harsh terrain, and only on 18 June did the commander of the 1st Division, Lieutenant Colonel José Félix Estigarribia, receive at Casanillo the news about the Bolivian invasion.[11]

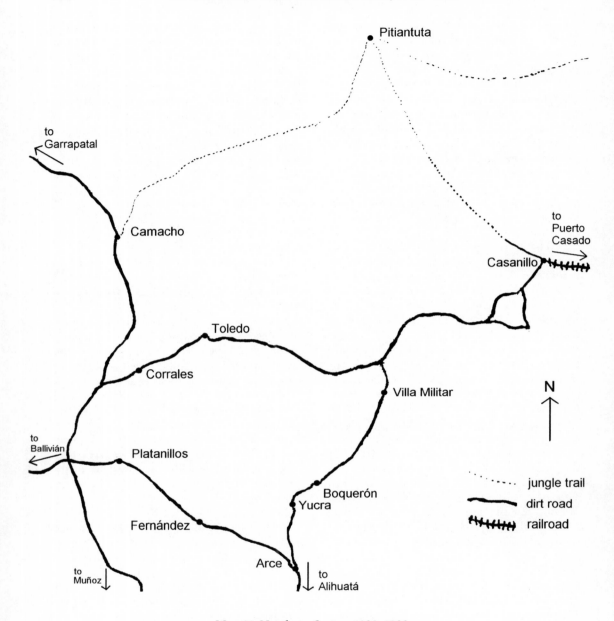

Map 21. Northern Sector, 1932–1933.

Before presenting the Paraguayan response, the action of Mayor Moscoso requires some examination. Why did he attack the handful of Paraguayan soldiers? When he received orders to occupy the place, he could only interpret them in a strictly military sense, namely, to drive out the existing garrison. Nevertheless, he stated afterwards that he had asked repeatedly for clarification of his orders and had received none. His divisional com-

mander had forwarded copies to him of the orders from the General Staff urging the importance of gaining control of Lake Pitiantuta, but Mayor Moscoso failed to receive any of the repeated orders from President Salamanca and from the General Staff prohibiting any combat or clash with Paraguayan units. Clearly a breakdown in the chain of communications had occurred. The jumbled confusion of orders, events, and coincidences that produced the capture by force of Lake Pitiantuta was not an exception, but proved endemic to the Bolivian army. Just a few months later a similar mix-up would have disastrous consequences for the siege of Boquerón.[12]

The confusion continued after La Paz heard of the capture of Pitiantuta. President Salamanca, who had insisted on avoiding any friction with Paraguayan units and had repeatedly given orders prohibiting any use of force, was outraged at the news. He instantly ordered the immediate withdrawal of the Bolivian detachment, but because the platoon did not have

a radio, messengers needed a week to take the order to Mayor Moscoso. Had the order been carried out, obviously the Chaco War could not have begun at this moment. As the days passed and no withdrawal took place, the General Staff submitted arguments that gradually eroded the initial decision of the president. The lack of water precluded any withdrawal to an intermediate position. Any withdrawal had to be to the nearest water well at the original starting place of Camacho and meant reopening the famous gap of nearly 200 kilometers between the 3rd and 4th divisions. The General Staff pro-

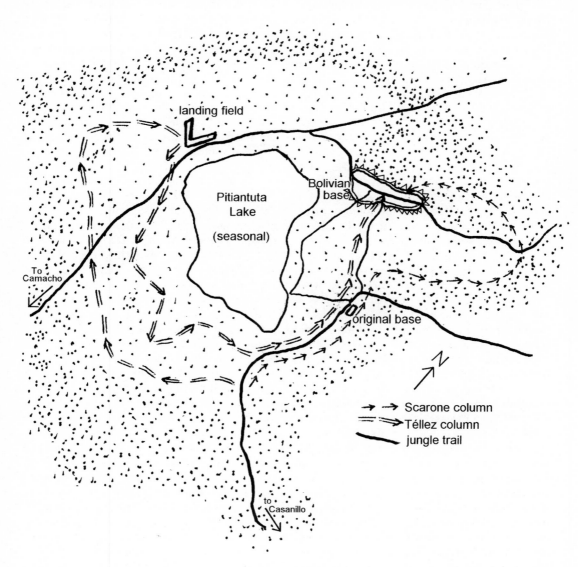

Map 22. Pitiantuta.

posed that since the Paraguayan buildings were on the east bank of the lake, Mayor Moscoso should abandon those buildings and relocate his forces to the west bank; the lake itself as a buffer zone presumably could mark the boundary between the two countries. The suggestions of the General Staff were rapidly losing touch with reality. As a deposit of rain water, the lake had been rapidly shrinking under the hot sun and might soon vanish altogether. Whatever the possibility of using the lake as a buffer zone had been, Mayor Moscoso had long since burned the Paraguayan buildings; his perplexity upon receiving the order to restore them to the Paraguayans can well be imagined. He picked a slight elevation to the northeast of the lake as the best site for his main camp. He put his soldiers to begin constructing an extensive system of fortifications. As more men dribbled in along the jungle trail from Camacho, he put them to cut trails through the jungle linking the main base with the outposts covering the approach from Paraguay to the east.[13]

Already the expedition of Mayor Moscoso was faithfully reflecting the structural flaws in the Bolivian army. One officer could start a war, but Mayor Moscoso alone could not win a battle. Records captured in the buildings revealed that as recently as 20 April the Paraguayan garrison had numbered 45 soldiers armed with machine guns. Because his 18 soldiers could not withstand the inevitable counterattack, he feared a repetition of the same fate that had befallen the garrison at Vanguardia in 1928. He promptly demanded reinforcements, but the lack of a radio meant that to obtain an answer required 15 days by messenger. Actually, the real problem was not poor communication but the shortage of soldiers. The 4th Division desperately tried to scrape together enough soldiers to send north as reinforcements. The men dribbled north in small groups and reached Pitiantuta after a harrowing march through the jungle. To his consternation, Mayor Moscoso found that the men brought some ammunition and very little food, so that as his garrison grew in numbers, his food supply dwindled. He did what he could to defend the position and put his men to dig an interconnected system of trenches and bunkers. He had his men remove the brush and trees in front of the main position to provide an open field of fire. He also

began to clear a landing strip to the west of his camp so that planes could land supplies.[14]

On 29 June a Paraguayan unit of 84 soldiers attacked the Bolivian position. Lieutenant Colonel Estigarribia had wanted to launch a counterattack as soon as possible, but the logistical support for a large force was still not ready. As a first step, he opted for a raid to test the Bolivian defenses. Ideally the detachment should capture Pitiantuta, but if resistance proved too strong, then its main mission changed to gather information on the Bolivian positions and defenders. In what seemed almost like second instinct for the Paraguayans, they stealthily slipped around the first Bolivian outpost and captured it from the rear in a surprise attack. The Paraguayans then approached the main defenses, but the Bolivian defenders fought back vigorously and began to counterattack. Running short of ammunition and without any more reserves to throw into the battle, the Paraguayan commander withdrew several kilometers back to the nearest water hole to await the arrival of the rest of his regiment.[15]

The attacking force had gained a good knowledge of the state of the defenses, but the failure to recapture Pitiantuta angered high Paraguayan officials who almost removed Lieutenant Colonel Estigarribia from command. At that time Pitiantuta was at the extreme limit of the Paraguayan logistics line, and consequently each additional soldier on the front increased the burden on the over-stretched supply line. The inhospitable jungle provided no sustenance, and unlike in the Amazon jungle, the Paraguayans had to bring water from distant wells to the thirsty soldiers. The Bolivians at Lake Pitiantuta had plenty of water, but they too were suffering tremendously from food shortages. Many of the men Mayor Moscoso received as reinforcements were sick with malaria and other tropical diseases. Most of the new arrivals were raw recruits, and the rest came from many different units and had never operated in unison before. Major Moscoso simply did not have the time or the means to shape this motley group into an effective fighting force. Already on 12 July in an attempt to make the food supply last, he had diminished the content of the meal portions: By the first day of the main Paraguayan attack, the Bolivians were on half rations and had flour for only two more meals. Clearly the only question was who would destroy the garrison first: the jungle or the Paraguayans.[16]

Captain Absón Palacios commanded the 400 Paraguayan soldiers Estigarribia sent to recapture Pitiantuta. With only a few mules to help carry equipment, the walk through the jungle left the soldiers exhausted and short of water. The most agile soldiers crawled stealthily at night to refill the canteens of the unit at the lake shore, and once his men quenched their thirst, the commander plotted his strategy. Although his reconnaissance information was spotty, Captain Palacios decided on a two-pronged offensive to trap the Bolivian garrison. While keeping a small reserve with him, he divided the rest of his force into two columns: The one under First Lieutenant Atilio Téllez had the mission of marching west of the lake until it reached the Bolivian supply trail to Camacho, while the other under First Lieutenant Ernesto Scarone attacked the main Bolivian position (Map 22). Captain Palacios himself stayed behind ready to rush his small reserve to any threatened point. On 15 July the column of Téllez set out at 0900 and one hour later stumbled upon the Bolivian supply trail. The column pushed east and ran into the Bolivian detachment that was clearing the field for a runway. Major Moscoso had ordered this detachment to be ready to repel any attack, but the Bolivians considered themselves safe so far in the rear and had failed to take any precautions. The surprise was complete for the Bolivians who hastily fled, and the Paraguayans easily captured the outpost and the landing strip. At this moment, Lieutenant Téllez had to decide whether to continue the march eastward along the northern border of the lake towards the Bolivian position, or more conservatively, to take up defensive positions in the path to prevent any Bolivians from escaping. In a thoroughly perplexing decision, he opted for returning to the original Paraguayan camp. As his men withdrew, the Bolivians regained the path to Camacho without having to fire a single shot. The plan of Captain Palacios to trap the entire Bolivian garrison had miscarried. Worse was still to befall the column of Lieutenant Téllez. One jungle trial inevitably resembles another, and soon the column was lost and wandered for hours until at last hunger and exhaustion forced them to stop for the night.[17]

Meanwhile, the column of Lieutenant Scarone had been advancing against the main Bolivian position along the east bank of the lake. Because the attacking column was slightly smaller than the defending force, the attack should have been a complete failure had not the Paraguayans enjoyed the decisive advantage of a superior weapon. The mud trails eliminated any possibility of bringing artillery, but mules carried one 81 mm mortar. The mortar proved to be decisive, because the Bolivian soldiers mistakenly concluded that the Paraguayans had heavy artillery. Although the Bolivians were safe in their underground bunkers, the double charges of the mortar shattered the morale of the defenders that afternoon of 15 July. The Paraguayans dispersed themselves widely and advanced close to the Bolivian defenses under the covering fire of the mortar. When the Paraguayan advance parties reported that ahead lay large earthen mounds and bunkers, Captain Palacios began to have second thoughts about the attack. He was confident his men could defeat the Bolivians in the trees and in the bush, but he did not want to slaughter the Paraguayans in charges against machine guns. He knew his one mortar could not make much of a dent on the underground bunkers, and most ominously, he had not heard anything from the column of Lieutenant Téllez. Late in the afternoon of 15 July, when his men were confident of successfully storming the main Bolivian trenches, he halted the attack and recalled his soldiers.[18]

Had he led his reserve to reinforce the attacking column, he probably could have overrun the Bolivian defenses that day, but only by taking heavy casualties. The fate of the other column worried him most, because he reasoned that only a very large force could have detained it. On 16 July Captain Palacios sent out a patrol to locate the missing column, which by then was just a few hours' march away. That morning Captain Palacios also ordered the column of Lieutenant Scarone back against the Bolivian base; as soon as the other column returned, he intended to hurl his combined forces against the Bolivian position. After a few hours the famished column of Téllez returned. After the men grabbed a quick bite to eat, Captain Palacios sent them to reinforce the attack of the Scarone column.[19]

In the morning under a covering barrage

of mortar fire the Paraguayan patrols approached the Bolivian defense lines. Seeing one Paraguayan patrol coming very near to a Bolivian trench, Major Moscoso went to investigate only to see that the Bolivian squad had fled. He promptly ordered another squad to man the position, but the very heavy fire from large numbers of Paraguayans convinced him that his hungry and ill-trained troops could not hold the position for long. Major Moscoso returned to his command post to prepare for an orderly withdrawal that night; in retrospect he should have abandoned the position immediately, even though many would have considered such a retreat as premature or cowardly. His men had no intention of waiting until the night of 16 July, and when the two Paraguayan columns launched their main attack at 1530, almost all the Bolivians abandoned their positions and fled into the jungle. As he toured the extensive system of trenches, he found that only 14 soldiers, the survivors of his original 18, were at their posts. "Upon verifying the shameful flight of almost all the officers and soldiers, I felt shame, anger, and hopelessness."[20] In an impulse of desperation, he ran toward the Paraguayan positions, but before they could kill or capture him, covering fire from his loyal 14 soldiers brought him back to his senses, and he managed to crawl back to the trenches.

Those few Bolivian soldiers still engaged in combat used the extensive network of trenches to change positions frequently and to fight off the attack until nightfall, when Mayor Moscoso led them down the long and tortuous jungle trail back to Camacho. Along the way he encountered many stragglers, but most of those who had fled never escaped alive from the barren forests. The remaining officers who had been among the first to flee were afraid of a court-martial. In a typical Latin American attempt to pin blame elsewhere, these officers invented the vicious rumor that the Paraguayans had captured Pitiantuta because Mayor Moscoso had spent all the time drunk and carousing with women. The false charges did not stick (no women had ever come to Pitiantuta), and Mayor Moscoco remained holding important positions for the rest of the war.[21]

Radio messages from the 4th Division reported the loss of Pitiantuta to La Paz, and the Bolivian government had to decide how to respond to the defeat. War was not inevitable yet. Paraguay had not announced its mobilization, and in Asunción some still believed that this was just another incident by isolated frontier troops. Thus a realistic option available to Bolivia was simply to make the accurate claim that the occupation of Pitiantuta had been the result of misinformation and confusion. In retrospect President Salamanca should have turned to diplomacy to extricate himself from this mess. But the pressures of the Great Depression, such as the drop in economic activity and government revenue, made the nationalistic outcries harsher and shriller than in the more sedate prosperous times. Salamanca, whose previous orders about Pitiantuta revealed a deep desire for peace, still had a chance to stop the train headed for war. However, the historical precedent of Vanguardia was too recent to ignore and provided a seemingly innocuous script to follow: Bolivia entered into negotiations only after having compensated for the loss of an outpost in the north with the capture of one position in the south.

As soon as he heard the news of the loss of Pitiantuta, Salamanca convoked an emergency meeting of his cabinet on the evening of 18 July. Instead of asking for a calm consideration of the best alternatives for Bolivia, he opened the cabinet discussion by proposing an immediate reprisal in the south in two days! After unanimous opposition from the army officers present, Salamanca relented and granted the army four days to counterattack. General Filiberto Osorio, the Chief of the General Staff, explained to the cabinet that the 4th Division was composed of barely 1,200 ill-trained and poorly supplied men and that any reprisal against an unknown Paraguayan force was foolhardy. Salamanca accepted as real the shortage of men, and as a solution he proposed opening a road through the forest to transfer part of the 3rd Division from the north to reinforce the 4th Division in the south. General Osorio insistently opposed the transfer, whereupon Salamanca cut off the discussion and said that this was an order! In a final challenge, General Osorio said he preferred to lose his position rather than obey the order; when the president asked: where would you go? Osorio replied: to the front with my men, whereupon the president accepted the transfer to the field.[22]

The removal of General Osorio still could not overcome the total opposition of the General Staff against making a hasty reprisal in the south. While indefinite defiance of the presidential order to attack was impossible, the General Staff hoped to delay long enough to gain time to provide some semblance of preparation for the army units in the front. As the days passed by without any results, Salamanca could no longer stand the "agonizing slowness."[23] President Salamanca summoned the ranking military officers to a meeting on the 25 July to find out why the Bolivian army had still not attacked. According to the president's own account

> I would prefer not to recall the details of that meeting, which you [General Osorio] appeared to have designed to force me to abandon my order for a reprisal. General Montes and General Quintanilla both stated that it was too soon to be thinking about reprisals until the 4th Division first received ample reinforcements. You, [General Osorio] were in a state of complete demoralization and twice proposed that Bolivia should turn to diplomacy to solve this conflict. [...] I will confess that in the meeting and against my usual habit, I treated you without any mercy and forced you almost brutally to follow the path that Bolivian honor demanded.[24]

Why had Salamanca suddenly changed from the peacemaker during Pitiantuta to the warmonger afterwards? The impersonal currents rushing the country into war were certainly strong, but in this week Salamanca was pushing harder than anybody else for war. Perhaps his self-fulfilling prophecy that gunshots would decide the boundary was becoming a reality. The army's delays in following his orders certainly contributed to his insistence on war, and with Bolivia's rich history of military coups, insubordination posed a danger. However, his statements and actions revealed that he was engaged in more than a power struggle with the generals. The obsessive desire to repeat the 1928 script of Vanguardia helps to explain his insistence on reprisals, but more than anybody else he was most vehemently determined to inflict a counterstroke. The above considerations put into perspective his decision to press for war, but the exact reasons that triggered his sudden change of mind remain a mystery.

Salamanca by his own words condemned himself for starting the Chaco War. The General Staff had desperately pleaded with him not to start the war or at the very least to grant enough time to prepare the frontier troops. The army high command always has the obligation to tell the civilian authorities (be they of the executive or legislative branch) that a war cannot be won or that a country needs more time to prepare. However, in Bolivia the General Staff was not completely free of blame. True, it had argued forcefully for a delay, but had never really stated its real reason for opposing the start of a war. The harsh truth was that the Bolivian army, no matter how long it prepared, would never be ready to wage war with its weakest and poorest neighbor. In the absence of few other salaried positions in the agrarian country, the army had become an employment agency for the middle class. Decades of corruption, favoritism, cronyism, and a myriad of other sins had left the Bolivian officer corps structurally flawed if not rotten. To try to remedy the many defects, the Bolivian government brought first a French military mission from 1906 to 1910 and then in 1911 a German military mission under General Hans Kundt.[25] In spite of the diligent efforts of the foreign missions, nothing could disguise the bitter truth about the Bolivian army. If the General Staff had told Salamanca that the army would never be ready to fight Paraguay, then even he had to pause. His outrage would have been no less, because he immediately had to ask: Why then do we need to have an army at all? The army, not willing to risk its institutional survival, refused to make the supreme sacrifice of its own extinction as the only way to spare Bolivia the ravages, suffering, expenses, and humiliation of the Chaco War.

The Siege of Boquerón and the First Paraguayan Offensive

Once President Daniel Salamanca ordered the army to capture Paraguayan outposts in the south, the drive toward war became unstoppable. Diplomats rushed into the fray, hoping to boost their careers by repeating the triumph over the Vanguardia incident of 1928, but little did they realize that the time for negotiations had long since passed. No less anxiously than the diplomats, Paraguay itself watched carefully for the Bolivian reaction. The Asunción government had only one card to play: full mobilization. After the debacle of 1928, Paraguay had organized a real General Staff whose primary duty was to prepare the entire country for war with Bolivia. Paraguay trained officers at home and in France, acquired a modest variety of weapons, and most importantly, created a workable plan to mobilize the reservists efficiently and rapidly. Unknown to Bolivia, Paraguay could place in the Chaco 16,000 trained and equipped reservists in 36 days.[26] Once Paraguay decided to mobilize, war was inevitable.

As the poorest country in South America and without the mineral wealth of Bolivia, a full mobilization was a costly and disruptive affair for Paraguay. If the measure turned out to be unnecessary, then Paraguay revealed to Bolivia its secret weapon; likewise a premature mobilization could make Paraguay appear to be the aggressor. Yet total passivity might signal to Bolivia that Paraguay was willing again to accept the humiliating outcome of the 1928 Vanguardia incident. In 1932 under no circumstances was Paraguay willing to exchange Pitiantuta for the return of any captured posts in the south. As Asunción sifted through the information coming from secret agents in Buenos Aires and La Paz (diplomatic relations with Bolivia had been broken earlier in the year), either an accumulation of signals or perhaps a single crucial report finally persuaded Paraguay that Bolivia was preparing to attack. On 23 July, or five days after the decision for war in La Paz, Paraguay announced its mobilization; already before that date hundreds of volunteers had spontaneously come to Asunción to offer their services: "The order for mobilization has been obeyed with the greatest enthusiasm."[27] Extensive newpaper coverage reporting the smooth start of the Paraguayan mobilization did not worry Bolivia in the least.[28]

Until the Paraguayans completed their mobilization, the numerically superior Bolivians were free to overrun most of the disputed territory. Although the Bolivian General Staff was busily trying to place more troops and supplies in the Chaco, La Paz was so confident of victory that it had decreed a partial mobilization only. The very long supply roads to the Chaco meant that sizable new units could arrive no earlier than in three months. Just sending replacements was a major struggle for the General Staff. The 4th Division at barely 1,200 men had to carry out the reprisals President Salamanca had so vehemently ordered. The first reports indicating that Paraguay could place as many as 8,000 soldiers on the field only emboldened President Salamanca, who on 23 July ordered the 4th Division "to continue the attack and to advance until the soldiers encountered serious resistance"; in that case they were to fortify themselves and to await the arrival of Bolivian reinforcements.[29]

The initial Bolivian sweep into the Chaco proved fairly easy. Against only light resistance, the Bolivians captured Corrales on 27 July and then Toledo on 28 July (Map 21). Paraguay had deliberately refused to reinforce its weak frontier posts to lure the Bolivians as far away as possible from their supply base of Muñoz and conversely to shorten the Paraguayan supply lines. The Paraguayan commander at Boquerón, however, decided to be more creative about his fighting withdrawal. He left only a fraction of his small force entrenched at Boquerón to face the Bolivian attack of 31 July. When these soldiers were about to be overrun, they fled noisily in utter panic. The triumphant Bolivians rushed the abandoned buildings in large groups and began to celebrate their victory in such excitement that they failed to notice that the rest of the Paraguayan unit was cleverly camouflaged in the jungle to the north. As soon as three high-ranking Bolivian officers arrived riding on horseback, the Paraguayans opened fire. Simultaneously a deafening barrage of machine gun and rifle fire mowed down the unsuspecting Bolivians, killing their commander among many others. By the time more Bolivian units arrived to clear the forest, the Paraguayan defenders had slipped away.[30]

In successive messages Salamanca urged the offensive forward as he strove to gain as much land as possible for the negotiations he naively expected to ensue soon. Whatever might have been the diplomatic justification, militarily the president was doing everything possible to rush the 1,200 soldiers of the 4th Division deep into the gradually forming jaw of the over 16,000 mobilizing Paraguayan soldiers. Finally on 2 August, after the insistent reports from Bolivian diplomats in Argentina confirmed the magnitude of the Paraguayan mobilization, the General Staff halted the advance and ordered the 4th Division to prepare to repel the coming Paraguayan onslaught.[31] The halt order was the least the General Staff could do, but in retrospect it should have ordered a partial withdrawal. Corrales was nearest to the Bolivian supply lines and farthest from the Paraguayan positions and thus afforded the best chance for a successful defense. Boquerón was the most vulnerable of the three positions, and Toledo was in an intermediate situation. Why didn't the General Staff recommend withdrawal? While holding on to Corrales only was politically unacceptable in Bolivia, making Toledo the main battleground evened the chances for Bolivia somewhat. Instead the General Staff mistakenly concluded that superiority in machine guns and aircraft sufficed to hold Boquerón until strong Bolivian reinforcements arrived.

Lieutenant Colonel Manuel Marzana took command of the forces at Boquerón and proceeded to fortify the position. A very methodical individual who was renowned for his blind obedience to orders, he very competently prepared Boquerón to face the assault. Although he had only 448 men, his unit had 13 heavy machine guns and 27 light ones, or the very high ratio of almost one machine gun per 11 soldiers. He also had three artillery pieces. His men constructed an intricate network of trenches and bunkers, and then they cleared the ground in front of the defenses to afford the machine guns wide open killing grounds. He established his outermost outposts over ten kilometers to the east and sent reconnaissance patrols in search of any Paraguayan activity. The telegraphic order from President Salamanca was categorical:

> Do not abandon Boquerón under any circumstances; better to die in its defense than to give the order to retreat. Shattering the Paraguayan offensive in this point would be enough to demoralize the enemy and above all would refute in the Western Hemisphere the Paraguayan propaganda about the inferiority of our troops.[32]

The Bolivian decision to fortify Boquerón left the next move to Paraguay. The decision was in the hands of Eusebio Ayala, who had just been inaugurated president on 15 August. In sharp contrast to Salamanca, Ayala was most hesitant to send his poor country into war, and in particular he knew that the country's small population could not withstand crippling casualties. Although he knew that diplomacy could not regain Boquerón, he psychologically refused to believe that only the god of war could return the disputed position to Paraguay. After much anguish and deliberation, on 1 September he at last ordered Lieutenant Colonel Estigarribia to recapture Boquerón. In a very rambling unsigned order, the Paraguayan president stated that he wanted the attack to be swift and that the troops not appear to be the aggressors. Once Boquerón was captured, the Paraguayan forces were to carry out a pursuit of the defeated enemy only if absolutely necessary; indeed after a short stay, Estigarribia should seek some excuse to evacuate Boquerón and return to the home base at Villa Militar. Afraid that Estigarribia might lack imagination, the president in the order suggested poisoned wells or infected barracks as good pretexts to justify the evacuation. After Estigarribia verified that the order had indeed come from the president, he called it "one of the most curious documents ever composed during the war."[33] The hesitation of Ayala to take up arms contrasted with the determination of Salamanca to pursue the offensive.

Fortunately for Paraguay, Estigarribia implemented the attack order according to military practices and not as part of a diplomatic minuet. Although he had under his command almost 10,000 soldiers, in reality he had brought less than half that number. As the Paraguayan units trudged forward through the trails, Bolivian planes reported their movements to Marzana. The Paraguayans, remembering the hurried flight of the Bolivian soldiers at Pitiantuta in July and just recently at the outermost outposts of Boquerón, were sure that the main Bolivian garrison would flee as soon as a determined attack began. Arriving late at night in front of Boquerón, the forward Paraguayan units did not have time for any reconnaissance and took up positions near the Bolivian trenches.

In a final preparation for the general assault on 9 September, the Paraguayan forces began repositioning themselves closer to the Bolivian front lines at 0530. Almost immediately problems emerged when the one unit that had to move through the thick forest reported little progress. For the rest of the units the open fields before Boquerón proved alluringly inviting, and at 0700 to the shouts of "Long Live Paraguay" the infantry began its final charge against the waiting machine guns. The Paraguayan artillery and mortars tried to provide a covering fire, but the shells fell short and ripped holes in the advancing lines. The Bolivians opened an almost continuous machine gun and rifle fire upon the Paraguayans, whose advancing lines collapsed under the murderous fire "like kernels falling from an ear of corn."[34] Eight times the Paraguayan officers rallied the soldiers to make one more attack, and each time with the same disastrous results. The Bolivian artillery joined the constant drone of the incessant machine gun fire; the artillery shells fell exactly among the huddled Paraguayans who still did not accept defeat. Only nightfall finally persuaded the Paraguayans to abandon any further attacks as hopeless.[35]

In a harbinger of the future, during the assault one Paraguayan unit had slipped around through the jungle and quietly blockaded the southern road leading to Arce; consequently, when the Bolivian high command sent reinforcements during the day, the Paraguayan unit kept the road closed. However, extreme thirst forced the Paraguayan unit to retreat hastily, and that night Bolivian troops were able to ride aboard trucks into Boquerón.[36] So ingrained was the assumption that the Paraguayans lacked the men and the weapons to sustain an attack, that the Bolivian corps commander believed that a quick counterattack was all that was needed to finish off the Paraguayans. Incredibly, the corps commander believed that the Bolivian forces in the area were adequate, even though Marzana was duly reporting that the Paraguayans enjoyed a large numerical superiority.[37] The unfounded optimism was contagious, and President Salamanca telegraphed: "The destiny of our Chaco depends on the successful defense of Boquerón."[38] With Bolivia not able to bring up sizable reinforcements for months, the tactical situation after the repulse of the Paraguayan assault of 9 September dictated an orderly evacuation to preserve the experienced men among the Bolivian troops.

For Paraguay Boquerón had become the first test of the war, and to achieve victory Estigarribia brought up the rest of his 10,000 men. The failed attack on Boquerón taught most Paraguayans never to attempt frontal assaults against automatic weapons, a lesson the Bolivians took years to learn.[39] Estigarribia decided to impose a formal siege and ordered his soldiers to surround Boquerón. His soldiers were still far from being skilled veterans who knew how to maneuver inside the jungle, so a full three days elapsed before the scattered units believed they had surrounded the Bolivian garrison. Meanwhile, the Paraguayan soldiers, unperturbed by the steady machine gun fire and using the bodies of their fallen comrades as cover, pressed closely to the Bolivian trenches at Boquerón. Expecting another attack, the Bolivian defenders kept firing at the Paraguayan lines, but already on the second day lack of shells silenced the Bolivian cannons. In contrast, the Paraguayan cannons at last found their range, just that same day killing seven and wounding ten defenders. However, it was the steady fire from the mortars that proved most deadly because of their high trayectory: The 81 mm mortars inflicted 70 percent of the Bolivian casualties during the siege. The dwindling garrison was in no position to resist for long the onslaught of the reinforced Paraguayan forces; if the ratio of defenders to besiegers had been 1 to 4 on September 9, by September 13 the ratio was 1 to 10.[40]

Once Paraguay showed its determination to establish a formal siege, the evacuation of Boquerón became the only rational military response. The commander of the Bolivian 4th Division soon "painted the situation as most serious" but his superior the corps commander far away in Muñoz "only saw the situation as delicate."[41] At La Paz Chief of Staff Osorio gave the local commanders authority to either resist or withdraw, but the optimism of the corps commander and the political needs of President Salamanca repeatedly cancelled any attempts to evacuate. Bolivian relief forces tried desperately to reach the encircled, and several times patrols managed to establish contact. A strong relief force broke the siege lines on 17 September and coincidentally disrupted a flanking Paraguayan attack, but brought few supplies. Bolivian airplanes in desperation dropped ammunition, food, and coca leaves. The ammunition generally shattered upon landing, and most of the air drops fell into the Paraguayan lines. The strategic equation demanded withdrawal, because as explained earlier, the Paraguayan mobilization had put on the field an army much larger than anything that Bolivia could bring to the front in months. Boquerón had given a good account of itself in the defense of 9 September, but because it was deep in the jaws of the Paraguayan offensive, the Bolivian government and the General Staff had to order the withdrawal of the garrison. Closer to the scene, the commander of the 4th Division ordered the evacuation, but his superiors cancelled the order before it reached the garrison.[42]

Dead bodies hung from Boqueron's barbed wire and piled up around its trenches; the Paraguayans set forest fires to try to lessen the horrible stench with smoke. Because La Paz was totally out of touch with reality, the decision to evacuate Boquerón fell by default to Lieutenant Colonel Marzana. For a commander, the moment can come when saving his unit takes precedence over carrying out his original mission. The groans from the growing number of wounded who were dying because of lack of medical supplies and the dwindling amount of ammunition and food left no alternative but to evacuate. To make things even more unbearable, the Paraguayan shells were targeting the water wells in Boquerón, so that his men had to grope carefully or walk longer distances under the mortar and artillery fire to try to retrieve the precious liquid. The only idea the Bolivian General Staff could imagine to help was to recall the earlier relief column and thus make the food rations last longer for the garrison left behind. Should Marzana evacuate his garrison with the departing relief force? If Marzana waited any longer, the growing number of seriously wounded precluded any escape. The decision to evacuate meant going against a whole career trained in total obedience, while he himself risked court-martial and execution. Command brings unsuspected responsibilities. Once an officer concludes that his unit faces capture or death unless he takes unauthorized actions, to save his men he has to assume any penalty or punishment.[43]

The successful escape of the relief column turned out to be the last chance the garrison had to evacuate. But Marzana—unlike Paraguayan commanders—could not break himself from blind obedience to orders given by distant superiors. His garrison was doomed, unless a miracle intervened. And a miracle almost happened on 24 September. Lieutenant Colonel Rafael Franco reported to Estigarribia that in Villa Militar the pond providing all the water for the Paraguayan troops at Boquerón was showing the first symptoms of spoilage. In no more than a few days the water of the pond would become undrinkable, so unless Paraguay captured the wells of Boquerón, the entire force would have to lift the siege and beat a shameful retreat home. Estigarribia decided to gamble, not on senseless frontal attacks, but on the increasing agility of his soldiers. On 26 September he ordered his men to move as close as possible to the Bolivian trenches in the hope of breaking through the defenses. Under a tremendous covering barrage from machine guns and mortars, the Paraguayans were able to crawl very near to the Bolivian lines. The shortage of ammunition among the defenders contributed to the success of the maneuver. Under orders from Marzana to conserve ammunition to the maximum, the random short bursts from machine guns could not deter the Paraguayans from inching ever closer to the Bolivian lines.

The days of the beleaguered garrison were coming to an end, but the Bolivian generals refused to recognize reality. In a meeting of leading generals on 27 September at Muñoz, the generals reached the conclusion that the garrison needed to hold out 10 more days to give reinforcements time to arrive. When planes dropped the order (and copies fell in the Paraguayan lines), at last Marzana recognized the hopelessness of the situation. It was too late to escape the tight noose the Paraguayans had established, but at least he could end the suffering of his men. He held a meeting of all his remaining officers, and all concluded that no further resistance was possible. Nineteen days of constant bombardment and attack had thoroughly shattered his men both physically and emotionally, and he felt he had no choice but to surrender the garrison on 29 September. As soon as the white flags fluttered, the Paraguayans yelled victory cries so loudly that even Bolivian outposts kilometers away heard the Guaraní yell of "piii–puuu!" The Paraguayans were supremely happy with their victory, but they were no less excited to tap the water wells of Boquerón to quench their thirst in the scorching hot climate.[44]

The Paraguayan soldiers could well use a

day of rest to recover from the exhaustion of the siege, but Estigarribia waited an excessive eight days. During the siege he had refused to deploy some units to the south because he did not have in mind any vigorous pursuit. He was worried about a surprise attack on his rear, and to eliminate this threat, he sent a strong detachment to drive the Bolivians from Toledo (Map 21). Thirty minutes of shooting on 2 October sufficed to send the Bolivians fleeing in panic from Toledo after they had set their buildings on fire. The Paraguayan detachment pressed west and seized Corrales as the Bolivians fled without firing a shot. Even after his rear was secure, Estigarribia still hesitated to push his pursuit, and thus he missed the opportunity to capture many of the demoralized Bolivian units. The ambiguous order of President Ayala of 1 September no doubt had a lingering effect, but the failure to take any steps for a rapid pursuit actually was the first manifestation of Estigarribia's ingrained aversion to bold moves. The capture of Boquerón had ripped such a large hole in the Bolivian defensive line that the Paraguayans still enjoyed the opportunity to seize many strategic positions before the slowly mounting momentum of the Bolivian mobilization made itself felt. Instead, Estigarribia idled away the time while the Bolivians set up defensive positions in the dirt road between Boquerón and Arce. By the time he finally sent some units south to Arce, they faced Bolivian roadblocks near Yucra. Against three divisions the isolated and demoralized Bolivian battalions stood no chance, and by 10 October the Paraguayans easily outflanked Yucra and forced the Bolivians to retreat south to the clearing at Campo de la Mula Muerta (Map 20).[45]

This last clearing was 11 kilometers north of Arce and held the main Bolivian defense line. An immediate pursuit seemed advisable before the Bolivians could complete their defenses, but remarkably on 13 October the order for the Paraguayan 1st Division was to rest. Eventually the Paraguayans brought up their artillery to pound the Bolivian defenses and then began probing attacks on 19 and 20 October. The next day as the Paraguayans continued to pin down the Bolivians in the front line, two Paraguayan regiments quietly hacked a path through the jungle in a flanking move. By noon the Paraguayans broke into the Bolivian rear for the first of many times during the war. As also

happened throughout the war, the surprise appearance in the Bolivian rear immediately provoked panic among the terrified defenders who fled in mass to Arce as soon as they heard the expression "Pilas (Bolivian slang for Paraguayans) in the rear." The spontaneous and swift flight saved most Bolivians from falling prisoner, but the disorganized rabble fleeing south could no longer pose any resistance to the Paraguayan advance. On 22 October Bolivian officers rallied some troops to defend Arce, but a few shells from the Paraguayan artillery sufficed to plunge the Bolivians into a panicky rout south to Alihuatá.[46] As night fell, the last Bolivian officers set fire to the huge arsenal they had hoped to use in the defense of Arce:

> In a few minutes the outpost displayed a fantastic spectacle, as thousands of bullets exploded. An almost blinding illumination lighted up the night and the glow invited our artillery to fire, not occasionally, but in a succession of rounds, as if announcing the requiem of an army, because what was withdrawing was little more than a shadow of its former self.[47]

Paraguayan troops entered Arce on 23 October but then halted. A patrol of thirty soldiers set out to explore the road south on 26 October and to its great surprise reached an abandoned and burning Alihuatá. Even La Paz "recognized the enemy superiority in every type of elements" and was authorizing the local commanders to withdraw as fast as possible to avoid the complete destruction of the Bolivian army.[48] With close to 14,000 soldiers in three divisions heading south towards Saavedra, Estigarribia was bound to "cut off the withdrawal by a flanking attack and sweep to the west of Saavedra. It is timely and necessary to begin an orderly defensive withdrawal to Saavedra and then back along the road to Muñoz before the enemy pressure intensifies as the way to avoid the misfortunes that befell us at Arce."[49] In any case, a speedy withdrawal was the only option left for the Bolivians who were only interested in reaching the Argentine border as fast as possible to desert. If Paraguay pressed forward fast to inflict a crushing defeat, the chance loomed that Bolivia might well abandon the war as hopeless.[50]

The capture of Alihuatá had not been in Estigarribia's timetable and if anything confirmed his fears that the Bolivians were laying a gigantic trap for his army. Convinced that Alihuatá was just bait to lure him deeply to the south, he concluded on the basis of no reliable evidence that a large Bolivian force lay to the west of Arce at Fernández or at least was gathering further west at Platanillos. Once his army had moved towards Saavedra, supposedly this large Bolivian force would strike in his rear and thus cut off his entire army from food, ammunition, and supply. How this fantastic idea entered the mind of Estigarribia has never been explained.[51] Instead of pressing with all his army south to Saavedra, he diverted the 1st and 3rd divisions to the east to counter the expected Bolivian counteroffensive. As soon as the small Bolivian units realized that a massive army was heading their way, they abandoned their positions, and the unopposed Paraguayans occupied Fernández and then entered Platanillos on 6 November. The almost nonexistent Bolivian presence powerfully suggested continuing the westward advance as far as Muñoz or even Ballivián. A swift advance to the Pilcomayo River at those points offered the easiest opportunity to trap the collapsing Bolivian army and probably to end the war in one brilliant strategic maneuver. The disintegrating Bolivian troops could offer no resistance, and the soldiers were obsessed with fleeing to the rear. When officers tired to rally their men, an epidemic of self-inflicted wounds decimated the ranks, and in one case a sergeant killed his lieutenant. If Estigarribia felt the drive to Muñoz or to Ballivián was too bold, then in the south just steady pressure from the remaining 4th Paraguayan Division sufficed to capture Saavedra and to trap the Bolivian army units to the southwest. Instead the order went out for this 4th Division to halt to rest. While officers amused themselves riding the captured horses of the Bolivians at Alihuatá, the precious opportunity to end the war was slipping away.[52]

The Bolivian fear of the unexpected appearance of Paraguayans in the rear had even reached La Paz and made the Bolivian General Staff worry about the exact meaning of the Paraguayan halt. "The lack of action by the enemy is dangerous, probably the result of preparations for encirclement of Saavedra or another concentration of his forces. In any case, we should not delay any longer our projected withdrawal."[53] Perplexed Bolivian officers tried to account for the excessively slow advance by blaming the French military influence on Paraguay. Many Paraguayan officers, including Estigarribia, had studied in the War College of France, and certainly the French predilection for trench warfare was one reason for the slow Paraguayan deployment. However, the personal preference of Estigarribia was not to pursue, and his failure to exploit the breakthrough after Boquerón was merely the first of many instances and also constituted his first major mistake.[54]

The argument can be made that not even the surrender of all the Bolivian army units east of Muñoz could have persuaded the La Paz government to accept peace, and indeed the war later demonstrated that only after many defeats did Bolivia come to the peace table. But even such argument requires not a halt but a relentless pursuit: Estigarribia had the obligation to inflict many crushing defeats as rapidly as possible as the best way to end the war. Already major Bolivian officers had become convinced that victory was impossible, and a major disaster so soon was bound to persuade the army that victory was impossible. After the loss of Boquerón, General Arturo Guillén became the new commander of the I Corps and soon telegraphed the following highly perceptive analysis to the General Staff:

> After exhaustive study and careful meditation, it is my duty to share with the General Staff the following reflections:
> What has occurred so far until today demonstrates beyond any doubt that the collapse of morale among the troops will continue and will extend to the new units formed with arriving reservists. A number of reasons, such as improvised officers, account for this poor morale. [...]
> Situation in general is serious. We lack everything. No matter who the corps commander is, the results will always be barren. The most carefully thought-out instructions can only fail miserably. If soldiers do not heed officers, war cannot be fought, nor can war be fought without all type of items needed for everyday use. [...]
> Even assuming that once we have obtained the large number of trucks—in particular water trucks—indispensable to resist in the staggered lines along the Muñoz–Saavedra road, even then, if we lose the present positions, we still could not hold on to Muñoz. [...]

If we lose Muñoz, then we could not conduct operations nor support troops in the stretch of Muñoz-Ballivián because of insurmountable difficulties such as the lack of outside links and the lack of sufficient water in that stretch.

In case we had to retreat to Ballivián [...] we could not rely on a single one of the soldiers who are now in the front, because they would reach Ballivián in a state of complete disintegration and with no will to fight. [...]

In accordance with the previous considerations, I believe the most correct approach is to try to seek a diplomatic solution before our situation becomes worse. The basic condition for talks is an immediate cease-fire so that we can at least retain the posts we still hold.[55]

General Guillén had revealed some underlying truths about the Chaco War. His prophetic message left no doubt about the outcome of the war. Unless Bolivia quickly rebounded, the methodical Paraguayan steamroller was sure to sweep away all resistance.

Hans Kundt and the Bolivian Counteroffensive

The incompetence of the Bolivian officers and especially of the high command was evident to all. During the Boquerón campaign, Bolivia had lost its best soldiers and the officers most familiar with the Chaco.[56] The loss of Boquerón had shocked La Paz, and the angry outcry was immense because the government had not even hinted at the possibility of a defeat. The search began not just for scapegoats but also for solutions. At rallies and demonstrations starting on October 4, the public clamored for the return of General Hans Kundt; soon a congressional resolution demanded the recall of the German general.[57] Except for his service in World War I, since 1911 this general had toiled patiently to build the Bolivian army, but a bloody coup in 1930 destroyed his home, and he had barely escaped alive to Germany. The soldiers remembered fondly how well he had looked out for their welfare, and most officers admired and even venerated him, although after the war they unanimously denied it. He seemed the only person able to save Bolivia from defeat, but should he fail, as a foreigner he made a convenient scapegoat. President Daniel Salamanca, who did not trust the

loyalty of his officer corps, valued the German general most as a guarantee against any army coup. When the Bolivian government formally requested the return of Kundt, the German communities in Buenos Aires and Asunción protested and demanded that the moribund Weimar Republic keep him home. After some hesitation, the German government stood aside, and General Kundt embarked on a very leisurely trip to Peru. Upon arriving at Lima, President Salamanca offered to fly him to Bolivia, but the general declined and took the winding railroad from Peru. He finally entered La Paz to an enthusiastic and joyful savior's welcome on 5 December 1932.[58]

Why had General Kundt delayed his arrival to Bolivia? Fear of flying was not a factor, and he had not taken the fastest passenger liners across the Atlantic. He well knew how fickle the Bolivian public could be and wanted to make sure that the country was ready to grant him absolute power to wage the war. Any worsening of the military situation of Bolivia increased his bargaining position with the Bolivian government. Once he was in La Paz, he secured independent authority over military operations and over the appointment of officers. Salamanca was most reluctant to grant such vast sweeping powers, but the immense public clamor left him no choice. The president consoled himself with the realization that he was safe from any military coup as long as Kundt was in command of the army.[59] Because after the war all the Bolivian officers depicted Kundt as a bumbling idiot who was responsible for the setbacks, just how competent was the German general? His Paraguayan opponents provided a more accurate assessment:

General Kundt is a man of will who knows his profession. He also knows the psychology of the Bolivians who will latch unto him like a life raft. In addition, if he knows us [the Paraguayans] and the Chaco well, then we are faced with an opponent we need to heed carefully. [...] The entry into action of such an experienced commander [...] can most certainly bring greater efficiency to the enemy army in the immediate future and even change altogether the present situation as time passes swiftly.[60]

The news that General Kundt was coming should have goaded the Paraguayans into a flurry of activity, but nothing could move the imperturbable Estigarribia to speed up the offensive against Saavedra. In contrast, some Bolivian officers were desperate to save face by halting the military collapse before the German general arrived. An orderly withdrawal to Muñoz instead of a collapse was possible only if the Bolivians held Saavedra long enough to allow the retreat of the troops to the south west near Nanawa. (Map 20). The Bolivian commanders hastened the arrival of the mobilized troops and erected defenses at Kilometer 7 of the road between Alihuatá and Saavedra. Along the entire road this was the only spot adequate to delay the Paraguayans. Although the site commanded the open plain to the north, the clearing provided a natural path for an outflanking movement to the west. As the Bolivian soldiers in growing numbers busily strengthened the defensive line at Km. 7, they also occupied the clumps of forest to the north in the middle of the clearing. In contrast to the feverish activity in the Bolivian defense line, only in the first days of November did a Paraguayan regiment of barely 900 men begin the leisurely stroll south from Alihuatá down the jungle road. To the soldiers' great surprise, the jungle gave way to a large plain at Km. 12. Ahead the Paraguayans saw islands of thick forest in the middle of the plain; patrols dimly could see to the south an unbroken line of jungle at the ridge on Km. 7.[61]

On November 5 the forward units of the Paraguayan regiment advanced across the field to try to capture the forested islands, but machine gun fire soon pinned down the center. The attacking units promptly began a flanking maneuver around the islands to the rear and moved so fast as to capture most of the Bolivian defenders. The next day the rest of the Paraguayan regiment arrived to support the expected advance south to Km. 7, but soon the soldiers realized they had fallen into a trap. Massed Bolivian artillery poured a constant fire into pre-plotted targets in the islands, while the Bolivian machine guns raked the Paraguayan positions. Snipers on top of the trees carefully spotted targets during the day and then fired at the Paraguayans during the night to keep them on edge at every moment. Casualties mounted, and to try to relieve the pressure on the pinned-down Paraguayans, Estigarribia moved a second regiment south from Alihuatá.[62]

Once the Bolivians realized they faced only a weak regiment, they decided to launch a counterattack with 3,500 men on 10 November. The plan called for the attacking force to go around the wide open field far to the west and then to enter the thick forest to the north to cut off the supply road of the Paraguayan regiment. Carrying out the sound plan was not easy, because the unbroken series of defeats and retreats had left the Bolivian soldiers so demoralized that they were extremely reluctant to abandon their trenches. Afraid to stray too far into the jungle, the Bolivians did not make the wide flanking movement to the west the plan called for. Instead, they turned too soon to cut off the road and emerged from the jungle just at the moment that the second Paraguayan regiment was heading south. As the arriving regiment repulsed the Bolivian flanking movement, the Paraguayan officers promptly realized the danger to their entire position and ordered the original Paraguayan regiment to retreat from the forested islands back to Km. 12. The mettle of the troops ultimately decided the outcome: A less vigorous Paraguayan response at the tactical level and a more aggressive Bolivian push could still have given the attackers a wonderful victory. Instead, the unexpected Paraguayan resistance destroyed any fighting spirit among the demoralized Bolivian soldiers, who all too quickly returned to their trenches to await the next Paraguayan offensive against Saavedra.[63]

Clearly a frontal attack could not dislodge the numerous and well-entrenched Bolivian defenders at Km. 7. Estigarribia recalled the two divisions from Platanillos, unaware that his action threw away the final chance to end the war. The hurried Bolivian concentration of troops at Km. 7 had left the rear unprotected, and only platoons stood in the way of Paraguayan divisions poised to advance from Platanillos to Muñoz. The danger was so real that for months afterwards Bolivian commanders continued to agonize about the danger to Saavedra if the Paraguayans attempted a wide enough westward movement. Thus, until then the successful defense at Km. 7 had been only a delaying action to make possible an orderly retreat of the Bolivian forces; indeed, the day after his arrival at La Paz, General Kundt ratified the order for the withdrawal to Muñoz. But as Kundt read the reports coming in from the front, the slowness of the Paraguayan pursuit stood out starkly. Bolivian officers repeatedly pleaded with him to stay at Km. 7, and he was most hesitant to dash their recovering desire to fight. A deciphered Paraguayan telegram postponing the attack on Saavedra clinched the argument, and on 7 December he canceled the evacuation order.[64]

The decision to hold Saavedra was momentous for Bolivia and was the first mistake of Kundt who had condemned the Bolivian Army to a very risky campaign of attrition in the eastern Chaco. A defense at Muñoz, as General Arturo Guillén had argued on 11 November, had the best chance of success and promised to spare Bolivia crushing defeats. Instead, the eastern Chaco was the region furthest from the Bolivian supply bases. But because each successive withdrawal increased the defeatism in the Bolivian army, stopping the Paraguayans at Km. 7 seemed the best way to restore morale among the flagging Bolivian soldiers. The possibility of preserving a Bolivian presence in the eastern Chaco also appealed to Kundt, who thus could enhance his prestige as the savior of Bolivia.[65]

On 8 December Estigarribia unleashed his long-awaited offensive. While the Paraguayan 2nd and 4th divisions tied down the Bolivians on the road to Saavedra, the 1st Division attempted to outflank the Bolivians to the west. The maneuver came a month too late, because the Bolivians had used the extra time to extend their defense line further west. Massed artillery hidden in the woods shattered the Paraguayan march across the clearing, and just the lead Paraguayan unit lost half of its men. Renewed Paraguayan attacks merely resulted in more bloody repulses until Estigarribia abandoned the offensive. The front between Km. 7 and Km. 12 settled into trench warfare from December 1932 until March 1933; localized raids and active patrolling ran up large casualty figures on both sides without altering the strategic stalemate.[66]

General Kundt and the Bolivian officers did not know that Estigarribia had lost any desire to renew the offensive, and they continued to worry needlessly about the defense of Saavedra. Because the western end of the defense line at Km. 7 still hung on air, the German general believed that a larger Paraguayan force could still carry out an outflanking movement. He

concluded that his two options were either to extend his line further to the west to block any wide Paraguayan sweep or instead to take the offensive himself. For the first time he had enough soldiers, because the partial Bolivian mobilization at last was bringing ample troops to the front and gave Bolivia a numerical superiority it retained for the rest of the war. Out of the arriving troops he organized the new 8th Division to open a new front in the north. In a series of swift attacks, the 8th Division drove a small Paraguayan unit out of Platanillos on 13 December 1932 and captured other nearby posts in the following days. The climax of this offensive came with the Bolivian recapture of Corrales on 1 January 1933. The logical next step was the recapture of Toledo, but General Kundt felt that further advance in that direction merely increased the Paraguayan logistical advantage. He already realized that the ability to supply his troops was the important factor affecting their success. The larger the Bolivian forces, the greater the strain on the supply line. Trucks had to carry cargoes by dirt road for at least one thousand kilometers from the nearest railroad head; in contrast the railroad heads of the Paraguayans were no more than 200 kilometers distant from the front. The border towns in Argentina provided gasoline and some foodstuffs, but the bulk of the supplies and all the equipment still had to come from the interior of Bolivia.[67]

Nanawa was the key to break the logistical and strategic stalemate. West of that point and sloping gently to the Paraguay River pastures suitable for grazing appeared. Even if the Paraguayans removed their herds from the ranches, the cattle of the Bolivians could survive on the ample grasses as was impossible to do on the scrub vegetation of the Chaco proper. Not having to bring fodder, the Bolivian trucks could then carry more food, gasoline, ammunition and weapons. The capture of Nanawa likewise made possible rapid advances either to the Paraguay River or to the north and threatened the entire Paraguayan defense system. For their part, Bolivian officers had long considered Nanawa ideal for an attack. Tactically, Nanawa offered an excellent field of fire for the Bolivian artillery, whose observers enjoyed the best view in the entire Chaco. General Kundt, who believed that the Paraguayans were sufficiently distracted with the Bolivian offensive to the north at Corrales, concluded that the moment to capture Nanawa had arrived.[68]

His assault plan called for three separate detachments to converge simultaneously from different directions and to advance after a heavy bombardment from artillery and airplanes (Map 23). In preparatory meetings Kundt met with the officers to see if they understood the plan and if they had any doubts or objections. Although Kundt encouraged open discussions, the presence of this decorated World War I hero was too intimidating to officers who knew only blind obedience; rather than raise misgivings, each one strove to be the most enthusiastic supporter of the plan. At 0600 on 20 January 1933 under a heavy barrage, the detachments on the south and in the center began crossing the large open fields; they were supposed to do everything possible to monopolize the attention of the Paraguayans. The intensity of the attack caught the defenders by surprise, and to stop the onrushing Bolivians, the Paraguayan commander sent all his reserves to the southern and central flanks.

The situation was perfect for the third Bolivian detachment to deliver the knockout blow against the weakly held northern flank. On the north the jungle came very close to Nanawa and thus offered an additional guarantee of surprise. The northern detachment had set out the night before at 2200, but soon lost itself in the thick woods. All the men had to pass though a narrow footpath made impassable by a torrential downpour. As dawn broke, the northern detachment heard the start of the attack on the southern and central flanks, but the wet and cold soldiers were still far from the battlefield. By then the Paraguayans had already detected the presence of the struggling and noisy Bolivians in the north. Not until the next day did the weary detachment finally emerge from the jungle to begin the attack. But by that time the Bolivian assaults on the south and the west had stalled, and the Paraguayans were free to shift units north to resist the attack on the second day. However, the defenders were down to their last five cartridges, and under orders to conserve ammunition, the Paraguayans spotted but did not shoot at the truck carrying General Kundt on his personal inspection of the front.

By the time Kundt found fresh troops to renew the attacks, three Paraguayan planes made risky landings in a partially cleared field to deliver boxes of ammunition. With the Paraguayans again able to fire back, the final Bolivian attack failed. Upon close observation, Isla Fortificada, a clump of thick woods, emerged as the key to Nanawa. In a final effort on 24 January, the Bolivian artillery rained 3,000 shells on this position, panicking its dazed defenders into flight. The Bolivian officer in front reported the flight of the Paraguayans but in an incredible omission did not send his men to occupy the abandoned Isla Fortificada. By the time headquarters received the report and promptly ordered him to attack immediately, it was already early the next day. During the delay Paraguayan officers forced their men at pistol point back to Isla Fortificada in time to repel the belated attack. Although raids and counter raids continued for several days, by 24 January it was clear that the campaign to capture Nanawa had failed.[69]

The setback at Nanawa in no way eliminated the need to stay on the offensive to keep the Paraguayans off balance, for otherwise they could launch an outflanking movement to force the Bolivians to withdraw to Muñoz. To keep the Paraguayans guessing as to the Bolivian intentions, Kundt opted for a series of attacks along the entire front, the two most important being those on Alihuatá and on Toledo. Aerial photographs reported the existence of a jungle trail to the west of Alihuatá; if the trail was widened, enough troops could pass to outflank the 1st Paraguayan Division at Km. 12 and thus end permanently the pressure on Saavedra. Kundt assigned the task to the raw recruits of the newly forming 9th Division, which began its advance on 10 February. As the 9th Division laboriously and slowly hacked its way through the dense jungle under stifling heat, to the northwest the 3rd Division was riding on trucks to Toledo.

The relatively easy capture of Corrales and nearby posts persuaded the Bolivian divisional commander that a push forward against Toledo (Map 21) had every likelihood of success, and this show of offensive spirit encouraged Kundt who readily assented to the operation. In reality, scarcity of gasoline for his water trucks had forced the Paraguayan commander, General Juan Ayala, to station only small detachments at the posts the Bolivians had captured so easily. At Toledo General Ayala decided to make a stand because its water wells eliminated the need for costly transport. He grouped his men into separate defense clusters instead of into one continuous line; his plan was to let the Bolivians advance unopposed through the gaps until the Paraguayans could open a murderous cross fire from their defense posts. The steady arrival of recruits increased the Paraguayan numbers, but the shortage of

officers made General Ayala hesitant to demand too much from his inexperienced men. He did launch a brief counterattack against Corrales to keep the Bolivians off balance and then withdrew in good order back to Toledo. On 10 February the Bolivians took up positions in front of Toledo and began an incessant artillery barrage. For the next 16 days a Bolivian

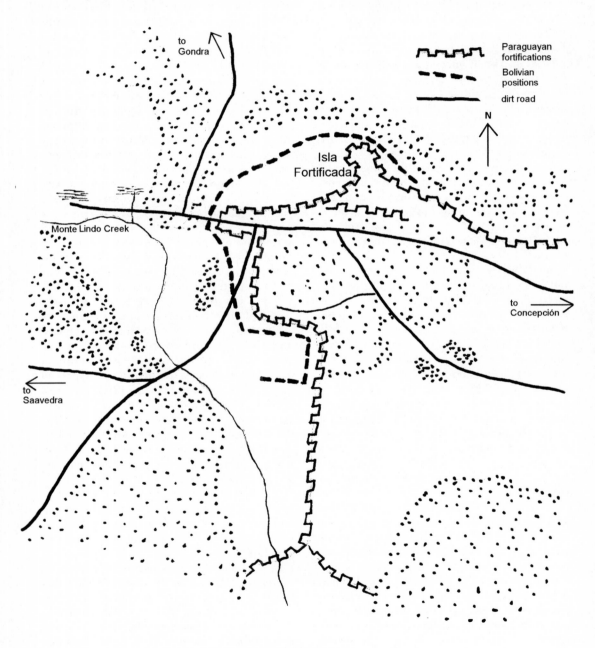

Map 23. Nanawa.

cannon fired on the average every two minutes; because the firing took place in a random manner, the horrendous waste of artillery shells had no other effect than to deplete the Bolivian stocks in the eastern Chaco permanently.[70]

On 25 February Bolivian bombers also came to pound the Paraguayan positions. The next day artillery delivered the fiercest barrage to provide cover for the first wave of Bolivian attackers. At 1300 the Bolivian troops enthusiastically ran forward through the gaps among the Paraguayan posts and plunged deeper into the trap; the Bolivians believed they were winning, but it was only good luck because at a critical point a Paraguayan heavy machine gun jammed. As the Paraguayans opened up a murderous barrage, the increasing crossfire gradually took its toll, and by nightfall volleys of concentrated rifle fire had pinned down the Bolivians. On 27 February the Bolivians resumed the attack but with much less enthusiasm than before, and in two charges they lost 1200 in dead, wounded, and missing. Sporadic combat took place on the following days, and on 2 March the Paraguayans were still expecting a final desperate assault from the Bolivians. The attack never came, as the utterly demoralized Bolivians refused to charge. The Bolivians later blamed the drunkenness of the commander for the disintegration of the 3rd Division, but the real reason was the Bolivian insistence on making disastrous frontal attacks.[71] Fortunately for the demoralized Bolivians, General Ayala did not immediately counterattack and waited some days before sending out patrols to gather information. One patrol returned on 9 March with a captured report that revealed the layout and the small numbers of the devastated Bolivian 3rd Division.[72]

General Ayala was surprised to learn the small size of the opposing force, and at last he ordered a counterattack on 10 March. He planned to tie down the Bolivians in the center, while larger forces marched to encircle the left and right flanks. Although the Paraguayan recruits were learning fast, they still had not mastered the complex maneuver of a double encirclement. As the barefoot soldiers struggled trying to find their way through the thick jungle, shots rang out in the center. Unknown to the Paraguayans, the frightened Bolivians had already decided to flee as soon as firing resumed. In the race to the rear, the Bolivians

abandoned considerable amounts of equipment and supplies; two regiments mutinied and stampeded down the road without their officers. Clearly Ayala had waited too many days after 2 March to launch the counterattack. Pursuit was no longer possible, because Ayala had to send all his trucks and some units to Estigarribia. The latter needed them as part of his efforts to try to rescue the Paraguayan 1st Division that was by this time trapped on Km. 12.[73]

The contrast between the Bolivian offensives at Toledo and at Alihuatá was most striking. While the 3rd Bolivian Division had been disintegrating at Toledo, the 9th Bolivian Division had been hacking its way through the jungle in stifling heat. Bolivian officers had believed that this undermanned division of just 1200 men was too small to challenge the large Paraguayan force believed to be stationed at Alihuatá. General Kundt reasoned otherwise, because he counted on Estigarribia removing forces from other fronts to hold off the Bolivian attack at Nanawa. Kundt was right because the Paraguayan 4th Division, originally stationed at Alihuatá, had departed to help the defenders at Nanawa and left behind only 250 soldiers. Meanwhile the commander of the 1st Division, Colonel Carlos José Fernández, had learned from prisoner interrogations that the Bolivians were carrying out a flanking maneuver around Alihuatá. In a serious mistake, Estigarribia refused to believe the reports from the 1st Division. Even when a patrol detected the 9th Bolivian Division near Alihuatá, the Paraguayan commander insisted on dismissing the movement as overblown aggressive patrolling. A major disaster was looming, but fortunately for the Paraguayans and for the first of many times during the war, a small Paraguayan unit held off a much larger Bolivian force starting on 10 March. The small Paraguayan garrison repulsed repeated attacks and inflicted casualties of nearly 200 before finally having to withdraw on 13 March. The constant Bolivian attacks should have persuaded Estigarribia to rush reinforcements while he still had time; just sending 500 soldiers would have sufficed to retain Alihuatá and to keep open the supply road south to the Paraguayan 1st Division. Instead, he did nothing, because he remained a prisoner of his conclusion that the failed campaign on Toledo had so drained the Bolivians that they were incapable of launching another offensive. Contrary to all evidence, he insisted on believing that only a weak patrol was responsible for the repeated attacks on Alihuatá.[74]

Estigarribia locked himself into an increasingly unreal view of the strategic situation. As early as 11 March, even while the Paraguayan garrison was still holding out at Alihuatá, Colonel Fernández had very presciently asked for permission to withdraw his 1st Division before the Bolivians captured its supply road, but a totally startled Estigarribia categorically refused. Fernández had ammunition for three days and food for six; and once the Bolivians gained control of his only supply road on 13 March, he knew that his division was headed for surrender unless he acted quickly. Fernández immediately sent his men up the road to Alihuatá to explore an escape route at Km. 22, where a narrow trail led off to the east to Gondra and linked up with the later famous clearing of Campo Vía. Fernández put soldiers to widen the trail feverishly so that his division could escape with all its equipment, but the mounting Bolivian pressure from the south at Km. 12 had become almost unbearable by 15 March. He set up a roadblock at Km. 31 to detain the southward push of the Bolivian 9th Division, which itself was under heavy attack from the north by the forces Estigarribia was at last starting to scrape together. Estigarribia had meanwhile created another unreal image that made him confident of trapping the Bolivians in Alihuatá. To complete his fantastic paper maneuver, he told Colonel Fernández that it was his duty and that of the 1st Division to hold out until relief arrived on 20 March. The assurances of future help recalled to Fernández the similar promises air dropped to the starving Bolivian garrison at Boquerón in September 1932, and he did not intend to repeat the mistake of the Bolivian Colonel Manuel Marzana. A direct order from Estigarribia made Fernández postpone his planned withdrawal on 15 March, but when no relief appeared, the divisional commander decided to act on his own. The Bolivian pressure increased on 17 March when an angry Kundt, unable to understand why his troops had still not closed the circle around the Paraguayan 1st Division, ordered the Bolivian forces to attack around the clearing to outflank the Paraguayan trenches at Km. 12; had Kundt intervened ear-

lier to take personal command of the offensive instead of relying on his subordinates, the Paraguayan 1st Division probably could not have escaped. That very night Fernández sensed that an overwhelming Bolivian attack was imminent. Realizing that his troops were fast reaching the limit of their endurance, he began the evacuation in defiance of Estigarribia's orders. The 3,000 men of the 1st Division silently left Km. 12 and made it back to Gondra without losing any of their equipment or weapons. The next day, after the rear guard of the division had taken the turn at Km. 22 and was marching east, the detachment holding the roadblock on Km. 31 retreated and safely rejoined the rest of the division at Gondra.[75] Estigarribia's failure to realize the fatal danger at Alihuatá almost cost him his best division, but fortunately the disobedience of his divisional commander turned what could have been a possible disaster into merely the loss of worthless real estate.

The Turning Point for Hans Kundt: The Battle of Nanawa

The capture of Alihuatá drove the Paraguayans away from Km. 12 and thus removed the long-standing threat of a flanking attack around Saavedra. The Bolivians could feel comfortable about retaining their positions in the eastern Chaco. Minor changes were still possible, but unless one side committed a major blunder, the war had reached equilibrium. The moment for a cease-fire and a boundary settlement based on the front line arrived for the first time since the war had begun. Eusebio Ayala, the president of Paraguay, had never accepted the war and was constantly looking for any excuse to end it. Estigarribia, with his vaunted caution and slow reactions, openly admitted Paraguay was on the defensive and was more than ready to halt the war that had already cost the small population of Paraguay more lives than it could bear. Daniel Salamanca, the Bolivian president, sensed the time was approaching for negotiations, and since April he urged General Hans Kundt to stay on the defensive unless an attack was sure to be successful. Unfortunately, the modest Bolivian advance had emboldened the

Bolivian officers who had no intention of ending the war prematurely. Their enthusiasm seemed genuine and persuaded Kundt to prosecute the war vigorously. By early 1933 the Bolivian army was large enough to overwhelm the Paraguayan defenders, provided of course, that Bolivia could put and support those soldiers in the Chaco. The 1,000 kilometer supply line had proved a formidable barrier, and reluctantly General Kundt refused to accept more troops because he simply could not feed them. In early April the scarcity of gasoline not only ruled out any offensive, but also forced putting his men on half rations.[76] The logistical nightmare after the capture of Alihuatá suggested that Bolivia should negotiate a boundary settlement along the existing front line.

Kunddt did not press hard enough to end the war and to turn over the conflict to the diplomats, and in any case he knew that the Bolivian government could not politically accept a cease-fire so far from the Paraguay River. Rather than concentrating all their efforts on defending the very exposed conquests at Alihuatá, Salamanca and the Bolivian officers could not resist testing the Chaco and its Paraguayan defenders one more time. The shameful collapse of the attack on Toledo and the failure to capture the Paraguayan 1st Division at Alihuatá did not prevent the Bolivian officers from dangerously overestimating their own capabilities.

The main dispute among the Bolivian officers was not over whether but over where to launch another offensive. The offensive could go to the north against Arce or to the east against Nanawa, and debate swirled over the two alternatives. Gradually most Bolivian officers came to accept that the capture of Arce was the best and easiest next step for the Bolivian army. Kundt was among those not convinced, but he did not want to dampen unduly the reviving offensive spirit of his formerly demoralized officers. Because the rains had made the roads in the low-lying lands leading to Nanawa virtually impassable, that objective remained out of reach for some time. Instead, once the downpours slackened, an offensive was possible on the firmer soils further to the north. The plan called for the 36th Regiment of the 9th Division to march around the jungle to outflank the Paraguayan position immediately north of Alihuatá, while the rest of this division

pushed north against the Paraguayan road-blocks up the road to Arce. From the west the 8th Division had the mission of tying down the Paraguayan defenders at Fernández so that they could not send reinforcements via the road to Arce. The always alert Paraguayans on the outskirts of Alihuatá caught wind of some impending move, and on 3 May abandoned their very vulnerable first defense line. They withdrew up the road to previously prepared positions just a few kilometers to the south of Arce.[77] In spite of this precautionary move, the Paraguayans were totally surprised when on 14 May the 36th Regiment emerged from a jungle path into the rear of the Paraguayan lines. The Bolivian commander, instead of promptly attacking with his 800 men, withdrew them ten kilometers while he himself marched back to obtain orders. Later General Kundt commented bitterly on this priceless lost opportunity: "The leadership of the 36th Regiment has nothing comparable in the military history of this campaign; it could not have been worse or more disastrous."[78] By the time the commander obtained the order to attack promptly, the Paraguayans had hurriedly gathered forces to mount repeated assaults on the 36th Regiment until it collapsed and fled in panic into the jungle with most of the men suffering excruciating deaths from lack of water.

The 9th Division tried to redeem its reputation by bloody frontal assaults on the entrenched Paraguayan positions south of Arce but only managed to run up high casualties. Any remaining hope of capturing Arce rested on the Bolivian 8th Division, which seemed to be enjoying good luck. The discovery of an old Indian trail promised to bring Bolivian troops to the rear of Fernández on the road to Arce. The extremely scarce local Indians had offered to lead the Bolivians who would thus be well positioned to capture both Fernández and Arce. As a further guarantee, the two best regiments in the entire Bolivian army were making this flanking move; the march started off with an amazing 16 kilometers covered the first day. Then things went wrong: "The trail takes another direction, the Indian guides vanish, the forest becomes too thick, the incessant rain turns the trail to mud."[79] By 31 May the bitter cold and torrential downpours had weakened the soldiers who were running out of food; the entire 8th Division was bogged down and the officers wanted to call it quits. On 1 June Kundt felt he had no choice but to halt the campaign.

The end of the offensive found the northernmost Bolivian outposts just a few kilometers south of Arce. Indispensable as this forward line had been to sustain the offensive against the Paraguayans, it lost all value once the offensive collapsed. Indeed, this exposed first line was downright dangerous, as the chief of staff of the 9th Bolivian Division pointed out on 10 June. The 9th Division was left with a very long exposed flank in the jungle to the west of the road Alihuatá-Arce; he urged a withdrawal to the original defense line just north of Alihuatá.[80] The divisional commander thought otherwise, among other reasons because "of the psychology of our troops, who consider any withdrawal to be a retreat and thus lose their confidence."[81] The divisional chief of staff had expressed a heresy, and he soon was sacked. In addition, political pressures dictated retaining every scrap of worthless Chaco real estate. Bolivian troops remained just south of Arce, offering themselves more like victims for whatever offensive the Paraguayans decided to mount. The decision in June to hold this furthermost front line was the first link in the chain of events that made possible the disaster of Campo Vía in December.[82]

No Paraguayan offensive was possible as long as General Kundt disposed of enough reserves to rush to any threatened area. If in April not all the Bolivians were convinced of the need for peace to end the costly stalemate, in May the disastrous failure of the offensive at Arce should have persuaded all Bolivians to seek a negotiated settlement. Bolivia, at the extreme limit of its supply lines, could not overwhelm the Paraguayans so near their bases. Kundt had inherited an army in shambles fleeing to the rear in December 1932 and had restored its will to fight, but without better officers he simply could not do more. The moment to call the diplomats again had come, but Kundt could not accept the fact that Bolivia had exhausted its abilities to mount offensives. Salamanca was so insistent on staying on the defensive, that Kundt demanded a direct presidential order forbidding any more offensives. The General also dangled the bait of the hope of a victory in the war and left the president in a quandary.

In retrospect Salamanca should have issued the formal order he had drafted, but he could not resist the political benefits that the bait of victory promised. For his part, Kundt should have insisted on ending the war at this moment, thus allowing him to leave with his reputation untarnished as the savior of the Bolivian Chaco.[83] But the General could not bring himself to admit that his years of work with the Bolivian Army had been largely in vain. In many ways he was the creator of the Bolivian army, and as a paternalistic teacher with bad pupils, he repeatedly gave them one more chance to improve their grades. His emotional attachment blinded him to the reality that with the existing personnel it was humanly impossible to do anything else to improve the Bolivian officers who if anything were beyond redemption. All the previous offensives had amply proven that the Bolivian units were incapable of independent initiative or of coordinated movements at any level. To worsen the problem, the shortage of skilled officers was already reaching critical proportions, and to try to compensate for the shortage, Kundt plunged deeper into the tactical minutiae of each unit, thus losing that general perspective indispensable for an army commander. He was always the teacher among his men and never lost the hope that his soldiers, after repeating the same mistakes many times, would finally learn how to perform correctly in combat. Many Bolivian officers did not share his optimism and vented their desperation by sending totally depressing reports to headquarters. Some of the reports turned out to be exaggerated, but in the main they were right. Kundt himself realized that the Bolivians units were afraid of the jungle and suffered an inferiority complex about the Paraguayans who seemed to thrive in the jungle. He himself admitted that "it had become practically impossible to make the Bolivian soldier leave his trenches."[84]

Kundt was just one step away from reaching the final and inevitable conclusion that the Bolivian army was incapable of any further offensive. For their part, the senior Paraguayan officers met at a strategy meeting in late June to consider possible offensives and concluded instead that the war had reached a stalemate. Estigarribia felt strongly that other than very localized actions, any offensive, no matter how promising, was simply beyond the resources of Paraguay. In any case, he concluded that Paraguay could not even think of any offensive until the outcome of the Bolivian buildup at Nanawa became clear. Implicit in the Paraguayan discussions was the assumption that even without the threat to Nanawa, the Bolivians were too strong to drive back. The situation was ripening towards a diplomatic settlement, and on 6 June a newspaper in Asunción floated the trial balloon of a peace without winners or losers. Kundt should have seized the newspaper article as the cue to press for a diplomatic solution, but misled by the false and in many cases duplicitous enthusiasm of his officers, he inclined towards renewing the attack on Nanawa. Only one officer still insisted on maintaining the pressure on Arce, and most sent written statements supporting the attack on Nanawa. At a final meeting on 30 June with all his commanders, Kundt gave them the opportunity to express any misgivings about the general plan or the specifics of the assault. Led by the sinister Lieutenant Colonel David Toro, once again the officers tripped over themselves to appear the most enthusiastic about the proposed attack. They were eager to disprove the Paraguayan news article of 6 June and were determined to show that victory in the Chaco was still possible. For Kundt to cancel the planned offensive in the face of such extraordinary support was beyond his capabilities. Emotionally involved in the growth of his former students, he decided to give them another chance. Kundt's first major mistake as commander had been to cancel the withdrawal to Muñoz in December 1932, and at this moment he made his second error of ordering the assault on Nanawa.[85]

Kundt was certainly taking a big gamble by returning to Nanawa, the scene of his earlier defeat in January. Misleading reports from Bolivian officers, especially from Lieutenant Colonel Toro, persuaded Kundt that the situation was ripe for a major breakthrough at Nanawa. The site offered the same attractions as in January, but by June the Paraguayans had enjoyed plenty of time to excavate an extensive defense network (Map 23). No surprise was possible, because captured prisoners and espionage had confirmed that Bolivia was massing for a major assault on Nanawa. Because the horseshoe shape of the defenses favored the attackers, in anticipation of a breakthrough the Paraguayans started to dig additional trench lines further to the rear. Aerial photography revealed these secondary defense lines, and Kundt mistakenly concluded that the Paraguayans at most planned to make a fighting withdrawal from Nanawa to their other lines in the rear. Wildly exaggerated reports about how Paraguayan officers needed to wield pistols to maintain discipline persuaded some Bolivian officers that the Paraguayans could not resist a massive attack. The Bolivian officer corps once again failed to realize to what extremes the Paraguayans were willing to go in their war of national survival.[86]

Kundt had prepared a sound plan of attack for the capture of Nanawa. The problem was not with the plan but with its implementation.[87] Although the Bolivians had only a slight superiority in the number of troops, their superior firepower and the horseshoe front gave them additional advantages. However, to make their firepower effective, the Bolivians had to coordinate the artillery shelling and the aerial bombardment with the deployment of tanks and flame throwers. The infantry had never trained with these new weapons before, and the scarce officers, who traditionally had fumbled the simplest infantry maneuvers, could not be expected to provide the necessary guidance and leadership. The tanks were an unknown variable; Bolivia had tried to use tanks to lift the siege of Boquerón, but they had always broken down before reaching the combat zone. The outrageous waste of shells at the failed attack on Toledo had so depleted the stocks in the eastern Chaco that Bolivia needed months to replenish its supply. Just the scarcity of artillery shells should have convinced Kundt of the need to postpone the attack indefinitely. The mandatory bombardment lasting many days to shatter the fortifications and to daze the defenders was simply not possible. Instead, the artillery had barely enough shells to lay down one brief barrage before having to shift to the rolling barrage that normally preceded the advancing infantry. Furthermore, the attack on Nanawa in January had revealed that the Paraguayan bunkers were built so solidly that they withstood even direct hits from small caliber artillery. The scarcity of shells was most acute for the few 105 mm. cannons, the only ones that could make a dent in the Paraguayan bunkers. Kundt was aware of the problem and counted on the forward observers to take maximum advantage of the excellent visibility to do very accurate plotting; unlike at Toledo, he expected each shell to score a direct hit at Nanawa. Furthermore, to spare the need for counter battery fire, he directed his bomber planes to destroy the Paraguayan artillery. As the preparations went forward, quietly sappers were tunneling under Isla Fortificada to plant a gigantic explosive charge; once this key bastion in the Paraguayan defense line was blown into the sky, Bolivian troops would pour though the breach and isolate the remaining defenders.[88]

The front line stretched nearly twenty kilometers and the Paraguayans realized that a concentrated Bolivian attack could probably pierce their defense lines. To stop these inroads, the Paraguayans kept in reserve sizable units that they would use only when the direction of the main Bolivian attack had become clear. As sunlight broke late in the short winter day of 4 July 1933, the Bolivian cannons and heavy machine guns opened fire. After a barrage of a half hour, the infantry prepared to storm the Paraguayan positions. Kundt had correctly concentrated his attack on the north and south sides of the horseshoe, although troops along the center did attempt some assaults. The advance in the south was the only one that had to go through thick jungle. Not surprisingly, the Bolivian troops got lost and confused, and by the time they reached the well-entrenched Paraguayan lines, the rolling artillery barrage had moved far north and left the Bolivian troops at the mercy of the Paraguayan machine guns. The flame throwers desperately hurled their fire beyond effective range until all their personnel died in the forest. The bloody repulse need not have been the end of the attack, because further to the east on the open plain, the supporting tanks had broken through the defense lines unopposed as the frightened Paraguayan soldiers scurried to safety from the iron monsters. For the first time the Bolivians had achieved the earnestly desired breakthrough, and victory was within their grasp. Inexplicably, no Bolivian infantry had accompanied the two tanks, and their commanders, feeling exposed and isolated, retreated; the Paraguayan infantry reoccupied their trenches and the tanks never returned; artillery fire and mechanical failure later immobilized them.

The diversionary attack in the center was

going as expected, and the outcome of the battle hinged on events in the northern front. The signal for the attack to begin was the detonation of the explosives under Isla Fortificada. Captured prisoners had alerted the Paraguayans about the subterranean excavations, but frantic soundings and diggings had failed to reveal any tunneling under the Paraguayan bastion. Independent of these reports, the Paraguayans had already decided to shorten their excessively long defense line and abandoned their forward positions at Isla Fortificada. At 0905 the explosive charges went off not under Isla Fortificada itself but under the recently abandoned forward trenches. The explosion created a large funnel shape hole in front of Isla Fortificada, which remained intact; in any case, the dynamite charge had been too small to shatter the bastion even if the sappers had placed it in the correct spot.

Under cover of the huge billowing cloud of smoke and dirt, the Bolivian infantry charged with exemplary courage across no-man's land. Although taking very heavy casualties, they managed to reach the line of trenches behind and to the north of Isla Fortificada. On the other side a huge tank cleared the path for the Bolivian infantrymen who likewise managed to complete the encirclement of Isla Fortificada. A decisive breakthrough appeared imminent, but the infantry stopped when direct artillery hits put the tank out of action. To try to stabilize the front, the Paraguayan divisional commander threw in all his local reserves into the battle. At this moment Estigarribia had to decide whether to throw in the army reserves to try to recover the lost positions. By 1400 Estigarribia had seen enough to conclude that the main Bolivian attack had come in the north; he threw in a first wave of reserves into the battle, and soon the Paraguayans had restored contact with the isolated company that continued to cling desperately to Isla Fortificada. The supposedly silenced Paraguayan artillery had converted the funnel depression in front of Isla Fortificada into a killing zone. In spite of the fearful slaughter, the day ended with the Bolivians still in control of the trenches to the north of Isla Fortificada. Estigarribia decided to take advantage of the Bolivians' fear of the dark to launch attacks with his last reserves at 0200 on 5 July. After ferocious hand-to-hand fighting, the

Paraguayan dexterity with machetes and hand grenades again carried the day. Kundt desperately sent reinforcements to try to hold the captured trenches only to see the remaining Bolivian defenders killed or captured.[89]

Some random attacks and intermittent shelling continued over the next days, but the battle was over by daybreak on 5 July. The carnage from the frontal assaults had been atrocious, and Bolivia lost some of its best soldiers in this battle. Estigarribia later described the carnage:

> On 14 July I personally inspected the battlefield and witnessed the most macabre spectacles of my entire life. In those areas where the Bolivians had broken our line and penetrated farthest into our defensive network, fragments of legs and arms blasted by our artillery were still hanging from the trees. In one spot a Paraguayan and a Bolivian soldier had died in mortal embrace when after ferocious hand-to-hand fighting the grenade the Paraguayan carried in his backpack exploded killing them both. This was clear from the fact that the hip of the Paraguayan was shattered next to the side of the pocket with the explosives.
>
> What I noticed afterwards was even worse. Because the battlefield was covered with so many cadavers, the order was to burn them. Instead of placing firewood among the cadavers to keep the fire going until they disintegrated, the soldiers simply piled up and drenched the dead bodies with kerosene. While the fuel lasted, the incineration proceeded smoothly, but when the kerosene ran out, an atrocious pile of human flesh remained charred and casting off an unbearable stench.[90]

Bolivian casualties were at least five thousand in captured, killed, or wounded, while Paraguayan losses were considerably smaller, with only 159 killed and about 400 wounded. More significant than the actual numbers was the impact on the Bolivian army that never really recovered from the failed attack. The superiority of the Paraguayan soldier became accepted dogma, when in reality only the Bolivian officers were inferior. Low self-esteem and recurrent bouts of depression became the norm for this demoralized army. Henceforth only vastly superior numbers and overwhelming firepower could tempt the Bolivian troops to challenge the numerically inferior but nimbler and supremely confident Paraguayans.[91] The battle of Nanawa also was the turning

point in Kundt's generalship. He had committed the blunder that at last allowed the Paraguayans to resume the offensive in the jungle regions of the eastern Chaco. However, complete disaster had not yet overtaken the Bolivian army, and Kundt could still partially redeem his reputation by concentrating not on retaining real estate, but on saving his army.

From Nanawa to the Battle of Campo Vía

At first sight the magnitude of the Paraguayan victory at Nanawa was not evident. Bolivia had not lost any ground because the Paraguayans, who had learned very well at Boquerón how costly were frontal attacks, did not counterattack. The fixed nature of the trench lines at Nanawa and throughout the theater of war was totally misleading. At Nanawa General Hans Kundt had lost his best soldiers and the reserves he needed to counter any Paraguayan offensive. The entire Bolivian army in the Chaco was ripe for the taking unless Kundt began orderly and staggered withdrawals, but unfortunately he refused to accept that Nanawa had been a disaster and continued to insist that the Paraguayans had been tremendously weakened by disproportionate losses. Kundt did not want to realize that the Bolivian 9th Division at the frontline south of Arce was his most exposed unit as its chief of staff had warned as early as June 1933. A timely withdrawal was the easiest way to avoid the danger hovering over the 9th Division and would have satisfied Salamanca's repeated pleas to shorten the defense lines by abandoning secondary positions. The retreat south could not halt at Alihuatá for long, because that position was likewise vulnerable to encirclement from the west. The clearing south of Alihuatá at Km. 31 offered the best chance to establish at least a temporary defense line. The final fall-back line of course was Km. 7 with its defensive network intact and its no less vulnerable western flank. Presumably, each successive fighting withdrawal should have weakened the Paraguayans, reduced the length of the Bolivian defense lines, and shortened the supply lines. Bolivia still had a chance of holding on to a slice of the eastern Chaco, and a stalemate at Km. 31 or more probably at Km. 7 — the original starting point for Bolivian offensive of 1933 — would spark negotiations to end the by then senseless war.[92]

No general likes to retreat and even less when abandoning territory is a confession of his failure. Rather than accept the strategic reality, Kundt deluded himself into believing that he could still save the eastern Chaco for Bolivia. Through his will power and detailed guidance he had earlier led the Bolivian army in its successful drive into the eastern Chaco, but those qualities were insufficient to keep the rapidly demoralizing Bolivian army intact on so many exposed fronts. As a worker who is desperately trying to plug up leaks in a dam about to collapse, Kundt insisted on seeing the problems purely at the tactical level. That he succeeded in prolonging the presence of the Bolivian army in the eastern Chaco until December reflected not just his abilities but also the exaggerated caution of Estigarribia and the hesitation of Eusebio Ayala, the Paraguayan president. Kundt had not failed to realize that his most dangerous opponent was the commander of the 1st Division, the forceful Colonel Rafael Franco. To keep the brilliant and dashing Colonel from wreaking havoc, Kundt tried to station his best units in front of Franco.[93]

The shelling at Nanawa was barely subsiding when on 11 July Colonel Franco began at Gondra the first of a series of Paraguayan moves to push the Bolivian Army towards its destruction. He had been the first to realize that Paraguay had regained the initiative and that Bolivia was on the defensive. At 0500 Franco led the 1st Division in a maneuver to open a jungle path around the Bolivian 4th Division. On 12 July the 1st Division cut off the supply road of the Bolivian 4th Division; quite ironically, this was the same trail that the Paraguayan 1st Division had used in March to escape encirclement. Water trucks could no longer reach the trapped Bolivian troops, but the extreme cold allowed the soldiers to stretch their remaining water supply. The Bolivian 4th Division promptly began hacking a path through the jungle north to Alihuatá, while Kundt stripped other fronts of units to try to save the trapped Bolivians. Kundt quickly deployed troops in Campo Vía to attack the 1st Division in its roadblock; he pulled troops from the north to help open at the other end

the path towards the escaping 4th Division. By the time Colonel Franco received enough reinforcements on 15 July to close the escape route, the entire Bolivian 4th Division had slipped away with all of its equipment. He pushed the Paraguayan 1st Division into the Bolivian rear as far as Campo Vía, thus giving Kundt the chance to trap the Paraguayans as the General rushed troops against this dangerous bulge in his line. Estigarribia refused to pour other divisions into the gap, and before Kundt could close his trap, Colonel Franco prudently abandoned the exposed bulge and was back in his original trenches in front of Gondra by 8 September.[94]

The cold climate and the repeated interventions of General Kundt had saved the 4th Division. The successful escape blinded Kundt to the gradual disintegration of the Bolivian army. Self-inflicted wounds, always frequent among Bolivian soldiers, reached epidemic proportions. The sick and the wounded when healed did not want to return to the front, and desertions continued at an alarming rate. Kundt introduced home leave as a way to bolster the collapsing morale of soldiers who had been continuously in the front for over a year, but he had to cancel the program immediately when only a third of the veterans reported back to duty. The only hope for the demoralized Bolivian army was to stay at easily defensible positions immune to flanking attacks. Instead, holding on to Alihuatá left the Bolivian army exposed to encirclement. The near loss of the Bolivian 4th Division should have served as a warning to Kundt that he had to begin an orderly withdrawal from Alihuatá. Kundt received one more warning, but this last one was no longer free of cost.[95]

To save the trapped 4th Division, Kundt had rushed troops from the front at Alihuatá, but he had not been able to return them because he needed those men to destroy the bulge Colonel Franco had created in the Bolivian line between Gondra and Campo Vía. Colonel Franco abandoned the bulge on his own by September 8 but his mere presence sufficed to tie down the Bolivian troops who could not return to their original positions at Alihuatá. Not only there, but throughout the eastern Chaco the Bolivian army was undermanned because of the impact of Nanawa. Kundt desperately tried to refill the depleted ranks of the units with raw recruits who had never fired a rifle before and lacked any experience in jungle warfare. The veterans were deserting sometimes in droves and the cases of self-inflicted wounds continued to multiply. The mounting indications of Bolivian weakness had become so overwhelming that even the cautious Estigarribia felt the time had come to launch a minor offensive.[96]

On 30 August the Paraguayans began an artillery bombardment and modest attacks to the north of Alihuatá to distract the Bolivian unit on the center. The lightly held front allowed the Paraguayans to surround first the Bolivian unit at Campo Grande and then another Bolivian unit at Pozo Favorito. As soon as the Bolivian Colonel David Toro heard the news, he decided to try to save Campo Grande by sending the only unit available, the Loa Regiment, in spite of orders from General Kundt not to move this unit without his express order. Right before the encirclement was completed on 12 September, the Loa regiment joined the other surrounded Bolivian troops at Campo Grande. With few other units nearby and none willing to march towards the Paraguayans, relief was impossible. On 15 September the trapped units surrendered, although timely intervention by Kundt managed to extricate the larger force that had been holding the road to Alihuatá.[97]

The loss of nearly two thousand men in dead and prisoners at Campo Grande and at Pozo Favorito was the final warning notice Kundt received. Again, his personal intervention had kept the disaster from being worse, but he could not single-handedly direct the movements of every Bolivian unit in the long front. The lack of a capable officer corps constantly crippled the Bolivian effort. Much different would have been Kundt's fate had he been able to rely on competent Chilean officers as happened during the last half of the war. As Kundt repeatedly complained, the Bolivian officers consulted him on trivial matters and instead took action on issues they needed to refer to him. The Bolivian officers consistently failed to strike the right balance between individual initiative and blind obedience. In contrast, Paraguayan teenagers fresh out of officer training school repeatedly led to victory small and even large detachments in very dangerous missions.[98] By October 1933, the Bolivian troops

were incapable of any offensive action and although still more numerous than the Paraguayans, were too thinly stretched to defend their positions. Demoralization was advancing even faster than before and was destroying any remaining fighting capability of the Bolivian troops. Sensing the impending doom, Kundt submitted his resignation. President Salamanca could not believe that the vaunted savior had failed to stabilize the front and refused to accept the resignation. Salamanca counseled Kundt to reinforce his positions and not to leave any long lines exposed; he also left to the discretion of the German general whether to evacuate Alihuatá. Bolstered by the President's backing, Kundt concluded that he still could rally the Bolivian army to make one last supreme effort. Instead of ordering the withdrawal back to Km. 7, he insisted on defending Alihuatá, not knowing that Paraguayan spies were promptly reporting his decision.[99]

Kundt's last mistake left a very long line exposed to flanking movements from the west around Alihuatá. Even the excessively cautious Estigarribia sensed the time was ripe for a major offensive, but President Ayala did not want any more attacks. With extreme difficulty Estigarribia had extracted permission from the Paraguayan president to launch the previous successful operations at Campo Grande and Pozo Favorito. President Ayala, always dreaming with negotiations, refused to authorize a new campaign. On the occasion of his visit to the front on 3 October to promote Estigarribia to the rank of general, the president at last relented and agreed to a new offensive. The delay had not been harmful, because Estigarribia was in no rush to begin the attack; only on 20 October did he issue the orders for an advance on Alihuatá and for a diversionary action on the Nanawa front. A surprise attack to the rear of the lines at Nanawa bagged 428 Bolivian prisoners, but the attack on a Bolivian flank near Nanawa failed. As Estigarribia had intended, the diversionary attack did prevent Kundt from drawing on troops in Nanawa to relieve the pressure on Alihuatá.[100]

The Paraguayan plan did not go much beyond capturing Alihuatá because in accordance with standard military practice, Estigarribia expected Kundt to withdraw his threatened troops southward to a place like Km. 31. Rather than reinforcing Colonel Franco, who was pleading for troops for another push west from Gondra to Campo Vía, Estigarribia hurled newly formed units against the Bolivian positions north of Alihuatá starting on 23 October. The pressure was so strong that the Bolivians began to construct a second line of defense just 5 to 6 kilometers to the north of Alihuatá. The attacks continued until early November and gave Kundt the opportunity to make an inspection tour of the front only to draw the false conclusion that the Bolivian 9th Division could hold the original defense line. The ferocity of the costly Paraguayan attacks impressed the Bolivians, who countered localized outflanking attempts and held the line as the piles of Paraguayan cadavers increased. Whole Paraguayan units perished in the frontal attacks, and although the casualties later were justified as part of the larger maneuvers in the battle of Campo Vía, these losses, the largest in the entire battle of Campo Vía, were needlessly high. Some Paraguayans had forgotten the lesson about the suicidal nature of frontal attacks, and if their purpose had been to capture one meaningless outpost, the sacrifice of so many lives was not justified. Smaller attacks and steady shelling could have kept the Bolivian troops pinned down no less effectively.[101]

Kundt had realized from the start the exposed position of the Bolivian 9th Division; while to the southeast the Bolivian 4th Division (facing Colonel Franco) sheltered the rear, no Bolivian divisions protected the main supply route of Alihuatá to Muñoz or the longer indirect road south to Saavedra. Kundt had been sending reinforcements to the 9th Division and was trying to collect a force at Km. 31 to cover any retreat south, but the Paraguayan pressure near Nanawa kept the troops tied down in that front. In the middle of November the Paraguayans captured an entire Bolivian regiment in the Nanawa area, while other Bolivian units simply abandoned their trenches and fled. The demoralized state of the Bolivian troops had brought the Nanawa front to the point of collapse, but for one last time Kundt dramatically intervened to stabilize the Nanawa front. In reality he should have begun the withdrawal from Nanawa, and all the effort he put into saving that post had diverted his attention away from the danger threatening the 9th Division at Alihuatá. In response to the desperate pleas for more troops to repel the Paraguayans, who kept coming through paths into the rear of the Bolivian lines, Kundt made the fateful decision to send many units from the 4th Division north to help in the defense of Alihuatá.[102]

Immediate withdrawal of the 9th Division to Km. 31 was the order Kundt should have sent. However, taking into consideration the criticism that he was interfering excessively in tactical matters and thus depriving his commanders of any chance to show initiative or to gain self-esteem, he left any decision about withdrawal in the hands of the divisional commander. Meanwhile aerial photography revealed that the Paraguayans had been hacking paths through the jungle west of Alihuatá. Daily pins on a table map showed the southern advance of the Paraguayan paths, although nobody suspected that smaller patrols had marched through narrow foot trails much farther south into the jungle. The Paraguayans soon cut off the main supply road to Muñoz from Alihuatá leaving the Bolivians dependent on the southern road to Saavedra. Either Kundt or the divisional commander needed to order the immediate withdrawal of the 9th Division to Km. 31. On 2 December the 9th Division reported that Paraguayan units of unspecified size had cut off the road to the south, and their appearance unleashed the by this time usual panic among the frightened Bolivians. Kundt authorized (but did not order) the withdrawal if the 9th Division was in real danger. Nothing happened until 6 December, when 200 Paraguayan soldiers reached the clearing at Km. 31 and set up a roadblock. A Bolivian artillery observer had counted one by one the weary and ragged infantry soldiers as they came out of the jungle and promptly had his battery pounding the Paraguayan force.[103] Bolivian units were pushing north to clear the roadblock at Km. 31 while the 9th Division was sending a motley force south to clear the road.

> Then ensued one of the typical events of the campaign. A not very numerous enemy detachment, without any transportation or logistical support, inserts itself between our units and finds itself in the cross fire. [...] in spite of everything, the enemy detachment retains its positions. [...] The Paraguayans have operated certainly with boldness and determination and in marked contrast to the lack of offensive spirit on our part.[104]

In desperation Kundt had brought up his last two tanks to blast their way through the

The satisfied if not contented look on the Bolivian prisoners of war suggests they may have preferred capture to fighting in the front line (Pablo Max Ynsfrán, ed., *The Epic of the Chaco: Marshal Estigarribia's Memoirs of the Chaco War;* Austin: University of Texas Press, 1950).

roadblock, but before they could arrive, the 9th Division had abandoned and torched Alihuatá on 6 December and was retreating southwest to join the 4th Division.[105] This withdrawal made needless any more attacks north on Km. 31, and these Bolivian units began a leisurely return to Km. 7, passing on the way Km. 22 whose future significance for saving the Bolivian army nobody could foresee.

Estigarribia with his attacks had merely been doing for Kundt the job the latter should have been doing on his own (withdrawing Bolivian troops to more defensible positions). In the retreat from Arce, the Bolivians had taken some losses, but not large enough to affect the course of the war. With each successive retreat of the Bolivian army, the advance became harder for the Paraguayans. A return to Km. 7, the start-

ing point of the 1933 campaign, was the most the Paraguayans could have hoped for, unless something dramatic changed the likely outcome.

As the 9th Division completed its withdrawal to the rear positions of the 4th Division, the Bolivians were unaware that Colonel Franco had already put in motion the plan that would seal their fate. At a meeting on 4 December with his field commanders, Estigarribia announced his decision to concentrate all resources in the offensive in the north. This statement dashed an earlier hope that a second division might be available to carry out a decisive breakthrough at Gondra. Colonel Franco felt stunned by this decision and with difficulty could obey the order. The commander of the 4th Division, Colonel Fernández (who had saved the 1st Division in March) felt so sorry for the clearly dejected Franco that as a consolation he offered to lend one and possibly two of the regiments of the 4th Division. Estigarribia listened to the conversation but did not make a single comment on the arrangement between the divisional commanders.[106]

Franco needed at least another division for the pursuit but not for the breakthrough itself because the Bolivians had dangerously depleted the lines in front of him to tend to crises in other parts of the front. Where many others had failed, he believed that he had found a way to break an enemy line by a frontal assault. On previous days his sly patrols had been able to come to within 10 or 20 meters of the Bolivian front trenches. Differing assumptions in each army accounted for this successful patrolling: While the Bolivians saw the last trench line as the end of their universe, the Paraguayans saw the trenches as the doorway for a safe entry into the jungle or into no-man's land. A clearing about 1500 meters long and 500 meters wide gave the Bolivian machine guns a great field of fire across the coarse vegetation that provided scant cover. Franco proposed to his officers and men a surprise attack to end the war, and they did not recoil in fear, because "with the Paraguayan soldier nothing is impossible."[107] He set the attack for December 7, but the crucial preparations had to take place on the night of 6 December.

After nightfall fell, his men had about two hours before 2200 when the full moon appeared to shed its reflected light on the clearing. Franco had his men crawl silently up to the Bolivian trenches and by 2200 he had two of the regiments of his 1st Division spread out across the clearing. At this moment began what the men considered the hardest task of staying awake so as not to reveal their positions by snoring. The men maintained absolute silence, and the forward positions kept themselves awake by overhearing the conversations of the Bolivian soldiers. As was their custom at night, every few minutes the Bolivian soldiers fired their machine guns towards the Paraguayan trenches; traditionally the Paraguayans were less wasteful with their ammunition and only replied after intervals of half an hour or longer just to let the Bolivians know the positions were not deserted. If the random fire of that night caused any casualties, no groans alerted the Bolivians. The mosquitoes and other insects meanwhile feasted on the Paraguayan soldiers stretched out in the field who could not defend themselves from their bites out of fear of revealing their positions.

Dawn finally was starting to arrive, and Colonel Franco, who had placed himself in the trench nearest the Bolivian front line, observed the whole process. Convinced that the Bolivians had not detected the deployment, he gave the signal for the four cannons of his division to fire a salvo as the signal the start of the attack. Upon hearing the exploding shells, all two regiments simultaneously jumped up and to the sound of the traditional Guaraní yell of "pi-iipuuu!!" ran the last 10 or 20 meters into the Bolivian trenches. The defenders in the first line were caught totally by surprise and Franco heard few shots. Of the firearms only pistols were useful in the hand-to-hand combat and the Paraguayans with their machetes soon had gained control of the frontline trenches. Before the Bolivians could attempt to hold their second line of trenches, the rest of the Paraguayans in the clearing had leapfrogged over those fighting in the first line and overpowered the defenders in the second line. By 1000 the Paraguayans had advanced 3,000 meters from their starting point and were on the verge of a breakthrough. The Bolivian commander threw in his last reserves to try to detain the avalanche at a hastily erected third line. Machine gun fire had stopped the advance, but fortunately the Paraguayans knew this terrain very well from past campaigns. Franco sent his reserve regiment through a foot path in the jungle that brought it to the rear of the Bolivian defenders who soon abandoned their third and last line. The road to Campo Vía all the way to Km. 22 was open. The 1st Division pressed forward 15 kilometers until sheer exhaustion and hunger finally forced Franco to order a halt. The next day his men resumed the advance and reached Km. 22, but because Estigarribia still refused to send reinforcements, no further advance was possible. For Franco the moment of his greatest triumph was also the moment of his greatest frustration: All he needed was one division to push south to Saavedra and trap the entire Bolivian army in the eastern Chaco.[108]

Seeing the chance of ending the war at one blow slipping before his eyes, Franco concentrated on defending the jungle path between Gondra and Campo Vía. He knew that the trapped Bolivian 4th Division to the north was sure to make efforts to escape through the thin line of his 1st Division. When it became clear that the trap also included the Bolivian 9th Division, the hope of ending the war at one swoop revived. Estigarribia was uncomfortable because the Bolivians had not behaved the way he had expected, and he was slow to realize the significance of the gap Franco had ripped open in the Bolivian front. At long last Estigarribia began releasing more units to reinforce the line Franco had deployed from Gondra to Campo Vía. At the same time the Paraguayan units in the north continued their march to the southwest to finish the encirclement of the Bolivian 9th and 4th divisions.

The slowness of Estigarribia's response gave some Bolivian soldiers time to escape but only by abandoning all their equipment. Kundt had reoccupied Km. 22 and also placed strong forces at the western end of Campo Vía facing Franco's troops at the eastern end of that clearing. On 8 and 9 December at least a thousand Bolivian soldiers traveling light managed to slip undetected through jungle trails back to safety at Km. 22. However, most Bolivian commanders, still unaware of the gravity of their situation, did not try to escape because they did not want to abandon their new artillery and shiny equipment or burn their trucks. Enough Paraguayan troops were in position on 10 December to beat back the ferocious Bolivian attacks to break the line of the 1st Division. Some Bolivians made it through, but their units suffered casualties of over 60 percent. The unusually savage attacks of the normally passive Bolivians were the result of their thirst, as they saw their water supplies dwindling. Abundant rains had quenched the thirst of the marching Bolivians in previous days, but by 10 December the life-bearing rains had vanished. Early in the morning of 11 December the Bolivians were surrendering in groups, and when two regiments spontaneously surrendered, the Bolivian commanders went through the formality of negotiating surrender to the Paraguayans at 1100.[109]

Over 10,000 Bolivians surrendered and left the Paraguayans with an impressive arsenal of new weapons and modern equipment. Like a plague of locusts the commanders of other Paraguayan units descended on the 1st Division to take a "souvenir" of the victory but in reality to find weapons and equipment for their poorly outfitted units.[110] While the haggling over the spoils continued, the magnitude of the victory at Campo Vía only gradually was becoming evident. The whole northern front of the Bolivian army had vanished, and the Paraguayans were free to advance with impunity towards the Pilcomayo River at Muñoz, thereby trapping the Bolivian forces facing Nanawa. The only option for the Bolivians was to flee rapidly to Muñoz and then to Ballivián; any talk of a fighting withdrawal was out of the question: "The defense of Km. 7 would mean the grave for the Bolivian army."[111] While the Bolivians rushed to escape in panic, the Paraguayans made almost no effort to pursue. Estigarribia had still not assimilated the magnitude of the victory, and inexplicably he resumed the passive stance of 1932. When he should have been driving his 8th and 7th divisions hard to reach Muñoz, he held them back. The Paraguayan soldiers, who believed that the war was won and over, began to celebrate prematurely, but the attitude of the soldiers can well be understood, for what else could they think and do if they were not allowed to advance? Only on 13 December did the 6th Division occupy Saavedra after it had been set on fire by the retreating Bolivians. Finally on 16 December the 6th Division received the order to proceed to Muñoz.[112]

Just like in the previous year, a cease-fire for Christmas was expected. Perhaps because of the approaching Christmas season or perhaps because of the magnitude of the victory, President Ayala concluded that the war was over and that the time for negotiations had arrived. The loss of life in combat might have affected him, although probably the desire to avoid bankrupting Paraguay in a long costly war was uppermost in his mind. His motives were certainly sound, and both countries were long overdue to call the diplomats to end the war. Instead of following the classical tradition of putting forward specific terms as prerequisites for a cease-fire, on 18 December Ayala merely proposed a cease-fire. Bolivian acceptance was never in doubt, indeed previously in late November General Kundt had for the first time urged Bolivia to accept any cease-fire, even before the final and decisive phase of the battle of Campo Vía had begun. As expected, Bolivia immediately accepted the proposal for a cease-fire to last 10 days. The cease-fire took effect on midnight of 19 December and all assumed that it would be renewed, as it was.[113] The Chaco War seemed to have come to an end.

13. The Chaco War:
The Second Phase, 1934–1935

Everyone can begin a war at his will but not finish it— Niccolò Machiavelli[1]

The truce that halted the Paraguayan advance on 19 December 1933 was "the worst political and military error that has ever occurred on Latin American soil."[2] The genuine pacifist desire of Paraguayan President Eusebio Ayala to end the fighting actually prolonged the war. The decision to grant a breathing space to Bolivia at its hour of greatest vulnerability was not a mystery but simply a blunder. In a striking deviation from classical diplomacy, Ayala failed to include territorial conditions into the truce offer. The omission of concrete peace terms was inexcusable for a civilian, but blame for the military consequences did not rest solely on the president. The main military responsibility rested upon General José Félix Estigarribia, who should have vehemently rejected the truce, as the dynamic Colonel Rafael Franco did when he learned of the proposal at a chance appearance at headquarters. Fearing similar outbursts from his field commanders, Estigarribia dropped any thought of sounding out subordinates. Instead, Estigarribia insistently stuck to his official excuse that he could do nothing about the truce because the president had imposed the decision.[3]

Only after the war did it become clear that loyalty to President Ayala had not been the main reason for Estigarribia's acceptance. In reality, the truce harmonized with his manner of conducting the war. The massive and unexpected victory at Campo Vía had overwhelmed Estigarribia's ability to assimilate events. The static warfare had suddenly given way to rapid movements and involved huge stakes: Up to this point, the offensives had been at most over divisions, but at this moment an entire Bolivian army was within the grasp of destruction. Paraguay regained the numerical superiority it had enjoyed in the early months of the war, and its troops refitted themselves with the piles of weapons, supplies, and ammunition the panic-stricken Bolivians cast away. The abundance of men and materiel made possible previously unimaginable offensive thrusts, but even before President Ayala consulted Estigarribia about the truce, the general had already decided not to pursue the Bolivians after the battle of Campo Vía. General Hans Kundt was the first one surprised with the Paraguayan immobility: "the whole military world expected an immediate pursuit carried out with every bit of energy and even if necessary to the last gasp of the last Paraguayan soldier."[4] In reality, not the Paraguayan soldiers but Estigarribia himself needed a pause to try to absorb the vastly changed situation. Just as in 1932 after the capture of Boquerón, again the general made the mistake of failing to advance rapidly after a battlefield success. His failure to pursue aggressively in December 1933 ended the first phase of the Chaco War and made possible a new war.

360

The New War and the Pursuit

The Bolivian public demanded a scape-goat for the disaster of Campo Vía, yet the Bolivian officers were reluctant to sacrifice General Hans Kundt. This last-minute loyalty came from the realization that they were primarily responsible for the repeated failures in the Chaco and that Kundt had frequently shouldered the blame and even covered up their mistakes. But if the government dismissed the German general, then who would bear the responsibilities for their failures? The reaction of the army startled Daniel Salamanca, and in hindsight the president should have shelved his desire to fire Kundt. In addition to the valid military reasons, political considerations required retaining the German general in command, because otherwise the Bolivian president irretrievably undermined his political position. Much as Salamanca had complained about the excessive independence of Kundt, paradoxically his insistence on removing the German general reduced the president's authority over the army, which henceforth felt free to ignore the government. Salamanca had tried to replace Kundt with a general loyal to the president, but Colonel David Toro, a seasoned political infighter, deftly blocked the appointment. In a masterful power play, Colonel Toro persuaded Kundt to appoint as his successor General Enrique Peñaranda, who took command on 13 December 1933. The officers took this action in defiance of Salamanca's wishes, and a confrontation ensued until the president unwisely backed down. However, the winner was not General Peñaranda, but rather Colonel Toro who emerged as the real power behind the throne. Without the formal responsibility of supreme command, Colonel Toro manipulated events according to his preferences from behind the scenes. He assembled a large number of loyal followers who did his every bidding, and for his part, General Peñaranda, who knew he owed his appointment to Colonel Toro, was most reluctant to challenge his subordinate. Soon General Peñaranda realized that orders lacking the blessing of Colonel Toro had no chance of being followed.[5]

The result was ironic, because Salamanca had reluctantly agreed to accept Peñaranda as commander on the assumption that at last Bolivia had found the forceful and dynamic leader needed to achieve victory. Instead, the fragmented command between Colonel Toro and General Peñaranda helps explains some of the Bolivian actions during the second phase of the Chaco War. Just ten days after Peñaranda became commander, he had his first violent clashes with Salamanca. The president should have replaced him immediately, but the fear of a military coup repeatedly made him desist from making any drastic changes in the army high command. Under these tense conditions, the officers and the president tried to create a new field army to replace the one lost at Campo Vía.[6]

This field army was actually the third one Bolivia sent into the Chaco and just in numbers was soon twice the size of Kundt's army. As will be recalled, because of logistical limitations Kundt had refused to accept more units in the Chaco, but as the withdrawal shortened the supply lines, Bolivia was better positioned to support a larger number of men. By calling up reservists from the years of 1917 to 1920 and by receiving conscripts of 1934, Bolivia regained numerical superiority over Paraguay by April. Not all went well with the recruitment, and most ominously 14-year olds and men over 50 began to appear in the ranks.[7] With so many men forcibly torn from their families and civilian life, the Bolivian units, never very aggressive, became even more cautious than before. At the tactical level the reservists had such a large stake in life back home that they were ready to retreat, flee, desert or surrender at any excuse. The reservists consumed huge amounts of cartridges and required massive artillery firing just to keep them from deserting. Sensing a psychological weakness, the Paraguayan soldiers routinely taunted the Bolivians and urged them to flee to escape capture or death.[8]

The natural caution of the older soldiers was aggravated by poor leadership. Throughout the war a sizeable percentage of officers performed poorly, in marked contrast to the Paraguayans whose officers generally performed splendidly. That the professional pre-war officers of Paraguay performed well was only natural; more remarkable was the blossoming of university students, sometimes teenagers, who after completion of officer training school displayed an extraordinary dedication to their duties. Instead, for reasons still not clear, Bolivia was never able to train an adequate number of officers. Even worse, the pervasive leadership failures suggested that the officer corps was so rotten than it had to be replaced.[9] The quick fix was to increase the number of soldiers in each unit, so that the same number of officers could lead a larger number of soldiers, but this stopgap formula only aggravated the leadership vacuum. A better solution emerged when the first of over 300 officers from Chile arrived in May. In January 1934 Bolivia had decided to hire Chilean officers, and once they reached their posts, the performance of these Bolivian units improved considerably. By allowing its officers to fight in Bolivia, Chile reaped economic and political benefits. Paraguay vigorously protested this hostile act and for a time suspended diplomatic relations with Chile.[10] More perplexing was the complete passivity of Argentina to this Chilean involvement. Argentina should have resented this intromission into its traditional sphere of influence and should have replied by stepping up the amount of assistance to Paraguay. Inexplicably, Argentina did nothing to offset the advantage that the Chilean officers had given Bolivia.[11]

New armament and equipment replaced the losses of Campo Vía, and Bolivia was well on its way to fielding a fairly formidable army to block any Paraguayan advance once the truce expired on 6 January 1934. But where exactly should Bolivia make its stand? The safest and most secure alternative was to conduct a staggered fighting withdrawal back to Villa Montes and the Parapetí River. As early as 1932 General Arturo Guillén had proposed this solution, the only one that guaranteed success but at the political and psychological cost of abandoning the Chaco to Paraguay without a fight. A significant Bolivian retreat was inevitable, because Paraguay retained a numerical superiority at the front line during the initial months of 1934. At least initially Bolivia had no choice but to withdraw rapidly, but as Bolivian reinforcements poured in, the question of their deployment resurfaced. Already troop congestion was appearing around Villa Montes and near the Parapetí River, and the temptation to reduce the crowding by deploying troops further south was too great to resist. Sites advantageous for the defense existed in many intermediate points, such as at Magariños, Linares, and Bal-

livián on the Pilcomayo River (Map 24). These and other positions further inland all could be outflanked, but any maneuver was bound to cost the Paraguayans casualties and time. A slim chance existed that Paraguayan carelessness might give Bolivia a chance to launch a surprise counterattack to reverse the unbroken string of defeats. But if the Paraguayans did not become careless, then the Bolivians could continue their fighting withdrawal in an orderly fashion back to their seemingly impregnable mountain defenses at Villa Montes.

Unlike the Bolivians who had frantically prepared for the resumption of hostilities, the Paraguayans believed that the war was over and had let their military posture deteriorate. An epidemic of leaves gripped the units as the men almost en masse returned home for some well-deserved rest. Although later he denied it, General José Félix Estigarribia for his part believed that the crushing defeat at Campo Vía had destroyed any ability of the Bolivian army to launch offensives. The news that General Kundt had been removed from command only confirmed the belief that the war was over; for propaganda reasons many in Paraguay proclaimed the erroneous view that the German general was the only person interested in prolonging the war. Discipline broke down in the units and a holiday atmosphere took over during the Christmas and New Year celebrations, the last ones for many of the men. The soldiers woke up from a dreamy and all too swift vacation to find the reality of war staring at them. Both officers and men with extreme difficulty abandoned the pleasures of civilian life for the savagery of war. Hardest of all was the recovery from the false sense of euphoria that the premature victory celebrations had left in their minds.

The Paraguayans were emotionally drained and were in no psychological condition to resume fighting immediately. President Ayala himself was in no mood for war, and he suggested a second extension of the truce. By then the Bolivian military prepartions were too obvious to deny, and Estigarribia rejected the president's suggestion. Curiously, Bolivian President Salamanca was tempted to seek an agreement both during and after the truce. The Paraguayan terms were vastly superior to those Bolivia received after the war, and just the chance to end the bloodshed seemed irre-

to
Santa Cruz

BOLIVIA

Amboro

Charagua

Parapetí River

Camiri

Santa Fe

27 de
Noviembre

Ingavi

to
Pitiantuta

Boyuibe

Mandyyupecua

Yrendagüe

El Cruce

Algodonal

Picuiba

Carandaití

La Faye

Capirenda

Siracuas

Villa Montes

Ybibobo

Garrapatal

El Carmen

to
Camacho

Lóbrego Road

Cururenda

to
Camacho

Esmeralda

ARGENTINA

Pilcomayo River

Guachalla

N

Ballivián

Conchitas

to
Platanillos

Bolivian
fortifications

Linares

dirt roads

Magariños

petroleum
fields

to
Muñoz

Map 24. Battlefields of 1934–1935.

sistible. Ayala sensed the ambivalence of his Bolivian counterpart and mistakenl concluded that fruitful negotiations might be imminent. To keep the door open, Ayala cabled Estigarribia not to press the Bolivian army hard unless ordered from Asunción. In their negotiating games diplomats love to move soldiers like pawns, but the Paraguayan general wisely ignored the request and uncharacteristically concentrated on resuming the offensive.[12]

Early in the morning of 7 January 1934 (after the expiration of the truce at midnight of 6 January) the Paraguayans resumed their offensive. Outwardly the situation they encountered resembled that of December. Abandoned weapons, equipment, and supplies littered the roads alongside countless cadavers. More fortunate were the Bolivian stragglers who, lost in the jungle since December, continued to surrender singly or in small groups. Effortlessly the Paraguayans marched unopposed and occupied one after another of the abandoned Bolivian posts. Estigarribia's belief that the truce had no harmful consequences seemed justified. On 8 January the Paraguayans entered Camacho, the last of the

Marshal José Félix Estigarribia, who commanded Paraguayan troops during the Chaco War (1932–1935) (*Epic of the Chaco*).

posts to have played any role in the previous years' warfare.

As the Paraguayans left behind the old battlefields forever, Colonel David Toro decided to make a first attempt to stop the Paraguayans at Magariños. The obstinacy of this colonel almost cost the Bolivians their entire 8th Division, which managed to make a panicky retreat barely in time to escape a Paraguayan encirclement. After entering Magariños on 10 February, the Paraguayan pursuit ground to a halt, not because of any Bolivian resistance, but because of torrential downpours. The dirt roads became mud canals and the rapidly multiplying vegetation quickly swallowed up any signs of foot paths. The rains continued into late February and effectively blocked any advance. The floods made supplying the front line troops impossible, and the mud halted the movement of trucks. Reluctantly Estigarribia had no choice but to order the advance to halt on 13 January at least until the worst rains subsided. More dangerously, he did not want to admit that the thirty-day window for easy pursuit after Campo Vía had ended [13]

The dense jungle also contributed to delay the Paraguayan advance. Left behind forever were the familiar battlefields of 1932 and 1933; the Paraguayan soldiers were marching into territory they had never visited. The Paraguayans lacked their own maps of the region, and the innumerable captured Bolivian maps all referred to areas left far in the Paraguayan rear. A thick and endless jungle loomed in front of the Paraguayan units, and quite prudently the cautious Estigarribia did not want to fall into a Bolivian trap or to have his men get lost. Only skilled scouts and extensive patrolling could slowly start to reveal a way through the thick jungle maze ahead.

As the Paraguayan units gradually felt their way forward, a clear pattern of troop deployment emerged and lasted until the end of the war. The geography imposed a separation of the army corps into two fronts. Running north from the Pilcomayo River lay the main front of combat: This line, gradually shifting westward but retaining its approximate north-south axis, became the main battleground. This "western front" contained the largest number of troops on both sides and experienced almost constant fighting; at times the intensity of the combat became so great that the positions returned to the trench warfare typical of first phase of the war. The second or "northern front" stretched north to the Parapetí River and appeared as the Paraguayan forces pushed northwest. The task of the Paraguayan II Corps was to protect the exposed flank of the other two Paraguayan corps facing west, but a passive role for the II Corps was inconceivable under the command of the forceful Colonel Rafael Franco.

To try to cut off the Bolivians, Franco had secretly begun to hack a trail west from Camacho to Cururenda on the Pilcomayo River (Map 24). On 27 February Bolivian planes flew low over the trail under construction, and the Paraguayans mistakenly concluded that the Bolivians had uncovered the secret. From separate reporting, the Paraguayans also learned that the Bolivians were building defense lines at Linares on the Pilcomayo River. When patrols came to scout Linares on 3 March, to their surprise they found that the Bolivians had abandoned their line of trenches the day before. The conclusion seemed inescapable that the Bolivians had hurriedly abandoned Linares as soon as they learned of Franco's trail in their rear. The Paraguayans also interpreted this hasty withdrawal as confirmation of the demoralized state of the Bolivians. In reality, not until 20 March did Bolivian aerial reconnaissance confirm the existence of Franco's trail, and the abandonment of Linares had not been hasty but had been part of the staggered withdrawal. Had the Paraguayans come sooner to Linares, the Bolivian garrison supposedly would have stood and fought, but by 2 March it had already guaranteed enough time for the construction of fortifications further in the rear, and its presence at the vulnerable position at Linares was no longer needed.[14] None of this was clear at the time to the Paraguayans, who were still left pondering the question: Did the Bolivians intend to resist anywhere?

Thrust and Counterthrust

The Bolivian garrison at Linares withdrew north to take up its assigned sector in the fortifications rapidly taking form at Ballivián. Had the Bolivians known early in March that Colonel Rafael Franco was pushing west through the jungle from Camacho (Map 24) to try to

cut off their rear, the still demoralized Bolivians were sure to have continued their headlong withdrawal perhaps as far as Villa Montes as had been their original intention. But unaware of the danger threatening their rear and confident that the jungle and the rains had finally slowed down the Paraguayan pursuit, the Bolivians settled upon Ballivián as a good place for a long defense. The troops soon had constructed a network of trenches and barbed wired that made a frontal attack on Ballivián suicidal. Inadvertently the fortifications began to loom so large in the minds of the Bolivian public, that any talk of withdrawing from this supposedly impregnable defense line became politically impossible for President Daniel Salamanca. The trenches stretched north initially for 20 kilometers and eventually for more than 40 kilometers, but whatever the length the terminus remained the same: The defensive line in the north faded into a dense mass of vegetation and hung on air. A gap of at least 60 kilometers of jungle separated the last trenches from the next solid Bolivian position to the north. Colonel Ángel Rodríguez, the only real brains of the Bolivian high command, regarded the gap as an opportunity rather than a danger. Aware of the Paraguayan preference for outflanking movements, he hoped to lure the Paraguayans into entering this impenetrable jungle and then trapping them by flanking attacks from the north and the south.[15]

The retreat north had shortened supply lines for Bolivia, which continued to purchase foodstuffs and many other non-military items from Argentina just across the Pilcomayo River. The I Corps under Colonel David Toro was the first Bolivian unit to be adequately fed and equipped in the Chaco War. But without hunger pangs to monopolize the men's attention, other basic instincts could surface. To raise the reviving morale of the inactive soldiers even higher, the Bolivian high command sent a plane with a madam and 13 prostitutes. Their arrival in Ballivián was an immediate sensation, but no instant gratification was possible for the poor soldiers who had to continue controlling their urgent sexual needs. First crack at the women went to the high-ranking officers who locked themselves in a house for days of nonstop riotous orgies. Once the commanders and staff officers of the I Corps had drunk themselves into total stupor, the women passed to the combat officers. Only after the officers had satiated themselves did they make the women available to the soldiers. Perhaps to preserve the scarce resource of a dozen women among thousands of soldiers, the officers rigorously restricted access by using the women as a reward for good behavior. Meticulously kept registers recorded the name of the officer who authorized the visit, the name of the soldier, and the time slot. Medical doctors labored in vain to check the rapid spread of venereal disease, but soon an even worse ailment was infecting the army. The prostitutes, wiser and more intelligent than almost all the Bolivian officers, had concluded that the war was lost and were whispering defeatist comments into the soldiers' ears. When the high command belatedly learned that the presence of the prostitutes rather than boosting

morale was having precisely the opposite effect, the women soon found themselves back on the way to Villa Montes. The immense regret of their many grateful clients in Ballivián can well be imagined, and the hasty departure of the women goaded many soldiers to join at the first opportunity the flow of deserters crossing the border into Argentina.[16]

The carousing of the high-ranking officers at Ballivián was rudely interrupted by the news that the Paraguayans were hacking a trail west from Camacho to Cururenda on the Pilcomayo. The Bolivians made the discovery on 20 March, and their most natural response would have been to abandon Ballivián and to take up defensive positions to the north at Cururenda. But Colonel David Toro did not want to abandon Ballivián because he realized the symbolic

Paraguayan light artillery. Whenever trucks could not penetrate the jungle or the mud, soldiers had to move and position the cannons (*The Epic of the Chaco: Marshal Estigarribia's Memoirs of the Chaco War*; Austin: University of Texas Press, 1950).

value it had acquired in the mind of the Bolivian public, and on the other hand Colonel Ángel Rodríguez wanted to try out his very ambitious plan. First he sent troops from Picuiba south to Garrapatal to pressure the rear of the Paraguayan II Corps. Secondly, he ordered the construction of a path through the jungle to try to cut off the Paraguayan II corps. The stakes could be high: If the Bolivians surrounded the II Corps, the other two Paraguayan corps risked collapse. The Paraguayans promptly detected the movements, and both Franco and Estigarribia ordered countermeasures.[17] They first halted work on the path to Cururenda and gave the highest priority to the destruction of the threat hanging over their northern front.

The results exceeded all expectations. Expecting considerable resistance, Colonel Franco sent a large force to drive the Bolivians from Garrapatal. On 27 March the Paraguayans surrounded the Bolivian front line south of Garrapatal and also captured 50 cases of ammunition the Bolivians had carelessly left exposed. The Paraguayans did not realize that they had seized the entire arsenal and mistakenly assumed that the defenders had many more stockpiles nearby. In reality, the Bolivians were down to their last 10 cartridges per soldier and were rapidly losing any will to fight. To make matters worse, the Chaco, like the Amazon, has the nasty tendency to affect the perceptions of individuals and sometimes even to drive them mad; one of these instances occurred at Garrapatal when a delirious Bolivian lieutenant colonel responded to the desperate situation by ordering his men to save the last cartridge to blow their brains out. Horrified junior officers raised the white flag and surrendered to the Paraguayans who took over 1200 prisoners. After securing Garrapatal on 28 March, the Paraguayans set up defensive positions many kilometers to the north.[18] Patrols and prisoner interrogations confirmed that no water sources existed between Garrapatal and Carandaití far to the northwest. The vast arid jungle stretching north of Garrapatal loomed as an impervious barrier against any southern Bolivian thrust.

Not only had the threat from the north disappeared, but the Paraguayans had also captured very valuable booty at Garrapatal. Among the more unusual items was a new code book for the Bolivian messages (the Bolivians had replaced all their codes after the disaster of Campo Vía). Even more significant was the capture of a map tracing out all the Bolivian paths, trails, and roads in the central and northern Chaco, including the long Lóbrego Road all the way to Villa Montes. Aerial reconnaissance had proven notoriously unreliable, so until this moment the Paraguayans obtained their topographical knowledge exclusively from foot patrols. With this map many new possibilities emerged, and for the first time Estigarribia sensed that his northern front could play a decisive role in shaping events at the western front. In another unexpected consequence, the mass surrender at Garrapatal had shocked the Bolivian public, and in an impulsive response President Salamanca had ordered Ballivián held at all costs.[19]

The insistence on defending Ballivián was sure to provide the Paraguayans with great opportunities, but the pathetic Bolivian performance at Garrapatal inadvertently induced the Paraguayans to let their guard down. By this time the Paraguayan soldiers come to consider themselves vastly superior to the Bolivians, but superiority did not necessarily imply that all resistance had collapsed. More dangerously, Estigarribia had not accepted the harsh truth that the truce had been a blunder, and he still deluded himself into believing that Campo Vía had so shattered the Bolivian Army that it was incapable of any coordinated action. And if the demoralized Bolivians tried to resist, he believed that a good shove and a push was all that was needed to gain a smashing victory, as Garrapatal seemed to confirm. He compounded his error by failing to recognize the many indications of a rapid Bolivian build-up. Not only were the Bolivians well supplied, but once again they vastly outnumbered the Paraguayans. Estigarribia was fundamentally right in believing that Paraguay could still prevail, but the days of a triumphal victory parade north were over, and any offensive was bound to require a long and costly campaign.[20]

On the Bolivian side, Colonel Rodríguez had seen the defeat at Garrapatal as a great opportunity to strike a counterthrust at the Paraguayans. He also knew that the Paraguayans faced arid terrain to the north and thus were unlikely to advance beyond Garrapatal. To guard this quiet sector he left behind only small detachments and secretly shifted the 9th Division from that front and placed it north of the Ballivián trenches precisely in the gap of 60 kilometers. He reinforced that division until it numbered 14,000 men, a force vastly larger than anything the Paraguayans had; indeed the entire Paraguayan I Corps barely numbered 7,000 men distributed in three undermanned divisions. The Bolivian plan called for waiting for the Paraguayans to outflank the Ballivián defenses through the unguarded gap to the north of the trenches. Once the Paraguayans began their outflanking movement, the Bolivian 9th Division would pounce on their rear and destroy them. Unfortunately for Rodríguez, the map captured at Garrapatal had revealed the existence of the long road called Lóbrego and persuaded Estigarribia to postpone any flanking movement around Ballivián into a more distant future. For the moment Estigarribia was content to have his troops march up the Lóbrego Road, under the expectation that eventually they would link up with the II Corps once again hacking a path westward from Camacho. He believed that either singly or jointly, the two Paraguayan advances were sure to crash into the Bolivian rear and to trigger a panicky flight from Ballivián.

Colonel Rodríguez went to Ballivián to direct his far-flung operations, but as the days passed, he realized that the Paraguayans were not behaving as he had expected. He finally concluded that if the Paraguayans did not come to him, he would have to lure them into a decisive battle. Any Bolivian forward movement risked a high chance of discovery, because the Paraguayans had a tradition of patrolling extensively ahead of their main units. Fortunately for Colonel Rodríguez, the Paraguayan overconfidence after the easy victory at Garrapatal filtered down to the forward soldiers, who became lax in their security and hugged the Lóbrego Road too closely. Colonel Rodríguez could thus carry out his plan to lure the Paraguayans into a decisive battle by offering his small 8th Division as bait. Once the Paraguayans had almost completed the predictable encirclement of his 8th Division, Rodríguez would unleash his large 9th Division on the flank of the Paraguayans to crush them. As a final precaution and to prevent any Paraguayan escape to the north towards the approaching Paraguayan II Corps, Rodríguez also

planned to move his 3rd Division in a southeasterly direction against the northern flank of the Paraguayans. If everything turned out according to his plan, he expected to surround and destroy the Paraguayan 2nd and 7th divisions.[21]

Unaware of the trap ahead, in mid May the Paraguayan 2nd Division confidently spearheaded the advance up the Lóbrego Road and was followed by the 7th Division. Soon the Paraguayans ran into the carefully prepared defensive positions of the Bolivian 8th Division. In a totally predictable manner, the Paraguayan 2nd Division avoided frontal assaults and duly began to hack a path through the jungle to the east to swing around the Bolivian 8th Division and cut if off. Colonel Rodríguez had been praying for just such a move, and he allowed the Paraguayans to advance far before stopping them cold just short of their objective. This ferocious last-minute defense when the Bolivians normally fled at this stage should have alerted the Paraguayans that something unusual was taking place. The commander of the Paraguayan 7th Division thought otherwise, and seeing his sister division tied down further up the road, he sent out patrols to reconnoiter a wider flanking movement to the east around both the Bolivian defenders and the bogged down Paraguayan 2nd Division. The patrols to their surprise uncovered several extensively traveled paths through the supposedly impenetrable forest, but the divisional commander, keenly aware of how easily the jungle plays tricks on the mind, dismissed their fears and claimed that they had let their imagination run wild. Consequently, the Paraguayan 7th Division abandoned the Lóbrego Road and set out on its very wide flanking maneuver through the jungle to the east. At last Colonel Rodríguez had everything in place to spring his trap, and on 18 May he brought the huge 9th Division forward from its rear bases. Advancing silently through the previously cleared paths, the 9th Division made a surprise appearance at Kilometers 57 and 60, effectively cutting off the Lóbrego Road. From this point on, the success of the Bolivian offensive depended on the ability of the divisional commander to take care of any unforeseen local complications.[22]

One obstacle immediately appeared: The Bolivians had trapped about 200 Paraguayans under Captain Joel Estigarribia (a distant relative of the commander José Félix) at Km. 58. A small covering force could have watched these Paraguayans until they finally surrendered after their food and water ran out, or the artillery could have pounded them into submission. Instead the divisional commander halted the advance of the rest of his troops until his forward units had first driven Captain Estigarribia's detachment from the road. The obsession with clearing this minuscule Paraguayan unit from the Lóbrego Road contrasted with the swift response of the Paraguayan 7th Division. Its commander, as soon as he heard that the Bolivians had blockaded the Lóbrego Road, immediately began to clear an escape route to the east. The 7th Division extricated itself from the trap without losing any men, equipment, artillery, or trucks, and on 21 May the 7th joined the rest of the Paraguayan I Corps further south on the Lóbrego Road.

The successful escape of the Paraguayan 7th Division did have the unfortunate consequence of leaving the Paraguayan 2nd Division isolated behind to face its fate. The latter should have fled at the same time and through the same path as the 7th Division, but the Chaco had affected the mind of its commander who had lost touch with reality and refused to retreat. The commander of the 2nd Division telegraphed triumphantly on 21 May at 1615 that he had repulsed all attacks. The I Corps commander, not wishing to overrule the person on the spot, hesitated to order the withdrawal. By 1800 when the general strategic situation had become abundantly clear, the I Corps commander ordered the withdrawal to begin that very night, but the delay of several hours was proving fatal. By then Bolivian troops had surrounded the 2nd Division, which suffered heavy casualties as it tried to fight its way out of the trap. The survivors reached safety on 23 May but only after having lost most of their equipment. Not all the units could escape, and on 24 May the remnants of two regiments surrendered. On 25 May the unit of Captain Estigarribia, which had been kept alive by air drops of ice blocks, also surrendered after its ammunition ran out.[23]

Bolivia captured 1400 soldiers, the single largest haul of Paraguayan prisoners in the entire war. The Paraguayans were the first to admit they had been surprised at what mistakenly became know as the battle of Strongest (a

road junction 90 kilometers to the northwest) and were angry with their intelligence services for failing to predict the Bolivian offensive. Specifically, the failure to detect the transfer of the large Bolivian 9th Division particularly galled them. The setback for the first time created a morale problem among the soldiers who began to desert in noticeable numbers. However, the Paraguayan defeat provided an invaluable lesson for both troops and commanders. Never again did the Paraguayans assume that the Bolivians were a beaten foe, and although Estigarribia could never bring himself to admit that the truce had been a blunder, this setback shook him out of any complacency. For their part, the troops slowly regained their morale and the deserters returned back to duty, their officers easily accepting the excuse that they had been "lost" in the jungle. Never again did the soldiers let their guard down, and relentless patrolling became immutable practice for the Paraguayans. In the inevitable postmortems after the defeat, Estigarribia and his fellow commanders soon found consolation: They could not understand how the massive numbers of Bolivians had failed to score a decisive blow.[24] The easy Paraguayan victory at Garrapatal had paved the way for a setback at Strongest, and it remained to be seen whether the Paraguayans could somehow turn their rare defeat into a smashing victory.

The Battle of El Carmen

José Félix Estigarribia later stated that the setback of Strongest had delayed the outcome of the war for six months. To the visible consternation of the Bolivians who had counted on a long respite, Strongest made no dent on the offensive spirit of the Paraguayans, who resumed the forward advance within days. Estigarribia ordered Franco to resume cutting the path to the west, but the Bolivians rushed troops to block the maneuver. Inconclusive fighting ensued, until by early July Estigarribia realized that the path to Cururenda could not provide the opportunity for a breakthrough. He decided to try a direct attack to Ballivián. On 8 July the Paraguayan III Corps launched a general offensive, but the frontal attacks against the Bolivian fortifications proved too costly in casualties. The Paraguayans began to desert across the Pilcomayo to Argentina, and Estigarribia had no choice but to halt the offensive on 13 July.[25]

The Paraguayans had taken heavy casualties and had exhausted themselves during these senseless frontal attacks. The situation was ripe for the Bolivians with their larger numbers to deliver a crippling counterblow to end the war once and for all. Colonel Ángel Rodríguez realized, however, that he lacked any troops to send on the offensive. The Bolivian commanders had learned that they needed an overwhelming numerical superiority to overcome the tactical skills and the leadership qualities of the Paraguayans. Just to hold a position required at least two Bolivians for each Paraguayan, and this assuming that the Bolivians were well fed and equipped and also en-

joyed overwhelming supporting fire from machine guns, cannons, and bombers. If these were the requirements for a successful defense, an offensive required at least three and preferably four Bolivians for each Paraguayan. The practical result was that 7,000 Paraguayans of the III Corps were tying down 18,000 Bolivians in the forty kilometers of trenches defending Ballivián. The remaining Bolivian troops in the Chaco barely sufficed to hold the rest of the fronts. Without any reserve, the Bolivians lacked the troops to mount a counterattack after the Paraguayan general offensive came to an end on 13 July.

Colonel Rodríguez proposed the abandonment of Ballivián as the only way to obtain the maneuver battalions he needed for an offensive. A secret and swift abandonment of

Paraguayan trenches at Ballivián. Lightly manned trenches like these tied down a much larger number of Bolivian troops (*The Epic of the Chaco: Marshal Estigarribia's Memoirs of the Chaco War;* Austin: University of Texas Press, 1950).

Ballivián would release many troops to launch a surprise attack further north against the unsuspecting Paraguayan I and II corps. But in the fragmented leadership of the Bolivian army after the departure of Hans Kundt, the proposal of Rodríguez was an invitation to debate and to negotiate. The first opposition came naturally from President Daniel Salamanca who knew all too well the political costs of abandoning Ballivián. After a long process of discussion with La Paz, President Salamanca finally authorized the army on 25 July to abandon Ballivián, but only within the framework of a general plan to launch an offensive. During Kundt's tenure the approval of the president confirmed any decision, but in the new Bolivian army no major action could take place without the approval of Colonel Toro, the commander of the forces at Ballivián. He vigorously opposed any withdrawal, and General Peñaranda, supposedly the commander of Bolivian forces in the Chaco, refused to overrule him. Peñaranda, while not a figurehead, saw his role mainly as that of a peacemaker between the warring factions of Toro and Rodriguez. The days turned into weeks without any decision on the withdrawal. The military reasons for abandoning Ballivián were so obvious that Estigarribia had expected the move as early as 2 June. He could not believe that the Bolivians were still in Ballivián in late June, and he was glad to see that after the failure of the Paraguayan general offensive of July, large numbers of Bolivians stayed pinned down in the fortified trenches at Ballivián.[26]

The Bolivian inability to launch a counteroffensive was not necessarily a major blunder and simply meant that the war for a second time had reached a stalemate, just as had happened in the months prior to Kundt's fatal attack on Nanawa in 1933. The Bolivians lacked the reserves to launch an offensive, and the Paraguayans lacked the numbers to pierce the Bolivian defenses. When war can no longer solve a dispute, the time has come to call in the diplomats. President Eusebio Ayala was sure to accept the present front line as the base for a permanent boundary between the two countries; presumably the diplomats would have authority to exchange pieces of worthless real estate to achieve a harmonious boundary that at least left the precious Ballivián in Bolivian hands. As a gambler fast losing all his chips,

President Salamanca had a final chance to save something from the debacle in the Chaco. He was ready to accept as Paraguayan almost all the territory Estigarribia's army controlled, but tragically for him and for Bolivia, he insisted on one last military operation. Desperately trying to cling to power, Salamanca was looking for political cover to bring the war to an end. The ultimate sacrifice a politician can make is abandoning his power for the good of his country, an action that automatically catapults him to the ranks of statesmen.

Salamanca was not ready to make the politician's supreme sacrifice and instead revived a pre-war plan for a Bolivian invasion through the north from Ingavi to the Paraguay River. The goal was to capture the slice of territory needed for access to a better port on the Paraguay River. Once the river port was captured, Salamanca could propose a permanent truce and he could sell the peace treaty back home with the argument that in exchange for worthless jungle in the eastern and central Chaco, Bolivia had gained a valuable outlet for its commerce with the world. Since the strip of territory was just unoccupied jungle, Salamanca could not see any vital Paraguayan interest at stake. He began to collect troops and created the III Corps to lead the offensive that would bypass the north Paraguayan front. All Bolivian officers properly joined ranks to oppose this fantastic presidential scheme, arguing correctly that it distracted resources away from the vital front and created logistical nightmares. But because the president had direct control over the units and supplies leaving La Paz, he began to divert some of the flow of reinforcements away from General Peñaranda and towards the new III Corps. Unknown to Salamanca, not only had he set in motion the events that determined his fate, but he had also unleashed the sequence of events that shaped the war until its end.[27]

When news of the new Bolivian III Corps and its intentions reached Paraguay, the reaction was immediate and not at all what Salamanca had predicted. Once the Bolivians reached the Paraguay River, what would keep them from going downstream either to attack the main cities of Paraguay or to cut off the supply lines of the army in the Chaco? What had seemed to Salamanca a harmless occupation was to the Paraguayans a deadly threat to their survival as a nation. The Asunción government and the field commanders unanimously agreed about the need to eliminate this mortal threat. Estigarribia developed a two-pronged plan to neutralize this northern Bolivian drive to the Paraguay River. Rather than block Ingavi, the natural jumping off point for any Bolivian advance, he decided to block the supply road to Ingavi at 27 de Noviembre. To accomplish this goal, he shifted the Paraguayan II Corps, which was still trying to open a path west through the jungle, eastward to Garrapatal. That sector had remained quiet since the capture of Garrapatal in March, and Estigarribia hoped that the unexpected arrival of the II Corps would make possible a swift advance north to seize the supply road at 27 de Noviembre. Once the Paraguayans had attained their goal, Estigarribia could plan at leisure on how best to take care of the isolated Bolivian garrison at Ingavi.[28]

Franco left behind a small covering force to distract the Bolivians, who did not suspect that the II Corps had quietly moved east to Garrapatal. From there he set out on 13 August expecting to encounter heavy resistance. Instead, he was happily surprised with the easy capture of Picuiba on 15 August. At the cost of 3 dead and 25 wounded, a forward detachment had overrun the Bolivian position and taken 450 prisoners besides abundant amounts of equipment, supplies, and weapons. The Paraguayans followed the Bolivian road north and the next day reached a fork in the road called El Cruce. Franco sent his 6th Division west towards Yrendagüe and the other division north towards 27 de Noviembre. On 17 August the Paraguayans reached both objectives, and with the capture of 27 de Noviembre, they had completed their original mission of blocking the supply road to Ingavi. The weak Bolivian resistance encouraged Franco to push his offensive to the maximum, and he asked Estigarribia for more trucks and reinforcements. Meanwhile to the west of Yrendagüe the Bolivians had hurriedly thrown up a defense line at Algodonal to try to detain the Paraguayans. A combination of flanking and frontal attacks soon shattered the Bolivians who lost over a thousand men in captured or killed; the Paraguayans also captured large amounts of ammunition and equipment when they occupied Algodonal on 22 August. Because the

Paraguayan drive depended on food and water coming all the way from Garrapatal, the inadequate supply was daily worsening the condition of the Paraguayan 6th Division. Franco believed outdated prisoner reports that at Carandaití the Bolivians had only 300 men and urged his soldiers to make one final effort. The 6th Division came to within five kilometers of Carandaití, but at the cost of heavy losses. Captured prisoners confirmed that the Bolivians had increased the garrison at Carandaití to over 3,000, considerably more than the weak 6th Division. The Paraguayan dash ground to a halt but not before surpassing all its original objectives.[29]

It would be some time before the Paraguayans could bring enough supplies and water to make possible a renewed effort on their north front. Because the western front was also relatively quiet, a period of inactivity seemed inevitable as both sides tried to refurbish their forces and pondered what move to take next. At this moment the Paraguayan president personally appeared to have a direct say on military operations. Throughout the war Estigarribia had always obtained the approval of Eusebio Ayala for any major military action; the president had often placed conditions or at the least had fixed the date for the start of the operation. The president had routinely toured the front, and in an extended visit to field headquarters from 24 to 28 August, he quite unexpectedly insisted on the immediate capture of Ballivián. As a politician, the President shared with his Bolivian counterpart the belief that the capture of Ballivián would mean the end of the war. Estigarribia and his staff officers in vain tried to explain to the president the futility of frontal assaults on Ballivián, but to no avail. Estigarribia went so far as to assert that in due time Ballivián will fall, but no military argument could sway the obstinate president. Finally on the last day of his visit a visibly angry president asked Estigarribia: "what would you do if I gave the troops the order to attack?"[30] Very calmly Estigarribia replied that he would then decide whether to obey the president as commander in chief or whether to ask to be relieved of command. Estigarribia had never raised the threat of a resignation before and it would fall like a bombshell in Asunción; as a politician Ayala had totally missed the military reasons but immediately understood the political argument. The president made a supreme effort to control his emotions and quietly boarded the plane for the return flight to Asunción. Estigarribia should have stood up to the president in the same manner when the truce proposal first appeared in December 1933, but at least this time the general's firm opposition prevented any rash political concerns from harming military operations.

During that same period, the Bolivian president likewise traveled to the front. The Paraguayans had shattered his plan to advance through Ingavi, and worse they were near the Parapetí River and Carandaití. Not only were the Paraguayans deep in the Bolivian rear and thus in a position soon to cut off the Bolivian army to the south, but the Paraguayans were near the petroleum fields. The rapid Paraguayan advance had sent La Paz and the Bolivian public into panic; more in response to these passionate political pressures than to any real military danger Salamanca had decided to visit his field commanders. All present except Colonel Toro agreed that the only solution was to abandon Ballivián and to use the released troops to launch a counteroffensive. The commanders overestimated the danger from Colonel Franco's II Corps and did not realize that the Paraguayan offensive in the north had ground to a halt. To Salamanca, the tentative withdrawal from Ballivián he had earlier authorized had become politically impossible after the rapid Paraguayan advance towards the Parapetí. The meetings took on a very gloomy look until Colonel Toro proposed a solution more congenial to the President. Besides holding Ballivián, Colonel Toro proposed leading troops in a march east to seize Garrapatal, in effect cutting off Franco's II Corps. Salamanca heartily agreed and gave Toro the necessary authorization on 29 August. The rest of the commanders were not happy with this unrealistic proposal, but they acquiesced for the simple reason that this was the first step necessary to abandon Ballivián. Once Toro became commander of the expedition, he lost control over the troops at Ballivián. Once Toro was out of the direct line of command, he could only protest against a withdrawal.[31]

Toro had originally intended to press from El Carmen to Garrapatal, but as expected, the Paraguayans blocked the paths leading east. No quick advance was possible through the jungle to cut off the Paraguayan II Corps. As an alternative, he stripped the troops from the El Carmen sector and trucked them through roads in the rear to Carandaití, which became his base of operations. He had swiftly positioned his troops to strike a surprise and devastating blow against the Paraguayans at Algodonal. However, he had run the very high risk of leaving unprotected large stretches of jungle in front of El Carmen, a situation that intensive Paraguayan patrolling soon reported to Estigarribia. Toro did not worry about any Paraguayan reprisals, and instead believed that his overwhelming numerical superiority was sure to win the smashing victories he needed to reach the presidency of his country. Bolivian commanders were all deeply enmeshed in politics, but Toro more than any other was truly a politician in an officer's uniform. His troops had arrived just in time, because the persistent Paraguayans had hauled their artillery to the front and began to shell Carandaití on 5 September in preparation for a large attack.

Just that day Toro ordered his troops to encircle the Paraguayan 6th Division, but not until 8 September did the Bolivians surround the Paraguayans. Toro greeted this initial success with frenzied rejoicing, even though he had not yet swallowed the coveted prize. Without a trace of modesty in his personality, on 9 September he announced that his victory resembled the German triumph at Tannenberg in World War I. That very same day, just as he was congratulating himself on his triumph, the Paraguayan 6th Division ruined the celebrations by quietly escaping through a gap. Toro was determined to have his victory, and undismayed he rushed reinforcements to prepare a second encirclement. But before he was ready to launch the maneuver, heavy rainfalls began on 18 September, the first downpour in five months. As the dirt roads turned into thick mud, the Bolivian offensive necessarily slowed and gave the Paraguayans several days to escape. However, the Paraguayans underestimated the threat from the huge army of Toro, and only withdrew to Algodonal where on 22 September the Bolivians again trapped the Paraguayan 6th Division. The Paraguayans launched desperate attacks until finally the 6th Division fought its way out, but not without suffering heavy casualties and losing some equipment. A chastened Franco pulled back his defense line near to Yrendagüe on 29 September and did everything possible to repel the next Bolivian attack. To the Paraguayans' surprise, Toro did not press forward with his huge army. Apparently the failure of the two prior attempts to encircle the Paraguayans had demoralized both him and the Bolivian soldiers. Toro bombarded headquarters with requests for reinforcements to complete his offensive and was quite content to proclaim to the public back home how much territory he had recovered.[32]

The triumphal announcements could not hide the fact that Toro's offensive had spent itself. Estigarribia decided that this was a good time to attempt to capture Ingavi. Units from the II Corps had been trying to push east from 27 de Noviembre but had always run into a strong Bolivian defense line. Estigarribia ordered the II Corps to keep up a steady pressure on the Ingavi front while he tried a very risky maneuver. Since 1932 only a platoon occupied Pitiantuta, and its orders were to withdraw if attacked by a superior force. For the first time Estigarribia decided to reinforce this distant outpost and made it the jumping off point for an attack on Ingavi. Setting out from Pitiantuta, a detachment of 150 soldiers supported by five trucks undertook the long march of 220 kilometers to the north through virtually impenetrable jungle trails. The Paraguayans completed the epic trek and surprised the Bolivian garrison. With the capture of Ingavi on 5 October, Paraguay prevented any Bolivian advance in the extreme north.[33]

The loss of Ingavi could still not prod the Bolivians to resume their offensive against the Paraguayan II Corps. Toro's request for massive reinforcements triggered an intense struggle within Bolivian ruling circles. Toro's successful advance had revived President Salamanca's earlier plan to strike via the north to reach the Paraguay River. While the president saw the plan as the as the last chance for an acceptable peace, Colonel Rodríguez saw in Salamanca's proposal a good opportunity to cut off the Paraguayan II Corps. If the Bolivians sent a large force east of Capirenda, they could cut off the Paraguayan II Corps near Garrapatal. The plan reduced Toro to a mere spectator, and predictably he insisted on being in command of any major offensive. Victories, no matter how meaningless or even harmful, impressed

public opinion at La Paz and made him a prime candidate for the presidency. As the power struggle raged among the army commanders and their president, the Bolivian army stood still. By the time Toro received the reinforcements for a renewed offensive, 46 days had elapsed.

The Bolivians had assumed that the Paraguayans would passively await the attack, when in reality even the proverbially cautious Estigarribia knew that he had to respond somehow to thrown the mounting Bolivian forces off balance. Where and how should Estigarribia attack? In a calculated gamble, he refused to reinforce the Paraguayan II Corps. As he explained to Colonel Franco "you will have the risky and difficult mission of getting the Bolivians to nibble after the bait."[34] The II Corps was the bait that Franco enthusiastically endangered in the dangerous mission of luring Toro's forces to the southeast. While the Paraguayan III Corps maintained steady pressure on the fortifications of Ballivián, the I Corps had the mission of breaking the Bolivian line further north near the El Carmen sector. The Paraguayans knew that Toro had stripped the El Carmen sector of units, and they counted on finding an undefended stretch through which one of their units could pass on the way to outflank the Bolivian division defending El Carmen. While the 1st Division distracted the Bolivians with frontal attacks, the 8th Division marched to the north of El Carmen at the same time that the 2nd Division did the same to the south. The objective of the two flanking divisions was the dirt road "V" which, branching off from the Lóbrego Road, was the only supply route to the Bolivian division defending El Carmen (Map 25). The front had become so long that the Bolivians cleared a second dirt road "S" to supply the southern sector. Because "S" branched off from "V," a road block of the latter necessarily trapped the entire Bolivian division.[35]

In the El Carmen front the Paraguayans initially enjoyed a slight numerical superiority over the Bolivian defenders but not enough to take any Bolivian defenses by frontal assault. Success hinged on finding an undefended route to the Bolivian rear, but the captured maps were inadequate and aerial reconnaissance was inconclusive. Estigarribia called on the 8th and 2nd divisions to send long-range patrols to dis-

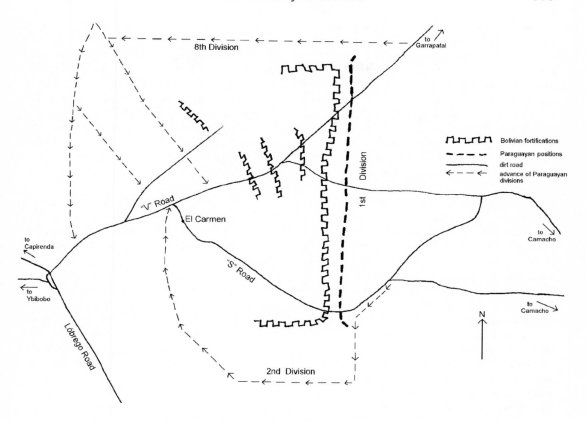

Map 25. Battle of El Carmen, November 1934 .

cover a way to the Bolivian rear. The commander of the 8th Division decided to send two small patrols to explore the northern area. Colonel Fernandez, the commander of the I Corps took charge of the organization of the patrol of the 2nd Division. He requested the divisional commander to send him the three best officers for the mission. Because coincidentally, all three were of equal rank and seniority, he asked them to pick their leader. Two of the three officers immediately proposed Gerónimo Vidal, and Colonel Fernández accepted their suggestion. Meanwhile the staff of the I Corps had busied itself concocting an elaborate plan for the patrol. The worst enemy was water: The Paraguayans had to haul their water from far in the rear and the only source of water on the Bolivian side was the well in El Carmen. In the past patrols had to turn back when their water supply became low, but Colonel Fernández and his staff believed they had found a solution. Each soldier received five canteens, the ideal number, while 32 carriers lugged 8 large water

cans for the 33 soldiers of the patrol. As soon as one water can was empty, a corresponding number of carriers would return to the base to report and to reduce the chance of detection by the Bolivians. Colonel Fernández emphasized that avoiding detection was almost as important as finding the way to the rear; the three officers requested that their orders be in writing to make sure they were absolutely clear about their mission.

Since this was not a combat patrol but a long-distance reconnaissance, the men were lightly armed. Officers normally carried submachine guns but for this mission they had only their pistols. The submachine guns went to three soldiers, and Mauser rifles armed the rest of the soldiers. Each man received only 100 cartridges or half their normal allotment, and even more significantly none received hand grenades. The Paraguayan soldier normally refused to go into battle without grenades, and for some assaults preferred to exchange their rifles and cartridges for extra grenades. This deliberate absence of grenades made the soldiers feel naked and more than anything else guaranteed that only a surprise Bolivian attack could force them into contact. On 31 October at 1430 Vidal's men set out and first marched about 4 kilometers down road "S" until they were one kilometer from the forward Bolivian positions. Walking parallel to the Bolivian line, they knew their chance of detection was greatest during this segment of their trip. They could have turned into the jungle sooner and avoided the Bolivians altogether, but then they would not have been able to discover the location of the southernmost Bolivian outpost. Because the Bolivians were used to aggressive patrolling by the Paraguayans in this sector, the patrol hoped that if detected the Bolivians would not attach any significance to this movement. Once the officers had concluded that they had left behind the last Bolivian outpost, the patrol turned west. By then night had fallen and with it came a torrential downpour, the first in a long time.[36]

Only Vidal gave the orders, but the enviable closeness of the three officers meant that the power of three minds worked harmoniously as one. As the officers huddled under the rainfall, they quickly expressed their doubts about being able to avoid contact with the Bolivians. The elaborate plan of the General Staff had been a very reasonable guide, but it needed some adjustments. Even if the patrol avoided running into Bolivians, skilled scouts were sure to spot mud tracks and other signs of troop movement in the water-soaked jungle. As a minimal precaution the soldiers were laboriously using the blunt end of their machetes to push aside rather than cut through the branches, but the scratching of the water cans against one ubiquitous plant sent off a loud shrill sound audible a long way off. The officers decided to send back the 33 water carriers on the morning of 1 November. The men of course stuffed themselves with water one last time and refilled their canteens; the officers made the calculated gamble that they would find ponds filled with the recent rain water. The officers also were aware of the natural tendency of the men to drop everything and to begin feverishly looking for ponds in the jungle once the canteens were almost empty. To the immense relief of the soldiers, at the end of a long and exhausting walk a pond 50 meters long greeted

them. The men drank heartily and replenished their canteens; unfortunately they knew that the shallowness of the pond (30 centimeters) meant that unless more rain fell, the pond would evaporate in a few days.[37]

During that day's march, the patrol found abandoned Bolivian positions; had the Bolivian troops stayed there instead of leaving with Colonel Toro, no reconnaissance patrol could have escaped detection. As recently as some weeks before the Bolivians had been present in large numbers at a deserted truck road running south from road "S." To cross this abandoned road, the patrol did not go in single file, and instead the officers scattered the men who then singly jumped by large steps across the road trying not to leave foot prints in the mud. On 2 November as the patrol advanced through the jungle, the men tried to use their machetes as little as possible to avoid leaving behind a visible path. The canteens they had refilled the night before still supplied adequate water, but the agonizing heat and the poor rations were weakening the men. During most of the war the soldiers carried canned cooked beef, which had the disadvantage of worsening their cravings for water. As a substitute, this patrol was testing a new canned ration comprised of hard tack (*galleta*) and salted peanuts. The Vidal patrol found that the concoction lacked nutritional value and made the men thirstier than the original canned corned beef. As the men staggered in for a night's sleep, the officers concluded that their patrol was in no condition to advance much farther.[38]

The next morning the men made a final effort, and soon the increasingly noisy sounds of trucks in the jungle rewarded their agonizing exertions. About noon the patrol came upon a glen 3 kilometers long and about 1.3 kilometers wide that aerial observation had reported existed next to road "V." The sound of truck traffic was strong, and upon hearing two hunting shots nearby, the officers decided that it was time to retreat quickly to report the findings to Colonel Fernández. The men walked back eagerly, because they were in a race to return to their base before either the malnutrition or the lack of water stopped them. On 4 November the patrol was again nearing the southernmost outpost in the Bolivian defense line; as an added precaution, Lieutenant Vidal decided not to return by their previous path, but to walk one kilometer further south through thick jungle. The additional effort was too much for many men, and even a night's sleep could not restore their energy. After a few hours walking on 5 November some soldiers and Vidal himself collapsed, but by then the patrol was very near the Paraguayan 1st Division, and enough survivors made it to safety. The strongest men returned with help to recover Vidal and their exhausted comrades. When Colonel Fernandez received the report of the safe return of the patrol, he was ecstatic and could not wait to send the entire 2nd Division down what was baptized as the Vidal trail.[39]

The final decision rested with Estigarribia who was relieved to hear from Vidal's patrol but was even more worried about the two patrols of the 8th Division. Although smaller than Vidal's patrol, their journeys had been more tortuous. On 4 November the patrol of Lieutenant Cecelio Escobar sent back a preliminary report with couriers who unfortunately exchanged shots with a Bolivian outpost. Even worse, the next day the second patrol crashed into a large Bolivian unit; the Paraguayans fled but one soldier was unaccounted for. Right then Estigarribia decided that he would have to cancel the operation unless the missing soldier appeared alive or was confirmed dead. If taken prisoner, even a simple interrogation would have revealed enough to the Bolivians to foil the offensive of Estigarribia. But fortune was beginning to show its preference to Paraguay, and on 6 November the 8th Division reported that the missing soldier had returned to base. Relieved as was Estigarribia, he still could not launch the offensive until he heard something more definite from Lieutenant Escobar. The expectation and anxiety mounted until on 7 November Estigarribia received the report that the patrol of Escobar had returned after having reached road "V." Since the Bolivians had seen only handfuls of Paraguayans in the skirmishes, Estigarribia concluded that they had failed to discern what his real intentions were, and he could safely launch the offensive.[40]

The risk in reality was much greater than Estigarribia believed. Colonel Rodríguez immediately concluded that the Paraguayans were preparing a flanking movement through the north, but the absence of any reports from the south left him unsure as to where the main Paraguayan blow would fall. The steady arrival of reinforcements had regained for Bolivia a numerical superiority over the Paraguayans. Rodríguez decided to place to the rear of the Bolivian defense line a division he began forming with new units and named Colonel Walter Méndez as its commander. Having a reserve force is a dogma of military doctrine, but in this case Rodríguez should have sent the new division either to the north or the south to extend the defense line. In reality the two ends of the Bolivian defense hung on air, and to the north the unprotected gap stretched 60 kilometers. To the south, the defenders at Ballivián were extending their line of fortifications, but at least 25 kilometers remained undefended.

Because Colonel Toro had taken so many troops away from the El Carmen front, Colonel Rodríguez could not do as much as he would have liked to parry the impending Paraguayan attack. Colonel Rodríguez had done everything possible to block the offensive of Toro, but the latter emerged victorious in the political in-fighting. Rodríguez was left with the slim hope that just maybe Toro's offensive might derail Estigarribia's attack on El Carmen. Toro was supposed to capture Picuiba and push further south and west into the Paraguayan rear. This offensive was fundamentally flawed, because only if Toro achieved extraordinary success could he neutralize the El Carmen operation. A simple glance at the map revealed that even if Colonel Franco's II Corps collapsed, the Bolivians had to traverse large distances before they reached any vulnerable point in the Paraguayan rear. And once more, intense rains delayed Colonel Toro's offensive, which finally began on 6 November. Because the Bolivians were trying to silently sneak around the front line, only on 8 November did the Paraguayan divisions become aware of the threatening maneuver. In spite of the overwhelming numbers of the Bolivians, twice the Paraguayan divisions escaped encirclement. The Bolivian capture of Yrendagüe on 10 November had been so fast that it had left isolated the Paraguayan garrison at 27 de Noviembre. This unit withdrew to Ingavi, along the way felling trees and setting up other obstacles to hinder any Bolivian attempt to recapture Ingavi. The Bolivians when they entered Yrendagüe on 10 November made the pleasing discovery that the Paraguayans had struck water after drilling wells. The abundant water heightened the danger of a serious Bolivian threat on this front, and Estigarribia had to decide whether to continue with his planned offensive on El Carmen or whether to shift units to stop Colonel Toro's offensive. After careful examination, Estigarribia concluded that Colonel Franco was capable of delaying Toro long enough to carry out a successful offensive at El Carmen.[41]

Fortunately for Toro's presidential aspirations, Estigarribia never wavered in his determination to sacrifice Yrendagüe and Picuiba for the sake of the offensive at El Carmen, although he moved up the attack date. Early in the morning on 11 November the Paraguayan 2nd Division set out silently through the Vidal trail in a narrow file, with mortars and machine guns as their heaviest equipment. Strung between every two soldiers was a box of 1000 cartridges. Ten-minute pauses after every hour of walking kept the men from collapsing in the exhausting heat. Separate teams of porters were shuttling water and food from the rear but soon fell behind in bringing the vital liquid to the men. On 13 November the 2nd Division reached the glen Vidal's patrol had earlier spotted, and to everyone's surprise found a large pond stretching along the glen (500 meters by 15 meters). The pond made the water porters unnecessary, and the soldiers requested more cartridges for the upcoming battle they expected to be particularly ferocious. The soldiers were already hearing truck traffic in the distance, and because the noise was increasing, they concluded that the Bolivians were already hastily fleeing. The lead unit hoped to reach road "V" in time to trap some escaping Bolivians. The divisional commander worried instead about how to hold his long front; and he feared that any trapped Bolivians would try to fight their way through one of the trails or the truck road leading south. Estigarribia was aware of the problem and had sent additional units behind the 2nd Division to help defend the long line of the Vidal path.[42]

The superb reconnaissance of the Vidal patrol had kept the 2nd Division undetected until it reached the designated truck road at 1600 on 13 November. Soon the Paraguayans realized that they had blocked not "V" but "S" road; thus in theory most of the Bolivian division could escape if it had not done so already.

Frantically the lead unit searched through a maze of Bolivian trails until at 1800 it wandered by accident into El Carmen. The sudden appearance of the Paraguayans so far from the front line caught by surprise the Bolivians, who were almost all staff personnel; the Bolivian commander fled hurriedly and abandoned his men, although some days later he was captured hiding in the jungle. Among the many items the Paraguayans captured were the entire archives of the division. With the captured documents and maps to guide them, the Paraguayans at last understood the Bolivian road network and the troop deployments. With night falling the Paraguayans could not reach their objective of road "V," but they made the amazing discovery that the well they had just captured at El Carmen supplied the water for the entire Bolivian division. In other words, all the Bolivians to the west of road "S" were without water and those along road "V" henceforth had to haul their water all the way from Lóbrego Road.

The silent deployment of the Paraguayan 2nd Division ranks as one of the great maneuvers of the war. To the north of the Bolivian defense line, the Paraguayan 8th Division clashed with Bolivian units the day after its departure on 10 November. Why the Paraguayan 8th Division hugged the Bolivian line so closely has not been explained, and in any case no surprise was possible when already on 11 November the Bolivians were expecting a large Paraguayan effort on the north. To counter the mounting Paraguayan pressure on the north, the Bolivian high command sent the new Méndez division down road "V" and gave it the task of extending the existing defense line westward. Once the Paraguayans had captured El Carmen on 13 November, to insist on rushing Bolivian troops east on road "V" was downright stupid. The high command should have promptly begun a swift evacuation, but unfortunately no commander wanted to take the politically risky decision of abandoning worthless real estate. When the Paraguayans heard the noise from the intense truck traffic on road "V," they mistakenly concluded that the Bolivians were making frantic efforts to evacuate all their forward positions. Not in their wildest dreams could the Paraguayans ever imagine that the Bolivians were rushing more troops into the trap. When the 2nd Division finally located and blocked the famous "V" road late at night on 15 November, Estigarribia felt the trap had shut too late.[43] To try to prepare the government for the bad news he sent the following telegram:

For President of the Republic
In spite of all the difficulties, today we finally blocked the second road, but I believe it was too late. In large part at least for now, we should not count on the anticipated success.
General Estigarribia[44]

He still retained the hope that if he hurried the northern pincer movement, the Paraguayans might still bag many Bolivian stragglers. To offset the Toro's gains in the east, Estigarribia desperately needed to inflict a crippling blow on the Bolivian forces at El Carmen. An early indication was encouraging. On 15 November the 2nd Division confirmed the disintegration of that part of the Bolivian defense line formerly supplied from road "S." These Bolivians had been the first to lose their water supply, and upon hearing the expression "pilas [Bolivian slang for Paraguayans] to the rear,"[45] the officers fled and the units collapsed as the men desperately searched the jungle for water. Finally the long-awaited news that the 8th and 2nd divisions had linked up at road "V" came at 1150 on 16 November. The moment had come to count the prisoners to see if the Paraguayans had trapped one division at least. The results exceeded all expectations, because the Paraguayans, at a cost of less than 100 casualties, had captured over 8,000 prisoners with all their equipment, weapons, and supplies. When the dead and wounded mostly from thirst were added, the Bolivians had suffered the loss of over 10,000 men.

The dry figures could not convey the immense human tragedy of this maneuver. The scenes among the Bolivians came out of Dante's Inferno. Soldiers hallucinated in their mad cravings for water; some dug holes in the sand searching for tubers and died in the effort. Some barely could crawl while others fought among themselves to drink the urine of a fellow prisoner. The Paraguayans brought water trucks, but the crazed Bolivians lunged forward in such desperation that the water was needlessly spilled. The Paraguayans then could do nothing but load the prisoners aboard trucks for a trip to the rear, but the dehydrated Bolivians kept sliding off the trucks. Initially the drivers stopped to try to res-

cue the fallen, but while the Paraguayans reloaded the men, more had fallen dead aboard the truck. Henceforth the drivers drove as fast as possible and stopped for no one; by then it was so dark that perhaps mercifully those that fell off were promptly crushed to death by the following trucks. Soon so many dead bodies littered the road that the Paraguayans named it in their Guaraní language the road of thirst.[46]

Had the heinous suffering become publicized, most certainly it would have powerfully affected the Bolivian public and helped pave a path to peace, as happened later at Picuiba. However, because the Paraguayans had executed the pincer movement so brilliantly, no survivors escaped to report the sufferings to the press. In the dark about the true human cost, the Bolivian public accepted a major defeat but still insisted on prosecuting the war. The immediate task was to save the threatened Bolivian troops at the Ballivián defense line. On 16 November the Bolivians began a hasty evacuation of Ballivián, but not without the predictable protest from Colonel Toro. The Paraguayan III Corps, long frustrated by the fortifications, lunged forward like an uncaged tiger against the withdrawing Bolivians and did not allow them enough time to set up a second fortified line at Guachalla (Map 24). The Paraguayans occupied that point on 21 November and then Esmeralda on 25 November. The Bolivian high command realized that the retreating troops had lost all will to fight and were in no condition to detain the Paraguayan advance up the Pilcomayo River. In desperation, the Bolivian high command transferred units from Colonel Toro's force to try to stem the onrushing tide of Paraguayans. The Bolivians were behaving just as Estigarribia had expected, and his careful plan to halt Toro at Picuiba by the thrust at El Carmen had worked perfectly. No less vigorous in the pursuit was Colonel Fernández, who hurled his I Corps into the huge gap the battle of El Carmen had left in the Bolivian defense lines. During the pursuit after El Carmen, at least another 10,000 men fell prisoner, and this without counting the many Bolivians who fled across the Pilcomayo River to desert in Argentina. The Paraguayans had accomplished the destruction of the third field army Bolivia had so laboriously created after the debacle of Campo Vía.[47]

Such a catastrophe was ideal for finger-pointing, and both the Bolivian public and the army demanded a scapegoat. President Salamanca, whose weariness with the war was already evident, was extremely angry with the army. After considering likely culprits, Salamanca decided to put all the blame on General Enrique Peñaranda, the nominal field commander. Salamanca flew to Villa Montes to dismiss General Peñarenda and to appoint a new commander. Other army officers were sure to oppose violently this change of command because they did not want their independent fiefdoms threatened. Salamanca should have recalled General Peñaranda to La Paz and there sacked him, or the president should have come to Villa Montes with a large police escort, as he had done in the past; the police, as the traditional rivals of the army, were sure to protect him. But Salamanca took none of the basic precautions, and the only possible explanation for his neglect was his subconscious desire to seek an end to an unmanageable situation. He could no longer shoulder the burden of the Chaco War which had physically and psychologically drained him. When he announced the changes in Villa Montes on 26 November, Colonel Toro launched a conspiracy to stage a military coup. Army units with clockwork precision and acting in perfect synchronization cut off all the escape routes of President Salamanca and quickly turned him into a helpless prisoner. As many quipped at the time, the first and only successful encirclement the Bolivian army completed was against its own president. The amazing efficiency of the Bolivian officers in domestic politics stood in stark contrast to their abysmal performance on the battlefield. A relieved Salamanca (long since reconciled to his bitter fate) duly resigned and handed the presidency over to vice president Luis Tejada Sorzano. He could not escape blame for his many blunders in the past, but at least he knew that the officers had spared him the additional humiliation of having to sign a peace treaty recognizing the loss of the Chaco. Salamanca returned to his home at La Paz, a broken and defeated man, no less a victim of the Chaco than the many ragged and crippled returning veterans.[48]

The Disaster of Picuiba

The burden of supporting Colonel David Toro's force placed excessive strain on the Bo-

livian supply lines. Along the Pilcomayo River and the Lóbrego Road the Bolivians had overcome the logistical difficulties, but the problems in the northern sector of the Chaco remained insurmountable. Only the capture of the water wells at Yrendagüe on 10 November prevented a total collapse in the Bolivian logistics, yet Toro insisted on pushing his men forward against the determined resistance of the Paraguayan II Corps. The exhausted Bolivian troops took a heavy beating and large casualties in their drive to reach Picuiba. By the time they entered Picuiba on 20 November, the capture of this place had become meaningless if not downright harmful. After the collapse of the front at El Carmen, the simplest analysis demonstrated that the Bolivians had to abandon their exposed positions at Picuiba, as even foreign newspapers were quick to point out. Picuiba was the place in the Chaco most vulnerable to an outflanking movement, because to the west stretched glens from Yrendagüe south to the Paraguayan positions near La Faye (Map 26). As the Paraguayans noted, soldiers did not have to use their machetes to traverse these glens. Even Colonel Toro recognized the danger, but correctly he saw in the glens an avenue to launch an attack. He requested either reinforcements to carry out an offensive or authorization to withdraw. The army commanders, who were virtually independent after the overthrow of the former president Daniel Salamanca, did not want a withdrawal to sully their new rule and instead somehow found units to reinforce Toro. West of El Carmen Bolivian resistance seemed to be stiffening, and the high command hoped to detain the Paraguayans long enough to establish a new defensive line around Cururenda (Map 24). Estigarribia had already detected the increasing Bolivian resistance and feared that his troops would get trapped in the maze of trenches defending Villa Montes. He was not going to repeat the blunder after Campo Vía of failing to pursue, but he did not want to sacrifice his scarce infantry in frontal assaults. In one of his most brilliant strategic decisions, on 21 November he ordered the 8th Division to walk from the western front to join Colonel Rafael Franco's II Corps.[49]

As the 8th Division recuperated from its long march on foot, Colonel Franco carefully prepared his counterstroke. The plan called first for the 8th Division to set out to capture

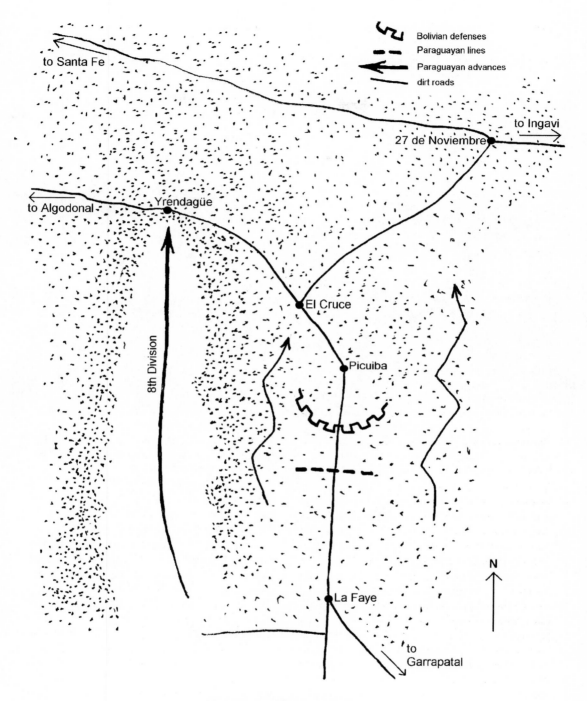

Map 26. Yrendagüe–Picuiba.

the wells at Yrendagüe. After the 8th Division had a lead of at least one day, then the other two divisions of the II Corps would enter the jungle to encircle the Bolivians by reaching the roads to the north (Map 26). On the night of 4 December the 8th Division began its march through the glens to Yrendagüe. Speed was vi-tally crucial, not just to surprise the Bolivians, but mainly because each soldier carried at most four canteens and had food rations for only three days. If the 8th Division did not capture the wells in three days, the soldiers would die of thirst, and the long march could easily turn into a suicide mission. About 40 kilometers

Paraguayan soldiers on the attack. Rapid advances through clearings like this one permitted victories otherwise impossible in the dense jungle of the Chaco (*The Epic of the Chaco: Marshal Estigarribia's Memoirs of the Chaco War;* Austin: University of Texas Press, 1950).

away from Yrendagüe, the soldiers halted to conserve their scarce water. A few hours later Colonel Franco by radio heard of the halt, and he ordered the division to resume the march immediately and not to stop walking until it had reached Yrendagüe where the soldiers would have plenty of water. The delay appeared to put the attack in danger, but later Franco learned that the halt had been a miracle. Just a few hours earlier, Bolivian troops had finished passing the glen as a short cut on the way south to Picuiba. Had the fresh Bolivian troops run into the haggard and thirsty Paraguayans, the whole attack plan would have failed.

Once Franco was sure that the 8th Division was near its objective, he felt he could safely order the two other divisions forward early on 7 December; however, he was already afraid that they might arrive too late to cut off the Bolivian retreat. Meanwhile at 0200 on 8 December the 8th Division emerged from the forest into a plain 6 kilometers long in front of Yrendagüe. According to prearranged plans,

the division had split up into small patrols and larger contingents under the desultory fire of Bolivian pickets. Rather than charge the Bolivian positions, Paraguayan units went to block the road to El Cruce. This maneuver was completed shortly after daylight began at 0530. The news that the Paraguayans had blocked the road to El Cruce sent the Bolivians, mostly wounded and convalescent men, into panic. After setting Yrendagüe on fire, the defenders fled west along the road to Algodonal. A general assault against collapsing resistance gave the Paraguayans control of Yrendagüe and its wells at 0715. The Paraguayans could not have captured the wells at a better moment, because one day before through sheer incompetence the Bolivian water trucks had failed to take the daily water ration to Picuiba. The Bolivians in Picuiba were already thirsty and anxiously waiting for the water trucks on 8 December when they heard that the Paraguayans had captured the wells.[50]

It is a testament to the enormous patient

endurance of the Bolivian soldiers that they did not immediately flee to the north in droves. The Paraguayans repeatedly commented that the war would have been much different had the Bolivian soldiers been well led; had General Hans Kundt commanded Chilean officers, a powerful force was sure to have emerged. At Picuiba by the rarest of coincidences, the officers in charge of the two Bolivian divisions were unusually competent. Quite revealingly, they held their positions in an interim capacity and their normal position was chief of staff. They were temporarily in charge because the nominal commanders of the two divisions had gone to the rear to participate in political intrigues and to enjoy the wild parties and banquets Colonel Toro was famous for. Of the two interim commanders, Lieutenant Colonel Félix Tabera had wanted to withdraw the division as early as 6 December. He believed a Paraguayan offensive to be imminent, and he knew his wretched and starving soldiers were in no condition to withstand any attacks. On 7 December he sent out patrols to confirm his belief, and they soon clashed with Paraguayan units. Tabera could not know that his patrols had run into the last part of Franco's maneuver to surround the Bolivians, yet he presciently concluded on the basis of fragmentary information that a major offensive had started. When he learned early in the morning of 8 December that the Paraguayans had captured the wells at Yrendagüe, he and his fellow divisional commander immediately requested permission to withdraw. Colonel Toro agreed to abandon Picuiba, because his fertile imagination fantasized that the retreating Bolivian troops were going to capture the Paraguayans supposedly trapped at Yrendagüe.[51]

Colonel Toro did not realize that the soldiers at Picuanda had already been one whole day without water, and to make the situation even more critical, 8 December proved to be one of the hottest days in an already scorching summer. The soldiers were simply too dehydrated and too malnourished to make a walk back possible. Men began throwing away their equipment, munitions, and weapons before collapsing. The sand was so hot that it burned the skin just by touching. When the ragged column reached the road junction of El Cruce that night, Colonel Tabera knew that his exhausted and unarmed men were in no condi-

tion to launch an attack to recover the well at Yrendagüe to the west. He promptly ordered all the artillery to continue retreating to 27 de Noviembre and to carry the weakest soldiers aboard its trucks. Radio communication with headquarters had been lost, although Toro dropped from airplanes messages repeating his earlier orders to attack and recapture Yrendagüe. So many soldiers had already died during the march of 30 kilometers from Picuiba to the road junction of El Cruce, that Tabera concluded that the infantry was in no condition to assault Yrendagüe. Not knowing how much longer the escape roads would remain open, he ordered the infantry to try to follow the artillery north to 27 de Noviembre in what was rapidly turning into a pathetic rout. The insubordination of Tabera saved many Bolivian soldiers, who with their last ounce of emotion yelled out thanks for this chance to escape alive.

Unknown to Tabera, extreme good luck had allowed the retreat north to continue unmolested. The two Paraguayan divisions carrying out the flanking movement were lost in the jungle and had still not blocked the escape roads. The Paraguayan threat remained as one more danger hovering over the thirsty and exhausted men who on foot were struggling to cover the 87 kilometers from Picuiba to 27 the Noviembre. As their desperation mounted and frustration reached unbearable proportions, many men went raving mad. In stark contrast to the Chilean officers who stayed with their soldiers, most Bolivian officers had long since abandoned their units and fled aboard the remaining trucks. In one disgraceful instance, Bolivian officers went so far as to mount machine guns aboard the trucks and to open fire on their own men to keep the soldiers from clambering aboard and overloading the trucks.[52] The leaderless men trudged north, only sustained by the hope that water trucks from 27 de Noviembre were coming to save them. Unfortunately for the dehydrated survivors, a combination of clogged roads and stark incompetence prevented the water trucks from delivering the vital liquid. In at least one case, an officer so hated Colonel Toro that to make the disaster reach catastrophic proportions, he deliberately sabotaged the supply efforts in an attempt to destroy Toro's chances to reach the presidency. Once stark reality shattered any illusions about the arrival of the water trucks, utterly dejected men started to fall behind and huddled under trees trying to find shade from the sun's furious rays. Others continued to laboriously drag themselves forward until they collapsed never to rise again. The lucky ones who had kept their rifles committed suicide in desperation. As in the battle of El Carmen, others died in an attempt to dig out juicy roots deep in the sands, while other men buried themselves in the sand before committing suicide. The two Bolivian divisions were suffering a horrendous agony, the most ghastly among the many tragic episodes of the Chaco War. The heavens took compassion on so much agonizing suffering and sent relief in a torrential downpour on the night of 10 December. Without these life-sustaining rains, none could have escaped alive.[53]

When Colonel Franco sent his covering force facing Picuiba to pursue the retreating Bolivians, the piles of abandoned equipment, trucks, weapons, and ammunition so clogged the road as to make any pursuit impossible. No trucks could drive through the chaos, and while normally nothing could stop the nimble Paraguayan infantrymen, the wreckage, the countless cadavers, and the groans of the dying paralyzed their advance. So many Bolivians had died in such hot temperatures that just the stench from the rapidly decomposing bodies was unbearable. The Paraguayans quickly tried to bypass the ghastly scenes, only to find even more nightmarish sites ahead on the road. The Paraguayans saved many agonizing Bolivians from death and took prisoner over two thousand survivors. Very few Bolivian officers fell prisoner, because these had fled ahead and abandoned their men. At last on 11 December one of the flanking divisions reached the road and at 27 de Noviembre promptly smashed the emaciated Bolivian regiment that had been trying to cover the disastrous rout. However, the survivors from Tabera's ragged column had already reached safety near the Parapetí River.

The failure to complete the encirclement did not have any adverse military effect. Besides the prisoners taken, at least ten thousand Bolivians perished or disappeared, and those who had survived were in no condition to return to the front in a long time if ever. The defeats under General Hans Kundt seemed bear-able compared to one catastrophe after another under the exclusively Bolivian leadership. The elimination of so many Bolivian units in one sweep had torn open such a huge gash in the front that Franco's II Corps was free to advance virtually unopposed.[54] The real impact of Picuiba was psychological, but in a different way than anyone had expected. The escape of enough survivors provided the first chance in the war for the Bolivian public to learn the truth about the Chaco. At El Carmen successful Paraguayan encirclement had prevented any Bolivians from recounting their horrible experiences, but instead Picuiba provided the press with many first-hand accounts of the disastrous retreat. The graphic accounts described the inhuman suffering and questioned the need to fight over a worthless wilderness. What most shocked the civilian public was that the blatant incompetence of the Bolivian officers had been responsible for the horrible suffering and the huge casualties. As a veteran explained, "No other action of the campaign had such a impact on the morale as the retreat from Picuiba"[55] Up to then the Bolivian public had insisted on driving out the Paraguayans from the Chaco, but the calamitous retreat from Picuiba paved the way for acceptance of much more modest aims. After years of nationalistic propaganda, public opinion shifted and became resigned to more limited aims. The new government of Luis Tejada Sorzano was determined to keep the fertile province of Santa Cruz and the oil fields of Villa Montes, but not the nearly worthless Chaco proper.

For the moment the initiative rested with the Paraguayans. How far would the Paraguayans advance after the collapse of the Picuiba front? The offensive was no longer just military but also political: Delegates from the province of Santa Cruz visited Colonel Franco requesting arms to set up an independent republic. The proposal promised to deprive Bolivia of its nearest source of food and to release all of the Paraguayan II Corps for its westward drive against Villa Montes. Colonel Franco enthusiastically supported the independence of Santa Cruz, but Estigarribia's position on the proposal was not clear. Delegations repeatedly visited President Eusebio Ayala, who ultimately rejected the idea, although as a goodwill gesture Paraguay released some Bolivian prisoners from Santa Cruz. Ayala's refusal to use

Santa Cruz as a lever to end the war was another of his blunders.[56] Bolivia gave no signs of wanting peace, and on the contrary, President Tejada declared a general mobilization on 10 December 1934. Henceforth all adult males were liable for military duty, and out of this huge human mass Bolivia proceeded to create its fourth field army, to replace the third one squandered away at El Carmen and at Picuiba. The Bolivian government was counting on overwhelming numbers of raw recruits to stop the Paraguayan breakthrough. Two races were on: One by Bolivians to send their new field army into the front, and the other by Paraguayans to reach Villa Montes and the oil fields. The proximity to this last prize gave the war for the first time a real meaning; as President Ayala explained "once we take the whole oil fields, it will be difficult to abandon them."[57]

For Bolivia, money was no problem, because the doubling of the price of tin, its main export, replenished the coffers of the Bolivian treasury. Instead Paraguay, with almost its entire adult male population already in the army, could not increase its forces and had tremendous difficulty finding replacements to try to keep the units from falling below strength. House-to-house searches in Asunción confirmed what all had suspected: All the able-bodied men were already in the field, and to try to alleviate the acute labor shortage, Paraguay distributed many Bolivian prisoners to work in farms and households. As the year 1935 approached, wrenching poverty, the constant problem of Paraguay, dogged its military effort. The country and the government were bankrupt and could not afford to continue the war much longer. The cattle herds were almost depleted and food to send to the soldiers was becoming scarce. The bright spot was the extraordinarily high morale of the Paraguayan soldiers, who having accomplished the impossible, were justifiably proud of their incredible victories. With the exception of cannons and artillery shells, the Paraguayan army had captured from its wealthy neighbor a lifetime supply of weapons and ammunition. But the exhaustion of its manpower and the near collapse of the Paraguayan economy made the limited and slow assistance from wealthy Argentina vital and decisive for the final Paraguayan offensive.[58]

The Struggle for the Andes Mountains

Reflections in the distance had fooled many a patrol in the Chaco, and the scouts of the Paraguayan I and III corps did not know what to make of fleeting glimpses behind clouds through the forest canopy to the north. Something loomed ahead beyond a surprisingly high ridge in the otherwise flat Chaco, and as more patrols marched north over the coming days, the murmuring increased as they too began to sense that something unusual lay ahead. Finally on a clear day no doubt remained in the mind of the Paraguayan soldiers as to what they had been glimpsing in the horizon. Enthusiastic about their discovery, the Paraguayan officers rushed to summon their commander José Felix Estigarribia to witness for himself. As General Estigarribia climbed a slight elevation, in the far distance he saw the Andes Mountains rising thousands of meters into the blue sky. The first view of the majestic elevations moved the Paraguayan soldiers who realized they were leaving behind the Chaco proper. The long journey that had begun in the mud trails of Boquerón had almost miraculously brought them across hundreds of kilometers of barren terrain to the Andes Mountains. Water became abundant in the tributaries of the Parapetí, cattle roamed grasslands, and small farmsteads began to appear. Technically and correctly from a strictly geographical perspective, the Chaco War was over.[59]

The incredible feat of reaching the Andes Mountains completely transformed the nature of the war. Nobody in their wildest dreams had ever imagined that small and impoverished Paraguay could have ever advanced so far against its large and rich neighbor. Even more tantalizing, for the first time Paraguayan troops were poised to capture petroleum fields and mineral deposits in the initial ranges of the Andes Mountains. From a meaningless struggle over worthless terrain the war transformed itself into a conflict over valuable petroleum deposits. Men had always been willing to die for petroleum, and the temptation for the Paraguayans living in the poorest country in South America proved irresistible. The Paraguayan soldiers had done the impossible to reach the Andes Mountains, and if they repeated their sacrifice a second time, the capture of the petroleum fields at last could free Paraguay from its otherwise inescapable poverty. The race was on to reach the petroleum fields before Paraguay exhausted its manpower.

An apparently unstoppable momentum drove the Paraguayan forces forward after the Bolivian disaster of Picuiba. The Paraguayan II Corps reached the Parapetí River on 16 January 1935, and another unit was fast advancing toward Santa Fe (Map 24) to consolidate the Paraguayan control over the south shore of the river.[60] The immediate question was: Should the II Corps halt at the Parapetí River or continue to press forward? The officer in charge of the leading Paraguayan unit sent the following telegraph to II Corps headquarters:

> After destroying the 47th Infantry Regiment, we gained control of Santa Fé at 20 hours on 17 January. Prisoners let us know that Charagua is defenseless. I request permission to push on and to capture that place with my troops. The enemy managed to set Santa Fe on fire, but the Gutiérrez warehouse with its supplies escaped unharmed.[61]

Colonel Franco, never one to pass any chance to strike, immediately saw the strategic opportunity and resolutely plunged forward. As the Bolivian commander facing the Paraguayans later confessed, at this moment the remaining Bolivian troops were in no condition to keep the II Corps from capturing Charagua and advancing with impunity far into the rear.[62] Colonel Franco had enough troops, but to maintain a fast pace forward, he needed more gasoline. Estigarribia had to decide whether to reject or to approve Franco's request. The ideal solution was to send the extra gasoline, but the argument that the entire front had to advance simultaneously was likewise a valid option. Instead of choosing between these two valid alternatives, in a totally surprising decision Estigarribia recalled many trucks away from Franco and sent them to support the flagging advance of the Paraguayan I and III corps. The order deprived the entire Paraguayan army of these trucks at a critical moment and gave extra time for the Bolivians to try to rebuild their shattered units. Why did Estigarribia commit such a blunder? Simple stupidity cannot be the answer, and very likely his natural reluctance to carry out an active pursuit con-

tinued to influence him. But this time there was more: Photographs of Franco and his II Corps prancing among the oil derricks and the refinery was something that Estigarribia did not want to see happen. He could not allow his dashing subordinate to bring the war brilliantly to a triumphant end. Estigarribia had thrown away the last chance to obtain valuable gains from an otherwise pointless war. Time was running out for Paraguay, because the worsening shortage of gasoline actually reflected Argentina's desire to reduce its assistance. Without Argentine gasoline, Paraguay could not continue the war unless it captured the oil fields and refinery at Camiri. Once again, as happened throughout the second phase of the war, the transfer of troops and resources at the precise moment between the II Corps and the other two corps determined the pace of the Paraguayan advance. Even without the trucks, Franco did not give up the struggle against fate and relentlessly drove his soldiers on foot against the panic-stricken Bolivians. In one final surge the II Corps captured Carandaití on 23 January, but afterwards human endurance could do no more and his exhausted men collapsed.[63]

By late January 1935 few could deny that the end of the war was approaching; Bolivia had irreparably lost the Chaco, and the Parapetí River was emerging as the geographical reference point but not necessarily as the final boundary between the two countries. How far north or south of the Parapetí River would the boundary run? Because the Parapetí River was the maximum claim of the Paraguayans, once the II Corps had reached its shores, Estigarribia considered the military offensive on that front finished. The thought that additional territory should be seized for purposes of negotiation did not cross his mind. As 1935 began, the lack of close cooperation between civilians and officers over the diplomatic implications produced adverse effects. Estigarribia refused to resupply Franco, whose II Corps halted near the Parapetí River to feast on the abundant crops and numerous cattle in this region. The harsh and hostile barrenness of the Chaco was behind them, because henceforth the Paraguayans could live off the land and thus ease the pressure on their long supply line and on the scarce food back home.

The abundant food did not compensate

for the shortage of gasoline, but had Estigarribia sent his remaining gasoline barrels to Franco, the II Corps soon would have captured the petroleum fields of Bolivia and given Paraguay the opportunity to build its prosperity. Estigarribia, as if trying to show that holding back the II Corps had not been a lost opportunity, furiously hurled his III and I corps forward against what he considered to be a crumbling Bolivian army. Although the Bolivians initially appeared to be putting up increasing resistance near the Pilcomayo, the advancing Paraguayans ran into more instances of Bolivian disintegration. On 28 December the Paraguayans surrounded Ybibobo on the land side. The trapped Bolivians panicked and tried to escape by swimming across the Pilcomayo River. After 200 drowned in the attempt, the shock was such that the remaining 2,000 men of the garrison meekly surrendered on 31 December in what was "their most humiliating defeat during the war."[64] The loss of Ybibobo was also strategically significant because it controlled one of the three passes across the first range of the Andes Mountains (the other two were Capirenda and Carandaití). On 11 January the Paraguayan I Corps reached Capirenda and surrounded its two Bolivian regiments. The garrison managed to escape but not without suffering at least 50 percent casualties; the Paraguayans counted at least 500 dead bodies and took nearly a thousand prisoners. These amazing successes brought the I Corps close to Franco's II Corps and opened the possibility of making wide flanking sweeps to the oil fields in the northwest while the III Corps kept the static Bolivians pinned down at Villa Montes. Estigarribia erroneously concluded that a direct dash against Villa Montes was the best and easiest way to reach the oil fields before the war ended. In a perverse way the easy Paraguayan victories at Capirenda and Ibibobo paved the way for a final Bolivian revival.[65]

The Bolivian high command harbored no illusions about stopping the Paraguayans in open maneuvers and concentrated all its efforts into completing a defense line at Villa Montes. These fortifications were the most complex and solid ever built for this war, and they eventually stretched over 43 kilometers and comprised a maze of trenches, bunkers, and barbed wire. Two networks of trenches manned by at least 17,000 men boasted 1,200 machine guns,

83 cannons, and 43 mortars. Formidable as the defense lines had been at Ballivián, these were even more impressive; and just like at Ballivián, the way to break them was by distant flanking movements. The General Staff of Argentina recommended making wide sweeps far to the north and crossing the Pilcomayo River to encircle Villa Montes and cut it off from supply roads to Santa Cruz and Tarija; only then could the Paraguayans capture Villa Montes. The accurate intelligence reports about the magnitude of the Bolivian fortified line at Villa Montes contrasted with the telegram printed earlier that Charagua was defenseless, but an unperturbed Estigarribia stubbornly insisted on making a direct assault on Villa Montes.[66]

His erroneous decision was incomprehensible from a military perspective. After he had threatened to resign in August 1934 when President Ayala demanded frontal assaults on Ballivián, in February 1935 Estigarribia insisted on costly frontal attacks. When his irreplaceable soldiers were dwindling, he had to husband every one of his men if Paraguay was to capture the petroleum fields.

His units took up positions in front of the Villa Montes defenses on 11 February and their appropriate task was to keep the Bolivians guessing about the exact direction of the main Paraguayan assault. But the next step was totally insane: After some days of testing the defenses, Estigarribia launched a massive frontal assault on 16 February. Miraculously, the Paraguayans broke through the outer defense line but not the inner network and soon found themselves trapped in a bulge. After a last massive attack on 20 February failed to crack the sides of the bulge, the heavy casualties at last forced Estigarribia to abandon the nearly suicidal attacks.[67]

In Estigarribia's defense, it must be said that he had not underestimated the superior tactics of the Paraguayan infantrymen who almost broke through the Bolivian front; indeed, only incessant firing from the massed Bolivian artillery blunted the Paraguayan attack. Estigarribia relearned the costly lesson from World War I that only intense shelling from high-caliber cannon could shatter bunkers. Throughout the campaigns artillery was the weakest arm of the Paraguayans, largely because their pre-war General Staff had concluded that cannons were not suitable for the Chaco.

In previous encirclements, the Bolivian artillery located in the rear always had the best chance to escape, so only small numbers of cannons had fallen into Paraguayan hands. For those captured pieces the Bolivians had not spiked or otherwise disabled, generally few shells remained. The scarce Paraguayan ammunition did not fit the Bolivian artillery, and the manufacturers refused to sell spare parts or extra shells.[68]

Until they could lay down artillery barrages, the Paraguayans ruled out any additional offensive at Villa Montes, but not all was unfavorable: Once again as previously at Ballivián, a small Paraguayan force tied down a many times larger number of Bolivians. On 16 March the Bolivians launched a counterattack to retake the bulge of February 20. The Bolivians took two days to close the bulge and straighten out their line but their performance was so chaotic that in the fierce combat Bolivian units ended up fighting against each other. The high Bolivian casualties confirmed their inability to conduct a simple operation over familiar terrain even with overwhelming superiority in numbers and artillery. The Paraguayans suffered 80 casualties and the Bolivians 500; the five-to-one ratio suggested the losses the Bolivians had to incur to make any advance against the Paraguayans. The trench warfare proved to be more than what many Bolivians could take, and in the thousands they fled south to desert in Argentina.[69]

With the bulk of the demoralized Bolivian army immobilized at Villa Montes, Estigarribia realized he had a chance to outmaneuver the remaining Bolivian units by flanking offensives. By this time all Paraguayans knew that time was running out for the war because of the dampening support from Argentina. The vote of Argentina against Paraguay in the League of Nations on 15 January was literally a stab in the back and brought the practical consequence of lifting the arms embargo against Bolivia but not against Paraguay. A League of Nations unable to stop the powerful dictators on a rampage in Asia and Europe instead vented its fury on tiny, poor, and weak Paraguay that it mistakenly labeled the aggressor.[70]

Meanwhile, a chastened Estigarribia regretted his January decision not to supply the II Corps on the Parapetí and belatedly tried to resume the advance on that front. Estigarribia

did not need to do much to urge Colonel Franco, who could never stay still and had only allowed his men enough time to recuperate before resuming the offensive. In what ranked among the most daring assaults of the war, at Boyuibe units of the II Corps calculated that if they ran fast enough across an open field, they could reach a heavily fortified ridge before an artillery barrage shattered them. The charge caught the artillerymen by surprise and the deadly barrage fell long. Once the Paraguayans set up their machine guns near the ridge, their superior tactical maneuvering drove the Bolivians from the fortified positions on 8 March. The Bolivians sent two fresh regiments to try to retake the ridges, but the steady and murderous fire from the Paraguayan machine guns turned the counterattack into a horrible carnage. Soon the field was littered with dead bodies, and dazed and stunned survivors surrendered in droves; the II Corps had shattered or destroyed at least five Bolivian regiments.[71]

The Paraguayans had once again proved their ability to inflict disproportionate losses on the Bolivians. However, the astounding victory turned hollow when the II Corps learned to its dismay that new Bolivian regiments had massed near Boyuibe to block the Paraguayan drive to the oil fields. The II Corps was stretched very thinly over a large front facing north and west, and its main units were separated by considerable distances. The opportunity of January to advance unopposed had passed, and in March Bolivia was sending regiments faster than Paraguay could destroy them.

Since 10 December 1934, when President Tejada had decreed a general mobilization, "The Bolivians are furiously recruiting all manpower from young to old and sending them without training to the Chaco."[72] In the cities, able-bodied men avoided military service, and when forcibly recruited, tried to escape during the train or truck ride to the front. Once in the front, they deserted in droves at the first opportunity, particularly those near Argentina whose frontier acted as a magnet for Bolivians. In some cases the officers placed light machine guns in the rear to prevent desertions. The endemic problem of self-inflicted wounds became so acute that the Bolivian high command ordered the execution of those who wounded themselves. The difficulty of recruiting from the cities forced Bolivia to press-gang illiterate Indians from the cold highlands for duty in the sweltering Chaco. More an armed rabble than real soldiers, these last-minute recruits were disposable troops. Bolivia stepped up its hiring of Chilean officers, but the scarcity of officers was so acute that Bolivia hired some Peruvian officers and at least one Mexican general who happened to be handily near by.[73] As usual, armament shipments poured into Bolivia and guaranteed that its forces enjoyed lavish equipment and weapons. Ample good food, that other indispensable component of troop morale, remained scarce, except in the tables of high officers whose wining and dining in sumptuous banquets became legendary.[74]

Since the Bolivian soldiers were little more than cannon fodder, the Bolivian high command did not want to waste time or resources on preparing them and instead counted on overwhelming firepower on the ground and in the air to halt the Paraguayans. The Bolivians enjoyed complete aerial supremacy throughout the war, but failed to make good use of its potential:

> Basically the inactivity of the Bolivian Air Force is due to lack of training. The pilots have neither the technical nor tactical knowledge. It is difficult to keep themselves oriented when flying, and frequently a pilot sent out on a bombing mission has bombed his own troops. [...] The pilots know very little of formation flying or dive-bombing. Practically all bombing is done while flying on a level plane and at rather high altitudes. The Bolivian pilot as a rule is not daring and has little initiative. [...] Attacks by airplanes equipped with machine guns have been insignificant.[75]

Shifting the II Corps' offensive to the north had the best chance of outflanking the massed Bolivian regiments at Boyuibe. The spectacular victory at this last place fooled both Franco and Estigarribia into concluding that because "the Bolivian morale is at a very low ebb," the II Corps did not need reinforcements to complete its advance.[76] The calculated gamble of the two commanders should have worked, had not Bolivian espionage in Buenos Aires reported the planned offensive and its scheduled start on 15 April. Bolivian diplomats had purchased the reports from officers of the General Staff of Argentina, yet the information was so detailed and abundant that it almost

seemed like somebody in Buenos Aires wanted the Paraguayan offensive to fail.[77] As some Paraguayans remarked, once the front line approached the oil fields of Bolivia, Argentina's support for Paraguay wavered. Unaware that he had been set up, Franco walked into a trap. Following the normally sound principle of concentration of forces, he shifted the 8th Division from Boyuibe to the north to join the forces at the Parapetí River for the drive to Charagua. He left behind the undermanned 3rd Division, barely the equivalent of one regiment, to defend the Boyuibe front. The Bolivian plan called for luring the Paraguayans into Charagua and then launching a massive attack against Boyuibe to cut off the II Corps from the rest of the Paraguayan army; the Bolivians intended to press forward to Carandaití and then to Yrendagüe and were sure to trap the Paraguayan troops that by then would be in headlong retreat from the Parapetí region. The goal was to inflict upon the Paraguayans a disaster of a comparable magnitude to what the Bolivians had suffered at Picuiba.

The Bolivian high command was more than ready to sacrifice Charagua and quietly shifted the main line of defense to the west in the mountain range. The Paraguayan offensive was set for 15 April, but as soon as observant scouts noticed that the Bolivians had abandoned the river shores, the Paraguayans began to cross the Parapetí way ahead of schedule on 12 April. Leaving one regiment behind to pretend to defend Charagua, the bulk of the Bolivian troops withdrew slowly and in good order to their prepared positions to the west in the mountain range. On 15 April the 8th Division pressed forward and easily outflanked the lone Bolivian regiment. The Bolivian defense line collapsed and late at night on 17 April the Paraguayans entered Charagua, and nothing seemed to be able to stop them. The Paraguayan capture of Charagua, a real town, had caused panic in Santa Cruz and made it very hard to restrain those in that frontier region who had been seeking Paraguayan support to declare independence from Bolivia. With Bolivia on the verge of disintegration, the political pressure became too strong for the Bolivian high command that had to unleash its offensive before it was ready.

On 16 April three Bolivian divisions moved forward to attack the undermanned Paraguayan 3rd Division at the Boyuibe front. With at least a 5-to-1 ratio and the element of surprise on its side, the Bolivians were in an ideal position to overwhelm the Paraguayan position and break the Paraguayan front in half. Fortunately for the Paraguayans, the combination of rugged terrain and thick woods proved too much for the raw Bolivian recruits who easily lost their way. It took the whole day for the Bolivian divisions to reach the Paraguayan line that had seemed so near, and only at nightfall did a few units engage in desultory firing; correctly the Bolivians postponed the attack for the next day, but they had already lost any chance of making a surprise attack. Colonel Franco admitted that the sudden appearance of three Bolivian divisions on his exposed flank did catch him by surprise, but he wisely used the few hours' advance notice to try to rush forces to the threatened front. He threw in his combat reserves, but when the Bolivian attack began at 0700 on 17 April under massive artillery shelling, the overwhelming force crashed through all the defensive positions. At the end of the day Franco frantically detained the Bolivians with a line he had hastily compiled out of administrative personnel, drivers, and wounded or convalescent soldiers. Franco gained time and slowed down the Bolivian assault that surprisingly never attained any momentum. The slow pursuit of the Bolivians did not fool Franco who knew that his thin makeshift line could not hold off the three Bolivian divisions for long. Estigarribia for his part had realized the danger and launched an offensive in front of the I Corps, in the hope that this diversionary attack would also draw Bolivian troops away from Boyuibe.[78]

Franco saw how exposed and vulnerable to encirclement his 8th Division at Charagua was, but rather than simply withdrawing it, he opted for a desperate solution. In a very risky move, he ordered the 8th Division to move south to attack the rear of the Bolivian advance. The much more numerous Bolivian 7th Division only needed to set up defensive lines to block the Paraguayan attack but decided instead to try a bolder move to trap the 8th Division. The Bolivians managed to surround part of the 8th Division on 22 April, and for a while it seemed that this proud Paraguayan unit, the victor in such famous battles as El Carmen and Picuiba, would finish its career by surrendering ignominiously. An undaunted Franco rushed rescue units, and the trapped Paraguayans with their superior infantry skills never despaired. After three days of clever maneuvering, the 8th Division lived up to its reputation and sprung free from the trap. The risky encounter had been too harrowing not for the Paraguayans but for the Bolivians, who were too exhausted from the strain to pursue the Paraguayans and instead watched them make a leisurely retreat back to the Parapetí River.[79]

Franco's strategy to wear down the Bolivians was to make them pay dearly for every piece of ground. The Paraguayan forces conducted an orderly and slow withdrawal, and were counterattacking at every opportunity to keep the Bolivians off balance. The Bolivians took heavy casualties when they finally began to cross the Parapetí River on 3 May. Not all the Bolivians units managed to cross that day, so at many points along the river front the Paraguayans continued to halt the crossings and to inflict casualties. The numerical superiority of the Bolivians was so great, however, that they continued moving forward as a slow steam roller, and if not stopped soon, the Bolivians could regain all the territory lost after the battle of Picuiba.[80]

The desperate maneuvers of Franco had so consumed every minute of his attention that proper reporting back to headquarters had suffered. At most the II Corps could only send incomplete and tardy reports; inadvertently Franco had dried up the information pipeline and deprived the Bolivian spies in Buenos Aires of fresh news. Without the help of their spies not only were the Bolivian commanders groping in the dark, but to even the contest on 2 May 1935 a Paraguayan patrol captured the order of battle of the Bolivians. At last Colonel Franco was in a position to deliver a fitting counterstrike. The new information allowed him to place his units in the most advantageous positions to block the Bolivian offensive. A passive defense did not suit his forceful temper, and he conceived the idea of another surprise attack on the Bolivian rear. Patrols had already discovered a secret trail to the Bolivian rear at Mandyyupecua, and Franco proposed to send the whole 6th Division through that path. The maneuver was risky, because not only were many Bolivian units in the area, but Bolivian planes engaged in regular reconnaissance. The 6th Division set out on 13 May with limited water and food; after avoiding all detection it destroyed the Bolivian position at Mandyyupecua on 16 May. The capture of this point tore open a gash in the Bolivian front, and the Bolivian high command dropped plans for any offensive south of the Parapetí River and hurriedly shifted units from that front to plug the gap. After some final maneuvering near Mandyyupecua, this front stabilized for the rest of the war. The last major Bolivian offensive to recover lost territory sputtered to an inglorious end.[81] "Defeatism was rampant in the upper ranks of the Bolivian military ... [and] the Bolivian commanders were primarily concerned with avoiding a fresh disaster."[82]

The spectacular failure of the Bolivian offensive could not hide certain basic facts. For the first time Bolivia had made a realistic power play to destroy an entire Paraguayan corps, and had Bolivia attained its goal, the entire Paraguayan front would have collapsed and would have forced a humiliating retreat back into the Chaco. Bolivia with its incomparably greater resources had raised the stakes and was no longer playing just for divisions but for entire corps. In the struggle for the petroleum fields, the Paraguayan David was not winning against the Bolivian Goliath. Each successive Paraguayan victory just meant facing larger numbers of Bolivians ahead. A nearly solid line of Bolivian troops blocked any advance, and with Paraguayan manpower running out, the end of the war was fast approaching.

Estigarribia knew that staying on the offensive was the only way to bring Bolivia to the peace table, and he also detected one final chance to reach the petroleum fields through Villa Montes. He believed that all that was needed to demoralize the defenders was for them to experience a substantial artillery barrage for the first time. Workers began stripping two river gunboats of their 120 mm. cannons and also removed the 196 mm. cannons from the shore batteries on the Paraguay River. The laborious transport of these large pieces required considerable time, but by then Paraguay hoped to have obtained enough shells from Argentina to be able to lay down a shattering barrage on the unsuspecting Bolivians. So far the 105 mm. cannon had been the largest piece used in the war. The Paraguayans counted on

either the thundering sound from the exploding 196 mm. shells or the shattering of bunkers like match boxes to send the Bolivians into panic. A few breaches in the line were all that the Paraguayan infantry needed, and as soon as the magic words of "Pilas [Bolivian slang for Paraguayans] in the rear" rang out, the Bolivians could be counted on to stampede to the Argentine border. Control of the oil fields and the Camiri refinery would deprive Bolivia of gasoline for its troops and would give Paraguay a virtually impregnable position to resist any counterattacks.[83]

Before the preparations for the final assault on Villa Montes were ready, fighting flared up at the Paraguayan outpost of Ingavi. As part of the Bolivian offensive against the Paraguayan II Corps, the Bolivian 6th Division approached Ingavi on 24 April. The Bolivians again were trying to open a path to the Paraguay River via Ingavi and Pitiantuta. Quite fittingly, the war in 1935 returned to its starting area of 1932. At Ingavi the Paraguayan garrison fought the attackers to a standstill. In expectation of receiving reinforcements, the Bolivian 6th Division did not retreat but remained virtually inactive 9 kilometers north of Ingavi. Then in the first days of June Estigarribia received news that the Bolivians were planning to mount a major drive to reach the Paraguay River before any cease-fire went into place. Whether the Bolivian intention was true or not, the Paraguayan II Corps rushed a detachment to Ingavi. The reinforced Paraguayans attacked and surrounded the collapsing Bolivian 6th Division. For one last time Paraguay announced a final encirclement with plenty of prisoners and captured weapons.[84]

The embarrassing disintegration of the 6th Division had a chilling effect on Bolivia and overcame any hesitation about accepting a truce. The well-founded belief that the Bolivian army was incapable of any significant offensive action took root. While Franco was rallying his men to make one final offensive in the sector of the II Corps, scouts reported that the Bolivian soldiers on the front did nothing but talk about the imminent peace; certainly the war was over for them even before the diplomats decreed an end. Although the planned offensive against Villa Montes had every probability of success, the exhaustion of manpower, and not excessively long supply lines as is usually stated, finally forced Paraguaya to accept a permanent cease-fire.[85] Any disaster risked costing Paraguay the Chaco, while any victory no matter how spectacular simply meant confronting a larger number of Bolivians ahead. An exhausted and impoverished Paraguay knew it could not continue in the war. Had President Eusebio Ayala not foolishly signed the truce in 1933 and had General Estigarribia husbanded his men more carefully, Paraguay could have captured the petroleum fields. But the men who could have made that smashing victory possible were dead and could not be replaced unlike the apparently inexhaustible Bolivians. On 12 June both sides accepted a truce and left to diplomats the task of constructing a secure peace. The negotiations lasted longer than the war, and not until 1939 did a final settlement appear. As expected, Paraguay received almost all the Chaco, but not Villa Montes and the oil fields in the Andes Mountains, while the province of Santa Cruz remained a part of Bolivia.[86]

Had Bolivia negotiated before the war or during the conflict, it would have received a much larger slice of the worthless Chaco. Did the Bolivian officer corps learn any lessons from the war? Seeing that diplomats and not generals would decide the final boundaries, the Bolivian army decided to make one last demonstration of its power before the cease-fire went into effect at noon on 14 June. The Bolivian high command ordered that at 1100 every gun in the front, from rifles to the largest cannons, was to open fire and continue shooting until noon. This impressive display of firepower was supposed to awe the Paraguayans into accepting harsher terms at the peace conference. For half an hour and for the first time in the war, firing took place along the whole front, with the heaviest cannonade taking place at the Villa Montes trenches. The dazzled Paraguayans did not know what to make of this huge fireworks display, and they too replied with their guns. How many soldiers were killed or wounded in this needless and totally irrational display of firepower? At 12 noon sharp the firing stopped. Soon after, in spite of Bolivian orders not to talk with the Paraguayans, both sides were fraternizing. Officers and soldiers were chatting as if after a sporting match; soon they were exchanging gifts and some developed lifelong friendships.[87] Clearly no hatred had ever existed between the two peoples, and the war had never been marked by the execution of prisoners and other atrocities that had so marred conflicts like the Mexican Revolution. Although the diplomats later took all the credit and one even received a Nobel peace prize, it was the fierce combat in the Chaco War that decisively ended a long-festering territorial dispute.

14. War Between Peru and Colombia

Famine makes greater havoc in the army than the enemy and is more terrible than the sword. — Flavius Vegetius Renatus[1]

In August 1932 as Bolivia and Paraguay were rushing to war over Boquerón in the Chaco, so were Colombia and Peru moving to a collision over Leticia in the Amazon. The Great Depression was responsible for starting not just the long Chaco War but also the briefer war between Colombia and Peru. After the initial clash in the Amazon over La Pedrera in 1911 (see chapter 2), the hostility between these last two countries seemed to have gradually dissipated. However, only weak diplomatic barriers stood in the way of renewed war, and these could not withstand the tensions and strains the Great Depression unleashed in Latin America.

Decisions for War

Chapter 2 had described the start of negotiations in Lima between Colombian minister to Peru Fabio Lozano Torrijos and the Peruvian Foreign Minister. In 1922 the two diplomats signed the Salomón-Lozano agreement defining the final boundary between Peru and Colombia. The agreement had opponents in both countries, and only in 1925 did the Colombian senate ratify the treaty. But Peruvian ratification proved even slower, because of violent opposition from Iquitos. The treaty seemed dead because Senator Julio César Arana of Iquitos ably blocked ratification. Simultaneously, Peru was conducting parallel negotiations with Chile to settle the long-festering Tacna-Arica dispute. Negotiations were extremely tense, and a war between Chile and Peru seemed likely to erupt at any moment. To cover Peru's northern front, dictator Augusto B. Leguía needed to end the boundary dispute with Colombia, and he finally forced the Peruvian senate to ratify the Salomón-Lozano treaty in December 1927. This treaty, which supposedly established the foundations for a permanent peace with Colombia, in reality created favorable conditions for an outbreak of war. The heart of the treaty was the Leticia trapezium, a strip of land given to Colombia between the Putumayo and Amazon rivers (Map 27). Although in compensation Peru received lands in the upper Putumayo River and bolstered its position against Ecuador, the inhabitants of Iquitos could still not accept the loss of Leticia. The Salomón-Lozano treaty soon proved its worth by contributing to the success of negotiations with Chile. Without the possibility of having Colombia as an ally, Chilean resistance to coming to terms with Peru collapsed. The agreement of 3 June 1929 confirmed Chile in its rule over the province of Arica and returned to Peru the province of Tacna. The threat of a war with Chile evaporated, and dictator Leguía could rightly be proud of having settled two very dangerous disputes. Peru was free to concentrate its efforts on its last remaining dispute, this time with Ecuador, the weakest and smallest of its neighbors.[2]

Unfortunately for Leguía, the majority of Peruvians saw both Salomón-Lozano and the treaty with Chile as betrayals. Discontent had long been mounting against his rule, and the opponents of the dictator could not resist using the two treaties to attack Leguía's rule. The critics never admitted that a weak Peru had scored diplomatic victories with the two treaties. The Great Depression finished undermining Leguía who fell from power in 1930, and his overthrow ushered in years of political instability for the country. The inhabitants of Iquitos had remained insistent in their desire to recover Leticia, and they hoped that the economic and political turmoil would provide an opportunity to repeal the Salomón-Lozano treaty.[3]

In this tense atmosphere, any incident could well spark a major confrontation over Leticia. The treaty had placed 400 Peruvian residents under Colombian rule, and until a substantial number of Colombian colonists settled in Leticia, Bogota's control over that jungle outpost remained shaky. Meanwhile, Colombia had to try to gain the trust of the resident Peruvians while it established a large garrison of soldiers and policemen. Colombia had taken formal possession of Leticia in August 1930, and shortly after relations with the Peruvian inhabitants got off to a bad start. The Treasury Ministry began collecting an export tax on the brown sugar the Leticia trapezium produced for the Iquitos market. The export tax made prohibitive the production of this sugar, and many very angry Peruvians lost their livelihood.[4] Not surprisingly, the hostility of a foreign population strikingly resembled the situation Bolivia had confronted in the Acre in 1900 (chapter 1). This historical precedent clearly indicated that a rich and populous Colombia needed to establish a large military presence to keep Leticia.

How large a force should Colombia station in Leticia? The 1911 agreement on the Peruvian withdrawal from La Pedrera had limited the police force to no more than 110 men, and for Leticia that figure seemed a minimum for the police force.[5] But La Pedrera bordered on the Caquetá River, and its fertile headwaters easily provided supplies; instead Leticia lacked any direct or easy link with the Colombian heartland. To guarantee its control over that jungle strip, Colombia had to station at least a company of 150 soldiers with machine guns

and artillery and preferably a battalion. The Peruvian garrison at Iquitos was just one day's steaming away downstream and could still threaten Leticia. Colombian officials did not fear the Iquitos garrison because it was rarely at full strength and its units spent most of their time patrolling the vast region. Any large-scale mobilization of the Iquitos garrison was sure to be noticed by the Colombian consul at that city or by visiting merchants.[6]

At Bogotá the senior officers in the War Ministry struggled to overcome the opposition of the Foreign and Treasury ministries to any substantial garrisoning of Leticia. The Foreign Ministry always believed passionately that the real defense of Leticia lay in the Salomón-Lozano Treaty and that any reliance on military force inevitably undermined trust in the paper treaty. The Foreign Ministry considered army units to be downright harmful, because they only served to antagonize Peruvians who would resent even more strongly the Colombian presence in the trapezium. Basic protocol did require that an army unit be present at the transfer of authority over the territory to Colombia on August 1930, so the Foreign Ministry with extreme reluctance accepted the dispatch of an army platoon and 20 policemen to Leticia.

In 1932 the Colombian commander of the Amazon region, Colonel Amadeo Rodríguez, concluded that his small force was insufficient for the defense of Leticia and as a substitute opted for a policy of tough-talking bluff. Aboard his lone gunboat, he traveled through the Putumayo and the Amazon rivers, always trying to awe the local Peruvians with his new weapons and his tough macho talk. He greeted visiting Peruvian boats with much firing of volleys into the air to show he had ammunition to spare and was eager to use it. He loved to strut into the lion's den at Iquitos, to show off how much better his shiny new gunboat was compared to the antiquated and derelict steamers of the Peruvian flotilla.[7]

The martial antics earned a healthy respect for Colonel Rodríguez among the Peruvians but not in Bogotá. An outraged Foreign Ministry pressed for the recall of Colonel Rodríguez's platoon from Leticia. In vain did senior officers at the War Ministry plead for keeping the platoon at Leticia, but the Treasury Ministry could not resist any chance to halt the

Map 27. Colombia–Peru, 1932–1933.

flow of money into the bottomless pit of the jungle. The expense of maintaining a garrison in the middle of the jungle seemed astronomical to a Treasury Ministry that was passionate about balancing the budget as the best way to fight the Great Depression. The high expenses had been much more important for preserving Colombian rule over Leticia than anyone realized at the time. Important as the weapons of the platoon were for the defense of Leticia, a greater impact came from the contracts Colombian officials had signed with Peruvians on both sides of the border. The Peruvian Amazon was experiencing the worst economic crisis in its history, and the contracts to supply the Colombian platoon and to work in Leticia were life-savers to many individuals otherwise trapped in abysmal jungle poverty.

When the platoon left, the supply contracts dried up. The mounting dissatisfaction with Colombian rule reached crisis proportions among the unemployed Peruvians already suffering horribly from the Great Depression. The removal of the platoon and of the tough Colonel Rodríguez gave local Peruvians the opportunity to retake what they considered theirs.

Army reservist Óscar Ordóñez and members of the Arana merchant house soon gathered a volunteer force of 212 men, mostly civilians but including the small Peruvian army detachment at nearby Chimbote. Rumors of an attack started to circulate in mid 1932, but Bogotá only haltingly began to consider sending reinforcements. Although Peruvians in the Amazon were very familiar with Leticia, Ordóñez himself visited the town again and brazenly drew maps and charts on the excuse that he was helping the trade in the region. He also carefully informed himself about the daily routine of the police force down to only 18 men. With this information, he now went to Iquitos to present the plan to a group of army officers headed by Lieutenant Colonel Isauro Calderón. Ordóñez knew them all well, because his father had been the commander of the Iquitos garrison as recently as 1930. Ordóñez wanted these officers to make sure that the Peruvian garrison of Iquitos did not attack him after he had captured Leticia. Once he was sure he enjoyed their support, he slipped out undetected from Iquitos and returned to the border to prepare the attack. Since no mobilization of the large Iquitos garrison had taken place, Colombian agents and merchants failed to detect anything suspicious.[8]

On 1 September 1932 at 0530 Ordóñez launched his attack on Leticia. Leaving nothing to chance, he had his men bring a cannon and a machine gun to awe into surrender the sleepy Colombian police force. The show of force was unnecessary, because the 15 Colombian policemen present at that moment had only twelve Mauser rifles. Resistance was in any case futile, because Peruvian rifle barrels woke up most of the policemen carelessly sleeping in the indolent tropical climate. A few policemen fired some shots before escaping, but neither side suffered any casualties or even wounds during the attack. The Peruvians arrested all the Colombians and released them at the Brazilian border town of Tabatinga a few days later. Ordóñez knew his operation had been a complete success, yet because he had not told his followers that they enjoyed the support of the Iquitos garrison, they still felt uneasy and feared that the Peruvian authorities might arrest them as trespassers.[9]

The seizure of Leticia caught both Lima and Bogotá by surprise and forced each capital to decide on a response to the unprovoked seizure of Leticia. The great faith the Foreign Ministry had in paper treaties inspired the belief that Peru would promptly repudiate the attack. Because the nearest forces to Leticia were Peruvian, Bogotá hoped that Lima would do the favor to Colombia of driving out the trespassers over the next few days. If domestic political pressures made this Peruvian cooperation impossible, then Bogotá was preparing to send its lone gunboat upstream carrying a company of soldiers. Provided Peru remained neutral, Bogotá expected the reinforcements to arrive in a couple of weeks to restore Colombian control over Leticia.

The decision for war or peace was in the hands of the recently elected President Luis Sánchez Cerro, an army officer who had led the revolt against Leguía. Lima received the news of the attack on the afternoon of 1 September, when Lieutenant Colonel Jesús Ugarte, the garrison commander and the prefect of Iquitos, recommended that he send a 50-man detachment to block any Colombian force from reaching Leticia until the Peruvian government decided what to do. Lima promptly ordered

Colonel Ugarte not to take any action, but this was the last order he received, because at Iquitos the army officers staged a coup and removed him from command in the morning hours of 2 September. In vain Colonel Ugarte pleaded that what the plotters wanted meant "a declaration of war for which we were not prepared."[10] The plotters ignored this first warning about the real risk of a disastrous war and chose Lieutenant Colonel Isauro Calderón, the ringleader of the plot to capture Leticia, as the new prefect and garrison commander.

On 2 September the civilian authorities rallied behind Colonel Calderón who insisted on keeping Leticia for Peru. On 4 September the commanders of the army, navy, aviation, and police units in Iquitos proclaimed their unanimous demand to keep Leticia. Popular demonstrations had begun on 1 September and continued with growing intensity during the following days as the inhabitants of Iquitos celebrated with intense joy the recovery of Leticia. Iquitos demanded a commitment from Lima to defend the annexation and refused to recognize the officials appointed by Lima to replace Calderón.

President Sánchez Cerro had tried to delay a decision on Leticia, but Iquitos was forcing his hand. As a junior officer he had served in Iquitos and had fond memories of his tour of duty in that jungle region. He too wanted to reincorporate Leticia and along with many shared the belief that the Salomón-Lozano treaty was invalid because it had been imposed by the dictator Leguía. At the same time, he feared that open defiance by Iquitos would trigger a revolt against his government and plunge Peru into a civil war. The political costs of returning Leticia to Colombia were immense, but vanity more than fear clouded the judgment of Sánchez Cerro. As a professional soldier, he knew that a Peru with inadequate amounts of rusting and obsolete weapons was not ready for war. Furthermore, the Peruvian finances were close to bankruptcy because of the Great Depression, and the country could not afford to buy new armament for a foreign adventure. Unfortunately the allure of fame proved irresistible to Sanchez Cerro who saw himself as destined to lead Peru into greatness. The deadline to reply to Colombia was 6 September 1932 when he either had to call the bluff of the Iquitos garrison or plunge into a war

General Luis Sánchez Cerro. As president of Peru in 1932, he took the country into a disastrous war with Colombia (Archivo Histórico Militar del Perú, Lima, Peru).

with Colombia over Leticia. Swept by the wave of nationalistic passions seemingly spreading like a ray of hope through an economically devastated country, Sanchez Cerro sealed his fate and chose war.[11]

Peru tried to hide the decision as long as possible from a Colombian government that refused to accept the inevitability of war. In Bogotá the Foreign Ministry never accepted the existence of war and constantly strove to delay and to halt the military operations. The Foreign Ministry regarded the military operations as a necessary evil to bring the Peruvians to the negotiating table where the real solutions would emerge. These civilian officials did not want to use the war to secure better terms from Peru.

Not only did Bogotá oppose the use of force, but it also lacked a credible military organization. Precisely the military weakness of Colombia had influenced President Sánchez Cerro's decision to keep Leticia. In the late 1920s Peruvian military attaché Zárate had revealed how puny were Colombia's military forces and the Peruvian minister in Bogotá

subsequently reported "That certainly before 1 September 1932 Colombia was practically unarmed [...] the army was in the same condition that our military attaché Coronel Zárate was familiar with, and if anything had perhaps worsened."[12] The absence of modern artillery, a navy, or an air force seemed to confirm the Colombian military weakness. The infantry was short of rifles and cartridges, while machine guns were scarce and old. The officer corps was small and the military structure was most rudimentary.[13]

Military Attaché Zárate and Peruvian diplomats also emphasized that the fundamental weakness of the Colombian military was the unwarlike nature of the people. Not only were the Colombians extremely peaceful, but the educated population spent all its time in publishing poems, philosophical disquisitions, and writing history. The intense cultural life in Bogotá of orchestra concerts, theatrical performances, poetry recitals, and public lectures convinced the less culturally inclined Peruvian army officers that a people of words, ideas, and music posed no military threat. Yet Lima had a similarly intense cultural life that had not prevented the rise of a technically proficient Peruvian army. The Peruvian officers finding no professional counterparts concluded that the people of Bogotá were too soft and verbose ever to want to wage a war.[14]

Colombia seemed to have every excuse to accept the loss of Leticia, but by 13 September the Peruvians were in for a surprise. Less than a week after President Sánchez Cerro's decision to keep Leticia, Colombian President Enrique Olaya Herrera decided to send a military expedition to the Amazon. The Peruvians at first could not believe that Colombia would actually fight and indeed in the initial weeks believed it was just a bluff to try to scare the Peruvians into a negotiated withdrawal. As Colombian military preparations in October left no doubt about their intention, Peru saw a precious opportunity to reap even more benefits out of this war. Peru devised a two-fold strategy. By keeping the Leticia trapezium, Peru in effect made the Putumayo River the boundary with Colombia. No negotiations were possible on this point, although Peru remained open to suggestions of compensation and perhaps even some face-saving territorial concessions further upstream. The moment Colombia accepted the Putumayo River as the boundary, the need for war ended. Should Colombia, however, insist on making a symbolic effort to retake the Leticia trapezium, then in response Peruvian officers felt that Peru should take the offensive to make the Caquetá River the northern boundary with Colombia. Many in the Peruvian army and in Iquitos had never reconciled themselves to the loss of La Pedrera in 1911 and still looked for an opportunity to regain that territory. Peru had learned from Chile in the War of the Pacific (1879–1883) that victories opened the possibility to gain territories far beyond the area originally in dispute. But Peru did not want to seem the aggressor bent on a war of conquest and preferred to wait until Colombia commenced hostilities before launching a counteroffensive to send Colombia reeling back to the Caquetá River.[15]

The Start of the Campaign: Tarapacá

The professional Peruvian army officers expected an easy initial victory over the motley force of poets, philosophers, historians, and writers Colombia was sending into the Amazon. The less polished and culturally handicapped Peruvian officers never realized that a writer of a classical sonnet can just as easily plot battlefield tactics, a philosopher can meditate on strategy, a historian who writes about campaigns can also lead them, and a novelist can imagine battlefield scenarios. The brutal and harsh side of combat had made the Peruvian officers overlook the subtler side of the art of war, but they could not ignore the large quantity of new weapons Colombia was frenetically buying. Colombian purchase missions in Europe and the United States had been acquiring practically every new weapon available on the market. The Great Depression initially had hurt the arms dealers or "merchants of death," who flocked to show their latest glossy arms catalogs to Colombian diplomats. The Peruvian military possessed largely pre–World War I weapons, while the Colombian military was acquiring the armament of the future World War II. Most disturbing was the acquisition of a navy. Although Peruvian diplomats succeeded in blocking some purchases such as two light cruisers from Spain, Colombia grad-

ually assembled a flotilla of destroyers, gunboats, and cargo vessels. As protection from air attacks, Colombia outfitted its merchant ships with heavy machine guns and antiaircraft cannons. When the specifications of the Colombian naval force reached the Peruvian commander at Iquitos, he panicked and urged Lima to send the destroyer *Lima* at once. The Peruvian high command dismissed this first alarm signal and refused to rush any naval vessel to the Amazon.[16]

Perhaps even more disturbing than the loss of naval supremacy was the rapid expansion of Colombian aviation. Many wealthy Colombians had become fascinated with aviation and since the late 1920s spent many hours of flight time practicing complex aerial acrobatics as a hobby. The thrill of flying had given meaning to the otherwise empty lives of these upper-class youths. The possibility of actually engaging in aerial dogfights and dropping real bombs was an irresistible prospect for these youths who wanted to fight in the war against Peru. Many German pilots of the civilian airline also volunteered to serve. Enjoying an abundance of skilled pilots, Colombia only needed to buy brand-new warplanes from the United States to acquire the most modern air force in South America. Without firing a shot, Colombia gained air supremacy over the Amazon region. Peruvian officers of the Army General Staff sounded the alarm: "We are losing the initial advantage we had gained by the surprise capture of Leticia," but Lima remained confident that Colombia posed no real threat.[17]

The spontaneous enlistment of the pilots reflected the mass outpouring of nationalist emotion that the loss of Leticia provoked in almost all sectors of the population. The outrage was not greater than in 1903 when Colombia felt betrayed by the U.S. occupation of Panama, but this time in 1933 the public knew that the country had a chance to avenge the injury. The demonstrations to save Leticia and the surge in public opinion caught President Enrique Olaya Herrera by surprise; his government never rid itself completely of the suspicion that it was willing to abandon Leticia for concessions elsewhere and had to take action in response to the collective nationalistic passion never before seen in Colombia. People lined up to donate their life savings, and couples contributed their wedding rings. The public eagerly subscribed to war bonds, and those citizens too poor to buy the smallest denomination pooled their funds to buy a war bond. Businesses and merchants made their facilities available for the war effort, and many landowners offered cattle, food, and installations to support the troops. The young and not-so-young flocked to join the army, and the flow of volunteers guaranteed more soldiers than the government needed for the campaign. Mass demonstrations in support of the war effort proliferated, and the crowds incessantly shouted the prophetic slogan "Sánchez Cerro will die, and Colombia will win."[18]

The universal reaction provided for the first time a common goal that all social classes, from the peasants to the wealthy, could share. Unlike the elite politics that had shackled the country until then, the cross-class alliances harbored the promise of a real democracy in Colombia. The military offered an avenue of political participation to previously marginalized groups in Colombia. The wild enthusiasm and spontaneous contributions of the Colombian public provided ideal conditions for any government determined to win a war. Paradoxically, the Colombian government, rather than pleased, felt threatened by the spontaneous outpouring of support. Previously in Mexico the political elite did not want to broaden popular participation and had blocked the attempt of General Bernardo Reyes to create an army reserve (chapter 5). So again in 1932 the Colombian government desperately was seeking any excuse to end the war and thus allow a return to the traditional monopoly the privileged elite had enjoyed over politics.

In Peru the popular response had been less enthusiastic, and Lima did not experience a frenzied outpouring of emotion like Bogotá's. Iquitos had genuinely celebrated the capture of Leticia, but this poor province lacked the means to support a war with Colombia. Not only was the population of the Peruvian Amazon too small to withstand the Colombian offensive, but its inhabitants, those most acclimatized to the tropical conditions, were the least determined to fight in combat. Troops from the highlands and the Pacific coast of Peru would have to do almost all the fighting, but these soldiers lacked the burning motivation of the Colombians to fight in the Amazon.[19]

For the majority of Colombians rushing to fight, the Amazon had an exotic quality and evoked images of romantic heroism, similar to what the Bolivians had felt when initially going into the Amazon to recover the Acre in 1900. For the Peruvians more familiar with the Amazon, the region evoked images of hunger, abandonment, and disease. But unlike smoldering Peruvian resentment towards Chile over the War of the Pacific, no deep hostility existed against Colombia. Pushing the northern border of Peru to the Putumayo evoked pride in Lima and throughout Peru, but when it came to donating money, health, and lives, most Peruvians were far from spontaneous. The government of Sanchez Cerro could always draw on that spirit of sacrifice and toil that has so characterized the Peruvian people since pre–Hispanic times, but the situation was the opposite of Colombia. While the Peruvian government had to prod the people into supporting the war, the Colombian people pressed their government to begin military campaigns.[20]

The Colombian public received with rapt attention the news about the military campaign, information for the first time readily available not just in the press but also on the radio. The newspapers were too eager to satisfy the public hunger for details, and soon the grand strategy to recapture the Leticia trapezium appeared in print. Colombia planned to make its main effort down the Putumayo River, and construction crews worked feverishly to improve the roads linking that river to the rest of Colombia. To provide a base for its airplanes, construction rapidly proceeded on installations west of La Pedrera. The goal was to send an ever growing flow of supplies, armament, and troops down the Putumayo River until the Colombians overwhelmed the outnumbered and poorly supplied Peruvian forces. The logistic reasoning was flawless and promised a resounding Colombian victory in less than a year because Peru could not deliver a similar volume of supplies into the Amazon. But Colombia did not want to wait so long for a smashing victory and was also preparing to send its new gunboats and troopships up the Amazon River. According to treaties signed with Brazil, both belligerent countries were free to navigate on Brazilian waters of the Amazon River. The logic of the grand strategy was impressive: As the Colombians pushed from the Andes Mountains down the Putumayo River, the naval expedition would push upstream and catch the Peruvians inside a deadly crossfire. Once Colombia drove the Peruvians from the Putumayo River, the road was then open to push into the Napo River and to cut off Leticia from Iquitos. An isolated Leticia "would fall like a ripe fruit," and Colombia could occupy all the territory north of the Amazon River.[21]

The first discordant note on the grandiose Colombian plans came with the appointment in early October of General Alfredo Vásquez Cobo as the commander of the expedition steaming up the Amazon River. At first glance the appointment seemed natural because as the Colombian minister to France, he had supervised the purchase of the European armament and of most of the ships. He had been a general in the Colombian civil wars of the nineteenth century and during his residence in Paris, the home of the victorious French Army, supposedly had learned the latest military advances. Politically the appointment was a coup for President Olaya Herrera of the Liberal Party, who needed a Conservative Party leader like Vásquez Cobo to share the blame in case the war turned out badly. The newspapers began to criticize Vásquez Cobo almost immediately and with good reason. Whatever he knew about nineteenth-century warfare was useless. The only thing he had learned in France was the expression "Artillery conquers and infantry occupies" a slogan the Colombian general repeated at nauseam as if making a tremendous revelation. In his scheme of warfare, aviation had no place, and he opposed constantly the attempts of the War Ministry to provide his expedition with warplanes.[22] A mature reflection upon the wartime activities of Vásquez Cobo suggests that his appointment was not just political insurance but also reflected the desire of Bogotá politicians who did not want the military offensive to advance too rapidly. From the perspective of Latin American military history, Vásquez Cobo figures prominently as the last gentleman-general to command an expedition. Rebel leaders continued to rise to high rank in Latin America, but never again would a government assign command of a military expedition to an amateur.

Commanders typically request more troops than any government can provide; by making supreme efforts, the War Ministry in Bogotá hoped to send about 1,200 soldiers from the Caribbean coast of Colombia to the city of Belém at the mouth of the Amazon River, where they would meet the empty ships sailing from France. To the utter consternation of Bogotá, Vásquez Cobo replied that he needed only 200 soldiers! After repeated exchanges of telegrams (most deciphered by Peruvian code breakers) Vásquez Cobo agreed to receive 300 soldiers and finally accepted 600; the War Ministry sent him 700 anyway, and he never complained. Once most of the ships had arrived in Belém in late December 1932, General Vásquez Cobo moved his base upstream to Manaus where he put his expedition into final shape. On 17 January 1933 his expedition departed Manaus but its destination was not the Putumayo River, as Bogotá wanted, but Leticia. Living close to the cannons in the ships and seeing how well-armed were the 700 soldiers on board had given Vásquez Cobo the sensation that nothing could stop these powerful forces. The modern firearms surpassed in lethality the muskets and machetes the peasants had used to butcher each other during the civil wars of the nineteenth century. Vásquez Cobo was confident his expedition could attack and capture Leticia by surprise and thus end the war, make him a national hero, and revive his presidential candidacy for the 1934 election at one swoop.[23]

Because Peru had placed its best artillery in Leticia and mined the surrounding waters, a direct attack on its garrison of over 1000 soldiers seemed a risky proposition. Perhaps bombardment from the planes could soften up the defenses, but likewise a lucky shot from a shore battery or an explosion from a mine could easily disable one or more of the ships and thus cripple the expedition. If the 700 Colombian soldiers tried to wade ashore, only overwhelming covering fire from the ships and planes could overcome the larger Peruvian garrison. Enjoying landing strips in Leticia and nearby spots, the few Peruvian planes had many opportunities to inflict crippling damage on the Colombian expedition. The probability of success lay with the Peruvians who had the chance to destroy the expedition and then to assume the offensive and push to the Caquetá River. Leticia seemed more like a trap to knock Colombia prematurely out of the war, and finally even Vázquez Cobo dropped his plan to attack Leticia; in an incredible telegram to Bogotá, he instead claimed that since Paris it had all along been his intention to attack Tarapacá first![24]

Rather than correcting the self-serving memory of Vázquez Cobo, the War Ministry was content to see the expedition turn right into the Putumayo River rather than continue up the Amazon River to Leticia. As the expedition neared the border of Colombia with Brazil, a hill appeared in the horizon rising almost like an island over the largely flat jungle canopy. As one of the few natural landmarks in this region other than rivers, the hill of Tarapacá had seemed a great boundary marker and its slight elevation made the hill a natural site for defense. The fleet dropped anchor on the Colombian side of the border and prepared for the attack on Tarapacá. The ships lowered hydroplanes into the water, and construction crews cleared a small temporary landing strip in the jungle. Aerial reconnaissance confirmed the presence of Peruvian troops at Tarapacá, but the thick jungle concealed their exact positions. Vázquez Cobo decided to send the Peruvians an ultimatum to withdraw or else face an attack the next day.

The Peruvian garrison consisted of 94 soldiers under the command of Lieutenant Gonzalo Díaz Rojas. The men had not had any contact with the outside world since 16 January and some were already sick. Besides their rifles, the garrison had one old machine gun; any hope for any successful defense rested on the two 75 mm Krupp cannons, but as 1894 models, they were obsolete and most of the shells had spoiled under the tropical conditions. When on 13 February 1933 the Colombian ships moved closer to Tarapacá, Lieutenant Díaz was able to get his usually inoperative radio equipment to send a telegram to Iquitos with the news. When a reconnaissance boat returned with depressing information on the vast size of the Colombian expedition, both Lieutenant Diaz and his artillery officer concluded that any defense was hopeless, and they decided to put in place arrangements for an orderly evacuation. On 14 February at 0830 a Colombian motor boat delivered an ultimatum to withdraw promptly, and in vain did the Peruvian commander try to gain time for a response from Iquitos. Three Peruvian planes arrived at

0900 to bomb the expedition, and Colombian planes scrambled to drive them off. The Colombian planes returned to their base, and Lieutenant Díaz realized they were preparing to make a bombing run from the air over his position. At 1000 he ordered a withdrawal back to a waiting motor launch in the Cotuhé River behind Tarapacá hill.[25]

As his men were beginning an orderly evacuation, one of his subordinates, Second Lieutenant Antonio Cavero, felt that Peruvian honor demanded making at least some resistance. Cavero drew his pistol and forced his detachment back to the trenches but other soldiers continued to follow Lieutenant Diaz. Meanwhile Colombian troops had landed further downstream and with their machetes were hacking their way through the jungle to the hill of Tarapacá. Lieutenant Cavero opened fire on them with his single machine gun but with so little effect that the unscathed Colombian troops continued to walk through the jungle barely noticing the irregular shooting. The firing by Cavero at last provided the Colombian spotters the target they had been striving to locate for their planes and the naval guns. The planes circled above Tarapacá and made their first bombing run. Although the bombs exploded mostly on top of the jungle canopy, they still managed to destroy dwellings and to shatter trenches. As the planes returned to reload bombs, the naval guns shelled the clearings the explosions had opened in the jungle. The soldiers of Lieutenant Cavero fled in panic and abandoned their weapons and equipment. A second bombing run finished demoralizing the Peruvian soldiers who became so afraid that when they reached the waiting motor boat of Lieutenant Díaz, they refused to come aboard out of fear it would be sunk by the planes or by the Colombian gunboats.[26]

Lieutenant Díaz calmed some soldiers into boarding the motor boat, but the rest of the terrified men preferred to trudge through the impenetrable jungle. A long ordeal through river and jungle awaited the soldiers on their retreat. Disease and malnutrition caused the worst ravages, and the fortunate ones who weeks later reached Leticia alive were in such a disastrous state that they never returned to active duty. But no hero's welcome awaited the men on their return. The news of the loss of Tarapacá stunned Iquitos, and almost immediately the search for a scapegoat began. Rather than seek the persons responsible for the weak defenses of Tarapacá, all the blame for the defeat fell on Lieutenant Diaz, who in a sickly condition was arrested and later died of illness in prison. Although after the war he was posthumously exonerated of any blame, the refusal of the Peruvian army to recognize the new nature of combat in the Amazon was sure to bring more setbacks during the war.[27]

General Vázquez Cobo was so excited with the victory that he ordered his men to sleep in the hill of Tarapacá instead of ordering them to pursue the retreating Peruvians. His excitement was still reflected the next day when he sent perhaps the most fanciful telegram in the military history of Latin America:

> I have just finished walking through the hill of Tarapacá, which had been transformed into a Gibraltar: Trenches with subterranean corridors and everything the art of war can teach. The fire of our ships and of our planes and the bold courage of the landing troops forced the Peruvians to flee and to leave behind six Krupp cannon of 75 mm with ammunition, considerable quantities of armament, machine gun ammunition, etc. Senior and junior officers and soldiers behaved according to the expectations of their renowned fame. Nothing new to report.[28]

Frequently the tropical jungle makes humans begin to lose touch with reality, and General Vázquez Cobo was an early victim of jungle delusions. To call thatched huts and mud trenches a Gibraltar was incredible and frankly ridiculous. He later revised his estimate of six Krupp cannon upwards to seven, when in reality only two existed. The fleeing Peruvians had dumped the two cannons into the river, and as soon as its waters receded, the Colombians dragged them out of the water. General Vásquez Cobo offered a large reward for the recovery of the missing cannons from the emerging mud flats of the Putumayo River, but the soldiers found only the wheels of one cannon.[29]

When Bogotá learned that not a single Colombian soldier had been killed or even wounded, the prestige of the general began to drop like a rock in water, and the excessively cynical public in Bogotá began to spread rumors about a sham battle for political purposes. But the lack of casualties could not hide from the Peruvians the harsh reality that they had lost Tarapacá, and in a tardy response, they repaired their remaining five planes in an attempt to cripple the Colombian ships. The Peruvian planes bombed the expedition but failed to hit anything because the ships were so cleverly camouflaged that they blended easily into the overhanging jungle canopy near the river banks. And a barrage of antiaircraft fire forced the Peruvian planes to drop their bombs hurriedly without properly sighting their targets, and as soon as Colombian pursuit planes took to the air, the Peruvian planes rapidly vanished. Similar air raids continued throughout the war, but other than providing some excitement, the planes never damaged the well-protected Colombian ships. However, the raids did have a tremendous psychological impact on General Vázquez Cobo, who experienced air bombardments up close: for the first time in his life he heard the sound and felt the shock waves from detonating bombs. Up to this moment he had repeatedly belittled aviation as a silly new contraption and continued to believe that real combat was with bayonets and machetes like in the nineteenth century, but the experience of bombardment suddenly converted him into a fanatical believer in air power:

> I believe Peru is concentrating near this area all its aviation for the purpose of attacking our ships and trying to obtain revenge for its defeat. Consequently I am requesting Your Excellency to concentrate here the largest number of planes possible, because this is the place Peru has picked to attack. If it were in my power, I would make come here every plane in Colombia.[30]

After so many prior obstacles from the always recalcitrant and stubborn Vázquez Cobo, this last telegram was too much for Bogotá and was the proverbial straw that broke the camel's back. The War Ministry began to ease him out of command by gradually transferring his units and ships to other sectors. As his forces dwindled away, eventually he returned to Bogotá to report on the situation, and the leadership of the offensive against Peru passed to other commanders. The Vázquez Cobo expedition had opened the entrance to the Putumayo River, and the grand strategy of driving the Peruvians out of the Putumayo River advanced forcefully as Colombian troops, supplies, and equipment poured down the Andes Mountains.

The Battle of Güepí

Curiously enough, both countries welcomed the Colombian attack on Tarapacá of 14 February 1933. For the Peruvians the Colombian attack was the long-awaited signal to shift to a planned offensive: once Colombian began hostilities, Peru was free to pursue its dreams of conquering the Caquetá River boundary of 1911. What the Peruvians had not anticipated was the swift fall of Tarapacá and the panicky flight of its garrison. The shattered Peruvian expectations forced Lima to reconsider its strategy and at least initially to postpone the plans for the offensive to the Caquetá River. Halting the offensive was not enough, however, because the Tarapacá attack had revealed the overwhelming superiority the Colombian forces enjoyed in material and firepower. Any careful analysis of this first clash confirmed that the side able to send and supply the largest military force into the Amazon would win. Logistics ruled this war, and Colombia with superior lines of communication easily outclassed Peru. The only military response possible for Peru was an orderly withdrawal in the face of overwhelming force. Every indication showed that Peru had to accept the Colombian demand to evacuate Leticia, yet General Sánchez Cerro insisted on bleeding his army to death in the inhospitable Amazon.

Because the Putumayo River was the most convenient transportation route, the capture of Tarapacá doomed the Peruvian garrisons upstream. To prevent any Peruvian attempt to recapture this strategic choke point, Colombian engineers worked feverishly to fortify Tarapacá on all sides. Colombia installed large caliber cannons able to rain destructive shell fire on any Peruvian ship at the very moment it left Brazil to cross into Colombian waters. Meanwhile the Colombian vessels of the Alfredo Vázquez Cobo expedition slowly began to move upstream, their main obstacle being the low waters of the river and not any Peruvian resistance. Once the rains returned in mid–March, the Colombia flotilla would steam west to Puerto Arturo, one of the two main Peruvian garrisons on the Putumayo (Map 27). The jungle affected the sense of reality not just of Vázquez Cobo but also of the Peruvians who began to refer to the modestly defended Puerto Arturo as another Gibraltar. The talk of the Gibraltar of the Putumayo did not dissuade the Colombians, who had already included Puerto Arturo in their plans. As the flotilla that had captured Tarapacá moved upstream and cleared other tributaries of the Putumayo River, the main Colombian force headed downstream from the Andes Mountains. The only Peruvian post on the upper Putumayo River was at the junction of the Güepí and Putumayo rivers. Although a small detachment of 80 ill-equipped soldiers guarded Güepí, Colombia had already deployed over 800 well-supplied soldiers on its side of the Putumayo in preparation for the attack. The War Ministry was so confident of victory that it had already decided to attack Güepí days before the capture of Tarapacá [31]

In preparation for the attack, Colombian troops established a base at Chavaco right across the river from Güepí and also occupied the islands overlooking the Peruvian positions (Map 28). Some of the islands were on the Peruvian side, but because the maps were unclear, Colonel Ricardo Rico, the Colombian commander, decided to occupy them all in mid February 1933. Very much aware of what an outcry the Foreign Ministry would make if it heard that Colombian forces had invaded Peruvian islands, he left unclear in his report what islands his troops had occupied. Indeed, army officers knew that a titanic struggle was raging in Bogotá. The Foreign Ministry wanted all combat localized in Leticia and did not want any attack on Peruvian territory. The Foreign Ministry never accepted the failure of diplomacy and refused to consider war a valid instrument to defend an invaded country. With extreme repugnance the Foreign Ministry had acquiesced in an attack on Tarapacá only because that territory was inside the Leticia trapezium. But because a frontal assault on Leticia risked defeat and went against all principles of strategy, the War Ministry insisted that the only correct military offensive was to drive out the Peruvians first from the Putumayo and then from the Napo river.

On 14 February 1933, the day Colombia captured Tarapacá, the War Ministry ordered Colonel Rico to attack Güepí as soon as his forces were in place. The anticipated rupture of diplomatic relations between Colombia and Peru also took place in the wake of the attack on Tarapacá. The government of Sánchez Cerro saw an opportunity to whip up the flagging support for the war effort and incited crowds to attack and loot the Colombian legation in Lima. Passions seemed at a fever pitch and diplomats of both countries transferred their efforts to the headquarters of the League of Nations in Geneva, Switzerland. At the League foreign diplomats superficially concluded that the danger existed of a much larger war, and their concerns sent the easily panicked Colombian Foreign Ministry rushing to secure from President Olaya Herrera the repeal on 16 February of the previous attack order.[32]

The news of the cancellation of the order demoralized the Colombian troops who had been anxiously waiting to attack for weeks. Chavaco and the Colombian outposts were on low-lying ground unlike the healthier Güepí on a slight elevation overlooking the river. Medicine and sanitation had improved immensely since the disastrous campaign of 1911, but Chavaco still had the reputation of being one of the unhealthiest spots in the upper Putumayo. While the Colombian soldiers in the sweltering heat fought against swarms of mosquitoes and all types of venomous insects and ferocious animals, the diplomats in Geneva leisurely delighted in the afternoon teas and cocktail parties of the League of Nations. While the soldiers at Chavaco ate a monotonous diet of boiled grains, the diplomats dined splendidly in banquets and reaffirmed their unshakable belief that negotiations rather than war was a much more civilized and certainly much more enjoyable way to settle differences between countries.

Despite the diplomats' idle chatter, the real work of solving the Leticia dispute fell to the soldiers. Bogotá could no longer withstand the pressure from the field and from the public to take action and on 22 February sent a second order to attack Güepí. Colonel Rico resumed his preparations, but just when his men were poised to move, he received a second order to suspend operations. His angry men could not understand why they were being wound up like a spring for combat and then suddenly unwound. This psychological torture was worse than the material discomforts, and the soldiers began to forward complaints to Bogotá. To calm his men who only wanted to fight, Colonel Rico returned most of them upstream to healthier and better supplied bases. He left behind a skeleton force composed of jungle-hardened veterans and continued to accumulate supplies and munitions at Chavaco; the boats that left with troops returned with cargoes. While most of the soldiers of Colonel Rico rested and replenished themselves in the cooler bases near the Andes Mountains, Colombia continued to pour material and men into the region; by March Colonel Rico had

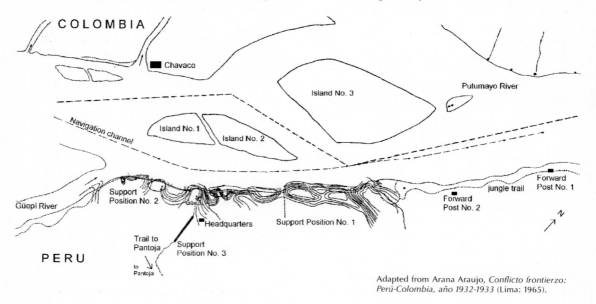

Adapted from Arana Araujo, *Conflicto frontierzo: Perú-Colombia, año 1932-1933* (Lima: 1965).

Map 28. Battle of Güepí, 26 March 1933.

available more than 1800 soldiers for combat in the Putumayo, a considerable increase over the 800 of early February.[33]

What had the Peruvians been doing to counter the mounting Colombian forces? Throughout the war Peru had an accurate and at times perfect knowledge of Colombian forces and intentions. Bogotá newspapers described in detail the Colombian plans, and deciphered telegrams confirmed the press reports; in any case the Colombian strategy stood out as the most logical and reasonable alternative. However, the information that would have been invaluable in another war was downright harmful to Peru. Knowledge of the rapid Colombian build-up demoralized the Peruvian defenders who saw confirmed their logistical deficiencies. Peru was unable to supply or reinforce properly the Güepí garrison. After the closing of the Putumayo to Peruvian shipping, a jungle trail of 114 kilometers linking Güepí to Pantoja in the Napo River became the lifeline for the garrison. Because Ecuador's base of Rocafuerte blocked the mouth of the Aguarico River, Peruvians could not use that water route and hence over the years had laboriously hacked a crude trail through the jungle. Just keeping the vegetation from swallowing up the narrow trail was an exhausting and never-ending task.[34]

To carry supplies the Peruvian army turned to civilian porters then common in the Andes Mountains, but these porters were unaccustomed to the tropical climate and quickly became ill. The porters also tended to pilfer the merchandise, worked at their own pace, and deserted at the first chance. Through extraordinary efforts the porters and soldiers had somehow lugged five machine guns through the trail to Güepí but not enough ammunition. Infantry soldiers could walk the trail, and their arrival gradually increased the garrison to around 230 men. However, to keep from sinking into the mud, the soldiers had to travel light, and none carried their normal complement of cartridges.[35] The officers realized that any credible defense required artillery but unfortunately the Pantoja commander telegraphed: "Impossible to send field cannons to Güepí, it takes five days in the trail and many swamps are 140 meters long; the porters cannot carry more than 30 kilometers."[36] In desperation, the commander of Güepí urged that

two pieces of artillery be flown in, as Colombia had done with some of its cannons, but Peru lacked suitable cargo planes. The heartbreaking pleas for help from Güepí came to an end on 9 March when the radio went dead and left the garrison abandoned to its fate.[37]

The future of the garrison at this moment depended not on its efforts but on the struggle raging in Bogotá. The popular mobilization had scared many politicians who joined the Foreign Ministry in trying to end the war at any cost. The peace party began to feed defeatist stories about the vaunted superiority of the Peruvian army and of its formidable armament. Critics dismissed Tarapacá as a fluke and warned that it was a Peruvian trap to lure the Colombians deeper into sure disaster in the jungle. The peace party could not stop expressing its awe at how completely the French officers had transformed the Peruvian army into a copy of the French army that had won World War I. The press dramatized the inevitable petty mistakes on the Colombian side and emphasized the shortages of some items on the front as proof that the campaign was headed for disaster. Any slight military embarrassment, no matter how trivial, was all that was needed to predict the destruction of the Colombian army.

Diplomacy could only offer to sugarcoat the loss of Leticia for Colombia, and President Olaya Herrera most reluctantly allowed the military campaign to resume but under extremely strict controls. Rather than give the commanders freedom to push on to Iquitos, the Colombian government imposed the pattern of using carefully measured doses of force to compel Peru to withdraw from Leticia. But war is an inherently unstable element and cannot be measured out precisely as weed killer to undesirable plants. The Colombian Foreign Ministry could not imagine anybody even thinking about a war for conquest when so many countries in the world had signed treaties outlawing war. Certainly the Foreign Ministry would have been shocked to learn that only the massive Colombian deployment in the Putumayo had prevented Peru from realizing its dream of seizing all Colombian territory south of the Caquetá River.

The War Ministry sent a third attack order to Colonel Rico on 18 March, but this time the preparations would take over a week because he had to transfer most of his forces from the headwaters of the Putumayo back to the unhealthy Chavaco. The navigation channel passed right in front of Güepí to the consternation of the Peruvians who could see for themselves the large number of Colombians deploying impressive armament. Colonel Rico mounted shore batteries in Chavaco and on the occupied islands in the river. All the vessels carried the latest model of heavy machine guns, and in addition, each of the two gunboats, the *Santa Marta* and the *Cartagena*, had brand-new cannons. Many soldiers carried automatic rifles, and the units were generously equipped with light machine guns. Ammunition was plentiful for all the weapons, and ample stocks remained in the camp.[38]

The superiority in firepower promised a resounding victory to the Colombians, but they had no way of verifying the size of the Peruvian forces. At the beginning of the war Colombian lookouts could easily see movement on the surface, but from early 1933 the Peruvians had been burrowing trenches, subterranean corridors and bunkers no longer visible from the other shore. The network of trenches soon stretched for kilometers and led to the Pantoja trail in the rear. Following the French lessons of World War I, the officers demanded even more trenches. The exhausted soldiers continued to dig the trenches, although some may have realized they were digging their own graves. However, by World War I standards, the defensive deployment seemed competent (Map 28). Downstream the farthest Peruvian position was Forward Post No.1 manned round the clock but only by 2 soldiers; a jungle trail paralleled the river bank to another small detachment (Forward Post No. 2), and from there the trail continued to the sloping elevations where the system of trenches began and where most of the Peruvian machine guns were lo-

Reservists in parade in Lima. In early 1933 General Luis Sánchez Cerro was sending poorly armed reservists to the Amazon to their certain death in the war with Colombia (Archivo Histórico Militar del Perú, Lima, Peru).

cated. The trenches stretched for over two kilometers until the mouth of the Güepí River. At that point a rocky prominence provided an ideal site for a second cluster of machine guns (Support Position No. 2). The remaining machine guns under Lieutenant Garrido Lecca guarded the rear at the entrance of the trail to Pantoja (Support Position No. 3). The large Peruvian force normally required a colonel as its ranking officer; but the colonel, probably sensing that command of this doomed garrison would be a blot on his career, had conveniently left to bring the reinforcements that never arrived. Command fell on the untested Captain Víctor Tenorio who had his headquarters close to the rearguard force of Lieutenant Garrido.

The Colombians were not aware of these troop dispositions because the Foreign Ministry had prohibited any reconnaissance by scouts or planes on the Peruvian side of the Putumayo River. Nevertheless, Colonel Rico was certain of success and he prepared his force to attack on Sunday 26 March 1933. He needed minimal information on the Peruvian positions, and on the afternoon of Saturday 25 March Colonel Rico sent a platoon under jungle veteran Captain Domínguez to explore. The current took the platoon much farther downstream than planned, and it failed to deliver a report. The failure of this reconnaissance attempt did not deter Colonel Rico, who woke up his men at 0300 on 26 March for the attack.

The first gunboat to depart was the *Cartagena* because it had the longest trip to make. The *Cartagena* had to land a company of soldiers upstream at the Güepí River while it was pitch dark; by going at half engine and keeping all lights off, the *Cartagena* escaped detection by Support Position No. 2 and waited for daylight to find a suitable landing site for the company. The maneuver by the *Cartagena* formed part of the double envelopment Colonel Rico had planned: While that company marched from the Guepi River, the main force advanced from the opposite direction. The gunboat *Santa Marta* ferried a company of soldiers across the river from Chavaco and landed quietly on the Peruvian side. This company captured the two soldiers in Forward Post No. 1 before they were able to send any warning signal. The company then marched through the Peruvian trail and successfully overpowered the small detachment at Forward Post No. 2. The

Colombian troops walked along the jungle trail close to the Putumayo River and parallel to them the *Santa Marta* steamed upstream ready to provide covering fire with its cannons and heavy machine guns.

Not a single shot had rung out yet, and the first explosions came only around 0830 when Colombian planes made their first bombing run over the Peruvian trenches. In a radical new departure, the planes circled overhead at a high altitude and then suddenly dived straight down to drop their bombs. The planes then quickly ascended in an almost vertical climb to escape machine gun fire which soon stopped because Captain Tenorio had sent the order not to waste scarce ammunition on shooting at the fast-moving planes. Once the airplanes had dropped all their bombs, the shore batteries and the *Santa Marta* began shelling the Peruvian positions. The Peruvian machine guns replied, but their bullets fell short and formed a harmless curtain of water far from the *Santa Marta* whose gunners carefully spotted trenches and either filled them with shrapnel or smashed them with direct hits. The explosion of the shells inside bunkers and covered trenches sent shattered beams and dirt flying meters up into the air. The Colombian troops continued to advance under the artillery barrage, but soon they ran into the machine gun nests of the Peruvian defenders. To the consternation of the Colombians, they were caught in a cross fire from Peruvian machine guns in the trenches and automatic rifles suddenly opening fire from tree tops. Colonel Rico who was aboard the *Santa Marta* sensed that the battle had reached a critical moment, and he ordered the *Santa Marta* close to the shore to bring its heavy machine guns to bear exactly on the Peruvian positions. Seeing the danger from the approaching gunboat, the Peruvian machine gunners desperately fired at the *Santa Marta* whose steel plating stopped the bullets. At this precise moment the missing platoon of jungle veteran Captain Domínguez suddenly emerged from the jungle and attacked the Peruvian position from the rear. The Colombian attackers and the gunboat immediately caught the Peruvians in a murderous cross fire. By 1000 the surviving defenders panicked and either surrendered or tried to flee desperately to the Pantoja trail in the rear. Meanwhile a tug boat pushed a barge loaded with troops across the river and the Colombians continued to overwhelm the Peruvian defenses.

As the Peruvian positions crumbled, a nervous Captain Tenorio was at a loss as to how best to respond. A defeat would blot his career, but withdrawal was out of the question because he knew what fate had befallen Lieutenant Diaz of Tarapacá. He wavered between different courses of action, and in a first burst of activity he sent written messages to his men containing the proverbial order "to fight to the death." After having completed his duty, he then abandoned headquarters and rushed to seek safety down the trail to Pantoja. Lieutenant Garrido was still defending the only escape route, and in spite of seeing his superior officer flee, the lieutenant did not succumb to the panic but continued to cover the retreat and did not stop firing his machine gun even after almost all his men had been killed. A Colombian soldier was about to kill Garrido and his last soldier, when Lieutenant Manrique, impressed by the bravery of the Peruvian officer, jumped into the line of fire and at considerable risk ordered the soldiers not to shoot at Garrido who became a prisoner.[39]

With the closing of the only escape route to Pantoja, the battle was won but not yet over. The gunboat *Cartagena* had landed its company on the south shore of the Güepí River and, in a similar manner to the *Santa Marta*, escorted them downstream to the mouth of the Güepí River. The Peruvian emplacements, still under the influence of "the fight to the death" order, tied down the Colombian troops, until the intense fire from the *Cartagena* distracted the defenders long enough for a Colombian platoon to reach the rear of the position. The Peruvians saw their escape route to the Pantoja trail cut off, and in desperation fled directly south into the thick jungle. Over the next few days, as the Peruvians realized that the Colombians were not executing prisoners (as often happened in the civil wars in Peru), the fugitives dribbled back and surrendered to escape certain death from starvation in the jungle. As nightfall approached, Colonel Rico halted any pursuit down the very narrow trail to Pantoja.[40]

The battle of Güepí was rich in tactical lessons, among others that the undisputed reign of the machine gun had come to an end. Aerial bombardment and artillery shelling could neutralize the fire from machine guns no matter how well ensconced in trenches. Machine guns and automatic rifles were key weapons to stop infantry attacks, but the bolt-action Mauser rifle failed to distinguish itself in the combat. The Mauser rifle, the lineal descendant of the musket that had been the faithful companion of the infantryman for centuries, was fast losing battlefield predominance to heavy weapons. Unquestionably the most important lesson was that firepower and mobility reigned supreme over the battlefield. Whenever the Peruvian defenders had changed positions in the trenches or had fired from tree tops, the Colombian advance had halted, but if the Peruvians stood immobile, heavy firing soon overwhelmed them.

Were these findings so surprising to the Peruvian high command? How did Peruvian officers expect 5 machine guns and 4 automatic rifles to stop the bombers, artillery, and naval cannons of the Colombians? The desperate pleas of the garrison for artillery and antiaircraft guns suggested that the defenders knew what fate awaited them. The response of sending more Peruvian soldiers actually compounded the problem: Not only did the new arrivals lack sufficient ammunition for their rifles, but each Peruvian soldier was an additional mouth to feed and put an added burden on the porters trudging through the jungle trail. Fascinating as were the tactical lessons, logistics trumped them all. The Colombians could bring and supply more men and material to Güepí than could the Peruvians to Pantoja. If the Peruvians could not adequately supply the base of Pantoja, how could they expect to supply Güepí accessible only through a nearly impassable jungle trail 114 kilometers long? The Peruvian forces, aware of the impeding attack on Güepí, were powerless to take any effective countermeasure in time. In such a desperate logistical situation, responsible military analysis demanded that Peru avoid a battle at Güepí and withdraw from an untenable position. Peru needed all its resources just to defend Pantoja; instead by insisting on fighting at Güepí, Peru lost all the equipment and munitions so laboriously accumulated in that place and over half of the garrison. The Colombians suffered only five killed (one from friendly fire) and 10 wounded. Not only were the Colombian losses insignificant, but the troops gained tremendous confidence and thirsted to finish the war with Peru. The shouts of "Long Live Colombia" resounded throughout the battle and after as the morale of the Colombian troops reached a fever pitch. The War Ministry urged rapid successive blows to destroy the remaining Peruvian defenders in the Putumayo River. The victory at Güepí gave Colombia the opportunity to bring the war to a quick and victorious conclusion. Public opinion back home went wild with the news of the victory, and those who had predicted a disastrous war temporarily faded from view.[41]

The Last Offensive

Colombia had used the Putumayo River as its main supply route for the war effort. The government worked feverishly to improve the roads leading to that river and by March 1933 also opened the Caquetá River as a second supply route. Even before the capture of Güepí on 26 March, Colombia acquired the capacity to increase its forces easily and also to rotate its troops between the healthier climate at the foot of the Andes Mountains and the Amazon jungle. As needed the army could move fresh and well-trained troops downriver to face the hungry and sickly Peruvian soldiers trapped in their steaming jungle outposts. In preparation for the final push to drive out the last Peruvian troops from the Putumayo, Colombia had established an air base at La Chorrera, just a few minutes flying time from the Peruvian base of Puerto Arturo. Slightly north of La Chorrera, a Colombia staging area at the mouth of the Campuya River was also rapidly appearing. The stocks of supplies and ammunition grew relentlessly at Campuya in anticipation of the main Colombian contingent coming for the attack on Puerto Arturo.[42]

Propaganda was the main defense of Puerto Arturo. Peruvians described this impregnable fortress as another Gibraltar and reported the arrival of large numbers of reinforcements. Agents planted rumors at the Ecuadorian post of Rocafuerte that Peru was preparing to launch a three-pronged counteroffensive from Pantoja to recapture Güepí. Although Bogotá dismissed the threat to Güepí as a fantasy, as a precaution the War Ministry halted the march of patrols down the Pantoja trail until a well-supplied force was ready.

Mules arrived to carry their fodder and cargoes on the jungle trail leading from Güepí to Pantoja, and construction crews worked to make the jungle trail suitable for mules pulling carts. The rainy season flooded the region and delayed operations, but by the start of May the Colombian troops and laborers had pushed south over 25 kilometers in the 114-kilometer jungle trail. Unknown to them, the Peruvian soldiers were making a similar effort to the north from Pantoja, but the Peruvians who lacked mules depended exclusively on human porters. Patiently Colombians and Peruvians hacked their way towards each other, but the work on the jungle trail was so slow and arduous that many weeks had to elapse before they encountered each other. Before then, combat was sure to break out elsewhere in the long front.[43]

Meanwhile an excessively cautious War Ministry postponed the planned attack on Puerto Arturo. Mistakenly concluding that the *Santa Marta* and the *Cartagena*, the two gunboats of the victory at Güepí, were insufficient to neutralize the shore batteries, the War Ministry decided to wait until they were joined by the flotilla slowly making its way up the Putumayo from Tarapacá. The War Ministry had seriously underestimated Colombian resources, because the quality and quantity of the artillery already in place vastly outclassed the old Peruvian cannons. No less decisively, Colombian air power had increased dramatically. Not only was the air base closer than the one at Güepí, but Colombia had acquired what some regarded as the largest air force in South America. The many planes made possible repeated bombing runs to pulverize Puerto Arturo and shatter its defenders into flight or surrender. Ironically, the first Colombian successes in breaking Peruvian coded messages contributed to the exaggerated caution. In a laconic deciphered telegram, the Peruvian commander of Puerto Arturo reported that he had a force of 960 men but did not make clear whether he included 120 Indian scouts and an undetermined number of civilian workers in this figure. Bogotá concluded that 960 was the right number, when in reality troop strength was only 652.[44]

Knowing the exact number of soldiers was in this case irrelevant, because the Peruvian commander had promptly sent back the most recent reinforcements. The new troops had come without a single grain of rice and the commander concluded that they would have been a burden when his garrison was already on half rations. And of his 652 soldiers, at least one-fourth could not fight because of sickness, partly because the supply of medicines had dwindled. Once again in the Amazon, large numbers of infantry are not only useless but actually harmful: Each additional soldier puts more strain on the supply network to feed him and to take care of him when he contracts tropical illnesses. Firepower and mobility were the essential components of victory in the Amazon jungle. The sickly and hungry Peruvian garrison trapped inside its World War I trenches lacked mobility, and their armament was only slightly better than that of the doomed defenders of Güepí. The three 75 mm Krupp cannons seemed at first sight formidable but as pre-World War I models, they lacked the range to reach the new Colombian artillery. Should

the three small naval 37 mm cannons survive the aerial bombardment, they might do some damage to landing barges but could not harm the Colombian gunboats with their 75 mm cannons. Seven old and rusting machine guns completed the armament of Puerto Arturo but they were no match for the shiny new models Colombia had bought.[45]

The Peruvian high command did realize that Puerto Arturo was vulnerable and hired Japanese technicians to install several modern artillery pieces. The Colombians to their relief deciphered a telegram reporting that the barge carrying the artillery pieces had sunk in a river and that attempts to rescue the cannon had caused the drowning of eight soldiers. However, the War Ministry was still not sure how formidable were the defenses already in place at Puerto Arturo and confirmed its decision to postpone any attack until the flotilla sailing upstream from Tarapacá arrived. Because of their draft, the armed merchant ships could not

In this allegorical photograph, Colombian president Enrique Olaya Herrera appears leading army officers in the war to recover Leticia in the Amazon from Peru in 1932–1933 (Plinio Mendoza Neira and Alberto Camacho Angarita, *El liberalismo en el poder;* Bogotá: Prag, 1946).

steam as far north as Puerto Arturo, but all the gunboats and the smaller craft could navigate the shallow waters. Furthermore, two brand-new gunboats, especially designed for combat in shallow waters, had just joined the Colombian fleet. The *Sucre* and the *Bogotá* carried 75 mm cannon and were vastly superior to the very reliable *Cartagena* and *Santa Marta*.[46]

The Peruvian high command was becoming increasingly worried about its crumbling defenses. To try to regain control of the river systems, a desperate Peru decided to play its last card. In a surprising move, Lima ordered the transfer of its two light cruisers, the *Grau* and the *Bolognesi*, to the Amazon. Warships of this magnitude had never reached the upper Amazon, and their draft excluded them from almost all the tributaries of the Amazon. During the rainy season these cruisers could reach Tarapacá but only down a narrow channel in the deepest part of the river and could not steam further upstream on the Putumayo. The naval guns of the cruisers were of a larger caliber than the artillery Colombia had set up in Tarapacá, but their extra range was useless: The moment a Peruvian warship left Brazilian for Colombian waters in the Putumayo, it entered the pre-plotted firing coordinates of the Colombian batteries. Rather than a suicidal charge against Tarapacá, most likely the Peruvian high command intended to send the two warships to Iquitos to act as floating batteries to try to save that city from falling into Colombian hands. Even in the Amazon River the fate of the two cruisers was far from promising: Colombian pilots had practiced long and hard learning to bomb ships rapidly twisting out in the open sea and would have no difficulty hitting these stationary cruisers in the Amazon. Accompanying the two warships came two Peruvian submarines, but whatever mission the submarines would play in the shallow waters of the Amazon tributaries has never been explained. Whatever spectacular fate awaited the cruisers, the Peruvian naval fleet heading for the Amazon was sure to write some memorable episodes in world military history.[47]

The normally cautious War Ministry in Bogotá remained confident that its bombers could take care of the Peruvian cruisers and eagerly looked forward to the campaign in the Putumayo. In early May President Olaya Herrera, in response to requests from his diplo-

mats, urged the capture of Puerto Arturo, preferably in a few days. His diplomats persuaded him that a quick victory would hasten serious negotiations at Geneva. Just as before the battle of Güepí, for the diplomats combat was a finely tuned valve they imagined they could turn on and off in response to the needs of the negotiating table. This time it was the War Ministry that pleaded for several weeks to complete the preparations for an overwhelming attack on Puerto Arturo. Orders went out to gather the strike force at Campuya and for the river fleet to hasten its trip up the Putumayo River. After some skirmishes near the mouth of the Algodón River, the gunboats pushed upstream in that river (Map 27). By 12 May the Colombian forces had captured all the Peruvian outposts in that tributary of the Putumayo River, including a large air base soon hosting many Colombian planes. The air base on the Algodón River was located roughly between Puerto Arturo and Iquitos; with difficulty the commanders struggled to restrain their pilots, each of whom wanted the honor to be the first to bomb Iquitos.[48]

Puerto Arturo was a doomed fortress. Its sickly and hungry garrison could not hope to stop the over 1000 infantrymen gathering for the attack. Not only had Colombia built an air base a few minutes flying time away, but the Peruvians had lost their air base on the Algodón River. Without control of the air or of the river, any defense of Puerto Arturo was impossible. The Peruvian government had so played up Puerto Arturo as another Gibraltar that the loss of this supposedly impregnable fortress would cause a profound shock and might even trigger a backlash against the war. To try to prepare Peru for a long war, President Sánchez Cerro was rallying young men to come and serve in the army. The government managed to recruit or press-gang almost 10,000 young men into going to fight to the Amazon. When lack of supplies forced local Peruvian commanders to refuse to receive more infantry, Sánchez Cerro insisted on sending 10,000 untrained men with rifles to the inhospitable region. Few would have survived hunger and disease to face the superior weaponry of the well-fed Colombians. Sánchez Cerro hosted a massive rally in Lima to try to cheer up the departing 10,000 recruits on 30 April 1933, but just as he was leaving, an assassin killed the president and plunged Peru again into political turmoil.[49]

Prior to his assassination, Sánchez Cerro had recalled General Óscar Benavides, the hero of La Pedrera (chapter 2, second section) from a diplomatic post in Britain and appointed him commander of all Peruvian forces on 11 April 1933. With this appointment Sánchez Cerro hoped to stabilize the collapsing Amazon front with Colombia. After the assassination of Sánchez Cerro, the Peruvian Congress chose Óscar Benavides to fill out the remainder of the deceased president's term. The appointment of the most prestigious Peruvian general as president seemed indispensable to Peru in its war with Colombia. As Benavides informed himself minutely about the front, he received the dangerous news that Ecuador was waiting for another Colombian victory, such as the capture of Puerto Arturo, to join Colombia as an ally against Peru. Even if Ecuador continued to hesitate, its willingness to allow free passage of Colombian troops through the Aguarico River meant the loss of Pantoja and the invasion of the Napo River. When the Colombian presidential candidate Alfonso Lopez Pumarejo, a good friend of Benavides since their mutual posting as diplomats in London, expressed a willingness to travel to Lima to seek peace, President Benavides enthusiastically accepted the proposal. In spite of publishing many fictional victory stories, the Peruvian army officers admitted that Colombia had gained the upper hand in the war, and they were eager not for peace but for a truce to rebuild their strength. At last on 24 May 1933 the diplomats could agree to sign a cease-fire in Geneva and the next day the truce went into effect.[50]

The Colombian commander who was ready to launch the assault on Puerto Arturo immediately "lamented militarily that we were not left with enough time to win the war"[51] a sentiment echoed throughout the Colombian forces in the Putumayo River. But in spite of the truce, the war was not over yet. Prior to the receipt of the news from Geneva, both sides had sent large detachments walking into the jungle trail between Güepí and Pantoja. The Colombian company was on a reconnaissance mission to try to verify a rumor about an impeding Peruvian offensive. The Peruvian detachment consisted of troops freshly arrived

from Iquitos and had been given the impossible mission of recapturing Güepí. In the French tradition of World War I trench warfare, after each attack a counterattack was mandatory. Although this tactic was impossible to apply in jungle warfare, Peruvian junior officers, fearful of the wrath of dogmatic superiors, mechanically inserted in their reports fictional accounts of counterattacks. Totally oblivious to the problems of supplying troops by jungle trail, Lima had incessantly demanded a counterattack at Güepí, and the Pantoja commander had no choice but to send this force of 3 machine guns and 83 men (about half were porters) up the jungle trail. The Colombian company was scattered through different jungle trails about 35 kilometers south of Güepí. A squad under the command of recently graduated Second Lieutenant Guillermo Aldana ran into the much larger Peruvian force, and a confused firefight broke out. The Lieutenant promptly sent a messenger to inform the rest of the company. To try to gain time to escape, he used the confusion to shout orders to his men calling upon the companies in the rear to come forward. When the Peruvians heard that companies were coming, they halted, whereupon Lieutenant Aldana saw the opportunity to press his luck with a wild gamble. He shouted out to the Peruvians to surrender before the Colombian companies arrived, and to his surprise a much larger Peruvian force threw down their weapons and surrendered. Lieutenant Aldana did not know how to guard the many ragged prisoners with his 9 soldiers. For the moment many Peruvians had not bothered to surrender and had fled into the jungle, and shortly after the rest of the Colombian company arrived.[52]

Gradually the Peruvians came out of the jungle to surrender and interrogations revealed their real motivation. They were all starving to death and were so exhausted that they were going to collapse anyway. They had stopped shooting because they could no longer lift their weapons, and many Peruvians had to be carried to Güepí in litters because they were too weak to walk. Yet these wretched-looking men were the fresh troops recently arrived in Pantoja, and if this was the best Peru could hurl against Colombia, the war was as good as lost.

Colombia enjoyed such an overwhelming military superiority that it was hard to believe that Bogotá and not Lima had been in a rush to sign the truce. Expecting some tough bargaining, the Peruvians had been surprised when at Geneva the Colombians enthusiastically accepted the terms dictated by the Peruvians. Essentially, Peru imposed on Colombia the obligation to withdraw from all Peruvian territory occupied during the campaign. The condition would have been a valid quid pro quo for a simultaneous Peruvian withdrawal from Leticia, but that was not the case. A League of Nations Commission paid by Colombia would administer Leticia for a year. All that Colombia had to show for the war effort was the recovery of Tarapacá and the closing of the mouth of the Putumayo to Peruvian navigation.

Militarily giving up these positions did not make sense but was not necessarily fatal as long as Colombia retained its superiority in firepower and mobility. The return of poorly supplied Peruvians to the trenches in Güepí did not alter the strategic equation, because Colombia could still drive them out again in any resumption of hostilities, but inevitably with much needless shedding of blood. The mouth of the Putumayo, the supply routes from the headwaters of the Caquetá and Putumayo rivers, and the many air bases all gave Colombia a logistic and strategic preponderance over Peru. Unfortunately, class politics came to reduce the Colombian military position to dangerously weak levels. Many politicians and members of the Colombian elite had never wanted the war and were most afraid of the democratic potential of a large army. For the Colombian elite to preserve its rigid control, the privileged few had to be the source of all benefits. Patron-client relationships and not merits earned in the battlefield were the only acceptable way to advance in Colombia. Barely had the diplomats signed the truce of 24 May 1933 when the Treasury and Foreign ministries were competing to see who could make the most drastic cuts in military expenses. Rather than maintaining large forces ready to pounce upon Peru should it decide to keep Leticia, Colombia rushed to demobilize.[53]

As expected, on 23 June 1933 Colombia handed over Güepí to Peruvian forces, and soon after most Colombian troops departed from the Putumayo River. Bogotá still had not learned the lesson that even after the signing of a formal peace treaty modest units should remain in place and even more so when only a cease-fire had been signed. As the Colombian troops vanished, Peru revived its plans for conquest. Peruvian army officers listed and identified the lessons of the war and by mid–June formed in their minds the idea that after making some changes, Peru could defeat Colombia. But the jungle remained the most formidable enemy and, in August 1933, budget overruns and the exhaustion of its men forced Peru to halt work on widening the jungle trails of Güepí-Pantoja and of Puerto Arturo-Santa Elena.[54] In spite of renewed efforts, three months later the commander of the Iquitos garrison admitted that "until today nothing has been accomplished as far as solidifying the security of our very lengthy frontier (around 1000 kilometers) with Colombia."[55]

The General Staff in Lima was undismayed and busily wrote many proposals on how to conduct the offensive should war with Colombia resume. In March 1934 the plans had taken form, but their only realistic measure was the recapture of Leticia then demilitarized and under League of Nations control. The recapture of Tarapacá was impossible, and a surprise bombardment could not knock out the Colombian air bases in the region. Any attack of Peru on the Colombian positions in the headwaters of the Putumayo was not just irrational but suicidal. Colombian espionage and code breaking did continue to improve, and soon the Colombian government acquired unmistakable proof of Peruvian preparations to renew hostilities. Rather than begin another mobilization and risk the predictable public outcry, the Colombian government decided to resume its armament purchases abroad quietly. More planes, more warships, more artillery, and more machine guns were sure to guarantee Colombian superiority in firepower and mobility. A financially poorer Peru could not match the arms purchases of its wealthier northern neighbor. Peru did acquire enough weapons to guarantee that any war would be bloodier than the first one, but never enough to put in doubt the inevitable Colombian victory.[56]

The election of a pro–Colombian president in Ecuador promised immediate Ecuadorian participation in any renewed war with Colombia. The old fear of a combination of bordering countries uniting against Peru reappeared for the last time. Negotiations shifted to Rio de Janeiro but failed to make progress as Peru insisted on keeping Leticia. The mandate of the League of Nations to administer Leticia was about to expire after one year and then Peru could reoccupy and fortify Leticia before a new Colombian expedition arrived. The Peruvian General Staff prepared the army units for an impeding clash: "The international situation, which had remained in status quo pending the outcome of the negotiations at Rio de Janeiro, seems to be approaching a crisis."[57] The man of destiny at this crucial moment was Peruvian President Benavides, who in 1911 had taken the unpopular decision of having to give up La Pedrera. Would the general give war another chance in 1934? As the general poured over the plans of the General Staff, he immediately detected their unreal nature. Just as in 1911, he rose to true heights of statesmanship and concluded that any war with Colombia would be disastrous for Peru. His decision for peace required an intense political struggle to secure approval for a very unpopular decision. Just moments before the mandate of the League of Nations was about to expire on 24 May 1934, the Peruvian delegation received orders to sign the agreement recognizing the Leticia trapezium as territory belonging to Colombia.[58] At the last minute peace had triumphed, but fears of a renewed outbreak of war in the Amazon jungle remained alive.

15. War Between Peru and Ecuador

Fight only when you are sure to win, without letting anyone know. — Sun Bin[1]

Without boldness and enterprising spirit on the part of the leader, the most brilliant victory will lead to no great success. — Carl Maria von Clausewitz[2]

The peace treaty Colombia signed with Peru in May 1934 seemed to many Peruvian officers to be just a truce. These army officers felt deeply humiliated by their shameful loss to Colombia, and they were looking for the first opportunity to redeem their sullied reputation. As Peru focused on the next war with Colombia, Ecuador saw the opportunity to encroach upon many Amazon territories. The collision course Ecuador chose meant that the next war in the Amazon would pit Peru not against Colombia but against Ecuador.

Mounting Tensions with Ecuador

The war with Colombia had exposed many weaknesses of the Peruvian army. Shortly after signing the cease-fire with Colombia on 24 May 1933, the General Staff in Lima ordered the field commanders to write extensively on the lessons learned from the war. The belief that hostilities would soon resume with Colombia gave a sense of urgency to the inquiry which, however, did not end once Peru accepted peace with Colombia on 24 May 1934. The Peruvian military had lost considerable face in the battles with Colombia and wanted to do everything possible to redeem its image. Officer training incorporated the lessons learned during the war, and gradually the Peruvian army

began to shift its emphasis away from French doctrine of trench warfare to new concepts of mobility and firepower.

The Peruvian army needed to change not just to win in any future conflict but also to justify its very existence. Peru had striven to professionalize its army and navy for decades, yet in contrast upstart Colombia seemingly out of thin air put on the field a more efficient military force in barely six months. Did the Colombian success argue for waiting until war broke out to create a military force? A dispassionate analysis indicated that the rapid Colombian mobilization was not a realistic alternative in the future. Colombia had been able to draw on many persons with prior military experience, yet their number remained inadequate. Colombia also had enjoyed the opportunity of purchasing modern weapons after the start of war, but even this country learned that not all arms exporters were willing to sell. The usual practice in the world was to halt all arms sales once combat begun; Peru did not want to run the risk of being caught again with obsolete weapons and decided to place orders abroad for new armament.[3]

After 1933 Peru engaged in the difficult and costly process of renewing its military doctrine and its armament. Ecuador decided to ignore these changes and instead believed that Peru was finished as a military power and as a

415

country. Ecuador drew on the published accounts of Colombian victories to conclude that Peru was irretrievably doomed to defeat in any of its wars. In 1933 and 1934 belittling Peru was essential politics for Ecuadorian leaders who needed to persuade their people to join the war with Colombia against Peru. However, the demeaning of Peruvian military capabilities became extremely dangerous after the agreement of May 1934 ended any possibility of a resumption of hostilities between Colombia and Peru. By then the anti–Peruvian agitation had gained Ecuadorian politicians so much popularity that they could not bring themselves to halt the publicity campaign. Even worse, Ecuadorian politicians came to believe their own propaganda and formed an exaggerated conception of their country's military power. The success of tiny Paraguay against a large Bolivia encouraged Ecuadorians to believe that they too could repeat the fabled exploits of the Chaco War. An arrogant Ecuador decided in 1935 to press across the unmarked border near the Zarumilla River (Map 29). This region seemed a good place to pick a conflict with Peru because in 1910 President Eloy Alfaro had obtained extraordinary results for Ecuador from his mobilization of an army in this same border.

The heavily forested and largely unoccupied Zarumilla region had served as a buffer zone between both countries. Ecuador built a bridge over the river and encouraged its farmers to push into the disputed territory. The final goal of the advance was the city of Tumbes, which had been in Peruvian hands since the early 1820s but which Ecuador claimed as its own. To counter Ecuadorian penetration, Peru sent a construction battalion to trace a road between Tumbes and the Zarumilla River. Ecuador protested the construction work and infiltrated small army units into the region; soon Peru countered by sending its own detachments, and already a clash seemed imminent in November 1935. On 4 March 1936 Ecuadorian tobacco growers attacked but failed to expel Peruvian tobacco growers from fertile river banks, and war seemed likely over this incident on the unmarked border.[4] Just like in 1911, Ecuador managed to go to the brink of war only to step back successfully with a status quo agreement of 6 July 1936. Both sides agreed to begin negotiations in Washington, D.C. under the sponsorship of the U.S. government;

on the ground, both Peru and Ecuador ordered their forces not to make any further advances.

The U.S. auspices evoked memories of the triple mediation of 1911 (chapter 2, section 1) and was a wonderful final opportunity for Ecuador to settle its boundary dispute with Peru on favorable terms. However, Ecuador did not want to accept the reality that the situation had vastly changed in the intervening 25 years and that essentially Ecuador stood alone. Peru had settled the border disputes with the rest of its neighbors, and no chance existed of creating or threatening to create a coalition against Peru. After the fiasco of the award by the King of Spain in 1911, Peru adamantly refused to arbitrate the dispute and rightfully insisted on direct negotiations as the only way to determine the boundary. For Peru, the remaining choices were starkly clear: either direct negotiations or war. Unfortunately, Ecuador did not want to admit these were the only two remaining options and instead used these final negotiations at Washington, D.C. for political grand standing back home. In 1937 Ecuador published diplomatic notes containing its outlandish territorial demands. Ecuador wanted to push the border in the Amazon considerably to the east in contrast to Peru that insisted on using the existing posts to draw a line in the jungle region. At play in the negotiations were not the minuscule strips near the Zarumilla River but vast stretches in the Amazon region.

The Amazon Region

In 1932 Ecuador had adopted a plan to establish its officials throughout the Amazon region, but in spite of enthusiastic support from the Ecuadorian Congress, action was slow at first. Ecuador took advantage of Peru's war with Colombia to move the post of Huachi downstream on the Pastaza River (Map 7). Other forward movements took place, but in spite of much prodding, Ecuador had not been able to advance far when both countries signed the status quo agreement on 6 July 1936.[5] An Ecuadorian commander decided on his own to disregard the agreement, and he moved his detachment from the Yaupi River down the Santiago River. Peruvian officials promptly told him that his detachment had to return to the Yaupi River in accordance with the status quo agreement. A committee of Indians delivered the message, but he replied that "he was in his territory and would not withdraw for any reason, and that he was not afraid of a land or river attack; he feared aerial attack, but soon airplanes would arrive to protect the detachment."[6]

The Ecuadorian commander had thrown down the gauntlet at the Peruvian officer, who prepared to attack. A Peruvian launch went upstream and in a surprise move captured the entire Ecuadorian unit without firing a shot on 17 July 1936 in what became known as the clash of Yaupi. Subsequently the Peruvians captured a second unit coming to reinforce the Ecuadorians. Peru later returned the prisoners but maintained control over the Santiago River as

Map 29. Pacific Ocean Sector, Ecuador-Peru.

far as the mouth of the Yaupi. Because of the small number of men involved (no more than 30 on each side) the incident might seem insignificant at first sight. But most ominous was the determination of Ecuadorian army officials to act independently of their orders from the Quito government. And from a purely military perspective, the clash at Yaupi confirmed an unbroken record of Peruvian victories over Ecuadorian units in the Amazon. In another ambush on 8 September 1937 Peruvians captured Ecuadorian soldiers who were trying to open communication from Yaupi to the Morona River.[7]

Undaunted by these setbacks, Ecuador did not give up on the Amazon and in 1938 continued implementing a policy of espionage and infiltration. Peruvian code breakers were already reading the Ecuadorian telegraph messages, but even without this additional help the Ecuadorian plan for advance in the Amazon had no chance of success. In an attempt to pressure Peru at the vulnerable Pantoja-Güepí trail, the Ecuadorian commander at Rocafuerte tried to make the jungle trail fall within Ecuador's territory. His harassment tactics failed, and Peruvian soldiers kept open the trail to Güepí. In spite of grandiose schemes, Ecuador's encroachments into the Amazon had been modest at best. The condition of the 26 Ecuadorian soldiers and one officer at Yaupi revealed why Ecuador had so little success in the Amazon:

> This poorly prepared officer and with scant knowledge of the military profession, seems more a farmer than an officer as his behavior demonstrates [...] The soldiers do not have the least concept of military discipline, because the officer for them is just a boss and they obey him like a boss. They state that they lost all loyalty to their garrison the moment the Ministry of Defense ignored them and fails to send them anything. They only think on the arrival of their replacements and enthusiastically await the day they can leave. [...] They don't care at all about the boundary question and even ignore what is the boundary with Peru. They actually think that all of the Santiago River upstream from the mouth of the Yaupí is Peruvian; they think for sure they will have to evacuate the position they hold once the diplomatic negotiations are concluded.[8]

The abysmal morale of the Ecuadorian troops who were supposed to defend Ecuador's claims revealed that the whole strategy of challenging Peru in the Amazon was fundamentally flawed. Ecuador had been unable to use the eastern slopes of the Andes to supply adequately its garrisons that felt forsaken in the vast Amazon jungle. Instead Peru, thanks to the completion of the Pichis Road over the Andes Mountains, for the first time could deliver substantial amounts of supplies and equipment from the interior of Peru to navigable rivers in the Amazon. The quantities of supplies were still dwarfed by what Colombia could deliver down its rivers but vastly exceeded anything that Ecuador could send. Before having fired a single shot, Ecuador had lost the logistics war with Peru.

The Ecuadorian posts on the Tigre, Corrientes, and Pastaza rivers did form a wedge into Peruvian territory, and Peru decided to use its logistical advantage to try to force those garrisons out in October 1939. Peru wanted to avoid the use of force and ordered its units to concentrate on depriving the Ecuadorian garrisons of any material assistance. Like the Yaupi garrison, the other Ecuadorian posts were in such weakened conditions that even if they did not withdraw, they could never pose any real resistance should hostilities ever begin.[9] The inability of Ecuador to reinforce and supply the Amazon region left the Zarumilla River as the only place to bring pressure upon Peru.

The Zarumilla Region

Ecuador's decision to threaten a war with Peru in the Zarumilla region had in its favor the precedent of Eloy Alfaro's successful bluff in 1910. The bordering province of El Oro was the richest in Ecuador and could easily feed and maintain troops. On the Peruvian side, the region was sparsely populated and virtually lacked a military presence. A show of force by Ecuadorian troops on Zarumilla seemed like a good way to bluff Peru. Ecuador hoped that the threat of being labeled an aggressor against a small country would finally convince Peru to accept the maximum Ecuadorian demands in the Amazon. Ecuador had to perform a delicate balancing act so as to pressure just enough to convince Peru into surrendering territory in the Amazon but not too much to push Peru into a war. The diplomats in Quito and the commanders in Zarumilla had to coordinate their actions meticulously if Ecuador's gamble was to stand any chance of success. At the negotiations in Washington, D.C., Ecuador presented exorbitant territorial demands in April 1937; Peru refused to accept them and ordered its army to prepare for mobilization in case of war. The crisis atmosphere soon dissipated as the diplomats returned to their unproductive talks.

The next year Ecuador took action on the ground and occupied the island of Matapalo in the channel of the Zarumilla River. Peru prepared for military action to recover the island, but the issue was muddled because both governments confused the names and locations of Matapalo and of Noblecilla, a neighboring island. In May 1938 Ecuador withdrew from Matapalo but kept previously unoccupied Noblecilla. The crisis dissipated again, but later the Foreign Ministry in Lima concluded from a careful examination of the maps that Noblecilla actually belonged to Peru.[10] The Ecuadorian occupation of Noblecilla became another aggravation for Peruvian officials who started to pay attention to this previously forgotten frontier. The long-postponed construction of roads and paths linking the Zarumilla region with Tumbes at last began. To avoid provocations, Lima did not station large army units in the region and instead left control of the zone in the hands of the Civil Guard (*Guardia Civil*), a national police force. The Civil Guard established its first posts in the disputed region in 1939, and although the network required another year to be complete, Peru for the first time began to have some control over this previously neglected border. The growing police presence gave Lima prompt first-hand information on Ecuadorian movements, but the close proximity also increased the risk of clashes between both countries.[11]

The incidents did not take long to appear. In July 1939 an Ecuadorian patrol killed two Civil Guards. In September units of both countries fought a skirmish, and in December an Ecuadorian unit opened machine gun fire on a Civil Guard post. In April 1940 two drunken Ecuadorian soldiers fired wildly into the Peruvian side, and constantly Ecuadorian airplanes flew over the region in another show of force. The immediate goal was to intimidate the Peruvian colonists into either naturalizing themselves as Ecuadorian or abandoning the region.

At times Ecuadorian patrols expelled Peruvian ranchers and tobacco growers from their lands by force and even arrested some settlers. Obviously the elimination of any Peruvian human presence would strengthen Ecuador's claim to the region during the negotiations.[12]

Ecuador enjoyed a position of strength because its army units in the province of El Oro were larger than the garrisons in the nearest Peruvian cities. The War Ministry in Lima repeatedly calculated that Ecuador could bring to the Zarumilla border a larger number of troops than Peru. The Civil Guard units served to restrict infiltration but could not stop any large invasion. Because Ecuador enjoyed the military advantage in this border, Peru risked the loss of cities such as Tumbes and maybe even Piura before reinforcements could arrive to stop the Ecuadorian invaders.[13] Any swift Ecuadorian capture of those cities could bring immense damage to Peru, because Ecuador could play the card of being the victim of a big aggressor and promptly demand an immediate cease-fire from gullible international mediators. Once in control of those cities, Ecuador could bargain a withdrawal for large stretches of Amazon territory. Facing such bleak prospects, the decision for the General Staff in Lima was not whether to go to war or not, but whether to prepare for war or not. The repeated incidents in the Zarumilla border during 1936–1939 convinced Lima that for basic self-defense it needed to prepare for war. Once Lima felt its northern provinces were safe from capture, the danger in prolonging negotiations disappeared. Negotiations could then continue perhaps indefinitely, but only if Ecuador stopped pressuring Peru on the Zarumilla border.

Preparations for War

The Peruvian army was deeply conscious of its poor performance during the war with Colombia. That war had caught Peru unprepared to fight, and the Peruvian General Staff was not about to repeat the same mistake. For any clash with Ecuador, the Peruvian General Staff insisted on careful preparations. But before beginning any preparations, Peru first had to define its main goal in a conflict. Little doubt existed that the purpose of any clash was to recuperate the lost territory in the Amazon region. Ecuador had pushed its outposts eastward during the 1930s until they encroached upon tens of thousands of square kilometers of Peruvian territory. But another consideration also existed. The Ecuadorian posts in the Amazon formed a saw-toothed line and made it impossible to draw distinct border between the two countries. Thus, a second Peruvian goal was not just to regain the status quo positions of 1936 but also to straighten the boundary line.[14]

In spite of the setbacks in the war with Colombia, Peru felt confident about its ability to expulse the Ecuadorian garrisons from the Amazon region. All prior clashes with Ecuadorians had ended in Peruvian victories, and as the previous section explained, the morale of the troops Ecuador stationed in the Amazon was pitiful at best. However, no matter how easily Peru overran the Amazon, something more was needed to force Quito to relinquish its claims. Peru concluded that to convince Quito of the need to abandon the Amazon, Peru had to inflict a traumatic defeat in the home provinces of Ecuador. Thus, although the main goal of any clash with Ecuador was the recovery of the Amazon territories, the Peruvian General Staff correctly selected the Zarumilla region to be the primary theater of operations. Both Peru and Ecuador could bring large forces into this region, and a decisive battle on this border was inevitable. For the Peruvian General Staff, the choice of the Zarumilla River was almost foreordained, because Ecuador was sure to pick this region for a build-up much like it had done in 1910. In actual practice, for Peru little difference existed between preparing to counter the expected Ecuadorian build-up and preparing to launch an offensive in the Zarumilla. However, each of the armed services staked out differing goals in any future war.

The Peruvian navy argued for "an unlimited war; all the resources of the nation concentrated to crush Ecuador."[15] In navy plans, Peru would first seize control of the sea, an easy task given that Ecuador had only one old warship. With control of the sea, the navy would land troops northwest of the Zarumilla River to capture Puerto Bolívar, the second largest port in Ecuador. The navy would then seize Isla Puná in preparation for a combined army-navy-air force operation to capture Guayaquil, the largest port and the richest city of Ecuador. The loss of Guayaquil was sure to convince Quito

that the war was definitely lost, but just for good measure, the navy also planned to seize the Galápagos Islands to bargain for more concessions from a defeated Ecuador. In the Amazon region the navy foresaw its gunboats easily crushing any Ecuadorian resistance.

The navy's classical conception of war and of the victor dictating treaty terms at the peace talks found support in the Peruvian air force. Although the air force then formed a part of the navy, the air force plan did not exude as much confidence as the navy's. However, the air force did share some of the enthusiasm of the navy and could not wait to send out its bombers to "make a massive attack on Guayaquil,"[16] though it admitted that the city offered few targets for air bombardment. The overwhelmingly agrarian society of Ecuador and the almost exclusive reliance of its army on infantry did not make for many military sites to bomb from the air. Even the interdiction of troop movements was not promising, because most roads to the Zarumilla border were no better than dirt paths burrowed through thick forests. Just like what happened to Bolivia in the Chaco War, aviation was unlikely to detect infantry movements under the forest canopy. As far as isolating El Oro province, whose trade almost all took place by sea, a naval blockade was the preferred option. Besides raids against minor military sites, the only real contribution the air force could make to the campaign was to destroy the railroad from Quito to Guayaquil, a necessary step in the capture of that last city.

Ultimately the Peruvian army had the final word on what type of war to wage. The General Staff did not share any beliefs in victory through sea or even air power and instead concluded that infantrymen would bear the brunt of the fighting. The success of infantry depended upon leadership, training, and equipment, and just the acute shortage of qualified officers ruled out any major offensives like those the navy contemplated. Serious shortages in modern machine guns and automatic rifles limited the firepower of the infantry. Peru was not a wealthy country and could not afford the classical warfare the navy proposed, but at the same time a passive defense at the Zarumilla River would never force Ecuador to renounce its claims to the Amazon territory. Consequently, an excessively cautious army decided upon a limited war at the province of El Oro rather than the destruction of Ecuador's army. With excessive pessimism, the army ruled out the capture of Guayaquil as simply beyond the budgetary and economic possibilities of Peru.[17]

The Peruvian army did not begin to dig trenches at Zarumilla as it had done with disastrous results at Güepí and instead planned on taking the offensive as soon as hostilities began. The Peruvian army at last broke with the French example of World War I and adopted a war of maneuver and firepower for its operations. Even if Peru had tried to remain purely on the defensive, the particular configuration of the Zarumilla border excluded such a possibility. South of the Zarumilla River a large bulge of Ecuadorian territory protruded to the west and reduced Tumbes to a narrow wedge or finger of Peruvian territory hugging the coast (Map 29). The simplest look at a map revealed the different routes Ecuador could take to outflank the Peruvian defenders at Zarumilla and imitate their Paraguayan precursors in the Chaco War. Depending on how bold the Ecuadorian commanders wanted to be, they could strike west to Sullana or to Piura in the Pacific Coast, or more modestly, swing north to Tumbes or to any other point west of the Zarumilla River. The Peruvian troops risked envelopment at many points, and only Peruvian naval supremacy prevented the Tumbes wedge from being an untenable position. The possibility was real that by a flanking movement a smaller Ecuadorian force could inflict a disastrous defeat on the larger Peruvian forces. The start of construction work on a highway from Cuenca to Loja in 1940 accentuated the danger. When completed, the road would give Ecuador "for the first time the capacity to move equipment and military units relatively quickly to the southern provinces."[18] Only by stationing many large units around the long and twisting border could Peru hope to prevent an embarrassing defeat. To learn these lessons first hand, the director of the War College, Colonel Eloy G. Ureta, took annual study trips to Tumbes province with his student officers.[19]

In fact, Ecuador enjoyed a clear numerical superiority in the border until early 1941. Historically Peru had stationed few troops in the Tumbes wedge and had kept its garrisons further south mainly in Lambayeque and Tru-

jillo. Deploying troops into the Tumbes wedge meant sending them into a trap unless the force was massive enough to counter any possible envelopment from the Ecuadorian bulge. The high risk of sending small numbers of soldiers into Tumbes province had influenced the decision to deploy only the national police or Civil Guard in this border region. Extensive patrolling by the Civil Guard would help to diffuse incidents and thus, at least the army hoped, make unnecessary a large army presence in the region. The Civil Guards served as effective representatives of the Peruvian government but did not have the menacing implications of combat battalions.

As each side erected a growing number of observation posts, they supposedly would stabilize the frontier, but not when Ecuador insisted on pushing its outposts into disputed territory. On 21 October 1940 Ecuador placed a garrison on Cerro Caucho and Peru promptly demanded its withdrawal. Complex negotiations ensued and Ecuador did prove willing to withdraw but not to renounce its policy of establishing additional posts to bolster its claims in the Zarumilla. In a remarkable statement on 23 October 1940, an Ecuadorian officer explained how the border line would be drawn:

> In vain have both governments spent millions on commissions and diplomatic meetings but without any useful results, because we here are the ones drawing the boundary lines in this way: Where you the Peruvians put a military post, we the Ecuadorians put another one. This means that where Peru places a post that is because it assumes that through that point passes the boundary line.[20]

Because Ecuador had been the first to establish frontier posts and Peru merely had responded, this frank confession implied that Ecuador felt free to enter any territory that Peru had not fortified. Peru sent more Civil Guard units to open additional posts, but the police could never prevent Ecuador from establishing another post in some unoccupied gap. In any case, Peru had already lost those lands. After half a century of experience, the Ecuadorian procedure in Zarumilla fit its long-term strategy in the Amazon. Essentially, Ecuador pushed outposts forward, but when Peru was about to make a military response, then Ecuador hurriedly turned to diplomacy and claimed it was the victim of aggression by its bigger neighbor, effectively securing a new status quo line. After diplomatic attention had subsided, then Ecuador repeated the process and this time started its encroachment from the status quo line. The only way Peru could stop Ecuadorian penetrations permanently was to build a fortified trench line 60 kilometers long on the Zarumilla border, but this alternative was not feasible for the vast Amazon region. And any decision to dig any trench line automatically cost Peru the lands that Ecuador had previously seized.[21]

The indiscreet statement quoted above by the Ecuadorian officer was the spark that put into action the Peruvian preparations for war; finally Peru realized that Ecuador had never intended to bargain in good faith. From the very start of the Ecuadorian advances, the commander of the Peruvian 1st Division had urged the creation of a new force, the "North Group," as the only way to regain the territories occupied by Ecuador. As a first step, Lima ordered the transfer of the 5th Battalion to Tumbes from Piura and the replacement of that unit by the 1st Battalion; As long as both battalions stayed near the coast, they were safe under the protection of the cannons of the Peruvian navy, but the moment Peru began to deploy these units into the Zarumilla border they risked entrapment by a sudden Ecuadorian flanking attack. Although the preparation for war had begun, Lima still hesitated and urged the commander of the 1st Division to complete the transfer of the 5th battalion to Tumbes "by gradual steps in such a manner as to call the least possible attention."[22] By themselves these two battalions were useless except as the vanguard of a large expeditionary force. Would Peru fight to recover its territories or would it accept the Ecuadorian fait accompli?

These two options were the only ones left because the Peruvian government finally concluded that diplomacy was useless to achieve a definite boundary. The Peruvian government still did not doubt the willingness of the Quito government to engage in productive negotiations, but the crux of the matter was that the Ecuadorian army was largely out of the control of the central government. Repeatedly the field commanders had taken decisions in direct defiance of orders from Quito. The Ecuadorian government was powerless to make its

officers comply with orders, while the officers did not stage a coup to rule through a military junta. A curious standoff ensued, with the Ecuadorian officers quite content to leave civilians running a government lacking any power to control the issue most vital for the survival of the country. The independence of the Ecuadorian army was compounded by its incredible arrogance. The Ecuadorian officers on the border loved to parade their brand-new automatic rifles in front of the Peruvian Civil Guards only poorly equipped with obsolete carbines and rusting Mauser rifles. The contempt the Ecuadorian army felt for the Peruvian army made them ignore the desperate suggestions from Quito to withdraw from the disputed territories before disaster befell on Ecuador. In speeches, newspapers and in the radio, Ecuadorian officials constantly belittled the Peruvian army; in some memorable broadcasts, the radio waves transmitted the sounds of hens to rub into the Peruvian listeners that their army was "chicken" and too afraid to face the powerful Ecuadorian army. These insults went right at the honor of the Peruvian officers who with difficulty restrained their impulses to lash out. The independence and arrogance of the Ecuadorian officers made negotiations futile, and only battlefield combat could end this absurd situation and return both sides to reality.[23]

By late December 1940 Peru was moving towards a momentous decision. The Secretary of War and the General Staff supported the request of the commander of the 1st Division to dislodge the Ecuadorian posts by force, but the army did not want to make a final commitment until after one last survey of the region. The General Staff sent the independent Inspector General of the army to visit the frontier region to make his own assessment. The President of Peru, Manuel Prado, had already made the decision in his mind when he talked to General Eloy Ureta in December 1940. Slightly ahead of the thinking in the army, President Prado ordered General Eloy Ureta to constitute a special interservice force to be called "North Group" whose mission was to dislodge the Ecuadorians from their posts in the Zarumilla. General Ureta did not wait for the arrival of the formal orders, and after his conversation with the president, he visited Colonel Monteza Tafur to ask him to be his chief of staff and to begin the arrangements to constitute the North Group. On 30 December 1940 the Inspector General presented a report urging strongly the use of force to dislodge the Ecuadorian posts. The whole military establishment was reaching a consensus on the need to attack; the final formality came on 11 January 1941 when the War Ministry formally created the North Group with full authority over all army, air force, and navy units operating in that theater.[24]

Since December 1940 General Ureta and Colonel Monteza Tafur had been trying to organize the North Group, which was supposed to be ready to attack by 25 May 1941. Mobilizing the troops proved much more difficult than anyone had imagined, and the North Group was still missing two infantry battalions, one cavalry regiment, one artillery battery, and one tank group. Chief of Staff Monteza Tafur promptly contacted President Prado when General Ureta was away inspecting the Zarumilla front. At a meeting with the army high command on 23 February, President Prado ordered the army to provide the additional units the North Group needed. The shortage of junior officers and noncommissioned officers was most acute,[25] and the only solution was to call up 3,400 reservists on 10 April. All the men were to report to their units in the North Group by 30 April, but the army bureaucracy proved incapable of handling this sudden inflow of reservists. The deadline of 25 May proved to be unrealistic and the General Staff postponed the deadline into an undefined date. A second call-up of reserves took place on 20 May, but the operation was badly bungled and these soldiers did not arrive until after the battle of Zarumilla was over. Consequently, the North Group had barely reached half its planned strength on 1 May and went into battle on 23 July with only 6,340 men to hold a front of over 60 kilometers. In a crucial tactical decision of unsuspected consequences, General Ureta positioned his troops several kilometers in the rear and kept the Civil Guard units holding the front line. He hoped to be able to transport his troops to the front on trucks in the roads that his engineers were having difficulty constructing.[26]

With ample troops, General Ureta was confident that he could repel any Ecuadorian attack but did not think he could dislodge the Ecuadorians from their outposts. Intelligence reports confirmed that the Ecuadorians had machine guns and automatic rifles in abundance. Instead, the Peruvian soldiers were acutely short of these weapons, and the ones they had were mostly old. Because almost all the region was heavily forested, Ecuadorian soldiers with their new machine guns and shiny automatic rifles could inflict a frightful carnage on charging Peruvian infantrymen. General Ureta knew that the Peruvian public could not stand to see its soldiers mowed down by machine guns as had happened to other countries in World War I or more recently to Bolivia and Paraguay in the Chaco War. This last war hung as an unspoken black cloud over Peruvian preparations. Just as Paraguay had halted and then hurled back much larger Bolivia at blood-soaked battles like Nanawa, the fear that Ecuador could inflict a humiliating defeat on bigger Peru was very real.

The Ecuadorian machine guns provided a formidable defense, and General Ureta knew he had to find some way to prevent the otherwise inevitable slaughter of his men. He personally inspected the Zarumilla River with his staff and watched as junior officers waded across the river near Chacras. General Ureta learned that the Zarumilla River was never deeper than 80 centimeters and many fords were much shallower. Neither the shallow waters nor the Ecuadorian machine gun bullets could stop his tanks from crossing the river and racing ahead to make a breakthrough at Arenillas (Map 29). This penetration would leave the Ecuadorian flanks exposed and with no option but to retreat hurriedly to escape encirclement. Thus, in one swift and relatively bloodless maneuver General Ureta hoped to make the Ecuadorian units abandon all their posts along the Zarumilla River.[27]

To increase the probability of success of this attack, he bolstered his field artillery of 75 mm cannons by placing the 105 mm battery, his heavy artillery, in front of Chacras. General Ureta also knew that many supposedly invincible plans had failed before in history, and in case a hail of machine gun fire still repulsed the initial infantry attacks, then he had two back-up options to break the Ecuadorian defenses. First, he ordered the Peruvian navy to prepare amphibious landings on the sea coast behind the Ecuadorian lines. Leaving nothing to chance in his quest for light casualties, he also ordered the air force to have a parachute unit ready to drop into the Ecuadorian rear. Whether the Peruvian soldiers came by sea or by parachute, General Ureta believed that the appearance of Peruvian troops into the Ecuadorian rear would demoralize the defenders and might even trigger a hurried retreat.[28]

The plan was ready but no action was possible until the North Group received its full complement of supplies, equipment, weapons, and trucks. The Lima bureaucracy was overwhelmed by these urgent requests so unknown in peace time, and once again the North Group had to appeal to President Prado to send the Inspector General of the Army on another observation visit to the front. The immediate goal was to convince this high official that the North Group was still inadequately supplied and thus in no condition to assume any offensive. If something was fundamentally wrong with the North Group, this high official was under obligation to state the objections and thus spare Peru from a humiliation like Bolivia's in the Chaco War. But if the plan was sound, then the blessing of the Inspector General would help secure the missing items and even more importantly would achieve the political goal of rallying the entire army behind the planned offensive campaign. In particular, the independent report of the Inspector General would dispel any doubt that North Group was an ill-conceived plan hatched by a coterie comprised of the Secretary of War, the General Staff, and the field commander. The Inspector General arrived unannounced on 4 July 1941 and later wrote a report supporting the North Group and its planned offensive completely.[29] His visit, which under normal circumstances would have had a far-reaching impact, was, however, overshadowed by totally unforeseen events the next day.

The Battle of Zarumilla

At dawn on 5 July 1941, reinforcements arrived at the Ecuadorian garrisons of Chacras (Map 29) and other border posts. At 1000 that day the recently arrived Ecuadorian troops marched to attack several Peruvian outposts of the Civil Guard. The policemen defended their positions long enough for army troops to come forward and finish repelling the Ecuadorian at-

tackers. Meanwhile gunfire broke out almost along the entire front. Bordering posts continued to exchange fire on 6 July, and then a relative quiet descended on the front. The attacks had caught Peru by surprise and their motivation remained unclear. Was Ecuador trying to test the Peruvian defenses? Did hot-heads in the newly arrived troops insist on showing off their superior firepower? The wild shooting could have been accidental, but sending Ecuadorian soldiers forward to attack required an order. Only after the war did the well-known arrogance of Ecuadorian officers emerge as the real reason for this impulsive attack.[30]

The Quito government realized that these attacks had made Ecuador look like the aggressor and provided Peru with an ideal casus belli. In anticipation of mounting tensions, the Foreign Ministry in Quito had revived the tripartite mediation by Argentina, Brazil, and the United States in May 1941. The tripartite mediation had been very useful to Ecuador in 1910, and the Foreign Ministry with new tactics at its disposal was confident of repeating the earlier success. After the clashes of 5–6 July, the mediators proposed that both sides withdraw their posts 15 kilometers to the rear. This same trick had brought wonderful results in 1910 and was certain to favor Ecuador again. An immediate acceptance of this proposal was the last remaining chance for Ecuador to halt the offensive Peru was planning to unleash on the border. Instead the high command in Quito raised objections, and the field commanders stated categorically they would not obey orders to withdraw.[31] The army was out of control and felt emboldened by the public rallies as large crowds poured out into the streets shouting the slogan "Tumbes, Jaén, Maynas," which encapsulated the extreme territorial demands. As Ecuador shouted publicly a war of conquest over whole provinces it had never ruled, Peru quietly let die the tripartite proposal to withdraw.

The Ecuadorian army rather than withdrawing to the proven safety of diplomatic defenses rushed reinforcements to the border. Vessels bringing troops from Guayaquil were arriving at the province of El Oro, and other units were coming by road from the cities in the Andes Mountains. As Peruvian intelligence reported the steady arrival of Ecuadorian reinforcements, it was only a matter of time before

Ecuador regained a numerical superiority over the North Group. In response to the incidents of 5–6 July and to the Ecuadorian buildup, the Peruvian War Ministry decided to transfer the last units allocated to the North Group to the front. This final deployment required time, and although many of the units, including the last tank formation, arrived too late to participate in the Battle of Zarumilla, the army was already fully committed to a war with Ecuador.[32] The final decision was in the hands of President Manuel Prado, who on 14 July 1941 authorized the North Group to take action: "If the means at your disposal allow you to guarantee success, then take advantage of the first opportunity to proceed to dislodge the Ecuadorian posts."[33] Coastwise shipping was starting to bring the last army units embarking in Lima, and the gradual process still required several months before the units reached their final positions. Vital supplies and equipment had still not arrived, so a very cautious General Ureta, who felt the fate of Peru resting on his hands, could promise an offensive no earlier than the middle of August.

Once again the Ecuadorians surprised Peru and launched another series of attacks on July 23. Except for some isolated shots, the front had been fairly quiet since July 7, but the Ecuadorians again sent troops to attack the Peruvian posts, and soon combat broke out along the entire front of the Zarumilla River. The motivations for these attacks remain no less murky than those of July 5–6, but their purpose probably was to test the Peruvian defenses. Accustomed to facing the wretchedly armed policemen of the Civil Guard, the local Ecuadorian officers still did not believe that they faced large and well-equipped Peruvian units. Ecuadorian spies such as the Consul in Piura did scare the Quito government with his reports of a large Peruvian buildup, but the local commanders had remained skeptical and dismissed the accurate reports as Peruvian propaganda. General Ureta brought up most of his infantry to repel the Ecuadorian attacks and for the first time unleashed his aviation and his artillery. By nightfall the Peruvians succeeded in occupying most of the disputed territory before intense machine gun fire tied them down and blocked any further advance.[34]

The fighting of the 23rd confirmed that the Ecuadorians relied exclusively on automatic rifles and machine guns for their firepower. General Ureta became convinced that a purely localized operation to recover the remaining Peruvian territory was militarily inadequate, because the thick forests were ideal for harassment and sniping. But he also coolly analyzed Ecuador's tactics and concluded that, even without the arrival of his remaining units, he could win a great victory. In the absence of any counter orders from Lima, he decided to take advantage of the blanket authorization in his 14 July order to launch a full offensive on 24 July. He concluded that the only way to regain the rest of the disputed territory without heavy casualties was to drive out the Ecuadorian forces from the entire region in one large offensive. Just trying to hold the ground would be a costly business, and he knew that the home public would not accept long casualty lists. General Ureta picked Chacras, the weakest point in the Ecuadorian defense line, to make his breakthrough.

Ecuadorian soldiers were already counterattacking and trying to recover the ground they had lost, and their machine gun nests ceaselessly poured a deadly fire on the pinned down Peruvian infantrymen. General Ureta knew he had to act fast to achieve a breakthrough before the Ecuadorian machine guns decimated his units. He sent forward more infantry units to make frontal advances on Chacras and Huaquillas (Map 29). He also gave his cavalry the mission of crossing the river between both towns and then splitting into two columns, one to make a flanking attack to the north on Huaquillas and another to the south on Chacras. A mortar unit was supposed to join the advancing infantry at Huaquillas, but heavy machine gun fire forced the mortar crew to withdraw to a protected site. At the new position the mortars resumed firing, and the Peruvian infantry tried again to advance as the cavalry coming from the south attacked the Ecuadorian flank. At 1800 on 24 July Huaquillas was in Peruvian hands.[35]

The capture of Huaquillas eliminated any threat from the north to the main Peruvian force trying to reach Chacras. The arrangements for the offensive attack were not ready until 1430 on 24 July when aerial bombardment began. The planes soon completed their bombing runs, but the artillery kept pounding the defenders for another two hours beyond the half-hour originally planned. The prolonged artillery barrage and in particular the explosions of the 105 mm shells in the thick forests finished demoralizing the Ecuadorian soldiers who still had not recovered from the aerial bombardments. No matter how beneficial in the long run, the prolonged artillery barrage delayed the infantry attack for over two hours. When the Peruvian soldiers finally set out, they were able to cross the Zarumilla River largely unopposed, because two Ecuadorian machine guns that controlled the best fords had withdrawn during the artillery barrage. As the Peruvians walked east, they soon were lost in the thick forest, and the units drifted apart. Two Ecuadorian automatic rifles opened fire to halt the advance to Chacras, while machine gun fire came from the north on the left flank. With squads lost in the woods in the dark and under fire, the Peruvian infantry halted for the night.

General Ureta did not know that his troops had voluntarily stopped for the night, and in the afternoon of the 24th he began to despair. He could not bear to imagine scenes of Ecuadorian machine guns mowing down the hapless Peruvian infantrymen, and he could not afford to wait longer for field reports. In his mind, the battle had reached its critical moment, and he had to break the Ecuadorian resistance soon or call off the offensive in a humiliating failure. He decided to hurl everything into one last attempt to shatter the Ecuadorian defenders. At 1600 on the 24th he ordered his dozen tanks with more infantry to rush to the attack as soon as possible. The infantry was able to cross the river that night, but the tanks only entered the battle early the next day.[36]

The decision of Ureta was not a panicky response but reflected a perhaps excessive concern for the welfare of his men who in reality were able to take very good care of themselves. Unknown to Ureta, the Peruvian cavalry that had separated from the detachment moving to attack Huaquillas had been marching south. The cavalry in its flanking movement encountered only light Ecuadorian resistance on the north side of Chacras. This cavalry unit had been the source of the firing the Peruvian infantrymen had heard to the north and which had convinced them to halt for the night. The cavalry pressed on and took advantage of the panic among the Ecuadorian defenders who were terrified at seeing horses they had believed

could not cross the thick forest. By 1900 the Peruvian cavalry had already captured Chacras, but the infantry reinforcements still believed it was in Ecuadorian hands and subjected Chacras to a bitter mortar barrage that sent the cavalry scurrying for cover back into the forest. The Peruvian infantry soldiers of the original attack resumed their advance as the sun was rising at 0530 on 25 July, and after overcoming a two-man Ecuadorian outpost, they entered Chacras at 0600.

The task of clearing the forests of isolated Ecuadorian detachments began as the tank column charged forward. The many bullets the Ecuadorians fired from their machine guns and automatic rifles bounced harmlessly off the lead tanks, and soon a procession of tanks crossed the shallow waters of the Zarumilla River. The tanks opened a path for truck convoys bringing additional infantry for the breakthrough. General Ureta had been reluctant to send his dozen tanks into thick forests, because Peruvian intelligence had reported the presence of anti-tank cannons. Inexplicably, Ecuador failed to deploy its anti-tank weapons, which later joined the considerable war booty captured by the Peruvians. The tanks kept casualties among the attackers to a minimum and deepened the demoralization of the already terrified Ecuadorian soldiers fleeing in droves to the rear.[37] The attack on Chacras was significant in many ways. For this single battle, Peru had deployed bombers, tanks, trucks, infantry, artillery, mortars, and cavalry; the combination of so many branches of the military made the engagement unique for Latin America.

The capture of Chacras also meant Peruvian victory in the battle of Zarumilla, because Peruvian forces could push east on the road to Arenillas and outflank the remaining Ecuadorian defenders.[38] As the Peruvian forces advanced east, the thick forest gave way to the cultivated fields of the fertile province of El Oro. The terrain was ideal for a blitzkrieg or lighting offensive and gave Peru maximum freedom to deploy its tanks, trucks, airplanes, and artillery. The capture of Huaquillas allowed the Peruvian troops to reach the coast and link up with patrol boats of the Peruvian navy. The intense aerial bombardment and artillery shelling actually inflicted little physical damage on the Ecuadorian defenders but instead had a profound psychological impact.[39] Soldiers who had never before experienced such a bombardment panicked, and although many continued to stand and fight, the disintegration of the Ecuadorian army began on 24 July. The Ecuadorian commanders, who had overestimated the capabilities of their infantry, were also shocked; the officers could not understand why the tide of battle had gone against them. Attempts to rally the fast disappearing troops for a defense of Arenillas failed, but the Ecuadorian commanders still hoped to save the situation by attacking Peruvian positions further south. Ecuador launched attacks at Vado Limón and in Cazaderos in the hope of at least drawing Peruvian pressure away from the collapsing Zarumilla front. If the attack at Cazaderos succeeded, Ecuador could still make an enveloping movement and wreak havoc on the Peruvian rear. Unfortunately Ecuador did not commit major forces to this last opportunity to reverse the outcome of the battle, and the troops General Ureta had wisely posted precisely in case of such an eventuality proved adequate to repulse the Ecuadorian attacks. By anticipating Ecuador's counter moves, General Ureta demonstrated that he had not just a material but also an intellectual superiority over the Ecuadorian officers.

Peruvian forces resumed their advance along the Zarumilla front on 25 July against rapidly crumbling Ecuadorian resistance. The only notable event that day was a brief encounter between the lone Ecuadorian warship, the *Calderón*, and the Peruvian destroyer *Villar*. In this unequal match, the unscathed destroyer seriously damaged the ancient *Calderón*, which, however, fled in time to reach a dry dock for lengthy repairs. The blockade of the coast remained in place, and the Peruvian navy continued to disembark troops on the sea shore and to clear small Ecuadorian detachments from the islands to the north.[40] On 28 July the War Ministry urged the Peruvian forces to advance as rapidly as possible before any cease-fire took effect. By then the Ecuadorian army had degenerated into a rabble trying to escape to the Andes Mountains. The Ecuadorian soldiers lost the last semblance of discipline and proceeded to loot the weathy towns of Arenillas, Santa Rosa, and Machala on 29 July. Drunken soldiers smashed doors and looted homes like an angry raging mob, and

the scenes of pillage recalled those of the Mexican Revolution. But unlike in Mexico, Peruvian troops were fast coming to save the grateful civilians from the otherwise uncontrollable rampage and to restore order. As soon as Peruvian troops were visible on the horizon, the last of the panic-stricken Ecuadorian soldiers vanished. Peruvian aerial reconnaissance confirmed that fleeing Ecuadorian soldiers had abandoned Machala, the capital of El Oro, and Santa Rosa, the other large town in the province. Rather than bomb these targets, cargo planes landed unopposed in their air strips and brought troops who occupied Machala and Santa Rosa on 31 July. At Puerto Bolívar no air strip was available, so Peru decided to test its airborne troops. In the first parachute attack in the history of Latin America, Peruvian paratroopers jumped from planes and captured Puerto Bolívar.[41]

The Peruvian offensive had been successful beyond all expectations. General Ureta's well-meaning and perhaps excessive concern for the welfare of his soldiers had led him to overreact, and rather than just capturing the Zarumilla region, his decision to hurl all his forces had destroyed the Ecuadorian army as an organized fighting force. Peruvian forces had occupied 1,000 square kilometers and effortlessly occupied El Oro, the richest province in Ecuador and the source of one-third of the government's revenue. Already on 24 July the leading citizens of Guayaquil had asked the Quito government to declare the city a free port and to withdraw the scarce army units to avoid an otherwise inevitable destruction. As the entire military position collapsed, the Ecuadorian high command confessed its total inability to defend Guayaquil. The prospect of an unopposed occupation of Guayaquil was bound to tempt the Peruvian army so pessimistic in its pre-war analysis. The government in Quito feared that "the capture of Guayaquil put the republic in the most serious danger of disintegration and foreshadowed, perhaps its partition,"[42] and talk of the "Polandization" or division of Ecuador began to surface. Victory was offering wonderful fruits, but inexplicably, the President of Peru refused to reap the unexpected and easy battlefield gains. A few days of war had been more productive for Peru than a century of diplomacy, but President Prado refused to recognize the barrenness of negotiations and wanted to end the war immediately.

Not the disappearing Ecuadorian army but the Foreign Ministry in Quito launched its very formidable weapons against the Peruvian military advance. For months before, the Ecuadorian diplomats had incessantly been playing the card of a small country as the victim of a big powerful neighbor and, after the start of hostilities, they constantly denounced Peru as the aggressor. But as the Ecuadorian army melted away, something spectacular was needed to trigger the diplomatic intervention of the United States. Already the Ecuadorian officers had invented an excuse for their total defeat, and without a moment of hesitation the Quito Foreign Ministry launched the ultimate weapon, the "Big Lie": The extraordinary Peruvian success had been the result of Japanese troops armed with the latest weapons. This totally unfounded accusation immediately caught the attention of the United States that demanded the halt of the Peruvian advance. President Prado faced the most momentous decision of his career and a turning point in the histories of Peru and Ecuador. Instead of opening up the front to any foreign military observers to disprove the Big Lie of Japanese troops and telling the United States firmly that Peru would solve its problems with its neighbors at its own pace, a panicky Prado, who never imagined that the recovery of a few strips of border would put all of Ecuador at Peru's disposal, capitulated. He agreed to a cease-fire at 1800 on 31 July and to another round of tripartite mediation, effectively plunging Peru into a costly and draining sixty-year effort to find a final negotiated settlement. Ecuador effectively used the false charges that Japanese troops had helped Peru win the war, and the Peruvian government agreed to the cease-fire when its troops had not completed all the mopping-up operations to secure the borders of the rich province of El Oro. The hasty cease-fire had not provided any means to keep Ecuadorian and Peruvian forces well separated from each other, and thus risked the resumption of incidents as in the past.[43]

The Quito government had tried to hide from the public the magnitude of the defeat at Zarumilla, but as word spread of the military disasters, the army of Ecuador felt obligated to redeem its reputation by some surprise attacks. The tripartite mediation emboldened the Ecuadorian officers who smugly believed that under the protection of the tripartite mediation they were safe from any Peruvian reprisals. The Ecuadorian attacks on Peruvian forces began on 5 August and culminated in the bloody ambush of a Civil Guard patrol on 11 September. Bitter fighting erupted in Panupali on 18 September and the cease-fire threatened to collapse. In reply, Peru sent its planes to bomb some military installations, and obviously the tripartite mediation intervened to find a more effective way to separate both sides. Talks resumed, and on 2 October 1941 both countries promised in the agreement of Talara to leave a large neutral zone between their forces.[44]

Technically the war was over, but Peru, very angry at the truce violations, had made good use of the time prior to the Talara agreement. The Peruvian army felt betrayed by the capitulation of President Prado and was furious at the surprise Ecuadorian attacks after the truce. The repeated violations of the cease-fire gave Peru the perfect justification to settle the Amazon border once and for all. The last section of this chapter and of this book traces the final efforts of Peru in the Amazon region.

The Last Offensive in the Amazon

Throughout the events leading up to the Battle of Zarumilla, Ecuador had left largely abandoned its garrisons in the Amazon. The neglect contrasted with the constant increase in its forces in the Zarumilla front; indeed, in the Pacific Coast, only in May of 1941 did the Peruvian forces finally outnumber the Ecuadorian units. The gigantic effort in the Zarumilla front had so drained Ecuador of resources that sending reinforcements to the Amazon became virtually impossible. Numerous indications also suggest that the Ecuadorian army had already written off the Amazon region as indefensible and hence not worth reinforcing. The lack of even minimal transportation to the Amazon region also persuaded the Ecuadorian army to concentrate its troops in the easily reached Zarumilla region. The above reasons contributed to the neglect of the Ecuadorian garrisons in the Amazon.

In May 1941 Quito sent one last contingent into the disputed Amazon region. The 20 soldiers and 1 officer were not reinforcements but merely replacements to try to fill the depleted Rocafuerte garrison (Map 7). The men initially rode down from Quito in trucks, but once the road became impassable, they had to trudge 10 days through a jungle path to Tena near the Napo River. If the men brought with them enough of their own money, they could rent a mule and buy food from colonists; the rest carried their own food and everything else on their backs. Quito had failed to send the officer any allowance for food, so he lent some of his own money to keep the soldiers from starving. Once the soldiers reached Tena, they were only a two-hours' walk away from the Napo River. At a trading post on this river the officer rented canoes for the voyage downstream to Rocafuerte. He also stocked up on provisions because nowhere else on the Napo River was food available for purchase. Aboard the canoes, tropical storms and torrential rains drenched the men who paddled down to their final destination in June. Actually, the route from Quito through Tena and down the Napo River to Rocafuerte was the best one linking Ecuador to the Amazon region. By comparison, the remaining routes to the other Ecuadorian garrisons were in a totally pitiful condition.[45]

In reality, Iquitos was the supply base for Rocafuerte and the entire Ecuadorian Amazon. The city of Iquitos and its nearby satellite towns gave Peru a considerable advantage over Ecuador which had never been able to establish any real urban center anywhere in the Amazon. In contrast to the Ecuadorian officials who prohibited upstream navigation by Peruvian vessels and blocked access to Peruvian merchants, Ecuadorian boats and launches were free to trade downstream at Peruvian towns. A river navigation company brought supplies to Rocafuerte regularly from Iquitos, while the small garrisons on other tributaries sent launches and canoes downstream to purchase food and supplies at Iquitos or at other Peruvian towns. Although Peru had ordered its garrisons not to help the Ecuadorian posts, the order did not apply to the Peruvian merchants who freely sold supplies to the Ecuadorian garrisons.[46] However, Quito was lax about sending money to pay the Peruvian merchants, for example in May 1940 the Rocafuerte garrison

"was suffering a complete scarcity of food."[47] To men already weakened by the jungle, the feeling of abandonment was utterly demoralizing. Quito routinely was late sending money and pay to the troops, and any supplies or equipment arrived late and usually incomplete, damaged, or spoiled. The men felt like marooned survivors in barren ocean atolls. Even officers broke down, such as one officer who had to be hospitalized in Iquitos and "is now suffering a tremendous moral depression and cries at every moment; his situation is similar to two other officers in the battalion."[48] An Ecuadorian captain at the Curaray garrison vented his frustration differently:

> Ever since the start of our trip, you have committed countless faults culminating last night in your verbal outbursts, which create discontent and indiscipline among the men [....] Neither my warnings nor the penalties I have imposed upon you have had any effect. Your discontent, laziness, and carelessness about everything of the service continues to increase at an alarming rate. Your productive usefulness borders on professional incapacity.[49]

Garrisons in such deplorable conditions and totally dependent on Iquitos for their survival had to avoid any clash with Peru at all costs. Instead, as previous sections had shown, Quito had insisted in pushing garrisons forward into Peruvian territory and beyond the status quo line of 1936. Ecuador was playing a dangerous game and risked that Peru might call the bluff. Lima actually was reluctant to make specific decisions about the Amazon and left the final shape of the campaign to the 5th or Jungle Division stationed in Iquitos. Lima gradually increased the strength of the 5th Division from 1,039 in November 1940 to 1,845 by July 1941, a number that was still vastly insufficient for that huge region. The 5th Division had to cover the front from the Brazilian border to the Cenepa and Santiago Rivers, and garrison duties left very few troops available for any offensive operation. Nevertheless, by February 1941 Colonel Antonio Santisteban, the commander of the 5th Division, felt confident that he had a sound plan to capture the Ecuadorian posts.[50]

Unlike Lima that was content with merely defending Amazon territory, the local commanders wanted to drive the Ecuadorians back to the Andes Mountains. The Peruvian troops never understood why Lima had tolerated the encroachment by Ecuador's puny units over the decades. The defeats in the war with Colombia also weighed heavily on the officers of the 5th Division who wanted to redeem their tarnished honor. The Peruvian troops likewise suffered the rigors of the climate, disease, and the jungle, but they considered their sacrifices as more than justified to expel the Ecuadorians from the Amazon. In spite of the hardships of the region, many Peruvian soldiers came to see in the bewitching Amazon their home; gradually settlements with families appeared near most of the Peruvian garrisons, unlike the Ecuadorian garrisons whose transient soldiers only dreamed of the day of their return to their homeland.

Incidents between Ecuadorian and Peruvian garrisons should have been rare, but the Ecuadorian practice of pushing posts further downstream had forced Peru to place a garrison opposite each Ecuadorian post. The close proximity necessarily generated incidents, but fortunately at Rocafuerte a verbal agreement with the Peruvian commander of Pantoja preserved peaceful relations between the two bordering posts. At Rocafuerte Ecuador had stationed a battalion, and although never at full strength, its around 200 soldiers comprised its single largest garrison in the entire Amazon region. Situated on an elevation in the north side of the Napo River, Rocafuerte commanded the mouth of the Aguarico River (Maps 7 and 27) and was supported by a small detachment on the south bank of the Napo River. Thick jungle stretched north from Rocafuerte until the Zancudo River, where at its mouth and further upstream on its left bank were two small Ecuadorian outposts. All these posts prohibited any Peruvian civilians from using the Napo, Aguarico, or Zancudo rivers; instead the Ecuadorians were free to trade with Iquitos as previously explained. The first Peruvian garrison was one kilometer downstream at Pantoja, which was also the terminus for the Pantoja-Güepí path made famous during the war with Colombia. Halfway between Rocafuerte and Pantoja was a gully that served as a "provisional" boundary line. Over the gully the men had built a wooden bridge covered with zinc shingles. Rather than garrison posts, Pantoja and Rocafuerte resembled a village stretched out along the river. Because Rocafuerte was the only Ecuadorian garrison in the Amazon to have women and children, social contact between families on both sides was easy. In addition, the Peruvian officers insisted on dropping by at the officer's mess hall in Rocafuerte almost every day to drink and talk with their counterparts, but the Ecuadorians rarely reciprocated the courtesy visits to the better stocked officers' club at Pantoja.[51]

War came to the Amazon fitfully, and the jungle environment imposed its own schedule on the operations. The first clash occurred on 10 July in the Tigre River when the Peruvian garrison of Bartra captured but then evacuated the nearby Ecuadorian post. The outbreak of hostilities in Zarumilla did not trigger attacks in the Amazon. Only on 31 July did Peruvian forces capture the Ecuadorian posts on the Curaray and the Corrientes rivers. Two Ecuadorian garrisons protected the mouth of the Yaupi River, and Peruvian forces overwhelmed both on 1 and 2 September. Many small Ecuadorian posts still remained, but the commander of the 5th Division knew that any permanent Peruvian success depended on the capture of Rocafuerte, the largest Ecuadorian garrison in the Amazon.[52]

Colonel Santisteban had rejected as unworkable the orders from Lima that called for the capture of only the two Ecuadorian outposts on the Zancudo River, an upstream tributary of the Aguarico River. Troops from Rocafuerte could easily navigate up the Aguarico River to reinforce those threatened outposts, and instead Peruvian troops had to slog through the muddy Pantoja-Güepi jungle trail. The transportation requirements made it mandatory for the Peruvians to attack Rocafuerte first, because once the Aguarico was open to Peruvian ships, the other outposts upstream near the Zancudo River would easily fall. The gunboat *Amazonas* arrived at Pantoja on 4 August bringing reinforcements; a second gunboat (undergoing repairs) was scheduled to bring more troops by the middle of August. In a bizarre twist only possible in the jungle environment, all the recently arrived Peruvian officers duly paid a courtesy visit to the officers' mess at Rocafuerte.[53]

The Ecuadorian garrison at Rocafuerte felt the mounting pressure and watched helplessly as war moved closer to that remote corner of the Amazon. Once news of the outbreak of hostilities at the Zarumilla front reached Roca-fuerte, the commander ordered the evacuation of all civilians and families. The women and children left the doomed garrison on 1 August after wrenching and tear-drenched separations from loved ones none ever expected to see alive again. In anticipation of the dreaded attack, for several weeks the commander had asked each of his officers to prepare and deliver a lecture on how best to improve the defenses of Rocafuerte. Although a transfer across the river to a slightly more defensible position seemed beneficial, the shortage of ammunition precluded any long resistance. The Ecuadorian garrison had several machine guns and seven automatic rifles for its defense, and its heaviest armament were two 47 mm cannons. To overcome the Ecuadorian defenses, the Peruvians had set up two batteries of 75 mm cannon at Pantoja. The Peruvian forces could also count on naval shelling from the gunboat *Amazonas* and bombing from Peruvian airplanes that routinely flew over the region.[54]

The 289 Peruvian soldiers at Pantoja under Lieutenant Colonel Armando Aguirre even after the arrival of the first batch of reinforcements barely exceeded the 200 soldiers at the Rocafuerte garrison. Not surprisingly, Colonel Aguirre wanted to wait for the arrival of the second gunboat bringing more troops before attacking Rocafuerte, but his orders were to attack promptly should any incident occur. The Ecuadorian soldiers had been celebrating a national holiday on 10 August, and a group of soldiers, possibly drunk, accidentally fired their rifles at 0400 on 11 August 1941 and then approached the first Peruvian guard post near the gully at Pantoja. Whatever the exact cause, both sides began shooting at each other at 0430 and the entire Peruvian garrison awoke to the sounds of gunfire. Colonel Aguirre promptly ordered his men to attack. His plan called for the 4th Infantry Company to set out immediately on the Pantoja-Güepi trail and after some hours of walking to turn west into the jungle to make an attack on Rocafuerte on its exposed northern flank. By the time daylight began, the 1st Infantry Company would make a frontal assault on Rocafuerte, but only after a heavy artillery barrage. The maneuver was highly risky, in case the Rocafuerte garrison counterattack at the growing gap between the two companies;

the Ecuadorians could overrun Pantoja because the Peruvians lacked any reserves. As a precaution, the commander sent the secret documents of the Peruvian garrison for safekeeping aboard the gunboat *Amazonas*. Excellent radio communications existed between the 75 mm batteries on land and the cannons aboard the gunboat, and soon after dawn intense barrages plastered Rocafuerte. The impact was so great on the Ecuadorian soldiers that they mistakenly believed that several gunboats, very heavy artillery, and waves of bombers were pounding Rocafuerte. Meanwhile the Peruvian artillery and the *Amazonas* continued to blast apart all the buildings in Rocafuerte.[55]

Fortunately for the Ecuadorians, aboard the *Amazonas* most of the shells for its 67 mm cannons had spoiled in the tropical weather, and the gunboat could maintain a steady shelling of Rocafuerte only with its secondary armament of 47 mm cannons. The 75 mm. cannons from the land batteries were more effective, and soon most of the buildings at Rocafuerte exploded into fragments. Under this covering fire, the 1st Infantry Company charged across the gully and at 0840 reached its first objective, but subsequently heavy machine gun fire pinned it down. The Peruvian artillery resumed an intensive fire to try to open a path for the pinned down 1st Infantry Company, but it seemed that until the 4th Infantry Company emerged from the jungle, no additional advance was possible. The Ecuadorians seemed to be extremely well ensconced in hidden trenches and underground bunkers in the elevations of Rocafuerte. To the surprise of Peruvian officials, at 0900 a major who was the second in command of the Ecuadorian garrison sent a message requesting to talk. He and his aide were promptly received, but the Ecuadorian officer was still under the impression that a truce could somehow be worked out. When the Peruvians demanded that Rocafuerte surrender, the Ecuadorian officer stated he first needed to obtain the approval of the garrison commander. The major sent a message urging the surrender of the garrison, only to learn from the returning messenger that the Ecuadorian commander had been among the first to abandon Rocafuerte.[56]

Without leadership from either its commander or the second-in-command, any chance of survival for the Rocafuerte garrison evaporated. When the 1st Company reached its second objective at 1000, some Ecuadorian soldiers sensed the inevitable and began to flee, but substantial resistance lasted until 1130 when the 4th Infantry Company suddenly poured out from the jungle to the north of Rocafuerte. The remaining Ecuadorian defenders, seeing their escape routes rapidly disappearing, hurriedly tried to flee into the jungle before the two Peruvian companies could open up a murderous crossfire. The Peruvians clambered up the elevations and were able to take about 30 prisoners by 12 noon. At 1225 the gunboat *Amazonas* saw hoisted over the highest elevation the Peruvian flag, and it has remained flying over the former Rocafuerte henceforth called Pantoja. The Peruvians had suffered minimal casualties, and except for the prisoners taken, almost the entire Ecuadorian garrison died, but not because of Peruvian action. Before the final Peruvian attack, many of the defenders escaped into the jungle where most eventually perished from hunger, disease, and the delirium called jungle madness. The Peruvian planes arrived two hours after the battle was over and did not get to drop their bombs.[57]

With the capture of Rocafuerte (renamed Pantoja), the Peruvian forces were free to advance at will up the tributaries of the Amazon. Low water impeded an immediate pursuit up the Aguarico River, but once rains raised the water level, the *Amazonas* steamed up the river on 13 August only to find that the Ecuadorians had abandoned their two outposts on the Zancudo River. After leaving detachments behind, the gunboat returned to Pantoja to begin the trip up the Napo River. Rarely did the *Amazonas* encounter any hostile fire, and the usual pattern was to find one abandoned Ecuadorian post after another. The repaired gunboat *Loreto* joined the persecution, and eventually a numerous Peruvian flotilla was busily pushing up every navigable river in the Amazon with almost virtual impunity. A reputation of invincibility preceded the Peruvian forces, and the Ecuadorians rushed to abandon almost all their positions. As one example of many, the Peruvian gunboats pushed 100 kilometers upstream

on the Napo River beyond Pantoja, and even more strikingly, scouts reported that no Ecuadorian troops stood between the Napo River and Quito.[58] Theoretically the road for a drive on Ecuador's capital was wide open, and if Ecuador could not make a successful defense where it enjoyed the greatest logistical advantages, how could it hold other regions in the Amazon?

Ecuadorian rule over the Amazon evaporated into the air, and nothing seemed to be able to stop the victorious 5th Division on its triumphant march to the Andes Mountains. The Peruvian General Staff saw in these victories a just punishment for the cease-fire violations of the Ecuadorians in the occupied province of El Oro. Because the detachments operated in relative isolation, Lima had a hard time communicating the orders to halt any further advance in the Amazon. As Peruvian troops overran Ecuadorian detachments at the Santiago and Yaupi rivers and pressed northward on the Cenepa, the initial elevations of the Andes Mountains began to loom in the background. Although a drive west from the jungle was not the optimal route to invade Cuenca, the position of Ecuador was precarious at best. With large Peruvian units facing Loja and the rich province of El Oro already under Peruvian occupation, Ecuador was on the verge of collapse, and only a slight push would give Peru control over most of Ecuador. Guayaquil was sending secret messages that the city would prefer to be ruled from Lima rather than from Quito, and a partition of Ecuador between Peru and Colombia had never before seemed so real. Military victory was offering Peru on a silver platter the opportunity to reshape the destinies of many countries, but President Prado preferred instead to fall into the trap of diplomatic mediations. Just like in the Zarumilla front, Lima halted the offensive too soon. Peru did not come out empty handed from the subsequent negotiations at Rio de Janeiro in 1942 and did receive a fair share of Amazon territory but at the very high price of arms races, lost economic opportunities, and constant tension over its border with Ecuador during the rest of the twentieth century.[59]

Conclusions

The Peruvian decision not to press for complete victory in 1941 seemed at first sight surprising if not simply stupid. Peruvian forces enjoyed such a commanding advantage, yet Peru in 1941 repeated Colombia's mistake of failing to press for complete victory in 1933. These two mistakes in no way were atypical or unusual for Latin America, as this book has shown. Indeed, the fundamental characteristic of warfare between countries in Latin America has been the extreme reluctance to engage in war and a willingness to stop a war at any moment. One consequence of this central characteristic has been that governments have been most reluctant to allow wars to impose solutions on international disputes. In Latin America, diplomacy and negotiations have been given every chance and every benefit of doubt, and war has been universally condemned as the worst possible catastrophe a country could suffer. Undoubtedly this philosophical approach is very appealing on humanitarian grounds, but its practical applications have brought greater problems and higher costs in resources and lives than just letting wars run their course. To show the absurdity of the situation, some examples from world military history suffice. How would World War II have turned out if the Allies, on the eve of making a breakthrough from the Normandy beachhead, had decided to declare a cease-fire and begin negotiations for the peaceful Nazi withdrawal from France? Or can anyone really believe that the Germans after making the breakthrough at Ardennes in 1940 would have halted their advance to negotiate terms with France and Britain? Yet on a corresponding scale events like these make studying the military history of Latin America quite frustrating.

If the only disadvantage of halting wars were to upset scholars, then this inconvenience would be a small price to pay for peace. But unfortunately, the consequences of ending wars prematurely have usually been adverse if not disastrous for the countries involved. The most pathetic example was, of course, the Chaco War's cease-fire in December 1933. The cease-fire doubled the duration of the war and caused horrendous human and material losses to both sides. A cease-fire when one side has gained superiority over the other is fatal, as the premature armistice of 11 November 1918 tragically demonstrated in World War I. For the sake of saving a few weeks' worth of lives and funds in 1918, humanity still has not ceased paying consequences a thousand times worse, not the least of which was World War II. Of course, the above statement does not mean that negotiations should never interrupt a war, and the two chapters on the Chaco War show several instances when a cease-fire was the best option for both sides. The optimal moment for a permanent cease-fire is when both sides have reached a military stalemate. When arms cannot provide a solution, the diplomats can safely come in without causing damage, but when dynamic offensives are providing a solution, war has to run its course. At worst, the exhaustion of all sides will finally bring an end to hostilities, as ultimately happened in the Mexican Revolution.

As Niccolò Machiavelli observed, it is not easy to end a war, and this book suggests that it is even harder to know *when* to end a war. A quick and easy formula would be a wonderful guide for rulers, but so far there is only one valid conclusion: When in doubt, let the war

433

run its course. In this book only two individuals have possessed the genius of knowing when to end wars without causing worse consequences than the war itself. The examples of Álvaro Obregón and Óscar Benavides are so rare that any reliance on the appearance of similar talents among the mediocre politicians who have generally ruled the Latin American countries is fanciful at best.

War is a reflection of a country's resources and abilities, and victory in the battlefield does provide an indication of the relative strength of a country in comparison with its opponent. This indicator is a rough guide, and more efficient measurements like GDP or educational levels do exist, but the ability of war to reveal the capacities of a country still stands. If some countries could not deploy troops effectively during a wartime crisis, those countries certainly could not exert a similar control in peacetime, as the cases in this book indicate.

The principle of letting wars run their course is equally valid to the many domestic insurrections in Latin America. When both sides finally realize that combat is useless, meaningful and productive negotiations will ensue, but not before. Unfortunately, the usual practice has again been constant cease-fires, truces, and halts in the fighting, so that a country suffers all the disadvantages of war but few of the benefits. Many of the stereotypes about mock conflicts and theatrical battles are real, yet a realization has not sunk in that this fake combat has been more harmful to those countries than real war. The sporadic and irregular warfare afflicting many parts of Latin America since independence in the 1820s has to be considered a major reason for the economic and social problems crushing the region.

Although a widespread popular stereotype has one general leading a dozen soldiers, a bloated officer corps was not the rule in Latin America in 1899–1941. Only after 1920 did Mexico suffer from an excessive number of officers, yet even there one general per hundred soldiers was the closest that reality ever came to the popular stereotype. Instead, when military campaigns took place, usually an acute shortage of officers manifested itself, and governments scrambled to find competent officers in sufficient numbers.

Once revolts began, no particular officer skills were needed to lead bands of rebels, while the crudest of weapons, such as machetes, muskets, obsolete rifles, or even wooden clubs sufficed to provide politicians with the demonstration of force they needed to hatch their never-ending deals. Politicians confidently believed they could maintain a strict control over this irregular warfare, when in practice these supposedly sham revolts and flexings of muscles easily degenerated into disorder and destruction. Murders, random killings, and even massacres were normal fare, and the opportunity to loot and go on a rampage was usually irresistible.

The rampant looting and butchery of most revolts reached the level of organized warfare only in Colombia, Cuba, Mexico, and Nicaragua during the years 1899 to 1941. The search for similarities among these four very different countries revealed a surprising characteristic: All four countries experienced U.S. influence in varying degrees. However, the U.S. influence took very different forms in these four countries, and as result each insurrection developed in a distinct manner.

In Colombia the U.S. involvement was weakest and was concentrated almost exclusively on the Isthmus of Panama. The U.S. presence was strongest in Mexico and Cuba, two countries closely tied to the United States by economic links and geographical proximity. Mexico had the largest direct U.S. investment, and Cuba had the largest in per-capita terms. Large numbers of American citizens had migrated either temporarily or permanently to Mexico and Cuba, and both countries increasingly fell under the U.S. cultural and technological zone of influence. None of those factors were present to any significant degree in Nicaragua, and instead military involvement accounted for the strong U.S. presence in that country.

In three ways the U.S. military impact in Nicaragua contrasted sharply with that in Mexico and Cuba. The most obvious difference among the three countries was the almost permanent stationing of U.S. marines for decades in a Nicaragua with a small population. In contrast, in Cuba with its larger population, the U.S. Army had kept a deliberately low profile and left occupation duties to locals. Secondly, in Nicaragua the United States labored for years to create a local constabulary, the later infamous Guardia Nacional. Because in its early years it espoused U.S. military values very deeply, it was, even more than the U.S.–created Rural Guard in Cuba, a powerful vehicle to make U.S. influence felt in Nicaragua. Lastly, and as part of U.S. efforts to organize the Guardia Nacional, the United States gave many weapons and cartridges as assistance to a wretchedly poor Nicaragua. As some readers may recall, during the later campaigns of the Mexican Revolution, the country was running out of resources to buy cartridges. Obviously, without ammunition the military campaigns in Mexico were in real danger of collapsing. In Nicaragua, on the other hand, U.S. largesse provided ample weapons and millions of cartridges that kept the war going and inadvertently made possible the insurrection against the U.S. marines. As will be recalled, captured weapons and stolen ammunition armed the Nicaraguan rebels.

Quite paradoxically, U.S. intervention to maintain peace in Nicaragua ultimately made possible the insurrection against the U.S. marines. Once the flow of weapons and cartridges to Nicaragua dried up, that poor country could not hope to sustain the warfare of the industrial age. The situation was different in Mexico and Cuba. Both countries had robust and expanding economies, and they could afford the warfare of the industrial age for a considerable time. Obviously neither country wanted an insurrection, but because economic expansion has to be accompanied by comparable growth in the police, the army and the navy, any laggardness or stinginess in enlarging and maintaining those forces left those countries vulnerable to upheavals. The U.S. intervention in 1906 arrived in time to stop the revolt in Cuba before it could gain momentum, and the subsequent creation of a Cuban army promised to prevent any future upheavals in the island. Although initially effective, the Cuban army soon found politics in the capital to be more profitable than chasing rebellious peasants of 1917 into their mountain strongholds. In the late 1950s these peasants at last found in Fidel Castro the leader they needed to launch a massive upheaval. In Cuba U.S. intervention had

postponed but not avoided a revolution, and Mexico without any comparable U.S. intervention to interrupt the revolt labored in vain to prevent the uprising of November 1910 from turning into a popular insurrection. Mexican rebels could draw on the accumulated resources of the previous economic expansion to sustain years of destructive warfare. When the United States finally sent troops into Mexico, the intervention was too limited and came too late to stop an ongoing insurrection, unlike in Cuba, where a U.S. occupation of the entire island eliminated any immediate possibility of a popular insurrection.

Mexico perfectly illustrated the case of an agrarian society just beginning its slow transformation into an industrial society. Scholars have begun to make fruitful comparisons between the Mexican Revolution of 1910–1929 and the War of Independence against Spain of 1810–1821. In reality, comparisons need to go back many centuries in time to the cataclysmic upheavals that leveled the marvelous pre–Columbian civilizations. Archeologists have often wondered how such brilliant and outwardly prosperous civilizations came repeatedly to such a violent and sudden end. The Mexican Revolution, the dying gasp of a gradually vanishing agrarian society, provides many clues as to how the seemingly wondrous Indian civilizations came crashing down. The struggle to return to the simple village life and to destroy the cities and their ruling elites was a familiar pattern in the ancient history of Mexico and repeated itself for the last time during the Mexican Revolution. Only this time the rebels could draw on large accumulated resources and also could cross the long U.S. border to acquire a steady flow of weapons and cartridges. But unlike in the pre–Columbian period, this time civilization won, and the cities, the necessary base of a central government, survived in Mexico. After 1930, the industrial society slowly and laboriously emerging in Mexico made impossible any revival of a violent insurrection. The airplanes and trucks of the industrial age banished the specter of domestic insurrection from most of Mexico and gave the country the opportunity to construct a better future in peace.

Chapter Notes

Prologue

1. Hugo Latorre Cabal, *Mi novela: apuntes autobiográficos de Alfonso López* (Bogotá: Ediciones Mito, 1961), pp. 261–262.

2. For a discussion of the hundred–thousand figure for deaths, see Charles W. Bergquist, *Coffee and Conflict in Colombia, 1886–1910* (Durham: Duke University Press, 1986), pp. 133–134.

3. José Fulgencio Gutiérrez, "A propósito de Palonegro," in Henrique Arboleda, *Palonegro* (Bucaramanga: Imprenta del Departamento, 1953), pp. xvii–xix; Leonidas Coral, *La guerra de los míl días en el sur de Colombia* (Pasto: Editorial Nariño, 1939), pp. 129–130, 174–175.

4. Leonidas Flórez Álvarez, *Campaña en Santander (1899–1900)* (Bogotá: Imprenta del Estado Mayor General, 1939), p. 46.

5. Joaquín Tamayo, *La revolución de 1899* (Bogotá: Banco Popular, 1975), pp. 36–41; Flórez Álvarez, *Campaña en Santander*, p. 104; Aída Martínez Carreño, *La guerra de los mil días* (Bogotá: Planeta, 1999), pp. 48, 50–54; Ary Campo Chicangana, *Montoneras, deserciones e insubordinaciones: Yanaconas y Paeces en la guerra de los mil dias* (Cali: Archivo Histórico de Cali, 2003), p. 86.

6. Julio Vengochea to Julio Durán, 22 October 1899, in José María Valdeblanquez, *Historia del Departamento del Magdalena y del Territorio de la Guajira* (Bogotá: El Voto Nacional, 1964), pp. 27–28; Tamayo, *La revolución*, p. 42; Flórez Álvarez, *Campaña en Santander*, pp. 36, 61. Because the *Hercules* was heavily guarded, the Liberals had to drop their plan to seize the gunboat by surprise, Domingo de la Rosa, *Recuerdos de la guerra de 1899 a 1902* (Barranquilla: Imprenta Departamental, 1940), pp. 17–18. The Liberals continued to lavish appointments until rank inflation became a problem. See Hermes Tovar Pinzón, "Tras las huellas del soldado Pablo," in Gonzalo Sánchez G. and Mario Aguilera P., eds., *Memoria de un país en guerra* (Bogotá: Planeta, 2001), pp. 154–156. Rebels in Cuba, Mexico, and Nicaragua routinely granted or took high officer rank.

7. Julio Vengochea to Julio Durán, 22 October 1899, in Valdeblanquez, *Departamento del Magdalena*, pp. 27–28.

8. This paragraph and the previous one rely on Tamayo, *La revolución*, p. 42; Flórez Álvarez, *Campaña en Santander*, pp. 99–100.

9. Tamayo, *La revolución*, pp. 42–43.

10. Valdeblanquez, *Departamento del Magdalena*, pp. 29–30; Flórez Álvarez, *Campaña en Santander*, pp. 100–102; Tamayo, *La revolución*, p. 43.

11. José María Vesga y Ávila, *La guerra de tres años* (Bogotá : Imprenta Eléctrica, 1914), pp. 177–185. For the guerrillas in Tolima, see El Comercio, *La guerra en el Tolima* (Bogotá: Imprenta Eléctrica, 1904). The more common meaning of the word "*la guerrilla*" in Spanish at that time was "an armed band or column," and the word was not usually synonymous with the modern term of "guerrilla warfare." See for example, "immediatamente levantamos una pequeña guerrilla que más tarde se llamó El Libres de Casanare cuando llegó a la categoría de batallón," Carlos Julio Chaparro Monco, *Un soldado en campaña* (Tunja: Imprenta Oficial, 1935), p. 20. Failure to understand the difference in the two meanings has been a source of considerable confusion in understanding the nature of the War of the Thousand Days.

12. Vesga y Ávila, *La guerra de tres años*, pp. 191–193; De la Rosa, *Recuerdos*, pp. 31–33; José María Valdeblanquez, *Biografía del señor general Florentino Manjarres* (Bogotá: Emilio Portilla e Hijos, 1962), p. 21; José Lázaro Robles, *Recuerdos de la Guerra de los Mil Días en las provincias de Padilla y Valledupar y en la Goajira* (Santa María, Colombia: Escofet, 1946), p. 11; Álvaro Ponce Muriel, *De clérigos y liberales; crónicas sobre la guerra de los mil días* (Bogotá : Panamericana Editorial, 2000), pp. 106–108.

13. Flórez Álvarez, *Campaña en Santander*, pp. 110–115; Rafael Uribe Uribe, *Documentos militares y politicos* (Medellín: Beneficencia de Antioquia, 1982), pp. 13, 16 (henceforth *DMP*).

14. Vesga y Ávila, *La guerra de tres años*, pp. 48–51; Martínez Carreño, *La guerra de los mil días*, pp. 86–87; Flórez Álvarez, *Campaña en Santander*, p. 103; Justo L. Durán, *La revolución del 99* (Cúcuta: El Día, 1920), p. 44.

15. This paragraph and the next two draw on Tamayo, *La revolución*, pp. 44–47; Flórez Álvarez, *Campaña en Santander*, pp. 117–128; Uribe Uribe, *DMP*, pp. 13–26; Martínez Carreño, *La guerra de los mil días*, pp. 66–75. Although General Villamizar was the nominal commander at Bucaramanga, the real spirit behind the valiant army defense of Bucaramanga was General Tobar of Piedecuesta fame. Failure to understand who was responsible for the victory later cost the government dearly.

16. Vesga y Ávila, *La guerra de tres años*, p. 90; Uribe Uribe, *DMP*, p. 35; Martínez Carreño, *La guerra de los mil días*, pp. 88–89. Had the railroad of Cúcuta extended to Zipaquirá, the northern terminus of the line from Bogotá, most if not all of the rebel campaigns in the Department of Santander would have been impossible, and the civil war probably would not have started. Cost/benefit analysis prevented the completion of that railroad across the Andes Mountains. But was the astronomical cost of building that railroad still not a bargain when compared to the loss of 100,000 lives and the savage destruction the country suffered during three years?

17. Vesga y Ávila, *La guerra de tres años*, p. 92 unrealistically has the bonfires burning to disguise the Liberals' withdrawal from Cúcuta to Tasajero, but his anti–Uribe Uribe hatred makes his testimony suspect. Uribe Uribe had been preparing trenches and other fortifications in the ridge, and rebels riding trains part of the way before walking up the ridge did not need bonfires to mislead the army troops. The rebels were vulnerable later when they abandoned their fortifications to start on the trip to Peralonso.

18. Flórez Álvarez, *Campaña en Santander*, pp. 168–169; Uribe Uribe, *DMP*, pp. 35–36.

19. This paragraph and the previous one rely on Martínez Carreño, *La guerra de los mil días*, pp. 93–94; Flórez Álvarez, *Campaña en Santander*, pp. 154, 179; Uribe Uribe, *DMP*, pp. 35–38, 51.

20. Flórez Álvarez, *Campaña en Santander*, pp. 165–168, 189–190 in detail demolishes the claims of anti–Uribe Uribe writers like Vesga y Ávila, *La guerra de los tres años*, pp. 97–98 and Durán, *La revolución del 99*, pp. 33–50 that General Herrera and not Uribe Uribe was responsible for the victory at Peralonso. The conclusions of Flórez Álvarez are supported by Martínez Carreño, *La guerra de los mil días*, pp. 94–97.

21. All sources, whether Conservative, pro or anti–Uribe Uribe, vie to present in the worst possible light the calamitous army retreat. See, for example, Max Grillo, *Emociones de la guerra* (Bogotá: Editorial Santa Fé, 1934), pp. 182–183 and Vesga y Ávila, *La guerra de los tres años*, pp. 99, 103–104, 135–142.

22. Grillo, *Emociones de la guerra*, pp. 236–241, 258–259; Chaparro Monco, *Un soldado en campaña*, pp. 27–28.

23. Víctor M. Salazar, *Memorias de la guerra (1899–1902)* (Bogotá: Editorial ABC, 1943), pp. 25–31.

24. Campo Chicangana, *Montoneras*, pp. 76–81; Ponce Muriel, *Clérigos y generales*, p. 127; Coral, *La guerra en el sur de Colombia*, pp. 148–153 ; Vesga y Ávila, *La guerra de tres años*, pp. 189–190.

25. Campo Chicangana, *Montoneras*, pp. 83, 252–254; Ponce Muriel, *Clérigos y generales*, pp. 130–131.

26. Salazar, *Memorias de la guerra*, pp. 36–44; Reports on Liberal expedition, 17–19 January 1900, Correspondencia del Presidente Sanclemente, vol. 17, folios 747–752, Archivo Histórico Nacional de Colombia (henceforth AHNC), Bogotá, Colombia; Armando Aizpurúa, *Biografía del General Manuel Quintero V.* (Panamá: Imprenta Nacional, 1956), pp. 35–58; Alex Pérez-Venero, *La guerra de los mil días en Panamá* (Panamá: Litho Impresora, 1979), p. 33; Belisario Porras, *Memorias de las campañas del istmo 1900* (Panamá: Imprenta Nacional, 1922), pp. 81–180; Patricia Pizzurno Gelos, *Antecedentes, hechos, y consecuencias de la guerra de los mil días en el Istmo de Panamá* (Panamá: Universidad de Panamá, 1990), pp. 154–159; Ruben D. Carles, *Victoriano Lorenzo* (Panamá: n.p., 1966), pp. 6–22.

27. Salazar, *Memorias de la guerra*, pp. 44–50; Aizpurúa, *Quintero*, pp. 35–58; Porras, *Las campañas del istmo*, pp. 232–250; Carles, *Lorenzo*, pp. 6–22;.De la Rosa, *Recuerdos*, pp. 66, 75. The details of the battle are far from clear; See Ricord, *Panama en la guerra*, pp. 86–91, 325 and also Pérez-Venero, *La guerra en Panama*, pp. 42–44.

28. Porras, *Las campañas del istmo*, pp. 287–312; Aizpurúa, *Quintero*, pp. 66–78; Carles, *Lorenzo*, pp. 26–28; De la Rosa, *Recuerdos*, pp. 68–70; Pérez-Venero, *La guerra en Panamá*, pp. 51–54; Ricord, *Panamá en la guerra*, pp. 98–104.

29. This paragraph and the previous two draw on: Governor Carlos Albán to President Manuel Sanclemente, Panama, 28 July 1900, Archivo José Manuel Marroquín (henceforth AJMM), Academia Colombiana de Historia (henceforth ACdeH), Bogotá, Colombia; Pizzurno Gelos, *Guerra en el Istmo*, pp. 160–165; Salazar, *Memorias de la guerra*, pp. 52–73; Porras, *Las campañas del istmo*, pp. 313–347; Aizpurúa, *Quintero* , pp. 79–102; Ricord, *Panamá en la guerra*, pp. 106–111; Pérez-Venero, *La guerra en Panamá*, pp. 56–51.

30. Flórez Álvarez, *Campaña en Santander*, pp. 212–219.

31. Lucas Caballero, *Memorias de la guerra de los mil días* (Bogotá: Instituto Colombiano de Cultura, 1980), pp. 44–45; Flórez Álvarez, *Campaña en Santander*, pp. 220–221.

32. Martínez Carreño, *La guerra de los mil días*, pp. 150–151; Grillo, *Emociones de la guerra*, pp. 228–233; Caballero, *Memorias*, p. 4; Chaparro Monco, *Un soldado en campaña*, p. 39.

33. Ponce Muriel, *Clérigos y generales*, pp. 127, 134–136.

34. *Ibid.*, pp. 136–139.

35. Campo Chicangana, *Montoneras*, pp. 97–101.

36. Coral, *La guerra en el sur*, pp. 162, 173, 178–179, 187; Ponce Muriel, *Clérigos y generales*, pp. 140–143.

37. Benjamín Latorre, *Recuerdos de campaña (1900–1902)* (Usaquén: Editorial San Juan Eudes, 1938), pp. 46–52; Campo Chicangana, *Montoneras*, pp. 227–229, and pp. 148–150, 156, 195, 252–253 for next paragraph. The *parte* published in *La opinión* (Bogotá), no. 90, 4 December 1900 gives figures of 800 soldiers and 2000 rebels including 500 Indians. As Campo Chicangana points out in pp. 226–227, this was the largest rebel force ever in central Cauca and could well have numbered 3,000 men.

38. Grillo, *Emociones de la guerra*, pp. 233–234.

39. Chaparro Monco, *Un soldado en campaña*, p. 46; Grillo, *Emociones de la guerra*, pp. 252–253, 257, 282.

40. Uribe Uribe, *DMP*, pp. 147–148, 163; Arboleda, *Palonegro*, pp. 15, 19–21; Flórez Álvarez, *Campaña en Santander*, pp. 242–270.

41. Uribe Uribe, *DMP*, pp. 154–155; Arboleda, *Palonegro*, pp. 23–25, 29; Flórez Álvarez, *Campaña en Santander*, pp. 271–278.

42. This paragraph and the next rely on Arboleda, *Palonegro*, pp. xii–xiii, 25, 31–38, 53, 67; Flórez Álvarez, *Campaña en Santander*, pp. 278–286.

43. Arboleda, *Palonegro*, pp. 60–64; Caballero, *Memorias*, pp. 48; Flórez Álvarez, *Campaña en Santander*, pp. 286–303.

44. Caballero, *Memorias*, pp. 50–51, 54–55; Uribe Uribe, *DMP*, pp. 175–180.

45. Grillo, *Emociones de la guerra*, pp. 327–346, 350–353; Uribe Uribe, *DMP*, pp. 180–184.

46. Grillo, *Emociones de la guerra*, pp. 362–366; Caballero, *Memorias*, 62–63; Uribe Uribe, *DMP*, pp. 185–190.

47. My conclusions about the two administrations are reinforced by a close reading of the Correspondencia del Presidente Sanclemente in the AHNC and the Archivo Marroquín in ACdeH. For the arguments supporting the palace coup see Luis Martínez Delgado, *Historia de un cambio de gobierno* (Bogotá: Editorial Santafe, 1958), pp. 37–70. A sickly General Próspero Pinzón, who was only 45 years old, died on 1 January 1901. He was then Minister of War, a post the Marroquín administration offered him after his triumphal return from Palongero. Pinzón was a close friend of Sanclemente, and only after he received the latter's permission had Pinzón with extreme reluctance accepted the post of Minister of War. On 27 May 1901 General Casabianca also died. *La opinión* (Bogotá) No. 108, 3 January 1901, no. 226, 28 May 1901.

48. A tendency exists in some writers, beginning with Tamayo in *La revolución*, to downplay or ignore military campaigns after the battle of Palonegro, and Bergquist in *Coffee and Conflict*, pp. 155–192 goes so far as to reduce the combat after July 1900 to guerrilla warfare. The failure of Colonel Leonidas Flórez Álvarez to complete his projected four-volume history of the War of the Thousand Days also unintentionally left the mistaken impression that all the important campaigns had taken place in Santander, the only region he covered in his first and only volume.

49. Pizzurno Gelos, *Guerra en el istmo*, pp. 108–111; Jorge Villegas and José Yunis, *La guerra de los mil días* (Bogotá: Carlos Valencia Editores, 1979), pp. 117–120, 262–265; *La opinión* (Bogotá) no. 342, 18 October 1901.

50. This and the previous paragraph draw on Valdeblanquez, *Departamento del Magdalena*, pp. 51–56; Durán, *La revolución del 99*, pp. 86, 100, 106–109, 124–125; Lázaro Robles, *Recuerdos*, pp. 26–27.

51. Valdeblanquez, *Departamento del Magdalena*, pp. 56–57; Uribe Uribe, *DMP*, pp. 199, 203–206.

52. This and the previous paragraph draw on Eduardo Santa, *Rafael Uribe Uribe* (Bogotá: Ediciones Triángulo, 1962), p. 342; Uribe Uribe, *DMP*, pp. 208–211; Valdeblanquez, *Departamento del Magdalena*, pp. 57–58.

53. The Cuban situation of 1895–1898 was totally different from what Uribe Uribe faced. (1)Large U.S. investments and the presence of many Americans in Cuba immediately attracted the attention of the U.S. public. (2) The strategic location of Cuba powerfully concerned the U.S. government, but in Colombia only the Department of Panama evoked a similar strategic interest. (3) The easily understood struggle of independence against colonial Spanish rule evoked strong sympathies in the United States. Instead decades of palace coups and sham revolts had made the U.S. public indifferent to the endemic turmoil in Latin America. (4) Building upon the previous factors, U.S. newspapers reported atrocities and savage behavior in Cuba in great detail in contrast to the sparse coverage of events in Colombia. (5) As far as actual fundraising for the Cuban war of independence, not wealthy patrons but Cuban working-class refugees in New York and in Tampa had provided the bulk of the funds for the revolt. Without a comparable Colombian community in the United States, Uribe Uribe lacked this vital source. (6) Those groups interested in the Panama Canal route might have contributed to Uribe Uribe, but his refusal to give away the canal closed that source. In conclusion, Uribe Uribe's fundraising mission to New York City was doomed to failure before he even arrived.

54. This and the previous paragraph draw on Santa, *Uribe Uribe*, pp. 343–350, 359–363; Uribe Uribe, *DMP*, pp. 263–292; Martínez Delgado, *Cambio de gobierno*, pp. 179–181, 195–196.

55. Santa, *Uribe Uribe Uribe*, pp. 363–364; Uribe Uribe, *DMP*, pp. 292–306.

56. President Cipriano Castro (henceforth PC) to General Celestino Castro (henceforth CC), Caracas, 2 September 1900, *Boletín del archivo histórico de Miraflores*, no. 5 (1960), p. 56 (henceforth BAHM).

57. PC to CC, Caracas, 16 March, 16 April, 1901, BAHM, no. 5(1960), pp. 70–71; Lázaro Robles, *Recuerdos*, p. 40.

58. Manifesto of Carlos Rangel Garbiras, Cúcuta, 18 July 1901, BAHM, no. 5(1960), pp. 75–78. Although the manifesto has many obvious deficiencies, President Cipriano Castro was too harsh when he labeled it "stupid," PC to CC, Caracas, 24 July 1901, *ibid.*, p. 78. The saga of governments in exile ready to return to power in their home country is a long one. Perhaps the most remarkable example came in April 1961, when Prime Minister José Miró Cardona and his cabinet appointees waited patiently in Miami for the success of the Bay of Pigs invasion. As soon as the regime of Fidel Castro collapsed, they were ready to fly to Havana to take office. Centuries before Niccolò Machiavelli had commented that exiles traditionally believed that their home country wants them back in power, but what was unique about the Bay of Pigs was that the U.S. government shared the same false assumption.

59. Telegrams of CC to PC, San Cristóbal, 26 July 1901, BAHM, no. 5(1960), pp. 79, 81. I have deduced the failure of some units to

arrive in time for the battle on 29 July from the easy escape to the border.

60. Uribe Uribe, *DMP*, pp. 306–314; Telegrams of CC to PC, San Cristóbal, 29 July–1 August 1901 and parte of 3 August 1901, *BAHM*, no. 5(1960), pp. 84–86, 89–93. Because the Venezuelan reports usually silence the participation of Colombian Liberals in San Cristóbal, the reconstruction of the battle presents unusual difficulties. The two paragraphs in the text present the most plausible account.

61. PC to CC, Caracas, 6 August 1901, CC to PC, San Cristóbal, 10 August 1901, *BAHM*, no. 5(1960), pp. 89, 96; Uribe Uribe, *DMP*, pp. 314–321.

62. Lázaro Robles, *Recuerdos*, pp. 40–41; Valdeblanquez, *Departamento del Magdalena*, pp. 67–69.

63. Lázaro Robles, *Recuerdos*, pp. 42–43; Valdeblanquez, *Departamento del Magdalena*, pp. 68–71.

64. The account in the following paragraphs on the battle of Carazúa rely on Lázaro Robles, *Recuerdos*, pp. 45–48, Valdeblanquez, *Departamento del Magdalena*, pp. 97–112, and *La opinión* (Bogotá), no. 344, 21 October 1901.

65. Pérez-Venero, *La guerra en Panamá*, pp. 65–72; Aizpurúa, *Quintero*, pp. 105–118; Carles, *Lorenzo*, pp. 34–50; *La opinión* (Bogotá), no. 265, 16 July 1901.

66. Guillermo Andreve Icaza, *Recuerdos de la Guerra de los Mil Días en el Istmo de Panamá 1899–1901* (Panamá: Editorial Universitaria Carlos Manuel Gasteazoro, 2005), pp.106–107, 109, 111, 115, 117, 122; pp. 73–74; Pérez-Venero, *La guerra en Panamá*, pp. 73–74; Carles, *Lorenzo*, pp. 51–52; De la Rosa, *Recuerdos de la guerra*, pp. 105–106.

67. Ricord, *Panamá en la guerra*, pp. 144–145; Pizzurno Gelos, *Guerra en el Istmo*, p. 170; Carles, *Lorenzo*, pp. 52–54; Andreve Icaza, *Recuerdos*, 118, 120, 128.

68. Pizzurno Gelos, *Guerra en el Istmo*, pp. 170–171; Carlos Albán to President Marroquín, Panama, 30 November 1901, AJMM, ACdeH; in his report to the President, Albán tried to hide his blunder in leaving Colón unguarded by placing all the blame for the loss of the city on the actions of the Panama Railroad Company. In another source of misinformation, Liberal writers such as the confusing De la Rosa, *Recuerdos de la guerra*, pp. 118, 121 have created the legend that the rebels' real intention was to delay Governor Albán long enough near La Chorrera for them to seize Panama City by surprise. The improbable scheme lacks coherence, and among other reasons, fails to take into account the presence of a modest garrison in Panama City more than adequate to hold the city until Governor Albán returned with the bulk of his forces.

69. Report of U.S. Consul H. A. Gudger, 25 November 1901, DUSCP, RG 59, NA. The U.S. Consul sensed a new stage had been reached in the U.S. presence in Panama: "The conditions as I saw them convince me that life is not safe on the trains crossing the Isthmus and that however much we may regret to do so, yet the awful moment has arrived when we should take a firm and decided stand."

70. De la Rosa, *Recuerdos de la guerra*, pp. 131–132; Pizzurno Gelos, *Guerra en el Istmo*, pp. 117–118, 128–130, 171–173; Andreve Icaza, *Recuerdos*, pp. 128–133. British and French warships supported the demands of the U.S. naval commander. U.S. forces occupied most of Colón, but French sailors landed in the French quarter of Colón on 29 November and withdrew on 1 December 1901.

71. Report of U.S. Consul H. A. Gudger, 7 December 1901, DUSCP, RG 59, NA; Pizzurno Gelos, *Guerra en el Istmo*, p. 131. An example of Colombian anger is the editorial in *La opinión* (Bogotá), no. 414, 20 January 1902.

72. PC to CC, 26 November 1901, Caracas, BAHM, no. 5(1960), p. 122.

73. Tamayo, *La revolución*, pp. 178–179.

74. Uribe Uribe, *DMP*, pp. 335–38.

75. *Ibid.*, pp. 366–69.

76. Martínez Delgado, *Cambio de gobierno*, pp. 197–198; Uribe Uribe, *DMP*, pp. 368–374.

77. *Ibid.*, pp. 352–354.

78. *Ibid.*, pp. 355–358, 365.

79. Uribe Uribe, *DMP*, pp. 343–47.

80. Lázaro Robles, *Recuerdos*, pp. 49–64; Valdeblanquez, *Departamento del Magdalena*, pp. 45–50, 84–87.

81. Caballero, *Memorias*, p. 80; Coral, *La guerra en el sur*, pp. 210–211; Ponce Muriel, *Clérigos*, pp. 182–183.

82. Coral, *La guerra en el sur*, pp. 224–227; Ponce Muriel, *Clérigos*, pp. 192–193, 200.

83. Caballero, *Memorias*, p. 83–85; Donaldo Velasco, *La guerra en el istmo*, 2 vols. (Panamá: Imprenta Santa Ana, 1903), 2: 1–25.

84. Latorre, *Recuerdos de campaña*, pp. 118–122; Ponce Muriel, *Clérigos*, pp. 192–193, 200, 209–210; Caballero, *Memorias*, pp. 86, 99. The at first sight exhaustive *Historia diplomática de Colombia* by Raimundo Rivas fails to discuss the war with Venezuela and the invasions from Ecuador.

85. Ricord, *Panama en la guerra*, pp. 164–167 has the longest discussion of the possible reasons for the Liberal invasion of Panama. However, I disagree with most of his conclusions. The fact remains that a Liberal faction was willing to grant anything the U.S. government wanted in a canal treaty and not only because the Panamanian Liberals desperately demanded the isthmian canal. Equally important, this faction of Liberals needed a big victory in Panama to overshadow the fame of Rafael Uribe Uribe.

86. Caballero, *Memorias*, pp. 99–100, 120–121.

87. Caballero, *Memorias*, pp. 114–120; Salazar, *Memorias de la guerra*, pp. 167–182; Donaldo Velasco to José Manuel Marroquín, Panama, 22 January 1902, AJMM, ACdeH.

88. Velasco, *La guerra en el istmo*, 2: 79–100; Caballero, *Memorias*, pp. 137–147, 167; Salazar, *Memorias de la guerra*, pp. 183–189; Aizpurúa, *Quintero*, pp. 144–149.

89. Salazar, *Memorias de la guerra*, pp. 191–192; Caballero, *Memorias*, pp. 223–225. Salazar, *Memorias de la guerra*, pp. 291–297 was the first to point out that Herrera could not have come up with this fantastic plan for a major operation on the Atlantic in October 1902. Because Bocas del Toro lacked any military value, Herrera's scheme to convert that isolated site into a base of operations on the Atlantic seems more plausible at the time of the Liberal invasion of Bocas del Toro in April 1902.

90. Report of U.S. Consul H, A. Gudger, Panama City, 10 March 1902, DUSCP, RG 59, NA; Velasco, *La guerra en el istmo*, 2: 117–125; Caballero, *Memorias*, pp. 152–154; Salazar, *Memorias de la guerra*, pp. 191–198.

91. This paragraph and the previous two draw on Velasco, *La guerra en el istmo*, 2: 139–169; Caballero, *Memorias*, pp. 161–163, 175–176; Salazar, *Memorias de la guerra*, pp. 235–238.

92. Latorre, *Recuerdos de campaña*, pp. 92, 172–74; Velasco, *La guerra en el istmo*, 2: 170–202; Caballero, *Memorias*, pp. 177–195; Salazar, *Memorias de la guerra*, pp. 238–251.

93. Valdeblanquez, *Manjarres*, p. 30; Uribe Uribe, *DMP*, pp. 507–509, 515.

94. This paragraph and the next two rely on Valdeblanquez, *Manjarres*, p. 30; Uribe Uribe, *DMP*, pp. 516–517, 520–523.

95. Valdeblanquez, *Manjarres*, pp. 50–53; Uribe Uribe, *DMP*, pp. 530–535. With that humane humor that so endeared him to his men, Uribe Uribe exclaimed upon realizing that the bullet had shattered his jacket and shirt: "Those Conservatives think that I have a huge wardrobe of clothes with me!" This, his final brush with death on the battlefield, confirmed that the bullet that could kill him had never been cast. Yet the envy that had always dogged his career finally inspired others to hack him to death with axes twelve years later, when as a senator he was approaching the Congressional palace. This savage and politically inspired assassination ranks among the most shameful episodes in Colombian history. Uribe Uribe's death deprived the country of intellectual talents it sorely needed to face its mounting problems.

96. Valdeblanquez, *Manjarres*, pp. 86–89, 93; Uribe Uribe, *DMP*, pp. 538–548, 567.

97. Salazar, *Memorias de la guerra*, pp. 225–235; Uribe Uribe, *DMP*, pp. 571–572.

98. Salazar, *Memorias de la guerra*, pp. 275–298.

99. Carles, *Lorenzo*, pp. 78–85; Salazar, *Memorias de la guerra*, pp. 306–326.

100. Velasco, *La guerra en el istmo*, 2: 210–238; Salazar, *Memorias de la guerra*, pp. 320–334.

101. The text has already mentioned a number of mistakes Governor Víctor Salazar made during the military campaigns. Given the almost impossible situation he faced and surrounded by incompetents, all those mistakes were understandable and could easily be overlooked had not four major errors also occurred during his governorship. (1) When the central government (recalling the *Lautaro* fiasco) suggested acquiring a second warship to supplement the soon to arrive gunboat *Bogotá*, Governor Salazar killed the proposal and prided himself on having saved the treasury this huge expense. As a prosperous businessman, he amply espoused the values of those who wanted to keep taxes low on the wealthy. A second warship would have been the kernel for a permanent navy, one that as chapter 14 shows, Colombia lacked until the war with Peru in 1932. A Colombian navy would probably have prevented war with Peru in 1932 and the loss of Panama in 1903. Although the dismantling of the *Bogotá* after his governorship cannot be blamed on Salazar, the action was completely in line with the views he strongly espoused of reducing military expenditures to a minimum to keep the wealthy from paying taxes. (2) For nearly a year the *Almirante Padilla* had pre-

vented the government from regaining control over Panama, yet neither Salazar nor any other Colombian took the next step in grasping the significance of sea power. If a decrepit steamship when armed with a few cannons could paralyze military operations, what could the modern warships armed with large caliber cannons do? The fearsome power of U.S. warships routinely loitering in Panamanian waters was immense, yet not once in his correspondence does Salazar tell Bogotá that at any moment the U.S. Navy could effortlessly end Colombian rule in Panama. During his visits aboard he is impressed with the U.S.S. *Wisconsin* but fails to report to Bogotá what its cannons can do. He wrote President Marroquín urging the Colombian congress to take the proper decision on the canal treaty, but how could it do so if Salazar did not say that ratification of the Herrán-Hay canal treaty (no matter how badly Colombia had been bamboozled in the negotiations) was preferable to having U.S. warships end Colombian rule in Panama. (3) and (4) These last two errors are closely intertwined. Salazar made the defeat of Liberals his single overriding goal, but his narrow definition left out the broader and more important goal of saving Colombian rule in Panama. Until the Panamanians reconciled themselves to rule from Bogotá, the presence of large garrisons was indispensable in the Isthmus, yet once the war was over, Salazar lost all interest in stationing troops in Panama. Instead, he approved of the rush to demobilize as quickly as possible and thus save treasury funds. His understandable obsession with the operations against the Liberals blinded him to the deterioration of support for Colombian rule. Like those situations that always precede Revolutions, the indispensable conditions were in place for a major political change but in no way made them inevitable as the scarcity of true Revolutions in world history attests. After the tragic death of Carlos Albán aboard the *Lautaro* in January 1902, only two persons remained who had the prestige and the capabilities to reconcile Panamanians to Colombian rule. One was the Liberal leader Belisario Porras, who although born in Panama, was more *Bogotano* than the locals of Colombia's capital. The thought of betraying Colombia was inconceivable to this honorable and highly dignified man who took nearly a decade to accept the independence of Panama as inevitable. Only a true act of statesmanship could have offered the governorship to the defeated Liberal leader Porras, and neither Salazar nor Bogotá ever considered such a brilliant move. The only other person left was Governor Salazar, who enjoyed high esteem in Panama and was a very effective administrator. Had he insisted on remaining at his post for at least another year or even for just five more months, his presence would have been enough to disrupt the plans of the conspirators. Instead when he left the governorship in the first days of January 1903, he formed part of that stampede of troops and officials rushing to abandon Panama as quickly as possible to return home. Salazar's natural desire to return to his native region was understandable and his business dealings clamored for attention, but his departure reinforced the impression that both he and Colombia were abandoning Panama because other things were more important. It should be noted that the real value of the Colombian garrisons in Panama was the profitable contracts for local merchants, but once this source dried up, the Panamanians were left desperately looking for economic alternatives. In a moment of economic and psychological vulnerability, the Panamanians fell prey to the United States that for a short time made them feel they were really important. For the most recent account of the independence of Panama, see Robert L. Scheina, *Latin America's Wars: The Age of the Professional Soldier, 1900–2001* (Washington, D.C.: Brassey's 2003), pp. 2–5.

102. Noticeable in this period was a trend to rely on a combination of coercion and economic incentives to obtain the necessary recruits. This emerging practice blurred the difference between joining the army either as conscripts or as volunteers. However, the trend did not become widespread throughout Latin America until after 1941.

Chapter 1

1. José Aguirre Achá, *De los Andes al Amazonas: Recuerdos de la campaña del Acre* (La Paz: Tipografía Artística Velarde, Aldazosa y Co., 1902), p. 172.

2. Lewis A. Tambs, "Rubber, Rebels, and Rio Branco: The Contest for the Acre," *Hispanic American Historical Review* 46 (1966): 259–260; Benjamín Azcui, *Resumen histórico de las campañas del Acre 1899–1903* (La Paz, Bolivia: Talleres de la Intendencia de Guerra, 1925), pp. 4–8; Aguirre Achá, *De los Andes*, pp. 15–16; Emilio Fernández, *La campaña del Acre 1900–1901* (Buenos Aires: Imprenta

de J. Peuser, 1903), pp. 11–15. Bolivians uniformly condemn the 1867 treaty; the criticism of contemporaries had some justification, because the chance still existed that Bolivia could assert control over the remaining part of the Acre. The failure of Bolivia to establish any official authority in the Acre over the next thirty years validated the judgment that the treaty of 1867 was a realistic recognition of Bolivian weakness.

3. William B. Sorsby to Secretary of State (henceforth SofS), 8 November 1902, La Paz, Despatches from U.S. Ministers to Bolivia (henceforth DUSMB), Record Group (henceforth RG) 59, National Archives, Washington, D.C. (henceforth NA); Frederick Willian Ganzert, "The Boundary Controversy in the Upper Amazon between Brazil, Bolivia, and Peru, 1903–1909," *Hispanic American Historical Review* 14(1934): 435; J. Valerie Fifer, "The Empire Builders: A History of the Bolivian Rubber Boom and the Rise of the House of Suárez," *Journal of Latin American Studies* 2(1970): 117; Robert L. Scheina, *Latin America: A Naval History, 1810–1987* (Annapolis: U.S. Naval Institute Press, 1987), pp. 117–118.

4. Luis Felipe de Castilhos Goycoechea, *O espirito militar na questão acreana* (Rio de Janeiro: Companhia Brasiliera de Artes Gráficas, 1973), pp. 27–28; Tambs, "Rubber, Rebels, and Rio Branco," p. 262; Azcui, *Resumen*, pp. 37–45; Aguirre Achá, *De los Andes*, pp. 154, 160–168; William B. Sorsbsy to SofS, 8 November 1902, DUSMB, RG 59, NA.

5. Charles Page Bryan to SoF, Petrópolis, 30 April 1902, Despatches from U.S. Ministers to Brazil (henceforth DUSMBR), RG 59, NA.

6. Tambs, "Rubber, Rebels, and Rio Branco," p. 265; Fernández, *La campaña del Acre*, pp. 107–110, 155; Elías Sagárnaga, *Recuerdos de la campaña del Acre de 1903; mis notas de viaje* (La Paz: Talleres Gráficos La Prensa, 1909), p. 50.

7. Aguirre Achá, *De los Andes*, pp. 16, 185; Azcui, *Resumen*, pp. 11–18. Leandro Tocantins, *Formação histórica do Acre*, 3 vols. (Rio de Janeiro: Conquista, 1961), 1: 169–187. Some accounts give 3 January as the date of the foundation. The original name of the capital was Puerto Alonso, in honor of the then president of Bolivia. After the fall of that president, even Bolivians were refering to the site as Puerto Acre, the present-day name. In a pun on the Spanish word for "shallow," Claudio de Araujo Lima wondered why the Bolivians did not promptly rename it "Puerto Pando" to impress the new president; See Claudio de Araujo Lima, *Plácido de Castro: um caudilho contra o imperialismo* (São Paulo, Companhia Editora Nacional, 1952), p. 102. However, upon deeper reflection, the meaning of the Spanish word does reveal the essential character of the president; see his evaluation at the end of this chapter.

8. Lima, *Plácido de Castro*, pp. 42–46; Tocantins, *Formação histórica do Acre*, 1:229–264; Fernández, *La campaña del Acre*, pp. 31–32, 124; Azcui, *Resumen*, pp. 18–20; Barbara Weinstein, *The Amazon Rubber boom 1850–1930* (Stanford: Stanford University Press, 1983), pp. 205–206.

9. Bolivia, *Memoria del Ministro de Relaciones Exteriores y Culto* (La Paz: Taller Topo-Litográfico Ayacucho, 1900), pp. xvi–xvii; Aguirre Achá, *De los Andes*, pp. 16–17; Azcui, *Resumen*, pp. 20–21; Lima, *Plácido de Castro*, pp. 46–48; Tocantins, *Formação histórica do Acre*, 2: 316–317; Goycochea, *O espiritu militar*, pp. 37–38, 40–41, 104–105.

10. Fernández, *La campaña del Acre*, p. 126, who in praising the president paradoxically condemns him: "El General Pando conocía palmo a palmo el teatro de las operaciones, sus elementos étnicos, su conformación topográfica, recursos y vías que conducen a él."

11. Olynto de Magalhães to Luis Salinas Vega, 19 June 1900, Rio de Janeiro, DUSMB, RG 59, NA.

12. Fifer, "Rise of the House of Suárez," p. 130; Fernández, *La campaña del Acre*, pp. 74–76, 90; Aguirre Achá, *De los Andes*, p. 147. I have calculated the distances from the detailed foldout map in Nicolás Suárez, *Anotaciones y documentos sobre la campaña del Alto Acre, 1902–1903* (Barcelona: Tipografía la Académica, 1928).

13. Sagárnaga, *Recuerdos de la campaña*, pp. 129–131; Fernández, *La campaña del Acre*, pp. 78–80, 84, 127–130; Azcui, *Resumen*, pp. 31–32.

14. Fernández, *La campaña del Acre*, pp. 80–81, 87, 91–104, 123; Tambs, "Rubber, Rebels, and Rio Branco," p. 268.

15. Aguirre Achá, *De los Andes*, pp. 140, 152–154, 156–158; Fernández, *La campaña del Acre*, pp. 131–132; Azcui, *Resumen*, pp. 46–56.

16. Aguirre Achá, *De los Andes*, pp. 158–165, 179–186; Azcui, *Resumen*, pp. 57–64.

17. Fernández, *La campaña del Acre*, pp. 135–139; Aguirre Achá, *De los Andes*, pp. 184, 186; Azcui, *Resumen*, pp. 64–65.

18. Fernández, *La campaña del Acre*, p. 105; Aguirre Achá, *De los Andes*, pp. 208–213; Azcui, *Resumen*, pp. 68–72.

19. Fernández, *La campaña del Acre*, pp. 140–141, 144–145, 154; Azcui, *Resumen*, pp. 68–72, 73–77.

20. Campaign Diary of Independencia Battalion, in Azcui, *Resumen*, pp. 23–25; the campaign diary has its own page numbering in the Azcui volume; Azcui, *Resumen*, pp. 78–79, 81–82, 91–92. This Azcui *Resumen*, published in the army printing press, is the nearest Bolivia came to issuing an official history, see Goycochea, *O espiritu militar*, pp. 90–91. None other than General Hans Kundt, a major figure in the Chaco War (see chapter 11), approved the publication; thus the book formed a link—not exactly auspicious for Bolivia—between the Acre campaigns of 1899–1903 and the Chaco War of 1932–1935.

21. Campaign Diary of Independencia, in Azcui, *Resumen*, pp. 27–30; Azcui, *Resumen*, pp. 82–86; Fernández, *La campaña del Acre*, pp. 148–154; Aguirre Achá, *De los Andes*, pp. 223–224, 229–232.

22. Fernández, *La campaña del Acre*, p. 157; Aguirre Achá, *De los Andes*, p. 232.

23. Azcui, *Resumen*, pp. 92–95; Fernández, *La campaña del Acre*, pp. 170–172; Aguirre Achá, *De los Andes*, pp. 236–238.

24. "Macacos! Isto não é briga é brincadeira." Azcui, *Resumen*, p. 95. In Book 2 of his *Discourses*, Niccolò Machiavelli has a whole chapter (26) on how counterproductive insults are; he makes it the duty of every commanding officer to prevent the troops from insulting the enemy.

25. Fernández, *La campaña del Acre*, pp. 173–174; Aguirre Achá, *De los Andes*, pp. 238–243; Azcui, *Resumen*, pp. 95–101, 103–105.

26. Aguirre Achá, *De los Andes*, pp. 252–253; Azcui, *Resumen*, pp. 111–116.

27. Azcui, *Resumen*, p. 194. The Bolivian army numbered 383 officers and 3350 soldiers, see "Information relative to the military establishment in Bolivia," 5 January 1903, DUSMB, RG 59, NA. The reference to Iquitos comes from a book I hope to complete on the Peruvian army.

28. Fernández, *La campaña del Acre*, p. 89; Azcui, *Resumen*, p. 135.

29. Secretary of State John Hay stated U.S. policy in the telegram of 3 May 1902: "The Government of the United States does not want to become a party to disputed questions between Bolivia and Brazil. You will use your best judgment in securing proper consideration for the interests of Amercian citizens whose rights may be affected." Diplomatic Instructions of the Department of State, Brazil, RG 59, NA. The Baron of Rio Branco completely undertood that once the American investors were taken care of, he had a free hand to solve the Acre dispute in Brazil's best interests.

30. E. Bradford Burns, *The Unwritten Alliance: Rio-Branco and Brazilian-American Relations* (New York: Columbia University Press, 1966), pp. 76–78; Azcui, *Resumen*, pp. 135–136.

31. Weinstein, *Amazon Rubber Boom*, pp. 176–177, 205–206; Azcui, *Resumen*, pp. 194–202; Charles Page Bryan to SofS, 17 April 1902, and 6 May 1902, Rio de Janeiro, DUSMBR, RG 59, NA.

32. Azcui, *Resumen*, pp. 136–139.

33. Lima, *Plácido de Castro*, p. 104; Azcui, *Resumen*, pp. 139–144; Goycochea, *O espiritu militar*, pp. 64–65. Lino Romero in his *El último combate en Puerto Alonso* (La Paz: Tipografía A.F. Palza, 1908) says nothing about his administration and claimed this pamphlet (among the rarest of publications on the Acre) was a fragment "del pequeño libro que pienso publicar sobre este asunto, " p. i. Perhaps not surprisingly, the promised book never appeared.

34. Lima, *Plácido de Castro*, pp. 102–105; Azcui, *Resumen*, pp. 140–144; Suárez, *Anotaciones y documentos*, p. 90.

35. Goycochea, *O espiritu militar*, pp. 59–63, 93–94; Lima, *Plácido de Castro*, pp. 105–108; Sagárnaga, *Recuerdos de la campaña*, pp. 62, 108; Suárez, *Anotaciones y documentos*, pp. 77–78, 92–95.

36. Lima, *Plácido de Castro*, pp. 115–118.

37. Azcui, *Resumen*, pp. 143–147; Lima, *Plácido de Castro*, pp. 122–124; Suárez, *Anotaciones y documentos*, pp. 134–138.

38. Azcui, *Resumen*, pp. 149–152; Lima, *Plácido de Castro*, pp. 125, 126, 135, 139, 141–142.

39. Tocantins, *Formação histórica do Acre*, 2:495–497.

40. Azcui, *Resumen*, pp. 149, 151–153; Lima, *Plácido de Castro*, pp. 144–150; Suárez, *Anotaciones y documentos*, p. 156.

41. Azcui, *Resumen*, pp. 153–154; Lima, *Plácido de Castro*, pp. 150–158.

42. Azcui, *Resumen*, pp. 154–163; Lima, *Plácido de Castro*, pp. 158–166.

43. Suárez, *Anotaciones y documentos*, pp. 110–118; Azcui, *Resumen*, pp. 174–184. In an attempt to cover up his failure to fortify Puerto Acre, Romero (*Último combate*, p. 1) claimed it had been besieged for six months.

44. Suárez, *Anotaciones y documentos*, pp. 118–121; Azcui, *Resumen*, pp. 183–184.

45. Suárez, *Anotaciones y documentos*, pp. 157, 161–162; Lima, *Placido de Castro*, pp. 180–181; Azcui, *Resumen*, pp. 183–186.

46. Lima, *Plácido de Castro*, pp. 181–182; Suárez, *Anotaciones y documentos*, pp. 150–154; Azcui, *Resumen*, pp. 186–191. The *Resumen* is the only Bolivian history of the entire Acre campaign and was sponsored by the German General Hans Kundt about whom chapter 12 has a lot to say. The sole flaw of the *Resumen* is its reliance on the fanciful historical speech of Federico Román for these and nearby pages of his book. Suárez wrote and published *Anotaciones y documentos* to demolish Román's self-serving and unreliable account; Azcui should have been more critical about using this very seductive source.

47. The account of the attack and seige of Puerto Acre relies on: Azcui, *Resumen*, pp. 173–174, 203–213; Lima, *Plácido de Castro*, pp. 189–218, and Romero, *Último combate*, pp 1–24. Plácido de Castro never received any public recognition for his exploits from the Brazilians. Paradoxically, the only time during his lifetime he received a hero's welcome and public ceremonies of appreciation was on a business trip to northern Bolivia: The former prisoners spontaneously wanted to thank him for his generous treatment that saved the lives of many of the wounded and sick.

48. Brazil had wanted to purchase the Bolivian Syndicate as early as October 1902. Talks to buy out the American investors, who had not spent a cent on the project, culminated in an agreement to sell on 26 February 1903, provided the Syndicate received "its money at once", and the Baron of Rio Branco had Brazil promptly pay on 10 March, Burns, *Unwritten Alliance*, pp. 82–83.

49. William B. Sorsby to SofS, 10 November 1902, La Paz, DUSMB, RG 59, NA; Charles Page Bryan to SofS, 21 November 1902, Rio de Janeiro, DUSMBR, RG 59, NA; Azcui, *Resumen*, pp. 217–219; Tambs, "Rubber, Rebels, and Rio Branco," p. 272.

50. William B. Sorsby to SofS, La Paz, 31 December 1902, No. 28, DUSMB, RG 59, NA.

51. The telegrams from the Bolivian minister Claudio Pinilla at Rio de Janeiro show the mounting Brazilian pressure. 7 January 1903—Comuniqué Ministro de Estado respuesta Bolivia, pidiendo neutralidad efectiva gobernador Manaos. Ministro de Estado dice expedida recomendación eficaz, considera entretanto conflicto latente;que continuará sublevación contra Bolivia e insiste proponer adquisición Acre cambio ventajas financieras, ferrocarriles, y obligándose entenderse Perú [Bolivian?] sindicato; 17 January 1903—Fui llamado a conferenciar con Ministro de Estado quien propuso como solución canje de territorios con la construcción del ferrocarril en el Madera, indemnización al sindicato y la suspensión de la expedición militar de Bolivia al Acre; 21 January 1903—Ministro de Estado me escribió que espera desistiremos expedición militar para que, si aun es tiempo, podamos entendernos amigablemente. Publicaciones prensa Argentina excitan Ministro de Estado. Se dieron órdenes alistar buques y enviar tropas Mato Grosso y Amazonas. DUSMB, RG 59, NA. At a meeting of 22 January with President Pando and the Bolivian Foreign Minister, the Brazilian Minister repeated these points, but subsequently in a Memorandum of 8 February 1903, Foreign Minister Eliodoro Villazón claimed Brazil did not ask for a halt to the expedition, when the telegrams could not have been clearer as to the requests of Brazil, DUSMB, RG 59, NA.

52. William B. Sorsby to SofS, La Paz, 14 January 1903, DUSMB, RG 59, NA; Azcui, *Resumen*, pp. 221, 228–229. Some sources have Montes leaving on a later date, but the U.S. Minister in Despatch No. 39 of 21 January 1903 gives the correct date of 19 January.

53. Azcui, *Resumen*, pp. 233–236; Sagárnaga, *Recuerdos de la campaña*, pp. 22–23, 38–39, 58–59.

54. William B. Sorsby to SofS, La Paz, 10 February 1903 with text of Brazilian ultimatum and 12 February 1903, DUSMB, RG 59, NA; Sagárnaga, *Recuerdos de la campaña*, pp. 84–85, 94–96; Tambs, "Rubber, Rebels, and Rio Branco," p. 272. The Bolivians estimated the number of Brazilian soldiers as high as 4,000; Goycochea, *O espiritu militar*, pp. 119 speaks of 2,891.

55. Brazil, *Exposição do Ministro das Relações Exteriores*, 27 December 1903; Tambs, "Rubber, Rebels, and Rio Branco," pp. 272–273; Ganzert, "Upper Amazon," pp. 438–439.

Chapter 2

1. Niccolò Machiavelli, *Discorsi sopra la prima deca di Tito Livio* (Milan:Biblioteca Universale Rizzoli, 1984), p. 352. Translation by author's wife.

2. Peru, *Arbitration between Peru and Chile; Appendix to the Case of Peru* (Washington, D.C.: National Capital Press, 1923), pp. 524–533; Arturo García Salazar, *Historia diplomática del Perú* (Lima: Imprenta

A. J. Rivas Berrio, 1930), pp. 85–87; George H. Bridgman to Secretary of State (henceforth SofS), La Paz, 8 March 1899, Despatches from U.S. Minsisters to Bolivia, Record Group (henceforth RG) 59, National Archives, College Park, Maryland (henceforth NA).

3. García Salazar, *Historia diplomática del Perú*, pp. 90–99; Mario Barros Van Buren, *La misión Eastman en el Ecuador* (Quito: Casa de la Cultura Ecuatoriana, 1966), pp. 37–29. Sentiment in favor of the partition of Bolivia remained strong at least as late as 1909: "Although Chilean public opinion is favorable to Bolivia in her present difficulties, the opinion is freely expressed that that republic has no raison d'être and that the best solution for her ever vexatious question of limits would be the partition of her territory among the bordering republics." U.S. Minister to SofS, Santiago, 5 August 1909, Case no. 534, Numerical File, RG 59, NA.

4. Pedro Portillo, *Acontecimientos relacionados con los ecuatorianos, colombianos y brasileros en los ríos Napo, Putumayo, Yurúa y Purús* (Lima: Tip. Del Panóptico, 1909), pp. 9–12; Guillermo S. Faura Gaig, *Los ríos de la Amazonía peruana* (Callao, Peru: Imprenta Colegio Militar Leoncio Prado, 1962), pp. 365–367.

5. Portillo, *Acontecimientos*, pp. 13–14; Faura Gaig, *Los ríos*, pp. 367–368.

6. The Peruvians called Bolognesi their camp on the mouth of the Torres Causano River, and writers refer to the engagement under either name. The spelling variant with an "a" of Torres Causana also exists.

7. Faura Gaig, *Los ríos*, pp. 370–372; Portillo, *Acontecimientos*, pp. 16, 18–20. The *Iquitos* was so heavily damaged, that by the time it was in condition to carry out a pursuit, it found no stragglers south of the Aguarico River. Apparently not a single Ecuadorean made it back by land to Rocafuerte.

8. Legación en el Ecuador al Ministerio de Relaciones Exteriores, Quito, 16 September 1904, Archivo Histórico Militar del Perú (henceforth AHMP), Lima, Peru; U.S. Department of State, *Papers Relating to the Foreign Relations of the United States 1904* (Washington, D.C., Government Printing Office, 1905), p. 297.

9. Note of the Brazilian Goverment to the Peruvian Legation, Rio de Janeiro, 2 June 1904, Despatches from U.S. Ministers to Brazil, RG 59, NA; Leandro Tocantins, *Formação histórica do Acre*, 3 vols. (Rio de Janeiro: Conquista, 1961), 3: 720; Portillo, *Acontecimientos*, pp. 29–31.

10. Faura Gaig, *Los ríos*, p. 531; Brazil, *O tratado de 8 de Setembro de 1909 entre os Estados Unidos do Brasil e a Republica do Peru* (Rio de Janeiro: Imprensa Nacional, 1910), pp. 25–26; Portillo, *Acontecimientos*, pp. 31–34.

11. Faura Gaig, *Los ríos*, pp. 531–32; Brazil, *O tratado de 8 de Setembro de 1909*, pp. 26–27; Tocantins, *Formação histórica do Acre*, 3: 732–733; Portillo, *Acontecimientos*, pp. 39–41.

12. Tocantins, *Formação histórica do Acre*, 3: 731, 745–747.

13. *Ibid.*, 3: 730–731, 748, 751.

14. On the poor state of the Brazilian navy and army, see "Reorganição Naval," *Correio da manhã*, 16 June 1904 and "Magna Questão," *Correio da manhã*, 25 June 1904 which contains the revealing statement "deploravéis condições da Armada Nacional, veiu corroborar o que não nos cançamos de dizer e repetir: não temos exercito, nem temos marinha de guerra."

15. Instituto Histórico e Geográfico Brasileiro, *Arquivos presidenciais, Rodriges Alves* (Rio de Janeiro: Instituto Histórico e Geográfico Brasileiro, 1990), pp. 50–51; F. B. Loomis to David E. Thompson, 1 August 1904, Diplomatic Instructions Brazil, RG 59, NA; Tocantins, *Formação histórica do Acre*, 3: 737–738.

16. Tocantins, *Formação histórica do Acre*, 3: 750.

17. Thomas Dawson to SofS, 18 March 1904, Despatches from U.S. Ministers to Brazil, RG 59, NA; John Hay to David E. Thompson, 10 May 1904, Diplomatic Instructions Brazil, RG 59, NA stated the U.S. position "you will express to the Minister of Foreign Affairs the earnest desire of the President that, in the interest of both parties, no armed conflict should arise."

18. David E. Thompson to SofS, 5 June 1904, Despatches from U.S. Ministers to Brazil, RG 59, NA.

19. Tocantins, *Formação histórica do Acre*, 3: 751–752.

20. David E. Thompson to SofS, 22 June 1904, Despatches from U.S. Ministers to Brazil, RG 59, NA. E. Bradford Burns, *The Unwritten Alliance: Rio-Branco and Brazilian-American Relations* (New York: Columbia University Press, 1966), p. 171 claims that "Rio-Branco succeeded … in using Washington's diplomatic pressure (in the dispute with Peru) to Brazil's advantage." Tocantins, *Formação histórica do Acre*, 3: 741–745 takes a similar position. The information and quotations in the text prove the opposite in this instance and also undermine the thesis of Burns about the existence of a tacit alliance between Brazil and the United States.

21. David E. Thompson to SofS, 13 July 1904, Despatches from U.S. Ministers to Brazil, RG 59, NA; U.S. Department of State, *Papers 1904*, pp. 109–111.

22. "Alto Juruá," *Jornal do comércio*, 3 Dec 1904; Faura Gaig, *Los ríos*, pp. 532–33; Tocantins, *Formação histórica do Acre*, 3: 760, 770–773.

23. David E. Thompson to SofS, 20 March 1905, Despatches from U.S. Ministers to Brazil, RG 59, NA.

24. Charge d'Affaires Seaone, son of the Peruvian Minister to Brazil, had made himself unwelcome in the Brazilian capital. "for a long period of time Chargé Seaone has been trying to pay court to Minister Rio-Branco's daughter. This has been objectionable to both the Minister and his daughter and the Rio-Branco house was months since a forbidden place for Seaone, since when he has persistently followed the girl on seemingly every possible occasion, making himself very obnoxious to both herself and her father." David E. Thompson to SofS, 11 September 1905, Despatches from U.S. Ministers to Brazil, RG 59, NA.

25. Peru, *Limites entre el Perú y el Brasil* (Lima: Talleres Tipográficos de La Revista, 1910), pp. iii–v; Brazil, *O tratado de 8 de Setembro de 1909*, pp. 33–39.

26. U.S. Department of State, *Papers Relating to the Foreign Relations of the United States, 1904* (Washington, D.C.: Government Printing Office, 1905), pp. 684–687.

27. J. Valerie Fifer, *Bolivia: Land, Location and Politics since 1825* (Cambridge: University Press, 1972), p. 142.

28. U.S. Department of State, *Papers Relating to the Foreign Relations of the United States, 1909* (Washington, D.C.: Government Printing Office, 1909), pp. 502–503; Fifer, *Bolivia*, pp. 145–147.

29. Minister of Foreign Relations of Bolivia to Bolivian Chargé d'Affaires at Santiago, 11 July 1909, La Paz, in Peru, *Arbitration between Peru and Chile; Appendix to the Case of Peru* (Washington, D.C.: National Capital Press, 1923), p. 554.

30. Bolivian Chargé d'Affaires to Minister of Foreign Relations, Santiago, 13 July, *Appendix*, p. 555.

31. Bolivian Chargé d'Affaires to Minister of Foreign Relations, Santiago, 17 July, *Appendix*, p. 555.

32. Bolivian Chargé d'Affaires to Minister of Foreign Relations, Santiago, 19 July, *Appendix*, p. 555. I have revised the translation based on the Spanish originals in *Ibid.*, pp. 559–560. Although initially some believed the telegrams were Peruvian forgeries, Charge d'Affaires Arce finally confessed their authenticy; see U.S. Minister to SofS, Santiago, 5 August 1909, Case no. 534, Numerical File, RG 59, NA.

33. U.S. Minister to Sof S, Lima, 27 July 1909 and U.S. Minister to SofS, Santiago, 5 August 1909, Case no. 534, Numerical File, RG 59, NA; García Salazar, *Historia diplomática del Peru*, pp. 174–175; Peru, *Appendix*, p. 557–559; Fifer, *Bolivia*, p. 145.

34. U.S. Minister to Sof S, Lima, 27 July 1909, Case no. 534, Numerical File, RG 59, NA; Peru, *Appendix*, p. 559.

35. For this and the next paragraph, see U.S. Department of State, *Papers 1909*, pp. 506–507; Fifer, *Bolivia*, pp. 145–147. In his last major action prior to his death, former President José Manuel Pando was instrumental in persuading Bolivians to seek and ratify an agreement with Peru. By saving Bolivia from a catastrophic defeat in a war with Peru, Pando partially compensated for his earlier disastrous decisions during the Acre war of 1899–1903 (see chapter 1).

36. Luis Larrea Alba, *La campaña de 1906* (Quito: n.p., 1962), pp. 129–132; Julio C. Troncoso, *Vida anecdótica del General Eloy Alfaro* (Quito: Editorial Santo Domingo, 1966), pp. 205–208.

37. Report of British minister of 15 January 1911, in George Philip, ed., *British Documents on Foreign Affairs*, Part I, Series D, *Latin America 1845–1914*, 9 vols. (Bethesda, Md.: University Publications of America, 1991–1992); 4:320–21; Larrea Alba, *La campaña de 1906*, pp. 133, 162–163; U.S. Department of State, *Papers Relating to the Foreign Relations of the United States, 1910* (Washington, D.C.: Government Printing Office, 1910), pp. 438–443; Troncoso, *Eloy Alfaro*, p. 230.

38. Legación en el Ecuador al Ministerio de Relaciones Exteriores, Quito, 19 January, 23 March 1910, AHMP; *Arbitration Between Peru and Chile: Appendix to the Case of Peru* (Washington, D.C.: National Capital Press, 1923), pp. 567–70; U.S. Department of State, *Papers, 1910*, p. 445.

39. Larrea Alba, *La campaña de 1906*, pp. 139–143; Daniel M. Masterson, *Militarism and Politics in Latin America; Peru from Sánchez Cerro to Sendero Luminoso* (Westport, Ct: Greenwood Press, 1991), pp. 26–30.

40. Reports from Quito Legation, April 1910, and Francisco Alaiza Paz Soldán to Oficial Mayor del Ministerio de Relaciones Ex-

teriores, Iquitos, 11 April 1910, 28 September 1911, AHMP; U.S. Department of State, *Papers, 1910*, pp. 445, 459.

41. Larrea Alba, *La campaña de 1906*, pp. 138–139, 156–158; Barros, *La misión Eastman*, pp. 50–52, 62, 66; Raimundo Rivas, *Historia diplomática de Colombia (1818–1934)* (Bogotá: Imprenta Nacional, 1961), p. 631.

42. U.S. Department of State, *Papers, 1910*, p. 457 and pp. 449–459, 461 for paragraph.

43. Larrea Alba, *La campaña de 1906*, p. 168: U.S. Department of State, *Papers, 1910*, pp. 472–476.

44. Report of British minister of 15 January 1911, in Philip, *British Documents on Foreign Affairs*, 4:322.

45. Ecuador, Ministerio de Relaciones Exteriores, *Documentos diplomáticos referentes al conflicto ecuatoriano–peruano; segunda serie* (Quito: Imprenta y encuadernación nacionales, 1910), pp. 27, 33–34; U.S. Department of State, *Papers, 1910*, pp. 469, 480–483, 484, 490, 495.

46. Report of British minister of 15 January 1911, Philip, *British Documents on Foreign Affairs*, 4:322–23; U.S. Department of State, *Papers, 1910*, pp. 504–507; Troncoso, *Eloy Alfaro*, p. 237.

47. As one example of close cooperation, the prefect in Iquitos reported on his decision to distribute Peruvian troops: "I have consulted with Arana who fully agrees with the dispositions I have taken." C. Zapata to Oficial del Ministerio de Relaciones Exteriores," Iquitos, 24 Mayo 1908, AHMP, Lima, Peru.

48. W. E. Hardenburg, *The Putumayo: The Devil's Paradise* (London: T. Fisher Unwin, 1912) and Norman Thomson, *The Putumayo Red Book* (London: N. Thomson and Company, 1914) were among the best contemporary accounts. For the unfolding of the Putumayo scandal, see Michael Edward Stanfield, *Red Rubber, Bleeding Trees: Violence, Slavery, and Empire in Northwest Amazonía, 1850–1933* (Albuquerque: University of New Mexico Press, 1998), ch. 7.

49. "La campaña del Caquetá," folio 129, AHMP.

50. Luis Forero Román, *La Pedrera: Relato del combate entre colombianos y peruanos en el año de 1911* (Bogotá: Editorial Bolívar, 1918), pp. 19–35. The expedition brought a new machine to lay mines in the Caquetá River, but mechanical malfunctions made it useless.

51. The civilian officials left the decision about how to react to the Colombian expedition in the hands of the Peruvian army and did not even provide a hint of guidance, see Minister of Foreign Affairs to Minister of War and Navy, Lima, 11 February 1911, AHMP.

52. "La campaña del Caquetá," folios 27–28, AHMP.

53. Peruvian Consul in Berlin to Foreign Ministry, 12 May 1911, AHMP; "La campaña del Caquetá," folios 28–29, AHMP; José Zárate and Alberto Ferreyros, *El Mariscal Benavides, su vida y su obra*, 2 vols. (Lima: Editorial Atlántida, 1976–1981), 1: 97–143.

54. Forero Román, *La Pedrera*, pp. 30–43; "Memorandum sobre los documentos relativos al Departamento de Loreto con ocasión de las cuestiones con Colombia respecto al Río Putumayo," 1911, AHMP.

55. Forero Román, *La Pedrera*, pp. 43–47, 130–132.

56. Francisco Alaiza Paz Soldán to President of Peru, Iquitos, 28 June 1911, AHMP.

57. Oscar R. Benavides to Prefecto del Departamento, La Pedrera, 15 July 1911, AHMP; "La campaña del Caquetá," folios 29–34, AHMP; Forero Román, *La Pedrera*, pp. 48–59. Forero Román, an eyewitness, captures vividly the emotions of the defenders who first believed that the Peruvian steamers were the reinforcements coming upstream from the Amazon. In 1911 and again in 1933, the Colombians easily won the literary war against the Peruvians.

58. "La campaña del Caquetá," folios 36–40, AHMP; Forero Román, *La Pedrera*, pp. 59–65; "Algunos datos sobre la campaña del Caquetá," 1911, AHMP; Zárate and Ferreyros, *El Mariscal Benavides*, 1: 148–157.

59. "La campaña del Caquetá," folios 39–46, AHMP; Forero Román, *La Pedrera*, pp. 63–72; Oscar R. Benavides to Prefecto del Departamento, La Pedrera, 15 July 1911, AHMP; Zárate and Ferreyros, *El Mariscal Benavides*, 1:157–161.

60. Francisco Alaiza Paz Soldán to President of Peru, Iquitos, 31 July 1911, AHMP. On 17 July, days after the battle had taken place, the prefect forwarded the telegraphic order he had just received to halt the Peruvian force, Francisco Alaiza Paz Soldán to Oscar Benavides, Iquitos, 17 July 1911, AHMP.

61. Francisco Alaiza Paz Soldán to Director Guerra — Lima, Itaya, 5 August 1911, AHMP.

62. Francisco Alaiza Paz Soldán to Oscar Benavides, Iquitos, 14 August 1911, AHMP.

63. "La campaña del Caquetá," folios 47–49, 60–61, AHMP; Francisco Alaiza Paz Soldán to Oficialía Relaciones, Iquitos, 17 September 1911. The government returned the 9th Battalion to the highlands in April 1912. Of the 282 men who had left the highlands in February 1911, about 100 men returned. A small number who fell in love with the Amazon stayed behind to serve in the small units scattered in the Peruvian Amazon.

64. *El comercio*, 3 September 1911. The plague seems to be related to the twenty-year flood and was not simply an intensification of the yellow fever, malaria, dysentery and other diseases endemic in the region . The Colombian unit sent to explore a nearby region had not contracted the disease. At least for the rest of 1911, the plague continued with the same if not greter virulence after the waters of the flood had receded.

65. Prefect Alaiza Paz Soldán to President of Peru, Iquitos, 16 August 1911, AHMP; Rivas, *Historia diplomática de Colombia*, p. 631.

66. Commander of the 5th Region, G. Álvarez, to Minister of War, Iquitos, 25 October 1911, AHMP. At least since August the prefect had complained about the declining customs revenue: Francisco Alaiza Paz Soldán to Oficialía Relaciones, Iquitos, 29 August 1911, AHMP.

67. Rivas, *Historia diplomática de Colombia*, pp. 628–28; "La campaña del Caquetá," folios 66, 68–69, AHMP. Not all the army officers accepted the decision to withdraw from La Pedrera, and Colonel G. Álvarez, the army commander at Iquitos, even went so far as to send a strong written protest in late 1911, AHMP.

68. Rivas, *Historia diplomática de Colombia*, p. 673.

69. Domingo Romero Terán, *Los traidores al Ecuador: Apuntes para la historia* (Quito: Talleres Gráficos del Servicio de Suministros, 1952), pp. 33–38; "Ecuadorean-Peruvian Boundary Dispute," No. 324, 19 August 1921, 2657-n-104, Military Intelligence Division (henceforth MID), Record Group (henceforth RG) 165, National Archives (henceforth NA) College Park, Md.; Commander of 5th Region, G. Álvarez to Minister of War, Iquitos, 25 October 1911, AHMP.

70. Francisco Alaiza Paz Soldán, "Instrucciones al Comisario del Río Morona Juan Francisco Chávez Valdivia," Iquitos, 28 April 1911, AHMP.

71. Prefect Francisco Alaiza Paz Soldán, "Reservadas. Instrucciones al Capitán Soderstrom, Jefe de las guarniciones establecidas en el Río Curaray," Iquitos, 22 June 1911, AHMP; Francisco Alaiza Paz Soldán to Oficial Mayor del Ministerio de R.R.E.E., Iquitos, 28 September 1911, AHMP.

72. Telegrams of 21 February and 8 March 1913 to War Ministry, AHMP; U.S. Department of State, *Papers Relating to the Foreign Relations of the United States 1913* (Washington, D.C.: Government Printing Office, 1920), pp. 1147–1151.

73. Romero Terán, *Los traidores al Ecuador*, pp. 38–41; Faura Gaig, *Los ríos*, p. 374. One account has the Indians justifying the massacre as a response to the looting of their huts and the raping of their women by the soldiers. Another account has the Indians claiming that the soldiers had taken Indian women captive and forced them to live in the army camp as concubines. As a justification for the massacre, those accusations do not seem credible, first of all because of the extreme friendship of the captain for the Indians. Also, the departure of soldiers to hunt in the jungle did not reveal a fear that any Indian women would flee during their absence. However, given the brutality of life in an Amazon naturally prone to atrocities, the looting of huts and raping of women has a ring of truth, and more likely occurred after the massacre and as reprisals by enraged soldiers at the killing of their comrades.

74. "Railways in operation or in project," Quito, 23 July 1906, Despatches from U.S. Ministers to Ecuador, RG 59, NA; Romero Terán, *Los traidores al Ecuador*, pp. 41–46; Teniente D. César Beleván, "Viaje a través de la selva ecuatoriana," 31 December 1917, paquete Ecuador, AHMP.

75. "Ecuadorean-Peruvian Boundary Dispute," No. 324, 19 August 1921, 2657-n-104, MID, RG 165, NA.

Chapter 3

1. Albert von Boguslawski, *Tactical Deductions from the War of 1870–1871* (London: Henry S. King, 1872), p. 69.

2. Although he will not approve what I wrote, I dedicate this chapter to whom I always consider my great and good friend: Alfredo Figueroa Navarro.

3. For the standard account of the origins of the dispute, see William D. McCain, *The United States and the Republic of Panama* (Durham, NC: Duke University Press, 1937), chapter 6.

4. Carlos H. Cuestas Gómez., *Panamá y Costa Rica: entre la diplomacia y la guerra* (Panama: Litho Editorial Chen, 1999), pp. 365–366.

5. George Philip, ed., *British Documents on Foreign Affairs*, Part II, Series D, *Latin America, 1914–1939*, 20 vols. (Bethesda, Md.:University Publications of America , 1989–1992) 2: 383.

6. Cuestas, *Panama y Costa Rica*, pp. 102–103.

7. Carlos Guevara Mann, *Panamanian Militarism: A Historical Interpretation* (Athens: Ohio University Center, 1996), pp. 47–55; Thomas L. Pearcy, *We Answer Only to God: Politics and the Military in Panama, 1903–1947* (Albuquerque: University of New Mexico, 1998), pp. 38–39, 45; McCain, *The United States and Panama*, ch. 3; Cuestas, *Panamá y Costa Rica*, pp. 123–141; Panama, Ministerio de Relaciones Exteriores, *Controversia de límites entre Panamá y Costa Rica*, 2 vols. (Panama: Imprenta Nacional, 1914–1921), 2:28.

8. Costa Rica, Secretaría de Relaciones Exteriores, *Documentos relativos al conflicto de jurisdicción territorial con la República de Panamá* (San José Imprenta Nacional, 1921), pp. 118–134, 237–241; Cuestas, *Panamá y Costa Rica*, pp. 123–141.

9. And looking into the future, as the Argentine Junta believed it could do with the occupation of the Malvinas (Falklands) Islands in April 1982.

10. "Military Information, Costa Rica," 1 February 1919, Costa Rican Occupation of the Almirante District," 9 March 1921, Correspondence and Record Cards of the Military Intelligence Division, (henceforth MID). Central America, RG 165, NA; Cuestas, *Panamá y Costa Rica*, pp. 119–123; Costa Rica, *Conflicto de jurisdicción*, pp. 226–227.

11. Cuestas, *Panamá y Costa Rica*, pp. 119–123; Panama, *Controversia*, 2:27–29; Cuestas, *Panamá y Costa Rica*, p. 375.

12. This paragraph and the next draw on: Panama, *Controversia*, 27–29; Cuestas, *Panamá y Costa Rica*, pp. 119–123, 216; Armando Aizpurúa, *Biografía del General Manuel Quintero V.* (Panamá: Imprenta Nacional, 1956), pp. 253–254.

13. Cuestas, *Panamá y Costa Rica*, pp. 177–179.

14. *New York Times*, 1 March 1921.

15. *New York Times*, 2 March 1921. See also, Philip, *British Documents on Foreign Affairs*, Part II, Series D, *Latin America, 1914–1939*, 2:385; Pearcy, *Politics and the Military*, p. 173.

16. *New York Times*, 13 March 1921.

17. Panama, *Controversia*, 2: 30–50, 73–76, 375; Cuestas, *Panamá y Costa Rica*, pp. 166, 168, 195–196, 198, 203–209; Aizpurúa, *General Quintero*, pp. 261–266.

18. Panama, *Controversia*, 2:31–32, 36–37; Aizpurúa, *General Quintero*, p. 266.

19. Panama, *Controversia*, 2:50–79, 103; Cuestas, *Panamá y Costa Rica*, pp. 202, 211–214, 221–224, 242; Aizpurúa, *General Quintero*, pp. 266–268.

20. Panama, *Controversia*, 2: 375; Cuestas, *Panamá y Costa Rica*, pp. 236–239, 242–254.

21. "Costa Rica, Service Report" 19 March 1921, MID, Central America, RG 165; Cuestas, *Panamá y Costa Rica*, pp. 240–241.

22. Panama, *Controversia*, 2: 127–129; Cuestas, *Panamá y Costa Rica*, pp. 309–321.

23. Panama, *Controversia*, 2: 130–131, 140–141; Cuestas, *Panamá y Costa Rica*, pp. 324–330.

24. "Costa Rican Occupation of the Almirante District," 9 March 1921, MID, RG 165, NA; Panama, *Controversia*, 2: 130–135, 141–142, 375; Cuestas, *Panamá y Costa Rica*, pp. 330–337. In contrast to the detailed Panamanian accounts, the Costa Rican sources do not make clear the exact date when President Acosta decided to invade Almirante; I have placed his decision in the most plausible place in the narrative.

25. "Costa Rican Occupation of the Almirante District," 9 March 1921, MID, RG 165, NA. I have preferred the conclusion of this report rather than the report of the U.S. military attaché in Costa Rica, who paints a dreadful picture of the Costa Rican military operations. Sitting in San José, all those negative reports were doubtlessly true, except for the suggestion that "the result of an attack on Bocas del Toro would have been doubtful." "Costa Rica, Service Report" 19 March 1921, MID, Central America, RG 165. The analysis of the capabilities of each side at Bocas del Toro validates the eyewitness conclusions of the report quoted in the text.

26. The well-read Porras drew on a classical Spanish saying in his telegram well worth quoting: "Panama, marzo 7 de 1921. Gobernador — Bocas del Toro. El gesto del Coronel Mosquera fué heroico y simpático; empero, bien meditado, vale más tender puente de plata que pase y se vaya el enemigo. Afectísimo, Belisario Porras." Panama, *Controversia*, 2: 137.

27. For the diplomatic correspondence, see U.S. Department of State, *Papers Relating to the Foreign Relations of the United States 1921*, 2 vols. (Washington, D.C.: Government Printing Office, 1936), 1: 175–228.

28. Philip, ed., *British Documents on Foreign Affairs*, Part II, Series D, *Latin America, 1914–1939*, 2:296; Cuestas, *Panamá y Costa Rica*, pp. 365–369; Panama, *Controversia*, 2: 471–476; Costa Rica, *Conflicto de jurisdicción*, pp. 204–206.

Chapter 4

1. Thomas Cleary, tr., *Mastering the Art of War: Zhuge Liang's and Liu Ji's commentaries* (Boston: Shambhala Dragon Editions, 1989), p. 52.

2. Louis A. Pérez, Jr., *Lords of the Mountain: Social Banditry and Peasant Protest in Cuba, 1878–1918* (Pittsburgh: University Press, 1989), pp. 63–66; Louis A. Pérez, Jr., "Supervision of a Protectorate: The United States and the Cuban Army, 1898–1908," *Hispanic American Historical Review* 52(1972): 253–254, 258.

3. Pérez, *Lords of the Mountain*, pp. 59–61; Lester D. Langley, *The Banana Wars: United States Intervention in the Caribbean, 1898–1934* (Wilmington, DE: Scholarly Resources, 2002), pp. 6, 9. U.S. War Department , *Informe sobre el censo de Cuba de 1899* (Washington: Government Printing Office, 1900), pp. 77, 189 gives the surviving Cuban population as 1,572,797.

4. Allan R. Millett, "The Rise and Fall of the Cuban Rural Guard, 1898–1912," *Americas* 29(1972): 192–193; Pérez, *Lords of the Mountain*, pp. 34–35, 118–121; U.S. War Department, *Censo de 1899*, p. 50. If urban is considered living in towns of 8,000 or more persons, the urban population was 32.5 percent, *Ibid.*, p. 82.

5. Millett, "Cuban National Guard," pp. 191–196; Charles Magoon to Secretary of War, Havana, 9 April 1908, box 755, Record Group (henceforth RG) 350, National Archives, College Park, Maryland (henceforth NA).

6. Louis A. Pérez, Jr., *Army Politics in Cuba 1898–1958* (Pittsburg: University Press, 1976), pp. 12–13, 16. Millett, "Cuban National Guard," pp. 195–196; David F. Healy, *The United States in Cuba, 1898–1902* (Madison: University of Wisconsin Press, 1963), pp. 191–193.

7. Pérez, *Cuban Army*, p. 16.

8. Charles E. Chapman, *A History of the Cuban Republic* (New York: Macmillan, 1927), pp. 148–149.

9. Not all Cubans were happy with the presence of U.S. troops, indeed sexual competition was certainly one factor fueling Cuban nationalism. Some popular verses (of which several variants exist) captured the mood as U.S. soldiers withdrew in 1902: "Se van los americanos/ con su banderita en la popa/ y quedan las cubanitas/ con la barriga en la boca." See Antonio Carbajo, *Un Cataruo de folklore cubano* (Miami: Language Research Press, 1968), pp. 76–77.

10. Leonard Wood diary cited in Millett, "Cuban National Guard," p. 196.

11. Robert F. Smith, *The United States and Cuba: Business and Diplomacy, 1917–1960* (New Haven, CT: College and University Press, 1960), pp. 18, 22–24; Healy, *The United States in Cuba*, pp. 175, 193–206, 208.

12. U.S. Department of State, *Papers Relating to the Foreign Relations of the United States, 1904* (Washington, D.C.: Government Printing Office, 1905), pp. 238–239; Louis A. Pérez, Jr., *Cuba Under the Platt Amendment, 1902–1934* (Pittsburgh: University of Pittsburgh Press, 1986), p. 149. General Carlos García Vélez stated: "The instruction which has been received by officers of artillery has been elementary, most elementary. [...] The function of the artilleryman has been limited to firing the cannon at nine o'clock. [...] Remember this, that our present corps of artillery knows nothing but infantry tactics." Stenographic Report of the Conference, 6 February 1907, Havana, box 129, RG 350, NA.

13. Chapman, *Cuban Republic*, pp. 161–162, 165, 172.

14. Major H. J. Slocum to Provisional Governor, Havana, 26 October 1906, box 755, RG 350, NA; Allan R. Millett, *The Politics of Intervention: The Military Occupation of Cuba, 1906–1909* (Columbus: Ohio State University Press, 1968), pp. 222–223.

15. Rafael Martínez Ortiz, *Cuba; los primeros años de independencia*, 2 vols. (Paris: Imprimerie Artistique Lux, 1921), 2: 777. For the public school system, see Healy, *The United States in Cuba*, pp. 179–182.

16. Millett, *Politics of Intervention*, pp. 50–53; Chapman, *Cuban Republic*, pp. 172, 177. The fullest account of the reelection is in Martínez Ortiz, *Primeros años de independencia*, 2:473–480, 487–613.

17. Millett, *Politics of Intervention*, p. 59; Chapman, *Cuban Republic*, pp. 191–193.

18. Millett, *Politics of Intervention*, pp. 59–60, 62, 105; Chapman, *Cuban Republic*, p. 193.

19. Statement of Pino Suárez of 19 February 1907, cited in Pérez, "Supervision of a Protectorate," p. 269. Wilfredo Ibrahim Consuegra codified this principle in 1914: "Por eso hay que tener muy presente, como lema que no falla: REVOLUCIÓN QUE ES BATIDA EN EL PRIMERO O SEGUNDO DIA DE SU COMIENZO, ES REVOLUCIÓN MUERTA. No se ha dado el caso todavía, de alguien que se haya incorporado a una partida revolucionaria en huída, en dispersión o durante un tiroteo." An extract (original capitalized) from his *Estudio acerca de la guerra de guerrilla* appears in Federico Chang, *El ejército nacional en la república neocolonial 1899–1933* (Havana: Editorial de Ciencias Sociales, 1981), p. 272.

20. Millett, *Politics of Intervention*, pp. 62–63, 222. Major H. J. Slocum to Provisional Governor, Havana, 26 October 1906, box 755, RG 350, NA. After the revolt was over and the danger had passed, all the militia volunteers promptly appeared to demand payment for the time they supposedly had spent on duty.

21. Millett, *Politics of Intervention*, pp. 61–62; Langley, *Banana Wars*, p. 37; Rafael Fermoselle, *Política y color en Cuba; La guerrita de 1912* (Montevideo, Uruguay: Ediciones Geminis, 1974), pp. 66–67.

22. Millett, *Politics of Intervention*, p. 71.

23. Consul Steinhart to Secretary of State (henceforth SofS), Havana, 8 September 1906, U.S. Department of State, *Papers Relating to the Foreign Relations of the United States, 1906*, 2 vols. (Washington, D.C.: Government Printing Office, 1909), 1:473–474; Millett, *Politics of Intervention*, pp, pp. 64, 72–73.

24. Roosevelt to Francis White, 13 September 1906, cited in Pérez, *Platt Amendment*, p. 97.

25. Millett, *Politics of Intervention*, pp. 64, 75–76; letter and telegram of August 1906, 812.24/199, RG 59, NA; Pérez, *Platt Amendment*, p. 97; Langley, *Banana Wars*, pp. 30, 32, 34–35.

26. U.S. Department of State, *Papers 1906*, 1: 482–483; Millett, *Politics of Intervention*, pp. 75–76; Langley, *Banana Wars*, p. 31.

27. Millett, *Politics of Intervention*, p. 94; I changed the spelling of Bacon to reflect the normal Spanish pronunciation.

28. Millett, *Politics of Intervention*, pp. 101–103; Pérez, *Platt Amendment*, pp. 101–102.

29. Charles E. Magoon to Secretary of War Taft, Havana, 31 December 1906, box 755, RG 350, NA. This document chronicles a turning point in Cuban history: "These people are apprehensive of a recurrence in Cuba of the dangers of militarism and consider it as great a peril in Cuba as it has been in other islands of the West Indies and in the countries of Central and South America. They call attention to the racial characteristics, traditions, etc., which they allege make it impossible for an armed force to be non-political or to assume the attitude of the soldiers of the United States towards political affairs. [...] They recognize that the authority to direct the police is vested in the Alcaldes and that, therefore, it would be impossible to secure united and uniform action throughout the Island at once and the same time; they admit the resulting hazard, but assert that the hazard is small compared with the danger from a large military force subject to the orders of a chief executive."

30. Millett, "Cuban Rural Guard, 1898–1912," pp. 201–202; Pérez, *Army Politics in Cuba*, pp. 24–25; Millett, *Politics of Intervention*, pp. 227–230.

31. Captain J.A. Ryan, "The Poltical Aspect of a Cuban Army," Havana, February 1907, box 129, RG 350, NA.

32. Pérez, *Army Politics in Cuba*, pp. 27–28; Millett, "Cuban Rural Guard," pp. 203–204.

33. Martínez Ortiz, *Primeros años de independencia*, 2: 836–837; Chapman, *Cuban Republic*, pp. 256–257. Magoon had previously appointed Pino Guerra head of the new army; See Decree No. 366 of 4 April 1908, Havana, box 755, RG 350, NA.

34. Charles Magoon to Secretary of War, Havana, 9 April 1908, box 755, RG 350, NA.

35. Millett, *Politics of Intervention*, p. 258.

36. Lt. Col. Robert Bullard, diary entry, 13 February 1909, cited in Millett, *Politics of Intervention*, p. 254.

37. John B. Jackson to SofS, Havana, 28 June 1910, 837.20/15, RG 59, NA; See also Major Henry Barber to Major H. J. Slocum, Havana, 3 February 1909, box 755, RG 350.

38. Department of State to Amlegation, 29 June 1910, 837.20/12, RG 59, NA.

39. John B. Jackson to SofS, Havana, 1 July 1910, 837.20/14, RG 59, NA.

40. Chapman, *Cuban Republic*, pp. 298–299; John B. Jackson to SofS, Havana, 1 March 1911, 837.20/21, RG 59, NA.

41. Fermoselle, *Política y color*, pp. 151–152; John B. Jackson to SofS, Havana, 1 March 1911, 837.20/21, RG 59, NA.

42. Chapman, *Cuban Republic*, pp. 275–276.

43. Millett, "Cuban Rural Guard," pp. 207–211; Pérez, *Army Politics in Cuba*, pp. 30–31.

44. John B. Jackson to SofS, 29 April 1910, 837.00/379, RG 59, NA; Mario Riera Hernández, *Cuba Libre 1895–1958* (Miami: Colonial Press, 1968), pp. 72–73; Fermoselle, *Política y color*, pp. 101–109, 131–138.

45. U.S. Department of State, *Papers Relating to the Foreign Relations of the United States, 1912* (Washington, D.C.: Government Printing Office, 1919), p. 243.

46. *Ibid.*

47. Memorandum of Law Officer, 13 May 1910, 837.00/390, RG 59, NA; Louis A. Pérez, Jr. "Politics, Peasants, and People of Color: The 1912 Race War in Cuba Reconsidered," *Hispanic American Historical Review* 66(1986): 529; Arthur M. Beaupré to SofS, Havana, 27 February and 23 March 1912, 837.00/575, 578, RG 59, NA.

48. Aline Helg, *Our Rightful Share: The Afro-Cuban Struggle for Equality* (Chapel Hill: University of North Carolina, 1995), pp. 201–203; Tomás Fernández Robaina, *El negro en Cuba: 1902–1958* (Havana: Editorial de Ciencias Sociales, 1994), pp. 86–88; Arthur M. Beaupré to SofS, Havana, 24 May 1912, 837.00/637, RG 59, NA; Fermoselle, *Política y color*, pp. 169–173.

49. British Vice-Consul to British Minister, Santiago de Cuba, 18 May 1912, 837.00/673, RG 59, NA; Arthur M. Beaupré to SofS, Havana, 24 May 1912, 837.00/637, RG 59, NA; Helg, *Our Rightful Share*, pp. 194, 201.

50. Arthur M. Beaupré to SofS, Havana, 23 March 1910, 837.00/578, RG 59, NA.

51. Helg, *Our Rightful Share*, pp. 195, 197, 200; Fermoselle, *Política y color*, p. 156.

52. Cited in Helg, *Our Rightful Share*, p. 196.

53. Arthur M. Beaupré to SofS, Havana, 20, 24 May 1910, 837.00/588, 637, RG 59, NA; U.S. Department of State, *Papers 1912*, p. 245; Pérez, "Race War," p. 531; Helg, *Our Rightful Share*, pp. 198–200.

54. British Vice-Consul to British Minister, Guantánamo, 23 May 1912, 837.00/673, RG 59, NA; U.S. Consul at Santiago to U.S. Minister, 25, 29 May 1912, 837.00/622, 675 RG 59, NA; Helg, *Our Rightful Share*, pp. 203–204.

55. Arthur M. Beaupré to SofS, Havana, 24 May 1912, 837.00/601, RG 59, NA; Helg, *Our Rightful Share*, p. 203.

56. U.S. Department of State, *Papers 1912*, p. 245; Pérez, "Race War," p. 536; Helg, *Our Rightful Share*, p. 199. General José de Jesús Monteagudo stated "that there are from two to three thousand negroes more or less armed and perhaps six or seven thousand unarmed negroes roaming Oriente province awaiting developments." Arthur M. Beaupré to SofS, Havana, 27 May 1912, 837.00/623, RG 59, NA.

57. Pérez, "Race War, " pp. 516–519, 522–524; Unpublished segment of Arthur M. Beaupré to SofS, 6 June 1912, 837.00/731, RG 59, NA; U.S. Navy Commander Fourth Division to Secretary of the Navy, Guantanamo Bay, 16 June 1912, 837.00/837, RG 59, NA. U.S. Navy personnel sometimes transcribed the usually uncoded messages of the Cuban army, and these intercepts fed into the reporting by U.S. officials on the Race War.

58. Helg, *Our Rightful Share*, pp. 207–208. A excellent introduction to the problems of the Spanish army is John Lawrence Tone, "The Machete and the Liberation of Cuba," *Journal of Military History* 62(1998): 7–28.

59. Arthur M. Beaupré to SofS, Havana, 20, 24 May 1910, 837.00/588, 637, RG 59, NA; Helg, *Our Rightful Share*, p. 203.

60. Pérez, "Race War, " pp. 533–535; Max Baehr to Beaupré, Cienfuegos, 24 May 1912, 837.00/623, RG 59, NA.

61. Chas. Ham to Ross E. Holaday, Palma Soriano, 25 June 1912, 837.00/877, RG 59, NA; Consul-General James Rodgers to SofS, Havana, 29 May 1912, 837.00/696, RG 59, NA; Arthur M. Beaupré, 4, 15 June 1912, 837.00/711, 772, RG 59, NA; U.S. Consul Ross E. Holaday to SofS, Santiago de Cuba, 15 July 1912, 837.00/905, RG 59, NA. Helg, *Our Rightful Share*, pp. 221–222; Fermoselle, *Política y color*, p. 158.

62. U.S. Consul Ross E. Holaday to SofS, Santiago de Cuba, 3 June 1912, 837.00/665, RG 59, NA. The paragraph also draws on Arthur M. Beaupré to SofS, 27 May 1912, 837.00/623, RG 59, NA, and U.S. Consult at Santiago to Beaupré, 27 May 1912, 837.00/626, RG 59, NA.

63. Helg, *Our Rightful Share*, p. 219. Compare U.S. Department of State, *Papers 1912*, p. 255 with Chapman, *Cuban Republic*, p. 311 who may be reporting a rumor when he mistakenly stated that U.S. Marines landed in Daiquirí on 31 May.

64. Proclamations of General Jose de J. Monteagudo, Santiago de

Cuba, 6, 11 June 1912, 837.00/745, 819; John A. Lejeune to Brigade Commander, Santiago de Cuba, 17 June 1912, 837.00/860, RG 59, NA; American Consular Agent Arthur Field Lindly to Beaupré, Baracoa, 14 June 1912, 837.00/ 827, RG 59, NA; American Consular Agent George Bayliss to American Minister, Antilla, 15 June 1912, 837.00/827, RG 59, NA; U.S. Consul Ross E. Holaday to SofS, Santiago de Cuba, 20 June 1912, 837.00/807, RG 59, NA.

65. Torriente to Colonel Machado, 26 June 1912, and District Commander to Brigade Commander, Guantanamo, 28 June 1912, 837.00/884, RG 59, NA; Riera Hernández, *Cuba Libre*, p. 72; Arthur M. Beaupré to SofS, Havana, 18 July 1912, 837.00/905, RG 59, NA; Commander Fourth Division to Secretary of Navy, Guantanamo Bay, 4 July 1912, 837.00/890, RG 59, NA; Helg, *Our Rightful Share*, pp. 224–225; Fermoselle, *Política y color*, p. 167.

66. Alejandro de la Fuente, "Myths of Racial Democracy: Cuba, 1900–1912," *Latin American Research Review* 34(1999): 50–52, 63–68; Helg, *Our Rightful Share*, pp. 198–199.

67. Louis A. Pérez, Jr., *Intervention, Revolution, and Politics in Cuba, 1913–1921* (Pittsburgh: University Press, 1978), pp. 5, 19; Hugh Gibson to SofS, Havana, 9 October 1912, 837.00/930, RG 59, NA; Chapman, *Cuban Republic*, p. 346.

68. Chapman, *Cuban Republic*, pp. 354–356.

69. Pérez, *Intervention*, pp. 20–25, 33–38; Chapman, *Cuban Republic*, pp. 357–358.

70. George Marvin, "Keeping Cuba Libre," *The World's Work*, vol. 34 (September 1917), p. 564.

71. Pérez, *Intervention*, pp. 11–19, 33–47. Shortage of U.S. Army troops for an occupation was a constraint upon U.S. policy makers who preferred to exhaust peaceful means. However, the U.S. Navy, with most of its units and personnel lacking a role in World War I, had enough bluejackets and marines to occupy Cuban coastal cities easily. The determining factor was the protection of the massive U.S. investment: If destruction of property became widespread in Cuba, Washington would have scraped together enough forces to restore order.

72. León Primelles, *Crónica cubana, 1915–1918* (Havana: Editorial Lex, 1955), pp. 245–247.

73. Pérez, *Intervention*, pp. 23–24; U.S. Department of State, *Papers Relating to the Foreign Relations of the United States, 1917* (Washington, D.C.: Government Printing Office, 1926), p. 359.

74. Luis Solano Álvarez, *Mi actuación militar* (Havana: Imprenta El Siglo XX, 1920), p. 63.

75. William E. González to SofS, Havana, 10 February, 12 March 1917, 837.00/1062, 1207, RG 59, NA; "La guerrita de febrero de 1917," *Boletín del Archivo Nacional de Cuba* 61(1962): 233–234; Primelles, *Crónica cubana*, pp. 248–249.

76. Marvin, "Keeping Cuba Libre," p. 563; Primelles, *Crónica cubana*, pp. 247–249, 251; Solano, *Mi actuación militar*, pp. 20–27.

77. U.S. Consul P. Merrill Griffith to SofS, Santiago de Cuba, 12 February 1917, 837.00/1113, RG 59, NA.

78. Pérez, *Intervention*, pp. 27–28. Solano, *Mi actuación militar*, pp. 27–41 provides the most detailed account of the rebel seizure of Camagüey.

79. Primelles, *Crónica cubana*, pp. 249–250; Pérez, *Intervention*, pp. 28, 159.

80. U.S. Department of State, *Papers 1917*, pp. 359, 367.

81. "La guerrita de 1917," p. 230; Solano, *Mi actuación militar*, pp. 43–68.

82. "La guerrita de 1917," pp. 227, 229; Chang, *Ejército nacional*, p. 38; William E. González to SofS, Havana, 19 February, 12 March 1917, 837.00/1104, 1207 RG 59, NA; U.S. Department of State, *Papers 1917*, pp. 356–358.

83. Telegrams of González to SofS, Havana, 19, 21, 23, 25, March 1917, 837.00/1104, 1117, 1126, 1137, RG 59, NA; Chapman, *Cuban Republic*, p. 375.

84. Primelles, *Crónica cubana*, pp 279–280; Pérez, *Intervention*, pp. 50–51; U.S. Department of State, *Papers 1917*, pp. 366, 368. This last source gives the date of the landing at Manzanillo as 24 February, as does Primelles, *Crónica cubana*, p. 280, unlike the date in Pérez, *Intervention*, p. 53; Merrill Griffith to SofS, Santiago de Cuba, 27 February 1917, 837.00/1180, RG 59, NA contains neither dates nor does it mention the landing.

85. Solano, *Mi actuación militar*, pp. 93, 96, 98, 136–137, 147, 152, 171–174. Solano, who should have known better, continued to argue that the cavalry charge was feasible when the tactic was suicidal against machine guns and almost always against Mauser rifles. See also Tone, "The Machete and the Liberation of Cuba," pp. 16–17, 26–28.

86. Commanding officer U.S.S. *Dixie* to Secretary of the Navy, Havana, 25 February 1917, 837.00/1185, RG 59, NA.

87. Solano, *Mi actuación militar*, pp. 206–213; Waldemar León, "Caicaje: batalla final de una revuelta," *Bohemia*, 30 June 1967, pp. 101–102; "La guerrita de 1917," pp. 238, 240–241; Primelles, *Crónica cubana*, pp. 268–273.

88. Solano, *Mi actuación militar*, p. 213.

89. Primelles, *Crónica cubana*, pp. 281–282, 284–285; Pérez, *Intervention*, pp. 60–61.

90. Pérez, *Lords of the Mountain*, pp. 177–183; British Embassy to State Department, 10 May 1917, 837.61351/8, RG 59, NA.

91. "Statement of Mr N. Arthur Helmar re Cuban situation," 28 March 1917, 837.00/1313, RG 59, NA.

92. William E. González to SofS, Havana, 29 March 1917, 837.00/1273, RG 59, NA.

93. "Political Conditions in Oriente Province," Caimanera, 22 May 1917, 837.00/1371, RG 59, NA; Pérez, *Lords of the Mountain*, pp. 186–187; Smith, *United States and Cuba*, pp. 18–190, 104–107.

94. The report merits reproduction in full: "1. The Cuban army at the present time is of little military value. The General Staff is largely a political organization and its main activities are along that line. Few officers take any real pride in the army from a military point of view, while the men who compose the army make little response to such training as they get. 2. The organization as it now exists is a greater menace to the safety of Cuba than it is a protection, and Cuba would profit by a complete demobilization both of its army and navy. The political activities and interests of both officers and men constantly threaten the peace of the island, and should political disorders occur, the army would only add to them, and be of little use in restoring order. 3. In addition to the above, the army is a heavy expense to Cuba and should be classed distinctly as a luxury and not as a necessity. Cuba would be better off with a thoroughly organized Rural Guard, which together with a sufficient force of coast artillery, could be controlled by one department, while the navy could be entirely abolished and an efficient Revenue Cutter Service substituted. 4. It is believed that should the above course be followed, tranquility could be more easily established and maintained in the island, a great source of discontent and a heavy burden of expense removed, and a dangerous and powerful weapon be taken from the hands of persons who are not qualified in any way to exercise the powers which have been entrusted to them." Major Albert Gallatin to the Director of Military Intelligence, Havana, 26 February 1919, Military Intelligence Division 2012, (henceforth MID), RG 165, NA.

95. Chang, *Ejército nacional*, pp. 103–104; "Influence of the Cuban army in the approaching national elections," Havana, 15 September 1920, MID 2012, RG 165, NA.

96. Major H. M. Hobson, "Reorganization of the Cuban Army," Havana, 23 May 1921, MID 2012, RG 165, NA. For the constant army involvement in partisan politics, see Pérez, *Army Politics in Cuba*, *passim*.

97. Pérez, *Lords of the Mountain*, pp. 177–188.

Chapter 5

1. Niccolò Machiavelli, *The Prince*, trans. W. K. Marriott (London: Everyman's Library, 1908), p. 97.

2. Santiago Portilla, *Una sociedad en armas* (México: El Colegio de México: 1995), p. 398; Miguel A. Sánchez Lamego, *Historia militar de la revolución mexicana en la época maderista*, 3 vols. (Mexico: Instituto Nacional de Estudios Históricos de la Revolución Mexicana, 1976), I: 34; Robert L. Scheina, *Latin America's Wars: The Age of the Professional Soldier, 1900–2001* (Washington, D.C.: Brassey's, 2003), p. 12. Of the 29,000, only 23,000 were combat personnel. The authorized but not budgeted figure of 40,000 frequently reappeared in discussions to give a false perception of strength.

3. Adolfo Duclós Salinas, *Méjico pacificado: El progreso de Méjico y los hombres que lo gobiernan* (St. Louis, MO, Hughes Press, 1904), pp. 223–224. The "First Reserve" was mainly an artificial construct presumably of 25,000 additional soldiers. Its two main components were the militia of the individual state governments and the *rurales* or federal mounted police budgeted at 2400 men. Memorandum from Department of War and Marine, December 1902, Despatches from U.S. Ministers to Mexico, Record Group (henceforth RG) 59, National Archives, College Park, Maryland (henceforth NA). Except for states facing Indian threats, the state militias existed only in paper and thus made meaningless the First Reserve. The *rurales* were notoriously inept and with a desertion rate of one-third, they were permanently undermanned and barely numbered 1,930 men in any average year from 1885 to 1910; See Paul J. Vanderwood, *Dis-*

order and Progress: Bandits, Police, and Mexican Development (Lincoln: University of Nebraska Press, 1981), pp. 110, 207.

4. Duclós Salinas, *Méjico pacificado*, pp. 224–234, 372–374; Alan Knight, *The Mexican Revolution*, 2 vols. (Lincoln: University of Nebraska Press, 1990), 1:49.

5. For the high esteem the army enjoyed, see, for example, Toribio Esquivel Obregón, *Mi labor en servicio de Mexico* (Mexico: Ediciones Botas, 1934), p. 49. A scholar rightly speaks of a "carefully constructed façade of army invincibility," Louis A. Pérez, Jr., "Some Military Aspects of the Mexican Revolution, 1910–1911," *Military Affairs* 43 (1979): 193.

6. David E. Thompson to Secretary of State (henceforth SofS), 8 February 1909, Case 8183/224–225, Numerical and Minor Files, RG 59, NA.

7. "Madero's Interview with Díaz," 25 May 1913, 812.00/17177, RG 59, NA; John Kenneth Turner, *Barbarous Mexico* (Austin: University of Texas Press, 1984), pp. 148–151; Paul Garner, *Porfirio Díaz* (Harlow, Great Britain: Longman, 2001), pp. 216–18; Charles C. Cumberland, *Mexican Revolution: Genesis under Madero* (Austin: University of Texas Press, 1952), pp. 81–84.

8. Knight, *Mexican Revolution*, 1:54.

9. Cumberland, *Genesis under Madero*, p. 85.

10. Turner, *Barbarous Mexico*, pp. 161–164; Hector Aguilar Camín, *La frontera nómada: Sonora y la Revolución Mexicana* (Mexico: Siglo XXI Editores, 1985), pp. 83–88; Knight, *Mexican Revolution*, 1: 57–73; Stanley R. Ross, *Francisco I. Madero: Apostle of Mexican Democracy* (New York: Columbia University Press, 1955), pp. 72–98.

11. Francisco I. Madero to his mother, 18 April 1910, in Francisco I. Madero, *Epistolario, 1900–1910*, 2 vols. (Mexico: Secretaría de Hacienda y Crédito Publico, 1985): 2: 122–123; *Ibid.*, 2: 126–27; "Madero's Interview with Díaz," 25 May 1913, 812.00/17177, RG 59, NA; Luis Lara Pardo, *De Porfirio Díaz a Francisco Madero: La sucesión dictatorial de 1911* (México: Instituto Nacional de Estudios Históricos de la Revolución Mexicana, 1985), pp. 147–48.

12. Turner, *Barbarous Mexico*, p. 166.

13. Friedrich Katz, *The Life and Times of Pancho Villa* (Stanford: Stanford University Press, 1998), pp. 53–54; Knight, *Mexican Revolution*, 1: 75–77; Cumberland, *Genesis under Madero*, pp. 121–123; Ricardo García Granados, *Historia de México; desde la restauración de la república en 1867 hasta la caída de Huerta*, 2 vols. (Mexico: Editorial Jus, 1956), 2: 111.

14. "Al ejército mexicano" November 1910, in Federico González Garza, *La revolución mexicana: mi contribución político-literaria*, (Mexico: A. del Bosque, 1936), pp. 465–67.

15. Antonio P. González and J. Figueroa Domenech, *La revolución y sus héroes*, 3rd ed. (Mexico: Herrero Hermanos, 1911), p. 93.

16. Paul J. Vanderwood, "Response to Revolt: The Counter-Guerrilla Strategy of Porfirio Díaz," *Hispanic American Historical Review* 56(1976) is the key scholarly article on the subject of this chapter; in pp. 571–573 he amply demonstrates that the Federal Army fought loyally for the regime until the end.

17. Peter V.N. Henderson, *Félix Díaz, the Porfirians, and the Mexican Revolution* (Lincoln: University of Nebraska Press, 1981), pp. 10, 16; Henry Baerlein, *Mexico: The Land of Unrest*, 2nd. ed. (London: Simpkin, Marshall, Kent & Co., 1914), pp. 224–225; Knight, *Mexican Revolution*, 1: 171–72. See also *Ibid.*, 1: 208–218 for a nuanced discussion of the role riots and the threat of riots played in the Mexican Revolution.

18. Katz, *Villa*, p. 123.

19. Vanderwood, *Bandits and Police*, pp. 110–115.

20. Report of military attaché Girard Sturtevant, Mexico City, 20 February 1911, Military Intelligence Division (henceforth MID), Box 1884, RG 165, NA; Vanderwood, "Response to Revolt," p. 556. General Félix Díaz, the president's nephew, was a very effective chief of police who benefited from a network of paid informants throughout the city. Requests to transfer this dynamic general to key combat commands later reached the president, who decided to keep his nephew in the sensitive position in Mexico City until May, when Félix became briefly governor of Oaxaca, Henderson, *Félix Díaz*, pp. 32–33.

21. Sánchez Lamego, *Época maderista*, 1: 191, 273–275; Knight, *Mexican Revolution*, 1: 172–175; Vanderwood, "Response to Revolt," p. 556; Baerlein, *Land of Revolt*, pp. 225–227; Henderson, *Félix Díaz*, p. 29.

22. Katz, *Villa*, pp. 89–90. The U.S. consul in Chihuahua City reflected the consensus when he telegraphed on 19 November 1910 (812.00/500, RG 59, NA) that "Many rumors current here relative to general uprising to occur about the twentieth [...] Is not probable that this state will take the initiative in such a movement."

23. Portilla, *Una sociedad en armas*, p. 398; Report of military at-

taché Girard Sturtevant to War College Division, Mexico City, 20 February 1911, MID, Box 1884, RG 165, NA; Pérez, "Military Aspects," p. 193; Vanderwood, "Response to Revolt," pp. 558–559; Baerlein, *Land of Unrest*, p. 245.

24. Michael C. Meyer, *Mexican Rebel: Pascual Orozco and the Mexican Revolution, 1910–1915* (Lincoln: University of Nebraska Press, 1967), pp. 17–18; Sánchez Lamego, *Época maderista*, 1: 49–52; Francisco R. Almada, *La revolución en el estado de Chihuahua*, 2 vols. (Mexico: Instituto Nacional de Estudios Históricos de la Revolución Mexicana, 1964–1965), 1: 169, 175–79; Knight, *Mexican Revolution*, 1:176. For a more charitable view of General Manuel Plata, see Vanderwood, "Response to Revolution," p. 561.

25. Portilla, *Una sociedad en armas*, p. 258. Did Urbano Zea have a glimpse at his personal fate? See note 29.

26. Sánchez Lamego, *Época maderista*, 1: 47–49; Portilla, *Una sociedad en armas* (México: El Colegio de México: 1995), pp. 238, 258; Vanderwood, "Response to Revolt," pp. 561–562; Almada, *La revolución en Chihuahua*, 1: 173; Guzmán, *Memorias de Pancho Villa*, p. 28.

27. Vanderwood, "Response to Revolt," p. 562.

28. Sánchez Lamego, *Época maderista*, 1:49; Almada, *Revolución en Chihuahua*, 1:173. The text follows the official reports. Barely a week later Colonel Samuel García Cuéllar captured the essence of the combat: "Hay dos versiones sobre este asunto; mientras los militares dicen que fueron muchos los que lo atacaron y por todas partes, los civiles dicen que fueron 50 ó 60 y que le tiraron solamente de las casas aspilleradas. La verdad del caso es: que al primero que mataron fue al Capitán 1o. y entonces entró el pánico y el sálvese el que pueda y unos se fueron por un lado con el Capitán 2o. y otros por otro con el teniente." Samuel García Cuéllar to Rafael Chousal, Pedernales, 2 January 1911, Box 33, Fondo Rafael Chousal (henceforth FRC), Archives of the Universidad Nacional Autónoma de México (henceforth UNAM), Mexico City, Mexico.

29. Sánchez Lamego, *Época maderista*, 1:47; Vanderwood, "Response to Revolt," p. 563. About a week later Orozco caught one of the civilian officials of Ciudad Guerrero in communication with the advancing column of General Navarro. The rebel chief also learned that a *jefe político* with Navarro's column had executed several civilians, including an uncle of Orozco. In reprisal and to teach a lesson, Orozco executed all ten civilian officials who had stayed behind in Ciudad Guerrero, including the deposed *jefe político* Urbano Zea. Orozco's keen business sense detected an opportunity for profit, and as the executions were coming to an end, he rounded up the wealthy merchants of the region and extorted money from them to spare their lives. See Meyer, *Orozco*, pp. 22–23, Almada, *Revolución en Chihuahua*, 1: 184–86, and Samuel García Cuéllar to Rafael Chousal, Ciudad Guerrero, 13 January 1911, Box 33, FRC, UNAM. Orozco's action was perhaps the earliest precedent for the endemic practice of executing all prisoners in later years. Extortion and protection payments were soon to become permanent characteristics of the Mexican Revolution.

30. Ellsworth Luther to SofS, Ciudad Porfirio Díaz, 24 December 1911, 812.00/594, RG 59, NA; Samuel García Cuéllar to Rafael Chousal, Pedernales, 2 January 1911, Box 33, FRC, UNAM.

31. Pascual Orozco to Francisco Salido, 11 December 1910, *El imparcial*, 19 February 1911. This very early accusation of robbery was not surprising and became a standard tactic of revolutionary leaders. If subordinates obeyed the leader, they were revolutionaries and could continue stealing, but if they disobeyed an order, then they were bandits; see Samuel Brunk, "The Sad Situation of Civilians and Soldiers: The Banditry of Zapatismo in the Mexican Revolution," *American Historical Review* 101(1996): 337–39.

32. Katz, *Villa*, pp. 87, 94–95, 99–100.

33. W. Dirk Raat, *Revoltosos: Mexico's Rebels in the United States, 1903–1923* (College Station, Texas A & M Press, 1981), p. 218.

34. *Ibid.*, p. 214. See chapter 8 of Raat's book for an exhaustive discussion of Madero's network.

35. Katz, *Villa*, p. 54 who very fittingly titles his chapter "The Revolution That Neither Its Supreme Leader Nor Its Opponents Expected"; Knight, *Mexican Revolution*, 1:176–183. As an example of the cold determination needed to start a revolt, Villa without a moment's hesitation killed informants prior to the 20 November target date to preserve secrecy; See Martín Luis Guzmán, *Memorias de Pancho Villa* (Mexico City: Editorial Porrúa, 1984), pp. 24–25.

36. Francisco I. Madero to his father, 18 April 1910, in Madero, *Epistolario, 1900–1910*, 2:316. To refer to Chihuahua as a "place" or locale, Madero used the word "foco" (cognate: focus), a term that loomed large in the debates over guerrilla strategy in the second half of the twentieth century.

37. Report of military attaché Gerard Sturtevant, 20 February

1911 and "Insurgent or revolutionary activity in Mexico," 24 March 1911, MID, Box 1884, RG 165, NA; "Defeat of the revolutionists in Tabasco and collapse of the revolutionary movement they engendered," 10 January 1911, 812.00/653; T. F. Serrano, *Episodios de la revolución* (El Paso: Modern Printing, 1911), p. 195.

38. Statement of Abraham González, *The Washington Post*, 1 January 1911.

39. Samuel García Cuéllar to Rafael Chousal, Pedernales, 2 January 1911, Box 33, FRC, UNAM. U.S. soldiers complained even more strongly about the bitter cold in Chihuahua during the Punitive Expedition in 1916, see for example, Clarence C. Clendenen, *Blood on the Border: The United States Army and the Mexican Irregulars* (New York: Macmillan, 1969), pp. 235–237, 244, 250.

40. General Juan A. Hernández to Porfirio Díaz (henceforth PD), Chihuahua, 7 December 1910, in Georgette José Valenzuela, *Últimos meses de Porfirio Díaz en el poder* (Mexico: Instituto Nacional de Estudios Históricos de la Revolución Mexicana, 1984), pp. 43–45.

41. González and Figueroa, *La revolución y sus héroes*, pp. 111–112.

42. Because most of the rebels retreated in good order, the army captured only 3 or 4 prisoners and handed them over to the local *jefe político*. The latter had them killed when they refused to reveal the rebels' plans. Word of the executions of Cerro Prieto reached Orozco who unleashed the reprisals at Ciudad Guerrero mentioned in note 29; See Samuel García Cuéllar to Rafael Chousal, Ciudad Guerrero, 13 January 1911, Box 33, FRC, UNAM. In some accounts the number of executed reached 200, Pérez, "Military Aspects," p. 192, while another, Katz, *Villa*, p. 85, speaks of "massive executions of revolutionary prisoners." Aldama, *Revolución in Chihuahua*, 1: 184 accepts the more moderate number of 19 executed, but admitted he could find the name of only one of the victims (different from Orozco's uncle), a figure much closer to that García Cuéllar reported. The executions of Cerro Prieto entered revolutionary lore as "la hecatombe de Cierro Prieto," Serrano, *Episodios de la revolución*, p. 213, because even though local officials had taken the action, the rebels blamed General Juan Navarro, the commander of the federal column. Curiously enough, Villa does not mention the executions, see Guzmán, *Memorias de Villa*, pp. 31–33, and later had to be reminded of them by Orozco in May 1911, *Ibid.*, p. 59. The question of how to punish General Navarro provoked the first major crisis in the Madero regime, as later pages will show.

43. Francisco P. Troncoso, *Campaña de 1910 a 1911* (Mexico: Secretaría de Guerra y Marina, 1913), pp. 19–32; Samuel García Cuéllar to Rafael Chousal, Pedernales, 2 and 13 January 1911, Box 33, FRC, UNAM; Serrano, *Episodios de la revolución*, p. 238.

44. Troncoso, *Campaña de 1910*, p. 33.

45. Samuel García Cuéllar to Rafael Chousal, Pedernales, 31 January 1911, Box 33, FRC, UNAM.

46. C.M. Leonard to SofS, Chihuahua, 7 January 1911, 812.00/646, RG 59, NA.

47. Report of military attaché Girard Sturtevant, 20 February 1911, MID, Box 1884, RG 165, NA.

48. "El amago de Orozco a Juárez y el no haber tomado la Ciudad son para mí un misterio todavía. Que pudo haber tomado Juárez, es indudable, y le bastaba sólo haberlo intentado, había sobre los dos puentes internacionales más de mil malos mexicanos hambrientos, esperando sólo que Orozco atacara por el frente, para atacar ellos por la espalda y saquear la población." Samuel García Cuéllar to Rafael Chousal, Ciudad Juárez, 23 February 1911, Doc. No. 2869, Colección Porfirio Díaz (henceforth CPD), Universidad Iberoamericana, Mexico City, Mexico (henceforth UIA); Serrano, *Episodios de la revolución*, pp. 242–261; Isidro Fabela, ed., *Documentos históricos de la Revolución Mexicana* (henceforth *DHRM*), 28 vols. (Mexico: Fondo de Cultura Económica and Editorial Jus, 1960–1976), 5: 244–245; Katz, *Villa*, p. 92; Meyer, *Orozco*, pp. 24–26.

49. Samuel García Cuéllar to Rafael Chousal, Ciudad Juárez, 23 February 1911, No. 2869, CPD, UIA.

50. *Ibid.*; additional extracts of this letter appear published in Katz, *Villa*, p. 89.

51. Report of consul C.M. Leonard, Chihuahua, 4 February 1911, 812.00/770, RG 59, NA.

52. Henry Lane Wilson to SofS, 2 February 1911, Gene Z. Hanrahan, ed., *Documents on the Mexican Revolution*, 8 vols. (Salisbury, NC: Documentary Publications, 1976–1983), 2:131.

53. The peasant masses in this region seemed to be waiting for the right moment ro revolt, and the capture of Nieves provided them with the signal to join the insurrection. Militarily, the capture of Nieves by 100 rebels was not a great feat: "La fuerza de seguridad pública se componía de 8 soldados de caballería y un subteniente, que hacían la vigilancia de todo el partido, soldados que carecían de toda instrucción militar. La guardia de cárcel se com-

ponía, así mismo, de 6 soldados y un sargento, individuos octogenarios unos, inválidos y dementes otros y en conjunto inútiles todos." Samuel Villareal to PD, Zacatecas, 1 March 1911, No. 5125, CPD, UIA.

54. Jefe Político Francisco del Palacio to Rafael Chousal, Torreón, 1 March 1911, Box 33, FRC, UNAM.

55. The standard source on this episode is Lowell L. Blaisdell, *The Desert Revolution: Baja California, 1911* (Westport, CT: Greenwood Press, 1986). For other military details, see Sánchez Lamego, *Época maderista*, 1: 183–188.

56. Report of military attaché Girard Sturtevant, 29 March 1911, MID, Box 1884, RG 165, NA.

57. The CPD at UIA contains many requests for machine guns. Even the old general Treviño was asking for four more machine guns, ibid. to PD, 22 April 1911, Monterrey, No. 7444, CPD, UIA.

58. Sánchez Lamego, *Época maderista*, 1: 93–94; Knight, *Mexican Revolution*, 1:183–187.

59. Parte del Coronel Agustín A. Valdés, 19 March 1911, Troncoso, *Campaña de 1910*, pp. 186–205.

60. Parte del Coronel Samuel García Cuéllar, 10 March 1911, Troncoso, *Campaña de 1910*, pp. 177–86.

61. Some accounts exaggerate the significance of the telephone line: (1)Colonel García Cuéllar already had a good general idea of the rebel positions; (2) if the line was down or the phone was otherwise inoperative, riders easily could have covered the six kilometers to bring the news, especially because the rebels had not yet surrounded Casas Grandes.

62. "Description of the battle of Casas Grandes," Chihuahua, 29 March 1911, 812.00/1222, RG 59, NA; Parte del Coronel Samuel García Cuellar, 10 March 1911, Parte del Coronel Agustín Valdés, 19 March 1911, Troncoso, *Campaña de 1910*, pp. 177–205; Sánchez Lamego, *Época maderista*, pp. 95–97; Juan Sánchez Azcona, *Apuntes para la historia de la revolución mexicana* (México: Instituto Nacional de Estudios Históricos de la Revolución Mexicana, 1961), pp. 198–200.

63. T. F. Serrano, *Episodios de la revolución*, p. 265; Sánchez Lamego, *Época maderista*, 1: 98–99; Almada, *Revolución en Chihuahua*, 2: 201, 204–205.

64. Sánchez Lamego, *Época maderista*, 1: 98.

65. General Lauro Villar to PD, Chihuahua, 13 April 1911, No. 6766, CPD, UIA; Troncoso, *Campaña de 1910*, p. 211; Serrano, *Episodios de la revolución*, pp. 276–77; Almada, *Revolución en Chihuahua*, 2: 219.

66. Knight, *Mexican Revolution*, 1: 182–183, 202. The timing and reasons for Díaz's acceptance of military defeat can be approximated. In spite of a flood of reports and letters reaching him, the documents did not provide a cohesive view of the nature and danger of the Madero revolt. The letters of his trusted aide Samuel García Cuellar, particularly that of 23 February quoted above (significantly enough in the Díaz and not the Chousal papers), began to open the president's eyes. When added to the countless requests for troops pouring in from many parts of the country, one War Department list of 27 March 1911 appears decisive. The "Estado que manifiesta el número de reemplazos que debían los Entidades Federativas en 1 de julio de 1910" (No. 8323, CPD, UIA) revealed that the states were behind 9,731 men in their annual levies. Only four entities (Aguascalientes, Morelos, Guerrero, and Tepic) had exceeded their quotas by a total of 399, which still left a shortfall of 9,332 for the country. One response to this alarming list was the decree of 11 April raising the pay of soldiers (Valenzuela, *Últimos meses*, p. 202), but the president knew that the game was up. The peasant masses had voted with their feet by fleeing the press gangs and by flocking to the banners of Madero; see Allen Wells and Gilbert M. Joseph, *Summer of Discontent, Seasons of Upheaval: Elite Politics and Rural Insurgency in Yucatán, 1876–1915* (Stanford: Stanford University Press, 1996), pp. 209–212.

67. Almada, *Revolución en Chihuahua*, 2: 205. Mostly junior offices formed the conspiracy known as the "complot de Tacubaya." The fullest account is in Portilla, *Sociedad en armas*, pp. 399–400.

68. John Womack, *Zapata and the Mexican Revolution* (New York: Vintage Books, 1968), pp. 67–82; Knight, *Mexican Revolution*, 1: 189–191; Francisco Pineda Gómez, *La irrupción zapatista, 1911* (Mexico City: Era, 1997), pp. 57–80; Valenzuela, *Últimos meses*, pp. 193–195.

69. General Lauro Villar to PD, Chihuahua, 8 April 1911, No. 6756 and 13 April 1911, No. 6766, CPD, UIA; Troncoso, *Campaña de 1910*, pp. 223, 238.

70. González and Figueroa Domenech, *La revolución y sus héroes*, p. 127; Serrano, *Episodios de la revolución*, 277–78; Troncoso, *Cam-*

paña de 1910, pp. 241, 245–247. In all fairness to General Navarro, he had asked for reinforcements on 20 March, *Ibid.*, pp. 221–222. However, after the small detachment from Casas Grandes reached Ciudad Juárez on 6 April, he limited himself in all his subsequent messages to requesting more ammunition–the only thing the garrison never ran out of.

71. General Lauro Villar to PD, 13 April 1911, No. 6766, CPD, UIA; González and Figueroa Domenech, *La revolución y sus héroes*, pp. 127–129; Hanrahan, *Documents on the Mexican Revolution*, 2: 298; Troncoso, *Campaña de 1910*, pp. 249, 262–65, 300.

72. Armistice of 23 April 1911, Hanrahan, *Documents on the Mexican Revolution*, vol. 1: 340.

73. Samuel García Cuéllar to Rafael Chousal, Ciudad Juárez, 23 February 1911, No. 2869, CPD, UIA; González and Figueroa Domenech, *La revolución y sus héroes*, p. 161; Sánchez Lamego, *Época maderista*, 1:105; Secretaría de Guerra y Marina, *Averigüación previa, instruída a solicitud del señor general Juan J. Navarro* (Mexico: El Republicano, 1913), pp. 53–58; Rafael Gama Martínez to PD, El Paso, 18 May 1911, No. 8678, CPD, UIA. Some accounts, such as Consul Lomelí's in Fabela, *DHRM*, 6: 413–414, claim the volunteers did not fight. The decisive testimony is of the rebel leader Giuseppe Garibaldi (grandson of the Garibaldi of fame in the unification of Italy), a personal witness to the valor of the civilian volunteers who fought longer than the soldiers, see Gonzalo G. Rivero, *Hacia la verdad: episodios de la revolución* (Mexico: Compañía Editora Nacional, 1911), p. 36.

74. Secretaría de Guerra, *Averigüación*, p. 8. The presence of parts of many units under one commander is a major reason why the text rarely designates the specific units; the reader who insists on these details can usually locate long lists in the volumes of Miguel A. Sánchez Lamego.

75. Rivero, *Hacia la verdad*, p. 36; Secretaría de Guerra, *Averigüación*, pp. 9, 165–66; Fabela, *DHRM*, 5: 363.

76. This possibility was not just speculation, and indeed years later U.S. troops drove out Villistas from Ciudad Juárez on 16 June 1919; See Clendenen, *Blood on the Border*, pp. 352–355.

77. Almada, *Revolución en Chihuahua*, 2:229; Secretaría de Guerra, *Averigüación*, p. 81; Serrano, *Episodios de la revolución*, p. 279.

78. Roque Estrada, *La revolución y Francisco I. Madero* (Guadalajara:n.p., 1912), p. 469; Telegram of Consul Tomás Torres, El Paso, 7 May 1911, Fabela, *DHRM*, 5: 364; Almada, *Revolución en Chihuahua*, 1:226; García Granados, *Historia*, 2: 156.

79. Rivero, *Hacia la verdad*, p. 11; Serrano, *Episodios de la revolución*, p. 281; Boynton to Attorney General, San Antonio, Texas, 9 May 1911, 812.00/1713, RG 59, NA; Consul Tomás Torres, El Paso, 8 May 1911, 8:30 a.m., Fabela, *DHRM*, 5: 368; Sánchez Azcona, *Apuntes*, p. 192.

80. My research confirms the explanation in Meyer, *Orozco*, pp. 29–31. Compare Katz, *Villa*, pp. 109–110, 850. The fullest exposition of the secret plot to attack Ciudad Juárez is in Guzmán, *Memorias de Pancho Villa*, pp. 51–53, where everything appears as carefully premeditated, but the account leaves out many events. The motivations for inventing the secret plot were very clear. As a politician, Villa wanted to take credit for the victory of Ciudad Juárez; likewise, he wanted to reveal the deviousness of Orozco. He also needed to construct a plausible narrative to excuse his insubordination against Madero after the battle.

81. Serrano, *Episodios de la revolución*, p. 286.

82. Report of Consul Antonio V. Lomelí, 26 May 1911, Fabela, *DHRM*, 6: 412–413; Rafael Gama Martínez to PD, El Paso, 18 May 1911, No. 8678, CPD, UIA; Colonel Edgar Steever to Adjutant General, 10 May 1911, 812.00/2034, RG 59, NA; this message ends with the annotation 5:17 p.m. and is different from the message in note 88.

83. Secretaría de Guerra, *Averigüación*, pp. 56, 74–75; Rivero, *Hacia la verdad*, p. 56; Serrano, *Episodios de la revolución*, p. 283.

84. Secretaría de Guerra, *Averigüación*, pp. 55–56; Rivero, *Hacia la verdad*, pp. 35, 56; Guzmán, *Memorias de Pancho Villa*, p. 55.

85. Serrano, *Episodios de la revolución*, p. 296.

86. Secretaría de Guerra, *Averigüación*, pp. 76–77; Consul Tomás Torres, El Paso, 10 May 1911, 9:00 a.m. and 14 May, Fabela, *DHRM*, 5: 374, 387–388; Katz, *Villa*, p. 111.

87. Rivero, *Hacia la verdad*, pp. 36–37.

88. Colonel Edgar Steever to Adjutant General, 10 May 1911, 812.00/2034, RG 59, NA.

89. Rivero, *Hacia la verdad*, pp. 18–19, 34.

90. Unsigned report, El Paso, 11 May 1911, No. 8515, CPD, UIA.

91. Meyer, *Orozco*, pp. 32–37. Roque Estrada, *Revolución*, pp. 471–480. For the supposed ordering of executions at Cerro Prieto,

see note 42. The insubordination of Villa and Orozco is a famous event in Mexican history; for the most recent scholarly discussion, see Katz, *Villa*, pp. 111–115; for Villa's version, see Guzmán, *Memorias de Pancho Villa*, pp. 59–61.

92. Report of Consul Marion Letcher, Chihuahua City, 15 May 1911, 812.00/1926, RG 59, NA. The 13 May report comes from Consul Marion Letcher, 812.00/1854, RG 59, NA.

93. In an otherwise fine account of the military operations, General Troncoso mars his narrative in the last page (*Campaña de 1910*, p. 317) by claiming that the Federal Army could have recaptured Ciudad Juárez. Such a maneuver was unrealistic, when the governor feared that Chihuahua City was in danger of rebel capture. Troncoso was making his contribution to the myth that the Federal Army had really not been defeated.

94. "The Evacuation of Torreón, May 15th, 1911," 812.00/2026, RG 59, NA. This paragraph draws also on Sánchez Lamego, *Época maderista*, 1: 142–43, on the unsigned report of 24 May 1911, No. 8349, CPD, UIA, and on García Granados, *Historia*, 2: 163–164.

95. "The Evacuation of Torreón, May 15th, 1911," 812.00/2026, RG 59, NA.

96. González and Figueroa Domenech, *La revolución y sus héroes*, pp. 165–66; see also Knight, *Mexican Revolution*, 1: 207–208.

97. The report to Consul William E. Alger, 23 April 1911, 812.00/1820 proved prophetic: "The taste of blood and pillage that thousands of bandits are getting over a great part of the country, in ever bolder abuses against all established institutions, whose bands have not even a muster roll or any other visible sign of connection with the Madero movement, is fast setting the country back to that chaos that prevailed over much of the Republic most of the time from 1811 to 1876. Thousands are getting daily object lessons in the facility with which wholesale robbery and murder and destruction of property can be carried on, and this knowledge will be an incentive to outlawry for another generation at least."

98. Telegram of Ambassador Wilson, Mexico City, 17 May 1911, Hanrahan, *Documents on the Mexican Revolution*, 2: 392; García Granados, *Historia*, 2: 163–164.

99. Luis E. Torres to PD, Hermosillo, 31 March 1911, Doc. No. 5517, CPD, UIA.

100. Aguilar Camín, *La frontera nómada*, pp. 153–54, 159–63.

101. Prefect Juan Roja to PD, 18 May 1911, Mazatlán, Doc. No. 8372, CPD, UIA.

102. J. R. Isunza to PD, Puebla, 16 May 1911, No. 8497, CPD, UIA.

103. Bernardino Ramírez to PD, 2 May 1911, No. 8339, CPD, UIA.

104. Luis D. Valdés to President, Morelia, 15 May 1911, No. 8139, CPD, UIA.

105. Francisco Pineda Gómez, *La irrupción zapatista, 1911*, pp. 133–139; Knight, *Mexican Revolution*, 1:190–191; Samuel Brunk, *Emiliano Zapata: Revolution and Betrayal in Mexico* (Albuquerque: University of New Mexico Press, 1995), pp. 36–38.

106. "Los que hayan conocido Cuautla, cuando vuelvan dirán: AQUI EN ESTE LUGAR EXISTIÓ CUAUTLA." Petition to Franciso I. Madero, Mexico City, 10 June 1910, Archivo de Francisco I. Madero, reel 19. Among historians, only Sánchez Lámego, *Época maderista*, 1: 270, mentioned "graves desmanes" after the rebel capture. The petition (name of petitioner illegible) demanded justice and came from a strong Madero supporter of modest origins ("soy muy humilde") and does not reflect the viewpoint of hacendados or a defense of land as do other accounts cited by Brunk, *Zapata*, p. 44; it is not one of the scare stories Womack, *Zapata*, p. 112 refers to. Because the many students of Zapata's career have not been aware of this first-hand testimony, it deserves quotation (atrocious spelling and grammar errors corrected as far as possible): "Al entrar los revolucionaríos a Cuautla, lo primero que estos han hecho es prender fuego a la Estación del F.C. Interoceánico, siguizendos[?] después con los carros cargados que estaban en el patio de dicha Estación, después siguieron con arrojar desde los altos del Hotel Mora todos los muebles y todo lo que en él había, dejando desde luego en la ruina a una pobre viuda que se mantenía con el arrendameinto de los cuartos del dicho hotel. En seguida quemaron porque sí, la casa de Don Teodoro Montero, que vive aquí en el Hotel Londres, después siguieron con la Admon. de Rentas, en seguida con el acto que nos conmovió hasta derramar lágrimas por la acción tan villana que fue cometida, quemando la casa de una Sra. Vda. del Dr. Ramírez, pues nos consta a todos los vecinos de Cuautla, que esta Sra. tiene una gran familia que al morir su esposo fue la unica herencia que como patrimonio para sus hijos y su esposa dejara este Señor, que los únicos males que hizo, fue durante su vida, curar gratis a los pobres, darles las medicinas de balde y

hasta regalarles dinero para sus alimentos. Esto nos ha conmovido y puede Ud. dirigirse a esta Sra. que vive en Cuautla para que le diga sus quejas.

Todas estas casas que relato, eran saqueadas antes de incendiarlas, pues los revolucionaríos dejaban al pueblo que saquearan. Siguieron después con la casa de comercio La Propaganda, después con el Hotel Providencia por el simple hecho de que eran españoles los dueños, cuando que Ud. siempre ha protegido a los extrangeros que en nada tiene que meterse con estas cosas; siguieron después con la tienda de abarrrotes de Don Félix Díaz, pobre español que después de incendiada su casa, fue víctima de martiríos terribles, habiéndolo llevado descalzo, por un pedregal hasta la presencia del Gral. Zapata, sin que bastaran para impedir estas villanías las imploraciones de su esposa que próxima a dar luz, iba entre los muchísimos prisioneros, tanto mexicanos como extranjeros que fueron llevados de la misma manera ante la presencia del General, el que ordenaba por lo pronto que se quedaran allí para ser fusilados. A las madres, las hermanas, las esposas, los hijos que iban a implorar piedad para aquellos tan desgraciados, en vez de ser oídos eran maltratadas y sacadas de su presencia. Esos cuadros capaces de conmover a un más criminal no tuvieron eco en los corazones de los jefes revolucionarios.

Después incendiaron el Hotel Francés, de una Sra. Bornacini, francesa de nacionalidad, residente aquí en el Restaurant Sylvain, Avenida 16 de Septiembre. Allí los heridos federales estaban curándose y vivos aún fueron quemados aquellos infelices, no después de haber saqueado hasta unos pescaditos que había allí en una fuente y las macetas y plantas del jardín. Siguieron después con la casa de un Sr. Lucio Montero que durante su vida, pues ha muerto ya, fue un amigo de su pueblo por quien siempre se interesó para que adelantara, dejando a la pobre viuda en la calle completamente, no sin haber pasado las vejaciones que sufrieron ella y sus hijas en el Cuartel General cuando fueron a implorar por uno de sus hijos que se encontraba en el Cuartel General para ser fusilado.

Siguieron con la Escuela de Niñas, que el único mal que cometía era permitir que en ella se instruyeran las niñas de la población, siguieron después con el palacio municipal, uno de los edificios más bonitos de la ciudad, y es curioso consignar que mientras se quemaba los revolucionaríos hacían blanco en la carátula del reloj público del mismo palacio."

107. Sánchez Lamego, *Época maderista*, 1: 196–99, 251–52, 255–56.

108. Report of military attaché Girard Sturtevant, 17 May 1911, Box 1885, MID, RG 165, NA. This confession finishes demolishing the myth that the Ciudad Juárez accords were premature because the Federal Army had not yet been defeated. Troncoso helped substantiate this myth in the last page of his book (see note 93). The myth became very popular among army officers like Victoriano Huerta and contributed to gather support for his coup. An echo of the myth appears even in Knight, *Mexican Revolucion*, 1:463–464. Of course, Madero himself, in what at the moment seemed like a masterful political maneuver, fed the myth with disastrous results when he stated "El Ejército Federal no ha sido vencido; fue vencido el dictador," *El tiempo*, 20 July 1911.

109. Garner, *Porfirio Díaz*, p. 220.

Chapter 6

1. Honoré de Balzac, *Maximes et pensées de Napoléon*, p. 76 (author's translation).

2. Stanley R. Ross, *Francisco I. Madero, Apostle of Mexican Democracy* (New York: Columbia University Press, 1955), pp. 185–187; Héctor Aguilar Camín, *La frontera nómada: Sonora y la Revolución Mexicana* (Mexico City: Siglo Veintuno, 1985), pp. 164–207, 221–232.

3. Report of military attaché Girard Sturtevant, 31 July 1911, Military Intelligence Division (henceforth MID), Box 1885, Record Group (henceforth RG) 165, National Archives, College Park, Maryland (henceforth NA).

4. "Detalle general del ejército, enero de 1912 , no. 1049, Fondo Revolución, Archivo General de la Nación, Mexico City. Although the budgeted strength of the army under Porfirio Díaz was also 29,000, the real figure was closer to 14,000.

5. For Cuautla, see note 106 in chapter 5.

6. "Conditions in Mexico and Considerations Attending Armed Intervention," 16 February 1912, MID, Box 1885, RG 165, NA.

7. Arturo Langle Ramírez, *Huerta contra Zapata: Una campaña desigual* (Mexico City: UNAM, 1981), pp. 17, 109, 113; Michael C. Meyer, *Huerta: A Political Portrait* (Lincoln: University of Nebraska Press, 1972), pp. 19–22.

8. Langle Ramírez, *Huerta contra Zapata*, pp. 19, 70, 102, 109–114; Miguel A. Sánchez Lamego, *Historia militar de la revolución mexicana en la época maderista*, 3 vols. (Mexico City: Instituto Nacional de Estudios Históricos de la Revolución Mexicana, 1976–1977), 2: 31–32; Report of military attaché Girard Sturtevant, 26 August 1911, MID, Box 1885, RG 165, NA. Captain Sturtevant accompanied Huerta during the first six days of the campaign and continued to follow the operation closely. Captain Sturtevant was merely fulfilling the duty of military attachés to report combat engagements. However, some authors mention his presence in a very sinister sounding way implying that ulterior U.S. motives were at play. Pineda Gómez, *La irrupción zapatista*, p. 164 goes so far as to make him a member of the General Staff of Huerta.

9. Huerta to President De la Barra, Jojutla, 13 September 1911, Langle Ramírez, *Huerta contra Zapata*, p. 102.

10. Peter V. N. Henderson, *Félix Díaz, the Porfirians, and the Mexican Revolution* (Lincoln: University of Nebraska Press, 1981), pp. 37–39.

11. Francisco Pineda Gómez, *La irrupción zapatista, 1911* (Mexico City: Era, 1997), p. 158.

12. Langle Ramírez, *Huerta contra Zapata*, p. 79.

13. Chargé Dearing to Secretary of State (henceforth SofS), 21 August 1911, 812.00/2299, RG 59, NA.

14. Pineda Gómez, *La irrupción zapatista*, pp. 155, 169, 175; Samuel Brunk, *Emiliano Zapata* (Albuquerque: University of New Mexico Press, 1995), p. 42; Ross, *Madero*, pp. 188–197. "Opinion prevalent among officers that Madero as private citizen has been presumptuous and a marplot." Telegram of 23 August 1911, 812.00/2304, RG 59, NA.

15. John Womack, *Zapata and the Mexican Revolution* (New York: Vintage Books, 1968), pp. 120–121; Brunk, *Zapata*, pp. 58–59; Pineda Gómez, *Irrupción zapatista*, p. 152; Sánchez Lamego, *Época maderista*, 2: 34–36.

16. Huerta to President De la Barra, Jojutla, 13 September 1911, Langle Ramírez, *Huerta contra Zapata*, p. 103.

17. Isidro Fabela ed., *Documentos históricos de la Revolución Mexicana* (henceforth *DHRM*), 28 vols. (Mexico City: Fondo de Cultura Económica and Editorial Jus, 1960–1976), 6: 62–74 reproduces major press articles.

18. Sánchez Lamego, *Época maderista*, 2:36–37; Langle Ramírez, *Huerta Contra Zapata*, pp. 58, 113. Ross, *Madero*, pp. 200–202. Madero in his letter of 2 November 1911, Fabela, *DHRM*, 6: 218–220, blamed Huerta for the military failure of the campaign against Zapata. Madero, who was increasingly losing even the most elemental political skills, was capable of one of the basest of maneuvers, as this letter shows. After he had delayed the launch of the offensive in August and then removed Huerta from command in October, Madero turned around and blamed Huerta for the failure of the offensive. By this accusation, Madero dropped down to the level of Secretary of Treasury José Limantour, who after years of constantly fighting to reduce the budgets and numbers of the Federal Army, then in his memoirs turned around and held the army responsible for not being able to put down the revolt against Porfirio Díaz. The accusation of Madero has also shaped the standard accounts of Huerta's campaign. Instead of admitting that Madero saved Zapata, the recall of Huerta is not mentioned and the Zapatista counteroffensive of late October is cited as proof that Huerta had failed miserably. In spite of the easy availability of the Langle Ramírez book, the Huerta campaign is barely noted as the necessary prelude to the Zapatista counteroffensive, see Ross, *Madero*, pp. 199–200 and Pineda Gómez, *La irrupción zapatista*, p. 177.

Subsequently the investigation of the War Committee of the Mexican Chamber of Deputies and press accusations exposed Madero's meddling in the Morelos campaign, Henderson, *Félix Díaz*, p. 45. From these very solid grounds it was only a small step to reach the wrong conclusion that the Federal Army had not been defeated during the revolt against Porfirio Díaz, see note 108 in chapter 5. Both the myth that the Federal Army had not been defeated and the fact that Madero had saved Zapata fed comfortably into the larger myth of the "iron hand " as the only possible solution to Mexico's disturbances, see Alan Knight, *The Mexican Revolution*, 2 vols. (Lincoln: University of Nebraska Press, 1990), 1: 385, 472.

19. Report of military attaché Girard Sturtevant, 27 October 1911, MID, Box 1885, RG 165, NA; Sánchez Lamego, *Época maderista*, 2: 60–62; Fabela, *DHRM*, 21: 28–33. Pineda Gómez, *La irrupción zapatista*, pp. 182–184 followed Womack, *Zapata*, p. 123 in giving the wrong dates for the attacks near Mexico City.

20. Womack, *Zapata*, pp. 157–158; Knight, *Mexican Revolution*, 1: 468; Brunk, *Zapata*, p. 73.

21. Womack, *Zapata*, pp. 400–404; Knight, *Mexican Revolution*,

1: 309. See Womack, *passim* for the traditional view of Zapata as the selfless leader who sacrificed all to fight for his people's land. Savage reprisals, looting, brigandage, and the rape and kidnapping of women remained standard operating practice for the Zapatistas in later years; See David G. LaFrance, *Revolution in Mexico's Heartland: Politics, War, and State Building in Puebla, 1913–1920* (Wilmington, DE: Scholarly Resources, 2003), pp. 67–68.

22. Knight, *Mexican Revolution*, I: 304–308, 310–311; Brunk, *Zapata*, pp. 32, 43, 65, 267 note 65, 269 n. 35; Brunk enriches but does not displace Knight's portrayal of Zapata.

23. Charles C. Cumberland, *Mexican Revolution: Genesis under Madero* (Austin: University of Texas Press, 1952), pp. 166–68.

24. W. Dirk Raat, *Revoltosos: Mexico's Rebels in the United States, 1903–1923* (College Station: Texas A&M University Press, 1981), pp. 243–45; Knight, *Mexican Revolution*, I: 251–254.

25. Cumberland, *Genesis under Madero*, pp. 189–190; Michael C. Meyer, *Mexican Rebel: Pascual Orozco and the Mexican Revolution, 1910–1915* (Lincoln: University of Nebraska Press, 1967), pp. 45–46.

26. Francisco R. Aldama, *La revolución en el estado de Chihuahua*, 2 vols. (Mexico: Instituto Nacional de Estudios Históricos de la Revolución Mexicana, 1964–1965), I: 239–41; William H. Beezley, *Insurgent Governor: Abraham González and the Mexican Revolution in Chihuahua* (Lincoln: University of Nebraska Press, 1973), pp. 94–95, 133–36. Villa said Madero offered him 25,000 (a truer reflection of his military worth in the revolt) but that he accepted only 10,000; see Martín Luis Guzmán, *Memorias de Pancho Villa* (Mexico City: Editorial Porrúa, 1984), pp. 62, 75.

27. Friedrich Katz, *The Life and Times of Pancho Villa* (Stanford: Stanford University Press, 1998), pp. 147–49. Because of his very hectic career, the willingness of Pancho Villa to return to civilian life has often been overlooked. Villa thus shared this rare trait with his nemesis, Álvaro Obregón; indeed, the two profoundly different men shared a striking number of similarities.

28. Beezley, *Governor González*, pp. 82, 94–95.

29. Meyer, *Orozco*, pp. 39–41; Aldama, *La revolución en el estado de Chihuahua*, I: 244–46.

30. Meyer, *Orozco*, pp. 46–47; Aldama, *La revolución en el estado de Chihuahua*, I: 276–82; Conrado Gimeno, *La canalla roja: notas acerca del movimiento sedicioso* (El Paso, Texas, n.p., 1912), pp. 14–15; Juan Figueroa Domenech, *Veinte meses de anarquía* (Mexico: n. p., 1913), pp. 88, 90, 145, 149; Knight, *Mexican Revolution*, I: 297–300; Ricardo García Granados, *Historia de México; desde la restauración de la república en 1867 hasta la caída de Huerta*, 2 vols. (Mexico: Editorial Jus, 1956): 2: 275.

31. Gonzalo González Ramírez, *Manifiestos políticos, 1892–1912* (Mexico: Fondo de Cultura Económica, 1957), pp. 558–563; Douglas W. Richmond, *Venustiano Carranza's Nationalist Struggle, 1893–1920* (Lincoln: University of Nebraska Press, 1983), p. 40.

32. Meyer, *Orozco*, pp. 50–52, 59–60; Knight, *Mexican Revolution*, I: 294; Consul Marion Letcher to SofS, Chihuahua, 7 March 1912, 812.00/3183, RG 59, NA; Guzmán, *Memorias de Pancho Villa*, pp. 68–69.

33. González Ramírez, *Manifiestos políticos, 1892–1912*, p. 541; Fabela, *DHRM*, 7:172–78.

34. González Ramírez, *Manifiestos 1892–1912*, pp. 540–546; Meyer, *Orozco*, pp. 62–66 and pp. 138–147 for an English translation of the "Pacto de la Empacadora." See also Knight, *Mexican Revolution*, I: 295–296.

35. Gimeno, *La canalla roja*, pp. 14–15; Consul Marion Letcher to SofS, Chihuahua City, 19 April 1912, 812.00/3730, RG 59, NA; Meyer, *Orozco*, pp. 67–69; Knight, *Mexican Revolution*, I: 301; Ramón Puente, *Pascual Orozco y la revuelta de Chihuahua* (Mexico: Eusebio Gómez de la Puente, editor-librero, 1912), pp. 82–84, 92–93. This last book, although hostile to Orozco, is a pleasure to read, and its analysis of Orozco's personality frequently rings true.

36. Consul Marion Letcher to SofS, Chihuahua, 20 February 1912, 812.00/2931, RG 59, NA.

37. "A los buenos mexicanos" by Inés Salazar, Braulio Hernández, and Emilio T. Campa, Chihuahua, 8 March 1912, 812.00/3561, RG 59, NA. See also, Meyer, *Orozco*, pp. 68–69. For the brief national popularity of Orozco in 1911, see Knight, *Mexican Revolution*, I: 289–290.

38. Raat, *Revoltosos*, pp. 245–248; Meyer, *Orozco*, pp. 70–71.

39. Sánchez Lamego, *Época maderista*, 3: 50–51; Knight, *Mexican Revolution*, I:321–322.

40. Figueroa Domenech, *Veinte meses de anarquía*, pp. 99, 103; "Notes on the Progress of the Revolution in the State of Chihuahua," March 1912, 812.00/3525, RG 59, NA; Almada, *Revolución en Chihuahua*, I: 316; García Granados, *Historia*, 2: 278–279.

41. The Military Attaché claimed that "there was no dynamite on the wild engine," Captain W. A. Burnside, "Encounter between the forces of Gen. Salas and Pascual Orozco," 30 March 1912, Box 1885, MID, RG 165, NA.

42. Meyer, *Orozco*, pp. 71–73; Figueroa Domenech, *Veinte meses de anarquía*, pp. 99–103; Almada, *Revolución en Chihuahua*, 1: 317–318; Hector Ribot, *La revolución de 1912* (Mexico: Imprenta Calle de Humboldt, 1912), pp. 39–43; Sánchez Lamego, *Época maderista*, 3: 52–54.

43. Figueroa Domenech, *Veinte meses de anarquía*, pp. 104–108, 118–119; Almada, *Revolución en Chihuahua*, 1: 318–319; Sánchez Lamego, *Época maderista*, 3: 55–56. Ambassador Henry Lane Wilson was among those who fell prey to the panic when he learned that eight wagons full of wounded soldiers had arrived in Mexico City. Without any direct information he predicted that "Torreón may be evacuated," see his telegram of 27 March 1912, 812.00/3402, RG 59, NA. Sánchez Lamego, *Época maderista*, 3:54, evaluated the outcome perceptively: "Las bajas sufridas por los federales parece que ascendieron al 9% del efectivo total de la División, por lo que no puede considerarse a esta batalla como un desastre."

44. Meyer, *Orozco*, pp. 73–75; Raat, *Revoltosos*, p. 248.

45. Report to the Parral & Durango Railroad Company, Parral, 8 April 1912, 812.00/3735, RG 59, NA; Sánchez Lamego, *Época maderista*, 3:56–58; Figueroa Domenech, *Veinte meses de anarquía*, p. 120; Guzmán, *Memorias de Pancho Villa*, pp. 68–73.

46. Report to the Parral & Durango Railroad Company, Parral, 8 April 1912, 812.00/3735, RG 59, NA.

47. Cumberland, *Genesis under Madero*, p. 196; Meyer, *Huerta*, p. 34; Knight, *Mexican Revolution*, I: 323, 325.

48. Juan José Tablada, *Historia de la campaña de la División del Norte* (Mexico: Imprenta del Gobierno Federal, 1913), 27–28; Figueroa Domenech, *Veinte meses de anarquía*, pp. 108–109, 122; Meyer, *Huerta*, pp. 34–35; Knight, *Mexican Revolution*, 1: 330.

49. Figueroa Domenech, *Veinte meses de anarquía*, p. 124; Victoriano Huerta to Francisco I. Madero, Torreón, 18 April 1912, in Fabela, *DHRM*, 7:320–23; García Granados, *Historia*, 2: 290–291. Knight, *Mexican Revolution*, 1: 325, 327 also points out that delay favored Huerta's campaign.

50. Sánchez Lamego, *Época maderista*, 3:58–59; Report of Manuel Cepeda, Cuatro Ciénegas, 15 May 1912, Venustiano Carranza Papers, folder 1, CONDUMEX, Mexico City, Mexico (henceforth AVC); García Granados, *Historia*, 2: 291.

51. Sánchez Lamego, *Época maderista*, 3:59–60.

52. Report of Manuel Cepeda, Cuatro Ciénegas, 15 May 1912, folder 1, AVC.

53. G.C. Carothers to American Consul, Torreón, 28 April 1912, 812.00/3826, RG 59, NA; Figueroa Domenech, *Veinte meses de anarquía*, p. 125–126.

54. Sánchez Lamego, *Época maderista*, 3:61–62; Figueroa Domenech, *Veinte meses de anarquía*, p. 125; Guzmán, *Memorias de Pancho Villa*, pp. 76–77.

55. Tablada, *División del Norte*, pp. 30–35; Figueroa Domenech, *Veinte meses de anarquía*, p. 126; Guzmán, *Memorias de Pancho Villa*, pp. 81–82.

56. Sánchez Lamego, *Época maderista*, 3:62–70; Figueroa Domenech, *Veinte meses de anarquía*, pp. 138–140; Thedore Hamm to SofS, 18 May 1912, Durango, Mexico, 812.00/4079, RG 59, NA.

57. Tablada, *División del Norte*, pp. 34–46; Figueroa Domenech, *Veinte meses de anarquía*, pp. 133–134; "Notes and Observations on the progress of the revolution," Chihuahua, 28 June 1912, in Gene Z. Hanrahan, *Documents on the Mexican Revolution* 8 vols. (Salisbury, NC: Documentary Publications, 1976–1983), 7: 99–100.

58. Tablada, *División del Norte*, pp. 43–51; Figueroa Domenech, *Veinte meses de anarquía*, pp. 136–138; "Informe revolucionario," 28 May 1912, Fabela, *DHRM*, 7:416; Meyer, *Orozco*, p. 82. Villa misrepresented this battle in Guzmán, *Memorias de Pancho Villa*, pp. 82–83 and unfairly criticized Huerta.

59. Tablada, *División del Norte*, pp. 61–62, 65; Figueroa Domenech, *Veinte meses de anarquía*, pp. 146–147, who states the mine destroyed a water car, while Consul Fletcher in Harahan, *Documents on the Mexican Revolution*, 7: 124 claims the mine exploded under a coal hopper. As early as 11 April, Madero had received warnings about powerful mines, Doc. 1648, Box 63, Francisco Madero Presidential Records, Archivo General de la Nación, Mexico City.

60. Captain W. A. Burnside, "Encounter at Bachincha," 24 July 1912, Box 1886, MID, NA; Tablada, *División del Norte*, pp. 68–71; Figueroa Domenech, *Veinte meses de anarquía*, pp. 150–151.

61. Marion Fletcher to SofS, Chihuahua, 29 August 1912, Hanrahan, *Documents on the Mexican Revolution*, 7:125–134; Figueroa Domenech, *Veinte meses de anarquía*, pp. 151; Knight, *Mexican Revolution*, 1: 331.

62. Telegram from U.S. Consul, 14 July 1912, Hanrahan, *Documents on the Mexican Revolution*, 7: 113; Alexander V. Dye to SofS, Douglas, Arizona, 31 July 1912, 812.00/4566, RG 59, NA; Sánchez Lamego, *Época maderista*, 3: 83.

63. Fabela, *DHRM*, 9: 114–119, 14: 68–73, 249–250; Sánchez Lamego, *Época maderista*, 3: 86–90; Meyer, *Orozco*, p. 87.

64. Fabela, *DHRM*, 8: 140–143, 156–158; Sánchez Lamego, *Época maderista*, 3: 91–99.

65. Manifesto of June 1912, in Fabela, *DHRM*, 7:494–95; Telegram of Colonel Edgar Steever, 14 July 1912, 812.00/4420, RG 59, NA; some of the information in Steever's telegram came almost verbatim from a telegram of the *comisario* in Naco, which is printed in Fabela, *DHRM*, 8:41–42. Alexander V. Dye to SofS, Doublas, Arizona, 8 August 1912, 812.00/4615, RG 59, NA; E. L. Bisset to Secretary of the Navy, Guaymas, Sonora, 4 September 1912, 812.00/4887, RG 59, NA.

66. Consul Thomas Edwards to SofS, Ciudad Juárez, 21 August 1912, 812.00/4715, RG 59, NA.

67. Aguilar Camín, *La frontera nómada*, pp. 212–214, 221, 237–239; Luis Hostetter to SofS, Hermosillo, 16 September 1912, 812.00/5070, RG 59, NA; Knight, *Mexican Revolution*, 1:328.

68. Feliciano Hill, *Biografía y vida militar del General Álvaro Obregón* (Hermosillo: Imprenta de M. F. Romo, 1914), pp. 5–6; Aguilar Camín, *La frontera nómada*, p. 243; Álvaro Obregón, *Ocho mil kilómetros en campaña*, 2 vols. (Mexico: Editorial Valle de México, 1988) 1: 36–49. This is a facsimile edition of the book published originally in 1917.

69. "Political Conditions in Northeastern Sonora," 18 September 1912, 812.00/5058, RG 59, NA; Obregón, *Ocho mil kilómetros*, 1:50–52; Sánchez Lamego, *Época maderista*, 3: 139–140.

70. Aguilar Camín, *La frontera nómada*, pp. 245–246; Obregón, *Ocho mil kilómetros*, 1: 52–57; Sánchez Lamego, *Época maderista*, 3: 110–111.

71. José María Maytorena, *Informe ante la XXIII legislatura* (Hermosillo: Imprenta del Estado, 1912), pp. 6–8; Report of Consul E. de la Sierra, Naco, Arizona, 22 January 1913, Fabela, *DHRM*, 8: 357; Aguilar Camín, *La frontera nómada*, p. 247.

72. Marion Letcher to SofS, Hanrahan, *Documents on the Mexican Revolution*, 7: 149–160; Sánchez Lamego, *Época maderista*, 3: 91.

73. Knight, *Mexican Revolution*, 1: 333, 382–383, 386–387. For the rampant banditry, see *Ibid.*, 1:352–367.

74. Cumberland, *Genesis under Madero*, pp. 202–204; Knight, *Mexican Revolution*, 1:474–476; Sánchez Lamego, *Época maderista*, 3:168–79; Henderson, *Félix Díaz*, pp. 50–63. The passivity of Félix Díaz and the strong opposition of the Mexican navy contributed decisively to the collapse of the revolt.

75. Aguilar Camín, *La frontera nómada*, pp. 265–268; Beezley, *Governor Gonzalez*, pp. 145–46; Knight, *Mexican Revolution*, 1: 458–459, 478–479; Richmond, *Carranza*, pp. 40–41.

76. Montgomery Schuyler to SofS, Mexico, 14 December 1912, 812.00/5728, RG 59, NA.

77. Cumberland, *Genesis under Madero*, pp. 206–207; Meyer, *Huerta*, pp. 44, 47; Knight, *Mexican Revolution*, 1: 473–474.

78. Meyer, *Huerta*, pp. 45–48; Knight, *Mexican Revolution*, 1: 480–481; Henderson, *Félix Díaz*, p. 70. Scholars have not devoted attention to the timing of the coup. The need to act before Woodrow Wilson took office seems to have been the trigger for unleashing the coup.

79. Sánchez Lamego, *Época maderista*, 3:187; Knight, *Mexican Revolution*, 1: 482–483; Henderson, *Félix Díaz*, pp. 73–74; Ross, *Madero*, pp. 282–285; Robert L. Scheina, *Latin America's Wars: The Age of the Professional Soldier 1900–2001* (Washington, D.C.: Brassey's, 2003), p. 17.

80. Meyer, *Huerta*, pp. 49–50; Cumberland, *Genesis under Madero*, pp. 49–50.

81. Sánchez Lamego, *Época maderista*, 3:189.

82. Henderson, *Félix Díaz*, pp. 75–76; Sánchez Lamego, *Época maderista*, 3: 188.

83. Meyer, *Huerta*, pp. 57–60; Knight, *Mexican Revolution*, 1: 483–487; Henderson, *Félix Díaz*, pp. 78–80.

84. Meyer, *Huerta*, pp. 61–67. Other than his biographer Meyer in his chapter 8, few other historians have dared present a more complete picture of Huerta; the majority of scholars have remained quite comfortable with the simplistic view of a savage and brutal reactionary; see Raat, *Revoltosos*, pp. 253–54.

85. Meyer, *Huerta*, pp. 69–82 has the most detailed scholarly discussion of the events surrounding the murders; Henderson, *Félix Díaz*, pp. 81–85 perceptively reviews the evidence.

Chapter 7

1. John R. Silliman to Secretary of State (henceforth SofS), 25 November 1913, 812.00/10050, Record Group (henceforth RG) 59, National Archives, Washington, D.C. (henceforth NA). The capitals are in the original.

2. Charles C. Cumberland, *Mexican Revolution: The Constitutionalist Years* (Austin: University of Texas Press, 1972), pp. 15–16; Michael C. Meyer, *Huerta: A Political Portrait* (Lincoln: University of Nebraska Press, 1972), pp. 64–68.

3. Juan Barragán Rodríguez, *Historia del ejército y de la revolución constitucionalista*, 3 vols. (Mexico: Instituto Nacional de Estudios Históricos de la Revolución Mexicana, 1985–1986), 1: 63–66; Mark T. Gilderhus, "Carranza and the Decision to Revolt, 1913," *The Americas* 25(1976): 299.

4. Cumberland, *Mexican Revolution*, pp. 16–19; Barragán, *Historia del ejército*, 1: 68, 72, 94–95, 98; Miguel A. Sánchez Lamego, *Historia militar de la revolución constitucionalista*, 5 vols. (Mexico: Instituto Nacional de Estudios Históricos de la Revolución Mexicana, 1956–1960) 1: 35–36, 39; Douglas W. Richmond, *Venustiano Carranza's Nationalist Struggle, 1893–1920* (Lincoln: University of Nebraska Press, 1983), pp. 44–45. I categorically reject the interpretation (originated in Huerta's propaganda) that Carranza really wanted to negotiate his recognition of Huerta in exchange for favors. The military preparations, the available evidence on negotiations, and Carranza's proverbial intransigence once he had made his mind up are all consistent with the account in these paragraphs.

5. Gilderhus, "Decision to Revolt," p, 307; Barragán, *Historia del ejército*, 1: 69–71. The self-appointed murderers of Abraham González were trying to curry favor Huerta. Rábago had merely sent the prisoner to Mexico City in response to a direct order from Huerta, but in the minds of many, including Pancho Villa, the general was responsible for the killing. See William H. Beezley, *Insurgent Governor: Abraham González and the Mexican Revolution in Chihuahua* (Lincoln: University of Nebraska Press, 1973), pp. 159–162.

6. Sánchez Lamego, *Historia militar*, 1: 39–49.

7. John R. Silliman to SofS, Saltillo, 31 March 1913, 812.00/7023, RG 59, NA.

8. Philip E. Holland to SofS, Saltillo, 25 March 1913, 812.00/7023, RG 59, NA.

9. *Ibid.; El ataque a la ciudad de Saltillo*, broadside dated 26 March 1913, 812.00/10937, RG 59, NA.

10. Sánchez Lamego, *Historia militar*, 1: 51–52; Cumberland, *Mexican Revolution*, pp. 77–78, 276–279; Richmond, *Carranza*, pp. 50–51, 71.

11. Sánchez Lamego, *Historia militar*, 1: 69–74.

12. Francisco R. Almada, *La revolución en el estado de Chihuahua*, 2 vols. (Mexico: Instituto Nacional de Estudios Históricos de la Revolución Mexicana, 1964–1965), 2:26–28; Michael C. Meyer, *Mexican Rebel: Pascual Orozco and the Mexican Revolution, 1910–1915* (Lincoln: University of Nebraska Press, 1967), pp. 96–100, 103; Samuel Brunk, *Emiliano Zapata: Revolution and Betrayal* (Albuquerque: University of New Mexico Press, 1995), pp. 82–89.

13. Álvaro Obregón, *Ocho mil kilómetros en campaña*, 2 vols. (Mexico: Editorial del Valle de México, 1988), 1: 61. For this paragraph, see also, Isidro Fabela, ed., *Documentos históricos de la Revolución Mexicana* (henceforth *DHRM*), 28 vols. (Mexico:Fondo de Cultura Económica, 1960–1976), 9:49–54, and Linda B. Hall, *Álvaro Obregón, Power and Revolution in Mexico, 1911–1920* (College Station: Texas A & M University Press, 1981), pp. 40–43. The fullest discussion is in Héctor Aguilar Camín, *La Frontera nómada: Sonora y la Revolución Mexicana* (Mexico: Siglo XXI, 1985), pp. 269–286.

14. Obregón, *Ocho mil kilómetros*, 1: 64.

15. Thomas Bowman to SofS, Nogales, 5 March 1913, 812.00/6612 RG 59, NA. Aguilar Camín, *Frontera nómada*, p. 287 first revealed the existence of this proposal. The Spanish text has not surfaced, but an English translation exists: "Hermosillo, March 4, 9:30 p.m. At this moment general meeting has just terminated between Governor Pesqueira, representatives of the Chambers of Commerce of Hermosillo and Guaymas, members of the State Legislature and Maderista chiefs. After lengthy discussions an agreement was arrived at whereby the State would maintain peace under the following conditions which will be made known to the Federal Government: 1. That the Federal Government will respect absolutely the sovereignty of the State. 2. That no federal troops shall be mobilized in direction of this State. 3. That all federal troops at present in the state of Sonora shall be retired. 4. That the Federal Government shall remit necessary funds to pay the irregular forces belonging to the State and which depend directly of the Executive. THE MAT-

TER OF RECOGNIZING THE CENTRAL GOVERNMENT WILL
BE DISCUSSED AFTERWARDS [capitals in the original] "Situation
on the West Coast of Mexico,"13 March 1913, 812.00/6974, RG 59,
NA. This crucial telegram should be read in conjunction with those
in Fabela, *DHRM*, 9:54–60.

16. Consul Simpich to SofS, Nogales, 11 March 1913, 812.00/6638,
RG 59, NA; Sánchez Lamego, *Historia militar*, 1:98–99. Obregón
with at least 2000 men needed 200,000 cartridges for an assault on
Guaymas at the rate of 100 cartridges per man. The number of 100
if anything was too low, because the soldiers were most reluctant to
enter into combat unless they carried at least 120 cartridges and
also knew that boxes with reserve cartridges were available. To escape the heavy weight of so much lead, the men ideally wanted to
carry no more than 50 cartridges and dumped the rest on their female companions, the *soldaderas*, who usually struggled under the
burden of bandoleers full of cartridges.

17. Aguilar Camín, *Frontera nómada*, p. 295 ignores the above
analysis and instead turns the intelligence reports around to try to
argue that because of the low morale of the federal troops, the rebel
leaders of Sonora committed a blunder by not attacking Guaymas.
In a surprising turn, on p. 296 the book then explains that the need
for customs revenue overrode the military justification for an attack
on Guaymas, when in reality both military and financial reasons
made mandatory the advance to the northern border. *Frontera nómada* is an attack on Obregón and Calles, and its use of code words
and double meanings shows that it forms part of an extensive liter-
ature designed to drive the PRI (*Partido Revolucionario Institutional*) from power. Although camouflaged with a scholarly apparatus, *Frontera nómada* is in the tradition of the delightful to read
partisan attacks, most notably José María Maytorena, *Algunas verdades sobre el General Álvaro Obregón* (Los Angeles: n.p., 1919).

18. Thomas Bowman to SofS, Nogales, 16 March 1913, 812.00/
6792, RG 59, NA; Obregón, *Ocho mil kilómetros*, 1:65–66, 69–77;
Sánchez Lamego, *Historia militar*, 1: 109–114.

19. In an interview he granted to the press after the battle of
Naco, General Ojeda blamed his defeat on the abandonment of key
posts by the Yaquis. Although some Indians may have fled during
the attack, the decisive desertion occurred on 18 March, weeks before the battle; see Commanding General, Southern Department, to
SofS, Fort Sam Houston, 19 March 1913, 812.00/6773, RG 59, NA.

20. Obregón, *Ocho mil kilómetros*, 1: 77–83; Simpich to SofS, 23
March 1913, 812.00/6834, RG 59, NA; Sánchez Lamego, *Historia
militar*, 1: 120, 122, 125–126.

21. Obregón, *Ocho mil kilómetros*, 1: 84–88; Sánchez Lamego,
Historia militar, 1: 124–128.

22. Obregón, *Ocho mil kilómetros*, 1: 89–99; Sánchez Lamego,
Historia militar, 1: 132–138.

23. Aguilera Camín, *Frontera nómada*, pp. 300–303, 308–319;
Cumberland, *Mexican Revolution*, p. 340.

24. Sánchez Lamego, *Historia militar*, 1:154–156; Obregón, *Ocho
mil kilómetros*, 1:102–105.

25. Report of U.S.S. *California*, 6 June 1913, Guaymas,
812.00/7814, RG 59, NA; Sánchez Lamego, *Historia militar*, 1:157–
162; Obregón, *Ocho mil kilómetros*, 1:105–110. The retreat turned
into a flight: "The general in command Barrón to effect his escape,
left his sword, epaulettes, cap, and personal baggage on the field."
Louis Hostetter to SofS, 13 May 1913, Hermosillo, 812.00/7542, RG
59, NA.

26. "The death losses of the troops did not exceed 100, this
[Obregón and Cabral] explain by stating that their men fought in
open order and were not massed together." Louis Hostetter to SofS,
17 May 1913, Hermosillo, 812.00/7608, RG 59, NA; Sánchez Lamego,
Historia militar, 1:162–164; Obregón, *Ocho mil kilómetros*, 1:110–113.

27. Report of U.S.S. *California*, 6 June 1913, Guaymas, 812.00/
7814, RG 59, NA.

28. Sánchez Lamego, *Historia militar*, 1:164–170; Obregón, *Ocho
mil kilómetros*, 1:113–115.

29. Report of U.S.S. *California*, 6 June 1913, Guaymas,
812.00/7814, RG 59, NA.

30. Among the booty was "28,000 pesos and all camp outfit of the
officers and men, even their clothing, private correspondence, in fact
they left everything they had." Louis Hostetter to SofS, 17 July 1913,
Hermosillo, Sonora, 812.00/8134, RG 59, NA; Obregón, *Ocho mil
kilómetros*, 1:115–125; Sánchez Lamego, *Historia militar*, 1: 176–186.

31. Obregón, *Ocho mil kilómetros*, 1: 100, 127, 132, 134, 169;
Sánchez Lamego, *Historia militar*, 1: 187–194.

32. Hall, *Obregón*, pp. 45–52.

33. Barragán, *Historia del ejército*, 1:185; Sánchez Lamego, *Historia militar*, 1:56; Cumberland, *Mexican Revolution*, p. 74; Ricardo
García Granados, *Historia de México; desde la restauración de la

república en 1867 hasta la caída de Huerta, 2 vols. (Mexico: Editorial Jus, 1956), 2: 391–392.

34. Lucio Blanco to Venustiano Carranza, 28 May 1913, carpeta
3, Papers of Venustiano Carranza, CONDUMEX, Mexico City
(henceforth AVC).

35. Venustiano Carranza to Lucio Blanco, Piedras Negras, 3 June
1913, carpeta 3, AVC; "Report on the Battle Ended the 4th inst."
Matamoros, 7 June 1913, 812.00/7755, RG 59, NA; Sánchez Lamego,
Historia militar, 1:91–96.

36. *Revista de Zacatecas*, 15 June 1913, no. 111. Because the Huerta
government kept out of the press any adverse news, periodicals are
generally useless for tracing military campaigns, but this issue of the
Revista de Zacatecas was published while Huerta officials, including
the censors, were absent.

37. Sánchez Lamego, *Historia militar*, 3: 9–11, 25; Barragán, *Historia del ejército*, 1:154–155; García Granados, *Historia de México*, 2:
384–385.

38. Telegram of Consul Theodore Hamm, 5 June 1913, 812.00/
7733, RG 59, NA.

39. "Diary of political events Durango consular district," by
Consul Theodore Hamm, 27 June 1913, 812.00/8449, RG 59, NA.
Perhaps the active participation of so many female looters intimidated the men who did not commit sexual excesses: "Department's
undated telegram relative to ravishing women in Durango just received. Except in very few isolated cases nothing of the sort occurred. Life and honor were respected much better than anticipated." Theodore Hamm to SofS, 25 August 1913, 812.00/8582, RG
59, NA.

40. Barragán, *Historia del ejército*, 1: 159.

41. Sánchez Lamego, *Historia militar*, 3: 25–40; Barragán, *Historia del ejército*, 1: 188–191.

42. "Report of general conditions along the Mexican border,"
no. 23, 29 August 1913, 812.00/8670, RG 59, NA.

43. "Report of general conditions along the Mexican border,"
no. 30, 16 October 1913, 812.00/9335, RG 59, NA.

44. Barragán, *Historia del ejército*, 1:248–249; Cumberland, *Mexican Revolution*, p. 46.

45. "Report of [...] attack on Monterrey," 31 October 1913,
812.00/9658, RG 59, NA.

46. Broadside of Pablo González, Guemez, Tamaulipas, 14 November 1913, Legajo 789, Archivo de Manuel W. González, CON-
DUMEX, Mexico City (henceforth MWG); "Report of [...] attack
on Monterrey," 31 October 1913, 812.00/9658 and "Experiences of
an American during the actions in and near Monterrey," 31 October 1913, 812.00/10306, RG 59, NA.

47. *El correo de Saltillo*, 28 October 1913; Barragán, *Historia del
ejército*, 1: 257–258.

48. Higinio Aguilar to Secretary of War, Ciudad Victoria, 14 November 1913, carpeta 6, MWG; Barragán, *Historia del ejército*, 1:
289–291, 695–697; Cumberland, *Mexican Revolution*, pp. 51–53.

49. Sánchez Lamego, *Historia militar*, 3: 163–171.

50. Barragán, *Historia del ejército*, 1: 292–294, 298–301; Sánchez
Lamego, *Historia militar*, 3:176–182; Cumberland, *Mexican Revolution*, p. 112.

51. Report of Salvador Mercado, Chihuahua, 18 May 1913, in
Sánchez Lamego, *Historia militar*, 2: 159–161; Almada, *Revolución
en Chihuahua*, 2: 32–33. Rábago became the governor of Tamaulipas and was in charge of the defense of Ciudad Victoria when that
city fell into rebel hands on 18 November. The antipathy Huerta felt
for General Rábago demoralized him and destroyed the effective-
ness of one of the rare aggressive commanders in the Federal Army.

52. Friedrich Katz, *The Life and Times of Pancho Villa* (Stanford:
University Press, 1998), pp. 205–206.

53. Report of Salvador Mercado, Chihuahua, 18 May 1913, in
Sánchez Lamego, *Historia militar*, 2: 161; Almada, *Revolución en
Chihuahua*, 2:34; Guzmán, *Memorias de Pancho Villa*, (Mexico City:
Editorial Porrúa, 1984), pp. 115–118; Luis and Adrián Aguirre Be-
navides, *Las grandes batallas de la División del Norte* (Mexico, Edi-
torial Diana, 1964), pp. 23–24; Katz, *Villa*, pp. 209–210, 212.

54. J. M. Amador to Juan Sánchez Azcona, El Paso, 6 October
1913, carpeta 4, AVC; Almada, *Revolución en Chihuahua*, 2:40–42;
Guzmán, *Memorias de Pancho Villa*, pp. 121–122; Aguirre, *Las
grandes batallas*, pp. 24–28; Federico Cervantes, *Francisco Villa y la
revolución* (Mexico: Instituto de Estudios Históricos de la Revolución Mexicana, 1985), p. 56.

55. Almada, *Revolución en Chihuahua*, 2:35–36; Meyer, *Orozco*,
pp. 104–105; Katz, *Villa*, pp. 213, 215.

56. "Conditions prevailing in Torreón from September 25 to October 11," 812.00/9658, and John R. Silliman to SofS, Saltillo, 16 October 1913, 812.00/9555, and "Report of Consulate's Courrier," 5

November 1913, 812.00/10022, RG 59, NA; Guzmán, *Memorias de Pancho Villa*, pp. 124–127; Aguirre, *Las grandes batallas*, pp. 29–45.

57. Katz, *Villa*, pp. 217–218; Guzmán, *Memorias de Pancho Villa*, pp. 127–128.

58. Barragán, *Historia del ejército*, 1: 266–267.

59. "Federal defeat at Torreón and occupation that city by rebels and reported early advance of revolutionists to attack Chihuahua in force is causing alarm among Federals here amounting almost to a panic." Marion Letcher to SofS, Chihuahua, 10 October 1913, 812.00/9162, RG 59, NA.

60. Evor Thord-Gray, *Gringo Rebel: Mexico 1913–1914* (Coral Gables, University of Miami Press, 1960), p. 67.

61. Aguirre, *Las grandes batallas*, pp. 46–52; Guzmán, *Memorias de Pancho Villa*, pp. 134–135.

62. Almada, *Revolución en Chihuahua*, 2: 49.

63. Meyer, *Orozco*, pp. 105–106.

64. "Report of general conditions along the Mexican border," 13 November 1913, 812.00/9947, RG 59, NA.

65. Aguirre, *Las grandes batallas*, pp. 53–69; Guzmán, *Memorias de Pancho Villa*, pp. 136–140; Almada, *Revolución en Chihuahua*, 2: 49–50.

66. "Report of general conditions along the Mexican border," 13 November 1913, 812.00/9947, RG 59, NA.

67. Thord-Gray, *Gringo Rebel*, p. 37.

68. *Ibid.*, p. 43. This book is the most insightful account of the whole battle; however, because he wrote decades after the event, I have relied for details and for the hours on reports and telegrams written shortly after or in some cases as the battle was unfolding.

69. Guzmán, *Memorias de Pancho Villa*, 145–148; Almada, *Revolución en Chihuahua*, 2: 51–53.

70. Almada, *Revolución en Chihuahua*, 2: 53–57; Barragán, *Historia del ejército*, 1: 269–270, 272; Aguirre, *Las grandes batallas*, pp. 70–73. Not surprisingly, Villa did not remember the battle the same way in Guzmán, *Memorias de Pancho Villa*, pp. 148–150. Besides the many inconsistencies in the version of Villa, his immense appreciation for Maclovio Herrera was a tacit admission of who had won this battle. Although since the days of John Reed many have described Villa as a military genius, whatever claim he has to military fame rests exclusively on what he did at Tierra Blanca against a federal commander who had broken almost every principle of war. Otherwise, hurling overwhelming numbers of men against the opponent remained the essential tactic in all his major battles.

71. Meyer, *Orozco*, pp. 106–107; M.E. Diebold to Secretary of War, El Paso, 22 December 1913, in Fabela, *DHRM*, 14: 418–423; *El noticioso* (Monterrey), 5 January 1914; Aguirre, *Las grandes batallas*, pp. 76–77.

72. For Meyer's criticicism of Mercado for not withdrawing to Torreón, see *Orozco*, p. 108.

73. Marion Letcher to SofS, Chihuahua City, 21 February 1914, 812.00/11043, RG 59, NA; Almada, *Revolución en Chihuahua*, 2: 58–61; Sánchez Lamego, *Historia militar*, 5:12–13.

74. Aguirre, *Las grandes batallas*, pp. 77–85; Sánchez Lamego, *Historia militar*, 3: 253–259; Almada, *Revolución en Chihuahua*, 2: 71–74; Guzmán, *Memorias de Pancho Villa*, 157–161; Cervantes, *Villa*, p. 85.

75. Pablo González to Venustiano Carranza, Matamoros, 12 January 1914 and Carranza to González, Navojoa, 14 January 1914, Carpeta 8, MWG; American Vice Consul to SofS, Ciudad Porfirio Díaz, 13 February 1914, 812.00/10899, RG 59, NA.

76. "Diary of Political Events, Durango Consular District, Installment #17," 16 December 1913, 812.00/10406, RG 59, NA.

77. Theodore Hamm, "Recent Military Movements about Torreón," 13 April 1914, 812.00/11706, RG 59, NA; Sánchez Lamego, *Historia militar*, 5: 14, 16, 22–25, 28.

78. U.S. Department of State, *Papers Relating to the Foreign Relations of the United States, 1914*, (Washington, D.C.: Government Printing Office, 1922), pp. 446–448.

79. George C. Carothers to SofS, El Paso, 10 February 1914, 812.00/10903, RG 59, NA.

80. Sánchez Lamego, *Historia militar*, 5:45–57; Theodore Hamm, "Recent Military Movements about Torreón," 13 April 1914, 812.00/11706, RG 59, NA; George Philip, ed., *British Documents on Foreign Affairs*, Part II, Series D, *Latin America 1914–1939*, 20 vols. (Bethesda, Md.: University Publications of Ameria, 1989–1992), 2: 36–37; Aguirre, *Las grandes batallas*, 86–123; Guzmán, *Memorias de Pancho Villa*, 193, 204–205, 220–221.

81. Sánchez Lamego, *Historia militar*, 5:59–75; Guzmán, *Memorias de Pancho Villa*, 234, 236, 238–240, 242–244; Aguirre, *Las grandes batallas*, 133–136. U.S. Consul Theodore Hamm reported the existence of considerable friction between generals Velasco and

Joaquín Maass "as to who was entitled to assume supreme command, with the resulting lack of cooperation and coordination of movements, which later cost the federal arms dear" 19 April 1914, 812.00/11703, an accusation repeated in Robert E. Quirk, *The Mexican Revolution, 1914–1915: The Convention of Aguascalientes* (Bloomington: Indiana University Press, 1960), pp. 25–26, and in Cumberland, *Mexican Revolution*, pp. 117–118. The extremely meticulous Sánchez Lamego does not mention this rivalry and reports that the second highest ranking officer was General Francisco Romero. The U.S. consul has the dates and other details wrong, but even without these obvious flaws, I still would have followed Sánchez Lamego. Personal rivalry would have been the perfect excuse to cover up embarrassing defects, but Miguel S. Ramos, *Un Soldado: Gral. José Refugio Velasco* (Mexico: Ediciones Oasis, 1960), does not mention it. Ignacio Muñoz, *Verdad y mito de la revolución mexicana*, 3 vols. (Mexico: Ediciones Populares, 1960–1962), 2: 179, 276–277 reports violent recriminations *after* the retreat to Saltillo, and garbled reports of those disputes probably influenced the consul's report.

82. Felipe Ángeles to Venustiano Carranza, 15 April 1914, San Pedro de las Colonias, in Barragán, *Historia del ejército*, 1:431.

83. Pablo González to Venustiano Carranza, 8 February 1914, carpeta 10, MWG. The reports about the kindness and weakness of González reached Villa, who used them as arguments in his disputes with Carranza, see Villa to Carranza, 30 May 1914, in Barragán, *Historia del ejército*, 1:431.

84. Sánchez Lamego, *Historia militar*, 5: 79, 92–104; Barragán, *Historia del ejército*, 1:471, 744–753; Cumberland, *Mexican Revolution*, pp. 119–120.

85. Supervising Inspector to Commissioner-General of Immigration, El Paso, Texas, 28 April 1914, 812.00/11806, RG 59, NA. A rebel agent reported "el pueblo del lado americano profundamente indignado hecho salvaje" Melquíades García to Isidro Fabela, 24 April 1914 in Fabela, *DHRM*, 2:62. According to Cumberland, *Mexican Revolution*, p. 120, the order to destroy came from Mexico City. That author sees indications that the Huerta regime had adopted "a modified scorched-earth policy." *Ibid.* In reality, the rest of the cases of destruction of buildings occured when federal troops were trying to make their escape from rebel attacks. At Piedras Niegras, "This consulate has received reliable information that General Guajardo had orders to evacuate [...] and burn the town as was perpetrated at Nuevo Laredo but declined to do so." American Vice Consul to SofS, 29 April 1914, 812.00/11808, RG 59, NA. A few days later the Carrancistas arrived and defeated the Federal garrison at Piedras Negras, but General Guajardo, who fled wounded into the mountains, never gave the order to destroy that town. In any case, no copy of the order imposing a scorched-earth policy has surfaced when its implementation required many messages to the scattered units. See also Alan Knight, *Mexican Revolution*, 2 vols (Lincoln: University of Nebraska Press, 1990), 2: 145, 164, 560n.954. Federal commanders could have ignored the scorched-earth order, but independent of whether the order was ever issued or repealed, at Nuevo Laredo the troops taking out their frustrations on civilian property clearly exposed the decay of the Federal Army.

86. Robert E. Quirk, *An Affair of Honor: Woodrow Wilson and the Occupation of Veracruz* (New York: Norton, 1967), pp. 89–92; Clarence C. Clendenen, *Blood on the Border: The United States Army and the Mexican Irregulars* (New York: Macmillan, 1969), pp. 158–161; Lester D. Langley, *The Banana Wars: United States Intervention in the Caribbean, 1898–1934*, 2nd. ed. (Wilmington, DE: Scholarly Resources, 2002), pp. 85–95.

87. George C. Carothers to SofS, 23 April 1914, El Paso, Texas, 812.00/11654, RG 59, NA. This part of the telegram appears published accurately in U.S. Department of State, *Papers 1914*, p. 485.

88. Quirk, *An Affair of Honor*, pp. 107–113, Langley, *Banana Wars*, pp. 97–101.

89. George Carothers to SofS, El Paso, 9 April 1914, 812.00/11461, RG 59, NA; Katz, *Villa*, pp. 336–338; David G. LaFrance, *Revolution in Mexico's Heartland: Politics, War, and State Building in Puebla 1913–1920* (Wilmington, DE: Scholarly Resources, 2003), p. 44; García Granados, *Historia de México*, 2: 418–419.

90. Guzmán, *Memorias de Pancho Villa*, pp. 250–251; Katz, *Villa*, pp. 343–344.

91. Sánchez Lamego, *Historia militar*, 5: 169–178; Barragán, *Historia del ejército*, 1: 474–475, 754–757.

92. Cervantes, *Villa*, pp. 139–141; Sánchez Lamego, *Historia militar*, 5:114–123; Guzmán, *Memorias de Pancho Villa*, pp. 253–257.

93. Sergio Candelas Villalba, *La batalla de Zacatecas* (Zacatecas: Gobierno del Estado, 1989), pp. 65–69. The events surrounding the break between the two men figure prominently in both contempo-

rary and scholarly accounts. For the most recent rendering, see Katz, *Villa*, pp. 343–348.

94. Sánchez Lamego, *Historia militar*, 5: 249–257; Aguirre, *Las grandes batallas*, pp. 156–164, 172–179; Guzmán, *Memorias de Pancho Villa*, pp. 304, 307–308, 317; Meyer, *Orozco*, p. 113; Candelas Villalba, *La batalla de Zacatecas*, pp. 79–108; Cumberland, *Mexican Revolution*, pp. 134, 136–137. The inability of the Huerta regime to reinforce or to recall the small garrison doomed Zacatecas. The revolutionary accounts want to inflate the number of federal troops to 12,000, *Ibid.*, pp. 71, 158, but such a high figure deprives the rebels of the three-to-one superiority they needed to guarantee a victory against a heavily fortified objective. Muñoz solves the problem by pitting 36,000 Villistas against 10,500 federals in *Verdad y mito*, 2: 209, 213, but he overestimates the original garrison and the reinforcements from San Luis Potosí, *Ibid.*, 2: 184, 189, and he mistakenly corrects another source confirming the 5,000 figure, 2:274. Muñoz was only a captain in the Federal Army who wrote many years after the event from memory. I have preferred to follow Sánchez Lamego who painstakingly lists each of the units in the original garrison and in the reinforcements.

95. Candelas Villalba, *La batalla de Zacatecas*, pp. 104–105. His men had enjoyed a day of looting when Villa finally stopped the rampage, Guzmán, *Memorias de Pancho Villa*, p. 318.

96. Katz, *Villa*, pp. 354–356; Guzmán, *Memorias de Pancho Villa*, pp. 324, 328. John F. Chalkley, *Zach Lamar Cobb: El Paso Collector of Customs and Intelligence during the Mexican Revolution 1913–1918* (El Paso: Texas Western Press, 1998), pp. 24–26 conclusively demonstrates that Villa could import U.S. coal freely in 1914 unlike in late 1915. Villa's sudden retreat from the drive to Mexico City was consistent with his traditional Chihuahua regionalism and was an early indication of his hesitation to grasp for national power.

97. Obregón, *Ocho mil kilómetros*, pp. 136–138, 152, 160, 173, 182–184, 201; Hall, *Obregón*, pp. 45–52.

98. Obregón, *Ocho mil kilómetros*, pp. 203–204, 209, 216.

99. Sánchez Lamego, *Historia militar*, 5: 279–291; Obregón, *Ocho mil kilómetros*, pp. 230–237.

100. Meyer, *Huerta*, pp. 208–211; Barragán, *Historia del ejército*, 1: 576–578.

Chapter 8

1. Marion Letcher to Secretary of State (henceforth SofS), Chihuahua, 21 February 1914, 812.00/11043, RG 59, NA. For other extracts from Letcher, see, Frederick Katz, *The Life and Times of Pancho Villa* (Stanford: Stanford University Press, 1998), p. 866n8.

2. Robert E. Quirk, *The Mexican Revolution, 1914–1915: The Convention of Aguascalientes* (Bloomington: University of Indiana Press, 1960), pp. 41–42; Martín Luis Guzmán, *Memorias de Pancho Villa* (Mexico: Editorial Porrúa, 1984), pp. 330–334. See the text of the Torreón agreement in Luis and Adrián Aguirre Benavides, *Las grandes batallas de la División del Norte al mando de Pancho Villa* (Mexico City: Editorial Diana, 1964), pp. 180–186.

3. Katz, *Villa*, pp. 356–357; Isidro Fabela, ed., *Documentos históricos de la Revolución Mexicana* (henceforth *DHRM*), 28 vols. (Mexico City: Fondo de Cultura Económica and Editorial Jus, 1960–1976), 15: 136–148; Guzmán, *Memorias de Pancho Villa*, pp. 358, 459–460.

4. Álvaro Obregón, *Ocho mil kilómetros en campaña*, 2 vols. (Mexico: Editorial del Valle de México, 1988), 1: 266–272; Guzmán, *Memorias de Pancho Villa*, pp. 357–360.

5. Obregón, *Ocho mil kilómetros*, 1: 272–275; "Delivery of Mexican Federal soldiers," Ciudad Porfirio Díaz, 28 September 1914, 812.00/13370, RG 59, NA.

6. Perhaps thinking he was safe after he had retired from the army in January 1914, Antonio Rábago did not leave Mexico City in time. In a vain attempt to placate Villa who needed a scapegoat to avenge the death of governor Abraham González, the Carrancistas arrested and handed over Rábago. After a drumhead court-martial in Chihuahua presided over by Villa, the former federal general was executed next to thieves; See *New York Times* 13 September 1914.

7. Richmond, *Carranza*, pp. 54–55, 77–78; Katz, *Villa*, pp. 445–446; Obregón, *Ocho mil kilómetros*, 1: 300–301; Ignacio Muñoz, *Verdad y mito de la revolución mexicana*, 3 vols. (Mexico: Ediciones Populares, 1960–1962). 2: 217, 221–223; Fabela, *DHRM*, 15: 154–155, 160–161; David G. LaFrance, *Revolution in Mexico's Heartland: Politics, War, and Sate Building in Puebla, 1913–1920* (Wilmington, DE: Scholarly Resources, 2003), pp. 48–49. In perhaps the only exception, in Colima 17 federal officers were executed in the hands of particularly vengeful revolutionaries; See George Philip, ed., *British*

Documents on Foreign Affairs: Reports and Papers from the Foreign Office Confidential Print Part II, Series D *Latin America 1914–1939*, 20 vols. (Bethesda, Md.: University Publications of America, 1989–1992), 2:75–76.

8. Obregón, *Ocho mil kilómetros*, 1: 274–283; Philip, *British Documents on Foreign Affairs*, 2:38–39.

9. Alfonso Taracena, *La verdadera revolución mexicana. Tercera etapa 1914 a 1915* (Mexico: Editorial Jus, 1972), pp. 21–22; Fabela, *DHRM*, 21: 86–95, 100–116; Richmond, *Carranza*, pp. 62–63; John Womack, Jr., *Zapata and the Mexican Revolution* (New York: Vintage Books, 1968), pp. 194, 197–212; Samuel Brunk, *Emiliano Zapata: Revolution and Betrayal in Mexico* (Albuquerque: University of New Mexico Press, 1995), pp. 113–114, 117–119.

10. Héctor Aguilar Camín, *La frontera nómada: Sonora y la Revolución Mexicana* (Mexico: Siglo XXI, 1985), pp. 398–410; Fabela, *DHRM*, 14: 100–105, 15: 110–117, 133–135; Guzmán, *Memorias de Pancho Villa*, p. 375; Katz, *Villa*, pp. 360–361.

11. U.S. Consul Louis Hostetter, "Conditions in Sonora," 26 July 1914, 812.00/12720, RG 59, NA. See also for this paragraph, Obregón, *Ocho mil kilómetros*, 1: 252, 259, 262–263.

12. U.S. Consul Louis Hostetter, "Conditions in Sonora," 26 July 1914, 812.00/12720, RG 59, NA. See also for this paragraph, Obregón, *Ocho mil kilómetros*, 1: 252, 259, 262–263.

13. U.S. Consul Louis Hostetter, "Conditions in Sonora," 26 July 1914, 812.00/12720, RG 59, NA. See also for this paragraph, Obregón, *Ocho mil kilómetros*, 1: 252, 259, 262–263.

14. U.S. Consul Louis Hostetter, "Conditions in Sonora," 26 July 1914, 812.00/12720, RG 59, NA. See also for this paragraph, Obregón, *Ocho mil kilómetros*, 1: 252, 259, 262–263.

15. Fabela, *DHRM*, 15:151–153.

16. Telegram of U.S. Consul Simpich, 9 September 1914, 812.00/13137, RG 59, NA. See also for this paragraph, Obregón, *Ocho mil kilómetros*, 1: 280–298.

17. *New York Times*, 11 September 1914; Linda B. Hall, "The Mexican Revolution and the Crisis in Naco: 1914–1915," *Journal of the West* 16(October 1977): 29.

18. Obregón, *Ocho mil kilómetros*, 1: 325–329; Guzmán, *Memorias de Pancho Villa*, pp. 402–403.

19. Fabela, *DHRM*, 15: 177–190; Guzmán, *Memorias de Pancho Villa*, pp. 402–412; Juan Barragán Rodríguez, *Historia del ejército y de la revolución constitucionalista*, 3 vols. (Mexico: Instituto Nacional de Estudios Históricos de la Revolución Mexicana, 1985–1986), 2: 84. For an exhaustive scholarly analysis of this episode, see Katz, *Villa*, pp. 364–371.

20. General Antonio I. Villarreal to Carranza, Monterrey, 23 September 1914, Leg. 42, Exp. 918, Ejército Constitucionalista (henceforth EC), Museo Nacional de Antropología e Historia (henceforth MNAH), Mexico City; Guzmán, *Memorias de Pancho Villa*, p. 414; Federico Cervantes, *Francisco Villa y la Revolución* (Mexico City: Instituto Nacional de Estudios Históricos de la Revolución Mexicana, 1985), pp. 258–260.

21. Fabela, *DHRM*, 15: 192–194; Guzmán, *Memorias de Pancho Villa*, pp. 412–414.

22. Report of U.S. Consul Theodore Hamm, Durango, 27 September 1914, 812.00/13429, RG 59, NA.

23. *New York Times*, 26 September 1914; Fabela, *DHRM*, 15: 190–192; Hall, "Crisis in Naco," pp. 29–30. One account merits quoting for its own merit and to illustrate many other clashes not so well chronicled: "La batalla de Martínez fue un acto imprudente y temerario. El jefe de esa columna sacrificada heróicamente en unas cuantas horas intrépido, casi feroz, confiaba en su arrojo personal, en su valor no desmentido, en su yo, en resumen; pero el efectivo de su columna era inferior numérica y militarmente a la del enemigo y hubo sobra de fé y de entusiasmos y falta de experiencia y el yo de aquel jefe demasiado joven cayó acribillado a balazos sobre el trípié de hierro de una ametralladora.

Después la confusión, el pánico, el sálvese él que pueda; plataformas de la Cruz Roja alcanzadas por los yaquis que remataban a los heridos a culatazos, oficiales y soldados degollados con los marrazos, la caballería que vuelve grupas al galope, los infantes que huyen despavoridos encumbrando cerros." Manuel Ortigoza, *Ciento catorce días de sitio: La defensa de Naco* (Mexico: Tipografía la Carpeta, 1916), p. 4.

24. "Report of General Conditions Along the Border," No. 82, 14 October 1914, 812.00/13545, RG 59, NA.

25. Ortigoza, *Defensa de Naco*, pp. 4–16; Plutarco Elías Calles, *Informe relativo al sitio de Naco* (Mexico City: n.p. 1932), pp. 13–15, 17–18; Hall, "Crisis in Naco," pp. 30–34; Guzmán, *Memorias de Pancho Villa*, pp. 508–509, 516–18; Clarence C. Clendenen, *The United States and Pancho Villa* (Ithaca: Cornell University Press, 1961), pp. 142–143.

26. Quirk, *Convention of Aguascalientes*, pp. 87–92; Barragán, *Ejército*, 2: 94–95.

27. The fascination with the Aguascalientes Convention has continued until today, but was not shared by the British diplomat: "Attention is at present chiefly being directed upon the convention at Aguascalientes, which appears closely to resemble the parliament of monkeys described by Mr. Kipling in the *Jungle Book*. The members arrive and take their seats, but the president of the body hardly has time to announce the subject for discusson before a wrangle begins; on several occasions revolvers have been drawn, and personal encounters have taken place amidst the most high-sounding phrases concerning liberty, legality, the eyes of the nation and of the world being upon them, etc. The whole thing is a grotesque parody of a serious discussion." Philip, *British Documents on Foreign Affairs*, 2:70.

28. Barragán, *Ejército*, 2: 112–114.

29. "Weekly Report on Political Conditions at Aguascalientes," 11 November 1914, 812.00/13914, RG 59, NA; Quirk, *Convention of Aguascalientes*, p. 121; Charles Cumberland, *The Mexican Revolution: The Constitutionalist Years* (Austin: University of Texas Press, 1972), pp. 176–180.

30. Fabela, *DHRM*, 1: 393–394; Leon Canova to SofS, Zacatecas, 8 October 1914, 812.00/13518, RG 59, NA; Barragán, *Ejército*, 2: 132–133, 180, 552; Guzmán, *Memorias de Pancho Villa*, pp. 460, 476; Cervantes, *Villa*, p. 357.

31. Philip, *British Documents on Foreign Affairs*, 2:81, 85; Obregón, *Ocho mil kilómetros*, 1: 363, 366.

32. Katz, *Pancho Villa*, p. 460. See also, Cumberland, *Mexican Revolution*, pp. 185–186.

33. Guzmán, *Memorias de Pancho Villa*, pp. 491–92; Muñoz, *Verdad y mito*, 2: 295–296; Barragán, *Ejército*, 2: 212–213; Cervantes, *Villa*, p. 361, 370–371; Obregón, *Ocho mil kilómetros*, 1: 388–389; Katz, *Villa*, p. 480.

34. George Carothers to SofS, El Paso, 16 December 1914, 812.00/14061, RG 59, NA; Francisco Villa to Emiliano Zapata, 22 September 1914, 10 November 1914 in Fabela, *DHRM*, 21: 124–125, 1:391; Womack, *Zapata*, p. 222; Brunk, *Zapata*, pp. 141, 144, 172.

35. Katz, *Villa*, pp. 478–480; Guzmán, *Memorias de Pancho Villa*, pp. 491–93.

36. Taracena, *Tercera etapa*, p. 137; Cervantes, *Villa*, pp. 371–372; Miguel A. Sánchez Lamego, *Historia militar en la época de la Convención* (Mexico: Instituto Nacional de Estudios Históricos de la Revolución Mexicana, 1983), p. 90.

37. Muñoz, *Verdad y mito*, 2: 308–311, 316–321; Taracena, *Tercera etapa*, pp. 138–139; Sánchez Lamego, *Historia*, pp. 91–92; Cervantes, *Villa*, pp. 372–375; Guzmán, *Memorias de Pancho Villa*, p. 520; Antonio Villarreal to Venustiano Carranza, 14 January 1915, Carpeta 24, Archivo Venustiano Carranza, Condumex, Mexico City (henceforth AVC). The refusal of General Villarreal to provide any additional explanation for his defeat other than this very brief report contributed to his disgrace. The main accusations against General Villarreal are in Emilio Salinas, *El desastre de Ramos Arizpe: Responsabilidades que resultan* (Mexico City: n.p., 1918), pp. 24–27. Muñoz, a former federal officer who fought for Villa in the battle, also puts all the blame on Villarreal in *Verdad y mito*, 2: 326–327.

38. Barragán, *Ejército*, 2: 179–180, 255, 311–312; Katz, *Villa*, pp. 484–485.

39. Barragán, *Ejército*, 2: 135–136; Antonio Rivera de la Torre, *El Ebano: Los 72 días de su heroica defensa* (Mexico: Imprenta del Departamento de Estado Mayor, 1915), pp. 6–7; "Situation—Tampico," 3 January 1915, 812.00/14259, RG 59, NA.

40. Sánchez Lamego, *Historia*, pp. 89, 92–93.

41. Barragán, *Ejército*, 2: 255–258, 562–563.

42. Sánchez Lamego, *Historia*, pp. 95–96; Guzmán, *Memorias de Pancho Villa*, pp. 553–554; Muñoz, *Verdad y mito*, 2: 330–331.

43. "Conditions in the Ciudad Porfirio Díaz, Coahuila, Consular District," 6 February, 12 March 1915, 812.00/14372 and 14689, RG 59, NA; Serapio Aguirre to Venustiano Carranza, Piedras Negras, 15 February 1915, carpeta 27, AVC.

44. Pablo González to Venustiano Carranza, San Juan, Nuevo León, 8 February 1915, carpeta 27, AVC; Barragán, *Ejército*, 2: 312–313; Muñoz, *Verdad y mito*, 2: 330.

45. Will Davis, "Taking of and Reentrance of General Diéguez into Guadalajara," 19 January 1915, 812.00/14482, RG 59, NA; Barragán, *Ejército*, 2: 213–216.

46. Obregón, *Ocho mil kilómetros*, 1: 398; Guzmán, *Memorias de Pancho Villa*, pp. 525–527; Quirk, *Convention of Aguascalientes*, pp. 140–141; Womack, *Zapata*, pp. 222–223; Bruck, *Zapata*, p. 157; Friedrich Katz, *The Secret War in Mexico: Europe, the United States, and the Mexican Revolution* (Chicago: University of Chicago Press, 1981), pp. 124–125. Most notable among the very last to switch sides

was Lieutenant Colonel Lázaro Cárdenas, who with his 400 men joined the Carrancistas at Sonora on 28 March 1915, Barragán, *Ejército*, 2: 507–510. Because Villa was still at the height of his power, Cárdenas's defection was not motivated by opportunism or political survival, but rather reflected courage to act on inner convictions even against adverse odds. This determination of Cárdenas later proved decisive during his famous presidency of 1936–1940.

47. Obregón to Carranza, Mexico City, 13 February 1915, box 2, exp. 34, Papers of Juan Barragán (henceforth JB), Universidad Nacional Autónoma de Mexico (henceforth UNAM), Mexico City; Obregón to Plutarco Elías Calles, Mexico City, 28 February 1915, Fondo Presidentes, Exp. 1, Inv. 755, Fideicomiso Calles-Torreblanca, Mexico City; Guzmán, *Memorias de Pancho Villa*, pp. 527–528, 536.

48. Allen Wells and Gilbert M. Joseph, *Summer of Discontent, Seasons of Upheaval: Elite Politics and Rural Insurgency in Yucatan, 1876–1915* (Stanford: University Press, 1996), pp. 268–279; Barragán, *Ejército*, 2: 245.

49. Jean Meyer, "Los obreros en la Revolución Mexicana: Los Batallones Rojos," *Historia Mexicana* 21(1971): 8–13; Richmond, *Carranza*, pp. 72–74. The agreement with the workers has been reprinted many times, see for example Fabela, *DHRM*, 16:41–43.

50. Salvador Álvarado, *Mi actuación revolucionaria en Yucatán* (Mexico: Secretaría de la Defensa Nacional, 1990), pp. 21–29; Barragán, *Ejército*, 2: 231, 248–250, 253; Wells and Joseph, *Summer of Discontent*, pp. 279–285.

51. Will Davis, "Second Evacuation of Guadalajara by General Diéguez (Carrancista) and Second Peaceful Occupation of Same by General Francisco Villa," Guadalajara, 15 February 1915, 812.00/14491, RG 59, NA.

52. Amado Aguirre, *Mis memorias de campaña* (Instituto Nacional de Estudios Históricos sobre la Revolución Mexicana, 1985), pp. 149–151; Taracena, *Tercera etapa*, p. 186; Guzmán, *Memorias de Pancho Villa*, pp. 542–545; Barragán, *Ejército*, 2: 217–221.

53. Sánchez Lamego, *Historia*, p. 96; Guzmán, *Memorias de Pancho Villa*, pp. 545–547.

54. Rivera de la Torre, *Ébano*, pp. 18–19; Barragán, *Ejército*, 2: 302–303, 565–566.

55. Rivera de la Torre, *Ébano*, pp. 11–14; Francisco Rivera, *Hechos históricos de la revolución constitucionalista hasta ahora desconocidos* (Mexico: n.p., 1959), pp. 7–8.

56. Rivera de la Torre, *Ébano*, pp. 20–21, 24–26; Barragán, *Ejército*, 2: 305–306, 569, 570, 574–575, 581–582.

57. Sánchez Lamego, *Historia*, pp. 96–98; Guzmán, *Memorias de Pancho Villa*, pp. 574–575; Muñoz, *Verdad y mito*, 2: 331. Barragán, *Ejército*, 2: 309–311 increased the number of machine guns to 100, reduced the number of cartridges to 2 millions, and declined to mention the sluices; he also did not give any precise dates.

58. Sánchez Lamego, *Historia*, pp. 96, 109; Guzmán, *Memorias de Pancho Villa*, p. 592; Muñoz, *Verdad y mito*, 2: 331–332.

59. Obregón to Carranza, 12 March 1915, Caja 3, Exp. 3, JB, UNAM; Barragán, *Ejército*, 2: 585–592.

60. Diéguez to Carranza, Ciudad Guzmán, 27 March, 1, 3, 11 April 1915, Zacoalco, 1 April 1915, Leg. 15 Exp. 350, EC, MNAH; Aguirre, *Memorias*, pp. 159–180.

61. Carranza to Obregón, 26 February 1915, Caja 2, Exp. 36, and Carranza to Obregón, 22 March 1915 and reply of 23 March, Caja 3, Exp. 5, JB, UNAM; Obregón to Carranza, 4 April 1915 , Leg. 32, Exp. 720, and José Siurob to Carranza, 4 April 1915, Leg. 40, Exp. 868, EC, MNAH. The Zapatista threat was not entirely unfounded: "Reinforcements and ammunition are being sent to Obregón constantly. If he should be defeated his retreat would be almost certainly cut off by the Zapatistas. It is a wonder that they have not also cut the line as they are known to have a considerable force at Otumba." John Silliman to SofS, Veracruz, 15 April 1915, 812.00/14860, RG 59, NA.

62. Guzmán, *Memorias de Pancho Villa*, pp. 560–561.

63. Obregón to Carranza, 8 April 1915, Leg. 32, Exp. 720, and Obregón to Carranza, 9 April 1915, Leg. 40, Exp. 68, EC, MNAH; Obregón, *Ocho mil kilómetros*, 2: 484–495, 518, 520, 528; Guzmán, *Memorias de Pancho Villa*, pp. 562–571.

64. Obregon to Carranza, Celaya 11 April 1915 and reply, 12 April 1915, Caja 3, Exp. 10, JB, UNAM.

65. Obregón, *Ocho mil kilómetros*, 2: 495–516, 530–531; Guzmán, *Memorias de Pancho Villa*, pp. 586–589. An American eyewitness confirmed the huge number of Villista casualties and saw that the cadavers "were strewn on both sides of the track as far as the eye could reach," Quirk, *Convention of Aguascalientes*, p. 225.

66. Diéguez to Carranza, Guadalajara, 18 April 1915, Leg. 15, Exp. 350, EC, MNAH; Will Davis, "Second Evacuation of Guadalajara," 20 April 1915, 812.00/15039, RG 59, NA.

67. Guzmán, *Memorias de Pancho Villa*, pp. 602–604. The nar-

rative of Guzmán stops at this point, thus depriving readers and scholars of a valuable inside account. Katz has put to rest any doubts about the reliability of Guzmán, see his *Villa*, pp. 830–832.

68. Gaston Schmutz to SofS, Aguascalientes, 23, 27 April , 6 May 1915, 812.00/14949, 14968 and 15014, RG 59, NA; Obregón, *Ocho mil kilómetros*, 2: 534–536.

69. Linda B. Hall, *Álvaro Obregón: Power and Revolution in Mexico, 1911–1920* (College Station: Texas A & M Press, 1981), p. 121. The execution of General Dionisio Triana about this time probably eliminated an important source, see Guzmán, *Memorias de Pancho Villa*, pp. 594–597. Other informants later appeared to help Obregón.

70. Aaron Sáenz, "La batalla de León," *Repertorio de la Revolución*, No. 5 (1960), pp. 151–152; Cervantes, *Villa*, pp. 454–456; Obregón, *Ocho mil kilómetros*, 2: 537–546, 552.

71. Gaston Schmutz to SofS, Aguascalientes, 24 May 1915, 812.00/15103, RG 59, NA; Cervantes, *Villa*, p. 457; Obregón, *Ocho mil kilómetros*, 2: 566–572. Although the paternity of the outstanding attack plan of 22 May is unclear, it seems to be the handiwork of Felipe Ángeles. It is just the sort of brilliant and complex plan to be expected from one of the very best graduates of the Chapultepec Military Academy, and it is in keeping with the battlefield career of General Ángeles. Doubtlessly the attack plan had input from Villa, most notably the idea of two soldiers riding the same horse. Instead the attack of 1 June, a documented Villa creation, was considerably bolder but lacked the intricate brilliance of the 22 May attack. Unfortunately for the Villistas, the 22 May attack was directed against Obregón, the only Carrancista general able to rise to the challenge of the outstanding plan, but even he needed a bit of good luck as the reader can verify by rereading the details of the day's action carefully.

72. Sáenz, "Batalla de León," pp. 152–156; Taracena, *Tercera Etapa*, p. 281; Cervantes, *Villa*, pp. 458–463; Obregón, *Ocho mil kilómetros*, 2: 547–597.

73. Sáenz, "Batalla de León," pp. 156–158; Muñoz, *Verdad y mito*, 2: 379–383; Cervantes, *Villa*, pp. 463–466; Obregón, *Ocho mil kilómetros*, 2: 597–605.

74. Obregón to Carranza, Lagos, 16 June 1915, Caja 3, Exp. 19, JB, UNAM; Gaston Schmutz to SofS, Aguascalientes, 17, 22 June 1915, 812.00/15292 and 15331, RG 59, NA; Cobb to SofS, El Paso, 26 September 1915, 812.00/16300, RG 59, NA.

75. John Silliman to SofS, Veracruz, 26 April and 21 May 1915, 812.00/14933 and 15051, RG 59, NA. To explain why Zapata did so little to help Villa between December 1914 and May 1915 requires some additional analysis. The huge martial display of Villa in Mexico City had easily impressed if not awed Zapata, who with more than ample reason believed that so many cannons and men guaranteed the defeat of Carranza. At the same time, Zapata did not see a danger in Villa, who was more than happy to let Zapata rule his fiefdom unlike the centralizing Carranza. The surprising recovery of the Carrancistas caught Zapata by surprise, but by the time he tried to help Villa it was too late to save his fellow warlord.

76. Brunk, *Zapata*, pp. 143, 177.

77. Pablo González to Carranza, Tepexpam, 28 June 1915, Leg. 21, Exp. 487, EC, MNAH; Fabela, *DHRM*, 16: 147; "Political Conditions,"Tampico, 29 June 1915, 812.00/15367, RG 59, NA; Quirk, *Convention of Aguascalientes*, p. 271.

78. "Conditions in the Piedras Negras Consular District," 19 June, 31 August 1915, 812.00/15291 and 16069, RG 59, NA.

79. Obregón, *Ocho mil kilómetros*, 2: 630–651; Gaston Schmutz to SofS, Aguascalientes, 7 July 1915, 812.00/15444RG 59, NA.

80. Zach Lamar Cobb to SofS, El Paso, 14 July 1915, 812.00/15445, RG 59, NA; Quirk, *Convention of Aguascalientes*, pp. 283–284; Obregón, *Ocho mil kilómetros*, 2: 652–651; Barragán, *Ejército*, 2: 393–394.

81. Fabela, *DHRM*, 16: 196–197; Quirk, *Convention of Aguascalientes*, p. 273.

82. Obregón, *Ocho mil kilómetros*, 2: 661–685; González vainly tried to justify the needless evacuation in his report to Carranza of 19 July 1915 from Ometusco, Caja 2, Exp. 5, JB, UNAM.

83. Obregón, *Ocho mil kilómetros*, 2: 666; Barragán, 2: 395–396.

84. G.C. Carothers to SofS, El Paso, 19 July 812.00/15490, RG 59, NA.

85. Obregón, *Ocho mil kilómetros*, 2: 667, 686–687, 717.

86. Cobb to SofS, El Paso, 14 July 1915, 812.00/15445, RG 59, NA; Marion Letcher to SofS, Chihuahua, 29 September 1915, 812.00/16449, RG 59, NA; Will Davís to SofS, Guadalajara, 9 November 1915, 812.00/16835, RG 59, NA; Alan Knight, *Mexican Revolution*, 2 vols. (Lincoln: University of Nebraska Press, 1990), 2: 332–333; Katz, *Secret War*, pp. 285–286; John F. Chalkley, *Zach Lamar Cobb: El Paso Collector of Customs and Intelligence during the Mexican Rev-

olution, 1913–1918* (El Paso: Texas Western Press, 1998), pp. 36–39. Cobb, in his messages to Washington, did not want to appear too passionate in his hostility to Villa, but occasionally glimpses surface: Describing "a black record" and "seeing the criminal nature of Villa and the criminal graft of his supposedly reputable supporters, I necessarily wish that our government might […] cut short his remaining career of crime, destruction of railroads and property essential to the near establishment of order." Cobb to SofS, El Paso, 26 September 1915, 812.00/16300, RG 59, NA.

87. Obregón, *Ocho mil kilómetros*, 2: 692, 698–703. For even cruder victories the admirers of Pancho Villa called him a Napoleon, but alas for Obregón, he never received the military fame he had so rightfully earned.

88. "Military activities," Monterrey, 4 September 1915, 812.00/16133, RG 59, NA; "Conditions in the Piedras Negras Consular District," 9 September 1915, 812.00/16151, RG 59, NA.

89. Obregón, *Ocho mil kilómetros*, 2: 703–712, 716.

90. George Carothers to SofS, El Paso, 9 October 1915, 812.00/16441, RG 59, NA; Villa, *Katz*, pp. 516, 523; Knight, *Mexican Revolution*, 2: 333; Will Davis, "Why many Villa Troops are keeping up the fight," Guadalajara, 9 November 1915, 812.00/16835, RG 59, NA. General Diéguez gradually moderated his extreme anticlerical practices, but not before he had aroused considerable Catholics opposition to Carranza in the state of Jalisco. The Catholic hostility in Jalisco to the Carrancistas foreshadowed the later Cristero Revolt of 1926–1929; See chapter 10.

91. The logistical nightmare of having to route all the units via Ciudad Juárez forced Villa to relent slightly from his original plan. He allowed General Juan Banderas to proceed south west from Chihuahua to northern Sinaloa, where Villa would join him for the victorious southern drive to Tepic and Jalisco. The two thousand men of Banderas made the grueling crossing of the Sierra Madre to El Fuerte, but their invasion of Sinaloa failed, and they retreated into southern Sonora to await the victorious Villa. After the collapse of the Villista invasion of Sonora, Banderas and the remnants of his force surrendered on 5 January 1916. Marion Letcher to SofS, Chihuahua, 7 October 1915, 812.00/16524, RG 59, NA; Francisco R. Almada, *La revolución en el estado de Chihuahua*, 2 vols. (Mexico: Instituto Nacional de Estudios Históricos de la Revolución Mexicana, 1964–1965), 2: 295; Knight, *Mexican Revolution*, 2: 334.

92. Obregón to Carranza, Torreón, 3 November 1915, Caja 3, Exp. 30, JB, UNAM; Frederick Funston to Adjutant General, Fort Sam Houston, 25 September 1915, 812.00/16310, RG 59, NA; Katz, *Villa*, pp. 516–518; Chalkley, *Cobb*, pp. 37–46. Technically but not politically Agua Prieta was the nearest rail head. Because the track passed through U.S. territory, Washington's approval was needed to move troops.

93. Louis Hostetter, "Maytorena's Government and the Yaquis," Hermosillo, 30 September 1915, 812.00/ 16467, RG 59, NA. A Mexican hostage who escaped "claims there are held in captivity there over 150 Mexican girls and women stolen from the different towns and villages. They are being treated most shamefully, Yaquis raping them in the streets and making them serve as slaves for the Yaqui women. The Yaqui women go around in silks and satins stolen in the raids made on different stores in the state." Louis Hostetter, "Maytorena and his Yaquis" Hermosillo, 21 September 1915, 812.00/16372, RG 59, NA. Revolutionary armies abducted females frequently, and the practice was not exclusive to the Yaquis.

94. "Weekly Report on General Conditions," 7 October 1915, 812.00/16457, RG 59, NA.

95. Louis Hostetter, "Conditions in Sonora," 6 October 1915, Hermosillo, 812.00/16468, RG 59, NA. When "a Yaqui stopped a young lady on the street and hugged and kissed her and worse, she screamed and some men ran to her assistance" but the policeman "said he was very sorry but had strict orders not to interfere with the Yaquis." *Ibid*.

96. Louis Hostetter, "Conditions in Sonora," 8 October 1915, 812.00/15470, RG 59, NA.

97. Marion Letcher, "Military movements," and "Death of General Tomás Urbina," Chihuahua, 15 September 1915, 812.00/16269 and 16270, RG 59, NA; *Vida Nueva* (Chihuahua) 14 September 1915; Katz, *Villa*, pp. 519–520, 522–523; Thomas H. Naylor, "Massacre at San Pedro de la Cueva: The Significance of Pancho Villa's Disastrous Sonora Campaign," *Western Historical Quarterly*, 8(April 1977), p. 126.

98. Frederick Funston to Adjutant General, Douglas, 3 November 1914, 812.00/167277, RG 59, NA; Naylor, "Sonora Campaign," p. 128; Elizabeth Salas, *Soldaderas in the Mexican Military: Myth and History* (Austin: University of Texas Press, 1990), pp. 39, 43–44; Katz, *Villa*, p. 525. Salas uses incidents like these to conclude in p. 45 of her book that "Villa proved the most vehement hater of the

soldaderas." Neither Katz, *Villa* nor the material gathered for this book support such an extreme characterization of his view toward the *soldaderas*. He exploited them as long as they were useful and then tried to dump them when they hindered his plans for victory; this practice he followed with everything else in his army. His attitudes to women outside the army fit the classic *machista* stereotypes. Just to mention some of the glaring traits, he had the contradictory combinations of abandoned wives, excessive courtesy and generosity to females, and even boyish embarrassment.

99. C. F. Leonard, "Villa Invasion of Sonora, Oct — Nov — Dec 1915," p. 3, Military Intelligence Division (henceforth MID), Box 1818, RG 165, NA. Naylor, "Sonora Campaign," p. 127 effectively debunks the authors whose excessive imagination likened Villa's invasion "to Hannibal's crossing of the Alps" with "snow clogged passes, arctic cold, and cannibalism," when the temperature at its coldest never came within ten degrees Farenheit of freezing. The imagination of the debunked authors contributed to create the legend of Pancho Villa when they described "the terrain as resembling a lunar landscape; towering crests devoid of all veggegation must be crossed; a trail cut from solid rock climbs to dizzying heights."

100. U.S. Department of State, *Papers Relating to the Foreign Relations of the United States 1915* (Washington, D.C.: Government Printing Office, 1924), pp. 771–772, 780–782.

101. "Weekly Report of General Conditions," 28 October 1915, 812.99/16667, RG 59, NA; Frederick Funston to Adjutant General, Douglas, 2 November 1915, 812.00/16689, RG 59, NA; Leonard, "Villa Invasion," p. 1.

102. "Report of Operations," November 1915, 812.00/16843, RG 59, NA.

103. Obregón to Carranza, Torreón, 3 November 1915, Caja 3, Exp. 30, JB, UNAM.

104. "Weekly Report of General Conditions," 4 November 1915, 812.00/16752, RG 59, NA.

105. George Carothers to SofS, Doublas, 10 November 1915, 812.00/16761, RG 59, NA; Naylor, "Sonora Campaign," pp. 130–131; Leonard, "Villa Invasion," pp. 2–3; Obregón, *Ocho mil kilómetros*, 2: 725–729; Clarence C. Clendenen, *Blood on the Border: The United States Army and the Mexican Irregulars* (New York: Macmillan, 1969), pp. 187–188.

106. George Carothers to SofS, Douglas, 6 November 1915, 812.00/16732, RG 59, NA; Naylor, "Sonora Campaign," pp. 131, 133; Leonard, "Villa Invasion," pp. 3–4.

107. George Carothers to SofS, El Paso, 20 November 1915, 812.00/16831, RG 59, NA; Obregón, *Ocho mil kilómetros*, 2: 735–737. In a rare and probably unique occurrence, after the battle of Alamito all the Yaqui prisoners were executed; See Aguilar Camín, *La frontera nómada*, p. 440. No doubt this extreme reprisal was vengeance for the impunity the Yaquis had enjoyed in Hermosillo under Governor Maytorena. For the Yaquis who later submitted to the government, manpower shortages forced the generals to resume the traditional practice of incorporating them into the ranks.

108. "Weekly Report of General Conditions," No. 140, 26 November 1915, 812.00/16890, RG 59, NA.

109. Almada, *La revolución en Chihuahua*, 2: 293–294; Naylor, "Sonora Invasion," p. 134; Obregón, *Ocho mil kilómetros*, 2: 738; Clendenen, *The United States and Pancho Villa*, p. 214.

110. "Weekly Report of General Conditions," 23 December 1915, 812.00/17030, RG 59, NA; Naylor, "Sonora Invasion," pp. 134–136; Obregón, *Ocho mil kilómetros*, 2: 739–749.

111. Leonard, "Villa Invasion," p. 5.

112. Thomas Edwards to SofS, and Cobb to SofS, 12 December 1915, 812.00/16942, RG 59, NA; Leonard, "Villa Invasion," p. 5; Naylor, "Sonora Invasion," pp. 136–148.

113. Obregón, *Ocho mil kilómetros*, 2: 751–755, who in his only significant omission in his memoirs declined to mention the U.S. role and placed all the blame on the Yaquis; Clenenden, *Blood on the Border*, pp. 190–191; U.S. Department of State, *Papers 1915*, pp. 839–848. In a characteristically American attempt to gain the friendship of the natives, the American civilians in violation of Mexican prohibitions gave arms and ammunition to the Yaquis, who repaid the kindness by attacking the Americans: "They themselves have brought about the evils from which they are now suffering," *Ibid.*, p. 849.

114. "Weekly Report of General Conditions," 31 December 1915, 812.00/17048, RG 59, NA; Knight, *Mexican Revolution*, 2: 373–374; U.S. Department of State, *Papers 1915*, pp. 859–864. The U.S. Consul heartily supported the campaign against the Indians. "In my opinion, the Yaquis will continue to be a menace to American and Mexican settlers in the Yaqui valley region, until a drastic, exterminating campaign is carried out against them. They are closely al-

lied to the late Arizona Apaches, similar to the latter in temperament, mode of warfare, and cruel practices. And the commonly circulated theory that the Yaqui is on the war-path because the avaricious white man has robbed him of his ancestral hunting ground is worse than fiction." Frederick Simpich to SofS, Nogales, 21 December 1915, 812.00/17023, RG 59, NA. For the sputtering offensive against the Yaquis from 1916 to 1919 and the truces, see Aguilar Camín, *La frontera nómada*, pp. 441–446.

115. Barragán, *Ejército*, 2: 525–530, 641–657.

116. Katz, *Villa*, pp. 537–538; Message from SofS, Washington, D.C., 18 December 1915, 812.00/17020, RG 59, NA. Many of Villa's family members went to El Paso for safety, Zach Lamar Cobb to SofS, 21 December 1915, 821.00/16982, RG 59, NA, where Customs Collector Cobb received them well. Cobb's message of 20 December 1915, printed in Chalkley, *Cobb*, p. 62 contributed to the welcome the U.S. extended to Villa. Just a month earlier Cobb "has taken the stand that the Villistas should be killed off, and that we should have nothing to do with any of them." Carothers to SofS, El Paso, 22 November 1915, 812.00/16870, RG 59, NA. Determined as Cobb was to eliminate Villa as a danger in Mexico, the Customs Collector harbored no thoughts of revenge and was quite content to achieve his original goal by the exile of Villa in the United States. Cobb emerges as an official even more remarkable than Chalkley's book suggests.

117. Katz, *Villa*, pp. 547–549; Knight, *Mexican Revolution*, 2:342–343.

118. Katz, *Villa*, pp. 561–562; Knight, *Mexican Revolution*, 2: 341, 359.

119. The clearest exposition of the attack itself is in John S. D. Eisenhower, *Intervention! The United States and the Mexican Revolution, 1913–1917* (New York: W.W. Norton, 1993), pp. 217–227. For the most recent scholarly account, see Joseph A. Stout, Jr., *Border Conflict: Villistas, Carrancistas, and the Punitive Expedition 1915–1920* (Forth Worth: Texas Cristian University Press, 1999), pp. 33–39.

120. Katz, *Villa*, pp. 569–570; Knight, *Mexican Revolution*, 2: 347–348; Hall, *Obregón*, pp. 145–146, 203.

121. Katz, *Villa*, pp. 572–573; Eisenhower, *Intervention*, pp. 241–249; Knight, *Mexican Revolution*, 2: 342–343.

122. Katz, *Villa*, pp. 577–578, 584; Eisenhower, *Intervention*, pp. 270–275; 289–290. The War Department decided to prohibit shipments of arms and munitions to Mexico on 1 May; U.S. Department of State, *Papers Relating to the Foreign Relations of the United States 1916* (Washington, D.C. Government Printing Office, 1925), pp. 790–791. The other government agencies adopted the new policy: "We have of late been refusing to allow any arms or ammunition to go to the de facto Government of Mexico, or to individuals and firms in that country, and have been refusing to permit the exportation of machinery or raw materials useful in the manufacture of munitions." Division of Mexican Affairs to SofS, 7 August 1916, *Ibid.*, pp. 794–795.

123. Barragán, *Ejército*, 3: 257–260. The clearest exposition is in Eisenhower, *Intervention*, pp. 290–299. Clendenen, *Blood on the Border*, pp. 303–311 presents the perspective of the U.S. Army, and Stout, *Border Conflict*, pp. 75–90 is the most recent scholarly account.

124. Katz, *Villa*, pp. 588–589; Cervantes, *Villa*, pp. 558–559; Barragán, *Ejército*, 3: 308–309; Stout, *Border Conflict*, pp. 107–108.

125. Katz, *Villa*, pp. 601–603; Eisenhower, *Intervention*, pp. 289–290; Barragán, *Ejército*, 3: 309; Stout, *Border Conflict*, pp. 117, 125–128. Treviño tried to explain away the defeat in his official report printed in Begonia Hernández y Lazo, *Las batallas de la plaza de Chihuahua* (Mexico: UNAM, 1984), pp. 67–84. The reports of the battalion commanders confirm the failures of Treviño, see "Parte que comprende la defensa encomendada en esta plaza al 9o. Batallón de mi mando, del 21 al 27 de noviembre de 1916," and Parte of 3 December 1916 in Papers of Jacinto Treviño, Box 4, exp. 17, UNAM.

126. Katz, *Villa*, pp. 625–632; Alfonso Taracena, *La verdadera revolución mexicana. Quinta etapa 1916 a 1918* (Mexico: Editorial Jus, 1979), pp. 37–38; Barragán, *Ejército*, 3: 481–482; Cervantes, *Villa*, p. 566; Stout, *Border Conflict*, pp. 135–136.

127. Katz, *Villa*, pp. 608, 632; Salas, *Soldaderas*, pp. 46–47. She finds the accusation that the slaughter was "evidence of a primitive, bestial mind," to be "harsh." In another fit of rage, he had the the town of Namiquipa punished by having his soldiers rape the wives of the inhabitants on 5 February 1917. Rapes had been an endemic plague since 1911, but by the collective rape at Namiquipa Villa once again showed his ability to go beyond the accepted limits of brutality and savagery.

128. For a full elaboration of this convincing argument, see Katz, *Villa*, pp. 611–613.

Chapter 9

1. Quoted in William E. Alger to Secretary of State (henceforth SofS), Mazatlán, 5 April 1914, 812.00/11543, Record Group (henceforth RG) 59, National Archives, College Park, Maryland (henceforth NA).

2. Alan Knight, *Mexican Revolution*, 2 vols. (Lincoln: University of Nebraska Press, 1990), 2: 334–336, 356–360 offers a lucid overview of Villa's later activities. For brief accounts, see Joseph A. Stout, Jr., *Border Conflict: Villistas, Carrancistas, and the Punitive Expedition 1915–1920* (Fort Worth: Texas Christian University Press, 1999), pp. 134–137 and Clarence C. Clendenen, *The United States and Pancho Villa* (Ithaca: Cornell University Press, 1961), pp. 305–314. The fullest scholarly account is in Friedrich Katz, *The Life and Times of Pancho Villa* (Stanford: University Press, 1998), chs. 16–18.

3. Douglas W. Richmond, *Venustiano Carranza's Nationalist Struggle, 1893–1920* (Lincoln: University of Nebraska Press, 1983), pp. 85–88; Berta Ulloa, *La encrucijada de 1915* (Mexico: El Colegio de México, 1979), pp. 17–26, 216–222; Knight, *Mexican Revolution*, 2: 407–411.

4. Linda B. Hall, *Álvaro Obregón: Power and Revolution in Mexico, 1911–1920* (College Station: Texas A&M Press, 1981), pp. 146, 156–157; Venustiano Carranza, *Informe* (Mexico: La Editora Nacional, 1917), pp. 202–204.

5. Katz, *Villa*, pp. 290–291; Elizabeth Salas, *Soldaderas in the Mexican Military* (Austin: University of Texas Press, 1990), pp. 43–44. Until official funds became available, American officers frequently had to pay with their own money the purchases to feed their men. See Clarence C. Clendenen, *Blood on the Border, The United States Army and the Mexican Irregulars* (New York: Macmillan, 1969), p. 222.

6. American Vice-Consul to SofS, Tampico, 15 June 1915, 812.00/15303, RG 59, NA.

7. Salas, *Soldaderas*, p. 64; See also Elena Poniatowska, *Las soldaderas* (Mexico: Ediciones Era, 2000), pp. 13–15.

8. One anti-Carranza account claimed that the Carrancista army had raped 50,000 women including 200 nuns. M.A. Spellacy to Secretary of Interior, Tampico, 30 July 1915, 812.00/15931, RG 59, NA. The Carrancista soldiers claimed they always gave money to the females for sex, because otherwise the soldiers were executed if any woman denounced them for rape, see "Report on fight at La Jarita, Mexico, 12 April 1915" 812.00/14932, RG 59, NA. Because repeated testimonies confirm the view that the Carrancistas (carefully excluding those Villistas who in 1913–1914 fought under the Carracista label) were the best disciplined army throughout the war, the figure of 50,000 might be more appropriate as the total for all sides. On the rape of the nuns and their resulting maternity, detailed denunciations appeared in the press; See Taracena, *Tercera etapa*, pp. 72–76.

9. Will B. Davis to SofS, Guadalajara, 28 June 1915, 812.00/15587 and Arnold Shankiin to SofS, Mexico, 4 September 1913, 812.00/8682, RG 59, NA. The *machistas*, who strenuously opposed female officers, seemed to have exacted their revenge when the word *coronela* entered the Spanish language with the connotation of a bossy and domineering woman.

10. Poniatowska, *Soldaderas*, pp. 15–17. Estimates inferred from analysis of descriptions and from Salas, *Soldaderas*, especially pp. 41–43, 47–49, 63–64.

11. "The empty shells from all over the Republic are being sent to Mexico City to be cleaned and reloaded," Frederick Funston to Adjutant General, Washington, D.C., 8 December 1916, 812.00/20105, RG 59, NA; U.S. Department of State, *Papers Relating to the Foreign Relations of the United States 1916* (Washington, D.C.: Government Printing Office, 1925), pp. 789–794; John Womack, Jr., *Zapata and the Mexican Revolution* (New York: Vintage Books, 1968), pp. 247–248; Samuel Brunk, *Emiliano Zapata: Revolution and Betrayal* (Albuquerque: University of New Mexico Press, 1995), p. 178; David G. LaFrance, *Revolution in Mexico's Heartland: Politics, War, and State Building in Puebla 1913–1920* (Wilmington, DE: Scholarly Resources, 2003), p. 80. On 3 June 1917 General Pablo González said that Mexico urgently needed ammunition and "that the national production is of decidedly inferior quality, insufficient, and extremely costly," U.S. Department of State, *Papers Relating to the Foreign Relations of the United States 1917* (Washington, D.C.: Government Printing Office, 1926), p. 1080.

12. Héctor Aguilar Camín, *La Frontera nómada: Sonora y la revolución mexicana* (Mexico: Siglo XXI Editores, 1985), pp. 329–324.

13. "Weekly report of general conditions along Mexican border,"

July 1916, 812.00/21243, RG 59, NA; Knight, *Mexican Revolution*, 2: 457. Will B. Davis, "Youthfulness of some Mexican Soldiers," Guadalajara, 26 September 1915, 812.00/16539, RG 59, NA mentions a soldier as young as seven years.

14. Generalization drawn from many testimonies and Knight, *Mexican Revolution*, 2: 455–459.

15. Meyer, "Los batallones rojos," *Historia mexicana*, 21(1971): 12–37; Knight, *Mexican Revolution*, 2: 320–321; Richmond, *Carranza*, pp. 72–74.

16. Charles Cumberland, *Mexican Revolution: The Constitutionalist Years* (Austin: University of Texas Press, 1972), pp. 397–398.

17. Isidro Fabela, ed., *Documentos históricos de la Revolución Mexicana*, 28 vols. (Mexico: Fondo de Cultura Económica and Editorial Jus, 1960–1976), 17:265 (henceforth *DHRM*); Taracena, *Quinta etapa*, pp. 73–74, 93–94.

18. Bevan to SofS, Tampico, 14 October 1915, 812.00/16476, RG 59, NA.

19. Richmond, *Carranza*, pp. 160–164; Womack, *Zapata*, pp. 274–321; Brunk, *Zapata*, pp. 194–221.

20. Knight, *Mexican Revolution*, 2: 478, 481–483; Richmond, *Carranza*, pp. 143–147. See Cumberland, *Mexican Revolution*, pp. 364–366, 370–372 for a more optimistic view of Carranza's control of the governors.

21. Clodoveo Valenzuela and Amado Chaverri Matamoros, *Sonora y Carranza* (Mexico: Editorial Renacimiento, 1921), pp. 372–375, 396–397 summarizes some of the corruption; Juan Barragán, who never found the time to write the final volume of his history of Carranza administration, appears deeply implicated in the charges. For a scholarly analysis of the corruption, see Knight, *Mexican Revolution*, 2: 459–463.

22. Álvaro Matute, *La carrera del caudillo* (Mexico: El Colegio de México, 1980), pp. 17–19; Womack, *Zapata*, pp. 322–330; Brunk, *Zapata*, pp. 222–229.

23. Douglas, *Carranza*, pp. 229–230; Fabela, *DHRM*, 18: 265–278.

24. Cumberland, *Mexican Revolution*, pp. 401–406; Douglas, *Carranza*, pp. 231–232; Knight, *Mexican Revolution*, 2: 489–491. Unfortunately, Knight ends his chronological coverage at this point, and thus he deprived scholars of a sure guide to the complex and turbulent events of the 1920s.

25. Fabela, *DHRM*, 18: 298.

26. Matute, *La carrera*, pp. 103–104.

27. Fabela, *DHRM*, 18: 383.

28. Valenzuela y Chaverri, *Sonora y Carranza*, pp. 185–209; Fabela, *DHRM*, 18: 393–394.

29. Fabela, *DHRM*, 18: 411–413, 435–439; Matute, *La carrera*, pp. 93, 100, 102.

30. José Rentería Jimeno to Álvaro Obregón, 5 June 1920, Fondo Álvaro Obregón, Exp. 149, Fideicomiso Calles-Torreblanca, Mexico City, Mexico (henceforth FCT).

31. Note of 21 April 1920, Archivo Plutarco Elías Calles, Exp. 86, FCT; U.S. Department of State, *Papers Relating to the Foreign Relations of the United States 1920*, 3 vols. (Washington, D.C.: Government Printing Office, 1936), 3: 143–145.

32. "Recopilación de datos relacionados con la revolucion de 1920," Archivo Plutarco Elías Calles, Exp. 86, FCT.

33. Valenzuela y Chaverri, *Sonora y Carranza* pp. 267–268, 271–273; Francisco Almada, *La revolución en el estado de Chihuahua*, 2 vols. (Mexico: Instituto Nacional de Estudios Históricos de la Revolución Mexicana, 1964–1965), 2: 348–349.

34. Pablo González, *El centinela fiel del Constitucionalismo* (Saltillo: Textos de Cultura Histórico-Grafica, 1971), pp. 442–474; José C. Valadés, *La revolución mexicana*, 10 vols. (Mexico: Manuel Quesada Brandi, 1963–1967), 7: 5; Matute, *La carrera*, pp. 116–118. This last author like most scholars emphasizes the virtual absence of combat, in contrast to some of the testimony included in the text. The ineffective Carrancista responses helped create the false impression that the campaign was a victory parade. Some have gone so far as to consider the military campaign to be sham combat. The rebels acted swiftly, brilliantly maneuvered units, and showed a determination to use force to prevent the revival of the bloody campaigning of the 1913–1916 period. The rebels proved to be true disciples of the Chinese sage Sun Tzu who valued most winning a war without fighting.

35. Valenzuela y Chaverri, *Sonora y Carranza*, pp. 376–377.

36. "Evacuation of Mexico City by the Federal Government," 9 May 1920, Military Intelligence Division Files: Mexico, Record Group 165, National Archives, Washington, D.C. (henceforth MID, RG 165, NA). See also for this paragraph, Valadés, *La Revolución Mexicana*, 7: 8–10.

37. "Evacuation of Mexico City by the Federal Government," 9 May 1920, MID, RG 165, NA.

38. John W. F. Dulles, *Yesterday in Mexico* (Austin: University of Texas Press, 1961), pp. 36–38; "Evacuation of Mexico City by the Federal Government," 9 May 1920, MID, RG 165, NA. According to the British diplomat, the collapse of the regime was complete: "in the official cars of the government, as well as on the Presidential Pullman, wine and loose women played a prominent part." George Philip, ed., *British Documents on Foreign Affairs*, Part II, Series D, *Latin America, 1914–1939*, 20 vols. (Bethesda, Md.: University Publications of America, 1989–1992), 2: 197.

39. "Parte que rinde el Coronel Fortunato Tenorio," Veracruz, 20 May 1920, Fondo Álvaro Obregón, Exp. 1489, FCT; Hall, *Obregón*, pp. 244–245.

40. González, *Centinela fiel*, pp. 597–613; Dulles, *Yesterday in Mexico*, pp. 36–39; Matute, *La carrera*, pp. 122–123; Valadés, *La Revolución Mexicana*, 7: 39, 42.

41. Report from secret informant, 16 May 1920, MID, RG 165, NA.

42. Dulles, *Yesterday in Mexico*, pp. 38–39, 55–59; Matute, *La carrera*, pp. 140–143.

43. Report from secret informant, 30 May 1920, MID, RG 165, NA; Dulles, *Yesterday in Mexico*, pp. 63–64.

44. Joseph Richard Werne, "Esteban Cantú y la soberanía mexicana en Baja California," *Historia mexicana*, 30(1980): 19–20; Katz, *Villa*, p. 720; Matute, *La carrera*, p. 150; Dulles, *Yesterday in Mexico*, p. 75.

45. Katz, *Villa*, pp. 721–724.

46. Valadés, *La Revolución Mexicana*, 7: 52–53; Katz, *Villa*, pp. 725–727.

47. "Principal Factors Menacing the Obregón Administration," p. 27, 4 March 1922, MID, RG 165, NA.

48. "Informe que rinde el C. General Brigadier Abelardo L. Rodríguez, Jefe de las Operaciones Militares en el Distrito Norte de la Baja California," Mexicali, Baja California, 15 February 1922, Exp. 189, Archivo Plutarco Elías Calles, FCT; Dulles, *Yesterday in Mexico*, pp. 75–76.

49. Werne, "Cantú," *Historia mexicana* 30(1980): 21–22; U.S. Department of State, *Papers Relating to the Foreign Relations of the United States, 1920*, 3 vols. (Washington, D.C.: Government Printing Office, 1935–1936), 3: 158–160, 246.

50. William C. Burdett, "Notes on Military Situation," 11 March 1920, Ensenada, Baja California, 812.20/26, RG 59, NA.

51. "Informe que rinde el C. General Brigadier Abelardo L. Rodríguez," Mexicali, Baja California, 15 February 1922, Exp. 189, Archivo Plutarco Elías Calles, FCT; U.S. Department of State, *Papers 1920*, 3:158–160; Matute, *La carrera*, pp. 152–154; Werne, "Cantú," *Historia mexicana* 30(1980):18, 23–24.

52. Matute, *La carrera*, pp. 185–186; WGBH Boston Public Television , "Mexico," 3 parts, 1988, part 1.

53. "Principal Factors Menacing the Obregón Administration," p. 9, 4 March 1922, MID, RG 165, NA; Luis Monroy Durán, *El último caudillo* (Mexico: José Rodríguez, 1924), p. 111.

54. Randall Hansis, "The Political Strategy of Military Reform: Álvaro Obregón and Revolutionary Mexico, 1920–1924," *The Americas* 36(1979): 207; Ernest Gruening, *Mexico and Its Heritage* (New York: D. Appleton-Century, Co., 1928), pp. 144–145; Monroy Durán, *El último caudillo*, p. 104; Enrique Plasencia de la Parra, *Personajes y escenarios de la rebelión Delahuertista* (Mexico, Universidad Nacional Autónoma de México, 1998), p. 104.

55. Hansis, "Political Strategy," p. 208; Plasencia de la Parra, *Rebelión Delahuertista*, pp. 9–10, 25, 27.

56. Katz, *Villa*, pp. 652–653. For the process of "landlord recovery" see Knight, *Mexican Revolution*, 2: 464–469. The most blatant case was the gradual return of the huge landholdings of the Terrazas family, an action that gave the impression that in Chihuahua the Revolution had changed nothing; see, Katz, *Villa*, pp. 649–651, 654, 749–755 especially the last page.

57. "Revolutionary activities," 8 December 1923, MID, RG 165, NA; Plasencia de la Parra, *Rebelión Delahuertista*, p. 19; Dulles, *Yesterday in Mexico*, pp. 182–191; Philip, *Latin America, 1914–1939*, 3: 260–261, 279–281. Upon reading a Mexican press article that said "We kill because we are assassins and we fail to respect the rights of others because we are ignorant of the first rules of civilization," the British diplomat felt vindicated by the confession and with undisguised satisfaction wrote: "At last Mexicans admit that they are unfit to govern themselves." *Ibid.*, p. 282.

58. Dulles, *Yesterday in Mexico*, pp. 192–196.

59. Fidelina G. Llerenas and Jaime Tamayo, *El levantamiento delahuertista: cuatro rebeliones y cuatro jefes militares* (Guadalajara: Universidad de Guadalajara, 1995), pp. 97–106; Hansis, "Political

Strategy," p. 225; Alfonso Taracena, *Verdadera revolución, 1922–1924* (Mexico: Editorial Porrúa, 1992), pp. 226–227.

60. Hansis, "Political Strategy," pp. 221–224; Plasencia de la Parra, *Rebelión Delahuertista*, pp. 104–111; Amado Aguirre, *Mis memorias de campaña* (Mexico: Instituto Nacional de Estudios Históricos de la Revolución, 1985), pp. 336–337.

61. Jaime Tamayo and Laura P. Romero, *La rebelión descabezada: el delahuertismo en Jalisco* (Guadalajara: University of Guadalajara, 1983), p. 21 and in particular Hansis, "Political Strategy," pp. 216–219, 224, 227–228.

62. George T. Summerlin to SofS, Mexico, 7 December 1923, 812.00/26612, and John Q. Wood to SofS, Veracruz, 13 December 1923, 812.00/26648, RG 59, NA; Plasencia de la Parra, *Rebelión Delahuertista*, pp. 35–37, 47.

63. Hansis, "Political Strategy,"pp. 224–225; Monroy Durán, *El último caudillo*, p. 108; Llerenas and Tamayo, *El levantamiento delahuertista*, pp. 111–113.

64. Plasencia de la Parra, *Rebelión Delahuertista*, pp. 42–43; George T. Summerlin to Sof S, Mexico, 22 December 1923, 812.00/26727, RG 59, NA; Llerenas and Tamayo, *El levantamiento delahuertista*, pp. 126–128.

65. Plasencia de la Parra, *Rebelión Delahuertista*, pp. 48–52.

66. "Insurrección De la Huertista —1923. Datos proporcionados por el Sr. José María Moreno," Archivo Amado Aguirre, box 3, exp. 9, Universidad Nacional Autónoma de Mexico, Mexico City (henceforth UNAM).

67. General Eugenio Martínez to president, 22 December 1923 and "Revolutionary activities," 15 December 1923, MID, RG 165, NA; John Q. Wood to SofS, Veracruz, 28 December 1923, 812./00.26712, RG 59, NA; Ygnacio Urquijo, *Apuntes para la historia de México, 1910–1924* (Mexico: Tipografía Moderna, 1924), pp. 109–110; Philip, *Latin America, 1914–1939*, 3: 285–286; Monroy Durán, *El último caudillo*, pp. 121, 126, 128–129; Fernando Ramírez de Aguilar, *Desde el tren amarillo; crónicas de guerra* (Mexico: Botas, 1924), pp. 34–38.

68. Amado Aguirre to Calles, 31 December 1923, Fondo Presidentes, Transcripciones 1923–1924, FCT; "Report on travel," 22 December 1923, MID, RG 165, NA; Valadés, *La Revolución Mexicana*, 7: 303; Urquijo, *Apuntes*, p. 110.

69. Obregón to Calles, 24 January 1924, Archivo Plutarco Elías Calles, exp. 5 of Álvaro Obregón, FCT.

70. "Insurrección De la Huertista—1923. Datos proporcionados por el Sr. José María Moreno," Archivo Amado Aguirre, Box 3, exp. 9, UNAM; see also Valadés, *La Revolución Mexicana*, 7: 320–321.

71. General Espiridión Rodríguez to Joaquín Amaro, 31 January 1924, Archivo de Joaquín Amaro, Serie 02, Sub 02, FCT; Valadés, *La Revolución Mexicana*, 7: 320–322.

72. John Q. Wood to SofS, Veracruz, 28 December 1923, 812.00/26712, RG 59, NA; Monroy Durán, *El último caudillo*, pp. 135–143; Plasencia de la Parra, *Rebelión Delahuertista*, pp. 60–61, 71–72, 74, 79; Dulles, *Yesterday in Mexico*, pp. 243–246.

73. U.S. Senate, *Shipment of Arms to Mexico*, Sen. Doc. No. 104 (Washington, D.C.: Government Printing Office, 1924), pp. 2–4; Plasencia de la Parra, *Rebelión Delahuertista*, pp. 121, 143.

74. "Insurrección De la Huertista—1923. Datos proporcionados por el Sr. José María Moreno," Archivo Amado Aguirre, box 3, exp. 9, UNAM.

75. Álvaro Obregón to Plutarco E. Calles, 4 February 1924, Archivo Plutarco Elías Calles, Álvaro Obregón, exp. 5, inv. 4038, FCT.

76. Álvaro Obregón to Plutarco E. Calles, Irapuato, 3 February 1924, Fondo Presidentes, Transcripciones, exp. 13, inv. 742, FCT.

77. Memorandum of 21 April 1924, Mexico City, leg. 3/3, Fondo Fernando Torreblanca (henceforth FFT), FCT; Monroy Durán, *El último caudillo*, pp. 160, 163; Aguirre, *Memorias*, pp. 338–339.

78. Valadés in *Revolución Mexicana*, 7: 325–327, who interviewed Estrada, accepted the General's claim of a double encircling maneuver to catch and destroy Obregón´s army in crossfire. Even if the rebels completed the encircling movement successfully, such a strategy was doomed to failure because the rebel forces lacked the artillery and the ammunition to stand and fight against the government troops in the open field. Too large for the simple task of ripping up the railroad track, the forces of Estrada and Diéguez were too small for a formal battle as Palo Verde confirmed. I have followed José D. Ramírez Garrido, *El combate de Palo Verde* (Mexico: Imprenta Núñez, 1925), pp. 10–12 who could see no purpose to the raid; this last military account is one of the finest of the Mexican Revolution.

79. The original order of Amaro ordering the attack in Poncitlán is in Ramírez de Aguilar, *Desde el tren amarillo*, pp. 77–80.

80. Plutarco Elías Calles, *Correspondencia personal*, 2 vols. (Mexico: Fideicomiso Calles-Torreblanca, 1991–1993), 1: 134–135; Monroy Durán, *El último caudillo*, p. 164; Memorandum of 21 April 1924, Mexico City, leg. 3/3, FFT, FCT; General Miguel González, "Estudio de las operaciones militares sobre Ocotlán," 31 March 1924, Mexico City, leg. 2/3, FFT, FCT. This official study admitted that "fueron de poca significación las bajas causadas al enemigo" but to avoid embarrassing the government claimed that "nuestras tropas sufrieron 402 bajas, 90 de los cuales fueron muertos." George T. Summerlin to SofS, Mexico, 15 February 1924, 812.00/27029, RG 59, NA, discusses the high casualties and the partial cover-up; see also Urquijo, *Apuntes*, p. 117. The political hesitation to hold superiors accountable seriously hampered the work of the study commission, Not surprisingly, the commission's report is not as revealing at it should have been. For additional extracts of the report, see Plasencia de la Parra, *Rebelión Delahuertista*, pp. 148–149.

81. "Evacuation of Guadalajara by Revolutionists," 11 February 1924, 812.00/27033, RG 59, NA; General Miguel González, "Estudio de las operaciones militares sobre Ocotlán," 31 March 1924, Mexico City, leg. 2/3, FFT, FCT. Although this study was disappointing, it appears to have been the first formal inquiry into a single battle. The *Averigüación* on the fall of Ciudad Juárez in May 1911 was done at the request of General Juan Navarro. The Madero administration also authorized but did not request the history of Francisco P. Troncoso *Campaña de 1910 y 1911*, which analyzed the entire Chihuahua insurrection.

82. Monroy Durán, *El último caudillo*, pp. 172–177; Ramírez Garrido, *Palo Verde*, pp. 19–20; Plasencia de la Parra, *Rebelión Delahuertista*, pp. 150–151.

83. Ramírez Garrido, *Palo Verde*, pp. 20–25; Monroy Durán, *El último caudillo*, pp. 177–179.

84. Ramírez Garrido, *Palo Verde*, pp. 25–29.

85. Monroy Durán, *El último caudillo*, pp. 178–179; Ramírez Garrido, *Palo Verde*, pp. 29–32.

86. *Ibid.*, p. 30.

87. "¡Ya nos llevó la chingada! Se acabó el parque" *Ibid.*, p. 32.

88. *Ibid.*, pp. 32–25. For the battle of Palo Verde, I have preferred the critical testimony of Ramirez Garrido published shortly after the battle to the later recollections of Estrada in Valadés, *Revolución Mexicana*, 7: 328–330.

89. Juan de Dios Bonilla, *Historia marítima de Mexico* (Mexico City: Editorial Litorales, 1962), pp. 645–652; O. Gaylord Marsh to Secretary of State, Progreso, Yucatán, 19 April 1924, 812.00/27226, RG 59, NA.

90. Philip, *Latin America, 1914–1939*, 3: 322–323; John Q. Wood to SofS, Veracruz, 6 January 1925, 812.00/27493, RG 59, NA.

Chapter 10

1. Alexis de Tocqueville, *The Old Regime and the Revolution*, trans. John Bonner (New York: Harper & Brothers, 1856), p. 22. A comparison with the French original made me prefer the British translation of Henry Reeve (London: J. Murray, 1888), p. 7 for the last phrase (after "individuals").

2. Martha Beatriz Loyo Camacho, "Joaquín Amaro y el proceso de institucionalización del ejército, 1917–1931," Ph.D. Dissertation, Universidad Nacional Autómoma de México, 1998, pp. 256–257; Jean Meyer et al., *Estado y sociedad con Calles* (Mexico: El Colegio de Mexico, 1977), pp. 256–257; Úrsulo Vásquez to President Calles, 27 May 1925, Archivo de Joaquín Amaro (henceforth AJA), serie 03, sub 07, Fideicomiso Calles-Torreblanca, Mexico City (henceforth FCT).

3. Meyer et al., *Estado y sociedad*, pp. 222–223, 235–236; Ernest Gruening, *Mexico and Its Heritage* (New York: D. Appleton-Century, 1928), pp. 274–277; Jean Meyer, *La Cristiada: la Guerra de los cristeros*, 3 vols. (Mexico: Siglo XXI, 1973–1974), 1: 99; Robert L. Scheina, *Latin America's Wars: The Age of the Professional Soldier 1900–2001* (Washington, D.C.: Brassey's 2003), p. 29.

4. Arthur L. Mayer to Secretary of State (henceforth SofS), 25 April 1926, "Movement of Troops to Guaymas, Sonora," Manzanillo, Colima, 18 September 1926, and Dayle C. McDonough, 17 November 1926, 812.00/27768, 27954, and 28078, Record Group (henceforth RG) 59, National Archives, Washington, D.C (henceforth NA); Meyer, *Cristeros*, 1: 107–109; Scheina, *Age of the Professional Soldier*, p. 30; Jim Tuck, *The Holy War in Los Áltos* (Tucson: University of Arizona Press, 1982), pp. 40–45.

5. "Report on the Mayo Indian Tribe," 26 April 1920, Nogales, 812.401/2, RG 59, NA.

6. "Yaqui Indian Uprising," 21 September 1926, 2657-G-605,

Mexico, Military Intelligence Division (henceforth MID), RG 165, NA; "Yaqui Uprising," 25 September 1926, Guaymas, 812.00/27958, RG 59, NA; *El Universal* (Mexico City), 27 September 1926, contains Obregón's personal account of the incident.

7. "The Yaqui situation," 21 October 1926, Guaymas, 812.00/28020, RG 59, NA; *El Universal* (Mexico City), 27 September 1926.

8. "The Yaqui situation," 6 November 1926, Guaymas, 812.00/28054, RG 59, NA; "The situation in Sonora," 2 February 1927, Guaymas, 812.00/28221, RG 59, NA; Loyo Camacho, "Joaquín Amaro," p. 253.

9. Telegram, 23 October 1926, Guaymas, 812.00/28007, RG 59, NA.

10. Naval attaché report, 26 October 1926, 2657-g-605, Military Intelligence Division, RG 165, NA; Colonel Vicente Torres to General Joaquín Amaro, Empalme, Sonora, 21 July 1927, AJA, Serie 03, Sub 02, FCT.

11. General Eduardo G. García to General Francisco R. Manzo, 19 January 1927, Guaymas, printed in *La Tribuna* (Guaymas) 20 January 1927; James R. Sheffield to SofS, 21 January 1927, Mexico City, 812.00/28203, RG 59, NA.

12. "The situation in Sonora," 2 February 1927, Guaymas, 812.00/28221, RG 59, NA.

13. Rubén García, "El Gral. Olachea liquida el problema Yaqui en Zamahuaca," *El Legionario*, no. 130, December 1961, pp. 15–16.

14. Colonel Vicente Torres to Joaquín Amaro, Empalme, Sonora, 21 July 1927, AJA, Serie 03, Sub 02, FCT.

15. Report of Consul Herbert S. Bursley, Guaymas, 6 July 1927, 812.00/28521, RG 59, NA.

16. West-central Mexico traditionally has been the source of the majority of the Mexican immigrants coming to the United States since 1900. The Cristero revolt accelerated a migratory movement already ongoing before the Mexican Revolution. The U.S. Consul noted "the large number of applicants for immigration visas, the majority of whom come from the Los Altos district, which is the most disturbed section. Many of these state that the constant crossing and recrossing of their lands by soldiers and rebels makes it impossible to continue to work and they therefore have to abandon their properties." See "Revolutonary Situation in Jalisco,"18 February 1929, 812.00Jalisco/44, RG 59, NA. The endemic structural problems of west-central Mexico cry out for detailed historical studies.

17. James R. Sheffield to SofS, Mexico, 11 January 1927, 812.00/28170, RG 59, NA; Meyer, *Cristeros*, 1: 131–133; "Campaign against Rebels," 29 March 1927, 2657-g-605, MID, RG 165, NA; Meyer et al., *Estado y sociedad*, pp. 219–220, 230–231; Tuck, *Holy War*, pp. 44–47.

18. Report of Consul Dudley G. Dwyre, 11 April 1927, 812.00/28332, RG 59, NA.

19. Tuck, *Holy War*, pp. 62–64. In a fit of rage the priest ordered the torching after he learned that his brother had been killed in the attack. For a less harsh account see Meyer, *Cristeros*, 1: 172–173.

20. "Campaign against the Rebels," 19 July 1927, 2657-g-605, MID, RG 165, NA; Dudley G. Dwyre to SofS, Guadalajara, 7 May 1927, 812.00/28412, RG 59, NA; Meyer, *Cristeros*, 1: 163–164.

21. "General Amaro arrived in Manzanillo," 20 April 1927, 812.00/28368, RG 59, NA.

22. Vice Consul E. W. Eaton to Sof S, Manzanillo, Colima, 4 June 1927, 812.00/28461, RG 59, NA.

23. Vice Consul E. W. Eaton to Sof S, Manzanillo, Colima, 11 June 1927, 812.00/28461, RG 59, NA.

24. Vice Consul E. W. Eaton to Sof S, Manzanillo, Colima, 30 June 1927, 812.00/28540, RG 59, NA.

25. "Resumen de la situación política y militar en la República julio de 1927," Archivo Aurelio Acevedo (henceforth AAA), box 2, Universidad Autónoma Nacional de México, Mexico City (henceforth UNAM); "Prospective Transfer of Troops from Sonora," 24 June 1927, Guaymas, 812.00/28489, RG 59, NA; Loyo Camacho, "Joaquín Amaro," pp. 254–255; Meyer, *Cristeros*, 1:194–195. 179–171.

26. Roderic A. Camp, *Mexican Political Biographies, 1884–1935* (Austin: University of Texas Press, 1991), p. 108; Meyer, *Cristeros*, 3: 199–200; Tuck, *Holy War*, pp. 105–107.

27. Meyer, *Cristeros*, 1:200–203; Tuck, *Holy War*, pp. 107–108.

28. Report No. 1745 of Military Attaché, 4 October 1927, 2657-g-605, RG 165, NA; Tuck, *Holy War*, pp. 95–96, 111–112; Meyer, *Cristeros*, 3: 173–201. Scholars are forever indebted to Meyer, who over decades patiently collected and preserved priceless information, which otherwise would have been lost. No less diligent has been Tuck in saving testimonies on the Los Altos region.

29. James Sheffield to SofS, Mexico, 1 June 1926, 812.002/193, RG 59, NA.

30. *Boletín municipal* (Mexico City), 1927, no. 33, p. 23; Arthur Schoenfeld to Sof S, Mexico, 23, 24 August 1927, 812.00/28659 and 28664, RG 59, NA.

31. "Forced military coup d´état," 25 October 1927, 2657–g–605 and Alexander J. McNab to Assistant Chief of Staff, G-2, 2657–g–605, MID, RG 165, NA; Arthur Schoenfeld to SofS, 3 October 1927, 812.00/28817, RG 59, NA; John W. F .Dulles, *Yesterday in Mexico: A Chronicle of the Revolution, 1919–1936* (Austin: University of Texas Press, 1961), pp. 344–351.

32. The conscientious American Consul William Jackson diligently collected evidence on this massacre, such as this testimony: "An American citizen, in charge of a private graveyard in Torreón, was called on by the military authorities to arrange for the burial of the dead. He reported to this office that none of the soldiers of the 16th Infantry Battalion were fully dressed. Most of the soldiers did not have on trousers, and though several had on shoes, the shoes were not laced, and only one soldier among those killed of the 16th Infantry had on his bandolier of cartridges, while all the dead of the 43rd Artillery were fully dressed with shoes, leggins, blouses, hats, bandoliers, and rifles. [...] The American who was called in to arrange for the burial, on seeing the bodies of a number of women and children, requested permission to have pine coffins made for them but was informed that this was not necessary, and it is surmised that they were buried in the same trench with the soldiers of the 16th Infantry Battalion." Report of Consul Jackson, 10 October 1927, 812.00/28857, RG 59, NA.

33. "Armed revolutionary movement," 11 October 1927, 2657–g–605, MID, RG 165, NA; *Boletín municipal* (Mexico City), 1927, no. 33, pp. 29–30.

34. Military Attaché Report no. 1781, 25 October 1927, MID, RG 165, NA.

35. "Armed revolutionary movement," 14, 18 October 1927, 2657–g–605, MID, RG 165, NA; Dulles, *Yesterday in Mexico*, p. 353.

36. Dwight Morrow to SofS, 16 July 1928, 812.00/29215 1/2, RG 59, NA; Meyer, *Cristeros*, 1: 204; 3: 114, 211–215, 244–248.

37. *Ibid.*, 1: 196–197, 3:109–111, 118–119, 215–221.

38. M.R. Olivas to Manuel J. Aguirre, San Gaspar de los Reyes, Jalisco, 14 August 1928, AJA, serie 03, sub 02, FCT; George Philip, ed., *British Documents on Foreign Affairs*, Part II, Series D, *Latin America, 1914–1939*, 20 vols (Bethesda, Md.: University Publications of America, 1989–1992), 5: 230–231; Meyer, *Cristeros*, 1: 167–168, 186–188, 214, 228, 3: 249–250, 252–254; Major Harold Thompson, "Memorandum for the ambassador," 812.00/29215 1/2, RG 59, NA; Scheina, *Age of the Professional Soldier*, p. 32. The sadistic extremes bear a striking resemblance to the atrocities occurring in Colombia from the late 1940s to the early sixties; See Germán Guzmán Campos, Orlando Fals Borda, and Eduardo Umaña Luna, *La violencia en Colombia*, 2 vols. (Bogotá: Carlos Valencia Editores, 1980), particularly chapters 8 and 9 in volume 1.

39. Meyer, *Cristeros*, 3: 255.

40. "Instrucciones a los jefes de operaciones en los estados de México, Morelos y Guerrero," Mexico City, 13 January 1928, AAA, Box 2, UNAM; Meyer, *Cristeros*, 1: 172–177, 214, 3: 120–121, 251–252, 260–264; Edward P. Lowry to SofS, Guadalajara, 2 March 1928, 812.00/Jalisco, RG 59, NA; Tuck, *Holy War*, pp. 52, 62.

41. Meyer, *Cristeros*, 3: 114–118; Tuck, *Holy War*, pp. 55–56, 100–104.

42. J. Trinidad Mora to Srta. M.M.Z., 11 August 1927, Exp. 49, Box 12, AAA, UNAM.

43. E. W. Eaton to SofS, Manzanillo, 6 February 1928, 812.00-Bandit Activities/1, RG 59, NA.

44. Dwight Morrow to Sof S, 16 July 1928, 812.00/29215 1/2, RG 59, NA.

45. Meyer, *Cristeros*, 3:204.

46. "Manzanillo attacked by revolutionaries," 26 May 1928, 812.00/Colima/6, RG 59, NA. Meyer, *Cristeros*, 1:231 Two boisterous dance parties lasting until 5:00 in the morning delayed the departure of the gunboat.

47. Dulles, *Yesterday in Mexico*, pp. 355–396, 404–435.

48. Memorandum of Robert B. Armstrong, Los Angeles, 14 February 1929, and Maurice W. Altaffer to SofS, Nogales, 19 February 1929, 812.00Sonora/24, 29, RG 59, NA; José C. Valadés, *Historia general de la Revolución Mexicana*, 10 vols. (Mexico: Manuel Quesada Brandi, 1963–1967), 8: 193–196; Lorenzo Meyer *et al.*, *Los inicios de la institucionalización, 1928–1934* (Mexico: El Colegio de Mexico, 1978), pp. 67–68; Dulles, *Yesterday in Mexico*, p. 441; Un observador, *La rebelión militar contra el gobierno legítimo* (San Antonio, Texas: n.p., 1929), pp. 26–27. Although pro-Calles, this anonymous work is the best contemporary source for the nature of the rebellion; the text also offers many delightful passages and keen insights.

49. Dwight Morrow to SofS, 18 March 1929, 812.20/75, RG 59, NA; Meyer, *Inicios 1928–1934*, pp. 68–69; *La rebelión militar*, p. 72.

50. Valadés, *Historia general*, 8: 204–205; Dwight Morrow to SofS., Mexico City, 4 March 1929, and James C. Powell to SofS, Torréon, 5 March 1929, 812.00Sonora/47, 314, RG 59, NA.

51. Dwight Morrow to SofS, Mexico City, 5, 7 March 1929, 812.00Sonora/ 76, 134, RG 59, NA; *La rebelión militar*, pp. 42, 43; Meyer, *Inicios 1928–1934*, pp. 71, 76–77; Valadés, *Historia general*, 8: 199, 202–203. Aguirre was captured on 20 March and, after a drumhead court martial, was executed the next day.

52. Dwight Morrow to SofS, Mexico City, 6 March 1929, 812.00Sonora/ 107, RG 59, NA; *La rebelión militar*, pp. 42–43; Meyer, *Inicios 1928–1934*, pp. 78, 81.

53. "Report No. 1," 12 March 1929, El Paso, Texas 812.00Sonora/ 372, RG 59, NA.

54. *La rebelión militar*, pp. 69–71; this author said in p. 29 that the Plan of Hermosillo "es un fárrago de vulgaridades y tonterías contradictorias," a judgment shared by scholars, see Meyer, *Inicios 1928–1934*, pp. 69–71.

55. Telegram of Ambassador Dwight Morrow, 8 March 1929, 812.00Sonora/166, RG 59, NA; Emilio N. Acosta, *Historia de la campaña de la columna expedicionaria del norte* (Mexico: Secretaría de la Defensa Nacional, 1996), pp. 75–77.

56. For the confused situation in Durango, see Meyer, *Inicios 1928–1934*, p. 78; on the failure to link up with the Cristeros, see Ellis A. Bonnet to SofS, Durango, 20 March 1929, RG 59, NA.

57. James C. Powell to SofS, Torréon, 18 March 1929, 812.00Sonora/524, RG 59, NA; Dwight Morrow to SofS, 15, 18 March, 1929, 812.00 Sonora/287, 337, RG 59, NA; Acosta, *Historia de la campaña*, pp. 76–81, 85–86; *La rebelión militar*, p. 65; "Report No. 2," 19 March 1929, El Paso, 812.00Sonora/436, RG 59 NA.

58. Dwight Morrow to SofS, 25, 26, March 1929, 812.00Sonora/ 414, 433, RG 59, NA.

59. Parte of Juan Andreu Almazán, Chihuahua, 10 April 1929, APC, Exp. 192, FCT; Dwight Morrow to SofS, 19 March 1929, 812.00/Sonora/355, RG 59, NA; Acosta, *Historia de la campaña*, p. 117.

60. Dwight Morrow to SofS, 1 April 1929, 812.00Sonora/475, RG 59, NA; Parte of Juan Andreu Almazán, Chihuahua, 10 April 1929, APC, Exp. 192, FCT; Acosta, *Historia de la campaña*, pp. 109–114.

61. Parte of Juan Andreu Almazán, Chihuahua, 10 April 1929, APC, Exp. 192, FCT; Acosta, *Historia de la campaña*, pp. 112, 115–116, 118.

62. Dwight Morrow to SofS, 2 April 1929, 812.00Sonora/481, RG 59, NA; Parte of Juan Andreu Almazán, Chihuahua, 10 April 1929, APC, Exp. 192, FCT; Acosta, *Historia de la campaña*, pp. 117–121.

63. Gus T. Jones, "Mexican Revolution," 9 April 1929, 812.00Sonora/715, RG 59, NA.

64. Dwight Morrow to SofS, 3 April 1929, 812.00Sonora/496, RG 59, NA; Parte of Juan Andreu Almazán, Chihuahua, 10 April 1929, APC, Exp. 192, FCT; Acosta, *Historia de la campaña*, pp. 121–124. The estimate of 2000 is Almazán's; Consul Myers believed Escobar had as many as 3000 men but the exact number did not matter: "They are worn out, have little ammunition, and morale entirely destroyed." Chihuahua, 5 April 1929, 812.00Chihuahua/ 26, RG 59, NA.

65. Consul William P. Blocker to SofS, Mazatlán, 11 March 1929, 812.00Sinaloa/12, RG 59, NA.

66. Consul William P. Blocker to SofS, Mazatlán, 28 March 1929, 812.00Sonora/559, RG 59, NA. All quotations in the next paragraph are from this source.

67. Besides Consul Blocker's militarily insightful report, the account also draws on *El Universal*, 26 March 1929 and *La rebelión militar*, pp. 71–72.

68. "Mexican Revolution, March 1929," San Antonio, 13 April 1929, 812.00Sonora/722, RG 59, NA.

69. Luis De Netto, "Report No. 8," El Paso, 30 April 1929, 812.00Sonora/ 922, RG 59, NA.

70. U.S. Department of State, *Foreign Relations, 1929*, 3: 400, 406; *La rebelión militar*, pp. 80–81.

71. E. W. Eaton, "Rebels evacuate Masiaca and retreat northward," Ciudad Obregón, 27 April 1929, 812.00Sonora/976, RG 59, NA.

72. *Ibid.* This is the most graphic report on the impact of air power.

73. "General Situation. Military," 21 May 1929, 2657-g-605, MID, RG 165, NA.

74. As Gorostieta himself recognized; See his letter to the bishops of 16 May in Meyer, *Cristeros*, 1: 316.

75. "Revolutionary Situation in Jalisco," 17 January, 18 February 1929, 812.00Jalisco/40, 44, RG 59, NA; Meyer, *Cristeros*, 3: 264; Dulles, *Yesterday in Mexico*, pp. 459–460; Tuck, *Holy War*, pp. 162–165.

76. Colonel Manuel Quiróz to Secretary of War, Encarnación, Jalisco, 26 December 1928, AJA, Serie 03, Sub 02, FCT; "Revolutionary Situation in Jalisco," 17 January 1929, and Raleigh A. Gibson, "Revolutionary Conditions in the State of Jalisco," 6 May 1929, 812.00Jalisco/40, 53, RG 59, NA; Meyer, *Cristeros*, I: 284–285, 304–305.

77. Joseph C. Satterthwaite, "Revolutionary Situation in Jalisco," 18 February 1929, 812.00Jalisco/44, RG 59, NA.

78. V. Harwood Blocker, Jr., "Political Conditions in the State of Colima," Manzanillo, 2 March 1929, 812.00Colima/34, RG 59, NA.

79. The army withdrawal may have influenced the erroneous characterization of the period of March–June 1929 as "Apogeo del movimiento cristero (de marzo a junio de 1929)" in Meyer, *Cristeros*, I: 286–320.

80. Tuck, *Holy War*, pp. 151–158; War Bulletin No. 7, March 1929, 2657–g–605, MID, RG 165, NA.

81. Enrique Gorostieta, "Orden Circular Num. 5," 14 March 1929, Box 1, exp. 3, AAA, UNAM. The reading of this document in its entirety reveals a Gorostieta more sympathetic to the Escobar revolt than what appears in Meyer, *Cristeros*, 1:286–287. A quotation from this document appears in *Ibid*, but not the following revealing statement by Gorostieta that "no he tenido inconveniente en conceder la Dirección del movimiento, al Jefe del nuevo pronunciamiento, nuestro aliado. En pliego aparte doy la manera de identificar a los Jefes y fuerzas del nuevo movimiento, que desde ahora son nuestros aliados."

82. General Heliodoro Charis to Secretary of War Joaquín Amaro, 17 February 1930, AAA, box 5, UNAM; "General situation," 21 May 1929, 2657–g–605, MID, RG 165, NA; V. Harwood Blocker to SofS, Manzanillo, 27 May, 18 June 1929, 812.00Colima/ 39, 40, RG 59, NA; Raleigh A. Gibson, "Revolutionary Conditions in Jalisco," 6 and 28 May 1929, 812.00Jalisco/53, 55, RG 59, NA.

83. V. Harwood Blocker, Jr., "Political Conditions in the State of Colima," Manzanillo, 11 July 1929, 812.00Colima/41, RG 59, NA.

84. Meyer, *Cristeros*, 3: 221–223. The murder of "El Catorce" was particularly repugnant to the local inhabitants because rivalries over female lovers had triggered it. For an excellent discussion of this controversial episode, see Tuck, *Holy War*, pp. 125–147.

85. The "Informe Extraoficial del Estado Mayor" of early 1929 graphically described the suffering at Zacatecas: "Las condiciones por las que atraviesan los soldados católicos son angustiosas: carecen absolutamente de ropa; no tienen víveres y se mantienen con nopales y carne cruda. De las rancherías elimináronse todas las posibilidades de obtener maíz u otros elementos de vida. De las poblaciones está prohibido por las autoridades militares la salida de toda clase de elementos de primera necesidad.

Los libertadores están diariamente solicitando parque pues son muy contados los soldados católicos que cuentan con una carrillera completa de tiros. Por centenares se cuentan los hombres de armas nuestros que carecen totalmente de parque. No han podido efectuarse mobilizaciones por falta absoluta de elementos de guerra." AAA, box 12, exp. 50, UNAM.

86. SofS to Amembassy, 1 June 1929, Gibson to SofS, 3, 5 June 1929, 812.404/984, 987, 994, RG 59, NA; Meyer, *Cristeros*, 1: 317–320.

87. Report no. 2424 of Military Attaché Gordon Johnston, 6 June 1929, 3020–d, MID, RG 165, NA. Not all the sources support the conclusion that Gorostieta planned to disband. I have taken the more charitable interpretation in the text as more consistent with his final action. For the controversy over his death and whether he was betrayed, see Tuck, *Holy War*, pp. 172–174.

88. "The bandit situation," 21 June 1929, 2657–g–605, MID, RG 165, NA.

89. "Informe general que hace el señor Fausto Pérez a la Liga de Defensa Religiosa," 24 December 1929, AAA, box 25, UNAM; Colonel Manuel Quiróz to Secretary of War, Lagos, Jalisco, 2 August 1928, AJA, Serie 03, Sub 02, FCT; Raleigh A. Gibson, "Revolutionary Conditions in the State of Jalisco," 5 June 1929, 812.00Jalisco/60, RG 59, NA; V. Harwood Blocker, Jr., "Revolutionary Conditions in the State of Colima," 18 June 1929, RG 59, NA; Raleigh A. Gibson, "Conditions in Jalisco," 22 August 1929, 812.00Jalisco/68, RG 59, NA; Dulles, *Yesterday in Mexico*, pp. 460–463; Tuck, *Holy War*, pp. 173–179.

90. For the most detailed account of "La Segunda" as the later Cristero revolt was known, see Meyer, *Cristeros*, 1: 323–386. The best summary is in Tuck, *Holy War*, pp. 180–189.

Chapter 11

1. Evaristo San Miguel, *Elementos del arte de la Guerra* (Madrid: Ministerio de Defensa, 1990), p. 437.

2. Richard Millett, *Guardians of the Dynasty* (Maryknoll, NY:

Orbis Books, 1977), pp. 25–36; Lester D. Langley, *The Banana Wars: United States Intervention in the Caribbean, 1898–1934*, 2nd ed. (Wilmington, DE: Scholarly Resources, 2002), pp. 49–70, 175–178.

3. Millett, *Guardians of the Dynasty*, pp. 41–52; Langley, *Banana Wars*, pp. 178–184.

4. U.S. officials were very slow to learn about Nicaragua, and even fifty years later CIA Director Bill Casey was mispronouncing the name of the country as "Nic-a-wha-wha"; See Bob Woodward, *Veil: The Secret Wars of the CIA 1981–1987* (New York: Simon and Schuster, 1987), p. 177.

5. U.S. Department of State, *Papers Relating to the Foreign Relations of the United States 1927*, 3 vols. (Washington, D.C.: Government Printing Office, 1941), 3: 345–347;" Anastasio Somoza, *El verdadero Sandino o el calvario de las Segovias*, 2 vols. (Managua, Nicaragua: Tip. Robelo, 1936), 1:27–32; R.R. Isaguirre and A. Martínez R., *Sandino y los U.S. Marines* (Tegucigalpa, Honduras: Omni Editores, 2000), pp. 109–116; Langley, *Banana Wars*, pp. 184–188; Millett, *Guardians of the Dynasty*, pp. 53–56; Gregorio Selser, *Sandino: General de hombres libres* (Mexico: Editorial Diógenes, 1978), pp. 134–140. The anti-Sandino bias in the Somoza book is no less pronounced than the pro–Sandino bias in the Selser book. The skilled historian can profitably use the two sources, because both publications are largely compilations of often the same documents.

6. Neill Macaulay, *The Sandino Affair* (Chicago: Quadrangle Books, 1967), pp. 48–61; Millett, *Guardians of the Dynasty*, pp. 63–64. For anti-Americanism, see Michel Gobat, *Confronting the American Dream: Nicaragua under U.S. Imperial Rule* (Durham, NC: Duke University Press, 2005), pp. 175–201, 206, 215, 253–254, 257–258.

7. Gustavo Alemán Bolaños, *Sandino: estudio completo del héroe de las Segovias* (Mexico: Imp. La República, 1932), pp. 16–17; Somoza, *El verdadero Sandino*, pp. 35–38; Macaulay, *Sandino Affair*, pp. 62–68. The Liberal generals had also wanted a U.S. military government, but they settled for the Tipitapa agreement as the best possible deal. For an explanation of the special circumstances that led the Liberals to consider a U.S. military occupation as the way to escape financial domination by Wall Street, see Gobat, *Confronting the American Dream*, pp. 125–145.

8. U.S. Department of State, *Papers, 1927*, 3: 444; Macaulay, *Sandino Affair*, pp. 73, 75.

9. Alemán Bolaños, *Sandino*, pp. 18–19; Somoza, *El verdadero Sandino*, pp. 57–58; Macaulay, *Sandino Affair*, pp. 69–72, 75–78; Bernard C. Nalty, *The United States Marines in Nicaragua* (Washington, D.C.: U.S. Marine Corps, 1962), pp. 15–16.

10. G.D. Hatfield, "Attack on Ocotal," 20 July 1927, Correspondence and Record Cards of the Military Intelligence Division, Central America, (henceforth MID), Record Group (henceforth RG) 165, National Archives, Washington, D.C. (henceforth NA); Somoza, *El verdadero Sandino*, pp. 50–55; Macaulay, *Sandino Affair*, pp. 78–82; Nalty, *Marines in Nicaragua*, pp. 16–17. For a Spanish translation of Hatfield's report, see Isaguirre and Martínez, *Sandino y los U.S. Marines*, pp. 145–149.

11. Alemán Bolaños, *Sandino*, p. 19; Somoza, *El verdadero Sandino*, pp. 55–57, 70–73; Macaulay, *Sandino Affair*, pp. 82–84, 95–96; Isaguirre and Martínez, *Sandino y los U.S. Marines*, pp. 322–324.

12. Somoza, *El verdadero Sandino*, p. 46; Macaulay, *Sandino Affair*, pp. 85–86; Alemán Bolaños, *Sandino*, p. 20; Selser, *Sandino*, p. 166.

13. Macaulay, *Sandino Affair*, pp. 70, 87–90.

14. Selser, *Sandino*, pp. 149–152, 166.

15. "Marine air tactics in Nicaragua," 12, 14 March 1928, MID, 165, NA; Alemán Bolaños, *Sandino*, pp. 41–42. Although Spanish translations of the report and some military attaché documents appear in Isaguirre and Martínez, *Sandino y los U.S. Marines*, pp. 172–177, this book has relied on the English originals.

16. Report of C.O. of 66th Company, 6 December 1927, MID, RG 165, NA. The marines tried to survive in the thick forest: "2. This patrol went out with the idea of staying several days and living off the country. This was impossible as there is nothing to be had in the way of foodstuffs with the exception of cattle. There are many cattle scattered over this area." Report of Lieutenant D. E. Wells, 19 December 1927, Ocotal, MID, RG 165, NA.

17. Report of Division Commander, 16 November 1927, "Statement of the Battle of Telpaneca," 19 September 1927, MID, RG 165, NA; U.S. Department of State, *Papers 1927*, 3:450; Millett, *Guardians of the Dynasty*, p. 86; Selser, *Sandino*, p. 193; Nalty, *Marines in Nicaragua*, pp. 17–18.

18. Reports of Sergeant Brown and Lieutenant Hunt of January

1927, MID, RG 165, NA; Macaulay, *Sandino Affair*, pp. 98–102; Millett, *Guardians of the Dynasty*, 86–87; Langley, *Banana Wars*, pp. 191–192.

19. "Chipote Operations 19 Jan to 30 Jan 1928," MID, RG 165, NA; Macaulay, *Sandino Affair*, pp. 98, 103–104; Selser, *Sandino*, pp. 171–172; Nalty, *Marines in Nicaragua*, pp. 20–22.

20. Langley, *Banana Wars*, pp. 192–194; Macaulay, *Sandino Affair*, pp. 105–106; Somoza, *El verdadero Sandino*, pp. 82–84.

21. Report No. 24 of Military Attaché Fred Cruse, 1 April 1928, MID, RG 165, NA.

22. Report No. 28 of Military Attaché Fred Cruse, 18 June 1928, and Report No. 57 of Military Attaché Fred Cruse, 6 October 1928, MID, RG 165, NA; Macaulay, *Sandino Affair*, p. 103.

23. "Summary of data [...] on engagement [...] on Coco River 7 Aug 1928," MID, RG 165, NA; Macaulay, *Sandino Affair*, pp. 123–125; Xavier Campos Ponce, *Los Yanquis y Sandino* (Mexico: Ediciones X.C.P. 1962), pp. 56–57, 83–84. Captain Matthew Ridgway, who in his *Memoirs* did not reveal the true nature of his mission, analyzed the performance of weapons in the tropical forest:

"The Springfield [a version of the Mauser fitted for .30 caliber bullets] has proved its superiority in all contacts at all ranges. However, in my opinion (Captain T. A. Austin, USA) a lighter arm firing lighter ammunition semi-automatically would be much more useful. A stainless steel barrel for tropical use would be an improvement. Rifles have been well cared for in the field.

Browning auto[matic] rifle has been a man-killer on the trail but effective when used. It is too heavy, for the average man, but carried on all mounted patrols. A field of fire permitting full use of its fire power is rarely found.

Bayonet of little or no use. Does not serve as a machete or knife. Seldom carried by patrols. Browning MC has been little used due to its weight and difficult packing on trails and is generally left in garrison.

Thompson sub-machine gun is the ideal weapon for bush warfare as ranges are always short. [...] an ideal weapon for conditions here. Its chief disadvantage is its rapidity of expenditure of ammunition. [...] The gun is carried under the arm, always ready, and it is almost impossible to surprise a Thompson sub-machine gun man. He always has his gun on his hip, ready to shoot, and can immediately put down a burst of fire while marching. This weapon is very popular with marines. [...]

Rifle grenade has been effectively used in nearly all contacts and has proved very valuable. Hand grenades useful on a number of occasions. [...] Its use is limited due to terrain and usual hit and run tactics of bandits. Recommended for use by officers and NCOs only." Captain Matthew Ridgway, "Notes on Military Operations of U.S. Naval Forces in Nicaragua," Managua, 30 October 1928, MID, RG 165, NA.

24. Report No. 10 of Military Attaché Fred Cruse, 10 September 1928, MID, RG 165, NA.

25. Escolástico Lara to Turcios, September 1928, and Report No. 71 of 17 December 1928, MID, RG 165, NA; Millett, *Guardians of the Dynasty*, p. 110; Selser, *Sandino*, pp. 183–184. Isaguirre and Martínez conveniently reproduce some of the Spanish press coverage in *Sandino y los U.S. Marines*, pp. 302–308.

26. Report No. 68 of Military Attaché Fred Cruse, 17 November 1928, and Report No. 80, 25 January 1929, MID, RG 165, NA; Campos Ponce, *Los Yanquis y Sandino*, p. 71.

27. Report No. 90 of Military Attaché Fred Cruse, 12 February 1929, Report no. 95, 22 February 1929, and Report No. 107, 20 March 1929, MID, RG 165, NA; U.S. Department of State, *Papers Relating to the Foreign Relations of the United States 1929*, 3 vols. (Washington, D.C.: Government Printing Office, 1943–1944), 3: 553, 567–568; Nalty, *Marines in Nicaragua*, p. 28; Michael J. Schroeder, "The Sandino Rebellion Revisited," in Gilbert M. Joseph et al. eds., *Close Encounters of Empire: Writing the Cultural History of U.S.–Latin American Relations* (Durham, NC: Duke University Press, 1998), p. 242.

28. Report No. 119a of Military Attaché Fred Cruse, 12 April 1929, MID, RG 165, NA. A longer extract of this report appears in U.S. Department of State, *Papers 1929*, 3: 562–563.

29. Campos Ponce, *Los Yanquis y Sandino*, pp. 77–78, 105–108; Macaulay, *Sandino Affair*, pp. 146–150; U.S. Department of State, *Papers 1929*, 3:565.

30. Campos Ponce, *Los Yanquis y Sandino*, pp. 113–118; Macaulay, *Sandino Affair*, pp. 156–159; U.S. Department of State, *Papers 1929*, 3: 580–590.

31. Macaulay, *Sandino Affair*, pp. 161–166.

32. Report No. 909 of Military Attaché Fred Cruse, 2 October 1930, MID, RG 165, NA; Macaulay, *Sandino Affair*, pp. 159–160, 165; Alemán Bolaños, *Sandino*, p. 62; Selser, *Sandino*, pp. 225–226.

33. U.S. Department of State, *Papers 1929*, 3: 564, 570–571, 576–578; Macaulay, *Sandino Affair*, pp. 150–151, 163; Alemán Bolaños, *Sandino*, pp. 42–42; Selser, *Sandino*, p. 216.

34. Millett, *Guardians of the Dynasty*, pp. 92–93; Macaulay, *Sandino Affair*, pp. 165–168; Alemán Bolaños, *Sandino*, pp. 63–64; Selser, *Sandino*, pp. 230–231, 237–238; Isaguirre and Martínez, *Sandino y los U.S. Marines*, pp. 400–401, 428–439.

35. Report No. 768 of Military Attaché Fred Cruse, 19 June 1930, MID, RG 165, NA; Millett, *Guardians of the Dynasty*, p. 92; Nalty, *Marines in Nicaragua*, p. 30.

36. U.S. Department of State, *Papers 1929*, 3:569–570, 574–576; Nalty, *Marines in Nicaragua*, p. 29.

37. Report No. 777 of Military Attaché Fred Cruse, 1 July 1930, MID, RG 165, NA; Macaulay, *Sandino Affair*, pp. 179–180; Somoza, *El verdadero Sandino*, pp. 178–179, 212–213, 230–231, 271, 287–288; Gobat, *Confronting the American Dream*, p. 241.

38. Report No. 1004 of Military Attaché Fred Cruse, 1 December 1930, MID, RG 165, NA.

39. Macaulay, *Sandino Affair*, pp. 183–185; Nalty, *Marines in Nicaragua*, p. 30.

40. Langley, *Banana Wars*, p. 209. For a nuanced portrait of the situation in the Atlantic Coast, see Charles R. Hale, *Resistance and Contradiction: Miskitu Indians and the Nicaraguan State, 1894–1987* (Stanford: Stanford University Press, 1994), pp. 52–56.

41. Macaulay, *Sandino Affair*, pp. 188, 196–198.

42. Millett, *Guardians of the Dynasty*, pp. 95–96; Macaulay, *Sandino Affair*, pp. 190–192.

43. U.S. Department of State, *Papers Relating to the Foreign Relations of the United States 1931*, 3 vols. (Washington, D.C.: Government Printing Office, 1946), 2: 810–812; Macaulay, *Sandino Affair*, pp. 192–196; Millett, *Guardians of the Dynasty*, pp. 94–95; Somoza, *El verdadero Sandino*, pp. 225–226.

44. Michael J. Schroeder, "Horse Thieves to Rebels to Dogs; Political Gang Violence and the State in the Western Segovias, Nicaragua, in the Time of Sandino, 1926–1934," *Journal of Latin America Studies* 28 (1996): 426–428. Alemán Bolaños, *Sandino*, pp. 69–70; Somoza, *El verdadero Sandino*, pp. 287–288, 302–303, 316, 340–341, 365–366; Macaulay, *Sandino Affair*, pp. 207–208, 211–213.

45. Somoza, *El verdadero Sandino*, pp. 201–202, 232–236; Macaulay, *Sandino Affair*, pp. 201–206, 214–215.

46. U.S. Department of State, *Papers 1931*, 2: 825–826, 828; Macaulay, *Sandino Affair*, pp. 215–218.

47. Schroeder "The Sandino Rebellion Revisited," pp. 229–231; Somoza, *El verdadero Sandino*, pp. 230–231, 236–237, 341–342, 405; Millett, *Guardians of the Dynasty*, p. 97; Selser, *Sandino*, pp. 250–258.

48. Alemán Bolaños, *Sandino*, pp. 75–77; Macaulay, *Sandino Affair*, pp. 220–223, 230–232; Somoza, *El verdadero Sandino*, pp. 356–358, 372. A vastly improved intelligence network made possible the offensive against Sandino's forces. The marines and the Guardia Nacional had been patiently trying to construct a network of spies and informants for years. By 1932 the authorities had neutralized the advantage Sandino had traditionally enjoyed on information. See Schroeder, "The Sandino Rebellion Revisited," pp. 237–238, 245.

49. Report No. 1925 of Military Attaché A. R. Harris, 27 January 1933, MID, RG 165, NA.

50. Report No. 1855 of Military Attaché A. R. Harris, 2 December 1932, MID, RG 165, NA. Gobat, *Confronting the American Dream*, p. 246. Among the defections was the Mexican José de Paredes who at last became disillusioned with the Sandino movement and returned to Mexico about this time; See *Gráfico* (Mexico City) 31 December 1932.

51. "Escamilla, in his operations against the bandits, will not be handicapped by any of the rules of civilized warfare, but will play the game according to the bandits' own rules. For example, known bandit sympathizers will be treated as such, without the formality of long trials attempting to establish their guilt." Report No. 1901 of Military Attaché A. R. Harris, 20 January 1933, MID, RG 165, NA.

52. Macaulay, *Sandino Affair*, pp. 238–247; Somoza, *El verdadero Sandino*, pp. 396–399, 409–412, 420–421, 426, 446–454; Selser, *Sandino*, pp. 259–272.

Chapter 12

1. Francisco Villamartín, *Nociones del arte militar* (Madrid: Ministerio de Defensa, 1989), pp. 466, 468; author's translation.

2. Bruce W. Farcau, *The Chaco War: Bolivia and Paraguay, 1932–1935* (Westport, CT: Praeger, 1996), p. 6. "Lunes 8 de mayo

[1933] hoy el rancho es pésimo en estos montes y bosques del Chaco no se encuentra nada, sólo existen bichos e insectos venenosos, sapos, etc. Martes 9 de mayo. Llueve todo el día; hoy es imposible de ranchear, el rancho es insoportable, todos los soldados protestan." Libreta de notas y de diario de Exaltación Garnica R. Rgtco. Chorolque 33 de infantería- 4a. compañía de ametralladoras, Natalicio González Collection, (henceforth NG), E 199 Spencer Memorial Library, University of Kansas (henceforth KU).

3. Antonio E. González, *Preparación del Paraguay para la Guerra del Chaco*, 2 vols. (Asunción, n.p., 1957), 2: 256–57. For a good description of the Chaco, see Dem Luis Vittone, *Tres guerras, dos mariscales, doce batallas* (Asunción: El Gráfico, 1967), pp. 218–222 and more briefly Farcau, *Chaco War*, pp. 5–6.

4. Harris Gaylord Warren, *Paraguay and the Triple Alliance: The Postwar Decade, 1869–1878* (Austin: University of Texas Press, 1978), pp. 59–61, 241–261. As a face-saving formula, Argentina agreed to submit the zone between the Verde and the Pilcomayo to arbitration; as expected, the award favored Paraguay, see *Ibid.*, pp. 281–283 and Farcau, *Chaco War*, pp. 6–7.

5. Bryce Wood, *The United States and Latin American Wars, 1932–1942* (New York: Columbia University Press, 1966), pp. 23–25, 96; Robert L. Scheina, *Latin America: A Naval History, 1810–1987* (Annapolis: U.S. Naval Institute Press, 1987), p. 124. General Hans Kundt seems to have been the first high officer to notice the colonial nature of the war for Bolivia; See his telegram to President Salamanca of 1 August 1933, Daniel Salamanca, *Documentos para una historia de la guerra del Chaco*, 4 vols. (La Paz: Editorial Don Bosco, 1951–1974), 3: 43.

6. Roberto Querejazu Calvo, *Masamaclay: Historia política, diplomática y militar de la guerra del Chaco* (La Paz: Gráfica E. Burillo, 1965), pp. 25–29. For the fullest military account, see Rafael Franco, *Memorias militares*, 2 vols. (Asunción, Paraguay: Nueva Edición, 1988–1990), 1: 5–35.

7. Juan B. Ayala, *La Guerra del Chaco hasta Campo Vía* (Buenos Aires: Artes Gráficas Aconcagua, 1958), p. 40; see also González, *Preparación*, 1:150, 363–365.

8. Ayala, *Hasta Campo Vía*, p. 39.

9. Salamanca, *Documentos*, 1: 75–99, 250 for this and the next two paragraphs. The following extract is revealing about attitudes to air power "Conversando confidencialmente hace poco con el Ministro de Relaciones Exteriores de Bolivia, doctor Julio Gutiérrez, he podido darme cuenta de que este Gobierno cifra sus mayores expectativas de éxito, para el caso de una agresión al Paraguay, en el poder y la eficiencia de sus elementos de aviación militar. En efecto, el Canciller me decía que si bien a Bolivia no le convenía embarcarse en la aventura de una guerra en la region pantanosa e insalubre del Chaco, en cambio, podría fácilmente, y con evidente beneficio para su causa, bombardear desde el aire la ciudad de Asunción." Carlos Concha to Ministro de Relaciones Exteriores, La Paz, 19 November 1931, Archivo Histórico Militar del Perú, Lima, Peru.

10. Salamanca, *Documentos*, 1: 217–220, 235. La Paz based its decision on oral accounts. The only written report is by the pilot Major Jorge Jordán and has a date of 6 June or forty days after the initial reconnaissance, a surprisingly long time. Army Major Óscar Moscoso claimed to have written his own report clearly stating that the Paraguayans already occupied the site, but no copies of this "smoking gun" have been found. For the controversy and possible cover-up, see David Alvestegui, *Salamanca: Su gravitación sobre el destino de Bolivia*, 4 vols. (La Paz: Fundación Universitaria Simón I. Patiño, 1957–1970), 3: 370–375 and Farcau, *Chaco War*, pp. 30–31. Zook prudently sticks to the written report of Major Jordán; See David H. Zook, *The Conduct of the Chaco War* (New Haven, CT: Bookman Associates, 1960), p. 69.

11. Natalicio Olmedo, *Acciones de Pitiantuta* (Asunción: Casa Editorial Toledo, 1959), pp. 9–10, who says the news reached Casanillo on 20 June, but the document he reproduces on the previous page says that the surviving soldiers gave the news to kilometer 145 of the railroad on 18 July; Ernesto Scarone, *Ataque y retoma del fortín Carlos A. López (Pitiantuta)* (Asunción: n.p, 1973), pp. 221–222; José Félix Estigarribia, *Memorias* (Asunción: Intercontinental Editora, 1989), pp. 27, 35. This is the best edition of his memoirs, because it was published from the Spanish original his daughter, Sor Guillermina Carmen Graciela Estigarribia, carefully preserved for decades.

12. Major Óscar Moscoso to commander of 4th Division, 16 June 1932, Pitiantuta, Salamanca, *Documentos*, 1: 279–281. For this controversy see Alvestegui, *Salamanca*, 3: 377–384. Zook, *Conduct*, p. 70 tries to be sympathetic when he states "Moscoso had been left with full initiative and disproportionate responsibility before history." That may be so, but the hypothesis needs to be considered

that Moscoso took advantage of the confusion in the orders to seize Pitiantuta on his own to bolster his career. To cover up his blunder later he could have invented the story of the existence of his earlier written aerial reconnaissance report. Because many documents have already disappeared, even the opening of Bolivian archives may not clear up this crucial point. Consequently this text has avoided being harsh on any one of the many possible culprits in this episode.

13. President to Jefe del Estado Mayor General, 21 September 1932, Salamanca, *Documentos*, 1: 343–48; Major Óscar Moscoso to commander of 4th Division, 26 July 1932, *Ibid.*, 1: 294–297 and see also 1:257–262. I have preferred the reports Moscoso wrote close to the events rather than his less reliable memoirs. Alvestegui, *Salamanca*, 3: 384–412 argues forcefully for the interpretation that the failure to deliver the withdrawal order to Moscoso reflected an army conspiracy.

14. Major Moscoso to commander of 4th Division, 30 June, 5, 26 July 1932, Salamanca, *Documentos*, 1: 284–298.

15. The fullest account is by the commander of the Paraguayan attack: Ernesto Scarone, *Contribución para la historia de la Guerra del Chaco: Reconocimiento en fuerza en Pitiantuta* (Asunción: n.p., 1963), pp. 64–94; See also his *Ataque y retoma*, pp. 112–115 and Olmedo, *Acciones de Pitiantuta*, pp. 14–16. Major Moscoso in his report of 30 June 1932 from Pitiantuta coincides in the essential points, Salamanca, *Documentos*, 1: 283–287.

16. Major Moscoso to commander of 4th Division, 26 July 1932, Salamanca, *Documentos*, 1: 294–296; Ayala, *Hasta Campo Vía*, pp. 89–90.

17. Scarone, *Ataque y toma*, pp. 149–159, 169–171; Olmedo, *Acciones de Pitiantuta*, pp. 35–40.

18. Angel F. Ríos, *La defensa del Chaco: Verdades y mentiras de una victoria* (Asunción: Archivo del Liberalismo, 1989), pp. 87, 126; Scarone, *Ataque y toma*, pp. 91, 127–136; Olmedo, *Acciones de Pitiantuta*, pp. 40–46.

19. Scarone, *Ataque y toma*, pp. 173–176; Olmedo, *Acciones de Pitiantuta*, pp. 46–50.

20. Major Moscoso to commander of 4th Division, 26 July 1932, Salamanca, *Documentos*, 1: 304 and also 300–309 for this and the following paragraph. Scarone and Olmedo, both participants in the battle, confirm in their accounts the essentials.

21. Salamanca, *Documentos*, 1: 240, 328–330.

22. President Salamanca to Jefe del Estado Mayor General, 21 September 1932, Salamanca, *Documentos*, 1: 343–48; Querejazu Calvo, *Masamaclay*, pp. 51–52. The U.S. ambassador to Bolivia soon was reporting the essence of the clash between Osorio and Salamanca; See Wood, *United States and Latin American Wars*, pp. 39, 420n6.

23. Salamanca, *Documentos*, 1: 347.

24. *Ibid.*, 1: 348.

25. "Affaire Bolivie," 6 April 1934, 7N 3390, Le Service Historique de l'Armée de Terre, Château de Vincennes, Paris, France (henceforth SHAT); Querejazu Calvo, *Masamaclay*, pp. 133–134.

26. Ríos, *Verdades y mentiras*, pp. 12, 14–16, 109–110.

27. Report No. 4609 of military attaché Frederick D. Sharp, 27 October 1932, Military Intelligence Division (henceforth MID), Box 1712, National Archives, Silver Spring, Maryland (henceforth NA).

28. Some Paraguayan units ended up near the Pilcomayo River and subsequently had to reembark to the Boquerón region, but in this instance the failure lay with the war plan rather than with the mobilization itself; Carlos Castañé Decoud, *Tres acciones tácticas de la guerra del Chaco* (Asunción: El Gráfico, 1962), pp. 21–22.

29. Estado Mayor transmitting presidential order to 4th Division, 23 July 1932, Salamanca, *Documentos*, 2:90.

30. Vittone, *Doce batallas*, pp. 226, 235; Aquiles Vergara Vicuña, *Historia de la guerra del Chaco*, 7 vols. (La Paz: Litografías e Imprentas Unidas, 1940–1944),1: 70, 74, 88–90; Carlos José Fernández, *La guerra del Chaco*, 7 vols. (Buenos Aires: Imprenta Militar, 1956–1976), 1: 88–93.

31. Salamanca, *Documentos*, 2:98.

32. Estado Mayor to I Corps, 22 August 1932, Salamanca, *Documentos*, 2:104.

33. Estigarribia, *Memorias*, p. 54; for this paragraph see also *Ibid*, pp. 49–50 and González, *Preparación*, 1: 91–92. Throughout the war President Ayala corresponded directly with Estigarribia, frequently bypassing the Secretary of War. The pre-war army General Staff disappeared when its members joined with Colonel Juan Ayala to organize the II Corps. Although some officers remained at Asunción under the Secretary of War to handle functions such as logistics, no independent body was left to provide military analysis. The lack of a source of independent military advice and analysis contributed to serious blunders by the Paraguayan government.

34. Franco, *Memorias militares*, 1: 52.

35. González, *Preparación*, 1:93, 99. The Paraguayan accounts emphasize the disaster, while Vergara Vicuña, *Historia de la guerra*, 1: 190–194 explains that the repulse of the forward Paraguayan detachment lacked decisive significance in itself and instead fed an exaggerated Bolivian optimism.

36. Details of these engagements are in Vergara Vicuña, *Historia de la guerra*, 1: 215–222.

37. Salamanca, *Documentos*, 2:106–110; Rios, *Verdades y mentiras*, pp. 15–16.

38. Salamanca, *Documentos*, 2:107.

39. Vittone, *Doce batallas*, p. 243.

40. Rios, *Verdades y mentiras*, p. 97; Vergara Vicuña, *Historia de la guerra*, 1: 192–199.

41. Carlos Quintanilla, I Corps commander, to Estado Mayor, 15 September 1932, Salamanca, *Documentos*, 2:109.

42. Vergara Vicuña, *Historia de la guerra*, 1: 239–240, 246, 289, 300, 302, 304.

43. Vicente Rivarola, *Memorias diplomáticas*, 3 vols. (Buenos Aires: Editorial Ayacucho, 1952–1957), 2:202; Vergara Vicuña, *Historia de la guerra*, 1:270–271; Querejazu Calvo, *Masamaclay*, pp. 77, 84, 86.

44. This and the previous paragraph draw on: Vergara Vicuña, *Historia de la guerra*, 1:265, 279–280, 296, 300, 302, 305, 321, 330; Querejazu Calvo, *Masamaclay*, pp. 88, 91–92; Farcau, *Chaco War*, pp. 50–60. For the best eyewitness account, see Heriberto Florentín, *Lo que he visto en Boquerón* (Asunción: Editorial El Foro, 1984), pp. 153–241.

45. Heriberto Florentín, *Más allá de Boquerón* (Rio de Janeiro: Imprensa do Exército, 1964), pp. 88–89, 103, 105; Vergara Vicuña, *Historia de la guerra*, 1:269, 333–336; M.G. de Zúñiga to I Corps, 2, 7 October 1932, NG, E 199, KU.

46. Order for 1st Division, 13 October 1932, NG, E 199, KU; Farcau, *Chaco War*, p. 74; Florentín, *Más allá*, pp. 111–112, 115–118, who is the best source for events from the fall of Boquerón to the clash at Km. 7. In contrast to the majority of books on the Chaco War, Florentín is a delight to read.

47. Franco, *Memorias militares*, 1: 62.

48. Estado Mayor to Quintanilla, 7 October 1932 (two messages), Salamanca, *Documentos*, 2: 120–21.

49. Estado Mayor to Jefe del Estado Mayor, 29 October 1932, Salamanca, *Documentos*, 2: 127–128.

50. Zook, *Conduct*, pp. 106–107; Farcau, *Guerra del Chaco*, pp. 70, 74.

51. The Bolivians planted a false message to show that large reinforcements were headed to Platanillos, Farcau, *Guerra del Chaco*, pp. 73–74, but the fact that Estigarribia seized on this false message rather than the many contrary reports demonstrates that he had already made up his mind to halt the pursuit and was simply looking for an excuse. Estigarribia, *Memorias*, pp. 74–76 fails to justify the action. It should be noted that he wrote his memoirs to create a view of the Chaco War that accounts for his mistakes. By exploiting other sources, this book escapes the influence of Estigarribia, an indispensable step to make possible an accurate reconstruction of the Chaco War for the first time.

52. Vergara Vicuña, *Historia de la guerra*, 1: 437–438, 484–486, 2: 279, 296–298, 308–312; 2: 320–321. Florentín, *Más allá*, pp. 114, 121–123; Alvestegui, *Salamanca*, 4: 118–120, 150–151, 155–156.

53. Estado Mayor to Jefe del Estado Mayor, 1 November 1932, Salamanca, *Documentos*, 2:128.

54. Telegram to Estado Mayor, 30 November 1932, Salamanca, *Documentos*, 2: 133; Alvestegui, *Salamanca*, 4: 118–120; Franco, *Memorias militares*, 1: 107–109.

55. Arturo Guillén to Estado Mayor, 11 November 1932, Salamanca, *Documentos*, 2:266–67; Paraguayan espionage in Buenos Aires had obtained a copy of this crucial message but without Guillén's name, Rivarola, *Memorias diplomáticas*, 2:243–244. Salamanca vainly tries to refute the message in Daniel Salamanca, *Mensajes y memorias póstumas* (Cochabamba, Bolivia: Editorial Canelas, 1976), pp. 31–33. Alvestegui, *Salamanca*, 4: 161–169 makes a final failed attempt to discredit the reasons in the telegram.

56. Vittone, *Doce batallas*, p. 243; "Notes sur le front paraguayen," 30 November 1933, 7N 3390, SHAT; Vergara Vicuña, *Historia de la guerra*, 2:268. Farcau, *Chaco War*, pp. 52–53, 63, 70 excessively emphasizes the negative impact on Bolivia of the loss of "the elite of the Bolivian army" and of the veteran troops familiar with the Chaco. The soldiers that went to help Major Moscoso defend Pitiantuta may well have been the elite of the Bolivian army, but they certainly were a very ragged and totally demoralized lot. Obviously bunching men from many different units into new formations contributed to the disaster at Pitiantuta, but the practice remained endemic throughout the war. And, as for the loss of the jungle veterans, even when the Bolivian army returned to familiar terrain in the Andes Mountains, its performance improved only in those units led by Chilean officers. Massive structural flaws in the Bolivian officer corps rather than the losses in the Boquerón campaign appear as the real explanation for the setbacks during the rest of the war.

57. Julio Díaz Arguedas, *Cómo fue derrocado el hombre símbolo* (La Paz: Fundación Universitaria Simón I. Patiño, 1957), pp. 38–39; Salamanca, *Documentos*, 2:119.

58. "Affaire Bolivie," 6 April 1934, 7N 3390, SHAT; Querejazu Calvo, *Masamaclay*, pp. 133–134; Salamanca, *Memorias*, pp. 25–27; Alvestegui, *Salamanca*, 4: 161–169, 175–177; Estigarribia, *Memorias*, pp. 81–82; Farcau, *Chaco War*, p. 136.

59. Querejazu Calvo, *Masamaclay*, pp. 134–136; Salamanca, *Memorias*, pp. 27–28.

60. Manuel Rojas A. to Minister of War, Asunción, 11 December 1932, NG, E 199, KU.

61. Vergara Vicuña, *Historia de la guerra*, 1: 441–442, 516–519; Florentín, *Más allá*, pp. 123–125; Manuel Rojas A. to Minister of War, 25 October, 30 November 1932, NF, E 199, KU; Alvestegui, *Salamanca*, 4: 155–156; Díaz Arguedas, *Cómo fue derrocado*, pp. 25–30.

62. Vergara Vicuña, *Historia de la guerra*, 2:313–323; Florentín, *Más allá*, pp. 125–132.

63. Vergara Vicuña, *Historia de la guerra*, 2:348–422; Florentín, *Más allá*, pp. 133–148.

64. Díaz Arguedas, *Cómo fue derrocado*, p. 37; Salamanca, *Documentos*, 2: 130, 135–136; Vergara Vicuña, *Historia de la guerra*, 2:653–656.

65. Castañé Decoud, *Tres acciones tácticas*, pp. 27–29.

66. *Ibid.*, pp. 27, 30–35; Alvestegui, *Salamanca*, 4: 189–195. The fullest account of the later engagements in this front is in Vergara Vicuña, *Historia de la guerra*, 2:423–461, 494–574.

67. Manuel A. Rojas, "Situación el 26 de diciembre de 1932," NG, E 199, KU; Ayala, *Hasto Campo Vía*, pp. 137, 150–151; Víctor Ayala Queirolo, *La incógnita de Platanillos* (Asunción: Imprenta Zamphirópolos, 1965), pp. 33–36.

68. Salamanca, *Documentos*, 3: 77–79.

69. The text on the first battle of Nanawa relies on Vittone, *Doce batallas*, pp. 266–270; Querejazu Calvo, *Masamaclay*, pp. 136–141; Sindulfo Barreto, *Nanawa: sector de los milagros* (Asunción: Editora Litocolor, 1985), pp. 345–359; Alvestegui, *Salamanca*, 4: 197–202; Farcau, *Chaco War*, pp. 100–103; Estigarribia, *Memorias*, pp. 84–86; the longest account is in in Vergara Vicuña, *Historia de la guerra*, 3: 255–402.

70. For Toledo, the text relies on Ayala, *Hasta Campo Vía*, pp. 169–182, Querejazu Calvo, *Masamaclay*, pp. 146–148, Vergara Vicuña, *Historia de la guerra*, 3: 410–470, and Salamanca, *Documentos*, 3: 84–85.

71. González, *Preparación*, 1: 331. The Paraguayans used the close proximity to wage psychological warfare effectively against the easily demoralized Bolivians: "Hoy martes [1933 febrero] 28 los pilas [Bolivian slang for Paraguayans] nos bochornan diciendo qué Bolivianos cojudos. Llamas del altiplano, vende patrias cocineros Gral. Kundt, qué cosa que les están dando. Sonso a qué se han venido. Váyanse pobrecitos se van a ver encerrados. […] Hoy martes 14 marzo […] en la tarde silencial, horas 6 los famosos pilas nos insultan. Bolivianos cojudos. Váyanse, que quieren hacer al fortín Toledo. Es vendido por el General Osorio. Huevones, vende patrias, ahí está General Kundt qué cosa les está dando. Está haciendo morir de hambre. Pobrecitos váyanse se van a ver encerrados. Quiere coca, quiere agüita." Libreta de notas y de diario de Exaltación Garnica R. Rgtco. Cholorque 33 de infantería- 4a. compañía de ametralladoras, NG, E 199, KU.

72. Ayala, *Hasta Campo Vía*, p. 185; González, *Preparación*, 2:106–107. The patrol had gone to the Bolivian rear to plug into telephone lines. Upon hearing in a conversation that an officer was setting out with a full report on the situation of the 3rd Division, the Paraguayan patrol set an ambush to capture the officer and the report.

73. Querejazu Calvo, *Masamaclay*, pp. 148–149; González, *Preparación*, 2:106–107; Ayala, *Hasta Campo Vía*, pp. 188–190; Estigarribia, *Memorias*, pp. 89–90.

74. Fernández, *La Guerra del Chaco*, 2: 219–249, 332; Querejazu Calvo, *Masamaclay*, pp. 179–183.

75. Fernández, *La Guerra del Chaco*, 2: 251–262, 3: 99–100. Incredibly, even in his memoirs Estigarribia continued to defend his fatally flawed plan; see his *Memorias*, pp. 90–92.

76. Salamanca, *Documentos*, 3: 24, 29, 31–35; Querejazu Calvo, *Masamaclay*, p. 200; Raúl Tovar Villa, ed., *Campaña del Chaco; El General Hans Kundt* (Oruro, Bolivia: Editorial de la Universidad Técnica de Oruro, 1969), pp. 94, 113.

77. Querejazu Calvo, *Masamaclay*, pp. 187–88; Tovar, *Kundt*, pp. 98–99; Ángel Rodríguez, *Autopsia de una guerra; campaña del Chaco* (Santiago, Chile: Ediciones Ercilla, 1940), pp. 89–90.

78. Tovar, *Kundt*, p. 101; Rivarola, *Memorias diplomáticas*, 2:343–344.

79. Tovar, *Kundt*, p. 104; this paragraph also draws on Salamanca, *Documentos*, 3: 29, 32–33.

80. Rodríguez, *Autopsia de una guerra*, pp. 90–91; Chief of staff of 9th Division Angel Rodríguez to division commander, 10 June 1933, Tovar, *Kundt*, pp. 13–14.

81. Commander of 9th Division Jacinto Reque Terán to I Corps commander, 11 June 1933, Tovar, *Kundt*, p. 16.

82. Rodríguez, *Autopsia de una guerra*, pp. 91–92.

83. Salamanca, *Documentos*, 3: 29, 34–35 and see in particular Salamanca to Kundt, 4 August 1933, Alvestegui, *Salamanca*, 4: 258–261. Already fed up with the constant political intrigues of the Bolivian officers, he had seriously considered resigning in June; See Tovar, *Kundt*, p. 110. The first offer to Salamanca to resign is of 17 September, and several followed afterwards, Salamanca, *Documentos*, 3: 51, 159, 162. Farcau, *Chaco War*, has followed too uncritically the post-war complaints of the Bolivian officers and thus is excessively and unjustly harsh with Kundt; See for example, pp. 106, 119, 123–125. More tantalizingly, Farcau, who admits that the later disasters under Bolivian officers were worse than anything under Kundt, twice mentions the term "foreign scapegoat" (pp. 166, 197) but failed to exploit this idea.

84. "Note confidentielle sur la guerre du Chaco," Paris, 21 June 1933, 7N 3390, SHAT. See also for this paragraph, Tovar, *Kundt*, pp. 106–107, 110, 112. The Bolivian recruit never lost the fear of the jungle: "Día 6 [de marzo de 1934] seguimos el trabajo de las posiciones, en la tarde fui por primera vez a traer el rancho, sentí el horror de la selva, en la noche vinieron a notificar que debía ir un soldado a presenciar el fusilamiento de los desertores (domingo). [...] Día 3 [de marzo de 1934] a primera hora salimos de patrulla 3 hombres, unos 4 kilómetros adelante, al salir tuvimos conocimiento de la muerte de un soldado nuevo con insolación." Copia de la libreta de guerra y diario del reservista Severino L. Menduina del regimiento Florida 12 de infantería, NG, E 199, KU.

85. Alvestegui, *Salamanca*, 4: 244–247; Franco, *Memorias militares*, 1: 81–86; Tovar, *Kundt*, p. 114.

86. Tovar, *Kundt*, pp. 111–112; Salamanca, *Documentos*, 3: 29–31.

87. Writing nearly a year later, Kundt stated:"To this very day I still believe that if all the orders had been followed, exactly as they were given, we would have achieved victory." Tovar, *Kundt*, p. 183.

88. Querejazu Calvo, *Masamaclay*, pp. 201–203; Tovar, *Kundt*, pp. 111–115; Salamanca, *Documentos*, 3: 88–90.

89. The smoke, the jungle, and the intense ferocity of the combat contributed to many discrepancies in the reporting on both sides; the text tries to reconstruct what happened from Tovar, *Kundt*, pp. 115–117; Estigarribia, *Memorias*, pp. 99–100; Querejazu Calvo, *Masamaclay*, pp. 203–206; Vittone, *Doce batallas*, pp. 288–291; Fernández, *La guerra del Chaco*, 3:122–140; Barreto, *Nanawa*, pp. 376–387, and Farcau, *Chaco War*, pp. 130–134.

90. Estigarribia, *Memorias*, p. 100.

91. Querejazu Calvo, *Masamaclay*, pp. 206–207; Fernández, *La guerra del Chaco*, 3:140–143. Salamanca said (Alvestegui, *Salamanca*, 4:259) that just at Toledo and Nanawa the casualties were five thousand. I have estimated the Bolivian casualties slightly higher than in the available sources to account for the acute shortage of troops after Nanawa.

92. Salamanca, *Documentos*, 3: 42–45. From a military perspective the withdrawal to Muñoz was the soundest course, as Kundt himself implies in Tovar, *Kundt*, pp. 152–153 and thus validating the prophetic analysis of Arturo Guillén of 11 November 1932 cited earlier in the text. Kundt believed that the abandonment of Alihuatá meant the loss of Saavedra and everything to the east of Muñoz. His fear was real if the Paraguayan commander had been Colonel Rafael Franco. But against the plodding Estigarribia, the Bolivians could delay the Paraguayans at Km. 31 for months and hold the old positions at Km. 7 for a long time and possibly indefinitely.

93. Had Franco commanded motorized units, he doubtlessly would have been called the Paraguayan George Patton. As students of General Patton may concede, a comparison between the careers of Patton and Franco suggests that mobility reflects more a commander's personality and state of mind than the speed of any particular transport vehicle.

94. Fernández, *La Guerra del Chaco*, 3: 143–151; Franco, *Memorias militares*, 1: 93–101.

95. Tovar, *Kundt*, pp. 127–128, 131: Farcau, *Chaco War*, pp. 126–127.

96. Salamanca, *Documentos*, 3: 57; Tovar, *Kundt*, p. 122; Franco, *Memorias militares*, 1:109–110, 127.

97. Report No. 4749 of M.A. Frederick D. Sharp, 22 September 1933, MID Box 1712, RG 165, NA; Tovar, *Kundt*, pp. 131–139; Fernández, *La Guerra del Chaco*, 3:168–189.

98. González, *Preparación*, 1:258, 2:261, 263; Tovar, *Kundt*, pp. 106–108, 112.

99. Salamanca to Kundt 17 October 1933 and reply of 18 October in Rivarola, *Memorias diplomáticas*, 3: 28–29 and in Salamanca, *Documentos*, 3: 51, 55–56.

100. Fernández, *La Guerra del Chaco*, 3: 204–211.

101. Tovar, *Kundt*, pp. 159–163; Fernández, *La Guerra del Chaco*, 3: 210–211, 230–231; Ayala, *Hasta Campo Vía*, p. 203.

102. Tovar, *Kundt*, pp. 38–39; Querejazu Calvo, *Masamaclay*, pp. 224–226.

103. Tovar, *Kundt*, pp. 43–44, 105.

104. *Ibid.*, p. 44.

105. The trailers carrying the tanks tried to return to Saavedra but became stuck in the mud. As the drivers enjoyed a leisurely breakfast, a Paraguayan patrol quietly emerging from the jungle captured the trailers and the tanks on 9 December; José Clemente Britos, *Fragmento de la batalla Zenteno-Gondra (Campo Vía)*, (Buenos Aires: Ediciones Niza, 1966), p. 96; Robert L. Scheina, *Latin America's Wars: The Age of the Professional Soldier, 1900–2001* (Washington, D.C.: Brassey's, 2003), pp. 89, 106.

106. González, *Preparación*, 2: 108–109; Franco, *Memorias militares*, 1:114–118 who corrects Fernández, *La Guerra del Chaco*, 3: 304–308.

107. Franco, *Memorias militares*, 1: 122.

108. *Ibid.*, 1: 119–126, 128–129. This is an extraordinary account of exceptional value. Franco had published an extract from his memoirs previously in *Campo Vía y Strongest* (Asunción: El Arte, 1967), pp. 7–81.

109. Salamanca, *Documentos*, 3: 65–68, 174–176, 196; Franco, *Memorias militares*, 1:137–141.

110. Querejazu Calvo, *Masamaclay*, pp. 238–241; Franco, *Memorias militares*, 1:153–154.

111. Tovar, *Kundt*, p. 59.

112. González, *Preparación*, 2:118–119, 121; Fernández, *La Guerra del Chaco*, 3: 356–373; Vergara Vicuña, *Historia de la Guerra*, 5: 170–171, 178–179, 256–259.

113. Franco, *Memorias militares*, 1:157–160; Fernández, *La Guerra del Chaco*, 3: 373–385.

Chapter 13

1. Niccolò Machiavelli, *Discorsi sopra la prima deca di Tito Livio* (Milan: Biblioteca Universale Rizzoli, 1984), p. 316. Translation by author's wife.

2. Aquiles Vergara Vicuña, *Historia de la guerra del Chaco*, 7 vols. (La Paz: Litografías e Imprentas Unidas, 1940–1944), 5: 221. Bruce W. Farcau, *The Chaco War: Bolivia and Paraguay, 1932–1935* (Westport, CT: Praeger, 1996), pp. 161–162 strongly defends Estigarribia from "vicious attack by the political opposition" over the truce. Vergara Vicuña as a Chilean artillery officer in the service of Bolivia was not politically motivated, and in addition his testimony is quoted approvingly by Estigarribia's loyal subordinate Raimundo Rolón in his *La guerra del Chaco: campaña de 1934*, 2 vols. (Asunción: Talleres Gráficos E.M.E.S.A., 1961–1963), 1: 22.

3. Rafael Franco, *Memorias militares*, 2 vols. (Asunción, Paraguay: Nueva Edición, 1988–1990), 1:157–164. Estigarribia made no formal objection to the truce proposal and its first extension but finally opposed a third extension; See José Félix Estigarribia, *Memorias* (Asunción: Intercontinental Editora, 1989), pp. 132, 135–137.

4. Raúl Tovar Villa, ed., *Campaña del Chaco, El General Hans Kundt* (Oruro, Bolivia: Editorial de la Universidad Técnica de Oruro, 1969), p. 177.

5. Daniel Salamanca, *Documentos para una historia de la guerra del Chaco*, 4 vols. (La Paz: Editorial Don Bosco, 1951–1974), 3: 171–198; David H. Zook, Jr., *The Conduct of the Chaco War* (New Haven, CT: Bookman Associates, 1960), pp. 194–195. Although generally superseded by Farcau's book, Zook's pioneering work still contains valuable insights and assessments.

6. *Ibid.*, 4: 233–234. The first Bolivian field army comprised the units lost in the fighting during the Boquerón campaign and retreat in 1932.

7. Report No. 4959 of Military Attaché (henceforth MA) Frederick D. Sharp, 28 August 1934, Military Intelligence Division (henceforth MID), Box 1714, Record Group (henceforth RG) 165, National Archives, College Park, Maryland (henceforth NA); Vergara Vicuña, *Historia de la guerra*, 5: 246–273; Julio Díaz Arguedas, *Como fue derrocado el hombre símbolo* (La Paz: Fundación Universitaria Simón I. Patiño, 1957), p. 61.

8. Copia de la libreta de guerra y diario del reservista Severino L. Menduina del regimiento Florida 12 de infantería, E 199, Natalicio González Collection (henceforth NG), Spencer Memorial Library, University of Kansas, Lawrence, Kansas (henceforth KU); Salamanca, *Documentos*, 4: 163–164. As one example, the Bolivian I Corps fired off a million cartridges in a few hours during minor combat operations. To feed this outrageous consumption of ammunition, Bolivia had to stockpile tens of millions of cartridges right in the front lines; whatever benefit the close proximity had on the morale of the troops, the mountains of captured cartridges proved invaluable to the Paraguayans who were very parsimonious with their ammunition.

9. Farcau, *Chaco War*, p. 173. A sympathetic Paraguayan officer blames the Bolivian decision to send university students into soldier ranks rather than into officer training school (as Paraguay did) for the shortage, but the problem went much deeper; Rolón, *Campaña de 1934*, 1: 285. Among other objections, this explanation fails to account for the poor performance of many pre-war Bolivian officers. Hopefully later studies will reveal what characteristics of the Bolivian society restricted the quantity and the quality of the officers. The problem was long-standing, and some episodes of the Acre campaigns of 1899–1903 foreshadowed the disasters of the Chaco War. Certainly involvement in national politics was one major factor in the poor performance of the Bolivian officer corps, but others, such as racism and elitism, were also present.

10. Vicente Rivarola, *Memorias diplomáticas*, 3 vols. (Buenos Aires: Editorial Ayacucho, 1952–1957), 3: 58, 114–119, 179, 225. The Chilean officers had absorbed the German army ethic and introduced the novel practice of always staying close to their soldiers. To the surprise of many, the Chilean officers bridged the supposedly abysmal differences of nationality, race, color, class, and language separating them from their men. Unlike the Bolivian officers who tended to stay in the rear and to flee at the first signs of trouble, the Chilean officers stuck with their soldiers whether to fight, to retreat, or to surrender. The danger lurked that upon capture the Paraguayans might execute the Chileans as mercenaries, but to the immense credit of Paraguay, it never sullied its war record and treated the Chileans like the Bolivian prisoners. As the Mexican Revolution cruelly demonstrated, once the execution of a few prisoners began, there was no stopping the momentum to kill large numbers of prisoners.

11. In response to a Bolivian protest, Argentina had withdrawn its military mission from Asunción on 15 August 1932, Angel F. Ríos, *La defensa del Chaco: Verdades y mentiras de una victoria* (Asunción: Archivo del Liberalismo, 1989), p. 107; Rivarola, *Memorias diplomáticas*, 2:173–174. Because the Argentine mission mainly trained officers, Bolivia hoped to deprive Paraguay of a critical element. But when Bolivia hired Chileans as replacement officers, Argentina made no comparable response and thus bears additional responsibility for prolonging the war.

12. Rolón, *Campaña de 1934*, 1: 27–32; Roberto Querejazu Calvo, *Masamaclay: historia política, diplomática y militar de la guerra del Chaco* (La Paz: Empresa Industrial Gráfica E. Burillo, 1965), p. 261; Estigarribia, *Memorias*, pp. 136–137.

13. Rolón, *Campaña de 1934*, 1: 32–39; Querejazu Calvo, *Masamaclay*, pp. 268–70.

14. Rafael Franco, *Campo Vía y Strongest* (Asunción, Paraguay: El Arte, 1967), pp. 89–92; Rolón, *Campaña de 1934*, 1: 60–64. Estigarribia, *Memorias*, p. 151, claims the idea for the trail was his, but because his extremely meticulous subordinate Rolón does not confirm the origin, I have followed Franco.

15. Díaz Arguedas, *Cómo fue derrocado*, pp. 70–71, 74–75.

16. Querejazu Calvo, *Masamaclay*, pp. 276–77; Rolón, *Campaña de 1934*, 1: 246.

17. Salamanca, *Documentos*, 4: 252–253; Rolón, *Campaña de 1934*, 1: 61–62, 246; Querejazu Calvo, *Masamaclay*, pp. 271–72.

18. Salamanca, *Documentos*, 4: 88–89, 254–256. Lieutenant Colonel Ángel Bavía still insisted on committing suicide, but with such bad luck that the bullet did not kill him. His men hid him for three days until the Paraguayans captured them all. Taken to the hospital at Camacho for surgery, he died three days later on 5 March. See Estigarribia, *Memorias*, pp. 157–158.

19. Rolón, *Campaña de 1934*, 1: 66–71; Salamanca to Peñaranda,

6 April 1934, Salamanca, *Documentos*, 4:257; Estigarribia, *Memorias*, p. 158.

20. Rolón, *Campaña de 1934*, 1: 83, 153.

21. *Ibid.*, 1: 123, 151–154; Querejazu Calvo, *Masamaclay*, pp. 285–86.

22. Rolón, *Campaña de 1934*, 1:126–139; Querejazu Calvo, *Masamaclay*, pp. 286–87.

23. Rolón, *Campaña de 1934*, 1: 136–37, 140–152; Querejazu Calvo, *Masamaclay*, pp. 287–291. In an angry book (as many on the Chaco tend to be), the commander of the 2nd Division tried to clear his reputation; See José Rosa Vera, *La batalla de Strongest frente a su tergiversación histórica* (Asunción: El Gráfico, 1966). However, Estigarribia, *Memorias*, pp. 166–167 confirms the errors of the 2nd Division's commander.

24. Farcau, *Chaco War*, pp. 179–181. Paraguayan prisoners were such a rarity that the Bolivians treated them extremely well and gave them considerable liberties; *Ibid.*, pp. 171–172, 238. Estigarribia, *Memorias*, p. 169 by accepting full responsibility for the defeat at Strongest conveniently avoided the need to recognize its two real causes: his acceptance of the truce in December 1934 and the false belief that after Campo Vía the Bolivian army was incapable of any serious resistance.

25. Rolón, *Campaña de 1934*, 1: 208, 211, 245–280; Querejazu Calvo, *Masamaclay*, pp. 291–293.

26. Salamanca, *Documentos*, 4: 294–299; Estigarribia, *Memorias*, pp. 171, 177.

27. Salamanca, *Documentos*, 4: 94, 98–100, 112.

28. Rolón, *Campaña de 1934*, 1: 289–292; Estigarribia, *Memorias*, pp. 172, 179–180.

29. Rolón, *Campaña de 1934*, 1: 325–339; Estigarribia, *Memorias*, pp. 184–186.

30. Rolón, *Campaña de 1934*, 1:355 and Estigarribia, *Memorias*, pp. 187–188 for rest of paragraph.

31. Díaz Arguedas, *Cóme fue derrocado*, pp. 74–78; Salamanca, *Documentos*, 4: 159–176.

32. Querejazu Calvo, *Masamaclay*, pp. 323–327; Vergara Vicuña, *Historia de la guerra*, 6: 1–102.

33. "Orden para el destacamento Palacios," Casanillo, 25 July 1932, NG, E 199, KU; Rolón, *Campaña de 1934*, 1: 292–293, 2: 19, 22–23.

34. Rolón, *Campaña de 1934*, 2: 70.

35. Report No. 5008 of MA Frederick D. Sharp, 23 November 1934, MID, Box 1712, RG 165, NA; Gerónimo A. Vidal, *Misión de la patrulla "Teniente Vidal" para la maniobra de "El Carmen"* (Buenos Aires: Gráficas Negri, 1968), pp. 89–91.

36. Ríos, *Verdades y mentiras*, p. 100; Vidal, *Misión de la patrulla*, pp. 39, 41–42, 49, 55, 105; Antonio E. González, *Preparación del Paraguay para la guerra del Chaco*, 2 vols. (Asunción: n.p., 1967), 2: 40, 229.

37. Vidal, *Misión de la patrulla*, pp. 57–59, 65; González, *Preparación*, 1: 173, 177–178, 2: 42. Generally, at least half of the Paraguayan soldiers carried machetes to clear the thick underbrush. The Paraguayans sometimes used the machetes in close combat. These instances and an unusually effective propaganda campaign helped terrorize many Bolivian recruits who lived in fear of having their necks slashed.

38. González, *Preparación*, 2: 269; Vidal, *Misión de la patrulla*, pp. 61–62, 72. The corned beef came in cans of 450 grams.

39. *Ibid.*, pp. 71, 75, 77, 79, 84.

40. Cecilio Escobar Rodas, *R. I. 18 Pitiantuta; aclaración sobre algunos acontecimientos de la guerra del Chaco* (Asunción: Artes Gráficas Zampirópolos, 1992), pp. 14–33; Rolón, *Campaña de 1934*, 2: 87–88.

41. Vergara Vicuña, *Historia de la guerra*, 6: 80–91; Eusebio Ayala to Vicente Rivarola, 21 November 1934, Rivarola, *Memorias diplomáticas*, 3:192–193; Report No. 5008 of MA Frederick D. Sharp, 23 November 1934, MID, Box 1712, RG 165, NA; Rolón, *Campaña de 1934*, 2: 103–107. Estigarribia, *Memorias*, pp. 197–198 makes the withdrawal from 27 de Noviembre to Ingavi appear to be a part of the original plan, when, as Rolón shows, the retreat was a good response to the unexpectedly fast Bolivian advance.

42. Vidal, *Misión de la patrulla*, pp. 85–90.

43. Estigarribia, *Memorias*, p. 199; Rolón, *Campaña de 1934*, 2: 99–103, 113–129.

44. Estigarribia, *Memorias*, p. 199.

45. *Ibid.*, p. 199; Zook, *Conduct*, p. 208.

46. Estigarribia, *Memorias*, pp. 200–201; Rolón, *Campaña de 1934*, 2: 129–143.

47. *Ibid.*, 2: 155–160, 163–172.

48. Díaz Arguedas, *Cóme fue derrocado* is the fullest account.

Many primary sources appear in Salamanca, *Documentos*, 4: 395–437.

49. Vergara Vicuña, *Historia de la guerra*, 6: 103–130; Querejazu Calvo, *Masamaclay*, pp. 369–371; Estigarribia, *Memorias*, pp. 202, 203.

50. Escobar Rodas, *Aclaración*, pp. 81–86; Félix Tabera R., *Picuiba* (La Paz: Editorial Don Bosco, 1960), pp. 268, 279–280.

51. Farcau, *Chaco War*, pp. 211–212; Tabera, *Picuiba*, pp. 253–255, 271, 317.

52. Report No. 5076 of MA Frederick D. Sharp, 15 January 1935, MID, Box 1712, RG 165, NA. No fighting occurred during the walk to 27 de Noviembre; as a cover up for the machine gunned bodies, the officers invented the story, uncritically repeated in Vergara Vicuña, *Guerra del Chaco*, 6: 505, that the first arriving Paraguayan soldiers butchered the dying stragglers. For an indignant refutation, see Ceferino Vega, *Guerra del Chaco: Yrendagüe-Picuiba* (Asunción; La Colmena, 1962), pp. 372–73.

53. Franco, *Memorias*, 2: 160; Tabera, *Picuiba*, pp. 271, 274, 290, 303–308.

54. Estigarribia, *Memorias*, pp. 204–205; Querejazu Calvo, *Masamaclay*, pp. 379–381; David Alvestegui, *Salamanca: Su gravitación sobre el destino de Bolivia*, 4 vols. (La Paz: Fundación Universitaria Simón I. Patiño, 1957–1970), 4: 600–603. The search for scapegoats soon led to the chiefs of staff who had saved the Bolivian divisions from total annihilation. Their army careers were over, but because of the acute shortage of officers they were quietly returned to the front. Toro wrote about his victories in the most megalomaniac book on the Chaco War and used his fictional successes to catapult himself into the presidency after the war.

55. Querejazu Calvo, *Masamaclay*, p. 380.

56. Report No. 5111 of MA Frederick D. Sharp, 15 March 1935 and Report No. 5146, 12 April 1935, MID, Box 1712, RG 165, NA; Bryce Wood, *The United States and Latin American Wars, 1932–1942* (New York: Columbia University, 1966), pp. 94–95; Franco, *Memorias*, 2:170, 172; Rolón, *Campaña de 1934*, 2: 339; Rivarola, *Memorias diplomáticas*, 3: 225, 265, 285. As he typically does with lost opportunities, Estigarribia remains vague about supporting the independence of Santa Cruz; See his *Memorias*, pp. 212, 216.

57. Eusebio Ayala to Vicente Rivarola, 23 February 1935, Rivarola, *Memorias diplomáticas*, 3: 264–265; Alvestegui, *Salamanca*, 4: 607–608.

58. Report No. 5102 of MA Frederick D. Sharp, 8 March, 1935, MID, Box 1712, RG 165, NA; Justo Rodas Eguino, *La guerra del Chaco: Interpretación de política internacional americana* (Buenos Aires: La Facultad: 1938), pp. 126, 129; Zook, *Conduct*, pp. 232–233; Estigarribia, *Memorias*, pp. 231, 214–216. The ties of friendship and even marriage that developed between the prisoners and their host families explain why possibly as many as several thousand Bolivians stayed behind in Paraguay after the war; See Farcau, *Chaco War*, pp. 171–172, 238.

59. Estigarribia, Memorias, p. 210; Rolón, *Campaña de 1934*, 2: 238.

60. Franco, *Memorias*, 2: 165–166.

61. Rolón, *Campaña de 1934*, 2: 323.

62. Tabera, *Picuiba*, p. 412.

63. Franco, *Memorias*, 2: 163, 169; Rolón, *Campaña de 1934*, 2: 332–334; Vera, *Yrendagüe-Picuiba*, pp. 415–418, 462.

64. Farcau, *Chaco War*, p. 221. For Ybibobo see also Rolón, *Campaña de 1934*, 2: 308.

65. Querejazu Calvo, *Masamaclay*, pp. 385–386.

66. Farcau, *Chaco War*, p. 224; Rolón, *Campaña de 1934*, 2: 313–314.

67. *Masamaclay*, pp. 383–385, 391–394; Zook, *Conduct*, pp. 229–230; Vergara Vicuña, *Guerra del Chaco*, 7: 79–88. As he likes to do to cover up errors, Estigarribia throws up numerous extraneous items to excuse the failure of his offensive through Villa Montes, see his *Memorias*, p. 212.

68. Rios, *Verdades y mentiras*, pp. 185–186; González, *Preparación*, 1: 120.

69. Report No. 5146 of MA Frederick D. Sharp, 12 April 1935, G-2 Regional File, Box 180, RG 165, NA; Vergara Vicuña, *Guerra del Chaco*, 7:164–177; Querejazu Calvo, *Masamaclay*, pp. 394–395.

70. Wood, *United States and Latin American Wars*, pp. 75–76, 85.

71. Report No. 5146 of MA Frederick D. Sharp, 12 April 1935, G-2 Regional File, Box 180, RG 165, NA.

72. Report No. 5102 of MA Frederick D. Sharp, 8 March, 1935, MID, Box 1712, RG 165, NA; Vega, *Yrendagüe-Picuiba*, p. 326.

73. Reports of MA Frederick D. Sharp: No. 5002 of 15 November 1934, No. 5102 of 8 March, 1935, No. 5163 of 31 May 1935, all in MID, Box 1712, RG 165, NA; M. A. Guy to Ministre des Affaires

Étrangères, La Paz, 12 March 1935, 7N 3390, Service Historique de l'Armée de Terre, Chateau de Vincennes, Paris, France. As soon as the food became poor or the marches too hard, the Bolivian recruits typically began to desert: see Libreta de notas y de diario de Exaltación Garnica R. Rgtgo. Chorolque 33 de infantería, NG, E199, KU. It became popular among Bolivian officers to pin their failures on the supposed flaws of the Indian conscripts, see for example, Salamanca, *Documentos*, 4: 173.

74. Ricardo M. Setaro, *Secretos de Estado Mayor* (Buenos Aires: Editorial Claridad, 1936), p. 49; Tabera, *Picuiba*, pp. 259–260; Salamanca, *Documentos*, 4: 85, 123. Salamanca himself gave an order on 7 September 1934 to stop the drinking among the officers but to no avail, *Ibid.*, 4: 157–159.

75. Report No. 2137 of MA John A. Weeks, 18 March 1935, MID, Box 1712, RG 165, NA. Rios, *Verdades y mentiras*, p. 191, is even more categoric:"En los espectaculares bombardeos de fortines y hospitales, algunas veces causaron media docena de bajas, entre muertos y heridos, pero nunca destruyeron un depósito de municiones ni de carburante, ni pudieron detener un convoy de camiones ni una columna de tropa. No levantaron un solo riel, ni detuvieron un solo convoy ferrocarrilero."

76. Report No. 5146 of MA Frederick D. Sharp, 12 April 1935, G-2 Regional File, Box 180, RG 165, NA.

77. Rodas Eguino, *Guerra del Chaco*, pp. 131–133. The tone of the Argentine staff studies changed so much from 1934 to 1935 and took on an almost deferential attitude towards Bolivia that the possibility arises that somebody was deliberately doctoring and feeding the later studies to Bolivia. Querejazu Calvo in *Masamaclay* published 1934 Argentine staff studies, but they lack the biting criticism and hostility of those of 1935 appearing in the book of Rodas Eguino, pp. 123–145. The 1935 staff studies with their utter pessimism about Paraguay's chances in the war certainly helped drive President Ayala to accept peace.

78. Franco, *Memorias*, 2: 171–172, 174–175; Rodas Eguino, *Guerra del Chaco*, pp. 133–135.

79. Franco, *Memorias*, 2: 177–178.

80. *Ibid.*, 2: 174–175.

81. Carlos Castañé Decoud, *Tres acciones tácticas de la guerra del Chaco* (Asunción: El Gráfico, 1962), pp. 58, 60, 63–64, 73–75; Franco, *Memorias*, 2: 179; Estigarribia, *Memorias*, pp. 222–223. As late as 19 May 1935 the Bolivian high command still refused to accept that its offensive had failed, a view that writers like Justo Rodas Eguino use to support the thesis that the sudden end to the war prevented a successful Bolivian counteroffensive, (see his *Guerra del Chaco*, pp. 136, 139–140, 154) when in reality the Paraguayans retained the initiative.

82. Farcau, *Chaco War*, p. 234. Zook shares the same conclusion, *Conduct*, p. 237.

83. Report No. 5164 of MA Frederick D. Sharp, 31 May 1935, MID, Box 1712, RG 165, NA; Salamanca, *Documentos*, 4:163; González, *Preparación*, 2: 7, 10, 22; Rodas Eguino, *Guerra del Chaco*, pp. 142–143; Ríos, *Verdades y mentiras*, p. 24; Rivarola, *Memorias diplomáticas*, 3:263, 266, 268; Robert L. Scheina, *Latin America: A Naval History, 1810–1987* (Annapolis: U.S. Naval Institute Press, 1987), p. 126. The naval shells did arrive at Asunción shortly before the war ended.

84. Franco, *Memorias*, 2: 191–193; Rolón, *Campaña de 1934*, 2: 360; Querejazu Calvo, *Masamaclay*, pp. 443–445. Estigarribia had saved for the right moment the propaganda tactic of exaggerating a victory. In a masterful move, he described an already smashing victory in even more glowing terms to a Bolivian public accustomed to expect new disasters. The exaggerated account of the victory ended any Bolivian hesitation to sign the final truce. See Estigarribia, *Memorias*, pp. 226–227.

85. Conventional wisdom has solidified into dogma the conclusion that excessively long supply lines impeded any further Paraguayan advance and forced Paraguay to the peace table. Some considerations refute this claim. (1) Water comprised the majority of the cargo, but because in the final campaigns the Paraguayans were near the Parapetí and Pilcomayo rivers, most soldiers were near enough to tributaries to obtain water without having to burden the supply line. (2) Besides benefiting from the considerable stores of food captured from the Bolivians, many Paraguayan troops for the first time could live off the land once they reached the fertile banks of the Parapetí River in 1935. It should be noted that the Paraguayan dependence on the Bolivian food supply remained constant, because the Paraguayan soldiers knew that the only way to eat well in the Chaco was to capture the well-stocked Bolivian field kitchens. (3) The Bolivian insistence on an outrageous waste of gunfire meant that the disasters of El Carmen and Picuiba yielded enough stocks

of ammunition for rifles and machine guns to last for a lifetime. Hand grenades and mortar shells comprised the bulk of the ammunition cargo; artillery shells were always too scarce to place a major burden on the supply lines. (4) The clothing the Paraguayans received quickly rotted in the Chaco even when of adequate quality. From the earliest battles the Paraguayans stripped the cadavers of Bolivians for usable and better clothes. The major victories yielded such large supplies of captured uniforms and clothes that Paraguay needed to send only specialized clothing items along the supply lines. (5) The capture of Bolivian field hospitals and pharmacies provided the best medical instruments and a huge supply of medicines for the Paraguayans fighting in the north. (6) Once near the Pilcomayo River, the Paraguayans could obtain food, gasoline, and other supplies from Argentina, reducing the need for bringing all these items from Paraguay. (7) The piles of weapons captured were so great, that the supply lines did not need to bring rifles, machine guns, pistols, and mortars. (8) Cattle and gasoline comprised the main cargo for the trucks going north in 1935. (9) Moderate amounts of food, some medicines, and miscellaneous items like spare parts rounded out the cargo. In conclusion, the Paraguayan field army of 1935 was much more self-sufficient than had been the case when the fighting took place inside the dry and inhospitable Chaco.

86. Franco, *Memorias*, 2: 193–195; Scheina, *Naval History*, p. 126. For the negotiations, the definitive account is Leslie B. Rout, Jr., *Politics of the Chaco Peace Conference, 1935–1939* (Austin: University of Texas Press, 1970), pp. 100–214; for a shorter account, see Wood, *United States and Latin American Wars*, pp. 98–166.

87. Estigarribia, *Memorias*, p. 229; Querejazu Calvo, *Masamaclay*, pp. 445–449.

Chapter 14

1. Flavius Vegetius Renatus, *The Military Institutions of the Romans* (Harrisburg, PA.: Military Service Publishing Co., 1944), p. 71. I cannot resist joining the centuries-old debate over the origin of Vegetius. In my reading of his book I found numerous passages revealing striking resemblances with some little-known traits of the Hispanic character. Consequently my conclusion is that Vegetius was from present-day Spain.

2. Bryce Wood, *The United States and Latin American Wars, 1932–1942* (New York: Columbia University Press, 1966), pp. 170–174; Ronald Bruce St. John, *The Foreign Policy of Peru* (Boulder: L. Rienner, 1992), pp. 160–168; Alberto Donadío, *La guerra con el Perú* (Bogotá: Planeta, 1995), pp. 73–91; Jorge Bailey Lembcke, *Recuerdos de un diplomático peruano 1917–1954* (Lima: Editorial Juan Mejía Baca, 1959), pp. 27–30, 42–43, 51, 54.

3. Daniel M. Masterson, *Militarism and Politics in Latin America: Peru from Sánchez Cerro to Sendero Luminoso* (Westport, CT: Greenwood Press, 1991), pp. 33–34, 39. Wood, *United States and Latin American Wars*, pp. 170–171 emphasizes how the Salomón-Lozano Treaty bolstered Peru's territorial claims against Ecuador. St. John, *Foreign Policy of Peru*, pp. 165–166 reveals that Ecuador felt betrayed by Colombia.

4. Ignacio Escallón, *Proceso histórico del conflicto amazónico* (Bogotá: Editorial Nueva, 1934), pp. 93–97; Donadío, *La guerra con el Perú*, pp. 123–126.

5. Antonio José Uribe, *Colombia y el Perú* (Bogotá: Editorial Minerva, 1931), p. 85.

6. Consul Rafael A. Vernaza D. to Minister of Foreign Relations, Iquitos, 1 June 1932, Archivo Diplomático y Consular de Colombia, (henceforth ADyC), Bogotá, Colombia; Carlos Uribe Gaviria, *La verdad sobre la guerra*, 2 vols. (Bogotá: Editorial Cromos, 1935–1936), 1:44–58.

7. Consul Rafael A. Vernaza D. to Minister of Foreign Relations, Iquitos, 1 June 1932, ADyC; Donadío, *La guerra con el Perú*, p. 126; Uribe Gaviria, *La verdad sobre la guerra*, 1:74–79.

8. Escallón, *Proceso histórico del conflicto amazónico*, pp. 41–46; Humberto Araujo Arana, *Conflicto fronterizo Perú-Colombia, año 1932–1933*, 3 vols. (Lima: n.p., 1965), 3: 42–43.

9. Donadío, *La guerra con el Perú*, pp. 119–123; Araujo Arana, *Conflicto fronterizo*, 3: 37–38, 43–50; Uribe Gaviria, *La verdad sobre la guerra*, 1:81–83.

10. Pedro Ugarteche, *Sánchez Cerro: Papeles y recuerdos de un presidente del Perú*, 4 vols. (Lima: Editorial Universitaria, 1979), 3:191. The paragraph also draws on *Ibid.*, 3:183–189 and Masterson, *Militarism in Peru*, pp. 43–47.

11. Donadío, *La guerra con el Perú*, pp. 133–141, 145–153, 158–168; Ugarteche, *Sánchez Cerro*, 3: 190–195, 203–212; Masterson, *Militarism in Peru*, p. 51.

12. Peruvian Legation to Ministry of Foreign Affairs, Bogotá, 3 October 1932, Guerra de Colombia (henceforth GdeC), tomo 7, Archivo Histórico Militar del Peru, Lima, Peru (henceforth AHMP).

13. Carlos Arango Vélez, *Lo que yo sé de la guerra* (Bogotá: Cromos, 1933), pp. 69–84, 119–129, 134–135.

14. Bailey Lembcke, *Recuerdos de un diplomático peruano*, pp 43–44; Arango Vélez, *Lo que yo sé de la guerra*, 40–41; Uribe Gaviria, *La verdad sobre la guerra*, 1: 16–17.

15. "Plan de Guerra — Aprobado por el Consejo de la Defensa Nacional en sesión de 30 de noviembre de 1932, " GdeC, Tomo 9, AHMP.

16. Colonel Víctor Ramos to Secretary of War, Iquitos, 26 October 1932, GdeC, tomo 8, AHMP; Alfredo Vázquez Cobo, *Pro-patria: La expedición militar al Amazonas en el conflicto de Leticia* (Bogotá: Banco de la República, 1985), pp. 63–66; Robert L. Scheina, *Latin America: A Naval History, 1810–1987* (Annapolis: U.S. Naval Institute Press, 1987), pp. 121–122.

17. "Informe no. 2, 16 November 1932," GdeC, tomo 8, AHMP.

18. Donadío, *La guerra con el Perú*, pp. 185–195. The words in the prophetic Spanish original were: "Sánchez Cerro morirá y Colombia vencerá."

19. José A. Vallejo, *Datos para la historia: El conflicto Perú-colombiano* (Santiago de Chile: Talleres Gráficos la Tarde, 1934), pp. 17–20; "Pero mejor sería , quizá, enviar cuerpos de tropa completos, con personal costeño y de todo el territorio de la República, para poder hacer una mejor selección de la gente de esta región que resultan inaparentes como soldados, por su débil contextura física (raquíticos), su temperamento apático, su incultura rayana en una ignoracia absoluta de la idea de Patria, etc." Fernando Sarmiento to Secretary of War, Iquitos, 7 April 1933, GdeC, tomo 9, AHMP.

20. U.S. diplomats confirmed the scant Peruvian desire for war with Colombia; See Wood, *United States and Latin American Wars*, p. 460n9. French military attaché Ronin captured the precise mood of the Peruvian public: "La situation du Pérou est assez sombre en effect. La guerre devient de plus en plus impopulaire. Je ne connais pas un Pérouvien qui partirait au front avec la joie que nous avions en 1914. Le peuple veut bien jouer au soldat sur la place publique mais l'idée de sacrifice s'arrête là." Rapport no. 339, Lima, 18 April 1933, 7N 3411, Le Service Historique de l'Armée de Terre, Château de Vincennes, Paris, France.

21. Uribe Gaviria, *La verdad sobre la guerra*, 1: 214, and also 210–213.

22. Donadío, *La guerra con el Perú*, pp. 221–227, 230–231; Uribe Gaviria, *La verdad sobre la guerra*, 1: 206–208.

23. Vázquez Cobo, *Pro-patria*, pp. 129–130, 209; Uribe Gaviria, *La verdad sobre la guerra*, 1: 183–185.

24. *Ibid.*, 232–234; Vázquez Cobo, *Pro-patria*, pp. 164–169, 207. At first glance the longer range of the expedition's cannons compared to the antique Krupp models of the Peruvians was supposed to make a Colombian victory certain, see Donadío, *La guerra con el Perú*, pp. 233–234, 239. Vázquez Cobo, *Pro-patria*, p. 218 says that the last Colombian official at Leticia gave valuable information on the site and the nearby islands that reaffirmed for Vázquez Cobo his conviction that a direct attack was possible. Whatever he may have understood from this conversation, the large islands in the Amazon River reduce the river channel in front of Leticia to modest proportions, as I observed in my visit to the region. Without considering the real danger of river mines that Vázquez Cobo dismissed, the ships' batteries would have to fire from the other side of the jungle-covered islands and hope to remain in range to shell Leticia. Unlike in Tarapacá on the Putumayo River, the location of the boundary line with Brazil right next to Leticia was another complication that also swayed President Olaya Herrera. As Uribe Gaviria conclusively explained in his book, a direct assault on Leticia was militarily unsound and doomed to failure.

25. Reports of Lieutenant Antonio Cavero, 15, 20 February 1933, Cotuhé and report of artillery officer, 15 February 1933, Cotuhé, GdeC, tomo 9, AHMP; Araujo Arana, *Conflicto fronterizo*, 3: 84–86; Uribe Gaviria, *La verdad sobre la guerra*, 1: 243; Vázquez Cobo, *Pro-patria*, pp. 253–258. I have preferred to follow the unpublished Peruvian reports rather than the confused account of Vázquez Cobo.

26. Reports of Lieutenant Antonio Cavero, 15, 20 February 1933, Cotuhé, and report of artillery officer, 15 February 1933, Cotuhé, GdeC, tomo 9, AHMP; Araujo Arana, *Conflicto fronterizo*, 3: 86–91.

27. Vázquez Cobo, *Pro-patria*, pp. 164–169; Araujo Arana, *Conflicto fronterizo*, 3: 91–102.

28. Vázquez Cobo to President Olaya Herrera, Tarapacá, 15 February 1933, Escallón, *Proceso histórico del conflicto amazónico*, p. 189.

29. Peruvian consul Carlos Farge to Commander of 5th Division, Pará, 23 March 1933, GdeC, tomo 7, and report of artillery officer,

15 February 1933, Cotuhé, GdeC, tomo 9, AHMP; Uribe Gaviria, *La verdad sobre la guerra*, 1: 241–243; Vázquez Cobo, *Pro-patria*, p. 333.

30. Vázquez Cobo to President Olaya Herrera, 19 February 1933, Uribe Gaviria, *La verdad sobre la guerra*, 2:19, 28–29.

31. Uribe Gaviria, *La verdad sobre la guerra*, 2:19, 28–29.

32. *Ibid.*, 2: 29–35.

33. Wood, *United States and Latin American Wars*, pp. 222–223 shows that Olaya Herrera caved in to U.S. pressure not to attack Güepí. When after six months of diplomatic pressure the United States had failed to obtain the Peruvian withdrawal from Leticia, it was inconceivable that by halting the attack Olaya Herrera could obtain anything, as he shortly after realized. Uribe Gaviria, *La verdad sobre la guerra*, 2: 42–47, 61–62.

34. Fernando Sarmiento to Secretary of War, Iquitos, 29 March 1933, GdeC, tomo 9, AHMP; Araujo Arana, *Conflicto fronterizo*, 2: 105–136; Vallejo, *Datos para la historia*, pp. 138–144.

35. Fernando Sarmiento to attack group for Güepí, Iquitos, 24 April 1933, and telegrams 28 March 1933, GdeC, tomo 9, AHMP.

36. Commander of Pantoja to Iquitos, 25 February 1933, and note of 9 March 1933, GdeC, tomo 9, AHMP.

37. Telegram from Güepí garrison to Iquitos, 28 February 1933, GdeC, tomo 9, AHMP.

38. The account of the battle relies on Araujo Arana, *Conflicto fronterizo*, 3: 116–137; "Diario de Guerra del cañonero *Cartagena*," in Álvaro Valencia Tovar, ed., *Conflicto amazónico 1932/1934* (Bogotá: Villegas Editores, 1994), pp. 287–303; Uribe Gaviria, *La verdad sobre la guerra*, 2: 62–74; Juan Lozano y Lozano, *El combate de Güepí* (Bogota: Imprenta municipal, 1933), pp. 1–30. This last author, serving as a lieutenant in the battle, was an excellent representative of the literary personalities that the Peruvian officers believed incapable of waging war. Lozano y Lozano wrote the best first-person account of any consulted for this book; hopefully one day it may be translated into English.

39. Arturo Arango Uribe, *180 días en el frente* (Manizales: Tipografía Cervantes, 1933), pp. 88–89, 135–136.

40. *Ibid.*, pp. 89–97, 137–138.

41. Uribe Gaviria, *La verdad sobre la guerra*, 2: 73–74, 85. For the always tricky problem of determining casualties, see the sensible comments on Güepí in Robert L. Scheina, *Latin America's Wars: The Age of the Professional Soldier, 1900–2001* (Washington, D.C.: Brassey's. 2003), pp. xiii–xiv, 111–112.

42. Uribe Gaviria, *La verdad sobre la guerra*, 2:104–105, 123.

43. Vallejo, *Datos para la historia*, pp. 125–126; Uribe Gaviria, *La verdad sobre la guerra*,, 2: 73, 75, 83–86, 104–105, 158, 160–162, 211.

44. Vallejo, *Datos para la historia*, pp. 138–144; Uribe Gaviria, *La verdad sobre la guerra*, 2: 95, 121–123, 145–146.

45. "Resumen de la situación en Nororiente, 10 April 1933, GdeC, tomo 9, AHMP; Vallejo, *Datos para la historia*, pp. 139, 141.

46. Uribe Gaviria, *La verdad sobre la guerra*, 2:107–108, 145–147.

47. Fernando Sarmiento to Secretary of War, Iquitos, 7 April and 8 May 1933, GdeC, tomo 9, AHMP; Uribe Gaviria, *La verdad sobre la guerra*, 2:147–148, 150, 187, 202; Araujo Arana, *Conflicto fronterizo*, 2: 66.

48. Fernando Sarmiento to Secretary of War, Iquitos, 29 March 1933, GdeC, tomo 9, AHMP; Uribe Gaviria, *La verdad sobre la guerra*, 2:194. 197–198; Araujo Arana, *Conflicto fronterizo*, 3:172–173; Vallejo, *Datos para la historia*, pp. 126–127, 139–140, 142; Scheina, *Naval History*, p. 122 and *Age of the Professional Soldier*, p. 112.

49. Donadío, *La guerra con el Peru*, pp. 277–278; Masterson, *Militarism in Perú*, p. 52.

50. Wood, *United States and Latin American Wars*, p. 245; Araujo Arana, *Conflicto fronterizo*, 3:156–157, 164–166, 176–179; Masterson, *Militarism in Perú*, pp. 52–53; Donadío, *La guerra con el Perú*, pp. 278–279, 284–286.

51. Efraín Rojas to Secretary of War, 24 May 1933, Uribe Gaviria, *La verdad sobre la guerra*, 2: 203.

52. Fernando Sarmiento to Secretary of War, Iquitos, 25 April 1933, and "Instrucción particular y secreta no. 100 al teniente coronel Carlos Lluncor para el ataque a Güepí, Iquitos, 12 May 1933, GdeC, tomo 9, AHMP; Uribe Gaviria, *La verdad sobre la guerra*, 2:224–226; Araujo Arana, *Conflicto fronterizo*, 3: 180–184; Vallejo, *Datos para la historia*, pp. 151–154.

53. Uribe Gaviria, *La verdad sobre la guerra*, 2:219–221, 227–228, 158–262 who accurately predicted the risks Colombia faced by a sudden and complete demobilization.

54. Coronel E. Montagne to Secretary of War, Iquitos, 16 August 1933, GdeC, tomo 8, AHMP; Araujo Arana, *Conflicto fronterizo*, 3:184–185.

55. Fernando Sarmiento to Secretary of War, Iquitos, 31 October 1933, GdeC, tomo 8, AHMP.

56. "Instrucciones para el Coronel Jefe del Estado Mayor General del Ejército," Lima, 13 February 1934, GdeC, tomo 8, AHMP; "Informe sobre la inspección general realizada en Nororiente," Lima, 12 March 1934, GdeC, tomo 8, AHMP; Bosquejo del Plan de Operaciones contra Colombia en el Teatro de Operaciones del Nororiente," Iquitos, 12 March 1934, tomo 8 AHMP; "Informaciones Militares de Colombia," Lima, 9 April 1934, GdeC, tomo 8, AHMP; "Plan de Guerra y Directivas Iniciales," Lima, 18 April 1934, GdeC, tomo 8, AHMP; Vallejo, *Datos para la historia*, pp. 190–194.

57. Circular No. 5 of Coronel Jefe del Estado Mayor General, Lima 7 April 1934, GdeC, tomo 8, AHMP.

58. Wood, *United States and Latin American Wars*, pp 230, 245.

Chapter 15

1. Sun Bin, *The Lost Art of War*, trans. Thomas Cleary (San Francisco: Harper, 1996), p. 69.

2. Roger Ashley Leonard, *A Short Guide to Clausewitz on War* (New York: Capricorn, 1967), p. 151.

3. Humberto Araujo Arana, *Conflicto fronterizo Perú-Colombia*, 3 vols. (Lima: n.p., 1965), 3: 186–188. I hope in a subsequent book on the Peruvian army to detail its transformation in light of the lessons from the war with Colombia.

4. Centro de Estudios Histórico-Militares de Peru, *Colección documental del conflicto y campaña militar con el Ecuador en 1941*, (henceforth CDCME), 7 vols. (Lima: Editora Ital-Peru, 1978–1979), I:5–25, 33–35, 116. This documentary collection is the finest and largest for any of the wars covered in this book. At least the first two volumes should be required reading for any student of this period of the history of Latin America. Unfortunately sudden budget cuts precluded publishing the final volumes dealing mainly with the Amazon campaign, even though most pages were already in galley proofs.

5. "Informe sumario sobre las invasiones y actividades de ecuatorianos en los principales ríos de nuestra region nor-oriental," 10 December 1935, Archivo Histórico Militar del Peru, Lima, Peru (henceforth AHMP).

6. Antonio Santisteban to Secretary of War, Iquitos, [?]15 July 1936, Comisión Catalogadora, AHMP.

7. "Síntesis histórica de los incidentes de límites," Comisión Catalogadora, AHMP; CDCME, 1: 35–37.

8. "Visita de clases peruanas a la Guarnición de Yaupi," 20 April 1939, Conflicto con el Ecuador 1937–1939, 5th Division, AHMP.

9. In a telegram of 29 July 1939, the commander of the Ecuadorian garrison in Huachi reported on his critical situation: "In light of the complete lack of food, the sickness of Lieutenant Yáñez, and the need for a radio receiver," he sent a party to return with supplies, but the large canoe capsized with the loss of life, food, munitions, money, radio receiver, and rifles, CDCME, 1: 229.

10. The word "island" is really a misnomer for the plots of land under dispute. The eastern border of both "islands" is the Zarumilla River, but dry river beds or dry creeks form the waters supposedly creating the islands on the other sides. As Map 29 shows, the islands are not near the sea or even surrounded by real rivers on all sides.

11. CDCME, 1: 63–68, 80, 121–122, 130–131.

12. *Ibid.*, 1: 160–162, 166, 169, 226.

13. *Ibid.*, 1: 172, 180, 182.

14. "Síntesis histórica de los incidentes de límites," Comisión Catalogadora, AHMP; "Estudio sintético sobre la situación de fronteras," 31 October 1939, Conflicto con el Ecuador 1937–1939, 5a. Division, AHMP.

15. CDCME, 1: 38, and 38–42 for rest of paragraph.

16. *Ibid.*, 1: 45, and 45–47 for rest of paragraph.

17. *Ibid.*, 1: 187–190.

18. Julio Tobar Donoso, *La invasión peruana y el protocolo de Río* (Quito: Editorial ecuatoriana, 1945), p. 115.

19. CDCME, 1: 268; Humberto Araujo Arana, *Antecedentes y choques fronterizos y ocupación peruana de territorio ecuatoriano en 1941–1942*, 3 vols. (Lima: Editorial Thesis, 1963–1969), 1:141–143.

20. CDCME, 2: 450.

21. "Síntesis histórica de los incidentes de límites," Comisión Catalogadora, AHMP.

22. CDCME, 2: 472.

23. Tobar Donoso, *Protocolo de Río*, p. 119; Miguel Monteza Tafur, *El conflicto militar del Perú con el Ecuador 1941* (Lima: Editorial Arica, 1976), p. 35; Felipe de la Barra, *Tumbes, Jaén y Maynas* (Lima: n.p. n.d), p. 38.

24. Monteza Tafur, *El conflicto militar*, pp. 32–36; Eloy G. Ureta, *Apuntes sobre una campaña 1941* (Madrid: Editorial Antorcha, 1953),

pp. 32–33. I have generally found Monteza Tafur's book more revealing than that of his commanding general Ureta.

25. The endemic shortage of junior and noncommissioned officers
did not reflect any particular negligence on the part of the army. As
in almost all of the countries of Latin America, the small size of the
middle class in Peru, and in particular of the lower middle class,
limited enormously the pool of qualified candidates.

26. Monteza Tafur, *Conflicto militar*, pp. 38–41, 59–62; Ureta,
Apuntes, pp. 44–45; Araujo Arana, *Choques*, 3: 34–36.

27. Monteza Tafur, *Conflicto militar*, pp. 48, 67; Ureta, *Apuntes*,
pp. 87–89.

28. Felipe de la Barra, *El conflicto peruano-ecuatoriano y la vic-
toriosa campaña de 1941 en las fronteras de Zarumilla y nor-oriente*
(Lima: n.p., 1969), pp. 61–63; Monteza Tafur, *Conflicto militar*, p.
58.

29. Monteza Tafur, *Conflicto militar*, p. 108; Ureta, *Apuntes*, pp.
52, 111–112 who gives 3 July as the date of arrival of the Inspector
General.

30. Ureta, *Apuntes*, pp. 111–113; Araujo Arana, *Choques*, 3:42–43.

31. Tobar Donoso, *Protocolo de Río*, pp. 179–182; *CDCME*, 2
:502–503, 523–524, 533, 538, 548–550.

32. Ureta, *Apuntes*, pp. 116–120, 135–136; Araujo Arana, *Choques*,
3:44–47.

33. *CDCME*, 3: 805–806.

34. "On July 31st Don Luis Vernaza and Dr. Leopoldo Izquieta
Pérez were commissioned by the local Chamber of Commerce to
hold a conference with Dr. Arroyo del Río in Quito, in order to
find out what the real situation of the country was, especially with
regard to the danger for the town of Guayaquil and the province of
Guayas. They flew to Quito and back on the same day and, with regard to their conference with the President, we have been able to
gather the news that Dr. Arroyo expressed his opinion that the
country had been shoved into war by the military element of the
country. This seems to confirm the opinion expressed in our letter
E–292 of July 30th, where we stated that this was supposed to have
been a political move brought about by the military element in
order to overthrow the government but that the situation got out
of control when real firing started between the two countries." Report by Military Attaché Lieutenant Colonel Frederick D. Sharp, 6
August 1941, Box 2772, G–2 Regional File, Record Group 165, National Archives, College Park, Maryland.

35. Monteza Tafur, *Conflicto militar*, pp. 141–147, 207; *CDCME*,
3: 836–837; Barra, *Campaña victoríosa*, p. 64.

36. Ureta, *Apuntes*, pp. 135–141; Araujo Arana, *Choques*, 3: 50–51,
69–89; Monteza Tafur, *Conflicto militar*, pp. 147–149.

37. Araujo Arana, *Choques*, 3:87–106, 212–219; *CDCME*,
3:877–880, 884–885.

38. The presentation of the battle differs from the traditonal interpretation best expressed in Barra, *Campaña victoríosa*, p. 61: "La
battalla consistió en un conjunto de operaciones parciales, sobre
objetivos limitados, si bien sincronizados en el tiempo y espacio,
pero eso sí desarrollándose cada una con maniobras tácticas sea
frontales o sea de desbordamiento." The extract reflects how the
scattered units fought but misses the significance of the drive for a
breakthrough at Chacras.

39. Tobar Donoso, *Protocolo de Río*, pp. 134, 247–248; Monteza
Tafur, *Conflicto militar*, pp. 208–210.

40. Araujo Arana, *Choques*, 2: 247–248. In Ecuadorian accounts,
the episode of the *Calderón* assumes epic proportions, cf. Rafael A.
Borja O., *El descalabro del 41* (Quito:Casa de la Cultura Ecuatoriana, 1978), pp. 99–124.

41. Ureta, *Apuntes*, p. 144; Araujo Arana, *Choques*, 1: 169–172, 2:
223–224, 3: 254–255. Ecuadorian writers console themselves by
ridiculing these efforts; for example, Tobar Donoso, *Protocolo de*

Río, p. 217: "Peru [...] uselessly showed off its acrobatic abilities in
aviation and parachuting, when no enemy capable of inflicing harm
was near."

42. Tobar Donoso, *Protocolo de Río*, p. 449.

43. Ernesto Yepes, *Tres días de guerra, ciento ochenta de negociaciones, Perú-Ecuador 1941–1942* (Lima: Universidad del Pacífico,
1998), pp. 53–53.

44. Borja, *El descalabro de 1941*, pp. 219–224; Araujo Arana,
Choques, 1:79–80, 2: 248–255.

45. Alonso Ordóñez, *Frontera provisional* (Quito: Casa de la Cultura Ecuatoriana, 1966), pp. 14–23. This Ecuadorian account is the
most human document of the war.

46. "Visita ocular a la guarnición de "El Infante," Pantoja, 14
February 1940, and General Felipe de la Barra to Secretary of War,
Lima 14 July 1914, Comisión Catalogadora, AHMP.

47. Telegram No. 32 to Quito of 4 May 1940, Rocafuerte,
Comisión Catalogadora, AHMP.

48. Telegram No. 34 to Quito of 4 May 1940, Rocafuerte,
Comisión Catalogadora, AHMP. See also for this paragraph Or-
dónez, *Frontera provisional*, pp. 49–50.

49. *CDCME*, 3: 885.

50. "Asuntos pendientes y sugerencias," Lima, 11 December 1939,
Conflicto con el Ecuador 1937–1939, AHMP; "Estado de las guarniciones peruans y ecuatorianas en el nor-oriente," Lima, February
1940, Comisión Catalogadora, AHMP; Barra, *Tumbes, Jaén y Maynas*, p. 62.

51. Ordóñez, *Frontera provisional*, pp. 46–47, 55–57; "Visita ocular a la guarnición de "El Infante," Pantoja, 14 February 1940,
Comisión Catalogadora, AHMP; "Informe sobre la actuación de la
5a. division durante la campaña librada contra el Ecuador en 1941,"
AHMP.

52. Monteza Tafur, *Conflicto militar*, pp. 242–243; "Informe
sobre la actuación de la 5a. division durante la campaña librada
contra el Ecuador en 1941," AHMP.

53. Monteza Tafur, *Conflicto militar*, pp. 240, 244; "Informe
sobre la actuación de la 5a. division durante la campaña librada
contra el Ecuador en 1941," AHMP; Ordóñez, *Frontera provisional*,
pp. 57–58; Guillermo S. Faura Gaig, *Los ríos de la Amazonía peruana* (Callao, Peru: Imprenta Colegio Militar Leoncio Prado, 1962),
p. 380.

54. "Informe sobre la actuación de la 5a. division durante la campaña librada contra el Ecuador en 1941," AHMP; Ordóñez, *Frontera
provisional*, pp. 58–62; Araujo Alonso, *Choques*, 3: 298.

55. Faura Gaig, *Los ríos*, pp. 381–382; "Informe sobre la actuación
de la 5a. division durante la campaña librada contra el Ecuador en
1941," AHMP; Ordóñez, *Frontera provisional*, indignantly rejects
the accusation of a drunken charge at p. 57 but partially under-
mines his argument at p. 28.

56. Faura Gaig, *Los ríos*, pp. 382–383; Monteza Tafur, *Conflicto
militar*, p. 245.

57. Araujo Alonso, *Choques*, 3: 297–298; Faura Gaig, *Los ríos*,
pp. 384–385; Ordóñez, *Frontera provisional*, pp. 87–90. This author
also relates in pp. 95–127 the nightmarish trek of the few survivors
(other than the prisoners taken by the Peruvians) who managed to
flee by land to Quito. His grissly descriptions contrast sharply with
what pampered tourists see today in their pre-packaged biodiver-
sity tours of the Amazon.

58. Tobar Donoso, *Protocolo de Río*, pp. 268–269; Araujo Alonso,
Choques, 3: 299–300; Monteza Tafur, *Conflicto militar*, pp. 242–
244.

59. Yepes, *Ciento ochenta de negociaciones*, pp. 123–124, 245–246,
417–422; Ronald Bruce St. John, *The Foreign Policy of Peru* (Boulder: L. Rienner, 1992), pp. 182–183.

Selected Bibliography

Achá, José Aguirre. *De los Andes al Amazonas: Recuerdos de la campaña del Acre.* La Paz: Tipografía Artística Velarde, Aldazosa y Co., 1902. (This is the best of several Bolivian memoirs on the first campaign in the Acre.)

Acosta, Emilio N. *Historia de la campaña de la columna expedicionaria del norte.* Mexico: Secretaría de la Defensa Nacional, 1996.

Aguilar Camín, Héctor. *La Frontera nómada: Sonora y la Revolución Mexicana.* Mexico: Siglo XXI, 1985. (This very detailed account of Sonora's role in the Mexican Revolution is well written and useful. Unfortunately, the author's agenda of trying to score hits against the then ruling political party in Mexico [the PRI] occasionally led the book astray. See note 17 in chapter 7.)

Aguirre, Amado. *Mis memorias de campaña.* Mexico: Instituto Nacional de Estudios Históricos sobre la Revolución Mexicana, 1985.

Aguirre Benavides, Luis and Adrián. *Las grandes batallas de la División del Norte.* Mexico: Editorial Diana, 1964.

Aizpurúa, Armando. *Biografía del General Manuel Quintero V.* Panama: Imprenta Nacional, 1956.

Alemán Bolaños, Gustavo. *Sandino: estudio completo del héroe de las Segovias.* Mexico: Imp. La República, 1932.

Almada, Francisco R. *La revolución en el estado de Chihuahua.* 2 vols. Mexico: Instituto Nacional de Estudios Históricos de la Revolución Mexicana, 1964–1965.

Alvestegui, David. *Salamanca: Su gravitación sobre el destino de Bolivia.* 4 vols. La Paz: Fundación Universitaria Simón I. Patiño, 1957–1970.

Arango Uribe, Arturo. *180 días en el frente.* Manizales: Tipografía Cervantes, 1933.

Arango Vélez, Carlos. *Lo que yo sé de la guerra.* Bogotá: Cromos, 1933.

Araujo Arana, Humberto. *Conflicto fronterizo Perú-Colombia, año 1932–1933.* 3 vols. Lima: n.p., 1965. (This publication compiles many documents and adds some running commentary. These volumes offer the fullest published Peruvian version on the war.)

Arboleda, Henrique. *Palonegro.* Bucaramanga: Imprenta del Departamento, 1953.

Ayala, Juan B. *La Guerra del Chaco hasta Campo Via.* Buenos Aires: Artes Gráficas Aconcagua, 1958.

Ayala Queirolo, Víctor. *La incógnita de Platanillos.* Asunción: Imprenta Zamphirópolos, 1965.

Azcona, Juan Sánchez. *Apuntes para la historia de la revolución mexicana.* Mexico: Instituto Nacional de Estudios Históricos de la Revolución Mexicana, 1961.

Azcui, Benjamín. *Resumen histórico de las campañas del Acre 1899–1903.* La Paz, Bolivia: Talleres de la Intendencia de Guerra, 1925. (This semi-official history of the Acre war is the fullest analytical narrative available. See also notes 20 and 46 in chapter 1.)

Baerlein, Henry. *Mexico: The Land of Unrest.* 2nd. ed. London: Simpkin, Marshall, Kent & Co., 1914.

Barra, Felipe de la. *Tumbes, Jaén y Maynas.* Lima: n.p., n.d. (This book by a noted Peruvian general and participant is the best brief account of the war.)

Barragán Rodríguez, Juan. *Historia del ejército y de la revolución constitucionalista.* 3 vols. Mexico: Instituto Nacional de Estudios Históricos de la Revolución Mexicana, 1985–1986. (Volume 1 provides the most readable account in Spanish of the revolt against Victoriano Huerta. The clearly written volume 2 covers the struggle against Pancho Villa. The author was a Carranza insider who wrote with the aid of many unpublished records.)

Barreto, Sindulfo. *Nanawa: sector de los milagros.* Asunción: Editora Litocolor, 1985.

Beezley, William H. *Insurgent Governor: Abraham González and the Mexican Revolution in Chihuahua.* Lincoln: University of Nebraska Press, 1973.

Bergquist, Charles W. *Coffee and Conflict in Colombia, 1886–1910.* Durham: Duke University Press, 1986. (This book is good on the social aspects of the War of the Thousand Days.)

Blaisdell, Lowell L. *The Desert Revolution: Baja California, 1911.* Westport, CT: Greenwood, 1962.

Brunk, Samuel. *Emiliano Zapata.* Albuquerque: University of New Mexico Press, 1995. (This book represents the start of a long-overdue reevaluation of Zapata's career.)

Burns, E. Bradford. *The Unwritten Alliance: Rio Branco and Brazilian-American Relations.* New York: Columbia University Press, 1966.

Caballero, Lucas. *Memorias de la guerra de los mil días.* Bogotá: Instituto Colombiano de Cultura, 1980.

Calles, Plutarco Elías. *Correspondencia personal.* 2 vols. Mexico: Fideicomiso Calles-Torreblanca, 1991–1993.

Campo Chicangana, Ary. *Montoneras, deserciones e insubordinaciones: Yanaconas y Paeces en la guerra de los mil días.* Cali: Archivo Histórico de Cali, 2003. (This was the most original book to come out of the commemoration of the centenary of the War of the Thousand Days. Although other writers had mentioned the participation of Indians, this author made innovative use of archival documents and oral histories to reconstruct in detail the Indian role in the Cauca campaigns.)

Campos Ponce, Xavier. *Los Yanquis y Sandino.* Mexico: Ediciones X.C.P., 1962.

Candelas Villalba, Sergio. *La batalla de Zacatecas.* Zacatecas: Gobierno del Estado, 1989.

473

Carles, Ruben D. *Victoriano Lorenzo*. Panama: n.p., 1966.

Castañé Decoud, Carlos. *Tres acciones tácticas de la guerra del Chaco*. Asunción: El Gráfico, 1962.

Centro de Estudios Histórico-Militares de Peru. *Colección documental del conflicto y campaña militar con el Ecuador en 1941*. 7 vols. Lima: Editora Ital-Peru, 1978–1979. (This publication is the most extensive source of documents existing for any war of the period 1899–1941. Unfortunately funds ran out before the final volumes on the Amazon campaign could be published. See note 4 in chapter 15.)

Cervantes, Federico. *Francisco Villa y la revolución*. Mexico: Instituto de Estudios Históricos de la Revolución Mexicana, 1985.

Chalkley, John F. *Zach Lamar Cobb: El Paso Collector of Customs and Intelligence during the Mexican Revolution 1913–1918*. El Paso: Texas Western Press, 1998.

Chang, Federico. *El ejército nacional en la república neocolonial 1899–1933*. Havana: Editorial de Ciencias Sociales, 1981.

Chaparro Monco, Carlos Julio. *Un soldado en campaña*. Tunja: Imprenta Oficial, 1935.

Chapman, Charles E. *A History of the Cuban Republic*. New York: Macmillan, 1927. (Although many of its views are now unfashionable, this lively classic still rewards the reader with many insights and nuggets of information.)

Clendenen, Clarence C. *Blood on the Border: The United States Army and the Mexican Irregulars*. New York: Macmillan, 1969.

Coral, Leonidas. *La guerra de los mil días en el sur de Colombia*. Pasto: Editorial Nariño, 1939.

Costa Rica, Secretaría de Relaciones Exteriores. *Documentos relativos al conflicto de jurisdicción territorial con la República de Panamá*. San José: Imprenta Nacional, 1921. (Many key documents are available only in this publication; unfortunately, it is less comprehensive than its Panamanian counterpart *Controversia*.)

Cuestas Gómez, Carlos H. *Panamá y Costa Rica: entre la diplomacia y la guerra*. Panama: Litho Editorial Chen, 1999. (Except for a few omissions, this book is the fullest scholarly treatment of the war.)

Cumberland, Charles C. *Mexican Revolution: Genesis under Madero*. Austin: University of Texas Press, 1952. (Although not as analytical as Alan Knight's book, this pioneering and very readable study has stood the test of time and still offers many easily understood insights into a turbulent period.)

———. *Mexican Revolution: The Constitutionalist Years*. Austin: University of Texas Press, 1972. (The second and last volume of the author's unfinished history of the Mexican Revolution still provides a good overview.)

Díaz Arguedas, Julio. *Cómo fue derrocado el hombre símbolo*. La Paz: Fundación Universitaria Simón I. Patiño, 1957.

Donadío, Alberto. *La guerra con el Peru*. Bogotá: Planeta, 1995. (This clearly written book is the most recent Colombian study on the war. Although the author used many unpublished documents, he concentrated on the political rather than the military side of the war.)

Dulles, John W. F. *Yesterday in Mexico*. Austin: University of Texas Press, 1961. (This easy-to-read chronicle is the best general narrative available in English for the years 1920 to 1936.)

Durán, Justo L. *La revolución del 99*. Cúcuta: El Día, 1920.

Eisenhower, John S. D. *Intervention! The United States and the Mexican Revolution, 1913–1917*. New York: W.W. Norton, 1993.

Escallón, Ignacio. *Proceso histórico del conflicto amazónico*. Bogotá: Editorial Nueva, 1934.

Escobar Rodas, Cecilio. *R. I. 18 Pitiantuta; aclaración sobre algunos acontecimientos de la guerra del Chaco*. Asunción: Artes Gráficas Zampirópolos, 1992.

Estigarribia, José Félix. *Memorias*. Asunción: Intercontinental Editora, 1989.

Estrada, Roque. *La revolución y Francisco I. Madero*. Guadalajara: n.p., 1912.

Fabela, Isidro, ed. *Documentos históricos de la Revolución Mexicana*. 28 vols. Mexico: Fondo de Cultura Económica and Editorial Jus, 1960–1976. (This collection emphasizes politics, although it contains a good number of documents on military campaigns.)

Farcau, Bruce W. *The Chaco War: Bolivia and Paraguay, 1932–1935*. Westport, CT: Praeger, 1996. (In the best tradition of diplomats who devote time to studying their host countries, this retired Foreign Service official has written the most recent study in English. He made a major contribution by rescuing the recollections of now deceased Bolivian veterans.)

Faura Gaig, Guillermo S. *Los ríos de la Amazonía peruana*. Callao, Peru: Imprenta Colegio Militar Leoncio Prado, 1962. (The author's intimate knowledge of the tributaries of the Amazon enhances the value of his reconstruction of military engagements.)

Fermoselle, Rafael. *Política y color en Cuba; La guerrita de 1912*. Montevideo, Uruguay: Ediciones Geminis, 1974.

Fernández, Carlos José. *La guerra del Chaco*, 7 vols. Buenos Aires: Imprenta Militar, 1956–1976. (This set was Paraguay's answer to Vergara Vicuña's work. Although Fernández has some good chapters, most of the volumes print raw data and regimental documents whose value is often not clear. Only a handful of unfortunate scholars will ever have to wade through these bulky volumes.)

Fernández, Emilio. *La campaña del Acre 1900–1901*. Buenos Aires: Imprenta de J. Peuser, 1903.

Fernández Robaina, Tomás. *El negro en Cuba: 1902–1958*. Havana: Editorial de Ciencias Sociales, 1994.

Fifer, J. Valerie. *Bolivia: Land, Location and Politics since 1825*. Cambridge: University Press, 1972. (Clear writing and attention to details make this book indispensable for understanding Bolivia's boundary disputes with Brazil, Paraguay, and Peru.)

Figueroa Domenech, Juan. *Veinte meses de anarquía*. Mexico: n. p., 1913.

Florentín, Heriberto. *Lo que he visto en Boquerón*. Asunción: Editorial El Foro, 1984.

———. *Más allá de Boquerón*. Rio de Janeiro: Imprensa do Exército, 1964.

Flórez Álvarez, Leonidas. *Campaña en Santander (1899–1900)*. Bogotá: Imprenta del Estado Mayor General, 1939. (Only the first volume was published of a projected four-volume official history of the war. The well-reasoned book has provided scholars with a wealth of data, yet it had the unintended consequence of misleading later writers into believing that the important battles took place only in Santander. See note 48 in the Prologue.)

Forero Román, Luis. *La Pedrera: Relato del combate entre colombianos y peruanos en el año de 1911*. Bogotá: Editorial Bolívar, 1918. (Because Peru never published its accounts of the war, this Colombian book is the only one existing on the decisive battle.)

Franco, Rafael. *Memorias militares*. 2 vols. Asunción, Paraguay: Nueva Edición, 1988–1990. (This is the best Paraguayan memoir by a high-ranking officer, and it is surprisingly easy to read.)

García Granados, Ricardo. *Historia de México; desde la restauración de la república en 1867 hasta la caída de Huerta*. 2 vols. Mexico: Editorial Jus, 1956.

García Salazar, Arturo. *Historia diplomática del Perú*. Lima: Imprenta A. J. Rivas Berrio, 1930.

Garner, Paul. *Porfirio Díaz*. Harlow, Great Britain: Longman, 2001. (This is the most recent scholarly survey of the Díaz regime.)

Gimeno, Conrado. *La canalla roja: notas acerca del movimiento sedicioso.* El Paso, Texas, n.p., 1912.

González, Antonio E. *Preparación del Paraguay para la Guerra del Chaco.* 2 vols. Asunción, n.p., 1957. (Much broader than its title suggests, this rambling and occasionally polemical book is unusually revealing.)

González, Antonio P., and J. Figueroa Domenech. *La revolución y sus héroes.* 3rd ed. Mexico: Herrero Hermanos, 1911.

González, Pablo. *El centinela fiel del Constitucionalismo.* Saltillo: Textos de Cultura Histórico-Grafica, 1971.

González Garza, Federico. *La revolución mexicana: mi contribución político-literaria.* Mexico: A. del Bosque, 1936.

González Ramírez, Gonzalo. *Manifiestos políticos, 1892–1912.* Mexico: Fondo de Cultura Económica, 1957.

Grillo, Max. *Emociones de la guerra.* Bogotá: Editorial Santa Fé, 1934.

Gruening, Ernest. *Mexico and Its Heritage.* New York: D. Appleton-Century, 1928.

Guzmán, Martín Luis. *Memorias de Pancho Villa.* Mexico: Editorial Porrúa, 1984. (For those who appreciate literary Spanish, this reliable account is a delight to read. See note 67 of chapter 8.)

Hall, Linda B. *Álvaro Obregón, Power and Revolution in Mexico, 1911–1920.* College Station: Texas A & M University Press, 1981.

Hanrahan, Gene Z., ed. *Documents on the Mexican Revolution.* 8 vols. Salisbury, N.C.: Documentary Publications, 1976–1983. (These volumes conveniently print many U.S. State Department reports.)

Hansis, Randall. "The Political Strategy of Military Reform: Álvaro Obregón and Revolutionary Mexico, 1920–1924." *The Americas* 36 (1979):199–233. (This pioneering article is fundamental to understand the De la Huerta revolt.)

Healy, David F. *The United States in Cuba, 1898–1902.* Madison: University of Wisconsin Press, 1963.

Helg, Aline. *Our Rightful Share: The Afro-Cuban Struggle for Equality.* Chapel Hill: University of North Carolina Press, 1995. (This book contains the most detailed scholarly account of the Race War of 1912 in Cuba.)

Henderson, Peter V. N. *Félix Díaz, the Porfirians, and the Mexican Revolution.* Lincoln: University of Nebraska Press, 1981.

Hernández y Lazo, Begonia. *Las batallas de la plaza de Chihuahua.* Mexico: UNAM, 1984.

Isaguirre, R.R., and A. Martínez R. *Sandino y los U.S. Marines.* Tegucigalpa, Honduras: Omni Editores, 2000.

Katz, Friedrich. *The Life and Times of Pancho Villa.* Stanford: Stanford University Press, 1998. (This monumental study is the most detailed scholarly account of Pancho Villa's career.)

———. *The Secret War in Mexico: Europe, the United States, and the Mexican Revolution.* Chicago: University of Chicago Press, 1981.

Knight, Alan. *The Mexican Revolution,* 2 vols. Lincoln: University of Nebraska Press, 1990. (This very analytical book is the classic history of the Mexican Revolution and is highly recommended. Volume 1 is indispensable to understand the insurrection against Porfirio Díaz and the gradual disintegration of the Francisco Madero presidency. Volume 2 takes the story through the years of Venustiano Carranza. See note 24 in chapter 9.)

LaFrance, David G. *Revolution in Mexico's Heartland: Politics, War, and State Building in Puebla, 1913–1920.* Wilmington, DE: Scholarly Resources, 2003.

Langle Ramírez, Arturo. *Huerta contra Zapata: Una campaña desigual.* Mexico City: Universidad Nacional Autónoma de México, 1981.

Langley, Lester D. *The Banana Wars: United States Intervention in the Caribbean, 1898–1934.* 2nd. ed. Wilmington,

DE: Scholarly Resources, 2002. (The author's close examination of U.S. Marine Corps sources sheds additional light on Sandino.)

Lara Pardo, Luis. *De Porfirio Díaz a Francisco Madero: La sucesión dictatorial de 1911.* México: Instituto Nacional de Estudios Históricos de la Revolución Mexicana, 1985.

Latorre, Benjamín. *Recuerdos de campaña (1900–1902).* Usaquén: Editorial San Juan Eudes, 1938.

Lázaro Robles, José. *Recuerdos de la Guerra de los Mil Días en las provincias de Padilla y Valledupar y en la Goajira.* Santa Marta, Colombia: Escofet, 1946.

Lembcke, Jorge Bailey. *Recuerdos de un diplomático peruano 1917–1954.* Lima: Editorial Juan Mejía Baca, 1959.

Lima, Claudio de Araujo. *Plácido de Castro: um caudilho contra o imperialismo.* São Paulo, Companhia Editora Nacional, 1952. (This is the best biography on Plácido de Castro.)

Llerenas, Fidelina G., and Jaime Tamayo. *El levantamiento delahuertista: cuatro rebeliones y cuatro jefes militares.* Guadalajara: Universidad de Guadalajara, 1995.

Lozano y Lozano, Juan. *El combate de Güepí.* Bogota: Imprenta municipal, 1933. (The literary charm of this classic makes it the best combat account encountered for the 1899–1941 period. See note 38 in chapter 14.)

Macaulay, Neill. *The Sandino Affair.* Chicago: Quadrangle Books, 1967. (This classic book is highly recommended.)

Madero, Francisco I. *Epistolario, 1900–1910.* 2 vols. Mexico: Secretaría de Hacienda y Crédito Publico, 1985.

Martínez Carreño, Aída. *La guerra de los mil días.* Bogotá: Planeta, 1999. (This book containing many first-person accounts is one of the most readable of those books published to commemorate the centenary of the War of the Thousand Days.)

Martínez Delgado, Luis. *Historia de un cambio de gobierno.* Bogotá: Editorial Santafe, 1958.

Martínez Ortiz, Rafael. *Cuba; los primeros años de independencia.* 2 vols. Paris: Imprimerie Artistique Lux, 1921.

Masterson, Daniel M. *Militarism and Politics in Latin America; Peru from Sánchez Cerro to Sendero Luminoso.* Westport, CT: Greenwood, 1991.

Matute, Álvaro. *La carrera del caudillo.* Mexico: El Colegio de México, 1980.

McCain, William D. *The United States and the Republic of Panama.* Durham, NC: Duke University Press, 1937. (Emphasizing the diplomatic aspects, this standard account is the most complete available in English on the war between Costa Rica and Panama.)

Mexico. Secretaría de Guerra y Marina. *Averiguación previa, instruída a solicitud del señor general Juan J. Navarro.* Mexico: El Republicano, 1913.

Meyer, Jean. *The Cristero Rebellion: The Mexican People between Church and State, 1926–1929.* New York: Cambridge University Press, 1976. (This edition is a great introduction for the English-speaking reader. However, only a fraction of the information contained in the three-volume Spanish edition cited below appears in the English translation; the French edition of 1974 is likewise slim.)

———. *La Cristiada: la Guerra de los cristeros,* 3 vols. Mexico: Siglo XXI, 1973–1974. (The lively account is a treasure trove of unique information on the Cristeros. See note 28 in chapter 10.)

Meyer, Lorenzo et al. *Los inicios de la institucionalización, 1928–1934.* Mexico: El Colegio de Mexico, 1978.

Meyer, Michael C. *Huerta: A Political Portrait.* Lincoln: University of Nebraska Press, 1972. (Victoriano Huerta has been extremely fortunate to find this methodical biographer who evaluates the general on evidence and not on revolutionary slogans.)

———. *Mexican Rebel: Pascual Orozco and the Mexican Revolution, 1910–1915.* Lincoln: University of Nebraska Press,

1967. (This detailed scholarly study carefully reconstructs the career of a powerful rebel leader.)

Millett, Allan R. *The Politics of Intervention: The Military Occupation of Cuba, 1906–1909.* Columbus: Ohio State University Press, 1968. (This careful study of the last U.S. occupation of Cuba uncovers the contradictions in U.S. policy to Cuba.)

_____. "The Rise and Fall of the Cuban Rural Guard, 1898–1912." *Americas* 29 (1972):191–213. (This article is indispensable to trace the evolution of U.S. military policy towards Cuba.)

Millett, Richard. *Guardians of the Dynasty.* Maryknoll, NY: Orbis Books, 1977. (As a history of the *Guardia Nacional*, the book presents the Sandino episode in a long historical perspective.)

Monroy Durán, Luis. *El último caudillo.* Mexico: José Rodríguez, 1924.

Monteza Tafur, Miguel. *El conflicto militar del Perú con el Ecuador 1941.* Lima: Editorial Arica, 1976. (The chief of staff of commanding general Eloy Ureta reveals many reasons for the Peruvian victory. See note 24 in chapter 15.)

Muñoz, Ignacio. *Verdad y mito de la revolución mexicana.* 3 vols. Mexico: Ediciones Populares, 1960–1962.

Nalty, Bernard C. *The United States Marines in Nicaragua.* Washington, D.C.: U.S. Marine Corps, 1962. (This book is the closest the U.S. Marine Corps came to publishing an official history of the Nicaragua intervention.)

Naylor, Thomas H. "Massacre at San Pedro de la Cueva: The Significance of Pancho Villa's Disastrous Sonora Campaign." *Western Historical Quarterly* 8 (April 1977): 124–150.

Obregón, Álvaro. *Ocho mil kilómetros en campaña.* 2 vols. Mexico: Editorial del Valle de México, 1988. (This is the outstanding military memoir to come out of the Mexican Revolution. Although the author decries his lack of literary talents, this very revealing book is easy to read. Volume 1 covers the revolt against Victoriano Huerta. Volume 2 describes his extraordinary campaign against Pancho Villa.)

Olmedo, Natalicio. *Acciones de Pitiantuta.* Asunción: Casa Editorial Toledo, 1959.

Ordóñez, Alonso. *Frontera provisional.* Quito: Casa de la Cultura Ecuatoriana, 1966. (Moving chapters on combat in the Amazon give extraordinary value to the best Ecuadorian memoir of the war. See notes 45 and 57 in chapter 15.)

Panama. Ministerio de Relaciones Exteriores. *Controversia de límites entre Panamá y Costa Rica.* 2 vols. Panama: Imprenta Nacional, 1914–1921. (Panama conveniently published many important documents on the war and its origins.)

Pearcy, Thomas L. *We Answer Only to God: Politics and the Military in Panama, 1903–1947.* Albuquerque: University of New Mexico, 1998.

Pérez, Louis A., Jr. *Army Politics in Cuba 1898–1958.* Pittsburgh: University of Pittsburgh Press, 1976. (This clearly written book is the standard scholarly account on the Cuban army.)

_____. *Cuba under the Platt Amendment, 1902–1934.* Pittsburgh: University of Pittsburgh Press, 1986.

_____. *Intervention, Revolution, and Politics in Cuba, 1913–1921.* Pittsburgh: University Press, 1978. (This is a careful scholarly analysis of an often neglected period in U.S.–Cuban relations.)

_____. *Lords of the Mountain: Social Banditry and Peasant Protest in Cuba, 1878–1918.* Pittsburgh: University of Pittsburgh Press, 1989.

_____. "Some Military Aspects of the Mexican Revolution, 1910–1911." *Military Affairs* 43 (1979): 191–194.

Pérez-Venero, Alex. *La guerra de los mil días en Panamá.* Panama: Litho Impresora, 1979.

Philip, George, ed. *British Documents on Foreign Affairs.* Part I. Series D. *Latin America 1845–1914.* 9 vols. Bethesda, MD: University Publications of America, 1991–1992.

_____. *British Documents on Foreign Affairs.* Part II. Series D. *Latin America, 1914–1939.* 20 vols. Bethesda, MD: University Publications of America, 1989–1992.

Pineda Gómez, Francisco. *La irrupción zapatista, 1911.* Mexico City: Era, 1997. (Although excessively favorable to Emiliano Zapata, this book provides the most detailed reconstruction of the Zapatista campaign against Porfirio Díaz.)

Pizzurno Gelos, Patricia. *Antecedentes, hechos, y consecuencias de la guerra de los mil días en el Istmo de Panamá.* Panama: Universidad de Panama, 1990.

Plasencia de la Parra, Enrique. *Personajes y escenarios de la rebelión Delahuertista.* Mexico: Universidad Nacional Autónoma de México, 1998. (This is a very valuable recent history by a Mexican scholar.)

Ponce Muriel, Álvaro. *De clérigos y liberales; crónicas sobre la guerra de los mil días.* Bogotá: Panamericana Editorial, 2000. (This book provides a good guide to the confused events in the southern part of the Department of Cauca.)

Poniatowska, Elena. *Las soldaderas.* Mexico: Ediciones Era, 2000.

Porras, Belisario. *Memorias de las campañas del istmo 1900.* Panamá: Imprenta Nacional, 1922.

Portilla, Santiago. *Una sociedad en armas.* México: El Colegio de México:1995. (This massive tome is the fullest presentation of the insurrection against Porfirio Díaz. The author included every known incident of violence in this encyclopedic book. The author also painstakingly prepared maps for each Mexican state to show the rising crescendo of combat for every month of the revolt.)

Portillo, Pedro. *Acontecimientos relacionados con los ecuatorianos, colombianos y brasileros en los ríos Napo, Putumayo, Yurúa y Purús.* Lima: Tip. Del Panóptico, 1909.

Puente, Ramón. *Pascual Orozco y la revuelta de Chihuahua.* Mexico: Eusebio Gómez de la Puente, 1912.

Querejazu Calvo, Roberto. *Masamaclay: Historia política, diplomática y militar de la guerra del Chaco.* La Paz: Gráfica E. Burillo, 1965. (This is the best one-volume history of the war in Spanish. Written by a Bolivian veteran of the war, the book is not biased against Paraguay and at times is actually too harsh on Bolivia.)

Quirk, Robert E. *An Affair of Honor: Woodrow Wilson and the Occupation of Veracruz.* New York: Norton, 1967. (This well-written study is the definitive book on the topic.)

_____. *The Mexican Revolution, 1914–1915: The Convention of Aguascalientes.* Bloomington: Indiana University Press, 1960.

Raat, W. Dirk. *Revoltosos: Mexico's Rebels in the United States, 1903–1923.* College Station: Texas A & M Press, 1981. (By studying a previously neglected area, the author sheds considerable light on the Mexican Revolution.)

Ramírez de Aguilar, Fernando. *Desde el tren amarillo; crónicas de guerra.* Mexico: Botas, 1924.

Ramírez Garrido, José D. *El combate de Palo Verde.* Mexico: Imprenta Núñez, 1925.

Ramos, Miguel S. *Un Soldado: Gral. José Refugio Velasco.* Mexico: Ediciones Oasis, 1960.

Ribot, Hector. *La revolución de 1912.* Mexico: Imprenta Calle de Humboldt, 1912.

Richmond, Douglas W. *Venustiano Carranza's Nationalist Struggle, 1893–1920.* Lincoln: University of Nebraska Press, 1983.

Ríos, Angel F. *La defensa del Chaco: Verdades y mentiras de una victoria.* Asunción: Archivo del Liberalismo, 1989.

(Although not a complete history of the war, this book, one of the few elegantly written books in Spanish on the war, provides crucial information to understand Paraguay's strategy.)

Rivarola, Vicente. *Memorias diplomáticas*. 3 vols. Buenos Aires: Editorial Ayacucho, 1952–1957.

Rivas, Raimundo. *Historia diplomática de Colombia (1818–1934)*. Bogotá: Imprenta Nacional, 1961.

Rivero, Gonzalo G. *Hacia la verdad: episodios de la revolución*. Mexico: Compañía Editora Nacional, 1911.

Rodas Eguino, Justo. *La guerra del Chaco: Interpretación de política internacional americana*. Buenos Aires: La Facultad, 1938.

Rodríguez, Ángel. *Autopsia de una guerra; campaña del Chaco*. Santiago, Chile: Ediciones Ercilla, 1940.

Rolón, Raimundo. *La guerra del Chaco: campaña de 1934*. 2 vols. Asunción: Talleres Gráficos E.M.E.S.A., 1961–1963. (Although occasionally it bogs down in tactical detail, this remains the most careful history from the Paraguayan side. Unfortunately, it covers only the year 1934.)

Rosa, Domingo de la. *Recuerdos de la guerra de 1899 a 1902*. Barranquilla: Imprenta Departamental, 1940.

Ross, Stanley R. *Francisco I. Madero: Apostle of Mexican Democracy*. New York: Columbia University Press, 1955.

Sagárnaga, Elías. *Recuerdos de la campaña del Acre de 1903; mis notas de viaje*. La Paz: Talleres Gráficos La Prensa, 1909.

St. John, Ronald Bruce. *The Foreign Policy of Peru*. Boulder: L. Rienner, 1992.

Salamanca, Daniel. *Documentos para una historia de la guerra del Chaco*. 4 vols. La Paz: Editorial Don Bosco, 1951–1974. (This source is indispensable to reconstruct events during the presidency of Salamanca and is much more reliable than the polemical memoirs of Bolivian generals.)

_____. *Mensajes y memorias póstumas*. Cochabamba, Bolivia: Editorial Canelas, 1976.

Salas, Elizabeth. *Soldaderas in the Mexican Military: Myth and History*. Austin: University of Texas Press, 1990.

Salazar, Víctor M. *Memorias de la guerra (1899–1902)*. Bogotá: Editorial ABC, 1943.

Sánchez G., Gonzalo, and Mario Aguilera P., eds. *Memoria de un país en guerra*. Bogotá: Planeta, 2001.

Sánchez Lamego, Miguel A. *Historia militar de la revolución constitucionalista*. 5 vols. Mexico: Instituto Nacional de Estudios Históricos de la Revolución Mexicana, 1956–1960. (Although containing many more details than Barragán, these volumes are useful mainly as a reference work for specialists.)

_____. *Historia militar de la revolución mexicana en la época maderista*. 3 vols. Mexico: Instituto Nacional de Estudios Históricos de la Revolución Mexicana, 1976. (This is one of a series of publications constituting the nearest Mexico came to issuing an official history of the Mexican Revolution. Although packed with valuable information, these three volumes, like the rest in the series by Sánchez Lamego, are not for beginning readers.)

_____. *Historia militar en la época de la Convención*. Mexico: Instituto Nacional de Estudios Históricos de la Revolución Mexicana, 1983. (Sánchez Lamego stopped his history of the Mexican Revolution with this brief volume. The author as always remained scrupulously fair to all participants and meticulously accurate in his details.)

Santa, Eduardo. *Rafael Uribe Uribe*. Bogotá: Ediciones Triángulo, 1962.

Scarone, Ernesto. *Ataque y retoma del fortín Carlos A. López (Pitiantuta)*. Asunción: n.p, 1973.

_____. *Contribución para la historia de la Guerra del Chaco: Reconocimiento en fuerza en Pitiantuta*. Asunción: n.p., 1963.

Scheina, Robert L. *Latin America: A Naval History, 1810–1987*. Annapolis: U.S. Naval Institute Press, 1987.

_____. *Latin America's Wars: The Age of the Professional Soldier, 1900–2001*. Washington, D.C.: Brassey's, 2003.

Selser, Gregorio. *Sandino: General de hombres libres*. Mexico: Editorial Diógenes, 1978.

Serrano, T. F. *Episodios de la revolución*. El Paso: Modern Printing, 1911.

Setaro, Ricardo M. *Secretos de Estado Mayor*. Buenos Aires: Editorial Claridad, 1936.

Smith, Robert F. *The United States and Cuba: Business and Diplomacy, 1917–1960*. New Haven, CT: College and University Press, 1960.

Solano Álvarez, Luis. *Mi actuación militar*. Havana: Imprenta El Siglo XX, 1920.

Somoza, Anastasio. *El verdadero Sandino o el calvario de las Segovias*. 2 vols. Managua, Nicaragua: Tip. Robelo, 1936.

Stanfield, Michael Edward. *Red Rubber, Bleeding Trees: Violence, Slavery, and Empire in Northwest Amazonía, 1850–1933*. Albuquerque: University of New Mexico Press, 1998.

Stout, Joseph A., Jr. *Border Conflict: Villistas, Carrancistas, and the Punitive Expedition 1915–1920*. Fort Worth: Texas Christian University Press, 1999.

Suárez, Nicolás. *Anotaciones y documentos sobre la campaña del Alto Acre, 1902–1903*. Barcelona: Tipografía la Académica, 1928. (The leader of the Bolivian rubber tappers provides a faithful reconstruction of his military campaign in the Amazon jungle.)

Tablada, Juan José. *Historia de la campaña de la División del Norte*. Mexico: Imprenta del Gobierno Federal, 1913.

Tamayo, Joaquín. *La revolución de 1899*. Bogotá: Banco Popular, 1975.

Tambs, Lewis A. "Rubber, Rebels, and Rio Branco: The Contest for the Acre." *Hispanic American Historical Review* 46 (1966):254–273. (The standard scholarly account in English neglected combat.)

Taracena, Alfonso. *La verdadera revolución mexicana. Quinta etapa 1916 a 1918*. Mexico: Editorial Jus, 1979.

_____. *La verdadera revolución mexicana. Tercera etapa 1914 a 1915*. Mexico: Editorial Jus, 1972.

_____. *Verdadera revolución, 1922–1924*. Mexico: Editorial Porrúa, 1992.

Thord-Gray, Ivor. *Gringo rebel: Mexico 1913–1914*. Coral Gables, FL: University of Miami Press, 1960.

Tobar Donoso, Julio. *La invasión peruana y el protocolo de Río*. Quito: Editorial ecuatoriana, 1945. (The obsession for blaming others for Ecuador's defeat makes most Ecuadorian memoirs notoriously unreliable, but this one by the foreign minister during the war is among the most trustworthy.)

Tocantins, Leandro. *Formação histórica do Acre*. 3 vols. Rio de Janeiro: Conquista, 1961. (A work of erudition, this comprehensive book reflects a deep love of the Acre and an even greater passion to seek out the truth in the many confused events of the Acre war. The book also provides the fullest Brazilian account of the boundary dispute with Peru.)

Tovar Villa, Raúl, ed. *Campaña del Chaco; El General Hans Kundt*. Oruro, Bolivia: Editorial de la Universidad Técnica de Oruro, 1969. (This straightforward first-person account by General Kundt provides the key to understand his campaigns.)

Troncoso, Francisco P. *Campaña de 1910 a 1911*. Mexico: Secretaría de Guerra y Marina, 1913. (Except for one major flaw in the last page [see notes 93 and 108 in chapter 5] this clearly written text is the best military account of the insurrection in Chihuahua. The author displayed greater abilities as an analyst and a writer than his successor, Miguel Sánchez Lamego.)

Tuck, Jim. *The Holy War in Los Áltos*. Tucson: University of

Arizona Press, 1982. (Inspired by Jean Meyer's magnum opus, this microhistory of one region reveals the dynamics of the Cristero Revolt. See note 28 in chapter 10.)

Turner, John Kenneth. *Barbarous Mexico.* Austin: University of Texas Press, 1984.

Ugarteche, Pedro. *Sánchez Cerro: Papeles y recuerdos de un presidente del Perú.* 4 vols. Lima: Editorial Universitaria, 1979.

U.S. Department of State. *Papers Relating to the Foreign Relations of the United States 1900–1931.* 83 vols. Washington, D.C.: Government Printing Office, 1901–1946.

Ureta, Eloy G. *Apuntes sobre una campaña 1941.* Madrid: Editorial Antorcha, 1953.

Uribe Gaviria, Carlos. *La verdad sobre la guerra.* 2 vols. Bogotá: Editorial Cromos, 1935–1936. (Very well written and clear, this is the fullest Colombian account of the war with Peru of 1932–1933 and was the nearest Colombia came to publishing an official history. Colombia easily outclassed Peru both in the battlefield and in books published about the war.)

Uribe Uribe, Rafael. *Documentos militares y políticos.* Medellín: Beneficencia de Antioquia, 1982. (This combination of documents and history is the single most valuable published source for the War of the Thousand Days. Because Uribe Uribe was such an incisive and clear writer, the text is eminently enjoyable. This is the best book in Spanish on the war.)

Valadés, José C. *La revolución mexicana.* 10 vols. Mexico: Manuel Quesada Brandi, 1963–1967.

Valdeblanquez, José María. *Biografía del señor general Florentino Manjarres.* Bogotá: Emilio Portilla e Hijos, 1962.

_____. *Historia del Departamento del Magdalena y del Territorio de la Guajira.* Bogotá: El Voto Nacional, 1964.

Valencia Tovar, Álvaro, ed. *Conflicto amazónico 1932/1934.* Bogotá: Villegas Editores, 1994.

Valenzuela, Clodoveo, and Amado Chaverri Matamoros. *Sonora y Carranza.* Mexico: Editorial Renacimiento, 1921.

Valenzuela, José. *Últimos meses de Porfirio Díaz en el poder.* Mexico: Instituto Nacional de Estudios Históricos de la Revolución Mexicana, 1984.

Vallejo, José A. *Datos para la historia: El conflicto Perú-colombiano.* Santiago de Chile: Talleres Gráficos la Tarde, 1934. (This highly critical but rambling account by a Peruvian officer exposes the flaws in Peru's effort to retain Leticia.)

Vanderwood, Paul J. "Response to Revolt: The Counter-Guerrilla Strategy of Porfirio Díaz." *Hispanic American Historical Review* 56 (1976): 551–579. (This scholarly article is an excellent analysis of the military obstacles hindering the régime.)

_____. *Disorder and Progress: Bandits, Police, and Mexican Development.* Lincoln: University of Nebraska Press, 1981.

Vázquez Cobo, Alfredo. *Pro-patria: La expedición militar al Amazonas en el conflicto de Leticia.* Bogotá: Banco de la República, 1985. (Although the book reproduces many valuable documents, the author fails to justify his many mistakes in the campaign.)

Vega, Ceferino. *Guerra del Chaco: Yrendagüe-Picuiba.* Asunción : La Colmena, 1962.

Velasco, Donaldo. *La guerra en el istmo.* 2 vols. Panamá: Imprenta Santa Ana, 1903.

Vergara Vicuña, Aquiles. *Historia de la guerra del Chaco.* 7 vols. La Paz: Litografías e Imprentas Unidas, 1940–1944. (This monumental work, the nearest Bolivia came to issuing an official history of the war, was written by a Chilean officer who fought in the Chaco War and who had total access to Bolivian records. The book is generally fair to both sides and is surprisingly well written, but its emphasis on chronicling every engagement may deter some fans of the Chaco War.)

Vesga y Ávila, José María. *La guerra de tres años.* Bogotá: Imprenta Eléctrica, 1914.

Vidal, Gerónimo A. *Misión de la patrulla "Teniente Vidal" para la maniobra de "El Carmen."* Buenos Aires: Gráficas Negri, 1968.

Villegas, Jorge and José Yunis. *La guerra de los mil días.* Bogotá: Carlos Valencia Editores, 1979.

Weinstein, Barbara. *The Amazon Rubber Boom 1850–1930.* Stanford: Stanford University Press, 1983.

Wells, Allen, and Gilbert M. Joseph. *Summer of Discontent, Seasons of Upheaval: Elite Politics and Rural Insurgency in Yucatán, 1876–1915.* Stanford: Stanford University Press, 1996.

Womack, John. *Zapata and the Mexican Revolution.* New York: Vintage Books, 1968. (This is the book to read for those who treasure the image of Zapata as the selfless and idealistic leader who took his people on a heroic struggle to recover their lands.)

Wood, Bryce. *The United States and Latin American Wars, 1932–1942.* New York: Columbia University Press, 1966.

Yepes, Ernesto. *Tres días de guerra, ciento ochenta de negociaciones, Perú-Ecuador 1941–1942.* Lima: Universidad del Pacífico, 1998.

Ynsfrán, Pablo Max. *The Epic of the Chaco: Marshal Estigarribia's Memoirs of the Chaco War.* Austin: Institute of Latin American Studies, 1950.

Zárate, José, and Alberto Ferreyros. *El Mariscal Benavides, su vida y su obra.* 2 vols. Lima: Editorial Atlántida, 1976–1981.

Zook, David H. *The Conduct of the Chaco War.* New Haven, CT: Bookman Associates, 1960. (As the pioneering scholarly study in English, this book has largely been superseded by Farcau's recent study. However, the English-speaking reader can still examine the older publication for additional details and valuable analysis.)

Index

Officers appear with their highest known rank